THE BERL

"Aimed at educated . . . . [Berlitz Travellers] Guides . . . . . . the flavor of foreign lands."
—*Entrepreneur*

"Filling a needed niche in guidebooks . . . designed to eliminate the cumbersome lists of virtually every hotel and restaurant . . . . Special out-of-the-way places are detailed. . . . The books capture the personality and excitement of each destination."
—*Los Angeles Times*

"There's a different tone to these books, and certainly a different approach . . . information is aimed at independent and clearly sophisticated travellers. . . . Strong opinions give these books a different personality from most guides, and make them fun to read."
—*Travel & Leisure*

"Aimed at experienced, independent travellers who want information beyond the nuts-and-bolts material available in many familiar sources. Although each volume gives necessary basics, the series sends travellers not just to 'sights,' but to places and events that convey the personality of each locale."
—*The Denver Post*

"Just the right amount of information about where to stay and play."
—*Detroit Free Press*

"The strength of the [Berlitz Travellers Guides] lies in remarks and recommendations by writers with a depth of knowledge about their subject."
                                        —*Washington Times*

"The most readable of the current paperback lot."
                                        —*New York Post*

"Highly recommended."
                                        —*Library Journal*

"Very strong on atmosphere and insights into local culture for curious travellers."
                                        —*Boston Herald*

"The [Berlitz Travellers Guides] eliminate cumbersome lists and provide reliable information about what is truly exciting and significant about a destination. . . . [They] also emphasize the spirit and underlying 'vibrations' of a region—historical, cultural, and social—that enhance a trip."
                                        —*Retirement Life*

"Information without boredom. . . . Good clear maps and index."
                                        —*The Sunday Sun* (Toronto)

CONTRIBUTORS

JAMES CLARK, whose travel articles have appeared in *The New York Times,* teaches university English in Heidelberg, where he has lived for 12 years.

JOHN DORNBERG has reported on Germany for more than 30 years and has been based in Munich since 1971. The author of several books, he is also a frequent contributor to *Travel & Leisure, Bon Appétit, National Geographic Traveler,* and the travel sections of *The New York Times* and the *Washington Post.*

JOHN ENGLAND, a freelance journalist, has been based in Bonn since 1972. He writes for British newspapers and magazines.

PETER HAYS, a resident of Germany since leaving Cheshire, England, in 1966, is a feature writer for German and English publications.

TED HECK, a freelance travel and sports writer who lived in Germany for five years, contributes regularly to American magazines and newspapers. He returns to Germany every year.

THOMAS LUCEY, a resident of Frankfurt for more than 25 years, is a freelance journalist. He has also been a newspaper and magazine editor and has contributed to two other travel guides.

PHYLLIS MÉRAS, travel editor of the *Providence* (Rhode Island) *Journal,* has contributed travel articles to newspapers around the country. She travels frequently in eastern Germany and is the author of three European guidebooks, including one to Eastern Europe.

DONALD S. OLSON, a freelance writer and editor, has written a guidebook to Berlin and contributed travel articles to many American magazines. The author of three novels, he has also had plays produced in New York and Europe.

DOUGLAS SUTTON, who has been living in Germany since 1974 and in Hamburg since 1978, is an editor with Deutsche-Presse-Agentur wire agency.

THE BERLITZ
TRAVELLERS GUIDES

THE BERLITZ TRAVELLERS GUIDE TO GERMANY

Fourth Edition

ALAN TUCKER
General Editor

BERLITZ PUBLISHING COMPANY, INC.
New York, New York

BERLITZ PUBLISHING COMPANY LTD.
Oxford, England

THE BERLITZ TRAVELLERS GUIDE
TO GERMANY
Fourth Edition

Berlitz Trademark Reg U.S. Patent and Trademark Office
and other countries—Marca Registrada

Published by Berlitz Publishing Company, Inc.
257 Park Avenue South, New York, New York 10010, U.S.A.

Distributed in the United States by
the Macmillan Publishing Group

Distributed elsewhere by Berlitz Publishing Company Ltd.
Berlitz House, Peterley Road, Horspath, Oxford OX4 2TX, England

ISBN 2-8315-1715-X
ISSN 1057-462X

Designed by Beth Tondreau Design
Cover design by Dan Miller Design
Cover photograph by Hans Wolf/The Image Bank
Maps by Mark Stein Studios
Illustrations by Bill Russell
Fact-checked in Germany by Clotilde Lucey
Edited by Donald S. Olson

Printed in the United States of America
1 3 5 7 9 10 8 6 4 2

THIS GUIDEBOOK

The Berlitz Travellers Guides are designed for experienced travellers in search of exceptional information that will enhance the enjoyment of the trips they take.

Where, for example, are the interesting, out-of-the-way, fun, charming, or romantic places to stay? The hotels described by our expert writers are some of the special places, in all price ranges except for the very lowest—not just the run-of-the-mill, heavily marketed places in advertised airline and travel-wholesaler packages.

We are *highly* selective in our choices of accommodations, concentrating on what our insider contributors think are the most interesting or rewarding places, and why. Readers who want to review exhaustive lists of hotel and resort choices as well, and who feel they need detailed descriptions of each property, can supplement the *Berlitz Travellers Guide* with tourism industry publications or one of the many directory-type guidebooks on the market.

We indicate the approximate price level of each accommodation in our description of it (no indication means it is moderate in local, relative terms), and at the end of every chapter we supply more detailed hotel rates as well as contact information so that you can get precise, up-to-the-minute rates and make reservations.

The Berlitz Travellers Guide to Germany highlights the more rewarding parts of the country so that you can quickly and efficiently home in on a good itinerary.

Of course, this guidebook does far more than just help you choose a hotel and plan your trip. *The Berlitz Travellers Guide to Germany* is designed for use *in* Germany. Our writers, each of whom is an experienced travel journalist who either lives in or regularly tours the city or region of Germany he or she covers, tell you what you really need to know, what you can't find out so easily on your own. They identify and describe the truly out-of-the-ordinary restaurants, shops, activities, and sights, and tell you the best way to "do" your destination.

Our writers are highly selective. They bring out the significance of the places they *do* cover, capturing the personality and the underlying cultural and historical resonances of a city or region—making clear its special appeal.

The Berlitz Travellers Guide to Germany is full of reliable information. We would like to know if you think we've left out some very special place. Although we make every effort to provide the most current information available about every destination described in this book, it is possible too that changes have occurred before you arrive. If you do have an experience that is contrary to what you were led to expect by our description, we would like to hear from you about it.

A guidebook is no substitute for common sense when you are travelling. Always pack the clothing, footwear, and other items appropriate for the destination, and make the necessary accommodation for such variables as altitude, weather, and local rules and customs. Of course, once on the scene you should avoid situations that are in your own judgment potentially hazardous, even if they have to do with something mentioned in a guidebook. Half the fun of travelling is exploring, but explore with care.

ALAN TUCKER
General Editor
Berlitz Travellers Guides

Root Publishing Company
350 West Hubbard Street
Suite 440
Chicago, Illinois 60610

CONTENTS

MAPS

THE BERLITZ TRAVELLERS GUIDE TO GERMANY

OVERVIEW

By John Dornberg

John Dornberg has reported on Germany for more than 30 years and has been based in Munich since 1971. The author of several books, he is also a frequent contributor to Travel & Leisure, Bon Appétit, National Geographic Traveler, *and the travel sections of* The New York Times *and* The Washington Post.

Germany is like a kaleidoscope or a jigsaw puzzle, a land that has baffled many travellers—the Germans included. None less, indeed, than the 18th-century poet and dramatist Friedrich von Schiller, second only to Goethe in stature as a bard and in influence on German literature and thought, once exclaimed rhetorically: "Germany? But where is it? I cannot find such a country. Where the political realm ends, the culture begins." That enigmatic description, written when the territory now called Germany was a patchwork of rival and often warring kingdoms, principalities, duchies, prince-bishoprics, and independent city-states, is as applicable today as it was 200 years ago.

What is Germany and who are the Germans? These are questions that instantly raise new ones: How many Germanys—one, two, a dozen, a score—and which ones?

It is not enough of an answer to speak merely of the former West and East Germanys, divided for 41 years and now reunited as the Federal Republic of 16 states in a country of 78 million with a territory of 138,000 square miles (nearly the size of Montana and somewhat larger than the United Kingdom and Republic of Ireland combined), of which the small city of Bonn on the Rhine will remain the capital until parliament and the government move to Berlin, probably toward the end of this decade. It skirts the issue of all the little Germanys—Baden, Bavaria, Hannover, Hesse,

Holstein, Schleswig, Brandenburg, Mecklenburg, Saxony, Thuringia, to name just a few—that as recently as 125 years ago were proud independent and sovereign states, some even so-called middle powers, with their own coinage, armies, foreign ministries, and citizenships.

For all its comparatively small size, this land in the middle of Europe is a mosaic of panoramas, as complex and variegated as a patchwork. Although it is a mere 80 minutes by air, or six and a half hours by train, from Munich in the Bavarian Alps to Hamburg near the North Sea—a distance of only 500 miles or so—geographically, architecturally, culturally, even linguistically, it can be like a journey between two different countries.

A trip to Trier on the Mosel river can be almost like a visit to Rome. A day in Nürnberg, Regensburg, Erfurt, or Lübeck will seem like one in the Middle Ages, a weekend in Augsburg a step back into the Renaissance. Or consider Frankfurt-am-Main, the financial center of Germany—indeed, of Europe—a modern metropolis of gleaming steel-and-glass skyscrapers, often derogatorily called "Bankfurt," "Mainhattan," or "Manhattan-am-Main." But within a short radius of this money capital where, they say, it is easier to find a syndicated billion-mark loan than a parking space, there are scores of picture-postcard villages with steep-roofed, half-timbered houses, romantic old market squares, and narrow cobblestone streets—each one a kind of three-dimensional travel poster, a spot where time seems to have stood still.

During an entire life span you could repeatedly travel the length of Germany, about 560 miles from the Danish border in the north to the Austrian and Swiss frontiers in the south, and its breadth, a scant 500 miles as the crow flies from the Rhine and the boundaries with France and the Benelux countries in the west to those of Poland and Czechoslovakia in the east, and still not see everything worth seeing. Nor will you be able to find a common German denominator, for there really is none. Its comparatively small size notwithstanding, Germany is a country of thousands of lifestyles and mores, hundreds of landscapes, scores of regions.

It is a land of craggy, snowcapped mountains and broad, expansive plains; of majestic rivers and sandy ocean shores; of lush, dark forests and vine-covered hills; bustling cities and idyllic hamlets; of graceful Gothic church spires and fairy-tale castles, but also of ugly factory chimneys and the cauldrons of heavy industry. Down south on the Bodensee (Lake Constance), which Germany shares with Austria and Switzerland, a microclimate creates a subtropical environment where even palm trees grow.

The people are as varied as the topography. The cliché image of *the German* invariably portrays a man in lederhosen, loden coat, and hat with goat's-hair tuft quaffing beer from a huge mug to wash down a mountain of sausages, sauerkraut, and baseball-size dumplings, or a buxom blond, blue-eyed woman garbed in a dirndl. But those are strictly stereotypes of Bavarian highlanders. No Berliner, Frankfurter, Hannoverian, Saxonian, or Rhinelander would be caught dead wearing such duds: It's like suggesting that all Americans wear cowboy hats and boots, bust broncos, and spend their leisure hours square dancing.

The same is true of cuisine. To speak of "German food" is a misnomer. There are no fewer than 1,000 kinds of bread, several hundred distinct *types*—not just brands—of beer, and scores of hams, sausages, and smoked meats, each one a local specialty. Bratwurst comes in a dozen varieties, shapes, and sizes, seasoned with a shelf-full of different spices. No Stuttgarter could survive without a helping of *Spätzle* to accompany the noonday meal. *Labskaus,* a mush of corned-beef hash mixed with red beets, may be the dish of the gods for a native of Hamburg or Bremen, but anathema to the Münchener, who swoons over *Weisswürste,* plump "white sausages" made of minced veal, various herbs, and grated lemon peel.

Nor (except in the written form, called *Schriftdeutsch*) can you really talk about a common language. There is *Hochdeutsch* (High German) and *Plattdeutsch* (Low German), which is very close to Dutch, Danish, and even English. The designations allude to the altitude and geography—Low German being the form spoken in areas close to the Low Countries—not to any refinements of grammar or pronunciation. Beyond those two basic distinctions you will encounter dozens of dialects—not simply accents—that, because they bristle with different words, phrases, and even grammatical constructions, border on being separate languages. To the untrained ear, a busload of Germans conversing in their native Bavarian, Berliner, Hessian, Rhinelandish, Saxonian, Swabian, Thuringian, and Westphalian tongues would sound like a Tower of Babel on wheels.

Of course there are great equalizers. One of them is the spate of Anglicisms that lace the lingo of advertising, business, finance, technology, science, and computerspeak. The other is the uni-language of nightly television. But don't count on that. Several years ago when the Bavarian broadcasting corporation produced a sitcom mini-series for the rest of the national network, station managers up north prudently inserted subtitles in *Schriftdeutsch*.

The Shaping of Germany

A description of this multifarious and complex land as a single country with clearly defined borders applied, until East and West Germany's reunification on October 3, 1990, to fewer than 80 years of its history.

That brief period began in 1871 when Prince Otto von Bismarck, the prime minister of Prussia, created a cohesive nation-state out of a crazy quilt of independent kingdoms, principalities, and dwarf-sized duchies. Called the Second German Reich, this hodgepodge was ruled by the Prussian kings (known as *kaisers,* or emperors). After World War I and the last kaiser's abdication, accompanied by the overthrow of the still-reigning kings of Bavaria, Saxony, and Württemberg—whose capitals were, respectively, Munich, Dresden, and Stuttgart—Germany became the democratic Weimar Republic, so named only because it was in the town of Weimar, one-time residence of both Goethe and Schiller, that the constitutional convention met; Berlin was the capital. The Weimar Republic gave way to the Third Reich, under the dictatorship of Adolf Hitler and the Nazis. The era of German unity came to an abrupt and destructive close after World War II with the formal establishment in 1949 of West and East Germany as separate sovereign countries. From August 1961 until November 1989 those two Germanys were divided by the grim Berlin Wall and a heavily fortified border. Then, miraculously, the Wall crumbled and opened up, and faster than anyone had expected or dared to predict East and West Germany moved toward reunification.

Germany B.C.E.

The first sign of human or prehuman life in what is now Germany goes back about 500,000 years: a fossil jaw, found in 1907 near Heidelberg, of an apelike fellow called Heidelberg Man. A cast of the original fragment is on display in that city's Kurpfälzisches Museum. The next indication of habitation is even better known: The remains of Neanderthal man, who lived 50,000 years ago near Düsseldorf in the Neander valley, were found there in 1856.

Celts, with a high level of civilization and culture, inhabited southern Germany long before the first Germanic tribes migrated from Asia into Central Europe, a process that began around 1000 B.C. and lasted more than 15 centuries. Although those early Germans were mentioned by a Greek navigator who sailed as far north as Norway, it was not until the time of Julius Caesar, who tried but failed to conquer them, that they entered clearly into recorded history.

Roman Germany

The bloodiest confrontation between Romans and Germans was the Battle of the Teutoburg Forest in A.D. 9, in which three of Augustus Caesar's finest legions were decimated by the Cherusci, a Germanic tribe led by the chieftain Hermann (Arminius). Hermann, sometimes confused with the mythological Siegfried, is celebrated as the arch-German hero. Although the Romans continued to clash with the Germanic tribes, they made no other serious attempts to penetrate more deeply into the Germanic territories. Instead, they colonized the areas south of the Danube and west of the Rhine, establishing strong military forts at Bonn and Xanten and major cities such as Augsburg, Cologne, Kempten, and Trier. Trier ultimately became known as the Rome of the North, a city as populous—with 100,000 people—in the time of Constantius I and Saint Helena, the parents of Constantine the Great, as it is today. To protect their territory, the Romans built the *Limes,* a defensive wall of stone, palisades, and fortresses some 300 miles long, which zigzagged in a generally southeasterly direction from Cologne on the Rhine to Regensburg on the Danube.

These two principal German rivers actually rise not far from each other—the Rhine in the Swiss Alps, the Danube in the Black Forest—but then run off in opposite directions: the Rhine generally northwestward past France and through the Netherlands to the North Sea, the Danube southeastward through Bavaria, Austria, Hungary, the Balkans, and a piece of the Soviet Union to the Black Sea.

A tour of this Roman Germany can be a rewarding journey for travellers with a penchant for antiquities. There is much left to see.

Xanten, a town on the Rhine between the Dutch border and Düsseldorf, was once a military city with a population of 15,000. Its ruins have been made into an archaeological theme park, with reconstructions of the Roman temples, barracks, private houses, and shops. **Cologne** (Köln) derives its name from *Colonia Claudia Ara Agrippinensis,* that is, Colony of Agrippina II, who was a great-granddaughter of Augustus Caesar, a sister of Caligula, the mother of Nero, and the niece as well as wife (third liaison for both) of Emperor Claudius. In A.D. 50 she badgered Claudius into elevating the town of her birth into a "retirement colony" for legionnaires-turned-merchants. Today Cologne abounds with remnants of its Roman past, the best of which are displayed in the Roman-Germanic museum.

Trier still has an immense Roman city gate, an amphitheater, several Roman baths, the palaces of Constantine and

Helena, and a fourth-century bridge used for modern traffic. In **Baden-Baden**, which Emperor Caracalla made into a health resort more than 1,700 years ago, you can see the Roman baths right underneath the gleaming tiles and chrome equipment of the modern spa. Remnants of the Limes, including a well-preserved fort, can be found north of Frankfurt. **Augsburg** (German for *Augusta Vindelicorum*, Citadel of Augustus in the Land of the Vindelicians) was founded in 15 B.C. as a fortified encampment and then became the provincial capital of Raetia. Nearby **Kempten**, first mentioned in A.D. 18 as Cambodonum, has remains of its Roman forum, walls, and a basilica. **Regensburg**'s Porta Praetoria, Germany's oldest town gate, was built in 179 under Marcus Aurelius and now forms part of a hotel.

The Germanic peoples living within the empire adopted many Roman customs, attitudes, lifestyles, and modes of thought that still distinguish them from their cousins farther east and north. In the late fourth and early fifth centuries, as Rome declined and neared collapse, the Germanic tribes from beyond the Limes expanded south and west. The Vandals, Lombards, and various Goths pushed into Italy and Spain. The Burgundii descended on the region of France that bears their name. Tribes from today's Denmark and the Elbe river valley, the divide between Western and Central Europe—Jutes, Angles, and western Saxons—crossed the sea to England. And there were the eastern Saxons and the Franks, who dominated what is now Germany itself.

The Holy Roman Empire

By the late seventh and early eighth centuries the face of Europe had been transformed by these various Germanic peoples. Rome itself was politically dead, with its remaining power vested in the eastern emperors at Constantinople. East of the Rhine, between the Limes and the advancing Slavs, lived the tribes that became the Germans of later times. West of the river a new realm, that of the Franks, had begun taking shape and expanding its territory under increasingly powerful kings. The most powerful, and important in the subsequent development of civilization, was Charles the Great, whom the French call **Charlemagne** and the Germans Karl-der-Grosse. On Christmas Day in 800 Pope Leo III crowned him emperor in Rome.

The title *kaiser* (meaning caesar) carried with it the implication that Charlemagne was the western Christian successor to the Roman emperors, and with that papal act the Holy Roman Empire (*das Heilige Römische Reich der Deutschen Nation*) was born. In name it lasted more than a millennium, until 1806, when Francis II of Austria, a Hapsburg, renounced the title under pressure from a new emperor then ruling Europe: Napoleon Bonaparte. Until the middle of the 16th century, 32 of these elected Holy Roman rulers were crowned in the cathedral at Aachen (Aix-la-Chapelle) while sitting on a stone throne that can still be seen there. Starting in 1562 the ceremony was held in the Frankfurt cathedral, followed by a gala coronation bash in the Römer (the town hall). For most of those ten centuries, however, the "empire" was largely a fiction. In fact, for a while, only the idea of it survived Charlemagne, for in 843 the West Franks seceded to form the nucleus of what became France, adopting Latin instead of Old High German as the base of their language. The realm of the East Franks went to one of Charlemagne's grandsons, Louis (Ludwig) the German. Though another grandson, Lothair, kept the title of Holy Roman Emperor, he got only a narrow strip of land running from Belgium through Burgundy into Italy—the "Middle Kingdom," over which the East and West Franks, alias the Germans and French, fought for centuries. Only when the imperial crown went to King Otto I in 962 did the empire revive—this time as a purely German affair.

But as Voltaire pointed out, this German Reich was "neither holy, nor Roman, nor an empire." It was largely an illusion, with grave long-term consequences for Germany, for in a sense the Germans are still paying the price. Prussia's Bismarck tried to reconstitute the Reich idea, albeit excluding the Austrians, whose Hapsburg rulers had been the Holy Roman emperors from 1273 to 1806.

One trouble with the Holy Roman Empire was that it was an anemic substitute for the unified monarchy that Germany lacked. Conversely, it became a major obstacle to the creation of such a monarchy. The kaisers were not only peripatetic, travelling from one castle to another with no place they could call a capital, but, having no real source of revenue, were politically impotent as well. Real power during most of the 1,000 years of the Holy Roman Empire rested not with the emperors but with the counts, dukes, margraves, electors, prince-bishops, and kings of the various German states. By the middle of the 17th century there were 350 of these states.

The Reformation

While other European countries were unifying under their kings and becoming major powers, the various Germanys, despite the imperial umbrella, became increasingly centrifugal. To complicate matters, there were also the deep religious divisions precipitated by **Martin Luther**, who appeared on history's stage on October 31, 1517, when he nailed his 95 theses attacking the Roman clergy and its abuses to the door of the castle church in Wittenberg. Thus began the Reformation, which altered the Germanys—and the rest of Europe—dramatically and forever. The Reformation accelerated the atomization of Germany into Protestant and Catholic dwarf states, each of whose local rulers determined the religion his subjects should practice. Moreover, it also triggered a century of violence that culminated in the Thirty Years' War (1618 to 1648), during which nearly every German town was sacked at least once and seven million people—one third of the population—were killed.

The Historical Legacy Today

Though the Germanys flourished culturally and economically during the millennium of the Holy Roman Empire and also in the years of the 19th century following its demise, politically they became increasingly provincial and parochial, a legacy that prevails even today. Each town, city, county, duchy, principality, and kingdom developed its own laws and lifestyle and cultivated its own customs, even costumes. Some, like Bavaria and Saxony, rose to become middleweight European powers in the 18th century, and one, Prussia (sometimes derisively referred to as "not a state with an army but an army with a state"), even became a heavyweight—so musclebound that by the second half of the 18th century King Frederick the Great was sitting down with Austria's Empress Maria Theresa and Russian Tsarina Catherine the Great to divide Poland and make colonial mincemeat of other independent countries of Eastern Europe. By 1870, when Prussia went to war against France, it was so powerful that it could impose hegemonial unity—a kind of "second Reich"—on the other German states. The eight decades of unity from 1871 to 1949, a period marked by jingoism, chauvinism, military conquest, and racism, failed to create a single picture from the jigsaw pieces. Today these local differences are being not only preserved but nurtured and encouraged. Cultivating local accents and dialects is a vogue. Provincial museums are sprouting. Hardly a day passes, especially in the balmier months of the year, without dozens of local religious, historical, and folk festivals taking place in small towns and the provinces.

But while diversity has its merits and is certainly colorful, it also contributes to a lack of national identity. That, and the collapse of the eastern German economy, have helped to foster the xenophobia, racism, and violence that have erupted, particularly in eastern Germany, since the 1990 reunification. The irony is that the neo-Nazis who shout "Germany for

Germans!" during their demonstrations and attacks on foreigners and asylum-seekers do not really know what it
means. East Germans were deliberately deprived of their
sense of Germanness during the 40 years of Communist
rule; West Germans sublimated it in the hyper-prosperity
and consumer consciousness of their postwar Economic
Miracle. The challenge, as the responsible political leaders
are now discovering, is not so much one of putting Germany
back together again, but of actually creating it.

Germany for Travellers

Given this diversity, small wonder that Germany is so hard to
describe. Which Germany? How many Germanys? They cannot be counted. Yet together they make it a fascinating and
rewarding country for travellers. Nothing is really far away,
but visiting Germany does require a *strategy,* for Germany
cannot be properly explored fully, or enjoyed to its maximum, in a week or two, or even in a month or two.

Instead, you should approach the country by selected
areas or a region, preferably with a cultural, historical, artistic, or scenic theme, and if that trip whets your appetite, plan
to return for a different view some other year. A week or two
spent hopping around from one place to another spanning
all points on the compass will be more frustrating than
pleasurable. Bear in mind, too, that with few exceptions the
really large cities offer the least, because virtually all of them
were reduced to rubble during World War II and are
reconstructions—sometimes good but more often bad—of
what they once were. Germany is at its best in the smaller
cities and towns, in the villages and countryside.

There are also numerous officially named, and sometimes
clearly marked, **touristic routes** that lead through the most
historic towns, the most picturesque villages, and the most
breathtaking scenery. They are the products of local and
regional tourism promoters who began plotting them out in
the 1950s and 1960s during the *Wirtschaftswunder* (Economic Miracle) years, when the Germans yearned for, and
started buying, the beetle-shaped cars they were exporting so
successfully. These itineraries—which avoid the no-speed-
limit multilane Autobahns—follow country roads and numbered federal highways (*Bundesstrassen*) through quaint old
villages with cobblestone streets and towns surrounded by
turreted medieval walls—offering proof not only that motoring can still be fun but also that there is still a Germany almost
as you imagined it to be.

By now there are more than 140 such routes, and quite a
number of them intersect. The oldest and most famous,

laid out more than 40 years ago, is the *Romantische Strasse* (**Romantic Road**), a 230-mile route between the Main river city of Würzburg, east of Frankfurt, and the Alpine town of Füssen, near Innsbruck, Austria. Others (some of which we have included in our descriptions of various regions) are: the *Deutsche Märchenstrasse* (**German Fairy Tale Road**), which begins at Hanau, just east of Frankfurt, and winds its way generally northward for more than 300 miles to Bremen; the *Bier und Burgen Strasse* (**Beer and Castle Road**), which starts just a little south of Nürnberg and then runs westward to the Neckar river and continues along that waterway north to Heidelberg; the *Deutsche Weinstrasse* (**German Wine Route**), a circular itinerary through the wine-growing region west of the Rhine between the cities of Mainz and Karlsruhe; the *Barockstrasse* (**Baroque Road**), a convoluted itinerary of dazzling Baroque monasteries and churches in Swabia, south of Stuttgart and north of Lake Constance; and the *Schwarzwald Hochstrasse* (**Black Forest Highway**) in the country's southwestern corner. Enthusiastically promoted with a plethora of literature, maps, and package deals by local boosters in the communities along their paths, all six rate very high with German vacationers themselves and reveal the country at its best. Moreover, they are easily and quickly accessible to anyone setting out with a rental car from Frankfurt airport, where most visitors arrive.

Berlin

Our more detailed discussion of Germany's attractions begins, ironically, with a city that for most of the postwar period was really two, symbolic of the country's Cold War division: Berlin. It is the only capital—in both the political sense and by the yardstick of global cosmopolitan values—a unified Germany ever had. It played the political role only during those eight decades of German unity; the global cosmopolitan one only during the 14 years of the Weimar Republic, by which time Berlin was the undisputed heart of literary, musical, theatrical, artistic, fashionable, scientific, and technological Europe and also the Continent's biggest metropolis. Now the Wall is gone and the city once again has been designated Germany's capital—though given the tens of billions of deutsche marks it will cost, the formidable logistics, the resistance of people who would prefer to remain in Bonn, and the fear that Berlin again will arrogate to itself the central powers undermining federalism that it had from 1870 until 1945, it will be the late 1990s, if not the next decade, before it becomes the actual seat of government. Still, Berlin is already girding to resume its roles as the country's cosmopolitan center and, with more than 3.4 million inhabitants, as the largest city in Europe between Paris and Moscow.

A half century of dictatorship, wartime devastation, postwar occupation, Cold War division, and isolation from the European mainstream have, of course, left their mark on Berlin. But it is one of the great cities of the world, and Berliners, in the face of adversity, are unique—in their spirit, their sense of humor, their love of art and culture, and their zest for life. The city's chic, carefree, tolerant, and enthusiastic atmosphere is infectious. No other German city has as many truly first-rate museums, art collections, symphony orchestras, opera houses, theaters, and cabarets, or as vibrant a nightlife.

Northern Germany

Northern Germany and the **Hanseatic Cities** are a world of their own. Not only is this the heartland of *Plattdeutsch*—Low German—it is also a region that looks to its Scandinavian neighbors across the Baltic, and across the North Sea to England. Indeed, Hamburgers are said to be more British than the British themselves.

It is a region of proud independence—other Germans call it cold aloofness—spiced by the lusty rambunctiousness that you find in all great harbor towns. **Bremen** and **Hamburg**, the latter Germany's second-largest city and Europe's second-biggest port after Rotterdam, were always and still are so independent that they are also *Bundesländer,* that is, states of the Federal Republic. **Lübeck**, pristine in its historic red-brick architecture, is famed not only as the birthplace of Thomas Mann and as the setting of his first novel, *Buddenbrooks,* but also for its marzipan. **Lüneburg**, southeast of Hamburg, became rich through the mining of salt—the white gold of the Middle Ages—and today is a perfectly preserved medieval town. **Schwerin, Rostock,** and the Baltic coastline of **Mecklenburg–West Pomerania** are the gems of Germany's northeast and are rapidly regaining their erstwhile popularity as travel and vacation destinations. All these cities—with the exception of Schwerin—were members of the Hanseatic League, the protective alliance of mercantile and seafaring city-states that dominated the trade of Europe from the 13th through the 17th centuries. **Schleswig-Holstein**, Germany's northernmost state, whose shores are washed by both the North Sea and the Baltic, is a land of brick architecture, dikes, windmills, and vast expanses of grazing pastures that remind visitors of the Netherlands and Denmark.

The Center

What we call the Center is the area bordered by the North German Plain to the north, the densely wooded Harz mountains and the states of Saxony-Anhalt and Thuringia to the east, the raw hills of the Rhön range—the highlands of Hesse—in the south, and the Westerwald and Sauerland ranges in the west, the latter laced by the lush, romantic valleys of the Werra, Fulda, Weser, Leine, Eder, and Lahn rivers. This is northern Hesse and Lower Saxony, the home base of the Guelphs, who inherited the duchy of Brunswick that became the kingdom of Hannover. Three Hannoverian kings—George I, II, and III—wore the crowns of both this and the English monarchies. **Hannover** has only a few reminders of its prewar splendor, as is the case with **Braunschweig** (Brunswick) and **Kassel**. But the region's smaller cities and towns—**Hameln**, famed for the Pied Piper legend, **Einbeck**, renowned for its beer, **Celle**, **Goslar**, and **Marburg** and **Göttingen**, the last two both university centers—are perfect gems of half-timbered architecture. North American visitors are still rare in this area, but the Danes, Swedes, Dutch, and English converge on it in droves.

Eastern Germany

The heartland of the former German Democratic Republic—Eastern Germany—is Bach-Handel-Luther-Goethe-Schiller country, especially the southern states of Thuringia and Saxony. The great men themselves are commemorated by the houses in which they were born or lived. **Eisenach**, where Luther attended school as a youngster and later translated the Bible, is also the birthplace of Johann Sebastian Bach, whose family home today is a magnificent museum. **Erfurt**, where Luther studied and became a friar, is the largest and best-preserved medieval city in all Germany, rich with treasures of art and architecture. In **Weimar**, capital of a duchy whose rulers lavishly patronized the arts and literature, Bach spent the first two decades of his musical career, and both Goethe and Schiller lived here in the late 18th and early 19th centuries. Their homes, now museums, are among the region's chief attractions. Handel's birth house in **Halle** is an important musical-instrument museum. The spirit of Luther is indelibly etched in the churches and castle of **Wittenberg**. Bach's name haunts **Leipzig**, where from 1723 to his death in 1750 he was music director of St. Thomas's Church. **Dresden**, the "Florence on the Elbe"—until the February 1945 air raid that turned it into a wasteland—still has its Zwinger palace, the most exquisite example of Baroque architecture in all Germany, and its famous Semper opera house, where Richard Wagner and Richard Strauss premiered many of their works.

For the more than 40 years of Germany's division, a journey to these areas entailed running an obstacle course of bureaucratic formalities and was accompanied by the chilling thrills of travelling behind the Iron Curtain. All that is now history. But another complication has arisen that will prevail for the next two to three years, if not longer. Eastern Germany is virtually fully booked up thanks to the paucity of good hotels and the droves of western German travellers seeking either to do business there or to see places from which they were barred during the country's division.

North Rhine

Moving back west, we then cover **Cologne** in the heart of the Northrhine–Westphalia area. Besides the obvious—the cathedral—steep yourself in the city's Roman past and save time to visit some of its dozen Romanesque churches, several of which predate Charlemagne by a couple of centuries. Of the city's many museums, the Roman-Germanic, with its treasures of Roman glass and sculpture; the Ludwig, renowned for its stupendous collection of modern and contemporary art; and the Wallraf-Richartz, loaded with 13th- through 19th-century paintings, are the most important. The *Altstadt,* the old city quarter, abounds with colorful taverns, all dispensing *Kölsch,* the tart, distinctive local beer.

The **Northwest**, that stretch of the Rhine around Cologne from Bonn to Düsseldorf, is the management and financial center of Germany's industrial heartland, and includes the medieval cities of Münster and Osnabrück as well as the surrounding Münsterland. Its attractions, however, are not the functional government buildings in Bonn or the corporate headquarters and banks in Düsseldorf. Besides being Beethoven's birthplace (naturally, the house is a museum), **Bonn** really *is* a charming provincial town worth more than a detour. **Düsseldorf** lures travellers with its many fine restaurants, the nightlife in its cobblestone Altstadt, its role as a center of contemporary art, and the Königsallee, one of Germany's most elegant (and expensive) shopping streets, a "miraculous kilometer" of conspicuous consumption. Though not a Rhineside city, **Aachen**, with its coronation cathedral, Holy Roman throne, and Charlemagne's bejeweled gold sarcophagus, is vital to understanding what the Rhine is all about. It is less than an hour west by car or train from either Bonn or Cologne, near the Belgian border. **Münster**, the **Münsterland** (with its profusion of moated castles), and 1,200-year-old **Osnabrück** are the heart of northern Westphalia and the cradle of Germanic national consciousness. It was in these two cities where the Peace of Westphalia, ending the Thirty Years' War, was negotiated and signed in 1648, and it was near Osnabrück, as recent excavations are proving, where Hermann (Arminius) defeated the Romans in A.D. 9. Both are cities of magnificent cathedrals and churches, colorful old quarters, and important museums.

Central Rhine

Of Germany's many wine-growing regions, one of the most idyllic (if you shut your eyes to the mobs of weekend and summer visitors) is the Moseltal, the **Mosel river valley**, which twists and winds from Trier near the Luxembourg border east to Koblenz, where it flows into the Rhine. The valley is important not only for connoisseurs of wine, who have long rated those of the Mosel on a par with the vintages of the Rhine, but for **Trier**'s Roman ruins and the picture-postcard medieval towns along the river. To appreciate this area fully, with perhaps a side trip to the Eifel hills and the backwoodsy Hünsruck region, driving is best, and you ought to spend a week.

Frankfurt deserves a better reputation. Derogatorily called "Krankfurt" and "Bankfurt," in the 1970s it was cited—like New York—as proof that cities as such were doomed. But it has rebounded. Alas, most Germans are either unaware of this or refuse to acknowledge it. Sure, there are bank skyscrapers, with more to come, but you will also find a reconstructed old quarter, villagelike neighborhoods, lush parks, one of Europe's best zoos, and fine museums supported by 11 percent of the municipal budget—more, proportionally, than any other city in the world spends on culture and the arts.

Frankfurt, moreover, is the ideal gateway for the Central Rhine region around it, an area encompassing far more than the **Rheingau** (best known for its wines), the cities of **Wiesbaden** and **Mainz**, and the central **Rhine river route**—site of the Mäuseturm and the Lorelei—south of Koblenz. It also includes the **Odenwald** (Oden Forest), where spring usually arrives a month before it comes to the rest of Germany; **Heidelberg**, popularized by Mark Twain in *A Tramp Abroad* and by Sigmund Romberg in *The Student Prince;* the loveliest and most dramatic segment of the **Castle Road**, along the **Neckar river**; and the **German Wine Route**, which introduces visitors to the wines of the Palatinate, less well known abroad than those of the Mosel and the Rheingau, and takes you close to the French border.

Bavaria

Northern Bavaria is the part of the former kingdom of Bavaria along and north of the Danube river (which bisects

Bavaria), today Germany's largest state geographically and its most important culturally and climatically. The **Danube region**, from Ulm to Passau via Regensburg, is almost a journey in itself, so rich in history, art, architecture, and verdant scenery that a few days hardly do it justice. North of it we focus on the best of **Franconia** ("Land of the Franks"). This area, more than half the size of Switzerland, is a microcosmic version of all of Germany's patchwork attributes. It was ceded to Bavaria by Napoleon as a reward for Maximilian I's loyalty and allegiance to France. No wonder that in Munich people still speak of Franconia as "the colony." Before Napoleon's act of largesse, Franconia was a crazy quilt of independent cities such as **Nürnberg** and **Rothenburg**; powerful church states and prince-bishoprics such as **Würzburg**, at the northern end of the Romantic Road, and **Bamberg**, one of the most beautiful towns in the entire country; and various margraviates and dwarf duchies such as **Bayreuth**, site of the yearly Wagner Festival, and **Coburg**, home of Queen Victoria's beloved Albert. To explore it all would take weeks. Our discussion concentrates on the highlights and a few selected routes.

The **Romantic Road** is the tourist route to which we have devoted a separate chapter. It is a route that will take you southward from Würzburg through such perfectly preserved, completely walled medieval cities as **Rothenburg**, **Dinkelsbühl**, and **Nördlingen**, across the Danube to 2,000-year-old **Augsburg**, and farther south to the Bavarian Alps, where you will find "Dream King" Ludwig II's 19th-century fairy-tale castle, **Neuschwanstein**.

Munich is Germany's "secret capital," the city toward which most tourists—several million annually—gravitate, and where most Germans—60 percent, according to various surveys—would like to live if they could. It has no match in art, music, cuisine, and the joys of life: a fulfillment of Bavarian King Ludwig I's dream to make his capital a city "of which all Germans will be proud." Alas, there is almost nothing in Germany except Berlin to equal its cost, though the visitor is likely to find the price worth paying.

Southern Bavaria (also called Upper Bavaria because it is higher in altitude) encompasses the Bavarian Alps, which stretch in jagged, snow-capped majesty along the Austrian frontier from Berchtesgaden, near Salzburg in the east, to the Allgäu district and the eastern tip of the Bodensee (Lake Constance) in the west. It is a land of beautiful lakes, highland pastures, neat mountain villages, Baroque churches topped by onion domes, and the castles built by the eccentric Ludwig II, whom the French poet Paul Verlaine gushingly called "the Sun King of the 19th century."

But Bavaria also means medieval towns such as Landshut, Burghaüsen, and Wasserburg.

Southwestern Germany

Stuttgart, once capital of the kingdom of Württemberg, is today the heart of Germany's technological belt and home of two of the country's most expensive and prestigious car brands, Mercedes-Benz and Porsche (BMWs are made in Munich). More important, however, it is the center of **Swabia**, a region that, to the north, includes the medieval city of **Schwäbisch Hall**, and, to the south, the lovely old university town of **Tübingen**, the German shore of Lake Constance, and the **Baroque Road**, which leads to the spectacular churches and monasteries of Zwiefalten, Ochsenhausen, and Weingarten.

The **Black Forest** and **Baden**, extending along the right bank of the Upper Rhine from Baden-Baden to the Swiss border, is Europe's oldest vacationland. Not only did the Romans come here for rest and recreation, but it was in the densely wooded hill country of the Schwarzwald (Black Forest) and its picturesque cuckoo clock–making villages that modern tourism began in the 19th century with the advent of the railroads. More important (at least for those who agree that half the fun of travelling is eating when you get there), this small niche of Germany, with its distinct regional cuisine partly influenced by neighboring France and Switzerland, boasts the best culinary delights the country has to offer, not to mention more starred and top-rated restaurants per capita and per square mile than any other region of Germany. To add to your pleasure, the best of them are in centuries-old inns. Our coverage includes the resort villages of Triberg, Hinterzarten, and Titisee, where you will find as many cross-country skiers in winter as hikers in summer, and, of course, the gold-plated spa and casino city of **Baden-Baden** as well as medieval **Freiburg im Briesgau**, with its magnificent Gothic minster.

To be sure, there is more to Germany than we can cover in this book: the Saarland (Germany's smallest state, bordering Luxembourg and France) and the Nahe river valley between the Mosel and the Rhine lie too far afield geographically to relate to our other regions. But there is more than enough variety and pleasure in each of the areas we do cover to lure you back again and again to other parts of the jigsaw puzzle that is Germany. Most of us who have observed and travelled in it for decades as journalists and writers are confident that the Germans will soon deal effectively with the problems that have arisen since reunification. The overwhelming majority of Germans, east and west, want the democratic and tolerant republic they now have. They are not going to let a tiny minority of radicals and extremists undermine or destroy it.

USEFUL FACTS

When to Go

Virtually any season is inviting for the visitor to Germany. In the Rhineland and the Altes Land along the Elbe, the showy blossoms of fruit trees brighten the landscape in April and May. Near Mannheim, May and June are asparagus time, when special menus feature that most springlike of vegetables in dozens of ways. Swollen streams rush and seethe in the Harz Mountains.

When summer days are hot and thundery, the lakes of Upper Bavaria and Mecklenburg provide refreshing swimming. Hamburg is hot, but there is cool sailing in the blue waters of the Baltic off Kiel and the island of Rügen.

September–October is grape-harvest time in the valleys of the Rhine, Mosel, and Danube rivers. *Altweiber Sommer* (Indian Summer) these fall days are called, when the gold of the grapevines and cornstalks flashes in the bright sun and there are wine festivals in the villages along the wine rivers. And late September and early October mean heavy beer drinking in Munich, of course—*Oktoberfest.*

November can be overcast. December may be, too, but it hardly matters, for the merriment of Christmas markets is everywhere. In Nürnberg, it's toy-market time.

Full-fledged winter brings with it in the Rhineland the gaiety of the carnivals preceding Lent. Munich celebrates with *Fasching;* the Black Forest with *Fasnet;* Cologne with *Fasteleer.* Skiers profit by the snow in the Black Forest and the Bavarian Alps; the more culturally inclined in city centers have a wide choice of operas and concerts and ballets to attend, not to mention castles and museums—sans crowds— to visit.

Entry Documents

Only a valid passport is needed for citizens of the United States, Australia, Canada, or New Zealand wishing to visit Germany for stays of three months or less. Identity cards are sufficient for British subjects.

Arrival at Major Gateways by Air

From almost anywhere in North America and the United Kingdom, flying to Germany is easy. Lufthansa, Germany's national carrier, offers nonstop service to Frankfurt from

Atlanta, Boston, Chicago, Dallas/Fort Worth, Detroit, Los Angeles, Miami, New York, Newark, San Francisco, and Washington, D.C. The airline also flies to Frankfurt from Houston with one stop. Connections can be made through Frankfurt to Berlin, Cologne/Bonn, Dresden, Düsseldorf, Hamburg, Leipzig, Munich, Nürnberg, Stuttgart, and other smaller German cities.

Lufthansa offers nonstop service to Düsseldorf and Munich from New York, and there is nonstop service from Miami and Los Angeles to Munich on joint Lufthansa-Lauda Air flights.

Lufthansa tickets will take air-weary travellers by **InterCity Express** train, in first class, from Frankfurt-am-Main or Düsseldorf airports along the Rhine to Cologne, Bonn, or Düsseldorf rail stations. The trip to Cologne from Frankfurt takes two hours; to Düsseldorf it's two and a half hours—only about an hour more than flying. A similar service operates between Frankfurt airport and the Stuttgart train station. The same rail service is available for the return journey for passengers departing Germany from Frankfurt on a Lufthansa flight. Reservations must be made when you book your plane tickets, however.

Airlines flying to Germany from the United States, in addition to Lufthansa, are American, Delta, Northwest, TWA, United, USAir, and the scheduled charter airline LTU. From Chicago American offers nonstop flights to Düsseldorf, Frankfurt, and Munich.

There is nonstop Lufthansa service to Frankfurt from Montreal, Toronto, and Vancouver, with connections to other points. Air Canada flies nonstop from Toronto and Frankfurt, and provides flights via Paris to Düsseldorf from Toronto. Canadian Airlines offers nonstop Toronto–Munich service as well as nonstop service from Vancouver to Frankfurt. From Calgary and Edmonton there are joint Canadian Airlines-Lufthansa flights to Frankfurt.

From Sydney Lufthansa flies nonstop to Frankfurt, with flights originating in Melbourne. Qantas flies to Frankfurt from Sydney and Melbourne via Bangkok, Thailand. Cathay Pacific's Frankfurt flights depart from Brisbane and Perth, as well as from Melbourne and Sydney, with a change of aircraft in Hong Kong. Air New Zealand flies to Frankfurt from Auckland via Los Angeles.

British travellers, like their North American counterparts, have an abundance of flights from which to choose. There is nonstop Lufthansa service from London to Berlin, Bremen, Cologne/Bonn, Düsseldorf, Frankfurt, Hamburg, Hannover, Munich, and Stuttgart. There is Lufthansa service as well to Frankfurt and Düsseldorf from Birmingham and Manchester, and British Airways service from those cities to several German destinations. British Airways and Lufthansa also fly from Glasgow to Frankfurt.

Getting in from the Airports

Efficient bus or train service links major German airports with the cities they serve. At Frankfurt there is a train station directly beneath the airport, with trains making the 11-minute run to the city center every ten minutes. There is also regular InterCity (IC) rail service from the airport station to many other cities in the country, and vice versa. Lufthansa operates hourly bus service from the airport to Heidelberg and Mannheim.

Munich's new airport, opened in 1992 and located more than 35 km (22 miles) from the city, has an S-Bahn (interurban train) platform on the lowest level of the terminal building, with service to the city center, a 40-minute ride, every 20 minutes. Düsseldorf airport also has a rail connection to the center of the city, and in all major cities bus service to and from the city is offered. This includes bus service from the Hamburg airport to Lübeck.

In Berlin, taxis and the number 109 bus are the links from Tegel airport to the city center; an S-Bahn operates from Schönefeld airport; a subway line (U-6) and the number 119 bus connect Tempelhof airport to the city center.

West German trains are punctual and efficient. A special high-speed InterCity Express (ICE) began hourly service between Hamburg and Munich in 1991, with stops in Göttingen, Kassel, Fulda, Frankfurt, Mannheim, Stuttgart, Ulm, and Augsburg. The train takes 6 hours between Hamburg and Munich—a trip that otherwise takes 8½ hours—and just an hour and 25 minutes from Frankfurt to Stuttgart—normally a 2½-hour trip. A more direct line linking Hamburg and Munich via Hannover, Fulda, Würzburg, Nürnberg, and Augsburg was introduced in 1992, reducing the total travel time to less than 6 hours.

A second high-speed train went into operation in 1992 on the Hamburg route, and two more—between Bremen and Hannover with links to Berlin and between Frankfurt and Hannover with links to Berlin—went into operation in 1993.

Frequent train service once more joins east and west, and though service continues to be slower in the east, it is somewhat better than it was before reunification. InterCity trains now connect the most important cities in west and east.

Before leaving for Germany, look into the German Rail passes and companion passes, possession of which will eliminate waits at ticket counters. They also will allow you to spread a fixed number of travel days—5, 10, or 15—over a month-long period. Both first- and second-class passes are sold, and they may be used on all trains, including the super-express InterCity trains, as well as on selected subways, buses, and ships. With them, reservations are not required (though they are advised). German Rail passes must be purchased before you leave home, however.

Further information is available from travel agents and, in the United States, from German Rail/DER Tours, 9501 West Devon Avenue, Rosemont, Illinois 60018, Tel: (708) 692-6300; European Rail Services/DER Tours, 3400 Peachtree Road Northeast, Atlanta, Georgia 30326, Tel: (404) 266-9555; and German Rail, 20 Park Plaza, Boston, Massachusetts 02116, Tel: (617) 542-0577. In Canada, contact German Rail/DER Travel, 904 The East Mall, Etobicoke, Ontario M9B 6K2, Tel: (416) 695-1211. In Britain, contact German Rail Passenger Sales, 18 Conduit Street, London W1R 9TD, Tel: (071) 290-1135.

Telephoning

The international telephone code for all of Germany is now 49. When calling from within Germany, dial zero before city codes.

Calling from west to east Germany has improved considerably, but still requires patience. All east German numbers were correct as of press time, but numbers there will continue to change.

Both local and long-distance calls can be made from all post offices and coin-operated street booths. Thirty pfennigs is the base charge for a local call from a booth; from a hotel it is considerably higher. A **Telefonkarte** (telephone card) will greatly simplify your long-distance and local calling and eliminate the need for coins. The cards, obtainable at any German post office, are sold in denominations of DM 20–50. To use, insert the card in any public *Kartentelefon* (card phone) and make your call; a meter tells you how much credit you have left on the card.

Addresses

Street names in eastern Germany were correct as of press time, but keep in mind that streets still bearing the names of heroes of the former Communist regime may change in the coming months.

Germany adopted a new nationwide system of postal codes in July 1993. The international postal code for Germany begins with a D (Deutschland) and is followed by five digits and the name of the city or town.

Local Time

Germany is nine hours ahead of Pacific Standard Time, six hours ahead of Eastern Standard Time, and one hour ahead of Greenwich Mean Time; during the changeover to daylight savings time there is a brief period when Germany is another hour behind or ahead. Sydney is ten hours ahead of Germany.

Electric Current

The electric current is 220 volts; North American appliances will require an adapter and adapter plugs.

Currency

The monetary unit of Germany is the deutsche mark, worth 100 pfennigs. Coins come in denominations of 5, 2, and 1 mark and in 50-, 10-, 5-, 2-, and 1-pfennig pieces; bills come in denominations of DM 1,000, 500, 200, 100, 50, 20, 10, and 5.

Tipping

In restaurants and cafés a service charge is added to the bill, but rounding out the total bill with an extra smaller amount is expected. Tipping is also expected by taxi drivers and porters and in beauty parlors. Be sure to carry small change for tipping attendants in some W.C.s.

Renting a Car and Driving

Germany has an outstanding toll-free road system with many superhighways where service stations are open 24 hours a day. The traffic signs are international. Unless marked otherwise, there is no speed limit on the Autobahns in Germany, but 80 mph (130 km/p/h) is the recommended speed. The standard in-town speed limit unless otherwise posted is 31 mph (50 km/p/h).

You can arrange to rent a car at the airport where you'll be landing when you purchase your airline ticket. Avis, Budget, ECP, Euro-Car, Euro-Rent, Hertz, Swiss Wheel, and Thrifty are among the car-rental companies operating in Germany. Arrangements for car leasing for short and long stays can also be made in North America through Auto-Europe, Box 1097, Camden, Maine 04843; Tel: (800) 223-5555. Most major credit cards are accepted for car rental in Germany. Liability insurance is required, but is usually included in the rental fee. Either a national or an international driver's license is also required.

Information desks for motorists are maintained at important border crossing points, including Wassersiebener Bucht near Flensburg (the E 3 from Denmark); Ellen near Emmerich on the motorway from Holland; and Kiefersfelden and Schwarzbach on the motorways from Austria. The major German automobile clubs also have some border offices and offices in large cities.

Road assistance is provided free of charge (except for the cost of the materials) by the Allgemeiner Deutscher Automobil Club (ADAC), which has emergency patrols on frequently travelled roads and motorways. There are orange emergency boxes at frequent intervals along all Autobahn routes.

Around Germany

By Bus. English-language bus tours following such popular touristic routes as the Grimm brothers' Fairy Tale Road and the Romantic Road (including half-timbered towns and villages like Rothenburg, Dinkelsbühl, Nördlingen, and towns in the former East Germany) are offered by Europa-Bus; bookings can be made by writing to Deutsche Touring, GmbH, Am Römerhof 17, D-60486 Frankfurt-am-Main, Germany, or call (69) 790-3251. Among operators providing package tours from North America (with air fare, accommodations, and some meals included) are American Express, Brendan Tours, Colette, Cosmos, DER Globus, Gogo Tours, Euro-Lloyd Tours, Maupintour, Olson, Tauck, Travcoa, and TWA Getaway Tours.

By Boat. From Cologne to Mainz, vineyards, castles, cathedrals, and half-timbered villages edge the stretch of the Rhine river where the Lorelei sing their seductive songs. Köln-Düsseldorfer (KD) River Cruises of Europe ply the Rhine, the Main, and the Mosel from April to October, making day trips as well as three- and four-day cruises from Cologne to Frankfurt and Trier. They also cruise the Elbe river between Hamburg and Dresden in the same months, with stops in Wittenberg and Meissen. At press time, new KD Rhine-Main-Danube Canal cruises from Nürnberg to Vienna or Budapest were scheduled to begin operation in spring 1994.

Information is available from **KD River Cruises of Europe** at 2500 Westchester Avenue, Purchase, New York 10577; Tel: (914) 696-3600 or (800) 346-6525. In Canada, c/o Holiday House, 110 Richmond Street East, Toronto, Ontario M5C 1P1, Tel: (416) 367-5860; c/o Holiday House, Hotel Vancouver, Suite 108, 900 West Georgia Street, Vancouver, British Columbia V6C 2W6, Tel: (604) 687-0380; or Tours Maison, 550 Sherbrooke Street West, Suite 1660, Montreal, Quebec H3A 1B9, Tel: (514) 842-8115. In England contact the G. A. Clubb Rhine Cruise Agency, 28 South Street, Epsom KT18 7PF; Tel: (037) 274-2033.

Other boat trips are offered by local tour operators in summer on Lake Constance, the Königssee in the Bavarian Alps, Hamburg harbor, and the Danube and Elbe rivers, as well as to the Frisian Islands of the North Sea; inquire locally.

Business Hours

There are mandatory closing hours for all stores and shops in Germany: 6:30 P.M. Monday through Wednesday, and Fridays; 8:30 P.M. Thursdays; 2:00 P.M. Saturdays, except the first Saturday of each month, when they remain open until 6:00 P.M. from October through April and until 4:00 P.M. May through September. Except at major railway stations and airports no stores are permitted to be open after these hours, nor on Sundays and holidays. Most stores and shops open at 9:00 A.M. A daily lunchtime closing from noon until 3:00 P.M. is common in shops in residential neighborhoods, smaller towns, and villages.

Bank hours are normally from 9:00 A.M. to 12:30 P.M. and from 2:30 to 3:45 P.M. weekdays (Thursdays until 5:30 P.M.).

Museums are almost always closed on Mondays. Hours otherwise tend to be from 10:00 A.M. to 5:00 P.M. year-round, with slightly longer hours in summer. Churches—even some of historic and architectural importance—are certain to be open only for Sunday services; for other hours it is wise to check with the local *Verkehrsamt* (tourist office).

Offices and shops are closed on New Year's Day, Epiphany (January 6), Rose Monday and Shrove Tuesday (Carnival), Good Friday, Easter Sunday and Monday, Labor Day (May 1), Ascension Day (May or June), Whit Monday (May or June), Corpus Christi Day (June), Assumption Day (August), German Unification Day (October 3), All Saints Day (November 1), the Day of Prayer and Remembrance (November), and Christmas Eve, Christmas Day, and the day after Christmas.

Tax Free Shopping

If you are a resident of a country outside the European Community (E.C.) you are entitled to a full refund of the Value Added Tax (*Mehrwertsteuer*) that is included in all your purchases exported from Germany. The tax was 15 percent or 7.5 percent (depending on the kind of item) at the time we went to press.

The procedure for obtaining this refund is as follows: All department stores and most major shops will issue a **Tax Free Shopping Check** (and fill it out for you) at the time of your purchase. Smaller shops and boutiques do not usually have these available, in which case you'll need to acquire a form called an *Ausfuhr- und Abnehmerbescheinigung* (a certificate of export) and have it filled in for each purchase you make. You can buy these forms at most larger stores selling office supplies (*Bürobedarf*). Should you have a problem obtaining one, check with the local tourist information office.

When you leave Germany, present the Tax Free Check or the Export Certificate with the receipt from the store and the *unused* goods themselves to the German Customs (*Zoll*) office at the point of exit. They will stamp your check. At major border crossings and most airports you can get your stamp from the customs office there and obtain your cash refund at the *Verkehrsbank*. In Berlin the refund service is provided by the Berliner Bank at the Tegel or Schönefeld airports.

For Further Information

German National Tourist Offices are located at 122 East 42nd Street, New York, New York 10168-0072, Tel: (212) 661-7200, Fax: (212) 661-7174; 11766 Wilshire Boulevard, Los Angeles, California 90025, Tel: (310) 575-9799; 175 Bloor Street East, North Tower, Toronto, Ontario M4W 3R8, Canada, Tel: (416) 968-1570; Nightingale House, 65 Curzon Street, London W1Y 7PE, England, Tel: (071) 495-3990.

—Phyllis Méras

BIBLIOGRAPHY

PETER ADAM, *Art of the Third Reich* (1992). Based on a television series made for the BBC in 1988, this is a riveting and lavishly illustrated examination of the ideo-art—painting, sculpture, architecture, films—of the National Socialists, most of which is hidden away and accessible only to scholars.

JEAN ANDERSON AND HEDY WÜRZ, *The New German Cookbook* (1993). Over 230 recipes, some traditional and some contemporary; the recipes are identified by region.

JOHN ARDAUGH, *Germany and the New Germans* (1987). A British Francophile's view of Germany before the fall of the Berlin Wall, with the emphasis on West Germany: How people think, lifestyles, social attitudes and opinions.

BABEL TRANSLATIONS, EDS., *Germany, A Phaidon Cultural Guide* (1985). An English translation of a German hardcover guide, indispensable for the traveller who wants additional background on the artistic, architectural, and cultural sights of the country.

ROLAND BAINTON, *Here I Stand: A Life of Martin Luther* (1950). A fascinating and meticulously researched account, regarded by many as the best one-volume Luther biography in any language. Illustrated with many woodcuts and engravings.

DENNIS L. BARK AND DAVID R. GRESS, *A History of West Germany* (1989). This brilliant and provocative two-volume study covers the period from 1945 to 1988, bringing postwar German history, and an all-star cast of diplomats and politicians, including Adenauer, Brandt, Strauss, Erhard, Heuss, Reuter, and many others, alive in vivid detail.

JULIUS BAUM, *German Cathedrals* (1956). Two hundred splendid photographs accompany a comprehensive and enlightening text describing Germany's cathedrals and explaining the various phases of German ecclesiastical architecture and sculpture in the Middle Ages.

FRANZ H. BÄUML, *Medieval Civilization in Germany 800–1273* (1969). A critical assessment by a highly regarded medievalist of the almost 500 years from the coronation of Charlemagne to the election of Rudolf of Hapsburg to the imperial throne.

HERBERT BAYER, WALTER GROPIUS, ISE GROPIUS, EDS., *Bauhaus 1919–1928* (1938; many times reprinted). This small book is required reading for anyone interested in modern art.

HEINRICH BÖLL, *Billiards at Half-Past Nine* (1962). A compelling novel by one of Germany's best-known writers about the compromises made by a rich German family during the Hitler years. Translated from the German.

———, *The Stories of Heinrich Böll* (1986). Spanning almost four decades of our own century, these stories by one of Germany's greatest writers blend wit with a large and tragic view of life. Translated from the German.

WILLY BRANDT, *My Life in Politics* (1992). The political memoirs of Willy Brandt, who died in 1992, reveal a man of vision, integrity, and determination. An active anti-Nazi, Brandt returned from war-time exile to become mayor of West Berlin, foreign minister, and ultimately chancellor of West Germany. He was awarded the Nobel Peace Prize in 1971. Translated from the German.

JAN CHIAPUSSO, *Bach's World* (1968). A rewarding exploration of the religious, philosophical, and social milieu of Bach's time and its effect on his development.

WALTRAUD COLES AND UWE KOREIK, *Simple Etiquette in Germany (East and West)* (1991). This useful introduction to basic German customs in east and west covers such diverse topics as meeting people, giving presents, the German home, and business etiquette.

GORDON CRAIG, *Germany 1866–1945* (1978). Beautifully written and indispensable for readers interested in Germany's recent past, this book by the Sterling Professor of Humanities emeritus at Stanford University remains the best single account of the turbulent political, cultural, and economic life of Germany during the years 1866–1945.

————, *The Germans* (1982). A highly readable and knowledgeable portrait of postwar Germany—a tour rooted in the past but with a contemporary view of religion, business and finance, literature, the role of women, academic life, the German-Jewish relationship, and the changing German language.

EDWARD CRANKSHAW, *Bismarck* (1981). An objective and highly readable life of Prince Otto Eduard Leopold von Bismarck, the first chancellor of the German Empire (1871–1890) and a seminal figure in Germany's Prussian past.

ROBERT DARNTON, *Berlin Journal 1989–1990* (1991). The first eyewitness account, by a noted historian, of the events that led to the opening of the Berlin Wall and the collapse of East Germany's Communist regime.

JOHN DORNBERG, *Munich 1923: The Story of Hitler's First Grab for Power* (British title: *The Putsch That Failed*) (1982). A dramatized, blow-by-blow re-enactment of Hitler's failed 1923 Munich "beerhall putsch" based on police documents, trial records, newspaper reports, a Bavarian parliamentary investigation, and the personal recollections of participants and eyewitnesses who were interviewed by the author.

JOHANN PETER ECKERMANN, *Conversations with Goethe* (1836). Early-19th-century Germany from the viewpoint of the most renowned German figure of the Enlightenment. "The best German book there is," according to Nietzsche. Translated from the German.

LOTTE EISNER, *The Haunted Screen* (1973). An intriguing survey of the great Expressionist films (*Nosferatu, The Cabinet of Dr. Caligari,* and *Metropolis* among them) produced during the Golden Age of German cinema, which lasted from the end of World War I to the advent of sound. Translated from the French.

ERIK ERIKSON, *Young Man Luther* (1962). The origins of a rebel; psychobiography at its best.

MARTIN ESSLIN, *Brecht: The Man and His Work* (1960). An acute and penetrating analysis of Bertolt Brecht, one of the most influential playwrights of the 20th century.

JOACHIM C. FEST, *Hitler* (1973). There are several good biographies about Hitler to choose from, including works by Robert Payne and John Toland, but Fest's is one of the best researched and most objective.

UTE FREVERT, *Women in German History: From Bourgeois Emancipation to Sexual Liberation* (1989). A fascinating collection of scholarly essays on the roles of women in 19th- and 20th-century German society.

OTTO FRIEDRICH, *Before the Deluge: A Portrait of Berlin in the 1920's* (1972). A comprehensive, fascinating portrait by a noted American journalist of the political, cultural, and social life of Berlin between the wars and the people who created and destroyed it.

MARY FULBROOK, *A Concise History of Germany* (1990). An unusually clear and informative guide to the twists and turns of German history, from the early Middle Ages to the present day, and the only single-volume history of Germany in English that offers a broad, general coverage of the main themes and topics.

H. F. GARTEN, *Modern German Drama* (1959). A lively and readable analysis of dramatists from Hauptmann to Brecht to the Swiss Dürrenmatt, exploring the art form that has served as Germany's main vehicle for spiritual, social, and political expression.

PETER GAY, *Weimar Culture: The Outsider as Insider* (1968). A brief historical introduction by a prominent scholar to the seminal between-the-wars epoch.

KARL GEIRINGER, *The Bach Family: Seven Generations of Creative Genius* (1954). Includes a large section on the life and work of Johann Sebastian Bach, tracing his various moves around and in Erfurt, Weimar, and Leipzig. Includes map, music, and index of compositions by members of the Bach family.

GÜNTER GRASS, *The Tin Drum* (1959). Perhaps the most famous novel about life in post–World War II Germany as it struggled to recover from the devastation of war and defeat. Translated from the German.

————, *Two States—One Nation?* (1990). In this caustic and compelling collection of short essays and public addresses,

Germany's most celebrated contemporary author argues against a united Germany. Translated from the German.

MARTIN GREGOR-DELLIN, *Richard Wagner: His Life, His Work, His Century* (1980). An entertaining and masterful analysis of the most controversial figure in the history of opera, from his early hardships and artistic frustrations to his subsequent triumphs. Translated from the German.

LEONARD GROSS, *The Last Jews in Berlin* (1982). Gripping true stories of a handful of Jews who remained in Berlin during World War II and managed to escape the Gestapo and SS by hiding out in the homes of non-Jewish German friends.

RICHARD HANSER, *A Noble Treason: The Revolt of the Munich Students Against Hitler* (1979). A dramatic account of the German resistance movement known as "The White Rose," founded by Hans Scholl and his sister Sophie when they were students at Munich University. The group's anti-Nazi leaflet campaign led to their arrest and trial for treason in 1943, and their subsequent execution in Munich's Stadelheim prison.

KARSTEN HARRIES, *The Bavarian Rococo Church: Between Faith and Aestheticism* (1983). Through careful analysis and lavish illustration, the reader is introduced to a wide variety of Bavarian churches as well as those features of the Bavarian Rococo that determine its particular style and set it apart from or relate it to the French Rococo and the Italian Baroque.

CHARLES W. HAXTHAUSEN AND HEIDRUN SUHR, EDS., *Berlin: Culture & Metropolis* (1990). Scholars in art history, film studies, literature, history, and sociology cover diverse aspects of Berlin in the 20th century, writing on such topics as cabaret, the celebration of Berlin's 750th anniversary, and the cultural contributions of Ernst Ludwig Kirchner, George Grosz, Alfred Döblin, and Christa Wolf.

FRIEDRICH HEER, *The Holy Roman Empire* (1968). In this excellent survey, a noted Austrian historian traces the Holy Roman Empire from the time of Charlemagne through the rise and decline of the Hapsburgs.

HEINRICH HEINE, *The Poetry and Prose of Heinrich Heine.* Edited by Frederic Ewen. In these writings, Heine, a product of the Napoleonic era and one of the country's literary greats, evokes the Germany of his day.

CHRISTOPHER HOGWOOD, *Handel* (1984). A famous conductor sketches a comprehensive and entertaining portrait of the developing character and career of Handel, from his early years in Halle and Hamburg to the heyday of opera and oratorio in London.

WERNER HÜLSBERG, *The German Greens: A Social and Political Profile* (1988). This in-depth analysis of Germany's Green movement is the first and most comprehensive account of what is perhaps the most successful radical movement of the 1980s. Translated from the German.

MICHAEL JACKSON, *The New World Guide to Beer* (1977). This comprehensive volume, recognized as the standard in its field, lives up to its name by covering the world, with Germany coming in for a lion's share of the *prosits*.

CHRISTOS M. JOACHIMIDES, NORMAN ROSENTHAL, AND WIELAND SCHMIED, EDS., *German Art of the 20th Century* (1985). Filled with breathtaking reproductions and illuminating essays covering the pre–World War I era through the "Golden Twenties," the Nazi period, and West German painting and sculpture of recent years. The book includes a chronology linking the major political/artistic/cultural events of 20th-century German history.

HUGH JOHNSON, *Atlas of German Wines and Traveller's Guide to the Vineyards* (1986). By one of the world's leading authorities on wine. Includes full-color photographs and maps, and a glossary of German wine terms.

HILDEGARD KNEF, *The Gift Horse* (1970). Berlin-born Knef, one of Germany's most popular postwar stars, reveals her considerable gifts as a writer in this best-selling account of her working-class upbringing in the Thirties, her involvement with a Nazi officer, and the subsequent twists and turns of her long career in theater and films.

KÄTHE KOLLWITZ, *The Diary and Letters of Käthe Kollwitz* (1988). This diary of one of the great German Expressionist artists explains much of the spirit, wisdom, and internal struggle that was eventually transmuted into her art.

J. KONRAD, *German Family Research Made Simple* (1989). If you're interested in tracing your German roots, this informative and easy-to-follow guide will make the task easier.

CLAUDIA KOONZ, *Mothers in the Fatherland: Women, the Family, and Nazi Politics* (1987). An eye-opening, groundbreaking study, compulsively readable and never less than fascinating; the first comprehensive history of the roles played by women in the Third Reich.

VICTOR LANGE, *The Classical Age of German Literature* (1982). A survey of the central, or "classical," period of German literature, with special attention to, of course, Goethe and Schiller, as well as Herder, Lessing, Richter, Wieland, and others.

————, ED., *Great German Short Novels and Stories* (1952). A Modern Library edition that provides a rich sampling of classic German short fiction, from Goethe's *The Sorrows of Young Werther* to Thomas Mann's *Death in Venice*. Works by Schiller, von Kleist, Heine, Annette von Droste-Hulshoff, Schnitzler, and Rilke are included. Translated from the German.

PETER LASKO, *The Kingdom of the Franks: Northwest Europe Before Charlemagne* (1971). An illuminating (and lavishly illustrated) study focusing on the misnamed "Dark Ages," a period with a highly developed civilization and culture, traces of which still survive.

SIEGFRIED LENZ, *The German Lesson* (1971). A bestseller when it first appeared, this powerful and moving novel explores Nazism and its aftermath in the North German provinces.

GOTTFRIED LINDEMANN, *History of German Art* (1971). A well-rounded survey in which the author discusses the special characteristics of German architecture, sculpture, painting, and the graphic arts, and describes the features that German art shares with the art of other European countries.

CHARLES S. MAIER, *The Unmasterable Past: History, Holocaust, and German National Identity* (1988). A study of West German attempts to come to terms with the Holocaust and the recent controversy surrounding conservative attempts to downplay the historical uniqueness of the German genocide against Jews and other minorities.

THOMAS MANN, *Buddenbrooks* (1902). A vivid and engrossing account of the transition of a Hanseatic (Lübeck) merchant family from 19th-century stability to early-20th-century uncertainty. The novel, banned by Hitler, endures as one of the classics of German literature. Translated from the German.

GEORGE R. MAREK, *Beethoven: A Biography of a Genius* (1969). A comprehensive and scholarly portrait that is intended, in the words of the author, to "help illumine the artist as a human being."

WILLIAM E. AND CLARE F. MARLING, *The Marling Menu-Master for Germany* (1971; many times reprinted). A comprehensive manual for translating the German menu into American English, so you won't confuse the *Hauptgerichte* (main courses) from the *Süss-Speisen* (desserts).

DAVID MARSH, *The Germans* (1990). A masterful and up-to-date account of the new, united Germany by the former chief German correspondent for London's *Financial Times;* especially interesting for its speculations on Germany's superpower prospects.

ANDREW MARTINDALE, *Gothic Art* (1967). One of the best available surveys of the period.

NANCY MITFORD, *Frederick the Great* (1970). Frederick, brilliant military strategist and statesman, scholar, musician, and patron of the arts, is sketched with wit and humor by the author, who draws almost all of her material from contemporary sources. With lavish illustrations.

CHARLES E. PASSAGE, *Friedrich Schiller* (1975). A brief and lively volume providing background for each of the nine dramas by the premier German dramatist of his time.

PIERRE RICHÉ, *Daily Life in the World of Charlemagne* (1978). A richly descriptive account of the world of the Carolingians, Riché's book focuses on the common people of the time, providing fascinating insights into, among other things, diet, medicine, methods of birth control, astrology, religion, drinking habits, superstitions, and hygiene.

JOHN ROWLANDS, *The Age of Dürer and Holbein: German Drawings 1400–1550* (1988). Although the emphasis is on Dürer and Hans Holbein the Younger, this work also surveys their contemporaries, including Lucas Cranach, Martin Schongauer, and Albrecht Altdorfer.

JEFFREY L. SAMMONS, *Heinrich Heine: A Modern Biography* (1979). The author shows how Heine arrived at poetic insight and a conception of humanistic responsibility in the face of obstacles not unlike those affecting dissident writers throughout the world in our own day.

HORST SCHARFENBERG, *The Cuisines of Germany: Regional Specialties and Traditional Home Cooking* (1989). Although it has some cookbook elements, Scharfenberg's book also provides much information about the food itself, as the title indicates. Translated from the German.

HELMUT SCHMIDT, *Men and Powers: A Political Retrospective* (1989). A bestseller in Europe, this book presents the personal insights and opinions of the former chancellor (1974–1982) of the Federal Republic of Germany, as well as a German perspective on the contributions of world leaders such as Leonid Brezhnev, Mikhail Gorbachev, Mao Zedong, Deng Xiao Ping, and presidents Nixon, Ford, Carter, and Reagan. Translated from the German.

HUBERT SCHRADE, *German Romantic Painting* (1977). The early- and mid-18th-century German Romantics were the first to exploit landscape as a theme in itself. The author, a leading German art historian, focuses on individual painters such as Caspar David Friedrich, Philipp Otto Runge, and Joseph Anton Koch.

PETER SELZ, *German Expressionist Painting* (1974). The first comprehensive study of one of the most important movements in 20th-century art, this book examines the work of the *Brücke* and *Blaue Reiter* artists working in Dresden and Munich between 1905–1914. Beautiful reproductions of paintings by Leon Kirchner, Oskar Kokoschka, Karl Schmidt-Rottluff, Max Pechstein, Max Beckmann, and others.

WILLIAM L. SHIRER, *The Rise and Fall of the Third Reich: A History of Nazi Germany* (1959, 1960). A three-volume account of the Hitler years in fast-paced, gripping, and exhaustively researched detail by a distinguished American foreign correspondent, news commentator, and chronicler of the contemporary world.

DONALD SPOTO, *Blue Angel: The Life of Marlene Dietrich* (1992). The life of the great German film star, who began her career in the theaters and cabarets of Weimar Berlin and went on to become a glamorous Hollywood icon under the tutelage of Josef von Sternberg, in juicy detail.

WOLFGANG STECHOW, *Northern Renaissance Art 1400–1600: Sources and Documents* (1966). An intriguing assortment of documents, contracts, and letters of the period, with the German section relating particularly to the work of Tilman Riemenschneider, Dürer, Grünewald, and Hans Holbein the Younger.

A.J.P. TAYLOR, *The Course of German History* (1946; 1962). First published shortly after World War II, Taylor's controversial reading of German history posits a direct line of development between the rabid anti-Semitism of Luther and that of Hitler. Although the book is dated, and generally discredited by historians, it provides an interesting, and often infuriating, perspective of the German "national character."

MARK TWAIN, *A Tramp Abroad* (1899). Twain's account of his travels in Germany are must reading for any visitor today, especially the hilarious chapter titled "That Awful German Language," in which he relates his attempts to cope with the grammar, syntax, and pronunciation of German.

MARIE VASSILTCHIKOV, *Berlin Diaries 1940–1945* (1987). A young aristocrat's life in wartime Germany; extraordinary reading.

HELMUTH JAMES VON MOLTKE, *Letters to Freya, 1939–1945* (1990). Lucid, compelling, often heartbreaking, this collection of letters from a young German aristocrat to his wife reveals how a man of great moral integrity responded to desperate times. The leader of the Kreisau circle of resisters, von Moltke was eventually executed by the Nazis. Translated from the German.

C. V. WEDGWOOD, *Thirty Years' War* (1962). The classic historical account of the religious wars that tore Germany asunder.

JOHN WILLET, *Art & Politics in the Weimar Period: The New Sobriety 1917–1933* (1978). Germany as a post–World War I center of a new cultural movement. Illustrated.

CHRISTA WOLF, *A Model Childhood* (1980). Wolf, one of the former GDR's best-known writers, examines her past as a member of the Nazi Youth Organization in this fictionalized account of a childhood spent under Nazism. Translated from the German.

—Donald S. Olson

BERLIN

By John Dornberg

It used to be claimed that you could get by with less sleep in Berlin than anywhere else in the world because of *Berliner Luft*—Berlin air. Enterprising souvenir merchants even sold it in cans to the gullible. Unfortunately, the air that Berliners breathe is not as bracingly pure as it once was, due to pollution. But one thing about the air has not changed: its electrifying quality. And you have to go to Berlin to experience that.

Few cities have made so much news and history. Berlin has usually been associated with something startling, stimulating, and significant, not just in politics but also in business, science, technology, art, theater, music, literature, cinema, fashion, and architecture.

Politically, the city has played many roles. It was the capital of the duchy of Brandenburg, which became the kingdom of Prussia in 1701 when Friedrich I crowned himself king. By 1871, Berlin was the capital of the Second German Reich, that of the kaisers; later it was the capital of the short-lived democratic Weimar Republic; and eventually it became the headquarters of Hitler's Third Reich. After the war Berlin was on the front line of the Cold War, the place where two ideologies, two political systems, and, indeed, two different worlds, met and occasionally collided. For 28 years the city's people were physically divided by the grim Berlin Wall.

The Wall began crumbling in November 1989. Today that ugly symbol of a dark era is gone, except for four small segments until now preserved as monuments (two of which will soon be gone) and broken fragments of it, mostly fake, being hawked near the Brandenburg Gate and at the former Checkpoint Charlie by souvenir vendors. The city is whole again, one immense metropolis, and by resolution of the *Bundestag,* Germany's parliament, on the road to becoming reunited Germany's capital not just in name but in fact by the late 1990s or early 21st century. Yet in many ways the Wall remains—"in people's heads," as Berliners say when speaking of the social, economic, and cultural differences between the city's western and eastern boroughs. And it remains in the physical scars of such wasteland real estate as Potsdamer Platz, once Europe's busiest square and now a huge, empty lot, deliberately carved by the Wall and its adjacent "death strip." Most of the physical scars undoubtedly will have disappeared by the year 2000.

The mental and emotional wounds of Germany's and Berlin's division, however, will take at least a generation to heal. And in a strange way those wounds are taking their toll. No longer is Berlin the Cold War city that alternately thrilled and chilled visitors with the feeling of being on the front line between two ideologies, a city to whose eastern boroughs one ventured with a sense of trepidation as well as anger at the machine-gun-toting guards. Today it is just Central Europe's largest city, with a fascinating past, an uncertain future, and a very troubling present marked by the urban problems facing every huge metropolis.

To be sure, at just over 750 years of age Berlin is an adolescent compared to other cities in Germany, some of which were medieval urban centers when Berlin was merely a frontier trading post. Youth notwithstanding, however, Berlin is special. It is delightfully kaleidoscopic, a vibrant city supercharged with high-voltage vitality and imbued with an optimism that seems to underscore its citizens' ability to survive all crises with humor and wit.

But it is not a city that can be mastered in three or four hours. To "see" Berlin may take three or four days; to figure out what makes it tick can take a lifetime.

Sheer size has something to do with this. In terms of population—3.5 million—Berlin is the largest city between Paris and Moscow. In area, 341 square miles, it is one of the biggest in the world. Nearly one third of it is covered by forests, such as the Grunewald, Spandau, Tegel, and Köpenick, as well as by farmers' fields. Parts of Berlin are still so bucolic that the city hosts the annual *Grüne Woche* (Green Week), Germany's biggest agricultural fair. Berlin has three large lakes, the Tegelersee, the Wannsee, and the Müggelsee, and two rivers, the Havel and the Spree. There are 113 miles of rivers and canals and about 1,000 bridges—more than in Venice. Before World War II the city was Germany's second-largest inland port, and both commercial shipping and pleasure boating are still common. A *Weisse Flotte* (White Fleet) of excursion steamers and ferries plies the waterways, and there are some 75,000 private pleasure boats registered in the city.

Life in Berlin is as diverse as its geography. You'll find not just one Berlin, nor even the two once divided by the Wall, but dozens: a jigsaw puzzle of neighborhoods, communities, impressions, moods, and scenes. Within the city limits there are still four 18th-century windmills, one of which was grinding grain as recently as 1980; 55 village churches dating from the 13th century; and 70 weekly outdoor produce markets.

To understand this diversity it helps to know that it was only in 1920 that Berlin became the huge metropolis it is today. That year nearly a dozen independent cities and 59 small towns were incorporated.

If the city has a common denominator, it is the distinctive Berliner dialect, plus a kind of braggadocio that other Germans call *Berliner Schnauze,* which, loosely translated, means "Berlin lippiness."

Berlin bleibt Berlin! "Berlin will always be Berlin!" So goes a popular saying. When it was coined in the 1960s after the Wall was built, it had a political meaning. Now that the Wall is just a bad memory it has a new meaning: Berlin, with more than 160 major and minor museums; 10 palaces, castles, and châteaux; three opera houses; eight symphony orchestras; six dozen theaters; and 8,000 restaurants, cafés, pubs, and night spots, is a continually fascinating city.

MAJOR INTEREST

The Brandenburg Gate and historic buildings
    along Unter den Linden
The Dom, St. Hedwigs-Kathedrale, and the Ma-
    rienkirche
Museumsinsel and the Pergamon Museum
Alexanderplatz, the Nikolaiviertel, and Platz der
    Akademie

The Tiergarten, the Reichstag, Schloss Bellevue, the
    Zoo
Museums in the Kulturforum complex
Kurfürstendamm and the Kaiser-Wilhelm-Gedächtnis-
    Kirche

Kreuzberg and the Airlift Memorial
Dahlem and its museums
Schloss Charlottenburg and its museums

Spandau and the Zitadelle Spandau
Treptow and the Soviet War Memorial
Köpenicker Forst, Grosser Müggelsee, and Schloss
    Köpenick

Grunewald and Wannsee

Potsdam (covered in the chapter on Bach and Luther
   Country, below) for Frederick the Great's
   Sanssouci

The City's History

The Wall that divided West from East Berlin from August 13,
1961, to November 9, 1989, did not mark the first separation
of this city. Indeed, Berlin started off as two small rival
trading settlements on opposite banks of the Spree river in
what was then the easternmost region of the Holy Roman
Empire, the March of Brandenburg.

This remote area had been settled by barbarian Germanic
tribes in the early part of the first century. By A.D. 500 they
had moved west and south, leaving the land to the Wends, a
Slavic people whose modern descendants, now called Sorbs,
still inhabit the Lausitz district southeast of Berlin. Throughout the Dark Ages the Wends and Germans battled frequently. In the eighth century Charlemagne conquered the
Wendish lands; by the tenth century, a coalition of Wendish
tribes had regained the territory.

In 1147 Emperor Conrad III, Duke Henry the Lion of
Saxony, and Count Albrecht the Bear joined forces against
the Wends and defeated them for good. Albrecht the Bear
settled the newly won land and, forging alliances through
marriage, became margrave of Brandenburg. His margraviate, or "march," meaning frontier zone, was the cradle of
what would become the kingdom of Prussia and, later, the
German Reich.

Germans soon began settling and reinforcing the forts the
Wends had built, one of which was the Zitadelle Spandau.
Around 1230 they founded two towns: Cölln on an island in
the Spree river, and Berlin on the river's northeastern bank.
Popular legend holds that the name Berlin may derive somehow from Albrecht the Bear, and it is true that the bear has
been the city's symbol for many centuries. However, most
city historians scoff at the idea and say that no one knows the
origin of the name or what it once meant. Although the two
towns profited from commerce on the east–west trade route
between Poznan in Poland and Magdeburg, they remained
bitter rivals. Each had its own *Rathaus* (City Hall) and was
surrounded by its own protective wall. Although only a few
yards of water divided them, the towns steadfastly rebuffed
attempts at amalgamation. It wasn't until 1307, when robber
barons were ravaging the March of Brandenburg, that they
agreed on a confederated union. A third city hall, where the

combined towns' councillors could meet, was built on the Lange Brücke (Long Bridge), now called Rathausbrücke.

Shortly after their union, Berlin-Cölln, with a population of some 5,000, joined the Hanseatic League, an alliance of Baltic and North Sea trading and shipping cities. Along with the land route that carried business to the town, the Spree gave Berlin-Cölln access to the Havel river, a tributary of the Elbe that empties into the North Sea, and an overland link was established with the Oder river, which flows into the Baltic Sea.

Berlin's history during most of the 14th and the early 15th century was tumultuous. In 1323 the last of Albrecht's descendants died without heirs, and ownership of the Brandenburg margraviate reverted to the Holy Roman emperor, Ludwig IV, who gave it to his son. Fifty years later Emperor Charles IV conferred the margraviate on his own son, Wenceslaus, who, in turn, gave Brandenburg to his brother Sigismund, who then transferred ownership to one of his most loyal supporters and lieutenants, Burgrave Friedrich von Hohenzollern. On several occasions during this period Brandenburg was also pawned to various moneylenders to finance the wars of its various owners.

Much changed with the advent of Friedrich and the Hohenzollerns, who were to rule Berlin, Brandenburg, and all of Germany (not to mention a good chunk of Europe) for the next 400 years. They were a South German clan with vision and a lust for power. They not only routed the robber barons and subjugated the gentry, but they also crushed the independent cities, including Berlin itself. Friedrich dissolved the merger of the two towns, disbanded their assembly of councillors, and forbade Berlin and Cölln to enter into alliances. He also confiscated substantial plots of land.

On one of those confiscated plots he laid the cornerstone for a grand palace, thus turning Cölln into his residence, seat of government, and capital of Brandenburg.

The Hohenzollerns, who also acquired Prussia to the east and territories as far west as Kleve on the Rhine, were among the first German rulers to adopt the views of Martin Luther and to make Protestantism their state's official religion. To this day less than 15 percent of Berlin's population is Catholic.

Although epidemics and starvation during the Thirty Years' War cut Berlin's population from 12,000 to 6,000, its political prospects continued to improve. Duke Friedrich Wilhelm, *der Grosse Kurfürst* (the Great Elector), who assumed office in 1640, consolidated and expanded the Hohenzollern lands and encouraged immigration. By 1677 religiously motivated French refugees had already settled in Berlin, and when Louis

XIV decided he could no longer tolerate the Calvinist Huguenots in Catholic France, the Great Elector offered them refuge in Protestant Brandenburg.

Of the 15,000 Huguenot immigrants who eventually came to Brandenburg, 6,000 settled in Berlin itself. By the time of the Great Elector's death in 1688, nearly one-third of the city's population was French. The Huguenots were granted the right of self-government and the right to found their own schools and churches. The Französischer Dom (French Cathedral) on Gendarmenmarkt, built in 1764 and now restored after more than 40 years as a World War II ruin, is one of their greatest legacies.

The French influence on the city's economic life, administration, armed forces, arts, sciences, language, educational system, and fashions was immense. To this day Berlin's curious dialect contains some French contributions. For example, Berliners still refer disparagingly to weak coffee as *Muckefuck,* which comes from the French expression *moka faux,* meaning a false mocha, or coffee substitute.

Yet when Friedrich Wilhelm died in 1688, Berlin was still a provincial town of fewer than 20,000, a backwater compared to London, Paris, Vienna, Prague, or Moscow.

His son, Friedrich I, changed all that. In 1701, after 13 years as duke and elector, he decided that the duchy should become a kingdom. He ordered royal insignia from a jeweler and, standing before a mirror, crowned himself king of Prussia. As a kingdom needs a proper capital, he then set out to create one. He merged Berlin and Cölln into a single city and hired some of the greatest German architects to expand and complete the Royal Palace (which was badly damaged during World War II and then demolished by East Germany's Communist regime in 1951). He also built the Zeughaus, or armory (now the Museum of German History) on Unter den Linden boulevard, as well as a number of summer palaces, including Schloss Charlottenburg, which has been restored following its devastation during World War II.

Although the city's territory was still limited to what is today the borough of Berlin Mitte (about 4.1 square miles), by the time Friedrich I died in 1713 the capital's population had grown to 60,000. Under his son, Friedrich Wilhelm I, known as the "Soldier King," and his grandson, Frederick the Great, Berlin became grander by the year. Stunning public buildings, and monuments such as the Brandenburg Gate, were erected along or near Unter den Linden. By 1790 Berlin had a population of 147,000.

The 19th century brought the Industrial Revolution and Prussia's transformation into the German Reich. This was an epoch of explosive growth for Berlin: Between Napoleon's defeat in 1815 and the start of World War I in 1914, the population grew tenfold, from 193,000 to 1.9 million. Yet despite incorporation of some surrounding towns and villages, the city's area was still only one-thirteenth of its present size. As well, some of Germany's largest industrial concerns—Siemens and AEG, electrical engineering companies; Borsig, the locomotive and steam engine manufacturer; Schering, the pharmaceuticals producer—were launched during this period. As many as 50 new factories started up each year. And to work in them, under grueling sweatshop conditions, hundreds of thousands of people streamed into the city.

The barons of industry built their factories to resemble medieval castles and cathedrals, with crenellated walls and spires. Berlin's industrialists also built villas and mansions that rivaled the royal palaces, prompting the kings and kaisers to build even grander edifices in an ornate style that critics dubbed "Reich braggadocio."

There was nothing ornate about the mass housing for the growing labor force: endless rows of five- or six-story buildings divided into dingy flats, most without plumbing, built around shaftlike inner courtyards. While Berlin was becoming Germany's biggest industrial center, it was also becoming Europe's largest tenement city. This aspect of Berlin life was eloquently portrayed in the art of Heinrich Zille and Käthe Kollwitz, as well as in the writings of Alfred Döblin, Joachim Ringelnatz, and Kurt Tucholsky.

Although the destruction of World War II, postwar reconstruction, and the urban renewal and renovation projects of the 1970s and 1980s have erased much of this tenement housing, you still can get a vivid idea of what it was like in the boroughs of Neukölln, Kreuzberg, Wedding, and Prenzlauer Berg. These areas are home to the typical *Kneipe,* a tavern that is the focus of a real neighborhood, or *Kiez,* as it's called in Berlin dialect. A good Kiez is an intersection with four corners and four taverns where wheat beer with a shot of corn schnapps flows like water.

There was a brighter side to life in the city. Impressionist painters Max Liebermann, Lovis Corinth, and Max Slevogt were at work; the Expressionist art of Max Pechstein, George Grosz, and Karl Schmidt-Rottluff was winning acclaim; and *Jugendstil,* or Art Nouveau design, was at its height. With two major opera houses, the Philharmonic orchestra, and the Deutsches Theater, the latter under the direction of Max Reinhardt, Berlin won international stature as a music and drama center. Leading scientists, including Albert Einstein, Max Planck, Fritz Haber, Walther Nernst, Adolf von Bayer, Robert Koch, and Emil Fischer, worked at various times in the city. And Berlin became one of the world's greatest museum cities, thanks to its matchless collections of painting, sculpture, and ancient art.

After World War I and the 1918 revolution, which toppled the kaiser and made Germany a republic, Berlin became *the* cosmopolitan crossroads of the Golden Twenties. Movie stars such as Marlene Dietrich, Greta Garbo, Peter Lorre, and Pola Negri and directors such as Fritz Lang, Ernst Lubitsch, F. W. Murnau, and Josef von Sternberg, working at the huge studios in suburban Potsdam-Babelsberg, made the city a cinema capital. Berlin was the home of Dadaist art; of artists Hans Arp, Max Beckmann, Max Ernst, Grosz, Paul Klee, and Schmidt-Rottluff; of the Bauhaus architects and designers, notably Walter Gropius and Ludwig Mies van der Rohe; of essayists, poets, and writers such as W. H. Auden, Arthur Koestler, Christopher Isherwood (whose *Berlin Stories* was the basis of the later play *I Am a Camera* and the play and film *Cabaret*), Heinrich Mann, Vladimir Nabokov, Carl von Ossietzky, and Kurt Tucholsky. Berlin was the stage for Bertolt Brecht, Kurt Weill, Erwin Piscator, Carl Zuckmayer, and Lotte Lenya. Wilhelm Furtwängler presided over the Philharmonic. The city had yet another opera house, and the local conductors were Bruno Walter, Otto Klemperer, and Erich Kleiber.

It was also in 1920 that Berlin became the sprawling metropolis that it is today. In October of that year eight independent surrounding cities, among them Charlottenburg, Schöneberg, Spandau, and Köpenick, plus dozens of smaller towns, were incorporated to create Greater Berlin.

Today, that period seems to many like a lost artistic and cultural paradise. It was lost, of course, because of Adolf Hitler and the Third Reich. Berlin, the mecca of culture and tolerance, became the center of anticulture and intolerance. In their racist megalomania the Nazis even began restructuring the city. Charlottenburger Chaussee (today called Strasse des 17. Juni), the extension of Unter den Linden west of the Brandenburg Gate, was doubled in width to accommodate the Nazis' military and political parades. Albert Speer, Hitler's favorite architect, drafted plans for a bombastic new city center near Tempelhof airfield. He envisioned, among other things, a railway station plaza 3,300 feet long and 1,000 feet wide, and a new triumphal arch so big that the Brandenburg Gate would have fit into it several times. Those plans were never realized, but other architectural relics of the Third Reich remain: Tempelhof itself, the Olympic Stadium, and some grim-looking government office buildings south of Unter den Linden.

Worst of all, Berlin became the caldron for World War II

and the Holocaust, a reign of terror and genocide that culminated in the city's own Götterdämmerung.

Of its 4.4 million prewar inhabitants, only 2.8 million remained in 1945, and the city was left a wasteland. Streets and squares, especially in the historic center, were strewn with dead bodies, burned-out tanks, and the debris of artillery attacks. Some 75 million cubic meters of rubble—one seventh of all the rubble in Germany—was in Berlin. Of the city's 245,000 prewar buildings, 50,000 were completely destroyed and as many again were near ruins. Transportation was at a standstill; public utilities were nonexistent. And once again Berlin, as it had been by the Russians during the Seven Years' War and by the French under Napoleon from 1806 to 1808, was under foreign occupation—first by the Russians alone, and from August 1945 on by the Americans, British, and French as well.

The situation was worsened by the conflicts between the wartime victors that led to the Cold War. The 1948 Soviet blockade, which the Western Allies met with an airlift called Operation Vittles that lasted nearly 11 months, was followed by the tragic June 17, 1953, workers' uprising in East Berlin, and finally by the construction of the Berlin Wall in 1961.

To this day, the scars and wounds of World War II, not to mention those of the Cold War, are more visible in Berlin than in any other German city. Many building façades, especially in the eastern boroughs, are still pockmarked with bullet holes from the street fighting in 1945, and large areas are still weed-covered lots on which nothing has been built or else wastelands created by the construction of the Wall.

Getting Oriented

Berlin's size, the distances between its most important sites, the legacy of the postwar division between Communist East and capitalist West, which resulted in a dramatic shift of cosmopolitan life, business, shopping, hotels, restaurants, theaters, and nightlife from the old center—Alexanderplatz, Unter den Linden, Leipziger Strasse, and Potsdamer Platz—westward to the area around and on Kurfürstendamm, all make it a difficult city to master.

Though Berlin is again one, with a single public transit network and with streets once divided by the Wall now connected as if the barrier had never existed, Berliners themselves still think in terms of West and East, and the differences between the two halves are—and will long remain—glaringly apparent. Immense investments over a period of many years will be needed to give central east Berlin, once the throbbing heart of the prewar city, the

urban glitter of the formerly western area around Kurfürstendamm. And even when the investments bear fruit, much of it
may become artificial. A good example is the planning for
Potsdamer Platz, where by the year 2000 large German and
Japanese industrial firms (Daimler-Benz and Sony) intend to
complete a vast office, residential, shopping, and entertainment center. The Italian architect Renzo Piano has just been
selected by Daimler-Benz to head its enormous project, and
the German-American Helmut Jahn for Sony's plot.

The logical way to explore a city is to start with its old
quarter. This historic center, traversed by Unter den Linden
boulevard and Karl-Liebknecht-Strasse, its east–west axis, is
the formerly eastern borough of **Berlin Mitte**, until 1990 the
political and commercial heart of East Berlin. On and
around this axis, its western end being the Brandenburg
Gate, its eastern one Alexanderplatz, are the quarter's most
important sights. But because of the paucity of hotels and
interesting restaurants, it is unlikely that you will be staying
here. The real "weight" of Berlin, that which thus far has
made and will for the next five to ten years make it the
throbbing, international city it is, is in the west, on and
around **Kurfürstendamm**, where most of the good hotels
are.

To make sense of western Berlin is also not easy, in part
because of its size and the fact that many of its sightseeing
highlights are some distance from its center, the Kurfürstendamm. This avenue runs on a northeast-to-southwest axis for
almost 3 km (2 miles) through the heart of west Berlin. Its
northeastern terminal, not far from Bahnhof Zoo, Berlin's
main railway station, is the **Europa-Center**, which itself is
more than 3 km (2 miles) southwest of the Brandenburg
Gate. This 22-story office, commercial, and shopping complex, topped by the huge revolving emblem of Mercedes-
Benz, is located in the center of Berlin's "downtown" area at
the convergence of Kurfürstendamm, Kantstrasse, Hardenbergstrasse, Budapester Strasse, and Tauentzienstrasse. As it
is one of central Berlin's tallest buildings, replete with 70
stores, 20 restaurants, five cinemas, cabarets, nightclubs, a
gambling casino, airline offices, and the Berlin tourist bureau, you can hardly miss it. An observation platform on the
20th floor provides a view of most of the city as well as a
sense of its layout.

Even if excursion-bus rubbernecking is not usually your
style, Berlin is where you should make an exception, for no
other mode will provide such an excellent overview of the
city. There are a variety of two- to four-hour tours of the entire
city, in both German and English, all covering the same basic
routes. Most have their ticket offices and departure points on

or just off Kurfürstendamm, within a few minutes' walk of the Europa-Center, or close to and on Alexanderplatz.

The best, fastest, and cheapest way to get around is by public transit, which is excellent throughout the city. Renting a car may seem inviting because of Berlin's size, but it is also an invitation to headaches. Traffic is always heavy, parking spaces are rare, and gridlock is common. Moreover, the layout of the city is so complex that you are bound to get lost, no matter how detailed your map. On the other hand, except for a few specific, relatively manageable areas such as Berlin Mitte and Köpenick, the Kurfürstendamm neighborhood, the Tiergarten district, the museums in Dahlem and around Charlottenburg Palace, and Spandau's Altstadt, walking tours can become endurance tests.

CENTRAL BERLIN

The 4.1-square-mile borough of **Berlin Mitte** is Berlin's historic heart, the spot where Cölln and Berlin were first settled in the Middle Ages. Later, it was the font of Prussian and German power, the district from which kings, kaisers, and also Hitler ruled. During the 40 years of postwar Germany's division, when East Berlin was the capital of the Communist East German Democratic Republic (GDR), this third-smallest of the city's 20 boroughs was East Berlin's political, economic, and cultural center. Within it are the entire city's most important sites: the Brandenburg Gate, Unter den Linden, the Deutsche Staatsoper, Humboldt Universität, the Deutsche Staatsbibliothek, the armory, the Museumsinsel, and Alexanderplatz, now dominated by the 1,200-foot TV tower, Berlin's tallest structure, nicknamed the "Speared Onion." Berlin Mitte also contains the Dom and St. Hedwig's, St. Mary's, and St. Nicholas's; the Gendarmenmarkt (known until recently as Platz der Akademie), with the Schauspielhaus theater and the French and German cathedrals; and the Rotes Rathaus, so called for its Neo-Renaissance red-brick façade.

In other words, when the devastated city was divided into four occupation sectors at the 1945 Potsdam Conference, the Soviets, and by inference East Berliners, got most of the nuggets. Moreover, though it seemed to take ages, most of it was rebuilt, restored, refurbished, renovated, and enriched with luxury hotels and restaurants, cafés, cozy taverns, special shops, department stores, theaters, and cinemas in an effort to make East Berlin as much a showcase of Communism as West Berlin became of capitalism.

The price of rebuilding a few streets, squares, museums, palaces, and monuments is evident in the neglect and decay, or the shoddy prefab restoration, typical of much of the rest of the eastern part of city. Moreover, for 28 of the more than 40 years that East Berlin was destined to play its role in the Cold War, it was a showcase within a cage, sealed off from West Berlin by the Wall with its bristling array of guard towers and barbed wire. Many would-be visitors wondered whether a visit was worth it, given the bureaucratic formalities, the surliness of the border guards, and the real or imagined restrictions on freedom of movement.

All that changed on November 9, 1989, when the Wall opened up and the two Berlins as well as the two Germanys began moving toward reunification. Yet at the same time some things have not changed. To be sure, the two Berlins are already being stitched back together. As just one example, the Rotes Rathaus is again, as it was before 1945, the city hall of all of Berlin as well as the seat of the burgomaster and his cabinet, called the Senate. Federal government agencies also have moved into a number of ministerial buildings of the former German Democratic Republic. But the scars of division and of the Wall will long remain, as will those of East Berlin having been the far poorer showcase and the capital of a far poorer country. How long? That depends on how fast the Germans and Berliners move ahead with their costly plans—DM 40 billion by the most optimistic estimates, thrice that according to the pessimists—to make Berlin not just a capital in name but in fact: the seat of government and parliament.

ON AND AROUND
UNTER DEN LINDEN

Unter den Linden is Berlin's most famous avenue. It runs from east to west for about a mile from Marx-Engels-Platz (known until 1951 as the *Lustgarten,* or Pleasure Garden), to Pariser Platz and the Brandenburg Gate.

The boulevard's pedigree goes back to 1573, when Elector Johann Georg laid it out as a bridle path from his palace to his hunting grounds in the Tiergarten. Three quarters of a century later, in 1647, the Great Elector ordered 1,000 nut trees and 1,000 lindens planted along the road. Although these were cut down in 1680 in order to pave the street and make room for residential and public buildings, the name Unter den Linden stuck, becoming official a century later when Frederick the Great widened the street into a parkway and again planted it with linden trees.

In the late 19th and early 20th centuries it was the unchallenged main street of Berlin, divided at midpoint by its intersection with Friedrichstrasse. Along its eastern end were the great palaces, the university, the opera, libraries, and other institutional buildings. The western half was lined by foreign embassies, elegant shops, luxury hotels, cafés, and restaurants. Wilhelmstrasse, now called Toleranz-Strasse (which intersects Unter den Linden close to the Brandenburg Gate), was the street of government, flanked by the presidential residence, the ministry of justice, and the Reich chancellory. To speak of "Wilhelmstrasse" in those days was like speaking of Pennsylvania Avenue or 10 Downing Street. By contrast, the intersection of Unter den Linden and Friedrichstrasse was the epicenter of Berlin's political, intellectual, cultural, and commercial life, the location of the Café Kranzler and the Café Bauer (the latter reborn in 1987 as part of the Grand Hotel).

In May 1945, after the bombs stopped falling and the guns were silenced, Unter den Linden was a bleak moonscape of craters and rubble, with only the charred, crumbling façades of gutted buildings still standing. The few linden trees that survived were soon cut down for firewood. Yet today Unter den Linden is again one of Berlin's finest boulevards, reconstructed almost as it was. Unfortunately its western half, although again lined with foreign missions, stores, and government offices, was rebuilt in faceless steel, glass, and concrete. But from Friedrichstrasse eastward virtually every building of note was recreated: Frederick the Great would hardly notice the changes. Even the 45-foot-high equestrian statue of "Old Fritz" stands in its proper place in the middle of the avenue. Erected in 1851, it was removed for safekeeping during World War II, then hidden for 35 years behind a clump of bushes on the grounds of Sanssouci palace in Potsdam because East Germany's rulers wanted no reminder of the Hohenzollerns and Prussia. In 1980, in an about-face, they allowed this monument to Frederick the Great to return to Unter den Linden.

The **Brandenburger Tor** (Brandenburg Gate), at the avenue's western end, is the very essence of Berlin. The huge gate—66 feet high, 204 feet wide, and 36 feet deep—was modeled after the Propylaeum on the Acropolis, and was officially opened in 1791. King Friedrich Wilhelm II attended the ceremony. Originally called the Friedenstor (Peace Gate), it assumed a more martial appearance two

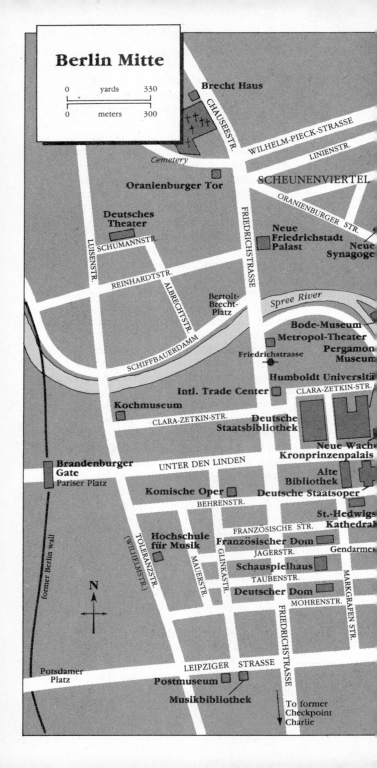

Berlin Mitte

| 0 | yards | 330 |
| 0 | meters | 300 |

Brecht Haus

CHAUSEESTR.

WILHELM-PIECK-STRASSE

LINIENSTR.

Cemetery

Oranienburger Tor

SCHEUNENVIERTEL

ORANIENBURGER STR.

Deutsches
Theater

FRIEDRICHSTRASSE

SCHUMANNSTR.

Neue
Friedrichstadt
Palast

Neue
Synagoge

LUISENSTR.

REINHARDTSTR.

ALBRECHTSTR.

Bertolt-
Brecht-
Platz

Spree River

Bode-Museum

Metropol-Theater

SCHIFFBAUERDAMM

Friedrichstrasse

Pergamon
Museum

Humboldt Universität

Intl. Trade Center

CLARA-ZETKIN-STR.

Kochmuseum

CLARA-ZETKIN-STR.

Deutsche
Staatsbibliothek

Neue Wach
Kronprinzenpalais

Brandenburger
Gate

Pariser Platz

UNTER DEN LINDEN

Alte
Bibliothek

Komische Oper

Deutsche Staatsoper

BEHRENSTR.

St.-Hedwigs
Kathedral

former Berlin wall

Hochschule
für Musik

FRANZÖSISCHE STR.

Französischer Dom

Gendarme

JAGERSTR.

TOLERANZSTR.
(WILHELMSTR.)

MAUERSTR.

GLINKASTR.

Schauspielhaus

MARKGRAFEN STR.

TAUBENSTR.

Deutscher Dom

N

MOHRENSTR.

FRIEDRICHSTRASSE

Potsdamer
Platz

LEIPZIGER STRASSE

Postmuseum

Musikbibliothek

To former
Checkpoint
Charlie

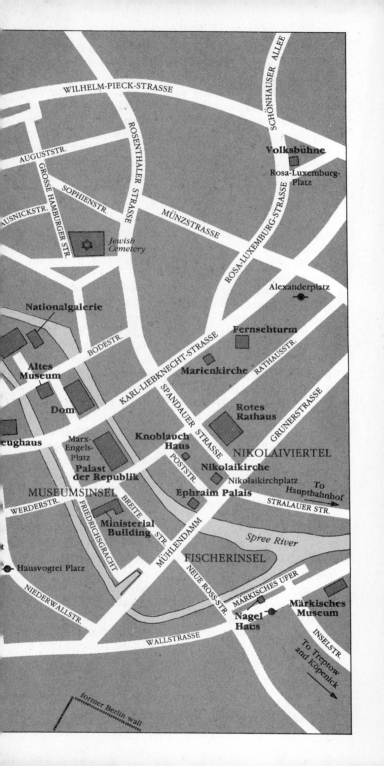

years later when it was crowned by the bronze **Quadriga**, a four-horse war chariot driven by the Goddess of Victory. The goddess was originally nude, but her appearance triggered so much indignation and so many ribald jokes that the sculptor, Johann Gottfried Schadow, clad her in a sheet of copper. She kept her vigil for 13 years, until 1806, when Napoleon marched triumphantly into Berlin. Like many conquerors before and after, he looted art, stating his own policy succinctly: "Take a nation's symbols, and you have it in your hands." Napoleon had the Quadriga dismantled and shipped to Paris, where it was mounted on the Arc de Triomphe. Eight years later, however, the Prussians marched into Paris and recaptured the Quadriga. It was taken to Jagdschloss Grunewald for repair, then replaced on the Brandenburg Gate in June 1814, with one small alteration: The Prussian eagle in the center of Victory's oak wreath was replaced with an Iron Cross.

Few structures have witnessed as many of the vicissitudes of German history as the Brandenburg Gate. In 1871 it was the backdrop for the victory celebration after the war with France and the establishment of the kaiser Reich. In 1919 leftist revolutionaries and government troops had a shoot-out around its Doric columns. Battalions of brown-shirted Nazi troops marched through it on the night of January 31, 1933, in a torchlight parade hailing Hitler's appointment as Reich chancellor. In May 1945, like the rest of Berlin, the gate and monument were in ruins. Reconstruction was not completed until 1958. The gate became the symbol of Berlin's division when the Wall was built in 1961, and of the city's reunification when it was opened to pedestrian traffic in 1989. The subsequent celebrations did so much damage to the Quadriga that in the spring of 1990 the monument was removed for renovation and repair and the gate sheathed in scaffolding. The scaffolding came down, and the refurbished Quadriga was restored to its position of honor in time for the Brandenburg Gate's bicentennial celebration on August 6, 1991, a gala show with Mozart music and fireworks. The only sour note was that the Prussian eagle and Iron Cross were back in place on Victory's wreath, eliciting protests from many in Germany who consider them to be symbols of Prussian militarism.

From the Brandenburg Gate back to Friedrichstrasse, where the main sights of Unter den Linden begin, is a ten-minute walk. Stay on the north side of the boulevard for a while. The Neo-Baroque structure at number 8 is the **Deutsche Staatsbibliothek** (German State Library), housing a collection of 5.5 million books, manuscripts, musical scores, etchings, and maps. Just past the library, at number 6, is **Humboldt Universität**, which has often been referred to

as the University of Berlin. Built in 1753 as a palace for
Prince Heinrich, the brother of Frederick the Great, it was
given to Wilhelm von Humboldt in 1809 when he founded
the university. Twenty-seven Nobel Prize winners have been
members of its faculty, and the philosopher Hegel taught
here. Statues of both Wilhelm and Alexander von Humboldt
flank the elaborate wrought-iron gateway.

Directly across Unter den Linden, at number 11, is the
Alte Bibliothek (Old Library), built between 1774 and 1788
by the Prussian architect Georg Friedrich Boumann according to plans drawn up by Joseph Fischer von Erlach for the
St. Michael wing of Vienna's Hofburg. Today the building
houses various university institutes.

A few paces beyond is the **Deutsche Staatsoper**, Berlin's
main opera house, commissioned by Frederick the Great,
designed by his favorite architect, Georg Wenzeslaus von
Knobelsdorff, and opened December 7, 1742, with a performance of Carl Heinrich Graun's *Caesar and Cleopatra*. One
of the world's oldest opera houses and a gem of Neoclassical
design, it was thrice destroyed and rebuilt: first by a fire in
1843, then by an air raid in 1943, and finally by bombs and
artillery in 1945. The present reconstruction dates from
1955. Erich Kleiber was one of its conductors and musical
directors, and Daniel Barenboim has been in that position
since the start of the 1992 season. For all its fame, it is just
one of three opera houses in Berlin. Its competitors are the
Komische Oper (Comic Opera) on nearby Behrendstrasse
and the **Deutsche Oper Berlin**, Bismarckstrasse 35, which
was the opera house of the city of Charlottenburg becoming
the Berlin municipal opera after Charlottenburg's 1920 incorporation into Berlin as a borough.

St. Hedwigs-Kathedrale, the squat domed structure (modeled on the Pantheon) behind the opera house, is the
Roman Catholic cathedral of Berlin and one of the few
Catholic churches in this predominantly Protestant city. Construction of the church (named for Hedwig, the beatified
wife of Duke Heinrich of Silesia) began in 1747, and the cast
of planners and architects was stellar: Frederick the Great,
Knobelsdorff, Johann Boumann, and the Frenchman Jean
Legeay. Although the Seven Years' War halted work, the
church was finally completed in 1772. It was destroyed by
fire during World War II and rebuilt in the early 1960s, with
its interior starkly simple and modern and the exterior
much as it used to be.

You can have lunch, coffee and pastries, or even dinner at
the **Opernpalais**, Unter den Linden 5, a complex of restaurants and cafés in the former **Prinzessinenpalais**. This was
the Baroque residence of the daughters of King Friedrich

Wilhelm III before their marriages. On a fair day you can sit on the terrace, which provides a splendid view of Unter den Linden's historic buildings.

Next to the café, at number 3, is the **Kronprinzenpalais**, a mid-17th-century mansion that was enlarged in 1732 for Frederick the Great when he was the 20-year-old crown prince in open rebellion against his tyrannical father, Friedrich Wilhelm I, known as the "Soldier King." For all his later impact on world history, as a teenager Frederick had no interest in government, in war, or in being a future king. His preferences were for art, literature, philosophy, and music (being a virtuoso flutist as well as a composer of chamber music). For this he was despised by his father, an extraordinarily coarse man whose main achievement was to make the Prussian army into an instrument of war, or as some have phrased it, "Prussia into an army with a state." Frederick reciprocated his father's loathing. In 1730, then 18, repeatedly abused and humiliated, he attempted to escape to England with his friend and lover, Lieutenant Hans Hermann von Katte. They were intercepted by the king's agents, however, and both imprisoned on charges of treason. Frederick was forced to watch Katte's beheading, but ultimately was himself released. In 1732, a year before his arranged marriage to Princess Elizabeth of Brunswick-Bevern (from whom he separated soon after), he moved into the Kronprinzenpalais. From then until the end of the monarchy in 1918, it served as the official residence of Prussia's and Germany's crown princes. Heavily damaged during the Battle of Berlin, it was finally rebuilt and reopened in 1969 for use as a government guest house. When Berlin becomes the seat of Germany's government, it will be the official residence of the German president and his staff.

On the other side of Unter den Linden, just east of the university at number 4, is the **Neue Wache** (New Guardhouse). This is one of Karl-Friedrich Schinkel's Neoclassical masterpieces, designed in the style of a Roman temple. After the 1918 revolution that toppled the kaiser and set the stage for the Weimar Republic, the Neue Wache became the Tomb of the Unknown Soldier, a memorial to the fallen of World War I. The East German regime turned it into a Monument against Fascism and Militarism, which it will remain.

The four-story **Zeughaus** (Armory), just past the Neue Wache at Unter den Linden 2, is the largest and best-preserved example of Baroque architecture in Berlin as well as the oldest public building on the avenue. It was completed in 1706 as an armory and gave a fairly clear indication of where Prussia was headed. For nearly a century and a half, from 1730 to 1877, it was used to store captured war matériel. It was then converted into a military museum and a hall of fame celebrating victories by Brandenburg's and Prussia's armies. In 1952 the East German government turned it into the **Museum für Deutsche Geschichte** (Museum of German History), a role it will continue to fill for a number of years until a new German history museum has been built.

THE MUSEUMSINSEL

The Museumsinsel (Museum Island) is a complex of museums and galleries at the east end of Unter den Linden. It was on this island that the town of Cölln was founded in the 1230s. It is also where Berlin's incomparable art collections, now shown in more than 50 museums, 28 of them under the administration of the Prussian Cultural Properties Foundation, had their start.

The origins of Berlin's hoard date back to the Brandenburg dukes and Prussian kings, who were lavish patrons and collectors of art. In the early 19th century the royal family sponsored the formation of museums open to the public. The first of these galleries, the Altes Museum, on the Museumsinsel, was built between 1824 and 1828, and opened in 1830, making it one of the world's oldest public art museums. Over the next 100 years the collections were expanded and four more museums were built on the island. Because the collections were state owned, their status remained unchanged during the years of the Weimar Republic and the Nazi Reich.

During World War II the museums were closed and most of their treasures evacuated to safer places: air-raid bunkers in Berlin, warehouses in the suburbs, salt mines in what later became West Germany. Toward the war's end, as the Allied armies advanced through Germany, the Americans and British confiscated the hidden art they found in their occupation zones, and the Russians did the same in the territory under their control.

More than 200 Old Master paintings were taken to the United States in 1945, exhibited around the country, and kept for many years. The Soviets shipped art to Moscow, where it remained until 1959. Many objects are still missing and presumed to be in Soviet or U.S. hands. By the time the wartime victors were willing to release the treasures, the Cold War was in full swing and both Germany and Berlin were divided. Prussia no longer existed as a legal entity, having been formally abolished in 1947 by the Four Power Allied Military Government. That raised the knotty question of who actually owned the Prussian treasures from Berlin's museums, and to whom they should be repatriated.

For the Soviets the answer was easy: They turned over their share to the Communist East German government, which restored most of the buildings on Museumsinsel. In West Germany the matter was finally resolved in 1961 with the creation of the Stiftung Preussisches Kulturgut (Prussian Cultural Properties Foundation), jointly owned by the Bonn government, the states, and Berlin. These are in building complexes in Dahlem, in and around Charlottenburg Palace, and the Tiergarten's Kulturforum.

That is why Berlin today has two of each kind of museum—one in the west and one in the east. Considering the haste and disorder with which some of the objects were evacuated during the war, it is also understandable why you may find the head of a statue in one part of the city and its torso in the other, the frame of one painting in the east and the picture itself in the west.

The two collections, now under one administrative hat, are moving toward gradual amalgamation, which will entail shifting entire divisions from one end of the city to the other and also building or completing construction of entirely new museum structures. The process will take many years—at least until the turn of the century—and cost billions of marks. And while the moves are going on, many museums and divisions may be closed, their treasures in storage.

Of the five original museums at the northern tip of the island—the Altes Museum, the Neues Museum, the Nationalgalerie, the Pergamon Museum, and the Bode Museum—all except the Neues Museum have been rebuilt since the war. Reconstruction of the Neues Museum, hampered by difficult soil and foundation conditions, is scheduled to begin in 1995. When completed, it will house all of Berlin's Egyptian collections. Hours for the Altes Museum, the Nationalgalerie, and the Bode Museum are Wednesday through Sunday from 10:00 A.M. to 6:00 P.M. The Pergamon Museum is open daily from 10:00 A.M. to 6:00 P.M.

The **Altes Museum**, the oldest museum in the complex, was built between 1824 and 1828 by Schinkel in Greek-temple style. At present it is being used for rotating exhibitions only. It will be closed for renovations and repairs starting in 1994, and after reopening will house the antiquities collections from the Pergamon Museum and Charlottenburg Palace. East Berlin's **Kupferstichkabinett** (Print Collection), an assemblage of 200,000 drawings, etchings, engravings, woodcuts, watercolors, and other kinds of graphic art from the 15th century to the present previously housed in the Altes Museum, moved to a new building in the

Tiergarten's Kulturforum in fall 1993. The collection will be joined there by the 400,000 pieces from the print collection in the Dahlem complex: For the first time since the war the 120 Botticelli drawings illustrating Dante's *Inferno* will again be under one roof.

The **Nationalgalerie**, built between 1866 and 1876 in the style of a Roman temple with Corinthian pillars, is set on a high base and approached by an imposing flight of stairs. Originally intended as a kind of festival hall for state receptions and royal ceremonies, it assumed its current role as the city's collection of 19th- and 20th-century art grew. It has a large collection of Neoclassical German sculptures, including works by Schadow, Rauch, and Tieck; paintings from the 18th, 19th, and early 20th centuries, among them the most important works by Adolf von Menzel, Anselm Feuerbach, and Hans von Marées; some fine Goyas; French and German Impressionists; and pictures by Corinth, Slevogt, Kokoschka, and Schmidt-Rottluff. It will close for a complete renovation in 1994, and after reopening will house the entire 19th-century collection, including works in the Galerie der Romantik, presently housed in a wing of the Charlottenburg Palace.

The **Bode Museum**, named for Wilhelm von Bode, director of the Berlin museums from 1872 to 1929, is a triangular two-story structure built in Neo-Baroque style. In it are eastern Berlin's Egyptian museum, the Museum of Pre- and Early History, the Early Christian–Byzantine collection, the numismatic collection, the sculpture collection, and the picture gallery. The Egyptian museum's mummies and collection of 15,000 papyrus rolls are among the best in the world. The sculpture collection is strong on German, Dutch, and French works from the 12th through 18th centuries. The Bode's **Gemäldegalerie** (Picture Gallery) features works by German, Flemish, and Dutch artists from the 15th through the 17th centuries, and English and French artists from the 18th. (The best examples of this period, however, are found in west Berlin's Dahlem complex.) The two picture galleries, with a combined lode of nearly 2,900 paintings from the 13th through the 18th centuries, will move to a new building in the Kulturforum, expected to be ready in 1996.

The largest and newest of the museums is the **Pergamon Museum**, completed in 1930. It takes its name from the huge altar from the ancient city-state of Pergamum, in what is today western Turkey. The vast two-story structure also contains the Antiquities Collection, the Islamic museum, the East Asian collection, the Folk Crafts museum, and the Western Asian museum. To see it all will take at least half a day. But most visitors make a beeline for the half-dozen main drawing cards on display: the Neo-Babylonian collections from the time of Nebuchadnezzar II, including the monumental Ishtar Gate, the Processional Way, and portions of Nebuchadnezzar's throne room; the gate from the Roman Market in Miletus; and the Pergamum Altar. The altar, dedicated to Zeus, ranks as one of the best-preserved examples of Hellenistic bas-relief. It was erected as part of a temple on Pergamum's Castle Hill between 180 and 160 B.C., when Pergamum was a powerful, independent city-state. Portions of it were found in 1871 during excavations at the city's Byzantine wall, and by 1880 almost the entire altar and temple had been dug up. The various sections were brought to Berlin in 1902, and it took curators until 1930 to reconstruct the altar. Enveloped in sandbags and concrete, it survived the World War II air raids. However, the Russians removed it to "protective custody" in Moscow in 1945 and did not return it until 1957. Two more years passed before the altar was reassembled and the museum reopened.

THE MARX-ENGELS-PLATZ AREA

This 1,200-by-600-foot square that extends south from the Altes Museum, called Marx-Engels-Platz since 1951, incorporates much of what used to be the Lustgarten, or Pleasure Garden. (The northern section of the square, in front of the Altes Museum, has been renamed Lustgarten.) Laid out in 1573 as an herb and vegetable garden for the ducal family, it was transformed into an ornamental garden in the 1640s, and then turned into a military parade ground by Friedrich Wilhelm I in 1715. Trees were planted here in the 1830s, a portion of the park was ceded to the Altes Museum, and in 1895, on the ground and foundations of an earlier church, work began on the Dom, Berlin's Protestant cathedral.

The **Dom**, 386 feet long, 240 feet wide, and 280 feet high, was completed in 1905, and is an example of ostentatious turn-of-the-century Neo-Renaissance style, with heavy overtones of Reich braggadocio. In many ways it resembles St. Peter's in Rome; in fact, it was considered the "Mother Church of Prussian Protestantism" and often called the "St. Peter's of the North." Many electors of Brandenburg and kings of Prussia are buried in its crypt.

Like everything else in the neighborhood, it was destroyed during the war, but East Germany's Lutheran Evangelical church authorities, with financial help from their brethren in West Germany, restored most of the exterior, and work on the interior was completed in 1993.

The square is flanked on the east by the ultramodern

steel, marble, and glass **Palast der Republik**, which occupies
the site of the former royal palace. Completed in 1976, the
new palace was the home of the *Volkskammer* (People's
Chamber), East Germany's parliament, and did double duty
as a community center, with cafés, restaurants, exhibition
halls, and a central auditorium and theater. Because of
asbestos contamination, the current plan is to destroy the
building. The entire area will be redesigned, and the Foreign Minisry will occupy one of the new structures.

THE ALEXANDERPLATZ AREA

Once one of Berlin's busiest squares, Alexanderplatz today
is the central shopping and commercial district of Berlin
Mitte. It bears no resemblance to what it looked like before
World War II.

To reach it, head east from the Dom, cross the Spree, and
continue along Karl-Liebknecht-Strasse. The left side of the
street is lined with shops, the right with a block-wide park
whose main features are the Marienkirche, the Fernsehturm,
and, on the right side along Rathausstrasse, the Rotes
Rathaus. The church and town hall are virtually all that
remain of the prewar district.

The **Marienkirche** (St. Mary's Church), at the foot of the
TV tower, is one of Berlin's oldest parish churches. Its
austere brick and stone exterior belies its ornate interior
decorations and furnishings. Begun in 1270 and first mentioned in town records in 1294, it was the centerpiece of
Berlin's Neumarkt (Newmarket Square) for the first century
of its existence. A fire devastated the church in 1380, but it
was rebuilt. The tower was added in the 16th century.

Among the art treasures inside is the *Totentanz* (Dance of
Death) mural—28 depictions of Death painted during an
epidemic of the plague in 1485 that were uncovered in the
course of restoration work 130 years ago. The church also
boasts a beautifully crafted 15th-century bronze baptismal
font, a Baroque pulpit from 1703, many elaborately carved
stone epitaphs, and a fine Neo-Baroque organ that is used
for frequent recitals.

The **Fernsehturm** (TV Tower), completed in 1969 and
dubbed the "Speared Onion," is 1,204 feet high. There is
room for 200 people on the observation platform and for
another 200 in the revolving **Tele-Café** above it, which
makes one complete circle every hour. Two high-speed
elevators, with altimeters for the amusement of passengers,
take you up into the "onion," from which on a clear day
you'll have a view extending 25 miles. The observation

platform and café are open daily from 9:00 A.M. to midnight. (Every second and fourth Tuesday they open at 1:00 P.M.) On weekends, holidays, and in the tourist season, crowds can be large.

Named for its red-brick color, the Renaissance-revival **Rotes Rathaus** was opened for its first town council session in 1865, replacing several older town halls in central Berlin, including the one that Cölln and Berlin built on the Lange Brücke when they formed their confederation in the 14th century. Since Berlin's enlargement in 1920 the Rotes Rathaus has served as both the borough and city town hall, and is once again the seat of Berlin's mayor, senate, and city-state administration. The city-state assembly moved to the Prussian Parliament building in 1993.

THE NIKOLAIVIERTEL

The St. Nicholas quarter, tucked between the southwest façade of the Rathaus and the Spree river, is the oldest part of Berlin, and was the heart of the frontier settlement of the early 13th century. It certainly looks old, with its narrow cobblestone streets and gabled medieval-style houses. But don't let appearances fool you. It's all brand new, as artificial as a movie set. A scant decade ago the little four-block neighborhood was still a wasteland, with only the gutted shell of the **Nikolaikirche** (St. Nicholas' Church), Berlin's oldest church, still standing. To prepare for the city's 750th anniversary, East German officialdom launched a crash program to create something "historic," with modern methods. The "ancient" houses here were built with prefab concrete slabs, then covered with cement and stucco, upon which craftsmen and artisans were free to indulge themselves with oriel windows, bartizans, Gothic arches, loggias, gargoyles, front stoops, helix ornaments, and the like.

The new "old" buildings added color and atmosphere to a city short on both. Moreover, the reconstruction and restoration of the church of St. Nicholas represent a remarkable achievement. It is now a division of the **Märkisches Museum** of Berlin history.

Even more remarkable was the re-creation of the **Ephraimpalais**, at the corner of Poststrasse and Mühlendamm. This richly ornamented Baroque mansion was built in 1765 for Veitel Heine Ephraim, a Jewish banker and financial adviser to the royal court. In 1935, during the Nazi era, the elegant town house was razed, supposedly to provide space for the widening of the Mühlendamm. Somewhat mysteriously, hundreds of its decorative elements were stored in various depots and warehouses, most in what became West Berlin. When East German authorities decided to rebuild the mansion, West Berlin provided some 2,000 sections of the house, which were melded with new pieces of stone masonry and stuccowork crafted on the basis of old photographs and illustrations of the structure. Today the Ephraimpalais is also a division of the Märkisches Museum, housing 17th- through 19th- century portraits and busts by a variety of artists. (Open daily from 9:00 A.M. to 5:00 P.M., Saturdays until 6:00 P.M.)

Completed in 1987, the Nikolaiviertel quickly became East Berlin's favorite residential and shopping district. Most of the new-old buildings are actually apartment houses, and specialty stores line the narrow cobblestone streets. There are numerous cafés, restaurants, and taverns to choose from, including **Zur Rippe**, at Poststrasse 17, which specializes in traditional Berlin dishes such as pea soup and sauerbraten.

THE GENDARMENMARKT AREA

Doubling back on Werderstrasse, the Nikolaiviertel's northern boundary, will take you across the Spree, the island, and the Spree canal, past the **Schinkelmuseum** in the **Friedrichs-werde Kirche** (an exhibition of Neoclassical sculpture), and into Französische Strasse. At the corner of Französische Strasse and Markgrafenstrasse, turn south and walk another block to the Gendarmenmarkt. All told, it should take you ten minutes.

The **Gendarmenmarkt** is named for the 18th-century gendarmes who had their barracks and stables here. One of Berlin's finest squares, it was the heart of the French quarter at the end of the 17th century.

Two magnificent churches, the Französischer Dom (French Cathedral) and the Deutscher Dom (German Cathedral), mark its northern and southern boundaries. The Schauspielhaus, another of Karl-Friedrich Schinkel's masterpieces, fronts the square to the west.

The **Französischer Dom**, a majestic example of late Renaissance–early Baroque style, was designed by two emigré French architects, Louis Cayard and Abraham Quesnay, and built between 1701 and 1705. It is still the main church of the Huguenot congregation. In the church tower you can visit the **Hugenottenmuseum**, a small collection of artifacts, applied art, and documents pertaining to the life of the French in Berlin at the turn of the 18th century. The museum is open Tuesday through Thursday and Saturdays from 10:00 A.M. to 5:00 P.M., and Sundays from 11:30 A.M. A carillon in the tower chimes at noon, 3:00, and 7:00 P.M.

The **Deutscher Dom**, a virtual twin of the French cathedral (and not to be confused with the Protestant Dom on Marx-Engels-Platz), was built between 1701 and 1708 according to plans drawn up by an Italian architect, Giovanni Simonetti. External reconstruction work was not completed until early autumn 1990, and it will be 1994 or 1995 before the interior will be ready to house the rotating art exhibitions officials have planned for it.

The **Schauspielhaus**, a jewel of Greco-Roman–revival style, was one of Schinkel's most notable structures. From the time it opened in 1821 until its destruction during the war, it served first as the Royal Court, then as the Prussian state theater. Since its restoration in 1987 it has been used as eastern Berlin's main concert hall. The **Restaurant Französischer Hof**, Jägerstrasse 56, offers French and international cuisine in an Art Nouveau setting. For lunch or dinner it's a delightful spot from which to view the square's architecture.

From the Gendarmenmarkt it is one block west back to Friedrichstrasse and three blocks north to Unter den Linden; from there it's a ten-minute stroll back to the Brandenburg Gate and the Tiergarten.

THE TIERGARTEN AREA

Tiergarten (literally, "animal garden") is the name of one of the largest of Berlin's nearly 50 public parks as well as of an entire borough. The eight-square-mile district is bordered by Berlin Mitte, the Brandenburg Gate, and Potsdamer Platz to the east, the Europa-Center and Bahnhof Zoo to the west.

Although one of the smallest and least populated of western Berlin's boroughs, it is also one of the richest in culture and interesting sights. Within its southern half are the Tiergarten itself; the zoo; the Reichstag building; Schloss Bellevue; the Siegessäule (Victory Column); the Soviet War Memorial; Congress Hall (a gift to Berlin from the United States); the Hansaviertel of modern architecture; the Kulturform complex, which includes the Philharmonic, the Neue Nationalgalerie, the Kunstgewerbemuseum (Museum of Applied Arts), the Bauhaus-Archiv, and the Staatsbibliothek (National Library); and the former German army headquarters building. The Landwehr canal and the Spree river cut across the borough. Its main thoroughfare, east to west, is the Strasse des 17. Juni.

To explore the Tiergarten you'll have to do quite a bit of walking, as public transportation in the area is not the best. The U-9 subway runs along the western periphery of the Tiergarten and stops at the Hansaplatz station, close to the

Hansaviertel and Bellevue Palace. The S-3 elevated train serves the Tiergarten station near the Strasse des 17. Juni as well as the Bellevue station, close to Bellevue Palace. A number of bus lines also provide access to the district; the most convenient is the number 100, which you can board either on Unter den Linden going west or near the Kurfürstendamm U-Bahn station going east. The shortest walk into the park and district is west from the Brandenburg Gate or northeast from the Europa-Center along Budapester Strasse, past the entrance to the zoo and the Inter-Continental Hotel.

The Tiergarten

The Tiergarten originally was a hunting preserve of the dukes and electors of Brandenburg. In 1717 it was transformed into a geometric, manicured Baroque-style park, only to be relandscaped in the manner of a freely growing, unstructured English garden by Prussia's greatest landscape architect, Peter Joseph Lenné, between 1833 and 1839. Dotted with numerous cafés and restaurants, it soon became Berlin's favorite recreation area. The park was also popular with the rich, famous, and powerful, who built their residences and embassies in its southern sector along Lichtensteinallee, Corneliusstrasse, and Tiergartenstrasse.

During the final month of World War II the Tiergarten was shelled into a virtual moonscape. What survived the fighting was ravaged that first postwar winter by desperate citizens who felled the remaining trees for firewood and planted cabbage and potatoes on the open spaces. Most of the foreign embassies lay in ruins, and their bricks and stones were carted off to rebuild the rest of the city. Only the Japanese embassy, recently turned into a German-Japanese cultural center, and the Italian embassy, built in the Fascist "Duce Style," survived. Use of the Tiergarten as a source for produce continued throughout the Berlin blockade and airlift. It was not until the spring of 1949, when the division of Germany was already a certainty, that replanting and relandscaping of the park began.

Today the Tiergarten is again an urban oasis of trees, shrubs, lawns, flower beds, ponds, idyllic little lakes sprinkled with rowboats, cafés, restaurants, and 15½ miles of paths and trails.

You can get a bird's-eye view of it all by climbing 285 steps to the observation platform of the **Siegessäule**, the victory column in the middle of the park on the traffic rotary called Der Grosse Stern (Big Star). The 224-foot-high Greco-Roman–style column, topped by a gilded Winged Victory, was built between 1869 and 1873 to commemorate Prussia's

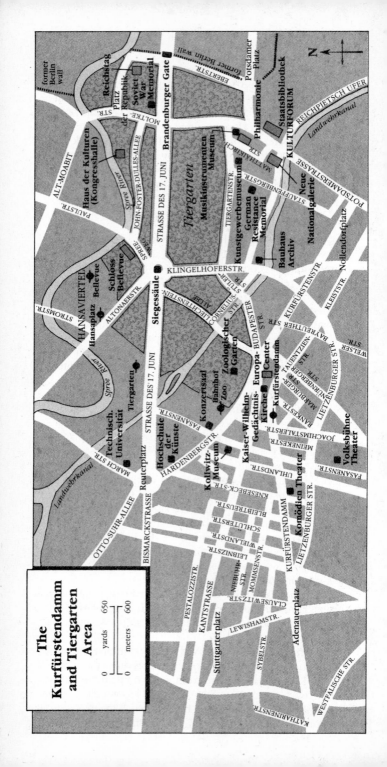

triumphs in the wars against Denmark, Austria and Bavaria, and France. Originally it was erected in front of the Reichstag, where it stood until 1938. That year, Albert Speer, Hitler's future minister of armaments, had the column moved to Der Grosse Stern on Charlottenburger Chaussee (now the Strasse des 17. Juni).

When originally laid out in the late 17th century, the **Strasse des 17. Juni** (the name commemorates the June 17, 1953, workers' uprising in East Berlin) was intended to be a coach road between the royal palace in Berlin Mitte and Schloss Charlottenburg, the new summer palace that Elector Friedrich III (later King Friedrich I) was building for his second wife, Sophie-Charlotte. In effect an extension of Unter den Linden, Strasse des 17. Juni cuts a 4-km (2½-mile) swath through the Tiergarten in an east–west direction, then changes its name to Otto-Suhr-Allee and continues on to the Charlottenburg palace.

Just north of the Brandenburg Gate, and easily visible from there, is the **Reichstag**, Germany's former parliament building. (Whether it will fill that role again when, as is planned, the Bundestag moves from Bonn to Berlin, supposedly by 1998, depends in part on what it will cost to restructure the interior to meet the needs of a modern legislature. Meanwhile it will be used for occasional celebratory sessions of the Bundestag.) A colossus measuring more than 450 feet wide, it was built in Neo-Renaissance and "Reich braggadocio" style between 1884 and 1894. (Kaiser Wilhelm I personally laid the cornerstone.) The Reichstag became the symbol of Hitler's destruction of democracy when it went up in flames on February 27, 1933. The Reichstag fire remains one of the unsolved mysteries of the Nazi era.

Capitalizing on popular indignation over the blaze, Hitler persuaded aging President Paul von Hindenburg, a World War I hero, to suspend all constitutional liberties and grant him full emergency powers. Within days, thousands of Nazi opponents all over Germany were arrested and put in prisons or hastily created concentration camps. Later that week Hitler and the Nazis handily won their first real majority in national elections. Along with the dying embers of the gutted Reichstag building, democracy disappeared in Germany.

Marinus van der Lubbe, a young Dutchman captured near the fire, was tried with three alleged co-conspirators—Bulgarian agents of the Communist International (Comintern), among them Georgi Dimitrov, who became the first prime minister of Bulgaria after World War II. The Bulgarians were acquitted, but van der Lubbe was sentenced to death and guillotined. Throughout his trial, van der Lubbe insisted that he had acted alone and on his own initiative.

The official Nazi version held that the fire had been a Communist plot. However, many suspected that van der Lubbe was a stooge and that the Nazis themselves had set the fire (using an underground passageway into the building to gain access), thereby giving Hitler a pretext for obtaining dictatorial powers.

Although the building was partly repaired and restored in the 1930s, Hitler's puppet Reichstag never convened in it again. The "world's highest-paid men's chorus," as the Third Reich's parliament was called, met in the nearby Kroll opera house to rubber-stamp the Führer's decisions. The Reichstag was severely damaged during World War II air raids. When the last German defenders of Berlin turned it into a fortress in April 1945, the Soviet army bombarded it with an estimated one million artillery shells. After the Russians captured the city, one of their first acts was to raise the Soviet flag over the building.

For years the Reichstag stood as a ruin. Reconstruction began in 1954 and was completed, after many delays, in 1972. Since then, in addition to serving as the occasional site of caucuses and formal celebrations of parliament, it has served as an exhibition hall.

There is probably no other spot in Berlin as weighted with politics and history as this easternmost edge of the Tiergarten. During the 28 years that the Wall divided Berlin, the Reichstag, one corner of which was a couple of feet from the Wall itself, represented a kind of outpost against Communism. The Brandenburg Gate was East Berlin's bastion against capitalism. These two symbols of Berlin and of Germany, flying the similar but dissimilar flags of the two Germanys, seemed to face each other like two huge warships. Now, as people move freely between the two, that feeling is gone.

Just 200 yards west of the Brandenburg Gate, on the Strasse des 17. Juni, is the **Soviet War Memorial**. Constructed in 1946 of marble from the ruins of the Reich chancellery, it bears the bronze figure of a Soviet soldier with fixed bayonet flanked by the two Red Army tanks that are said to have been the first to reach Berlin in 1945. The monument, once guarded by two Soviet troopers, is now under the surveillance of Berlin police.

A 20-minute walk northwest from the Soviet memorial will take you to the Spree river embankment, John-Foster-Dulles-Allee, and the **Kongresshalle**, now called the *Haus der Kulturen der Welt*. Designed by U.S. architect Hugh Stubbins for the 1957 Interbau architectural exposition, it was a gift of the U.S. Congress to the people of Berlin. Local wagsters dubbed it the "Pregnant Oyster" because of the shape of its roof. In 1980 the roof came crashing down, killing one person and injuring a dozen others. After repairs and reconstruction it reopened as the "House of World Cultures," an exhibition hall for rotating shows of non-European art and as a conference and concert center.

A ten-minute stroll along the Spree embankment or John-Foster-Dulles-Allee will bring you to **Schloss Bellevue**, a Neoclassical château built in the 1780s for Prince Ferdinand, the younger brother of Frederick the Great. Although severely damaged during World War II, the château was completely restored in 1959. Since then it has served as the Berlin residence of Germany's federal president. When the government moves to Berlin and the president into the Kronprinzenpalais on Unter den Linden, Bellevue will be turned into a guest house for visiting foreign dignitaries. It is not open to the public.

From Schloss Bellevue it's a ten-minute walk north and west to the **Hansaviertel**, a residential and shopping district that is a prime example of 1950s architecture and urban planning. In fact, the district's mixture of high-rise apartment houses, boxlike single-family dwellings, churches, and stores was built as an exhibit for the 1957 Interbau exposition. Leading modern architects of the day, including Egon Eiermann, Walter Gropius, Oscar Niemeyer, Alvar Aalto, and Arne Jacobsen, are represented here.

The biggest attraction in the southern half of the Tiergarten is the **Zoologischer Garten** (there is also a zoo in east Berlin). Entry, however, is not from the Tiergarten itself: The main gate is at Hardenbergplatz, just east of Bahnhof Zoo; the side gate, called the Elefantentor, is on Budapester Strasse, virtually across the street from the Europa-Center. (There is no way you can miss the Elefantentor—it resembles a Chinese temple portal with its columns supported by two stone elephants.)

Berlin's Zoologischer Garten is not only the largest zoo in the world, with more than 11,000 animals representing 1,575 species, it is also one of the oldest, dating back to 1841, when Prussia's King Friedrich Wilhelm IV consigned his collection of animals to the city. The **Aquarium**, just inside the Elephant Gate, houses another 10,000 animals, among them fish, amphibians, reptiles, and insects. It's best to get a combined ticket for both. Zoo and aquarium both open at 9:00 A.M. daily; the aquarium closes at 6:00 P.M., the zoo at dusk or 7:00 P.M., whichever comes first.

The Kulturforum Complex

From the zoo it is a one-mile walk back east along Budapester Strasse, northeast along Stülerstrasse to Tiergartenstrasse, then east again to Berlin's Kulturforum. Virtually everything in this area was destroyed during the war. Now the Philharmonie, the Staatsbibliothek, the Neue Nationalgalerie, the Kunstgewerbemuseum, the Musikinstrumenten Museum, and the Kupferstichkabinett are clustered here.

The **Philharmonie**, on Kemperplatz, home of the Berlin Philharmonic Orchestra, is one of the city's most daring pieces of contemporary architecture. Designed by Bremen architect Hans Scharoun and completed in 1963, it is an asymmetrical structure with a tentlike roof. The hall itself, with seating for 2,000, is pentagonal in shape, and the stage is in the center, so that half the audience looks at the backs of the musicians. That arrangement caused a furor at first, but was soon accepted because of the excellent acoustics.

Scharoun also designed the nearby **Staatsbibliothek** (State Library), at Potsdamer Strasse 33, which houses the remnants of the Prussian National Library along with newer acquisitions—some 3.5 million books at present (with space for another 4.5 million), as well as a huge periodicals department.

Mies van der Rohe's **Neue Nationalgalerie**, at Potsdamer Strasse 50, just across from the library, is a stunning steel-and-glass pavilion-like structure that was completed in 1968, a year before the architect's death. Until about 1994 or 1995 the art collection here will consist of paintings, sculptures, and graphics from the late 19th and 20th centuries. Then the 19th-century works will move to the Nationalgalerie on Museum Island, while the Neue Nationalgalerie will show only 20th-century art and special rotating exhibitions. Contemporary art will be shown in the **Hamburger Bahnhof** on Invalidenstrasse. That oldest Berlin railway station (built in 1847) has been a museum and exhibition hall since 1906. It has been under reconstruction for a number of years and is expected to open as a division of the National Gallery in 1994.

The new **Kupferstichkabinett** (entrance on Matthäikirchplatz), housing both the western and eastern print collections, opened in the fall of 1993.

The architecture of the **Kunstgewerbemuseum** (Museum of Applied Arts), at Tiergartenstrasse 1, was thoroughly panned when it opened in 1987: People complained that it looked like a cross between a fortress and a power plant. Be that as it may, its collection is superb—with examples of every kind of European applied art from the Middle Ages through the 20th century.

At the **Musikinstrumenten Museum**, at Tiergartenstrasse 6, you will find a collection of musical instruments from around the world, dating from the early 16th to the 19th century.

All the museums are open daily, except Mondays, from 9:00 A.M. to 5:00 P.M., and from 10:00 A.M. on Saturdays and Sundays.

The Kulturforum also includes the **Bauhaus-Archiv**, Klingelhöfferstrasse 14, a building completed in 1978 after a design by Walter Gropius. It exhibits architectural models, designs, drawings, paintings, furnishings, ceramics, textiles, and numerous other objects by the leading architects, artists, and designers of the famous Bauhaus School, including Wassily Kandinsky, Paul Klee, Oskar Schlemmer, Lyonel Feininger, Walter Gropius, and Ludwig Mies van der Rohe. (Open daily except Tuesdays, 11:00 A.M. to 5:00 P.M., Fridays until 8:00 P.M.)

If you walk one block west on Tiergartenstrasse you'll come to the **Gedenkstätte Deutscher Widerstand** (German Resistance Memorial) on Stauffenbergstrasse, named for Claus Graf Schenck von Stauffenberg, the Wehrmacht colonel who planted a bomb in Hitler's Eastern front headquarters on July 20, 1944. The street used to be called Bendlerstrasse, and the grim, gray building at number 14 was the **German War Office**, where Stauffenberg and three of his co-conspirators were executed when the plot failed. A memorial to the four men stands in the courtyard where they were shot. The third floor of this old war-ministry building, which now houses various municipal offices, is devoted to a permanent exhibition of documents and artifacts dealing with the resistance movement. It is open Monday through Friday from 9:00 A.M. to 6:00 P.M., and Saturdays and Sundays until 1:00 P.M.

ON AND AROUND THE KURFÜRSTENDAMM

The Kurfürstendamm—Ku'damm for short—runs southwest from the zoo and southwestern tip of the Tiergarten. This is Berlin's grandest commercial avenue: two miles of conspicuous consumption, round-the-clock entertainment, pleasant strolling, and fascinating people-watching. In many ways it symbolizes what West Berlin was during the dark years of the Cold War—both a *Frontstadt* (front-line city) and a showcase of capitalism. The boulevard is lined with the city's most expensive shops; dozens of restaurants, cafés, and night spots; numerous cinemas and theaters; and some of Berlin's best hotels, including its most luxurious, the Bristol Hotel Kempinski, at Kurfürstendamm 27. The Ku'damm was and is to Berlin what the Champs-Elysées was and is to Paris.

The avenue's name derives from *Kurfürst,* meaning elector, and *Damm,* meaning causeway. The duchy of Brandenburg's elector Joachim II had it laid out in the 1540s as a carriageway between the ducal palace in Berlin-Cölln and his hunting château in the Grunewald. Not until nearly 350 years later, in 1881, at the instigation of Prussia's and the German Reich's prime minister, Otto von Bismarck, was it turned into a 175-foot-wide parkway, divided along its length by a broad strip of grass and trees. Although removed from what was then Berlin's governmental, financial, and cultural center, it soon became one of the city's most vibrant and sought-after strips of real estate. There were so many cafés, in fact, that American novelist Thomas Wolfe described the Ku'damm as "the biggest coffeehouse in Europe."

One of the boulevard's most famous cafés is the **Café Möhring** at Kurfürstendamm 213, a favorite hangout of politicians and intellectuals in the early years of the century. Among its habitués were Reich chancellor Theobald von Bethmann-Hollweg, Russian playwright Maxim Gorky, German writers Gottfried Benn and Frank Wedekind, and the painter-poet Else Lasker-Schüler.

Unfortunately, half of the Ku'damm's *Jugendstil* (German Art Nouveau) buildings were destroyed during World War II and replaced by nondescript steel-and-glass structures, so if you're looking for interesting turn-of-the-century architecture, the supply here is a bit skimpy. The rewards are greater on the streets that intersect the Ku'damm, especially Meinekestrasse, Fasanenstrasse, Uhlandstrasse, Knesebeckstrasse, Bleibtreustrasse, Schlüterstrasse, and Wielandstrasse.

If you want a respite from the commerce and consumption, visit the **Käthe-Kollwitz-Museum** in the late-19th-century villa at Fasanenstrasse 24, just off the Ku'damm itself. The museum houses a collection of 100 lithographs, 70 drawings, and 15 bronze sculptures by this Berlin artist, who, in the late 19th and early 20th century, depicted the misery of poverty, hunger, and war more movingly than anyone of her generation. (Open daily except Tuesdays from 11:00 A.M. to 6:00 P.M.)

In the adjacent villa at Fasanenstrasse 23, the **Wintergarten Café im Literaturhaus** is a delightfully calm and dignified refuge from the hustle and bustle of the avenue, good for a coffee break, a light lunch, or even dinner. They serve breakfast until 1:00 P.M. and stay open until 1:00 A.M.

The best way to see the Ku'damm is to start at the Europa-Center, stroll up one side to where it ends at the intersection of Katharinenstrasse and Westfälische Strasse, then cross over and amble back on the other side. You can explore the cross streets according to your mood and fancy. If the distances seem a bit daunting, don't worry: The myriad eateries and watering places along the route provide ample opportunities to recharge your batteries. Moreover, the buses that run along it—numbers 109, 119, and 129—have a special "Ku'damm" rate of DM 1.5, one-way.

The only "must see" monument on the boulevard is the **Kaiser-Wilhelm-Gedächtnis-Kirche**, or Kaiser Wilhelm Memorial Church, just west of the Europa-Center. Begun in 1891 to mark the 20th anniversary of the Second German Reich, and completed in 1895, it originally was a Neo-Romanesque structure. Wartime raids leveled all but the western spire and portal, however, which eventually were preserved as a memorial to peace. (Berliners, who find humorously cynical names for nearly all their public edifices, call it the "Hollow Tooth.")

For more than a decade after the war there was endless debate about what to do with the ruin. In 1959 Egon Eiermann, one of Germany's leading modern architects, was commissioned to build a new church around it. His complex consists of a hexagonal flat-topped belfry tower, an octagonal central church building, a sacristy, and a chapel. The walls of the complex are a concrete honeycomb with 20,000 spaces filled by glass mosaics created by the French glass artist Gabriel Loire of Chartres. The bronze crucifix in the main church building is based on a pencil sketch by the early 20th-century German sculptor Ernst Barlach.

KREUZBERG

You can still get a vivid idea of what living conditions were like in Berlin's 19th-century tenement areas in the boroughs of Wedding, Neukölln, and especially Kreuzberg.

Located southeast of the Tiergarten, and bordered on the north and northeast by Berlin Mitte, Kreuzberg is just four square miles in area. However, with a population of 130,000 it is the borough that most closely resembles the original scene: run-down, neglected, and crowded. But it is also where Berlin's cultural, subcultural, and countercultural renaissance began in the 1970s. This is where the *Neue Wilden* (New Wild) artists had, and in some cases still have, their studios. It is also the borough of punkers and skinheads, of squatters and revolutionaries, of the old and impoverished, of people seeking alternative lifestyles, and of Turkish "guest workers," who account for one-third of the district's population.

To be sure, opinions about Kreuzberg vary. Some call it a

"zoo," others liken it to New York City's East Village, and still others consider it "an intellectual prison." The common denominator here is variety. Art galleries, bookshops, second-hand emporiums, health-food stores, boutiques, hole-in-the-wall theaters, kebab stands, and countless dives line shabby streets dwarfed by 19th-century tenement blocks. From the Möckernbrücke subway stop in the west to the Schlesisches Tor station in the east, from the Kochstrasse stop at the district's northern periphery to the Platz der Luftbrücke stop and Tempelhof airfield on the southern edge, Kreuzberg is Berlin at its wildest and most confusing.

The easiest and fastest way to get into Kreuzberg is by subway. The U-1 travels west–east through the borough to the Schlesisches Tor station. The U-6 line runs through Kreuzberg on a north–south axis. The U-8 subway's northern stop in Kreuzberg is Moritzplatz; it then runs southeast through the borough and intersects with the U-1 at Kottbusser Tor. The U-7 line runs generally southeast.

The art scene in Kreuzberg is represented by a string of commercial galleries on Oranienstrasse, as well as on and around Chamissoplatz, near the Platz der Luftbrücke. Two of the most interesting cafés in the district are the **Café Jedermann,** Diefenbachstrasse 18, open from 9:00 A.M. to 2:00 A.M., and the **Café,** Muskauer Strasse 23, open from 11:00 A.M. to 3:00 A.M., with breakfast served as late as 4:00 P.M. The borough is also going upmarket with a profusion of medium- to high-priced restaurants and bistros, not to mention skyrocketing rents. The most established spot, and a popular hangout for artists, is the **Exil,** at 44a Paul-Lincke-Ufer, near the Kottbusser Tor station.

Kreuzberg is also home to five unusual museums and to what in many respects is the city's most important postwar monument. The first of the museums, the **Berlinische Galerie,** located in the Martin-Gropius-Bau, Stresemannstrasse 110, at the northwest tip of the borough, is devoted entirely to late-19th- and early-20th-century Berlin visual arts: painting, sculpture, graphics, design, architecture, and applied art. Only the Brücke group of Expressionists is not included in the collection, as the Expressionists have their own museum: the Brücke, near the Dahlem complex (see below). The collection is especially strong in Dada art, Berlin Realism of the 1920s, and late-19th-century Impressionists who lived and worked in Berlin, and the building itself is almost as interesting as the exhibits. It was designed in the early 1880s by Walter Gropius's uncle, Martin Gropius, as Berlin's museum of applied art, and was reconstructed after its near-total destruction during World War II. Hours are 10:00 A.M. to 8:00 P.M. daily, except Mondays.

Next to the Martin-Gropius-Bau and adjacent to a remnant of the Wall is what at first appears to be a vast empty lot. But it is a space of horror. The Prinz-Albrecht Palais and other buildings that stood here were the offices of the Gestapo, the SS, and the Reich Head Security Office, where Heinrich Himmler, Reinhard Heydrich, and Ernst Kaltenbrunner had their headquarters. This was the Third Reich's most feared address, the focal point of Nazi terror, and the place where the Holocaust was planned. Subterranean bunkers, prison and interrogation cells, and other cellars of the mansions, hotel, and school that once stood there and became the SS and Gestapo buildings from 1933 to 1945, were excavated in the 1980s and later integrated into a documentary exhibition, the **Topographie des Terrors** (Topography of Terror), detailing the entire history of Nazi terror. (Open daily except Mondays from 10:00 A.M. to 6:00 P.M.)

Just a few yards from the northwestern corner of the site is the reconstruction of the **Preussischer Landtag** (Prussian Parliament Building), which, since completion, has become the Berlin City-State Assembly building.

Due north of it, between Potsdamer Platz and Toleranz-strasse (as Wilhelmstrasse in eastern Berlin is now called), municipal archaeologists have unearthed remnants of the Führer's bunker, complete with furnishings and artifacts. It is part of the underground network in which Hitler, Goebbels, other Nazi bigwigs, and their staff had their headquarters during the last weeks of the war. Most of the labyrinth was blown up by the Soviets in 1945. The city has placed the bunkers under monument protection but sealed them off from public viewing.

Two blocks south of the Kochstrasse subway station (U-6 line) at Lindenstrasse 14 is the **Berlin Museum**. The museum's displays of art, furnishings, porcelain, handicrafts, and artifacts will tell you everything about Berlin and its history you could possibly want to know. The building itself is a gem of Neoclassical architecture that was completed in 1735 and served as the city's supreme appellate court for two centuries. From 1816 to 1822 one of the justices was E. T. A. Hoffmann, the painter, composer, conductor, and author of fantasy tales, on whose life and stories the opera *Tales of Hoffmann* is based. Crammed with the bric-a-brac of Berlin's history, the museum is also a great spot for a snack or lunch. The **Alt-Berliner Weissbierstube**, on its main floor, serves seven varieties of *Berliner Weisse,* the local wheat beer, and an array of Berlin specialties such as *Soleier* (hard-boiled eggs pickled in salt brine), *Rollmops* (pickled herring), *Hackepeter* (sharply seasoned raw ground meat served on a piece of bread or crisp roll), and *Sülze* (jellied meat). The museum is open daily, except Mondays, from 10:00 A.M. to 10:00 P.M.; the pub is open Tuesday through Friday from 11:00 A.M. to 6:00 P.M., Saturdays and Sundays until 4:00 P.M.

Near the Kochstrasse station at Friedrichstrasse 44, on the corner of Kochstrasse and Friedrichstrasse, the **Haus am Checkpoint Charlie** contains an impressive collection of vehicles and equipment used by East Berlin refugees to flee over, tunnel under, ram through, and get around the Berlin Wall and the East–West German border. Among the exhibits are pint-size automobiles with hidden compartments for refugees, fake U.S. and Soviet army uniforms, and pieces of the hot-air balloon in which two East German couples and their four children floated over the border in 1979. The museum is a tribute to human wit, courage, and ingenuity. Museum hours are 9:00 A.M. to 10:00 P.M. daily.

Though Checkpoint Charlie on Friedrichstrasse, the erst-while crossing between the American and Soviet sectors, does not exist anymore, many of its grim accoutrements—a watchtower, segments of the Wall, pillboxes, barbed wire— have been preserved and are under monuments protection. The museum acts as curator of these Cold War relics, which will be integrated into a new "American Business Center" on Friedrichstrasse.

Take the U-6 from Kochstrasse to Hallesches Tor and trans-fer there to the westbound U-1, taking it to the Möckern-brücke stop near the **Museum für Verkehr und Technik** (Museum of Transport and Technology), at Trebbiner Strasse 9. Housed in Kreuzberg's 19th-century market hall, icehouse, and the locomotive yard of the Anhalter freight train depot, the museum's exhibits include one of Otto Lilienthal's origi-nal gliders; Baron von Drais's wooden *Laufrad* (the world's first bicycle); and early steam locomotives. It is open 9:00 A.M. to 5:30 P.M. Tuesday through Friday, and 10:00 A.M. to 6:00 P.M. Saturdays and Sundays.

Few structures are more symbolic of the division of Berlin than the **Luftbrückendenkmal** (Airlift Monument), on Platz der Luftbrücke at the entrance to Tempelhof airfield. The 65-foot-high stone memorial, with its three towering arches symbolizing the three air corridors that linked West Berlin with the Western occupation zones of Germany during the 1948–1949 blockade by the Soviets, is a tribute not only to the airlift itself, which kept the city alive, but also to the 31 American and 41 British servicemen who died in the line of duty during the operation.

The Soviet blockade of West Berlin had its roots in the Western Allies' decision, on June 20, 1948, to introduce the deutsche mark into the three western sectors of Berlin. The Anglo-American answer to the blockade was "Operation Vittles," the airlift that lasted nearly 11 months until the U.S. and Soviet governments negotiated a settlement of the dispute. During the operation American transport planes alone made 277,728 flights into the city.

Tempelhof, the focal point of the airlift, is virtually in the middle of the city, and has a history going back to the earliest days of aviation. Indeed, it actually predates airplanes. In 1883 Arnold Böcklin, a Swiss landscape painter who was also an inventor, experimented on the site with two motorless biplanes, which he failed to get off the ground because of high winds. In 1908 the Wright brothers demonstrated one of their planes here with a 19-minute flight. In 1923 Tempelhof, which takes its name from a 13th-century church built by the Knights Templars, became Berlin's central airport. In 1975 the city's civil air traffic was routed to Tegel because the Tempelhof runways, surrounded by apartment houses, shops, office buildings, a public park, and a sports stadium, could not be extended to accommodate wide-bodied jetliners. For the next 15 years it was used exclusively by the U.S. Air Force. Since early 1991 the airport has again been used for commercial flights, all of them on regional and feeder lines.

SCHÖNEBERG

This borough, just west of Kreuzberg and Tempelhof and south of the Tiergarten, was the "capital" of West Berlin. Once a rich farming area, it became an independent city in 1898 and had a population of well over 200,000 when it was incorporated into Berlin in 1920.

Rathaus Schöneberg (also the name of a subway station on the U-4 and U-7 lines, which intersect here), the borough's city hall, is a massive structure that could easily be mistaken for a factory. It was the seat of West Berlin's city-state government from December 1948 until reunification. The building's 230-foot clock tower houses the Liberty Bell, a replica of the bell at Independence Hall in Philadelphia. The bell was a gift of the American people to the people of Berlin, and the signatures of 17 million Americans who contributed money for it during the 1948–1949 Crusade for Freedom are preserved in a book in the tower. The ten-ton bell is rung daily at noon and on special occasions.

It was from the tower balcony facing the square that, on June 26, 1963, President John F. Kennedy delivered the memorable speech in which he said: "All free men, wherever they may live, are citizens of Berlin, and, therefore, as a free man, I take pride in the words '*Ich bin ein Berliner*.' " Berliners have revered him ever since.

AWAY FROM THE CENTER

THE DAHLEM MUSEUMS

From Rathaus Schöneberg, or elsewhere in the inner city, it is a 20- to 30-minute subway ride southwest on the U-2 line to the Dahlem-Dorf station, the heart of the great museum area in the leafy residential district of Dahlem.

West Berliners love to confront visitors with a riddle: Who are the city's two most famous residents? The answer: Queen Nefertiti and The Man with the Golden Helmet. The bust of Nefertiti, the world's most beautiful and most photographed woman (even if she does have one eye missing), is the centerpiece of western Berlin's Ägyptisches Museum (Egyptian Museum), near Charlottenburg Palace. Although its authenticity is now doubted, *The Man with the Golden Helmet* is by far the most popular "Rembrandt" in west Berlin's Gemäldegalerie (Picture Gallery), one of the main attractions in the Dahlem museum complex.

The Dahlem complex, one block south of the Dahlem-Dorf subway station, with entrances at Arnimallee 23 and Lansstrasse 8, includes the Skulpturengalerie (Sculpture Gallery), the Gemäldegalerie, the Museum für Völkerkunde (Ethnographic Museum), the **Museum für Indische Kunst** (Museum of Indian Art), the **Museum für Islamische Kunst** (Museum of Islamic Art), and the **Museum für Ostasiatische Kunst** (Museum of East Asian Art). But with the amalgamation of the city's western and eastern collections in the coming years some of this will change.

The **Skulpturengalerie**, covering two floors in the Lansstrasse building, is full of spectacular pieces dating from the Early Christian–Byzantine period through the 19th century. Among the greatest treasures here are wood carvings by Tilman Riemenschneider and other German masters and works by such Italian sculptors as Giovanni Pisano, Donatello, and Bernini.

The **Gemäldegalerie**, located on two floors and in three wings of the Arnimallee building, is a treasure trove of

European painting from the Middle Ages through the Neo-classical period. The German masters represented here include Albrecht Altdorfer, Lucas Cranach the Elder, Hans Holbein the Younger, and Albrecht Dürer. In the Dutch and Flemish division are 25 Rembrandts and 19 Rubenses. In addition there are major works by Hieronymus Bosch, the Brueghels, Sir Anthony Van Dyck, Jan Van Eyck, Hugo van der Goes, Frans Hals, Hans Memling, Jan Vermeer, and Rogier van der Weyden. The Italian section includes a dozen paintings by the Bellinis—father Jacopo and sons Giovanni and Gentile—seven Botticellis, and Giottos, Tintorettos, Titians, and Raphaels. The Spanish school is represented by, among others, El Greco's haunting *Mater Dolorosa* and Diego Velázquez's *Three Musicians*. The entire collection, together with those on the Museumsinsel, will move to a new building on the Kulturforum site in 1996.

The **Museum für Völkerkunde**, whose entrance is on Lansstrasse, is one of the most important ethnographic museums in Europe. Unfortunately, only a small portion of the collection, which is divided into five sections—pre-Columbian American, African, Southeast Asian, East Asian, and Pacific South Seas art—is on permanent display.

If, after having visited these four museums, your legs, back, and eyes are still in working order, proceed to the museums of Indian, Islamic, and East Asian art. All the Dahlem museums are open Tuesday through Friday from 9:00 A.M. to 5:00 P.M.; weekends from 10:00 A.M.

About a half hour's walk from the Dahlem complex, at Bussardsteig 9 near the edge of Grunewald forest (see Green Berlin and the Lakes, below), you will find the **Brücke Museum**, named for *Die Brücke* (The Bridge), a group of early-20th-century German Expressionists. Virtually all these artists, who collaborated between 1905 and 1913, are represented, including Erich Heckel, Ernst Ludwig Kirchner, Otto Mueller, Emil Nolde, Max Pechstein, and, not least, Karl Schmidt-Rottluff, whose own collection of paintings, a gift to the city, comprises the body of this collection. Hours are 11:00 A.M. to 5:00 P.M., daily except Tuesdays.

SCHLOSS CHARLOTTENBURG AND THE MUSEUMS

It was not until the late 17th century that the electors of Brandenburg began to build grand residences, but once started they freely indulged in ostentatious pomp and conspicuous Baroque consumption. Most of their lavish digs

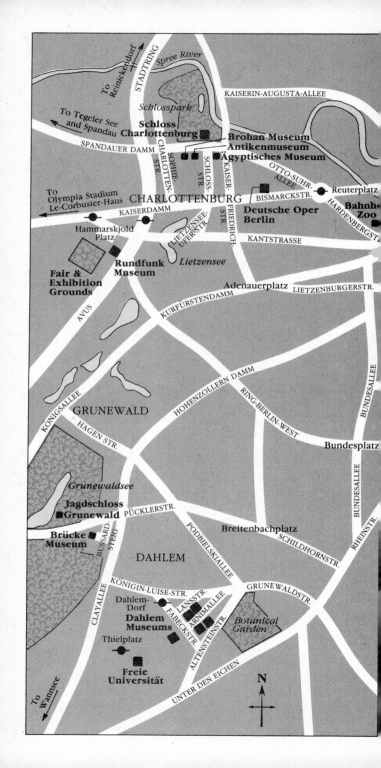

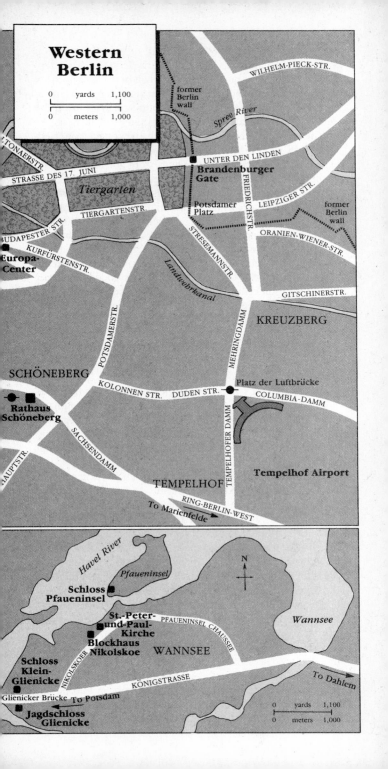

Western Berlin

0   yards   1,100

0   meters   1,000

WILHELM-PIECK-STR.

former Berlin wall

Spree River

UNTER DEN LINDEN

Brandenburger Gate

FRIEDRICHSTR.

LEIPZIGER STR.

former Berlin wall

ALTONAERSTR.

STRASSE DES 17. JUNI

Tiergarten

TIERGARTENSTR.

Potsdamer Platz

ORANIEN-WIENER-STR.

BUDAPESTER STR.

KURFÜRSTENSTR.

Europa-Center

STRESEMANNSTR.

Landwehrkanal

GITSCHINERSTR.

POTSDAMERSTR.

MEHRINGDAMM

KREUZBERG

SCHÖNEBERG

KOLONNEN STR.   DUDEN STR.

Platz der Luftbrücke

COLUMBIA-DAMM

● **Rathaus Schöneberg**

SACHSENDAMM

TEMPELHOFER DAMM

HAUPTSTR.

TEMPELHOF

Tempelhof Airport

RING-BERLIN-WEST

To Marienfelde

Havel River

Pfaueninsel

N

Schloss Pfaueninsel

St.-Peter-und-Paul-Kirche

PFAUENINSEL CHAUSSEE

Wannsee

Blockhaus Nikolskoe

NIKOLSKOER

WANNSEE

Schloss Klein-Glienicke

KÖNIGSTRASSE

To Dahlem

Glienicker Brücke   To Potsdam

Jagdschloss Glienicke

0   yards   1,100

0   meters   1,000

were damaged during World War II; nearly all have been restored. The most dazzling palace is **Schloss Charlotten-burg** in Charlottenburg borough, a half-hour walk north of Kurfürstendamm and its intersection with Adenauerplatz, or about ten minutes on foot along Otto-Suhr-Allee from the Richard-Wagner-Platz subway station on the U-7 line.

The building was commissioned in 1695 by Elector Fried-rich III (King Friedrich I) as a summer palace for his second wife, Sophie-Charlotte. Many wings were added in the 18th century, along with a manicured park, little pavilions, and various museums. Even a cursory visit fills up half a day. The ornate historic apartments, which can be seen only on guided one-hour tours, are open from 9:00 A.M. to 5:00 P.M., daily except Mondays, and Thursdays to 8:00 P.M. Tours start about every 20 minutes; the last one begins at 4:00.

During the 220 years that the Hohenzollern clan used the palace, the interior decor and furnishings underwent many changes to suit changing tastes. But as frugal Prussians, they never threw anything away. Instead, each generation stored its forebears' household goods in Berlin's environs. As a result, the furniture survived the 1943 air raid that almost completely destroyed Schloss Charlottenburg, and postwar restorers could re-create the palace's interior as it had been during Sophie-Charlotte's time.

The queen was addicted to Oriental decor, which was then quite the rage. As you are shepherded through the more than 70 rooms and hallways open to the public, you'll see nearly a dozen decorated in East Asian motifs, including one chamber whose walls are entirely covered with Oriental porcelain.

Charlottenburg began rather modestly. The original cen-tral building, crowned by an elegant 165-foot copper dome upon which stands a gilded figure of Fortuna, was a summer "cottage" with only a dozen rooms. But Sophie-Charlotte was a brilliant hostess who gave lavish parties and balls, for which she needed more space. Extension of the central building and the addition of the Orangerie began in 1701. Another wing was built between 1740 and 1746 by Frederick the Great's favorite architect, Georg Wenzeslaus von Knobels-dorff, and in 1790 a court summer theater was added. Today the façade of the entire palace complex, though only two stories high, is a mind-boggling 1,666 feet long.

The immense bronze equestrian statue in the center of the courtyard is of Duke Friedrich Wilhelm of Brandenburg, the Great Elector. Unveiled in 1703, it ranks as one of the finest examples of Baroque bronze sculpture in Europe. Its present location, however, is strictly postwar. Originally it stood on the Lange Brücke in Berlin Mitte, and later was moved to the front of the royal palace that is no more. In 1943, just before the first devastating Allied air raid on the city, the statue was removed by river barge to safety. Unfortunately, the barge sank in Tegel harbor. The statue was recovered in 1949 and erected in front of Schloss Charlottenburg in 1952.

The **Schlosspark** was laid out in 1697 in the neatly manicured French Baroque style. In the 19th century Lenné, the landscape architect of the Tiergarten, turned it into a less formal English-style garden. Part of it was then restored to its original Baroque form after World War II. The two principal buildings in the park are the **Schinkel Pavilion**, executed in the style of a Neapolitan villa, and the **Belvedere**, a late Rococo–style teahouse completed in 1788. The Schinkel Pavilion contains fine examples of late-18th-century furnishings. The Belvedere has a collection of 18th- and 19th-century china from Berlin's state-owned Royal Porcelain Manufactory.

The Charlottenburg Museums

Four museums that form part of the Prussian state collections are at Schloss Charlottenburg, two in the palace itself and two across the street in the former royal armory and the palace guards' barracks. Before visiting them you might want to fortify yourself with a light lunch in pseudo-royal surroundings at the **Kleine Orangerie**, Spandauer Damm 20, a moderately priced restaurant adjacent to the western Orangerie wing of the palace. Game dishes are among the restaurant's specialties.

The **Galerie der Romantik**, a division of Berlin's Nationalgalerie, is in the long Knobelsdorff wing of the palace and contains a fine collection of German Romantic painting. Caspar David Friedrich (1774–1840) and Carl Blechen (1798–1840) are each represented by 23 pictures. Though best known as an architect, Karl-Friedrich Schinkel (1781–1841) was a talented illustrator and painter as well; more than a dozen of his landscapes and pictures of imaginary Gothic cathedrals are on exhibit here.

At the opposite end of the long palace façade, in the former court theater, is the **Museum für Vor- und Frühgeschichte** (Pre- and Early History), housing a collection of art and artifacts from the Paleolithic, Mesolithic, and Neolithic cultures of Asia Minor as well as from the Bronze and Iron ages in Brandenburg.

The **Ägyptisches Museum**, at Schloss Strasse 70, across

the street from the palace, is the home of Queen Nefertiti, whose polychrome limestone bust draws an estimated half-million visitors a year. This 3,350-year-old sculpture alone is worth the visit, because Nefertiti, wife of Ikhnaton, was surely one of the greatest beauties of all time, and also because the bust is one of the finest pieces of art extant from the Amarna period. But there is much else to see in the museum, including an ebony bust of Queen Tiy, a green stone head of a priest, several mummies, and artifacts of daily life dating back some 5,000 years.

The **Antikenmuseum**, at Schloss Strasse 1, directly across the Schloss Strasse parkway from the Ägyptisches Museum, is a dazzling repository of art from the Minoan and Mycenaean periods through early Byzantine times, including Greek vases and amphoras, bronzes, jewelry, worked gold, and ivory carvings.

The Ägyptisches, Antiken, and Pre- and Early-History museums are open daily, except Fridays, from 9:00 A.M. to 5:00 P.M., and weekends from 10:00 A.M. The Galerie der Romantik is open daily except Mondays from 9:00 A.M. to 5:00 P.M., and weekends from 10:00 A.M.

You can buy replicas of some of the best pieces in west Berlin's state museums at the **Gipsformerei** on Sophie-Charlotten-Strasse 17–18, just beyond the west end of the palace grounds. This museum-sponsored workshop has more than 7,000 molds of the most famous sculptures and bas-reliefs in Berlin (and elsewhere), from which copies in plaster, synthetic stone or resin, and bronze can be cast. It keeps some of the more popular items in stock. A catalogue is available, and the Gipsformerei will also ship. Small stock items start at around DM 40; a copy of the head of Nefertiti goes for about DM 1,500. Open Monday through Friday, 9:00 A.M. to 4:00 P.M.; Wednesdays to 6:00 P.M.

Fans of Art Nouveau and Art Deco will want to take a look at the **Bröhan Museum**, Schloss Strasse 1a, adjacent to the Antikenmuseum. This stunning collection of paintings, furniture, china and glassware, and jewelry from the turn of the century to the 1930s was amassed by Berlin businessman Karl H. Bröhan, who donated it to the city in 1984. Open Tuesday through Sunday, 10:00 A.M. to 6:00 P.M., and Thursdays until 8:00 P.M.

OUTLYING AREAS

SPANDAU

The formerly independent town of Spandau, half a century older than Berlin itself, now one of its 20 boroughs, and best known perhaps for its Spandau prison, is situated at the westernmost edge of the city and is well worth a day's exploration. Getting there is easy. Take the U-7 subway westbound; the last two stops on the line, Zitadelle and Altstadt Spandau, are where the attractions are.

Zitadelle Spandau is a thick-walled medieval castle built on the foundations of one of Albrecht the Bear's 12th-century fortresses. The present complex, moated on three sides and bordered on the fourth by the Havel river (more of a lake here), was begun by Elector Joachim II in 1560 and completed in 1594. Since then it has remained virtually unchanged, a perfect example of Italian military engineering; indeed it was an Italian, Francesco Chiaramella di Gandino of Venice, who was its principal architect. Until the age of modern artillery it was virtually impregnable.

The citadel played a key role in the 17th- and 18th-century wars in which Brandenburg and, later, Prussia were involved. Twice it was captured—by the Swedes during the Thirty Years' War and by Napoleon in 1806—but each time without battle. The Juliusturm, the castle's central tower, is its oldest part, dating to 1200. The 19th-century kaisers used it as a kind of German Fort Knox, a storage depot for the five billion gold francs they wrested as "reparations" from France after the Franco-Prussian War of 1870–1871. What remained of the hoard after World War I was returned to France in accordance with the Treaty of Versailles.

Most of the buildings in the complex are open to visitors. The most rewarding is the Renaissance-style **Palast**, once the main living quarters of the fortress and now the home of Spandau's **Heimatmuseum** of local history. The collection is actually far less parochial than its name suggests and includes objects dating to the 10th and 11th centuries, when the Slavic Wends inhabited the area. The lower parts of the building incorporate 13th- and 14th-century tombstones with Hebrew inscriptions that were taken from Spandau's Jewish cemetery during a pogrom in 1348.

In the fortress commandant's house is the **Zitadellen-Schänke**, a rustic inn and restaurant that serves lunch and dinner as well as medieval-style banquets (the waiters and waitresses dress as knaves and wenches).

A ten-minute walk southwest from the citadel's main gate will take you to the heart of Spandau's **Altstadt** (Old City), where many 18th-century burgher houses have been restored in recent years. The Altstadt also has remnants of the city's medieval defensive wall, and most of its streets are cobblestoned. The **Nikolaikirche**, on Reformationsplatz, is an early-15th-century brick Gothic structure built on the foundations of an even earlier church, and is typical of the style of Brandenburg. The bronze baptismal basin was cast in 1398; the Renaissance altar dates from 1582.

TREPTOW

This borough, which stretches southeast from Berlin Mitte along the Spree, is named for a fishing village first documented in 1568. In the late 19th century the area around the old town was turned into the English-style **Treptower Park**, and it has been a popular recreation area ever since. Today one of its main attractions is the **Sowjetisches Ehrenmal** (Soviet War Memorial) and military cemetery. Created in the late 1940s, this is the largest Soviet military monument outside the former U.S.S.R. Five thousand Soviet soldiers killed in the Battle of Berlin are buried here. Although the sculpture is executed in strict Socialist Realism style and the architecture is monumentally Stalinist, the memorial is poignantly moving. On the avenue leading to the entrance is a figure of Mother Russia carved from a 50-ton block of granite. Birches line the broad path to a "Grove of Honor," and two walls of red granite symbolize flags lowered in mourning. Atop the cylindrical mausoleum stands a 38-foot-tall bronze figure of a Red Army soldier cradling a small child in one arm and brandishing a sword with which he has just smashed the Nazi swastika.

To get to the park, take any westbound S-Bahn from the Friedrichstrasse or Alexanderplatz stations to the Ostkreuz stop and transfer to any southbound line (S-8, S-6, S-9, or S-10) to Treptower Park. It is a five-minute walk along Puschkinallee from the station to the memorial.

KÖPENICK

Stronghold of the 12th-century Wendish Prince Jaczso, Köpenick predates even Cölln-Berlin. A separate city until its incorporation into Berlin in 1920, it is now the largest of the city's boroughs, and still its most pastoral. The **Köpenicker Forst** and **Grosser Müggelsee** are, respectively, Berlin's largest municipal wood and lake: a vast area for hiking, boating, and escaping from the urban landscape. To get there take the eastbound S-3 S-Bahn from Bahnhof Zoo, Friedrichstrasse, Marx-Engels-Platz, or Alexanderplatz to the Köpenick stop.

Schloss Köpenick, south of the train station (walk or take the number 168 or 169 bus), occupies the site of Prince Jaczso's fortress and is the oldest surviving palace in Berlin. It was completed, in Renaissance style, in 1571 and served as a hunting château for Elector Joachim II. In the early 18th century King Friedrich I added two Baroque-style wings. The court-martial that condemned Frederick the Great and his friend Lieutenant Katte was held here in 1730. In October 1760, during the Seven Years' War, Russian troops plundered the château, and soon after that it went into a long decline. Virtually undamaged during World War II, the palace and its park have enjoyed a renaissance since 1963, when the administrators of the East Berlin state museums turned the richly decorated structure into the **Kunstgewerbemuseum** (Museum of Applied Arts). The collection of furniture, porcelain, glass, and goldsmith work here includes more than 900 years of European decorative art, from the Middle Ages to the present. The museum is open Wednesday through Sunday from 10:00 A.M. to 6:00 P.M. The **Schlosscafé**, open daily except Mondays from 2:00 to 6:00 P.M., is a delightful place to take a coffee break and indulge in some calorific Berlin pastry.

Köpenick's Neo-Gothic red-brick **Rathaus**, a five-minute walk north of the palace in the direction of the S-Bahn station, would hardly be worth a glance were it not for Wilhelm Voigt and the playwright Carl Zuckmayer, who immortalized him in the drama *The Captain of Köpenick*.

In the fall of 1906, Voigt, a down-and-out shoemaker, found an imperial guards captain's uniform in a pawn shop. He put it on and strolled out of the shop, looking and feeling like a new man. And he was. On the street he spotted a squad of 12 soldiers, took charge of the troop, marched them to the nearest train station, and rode with them to Köpenick. There Voigt and his soldiers proceeded to the Rathaus, arrested the mayor, and confiscated the municipal treasury. With the cashbox under his arm, the fake captain ordered his soldiers to release the mayor after half an hour and then take the rest of the day off. He strutted back to the station, boarded a train, and disappeared. The story of the Hauptmann von Köpenick, or "Copper Captain," as he was called in the Anglo-American press, made headlines around the world.

But Voigt wasn't after the money: He wanted blank identity papers. When he didn't find any in the heavy cashbox, he surrendered to the police. He was tried for robbery and impersonating an imperial officer, was sentenced to four years in prison, and served two. For the rest of his life the cobbler earned a good living by appearing in uniform for a fee.

Zuckmayer turned the episode into a hit play in 1931 and in the 1950s wrote the script for a prizewinning movie starring Heinz Rühmann, then Germany's leading comic actor. The incident gave the German language a new word—*Köpenickade,* a caper that plays on gullibility and blind respect for uniforms and military authority. To Berliners east and west, the phony Captain of Köpenick is still a hero. The room with the Köpenick municipal safe has been turned into a small museum and is open daily, including weekends. The Rathaus is still the borough city hall.

SPECIAL SIDE TRIPS
Village Churches

Within Berlin are 55 stone *Dorfkirchen,* or village churches. Seven were built in the early 13th century, before the founding of Berlin itself, by the Knights Templars. Two of the most interesting are in the districts of Marienfelde and Buckow, both part of Tempelhof borough. To reach them take the southbound S-2 elevated train from the Friedrichstrasse, Unter den Linden, or Anhalter Bahnhof S-Bahn stations in Kreuzberg to the Marienfelde station; from there, it's not far by bus to either of these little chapels.

The **Dorfkirche Marienfelde**, consecrated in 1220, is the oldest village church in Berlin. A Gothic structure built of massive granite blocks, it is located on the tree-shaded, cobblestone village square just off Marienfelder Strasse on a little street named, appropriately, An der Dorfkirche. To get there take the S-2 to the Marienfelde station, then transfer to the number 179 bus going south on Marienfelder Allee. The church is about one mile from the station; the bus stops right at the corner leading to the square.

The **Dorfkirche Buckow**, about four miles east of Marienfelde, was built around 1250, and still has five 13th-century stained-glass windows. There are also wall frescoes and gravestones dating from the 14th century. To get there, take the number 172 bus from in front of the Marienfelde church east to the Buckow village center. The bus stops right in front of the church.

To return to central Berlin, take the number 172 bus east to the Johannisthaler Chaussee subway station on the U-7 line, where you can catch a westbound train to the Adenauerplatz station on the Kurfürstendamm.

Green Berlin and the Lakes

Vast expanses of Berlin are as pastoral as a landscape painting. The Grunewald is 12 square miles in area; the Spandau and Tegel forests are somewhat smaller. (Köpenicker Forst, discussed above, is the largest, at 22 square miles.) The tourist office in the Europa-Center and the information center at Hardenbergstrasse 20 provide guidebooks to and maps of the marked trails.

The **Grunewald**, in the southwest corner of the city, is bordered on the west by the Havel river and one of the lakes, the **Grosser Wannsee**. The forest begins just beyond the western end of the Kurfürstendamm, which becomes Königsallee and winds southward through the eastern half of the forest. From the Dahlem museum area or the Dahlem-Dorf station on the U-2 subway, walk northwest to the Brücke Museum and you are at the edge of the forest. The forest is rewarding not only for its greenery and excursion-boat facilities but also for sheltering several of Berlin's most interesting smaller châteaux and royal mansions.

Jagdschloss Grunewald was built for Elector Joachim II in 1542. The hunting château, situated idyllically on the shore of the little **Grunewaldsee**, was restored to its original Renaissance appearance in 1963 and is now a museum. Among its holdings are paintings by German and Flemish masters, including pictures by both Lucas Cranachs (the Elder and the Younger), Barthel Bryn, Jacob Jordaens, Antoine Pesne, and Rubens. There are also 16th- to 18th-century furnishings, hunting trophies, and weapons. The museum is open daily, except Mondays, from 10:00 A.M. to 6:00 P.M. April through September; until 5:00 P.M. in March and October; and until 4:00 P.M. November through February. For sustenance, try the **Forsthaus Paulsborn**, a delightfully rustic forest inn right by the lakeside. It is open for lunch and dinner in the summer, lunch only in the winter, and for breakfast, starting at 9:00 A.M., every Sunday.

To see more châteaux and the Wannsee, head to the southern part of the Grunewald. Take either the S-3 or S-5 elevated train from Bahnhof Zoo or the S-1 from Friedrichstrasse, Unter den Linden, or Anhalter Bahnhof; all three lines go to the Wannsee station. From there you can either walk due west along Königstrasse or north along the lakeshore, or board the number 114 or 116 bus.

Both the shore road (called Am Grossen Wannsee) and the number 114 bus (which you can board at the S-Bahn station and take to the Löwendenkmal stop) pass the **Gedenkstätte Haus der Wannsee-Konferenz** (House of the Wannsee Conference Memorial), Am Grossen Wannsee 56–58. This is the mansion, built in 1915 for a Berlin industrialist, then sold to the Security Service of the SS as a guest house, where in January 1942 top Nazi officials, including Adolf Eichmann and Reinhard Heydrich, met to plan the systematic destruction of European Jewry. On January 20, 1992, the 50th anniversary of the heinous conference, the house opened as a memorial and study center with a permanent exhibition on the "Final Solution." The exhibition documents the conference itself, the events leading up to it, and its consequence: the Holocaust. There is also an education department where seminars and workshops are held, and a multimedia library on Jewish history, anti-Semitism, Nazism, and neo-Nazism. (Open Tuesday through Friday, 10:00 A.M. to 6:00 P.M.; weekends 2:00 to 6:00 P.M.)

The four main attractions at the western end of Königstrasse are the Glienicker Brücke, Jagdschloss Glienicke, Schloss Klein-Glienicke, and the DEFA Film Studio in Potsdam-Babelsberg. The **Glienicker Brücke**, a bridge that crosses the Havel river to Potsdam, became famous during the spy-trading days of the Cold War. This is where Soviet KGB Colonel Rudolf Abel went east (although he actually walked west by the compass) in exchange for U-2 pilot Gary Powers in 1963, and where Soviet human rights activist Anatoly Sharansky walked to freedom in 1983. Until November 1989, the bridge could be used only by Western and Soviet military and diplomatic personnel. Now it is a main route between southwestern Berlin and Potsdam. (For our discussion of Potsdam see the Bach and Luther Country chapter.)

The **DEFA Film Studio**, August Bebel Strasse 26–52, in the Potsdam suburb of Babelsberg, just beyond the Berlin city limits, is the embodiment of German movie history. Dietrich, Garbo, Lorre, Lang, von Sternberg, and Billy Wilder were only a few of the stars and directors who worked at what is still one of the world's largest film production sites, making such classics as *The Blue Angel, Metropolis,* and *The Cabinet of Dr. Caligari,* until the rise of Hitler and Nazism forced them to emigrate or flee to Hollywood. In its heyday the studio was known as the Universum Film Studio (Ufa), but after World War II and its nationalization by the East German regime, the studio became known by its present name, DEFA. Reunification put a virtual end to film production here, but a French investment conglomerate, Compagnie Générale des Eaux (GCE), has bought it and plans to turn it into a media center. Meanwhile, tours of the site, replete with visits to the props warehouses, cutting rooms, walks through sets, film showings, and demonstration shoots with actors and stuntmen have made the studio a magnet for busloads of visitors, especially on weekends. The best way to get here is to continue past the Wannsee station on the S-3 to the next stop, Griebnitzsee, and there either catch the number 693 bus, which drops you right in front of the main entrance. Or you can walk west on Rudolf Breitscheid Strasse to its intersection with August Bebel Strasse, and there turn left (about a 20-minute walk). Open daily from 9:00 A.M. to 5:00 P.M. To enjoy the full tour visitors are advised to arrive by 3:00 P.M.

Jagdschloss Glienicke, just south of the Glienicker bridge, was built as a hunting lodge for Brandenburg's Friedrich Wilhelm, the Great Elector, in 1682. A gem of the Baroque style, it has served since 1963 as a live-in adult education center. Only the grounds are open to visitors.

Schloss Klein-Glienicke, across the street, is situated in one of Berlin's most beautiful parks, landscaped by Peter Josef Lenné in 1816. The château, originally a small country mansion belonging to a wallpaper manufacturer and then to a chancellor of Prussia, was enlarged and rebuilt in its present form by Schinkel to serve as a summer residence for Prince Karl, a son of King Friedrich Wilhelm III. Neoclassical in style, it has a central building with two wings that enclose an Italian-style courtyard. Prince Karl was an inveterate globe-trotter who brought back hundreds of souvenirs from his travels to Italy, Greece, and Asia Minor. He had them all imbedded in the château's exterior walls, where they can be seen today. One is an old Persian gravestone. The late shah of Iran, on a visit to West Berlin in 1967, pointed out that it was upside down; apparently Prince Karl could not read Persian.

A stroll north through the park or on the path along the Havel river embankment will take you to **St.-Peter-und-Pauls-Kirche** and **Blockhaus Nikolskoe**. The onion-domed church and the log house, which looks as if it is right off the Siberian taiga, were built by King Friedrich Wilhelm III in honor of his son-in-law, Tsar Nicholas I, who married Prussia's Princess Charlotte in 1817. The church, consecrated in 1837, was a 20th wedding anniversary gift. The log house, named for Nicholas, was a present from the king to the couple in 1819. A fire destroyed it in 1984; it was reconstructed and is now a popular restaurant, serving strictly

German, not Russian, food. This transplanted piece of Russia provides a panoramic view of the Havel, the Wannsee, and the Pfaueninsel (Peacock Island), site of one of Berlin's strangest châteaux, **Schloss Pfaueninsel**. A ferry will take you there; the landing is just below the Russian church.

For centuries the island has been a famous scenic spot. Toward the end of the 17th century it belonged to an alchemist named Johann Kunkel von Löwenstern, who was supposed to make gold there for the Great Elector. Instead he produced beautiful ruby-colored glasses and goblets, examples of which are on exhibit in the palace. When the Great Elector died in 1688, Kunkel left to ply his trade in Sweden, and the island was all but forgotten until 1793. Then Friedrich Wilhelm II bought it from Kunkel's heirs, intending to use it as a hideaway for himself and his mistress, Wilhelmine Encke, the Countess Lichtenau. Together they designed the château to resemble the ruin of a Roman country house, with Romanesque elements. They did not have much use of it, however—the king died in 1797. But his son, Friedrich Wilhelm III, and his consort, Queen Louise, loved the place and used it as a summer retreat. During their reign peacocks were brought to the island, and Lenné landscaped the grounds. The palace is open daily except Mondays from 10:00 A.M. to 4:00 P.M., April through October. It is closed November through March.

From the island you can catch the number 1 steamer, part of the city's public transit system, back to the landing at the Wannsee S-Bahn station, and from there transfer to the number 2 steamer route, which will take you all the way back to Spandau for connections to the U-7 subway line. Or you can transfer to another boat and travel on the **Tegeler See** to the Tegel forest and Schloss Tegel.

If you happen to be in the Wannsee area on a Sunday between May and October, be sure to visit the Düppel village museum, **Museumsdorf Düppel**, at Clauertstrasse 11, about a half-hour walk east of the Wannsee S-Bahn station (bus number 211 will also take you close). The museum consists of a reconstruction of a medieval farming hamlet, based on excavations made by archeologists of the Museum of Pre- and Early History. The various structures here house furnishings, tools, and artifacts of the period, and there are demonstrations of 13th-century handicrafts and lifestyles. Open Thursdays 3:00 to 7:00 P.M., Sundays 10:00 A.M. to 5:00 P.M., April through September.

Schloss Tegel, at Adelheidallee 19–20 (a mile north of the Wannsee boat landing, and near the Tegel station on the U-6 subway line), is also called the **Humboldt Schlösschen**. Built in 1550 for the court secretary of Elector Joachim II, it was later used as a hunting château by the Great Elector. In 1766 it became the property of Georg von Humboldt, father of Alexander, the famous naturalist, and Wilhelm, the equally famous statesman, philosopher, and educator.

Wilhelm von Humboldt commissioned Schinkel to reconstruct the house in the Neoclassical style for his use as a private residence. He, Alexander, and many of their descendants are buried in the family mausoleum on the grounds not far from an 800-year-old oak under which, according to legend, Margrave Albrecht the Bear often napped. The mansion and surrounding park are still owned by the Humboldt family. The house is full of family heirlooms and memorabilia documenting the life and work of both Wilhelm and Alexander.

Wilhelm von Humboldt established Berlin's university and created Germany's public education system. He was also an art collector, with a special interest in Greek and Roman sculpture. Unfortunately, many pieces in his collection were lost during World War II (although some mysteriously reappeared in East Berlin). Until mid-1990 most of the artworks in the mansion were copies, but the East Berlin authorities began returning them and the collection is once again complete. (Open Mondays only from 10:00 A.M. to noon and 3:00 to 5:00 P.M.)

From the Humboldt mansion it is a 10- to 15-minute walk (or two minutes on any of the bus lines) back to the Tegel subway station, where you can catch the U-6.

GETTING AROUND

When to Go

The best months to visit Berlin are May through October. The weather in March and April can be fickle, and from November through February it can get grim. Berlin usually has a bracing, temperate climate, with low humidity. Few days are either scorchers or arctic, but you can count on one or the other at least once in a season.

Whatever the season, be sure to reserve hotel accommodations well in advance. Berlin's calendar is crammed with trade fairs, festivals, conventions, and congresses. There have been occasions in recent years when hoteliers have put cots and folding beds in lobbies and hallways to accommodate overflow guests. The busiest times are the Green Week agricultural show in late January to early February, the International Film Festival in the second half of February, the International Tourism Bourse (ITB) in early March, the Berlin Festival Weeks in September, and the biannual International Radio-TV-Electronics Exhibition during the last week of August and the first week of September.

Arrival at Major Gateways

The best way to get to Berlin is by plane or by car. Rail connections from cities in western Germany are few (about 40 trains a day from a dozen different cities, most with one or two transfers) and the journey is arduously long. Bahnhof Zoo, five minutes' walk from the Europa-Center, is the main terminal in the west and center; Bahnhof Lichtenberg and Hauptbahnhof are the main terminals in the eastern part of the city.

Tegel airport, northwest of the city center, is serviced by Delta, American, TWA, United, British Airways, Dan Air, Air France, Alitalia, KLM, SAS, Swissair, Austrian Airlines, and Lufthansa. Aeroflot, Austrian Airlines, El Al, Japan Airlines, and Singapore Airlines fly into Schönefeld airport. Various regional and feeder carriers, as well as Lufthansa, service Tempelhof airport, located in the borough of Kreuzberg.

The number 109 bus runs between Tegel and central Berlin, stopping along Kurfürstendamm, at Bahnhof Zoo, and at the hotel area on Budapester Strasse. Departures are every 10 minutes and the ride into the city takes 40 minutes. A cab to the center from Tegel costs about DM 35. S-Bahn number 9 operates from near Schönefeld airport in the southeastern part of the city, with stops at Alexanderplatz, Friedrichstrasse, and Bahnhof Zoo. The cab ride from Schönefeld costs about DM 50 to the center. From Tempelhof there is a subway connection (U-6) to the center as well as bus service (numbers 119, 184, and 341). The cab ride costs about DM 15.

There are four Autobahn routes from western Germany, three from the east to Berlin. Driving time from Frankfurt or Munich takes from six to eight hours, depending on traffic conditions.

Public Transit

Berliners claim theirs is the best in Germany, if not the world. Their penchant for boasting notwithstanding, the claim has some validity.

The system consists of U-Bahn subways, S-Bahn elevated trains, buses (including many double-deckers), streetcars (in east Berlin only), and steamers on many rivers and lakes. Multiple-ride and 24-hour tickets provide use of and free transfers among all systems.

The U-Bahn has nine lines. Service during peak hours is every two and a half minutes; off peak, trains run every five to seven and a half minutes. Late at night service is reduced to a train every ten minutes. (Note that in late 1993 the U-Bahn underwent some renumbering and rerouting.)

The network operates on an honor system, backed by spot inspections: You obtain tickets from dispensing machines or ticket windows and cancel them in meters at platform entrances or on buses. The fine for not having a canceled ticket is DM 60. A single ride costs approximately DM 3.2; four-ride tickets cost approximately DM 11. The best bargains are 24-hour tourist passes, costing DM 12, which allow unlimited use of all conveyances; they are for sale at most dispensing machines, the tourist-office counter at Tegel airport, the BVG-Kiosk Zoo, on Harden-bergplatz, and from ticket windows in the following subway stations: Zoo, Kurt-Schumacher-Platz, Richard-Wagner-Platz, and Rathaus Spandau.

Taxis

Although there are more than 6,000 cabs licensed in Berlin, you can never get one when you need it. They can be hailed on the street or ordered by phone at the following numbers: 21-01-01, 21-02-02, 26-10-26, and 690-22. A one-mile ride costs about DM 7.5.

ACCOMMODATIONS

The hotel rates listed here are 1994 projections for double-bed, double-occupancy rooms, with a range from low to high whenever possible. Prices are given in deutsche marks (DM). Basic rates are always subject to change, so please verify the price when you are booking. Breakfast is usually included in the price of a room.

Berlin's phone system has been reunited since June 1992. The city code for all of Berlin is now 30. When phoning Berlin from within Germany precede the city code with a zero.

The Kurfürstendamm Area

If you can afford it, "*die beste Adresse*" in town is the ► **Bristol Hotel Kempinski**, in the center of the action. Totally destroyed during the war, rebuilt in 1952, and thoroughly renovated in 1980, the Bristol has all the ambience of a grand hotel, and its guest list reads like *Who's Who*.

Kurfürstendamm 27, D-10719 Berlin. Tel: 88-43-40; Fax: 883-60-75; in U.S., Tel: (800) 237-5469; Fax: (314) 434-6484. DM 470–530.

East on the boulevard, and easy to miss because terrace

cafés flank the entrance, is the ▶ **Hotel am Zoo**, a favorite among visiting journalists, and not just because it's close to their Berlin editorial offices. It's the size—130 rooms—and the courteous, efficient service. Rooms have a pleasing modern elegance. The best face the avenue, and some even have little balconies from which to watch the show below.

Kurfürstendamm 25, D-10719 Berlin. Tel: 88-43-70; Fax: 88-43-77-14. DM 300–370.

Meinekestrasse is a small side street that intersects the Ku'damm across the avenue from the Hotel am Zoo. In what used to be an upper-class apartment house you'll find the ▶ **Hotel Meineke**, a small family-run establishment with some of the advantages of a *Pension* and none of the disadvantages. The 60 rooms are high-ceilinged and large, the furniture comfy, the breakfast chamber a delight of Neo-Baroque decor with crystal chandeliers.

Meinekestrasse 10, D-10719 Berlin. Tel: 88-28-11; Fax: 882-57-16. DM 215–240.

Right next door, in a splendid Belle Epoque building, is the moderately priced ▶ **Hotel Residenz**, a reincarnation of old Berlin. Although functionally modern, all 85 rooms are agreeably large, and many have elaborate stucco ceilings. Its **Grand Cru** dining room is one of the city's better French restaurants.

Meinekestrasse 9, D-10719 Berlin. Tel: 88-44-30; Fax: 882-47-26. DM 266.

Joachimstaler Strasse, which intersects the Ku'damm just west of the Gedächtniskirche and the Europa-Center, is noisy, but you couldn't be more centrally located. And nothing beats the ▶ **Art Hotel Sorat** for living with and in an ambience of modern art and design. In fact, German designer Wolf Vostell has turned the entire establishment into a kind of live-in avant-garde gallery.

Joachimstaler Strasse 28/29, D-10719 Berlin. Tel: 88-44-70; Fax: 88-44-77-00. DM 260–285.

The atmosphere is strictly old-worldly up the street in the ▶ **Hotel Hardenberg**, a converted and modernized turn-of-the-century burgher's house with only 34 rooms, each appointed differently.

Joachimstaler Strasse 39/40, D-10623 Berlin. Tel: 882-30-71; Fax: 881-51-70. DM 255–280.

Moving west on the boulevard, you will find *Pensionen* and small, so-called *Hotelpensionen* on intersecting cross streets. Because many smaller hotels have reception and lobby areas on the second, or *belle-étage,* floor of these converted apartment buildings, the distinction between hotel and pension is not always discernible. But there *is* a difference.

Hotels have key desks and concierges on duty; in a pension you are handed room and front-door keys for the duration and left to your own devices. The *Hotelpension* is a hybrid of the two, without a concierge but with a few hotel-type amenities. Both *Pensionen* and *Hotelpensionen* are almost endemic to Berlin, and the best are on and right off the Kurfürstendamm.

The ▶ **Hotelpension Dittberner**, on the fourth floor of a turn-of-the-century building, will give you the impression that you've entered an art gallery, for it is full of works by contemporary Berlin painters that proprietress Elly Lange and her husband Ludwig, an art dealer, collect and exhibit. Among the keys handed to guests is one to the cagelike elevator. Eighteen of the 20 rooms have private baths or showers; 13 are without a private toilet.

Wielandstrasse 26, D-10707 Berlin. Tel: 881-64-85; Fax: 885-40-48. DM 110–180.

The ▶ **Hotel Bogota**, in a reconstructed early-20th-century apartment house, is strictly functional in its decor, and located on a quiet cross street of the Ku'damm. Only 60 of the 120 rooms have private shower and toilet; 13 have showers only; 47 have no bath or toilet.

Schlüterstrasse 45, D-10707 Berlin. Tel: 881-50-01; Fax: 883-58-87. DM 110–190.

Back on the Ku'damm, between Wielandstrasse and Schlüterstrasse, you'll find the ▶ **Askanischer Hof**. Established in 1925 by connecting two grand *belle-étage* apartments in adjacent houses, it has been a favorite of film and stage folk for decades. Arthur Miller was a guest not too many years ago, as was Heinz Rühmann, the character actor who played the lead role in *The Captain of Köpenick*. Many movies have been made in its opulent Art Nouveau salon and suites. All 17 rooms have private baths or showers, but two are without private toilet.

Kurfürstendamm 53, D-10707 Berlin. Tel: 881-80-33; Fax: 881-72-06. DM 250–280.

The Budapester Strasse Area

The southern boundary of the Tiergarten became a hotel street specializing in the luxury and first-class category not long after the building of the Wall. Among the properties here the ▶ **Schweizerhof** is popular, in part because it can boast Berlin's largest indoor hotel pool, replete with ozone-bubble thermal baths and a balneological department to cure whatever you think ails you. All 430 rooms were recently renovated and redecorated. The atmosphere is a bit sterile, but the Swiss cuisine in the hotel's **Schweizerhof Grill** is great.

Budapester Strasse 21–31, D-10787 Berlin. Tel: 269-60; Fax: 269-69-00; in U.S., Tel: (800) 237-5469; Fax: (314) 434-6484. DM 345–495.

Just south of Budapester Strasse is another group of first- and luxury-class hotels. The ▶ Ambassador offers the best in service and amenities at manageable prices. Whatever the 200 rooms may lack in spaciousness is compensated for by the large bathrooms. The pool on the top floor is decorated in "tropical Caribbean" style, and there is also a fitness center with solarium.

Bayreuther Strasse 42–43, D-10787 Berlin. Tel: 21-90-20; Fax: 21-90-23-80. DM 310–350.

Out of the Center
One of the newer additions to the first-class category is the 78-room ▶ Seehof, idyllically situated just east of the trade-fair grounds on the banks of the Lietzensee, one of Berlin's smaller lakes. The rooms could be a little larger, but they have all the conveniences and amenities, and when the city is not overcrowded you can choose between a room with modern or traditional furnishings. The service is personal, there's a terrace restaurant and garden bar facing the lake, and for all the pastoral ambience you are within easy walking distance of Charlottenburg palace and only a block from a subway station with a connection to the Ku'damm.

Lietzensee-Ufer 11, D-14057 Berlin. Tel: 32-00-20; Fax: 32-00-22-51. DM 320–420.

The Unter den Linden Area
For reasons having to do with the Cold War there was a long-held opinion that East Berlin couldn't possibly have a hotel worth recommending (except maybe to your worst enemy). But long before the Wall crumbled the then state-owned In-terhotel chain had been doing its utmost, and with consider-able success, to dispel that idea.

Indeed, the grandest and most luxurious hotel in Berlin is the ▶ Grand-Maritim, on the block between Behrenstrasse and Unter den Linden. Opened in 1987, it is an eclectic blend of Belle Epoque and Postmodern architecture. The Grand is everything its name implies. A splash of marble, thick carpeting, beautifully crafted period furniture, warm wood paneling, exquisite filigree stuccowork, crystal chande-liers, and subdued lighting from polished brass lamps with silk shades are some of its best details. Fresh flowers, mostly orchids from the hotel's own greenhouse, decorate the 350 rooms, apartments, and suites. Down pillows and comforters complement soft linens on the beds. Guests have use of the marble swimming pool, saunas, solarium, and squash courts, and classical music plays around the clock on one of the four in-house channels.

Friedrichstrasse 158–164, D-10117 Berlin. Tel: 232-70; Fax: 23-27-33-62; in U.S., Tel: (800) 237-5469; Fax: (314) 434-6484. DM 480–580.

The latest addition to the ranks of hotels in and near Berlin's historic center is the splendid ▶ **Berlin Hilton International,** a Postmodern-style building with cozily furnished rooms, adjacent to the Gendarmenmarkt, the French and German cathedrals, and the Schauspielhaus. There are seven different restaurants here—from a beer cellar with a bowling alley to a top-rated gourmet eatery.

Mohrenstrasse 30, D-10117 Berlin. Tel: 238-20; Fax: 23-82-43-24; in U.S., Tel: (800) 445-8667. DM 355–525.

Right across from the Palast der Republik you will see the huge, modern, Swedish-designed ▶ **Radisson Plaza Hotel.** The ambience in the 600 rooms is uniformly modern, with a warm Scandinavian touch. You have a choice of ten restaurants in the house.

Karl-Liebknecht-Strasse 3, D-10178 Berlin. Tel: 238-28; Fax: 23-82-75-90; in U.S., Tel: (800) 237-5469; Fax: (314) 434-6484. DM 380–490.

DINING

Berlin has more than 7,000 restaurants, cafés, pubs, dives, and eateries—6,000 in western Berlin, 1,000 in eastern Berlin. Berliners, it seems, never eat at home. It also seems they need no sleep. In no other city in Germany do establishments stay open and serve food as late. There are no closing laws, no last calls. Most places call it quits at 1:00 or 2:00 A.M.; some stay open much later.

There is a distinct Berlin cuisine; it sticks to the ribs and is not to everyone's liking. A *Bulette* is a cold meatball, Berlin's version of the hamburger, that usually is eaten as a snack. *Eisbein*—with sauerkraut, naturally—is pickled pig's feet. *Bockwurst* is a very chubby hotdog, smothered in curry-ketchup sauce or served with potato salad. *Erbsensuppe,* sometimes called *Erbspüree,* is thick pea soup, frequently served with pieces of bockwurst or bacon in it. The *Schlacht-platte* is a platter of blood sausage, liverwurst, boiled beef, and hunks of pork kidney.

For slightly more sophisticated appetites there is *Schlesisches Himmelreich,* consisting of either roast goose or roast pork with potato dumplings and sweet-sour gravy containing dried fruit. *Königsberger Klopse* are veal meatballs, sometimes with pieces of herring ground in, in a caper sauce. *Aal grün mit Gurkensalat* consists of stewed eel in an herb, onion, and sour-cream sauce, accompanied by cucumber salad. A *Berliner* is a person and also a doughnut without a hole, filled with jam and sprinkled with sugar.

Beer is the beverage of Berlin, specifically *Weissbier,* brewed with wheat instead of barley malt and officially called a *Berliner Weisse.* Less officially it is known as a *Molle* or *Kühle Blonde* (cool blonde). With a dash of raspberry syrup it becomes a *Berliner Weisse mit Schuss.* Besides modifying the tartness of the beer, the syrup gives it a Champagnelike effervescence, which may explain why it is always served in a bowl-like chalice.

Finally, the city probably has more foreign than German restaurants, from simple Turkish *kebab* stands to fine French dining rooms. The profusion of French restaurants should come as no surprise given the role the Huguenots played here in the 17th and 18th centuries.

However, Berlin is definitely not Germany's culinary capital. The Gault-Millau guide awards 23 Berlin restaurants toques, but only eight of these have earned two or more, and all of those are in residential areas or at hard-to-reach edges of the city; moreover, two of them are Italian. The German Michelin is far less charitable. It awards a mere five places stars, and gives only one of them a two-star rating.

WESTERN BERLIN

Gourmet and Foreign Restaurants

Though it may seem like a journey to the end of the world, **Rockendorf's Restaurant**, at Düsterhauptstrasse 1 in Waidmannslust, Reinickendorf borough, 12 miles north of the city center, is certainly worth the trip. Here, Siegfried Rockendorf has converted a lovely villa into what is indubitably Berlin's finest—and also most expensive—restaurant. The moment you have been seated by Rockendorf's wife, Ingeborg, the maestro himself approaches your table to describe the menu. There are no à la carte choices, only multicourse prix-fixe menus that change daily. At lunch you can select either the three- or the six-course presentation, at dinner the six- or nine-course program. The wine list has more than 200 selections. Closed Sundays and Mondays and for four weeks in July and August. Tel: 402-30-99.

Frühsammer's Gasthaus, at Matterhornstrasse 101, near the Grosser Wannsee at the southern tip of the Grunewald forest, is almost as far away. Young Peter Frühsammer, whose wife, Antje, is the hostess and oversees the staff, approaches German and French dishes in a creative nouvelle style. You are not bound to a prix-fixe menu here, though one or two are offered daily, and 300 wines are listed. Open for dinner only. Closed for two weeks in January, three in July. Tel: 803-80-23.

Franz and Dorothea Raneburger, both Austrians, moved to Berlin in the early 1980s and opened the **Bamberger Reiter** at Regensburger Strasse 7, a turn-of-the-century corner wine tavern in a residential/commercial neighborhood just two subway stops south of Bahnhof Zoo. Today their restaurant is one of the city's best, frequented by young professionals and intellectuals, scientists, and musicians. The late Vladimir Horowitz was served Dover sole when he ate here, but Raneburger's repertoire, which he performs with a staff of five in the kitchen, goes far beyond such simple fare. The decor is rustic, with parquet flooring and a growing collection of antiques to make diners feel at home. Dinner only; closed Sundays and Mondays and January 1–15. Tel: 218-42-82.

Karl Wannemacher came to Berlin from a town on the Saar-Luxembourg border in the mid-1970s and eventually opened his own restaurant, the 25-seat **Alt Luxemburg**, at Windscheidstrasse 31. The exquisite fare is a blend of French, Luxembourgian, and Saarland cuisine, with occasional touches of Berlin nouvelle style to remind you where you are; the restaurant is wood paneled, with lots of mirrors and antique furnishings Karl's wife Ingrid has collected. Dinner only; closed Sundays and Mondays, the first three weeks in January, and three weeks in July. Tel: 323-87-30.

Several Berlin restaurants offer proof that good French food can be found at moderate prices. One example is the **Restaurant Le Paris**, at Kurfürstendamm 211, in the Maison de France, the French cultural center. Open daily for lunch and dinner. Tel: 881-52-42.

The **Paris Bar**, at Kantstrasse 152, is not a bar but a restaurant; it is also *the* hangout of the city's artists, writers, filmmakers, and theater people. The place is reminiscent of a French working-class bistro. Open from noon to 2:00 A.M. Tel: 313-80-52.

Every Berliner has a favorite Italian restaurant among the 800 or so in the city. One of the best is **Ponte Vecchio**, at Spielhagenstrasse 3, not far from Schloss Charlottenburg. Proprietor-chef Valter Mazza is from Tuscany, and he emphasizes Tuscan regional cuisine. His is one of the few Italian restaurants in Germany with a Michelin star, not to mention three Gault-Millau toques. Open for dinner only. Closed Tuesdays and most of July. Tel: 342-19-99.

One of Berlin's newer culinary additions, getting rave reviews and serving exquisitely prepared nouvelle cuisine at moderate prices (a three-course dinner for two will cost about DM 120 before beverages), is the simply decorated Trio, Klausenerplatz 14, diagonally across the boulevard from Charlottenburg palace. Dinner only, closed Wednesdays and Thursdays and three weeks in June and July; Tel: 321-77-82.

Hotel Restaurants

The best are: **Zum Hugenotten**, in the Inter-Continental Hotel (near the Zoologischen Garten at Budapester Strasse 2), where the cuisine is classically French, Tel: 26-02-11-41; **Park Restaurant**, in the Steigenberger Hotel (Los-Angeles-Platz 1, south of the Kaiser-Wilhelm-Gedächtnis-Kirche), serving Asian cuisine, Tel: 210-88-55, dinner only; **Kempinski Grill and Lobster Bar**, in the Bristol Hotel Kempinski (Kurfürstendamm 27), serving lobster and fish, Tel: 88-43-40; the **Schweizerhof Grill**, in the Hotel Schweizerhof (Budapester Strasse 21–31, across from the zoo), serving Swiss cuisine, Tel: 269-69-00; and **Grand Cru**, in the Hotel Residenz (south of Kurfürstendamm at Meinekestrasse 9), offering French cuisine, Tel: 88-44-30.

Traditional Berlin Food

There are hundreds upon hundreds of restaurants, inns, and pubs serving what is generally called *Deutsche* or *Berliner* or *gut-bürgerliche* (bourgeois) *Küche*. Prices in most are moderate, as, alas, are culinary skills. On or near the Kurfürstendamm there are quite a few; most stay open until 1:00 or 2:00 A.M.

The **Schultheiss Bräuhaus**, at Kurfürstendamm 220, is the main beer hall of Berlin's leading brewery. With its bare wood tables and huge portions, **Hardtke**, at Meinekestrasse 27, is typical of old Berlin restaurants. The **Mommsen Eck**, in Charlottenburg at Mommsenstrasse 45, was established in 1905 and is famous for its 100 brands of beer, which you can enjoy out in the beer garden. Although the **Alt Berliner Schneckenhaus**, at Viktoria-Luise-Platz 12a, near the U-Bahn station of the same name, is a bit pricey, it's hard to beat for atmosphere: The place is crammed with Victorian and Wilhelminian furniture. A little farther afield in the Wilmersdorf district, the **Wirtshaus Zum Nussbaum**, at Bundesplatz 5, is a bargain if you're looking for Berlin specialties such as *Schlesisches Himmelreich* or potato pancakes served with onions, bacon, and pumpkin purée.

Kneipen and In Places

More than 4,000 spots fall under the general heading of *Kneipe*. While the term originally meant a corner tavern in a blue-collar neighborhood, today it includes just about any place where people eat, drink, meet friends, or simply hang out.

Kneipen close to and around the Kurfürstendamm are the **Cour Carree** (Savignyplatz 5), where billiard and card tables are among the attractions; **Zwiebelfisch** (Savignyplatz 7), which is popular with literati; **Die Kleine Kneipe** (Wielandstrasse 45), popular for its billiard tables as well as its stews and sandwiches; and **Dicke Wirtin** (Carmerstrasse 9), which serves good thick soups.

Among the in places that are likely to stay in for a while are the already mentioned Paris Bar; the **Ax Bax** (Leibnizstrasse 34), popular among the artistic set for its cold buffet; **Dschungel**, or Jungle (Nürnberger Strasse 53), which continues to attract the New Wild painters; **Chez Alex** (Kurfürstendamm 160), favored for its piano bar, but rather pricey; **Café EinStein** (Kurfürstenstrasse 58), where the upper-crust leftist intellectual crowd gathers and the novelist Günter Grass may show up to read from a work in progress; and **Exil**, an expensive eatery for successful artists and literati in Kreuzberg (Paul-Linke-Ufer 44a).

Breakfast

Breakfast, definitely not of the "power" variety, has been a Berlin craze since the late 1980s. At latest count some 300 cafés, bistros, and pubs serve variations of the morning meal at the oddest of hours.

Café Voltaire (near the Charlottenburg S-Bahn stop at Stuttgarter Platz 14) serves a choice of French, English, or Dutch breakfasts. **Zillemarkt** (Bleibtreustrasse 48, next to the Savignyplatz S-Bahn stop) is renowned for gourmet ice-cream concoctions and offers Champagne breakfasts until 2:00 P.M. **Miami** (Kurfürstendamm 100), with billiard and card tables, is open round the clock and starts serving breakfast at 4:00 A.M. **Café Leysieffer** (Kurfürstendamm 218) helps start the day with a breakfast of smoked salmon, Parma ham, fresh baguettes, and Champagne. Most hotels also include a scrumptious breakfast buffet in the price of your room.

Cafés

The word is overused in Berlin, where it can apply to anything from a gay bar or jazz cellar to a place serving *Kaffee und Kuchen*—coffee and German pastries. We have the last in mind here.

The incarnation of the Berlin café is still **Café Kranzler** (Kurfürstendamm 18), which is usually crowded with matronly ladies wolfing down two (never just one) pieces of cake topped by mounds of whipped cream. **Café Möhring**

(Kurfürstendamm 213) was a favorite hangout of the bohemian and bourgeois Kurfürstendamm crowd in the early part of this century, and has two other locations on the avenue: at Kurfürstendamm 234 and Kurfürstendamm 161–163. **Café Huthmacher** (Hardenbergstrasse 29d, second floor) offers daily teatime dancing at 3:30 P.M. in addition to fine pastries.

EASTERN BERLIN

The choices in Berlin Mitte and elsewhere east of the former Wall are still somewhat limited: 45 years of Communist rule and isolation from the western culinary world have left a void that will take a while to fill. Here are our best choices.

Gourmet Restaurants

The Grand-Maritim hotel's **Le Grand Restaurant Silhouette**, at Friedrichstrasse 158–164, matches the best in the west, in both decor and creative, impeccably prepared nouvelle-style French and German cuisine. And it surpasses all competitors in friendliness and service. Lunch or dinner here is memorable, but very expensive. Besides the à la carte selections, you will be offered a daily six-course prix-fixe menu. The wine list has 300 labels, among them some otherwise unobtainable whites from eastern Germany's own wine-growing region along the Saale and Elbe rivers. There is low-key piano music until 10:00 P.M., and after that a combo with singer always performs, usually until 1:00 A.M. Open for dinner only; closed Sundays. Tel: 232-70.

For elegant dining in a stunning setting right on the Gendarmenmarkt, the **Französischer Hof**, Jägerstrasse 56, is hard to top. Though a Communist-era reconstruction, the dining room seems genuinely Art Nouveau. The wine list includes some hard-to-get vintages from the eastern German vineyards along the Elbe and Saale-Unstrut rivers. Tel: 229-39-69.

The **Opernpalais**, Unter den Linden 5, in the Prinzessinenpalais, is a complex of restaurants. The **Königin Luise** (dinner only and closed Mondays) serves international food in elegant Baroque surroundings, whereas the **Fridericus** (open daily for lunch and dinner) offers regional specialties and grilled fish dishes. The **Operncafé** serves breakfast from 8:30 A.M. to noon, and coffee, cake, and the like from noon to midnight. Tel: 238-40-16.

If you wish to dine in genuine Rococo surroundings, go to the **Ermeler Haus**, at Märkisches Ufer 10–12, right on the Spree canal and about four blocks southeast of Alexanderplatz. This 16th-century mansion was renovated in the 18th century and turned into a restaurant in the 1960s. Tel: 279-40-28.

German and Berlin Food

In many respects eastern Berlin has been the better turf for real local and regional food because it remained closer to "Germany as it used to be"—for better or for worse.

You will find historic surroundings and honest food at **Zur Letzten Instanz** (Waisenstrasse 14–16, south of Alexanderplatz). The name means "Court of Last Resort" and comes from the location of this 360-year-old house next to the former appeals court. The menu reads like a legal proceeding: *Anklage* (indictment), *Kreuzverhör* (cross-examination), *Plädoyer* (closing argument). Among the specialties are fried herring with onions, fried potatoes and cole slaw, and jellied meat with hash browns.

A number of similar establishments can be found in the Nikolaiviertel, although all are housed in reconstructions. **Zum Paddenwirt** (Nikolaikirchplatz 6) is worth trying. **Zur Rippe** (Poststrasse 17) serves dishes based on historic Berlin recipes. The **Bierschänke in der Gerichtslaube** (Poststrasse 28), with its vaulted ceilings and medieval furnishings, serves traditional Berlin dishes such as Eisbein and pork roasts, with lots of sauerkraut.

Kneipen and In Places

Communist rule and the Wall may have left their mark on Berlin in many ways, but *Kneipenleben* (café life) remained unchanged. **Zum Trichter** (Schiffbauerdamm 6–7) is the favorite *Kneipe* of the adjacent Berliner Ensemble Theater, as popular with actors and staff as it is with the after-theater crowd.

Venturing a bit north of Unter den Linden, you'll find the **Hafenbar** at Chausseestrasse 20, the extension of Friedrichstrasse. Dimly lit, it attracts the younger generation, who come to dance. Still farther afield, in Prenzlauer Berg borough, there's the **Alt-Berliner Bierstube** (Saarbrücker Strasse 17, near the Senefelderplatz subway station), which attracts the alternative-lifestyle crowd. The **1900** (Husemannstrasse 1) is a popular hangout for actors, painters, television people, and folks from the neighborhood.

Cafés

During the day the **Operncafé** on Unter den Linden is a great spot for coffee and pastries; in nice weather the terrace and garden are open. At **Café Bauer**, in the Grand Hotel at the corner of the Friedrichstrasse and Unter den Linden, the pastries are divine. In the afternoon a string orchestra performs.

ENTERTAINMENT AND NIGHTLIFE

With three opera houses, six symphony orchestras, scores of theaters, and some of the country's wildest nightlife, there is no way to run out of after-sightseeing things to do in Berlin. Language may be a bit of a problem for the theater, but in both west and east Berlin you will find musical and revue theaters where the spoken word is not so important.

To find out what's doing and where, check the monthly *Berlin Programm,* available at the tourist office in the Europa-Center, at newsstands, in large bookstores, and from hotel concierges; or the fortnightly program magazines *Zitty* and *Tip,* sold at newsstands.

All theaters, opera houses, concert halls, and cabarets have box offices where you can buy tickets up to an hour before the performance. You can also reserve by phone. For a small fee, hotel desks and any of the central ticket agencies will also obtain tickets for you.

Ticket agencies close to the Kurfürstendamm are **Theaterkasse Centrum**, Meinekestrasse 25, Tel: 882-76-11; **Theaterkasse im Europa-Center**, Europa-Center, Tel: 261-70-51; **Ottfried Laur**, Hardenbergstrasse 6, Tel: 31-37-70-07; **Theaterkasse Kiosk am Zoo**, Kantstrasse 3, Tel: 881-36-03; the **Wertheim** department store, Kurfürstendamm 231, Tel: 882-53-54; and the **KaDeWe** department store, Tauentzienstrasse 21, Tel: 218-10-28. For half-price tickets to same-day shows, try **Hekticket**, at Ku'damm 14 or Rathausstrasse 1 (Alexanderplatz), Tel: 242-67-09.

Opera and Musical Theater

The **Deutsche Oper Berlin** (Bismarckstrasse 35) is western Berlin's opera house. The season runs for ten months, with repertory performances nightly. The ticket office is open Monday through Saturday 11:00 A.M. to 7:00 P.M., Sundays from 10:00 A.M. to 2:00 P.M., and one hour before performances; Tel: 341-02-49. Write for reservations to: Kartenbüro der Deutschen Oper Berlin, Bismarckstrasse 35, D-10627 Berlin.

Theater des Westens (Kantstrasse 12) is an operetta and musical theater. The box office is open 10:00 A.M. to 6:00 P.M. Monday through Saturday, Sundays from 3:00 to 6:00 P.M., and one hour before performances. Tel: 31-90-31-93.

East Berlin's **Deutsche Staatsoper** (Unter den Linden 7) also has a ten-month season. Daniel Barenboim is now its general music director. The box office is open Monday through Saturday noon to 6:00 P.M., Sundays 2:00 to 6:00 P.M., and one hour before performances. Tel: 200-47-62.

The **Komische Oper** (Behrenstrasse 55–57, adjacent to the main entrance of the Grand Hotel) is in a league all its own, thanks to Walter Felsenstein, who, as general manager and director from 1947 until his retirement in the 1980s, built it into one of the world's greatest houses. Box-office hours are Monday through Saturday noon to 5:30 P.M., Sundays 1:00 to 4:30 P.M., and one hour before performances. Tel: 220-27.

The **Friedrichstadtpalast** (Friedrichstrasse 107) is east Berlin's variety and musical revue theater. Box-office hours are noon to 7:00 P.M. daily and one hour before performances. Tel: 28-46-64-74.

Musicals and operettas are performed on a repertory basis in the **Metropol-Theater** (Friedrichstrasse 100–102). The box office is open Monday through Saturday 10:00 A.M. to 6:00 P.M. and one hour before performances. Tel: 20-36-41-17.

Cabaret

A *Kabarett* in Germany is a night spot offering food, drink, and entertainment in the form of a politically and socially satirical floor show. To appreciate the humor you should have a fluent command of German and, in Berlin, of the local dialect.

The best ones are **Die Stachelschweine**, or The Porcupines (lower level of the Europa-Center), advance ticket sales Monday through Friday 10:30 A.M. to 12:30 P.M. and 4:00 to 7:00 P.M., Tel: 261-47-95; **Die Wühlmäuse**, or The Voles (Nürnberger Strasse 33), box office open Monday through Saturday 10:00 A.M. to 8:00 P.M. and Sundays 3:00 to 8:00 P.M., Tel: 213-70-47; and **Die Distel**, or The Thistle (Friedrichstrasse 101), box-office hours Monday through Friday noon to 6:00 P.M., Tel: 200-47-04.

NIGHTLIFE

Berlin has always been famous, or infamous, for its nightclubs, discos, dance spots, jazz clubs, and transvestite shows—not to mention prostitution, on the streets and in brothels. After the Wall went up, almost all of this activity gravitated to western Berlin, where most of it remains.

La Vie en Rose, in the Europa-Center, has a show that begins at 10:00 P.M. and gets rave reviews. Reservations are essential; closed Mondays; Tel: 323-60-06. At the **New Eden**

(Kurfürstendamm 71), open daily except Sundays, 9:00 P.M. to 4:00 A.M., the emphasis is on striptease.

Chez Nous (Marburger Strasse 14) offers the city's best transvestite show at 8:30 and 11:00 P.M. Tel: 213-18-10.

The **Big Eden** (Kurfürstendamm 202) is *the* disco for the younger crowd, with ear-bursting music. The **Metropol** (Nollendorfplatz 5, near the Nollendorfplatz U-Bahn station), a former operetta theater, and the **Coconut** (Joachimsthaler Strasse 1–3, close to Bahnhof Zoo) are similar. The mid-life-crisis and sensitive-ears crowd prefers **Coupé 77** (Kurfürstendamm 177), which is decorated like an Orient Express railway car, and **Annabelle's** (Fasanenstrasse 64, on the south side of Lietzenburger Strasse). Both are quite expensive.

Jazz is best at **Flöz** (Nassauischestrasse 37, two blocks east of Uhlandstrasse); **Ewige Lampe** (Niebuhrstrasse 11a, a short walk from the Savignyplatz S-Bahn stop); and **Quasimodo** (at Kantstrasse 12, close to the Theater des Westens). All have varying programs, including modern and rock jazz, blues, New Wave, and reggae. **A Trane** (Bleibtreustrasse 1, near the Savignyplatz S-Bahn shop) is an important new addition to Berlin's jazz scene. Major acts appear regularly, and the decor is cool. For folk music, try **Go-In** (Bleibtreustrasse 17).

SHOPS AND SHOPPING

Berlin is a consumer city incarnate, and, since the Bundestag voted to make it the capital in fact and not just in name, it has become Germany's most expensive. In addition to international names like Cartier, Louis Vuitton, and the inevitable Rosenthal, the city has a profusion of indigenous craftsmen and designers.

Kurfürstendamm is a mixed scene, with discount stores and by-appointment-only jewelry stores, designer clothiers, and chic men's tailors competing for attention. Serious shoppers usually find the streets that intersect the Kurfürstendamm—including Fasanen, Uhland, Knesebeck, Bleibtreu, Schlüter, Wieland, and Leibniz—more rewarding. Lietzenburger Strasse to the south and Mommsen, Niebuhr, and Kant streets to the north are also worth exploring.

The district on and around **Tauentzienstrasse** is where the biggest department stores are located. There are also interesting shops on the streets that intersect Tauentzien—Rankestrasse, Marburger Strasse, and Nürnberger Strasse.

Alexanderplatz in Berlin Mitte is slowly regaining some of its prewar importance as a shopping area. Friedrichstrasse will be chic and expensive in about three to five years.

Women's Fashions

All the top German designers are well represented on and around the Ku'damm. **Horn** (Kurfürstendamm 213) carries designs by Munich's Manfred Schneider, Cologne's Uta Raasch, and Hamburg's Wolfgang Joop. **Jil Sander** of Hamburg, Germany's most successful designer, has a boutique at Kurfürstendamm 48. **Ritter Moden** (Kurfürstendamm 216) offers Munich's Escada Line; **Zenker** (Kurfürstendamm 45) carries Bogner casuals and sportswear. **Diana Piu** (Kurfürstendamm 72) shows her own collection. **Anna von Griesheim** (Pariser Strasse 44, south and parallel to the Ku'damm) shows and sells her own sleek designs at a small shop on this trendy Charlottenburg street. **Molotow** (Gneissenaustrasse 112), in the heart of Kreuzberg, is a sales and showroom for 35 up-and-coming Berlin fashion designers.

Menswear

Braun & Co. (Kurfürstendamm 43) and **Sabo & Sabo** (Kurfürstendamm 193) are Berlin's answer to Brooks Brothers, while **Mientus** (Kurfürstendamm 52) leans more toward Italian fashions. **Selbach** (Kurfürstendamm 195) is for those who are (or think) young. Other top-of-the-line menswear shops on the boulevard are **Heinz Brand** (Kurfürstendamm 184), **Kurt Heinemann** (Kurfürstendamm 35), and **Leo Kirsch** (Kurfürstendamm 64–65).

Children's Apparel

Elephant's Knot (Meinekestrasse 8) carries Baby Dior, Floriane, Les Enfants Terribles, and Missoni designs. **Cinderella** (Kurfürstendamm 45) is a little less pricey.

Leather and Shoes

Etienne Aigner is at Kurfürstendamm 197. **Budapester Schuhe** (Kurfürstendamm 199) features handmade Hungarian footwear. **Scarpa Moda** (Kurfürstendamm 52) specializes in the latest shoe fashions. **Konrads Lederaccessories** (Pariser Strasse 59) specializes in avant-garde designer leather goods—purses, bags, belts, and more—created on the premises.

Jewelry and Watches

Nürnberger Strasse is lined with jewelry shops. For innovative design and top-of-the-line gold work, visit shops on Uhlandstrasse and Bleibtreustrasse. **Galerie Lalique** (Bleibtreustrasse 47) has handmade creations by 40 goldsmiths. **Juwelier Hülse** (Kurfürstendamm 42) represents Blancpain and Audemars-Piguet; **Axel Sedlatzek** (Kurfürstendamm 45) carries Rolex and Patek Philippe watches. Both are also fine jewelers. So are **Juwelier Alt** (Kurfürstendamm 26a); **Wurz-bacher** (Kurfürstendamm 36); **Paco** (Fasanenstrasse 73); and **Heinz Wipperfeld** (Budapester Strasse 30).

Porcelain and Glass

The **Rosenthal Studio-Haus** is at Kurfürstendamm 226, and **Hutschenreuther**, Rosenthal's chief competitor, is at Eisenacher Strasse 36. **Helmut Trimberg** (Kurfürstendamm 214) features Meissen.

But for the best, shop at the showroom of **KPM**, Königliche Porzellan Manufactur, the state porcelain factory (Kurfürstendamm 26a). Founded as a private enterprise in 1751, KPM was taken over by Frederick the Great and the Hohenzollern dynasty in 1763 and has remained Prussia's answer to Meissen ever since. KPM porcelain is all handmade and hand-painted in the original workshops (open to visitors) at Wegelystrasse 1, near the Tiergarten. Most patterns are from the 18th and 19th centuries—and prices are *königlich* (royal).

Comestibles

Berlin's, and possibly the world's, greatest food emporium is on the sixth floor of **KaDeWe** department store (Tauentzienstrasse 21). KaDeWe stands for *Kaufhaus des Westens,* or Department Store of the West. This has nothing to do with the city's postwar division, but instead reflects the fact that when the store was established in 1912 it was on Berlin's western outskirts. Twenty-five thousand different comestibles are displayed in more than 50,000 square feet of space here. Among the delicacies are 1,800 varieties of cheese and 400 kinds of bread, baked fresh daily; some 60 different salads prepared hourly; vegetables and fruit imported from every continent; a meat counter that seems as long as a football field; and 18 huge tanks containing live fish and seafood that is flown in thrice weekly, then caught and cleaned before customers' eyes. Fauchon's of Paris, Gaston Lenôtre, and Milan's cheese specialist Peck all have shops where they prepare and sell their own goodies.

Art and Antiques

West Berlin abounds with art galleries—180 at latest count—not to mention antiques stores and scores of bric-a-brac shops. Moreover, it has become a leading art-auction center, thanks to two energetic art promoters, Bernd Schultz and Peter Graf zu Eltz, who have turned the semiannual dispersals at the **Villa Grisebach** (Fasanenstrasse 25) into the most important on the Continent for German modern and classical art.

The best little neighborhood for galleries representing

contemporary artists is the one-block stretch of **Fasanen-strasse** between Kurfürstendamm and Lietzenburger Strasse.

Rudolf Springer (Fasanenstrasse 13), Berlin's best-known dealer, has been on the scene for some 40 years. Springer represented Max Ernst, Joan Miró, and Pablo Picasso in the early 1950s, and began showing Georg Baselitz, Jörg Immendorf, Markus Lüpertz, and A. R. Penck in the late 1960s and early 1970s. **Galerie Redmann** (Kurfürstendamm 199) represents many American artists, especially from the Northwest. **Pels-Leusden Galerie** (in the Villa Grisebach) alternates exhibitions of German classic and modern art, and is a good source for works by Lovis Corinth, Käthe Kollwitz, Franz Marc, August Macke, and Erich Heckel. **Volker Westphal** (Fasanenstrasse 68) carries 19th- and 20th-century art, with an emphasis on French and Berlin-based painters. **Galerie Wewerka** (Fasanenstrasse 41a) emphasizes abstract painting as well as performance art. **Gerda Bassenge** (Bleibtreu-strasse 19) features work that ranges from the 15th through 20th centuries, including etchings and drawings by Dürer and Rembrandt, as well as works by Chagall, Beckmann, Kollwitz, Liebermann, and Nolde. **Galerie Brusberg** (Kurfürstendamm 213) is strong on the top international names of contemporary as well as classical modern art. **Galerie Ludwig Lange** (Wielandstrasse 26) represents some of the best Berlin-based abstract and minimalist painters, and is known especially for contemporary sculpture. **Galerie Raab** (Potsdamer Strasse 58 in the Tiergarten borough) is credited as the discoverer and principal backer of the Berlin Neue Wilden, and still represents the avant-garde.

Antiques and Classical Art

The best and most expensive stores and galleries are on Fasanenstrasse, Bleibtreustrasse, Schlüterstrasse, and Mommsenstrasse; more line both sides of Keithstrasse between Budapester Strasse and Kleiststrasse. The quality of merchandise and prices go down a notch or two on Motzstrasse, Eisenacher Strasse, and Kalckreuthstrasse; more middle-of-the-market wares are available along Pariser Strasse and on Ludwigkirchplatz.

Bric-a-Brac, Junk Shops, Flea Markets

Pestalozzistrasse, north of and parallel to Kantstrasse, is packed solid with bric-a-brac shops between Schlüterstrasse and Wilmersdorfer Strasse. Most are open from 3:00 to 6:00 P.M. weekdays, 10:00 A.M. to 2:00 P.M. on Saturdays.

Huge flea markets are held every Saturday and Sunday on the Strasse des 17. Juni in the Tiergarten, as well as on Linkstrasse near Potsdamer Platz.

THE NORTH
HAMBURG, BREMEN, SCHLESWIG-HOLSTEIN, LÜBECK, ROSTOCK

*By Douglas Sutton
with John England*

Douglas Sutton, the author of the sections on Hamburg, Schleswig-Holstein, and Mecklenburg–West Pomerania, is a U.S. journalist who has lived in Hamburg since 1978. An editor with the Deutsche-Presse-Agentur (DPA) wire agency, he has also written about Hamburg for the International Herald Tribune, *the* Financial Post, *and other publications. John England, who created the Bremen, Lübeck, and Lüneburg sections, is also the author of the Northwest and Mosel Valley chapters.*

Travellers sometimes have difficulty connecting the northern part of Germany with the cliché images of "typically German" landscape and culture. There are no snowcapped Alpine mountains, no lederhosen-clad men quaffing huge steins of beer, no scenic winding river valleys lined with vineyards and dotted with romantic castles, and hardly any early medieval towns with ancient walls and church-steepled skylines.

Northern Germany is a different countryside, with associations of another nature—a historical and cultural amalgam of Germanic, Slavic, Scandinavian, and Dutch influences. The landscape, both in the Schleswig-Holstein region (which lies between the North Sea to the west, the Baltic Sea to the east, and the Elbe river to the south), as well as in a good deal of the Lower Saxony region (just south of the river and inland from the Baltic in what used to be East Germany), is mostly flat and

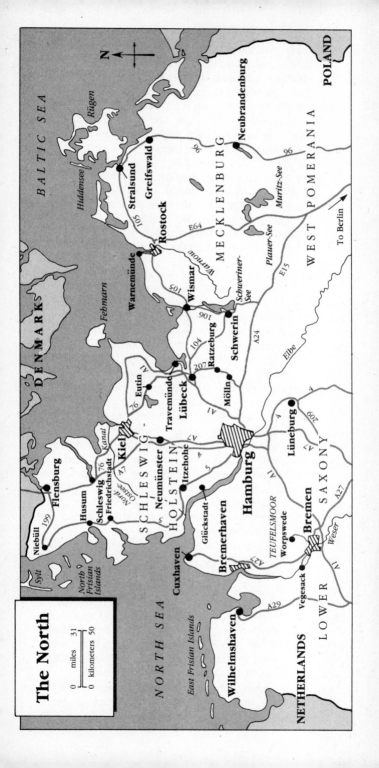

windswept, characterized by marshlands, glacial lakes, and the birches usually associated with Scandinavia. On the North Sea side, you'll find dikes and canal systems for which Dutch know-how was imported three centuries ago. Here and there south of the Elbe river, you'll run across "round villages," settlements of half-timbered Saxon farmhouses arranged in a circle for defensive purposes, evidence of the influence of Slavic settlements a millennium ago.

A dominant characteristic of the region is its long tradition of trade and commerce. Hamburg, Bremen, Lüneburg, Lübeck, and Rostock all belonged to the Hanseatic League, which in medieval times was the most powerful commercial network linking the eastern Baltic regions, Scandinavia, and northern Germany. Hamburg, Bremen, and Lübeck still retain the term *Hansestadt* (Hanseatic City) in their official titles.

Hamburg officially calls itself the "Free and Hanseatic City of Hamburg," and many people consider it the most cosmopolitan and colorful of all German cities. A city-state steeped in international trade traditions because of its busy harbor, Hamburg is also alive with artistic and cultural attractions and an entertainment scene that can provide round-the-clock merrymaking. As the country's second-largest city, and one that is very much "in," Hamburg is a good point of departure for exploring the other major cities and sites in the north.

Though less than half the size of Hamburg, **Bremen** (with its seaport, **Bremerhaven**, some 30 miles to the north) is equally steeped in seafaring and world-trade traditions. Situated on the Weser river, Bremen is a major industrial city-state (shipbuilding, electronics, vehicles), but also boasts some architectural gems that survived the bombing of World War II—chiefly Gothic and Renaissance structures such as the Rathaus and the cathedral. Attractive side streets attest to the city's merchant and trading heritage.

Dotted with colorful harbor towns and villages that have retained their Danish and Dutch heritage, **Schleswig-Holstein**, Germany's sea-girt northernmost state, provides an intriguing backdrop for the internationally known Schleswig-Holstein Music Festival, held at various sites throughout the state every summer. The coastal scenery and white sand beaches of **Sylt**, the most popular of the **North Frisian Islands**, have attracted northern Europeans for decades, if not centuries. Boat tours of the islands and fjords of Schleswig-Holstein add to the briny flavor of this former Viking domain.

For those seeking the most traditional Hanseatic city atmosphere, **Lübeck**, once the capital of the Hanseatic League, is unsurpassed. With its medieval walls, church spires, and narrow cobblestone passageways, this small city in Schleswig-Holstein looks and feels like a living illustration of the Middle Ages. Lübeck offers nourishment for body and mind alike: Marzipan was created here, and when walking the streets you'll recognize sites from books written by the city's two most famous authors, the brothers Thomas and Heinrich Mann.

The oversized small town of **Lüneburg**, with its German Gothic and Renaissance-style buildings and medieval market square, is an architectural treasure. Its commercial character is rooted in its membership in the Hanseatic League as well as in its former role as an important salt-trading center. About a 40-minute train ride southeast of Hamburg, Lüneburg is an attractive alternative to the big city for an afternoon outing.

The reunification of Germany has brought with it one major discovery for even the most experienced travellers: **Mecklenburg–West Pomerania**. This northern part of the former East Germany was perhaps the best-kept secret in the East before the Wall fell in 1989, but has since become a popular destination for visitors who are enthralled by its landscape and once-inaccessible cities. Visitors should be aware, however, that reunification has not made life any easier for Germans in "the new lands" (the politically correct term used for former East Germany). Unemployment is high and so are the social frustrations.

About 250 km (155 miles) across and bordered by Schleswig-Holstein and Lower Saxony to the west, Brandenburg to the south, and Poland to the east, Mecklenburg–West Pomerania treats visitors to a landscape of gently rolling hills and glacial lakes in its center and a picturesque and at times rugged Baltic Sea coastline in the north. Its main cities—the capital, **Schwerin**, nestled among several lakes, and, like a string of pearls along the coast, the Hanseatic League ports of **Rostock** (the major one), **Wismar**, **Stralsund**, and **Greifswald**, with several traditional seaside resorts sprinkled in between—taken together, offer a cultural and historical heritage equal to their already well-known counterparts in western Germany.

Mecklenburg–West Pomerania is one of the least-populated regions of Germany. Along backcountry roads flanked by farmlands, lakes, and forests, travellers can get a feeling of wide-open spaces that few other areas of Germany offer. But then, in stark contrast to the restful beauty of the countryside, they'll be stimulated by the cities—with their formidable North German Gothic churches, castles, medieval fortifications, and trading ports—as well as by a population busily going about the business of recovering from four decades of Communist rule.

HAMBURG

The *Freie und Hansestadt Hamburg*—Free and Hanseatic City of Hamburg—is baffling, not only to the visitor, but, often enough, to its own residents. Its many different faces are so often at cross-purposes that visitors may go away with several different impressions of the city, each true yet taken as a whole failing to render one valid description.

"To write about Hamburg . . . means to write about something withdrawing and denying; it means describing a city that readily lets you grasp it in order to make itself unfathomable," wrote German author Gerhard Mauz.

Hamburg is a bustling place where many different attractions will compete for your attention, be it the arts, the entertainment, the parks, and inviting old neighborhoods, or the action along the *Waterkant* (water's edge) on the Elbe river. With its strongly international flair, the city is often called Germany's "gateway to the world."

Putting Hamburg's statistical parameters down on paper is easy enough, and one of the temptations in trying to describe the city is to quantify it. It has more bridges than Venice and Amsterdam combined, and with more than 80 consulates ranks second in the world behind New York City in that category. It is Germany's media capital; it has Europe's second-busiest port and, with 1.6 million residents, is Germany's second-largest city after Berlin.

It is not just a city, in fact, but also one of Germany's 16 federal states, and encompasses 294 square miles. Located on the Elbe river about 100 km (62 miles) from the North Sea, the city looks back on nearly 1,200 years of history, during which it developed from an obscure fishing settlement to one of the most wealthy and powerful cities in the Hanseatic League. Its original name, when it was established as a Christian outpost in 831 by the missionary Saint Ansgar, was "Hammaburg," a combination of the Old Germanic *Hamma* (marshland) and *Burg* (fortress).

One of the labels that applies accurately enough to Hamburg is *amphibious*. There are miles and miles of Elbe river shorefront and a huge (40-square-mile) bustling port area, in addition to the 450-acre Alster lake in the middle of the city, the Alster river that feeds it, and an extensive network of canals that connect many of Hamburg's neighborhoods.

Is Hamburg a cold, gray, commercial city? Yes. "A city of bancos," sneered Heinrich Heine, who freeloaded off his uncle Salomon Heine, a wealthy Hamburg banker.

A surprising, fun-loving city? Yes. "It was simply, madly wild," said Paul McCartney of Hamburg in the early 1960s, when the Beatles were getting their act together in the St. Pauli quarter's red-light Reeperbahn district.

Hamburg is also a city of high culture—museums, theaters, and opera—and genteel turn-of-the-century neighborhoods characterized by tree-lined streets and patrician mansions. "Hamburg is a beautiful city, but perhaps a bit smug," former chancellor Helmut Schmidt, a native son, once commented.

For each label you are tempted to attach to Hamburg the city readily supplies you with evidence to the contrary. Your best bet is to take in Hamburg in its *Gesamtheit,* its entirety of contradictory appearances.

MAJOR INTEREST

Rathaus (Town Hall)

Shopping arcades, downtown and Binnenalster (the inner lake) neighborhoods

Speicherstadt (Free Port warehouse city)

Churches of St. Jacobi, St. Katharinen, St. Michaelis

Museum für Hamburgische Geschichte (Hamburg Historical Museum)

Strolls in Aussenalster (the outer lake) neighborhoods

Boat tours of Alster lake and canals

Jugendstil and porcelain collections, Museum für Kunst and Gewerbe

Baroque Christianskirche, Altona

Nightclubs and red-light district of the Reeperbahn, St. Pauli quarter

Clipper ship *Rickmer Rickmers,* with museum of maritime history

Elbe river and boat tours of the harbor

Seafaring museums, Altona and Övelgönne

The Historic City Center

Hamburg was once surrounded by defensive walls. Today there is little evidence of these fortifications, which were torn down in the 18th and 19th centuries, yet many of the names remain as a reminder of where Hamburg's early

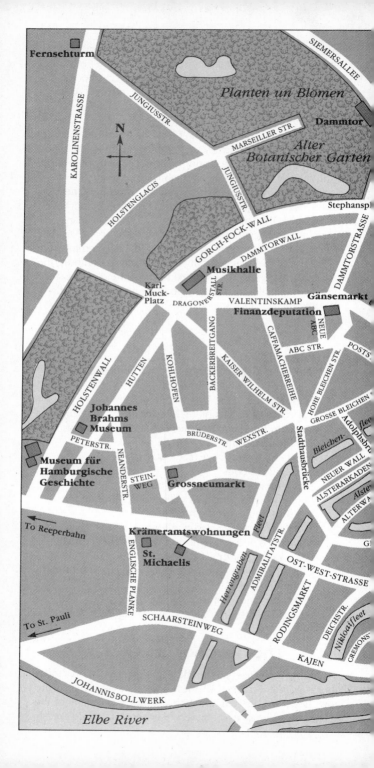

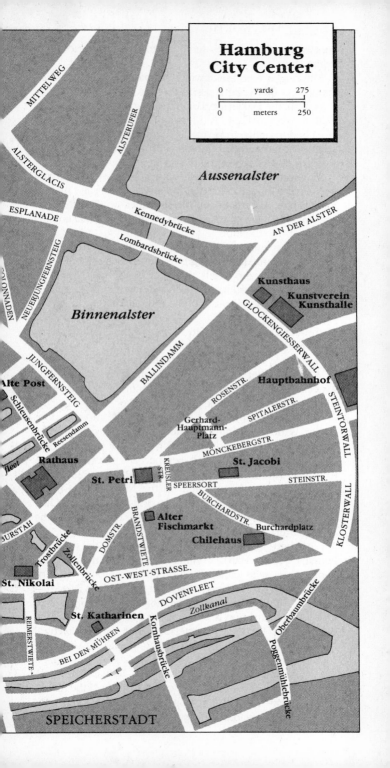

Hamburg City Center

0   yards   275

0   meters   250

MITTELWEG

ALSTERGLACIS

ALSTERUFER

ESPLANADE

Kennedybrücke

AN DER ALSTER

Aussenalster

NEUERJUNGFERNSTEIG

Lombardsbrücke

COLONNADEN

Kunsthaus

Kunstverein
Kunsthalle

GLOCKENGIESSERWALL

Binnenalster

BALLINDAMM

JUNGFERNSTEIG

Alte Post

ROSENSTR.

Hauptbahnhof

STEINTORWALL

Schleusenbrücke

Reesendamm

Gerhard-
Hauptmann-
Platz

SPITALERSTR.

MÖNCKEBERGSTR.

fleet

Rathaus

St. Petri

KREUSLER
STR.

St. Jacobi

SPEERSORT

STEINSTR.

KLOSTERWALL

BURCHARDSTR.

BRANDSTWIETE

Alter
Fischmarkt

Burchardplatz

BURSTAH

Trostbrücke

Zollenbrücke

DOMSTR.

Chilehaus

St. Nikolai

OST-WEST-STRASSE..

DOVENFLEET

REIMERSTWIETE

St. Katharinen

Zollkanal

Obertbaumbrücke

BEI DEN MÜHREN

Kornhausbrücke

Poggenmühlebrücke

SPEICHERSTADT

roots were planted; they serve to define the historic center of the city.

The ring around the downtown area includes (clockwise, starting on the western perimeter) the Holstenwall, Gorch-Fock-Wall, the Esplanade, Lombardsbrücke, Glockengiesser-wall, Steintorwall, and Klosterwall. The southern boundary stretched roughly from today's Oberbaumbrücke on the southeast perimeter to the Johannisbollwerk on the southwest, and is defined by the riverfront.

Intersecting this semicircle on a northeast to southwest axis are the **Binnenalster** (the inner Alster lake) and the two main canals, **Alsterfleet** and **Bleichenfleet** (which eventually becomes the Herrengrabenfleet), both of them channeling the Alster into the Elbe.

Using the canals for orientation, two walking tours of the city center immediately suggest themselves: one on the east side of the lake and canals, the other on the west. For both, the convenient starting point is **Jungfernstieg**, the street that forms the southern border of the Binnenalster.

At the extreme southeastern corner of the Binnenalster is the Reesendammbrücke, a good place to pause at the start of your eastside walking tour. The point marks the spot where, in 1235, a miller named Reese dammed the meandering Alster river, flooding the meadowlands in the river valley to the north and creating the great Alster lake.

As you gaze around the Binnenalster the most obvious feature is the architectural harmony provided by department stores and office buildings, chiefly the work of the 19th-century architects Gottfried Semper and Alexis de Châteauneuf. Three buildings that stand out are the gleaming white Hotel Vier Jahreszeiten on the Neuer Jungfernstieg and, a few doors farther up, the Classical-style Übersee Club. Facing opposite, on the Ballindamm side of the lake, is the headquarters of the Hapag-Lloyd company.

From here it is just a minute's walk south to the towering **Rathaus** (Town Hall). Completed in 1897, the German Renaissance–style Rathaus is the sixth in Hamburg's history. Its size alone—647 rooms (more than Buckingham Palace)—is not its only impressive feature, however. Built on marshy ground, its foundation is laid on the trunks of 4,000 oaks. The German Neo-Renaissance exterior belies the architectural diversity of the interior: Rococo-, Baroque-, and Classical-style rooms and hallways.

Reminiscent of Venice are both the **Rathausplatz** and, across the Alsterfleet canal, the covered arcade of the **Alster-arkaden**, with its clothing shops, jewelry stores, and boutiques. Both were intended by Châteauneuf, who presented his designs after the Great Fire of 1842, to evoke the piazza San Marco.

Entire books have been written about the Great Fire. One of its ironies was that Hamburg, in 1676, established Europe's first fire-insurance company. The material damage caused by the four-day conflagration — one-eighth of the city's population was left homeless — far surpassed the coverage that the Hamburg fire insurance association could offer and wiped the company out. In the aftermath of the catastrophe, it even looked for a while as if the city would be financially ruined. But the banker Salomon Heine put his entire fortune on the line to guarantee new credits to help the city rebuild. Heine, whose own mansion was devoured in the flames, asked, "Did the Elbe river burn up? No? Well then, nothing has been lost."

From Rathausplatz, the next point of interest, a few blocks up the hill on Mönckebergstrasse to the east, is Hamburg's oldest church, **St. Petri**. The Neo-Gothic building here dates only to its reconstruction after the Great Fire, but its foundations go back to sometime around 1050. On the corner of Speersort and Kreuslerstrasse, in the parish basement, visitors can see the foundation of the Bishop's Tower, built in 1040, the first stone fortification north of the Elbe river.

In fact, the immediate area, from here across Domstrasse and Speersort to the **Alter Fischmarkt** (Old Fish-Market), was the location of the original Christian mission, established in the year 831 on the order of Ludwig the Pious, a son of Charlemagne. Today the site is an open-air parking lot.

East up the Speersort a few blocks away is the church of **St. Jacobi**, which dates from the year 1255 but was almost totally destroyed during World War II. Luckily, what was rescued was one of Hamburg's musical treasures — the Baroque organ built in 1693 by Arp Schnitger, a master craftsman who in his day built some 150 organs. Johann Sebastian Bach gave a two-hour concert on a Schnitger organ in Hamburg in 1720 — at another church, St. Katharinen — and exclaimed, "The beauty and virtuosity of the sounds it makes cannot be praised enough!" The 60-register instrument at St. Jacobi is one of only two surviving Schnitger organs in Germany.

The jump from religion and music to commerce and an architectural treasure is a matter of a few blocks, across Speersort and south on Burchardstrasse to Burchardplatz, where the **Chilehaus**, a wedge-shaped, red-brick counting house, takes up an entire city block. Completed in 1930 by architect Fritz Höger, the building evokes a merchant ship, symbolic of Hamburg's role in world commerce.

Red brick dominates much of Hamburg's architecture.

This was the intention of the city's building director during the 1920s, Fritz Schumacher, who wanted to revive North German brick architecture, and who himself designed several buildings downtown as well as entire neighborhoods of low-income housing in Hamburg's outer districts.

The epitome of red-brick architecture is found across the busy Ost–West-Strasse and down toward the port. There, rising on the other side of the Zollkanal and stretching westward for more than a mile, is the **Speicherstadt**, or free-port warehouse city, which was completed in 1888. The political significance of the city's free-port status lies in the fact it was given to Hamburg by Reich Chancellor Otto von Bismarck to lure the city into the Prussian customs union.

The area's seven- and eight-story warehouses, decorated with Gothic-style towers and balconies, provide ten square miles of storage space—for Persian carpets, coffee, tea, cocoa, silk, cotton, rubber, and an array of spices. It is here that you can sense this city's worldwide trading spirit and exult along with prominent 18th-century merchant Caspar Voght: "I am the first merchant to import coffee from Mocca, tobacco from Baltimore, cocoa from Surinam, and rubber from Africa."

It's best to experience this "port within a port" by crossing the Zollkanal at the Poggenmühlebrücke south of the Chilehaus and then walking west among the tall warehouse buildings, recrossing the canal at the Kornhausbrücke, where across the street is the 14th-century church of **St. Katharinen**. Downstairs in the Late Gothic structure, a slide show depicting a thousand years of Hamburg history is shown several times a day.

What little downtown Hamburg has to offer in the way of authentically old buildings (repaired after the destruction of the war) is found a few blocks west of the church. First up are the half-timbered 18th-century warehouses at the Reimerstwiete; another block farther west are **Cremonstrasse** and **Deichstrasse**, which traverse both sides of the curving Nikolaifleet and along which the buildings date back to the 17th and 18th centuries.

Both Cremonstrasse and Deichstrasse feature several traditional old-style restaurants, among them Nikolaikeller, Deichgraf, and Alt Hamburger Aalspeicher. More important, these two streets give you a feeling for what Hamburg must have looked like before the Great Fire of 1842, and before the three weeks of carpet-bombing 101 years later. Deichstrasse is where the Great Fire broke out—the restaurant **Zum Brandanfang** ("Where the Fire Began") marks the spot. The buildings here also typify the merchants' quarters of the period unique to Hamburg, in which warehouses were built right on the edge of the canal so that goods could be lifted off the boats by pulleys.

From here, crossing to the north side of the Ost–West-Strasse via a pedestrian overpass, you come directly to Hamburg's starkest reminder of July 1943: the towering, charred Gothic steeple—its original color was yellow—of **St. Nikolai.** Completed in 1874, the Gothic-style church is today a blackened skeleton reminding passersby of the horror of war. One block east is the Trostbrücke, on which two statues mark the spot where "old" (on the northeast side) and "new" (on the west) Hamburg were linked in the 13th century. One statue is of Saint Ansgar, the canonized archbishop who founded Hamburg in 834, and the other is of Count Adolf III, who set up the New Town in 1188. To the east across the way is the **Zollbrücke,** built in 1633, Hamburg's oldest surviving bridge.

The Trostbrücke also marks the spot where Germany's first stock exchange was founded in 1588. The present exchange (the original burned down in the Great Fire) is several blocks farther north, a Classical-style building erected in 1841 behind the Rathaus, and located just a few blocks south of Jungfernstieg, where we began.

The second walking tour, beginning back at Rathausplatz near Jungfernstieg, covers the west side of the Bleichenfleet and the Alsterfleet. Across the Schleusenbrücke two blocks northwest on Poststrasse is the towered Tuscan Renaissance **Alte Post** (Old Post Office) building. Built in 1847 from a design by Alexis de Châteauneuf, it is now a shopping arcade filled with art galleries, bookstores, and clothing shops.

Turn left at Grosse Bleichen Strasse and head southwest on Wexstrasse through a nondescript area of office buildings to reach the next hospitable attraction, the **Grossneumarkt.** This tree-lined oasis of restaurants and night spots has two streets worth looking at. A block north of the market square is **Brüderstrasse,** consisting entirely of Classical-style buildings from the last century. Cobblestoned **Peterstrasse,** two blocks farther west, is lined with restored 17th- and 18th-century red-brick town houses. The **Johannes Brahms Museum** at the western end of Peterstrasse is not his birthplace—that is a few streets over, in Speckstrasse—but it is in the neighborhood where he grew up.

Four blocks to the south of Peterstrasse, Hamburg's most famous landmark sits high atop a hill on Ost–West-Strasse: the towering church of **St. Michaelis.** Dating to the 18th century, it was twice badly damaged by fire, once in 1750 and again in 1906. The Baroque-style "Michel" easily wins the prize as Hamburg's most beautiful church. Its interior is a symphony of white and gold, dazzling when the sun shines through the stained-glass windows.

One block to the south are the **Krämeramtswohnungen**, the city's last remaining 17th-century apartment buildings, which form a courtyard and were built for the widows of the mercers' guild members. It's worth taking a quick walk among the half-timbered houses—there is also a museum devoted to the interiors of the period.

One museum that should not be missed (it's a ten-minute walk northwest to the Holstenwall) is the Fritz Schumacher–designed **Museum für Hamburgische Geschichte** (Hamburg Historical Museum), which houses, among other things, an exact replica of a 17th-century merchant's home. Most informative are the scale models of Hamburg's development from the earliest times onward, filling in all the present architectural gaps in the downtown area.

The history museum is especially worth a visit if you have German ancestors and want to do genealogical research. In the museum's office of historic emigration, staff members have access to passenger lists of all the people who shipped out of Hamburg from the 1850s to about 1930. There are literally hundreds of thousands of names on record, and, more important, records of the cities and towns from which the emigrants originally came. The service costs a slight fee, and you should bring records with you that indicate the approximate date that your ancestors left Germany. North of the building parallel to the Holstenwall the museum's parklike grounds contain statues and stone gateways from homes and gardens of the past couple of centuries.

At Karl-Muck-Platz (where Hamburg's concert hall, the Baroque-style **Musikhalle**, is the chief landmark), turn east and head downhill on Dragonerstallstrasse, pausing at a little side street, **Bäckerbreitgang**, to see a row of half-timbered houses from the 18th and 19th centuries. Still heading east, down Valentinskamp past Dragonerstallstrasse, you'll soon reach the Gänsemarkt. The most imposing structure on the southwest side of the square is another Schumacher building, the **Finanzdeputation** (Treasury). A block east and you're back at Jungfernstieg.

The Alster

Downtown is about business and commerce and shopping and history, not a place to contemplate Mother Nature. But you need only travel just outside the old city limits to see Hamburg's wealth of tree- and garden-ornamented residential areas.

For example, there's the **Alter Botanischer Garten** and

the adjoining **Planten un Blomen** park outside the northwest perimeter of the Gorch-Fock-Wall and Stephansplatz. Besides the greenery, the chief landmark here is the **Fernsehturm** (TV Tower), which has an observation platform and a revolving café offering a spectacular view of the downtown area and the vast Elbe harbor.

There is more greenery along the Alster river and the Aussenalster, the outer lake. You can walk or bicycle all the way from the Aussenalster to the source of the river, some 25 km (16 miles) northeast of downtown Hamburg, along the **Alster Wanderweg** (hiking path).

However, you'll probably settle for hiking around the **Aussenalster**, which is surrounded by parks and footpaths. Along the way are any number of cafés, some doubling as sailboat marinas, where you can rest and get refreshment. "It's the Elbe that makes us wealthy," wrote the 18th-century poet Friedrich von Hagedorn, "and the Alster that teaches us to be sociable." To this day, the Alster—referred to as the "pearl of Hamburg"—remains the focal point of recreational activity: sailing, rowing, and windsurfing, and, around the shores, walking paths and parks as well as cafés.

The distance around the lake is about 7 km (4 miles). But there are several inviting stops along the way. One of the most favored is **Bobby Reich's** boat marina at the northern tip of the lake, just east of the Krugkoppelbrücke. From here, looking south, you have a panorama of the lake and the downtown skyline. Other favorite rest stops on the circuit around the Aussenalster include the **Mühlenkamper Fährhaus**, one of Hamburg's most popular and pricey restaurants, and the **Uhlenhorster Fährhaus**.

If you do walk the entire circuit, you'll also see a turquoise-colored mosque on the Schöne Aussicht; it's used by the many Muslims (chiefly Iranians and Turks) who live in Hamburg. You can also enjoy the Alster by boat. A fleet provides regular transportation (April to October) between Jungfernstieg and the neighborhood of Winterhude, some three miles upriver (for more on Winterhude, see the Neighborhoods below). These shallow-bottomed boats zigzag their way up and down the Alster, linking both shores and giving visitors plenty of time—about 40 minutes for, say, a trip between Jungfernstieg and the Krugkoppelbrücke—to take in the scenery.

A good way to get a feeling for both the Alster and some of its neighborhoods would be to take an even longer boat ride—about an hour—all the way to the last stop, at the Winterhude Fährhaus, about a mile north of the Krugkoppelbrücke. Across the river you'll notice the 18th-century village church of **St. Johannis**, in the Eppendorf district.

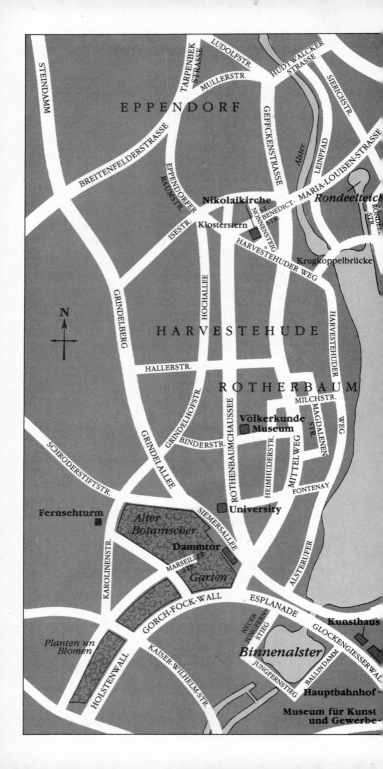

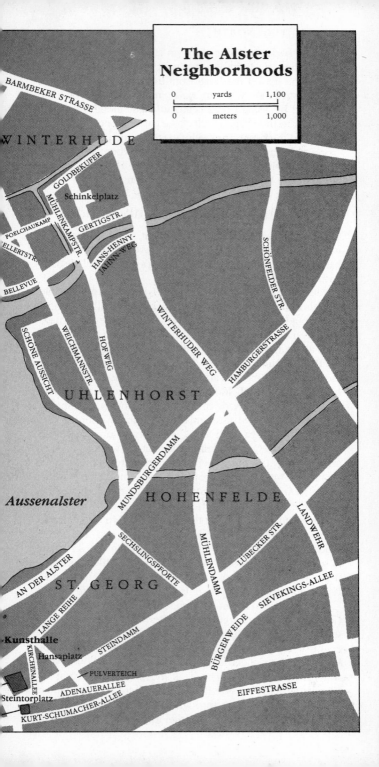

The Alster Neighborhoods

0 — yards — 1,100

0 — meters — 1,000

BARMBEKER STRASSE

WINTERHUDE

GOLDBEKUFER

Schinkelplatz

MÜHLENKAMPSTR.

GERTIGSTR.

POELCHAUKAMP

ELLERTSTR.

HANS-HENNY-JAHNN-WEG

BELLEVUE

SCHÖNFELDER STR.

SCHÖNE AUSSICHT

WEICHMANNSTR.

HOF WEG

WINTERHUDER WEG

HAMBURGERSTRASSE

UHLENHORST

MUNDSBURGERDAMM

Aussenalster

HOHENFELDE

SECHSLINGSPFORTE

MÜHLENDAMM

LÜBECKER STR.

LANDWEHR

AN DER ALSTER

ST. GEORG

LANGE REIHE

SIEVEKINGS-ALLEE

STEINDAMM

BÜRGERWEIDE

Kunsthalle

Hansaplatz

KIRCHENALLEE

PULVERTEICH

ADENAUERALLEE

EIFFESTRASSE

Steintorplatz

KURT-SCHUMACHER-ALLEE

To get back downtown you can take the boat, or the U-1 subway line at Hudtwalckerstrasse, just one block east of where you get off the boat; from there, it's five stations to Jungfernstieg. Or you can walk, in which case you'll be rewarded by going down **Leinpfadstrasse** along the river's east bank to the Krugkoppelbrücke (where, once again, you can board the boat). The Leinpfad (the name literally means "rope path," and refers to the path made when people used to tow the riverboats upstream), one of Hamburg's finest addresses, is lined with villas and mansions.

The Aussenalster Neighborhoods

The debate rages on about whether it is something to be welcomed or condemned, but in any event it seems unstoppable: the gentrification of Hamburg's residential districts around the Alster lake.

You can form your own opinion when you tour the old neighborhoods around the lake. Such a tour will reveal that the spread of gentrification is uneven—some areas have gone to the upwardly mobile and some haven't.

As an example of the latter, there is the western section of the **Rotherbaum district**, in the Hamburg university area on the west side of the lake along Grindelhofstrasse. Here you'll find the usual scruffy-looking student pubs and cafés, bookstores and record shops, and one good cinema, the Abaton Kino, where an old foreign-language film is bound to be showing. This area used to be Hamburg's principal Jewish neighborhood. On Grindelhofstrasse at the western edge of the university campus a memorial park features the ground layout of a synagogue destroyed by Nazis during the November 1938 *Kristallnacht* pogrom. Farther up the street, on the same side, is a former Torah-Talmud school.

The gentrification of Rotherbaum is more in evidence along Mittelweg, which runs north–south two and three blocks in from the lake, and particularly in the so-called **Pöseldorf** section along the perpendicular **Milchstrasse**, a street lined with discos, wine shops, clothing stores, and fashionable restaurants. Pöseldorf is a good nightlife venue.

While you're in the neighborhood you might want to visit Germany's second-largest (after Berlin's) ethnology museum, the **Museum für Völkerkunde**, at the corner of Binderstrasse and Rothenbaumchaussee, three blocks west of Mittelweg. It contains extensive collections of South Seas and African artifacts, as well as the largest collection of Siberian artifacts outside Russia. From here you can either continue walking north through the next gentrified neighborhood, **Harvestehude**, or take the subway (U-1 line), boarding at the Hallerstrasse stop on Rothenbaumchaussee and getting off at the next stop, Klosterstern.

This puts you right in the middle of one of Hamburg's smartest neighborhoods. Angling northwest from Klosterstern into the Eppendorf neighborhood and lined with cafés, restaurants, art galleries, antiques shops, boutiques, and bookstores is **Eppendorfer Baumstrasse**. Here you won't find the patrician town houses of Rotherbaum, but instead a colorful array of four- and five-story *Jugendstil* (Art Nouveau) apartment houses.

Just east of Klosterstern on St. Benedictstrasse is the modern **Nikolaikirche**, built after the war in remembrance of the downtown church of the same name, now a war memorial. Inside the newer church is an altar painting by Oskar Kokoschka.

If you continue east on St. Benedictstrasse you'll come to a bridge spanning the Alster river just above the point where it enters the lake. Crossing the bridge and continuing on what is now Maria-Louisen-Strasse, you'll soon come to a major north–south street, Sierichstrasse, and a circle of imposing turn-of-the-century mansions to your right on what is called the **Rondeelteich** (Round Pond). Because Sierichstrasse is a major traffic artery—beautifully tree-lined, but noisy—continue around to the right on Rondeelstrasse, which then turns into **Bellevue** heading south. The name needs no explaining; as you follow Bellevue back to the northern tip of Alster lake, a panorama of the downtown skyline opens up across the lake.

You'll find another interesting neighborhood a few blocks east of Bellevue. Walking east on Gellertstrasse and then Poelchaukamp will take you to the southeastern edge of the **Winterhude district**, mentioned above in connection with boat trips on the lake. It's less trendy and upscale than Eppendorf and Harvestehude, but there is plenty of entertainment here, particularly in the grid of streets east of the Mühlenkamp bounded by Goldbekufer to the north and Gertigstrasse to the south. **Schinkelplatz**, alive with down-to-earth taverns, restaurants, and small specialty stores, is the heart of the action.

If your legs give out from all the walking, you can simply hop on the number 108 bus heading south on Mühlenkampstrasse and ten minutes later you'll be back at the Hauptbahnhof (main railroad station), on a route that takes you through three more neighborhoods on the east side of the Alster: Uhlenhorst, Hohenfelde, and St. Georg.

It's worth touring the **St. Georg neighborhood** (though it's advisable to do it by day). This is the one area of Hamburg that has seen hardly any gentrification at all, and so gives you an idea of how some of the other neighborhoods used to look. Also, many Hamburgers say these blocks between Steindamm and the lake northeast of the main train station—their center-piece being **Hansaplatz**—are a less touristy, and therefore more authentic, version of the red-light St. Pauli district, complete with hookers walking the streets (particularly Lange Reihe), small grocery shops, vegetable stands, pubs, and kiosks, all in a seedy, run-down setting.

This is also one of Hamburg's most polyglot areas, where Turkish merchants and snack shops compete with Italian, Greek, Yugoslav, and Lebanese shops. But there's no sense in romanticizing this area; prostitution goes hand in hand with petty crime and a hard-drug scene, and the down-and-out sleep off their latest binge in doorways.

St. Georg also has an intellectual side, and boasts Hamburg's three chief art museums: the Kunsthalle and the Kunsthaus/Kunstverein, across Glockengiesserwallstrasse from the Binnenalster northwest of the Hauptbahnhof; and the Museum für Kunst und Gewerbe, south of the station.

The **Kunsthalle**'s collection ranges from the carved 1383 triptych altar of the St. Petri church executed by Meister Bertram to works by Philipp Otto Runge, Edvard Munch, Edouard Manet, and Caspar David Friedrich (including his masterpiece *The Wanderer over the Sea of Mist*). The **Kunsthaus/Kunstverein** showcases the work of current professionals and unknown artists in a series of changing exhibitions.

At the **Museum für Kunst und Gewerbe** (Museum of Decorative Arts and Crafts), a block south of the Hauptbahnhof on Steintorplatz, one of the main attractions is the *Jugendstil* collection, with its "Paris Room" from the 1900 World Exhibition. The museum also features stage designs by Oskar Kokoschka, a faïence and porcelain collection, and antique musical instruments. East Asian and Islamic arts and crafts are also part of the permanent collection.

St. Pauli and Altona

Visiting Altona and St. Pauli, west of the inner city, you may feel as if you've wandered into a different place altogether—which is exactly what you have done. Altona was only incorporated into Hamburg in 1937. For the 400 or so years before that it was often locked in fierce competition with the immensely wealthy and powerful Hanseatic trading city right outside its gates. St. Pauli was a kind of buffer zone between the two, and with its fishing harbor, its working-class neighborhoods abounding in taverns, and its red-light district on the Reeperbahn catering to the world's merchant seamen, it developed a character all its own.

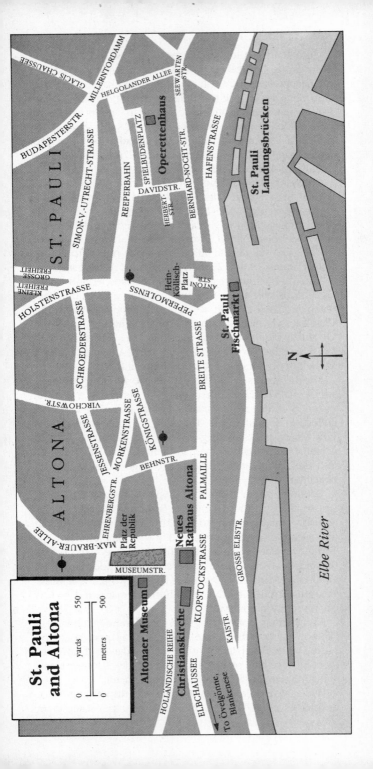

Accentuating **Altona**'s difference was the fact that at one point in the 17th century it was under Denmark's rule, and the second-largest Danish city after Copenhagen. The Danish rulers, never able to subdue Hamburg, set about establishing commercial and civic freedoms and privileges to help Altona compete with its rival. Around 1800, at the height of its economic might, Altona had a merchant fleet larger than Hamburg's, and it was around this time that most of its imposing buildings were built.

Today Altona is a largely working- and middle-class residential area where leftist intellectuals and artists feel at home. Particularly the little side streets just west of the Altona train station (the Hahnenkamp and the Hohenesch) have the typical Altona flavor of modest shops and taverns.

The best way to tour Altona is to take one of the rapid-transit trains (S-1, S-2, or S-3) from St. Pauli Landungsbrücken a bit southwest of the Michaeliskirche and get off three stops later at the Altona train station. From there, head south across the street to Platz der Republik, where the Classical-style **Neues Rathaus Altona** dominates the scene. Originally built as a railway station in 1844, it was converted to its present town hall status in 1898. A statue of Kaiser Wilhelm I on horseback stands guard out front.

On the west side of the park is the **Altonaer Museum**, which, like its Hamburg counterpart, provides a colorful overview of the town's seafaring history, including a valuable collection of figureheads. The daily life and customs of the Elbe valley and Schleswig-Holstein are illustrated through costumes, artifacts, old toys, and embroidery. The museum also has an authentic peasant's cottage housing a small restaurant.

Continue south from the Altonaer Museum to Königstrasse, then west a block to the Baroque **Christianskirche**, arguably equal in beauty to Hamburg's St. Michaelis. Named after Denmark's King Christian VI, it was completed in 1738. Old gravestones surround the church; on the south side is the grave of Hamburg's most celebrated poet, Friedrich Gottlieb Klopstock, whose most famous work, the *Messias,* was put to music by Georg Philipp Telemann and had its premiere in Hamburg in 1759.

After visiting Klopstock's grave, Heinrich Heine remarked, "I know of no other place where a dead poet could be buried better than [Hamburg]," then added a dig characteristic of his love-hate relationship with the city: "However, as a living poet, living there is much more difficult."

Heine at least knew the area he was disparaging, since he had stayed at his wealthy uncle's country estate, about a five minutes' walk west of the Christianskirche on Elb-chaussee. Today a modest yellow "garden house" that Salo-mon Heine had built on the grounds still remains. The spot marks the start of several miles of palacelike man-sions that the merchants of Hamburg and Altona built overlooking the Elbe all the way west to Blankenese (for which see below).

Retracing your steps on Elbchaussee, you first come to Klopstockstrasse and then pass the Rathaus before reaching the **Palmaille**, a tree-lined boulevard flanked on both sides by pure Classic-style houses designed by Danish architect Chris-tian Frederik Hansen. The street's name derives from the fact that it was first laid out in the mid-17th century as a play-ground for ball games—*palla* (ball) and *maglio* (bat).

At the eastern end of the Palmaille you'll come to Behn-strasse, where you turn left and backtrack one block to the Königstrasse rapid-transit station. From here you can take the S-1, S-2, or S-3 train back downtown.

Or you can get off in the **St. Pauli district** at the first station, the **Reeperbahn** stop, to see the "world's most sinful mile," as the boulevard is sometimes called. Many people also call it boring, saying that the live-sex shows and strip-tease acts lack the joie de vivre and humor of their French counterparts and in no way justify the horrendous prices charged for drinks. One of the landmarks in the district is the red-brick Davidswache police station, and just up Da-vidstrasse is the infamous little **Herbertstrasse**, an alleyway where ladies of the night display themselves in windows.

You'll also notice that there's a certain amount of legiti-mate entertainment on the Reeperbahn (its name means "Ropers' Lane," a reference to the place where rigging for sailing ships was once manufactured). The **Operettenhaus**, at Spielbudenplatz 1, expects to be showing *Cats* for several more years, and plans are on the drawing board for reviving the live-music clubs that were once as much a hallmark of the area as the sex trade. This street, after all, is where the Beatles starred before anybody outside of Liverpool had ever heard of them.

Along the Elbe

The most lasting impression visitors are likely to take home from Hamburg is a vision of its harbor and the hum of activity on the Elbe river's banks. The main attraction—in fact, the gravitational point of touring activity—is at the **St. Pauli Landungsbrücken**, a 2,300-foot-long floating landing stage where **boat tours** of the harbor and downriver excursions to the scenic former fishing villages of Övelgönne and Blankenese embark. It's also the terminal for ferry service to Harwich, England.

The St. Pauli Landungsbrücken building, with its clock-tower, is one of Hamburg's best-known landmarks. Just east of the landing stages is the **Rickmer Rickmers**, a 19th-century clipper ship now serving as a museum of maritime history.

The huge port itself—the second largest in Europe, em-ploying more than 50,000 people and handling some 16,000 ships a year—goes back more than 800 years. On May 7, 1189, Holy Roman Emperor Frederick Barbarossa issued an edict granting free-trading privileges to Hamburg. Each year in early May visitors to the city can take part in huge celebra-tions of the event all along the riverfront.

Hamburg's harbor is an open tidal port in which the North Sea tides influence the level of the Elbe river. Just southeast of Hamburg, the Elbe splits into two arms, the Norderelbe and Süderelbe, forming a kind of circle that closes again across from the Fischereihafen. The area inside this circle is a giant network of quays, warehouses, and giant floating drydocks.

The best way to enjoy the harbor is to take a **boat tour** from the Landungsbrücken, which takes about one hour. An English-language tour (daily, March to November, at 11:15 A.M.) departs from pier number 1, near the Rickmer Rick-mers. The tour includes the Speicherstadt as well as the main port itself, where your tiny boat will be dwarfed by the huge ocean freighters it passes. You'll gain an appreciation for the role the Hamburg port plays not only in the city's economy, but also in Germany's foreign trade as a whole.

Some of the best fun year round, albeit only on Sunday mornings, is at the **St. Pauli Fischmarkt**, about a half-mile west of the landing stages. The fishing boats berth at dockside to sell their catch, and a variety of seafood is on sale at booths. The St. Pauli Fischmarkt is also a huge flea market and open-air bazaar where everything from clothing and live poultry to Chinese umbrellas, potted plants, and herbs and spices is sold.

True appreciation of Hamburg's "amphibious" existence comes with visiting, besides the harbor and the fish market, the string of districts on the Elbe's banks, which stretch northwest from downtown and have over time become incorporated into the city proper. These include Altona, Ottensen, Othmarschen, Nienstedten, and, finally, about 12 km (7½ miles) to the west, Blankenese.

Bicyclists and hikers can cover the entire distance along a specially marked route starting from the Landungsbrücken.

If you're driving you'll head out along the **Elbchaussee**. Atop a ridge overlooking the river is Germany's most famous stretch of mansions, belonging to merchants, bankers, and shipping-line owners.

You can also get out to Blankenese by boat—about a 50-minute ride—starting from the Landungsbrücken. The rapid-transit train (S-1), starting from the same place, is faster, of course, but not nearly as scenic.

The boat glides past the St. Pauli and Altona districts with their hilltop churches and buildings. Leaving the downtown areas behind, you'll see much more greenery in the outer districts as you steam downriver toward Blankenese. Stops along the way include Övelgönne and Teufelsbrück, where passengers can debark to see the sights and then catch the next boat downstream.

At **Övelgönne**, just west of Altona, is the **Lange Jammer**, a row of restored 250-year-old houses and a private maritime museum. Teufelsbrück has a large park, the **Jenischpark**, where the chief attractions are the **Jenisch-Haus** and the **Ernst-Barlach-Haus**. The former, a Classical white mansion built in 1932, is now a "museum of upper-class living" devoted to the life and times of 19th-century politician and banker Senator Johann Martin Jenisch. Set amid spacious lawns and wooded grounds, the Ernst-Barlach-Haus features more than 100 paintings, 20 wood sculptures, and more than 300 drawings by this North German Expressionist.

The tour boat's final stop is **Blankenese**, another former fishing village hugging the side of the Sullberg hill. It's fun simply to get lost among the labyrinthine tangle of walkways winding past thatched-roof cottages, many of them 18th-century structures and each with its own tiny garden plot. At the top of the Sullberg is a restaurant, also called **Sullberg**, offering a grand view of the Elbe river below. Nearby, on the Elbterrasse pathway, is the **Dreehus**, a three-family dwelling built around 1800.

A final point of interest is the **Willkomm-Höft**, or welcoming point, in Schulau, about 8 km (5 miles) west of Blankenese by boat. At a restaurant here passing ships are hailed by a playing of the national anthem of the country where they originate and by a saluting of their colors. There's also a small museum with a collection of ships in bottles.

GETTING AROUND

Hamburg's Fuhlsbüttel airport is a relatively short distance north of the city's downtown area. Barring traffic, a taxi ride downtown takes 20 minutes and costs around DM 30. The airport bus leaves every 20 minutes between 6:22 A.M. and 10:42 P.M. from the three passenger terminals to the Hauptbahnhof; it costs DM 8. A third option is to take the number 110 bus (fare DM 3.20), which leaves every ten minutes for the Ohlsdorf station on the U-1 line; from there you can ride the U-Bahn (subway) downtown. What you save in money this way you'll lose in time.

If you're arriving by train, remember that the Hauptbahn-hof is not the final stop. Other stops in the city are the Dammtor, a few minutes away, and the Altona Bahnhof at the end of the line. As a rule, trains arriving from the south, for which Hamburg is the end of the run, will go to Altona. Trains headed for or arriving from Scandinavia stop only at the Hauptbahnhof. It is wise to check with the train conduc-tor about where your train will be stopping in Hamburg. If your hotel is in the Rotherbaum area or on the west side of the Alster lake, for example, you should get off at the Dammtor station.

The two Autobahn links are the A 1 (Lübeck to Bremen), and the A 7 (Hannover to Flensburg). The A 1 exits for the city are the HH-Horn and HH-Veddel; the A 7 exits are the HH-Schnelsen, HH-Stellingen, and HH-Bahrenfeld. The roads leading downtown are clearly marked "Centrum."

Once you've arrived, you'll do your nerves a favor by using mass transportation instead of driving around the city. If you do drive, remember that three major "ring" roads circle the city. Ring 1, the innermost one, follows the old wall fortifica-tions; Ring 2 cuts through the neighborhoods between down-town and the airport; Ring 3 links up with the districts on Hamburg's outer city limits.

Hamburg has a well-developed network of buses, sub-ways, and rapid-transit trains, which run both above and below ground. The U-Bahn runs on the honor system—if you're caught riding without a ticket (*schwarzfahren,* or "riding black") the fine is DM 60. Tickets for the U-Bahn (U-1, U-2, and U-3) and for the S-Bahn (rapid-transit trains; five main lines, S-1–S-5) are available at the stations from vending machines and in some cases from a clerk. More and more bus stops also have vending machines, although most people still buy their tickets from the driver. To determine your fare, consult the map with rings portraying the zones you'll be travelling to, and then push the corresponding button.

You'll probably want to stay within Zone 1 and Zone 2 to see most of Hamburg's sights. If you think you'll be doing a lot of U-Bahn and bus riding on a given day, get a *Tageskarte,* valid for the whole day for all transportation services.

When packing for Hamburg, think of one element: water. Hamburg's weather year-round is generally a succession of variations on precipitation. It is foggy and rainy in November through February; blustery and rainy from March through May; drizzly and on the humid side from June through August; and sunny with intermittent showers in September and October. Hamburg's people just shrug about the generally moist climate, borrowing the British maxim to the effect that there is no such thing as poor weather—only the wrong clothing.

Hamburg is one of Germany's foremost bicycling cities, with special paths in many of the downtown and Aussenalster districts. Rentals are available from the tourist information office in the Bieberhaus at the Hauptbahnhof.

Hamburg is a terminus for Elbe river cruises on the KD line; the cruises overnight at various places in Germany, including Dresden, with land tours available. See Useful Facts (Around Germany) for contact information.

ACCOMMODATIONS

The hotel rates listed here are 1994 projections for double-bed, double-occupancy rooms, with a range from low to high whenever possible. Prices are given in deutsche marks (DM). Basic rates are always subject to change, so please verify price when you are booking. Breakfast is usually included in the price of a room.

The telephone area code for Hamburg is 40, preceded by a zero if you are calling from elsewhere in Germany.

Downtown

The ► **Vier Jahreszeiten** (Four Seasons), overlooking the Binnenalster, qualifies as one of the world's legendary hotels. Luxury has its price, of course, but if you can afford it, then go ahead. It's close to downtown shopping, and its **Restaurant Haerlin,** with a 35,000-bottle wine cellar, is justifiably famous.

Neuer Jungfernstieg, D-20354 Hamburg. Tel: 349-40; Fax: 349-46-02. DM 465–595.

Up around the corner is the ► **Baseler Hof,** several cuts below in price and quality but still an oasis of old-European-style comfort only a few minutes' walk from the downtown attractions. A room toward the rear of the hotel will be much quieter than one facing the busy street but won't have a view.

Esplanade 11, D-20354 Hamburg. Tel: 35-90-60; Fax: 3590-69-18. DM 180–200.

Centrally located for shopping and downtown attractions, the ► **Ramada Renaissance** also ranks high in terms of luxury and comfort.

Grosse Bleichen, D-20354 Hamburg. Tel: 34-91-80; Fax: 34-91-84-31. DM 325–455.

The ▶ **Hamburg Marriott Hotel** is another convenient and comfortable choice that offers a full range of services.

ABC Strasse 52, D-20354 Hamburg. Tel: 350-50; Fax: 35-05-17-77. DM 350–380.

Around the Alster

Hamburg's one high-rise hotel, the ▶ **SAS Plaza Hotel**, provides unsurpassed panoramic views of the lake. In some ways it offers the best of two worlds: It is walking distance both to downtown and to the neighborhoods on the west side of the lake. And if you arrive by train you can get off at the Dammtor station, only a few minutes' walk away.

Marseiller Strasse 2, D-20355 Hamburg. Tel: 350-20; Fax: 35-02-33-33. DM 330–410.

The new luxury-class ▶ **Elysée**, a few blocks north, is at the southern edge of the quieter Rotherbaum neighborhood, and is within walking distance of the university.

Rothenbaumchaussee 10, D-20148 Hamburg. Tel: 41-41-20; Fax: 41-41-27-33. DM 310–370.

Clean and comfortable accommodations are offered nearby in the ▶ **Haus Heimhude**, located on a quiet tree-lined street surrounded by the patrician Rotherbaum neighborhood's turn-of-the-century town houses, one of which this *Pension*-style house once was.

Heimhuder Strasse 16, D-20148 Hamburg. Tel: 44-27-21, Fax: 44-74-27. DM 180.

Close to the western shores of the Aussenalster is the ▶ **Inter-Continental**. Most of the rooms offer panoramic views of the lake, and a gambling casino is located on the premises. Situated just a short walking distance from the nightlife neighborhood of Pöseldorf, in Rotherbaum, the Inter-Continental is a place to see Hamburg's trendy fun-seekers.

Fontenay 10, D-20354 Hamburg. Tel: 41-41-50; Fax: 41-41-51-86. DM 325–510.

Another peaceful tree-lined side street a few blocks north is the setting for the refined ▶ **Garden Hotels Pöseldorf**, a recent effort to fill a gap in the near-luxury category in Hamburg's hotel landscape. Located around the block from the Pöseldorf nightlife scene, the two houses (both under the same management) are also just a few minutes' walk from the lake.

Magdalenenstrasse 60, D-20148 Hamburg. Tel: 41-40-40; Fax: 41-40-420. DM 320–380.

Located in the turn-of-the-century neighborhood of Harvesthude, midway between the lake and Eppendorfer Baum, a popular shopping street, is the small, quiet ▶ **Pension am Nonnenstieg**.

Nonnenstieg 11, D-20149 Hamburg. Tel: 47-38-69; Fax: 48-06-49-49. DM 100–185.

A block away is the ▶ **Hotel Smolka**, a modest establishment in a charming neighborhood a few minutes' walk from the Klosterstern U-Bahn (U-1) line.

Isestrasse 98, D-20149 Hamburg. Tel: 47-50-57; Fax: 47-30-08. DM 225–280.

On the eastern shore of the Aussenalster three hotels that face the lake are conveniently located close to a variety of nearby attractions. The ▶ **Atlantic-Hotel Kempinski**, Hamburg's second most prestigious abode after the Vier Jahreszeiten, offers all the comforts of a traditional grand-style hotel, as well as its **Atlantic Restaurant**. Out front on the lake is a landing for the canal boats that ply the Alster. Just behind this noble hotel is the seedy but colorful St. Georg district.

An der Alster 72–79, D-20099 Hamburg. Tel: 288-80; Fax: 24-71-29. DM 370–480.

A few hundred yards farther north is the ▶ **Hotel Prem**, smaller and simpler than the luxury-class hotels but offering guests warm, individualized attention. The hotel restaurant is excellent (see Dining, below).

An der Alster 9, D-20099 Hamburg. Tel: 24-54-54. Fax: 280-38-51. DM 220–300.

In the same vicinity is the ▶ **Hotel Bellevue**, another smaller establishment known for its fine restaurant (see Dining, below) and courteous service.

An der Alster 14, D(W)-2000 Hamburg 1. Tel: 24-80-11; Fax: 280-33-80. DM 230–270.

Also in the St. Georg district, and right across the street from the Hauptbahnhof, is the ▶ **Europäischer Hof**, with first-rate services and accommodations favored by out-of-town theatergoers; the city's main stage, the Deutsches Schauspielhaus, is a few doors away.

Kirchenallee 45, D-20099 Hamburg. Tel: 24-82-48; Fax: 2482-47-99. DM 240–340.

Elbe River Hotels

For those whose fascination with the busy Hamburg harbor extends to wanting to stay close by, the ▶ **Hotel Hafen Hamburg**, a converted former seamen's mission on a hillside near the St. Pauli Landungsbrücken, is the place to be.

Seewartenstrasse 9, D-20459 Hamburg. Tel: 31-11-30; Fax: 319-27-36. DM 186–206.

Out in Blankenese, the best address on the Elbe is the quiet, charming ▶ **Strandhotel**. It is very small—only 16 rooms—so call in advance to confirm your reservation.

Strandweg 13, D-22587 Hamburg. Tel: 86-13-44; Fax: 86-49-36. DM 290–340.

DINING

Hamburg's restaurant scene is a mixture of quantity, diversity, and quality. With 4,000 restaurants, Hamburg is not a town where a visitor is likely to go hungry; and, reflecting the city's internationalism, virtually every nation on the globe is represented in one way or another in Hamburg's eateries.

As might be expected, given Hamburg's seafaring tradition, fish plays a big role in the indigenous cuisine, and most of the top restaurants offer traditional German dishes as well. A handful of its dining establishments have won acclaim beyond Germany's borders.

One of those is the **Restaurant Haerlin** in the Vier Jahreszeiten. Like the hotel, the restaurant is a haven of luxury where service and food compete for accolades. The menu balances fish, fowl, and meat dishes in a variety of presentations. Neuer Jungfernstieg 9–14. Tel: 349-41.

Down on the Elbe waterside, where fishing boats come and go by day and prostitutes ply their trade at night, is what is widely regarded as Hamburg's best seafood place, the **Fischereihafen-Restaurant Hamburg**. Patrons usually start with a *Krabbensuppe* (crabmeat soup), then proceed to filet of red flounder, one of the house's specialties, served with a choice of French and German wines. Grosse Elbstrasse 143, in Altona. Tel: 38-18-16; Fax: 38-93-02.

The **Historischer Gasthof Anno 1750** lets you enjoy both Old World charm (at modern-day expense-account prices) and a well-rounded, top-quality menu that includes *Leberknödelsuppe* (liver dumpling soup), herring dishes, steak, and filet of pork served with salads and ample helpings of fried potatoes. The beer is brewed on the premises. Closed Sundays. Ost–West-Strasse 47. Tel: 33-00-70; Fax: 32-38-40.

Located across the street to the west of St. Michael's church, the **Old Commercial Room**, a restaurant whose name needs no translating, looks and feels like the captain's quarters of an 18th-century sailing vessel. It lays claim to serving the best *Labskaus,* a local dish that consists of corned beef, herring, pickles, and mashed potatoes, topped with a fried egg. Patrons usually start with the *Aalsuppe* (eel soup). Englische Planke 10. Tel: 36-63-19; Fax: 36-68-14.

A few blocks away, at **Zum Alten Rathaus**, diners who love herring will find themselves in 17th heaven: The restaurant offers herring dishes served in 17 different sauces. Sweet-and-sour roast goose is another specialty, as are its rice dishes. Closed Sundays. Börsenbrücke 10. Tel: 36-75-70; Fax: 37-30-93.

Those searching for Hamburg's top restaurant (and willing to pay handsomely) will head west on the Elbchaussee toward Blankenese and the converted 19th-century estate housing **Landhaus Scherrer.** Among the specialties of chef Heinz Wehmann are breaded cod in tarragon sauce served with sauerkraut, stuffed kohlrabi served with lobster, and asparagus in a vermouth sauce. Closed Sundays. Elbchaussee 130. Tel: 880-13-25; Fax: 880-62-60.

Outside of downtown Hamburg, but not so far out as the Elbchaussee, are two well-established Eppendorf-district restaurants, best reached by taking the U-1 or U-3 subway to the Hudtwalkerstrasse stop and then walking over the bridge toward the St. Johannis church. One is **Fish Sellmer,** which has established itself as one of the city's best fish restaurants, with very reasonable prices (Ludolfstrasse 50; Tel: 47-30-57). Across the street is the smaller, equally popular **Brahms-stuben,** with 19th-century bourgeois decor and specializing in traditional German dishes (Ludolfstrasse 43; Tel: 47-87-17; closed Mondays).

Hamburg's most "in" restaurant is the **Mühlenkämper Fähr-haus** (on the Alster boat line), which specializes in herring, risotto, and beef tenderloin dishes —at very upmarket prices. Hanns-Henny-Jahnn-Weg 1; Tel: 220-73-90; Fax: 220-69-32; closed Saturdays, Sundays, and holidays.

Also on the eastern shore of the Aussenalster are the restaurants of the Prem and Bellevue hotels. **La Mer,** in the Prem, specializes in fish (An der Alster 9; Tel: 24-17-26; on weekends, open evenings only), while the cozy **Pilsener Urquell-Stuben,** in the Bellevue, offers top-rated traditional German dishes and the famous Czech beer for which the restaurant is named. An der Alster 14. Tel: 24-80-11.

NIGHTLIFE

With the possible exception of Berlin, no German city can match the diversity of Hamburg's nighttime entertainment. As one popular song notes, "in Hamburg the nights are long"; indeed, the partying can last until dawn, and the variety is overwhelming. From Puccini at the Staatsoper to punk rock at any number of live-music clubs, from glittering Postmodern discotheques to 1940s-style gin 'n' jazz dives, from musicals to bawdy live-sex shows, Hamburg's night action bubbles with excitement.

As your tour of Hamburg's various districts has already confirmed, the action is not confined to the downtown district area, but is spread around St. Pauli and the Aussenalster, St. Georg, Rotherbaum, Harvestehude, Winterhude, and Uhlenhorst. In general, the "serious" artistic entertainment (operas, concerts) is located in the downtown area, while lighter entertainment is to be found elsewhere. The following is a sampling of highlights in what Hamburg citizens call *die Szene* (the scene).

Discotheques

The international set meets at the **Top of the Town**, atop the SAS Plaza Hotel, which glitters like the lights of the city 26 floors below (open till 4:00 A.M. daily except Sundays; Tel: 350-20). On the alternative, low-life side, the **Madhouse** (Valentinskamp 46; Tel: 34-41-93) will blow out your eardrums with its sound system, and the dance floor is crowded with all manner of interplanetary visitors.

Live-Music Clubs

Hamburg's live-music scene is experiencing a revival, with most of the emphasis on rock music and jazz, mostly Dixieland. Some places offer both, which is the case at the **Fabrik** in Altona (Barnerstrasse 36; Tel: 39-10-70), a former factory converted into a smoky concert hall that is frequented by Hamburg's leftist/intellectual community. Top U.S. and European artists regularly appear here, and it's the one place in town where the entire spectrum of jazz, not just Dixie, is played.

The most popular Dixieland place is the **Cotton Club**, just off the downtown area's Grossneumarkt (Alter Steinweg 10; Tel: 34-38-78). Another club offering Dixieland and small jazz combos is **Birdland**, bordering on the Eppendorf neighborhood (Gärtnerstrasse 122; Tel: 40-52-77). Across town, on the other side of the Alster lake in the Uhlenhorst district, a good bet is **Dennis' Swing Club**, where Dennis Busby, an expatriate American, has been entertaining people at his piano for more than 20 years (Papenhuder Strasse 25; Tel: 229-91-92).

Rock music fans also have a variety of places to choose from. The Fabrik, described above, offers both jazz and rock, so it's best to check first. Among the places featuring rock groups only, one of the most popular, in the university district of Rotherbaum, is **Logo** (Grindelallee 5; Tel: 45-36-84). Another, near the Hauptbahnhof, is **Markthalle**, a flower market hall converted into a rock music center (Klosterwall 9–12; Tel: 33-94-91).

In St. Pauli, both jazz and rock music await you at clubs on two parallel streets north of the Reeperbahn rapid-transit station: the Kleine Freiheit and the Grosse Freiheit. The latter, where the Star Club of early Beatles days was located, is making a comeback after some years in the doldrums (the Star Club burned down). The closest you'll come to the Beatles' turf is **Grosse Freiheit 36** (same address, Tel: 319-36-49), which stands across the street from the former Star Club. Rock music is the main fare here, as it is in the basement called **Kaiserkeller**, where the Beatles sometimes played. At **Blockhütte**, meanwhile, you might catch anything—jazz, rock, or country (Grosse Freiheit 64; Tel: 31-08-01).

Shows
Probably the most popular show in town is at the **Hansa Theater** (Steindamm 17; Tel: 24-14-14), which offers an old-fashioned variety mixture of song and dance, juggling acts, sword swallowers, you name it.

Fun, and naughtily entertaining, is Hamburg's most popular transvestite show, **Pulverfass** (Powder Keg), in the St. Georg district (Pulverteich 12; Tel: 24-97-91).

A club offering a little of everything, including audience participation, is **Schmidt** (Spielbudenplatz; Tel: 31-12-31), near the Reeperbahn.

If your German is good enough and you like political satire, you'll enjoy **Mon Marthe**, in the Eppendorf district, featuring local Hamburg cabaret artists as well as acts from around Germany (Tarpenbekstrasse 65; Tel: 47-54-02).

Dancing
A review of Hamburg's nightlife is not complete without mentioning one popular institution: the **Café Keese**, an old-fashioned dance hall where, under the motto "Ball Paradox," the dancing to live orchestra music is ladies' choice. Coats and ties are required for men, dresses for ladies. Once each hour, the men can choose dance partners (Reeperbahn 19; Tel: 31-08-05).

SHOPS AND SHOPPING
A visitor could spend an entire day in Hamburg's downtown shopping area and not cover even half of everything there is to see. Hamburg is Germany's leader in creating the labyrinthine *Einkaufspassagen* (shopping arcades), a development attributable in part to mercantile showmanship and in part to Hamburg's often inclement weather. The arcades, some of the more popular of which draw up to 20,000 visitors per day, generally feature the predictable international boutiques and brand names, and have all but supplanted any authentic local Hamburg shops. There are nine arcades in the areas adjacent to the southern part of the Binnenalster.

A block west of the Binnenalster is the **Gänsemarktpassage**, which links the Colonnaden with the Gänsemarkt. Across the latter, on ABC Strasse, is the **Gerhofpassage**, which leads toward Poststrasse, where the **Hanse-Viertel**, the largest of all the arcades, is located. Emerging from the Hanse-Viertel on Grosse Bleichen Strasse, you have a choice of two arcades—the **Alte Post** and the **Kaufmannshaus**. There's the small **Galleria** on the Neuer Wall, while two other arcades can be entered from Jungfernstieg: the **Hamburger Hof** and the **Alsterarkaden**. A few blocks east of the lake is the **Landesbank Galerie**, at Gerhard-Hauptmann-Platz.

In addition to the arcades, there are the two chief *Fussgängerzonen* (pedestrian zones): the **Colonnaden**, west of the lake, and the **Spitalerstrasse**, on the east side, which branches off at Gerhard-Hauptmann-Platz from Mönckebergstrasse.

BREMEN

The Hanseatic port city of Bremen, on the Weser river 120 km (75 miles) southwest of Hamburg, is a place where ancient buildings tell the story of its development over the centuries as a hard-working and determinedly independent community. It is also a lively and bustling hub of shipping, commerce and industry, art, museums and theater, good shopping, excellent eating and drinking spots, green riverbanks and parks— and friendly local people who give the lie to the cliché that North Germans are cool and unapproachable.

The city offers river and harbor boat trips, including an excursion downriver to the North Sea town of Bremerhaven, as well as interesting day excursions to the art colony of Worpswede, on the **Teufelsmoor** (Devil's Moor) north of Bremen, a lonely land of old peat diggings. Bremen, the northern terminus of Germany's **Märchenstrasse** (Fairy Tale Road), is also a good starting point for exploring the northern part of the route. (Contact the German National Tourist Office for details.)

MAJOR INTEREST

St. Peter's Cathedral
Rathaus
Altstadt
15th–18th century "dollhouses" of the Schnoor
    district
Museums
Weser river and port
Old tavern-restaurants

River excursions

Bremerhaven

Deutsches Schiffahrtsmuseum
Open-air museum of 17th-century farmhouses
Zoo am Meer

Although it's more than 100 km (62 miles) south of the North Sea (Bremerhaven is its deep-water port at the mouth of the Weser), Bremen is very much about ships and their cargoes. Its port provides work to more than 40 percent of its population of 545,000. Germany's oldest maritime city and its second-leading port after Hamburg, Bremen is more than 1,000 years old; its market rights date from 965.

Bremen became a member of the Hanseatic League in 1358 and an Imperial Free City in 1646. The landmark on its market place, a 30-foot-high stone figure of Roland, a knight armed with sword and shield, dates from 1404, and is a symbol of independence and will for freedom from the rule of princes. Exhibits at the **Focke-Museum**, Bremen's state museum at Schwachhauser Heerstrasse 240, east of the Hauptbahnhof (main train station), trace the city's municipal, ecclesiastical, and maritime history, with many models and pictures of ships as well as displays of bourgeois home decor, porcelain, and costumes.

Together with Bremerhaven, downstream to the north, which was founded as Bremen's deep-water port in 1827 after the Weser had become so silted up that only small boats could navigate the waterway, the city constitutes the smallest German state. Just over 100 years ago, however, a harbor engineer named Ludwig Franzius solved the silt problem by straightening and narrowing the Weser. The river then flowed faster, washing the silt into the sea and reopening the city to big ships. By that time, unfortunately for Bremen, the port of Bremerhaven had become (and still is) a keen trade competitor with the city that spawned it.

Each of the two ports, among the fastest and most technically advanced in the world, now has its individual specialties: Bremerhaven handles fish, tropical fruits, autos, and containers; Bremen deals mainly with mixed cargoes, especially coffee beans, tobacco, and cotton. Every second cup of coffee drunk in the country comes from Bremen.

The Bahnhofsplatz Area

Most of Bremen's compact oval Altstadt, originally a walled semi-peninsular enclave with the Weser along the south side and the moatlike Stadtgraben along the north, is now a pedestrian zone. The best introduction to it is the excellent 90-minute guided walking tour offered by the city tourist information office; Tel: (421) 30-80-00. The office, well stocked with maps and booklets, is in a pavilion on Bahnhofsplatz, directly opposite the Hauptbahnhof, only a few minutes' walk northeast of the Altstadt. The daily tour, which starts from the office at 2:30 P.M. (May through October), is also available in English.

Next to the station to the northwest is Bremen's noted **Übersee Museum** (Overseas Museum), housing collections of ethnological artifacts from the South Seas, Australia, South and East Asia, Africa, and the Americas as well as the Bremen-Weser region. The hotels ▶ **Zur Post** and ▶ **Mercure-Columbus**, on Bahnhofsplatz, are handy to the station, the museum, and the tourist office. Behind the station to the northeast is the spacious Bürgerpark, where the ▶ **Bremen Park Hotel**, one of Bremen's top accommodations, is located. Horse-drawn carriages tour the park on Sundays at 11:00 A.M. and Wednesdays at 3:00 and 4:00 P.M., leaving from the Marcusbrunnen (fountain) near the hotel.

Between Bahnhofsplatz and the Altstadt to the southwest are the city's other luxury-class hotel, the ▶ **Bremen Marriott**, on the pedestrian Hillmannplatz, and the highly recommended gourmet (lunch only) **Grasshoff's Bistro**, at Contrescarpe 80 (next to the Hillmann-Passage); Tel: (421) 147-40. From here, you only have to cross a moatlike arm of the Weser to get to the Altstadt, at Am Wall, the northern perimeter of the old semicircular city fortifications, by the Herdentor bridge at the site of one of Bremen's eight medieval gates.

THE ALTSTADT

The first stop after that, in the Altstadt proper, is the narrow Sögestrasse (in old local dialect, Sow Street). Butchers used to keep their pigs on the street in the Middle Ages, and the practice is commemorated by a bronze swineherd with sows and piglets at the street's corner with Knochenhauerstrasse, which runs east–west here. A two-block walk south along Sögestrasse brings you to the 13th-century **Liebfrauenkirche** (Church of Our Lady). The former church of the city council, it has some fine medieval murals and stained-glass windows. Another short stroll in the same direction takes you into the **Marktplatz** (no longer used as a market), with its statue of Roland standing guard next to the streetcar line outside the Rathaus.

The Rathaus

The main Gothic structure of the impressive three-story Rathaus, which was untouched by World War II, was built in 1405. A Weser Renaissance façade was added in 1612. (For more on Weser Renaissance, see under Hameln in The Center chapter.) On the first floor is a huge banquet hall with high arched windows, ornate wooden carvings, and models of old sailing ships suspended over its long tables.

While Bremen is well known for its beer, it is also Germany's leading wine transshipment center, and down in the Rathaus basement its famous **Ratskeller-Bacchuskeller** restaurant offers a choice of 600 different German wines. Its cellars hold almost one million bottles of German wine alone. Some of the vintages are centuries old, and you had better ask the price. For example, a bottle of a fine German white wine, vintage 1947, can be had for a mere DM 4,400. Tel: (421) 32-16-76.

The vaulted cellar restaurant can seat up to 600 and serves a wide choice of good, hearty food, with fish dominating the menu. You can also enjoy a good North Sea *Scholle* (plaice) at the **Deutsches Haus**, a fish restaurant next to the Rathaus at Am Markt 1. Tel: (421) 32-65-53.

Before leaving the Rathaus area, take a look at the amusing *Bremer Stadtmusikanten* (Bremen Town Musicians) statue at its west entrance, portraying in descending pyramidical order a cockerel, a cat, a dog, and an ass. The group, from the Brothers Grimm fairy tale, was created in 1953 by local sculptor and graphic artist Gerhard Marcks, who felt Bremen should play up its connection with the Fairy Tale Road. The Gerhard Marcks House, Am Wall 208, is dedicated to his works. The **Kunsthalle** (Art Gallery), whose main holdings are 15th- to 20th-century European paintings and 17th- to 20th-century sculptures, is at Am Wall 207.

The Dom

Bremen's Dom St. Petri (St. Peter's Cathedral), next to the Rathaus to the southeast, has a history as a church site going back 1,200 years; construction of its Gothic main building was begun in 1042. A Lutheran church since the Reformation, it was damaged in World War II, and it took 15 years to restore it to its former glory. Special points of interest include a 16th-century Madonna and Child at the chancel, pulpit carvings from the same century, an 11th-century crypt with a 13th-century font (the "Lion's Bowl"), and a Gottfried Silbermann organ dating from 1744.

Excavation work for a new heating system in the early 1970s uncovered a medieval cemetery containing the graves of 22 bishops. The vestments, miter, and crosier of Bremen's first bishop, which were in incredibly good condition, are now on display in the cathedral **museum**, which also houses medieval murals, stone relics, sculptures, and other treasures found by the excavators. For a chill, visit the cathedral's *Bleikammer* (Leaden Chamber), which contains several mummified corpses believed to have been recovered from dunes along the Weser.

The Market Place

On the Marktplatz directly opposite the Rathaus is the Schütting, Bremen's chamber of commerce, which bears an inscription above its doors that sums up the city's can-do philosophy; in regional dialect, it says, *"Buten un binnen, wagen un winnen"* ("Outside the country and in, dare and win"). The less attractive modern steel-and-glass building on the east side of the market place is the Haus der Bürgerschaft, the state parliament. The ▶ Überseehotel, favored by business travellers, is on Wachtstrasse, just south of the Marktplatz.

Böttcherstrasse

Böttcherstrasse, one block to the south and west, is a narrow medieval street that has been a noted arts-and-crafts center since the 1920s. Its late patron, Ludwig Roselius, made his fortune in coffee. You can see his collection of medieval art in the 16th-century **Roseliushaus**, at Böttcherstrasse 6. The **Paula Modersohn-Becker-Haus**, at Böttcherstrasse 8–10, was named after one of the founders of the Worpswede art colony (see Day Trips from Bremen, below), and features many of her works. Workshops and stores of goldsmiths, silversmiths, and other artisans and craftspeople occupy many of the street's interesting nooks and crannies.

A carillon of Meissen porcelain bells, perched high up next to the Roselius house, chimes at noon, 3:00 P.M., and 6:00 P.M. Beer glasses clink all day long at the **Spitzen Gebel**, a tavern behind the Schütting with a genuine Old Bremen atmosphere.

The pedestrian tunnel at the southern end of Böttcherstrasse brings you to the Martini *Anleger* (river piers) for 75-minute harbor **boat trips**. Boats depart daily, March through October, at 10:00 A.M., 11:30 A.M., and 3:15 P.M., with a 4:40 P.M. departure subject to demand.

Evening riverboat parties on the Weser are run every first

and third Saturday, April through October, leaving the piers
at 7:15 P.M. for a run downstream, with an ice-cold schnapps
as a welcome-aboard *Aperitiv* before a generous cold buffet.
Book well in advance, if possible, through the tourist information office. Bremen's **Kajenmarkt**, a lively flea market
featuring a fish auction, arts and crafts, a market crier, and
live music, is held next to the piers every Saturday from 8:00
A.M. to 2:00 P.M.

The Schnoor District and Nightlife

Across Balgebrückstrasse, a block south of the cathedral, is
the charming Schnoor district, on the river at the southeastern end of the Altstadt. Bremen's oldest, still-intact residential quarter of 15th- to 18th-century "dollhouses" on narrow
streets and alleys, the Schnoor is packed with cozy inns,
coffee shops and restaurants, arts-and-crafts workshops, antiques stores, boutiques, and galleries.

Night owls are well catered to in Bremen by a multitude of
pubs (several of them offering jazz) and discos. Bremen's
oldest "in" disco, the **Lila Eule** (Lilac Owl), is at Bernhard-
strasse 10. *Schickeria* (the chic crowd) restaurants include the
Topaz, Violenstrasse 13, and **Jan Tabak**, Weserstrasse 93.

Day Trips from Bremen

Vegesack, a small 18th-century town on the Weser river
about 35 km (22 miles) northwest of Bremen, is where many
sailing-ship captains built their retirement homes. Today the
harbor area is full of faithfully restored old houses and
narrow alleys. The town also has many stores and boutiques,
and no fewer than 50 hotels, restaurants, cafés, and pubs.

A ten-minute walk north from the harbor through the
green Schönebeck Aue brings you to **Schloss Schönebeck**, a
17th-century brick-and-timber *Wasserschloss* (moated castle)
that is now the Heimatmuseum (museum of local history).
Closed Mondays, Thursdays, and Fridays.

Half-hourly trains from Bremen's Hauptbahnhof take
about 25 minutes to Vegesack, and the round-trip fare is
about DM 7.20.

The attractive art colony of **Worpswede**, on the Teufelsmoor, 20 km (12½ miles) north of Bremen, celebrated its
centenary in 1989. It has 22 mostly private arts-and-crafts
galleries in which to browse, about half of them concentrated in what the locals call the "magic triangle," formed by
Bergstrasse, Findorffstrasse, and Hembergstrasse in the village center. The **Ludwig-Roselius-Museum**, with exhibits of
archaeological finds from around Europe, ranging from the

late Stone Age to the Vikings, is on Lindenallee, which runs south from Bergstrasse. The tourist information office is at Bergstrasse 13.

To get to Worpswede by car from the center of Bremen, drive north via Schwachhauser Heerstrasse–Horn–Lilienthal on *Landstrassen* (regional highways) L 133/L 153. The number 140 bus from the Hauptbahnhof takes 45 minutes to Worpswede; the round-trip fare is about DM 8.60.

The Deutsche Märchenstrasse (**German Fairy Tale Road**), which begins in Hanau, near Frankfurt, where the Brothers Grimm were born, ends in Bremen after winding north some 600 km (372 miles) through the towns and countryside that inspired their *Märchen*. (We cover the route in our next chapter, The Center.) A day trip south from Bremen on the B 215, involving a total of about 200 km (124 miles) for the entire trip, would include **Verden an der Aller**, with its 1,000-year-old cathedral and a Märchenpark featuring seven fairy tales in life-size pictures; **Nienburg**, with an historic Altstadt and medieval fortifications surrounded by woods, heath, and moor; and **Minden**, on the Weser river and the Mittellandkanal, with another 1,000-year-old cathedral, the Schachtschleuse (a great lock linking the canal and river), and the Kanalbrücke (aqueduct) over the canal.

BREMERHAVEN

Bremerhaven, 65 km (41 miles) north of Bremen at the mouth of the Weser river, is well worth a day trip from Bremen. Its attractions include the Deutsches Schiffahrts-museum (German Maritime Museum), an open-air museum of 17th-century farmhouses, excellent seafood restaurants at the harbor, and a marine zoo. Bremerhaven is also a departure point for day boat trips to the North Sea island of Helgoland, and is handy for visits to the historic port and spa of **Cuxhaven**, about 40 km (25 miles) due north on the A 27 Autobahn or state highway B 6.

In historical terms, Bremerhaven is a mere infant—only 163 years old. Founded by Bremen *Bürgermeister* (Mayor) Johann Smidt, the new town quickly became a major maritime gateway to Germany, the home port of a big fishing fleet, and an important fish market.

Because of European Community limits on fish catches, Bremerhaven's own fishing fleet has shrunk to about a dozen vessels. But the city switched successfully to fish processing and handling cargoes from foreign fishing boats some years ago, and is now one of Europe's leading trans-shipment centers for fish. The traditional trade in fish employs about 55,000 of the city's population of 131,500. The main port also embraces Europe's largest enclosed container terminal.

The City Center

The long, narrow city center extends north–south along the riverfront, and most things worth seeing—except for the main Fischereihafen (fishing harbor) and the farmhouse museum—are only a short walk from **Theodor-Heuss-Platz**, the town square, with a statue of founding father Johann Smidt at its center and the Stadttheater on its riverside flank. The comfortable tourist and business traveller's ▶ **Nordsee-Hotel Naber** is on the north side of the square. Seagulls provide early morning wake-up calls.

Just around the western corner of the hotel, running north–south, is **Bürgermeister-Smidt-Strasse**, the city's main street, which is lined with stores, including the big Columbus-Center shopping mall on its west side. The local tourist office (Tel: 471-430-00) is on the center's first floor, well marked by many signposts that also point the way to stairs down to the open-air section of the **Deutsches Schiffahrtsmuseum** on the Alter Hafen (Old Harbor).

The first ship in the museum's dock is the U-boat *Wilhelm Bauer,* a World War II-era Type XXI German submarine launched in January 1945 and scuttled by her crew at the war's end. Raised in 1957, she has been a floating technical museum since 1984 and can be toured daily April through October.

The other ships in the dock include a whale-catcher, a deep-sea tug, a former navy PT boat, and an Elbe river lightship. The three-masted bark **Seute Deern** here is a good floating restaurant specializing in herring and crabmeat cocktails. The museum building itself is about 100 yards to the south. Its halls are crammed with models and pictures and parts of old ships, including the only preserved Hanseatic *Kogge,* which dates from 1380. This single-sailed, shallow-draught ship never put out to sea; instead she was torn loose from her Bremen fitting-out dock by a freak flood tide and sank. Found and raised in 2,000 pieces in 1962, she was reassembled and then submerged in a special conservation tank. You may be able to see the ship out of its tank in the year 2000. For now, you'll have to make do with an indistinct view of her in the greenish gloom of her preservative bath.

A short walk north along the riverfront Deich Promenade brings you to the **Zoo am Meer**, containing marine animals, including polar bears, seals, and sea lions. The **Nordsee Museum**, with exhibits of sea animals and plants, is back past the maritime museum and the radar tower between the Weser ferry terminal and the double locks of the Fischereihafen.

The open-air **Farmhouses Museum** is at Parkstrasse 9 in the Stadtpark Speckenbüttel, on the northern edge of the city. Take bus line number 2 from Theodor-Heuss-Platz to the Parktor stop; the ride takes less than 15 minutes.

The best seafood meals in Bremen are said to be found in Bremerhaven, and the best in Bremerhaven are to be had at the **Natusch** restaurant, Am Fischbahnhof 1, on the Fischerei-hafen south of the city; Tel: (471) 710-21. (It's best to take a cab.) The Natusch, which is closed Mondays, has a dark, cozy, old sailing-ship atmosphere. Owner Lutz Natusch buys freshly landed fish daily at the nearby Fischauktionshalle. Early birds interested in seeing a weekday auction should get to the hall before 7:00 A.M.

—*John England*

SCHLESWIG-HOLSTEIN

Schleswig-Holstein, Germany's northernmost *Bundesland* (federal state), is a windswept landscape of gently rolling hills, meandering streams, glacial lakes, fjords, sand dunes, and flat marshlands. The state hymn describes the land as *Meerumschlungen* (embraced by the sea), and the sea does indeed play a prominent—if not always benign—part in the lives of Schleswig-Holstein's two-and-a-half million inhabitants. Sandwiched between the Nordsee (North Sea) to the west and the Baltic Sea (which the Germans call the Ostsee) to the east, the countryside of Schleswig-Holstein is dotted with picturesque villages, towering Gothic cathedrals, moated castles, windmills, and thatched-roof farmhouses surrounded by grazing sheep and cattle. The state shares a border with Denmark to the north and the German state of Mecklenburg–West Pomerania to the southeast. Its economy, as one might expect, is still based on farming, fishing, and shipbuilding.

But for all its peaceful appearance, Schleswig-Holstein has a dramatic history, both historically and topographically. Unleashed by the North Sea, devastating tidal waves known as *Mannsdränke* (drownings of men) have over the centuries washed away significant portions of the land and its inhabitants. Though protected by a costly and sophisticated system of dikes and dams, Schleswig-Holsteiners still keep an anxious eye out when a winter storm whips up the sea, always on the ready to make a dash for higher ground.

The human history of Schleswig-Holstein is equally dramatic and has provided archaeologists with a gold mine of artifacts dating back to prehistoric times. Mummified corpses sacrificed to pagan deities and found preserved in peat bogs have been the object of anthropological studies, as has Haithabu, a once-thriving ninth-century Viking trading outpost near the city of Schleswig. A thousand years ago the Vikings hauled goods bartered and booty plundered in Baltic sea raids overland from Haithabu to the Treene river and sailed from there to the North Sea.

Schleswig-Holstein's history after the Vikings was shaped by two major struggles. The first, which took place about a thousand years ago, was a campaign to Christianize the region. Several Gothic cathedrals, made of brick and dwarfing the tiny towns where they were built, are a legacy of that period. The other struggle was political in nature and saw Germanic dukes battling Danish kings for ownership, with Sweden occasionally joining in the fray. The land changed hands several times over the centuries, with the struggle finally ending in 1864 when what was then Prussia claimed Schleswig-Holstein as its own. But Denmark's influence on the state's culture and history was a lasting one, and is reflected today by the many Danish place names, customs, and by a Danish-speaking minority.

Schleswig-Holstein, comprising a fairly compact area (about 96 miles from north to south and between 80 and 160 miles from coast to coast), yields up its many architectural, cultural, and historical treasures amid a landscape that is both peaceful and unspoiled. It can be explored in just a few days, but as its charms slowly unfold it may keep a visitor much longer.

Every summer from late June to mid-August music lovers from Germany and throughout Europe flock to the annual **Schleswig-Holstein Musik Festival**, founded and still run by pianist Justus Frantz. Top-echelon conductors, soloists, and ensembles perform in venues ranging from cathedrals and castles to country estates and simple barns scattered around the state. For program information and advance ticket sales, contact: Schleswig-Holstein Musik Festival, Kartenzentrale, Postfach 3840, D-24105 Kiel; Tel: (431) 56-70-48; Fax: (431) 56-91-52.

Probably the best way to explore the region is by car. There are train connections to all the destinations described below, but train travel requires careful planning, as some of the destinations are off the main railroad lines and service to them is infrequent.

The itinerary we have chosen uses Hamburg as its starting point and moves in a northerly, clockwise direction to Glückstadt on the Elbe river, Friedrichstadt, and the coastal town of Husum. After briefly exploring Nordstrand and Sylt, two of the Nordfriesische Inseln (North Frisian Islands), we turn east to Flensburg, and then south to Schleswig, Eutin, and Lübeck, which is treated separately below. From Lübeck it's an easy return trip to Hamburg, or you may want to proceed on to Mecklenburg–West Pomerania in the former East Germany (see the section on Rostock and the Baltic Coast at the end of this chapter).

MAJOR INTEREST

Coastal and lake scenery with fjords, windmills, and dikes
Viking, Danish, and Dutch past
Gothic churches and red-brick architecture
The Schleswig-Holstein Music Festival
Local fish specialties (matjes herring)

Glückstadt (coastal town on the Elbe river)
St. Laurentius cathedral in Itzehoe
Nord-Ostsee-Kanal connecting the North Sea to the Baltic

Friedrichstadt
Canals and Dutch architecture from the 17th and 18th centuries
St. Christophorus cathedral

Husum
Colorful harbor town on the Wattenmeer sea
Theodor Storm house and museum
Nissenhaus Museum (exhibit on dike building and tidal storms)

The North Frisian Islands
Boat tours of the main islands
Sylt (resort island with sandy beaches, sunbathing, camping)

Emil Nolde museum in Seebüll

Flensburg
Nordertor (16th-century gate) and restored buildings in old city center
St. Nikolai-Kirche, Heiliggeist-Kirche, St. Marien Kirche

Glücksburg (popular seaside resort on Flensburg fjord)

Schloss Glücksburg (16th-century moated castle)

Schleswig

Schloss Gottorf (medieval religious art, modern German art)

Nydam Hall (museum of Schleswig-Holstein's early history)

Haithabu (reconstructed Viking settlement and museum)

St. Petri cathedral, with 16th-century Bordeshom Altar

The Holsteinische Schweiz (Schleswig-Holstein's lake country)

Eutin, the "Weimar of the North" on Great Eutin Lake

THE WEST COAST

Glückstadt, an Elbe river coastal town about 50 km (31 miles) northwest of Hamburg on federal highway B 31, is a prime example of Denmark's influence in Schleswig-Holstein's history. Danish king Christian IV established the town in 1617 to compete for shipping trade with Hamburg. "If matters proceed fortunately," the king proclaimed, "then Glückstadt will become a city and Hamburg a village."

But *Glück* (luck) evidently wasn't on the king's side. Although Glückstadt became a major whaling center, it suffered more than its share of misfortunes through fire and flood and never became the metropolis envisioned by Christian. It remains a town, but a charming one, with a variety of well-preserved Renaissance, Baroque, and red-brick Gothic buildings.

Especially worth seeing are the 17th-century **Stadtkirche** (City Church); the Baroque-style **Rathaus**, rebuilt in the 19th century to its original 1642 design; and the 17th-century **Brockdorf Palais**, which now houses a **museum** devoted to whaling and local history. All three buildings are on the main market square.

Glückstadt is well known to fish lovers as the home of the original *Glückstadter Matjes,* young herring seasoned in saltwater in wooden casks. Every June a matjes festival is held in Glückstadt to celebrate this briny delicacy, and one of the best restaurants in which to sample them is the **Ratskeller** on the main market square.

The history of **Itzehoe**, a short 20-km (12-mile) hop to the north of Glückstadt, dates back to 810 when Charlemagne established it as a military outpost during his campaign against the Slavs and the Danes. Visitors come mainly to see the church of St. Laurentius, completed in 1718, with its mighty square-shaped tower and the decorated copper and pewter tombs of 17th- and 18th-century Schleswig-Holstein nobility.

Friedrichstadt, some 80 km (50 miles) northwest of Itzehoe, is a genuine oddity in Schleswig-Holstein's history. To reach this "little Amsterdam" at the confluence of the Treene and Eider rivers, take the B 431 to Meldorf, outside of which you have to cross the Nord-Ostsee-Kanal by ferry (free of charge, but involving waits of up to an hour or more, depending on the traffic). Completed in 1895, the canal is the shortcut between the North and Baltic seas and is the third-busiest canal in the world after Panama and Suez. From Meldorf, state highway B 5 heads due north toward Heide. Ten kilometers (6 miles) south of Husum, watch for the B 202 highway and turn east to Friedrichstadt.

As you pass through the region you'll notice that the fields of rapeseed and barley as well as the pasturelands are curved upward for miles on end. This is man-made land, called *Kooge,* that up to a few hundred years ago was covered by water. Two of the catastrophic tidal storms, the Mannsdränke, one in 1362 and another in 1634, literally changed the map of the entire area, washing away miles of land, burying scores of villages, and drowning thousands of people. On each occasion, Schleswig-Holsteiners painstakingly reclaimed the land piece by piece from the sea. A local saying here—*"Wer will nicht deichen, muss weichen"*—can be roughly translated as "He who doesn't build a dike will have to take a hike," and the work to protect the land with dikes from the shallow Wattenmeer (*Meer* means sea) continues to this day.

Friedrichstadt

Building dikes and canals is, of course, a specialty of the Dutch, which is why Friedrichstadt belongs on any tour of the region. Its origins and its appearance today are distinctly Dutch. In 1621 Duke Friedrich III of Gottorf permitted religious refugees from Holland (a reformist sect of Dutch Calvinists called *Remonstranten)* to build a town bearing his name. Friedrich's motives were more commercial than religious. He had seen how his Danish rival Christian IV set up Glückstadt four years earlier and similarly hoped that Friedrichstadt would become a major metropolis. It didn't, but it has survived as a remarkable set piece of 17th- and 18th-century Dutch architecture.

The compact town (only about a mile in circumference), its tree-lined cobblestone streets surrounded by small canals or the Treene river, is bisected by the larger, east–west Mittelburggraben (which roughly translates as "City Center Canal"). A good place to begin a walking tour is the Marktplatz (Market Square) south of the Mittelburggraben. The tourist information office at Am Markt 9 provides maps, brochures, and help in finding accommodations.

Among the many highlights on the Marktplatz itself are the three- and four-story gabled Dutch Renaissance houses. The pedestrians-only Prinzessenstrasse leads south from the Markt past a number of architectural landmarks, including the twin-gabled **Doppelgiebelhaus**, built in 1624 and today housing a shop that sells Dutch faïence tiles and hand-crafted items, and the **Paludenhaus**, the 17th-century home of a wealthy merchant. Prinzessenstrasse continues to Am Fürstenburgwall where, half a block to the west, the local history museum is housed in the **Fünfgiebelhaus**.

One of Friedrichstadt's most famous churches is the late Classical-style **Remonstrantenkirche**, completed in 1853 and located a block southeast of the Marktplatz. The church's light and airy interior is framed by Corinthian columns, high-arched windows, and a massive pewter chandelier that hangs above the altar.

More austere is the Danish **Mennonitenkirche** (Church of the Mennonites), located in a rear wing of the red-brick **Alte Münze** (Old Mint) on the south side of the Mittelburggraben canal just west of the Marktplatz. The church, consecrated in 1708, consists of a single modest room. Directly across from it, on the northern side of the canal, is **St. Christophorus**, completed in 1649 and known primarily for its altar painting by Jurriaen (Jürgen) Ovens. A student of Rembrandt and the court painter for Friedrich III, Ovens is buried in the church. A number of the church's fittings—the wood-carved pulpit, the black marble baptismal font, and the bells—were rescued from churches destroyed by the 1634 flood on the North Frisian island of Nordstrand.

Walking eastward along Am Mittelburgwall on the northern side of the canal brings you to two of the town's best hotels. The ambience in the ▶ **Holländische Stube**, Mittelburgwall 22, with its steep wooden stairways in three adjoining 17th-century town houses, is distinctly Dutch. The rooms in the hotel, which claims Louis Philippe, later a king of France, as its most famous guest, look out on the tree-lined canal or an interior courtyard in the rear. And the hotel's restaurant, specializing in salmon, flounder, matjes herring, and lamb-chop dishes, ranks as one of the town's favorite dining spots. A few doors down at Mittelburgwall 4–8 is the pricier but better appointed ► **Aquarium** hotel, owned by the Ringhotel chain, with an indoor swimming pool and banquet facilities.

More modest alternatives are the ► **Stadt Hamburg**, Am Markt 7; the ► **Herzog Friedrich**, on Schmiedestrasse; and the ► **Holsteinisches Haus**, Am Eiland 1–3. The last is close to the train station, but also near a traffic-filled street.

Friedrichstadt can be seen from the water as well as by foot. At the northeast corner of town, on Treeneufer, rowboats and paddleboats can be rented, allowing you to explore the canals on your own. Günther Schröder, at Treeneufer 1, offers excursion boat tours of the canals and the Treene river every half hour.

Husum

Theodor Storm, a 19th-century native son who wrote tales about this sea-girt windswept region, called the fishing port town of Husum "the grey city by the sea." But Husum, about 20 km (12 miles) north of Friedrichstadt on the B 5, is far from being drab, and is worth a visit for its colorful harbor and small downtown area. In early spring visitors flock to the town **Schloss**, a 17th-century castle on Neustadt, to view the violet-colored carpet of crocuses that covers the entire grounds.

Hafenstrasse, with its cafés, boutiques, and restaurants, runs east–west along the harbor and is a popular gathering spot. Conveniently located here is the modest ► **Obsens-Hotel**, with rooms looking out over the harbor. Four blocks north, at Neustadt 60–64, is the elegant and much pricier ► **Theodor Storm Hotel**.

Visitors with a literary bent seek out Theodor Storm's house. Storm wrote some 50 novellas, but it is his last work, *Der Schimmelreiter* (*The Rider of the White Horse*), describing the adventures of a *Deichgraf*, the local official in charge of building and maintaining the dikes, which has become required reading for German high school students. The 18th-century two-story brick **Theodor Storm Haus** at Wassereihe 33 (one block north of Hafenstrasse) is a museum dedicated to the writer.

Norderstrasse, a few blocks south of Neustadt, is a lively pedestrian zone filled with shops and cafés. The well-respected **Ratskeller** restaurant here is located in the cellar of the **Altes Rathaus** (Old Town Hall), where tourist information, maps, and hotel reservation services are available.

The **Nissenhaus Museum**, two blocks south of Norderstrasse on Nissenstrasse, is one of Germany's few privately funded museums. Devoted to local North Frisian culture, the museum was founded on the estate of Ludwig Nissen, a local shoeshine boy who emigrated to America in the last century and made a fortune as a diamond trader in New York. Scale models and reconstructions of dikes, artifacts from towns swept away in the Mannsdränke, and a photography exhibit showing the devastation wrought by a major tidal storm in 1962 all dramatically underscore the ever-present threat of the sea.

As you look out on the shallow **Wattenmeer**, the very idea of a murderous tidal wave seems like so much *Sturm und Drang* hyperbole, especially during ebb tide, when the mud flats stretch as far as the eye can see and groups of hikers tramp barefoot through the sand-and-mud mixture called *Schlick*. There is no thundering surf to be seen, no crashing waves, and at times it is difficult to make out where the land ends and the sea begins. Some dreamlike farmhouses may appear to be far out at sea. These farmhouses lie atop low-lying elevations called *Halligen,* which are dispersed among the main North Frisian Islands. The word *Watte* translates as shallows, shoals, mud flats, and sand banks, and depending on tidal conditions, the Wattenmeer is all of these.

THE NORTH FRISIAN ISLANDS

The entire Wattenmeer region, which includes the North Frisian Islands, is a national park and serves as a major sanctuary for birds, seals, and diverse marine, plant, and animal life. (The *West* Frisian Islands lie off the coast of the Netherlands, and the *East* Frisians are located along the German coast west of Bremerhaven.) If slopping through the mud is not your idea of fun, you can visit the North Frisian Islands—Nordstrand, Pellworm, Föhr, Amrum, and Sylt—and the Halligen by taking one of the boat excursions that leave from Husum's harbor, the island of Nordstrand, or from the town of Dagebüll, 40 km (25 miles) farther north. During the April–October season there are several daily tours from Husum, varying in length and price. For information about the available boat tours in the area, contact: Wilhelm E. F. Schmid, Am Aussenhafen, D-25813 Husum; Tel: (4841) 20-14-16.

Nordstrand, the closest island, is linked to the mainland by a narrow causeway, and is a 10-km (6-mile) drive north from Husum. No matter which direction you look on Nordstrand, the horizon is delineated by the flat elevation of dikes. Historical memory runs deep in this area. In 1634 a tidal storm swept away 19 churches, 1,300 houses, and drowned 9,000 people while washing away so much of the mainland that Nordstrand and Pellworm, an island a few miles to the west, were left in its wake. The beaches on Nordstrand consist of the same *Schlick* found everywhere in the Wattenmeer region. The dike-enclosed interior of the island is pastureland.

If it's sand and surf amid a livelier resort atmosphere you're after, you'll find it on Sylt, Germany's most popular island. To get there, continue north from Husum on the B 5 to Niebüll, where you load your car onto one of the several trains that connect Sylt to the mainland via the Hindenburg-damm causeway (DM 116 per car, round trip). It's a 30-km (19-mile) train ride from Niebüll to Westerland, Sylt's main town.

Sylt

A narrow strip of an island, some 24 miles north to south and generally less than a mile wide, Sylt is a favorite vacation retreat for Germany's wealthy industrialists and film and entertainment stars. Its eastern coastline is a quiet landscape of marshlands, mud flats, and wildlife sanctuaries, while its western side is characterized by extensive white-sand beaches, steep cliffs, and sand dunes. It's anyone's guess how much longer the island will be here, since thus far nobody has figured out a way to stop the North Sea from eventually washing it away.

Sylt's scenic west-coast beaches, with their crashing surf, stand in dramatic contrast to the flat shallows that characterize most of the Wattenmeer region, and are popular vacation spots for northern Europeans. This is one place where nudism, or what the Germans call *Freie Körper Kultur* (Free Body Culture), is definitely not frowned upon. If you're in the mood to let it all hang out, you'll find designated nudist beaches marked "FKK" every two or three miles along the island's western coastline. For privacy and protection against the wind and the sun, *Strandkörbe* (wicker basket chairs) can be rented at all the beaches.

Sylt vacationers are, by and large, an active crowd. Many will spend the day sunbathing, of course, but many more will be out hiking along the shoreline, no matter what the weather. After striding for miles against the wind, they'll stop at a café for a bracing *Tee mit Rum* (tea laced with rum) before heading back. (Another favorite drink on Sylt is the *Pharisäer,* or Pharisee, much like an Irish coffee. The name reputedly comes from a pastor who, discovering his parishioners sneaking shots of whiskey and rum in their coffee rather than drinking in front of him, called them Pharisees.) There are camping facilities all along the coast, mostly filled with vans instead of tents (nightly charge). Boat trips depart from the harbor at List on the island's northern tip or from Hörnum at its southern tip. Before casting their rods, fishermen must purchase a license from one of the community administration centers (*Gemeindeamt*) scattered around the island at Keitum, Morsum, Hörnum, Rantum, List, Wenningstedt, and Tinnum.

There are a handful of towns on Sylt, most of them catering to the tourist trade. The main town, **Westerland**, is filled with unimaginative concrete-and-glass hotels that don't have much aesthetic appeal, but the town is centrally located on the island and offers more amenities than any of the others. Advance booking is a must if you are planning to visit between May and October. Golf, tennis, and a fairly lively night scene add to Westerland's appeal.

On Strandstrasse, the pedestrians-only street in the middle of Westerland, the reasonably priced 55-room ▶ **Hotel Roth** caters to a mixed crowd of vacationers who don't expect much in the way of frills or luxury. Next door, at Strandstrasse 2, a country-house atmosphere prevails in the more intimate—and more expensive— ▶ **Hotel Stadt Hamburg**, which also has one of Westerland's better seafood restaurants. Two blocks to the north of Strandstrasse, at Johann-Möller-Strasse 30, is the much smaller ▶ **Hotel Atlantic**, with a swimming pool and sauna. The exclusive ▶ **Hotel Sylter Seewolf**, two blocks to the south of Strandstrasse at Bötticherstrasse 13, provides a wide range of comforts and services. On Bomhoffstrasse, just off Strandstrasse, the small ▶ **Residenz Rezai** has rooms decorated with antiques.

If the crowded scene in Westerland isn't to your liking, try the towns of Keitum and Kampen. **Keitum**, 3 km (2 miles) to the east, is a quiet village of thatched-roof houses, with just enough shops and restaurants to keep ennui at bay. Intimate, country-style accommodations can be found in guest houses such as the ▶ **Wolfshof**, ▶ **Seiler Hof**, and ▶ **Groot's Hotel**.

Many of Germany's wealthiest citizens have chosen **Kampen**, 6 km (3½ miles) north of Westerland, as the spot to build their vacation homes. The ▶ **Hotel-Pension Wuldehof** in Kampen is a thatched-roof country house that faces the mainland to the east, while the ▶ **Hotel Rungholt**, a 100-bed establishment set among the dunes, looks out toward the North Sea.

Before heading east, visitors with an interest in modern German art may want to make a short detour to the hamlet of **Seebüll**, about 15 km (9½ miles) northeast of Niebüll. Emil Nolde, one of Germany's greatest Expressionist painters, was banished to this tiny town by the Nazis, who considéred his art "decadent"; it was a rather ironic twist of fate, as Nolde was one of the few major German painters who actually joined the party in its earliest years. The **Nolde Museum**, open daily from 10:00 A.M. to 6:00 P.M., March to October only, contains more than 200 of Nolde's "unpainted" works. Forced to work in secret, the artist sought to avoid the telltale smell of turpentine associated with oil paintings by turning to watercolors. Drawing on the local landscape for inspiration, Nolde painted 1,300 pictures, all of them small enough to be easily hidden. The story of his exile is told by Siegfried Lenz in his novel *The German Lesson*.

EASTERN SCHLESWIG-HOLSTEIN
Flensburg

Located near the Danish border at the western tip of the Flensburg fjord, some 40 km (25 miles) east of Niebüll on the B 199 highway, Flensburg is steeped in the Danish and German rivalries that mark so much of Schleswig-Holstein's history. The city's history as a center of Baltic Sea shipping, commerce, and culture goes back a thousand years, during which time Flensburg and nearby Schloss Glücksburg (see below) alternately belonged to Danish kings and the dukes of Schleswig. In Germany Flensburg is still known as the "Rum City" because of its role 200 years ago as a center of sugar cane trade with the Danish West Indies.

Norderhofenden, a street on the west side of the harbor, and the nearby pedestrians-only Holm, Grosse Strasse, and Norderstrasse, contain most of Flensburg's historical landmarks. The tourist information office at Norderstrasse 6, where brochures and maps in English can be obtained, is a good place to begin a walking tour.

One of the city's landmarks, the ▶ **Flensborg-Hus** at Norderstrasse 76, also serves as a simple, comfortable hotel (most rooms have a bath and toilet). It was built in 1725 as an orphanage, and has a monogram of Danish king Friedrich IV above its gateway. Flensburg's most famous landmark, the **Nordertor** (Northern Gate), is a few hundred yards to the north. The brick stepped-gable structure, dating back to 1595 (when the old city center was surrounded by fortifications), is decorated with Flensburg's coat of arms—as well as those of Danish king Christian IV.

A block east of the Nordertor is Schiffsbrücke, a street facing the waterfront. The **Schiffahrtsmuseum** at number 39 provides an introduction to Flensburg's seafaring history with a collection of ship models and nautical instruments. Souvenirs from seamen returning to Flensburg from all corners of the globe provide the decoration in **Piet Henningsen**, the town's oldest and best-known seafood restaurant, located a few doors south of the museum. Reservations are advisable; Tel: (461) 245-76. The area south along the harbor from here, with its red-light bars and run-down brothels, still carries the boozy flavor of the rough-and-tumble world of sailors.

Schiffsbrücke, as it heads south, becomes Norderhofenden and then Süderhofenden. At Süderhofenden 38 is another centrally located hospice, the ▶ **Flensburger Hof**. Set back from the busy street, the modern concrete-and-glass hotel is one of the most comfortable in the city.

Two very different landmarks, just across the street from one another on Friedrich-Ebert-Strasse, are several hundred years apart in terms of architectural design. The **Deutsches Haus**, a Bauhaus-style building from 1929, serves as Flensburg's main concert hall, while the **Kloster zum Heiligen Geist** (Monastery of the Holy Ghost) is a 13th-century Franciscan monastery.

A block north, on Dr. Todsen Strasse, is Südermarkt and the beginning of Holm, a pedestrians-only street. On Holm and Grosse Strasse you'll find most of the painstakingly restored architectural and historical gems of Flensburg's old city center. At Südermarkt itself is the Gothic **St. Nikolai-Kirche** (St. Nicholas' Church), built of red brick in 1390 and containing the largest organ in Schleswig-Holstein: a 66-register, 5,000-pipe instrument built between 1604 and 1609 by Nicolaus Maas, a master organ builder from Stralsund.

Flensburg's Danish-speaking minority is served by the **Heiliggeist-Kirche** (Church of the Holy Ghost) on Grosse Strasse, which since 1588 has held its services in Danish. The small and simple twin-naved brick church was built in 1388. The **St. Marien Kirche** (Church of St. Mary), also located on Grosse Strasse, about a block south of the information office, was begun in 1284 and completed in 1445. Its 16th-century high altar, built by Hans Ringer, is one of the finest Late Renaissance altars in northern Germany.

Holm and Grosse Strasse are lined with cafés, shops, restaurants, and one very convenient hotel, the ▶ **Stadt Hamburg**, whose rooms look out over the *Fussgängerzone* (pedestrian zone). At Holm 19–21 a courtyard on the east side of the street leads to several boutiques and an outdoor restaurant, the quiet tree-shaded **Borgerforenigung** (Danish for "citizens' association"), where many Danish dishes are on the menu; Tel: (461) 233-85. The **Börsenkeller**, located on Grosse Strasse in what was once the city's stock exchange building, specializes in seafood. Closed for lunch on Sundays; Tel: (461) 233-38. On the same street, in a restored

18th-century house next to the tourist office, is another recommended restaurant, the **Alt-Flensburger Haus**. The atmosphere here is cozy but the prices high. Closed Sundays; Tel: (461) 264-64. It's best to reserve at all three restaurants.

Glücksburg

For centuries the region northeast of Flensburg was caught in a tug-of-war battle for ownership between the kings of Denmark and the dukes of Schleswig. The only thing the combatants had in common, though not concurrently, was a strategically sited *Schloss* (castle) in Glücksburg, about 10 km (6 miles) northeast of Flensburg. Now, of course, it's vacationers rather than soldiers who descend on Glücksburg: The town has become one of the most popular seaside resorts on the Flensburg fjord. From Flensburg you can reach Glücksburg by car (a 15-minute drive) or by taking one of the boats of the Viking Reederei line (Neue Strasse 6–8; Tel: 46-276-86) that leave Flensburg harbor for excursion tours of the fjord. During the April to October season boats depart on the hour from 8:30 to 11:30 A.M. and from 1:00 to 5:00 P.M. daily. The trip to Glücksburg (via Kollund) takes about an hour.

Schloss Glücksburg is a gleaming white four-story *Wasserschloss* (moated castle) with a red-tile roof and octagonal towers at each of its four corners. Built on the orders of Duke Johann the Younger and completed in 1585, the Renaissance castle served as the seat of power for the Schleswigian dukes and the Danish kings—depending, of course, on who was currently in power. Danish king Christian IX (1818–1904), whose descendants still inhabit the castle, was dubbed the "grandfather of Europe" after his grandsons became the kings of Denmark, Norway, Greece, and England, as well as the tsar of Russia. About 20 rooms on two floors of the castle are open to the public, the most splendid being the small **Rote Saal** (Red Hall), where *lieder* concerts and string-quartet recitals are given during the annual Schleswig-Holstein music festival, usually in July.

Schleswig

Museums—especially the two dealing with the early and Viking past of Schleswig-Holstein—and the most famous cathedral in the state are good reasons for visiting the city of Schleswig, on the northern end of Schlei fjord, some 40 km (25 miles) south of Flensburg on the A 7 Autobahn.

About 1½ km (1 mile) west of downtown Schleswig is

Schloss Gottorf, the residence of the dukes of Gottorf, built over a 200-year period from the early 1500s to the early 1700s. The first period of construction was carried out with the help of Italian and Dutch craftsmen; later, the Swedish Baroque architect Nikodemus Tessin took over the design. In the castle **museum** you'll find a comprehensive collection of medieval religious artifacts, paintings, and triptychs—some of them rescued from churches destroyed in North Sea floods, others salvaged from churches secularized in the wake of the Reformation. A separate building on the castle grounds is devoted to modern German art and features paintings by Nolde, Oskar Kokoschka, and Max Beckmann as well as sculptures by Ernst Barlach.

Another museum located on the grounds of Schloss Gottorf, **Nydam Hall**, has a fascinating—if grisly—collection of mummified corpses found in the peat bogs of the region. Thanks (or not, depending on your viewpoint) to the chemicals in the peat, some of these ancient folk are remarkably well preserved. Their endings, however, must have been anything but peaceful: Evidence suggests that many were sacrificed to pagan deities. The lives of Schleswig-Holstein's early inhabitants are documented by a collection of clothing, weapons, tools, pagan icons, and handicrafts, some dating back 2,000 years, as well as a 70-foot-long wooden boat from the fourth century A.D. (The Schloss Gottorf complex, including the three museums, is open daily from 9:00 A.M. to 6:00 P.M.)

Anyone with even a passing interest in the Vikings and their culture will want to visit **Haithabu**, on the southern shore of Schlei fjord. Haithabu—a Viking name meaning "town on the heath"—was the site of one of the most important Viking trading towns in the Baltic region. From the Baltic Sea the Vikings sailed down the Schlei fjord to Haithabu, the point from which they carried their goods and booty overland about a dozen miles west to the Treene river and on to the North Sea. The cluster of rough wooden buildings at Haithabu are reconstructions of the kind of structures the Vikings built in the ninth century. The **Wikinger Museum Haithabu** (Vikings' Museum), opened in 1985, provides further insights into the area's Viking past with archaeological finds from the site, including a Viking ship. There is a 30-minute film, "The World of the Vikings," with soundtracks in German, English, Danish, and French. (Open daily 9:00 A.M. to 6:00 P.M.)

On the northern shore of Schlei fjord is the town of **Schleswig**, dominated by the 350-foot spire of **St. Petri** cathedral. The cathedral's most famous feature is the Late Gothic **Bordeshom Altar**, with 22 panels and 398 figures carved in oak by master craftsman Hans Brüggemann between 1514 and 1521. These carvings reflect both North German and Dutch Gothic influences; one panel was clearly influenced by Albrecht Dürer's engraving *The Descent from the Cross*. A student of Rembrandt's, Jürgen Ovens, whose work is also found in the church of St. Christophorus in Friedrichstadt, painted the *Victory of Christianity* over the cathedral's Kielmannseck altar.

Schleswig (population 32,000) is a town of quiet pleasures. Marktplatz (Market Square) and its adjacent side streets, zoned for pedestrians only, contain restaurants, shops, and cafés. Located a block north of the cathedral, Schleswig's **Rathaus**, a Franciscan monastery in the 13th century, was converted to a paupers' home when the Reformation swept Catholicism out of the region. Restoration work carried out in 1983 uncovered a 13th-century mural painting of the Crusades.

A good seafood meal (salmon, plaice, matjes) can be had in Schleswig at the cozy **Senator Kroog**, also on Rathaus Markt. Rooms with waterfront views are available at the ▶ **Strandhalle Hotel** at Strandweg 2. A three-hour boat tour of the Schlei fjord leaves from Schleswig's harbor daily at 2:00 P.M. during the April–October season. (For more information on the boat tour contact Bischoff's, Gottorfdam 1; Tel: 4621-231-19.)

THE LAKE DISTRICT

A placid, rural landscape of farms, hills, and lakes unfolds as you head southeast toward Lübeck from Schleswig via federal highway B 76 into the gently rolling hill region known as the *Holsteinische Schweiz* (Holstein's Switzerland). The hilly terrain, with some 140 lakes, was carved out by glaciers during the last Ice Age. Camping facilities (dominated by recreational vehicles) are located on or near many of the lakes, and at most of them small boats can be rented.

After some 63 km (39 miles) you'll reach Kiel, the state capital, whose shipyards built U-boats during World War II. Old Kiel was totally destroyed by Allied bombers, and the postwar rebuilding created a city of modern but monotonous brick buildings.

A short detour 15 km (9 miles) west of Kiel on B 4 will bring you to **Molfsee**, where thatched-roof farm houses, a windmill, and arts, crafts, and cooking exhibits convey an impression of rural 17th-century life at the 100-acre **Freilichtmuseum** (Open Air Museum).

Continuing southeast through the lake district from Kiel,

route B 76 passes through an area with any number of picturesque waterside towns. The most attractive of these is **Eutin**, 50 km (31 miles) from Kiel, overlooking the Grosse Eutiner See (Great Eutin Lake). Dubbed the "Weimar of the North" because of its rich cultural heritage, Eutin was the birthplace of opera composer Carl Maria von Weber. Every summer the town stages an open-air music festival devoted to Weber's works. The 13th-century Gothic church of **St. Michaelis** is also the venue for year-round musical programs, particularly organ concerts played on its new 35-register Metzler organ. The 32-room ▶ **Voss Haus** hotel here has comfortable rooms looking out over the lake.

Plön, 15 km (9 miles) west of Eutin and about 55 km (34 miles) northwest of Lübeck, is surrounded by 12 lakes, large and small, and is another good base for exploring the region.

LÜBECK

Lübeck, once known as the Queen of the Hanseatic League, is a fine old city of red brick, spires, and towers on the river Trave near the Baltic coast of Schleswig-Holstein, about 40 km (25 miles) southeast of Eutin via the B 76 and B 207, and 65 km (41 miles) northeast of Hamburg via the A 1 Autobahn. About one-fifth of Lübeck's historic Altstadt was destroyed in an air raid in 1942, but it still has more intact buildings from the 13th to the 15th centuries than all other northern German cities combined. Some 1,000 of the old town's buildings are protected historical sites—Lübeck dates from the 12th century—and UNESCO has placed the city on its World Heritage list of international monuments alongside bigger cities like Florence, Amsterdam, and St. Petersburg.

Lübeck is still an important maritime trading center, with a population of about 225,000, and competes with Rostock for honors as Germany's biggest port on the Baltic. The Lübeck area, with excellent sea links for travellers to Scandinavia and connected by canal to the Elbe river (and via that busy waterway to the North Sea), is also a center for heavy industry. The city's medical university, founded in 1973, is an important research, teaching, and medical-care center.

The charming historical character of the city—which began as a trading settlement in 1143, was destroyed by fire in 1157, and was refounded by Saxony's Duke Henry the Lion in

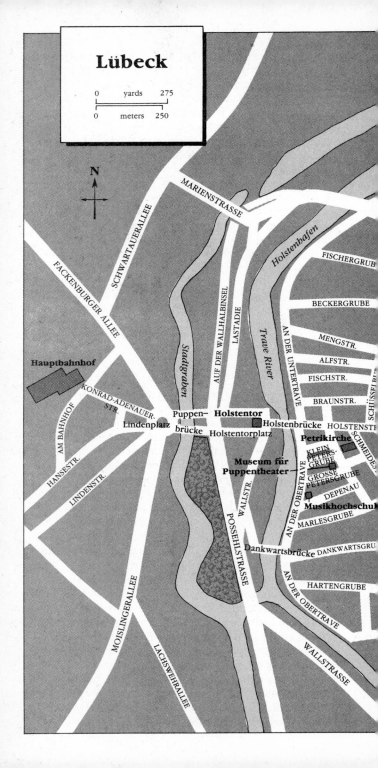

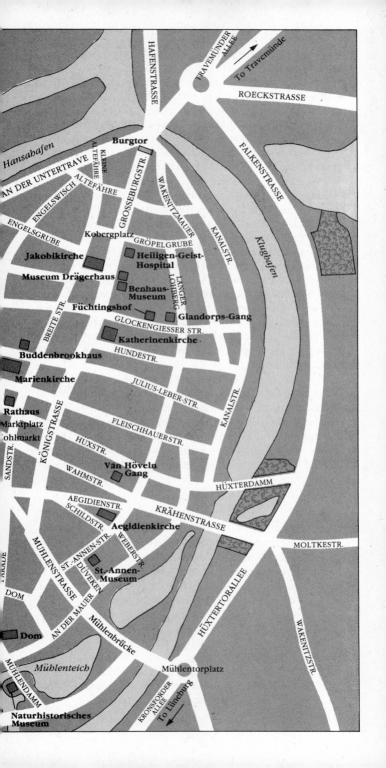

1159—is what draws most visitors. Lübeck's waterbound Altstadt, situated on an island, offers fascinating walks through its past, enshrined in its medieval Rathaus and Markt; its Dom (cathedral), Marienkirche, and other churches; its 15th-century twin-towered Holstentor (Holsten Gate) and Burgtor (Castle Gate); its six old *Salzspeicher* (salt warehouses); its old red-brick gabled houses lining narrow cobblestone streets and alleys; and its two most famous and historic restaurants: the elegant and formal Schabbelhaus, which occupies two Renaissance houses, and the Haus der Schiffergesellschaft (Seamen's Guild House), built in 1535, the property of 49 sea captains, and offering hearty traditional sailor's dishes.

Lübeck's cultural scene is a lively one. The hometown of Nobel Prize winner Thomas Mann, the city is well known for its Musikhochschule (Academy of Music), which plays a leading role in Schleswig-Holstein's annual summer music festival. In Lübeck, the music festival opens with a concert in the cathedral in June and closes with a grand finale in August, in the Marienkirche. The city is also well known for its museums, two of which show how local people lived up to the 19th century; and for its marzipan, its *Rotspon* (red wine), its many good cafés and restaurants, and its great variety of shopping.

The city also offers enticing day trips to Travemünde, Lübeck's freight and Scandinavian ferry-boat port (not to mention a lively beach resort) on the Baltic, only 20 km (12½ miles) to the north; and to Lüneburg, the old Hanseatic League salt-producing town, about 100 km (62 miles) to the south, whose shipments of the "white gold" to Lübeck helped secure for it the leadership of the Hanseatic League in the mid-14th century.

MAJOR INTEREST

Rathaus and Markt
Marienkirche, Katherinenkirche
Buddenbrookhaus (birthplace of Thomas Mann)
Schabbelhaus museum and restaurant
Burgtor and Holstentor (old fortified gates)
Heiligen-Geist-Hospital (medieval hospice)
Schiffergesellschaft (historic seamen's restaurant-
     tavern)
Behnhaus Museum (19th–20th century art) and Mu-
     seum Drägerhaus
Füchtingshof and other Baroque almshouses
16th–18th-century salt warehouses (Salzspeicher)
Puppet Theater Museum
Musikhochschule

Naturhistorisches Museum (natural history museum)
Altarpiece collection in the St.-Annen-Museum
Marzipan at Café Niederregger

Day trips to Travemünde and Lüneburg

Lübeck's compact **Altstadt**, the focus of the traveller's attention, occupies an oval-shaped island a little over a mile long (north to south) and less than a mile wide (east to west) and girted by a zigzagging ring road that changes its name several times on its route around the inner town. This island, between the Trave and Wakenitz rivers, is where the city began as a trading settlement. Eight bridges span the encircling, moatlike Trave river and Klughafen waterways, connecting the old town with greater Lübeck; only about 12,000 of Lübeck's residents live on the island.

The Rathaus, Markt, and Marienkirche are next to each other roughly at the center of the old town, surrounded by shopping streets. Breite Strasse, the main pedestrian shopping street, runs past them on their eastern side. Königstrasse is a block east of Breite Strasse.

At the northern end of Königstrasse is the Heiligen-Geist-Hospital, on Kobergplatz, and a few blocks north of it is the Burgtor gate. The Holstentor, the better-known old fortified gate, is on the western side of the island. The cathedral is at the island's southern tip.

One of the city's three tourist information offices is located on the north side of the Markt; Tel: (451) 122-81-06. The other two offices are at Beckergrube 95, three blocks north of the Markt (Tel: 451-122-81-09), and at the Hauptbahnhof, or main railroad station (Tel: 451-122-81-07), at the western end of Konrad-Adenauer-Strasse, on the "mainland" just half a mile west of the Markt across the Puppenbrücke. (The Puppenbrücke, or Dolls' Bridge, with its seven stone figures of classical gods and goddesses, was given its name by irreverent local folk.)

The tourist office offers a two-hour guided walking tour of the Altstadt, well worth taking for initial orientation. The tour starts outside the Markt tourist office in summer at 11:00 A.M. and 2:00 P.M. Monday through Saturday, and at 11:00 A.M. on Sundays and public holidays. The tour is in German, but the guides are usually happy to explain the main points in English. Individual tours can be arranged in any of ten languages, as well as to focus on such special interests as churches, museums, or Mann. The tourist office has a good free booklet in English with maps outlining three walks lasting from one to four hours. The longest tour includes visits to seven museums.

Several operators run riverboat trips around the old town or the port from piers on the north and south sides of the Holstentorbrücke on the east bank of the Obertrave, as well as just north of the bridge on the west bank of the river.

The Markt and the Rathaus

The Markt and the Rathaus, a bit west of the exact center of the Altstadt, are good starting points for touring Lübeck on foot. The spacious **Marktplatz** is filled every Monday and Thursday with colorful stalls selling meat, fruit, vegetables, cheese, bread, and handicrafts. In December, the square is given over to a big daily Christmas market stocked with sweets, cakes, and other goodies.

The foundation stone of the multi-winged **Rathaus**, which stands on the north and east sides of the Markt above attractive brick arcades that allow easy access between the north side of the marketplace and the pedestrian precinct of Breite Strasse (see below), was laid in 1230. The present-day building, topped by slim turrets, is a mixture of Gothic and Renaissance, with high red-brick walls decorated with black glazed-brick courses and round panels emblazoned with coats of arms. Its south-facing wall, built in 1435, is pierced by two large vent holes to allow passage for the keen Baltic wind. The town hall's main entrance on Breite Strasse has a pointed arch made of green glazed bricks that are believed to date from 1350. Circular bronze fittings on the door wings show Kaiser Karl IV surrounded by seven electors. One of the fittings is a 14th-century Gothic original, the other a cast copy. The splendid Dutch Renaissance stone staircase at the front of the building was designed by Tönnies Evers the Elder and completed in 1594.

Dominated by black glazed-brick arches built in 1887, the small entrance hall of the Rathaus is heavy modern Gothic Revival, but the furnishings and decorations of the big audience hall on its ground floor, the former Hanseatic high court, are pure Rococo, dating from 1754 to 1761. Allegorical paintings by Stefano Torelli depict the liberal arts, trade, freedom, mercy, harmony, industry and abundance, vigilance, intelligence, moderation, and discretion. A tall 18th-century iron stove with a decorative brass fretwork screen was the only heat source for the hall—which is now used for receptions, honors, awards, and concerts—until 1963. People tried by the court used to leave it by one of two side-by-side doors, depending upon the court's verdict. Those acquitted exited left; those found guilty and sentenced to jail or execution went to their fate by the right-hand door. Both doors have stone steps; those on the right are worn down much more than the ones on the left.

Underneath the Rathaus at the north side of the Markt is the informal and spacious **Ratskeller** restaurant, which serves a wide range of meat, fish, and vegetarian dishes at very reasonable prices. Try the *Labskaus,* a traditional seaman's meal of potato and corned beef mashed together with a fried egg on top, and garnished with fresh salt herring and pickles. Another typical local meal is pork and cabbage. The Ratskeller is also known for its *Holstein Ente* (duck) with apple slices. The house brews its own beer, known as *Lübsch.* Tel: (451) 720-44.

Try a glass of Lübeck's *Rotspon,* a French Bordeaux that the city has been importing since the 13th century. French officers of Napoleon's army, which occupied Lübeck in 1806, found that Bordeaux wines stored in the city's cellars tasted much better than the same wines at home. An explanation has never been found, but it is believed that Lübeck's climate and the temperature in its wine cellars has an improving effect on the wines. The word *Rotspon* comes from the North German dialect word *Span,* which means a wooden chip, referring to the wooden casks in which red wine was originally stored.

After visiting the Rathaus, walk along bustling **Breite Strasse**, which leads north to the Marienkirche. Or take a coffee break at the big **Café Niederegger**, on Breite Strasse opposite the Rathaus. The café was founded in 1806 by Johannes Niederegger, whose firm is now the major producer of the marzipan for which Lübeck is internationally known, employing a staff of 600 to make about 30 tons of the sweet stuff every day.

Local legend has it that Lübeck marzipan was created in 1407 during a famine, when there was no grain available for making bread; the city fathers are said to have told bakers to make bread out of almonds. Racks of marzipan-to-go in all shapes and sizes, from pigs and clowns to floral arrangements and baskets of fruit, fill the entrance hall of the café. Although marzipan cake is the house specialty, there are plenty of other mouth-watering goodies on sale.

NORTH OF THE MARKT
The Marienkirche Area

The nearby 14th-century **Marienkirche** (St. Mary's Church), just north of the Rathaus, is Lübeck's most outstanding example of brick Gothic, and was the model for many other churches in the Baltic area. Built over a span of 100 years by citizens who aimed to outdo the city's cathedral (see below), the Marienkirche ended up being Germany's third-largest church, with a 120-foot-high central nave and the highest brick vaulting in the world. The ambitious townspeople built the church's twin towers—two of the seven church spires which are Lübeck's "trademark"—to a height of 406 feet, 32½ feet taller than the cathedral's two towers. The church was badly damaged in the 1942 bombings. Its bells crashed down and embedded themselves in the stone floor of its south tower—in which state they have been left as a reminder and warning of the horrors of war.

A beautiful astronomical clock built in 1566 was also destroyed. It was replaced with a faithful copy that presents a parade of figures every day at noon. The church, where the great Baroque organist Dietrich Buxtehude (1637–1707) played for almost 40 years (he counted Handel and Bach among his pupils), has the largest mechanical organ in the world (8,512 pipes and 101 stops), built by Lübeck craftsmen in 1968. Like most other big churches in the city, the Marienkirche stages superb organ concerts at various times throughout the summer and fall. (Every day during summer there is at least one organ concert in one of the churches. Ask at a tourist office for the current schedules.)

Mengstrasse, a narrow cobblestone street of handsome gabled merchants' houses on the north side of the Marienkirche (reached via the arcade of the 15th-century Kanzleigebäude, the former Rathaus chancellery), is known not just for its Schabbelhaus restaurant. At number 4, on the north side of the street just west of Breite Strasse, is the **Buddenbrookhaus**, which was once the property of Thomas Mann's family, leading merchants of the city. Mann (1875–1955), winner of the 1929 Nobel Prize for Literature, was born in the house and made it world-renowned with his novel *Buddenbrooks*. The 13th-century house was rebuilt in 1758 and, except for its façade, was almost completely destroyed during World War II. It is now a museum devoted to the Mann brothers.

The **Schabbelhaus** restaurant, a short walk to the west of the Buddenbrookhaus at Mengstrasse 48–50, owes its name to a wealthy master baker and confectioner named Heinrich Schabbel, who bequeathed 125,000 goldmarks to the city on condition that it establish a museum for Lübeck antiquities. The city bought a patrician house at Mengstrasse 36 and filled it with valuable furniture. Later, city officials also installed a wine tavern that became a popular meeting place. The house was bombed in the 1942 air raid, and postwar reconstruction was not possible. But the Schabbelhaus idea survived, and in the 1950s the city bought the properties the restaurant now occupies.

The new Schabbelhaus was equipped with antique furniture from old merchants' houses and on loan from Lübeck's municipal museum. The stylish restaurant, which serves regional and international dishes, can seat up to 200 in its various rooms and is a favorite lunch spot for local businessmen and visiting state politicians from Kiel. Open noon to 2:30 P.M. and 6:00 to 9:30 P.M. daily except Sundays. Reservations are recommended; Tel: (451) 720-11.

Das Kleine Restaurant, to the west along the Trave at An der Untertrave 39, part of the ring road, is in a 300-year-old red-brick building with Renaissance stepped gables and a rustic interior decor featuring dark-brown ceiling beams and light oak furniture. The restaurant offers refined regional specialties such as terrine of duck with a honey and pepper sauce and delicate fish dishes such as salmon and sole. A wide choice of German and French wines is also available. Reservations recommended; Tel: (451) 70-59-59; closed Saturday evenings and Sundays. Another good restaurant, the **Wullenwever**, at Beckergrube 71, three blocks northwest of the Markt, is housed in a 400-year-old former brewery. It offers regional dishes, especially fish, and a choice of 150 wines. Reserve; Tel: (451) 70-43-33; closed Sundays and Mondays.

If you prefer to stay at a quiet, informal, well-located hotel in the center of the old town, the 50-room ► **Alter Speicher**, the biggest and most modern hotel in the Altstadt, is located on the Beckergrube in two neighboring buildings. One is a faithful copy of a former gabled warehouse that occupied the site until it burned down in 1980. The new building was completed in 1989. The hotel lives up to its claim of providing first-class accommodation and service at "civil" prices. It also has a bar and a cozy pub named **Spökenkieker** (an old North German dialect name for a fortune-teller who is not to be taken seriously), as well as the rustic **Winzereck** (Vintner's Corner), a good restaurant serving generous portions of regional dishes, with a summer-garden café for light snacks.

In this sector of the Altstadt the streets are linked by passageways, and you may find yourself zigzagging as you explore neighborhoods filled with *Wohnhöfe* (courtyards), antiques shops, cafés, and bookstores.

The North Gate

By heading in a northerly direction, taking Engelwisch and then Grosse Altefähre street, you'll reach Grosse Burgstrasse. This brings you to the brick **Burgtor** (Castle Gate) and the Burgtorbrücke at the junction of two waterways, the

Hansahafen and the Klughafen, the latter a long, narrow harbor at the northeast corner of the island. The original Burgtor, built in 1444, was Lübeck's fortified northern city gate. It once guarded a small isthmus—now cut by a canal between the two harbors—that was the only means of access to the city by land. The remains of the old wall extend down around the eastern side of the old inner city as far as the Mühlentor, at the Mühlenbrücke, and now serve as a long parking lot. To the east is the former customs house, and next to the gate to the west is the red-brick Burgkloster (monastery) whose origins date from 1227. None of the buildings is open to the public.

The Heiligen-Geist-Hospital Area

From the Burgtor, head south on Grosse Burgstrasse. Two blocks away, on the left side of the street, stands the **Heiligen-Geist-Hospital** (Hospital of the Holy Spirit), founded by some rich and philanthropic local citizens in 1230 and completed 60 years later. You will recognize it by its four slender turret spires and its spired belfry. The hospice, one of the oldest social institutions in Europe as well as one of the most important monumental buildings of the Middle Ages, was converted to a shelter for elderly men and women in the early 19th century, when rows of 130 small wooden cabins with no ceilings were built in its big hall. The cabins, now empty but still intact, come to life again each Christmas, however, when they are used as stalls for an arts-and-crafts market.

The building's huge vaults were used for centuries to store a wide variety of goods, but are now occupied by an excellent wine restaurant, **Historischer Weinkeller unter dem Heiligen-Geist-Hospital**. The restaurant has two dining areas: the informal Bürgerkeller, serving regional dishes, and the more formal Weinkeller, with silver table service and haute cuisine. The wines come from the best vineyards in Europe, and the house also has some vintages from California. Both restaurants are open for lunch and supper daily except Tuesdays (until 1:00 A.M., but cold dishes only after 11:00 P.M.). Reservations are recommended; Tel: (451) 762-34.

For a good—and "different"—lunch head over to the **Schiffergesellschaft**, a block west of the Heiligen-Geist-Hospital across Kobergplatz. The house, with its narrowly stepped gables, is one of Lübeck's most beautiful buildings, and has a classic, big tavern-restaurant up front and more elegant dining rooms toward the rear. The original building on the site was first chronicled in 1292; the Society of

Skippers acquired it in 1535, after which they pulled it down and built the present house.

The front dining area, a big hall that was once the skippers' convention room, is supported by painted wooden beams and carved posts, and is filled with long wooden tables at which guests sit on high-backed oak benches under big models of sailing ships suspended from the ceiling. It's fun—and the food is good, too. Regional specialties and seamen's dishes like those at the Ratskeller, including *Labskaus,* are the feature of the extensive menu (the prices are higher here). A wide range of beers is available, and the restaurant has a good wine cellar. Reservations are recommended for dinner; Tel: (451) 767-76. Closed Mondays.

Across the street from the restaurant is the famous **Jakobikirche** (St. James's Church). The church, dedicated to seamen, dates from 1227 and has an altar built in 1698 as well as two historic organs—one of them, built in 1504, is among the oldest in Europe. The Jakobikirche also contains a lifeboat from the ill-fated German four-masted training ship *Pamir* (which sank in the Atlantic in 1957 with the loss of all hands) as a memorial to her 80 dead.

Lübeck's collection of 19th–20th century paintings, including works by Johann-Friedrich Overbeck, Caspar David Friedrich, Edvard Munch, Max Liebermann, Lovis Corinth, and Max Beckmann, is displayed at the **Behnhaus-Museum,** in one of the city's finest 18th-century burgher houses at Königstrasse 11, across the street from the Jakobikirche. The neighboring **Museum Drägerhaus,** at Königstrasse 9, traces the art and cultural history of middle-class urban life in Lübeck from 1750 to 1914, using displays of contemporary art and objets d'art, furniture, and clothing. A special section devoted to Thomas Mann and his elder brother, Heinrich (also a writer—the film *The Blue Angel,* which made Marlene Dietrich a star, was based on one of his books), contains documents and letters connected with their lives and work, including the original manuscript of *Buddenbrooks.*

The **Füchtingshof,** Glockengiesserstrasse 23, just east of the Behnhaus museum, is the largest and most attractive of Lübeck's several almshouses, and was built by 17th-century city councillor Johann Füchting for the widows of seamen and merchants. It has a richly ornamented Baroque portal leading to a peaceful, secluded courtyard with houses still occupied by widows. The city's oldest almshouses are also on this street: the **Glandorps-Gang** (number 41) and the **Glandorps-Hof** (numbers 49–51), built in 1612 for the widows of merchants and craftsmen.

Also well worth seeing is the medieval museum-church,

the **Katherinenkirche** (St. Catherine's Church), at the corner of Königstrasse and Glockengiesserstrasse. The towerless church—a former Franciscan monastery completed in 1370, secularized in 1806, and now belonging to the city—is one of the most significant brick churches in northern Germany, and is being restored to its original form. The church roof is an original wooden structure, and the floor is covered by centuries-old tombstones. The side aisles have beautiful Baroque chapels. Noteworthy works of art inside the church include *The Raising of Lazarus* (1578) by Jacopo Tintoretto and a Late Gothic triumphal cross group. Niches in the church's west façade, on Königstrasse, contain a figure cycle called *The Community of Saints,* sculpted by Ernst Barlach and Gerhard Marcks.

SOUTH OF THE MARKT
The West Gate

The **Holstentor** lies on the Wallhalbinsel (Wall Peninsula) on Holstentorplatz, two blocks west of the Markt, on the far side of the short Holstenbrücke (bridge) crossing the Obertrave river. Built in 1469–1478 by *Ratsbaumeister* (city architect) Heinrich Helstede, the Holstentor, with walls up to 11 feet thick, was once a fortified gate with 30 guns guarding the Holstenhafen (the city's western harbor) and the western entrance to Lübeck. It now houses the **local history museum** (closed Mondays), whose exhibits include a model of Lübeck as it was in 1650; models of Hanseatic *Kogge,* or cogs (single-sail vessels); and medieval torture instruments. Built on a mound of peat that was unable to withstand its heavy load, the southern tower subsided slightly and the gate inclined westward. During following centuries the tower sank more and more, so that today some of the lowest "loopholes"—once used for shooting and as a source of light—are now a couple of feet below the surface.

The six old **Salzspeicher** (salt warehouses), which stored consignments from Lüneburg for shipment (mainly) to Scandinavia, where most of it was used to preserve fish hauls, are south of the ancient gate. The oldest, nearest to the Holstentor, dates from 1579, while the next three were built about 1600, and the last two about 1745. The buildings are now occupied by a department store.

A good view of the Holstentor and the rest of Lübeck's romantic skyline is offered by the ▶ **Mövenpick Hotel**, only a two-minute walk due west of the gate on Auf der Wallhalbinsel. The quiet 197-room hotel, considered the best in town, is favored by visiting business travellers for its good conference and seminar facilities, and is also popular with well-to-do tourists. Its excellent restaurant offers local specialties, especially fish dishes, as well as an international menu, and its **Duell Pub** has a classic English decor and atmosphere.

A quiet family hotel nearby is the medium-priced 54-room ▶ **Hotel Excelsior**, on Hansestrasse, at its junction with Lindenplatz, only a few minutes' walk west.

Directly opposite the salt warehouses, on the east bank of the Obertrave not far from the Musikhochschule, is the medium-priced 46-room ▶ **Hotel Jensen**, whose restaurant offers 40 different fish dishes every day. This quiet family hotel has no bar, but provides 24-hour front-desk service.

From mid-April to mid-October an elevator takes visitors to the top of the landmark tower of the 13th-century **Petrikirche** (St. Peter's Church), a short walk east of the Holstentor on Schmiedestrasse, for a great bird's-eye view of the Altstadt.

Just west of the Petrikirche is Lübeck's privately owned **Museum für Puppentheater** (Puppet Theater Museum), in three old houses at Kleine Petersgrube 4–6. Its exhibits include almost 2,000 puppets from Europe, Africa, and Asia, with an emphasis on 19th-century models, in what is claimed to be the largest private collection of its kind in the world. The museum, which offers guided tours in English upon request, stages daily puppet-theater performances.

The **Musikhochschule**, which runs an open house for visitors, who may listen to lessons, is situated in a graceful 200-year-old Baroque-style former merchant's house at Grosse Petersgrube 21, one block south of the puppet theater. The houses on the street numbered 7–29 offer a fine display of various architectural styles ranging from Gothic to Baroque through Rococo to Neoclassical.

The Romanesque **Dom**, a three-aisle basilica with piers at the southern end of the island, is the oldest church in Lübeck. It was the Episcopal church of Henry the Lion, who founded it in 1173 on the site of an earlier wooden church. A Gothic chancel and choir were added in the 13th–14th centuries. Its huge *Triumphkreuz* (Triumphal Christ on the Cross) was completed in 1477 by Lübeck wood-carver Bernt Notke (1440–1509), the leading master of the Late Gothic in the Baltic region.

The **Naturhistorisches Museum** (Natural History Museum), on the south side of the cathedral overlooking the Mühlenteich, has three floors filled with exhibits of animals, birds, fish, insects, plants, minerals, rocks, and fossils. Its ethnological collection is based on objects brought home by Hanseatic merchants from journeys abroad. The *Völker-*

kundesammlung, a collection of objects ranging from gold arm bands to carpets and tapestries to saddles and weapons, is in the **Zeughaus**, on the cathedral's north side at Grosser Bauhof 12. The Zeughaus is a fine old building that was constructed in 1594 as a grain store.

Lübeck's museums are well known for the quantity and quality of their exhibits. What is now the **St.-Annen-Museum** is housed in a former Augustinian convent built in 1502–1515; after the Reformation the convent became an almshouse, then a prison. It has been Lübeck's museum for art and the history of art, to about 1800, since 1915. Its prize exhibits are an important altarpiece collection, with contributions by Bernt Notke and Hans Memling. The museum, at St.-Annen-Strasse 15, two blocks northeast of the cathedral, also holds frequent exhibitions of contemporary art.

The 13th-century **Aegidienkirche**, on the corner of Aegidienstrasse and Schildenstrasse, a block north of the St.-Annen-Museum, has Gothic wall murals and a choir dating from 1587 that was carved by Tönnies Evers the Younger.

A block north of the Aegidienkirche, at Wahmstrasse 73–77, you'll find the **Von Höveln Gang**, an old almshouse dating from 1792.

Located across the Trave river outside the southeast perimeter of the Altstadt, about 200 yards or so south of Mühlentorplatz on Kronsforder Allee, lies the ▶ **Kaiserhof**, a peaceful, friendly, medium-priced hotel formed out of two attractive merchants' villas. The 140-bed hotel offers free use of a sauna, steam bath, and indoor swimming pool; its solarium costs extra. Its restaurant has only a limited supper menu, and closes at 9:00 P.M., but its small bar stays open as long as guests want it to. The Kaiserhof has two guest houses one block to the south; the rooms are comfortable but rather pedestrian, so ask for a room in the *Haupthaus* (main building).

DAY TRIP FROM LÜBECK
Travemünde

Travemünde, founded as a fishing village at the mouth of the river Trave on the Lübecker Bucht (bay) in 1187, is a district of Lübeck located some 20 km (12½ miles) to the northeast via the fast-moving B 75. It is also a lively place that offers something for everyone. First, it is a typical and very popular Baltic coast resort (for fun and for health cures), with a nearly three-mile-long beach of fine, golden sand dotted with 1,700 municipally owned *Strandkörbe,* rentable wicker beach chairs with upholstered bench seats for two and an adjustable hood that protects against sun, rain, and wind—a German invention.

Travemünde also has a busy nightlife, with plenty of bars and discos and a casino. It is a major shipping port and a gateway to Scandinavia, with huge Baltic ferries running to and from Denmark, Sweden, Finland, and Poland.

Travemünde's long north–south **Strandpromenade**, with the casino situated at its midpoint; the Nordermole, at the mouth of the Trave; and the Vorderreihe, the town's main street on the west bank of the river, south of the Norder-mole, are all lined with shops, cafés, restaurants, and bars, and offer agreeable strolls or open-air coffee breaks while you watch the big ferries moving to and from the Skandina-vienkai (Scandinavian Quay). The 35-floor tower of the upmarket ▶ **Maritim Strand Hotel**, which dominates the southern end of the beach and is now Travemünde's main architectural landmark, offers panoramic views of the town, harbor, and bay from its **Dach Restaurant** (Roof Restaurant), a gourmet establishment serving international dishes along with a wide choice of fine wines.

The Maritim as a place to stay is better suited for business travellers with generous expense accounts than for tourists. But Travemünde does have a number of comfortable, quiet, middle-class establishments like the 30-room ▶ **Hotel Atlantic**, on Kaiserallee, which runs parallel to the Strandpromenade north of the casino. The hotel does not have a view of the sea, but is very near the beach. A small bar serves snacks until 11:00 P.M.

Travemünde's busy yacht harbor, on the east side of the Trave opposite the Nordermole, stages the internationally known Travemünde Woche regatta at the end of July and beginning of August, an annual event that attracts big-time yachters from around the world. The regatta is both a folk festival and a sparkling society gathering. The week ends with a grand fireworks display that lights up Lübeck's seven church spires, to the southwest.

The four-masted sailing-ship *Passat,* the sister ship of the lost *Pamir* (see Lübeck), is moored among the yachts in the Passathafen (harbor). Now a floating youth hostel, she can be reached by a small ferry that runs frequently between the two riverbanks from a pier on the Nordermole, near its junction with the Strandpromenade. Small cruise-boat operators offer excursions up and down the river and around the harbors, and the big ferry lines sail out on day trips on the Baltic. The tourist office at Strandpromenade 1b has all the details; Tel: (4502) 18-04-30.

There are hourly trains from Lübeck's Hauptbahnhof to Travemünde's Strandbahnhof, which is located opposite the casino just a short walk west of the beach. There is also a good private bus service (LVG) between Lübeck and Travemünde that runs every 15 minutes during rush hours and every 45 minutes in off-peak periods. The bus (no number) leaves Lübeck from the Holstenhafen.

—John England

LÜNEBURG

The interesting old salt town of Lüneburg, about 100 km (62 miles) south of Lübeck along the Alte Salzstrasse (Old Salt Road; now the B 207–B 209), lies on the river Ilmenau at the northern edge of the Lüneburg heath. (Lüneburg is only 36 km/22½ miles southeast of Hamburg on the B 4.) Founded about 1200, and sponsored by Henry the Lion, the town garnered great importance from its salt pits, and in the second half of the 14th century it was made a member of the Hanseatic League. Salt was transported to Lübeck by horse and cart as well as via the Stecknitz canal, which became part of the Trave-Elbe canal in 1900.

Its trade in salt—which in the Middle Ages was the only means of preserving food and was almost worth its weight in gold—made Lüneburg one of the richest towns in Germany. Salt revenues paid for construction of magnificent public buildings like its Rathaus, on the old Marktplatz, dating from 1230; a cathedral and other impressive churches; and splendid **gabled town houses** that today are almost the only example of North German Gothic brick architecture still wholly intact.

Lüneburg, now with a population of about 60,000, commemorated the salt that it produced for more than 1,000 years—until 1980—by building the **Deutsches Salzmuseum** (German Salt Museum) at the last salt mine to close, at Sülfmeisterstrasse 1, about five blocks southwest of the Marktplatz. Open daily; guided tours last about an hour.

You should begin your tour of Lüneburg, however, by visiting the **Rathaus** (closed Mondays), on the north side of town, one of the most attractive medieval town halls in northern Germany and the largest preserved Rathaus in the country as a whole. It has a handsome Baroque façade built between 1706 and 1720, with a large clock and belfry tower in which Meissen porcelain bells ring out the hours, and richly furnished rooms and halls, enhanced by wall and ceiling murals and stained-glass windows that date from the 14th to 16th centuries.

Guided 90-minute walking tours in German start daily, April through October, at 11:00 A.M. at the tourist information office (Tel: 4131-322-00), located in the arcade underneath the Rathaus facing the Marktplatz (where a fruit and vegetable market is held on Wednesdays and Saturdays). Tours in other languages can be arranged. Daily 90-minute bus tours start at the tourist office at 3:00 P.M.

The **Lüneburger Heide** (heath) is on the town's southern border. Local tour operators offer day trips to this popular excursion area (at its best in August when the heather blooms) by bus, canal, riverboat, and a train called the Heide Express. Details are available at the tourist office.

The Salzmuseum is one of five museums in Lüneburg (including the Rathaus) well worth visiting if you have the time. The others are: the Museum für das Fürstentum Lüneburg (Museum of the Principality of Lüneburg), at Wandrahmstrasse 10, on the Ilmenau river about six blocks southeast of the Marktplatz; the Brauereimuseum (Brewery Museum), at Heiligengeiststrasse 39, four blocks south of the Marktplatz; and the Ostpreussisches Landesmuseum (East Prussian Culture Museum), at Ritterstrasse 10, one street south of Heiligengeiststrasse.

Am Sande, the town's second main square, is four blocks south of the Marktplatz. A new hotel, opened in 1989 and built in pleasing harmony with its ancient surroundings, is the medium-priced ▶ **Bergström**, on Bei der Lüner Mühle along the banks of the river Ilmenau. Nearby is the 18th-century Alter Kran (Old Crane), the town's landmark. The hotel's **Brasserie** restaurant and its **Greenhouse** café, overlooking the river, have big window walls providing views of half-timbered old warehouses across the narrow waterway.

Lüneburg also has historic red-brick tavern-restaurants, among them the 500-year-old **Kronen Brauhaus**, at Heiligengeiststrasse 39–41, which offers good beer and hearty country fare in rooms with medieval beams or, in summer, in its beer garden.

Although trains from Lübeck to Lüneburg run every 45 to 60 minutes, travelling by car allows you to stop by the picturesque towns of **Ratzeburg**, a few kilometers west on the B 207 and about 32 km (20 miles) south of Lübeck, and **Mölln**, on the B 27 about 40 km (25 miles) south of Lübeck.

—John England

ROSTOCK AND
THE BALTIC COAST

Visitors to Rostock, if they have already been to such cities as Bremen or Hamburg, may get a feeling of déjà vu on their first encounter with the city. Like those famous western German port cities, Rostock, which is located in the state of Mecklenburg–West Pomerania in what used to be East German territory about 20 km (12 miles) inland from the Baltic seacoast on the Warnow river, is also a *Hansestadt* (Hanseatic City), with all that that implies—a daily life influenced chiefly by shipping and by the city's mercantile contacts with distant corners of the globe for more than 500 years.

But Rostock is different in a number of ways. For one thing, its origins are Slavic, the first settlement in the area having been by Slavs in the 12th century. Though Germanic tribes drove out the original settlers in the early 1200s, the Slavic name for the site, Roztoc, or "river widening," has survived, aptly describing the city's setting on the meandering Warnow river, which here becomes a wide, natural deepwater basin that forms the northern boundary of the historic city center (*Innenstadt*).

With a population of 250,000, Rostock is smaller in size and more relaxed than its bigger western German counterparts. Its historic core, an oval-shaped area roughly two kilometers (east to west) by one kilometer (north to south), can be explored easily in a couple of days.

Despite its faltering shipbuilding and trade industries Rostock, with its museums, theaters, and concert halls, remains a place of culture. And, with its nearby seaside resort district Warnemünde (which we discuss later), Rostock is definitely a city that gives its residents a convenient excuse to have fun.

At the moment, however, it's a city busily going about the transition to a capitalist economy, a change that isn't coming easily. The port, which was East Germany's "gateway to the world," is feeling the cold wind of competition from the better-equipped and more conveniently situated ports at Bremen and Hamburg (154 miles and 104 miles to the southwest, respectively). Its shipbuilding industry, too, is in the midst of restructuring, with workers being laid off and, whenever possible, being retrained for higher-skilled jobs. Problems there are, and with the problems has come some violence. In 1992 Rostock hit the headlines when local neo-Nazis began the rioting and attacks on refugees that quickly spread to other economically hard-hit cities in the east.

In its seven centuries of history Rostock has survived hard times, including trade wars in the Baltic region, and military wars on the Continent. It recovered from occupation by French troops during the Napoleonic Wars, and it was rebuilt, though not completely, after the devastation of World War II (which left about 40 percent of the city in ruins). Now it is in the midst of revamping its entire economic and political life, a process in evidence everywhere, and one about which Rostockers are eager to share their opinions with visitors from the West.

Midway between Lübeck and Rostock are the cities of **Wismar**, on the Baltic coast, and **Schwerin**, the state capital and oldest city in Mecklenburg–West Pomerania. Rostock is a convenient base for exploring both, although you may wish to make them part of an itinerary that begins in Hamburg, continues on to Lübeck, and from Lübeck follows a northeasterly route to Rostock, **Stralsund**, the island of **Rügen**, and **Greifswald**, the last Hanseatic city in our tour of Mecklenburg–West Pomerania. (See the Getting Around section at the end of this chapter.)

MAJOR INTEREST

Rostock
Rathaus
Nikolaikirche and Petrikirche
Marienkirche, with 15th-century astronomical clock
Cloister of the Holy Cross (Cultural History Museum)
Kröpeliner Tor (old city gate and museum)
Warnemünde sea resort

Schwerin
Cathedral
Schelfstadt district and the Nikolaikirche
Schlachtermarkt (open-air market)
Historical museum
State theater
Staatliches Museum (major collection of 17th-century
    Dutch landscape painting)
Schwerin Castle

Wismar, Stralsund, and Greifswald (Hanseatic cities
    on the Baltic coast)
Rügen, Germany's largest island, with magnificent
    scenery

ROSTOCK
The Historic City Center

The fairly compact downtown area of Rostock was developed from east to west, the oldest part being the Alter Markt in front of the Petrikirche (St. Peter's Church), which dates to 1218. The western sections of the historic center stretching to the Kröpeliner Tor (city gate) were developed by the 1270s, so that Rostock historians speak of "old" and "new" parts of the center.

Because it is fairly close to the dividing line between the "old" and "new" sections of the historic city center, a good place to start a walking tour is the **Neuer Markt** square in front of the Rathaus. Unfortunately, Rostock's rich architectural heritage was allowed to deteriorate during the city's years under Communist rule, and some of it is in danger of being lost completely. You'll notice this almost immediately as you head into the older part of the city.

The Neuer Markt buildings are faithful reconstructions of the typical 17th- and 18th-century gabled North German Gothic houses that were flattened by bombs during World War II. On the east side of the square, lined with cafés, bookstores, and clothing shops, the first eye-catcher is the **Rathaus**, a peculiar mixture of Gothic and Baroque styles. The seven Gothic spires belong to the original 15th-century building. All but covering up this building is the pink-and-white Baroque decorative structure, topped by a clock and built in 1727–1729. Located close to the Rathaus, at Neuer Markt 2, is the ▶ **Hotel Sonne**, a 128-room hotel that offers clean but very basic accommodations (none of the rooms has private bath or toilet); it was formerly used by seamen on shore leave.

South down busy Steinstrasse, the next major landmark is the massive brick **Steintor** (Stone Gate), dating to around 1270, with a steeplelike roof and one of the former 22 gates to the walled city. Today only sections of the medieval walls around Rostock remain intact, but one section can be seen by walking downhill from in front of the Steintor along Ernst-Barlach-Strasse for a few hundred yards, passing by the hexagonal **Lagebuschturm** (tower) and then turning left through the oldest gate, the **Kuhtor** (Cow Gate), built in 1262.

Downhill along Kleine Wasserstrasse is where the shock of neglected architecture will start to make itself felt. Everywhere you look in the "old" part of the historic center you will see small blue-and-white signs on poorly maintained buildings declaring them to be architectural landmarks that cannot be razed. Just where the money will come from to restore these buildings—the Communist regime expended its resources building the gigantic, drab prefabricated housing districts outside the downtown area—remains to be seen.

As you move eastward from Kleine Wasserstrasse you'll first cross Grubenstrasse; in the city's early years this was actually an arm of the Warnow river that formed a defensive moat for the oldest section of Rostock to its east. Heading uphill from Grubenstrasse along Am Wendländer Schilde you'll spot the unusual roof of the **Nikolaikirche** (St. Nicholas' Church), with windows and balconies of some 20 apartments for church employees in its upper level. The church, dating from the 13th century, was badly damaged during World War II, and now serves as a community center. The next church, **Petrikirche**, is reached by heading north along Altschmiedestrasse; it, too, is still a ruin. Its site, the **Alter Markt**, is where the area's first Germanic settlement was located. Construction on the church began in 1252; a spire was added in the early 16th century, but the upper half was destroyed in the war and has not been rebuilt.

A tour of this area will pass a few restored architectural gems, which vividly signal the area's potential. In fact, Rostock university students prefer to live in this area for its no-nonsense neighborhood life—and low rents.

Heading downhill from the Alter Markt, first along the street known as Sackpfeife, and then Harte Strasse—where refreshment beckons at the simple but atmosphere-laden **Altstaedter Hof** tavern—you'll again hit Grubenstrasse. Walk southward on this for two blocks until reaching Weissgerberstrasse, then turn left on Kleine Wasserstrasse for a block until it intersects with Grosse Wasserstrasse. On this street you'll find two beautifully restored examples of gabled North German Gothic brick houses. One is the **Kerkhofhaus**, a patrician family's residence dating to the 15th century and now serving as a city archives office. A few doors down, and similar in style and period, is one of the most fashionable tavern-restaurants in Rostock, the **Krahnstövers Kneipe**. One block west are the Rathaus and Neuer Markt, where our tour began.

The second suggested walking tour has more variety, filled as it is with architectural and historical landmarks restored after the war. Starting at the Neuer Markt, you head down the east–west pedestrian zone, Kröpeliner Strasse. The **Marienkirche** (St. Mary's Church) is just north of the street. This church was spared from destruction during the war thanks to its custodian and his daughter, who labored heroically to put out a fire caused by a bomb.

Construction on the church began around 1290; its completion—the final touches to a 270-foot steeple—was recorded almost 500 years later, in 1796. While the Late Gothic oak-wood triptych altar dating to the early 16th century is a major attraction, the real treasure here is the **astronomical clock**, completed in 1472 and still operating. During the war city officials wanted to have it dismantled to spare it possible damage, but the clockmaster refused, saying it could never be put back together again. A thick wood-and-masonry wall was built around it for protection, and it survived intact, as did the entire church, during the 1942 bombing raids.

Outside the church, an inviting café in which to rest is the **Alte Münze** (Old Mint), the name recalling the site where Rostock, having received the right in 1325 to produce its own coins, had its mint. The city minted gold, silver, and copper coins until 1864.

Examples of such coins can be seen at the Museum of Cultural History; but first, if you keep walking westward along Kröpeliner Strasse, you'll come to **Universitätsplatz**. In front of the university is a fountain called "Joy of Life," depicting men, women, children, and animals cavorting in various poses and positions. Many Rostockers refer to the work, which was completed in 1980 by sculptors Jo Jastram and Reinhard Dietrich, as the "Porno Fountain."

North, across from the square, is the **Fünf Giebel Haus** (Five Gable House), five buildings containing apartments, cafés, restaurants, and boutiques that were built in 1986 in a modern architectural derivative of the gabled Gothic-style houses.

On the west side of the square is the **university**, founded in 1419 and the oldest in northern Europe. The current Neo-Renaissance building dating to 1866 counts as one of the visual highlights on the square along with, on its south side, the **Barocksaal** (Baroque Hall), site of the residence of Mecklenburg's Duke Friedrich Wilhelm. Built under the supervision of French architect Jean Legeay in 1750, the Barocksaal today serves as a concert hall.

One further feature of Universitätsplatz is a statue of Rostock's most famous native son, Gebhard Leberecht von Blücher, the German general known as "Marshall Forward" in commanding German forces against the French during the Napoleonic wars.

To continue the tour, walk diagonally to the southwest along Klosterhof, a cobblestone street that leads through a brick portal to an oasis of quiet: the former **Klostern zum Heiligen Kreuz** (Cloisters of the Holy Cross), which now houses Rostock's **Museum of Cultural History** (open 10:00

A.M. to 6:00 P.M.; closed Mondays) and features models of Rostock's development over the centuries, collections of medieval artifacts, and Dutch landscape paintings. The original cloisters was a gift to the Sistine order of nuns in 1270 from Queen Margarete of Denmark after she survived a shipwreck near Rostock; the simple two-story complex now housing the museum dates back to the 1300s; the Gothic-style **Heiligen Kreuz Kirche** (Church of the Holy Cross) here was completed around 1360.

After leaving the cloisters area head along a gravel path to the nearby wall to the south, where a door lets you through to the park on the south side. Here you head west along the outside of the wall in a clockwise curve that, after a few hundred yards, brings you to perhaps the city's most famous architectural landmark, the **Kröpeliner Tor**, a high (170 feet) Gothic brick tower and gate built in 1280. The mighty structure today, as a branch of the cultural history museum, houses a museum on Rostock history.

This marks the westernmost point of the historic center of Rostock, which more or less contained the city's entire population until the early 19th century, when the outlying districts started to be established. From here you should walk north about a block to Lange Strasse in front of the city's most prestigious hotel, the ▶ **Hotel Warnow**, which meets Western-level standards of comfort at Western-style prices. The hotel features four restaurants, a bar, boutiques, and conference rooms. Rooms facing south have a view of the Kröpeliner Tor; rooms on the north face traffic-filled Lange Strasse but enjoy a vista of the harbor area.

Stopping at the corner of busy **Lange Strasse** you can gaze for over a kilometer eastward at a canyon of tall brick buildings that was a Stalinist vision of Proletariat Heaven: These solidly built and spacious apartment buildings were a propaganda project in the early 1950s to prove how well Communism took care of its workers.

Cross over Lange Strasse and head north, down the hill of Fischerstrasse toward the Warnow river. You're entering the **harbor district**, of which at first you'll see precious little, mostly empty areas now used as parking lots. Beyond the railroad tracks running next to Am Strande you'll see big oceangoing freighters berthed at the docks. Go east a bit on Am Strande and you'll find, at the corner of Badstüber-strasse, an open-air market with snack stands and booths offering a flea-market variety of items.

From here, it's worth exploring the gridwork of streets formed by Schnickmannstrasse and Wokrenterstrasse running north–south, and intersected in an east–west direction by one street with three different names: Auf der Huder, Beim

Hornschen Hof, and Pläterstrasse. You'll notice that this district contains entire blocks of modern prefabricated apartments built in a style derived from the old warehouses that once made up the harbor district. A few of the old structures remain here and there, most of them crumbling, but one—which houses the Rostock tourist information office—has been restored. The tourist office, at Schnickmannstrasse 13/14, organizes guided walking tours—in English on request—and also helps in finding room accommodations and reserving theater tickets. (Open Monday through Friday, 9:00 A.M. to 6:00 P.M., Saturdays 9:00 A.M. to 4:00 P.M.; in the summer months open on Sundays as well, 10:00 A.M. to 4:00 P.M.; Tel: 38-15-24-56.)

Wokrenterstrasse is Rostock's main contribution to the fight for architectural preservation, featuring an entire row of restored 16th- and 17th-century gabled houses. Two are worth particular mention: The first, the Late Gothic house at number 40, now headquarters for Rostock's architects' association, is a *Baumhaus* (tree house); the name describes a construction method whereby a single mighty oak tree trunk running from the cellar to the upper stories served as the sole supporting pillar. It is one of the few houses of its kind remaining in northern Germany.

The other special attraction on Wokrenterstrasse, at the corner of Strandstrasse, is Rostock's most famous port-district tavern, **Zur Kogge** (a *Kogge* was a small medieval sailing vessel). Decorated with fishermen's nets, ships' wheels, and various other nautical paraphernalia, Zur Kogge thrives on a custom called "ringing the bell": If you ring the brass bell at your table once it means you're buying a round for those at the table. Ring it twice and you buy a round for all the patrons in the house.

To get back to the original starting point, the Neuer Markt, walk a block farther east to Lagerstrasse and then turn right, going uphill until you again reach Lange Strasse. You can cross over there at the Marienkirche, a block away from Neuer Markt.

If you are looking for a hotel in Rostock that is something more than the Hotel Sonne but less than the Hotel Warnow, the 17-room ▶ **Gastmahl des Meeres**, at August-Bebel-Strasse 111, is clean and comfortable in a 1950s Socialist Realism kind of way. Convenient to city center touring but somewhat noisy because of two busy traffic streets, the hotel features one of the city's top seafood restaurants. Another possibility is the more modern 73-room ▶ **Hotel am Bahnhof**, located across from the Rostock train station on Adenauer Platz, a ten-minute streetcar ride from the Neuer Markt and Rathaus.

Warnemünde

What Travemünde is to Lübeck, Warnemünde is to Rostock—a nearby port and seaside resort, located about 25 km (16 miles) to the north. Trains leave the Rostock Hauptbahnhof (south of the Innenstadt) for Warnemünde about every ten minutes, and the ride itself is about 25 minutes. For many travellers, staying in Warnemünde—the name describes the Warnow river's estuary at the Baltic Sea—is a good way to "do" Rostock: It's convenient for going into Rostock for sightseeing, and when the day is over, it's a quiet and relaxing retreat from the city.

With its clean and sparkling beach and cozy network of streets filled with cafés, boutiques, restaurants, and small hotels, Warnemünde is so popular that getting accommodations here in the summer can be a problem. However, now that private enterprise is getting established, more and more bed-and-breakfast accommodations are becoming available. The four-star ► **Hotel Neptun** is located directly on the beach at Seestrasse 19, and every one of its 350 rooms has a view of the Baltic. Two restaurants, an indoor swimming pool, fitness rooms, and a sauna make this hotel a favorite. The 95-bed ► **Strandhotel**, also on the beach, at Seestrasse 12, offers simple rooms without bath or toilet but is convenient to the town's main restaurant and shopping area.

A bit to the west, at Strandweg 17, you'll find the recently-renovated ► **Stolteraa**, a traditional-style seaside hotel and a favorite of many long-time Warnemünder vacationers (some of its 18 rooms have baths and toilets).

For help in getting accommodations, check with the local Warnemünde tourist information office, located at Heinrich-Heine-Strasse 17; Tel: (381) 511-42.

SCHWERIN

Schwerin, the state capital of Mecklenburg–West Pomerania, with about 130,000 people, stands out from the rest of the region. While the nearby Hanseatic cities—Hamburg to the west, Lübeck to the northwest, Wismar to the north, and Rostock to the northeast—have a mercantile feel to them, and the towns and villages all around Schwerin are rustically simple, Schwerin has a fairy-tale quality to it.

Established in the year 1160 by Henry the Lion, Schwerin is Mecklenburg's oldest city and the second-oldest German city east of the Elbe river (after Lübeck). The city's name derives from "Zuarin," the name Slavic tribes two centuries earlier had given their fortress at the site, a word roughly meaning "abundance of plants and animals." Schwerin's history as a seat of power both for North German nobility and for religious authorities belies a certain provinciality stemming from its rural setting. While the Baltic seacoast cities hum with the activity of shipping and foreign trade, people in Schwerin, some 31 km (19 miles) south of the coast, admit that their city has a slower pace, and are happily disinclined to follow trends elsewhere. The city never joined the Hanseatic League, for example, and never had much industry. With only a tiny *Graben* (waterway) to link it to the Baltic seaport of Wismar to the north, it was bypassed by the major Hanseatic trade routes.

There is no debating, however, that Schwerin is one of the most beautiful cities in Germany, east or west. First, there is the setting of gently rolling hills nestled among seven lakes. Particularly in the summer, you seem to see blue water and green tree-lined shores everywhere you look. The lakes, which formed a natural defensive barrier, also provided Schwerin with the fish on which—along with agriculture— its economy was based.

Then there's the architecture: a lot of North German Gothic, like everywhere else in the region, to be sure—but also a rich mixture of Baroque, Neo-Renaissance, Neoclassical, and timber-and-brick, linked by cobblestone streets and punctuated by inviting parks and market squares. The crowning glory of this architectural abundance is the city's landmark, the huge French Renaissance–style Schwerin Castle, built on an island and easily qualifying as northern Germany's answer to Bavaria's Neuschwanstein. The city suffered virtually no damage during the war so it is a real showcase of these many different architectural styles.

Unless you choose to start by looking at Schwerin Castle, a good place to begin a walking tour of Schwerin is at the **Marktplatz** (Market Square), in the center of the city; it's best suited for taking off in whatever direction you choose. You can obtain maps from the tourist information office at Am Markt 11. One of the best—albeit strenuous—ways to get your bearings is to go just north of the market to the **Schweriner Dom** (cathedral) and climb the spiraling steps in its steeple to the lookout platform for an aerial view of the town.

The Gothic cathedral, located on a slight elevation above the market square, is the most imposing structure in Schwerin after the castle. Construction on it began around 1270, or about 110 years after Schwerin was established, and its completion was recorded in 1416. Initially the seat of a Roman Catholic bishopric, after the Reformation the cathedral allied itself with the Lutheran church (in 1552). The current steeple was built in 1889; 220 steps up bring you to the observation platform.

One block west of the market square and cathedral is Mecklenburgstrasse, a pedestrian zone worth looking at both for its stores, shops, and cafés as well as for its Neo-Renaissance post office building. If you head north from here you'll come to a man-made lake, the **Pfaffenteich**, where the sight most likely to grab your attention, on the southwest side, is the gleaming white 1844 Tudor-Gothic **Arsenal** building, designed by Georg Adolf Demmler, Schwerin's court architect during the 1840s, who also gave the Rathaus on the main market square its Tudor-style façade. More than any other person it was Demmler who, encouraged by Grand Duke Friedrich Franz II of Mecklenburg, had the greatest influence on the way Schwerin looks.

It's worth walking around the Pfaffenteich, going up the west side along tree-lined Karl-Marx-Strasse to the farthest point north—just a few hundred yards—to Spieltordamm, from which, looking southward, you get the best panoramic view of the medieval city skyline. Conveniently located on the west side of the lake, at Karl-Marx-Strasse 12–13 is the 32-room ► **Hotel Niederländischer Hof**. Equally convenient are two hotels on nearby Grunthalplatz, in front of the Hauptbahnhof (main train station). The ► **Hotel Stadt Schwerin** is the area's most comfortable and modern, its well-appointed rooms meeting Western standards of comfort; the ► **Hotel Reichshof** offers simpler accommodations (not all rooms have bath or toilet).

As you keep walking around the Pfaffenteich in clockwise fashion and start heading south on August-Bebel-Strasse on the eastern side of the lake, look for Gaussstrasse and turn left. This brings you into the **Schelfstadt** district of the city.

In local dialect, *Schelf* variously meant "flat island" or "bulrush," and it was in this area that in 1705 the **Neustadt** (New City) was established on the orders of Duke Friedrich Wilhelm to accommodate a rising population. This residential area rich in half-timbered houses also features the attractive Baroque-style **Nikolaikirche** (St. Nicholas' Church), completed in 1713 and popularly referred to as the "Schelfkirche." Among the nobility entombed here is Sophie Louise, the wife of the first king of Prussia, Friedrich I. In the center of the Schelfstadt district, at Apothekerstrasse 2, is the very small (11 beds) ► **Hotel Nordlicht**.

Walking a few blocks south of the church along Puschkinstrasse, you'll find yourself back at the Marktplatz. On the northeast corner of the square look for an arched passageway leading to another nearby square, the **Schlachtermarkt**, an open-air marketplace lined on all sides by restored half-timbered houses. Any number of restaurants are located here, including what is widely regarded as Schwerin's best, **Zum Goldenen Reiter,** where roast duck is the specialty.

A block farther east, at Grosser Moor Strasse 38, is the **historical museum** (closed Mondays), located in a restored half-timbered house built in 1720. Besides depicting the city's development, it's also the venue for art exhibitions. And as you walk down the slight slope of Grosser Moor you'll see a complex of white buildings called the **Marstall,** where the Mecklenburg dukes kept their horses and carriages. Today the buildings house the cultural and social welfare ministries of the state of Mecklenburg–West Pomerania.

At this juncture you can opt for a scenic ride on one of the boats of the **Weisse Flotte** (White Fleet), located a few minutes' walk south of the Marstall on busy Werderstrasse. The excursion takes you around various points of the large **Schweriner See** (lake) for a waterside view of the city.

The best is saved for last: Three more major attractions await as you head southwest along Werderstrasse and come to the Alter Garten square: the Neo-Baroque Staatstheater completed in 1886; the Neoclassical Staatliches Museum; and then, south across a bridge on a small island, Schwerin Castle.

The **Staatstheater** (State Theater), completed in 1886, has a special place in Schwerin's history: It was the first public building to have electric lights, and it was at the time one of the most technically advanced stages anywhere in Germany. Today it is Schwerin's main stage for opera, ballet, operettas, and musical productions.

The **Staatliches Museum** (State Museum), completed in 1882, is well worth a visit for its collection of 17th-century Dutch landscape paintings and drawings acquired by Duke Christian Ludwig II and his son Duke Friedrich. The other major attraction is its collection of Meissen porcelain.

Schwerin Castle is large enough for several functions. It serves as the seat of the Mecklenburg–West Pomerania state parliament, is a local history museum in its own right, and also contains a gallery of Mecklenburg landscape paintings that shouldn't be missed. There's also a café.

Built on the small island that was the original site of the Slavic Zuarin settlement in the ninth century, Schwerin Castle evolved over the centuries from a small fortress into the seat of power of the Mecklenburg dukes. But it was not until the mid-1800s that the present structure was built, following a decision in 1837 by the ruling family to move its residence to Schwerin from the Ludwigslust palace, about 15 miles south of the city.

Various men, including the renowned Dresden architect

Gottfried Semper, had their hand in the castle's planning, but the main design—albeit on his third try after the first two drafts were rejected by Duke Friedrich Franz II—stemmed from Demmler, who drew his inspiration from French châteaux in the Loire river valley. Demmler himself was not in charge at the time of the castle's completion; in 1857, after 14 years' construction, he was fired for having taken the wrong side in the ill-fated revolutionary struggles of 1848.

Today a tour of the castle covers some 18 rooms—more are in the process of being restored. Highlights of the tour include the pretentious throne room designed by August Stüler (a student of Berlin's historical-style movement), the octagonal Flower Room, the Rococo-style Tea Room, and the dark wood-paneled Banquet Room.

As you walk back to the city center via Schlossstrasse you probably won't be able to resist stopping in at the wonderfully romantic **Café Prag**, at the corner of Buschstrasse. But before you do, turn around for one of the most rewarding prospects in the city: the cobblestone street lined by Classical buildings now housing various state ministries and, in the distance, gleaming white Schwerin Castle with its turrets and towers.

Travellers wishing to stay overnight in Schwerin—if any rooms are to be had—have two alternatives to the hotels mentioned above. The ► **Hotel "Am Heidberg,"** at Rogahner Strasse 20, was one of the first hotels to be redecorated and modernized (in 1991) after the collapse of the Communist regime, and offers clean, comfortable accommodations. Another good choice is the 25-room ► **Strandhotel**, located in Zippendorf, on the southern shore of Schwerin lake. A scenic and quiet alternative to the city's hotels, the Strandhotel offers lakeside rooms that provide a view of the downtown skyline a few miles to the north.

OTHER HANSEATIC CITIES

Besides the two chief cities of Schwerin and Rostock, well worth brief visits are three smaller but equally rewarding cities along the Baltic coast: Wismar, Stralsund, and Greifswald. If you're heading for the island of Rügen, Stralsund will be on your route.

Wismar

Wismar, located about 53 km (33 miles) east of Lübeck, and about 75 km (47 miles) west of Rostock, has more than its

share of architectural gems existing right alongside collaps-
ing architectural ruins. The market square of this city of
60,000 people is framed on all four sides by wonderfully
restored two- and three-story buildings combining German
Gothic and Classical styles. The prime example of the latter,
a six-gabled brick house on the southwest side of the market, is the inviting **Alter Schwede** (Old Swede) restaurant,
which recalls that between 1648 and 1803 Wismar belonged
to Sweden.

Wismar also has three massive churches, although only
one is actually intact (the other two are in ruins). While the
Nikolaikirche (St. Nicholas' Church), built between 1380
and 1403, was not damaged in the war, the 15th-century
Georgenkirche (St. George's Church) now stands as the
largest church ruin in all of Europe. The **Marienkirche** (St.
Mary's Church), of the same generation as the other two,
now consists of nothing more than a 250-foot-high steeple—
the rest of the site is a parking lot.

As a member of the formidable Hanseatic League, Wismar—unlike nearby Schwerin to the south, to which it is
linked by a small waterway—was a bustling city of shipping
and commerce. Down by its scenic port, now mainly visited
by smaller merchant ships and fishing vessels, the Lohberg
waterfront is the showcase for reconstructed brick-and-
timber and gabled houses dating back to the 1500s, while the
nearby **Wassertor** (Water Gate) is a fine example of mid-15th-
century Late Gothic construction.

Stralsund, population 76,000, lies some 73 km (45 miles)
northeast of Rostock on the coast opposite Rügen island. It
was established in 1234, and joined the Hanseatic League in
1259. Early on, construction got started on its major architectural landmarks: the **Marienkirche** (1298), the **Johannis-
kloster** (Cloister of St. John) of the Franciscan order (1250),
the **Nikolaikirche** (1276), and the **Rathaus** (late 13th century), the predominant style of all being North German
Gothic.

The best view of Stralsund—and of the island of Rügen
over the narrow Stralsund Sound—must be earned by climbing more than 300 steps to the top of the 330-foot steeple of
the Marienkirche. Another attraction is the **Meeresmuseum**
(Sea Museum), which was the former East Germany's only
museum devoted to all facets of oceanography.

Rügen, Germany's largest island, covering nearly 600 square
miles northeast of Stralsund, also qualifies as the most
scenic. Virtually off-limits to Western visitors under the Com-

munist regime, the island is now experiencing an unprecedented boom in tourism as Westerners pour in trying to see
whether the island is as inviting as its reputation. Nobody
goes away disappointed by the scenery, though they may be
less than satisfied with their lodgings, as hotel accommodations meeting Western-style standards were not a high priority of the former regime.

That magnificent scenery makes up for it. The gleaming
chalkstone cliffs (which Caspar David Friedrich painted
many times); the great diversity of plant and animal life in its
landscape of forests, marshlands, gentle hills, and lakes; and
the clean white sandy beaches hold the same charm for
people now that they did for wealthy Berliners who all but
kept the island to themselves in the last century.

The other attractions of Rügen include several old seaside
resort towns, **Binz** and **Sassnitz** being the most famous (and
offering the most accommodations); the castles at Granitz
and Ralswieck; the lighthouse at the island's northernmost
tip, Kap Arkona; and the tiny scenic fishing harbors that dot
the coastline. And for nostalgia there's the **Rasende Roland**
(Racing Roland) steam railroad, which tuckers along its
narrow-gauge track, laid down in 1895, at the breathtaking
speed of about 20 miles per hour, connecting Putbus and
Göhren. For those who really like to get away from it all, the
narrow sliver of island called **Hiddensee**, just northwest of
Rügen, is absolutely free of automobiles, and is the burial
site of author Gerhart Hauptmann, who did much of his
writing here.

Greifswald, situated about 39 km (24 miles) southeast of
Stralsund, is best known to outsiders as the birthplace of
Romantic artist Caspar David Friedrich, who made the 13th-
century cloister ruins at nearby Eldena the subject of one of
his paintings. Like the other Hanseatic port cities, Greifswald
(population 64,000) is rich in Gothic brick architecture, its
showpieces being the 1738 **Rathaus**, the 13th-century **St.
Nikolai Dom** (St. Nicholas' Cathedral), and the brick-and-
timber hospital known as **St. Spiritus**.

GETTING AROUND
For information on Hamburg, see the section on Hamburg,
above.

Bremen and Bremerhaven
Major international airlines do not fly directly to Bremen
from overseas airports, but Lufthansa has frequent connecting flights between Bremen and Frankfurt, Germany's busi-

est gateway. Air Bremen, the local airline, operates daily service between Bremen and London and Brussels, as well as to many other European cities (although not Paris). Hamburg's international airport is 120 km (75 miles) away, and there is hourly InterCity express train service between the two cities.

Bremen airport lies about 5 km (3 miles) south of the city, or a 12-minute ride on streetcar number 5 (DM 3) that takes you to the Domsheide stop, next to the cathedral, or to Bahnhofsplatz. The taxi fare into the city is DM 15. The airport has only one exit, and both the streetcar stop and the taxi stand are located directly outside it.

Bremen has six streetcar and 42 bus lines servicing the city and suburbs, and offers up to two days of unlimited travel on the entire network for DM 6.60. On weekends, up to four persons can travel on one ticket. All major international car rental firms have offices in Bremen.

Daily sightseeing bus tours of Bremen (duration about two hours) begin at the central bus depot on Bahnhofsplatz at 10:30 A.M., May through October. Bremen is "bicycle friendly," and you can rent bikes at the *Fahrrad* (bicycle) station on the east side of Bahnhofsplatz, which has maps showing bicycle paths in and around the city.

Bremerhaven has seven metropolitan bus lines, and is easy to get around in. The city's radio-taxi service is also good; Tel: (421) 400-04.

Schleswig-Holstein

The major airport in the region is at Kiel, and Lufthansa, flying from Frankfurt, is the only major carrier providing service to the area. There are excellent train connections between Hamburg and Sylt, on the west coast, Hamburg and Flensburg, and Hamburg and Lübeck (see below). There are three Autobahn routes, all of them originating in Hamburg. The A 23 heading northwest from Hamburg becomes state highway B 5 after Heide (about 100 km/62 miles north of Hamburg) and continues up to Niebüll near the Danish border on the west coast; the A 7 between Hamburg and Flensburg (about 160 km/99 miles) traverses the middle of the region; and the A 1 heads northeast past Lübeck as far as Oldenburg. The federal highways (marked "B") are well-paved. It's possible to drive into Schleswig-Holstein from Bremen/Bremerhaven, or the reverse, bypassing Hamburg, by crossing the Elbe river by car ferry at Wischhafen or Glückstadt. There are also KD boat cruises between Hamburg and Kiel that travel through Schleswig-Holstein on the Elbe and the Nord-Ostsee-Kanal (see Around Germany in the Useful Facts section).

Lübeck

Lübeck's airport only serves small aircraft. Hamburg's international airport is 65 km (41 miles) away. There are daily feeder flights between the two cities, but trains between Hamburg and Lübeck run every 30 minutes and the journey takes only a half hour. Lübeck is also on the InterCity and EuroCity railroad network, linking the town with the rest of Germany and Europe. Its big ferry port at Travemünde makes Lübeck a gateway to Scandinavia.

The town has no subway, but its many bus lines and the frequency of service make it easy to reach all districts and suburbs. Bus tickets are bought from the driver, and multi-journey tickets are available at a discount. The taxi service is also good; Tel: (451) 811-12 or 22.

Rostock and the Baltic Coast Cities

Depending on your inclination—and your starting point—there are various routes to follow, both by train or by car, to cover the major destinations in Mecklenburg–West Pomerania and the former East German Baltic coast. From Berlin there are several trains a day heading to Schwerin, Rostock, and Stralsund; if you are in the western part of Germany, several trains each day leave Hamburg and Lübeck for those same destinations.

If you are driving, one thing to remember is that the seemingly short distances between the points on your itinerary are deceiving in terms of how much travel time to calculate. The back roads, while scenic, are often bumpy and narrow, and it's difficult to pass slower vehicles on them; they also lead through every little town where traffic can get snarled.

Lübeck to Wismar along the B 104 and B 105 is about 53 km (33 miles); from Wismar to Rostock along the B 105 is about 75 km (47 miles); and from Rostock to Stralsund on the B 105 it is another 75 km (47 miles). Lübeck to Schwerin going southeast on the B 104 is roughly 73 km (45 miles), while Schwerin to Wismar, due north on the B 106, is about 33 km (20 miles).

From Hamburg, if you're driving first via Lübeck, add about 65 km (40 miles) to the expected travel distance to Wismar, Rostock, and Stralsund. The fastest road connection between Hamburg and Schwerin, about a two-hour drive, is the B 24 Hamburg–Berlin Autobahn; get off at the Ludwigslust exit and head north on the B 106.

From Berlin, the distance to Schwerin going northwest on the B 24 Autobahn is about 165 km (103 miles); to Rostock, first on the B 24 Autobahn and then on the B 25 at Wittstock, the distance is about 208 km (130 miles).

ACCOMMODATIONS REFERENCE
(For Hamburg accommodations, see the Hamburg section earlier in this chapter.)

Among the rapid changes taking place in the formerly East German Baltic region, one is of particular benefit to travellers: Hotel accommodations, though still lagging behind Western standards, are being steadily improved, both in terms of overall capacity and of comfort. Though it is advisable to make reservations well ahead of time, particularly in the summer, travellers can get on-the-spot help from the efficient and well-organized room-reservation agencies in the tourist information offices of each city (for a list of addresses and telephone numbers for the major Mecklenburg–West Pomeranian cities, see the end of this section).

Although our eastern Germany hotel information was correct as of press time, east German telephone numbers will continue to be changed in 1994. Despite considerable improvements, calling from western to eastern Germany still remains a problem. Phone lines are crowded during weekday working hours, so try calling during lunchtime (noon to 2:00 P.M.) or later in the evening. Even dialing correctly you may get a wrong number, a problem familiar to east Germans. Eastern German hotels in general are overbooked these days—packed with west German and other businesspeople trying to gain a timely commercial foothold in the former GDR. In addition, hotels now owned by the Treuhandanstalt, the government's privatization agency, are uncertain about their future—some may be closed, others sold.

The hotel rates listed here for all cities in the North are 1994 projections for double-bed, double-occupancy rooms, with a range from low to high whenever possible. Prices are given in deutsche marks (DM). Basic rates are always subject to change—especially in the former East Germany, as hotels transfer ownership and work to upgrade their quality—so please verify price when you are booking. Breakfast is usually included in the price of a room.

For eastern Germany the international telephone country code is now the same as for western Germany, 49. If you are calling from within Germany precede the city code with a zero.

▶ **Alter Speicher.** Beckergrube 91–93, D-23552 **Lübeck.** Tel: (451) 710-45; Fax: (451) 70-48-04. DM 180–220.

▶ **Aquarium.** Mittelburgwall 4–8, D-25840 **Friedrichstadt.** Tel: (4881) 691; Fax: (4881) 70-64. DM 156–196.

▶ **Bergström.** Bei der Lüner Mühle, D-21337 **Lüneburg.** Tel: (4131) 30-80; Fax: (4131) 30-84-99. DM 110–230.

▶ **Bremen Marriott**. Hillmannplatz 20, D-28195 **Bremen**. Tel: (421) 176-70; Fax: (421) 176-72-38. DM 280–320.

▶ **Bremen Park Hotel**. Im Bürgerpark, D-28209 **Bremen**. Tel: (421) 340-80; Fax: (421) 340-86-02. DM 435.

▶ **Flensborg-Hus**. Norderstrasse 76, D-24939 **Flensburg**. Tel: (461) 261-05. DM 98–108.

▶ **Flensburger Hof**. Süderhofenden 38, D-24937 **Flensburg**. Tel: (461) 173-20 or 29; Fax: (461) 173-31. DM 190.

▶ **Gastmahl des Meeres**. August-Bebel-Strasse 111, D-18055 **Rostock**. Tel and Fax: (381) 223-01. DM 145–175.

▶ **Groot's Hotel**. Gaat 5, D-25986 **Keitum/Sylt**. Tel: (4651) 933-90; Fax: (4651) 329-53. DM 240–270.

▶ **Herzog Friedrich**. Am Stadtfeld/Ecke Schmiedestrasse, D-25840 **Friedrichstadt**. Tel: (4881) 17-71; Fax: (4881) 10-27. DM 98–180.

▶ **Holländische Stube**. Mittelburgwall 22, D-25840 **Friedrichstadt**. Tel: (4881) 72-45; Fax: (4881) 71-26. DM 135.

▶ **Holsteinisches Haus**. Am Eiland 1–3, D-25840 **Friedrichstadt**. Tel: (4881) 209; Fax: (4881) 79-93. DM 120.

▶ **Hotel Atlantic**. Kaiserallee 2a, D-23570 **Travemünde**. Tel: (4502) 750-57; Fax: (4502) 735-08. DM 140–220.

▶ **Hotel Atlantic**. Johann-Möller-Strasse 30, D-25980 **Westerland/Sylt**. Tel: (4651) 60-46; Fax: (4651) 283-13. DM 205–385.

▶ **Hotel am Bahnhof**. Adenauer Platz, D-18055 **Rostock**. Tel: (381) 363-31; Fax: (381) 346-79. DM 165–195.

▶ **Hotel Excelsior**. Hansestrasse 3, D-23558 **Lübeck**. Tel: (451) 826-26; Fax: (451) 88-09-99. DM 130–190.

▶ **Hotel "Am Heidberg."** Rogahner Strasse 20, D-19061 **Schwerin**. Tel: (385) 61-11-36; Fax: 61-11-20. DM 136.

▶ **Hotel Jensen**. Obertrave 4–5, D-23552 **Lübeck**. Tel: (451) 716-46; Fax: (451) 733-86. DM 155–195.

▶ **Hotel Neptun**. Seestrasse 19, D-18119 **Rostock-Warnemünde**. Tel: (381) 54-60; Fax: (381) 540-23. DM 358–418.

▶ **Hotel Niederländischer Hof**. Karl-Marx-Strasse 12–13, D-19055 **Schwerin**. Tel: (385) 55-52-11; Fax: (385) 86-59-44. DM 210.

▶ **Hotel Nordlicht**. Apothekerstrasse 2, D-19053 **Schwerin**. Tel and Fax: (385) 86-47-47. DM 145.

▶ **Hotel-Pension Wuldehof**. Wulde Schlucht 5, D-25999 **Kampen/Sylt**. Tel: (4651) 410-51; Fax: (4651) 410-52. DM 230–290.

▶ **Hotel Reichshof**. Grunthalplatz 15–17, D-19053 **Schwerin**. Tel: (385) 86-40-45. DM 100–164.

▶ **Hotel Roth**. Strandstrasse 31, D-25980 **Westerland/Sylt**. Tel: (4651) 50-91; Fax: (4651) 50-95. DM 153–185.

▶ **Hotel Rungholt**. Kurhaus Strasse 35, D-25999 **Kampen/Sylt**. Tel: (4651) 44-80; Fax: (4651) 448-40. DM 300–370.

▶ **Hotel Sonne.** Neuer Markt 2, D-18055 **Rostock**. Tel: (381) 33-70; Fax: (381) 337-80. DM 69–99.

▶ **Hotel Stadt Hamburg.** Strandstrasse 2, D-25980 **Westerland/Sylt**. Tel: (4651) 85-80; Fax: (4651) 85-82-20. DM 260–300.

▶ **Hotel Stadt Schwerin.** Grunthalplatz 5, D-19053 **Schwerin**. Tel: (385) 55-52-61; Fax: (385) 81-24-98. DM 270.

▶ **Hotel Sylter Seewolf.** Bötticherstrasse 13, D-25980 **Westerland/Sylt**. Tel: (4651) 80-10; Fax: (4651) 801-99. DM 202–265.

▶ **Hotel Warnow.** Lange Strasse 40, D-18055 **Rostock**. Tel: (381) 451-97-01; Fax: (381) 459-78-00. DM 240–270.

▶ **Kaiserhof.** Kronsforder Allee 13, D-23566 **Lübeck**. Tel: (451) 79-10-11; Fax: (451) 79-50-83. DM 180–225.

▶ **Maritim Strand Hotel.** Trelleborgallee 2, D-23570 **Travemünde**. Tel: (4502) 8-90; Fax: (4502) 744-39. DM 328–368.

▶ **Mercure-Columbus.** Bahnhofsplatz 5, D-28195 **Bremen**. Tel: (421) 141-61; Fax: (421) 153-69. DM 175–255.

▶ **Mövenpick Hotel.** Auf der Wallhalbinsel 1–5, D-23554 **Lübeck**. Tel: (451) 150-40; Fax: (451) 150-41-11. DM 195–235.

▶ **Nordsee-Hotel Naber.** Theodor-Heuss-Platz 14–18, D-27568 **Bremerhaven**. Tel: (471) 487-70; Fax: (471) 487-79-99. DM 185–230.

▶ **Obsens-Hotel.** Hafenstrasse, D-25813 **Husum**. Tel: (4841) 20-41; Fax: (4841) 20-44. DM 140.

▶ **Residenz Rezai.** Bomhoffstrasse 3, D-25980 **Westerland/Sylt**. Tel: (4651) 60-16; Fax: (4651) 60-19. DM 200–390.

▶ **Seiler Hof.** Gurtstig 7, D-25980 **Keitum/Sylt**. Tel: (4651) 310-64; Fax: (4651) 353-70. DM 250–305.

▶ **Stadt Hamburg.** Grosse Strasse 59, D-24937 **Flensburg**. Tel: (461) 126-11; Fax: (461) 14-40-70. DM 90–110.

▶ **Stadt Hamburg.** Am Mark 7, D-25840 **Friedrichstadt**. Tel: (4881) 398; Fax: (4881) 76-07. DM 120.

▶ **Stolteraa.** Strandweg 17, D-18119 **Warnemünde**. Tel: (0381) 532-32. DM 100–180.

▶ **Strandhalle Hotel.** Strandweg 2, D-24337 **Schleswig**. Tel: (4621) 90-90; Fax: (4621) 90-91-00. DM 150–180.

▶ **Strandhotel.** Am Strand 13, D-19063 **Schwerin**. Tel: (0385) 21-30-53; Fax: (0385) 32-11-74. DM 125–150.

▶ **Strandhotel.** Seestrasse 12, D-18119 **Warnemünde**. Tel: (0381) 523-36. DM 120.

▶ **Theodor Storm Hotel.** Neustadt 60–64, D-25813 **Husum**. Tel: (4841) 30-85; Fax: (4841) 819-33. DM 150–190.

▶ **Überseehotel.** Wachtstrasse 27–29, D-28195 **Bremen**. Tel: (421) 360-10; Fax: (421) 360-15-55. DM 180–240.

▶ **Voss Haus.** Vossplatz 6, D-23701 **Eutin**. Tel: (4521) 17-97; Fax: (4521) 13-57. DM 165–200.

► **Wolfshof**. Osterweg 2, D-25980 **Keitum/Sylt**. Tel: (4651) 34-45; Fax: (4651) 311-39. DM 200–290.

► **Zur Post**. Bahnhofsplatz 11, D-28195 **Bremen**. Tel: (421) 305-90; Fax: (421) 305-95-91. DM 230–290.

For further information and help with room reservations throughout Mecklenburg–West Pomerania, contact the tourist information office in the following cities and towns:

- Am Markt, D-18528 **Bergen** (Rügen). Tel: (3838) 211-29.
- Bahnhofstrasse 38, D-18609 **Binz** (Rügen). Tel: (38393) 51-91.
- Schuhhagen 22, D-17489 **Greifswald**. Tel: (3834) 34-60; Fax: (3834) 684-92.
- Türmstrasse 11, D-17033 **Neubrandenburg**. Tel: (395) 22-67.
- Schnickmannstrasse 13/14, D-18055 **Rostock**. Tel: (381) 252-60.
- Hauptstrasse 70, D-18546 **Sassnitz** (Rügen). Tel: (38392) 223-63.
- Am Markt 11, D-19055 **Schwerin**. Tel: (385) 81-23-14; Fax: (385) 86-45-09.
- Alter Markt 15, D-18439 **Stralsund**. Tel: (3831) 25-22-51.
- Heinrich-Heine-Strasse 17, D-18119 **Rostock-Warnemünde**. Tel: (381) 522-32.
- Am Markt 11, D-23952 **Wismar**. Tel: (3841) 29-58; Fax: (3841) 29-58.

THE CENTER

By Peter Hays

Peter Hays, a resident of Germany since leaving Cheshire, England, in 1966, is a feature writer for German and English publications.

Popularly, the river Main, dividing northern from southern Germany, is known as the "Weisswurst Equator." The spicy veal sausage, a traditional delicacy of the South, has proved to be a better way to distinguish North from South than anything geographers can muster.

What we call "The Center" might well be expected to straddle these two halves of Germany, but the whole area actually lies north of the Great Sausage Divide. From a strictly geographical point of view, only our center's southernmost reaches, in particular the volcanic **Vogelsberg** plateau, really qualify as central territory. The **Harz Mountains,** to the east, were bisected for decades by a stretch of the Iron Curtain. Between this range and the **Weser river valley** on the region's western fringe, forested uplands slope down gently from the **Hessisches** (Hessian) **Bergland** to the North German Plain. Hannover, Celle, and Braunschweig (Brunswick), near the plain's edge, are unmistakably northern cities where *Hochdeutsch* (High German), at its purest, is spoken.

Often enough, the center-stage role this region has played has had more to do with politics than geography. During medieval centuries the *Welfen,* internationally known as the Guelphs, ruled large parts of it from their bases in and around Goslar, Braunschweig, Celle, and Hannover. Thanks to shrewd marriage policies, the dynasty managed to intertwine its lineage with that of the British Stuarts. In 1714 this led to the Hanoverian Elector Georg Ludwig, a Guelph descendant, succeeding Queen Anne as Britain's King George I. For the next 123 years Hanoverian monarchs held sway simultaneously in Westminster and their home duchy

The Center

0	miles	20
0	kilometers	32

To Bremen

To Hamburg

E234

Aller River

E45

3

214

6

Leine River

Celle

E30

214

To Berlin

Hannover

E30

7

Braunschweig

E83

217

3

Salzgitter

Wolfenbüttel

Weser River

Hildesheim

4

Hameln

6

82

E45

Bodenwerder

Goslar

241

Bad Harzburg

Altenau

64

Einbeck

Clausthal-Zellerfeld

242

Torfhaus

Leine River

83

SOLLING

Lerbach

Sieber

27

64

Weser River

3

Bad Lauterberg

HARZ MOUNTAINS

27

68

Reinhardswald

80

Sababurg

Göttingen

E331/44

83

E45

80

THURINGIA

Warburg

7

Hannoversch Münden

Kassel

49

7

Gotha

252

83

27

E40

3

E45

Eisenach

To Leipzig and Dresden

N

Marburg

62

E40

3

Lauterbach

254

Herbstein

Fulda

45

275

VOGELSBERG

40

276

Steinau

3

Gelnhausen

Hanau

Frankfurt-Am-Main

E42

Berlin

Rhine R.

Frankfurt

Danube R.

(later kingdom). At the time, this part of Germany was as close to the hub of British Empire affairs as many an English province. Though little Georgian prestige has lingered here, the region has not faded from the royal scene completely. Members of the House of Windsor, notably Queen Elizabeth II and Prince Charles, are regularly sighted on both official and informal visits to the land of their Hanoverian forebears.

Major trade routes have always crisscrossed the center region. In the days of the Hanseatic League, for instance, Goslar lay on the Hanse merchants' road from Lübeck to Padua, Italy. Walled little towns like Herbstein, much farther south, offered a safe night's sleep for long-distance traders on their way from Leipzig to Frankfurt-am-Main. By the same token, today's truckers, en route from, say, Hamburg to Stuttgart, feel they are at the halfway point when they stop for a mug of Autobahn coffee just south of the steep Kasseler Berge.

It's best to take a two-pronged approach to this region. Start by visiting the cities and towns that ring the forested mountains of the Weserbergland and the Vogelsberg, from Celle in the north to Marburg in the south, which will put you in the historical picture. After that, you may feel like diving inside those rings, into the pages of a storybook. Meandering upriver from Hameln (Hamelin) along the Weser will take you into Sleeping Beauty country: the dark, still quite forbidding forests in which some of the best-known German folk and fairy tales are set.

MAJOR INTEREST

Hannover
Celle and its medieval architecture
Braunschweig and its historic backwaters
Goslar and the Harz Mountains

The Land of Fairy Tales and the Brothers Grimm
Einbeck
Hameln and the story of the Pied Piper
Bodenwerder and the Baron Münchhausen
Hannoversch-Münden
The Reinhardswald and Sleeping Beauty
Kassel
Marburg and the Romantics
Hanau, birthplace of the Brothers Grimm

HANNOVER

Lower Saxony's state capital is a good base from which to explore the Center proper, especially if you happen to be on the rebound from a Hanseatic city tour. Hamburg to Hannover (the German spelling) is a comfortable 90-minute Autobahn hop. A good map and some astute navigating to the freeway called the Messe Schnellweg will assure you of smooth entry into town, because city planners have pandered to the motorist with a network of urban superhighways. You may be tempted to cruise right into the heart of the city. But beware: Parking is tight. Instead, turn right down Hans-Böckler-Allee and leave your car in the neighborhood of the **Congress-Centrum**, where there is far more space.

Hannover's city center suffered a great deal of bomb damage during World War II. Stately buildings such as the Oper and the Leineschloss, of which enough survived to warrant restoring, are generally lone period pieces, separated by several blocks of modern façades. To conjure up some semblance of cohesion, the authorities had a broad red stripe, over 4 km (2½ miles) in length, painted along the city pavement. Its loops and squiggles lead to some three dozen interesting buildings and monuments. Consecutive numbers on the pavement should match those of a companion booklet (obtainable at the tourist offices in the Neues Rathaus or the main train station), but fail to do so in many cases. The stripe is badly faded and, here and there, completely erased. Discovering the remains of Old Hannover under your own steam can be just as much fun.

Suggesting the **Hauptbahnhof** as your point of departure may not sound all that exciting. But this is as central a railway station as you can imagine, with plenty of atmosphere. The transcontinental Milan–Copenhagen and Paris–Moscow express trains both stop here. The station's exterior deserves more than just a glance. One of the most palatial you are likely to see in any town, it is a proud, escutcheoned edifice designed on Classical lines and similar to the nearby **Opernhaus** (Opera House). Both were the work of Hannover's official architect, Georg Ludwig Laves, in the first half of the 19th century. A statue of King Ernst August, who commissioned the work, rides high in front of the station. At the Vienna Congress in 1814 the Guelph electorate of Hannover had been promoted to kingdom. It survived as such until 1866, when Ernst August's blind son, King Georg V, lost a decisive battle to his cousin, King Wilhelm I of Prussia, whereupon Hannover became a Prussian province—as did the ancient bishops' seat of Hildesheim (a few kilometers south), famed for the 1,000-year-old climbing rose (*Rosenstock*) still thriving in its cathedral's crypt, and now earmarked as a World Heritage town by UNESCO.

From Hannover's main station to the sweeping curve formed by the river Leine and the Friedrichswall highway are some 3 km (1½ miles) of pedestrian zones to stroll in. Modern urban designers have done their best to create boulevards and squares that invite you to linger. Department stores and fast-food establishments have, unfortunately, replaced patrician architecture, but **Georgstrasse**, the **Kröpcke** (the liveliest square), and **Karmarschstrasse** still seem to work the same magic as in prewar times. This area is nearly always teeming with window-shoppers, knots of chatting students, street musicians, and teenage daredevils on skateboards.

A fragment of medieval Hannover awaits you down by the Leine river. A couple of half-timbered houses on Kramerstrasse and Burgstrasse date as far back as the 16th century. A stone arch, the **Marstallstor**, is all that remains of the royal stables built in 1714. The graffiti on it almost eclipse the sculpted coat-of-arms of King George I of Great Britain and Hanover. On the river are a few cafés, their beer gardens basking in the last of the day's sunshine. From here you'll have a good view of the 17th-century **Leineschloss**'s riverside façade, just a short walk from the Marstalltor along the Klostergang on the banks of the Leine. It was here, in 1701, that Electress Sophie was designated successor to the British throne by London's emissary, the earl of Macclesfield. Shortly after Queen Anne's death in 1714, Sophie died too. The British crown thereupon passed to her son Georg Ludwig.

Lackluster rebuilding has recently given way to restoration by stonemasons trained to work in the old-fashioned way. A good example is the **Leibnizhaus** in one of Hannover's most elegant squares, the **Holzmarkt** (down Schlossstrasse, which branches off the riverside Klostergang). The ornately fronted Renaissance house that the mathematician and philosopher Gottfried Wilhelm Leibniz lived in from 1698 on now serves as a scientists' conference center. Equally stylish is the nearby **Ballhof**, built as a badminton hall for Duke Georg Wilhelm in the 17th century, and now a theater (a short stroll, via Burgstrasse, from the Holzmarkt). The **Altes Rathaus** (Old Town Hall), with its Gothic pinnacle gables and pottery friezes, has its own restaurant, the **Ratskeller**, which is renowned for its chanterelle dishes. Dining here, you are quite likely to witness medieval-style banquets re-enacted for the benefit of large tourist groups. Down Schmiedegasse is the candlelit **Brauhaus Ernst August**, where you can have a glass or two of top-fermented *Hannöversch Pils,* Hannover's celebrated beer, available only here. Meals are served until 1:00 A.M. on weekdays and 3:00 A.M. on weekends. Popular eateries also include the vegetarian meeting place **Hiller**, on Blumenstrasse close to the station.

South of the **Friedrichswall** highway the cityscape opens

onto spacious greens and parks, ornamental lakes such as the **Maschsee** (a 25-minute walk, via Karmarschstrasse and Maschpark, from the main station), and majestic squares such as **Waterlooplatz**. The column here, another Laves masterpiece, commemorates the June day in 1815 when Napoleon was defeated by the combined efforts of an unprecedented alliance. A minor monument in front of the **Hauptstaatsarchiv** (Capital Archives) depicts Count Carl von Alten, a German general who led an English infantry division at the battle. Anglo-Hanoverian cooperation has continued: The city hosts an annual "British Week," which features pop stars such as Rod Stewart.

Hannover's many museums attract a large number of *Bildungsbürger,* or culture vultures. Be sure to visit the **Sprengel Museum** on the banks of the Maschsee. It houses a collection of contemporary art, with works by Marc Chagall, Picasso, Max Beckmann, Emil Nolde, and Paul Klee. The museum is named after its patron, the local chocolate manufacturer Dr. Bernhard Sprengel, who donated his private collection and a considerable sum of money to the city of Hannover in 1969. Sprengel started collecting in 1937; a Third Reich exhibition of "Degenerate Art" in Munich that year so dismayed him that he promptly bought two watercolors by one of the abused artists, Emil Nolde.

Hannover's most regal feature is a short tram ride (on the number 1 line) away from the city center, in **Herrenhausen**, an area that boasts the country's finest example of an early Baroque park. Laid out like a geometrician's idea of floral embroidery, the **Herrenhäuser Garten**'s 120 acres of horticultural symmetry would be best appreciated from a hovering helicopter. The view from a special visitor's "panorama terrace" is almost as impressive, however. Miles of hornbeam hedges and box trees shorn like poodles frame potted plants (including a 327-year-old Viennese pomegranate shrub), flower beds, lawns, and gravel paths arranged to reflect gardening styles from Renaissance to Rococo, with some flowery Islamic frills thrown in. The original planting dates from the time of the Thirty Years' War, but Herrenhausen owes most of its charm to the period of Hanoverian ascendancy. Electress Sophie, who had a lot of say about its design, called the park "my life," and in fact died while on one of her regular walks through it.

Nowadays, open-air plays are staged within the **Heckentheater**'s immaculately trimmed hedges, and dazzling Baroque-style firework displays are accompanied by high-decibel renditions of Handel's "Music for the Royal Fireworks" and other pieces. No entrance fee is charged, except during the illuminations, which you can see after dusk (on Wednesdays, Fridays, and Saturdays during the summer). The main grounds open at 8:00 A.M. and close at 8:00 P.M. in the summer, 4:30 P.M. in the winter. The **Georgengarten** section is open round the clock.

Many of the city's hotels, more attuned to business folk than tourists, are located on the outskirts of the city within easy reach of Autobahn and airport. More centrally located hotels include the prestigious ▶ **Kastens Hotel Luisenhof**, with its family atmosphere rooted in more than 100 years of traditional service, and the ▶ **Intercontinental**, a premier hotel geared to executive demands.

If you leave town along the Friedrichswall, you can stop at the (relatively) new **Rathaus** for some farewell bombast. Designed by a Berlin architect at the turn of the century, its Neo-Gothic dome and turrets were more to the liking of Kaiser Wilhelm II than to that of many Hannoverians. Its dizzying entrance hall contains four scale models of the city, each from a different period. One, of half-timbered Hannover in the year 1689, will give you an inkling of what to expect in Celle.

CELLE

The fables woven around Britain's royal family by today's tabloids are pretty tame stuff compared to the real-life dramas their Hanoverian ancestors played out. So read on, or, rather, drive northeast on highway B 3 to Celle, which is 40 km (25 miles) from Hannover. (A two-story parking garage as you enter town is signposted "Hallenbad.") There, the Herzogschloss, encircled by the river Aller, one of its tributaries, and a stretch of moat, faces some 600 wood-frame houses, most of them listed as historic monuments, lining a compact grid of streets much as they did more than 300 years ago. The original settlement two miles upstream was shifted here lock, stock, and beam by order of Duke Otto the Severe in 1292. The move gave the citizens better protection from marauding barons, and explains the orderly layout, an early example of urban planning.

From here the dukes of Celle ruled their share of Guelph territory, including Hannover. Not until 1705, at the death of Duke Georg Wilhelm, Electress Sophie's brother-in-law, was the seat of government transferred from Celle to Hannover. During Georg Wilhelm's reign the Hanoverian dynasty acquired a Macbethian flavor. The duke's daughter Sophie Dorothea was coupled with his nephew Georg Ludwig, Britain's future King George I, in a dynasty-buttressing marriage. It was a mismatch from the start. Sophie Dorothea took an aristocrat, Philip von Königsmark, as a lover. When news of the affair leaked out, von Königsmark was murdered in Hannover's **Leineschloss**, supposedly on Georg Ludwig's orders. After divorcing his wife, Britain's monarch-to-be banished her to grim **Schloss Ahlden** on the river Aller, some 20 miles northwest of Celle. There, Sophie Dorothea languished until her death in 1726. During her 30 years of confinement she was never once allowed to see her two children: Sophie Dorothea, who later gave birth to Prussia's Frederick the Great, and Georg Augustus, Britain's future George II.

Georg Ludwig, it seems, took some time settling in as George I in London. He never bothered to learn English, conversing instead in French with his new courtiers. After the absolute power he had wielded in Hannover, he also had to accustom himself to his new subjects' watchful parliament.

When Prince Charles, who is said to take the Royal Hanoverian motto *ich dien* (I serve) particularly seriously, occasionally turns up in Celle, Union Jacks galore are unfurled to welcome this not-so-distant relative.

From the Hallenbad parking garage it is a five-minute walk through the Französischer Garten to the **Herzogschloss**. The ducal palace may not match Buckingham Palace for size, but it certainly is as elegant. The palace is a refined edifice of Weser Renaissance pedigree, with deliberately asymmetrical windows (for *Weserrenaissance,* see Hameln, below), and is featured on one of Germany's 30-pfennig stamps. Its beautifully stuccoed **theater**, the oldest of its kind in Germany, has been in use since 1670, and Celle's municipal ensemble performs here almost nightly. The ten-month repertory season includes works by Molière, Calderón, Lessing, and Wilde, as well as contemporary dramatists such as Bodo Strauss.

When Celle's royal residents moved to Hannover in 1705, the city fathers were given the choice of a prison-cum-lunatic asylum or a university as the city's next tenant. They opted for the former, reputedly because they saw students as a greater threat to public morals. The economic slump that ensued is one of the main reasons for Celle's present wealth of medieval architecture: Funds were not available to replace what later generations tended to scorn as peasant housing.

In those days the **Lüneburger Heide**, 48 km (30 miles) northwest of the city via the B 3 and now a juniper-dotted heathland, was covered with oak forests that grew slowly and sturdily in the sandy soil. Celle's medieval builders used whole oak trunks as foundation posts. Pointed gables added to the haughty demeanor of the long rows of tall town houses. Tradesfolk evidently thought wattle, daub, and timber anything but fashionable, and at one end of the **Markt**, one of the Altstadt's pivotal streets, there are still some façades they plastered over in order to distinguish them from those of their *Ackerbürger,* or town-peasant neighbors. Take a short stroll around the **Rathaus** opposite. Pillars and gray brickwork painted on the side are signs of Celle's relative impoverishment at a time when other, wealthier towns were indulging in extravagant Baroque adornments. Note, too, in a niche near the entrance, a painted plaster miniature of the town hall's bearded medieval masterbuilder Reisz in profile, and, hanging from the front wall, the iron rod with which the merchants of old measured out their cubits of cloth.

In Celle, individual house owners, who receive minimal tax relief for their efforts, have forked out considerable sums to restore their homes. **Zöllnerstrasse**, **Poststrasse**, **Neue Strasse**, and the **Stechbahn** (the former jousting field) comprise the focal point of the touristy part of town. A short walk from the Schloss, they are crammed end to end with fine half-timbered specimens, and you can spend hours attempting to decipher the dozens of repainted and recarved inscriptions on the beams. Some are in Hochdeutsch, others in *Platt,* northern Germany's Anglophonic dialect. A long inscription above the windows of the **Lateinschule** (Latin School), on Rolandstrasse—in Latin, naturally enough—exhorts young scholars to heed their elders' pearls of wisdom.

It's easy enough to determine the period of the houses, as many have the date of construction neatly carved into one of their front beams. At the corner of Poststrasse and Rundestrasse stands the town's most profusely decorated burgher residence, **Hoppener Haus** (dated 1532), with its lewdly allegorical wooden reliefs. Next to it is a less ornate house built, according to the first owner's carved caption, "out of necessity, not pleasure," at the end of the Thirty Years' War. Next door is an even plainer building, dated 1701. It should come as no great surprise that twice a day—at 6:30 A.M. and 6:30 P.M.—a bugler's brief chorale drifts down the Stechbahn from the spire of the **Stadtkirche** (City Church).

Quite a few Hamburgers and Hanoverians travel to Celle to do their Saturday shopping. In the center of the compact Altstadt, along **Bergstrasse** and the **Grosser Plan**, in particular, a motley band of grocers and old-time purveyors thrive. **Huths Kaffee** has been roasting its own coffee since 1851. In the **Café Kiess** you can sample *Schweineöhrchen,* traditional Danish pastries shaped like pigs' ears. Both establishments are on the Grosser Plan. A couple of medieval blocks away, in the Stechbahn, the **Löwenapotheke** has been in the pharmacy business for well over four centuries. Duck down into the **Ratskeller** beneath the town hall chambers on the Markt and try some *Niedersächsische Hochzeitssuppe* (Marriage Soup), a beef broth with asparagus tips and noodles still served on occasion at local weddings. The town's premier hotel, ► **Der Fürstenhof,** has been known for its various duck dishes ever since it had access to the *Endtenfang,* a ducal pond originally patrolled by duck-catchers who kept Georg Wilhelm supplied with his favorite fowl. Today the chefs use only free-range birds. A recent addition is the ► **Hotel am Stadtgraben,** on Fritzenwiese on the northeastern edge of the Altstadt. It has only 16 rooms, all of them opulently furnished with antiques.

BRAUNSCHWEIG

As you approach what the Anglo-Saxon world calls Brunswick on B 214 from Celle, to the southeast, you will see that lush dairy pastures are being slowly but surely enveloped by the city's industrial outskirts. The puffing factory chimneys are one of the less attractive ways that once-aristocratic Braunschweig now makes its presence felt. This city of 250,000 people, only 42 km (26 miles) east of Hannover, has gone through some tough times. World War II bombing flattened most of the noble architecture of this former capital of the Guelph duchy of Brunswick. Today it is hard to picture that ducal heyday, when Braunschweig ranked as one of the country's centers of culture. Gotthold Ephraim Lessing's *Emilia Galotti,* Germany's first non-Classical tragedy, had its premiere here in the **Hoftheater** (since replaced by the **Staatstheater**) in 1772, as did Goethe's *Faust I* in 1829.

The postwar decades saw a shift in emphasis. Braunschweig is the home of Rollei cameras, and has made the most of its technical and scientific traditions. The nation's civil aviation authority is based here. So is the **Physikalisch-Technische Bundesanstalt** (Federal Institute of Physics and Metallurgy), which possesses the world's most accurate atomic clock. The country's oldest polytechnic school, an offshoot of the Collegium Carolinum founded in 1745, now has more than 14,000 students in some 100 disciplines.

All this has had very little effect on tourism to the city. Recent promotional drives, which labeled Braunschweig "The Likeable City," were aimed at widening the former capital's appeal. What the image-makers call "islands of tradition" do exist amid the concrete sea of office blocks, department stores, and parking lots. Follow the "Stadtmitte" signs to **Burgplatz,** one such enclave right in the center of the city.

Braunschweig is at its most medieval here, thanks to the awe-inspiring **Dom St. Blasius** (Cathedral of St. Blasius), which rears up opposite the **Burg** (Castle) **Dankwarderode**. Cathedral and castle are both testimony to a 12th-century building spree unleashed by the Guelph heavyweight Heinrich der Löwe (Henry the Lion). He and his cousin Frederick Barbarossa, the rival Hohenstaufen clan's red-bearded Holy Roman emperor, were two of the Middle Ages' most flamboyant figures. In youth and early manhood they were friends and even allies, but in 1176 they clashed on matters of principle and power. Henry was consequently stripped of his Bavarian and Saxon holdings by Frederick and exiled for three years in England. On his return he retired to Braunschweig.

During that period, English and German royalty were closely entwined. Henry the Lion's wife, Maud, was the daughter of England's Henry II and Eleanor of Aquitaine. Today Maud and Henry lie side by side in a delicately sculpted tomb in the Romanesque Dom St. Blasius. The discreet sculptor saw to it that the duke was portrayed as being several inches taller than his spouse, when in fact the opposite was the case. Maud, who was married off at the age of 12, grew to outstrip her husband by about eight inches. On the tomb Henry is shown clutching a model of the cathedral. Among St. Blasius's main delights is the barley-sugar twist of the pillars, which foreshadows Tudor fluting.

The castle, across the square, now holds a fine collection of Guelph treasures, including the 800-year-old bronze lion that Henry made the Guelphs' heraldic symbol. The one atop the pedestal in the square is a more recent replica.

Excellent à la carte meals followed by stylish slumber under 500-year-old oak beams can be had in the city's pricey ▶ **Hotel Ritter St. Georg**, on Alte Knochenhauerstrasse. The St. Georg is on an historical par with the ▶ **Hotel Stadtpalais**, formerly the Beata Maria Virginalis orphanage but now a sumptuously appointed hotel on Hinter Liebfrauen. For more down-to-earth fare, head for the eastern loop of the city Ring. This part of town is called the **Magniviertel** after the bomb-torn **St. Magni-Kirche** (Church of St. Magnus). In spite of its name, the **Altstadt Bierhaus** near the Magnitor regales its patrons with Greek snacks and taped pop music. A lot of the surrounding *Gasthäuser* (inns) go in for traditional dishes. If possible, sample the variations on the culinary theme of kale and asparagus, two regional specialties, during their respective seasons: the former from October to December (the cabbage tastes best if harvested after a hard frost), the latter usually from mid-May to the end of June. Farther north on Meinhardstrasse along the city Ring, **Cellarius**, a gourmet restaurant in the vaults of the Neustadt

Rathaus, has recently reopened. Also back in business is the **Gewandhaus Keller**, an eatery steeped in local history, on the Altstadtmarkt near Burgplatz.

Any tour of Braunschweig's surroundings should include a visit to the **Bibliotheca Augusta** in **Wolfenbüttel**, a few miles south of Braunschweig on the B 4. The world-famous Baroque library made the headlines in 1983 when it was decided to give the 12th-century Gospels of Henry the Lion, commissioned by the monarch as a present for Braunschweig's Cathedral of St. Blasius, a permanent home here. The states of Lower Saxony and Bavaria, the federal government, and an industrial trust forked out a grand total of DM 32.5 million for the beautifully illuminated masterpiece—the highest price ever paid for a single book. The library is named after local Duke August the Younger, one of the greatest scholars and bibliophiles of his day. When he died in 1666, at age 87, the "prince of peace" had amassed some 130,000 imprints. Subsequent librarians, such as the 18th-century dramatist and critic Gotthold Ephraim Lessing, were recruited from the highest literary ranks. One of many famous visitors was Giacomo Casanova, who rated the seven days he spent browsing through dozens of volumes here "among the happiest in my life." Today the library has more than 350,000 books, including some 13,000 Bibles in different languages, on display. Many of the incunabula are unique. One of the most valuable is Ulrich Boner's *Edelstein,* printed in Bamberg by Albrecht Pfister in 1461.

GOSLAR

Leave Braunschweig heading south via B 4 (followed by a short spell on B 82) for Goslar. Thanks to its status as a hospital town during World War II, Goslar's core of medieval buildings, many of them more than 400 years old, is on a par with Celle's. Whichever of the crooked, cobbled lanes you head down, you are more than likely to end up in the central **Marktplatz**. Do not miss the mechanical movie—the glockenspiel—there. In the course of four daily performances (9:00 A.M., noon, 3:00 P.M., 6:00 P.M.) starring life-size figures on the 19-bell carillon facing the **Rathaus**, a knight-errant called Ramm emerges mounted on a horse that paws the ground and unearths a rich lode of silver. The horse may well be a piece of poetic license, but the fact remains that from the year 969 on, large quantities of lead, silver, gold, copper, zinc, and other nonferrous metals were mined on the nearby **Rammelsberg**. By the end of the last millennium, a veritable gold and silver rush was on, and, according to one chronicler, Goslar rated as "the fairest and wealthiest city in the whole of Saxony."

From the outset silver was smelted under imperial license. Generations of troubleshooting Holy Roman emperors certainly stashed away a lot of it. With the coins talented artisans minted for them, umpteen feuds and political showdowns were funded. Meanwhile, the miners themselves often spent a grueling week at a time down in the shafts.

Those early Holy Roman rulers were as nomadic as bedouins, with castles all over Western Europe. But Heinrich (Henry) III seems to have had a genuine soft spot for Goslar, and it was during his reign that the **Kaiserpfalz**, a short walk via Hoher Weg from the Rathaus, was built. By 1056 the palace had attained its present enormous dimensions: a two-story stone structure 178 feet long and 60 feet wide, the world's largest secular example of pure Romanesque style. Countless sessions of the *Reichstag* (the Imperial Diet) were held here. Henry III is buried in Speyer, but his heart remains enshrined in Goslar's **Ulrichskapelle** (Chapel of St. Ulrich), adjoining the Kaiserpfalz. In later centuries the palace either fell into disuse or served intermittently as a courthouse, jail, and granary. Kaiser Wilhelm I donated millions for restoration work in 1871 and turned the Kaiserpfalz into a kind of German shrine. As a result, it bristles with the symbolism of a more glorious age: In the imperial hall huge murals, vaguely reminiscent of a Wagnerian opera set, glorify a millennium of Teutonic myths.

Ore was mined until a few years ago. As early as the 13th century, after the decline of imperial influence, the increasingly independent and powerful burghers joined the Hanseatic League, bought the duchy of Brunswick's tithing rights to the mine, and soon enjoyed their own coinage privileges. Periods of slump included part of the 15th century, when the mine shafts (you can book guided tours down them at the tourist office in the main square) were continually flooded. That problem eventually was solved by Thuringian engineers.

The miners themselves never benefited much from their work. Back in the Middle Ages their houses, now so picturesquely restored on **Glockengiesserstrasse** and similar lanes, were humble, smoke-filled abodes without chimneys. The affluent classes consisted mainly of merchants, brewers, artisans, and patrician farmers, whose guilds had a lot of political clout. One of the most powerful, the cloth merchants', operated from the ▶ **Kaiserworth** (in the Marktplatz), now a hotel-cum-restaurant with some fine old vaulting and atmosphere to match. One corner of the building has a worn ledge at its base; guild bosses once sat persistent debtors there and then made them walk the breadth of the square with their breeches down, to the jeers of the populace. The bronze fountain nearby is more than 700 years old. One of its gargoyles graphically portrays the Old Testament story of Jonah; interestingly, the marine monster shown regurgitating Jonah bears scant resemblance to a whale.

Goslar is still good at grand gestures. Opposite the **Marktkirche** (Market Church), on the Marktplatz, is the highly respected restaurant **Das Brusttuch**, where diners ensconced behind mullioned windows and a decorative façade are given rolled-up menus fastened with a red seal; Tel: (5321) 210-81. Slightly more affordable eateries include the **Butterhenne** on the main square, which specializes in barrel-fresh sauerkraut, venison, and salted hamshank, and **Die Worth**, on the main market square, which specializes in Harz mountain fare. The town's most lauded hotel, ► **Der Achtermann**, does a brilliant Disneyland impression of the Middle Ages, with sundry halberds, muskets, and suits of armor lining its walls. Bits of roughly hewn masonry, originally part of the town fortifications, are still visible inside the hotel.

THE HARZ MOUNTAINS

A short, ear-popping climb south via B 241 from Goslar will bring you to the heart of this gently undulating range. The densely forested humps, which rarely rise above 800 meters (2,600 feet), are just about rugged enough to figure as a skiing option in the winter and as a favorite hiking area in the summer. From Clausthal-Zellerfeld take the scenic mountain road, B 242, via Altenau, to **Torfhaus**. The broad swaths of treeless no-man's-land snaking through the forest are all that remain of the formerly lethal border with East Germany.

Through one of the very popular pay telescopes scattered around this area you can pick out **the Brocken**. Crowned by a communications antenna, the legendary granite peak (one of the few taller than 3,300 feet) towers over the eastern portion of the Harz. Since reunification the narrow-gauge **Brockenbahn** has started running again. You can catch the little train at Drei-Annen-Hohne and travel all the way up to the Brocken plateau. Then stay on board for the run down to **Wernigerode**, a spa to the east of what used to be the border. Wernigerode's Baroque-style castle is now open to the public. (For more on Wernigerode and the eastern Harz Mountains see our chapter on Bach and Luther Country.) Superstition had it that every Walpurgis Night, May 1, hordes of witches, described poetically in Goethe's *Faust,* smeared themselves with a secret ointment and then flew up to the Brocken on winged horses, cats, rams, brooms, hayforks, and even shovels to celebrate their sabbath. Since those wild Harz days, when backwoodsmen still roamed the hills, sleek and efficiently run spas such as **Bad Harzburg** and **Bad Lauterberg** have proliferated. The spas tend to attract health-conscious visitors who pop pills, follow strict diets, and walk a network of forest trails signposted to the point of urbanity.

To leave this well-beaten and sophisticated track, head for the broad wedge of hill country that slopes down on either side of the **Auf der Acker** ridge. Life in secluded villages such as **Sieber** and **Lerbach** still revolves around lumber-jacking and other kinds of forestry work. Although you won't find quite the same love of pageantry here as you will, say, in Bavaria, local customs are kept alive by folk groups like the one in Lerbach. On festive occasions young men and women don their traditional costumes for a spirited session of whip-cracking, singing, and dancing. Their distinctive yodeling, a means of communicating in the dense forest, is also a sort of high-pitched narrative. The very rural ► **Akzent-Hotel Sauer-brey**, run by the same Lerbach clan for the past five genera-tions, has its own little theater-cum-beerhall that regularly puts on folk plays and fairy tales for children. The present owner remembers how his father would spend weeks on end in the forest burning charcoal to sell. The charcoal burners are no more, but every August **Altenau** hosts a lengthy *Köhlerfest* in remembrance of its vanished craft. It takes weeks to construct and stoke the old-fashioned kiln, with the festivities lasting just as long.

GÖTTINGEN

For a modern city of 130,000, Göttingen, 110 km (68 miles) south of Hannover, has a remarkably large and lively **Alt-stadt**. The base of the ramparts is intact enough to challenge early-morning joggers to a long, looping run. Mind you, for several postwar decades the Altstadt's main medieval feature was the bout of rush-hour jousting by knights in gasoline-powered tin. Eventually, the city council stepped in and "becalmed" its central grid of streets, turning them into a pedestrian zone. So now, while Greater Göttingen throbs away, life in this inner haven of shops and open-air cafés has been decelerated to a pace that would upset no one in the sleepy Harz villages less than an hour's drive to the north.

The Altstadt, encompassing a crush of noble avenues, crooked alleys, and quiet courtyards, has benefited from the lack of exhaust fumes. Classical façades abound, including that of the still handsome **Aula** in Wilhelmsplatz, formerly one of the centers of the **Georgia Augusta University**, which recently moved most of its faculties to the outskirts of the city. With its magnificently pillared early-19th-century Great Hall, the Aula is comparatively new. Its architectural forebears, such as the row of half-timbered houses down **Paulinerstrasse**, date to the 15th and 16th centuries. There is a reason for the age gap. In 1536, when other German universities were already thriving academic communities, Göttingen made its first application to its imperial overlords for permission to build a university. Prospects were good, until Göttingen joined the *Schmalkaldischer Bund,* an alliance of Protestant towns and principalities committed to overthrowing the Holy Roman Empire. After the Protestants' defeat, Göttingen, along with many of its allies, had to eat humble pie. Envoys travelled to the court of Emperor Charles V to beg his forgiveness. Payment of 10,000 gold florins averted the *Reichsacht,* a decree that would have practically outlawed the town. A long period of economic decline ensued, and it wasn't until 1733 that Britain's King George II, alias Hannoverian Elector Georg Augustus, inaugurated and funded the university named for him.

The university has made up for its late start, claiming some 30 Nobel Prize winners as its own. The whole town is dotted with more than 250 marble plaques. Posted on house walls, they honor the prominent academics and alumni who resided or lodged there. The chemist and physicist Otto Hahn, who later regretted splitting the atom with fellow scientist Lise Meitner, lived at Gervinusstrasse 5 from 1953 on. Germany's "Iron Chancellor," Otto von Bismarck, a law student here, spent 1832–1833 at Bürgerstrasse 27a, the last remaining of the ramparts' 30 watchtowers. The poet Henry Wadsworth Longfellow studied belles lettres here for a year in 1829 and is remembered by a plaque at Rote Strasse 25. The boisterous law student Heinrich Heine, who was expelled from Georgia Augusta for six months after challenging an acquaintance to a duel, lodged at five different addresses between 1820 and 1825. Originally, four plaques commemorated him. Today only the one at Weender Strasse 50 remains. Locals put the others' disappearance down to the scathing descriptions of academic life with which young Heine, later to become one of the country's most acclaimed poets and writers, spiced his *Harzreise* (*Travels in the Harz*). The very first sentence sums up his feelings: "The town of Göttingen, famous for its sausages and university . . ."

Almost in the same line, though, Heine praised "the very good beer" in the city's Rathskeller. He often balked at the "iron paragraphs of Roman jurisprudence" he had to memorize, although he eventually earned a doctorate in law. Very probably Heine preferred a favorite German student discipline: beer-mug philosophy. In a wide range of Göttingen *Kneipen* (pubs), you can eavesdrop on an interesting mix of bright thoughts and platitudes. Down in the vaulted cellars of the crenellated **Altes Rathaus**, the **Rathskeller** itself has kept good wines and brews on tap since the 14th century. Today it specializes in *Deutsche Küche,* which translates as an emphasis on fresh cuts of meat and a variety of the region's spicy sausages. Up above, the old town hall's main hall, used for New Year receptions and official functions, is a beautiful blend of medieval beams, late-19th-century frescoes, heraldic friezes, and Gothic windows.

The **Zum Szültenbürger** restaurant on Prinzenstrasse has a cozy, unaffected feel to it, and caters to an international clientele in the sense that students bring along any newly arrived overseas friends and treat them to the town's most affordable snack: *Schmalzbrot,* thick slices of bread spread with dripping. The **Junkernschänke**, a stylish joint with Renaissance carvings, at Barfüsserstrasse 5, attracts the moneyed class of students and lecturers out to impress. Tel: (551) 573-20; closed Mondays. Considered an "underground" establishment by the trendy set, the basement-level **Con Cave**, easy to overlook down a passageway off Groner Strasse, often offers live folk music and student mini-theater. Regulars divide their time between quiet card games and heated discussions. **Zum Altdeutschen**, on Prinzenstrasse, treats you to generously filled baguette sandwiches and *Pils*.

With any luck you may witness an academic ritual in Göttingen as quaint as any of the surrounding hill country's folk customs. Upon receiving their doctorates, graduates are wheeled out in flower-bedecked carts to kiss the bronze **Gänseliesel** statue opposite the Altes Rathaus. At the turn of the century dozens of competing sculptors offered designs for a suitable monument. The "Goose Maiden," erected in 1901, won over more orthodox suggestions — thanks to a strong student lobby.

THE LAND OF FAIRY TALES

The country roads heading northwest from Göttingen up into the **Weserbergland** should be guarded by gossamer checkpoints with elfin sentinels on duty. Travellers who follow them will soon find themselves entering the land of Snow White and the Seven Dwarfs and deep, dark forests like the **Solling** that have lost none of their mystery. The brooks and rivers hurrying down hillsides to meet the Weser river all seem to have age-old tales to tell; even the smallest town prides itself on its stock of fables and legends. Local storytellers have been skillful weavers of fact and fiction for centuries, often providing the raw material on which writers like the Brothers Grimm embroidered. Hanau, the Grimms' birthplace, more than two hours' drive south of Göttingen, is the starting point of an officially designated **Deutsche Märchenstrasse** (German Fairy Tale Road), which meanders north to coastal Bremerhaven. We suggest you reverse the route's sequence of towns and head south down it, using it merely as a rough guide (with pertinent and entertaining literature at all the municipal tourist offices along the way). From Göttingen take the B 3 north to Einbeck. This *Bundesstrasse* (federal highway), followed by the B 64, B 240, and the B 83, will get you to Hameln. You can pick up the Fairy Tale Road there.

· Einbeck

If you skirt the eastern edge of the Solling on the way from Göttingen to Hameln, it is worth making a detour to see this half-timbered old town, where some 400 Gothic- and Renaissance-style houses still stand, their beams crooked with age and covered with carved reliefs. Their entrances are unusually large, but for practical reasons: In the Middle Ages some families brewed beer at home and stored their hops on the top floor, and it was through the front entrance that the town's master brewer delivered and fetched the jointly owned vats needed for the job. In an early cooperative scheme, Einbeck's burghers pooled their *Ainpöck'schen Bier,* as it was called, and exported it as far afield as Stockholm and Amsterdam. During a Reichstag in Worms, Martin Luther allegedly did a short commercial for their brew, raising a tankard and calling it "the best one knows." Local people never tire of telling visitors that Munich's Hofbräuhaus started in 1589 with imported Einbeck beer. Sixteenth-century Bavarian brewers were so impressed by it that they stopped mixing spices in with their hops and malt. It was also in Bavaria that *Ainpöck'schen* was slowly but surely abbreviated to *Bock,* the present name, by that region's guttural dialect.

Guided tours of the modern brewery are popular because any beer sampled en route is free of charge. But a more historical approach is to down your Bock in **Zum Brodhaus**, the former bakers' guild headquarters on the Marktplatz and now one of the oldest inns in town. The regulars here prefer Pils; they find Bock too sweet.

Einbeck was nearly destroyed at the end of World War II.

U.S. soldiers were amazed when they saw swastikas on a house at Tiedexer Strasse 8, on a chest in the Rathaus, and, most conspicuously, on an escutcheon outside Zum Brodhaus. Sickened by the sight, their commanding officer was about to have the town shelled when one Heinrich Keim, who later became the mayor, did some eloquent explaining to save Einbeck: During the Middle Ages a patrician family, the von Ravens, had cherished the swastika as a symbol of fertility and prosperity. (That, indeed, was its meaning to the ancient Romans, who called it the *crux gamata*.)

From Einbeck it is another 50 km (31 miles) to Hameln (in English, Hamelin), southwest of Hannover.

Hameln

Even on weekdays (from spring to late autumn) Hameln's two main pedestrian thoroughfares, **Bäckerstrasse** and **Osterstrasse**, are crowded with day trippers admiring the town's lavishly ornamented stone façades. The unusual carvings of masks, pyramids, and gargoyles gave rise to the architectural term *Weserrenaissance*. One alley, **Bungelosenstrasse**, seems strangely unaffected by the bustle: It was here, on June 26, 1284, that the Pied Piper was last seen with 130 children in tow, and to this day the locals respect an unwritten rule that forbids music of any kind to be played on this eerie back street.

With the wedding-cake splendor of the 17th-century **Hochzeitshaus** as a backdrop, the mysterious event is enacted every Sunday at noon by a group of costumed residents. The play in the market square sticks closely to the Grimms' version: A young journeyman, resplendent in a gaudily hued doublet, drifts into town, rids it of a plague of rats by luring them into the River Weser with a tune on his silver flute, and then, denied his fee, leads the children away with another enticing tune. Historians speculate that the fairy tale is based on fact, probably an exodus of young colonists to Moravia or Pomerania.

The town, understandably, prefers not to quibble with the Grimm tale: It attributes more than half its tourist revenue to the legend. Indeed, there is not a souvenir shop without a supply of fluffy toy rats. The **Rattenfängerhaus** (Rat Catcher's House) restaurant, at Osterstrasse 28, serves *Rattenschwänze* ("rat tails"), really pork filets flambéed with Calvados; Tel: (5151) 38-88. **Zur Krone** offers larger groups *Ratten-Nester,* a similar meat dish (which must be ordered ahead through the tourist office). A ubiquitous chaser in most taverns and restaurants is *Rattenkiller* (Rat Killer), a highly potent bitters.

Bodenwerder

A couple of years ago, this tiny town on the Weser river, 25 km (16 miles) south of Hameln via the B 83, celebrated its 700th anniversary; its oldest houses lean crookedly along the river's leafy left bank. From the riverboat pier (there is regular service from Hameln) a narrow street leads to the manor in which Baron Karl Friedrich Hieronymus von Münchhausen was born in 1720. Most of the building is the city hall, but one small chamber serves as a **museum** brimming with Münchhausen memorabilia, each piece with a baronial tale to tell. Part of an iron stove on display has the British crown embossed on it—not so surprising, as young Hieronymus was born in the heady Anglo-Hanoverian era. In fact, his father held the rank of "Royal Mounted Great-British Lieutenant-Colonel." A page at the duke of Brunswick's court at the age of 12, young Münchhausen soon followed in his father's footsteps and, as an officer in the Brunswick Regiment, saw years of action in Turkey, Russia, and Finland. In 1750, he returned to Bodenwerder with several citations for gallantry, and remained as lord of the manor. From then on, Münchhausen's life became rather humdrum, and the baron evidently relieved the tedium by amusing relatives and friends with far-fetched accounts of his wartime experiences.

The manor grounds used to stretch as far as today's **Café Berggarten,** which has a fine view of the Weser snaking its way through the Weserberg hill country. Von Münchhausen would invite his friends to the adjoining tower for hour upon hour of storytelling. Down at the museum, you can see the battered old megaphone with which the baron called down to the manor for more ham and wine during such sessions. Münchhausen never wrote down his stories: This was done, apparently without his knowledge, by business-minded scribes with a keen ear for best-selling material. The first collection was published in English, under the title *Baron Münchhausen's Narrative of His Marvellous Travels and Campaigns in Russia.* In England the volume proved to be extremely popular. Translated into German, the baronial bard came out as *Der Lügenbaron* (the lying baron). The harsh title seems to have upset him, even though he deliberately exaggerated his tales to the point of fantasy. Often enough, they were meant as parodies of the usual war veterans' bragging. A classic example: Münchhausen cruises over enemy lines on a cannonball.

The recent film based on the marvelous campaigner's adventures ran for only a couple of days in Bodenwerder. The townsfolk seem to prefer the uproarious Münchhausen sketches as performed by local actors in front of the **Rathaus** (at 3:00 P.M. on the first Sunday of each month from May to October). The biggest event of the year is the *Lichterfest* (on the second Saturday in August), when a Münchhausen stuntman on a lightweight cannonball is towed over the town by helicopter. Some 50,000 spectators usually turn up.

Hannoversch-Münden

From Bodenwerder the B 83 and then the B 80 follow the Weser upstream (south) for 120 km (72 miles) to Hannoversch-Münden, a leisurely 90-minute drive away. (On some maps it may appear simply as "Münden," between Göttingen and Kassel.) In the **Rotunda** here, formerly one of the town's fortified towers, you can sign a chit of paper renouncing any claim to compensation in case of injury and then climb up a series of ladders to the topmost rafter. Through a hatch you'll have a sparrow's-eye-view of yet another medieval gem: some 700 mostly half-timbered houses crammed into a triangle formed by the confluence of the rivers Weser, Fulda, and Werra. Nothing much has changed here since Dr. Johannes Andreas Eisenbart, another of the region's colorful characters, walked the streets below.

Eisenbart was an 18th-century itinerant medic who hired jugglers, tumblers, and fire-eaters to herald his rounds through the villages. Due not least to this approach, he was regarded as a kill-or-cure charlatan by his critics. Allegations were made of horrific operations, including the extraction of gallstones with forceps the size of coal tongs. An inscription on the house at Lange Strasse 79, in which he died, seeks to put the record straight: "He was not as reputed." Recent research has revealed that Eisenbart treated penniless patients free of charge and successfully pioneered the removal of eye cataracts. The doctor is buried outside the **Aegidienkirche**. His headstone describes him as "Royal British, Electoral-Brunswickian, Privileged General Practitioner."

An Eisenbart play reminiscent of the Pied Piper capers is performed on intermittent Sundays from late spring to late summer at 11:15 A.M. in front of the **Rathaus**.

The Reinhardswald

From Hannoversch-Münden a secondary road climbs via the hamlet of Hilwartshausen toward the Reinhardswald. These darkly inviting hill forests flanking the upper Weser river valley, including the **Bramwald**, are among Germany's best-kept secrets. The Reinhardswald is still a magical world of fir-scented, sun-dappled glades, where any of the toadstools could be the Fairy King's throne.

From Hannoversch-Münden follow the signs northwest to Sababurg. After about 8 km (5 miles), you'll feel the almost primeval forest begin to close in on you. Some of the oaks and beeches are more than 700 years old. One of the world's oldest game reserves, a 530-acre area set aside by a local count in 1589 and containing endangered species such as the auroch and bison, is here as well.

Six-hundred-year-old **Sababurg** would be perfectly hidden here were it not for the many signposts. Part of its Schloss (castle), said to be the one Jacob Grimm used as the locale for his tale of Sleeping Beauty, is in ruins, draped with climbing roses. It is often a summer venue for open-air concerts and the like. The other attraction hereabouts is a hotel-cum-restaurant named after Sleeping Beauty (▶ **Dornröschen-Schloss-Sababurg**), where Old World charm comes at a price. This has long been a popular spot for wedding receptions and even has its own registry office. The Schloss is well signposted and only a 30-minute drive from Hannoversch-Münden (take B 80 north for 9 km/5½ miles to the hamlet of Veckerhagen, where you turn left). From here as far south as Hanau you will be travelling through the landscape in which the Brothers Grimm set most of their fairy tales.

KASSEL

This city, spread across several steep hills overlooking the Fulda valley some 50 km (31 miles) southwest of Göttingen, had the misfortune to be saddled with a large tank and locomotive factory during World War II. Bombing reduced most of its once elegant districts to rubble. For a taste of what remains of Old Kassel take a tram from the Hauptbahnhof (main train station) up to the ▶ **Schlosshotel Wilhelmshöhe**, which still sports its turreted **Löwenburg**, built in the 18th century on the lines of a Scottish Highland castle. Friedrichsplatz, at the bottom of Treppenstrasse's flights of steps, is adorned by one of the region's finest Neoclassical buildings, the **Museum Fridericanum**. Every five years the museum hosts the *Documenta,* a 100-day festival of contemporary art that has brought Kassel postwar fame (the next one will be held in 1997). Shortly before his death, the artist and environmentalist Joseph Beuys, a *Documenta* regular, began a "7,000 Oaks" campaign: He planted oak trees in and around the city, marking each tree with a small block of basalt like the one in front of the museum. One of the square's less conspicuous attractions is a 3,300-foot brass rod that the artist Walter de Maria, one of Beuys's contemporaries, drove vertically into the ground.

The Fridericanum once housed the Hofbibliothek (Court Library), where Jacob and Wilhelm Grimm worked as librarians in their mid-twenties. The brothers had spent the early part of their childhood in Steinau an der Strasse (see below), but after their father's untimely death they were sent to live here with an aunt who was a lady-in-waiting at court. After completing their studies in Marburg, the brothers returned to Kassel. At one of the markets on the outskirts of town they met Dorothea Viehmann, a housewife who seems to have been a gifted storyteller. In her youth she had learned dozens of tales from the soldiers and merchants who passed through her father's inn, **Die Knallhütte** (still in business today), on their way south to Frankfurt-am-Main. The Grimms would invite Dorothea up to their rooms at the corner of Marktgasse and Wildemannsgasse, where she supplied them with the raw material for roughly a third of the stories they later published. There was no fee involved. Instead, the brothers would bring out their best china and serve tea. Dorothea, a woman of modest means, regarded the pleasure of stirring her tea with a silver spoon as sufficient recompense, we are told.

The house the Grimms lived in no longer stands. But there are twin statues in the little square named after them at the eastern end of Wilhelmshöher Allee, Kassel's main street. The brothers were inseparable to the end of their days, Jacob, a bachelor, even moving in with Wilhelm and his wife.

MARBURG

Marburg, 80 km (50 miles) southwest of Kassel via B 3, has one of the region's most ancient pedigrees. Its municipal records date back to the beginning of the 12th century. The town's core of venerable buildings, on a hill overlooking the Lahn river, emerged from World War II unscathed, and life in the **Altstadt** still has a tranquil, academic flavor. Nearly a quarter of Marburg's 70,000 inhabitants are students at its university, founded in 1527. It was here that Martin Luther and the Swiss church reformer Ulrich Zwingli met for talks that failed to bridge the doctrinal gap between them. From the **Schloss**, the Altstadt's crowning 15th-century glory, you'll have a splendid view of the Lahn hills. Getting into the hills from the river entails a steep climb up cobblestone lanes and more than 400 steps. During their sojourn here as law students, from 1802 to 1805, the Grimm brothers lodged about halfway up, at the corner of Barfüsserstrasse and

Wendel Gasse. The building, with a shoe shop on the ground floor, is marked by a plaque.

The old part of town, something of a maze, is where Marburg's 16,000 university students spend a fair portion of their après-lecture time. Favorite haunts include the **Destille** on Steinweg, famous for its Tequila Sunrises, and **Cavete**, also on Steinweg, a jazz tavern where the late Chet Baker and Elvin Jones once performed. Except on weekends, when an endless stream of provincial shoppers climbs the hill from the parking lots, life is a placid round of baguette-crunching and wine-sipping. The last political demonstration, in which stark-naked students protested cuts in grants, took place more than a decade ago.

Jacob and Wilhelm Grimm apparently found early-19th-century Marburg idyllic. Walk up through the fragrant gardens, aflutter with butterflies, to the **Forsthof**, now a residence hall, where the brothers had their tutorials with Professor Friedrich von Savigny. The good professor introduced them to his brother-in-law Clemens von Brentano, a member of the Heidelberg school of Romantic writers and a collector and publisher of German folk songs. The association furthered their career, much as Dorothea Viehmann did later.

Down in the *Unterstadt* (Lower Town) do not miss the **Elisabethkirche**, named after the city's patron saint, Elisabeth von Thüringen. At the beginning of the 13th century, Elisabeth, the 20-year-old widow of that state's duke, became Marburg's titular ruler. Instead of exploiting the position as had many of her predecessors, she gave up all her worldly goods and spent her short life tending to the sick and aged. Elisabeth was canonized in 1235. In the sacristy you can see the glittering gold shrine, studded with jewels, that contained her remains, which disappeared during Reformation looting. Grimm connoisseurs identify it as the model for Sleeping Beauty's glass coffin. Latter-day pilgrims to the shrine have included the British royal family, who are Elisabeth's distant relatives.

HERBSTEIN

A pleasant cross-country drive east from Marburg along B 62 and B 254 as far as Lauterbach will lead you back to the heart of Fairy Tale Country. This part of the B 275 climbs south from Lauterbach to the **Vogelsberg**, a bumpy plateau formed by volcanic activity some 30 million years ago. Herbstein, a quiet farming community in the process of restoring its medieval architecture, came to fame as the geographical center of the erstwhile West Germany. In 1978 a TV network found that a map of the country, cut out along its borders and then mounted on cardboard, could be spun on a perfectly horizontal plane only if pivoted almost exactly where Herbstein is. The village presented its visitors with certificates proudly proclaiming its central location (50° 32′ 18″ latitude and 9° 21′ 41″ longitude). An inscribed stone was even erected at the exact spot: south of Herbstein on the road to Altenschlirf. Since reunification the village of Niederdorla in Thuringia has inherited the title of "Germany's hub."

The weaving of legends is an age-old local craft here. Herbstein's name, for example, is said to derive from the ancient Harras, a knight who ruled the area. Harras had the suitors bidding for his daughter Hermengilde's hand engage in a formidable contest. The first to shoulder a huge basalt rock up to the castle could marry Hermengilde. Hugo, his daughter's favorite, almost made it to the portcullis but then collapsed. With his dying breath he uttered the words *herber Stein*—which translates roughly into the genteel expletive "dratted stone."

Volcanic rocks, which came in handy during the village's restoration work, still dot the surrounding fields. **Hoherodskopf**, one of the nearby hills, is probably where the ancient volcano's crater once opened. It was here that the eighth-century missionary Boniface, who was born in Devon, England, did some of his early preaching. Boniface had received papal authority to evangelize the German tribes in 718; by 754 he was the archbishop of Mainz. He and 53 companions were martyred in Frisia three years later.

Ten years before his death Boniface had instructed one of his pupils, Sturmius, to have an abbey built in **Fulda**, 25 km (16 miles) east of Herbstein. Along with its counterparts in Orleans, Tours, and St. Gallen, the abbey school had become one of the Continent's theological centers by 814, the year of Charlemagne's death. Christianity was spread throughout central Germany from here. Today the abbey's foundations lie under Fulda's **Dom** (cathedral), in whose crypt Boniface is buried. Built between 1704 and 1712, the Dom is the focal point of one of Germany's finest Baroque town centers, which throbs and buzzes with life on market days.

STEINAU AN DER STRASSE

The B 27 and B 40, running south from Fulda, return you to the Fairy Tale Road in Steinau. This town, close to Frankfurt-am-Main to the southwest, was once the first-night stop for merchants on their way from Frankfurt to Leipzig. When the town gates were bolted at dusk, the highway robbers known to lurk in the spooky **Spessart forest** nearby must have felt well and truly locked out—the walls of the Renaissance **Schloss** are more than 90 feet high. In fact, the whole of this tiny town has a fortified feel.

The Grimm family moved here from Hanau when Jacob and Wilhelm were six and seven years old, respectively. During the five years their father was a magistrate in the **Amtshaus** (now the **Heimatmuseum**), the boys led a carefree and sheltered life. One of their favorite haunts was the spring down by the town wall—follow the sign reading *Stadtborn* to visit it. Jacob and Wilhelm probably felt the same way about their surroundings as their brother Ludwig Emil, who later illustrated many of their books. Looking back on those romantic days as an adult, he recalled "Steinau, nestling between two hills, [as] the wonderland of my childhood."

When their father died in 1796 the Grimms fell on hard times. The widow Grimm had very little money and six children to feed. To help out, her well-to-do sister, Henriette, at Kassel's court, took charge of Jacob and Wilhelm, who bade a sad farewell to Steinau. The town has kept their memory alive, and the **Brüder-Grimm-Gedenkstätte** (Grimm Memorial) in the Amtshaus is amply stocked with their writings, including the erudite philological volumes of their later years. In the market square, opposite the fountain embossed with characters from their best-known folk tales, the **Steinauer Marionettentheater** regularly performs their stories with beautifully carved puppets. One of the cozy taverns, **Zum Weissen Ross**, even serves (on request for larger groups) the brothers' favorite boyhood dishes: pea soup followed by wine-flavored mousse with vanilla sauce.

GELNHAUSEN

With its steep lanes and two main squares, **Untermarkt** and **Obermarkt**, set on different levels, you need considerable time and stamina to explore this old hillside town between Steinau and Frankfurt. But a walk around Gelnhausen chronicles a millennium of German history. Down on the banks of the Kinzig river are the remains, including some still elegant arches, of the **Kaiserpfalz** (palace) built for Emperor Friedrich I of Hohenstaufen in the 12th century. It was during the convening of Reichstag here in the year 1180 that Barbarossa parceled out the territory of his cousin and rival Henry the Lion—a fateful decision that triggered Germany's *Klein-*

staaterei, its division into hundreds of small states. The Kaiserpfalz grounds are open daily except Mondays.

Opposite the palace grounds, in the former fortifications, is the **Hexenturm**, a tower in which alleged witches and heretics were held prisoner by the Inquisition and its torturers during the Middle Ages.

The former synagogue in Brentanostrasse, built in 1601 and destroyed in 1938, has been reconstructed as a venue for lectures and exhibitions. It still contains one of the very few Baroque Torah shrines left in Europe, the inscription on which, in both Hebrew and German, reads, "In the years of hatred our Jewish citizens were deported and their place of worship desecrated. In the hope of reconciliation, this building was dedicated to the spirit of peace and culture on September 25 in the year 1986."

On **Kuhgasse** you can see the oldest half-timbered house in the state of Hesse (which you entered north of Kassel). It is Gothic in style and dates to 1340. The bust in the Untermarkt potrays Philipp Reis, born on Langgasse in 1834. Along with Alexander Graham Bell and Charles Boursel, he is one of the telephone's pioneers.

For some historic accommodations try the ▶ **Grimmelshausen-Hotel** in Schmidtgasse, where Johann Jacob Christoph von Grimmelshausen was born in 1621. As a 13-year-old he watched as imperial troops sacked the town and had to flee to Hanau with his grandfather. Soon afterward, he was pitched into the atrocities of the Thirty Years' War. He survived some nine years in the thick of the fighting, serving as a groom, imperial musketeer, and regimental clerk. In 1669 Grimmelshausen published *Der Abentheurliche Simplicissimus,* the first German-language novel. His account of a disingenuous young man enlightened and toughened by the horrors of war is allegorical and satirical, but not all that fictional. Simplex, the book's hero, relives much of what Grimmelshausen himself went through. The novel has since been translated into more than a hundred languages, including Chinese.

HANAU

Fifteen km (9 miles) southwest of Gelnhausen the ragged skyline of Hanau's 1950s architecture rises to meet you. Within the town a semblance of an Altstadt—just enough for you to picture yesteryear's Hanau—has recently been restored. One of the most ornate buildings is the **Rathaus**, which faces a huge monument honoring Jacob and Wilhelm Grimm. Hanau has made the most of the fact that the brothers were born here, even though they soon moved on to Steinau with their parents. After their years in Kassel and Marburg, the brothers pursued academic careers in Göttingen, as we have noted, and finally Berlin. There they lived busily ever after, immersed in compiling a comprehensive German dictionary. Wilhelm got as far as the letter D; Jacob, who died four years later in 1863, continued as far as *Frucht,* the word for fruit. They were buried side by side in Berlin's Schöneberg cemetery. By the time subsequent generations of academics had completed their dictionary, in 1960, *Der Grimm* was 35,000 pages long.

Frankfurt-am-Main lies just to the west of Hanau.

GETTING AROUND

The region lies within a heart-shaped network of major Autobahns: Hannover to Kassel; Kassel to Paderborn; and Bielefeld to Hannover. These Autobahns are convenient enough to be useful for A-to-B driving but do not encroach on the scenic interior. Motoring in the region is a pleasure: Country roads and remote forest roads are relatively free of traffic, thanks to the Autobahns.

Hameln, Bodenwerder, Hannoversch-Münden, Kassel, and Marburg are connected to the main Munich–Hannover railroad line by some of the fastest stretches in Germany's rail network, but there is no line up the Weser river valley. Nature lovers see this as a blessing.

One of the most enjoyable ways to explore the area is by riverboat on the Weser. **Oberweser Dampfschiffahrt**, the biggest of several shipping companies, runs a scheduled service from the end of April to the beginning of October. Vessels call at most of the villages and towns between Hameln and Bad Karlshafen. Downstream travel (to the north) is considerably faster than upstream travel; for example, the trip from Karlshafen to Bodenwerder takes seven hours, while the return trip can take up to 12 hours. During periods of low rainfall there are some very shallow stretches of river, and schedules cannot always be maintained. For information contact: Oberweser Dampfschiffahrt, Inselstrasse 3, D-31787 Hameln; Tel: (5151) 220-16; Fax: (5151) 230-40.

ACCOMMODATIONS REFERENCE

The hotel rates listed here are 1994 projections for double-bed, double-occupancy rooms, with a range from low to high whenever possible. Prices are given in deutsche marks (DM). Basic rates are always subject to change, so please verify price when you are booking. Breakfast is usually included in the price of a room.

City telephone codes must be preceded by a zero if you are calling from elsewhere in Germany.

▶ **Der Achtermann.** Rosentorstrasse 20, D-38640 **Goslar.** Tel: (5321) 210-01; Fax: (5321) 427-48. DM 238–328.

▶ **Akzent-Hotel Sauerbrey.** Friedrich-Ebert-Strasse 129, D-37520 **Osterode-Lerbach.** Tel: (5522) 509-30; Fax: (5522) 50-93-50. DM 120–150.

▶ **Dornröschen-Schloss-Sababurg.** D-34369 **Hofgeismar Sababurg.** Tel: (5671) 80-80; Fax: (5671) 80-82-00. DM 180–300.

▶ **Der Fürstenhof.** Hannoversche Strasse 55/56, D-29221 **Celle.** Tel: (5141) 20-10; Fax: (5141) 20-11-20. DM 220–400.

▶ **Grimmelshausen-Hotel.** Schmidtgasse 12, D-63571 **Gelnhausen.** Tel: (6051) 170-31; Fax: (6051) 170-33. DM 75–140.

▶ **Hotel Ritter St. Georg.** Alte Knochenhauerstrasse 11–13, D-38100 **Braunschweig.** Tel and Fax: (531) 130-39. DM 220.

▶ **Hotel am Stadtgraben.** Fritzenwiese 22, D-29221 **Celle.** Tel: (5141) 10-91; Fax: (5141) 240-82. DM 190–260.

▶ **Hotel Stadtpalais.** Hinter Liebfrauen 1a, D-38100 **Braunschweig.** Tel: (531) 24-10-24; Fax: (531) 24-10-25. DM 298–328.

▶ **Intercontinental.** Friedrichswall 11, D-30159 **Hannover.** Tel: (511) 367-70; Fax: (511) 32-51-95; in U.S., Tel: (800) 327-0200. DM 300–545.

▶ **Kaiserworth.** Markt 3, D-38640 **Goslar.** Tel: (5321) 211-11; Fax: (5321) 211-14. DM 140–240.

▶ **Kastens Hotel Luisenhof.** Luisenstrasse 1–3, D-30159 **Hannover.** Tel: (511) 304-40; Fax: (511) 304-48-07. DM 248–348.

▶ **Schlosshotel Wilhelmshöhe.** Im Schlosspark 2, D-34131 **Kassel.** Tel: (561) 308-80; Fax: (561) 308-84-28. DM 210–220.

BACH AND LUTHER COUNTRY
IN EASTERN GERMANY

By Phyllis Méras

Phyllis Méras, travel editor of the Providence (Rhode Island) Journal, *contributes travel articles to newspapers around the country. She travels frequently in eastern Germany and is the author of three European guidebooks, including one to Eastern Europe.*

Now that there is a united Germany, the eastern central section of the country—the towns and cities of Bach, Luther, and Goethe—are once again freely open to visitors. The Communist regime's stiff regulations, which discouraged travel in eastern Germany for all but the most dauntless of travellers, are things of the past. There are, however, still challenges to be met by the visitor to this newly accessible area. Though prepayment for accommodations is no longer required, it is *essential* to make room reservations well in advance. Bankers, real-estate developers, industrialists, and other entrepreneurs from the West now spend the work week in eastern Germany, filling the rooms in the limited number of hotels. In addition, many old hotels have been closed for refurbishment. Until new ones can be built, finding a room for the night in a major eastern German city— especially on a weekday—is not easy. Although it is now possible to stay with families, even such relatively inexpensive bed-and-breakfast places are in short supply. Thus, a trip to the east should be well thought out, with your itinerary carefully planned.

Eastern Germany (detail)

miles
0 ——————— 20

kilometers
0 ——————— 32

Berlin

Rhine R.

Frankfurt

Danube R.

E30

Braunschweig

Magdeburg

Elbe River

Former East
German border

E30

H A R Z
M O U N T A I N S

81

Elbe River

Saale River

184

Dessau

Wernigerode

Quedlinburg

6

180

Lutherstadt
Eisleben

E49

Halle

Saale River

Nordhausen

80

80

4

247

Mülhausen

Naumburg

Ilm River

87

E49/51

Erfurt

Weimar

7

Eisenach

Gotha

7

E40

Gera

Arnstadt

Ilm River

Saale River

4

Gera River

Thüringer Wald

To Nürnberg

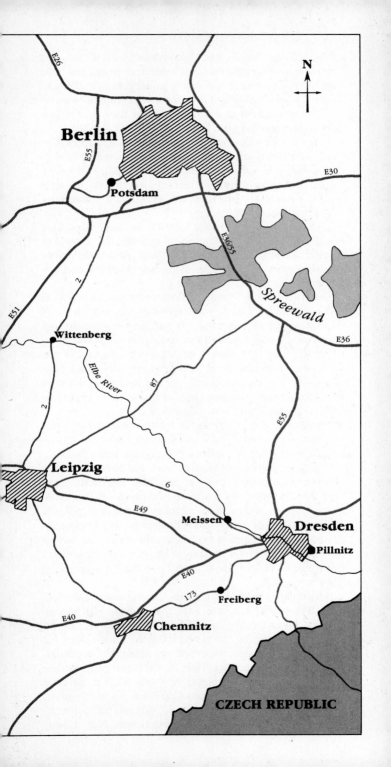

The traveller to the east should bear in mind, too, that while the postwar rebuilding of western Germany has been virtually completed, in the east it is just getting under way. There is scarcely a city or town whose streets are not torn up and where scaffolding does not conceal many of the fine Renaissance and Baroque façades.

In the countryside, though many polluting industries have been shut down and incentives are now being offered to householders to substitute oil or gas as heating fuel for the brown coal whose smoke for years clouded the sky, the air is not yet clear. It will take time, too, to bring back waterways killed by chemical wastes.

And because, in the past, tourism from English-speaking lands was minimal and English, in general, was given low priority as a language, it can still be difficult to find English-language tours or English-speaking help in hotels and restaurants.

Germany's reunification has not been painless. Not all residents of the east favored reunification, and many of those who did, now that there is a single Germany, are not so certain it was a good idea. Hundreds of thousands of easterners have lost their jobs. Many are resentful of the westerners who now head their factories, banks, and businesses—and who, presumably, are teaching them the ways of a free-market economy, but who are often imperious and inconsiderate in the way they do it.

Alcoholism, too, is a problem for the jobless. The drugs that were never available for East German marks can now be bought with western currency. Petty crime, never before a problem in the heavily policed east, has now become a concern, though still a minor one. Also worrisome have been neo-Nazi skinhead attacks on foreigners—Poles, Romanians, Gypsies, Vietnamese, Africans, Turks, and political asylum-seekers of other nationalities who are being supported by the federal government. The issue has shaken German politics, and it remains to be seen how the country as a whole will handle the problem now that it has spread to cities in the west.

Nonetheless, Saxony, Thuringia, Brandenburg, Mecklenburg–West Pomerania, and Saxony-Anhalt are rich in culture and historic cities, among them Berlin (see our Berlin chapter) and Leipzig, renowned since the Middle Ages for its trade fairs; Dresden, whose incomparable Baroque buildings, demolished in World War II, are being painstakingly restored; and Potsdam, home of Sanssouci, the dazzling showplace built by the Prussian king Frederick the Great. In eastern Germany's little towns and villages, half-timbered medieval houses crowd cobblestone streets. High Gothic churches tower over marketplaces. Castles loom on forested hillsides. Music seems to be everywhere in the air. Raphael's *Sistine Madonna* and Giorgione's *Sleeping Venus* are in Dresden, along with one of the world's finest collections of porcelain and royal jewelry. Then there is Luther's birthplace at Eisleben; Handel's birthplace in Halle; Eisenach, where Johann Sebastian Bach was born; Arnstadt and Mühlhausen, where he played the organ; Wittenberg, where Protestantism began; Weimar, where Johann Wolfgang von Goethe and Friedrich Schiller wrote; and Gotha, once ruled by Queen Victoria's sons. There is Naumberg, with its medieval cathedral; the Hanseatic towns of Stralsund and Rostock on the Baltic Sea (for which see our chapter on The North); the sylvan Spreewald with its winding waterway; the wildflowers of the Harz Mountains; half-timbered Quedlinburg and Wernigerode as well as rebuilt Halberstadt; the Thuringian forest; and the Elbe valley with its brown-gold river.

Only a few of these attractions—the major cities of Leipzig and Dresden, as well as those with close connections to Frederick, Luther, Bach, Handel, and Goethe, and the picturesque villages in the eastern Harz mountains—are discussed here, but the adventurous visitor to eastern Germany should consider exploring further. It will be a rewarding experience.

MAJOR INTEREST

Potsdam
Sanssouci
Schloss Cecilienhof

Wittenberg
Sites associated with Martin Luther
Schlosskirche and Stadtkirche
A stroll along Collegienstrasse
Renaissance Rathaus

Halle
Handel house
Gothic and Romanesque towers
Halloren Museum

Lutherstadt Eisleben
Luther birth house and death house
Petri-Pauli-Kirche and Andreaskirche

Quedlinburg
Fachwerk (half-timbered) houses in the Altstadt
Schlosskirche

Wernigerode
Colorful town in the eastern Harz mountains

Eisenach
The Wartburg
Reuter-Wagner Museum
Georgenkirche
Bach and Luther houses

Gotha
Schloss Friedenstein

Mühlhausen
Museum of the Peasants' War
Marienkirche

Erfurt
Dom
Augustinerkirche
Severinkirche
12th-century Krämerbrücke
Thuringian folk art museum

Weimar
Goethe and Schiller houses, Altstadt
Lucas Cranach the Elder altarpiece, Stadtkirche
Franz Liszt house

Leipzig
Altes Rathaus
Naschmarkt
Thomaskirche
Bach archives, Bose house
Neues Gewandhaus

Dresden and Environs
The Albertinum museum
The Zwinger museum
Semper Oper
Summer palace of Pillnitz
Albrechtsburg and Dom, Meissen
Display rooms of the Meissen factory
Cathedral and town of Freiberg
Traditional wooden-toy carvers in Seiffen

Saxon Switzerland

We begin at Frederick the Great's palace in Potsdam, just
outside Berlin, then move southwest into Luther and Handel
territory, first Wittenberg, then Halle and Eisleben, near
Leipzig. From here we turn north and west to reach

Quedlinburg and Wernigerode, two special villages in the eastern Harz mountains.

Bypassing Leipzig for the moment, we continue on to Eisenach, on the former West German border. From Eisenach—of interest for both Luther and Bach—we follow the northern edge of the Thuringian forest eastward through towns famous for their association with Bach: Gotha, Mühlhausen, Erfurt, Arnstadt, and Weimar (this last also a Goethe shrine).

From this point the route heads east back toward Leipzig, and after Leipzig we end still farther east at Dresden and Meissen on the north–south route between Berlin and Prague.

POTSDAM

In Potsdam, 30 km (19 miles) southwest of Berlin Mitte, Frederick the Great of Prussia, longing for a restful place, built a summer palace near the Havel river that is one of Europe's loveliest 18th-century royal dwellings. The center of this historic town was severely damaged in 1945, and is only now being rebuilt for its 1,000th anniversary in 1993. But Frederick's country palace survived the war relatively intact. Indeed, it was to Schloss Cecilienhof, on the grounds of Sanssouci, that Harry Truman, Joseph Stalin, and Winston Churchill (and his successor as British prime minister, Clement Attlee) came for the Potsdam Conference of 1945, which decided the postwar fate of Germany.

Small by the standards of its day—**Sanssouci** was built between 1745 and 1747—Frederick the Great's golden ten-room summer palace (plus a vestibule and a marble hall) is an architectural and decorative gem. It seems to bring the outdoors indoors in a near-miraculous way.

Frederick wrote poetry and prose and played the flute, for which he composed concertos. Bach wrote his "Musical Offering" for Frederick in 1747. Though often curt to people, he was devoted to animals and to nature. Indeed, he asked to be buried in the garden here beside his beloved greyhounds. Instead, he was interred first in the Garnisonkirche (Garrison Church) in Potsdam (destroyed in World War II), where his father, Friedrich Wilhelm I, whom he abhorred, was also buried. Then his remains were moved to Württemburg. And at last, in 1991, they were finally brought here.

Frederick drew the plans for Sanssouci himself, setting his palace at the top of a terraced vineyard. He wanted a single-story structure so he could open his doors and step out into the garden. To transform his design into reality he selected an old friend, Georg von Knobelsdorff, an army officer turned architect. From the garden entrance, guests entered a long, low, narrow building with a center dome and mounted a graceful flight of stairs. There, between the long windows of the façade, 36 caryatids lean outward. At the north entrance, where today's visitors enter, Frederick's guests who arrived by coach would, stepping out, look through a semicircular colonnade of Corinthian pillars to a view of artificial Roman ruins in the distance.

The palace itself was constructed in what has come to be called "Potsdam Rococo." Bacchus and nymphs dance in relief above the doors in its cheerful entrance hall. Flora, goddess of flowers, looks down from the painted ceiling. In the art gallery, paintings from the school of Jean-Antoine Watteau and sculpture and busts (including a bust of Frederick made from his death mask) line the walls. Off Frederick's library—filled in his day with more than 2,000 books in French, for he admired everything Gallic—are his study and bedroom. Though the furniture is Rococo, the rooms themselves have since been rebuilt in Classical style. It was in the alcove here, sitting in his wing chair, that Frederick died in 1786, at the age of 74. The French clock that he always took great care to wind himself is said to have stopped at the moment he died.

The ceiling in the bright music room, which especially seems to bring nature indoors, is gaily painted with spiders and birds, baskets of flowers, and dogs chasing rabbits. Murals inspired by Ovid's *Metamorphoses,* done by the French painter Antoine Pesne, visually expand the walls.

In the reception room, with its ceiling mural depicting Flora and Zephyr (the god of wind), the king thoughtfully hung French paintings that he liked, so that those awaiting an audience could wile away their time fruitfully.

Frederick had the central hall of his palace fashioned after the Pantheon in Rome, with Carrara marble columns. The guest rooms are off it—the decor in one based on the paintings on Chinese porcelain; a second done in blue; a third in red. Finally, there is the Voltaire room, with a bust of the French philosopher scrutinizing the parrots portrayed on its lemon-yellow walls.

A great admirer of Voltaire, Frederick corresponded with him for years and invited him to move to his court so they could talk of matters the king considered important— primarily philosophy and literature. Voltaire came and stayed for a while, but the pair quarreled and the philosopher left.

"He is like a lemon," Frederick remarked afterward. "You can press out the juice and throw the rest away."

The number of visitors allowed to enter the palace each day is limited to 1,700, and all must enter on guided tours. Therefore it is advisable either to be at the booking office at the palace itself before 10:00 A.M. or to take a bus tour from Berlin that includes admission. (During the summer tourist season these are offered once a day in English.) Information on such tours is available from the Potsdam Information Office, Friedrich-Ebert-Strasse 5, Tel: (331) 211-00, or in Berlin at the tourist information office in the Europa-Center, Budapesterstrasse 45, Tel: (30) 262-60-31; Fax: (30) 21-23-25-20.

If you decide to arrive early in Potsdam, and buy your ticket yourself, you can tour the grounds and its many attractions while you wait your turn to get into Sanssouci.

A stroll through the extensive grounds of the palace is as important a part of a visit to Sanssouci as seeing its buildings. At the foot of the stairs to the garden, the great fountain plays. Down the Hauptallee from the fountain is the obelisk portal entrance to the park, with two goddesses—Flora again, and Pomona, the goddess of fruit—standing on a wall beside Corinthian columns. In the Neptune grotto, the god of the sea brandishes his trident over a Baroque arch set against a backdrop of trees.

Above the grotto rises the **Bildergalerie** (Picture Gallery), said to be the first building ever constructed solely for the purpose of exhibiting works of art. Here (open to the public) are paintings by Peter Paul Rubens, Lucas Cranach the Elder, Guido Reni, Caravaggio, and Anthony Van Dyck.

On the west side of Sanssouci is the **Orangerie**, built in Italian Renaissance style in the 19th century by Friedrich Wilhelm IV. Inside, the decoration is French Regency and Empire, and copies of 47 Raphael paintings hang on the walls.

Also west of Sanssouci is the extensive **Neues Palais** (New Palace), whose construction, just after the Seven Years' War with France, Austria, Russia, Saxony, and Sweden had exhausted the nation's treasury, dismayed Frederick's subjects considerably. The king, who himself called this enormous brick palace (with a marble concert hall 100 feet long and a Grotto Hall decorated in marble and glittering quartz) ostentatious, evidently thought it was important to build it to show off the powers of his state.

There is a charming little **Chinese teahouse** with a tent-shaped roof, treelike columns, gilded sculptures, and, on the roof, a statue of a Mandarin sitting beneath a parasol. This was a period of great admiration for things Chinese all across Europe, for China seemed to Europeans, from the little they knew of it, a paradise on earth. The teahouse, designed by John Büring, is one of the finest examples of chinoiserie.

Schloss Cecilienhof, now part first-class hotel, part historical museum, is a 1913 copy of an English country house built on the palace grounds for Kaiser Wilhelm II's son, Crown Prince Wilhelm, and his wife, Cecilia. Thirty-six rooms of the palace were renovated and used for the Potsdam Conference. Today only a few are open to the public (see also Staying in Potsdam, below). The Soviet delegation to the conference met in the former study of the crown princess. The crown prince's paneled smoking room became the working room of the American delegation. (It was here, reportedly, that Truman learned of the successful completion of the atomic bomb with a telegram declaring cryptically, "A baby is born.") Churchill worked at the writing desk in the crown prince's blue study for a few days before Attlee's Labour Party came into power and Attlee succeeded him.

Other late additions built by Friedrich Wilhelm IV in the 19th century on the palace grounds include **Charlottenhof,** a little palace designed by Karl-Friedrich Schinkel in the 1820s in villa style (its wide lawns, maples, copper beeches, lindens, and extensive flower beds were largely laid out in their present form by master landscape artist Peter Joseph Lenné); the Römische Bäder (Roman Baths), the Fasanerie (Pheasantry), the Friedenskirche (Peace Church), and a number of gardens.

To the east of the palace grounds, in the town of Potsdam itself, the dome of the **Nikolaikirche** (St. Nicholas' Church), built by Schinkel in 1849 but bombed in World War II, has been restored along with **Wilhelm-Staab-Strasse,** a Baroque street. There are the little houses of the Dutch quarter to see; the Russian colony built for singers from Russia at Friedrich III's court; the reconstructed 1752 Rathaus topped by Atlas holding the world on his shoulders; and the **Brandenburger Tor** (Brandenburg Gate) of 1770—not, of course, to be confused with the gate of the same name in Berlin.

Potsdam is an easy day trip from Berlin by S-Bahn, bus, or train, and from April to October there are Weisse Flotte Potsdam excursion boats several times a day from the Wannsee. The Potsdam bus station, train station, and boat dock are all at the edge of the main town, with bus and tram service to the palace grounds.

Staying and Dining in Potsdam

The historic ▶ **Travel Hotel Schloss Cecilienhof**, built in English country-house style for the family of the crown prince at the beginning of World War I, is the place to stay in Potsdam. It was here that the Potsdam Agreement was signed in 1945. Much of the palace—42 rooms, many of them elegant and with garden overlooks—is now a hotel. Tours of the city can be arranged at the hotel; some English is spoken. There is good dining in the Cecilienhof dining rooms.

The ▶ **Mercure Hotel An der Havel** on Lange Brücke is an expensive, but less charming, possibility. Some English is spoken and its **Havelland Grill** offers fine fare. Other popular restaurants are the **Gastätte Pegasus** in the Klub der Kunstler und Architekten "Eduoard Claudius" near the Hotel Potsdam, at Schloss Strasse 14, Tel: (331) 215-06, closed Sunday evenings; the **Gastmahl des Meeres** at Brandenburger Strasse 72; the **Klosterkeller** at Friedrich-Ebert-Strasse 94, Tel: (331) 212-18; and **Zum Garde-Ulanen** at 13 Jägeralle, Tel: (331) 212-61.

Pleasant cafés are the **Drachenhaus** in Park Sanssouci and the **Kleines Schloss** in Park Bobelsberg.

WITTENBERG

About 75 km (47 miles) south of Potsdam via the B 2, about halfway to Leipzig, is Wittenberg, where, in 1517, Martin Luther posted his 95 theses—the foundation of Protestantism—on the castle-church door. The original door was destroyed in a 16th-century fire; a bronze 19th-century door engraved with the theses has replaced it.

Martin Luther came to Wittenberg in 1508 to study and teach at its university. Before long he was one of its most popular professors, and the reputation of the university had spread far and wide. But Luther was outraged by the practice of selling indulgences—as he saw it, buying pardon for sin through contributions to the Church. The poster he tacked on the church door took issue with the practice.

The sale of indulgences, however, was profitable to the Church, and the enthusiasm with which Luther's theses were received (unbeknownst to him, they were translated from Latin into German and were widely distributed) was disturbing. He was summoned to Worms to explain himself to Holy Roman Emperor Charles V. On his return, his supporter-benefactor, Saxon elector Friedrich the Wise, fearful that Luther might be in danger, whisked him off to Wartburg castle in Eisenach (see below).

But Wittenberg was Luther's home, and it was here that he returned from Eisenach. While he was gone his priestly colleagues had been rewriting the rules. One change allowed priests to marry, and on a bright spring day at the door of the **Stadtkirche** (Parish Church) of St. Mary, which still towers behind Wittenberg's Marktplatz, the priest and monk Martin Luther married a former nun, Catherine von Bora.

If you visit that Gothic church today you will see Luther preaching on a panel of the altar triptych that his friend and fellow Wittenberg resident, Lucas Cranach the Elder, is said to have painted (Luther sometimes was a substitute preacher in the church). Luther is also depicted as Junker Jörg—the knight he was disguised as in the Wartburg. His wife Catherine, his protector Friedrich the Wise, and his friend, adviser, and professor of Greek, Philipp Melanchthon, are also depicted on the altarpiece. Wittenberg today is remembered not only for Luther, in fact, but also for Melanchthon and the Cranachs, father and son.

An amble along mile-and-a-half-long **Collegienstrasse** is a pleasant way to spend an afternoon. A good starting place, less than a ten-minute walk from the railway station, is the oak tree marking the site where Luther burned the papal bull threatening him with excommunication. It stands beside a well in a little park at the first crossing going into town. Farther along on the left, across a tree-shaded courtyard, is the **Augusteum**, the Augustinian monastery where first Luther the priest and, after the dissolution of the monasteries, Luther the married man, lived with his family. Today the monastery is filled with Reformation-period exhibits: richly decorated Bibles, prints, coins, medals, and drawings. In Luther's room is a pulpit from which he preached, and the platform from which he lectured to his students.

Still farther along is the house where Melanchthon, page by page, checked Luther's translation of the New Testament, sent to him from the Wartburg. At number 29 Collegienstrasse, the Wittenberg tourist information office sells maps showing the sites along Wittenberg's most famous street.

In the **Marktplatz**, monuments to both Luther and Melanchthon stand in front of the High Renaissance **Rathaus**, with its striking two-story portico. From the town hall balcony sentences for malfeasance were issued, and in the marketplace itself executions were carried out. Modern-day strollers often sit for a while on park benches in the Marktplatz to enjoy a sausage or an ice-cream cone and watch the passersby.

Beyond the Marktplatz, which is edged with gabled Renaissance houses, Collegienstrasse becomes Schlossstrasse and leads to the **Friedenskirche**. En route, on the left hand side at the corner of Elbstrasse, the workshop of Lucas Cranach the Elder, mayor and councillor of the town as well as painter and friend to Luther, is now an apothecary.

In its present form the **Schlosskirche** (Castle Church), which has been many times destroyed and restored, is largely 19th century. Friedrich the Wise is buried here beneath an early German Renaissance bronze plaque by the Nürnberg sculptor Peter Vischer the Younger. On one side of the church are Melanchthon's remains; on the other, under the Late Gothic altar, are those of Luther.

It is probably better not to stay overnight in Wittenberg but to come here on a day trip from Berlin or Leipzig. If you do stay over, the best accommodation as this book went to press was the little ▶ **Goldener Adler**. (As always in eastern Germany, be sure to book in advance.) The newly opened ▶ **Waldhotel Vogel** is a five-minute drive outside of town.

The best dining possibilities in Wittenberg are at the **Goldener Adler** hotel, Tel: (3491) 20-53, and the **Ratschänke** at Markt 14, Tel: (3491) 503-51, where trout from the nearby Fläming Hills is the specialty (closed Mondays).

HALLE

Southwest of Wittenberg, and only about 30 km (19 miles) west of Leipzig, is Halle, where George Frederick Handel was born in 1685, and where, at the sprawling yellow **Händel-Haus** at Nikolaistrasse 5, pictures and documents (in German but with an English tape available) tell of his defiance of his father's wish that he become a lawyer, and of his musical studies. They recall his education at Halle's university, his post as cathedral organist at 17, and his quitting Halle for Hamburg, then Italy, and finally England, where he spent the greater part of his life. Period musical instruments are on display in the house, and visitors are treated to recorded selections from his work. A Handel festival is an annual June event in town.

Halle's other appeals are its skyscape at dusk and its elaborately decorated turn-of-the-century houses. All around the Markt are towers—the two Gothic and two Romanesque towers, joined by a bridge, of the **Marktkirche**, where Bach's oldest son, Wilhelm Friedemann Bach, was the organist for 18 years. The Late Gothic **Roter Turm** (Red Tower) also rises here, with a statue of Roland, symbolizing the town's independence, at its foot. A statue of Handel also stands in the square. Lamentably, a tram crosses the marketplace, and by daylight its tracks and overhead cables destroy the illusion of antiquity the towers otherwise offer.

Handsome town houses rise along Schmeerstrasse and on Rannischestrasse, both in the neighborhood of the market square, but again the omnipresent trams intrude.

For centuries Halle was renowned for the *Halis* (salt springs) from which it takes its name, and at its **Halloren Museum**, at Mansfelder Strasse 52, one Sunday morning each month, the stunning silver drinking-cup collection of its old salt workers' guild is displayed. To find out which Sunday the silver is shown, check with the Halle tourist information office in the Roter Turm on the Marktplatz.

As a leading industrial city and railroad junction, Halle suffered considerably during World War II. Much rebuilding and demolition of badly damaged structures still go on, but half-timbered buildings on narrow lanes still provide glimpses of the Halle of the Middle Ages. Until recently, with brown coal firing many Halle factories, air pollution was a major problem; now it is getting better.

Staying and Dining in Halle

The ▶ **Maritim Hotel Stadt Halle**, across from the railway station, is an enormous edifice designed in Eastern European Modern, but its location is convenient and, room by room, it is being remodeled. The little ▶ **Hotel Rotes Ross** on Leipzigerstrasse is the other centrally situated hotel possibility. Because this is a city crammed with businessmen from the west, it is essential to book well in advance, especially for a weekday visit.

Restaurants worth trying, in addition to the **Saline** in the Stadt Halle, Riebeck Platz 4, Tel: (345) 88-80, are the **Haus am Leipziger Turm**, Am Waisenhausring 16, Tel: (345) 289-07; the **Weinhaus Bacchus**, at Rathausstrasse 14, Tel: (345) 66-81-54; and **Kruger's Gute Stube**, Steinweg 41–42, Tel: (345) 299-38.

Lutherstadt Eisleben

It was in the pretty little Harz mountain town of Eisleben (population 27,000), 21 km (13 miles) west of Halle, where blue and rose and yellow stucco houses with high-pitched roofs front on the market square, that Luther was born in 1483. His father was a copper miner; before Martin was a year old the family moved to neighboring Mansfeld, which was more of a mining center.

Though Luther spent only the first months of his life in the square little Franconian **Geburtshaus** (birth house) near the Markt (now reconstructed), Lutherstadt Eisleben (the "Lutherstadt" was added to the name in 1946) proudly lays claim to his birth. He was baptized in the **Petri-Pauli-Kirche** (Church of Sts. Peter and Paul); he died in the town archivist's house at the top of the Marktplatz; and his body lay in state at the **Andreaskirche** (St. Andrew's Church), which towers over the Marktplatz.

Both Luther houses—the Franconian-style birth house, where an 1817 Johann Gottfried von Schadow bust of the Reformer sits in the garden, and the Gothic-style death house—have been painstakingly restored and furnished, albeit sparsely, in 16th-century style.

Of particular interest in the Geburtshaus are period paintings of supporters of the Reformation as well as the gleaming golden swan that became Luther's symbol. The swan alludes to the martyred Czech Reformer Jan Hus's cry 68 years earlier at the stake: "You are roasting a goose, but after me there will come a swan you will not be able to roast." (In Czech, *hus* means "goose.") There is a kitchen with iron pots and wooden buckets on the ground floor, along with old copper-mining tools and copies of Lucas Cranach the Elder's portraits of the Reformer's forbidding-looking parents, Hans and Margaretta Luther.

Luther died of a heart attack on the way back to his home in Wittenberg after settling a dispute between two landgraves of Mansfeld. In the little room where he stayed before he died are a curtained bed, a chest, and a washstand. Elsewhere in the house are the cloth that covered his coffin and a copy of one of the last letters he wrote to his wife.

A text in English describes the displays in both the Geburtshaus and the death house. To enter the Petri-Pauli-Kirche arrangements must be made through the town's information bureau or by knocking on the pastor's door across from the church. Renovation, however, was under way at press time.

In the marketplace, which is edged with half-timbered and gabled houses, stands a turn-of-the-century statue of the Reformer.

As Lutherstadt Eisleben is only 50 km (31 miles) from Leipzig, it makes for an easy day trip. Accommodations, except for bed and breakfasts, are limited, but those can be found through the Fremdenverkehrsverein, Halleschestrasse 6, Tel: (3475) 60-21-24; Fax: (3475) 60-26-34.

THE EASTERN HARZ MOUNTAINS
Quedlinburg

To reach Quedlinburg, a fairy-tale town of half-timbered pink-and-gold dwellings lurching along cobblestone lanes, take highway B 180 north from Lutherstadt Eisleben and turn west onto route B 6 near Aschersleben; the total distance is about 54 km (33 miles).

If the town's name sounds familiar, it's because Quedlinburg attracted international attention a few years ago when religious and historical treasures stolen from it during World War II by an American GI suddenly resurfaced—put up for sale by the GI's heirs. The "Quedlinburg Treasure,'" which includes a reliquary shrine, a 10th-century bejeweled beard comb that belonged to Heinrich I (Henry the Fowler), the first German king, and a 15th-century gospel book, was returned in 1993 to the cathedral of St. Servatius (see below), where the objects had lain for centuries in the crypt.

For nearly 200 years, from Heinrich's refounding of Charlemagne's empire here in the tenth century, Quedlinburg was Germany's imperial city. More gatherings of kings, emperors, and church dignitaries were held in Quedlinburg than in any other German town. Quedlinburg was also one of Germany's major trading cities, a member of the Hanseatic League and the equal of Cologne, Mainz, and Magdeburg. It survived World War II unscathed.

Until reunification, Quedlinburg was considerably more run down than Goslar, in the western Harz mountains, and Wernigerode, its neighbor in the eastern Harz region (see below), towns that, like Quedlinburg, are known for their *Fachwerk* (half-timbered) buildings. But on virtually every street and square in Quedlinburg these days, scaffolding signals that major restoration efforts are underway.

Today, although Quedlinburg's population of 28,000 extends far beyond the winding picturesque streets of the **Altstadt** (Old Town), it's the Altstadt that makes the town remarkable. The half-timbered buildings span so many centuries and are so varied that they amount to a virtual textbook in the art of German Fachwerk. There are some 1,500 half-timbered houses still standing.

Above many of the house portals carved ribbons of wood bear the names and the dates of the first owners or biblical texts in Old German script, or are decorated with symbols— the sun, palmettos, and hexagons were the most popular. On what was once the town piper's house, at Marktkirchof

7–9, a trumpet is carved into the tower beam. At Lans Gasse 29, carved rope strands emblazon the façade of a notable Renaissance house.

The **Haus Grunhagen**, built in 1701 on the Marktplatz, with its ground-floor doors and windows like open, yawning mouths, is among the town's Baroque masterpieces. Diagonally across from it, on Marktplatz, Abundantia, the town's goddess of good luck, is carved above Quedlinburg's Renaissance **Rathaus** and a 14th-century statue of Roland signifies the town's independent status. Turn-of-the-century stained-glass windows inside the Rathaus depict the Saxon duke, Heinrich, receiving the German crown, and murals recount later episodes in Quedlinburg's history. At the other end of the Marktplatz there is a modern statue of the Münzenbergen musicians who used to come down from the hills behind the town to play on market days.

Other fine Fachwerk structures line Mühlgraben and can be seen along Schuhof, the former shoemakers' alley, and the Hölle. Along Breitestrasse and Schmalestrasse are 16th- and 17th-century houses whose window shutters became sales counters by day. The oldest house in town, at Steinbrucke 1, shows the goddess Flora scattering her flowers. Church spires in varying states of repair rise everywhere.

By following the street almost opposite the Hotel Bar on the Marktplatz and then turning left on Hohestrasse, you reach the little **Finkenherd** (Finch Rookery), a golden-yellow Fachwerk structure built in the 17th century on the legendary spot where Henry the Fowler is said to have been surprised while hunting birds and offered the German crown. Nearby, in the **Feininger Art Gallery**, at Finkenherd 5a, more than 100 engravings, lithographs, etchings, and paintings by the American artist Lyonel Feininger are displayed. The artwork was left behind with a friend and fellow teacher at Germany's Bauhaus School of Applied Art and Architecture when Feininger, who had left the United States to teach at the Bauhaus, heard that his work had been labeled "*entartet*" ("decadent") by the Hitler regime and fled his post in Germany to return to America in 1938.

At Schlossberg 12 is the half-timbered house where the fervid 18th-century poet Johann Gottlieb Klopstock lived. Klopstock is remembered today for his poem "Messiah," which was set to music by Georg Philipp Telemann. Close by at Wordgasse 3 is the Ständerbau, dating from 1310, which today houses the **Fachwerkbaumuseum** (Museum of Half-Timbering).

The **Schlossberg** (Castle Hill), with the 12th-century Romanesque cathedral of St. Servatius (also known as the Schlosskirche, or Castle Church) and Renaissance **castle** (closed for restoration at press time), rises above Schloss-platz and Wordgasse.

St. Servatius is a simple, graceful church whose historical association with Heinrich I eventually led to its appropriation by the Nazis. Heinrich I and his wife, Mathilde, were both buried in the cathedral crypt. Though Heinrich's remains later disappeared, Mathilde, who was canonized for her charitable work and her founding of a convent school, is still buried here. (The castle museum across the courtyard was for many centuries the residence of the abbess of the convent school founded by Mathilde.) It was in this cathedral crypt that the objects constituting the "Quedlinburg Treasure" were stored.

In Hitler's days the SS leader Heinrich Himmler transformed the Schlosskirche into a shrine dedicated to the National Socialist Party. Himmler had the religious furnishings removed and replaced the crucifix on the altar with a swastika. Because Heinrich I had been the founder of the first German Reich (the Holy Roman Empire), and Hitler viewed himself as the founder of the Third Reich, the church became the center of an SS cult. On the anniversary of Heinrich I's death Himmler would come to stand vigil in the cathedral crypt.

The Schlosskirche has been reconsecrated as a church, but the same nationalistic symbology used by the Nazis to link Heinrich I and the Third Reich may have played a part in the neo-Nazi riots and attacks on refugees that shook Quedlinburg (and other towns in Germany) in 1992.

For overnight stays in Quedlinburg try the newly renovated ▶ **Quedlinburger Hof** near the railway station, or ▶ **Zur Goldenen Sonne** in the Neustadt (New City). There are also bed-and-breakfast establishments.

There is good dining at the two hotels, and also at the **Goldener Ring**, Neuer Weg 1, Tel: (3946) 22-66 (closed Mondays); the **Munzenberger Klause**, Polle 22, Tel: (3946) 29-28 (closed Mondays); the **Schlosskrug am Dom**, Schlossberg 1, Tel: (3946) 28-38 (closed Mondays); and the **Ratskeller**, Tel: (3946) 27-68 (closed Wednesdays). To watch the life of the town, take a long afternoon coffee break out of doors at the **Café am Markt**, or at the **Café Finkenherd** on Hohestrasse.

Wernigerode

Located about 30 km (19 miles) west of Quedlinburg on route 6, Wernigerode is one of the most colorful villages in the Harz mountains. With its red-roofed half-timbered houses, its red-

and-blue and green-and-gold twin-turreted town hall on the marketplace, and its 19th-century Baroque-style castle set against a backdrop of mountains, Wernigerode has been charming visitors since the 1920s.

Even in the grim days of the German Democratic Republic Wernigerode sparkled in a way few other towns or cities in East Germany did. The GDR declared its old town center a national monument and restored it. For East Germans it became a favorite wedding and honeymoon spot.

Now, with Germany reunited, and with Wernigerode just a few miles from the former border, it is again attracting visitors in the hundreds of thousands. And with good reason. Wernigerode has more than 200 half-timbered houses to show off and offers fine walks along mountain paths.

In case you're wondering why so many shops here sell souvenir *Hexen* (witches), it's because the witches in Goethe's *Faust* flew to the nearby **Brocken**, the rocky height west of town, on Walpurgis Night for their annual revels with the Devil. Although it is now crowned by a devilishly ugly communications antenna, you won't need a broomstick to visit the Brocken plateau yourself. It is easily reached by taking the narrow-gauge train known as the Brockenbahn. The train runs west from Wernigerode, up the Brocken, and continues on to Drei-Annen-Hohne near Goslar in the western Harz Mountains (for which see The Harz Mountains section in our chapter The Center).

Among Wernigerode's lode of richly decorated houses the most fascinating is the 17th-century Baroque **Krummelische Hause** (Krummel House), at Breitestrasse 72, where a woman astride a crocodile was carved to represent America and another riding a fantasy animal symbolized Africa. Festooned above the doorway are carved garlands and cherubs' heads. The aptly named **Kleinstes Haus** (Smallest House) at Kochstrasse 43 is little more than nine feet wide. The house at Breitestrasse 72, built in 1674, has carving on every inch of it. More elegant carving may be seen on the façade of the 15th-century **Haus Gadenstadt** behind the Oberpfarrkirche, Wernigerode's principal church. The **castle**, reached by a pleasant climb through the woods above the town, houses a **museum** of feudal history.

Wernigerode abounds in attractive hotels and restaurants. The largest and grandest hotel is the ► **Weisser Hirsch**, at Markt 5. The recently renovated and substantially enlarged ► **Travel Hotel Gothisches Haus**, with an impressive half-timbered façade overlooking the Markt, has 102 rooms. Smaller and less expensive is ► **Zur Post** at Marktstrasse 17.

The ▶ **Hotel Deutsche Eiche** at Mühlental 36 has a pleasant setting but is a 15-minute walk from the center of town.

There is good food at the **Altstadt Klause**, Unteregengasse 14, Tel: (3943) 325-33, and **Zur Tanne**, Breitestrasse 59, Tel: (3943) 325-54. The **Café Wien** at Breitestrasse 4 charms with its 16th-century exterior and is the best place for *Kaffee und Kuchen*.

EISENACH

It has often been said that this town near the former West German border in the Thüringer Wald (Thuringian Forest), about 53 km (33 miles) west of Erfurt on the B 7 or Autobahn A 4, has been thrice blessed: Here Luther spent both his teenage years and the months in which he translated the New Testament from Greek into German; here in 1685 Bach was born; and here, in 1842, Richard Wagner saw the castle-fortress that rises above Eisenach and, inspired by it, wrote *Tannhäuser*.

Though World War II wreaked considerable damage on it, Eisenach, being relatively small (population 55,000), has had enough restoration so that much of it looks today as it must have looked in the 17th century. Its half-timbered houses are nestled in the valley below the forest of oaks and birches and lindens. From the **Wartburg**— once the castle home of the landgraves of Thüringen—you can look down on these pretty pastel houses with their red tile roofs.

From the spring of 1521 until December of that year, Luther remained in the hilltop castle above Eisenach. Charles V, the devoutly Catholic emperor of the Holy Roman Empire, had called the reformer-monk to Worms and ordered him to recant his criticisms. When Luther refused, he was declared a "notorious heretic." Though he was given a safe-conduct to return to his home in Wittenberg, the emperor vowed that action would be taken against him later. En route home Luther was "kidnapped" and spirited off, blindfolded, to the Wartburg. There his protectors had him discard his monk's robe for a knight's garb, grow his hair and a beard, and assume a knight's name and identity: He became "Junker Jörg." For nine months he was kept in the Wartburg in hopes that, while he was away, the furor over his activities would subside.

His small, simple room at the Wartburg looks today largely as it was then, furnished only with a table and a green tile stove, the whale vertebra he used as a footstool, a copy of the copper engraving his friend Lucas Cranach the Elder did of him as Junker Jörg, and Cranach paintings of Luther and Melanchthon hanging on the wall. In this room, Luther translated the New Testament from Greek into German in ten weeks, and in so doing virtually created the modern German language.

He was not happy in the Wartburg, however, the view of wind-tossed trees and spacious valley and red-tile village roofs below notwithstanding. He felt guilty being away from the people he thought he should be serving. When bats wheeled about the nearly deserted castle and owls hooted, he wondered if they were the Devil incarnate. (An ink spot on the wall of his room is said to have been made when he threw ink at the Devil.) Conquering his guilt and anxiety, he worked assiduously, and the visitor to the Wartburg today will find, on the table in his room, a copy of the German New Testament he prepared here.

On guided tours of the castle you also visit the Late Romanesque hall with a cross-vaulted ceiling that has been restored to give it the 12th-century look of the landgraves' time, and you will see the bright mid-19th-century frescoes that recount the history of the landgraves. Devotees of music and culture, the landgraves' hospitality to the minnesingers of medieval Germany was renowned, and the *Sängerkrieg* (a contest among minstrels) said to have been held in the fortress so captivated Wagner, visiting in the 19th century, that he made it an integral part of *Tannhäuser*.

Bright frescoes and murals recall the Sängerkrieg and the life of Saint Elisabeth of Hungary, the landgrave's wife who, as Elisabeth of Thuringia, performed great acts of generosity and mercy in the 13th century. Fifteenth- and 16th-century carvings and sculpture are also on display, and in the Jubilee Hall, notable for its acoustics, concerts are held in summer.

En route into town from the Wartburg you pass the **Reuter-Wagner Museum**, a villa at Reuterweg 2 that houses a collection of Wagner memorabilia said to be second only to the Wagner collection in Bayreuth in size, but of minimal interest to any but Wagner aficionados.

The musical memorabilia of Bach present quite a different story, however. From 1662 to 1741 Eisenach was a Saxon duchy whose rulers, like the Thüringen landgraves before them, were patrons of the arts. Though they had little money to pay musicians, year after year they invited them to their court. Most of the musicians soon went on to better-paying positions elsewhere, but not Johann Ambrosius Bach. And that was how it happened that Johann Sebastian Bach was born in Eisenach in 1685 to Johann Ambrosius and his wife, Elizabeth. Johann Sebastian was christened in the simple little **Georgenkirche** (St. George's Church), whose wrought-iron gate on the marketplace bears both his entwined initials and the cross and heart of Luther. (To earn his keep as a schoolboy in Eisenach, Luther sang in the choir and, later, as a fiery preacher, spoke from its pulpit.)

Though 12th-century in its original incarnation, the Georgenkirche bears few reminders of that period today. Heavily damaged in World War II, the interior is gray and gold with biblical texts in gold gleaming from its walls. It is notable for its 17th-century paintings of Luther and his reformer forerunner Jan Hus; of Luther's patron and protector, Friedrich the Wise; and of Holy Roman Emperor Charles V; for its Baroque pulpit; and for its 4,835-pipe organ.

Relatively little is known of Bach's early years in Eisenach, except that he sang a joyous soprano in church and was taught to play stringed instruments by his father and the organ by his uncle. When he was nine, his mother died; his father died a year later, and the young Bach was sent to live with an older brother. Although it is *not* a house in which he ever lived, Bach is remembered in Eisenach in the mustard-yellow, late-17th-century **Bachhaus**, at Frauenplan 21, not too far from the church.

The house, furnished much as it would have been in Bach's day, is filled with old engravings, letters, and documents about the Bach family. An English-language text explaining the displays is available. On the ground floor is a museum of Baroque instruments: lutes, cornetti, a viola da gamba, flutes, piccolos, a harpsichord, and a clavichord. A visit to the house—even if you are alone—is always accompanied by Bach music (live or recorded) played on one or more of these instruments.

Open to visitors, too, is the **Lutherhaus**, where, for two years, the teenaged Luther lived with family friends, the Cottas, and attended Latin school. The little, lopsided, 500-year-old half-timbered house at Lutherplatz 8, now the property of the German Evangelical Church, has, over the years, been put to different uses. It has had a stocking factory on the ground floor and has been a restaurant, but now it contains documents, illustrated Bibles of Luther's day, and memorabilia of his school years. The two small rooms that were his, with their windows angled for light, are furnished frugally, as they would have been in Luther's day.

Eisenach's other principal visitor attractions are the elegant Baroque palace museum of blue Thuringian porcelain, on the marketplace; the Romanesque **Nikolaikirche** (St. Nicholas' Church) on Karlsplatz; the 16th-century Late Gothic red Rathaus; and the many half-timbered dwellings that line the town's winding streets.

Staying and Dining in Eisenach

High up at the Wartburg castle, where Luther was forced to hide, visitors may now stay, too, at the ► **Wartburg Hotel,** a small hotel with a splendid view of the red tile roofs of the city below it. The Wartburg dining room features wild game and Thüringen specialties in a hunting-lodge atmosphere. Reservations required; Tel: (3691) 51-11.

Conversely, in the city below, but offering a superb view up to the Wartburg, is the ► **Fürstenhof** (formerly the Stadt Eisenach), at Luisenstrasse 11. The ► **Christliches Hospiz Glockenhof** at Grimmelgasse 4 is another possibility.

Satisfying fare—in addition to that served at the Wartburg Hotel—is offered at **Alt-Eisenach,** Karlstrasse 51, Tel: (3691) 760-88; at the **Hotel Berghof,** Am Burschenschaftsdenkmal, Tel: (3691) 37-46; **Mičik's Spezialitaten Restaurant,** Marienstrasse 4, Tel: (3691) 763-85; and the **Café-Restaurant Lackner** at Johannistrasse 22, Tel: (3691) 62-45-50. **Konditerei** and the **Kafe Bruheim** opposite the Bachhaus, and the **Boulevard Café** near Frauenplan, offer good cake and coffee.

Gotha

Twenty-eight kilometers (17 miles) east of Eisenach, Gotha, at the entrance to the Thüringer Wald, is today a largely modern city of 58,000. Its limited attractions include, again, old houses and the red Rathaus (Town Hall) at the market square, as well as the early Baroque **Schloss Friedenstein** above the city.

This 17th-century palace, with its immense courtyard and surrounding park, contains an extensive gallery of work by the 18th-century French sculptor Jean-Antoine Houdon; a roomful of Cranachs; Roman, Egyptian, and Greek artifacts; a **museum of the Middle Ages;** a **theater museum** with stage machinery from Baroque days; a 17th-century ivory collection; a globe collection; and richly decorated drinking vessels of the Baroque era. The palace interior itself is elaborately decorated with stucco garlands and gods, parquet floors, and gleaming crystal chandeliers.

The *Almanach de Gotha,* the registry of royal lineage that the world's royals hold in reverence, was started here in 1763. The court of Gotha in those days was small and quiet. (The disappointed English biographer James Boswell, stopping here in 1764, described the duke and duchess as "plain old people.") Members of the Saxon royal house were literary and scientific in their interests. French was the household language, and it was in French that the first

Almanach, largely an astronomical calendar, was written. The next year, the *Almanach* was expanded to include the genealogy of the house of Saxony and a list of the emperors of Germany.

By 1765 the considerably expanded *Almanach* was being printed in German and was filled with amusing anecdotes and such assorted information as the names of the best confectioners in Paris and the ambassadors of the leading nations. Though the *Almanach* still exists, it is no longer printed in Gotha and bears little resemblance to what it was when every duke born in the world was listed in it.

The last dukes to reside here were sons of England's Queen Victoria, invited at the turn of the century to rule the dukedom because there were no male heirs in Gotha. Albert, the queen's consort, was, after all, a prince of Saxe-Coburg-Gotha.

Gotha is also known as a town where the painter Lucas Cranach the Elder stayed for a time with his daughter, who was married to the burgomaster. His symbol, a crested, winged snake, and the bag that was the symbol of his son-in-law still embellish the house they occupied on the Hauptmarkt.

Mühlhausen

Genius, as Bach knew, does not pay the rent. Nor is it always recognized. And that is why Bach, after squabbling with the church officials in Arnstadt over money and his playing, accepted a post as organist at the parish church of **St. Blaise** in Mühlhausen, 37 km (23 miles) northwest of Gotha on route B 247. Today that soaring Gothic church is being restored. The visitor tends to be urged, instead, to visit the 14th-century **Barfüsserklosterkirche** (Barefoot Friars' Church), now a museum devoted to the 1525–1526 German Peasants' War, for it was here in Mühlhausen that the clergyman Thomas Münzer urged his farmer parishioners to fight taxation by the Church and the outrageous demands of their feudal landlords. The museum exhibits clothes of peasants and dukes, craftsmen and patricians of the day, and the pitchforks and scythes that were the peasants' weapons.

Beside St. Blaise's and the Peasants' War museum in Mühlhausen, there is the **Marienkirche** (St. Mary's Church), where Münzer was a clergyman. It is notable for its 1510 Gothic altar by a pupil of Tilman Riemenschneider and for the little white-and-gold screened area, built in 1608, in which town council members—and no one else—could sit during church services. There are also the 16th-century

Rathaus and several other churches to see—most only from the outside—and half-timbered houses on the town's narrow lanes.

ERFURT

One of the oldest cities in Germany, and one of the best-preserved, least war-damaged of all, Erfurt was a bishopric in 742. By the ninth century it was a prosperous trading post thanks to its location on the salt route between the north and south as well as on the road from Spain to Russia. It was even permitted to hold fairs, an honor that later was given to Leipzig. Today it is the capital of the state of Thuringia.

When 17-year-old Luther arrived here as a student in 1500, Erfurt, about 25 km (16 miles) due east of Gotha on what is now route 7, was called "Little Rome" for its 40 churches and 13 monasteries. There were monks and nuns and priests everywhere, attracted by Erfurt's notable university, which, founded in 1392, was one of Germany's first.

The university is no more, having been closed in 1816 (though efforts are underway to revive it), but there are still 22 churches and one monastery, and it is above all to see two of those churches, the Catholic Dom (cathedral) and the Lutheran Severikirche (Church of St. Severus), that visitors come to this medieval city on the Gera river. To reach them, set side by side high on the Domhügel, a hill near the center of town, there are 48 stone steps to climb, but no one seems to mind.

The **Dom** was started in the 12th century and rebuilt in the 14th century in Gothic style. It is constructed on arches of stone that in their day were innovative indeed. Its 15th-century stained-glass window—blue, gold, rose, and red—is, art historians say, one of the most precious in all of Germany. There is an enormous 12th-century mural of a red-cloaked Saint Christopher; a 16th-century Peter Vischer the Younger bronze titled *Coronation of the Virgin;* a 12th-century Romanesque Madonna; and a distinctly modern-looking 12th-century bronze candelabrum. And from one of the cathedral towers, the second-largest bell in Germany, the Gloriosa (weighing more than 13 tons and surpassed in size only by the bell in Cologne's cathedral), rings out on Christmas and Easter. It was in this cathedral that Luther was ordained, in 1507.

Beside it, the gracefully spired **Severikirche**, built in the 14th century, is known for its Late Gothic baptismal font and for the 14th-century reliefs on its altar.

Though Luther entered Erfurt university in the faculty of

arts, received his master's degree in arts, and began after that to study law, his life plan was irrevocably changed, so the story goes, one July afternoon in 1505.

Walking in the countryside, he was caught in a thunderstorm. Instead of seeking cover he hurried on through the lightning and thunder and downpour, for he was only a half mile from town. But there in the open country a lightning bolt seared the ground beside him—close enough to knock him down. Though uninjured, he was terrified. Realizing how close he had come to death, he promised himself to God. Two weeks later Luther changed his course of study at the university to theology and entered the **Augustinerkloster** on Augustinerstrasse. Today's followers of Luther in Erfurt visit the cathedral where he was ordained, walk in the monastery's Renaissance courtyard, and go to the Gothic **Augustinerkirche** (Church of St. Augustine), where as a young man seeking salvation Luther often flung himself on the cold stone floor.

Erfurt suffered relatively little damage in World War II (500 houses were destroyed but only three of historic value). The monastery, however, was struck by a bomb, and reconstruction has been necessary.

The visitor arriving here by train faces a short walk directly down Bahnhofstrasse past the 12th-century Gothic **Predigerkirche** (Preacher's Church) to the central square and main shopping area of the town, **Der Anger**. In an imposing Baroque building—once the weighing house—where Bahnhofstrasse meets Der Anger is the **Anger Museum** of Thuringian pottery and medieval art.

Across Der Anger is Hermann-Johann-Strasse, which leads in turn to the Fischmarkt in the Altstadt. If you continue west from the Fischmarkt down Marktstrasse you'll come to the Domplatz. In the opposite direction, the street beside the elaborately decorated 19th-century Rathaus goes down to the Gera river. If you cross the Anger and turn left, then make a right at the Wigbertikirche, you will reach the **Barfüsserkirche** on Barfüsserstrasse, where Luther preached one of his last sermons and which is now used for organ recitals.

Around in Erfurt

Commercial town that Erfurt was, its enterprising tradesmen built homes and shops on the bridge that crossed its river as part of the Russian route. This 12th-century **Krämerbrücke** (Tradesman's Bridge), not unlike Florence's Ponte Vecchio, still stands, with art and antiques for sale today in what were goldsmiths' and spice merchants' shops in the Middle Ages.

It is the only bridge of its kind north of Italy. From either the span itself or the park below, where the pastel-colored half-timbered houses on top are reflected in the Gera, the bridge is a picturesque sight.

Picturesque, too, are the elaborate Renaissance façades of Erfurt's patrician houses, many of them built from the trade in woad, a locally produced blue vegetable dye that, to the sorrow of the town's businessmen, was displaced when indigo was brought back from the Far East.

Erfurt's most prosperous periods were in the 14th and early 15th centuries and again in the mid-16th century. These were the years of structures like the golden-yellow 1562 **Haus zum Roten Ochsen** (House of the Red Oxen), on the Fischmarkt, embellished with the carving of an ox over the door, a frieze of muses, the heads of gods—and with the Devil on the pediment. (If the Devil saw himself, he would be afraid and stay out of a house, or so it was thought then.) Another Fischmarkt treasure is the step-gabled **Haus zum Breiten Herd** (House of the Broad Hearth; 1582), with its colorful reliefs illustrating the five senses—a woman looking in a mirror, playing music, smelling a rose, eating an apple, and touching a bird. Two other fine Renaissance houses are the **Alter Schwan** (Old Swan), on Gotthardstrasse near the Krämer bridge, and the Gothic **Haus zur Hohen Lilie** (House of the Tall Lily; 1538), on the Domplatz. The 1604 **Haus zum Stockfisch**, on Johannesstrasse, also has a façade worth seeing. Near it, on Juri-Gagarin-Ring, is a good museum of Thuringian folk art, including carnival masks, toys, Christmas decorations, and farm implements from Thuringia's past. Set on the river in Erfurt's Little Venice, the **Bursa Pauperum**, now privately owned, was a hostel for needy students in the Middle Ages.

Michaelisstrasse, in the Altstadt, is the location of a number of venerable buildings. The Early Gothic **Michaelis-kirche** (Church of St. Michael), where Luther preached in 1522, dates from the 13th century, the **Haus zum Goldenen Stern** (House of the Golden Star) from the 15th, and the few remaining ruins of the university from the 14th.

A curiosity of some of Erfurt's old houses is a round hole in the façade. University professors' wives would place a wisp of straw there on the days they brewed beer, signaling neighbors to come in and have some.

In the quarter off Marktstrasse around the half-timbered, sprawling **Waidspecher Theater**, once a woad warehouse, many of the dwellings of the past have been reconstructed. Among those partly salvaged (its 16th-century door and the Renaissance painting in one of its rooms are original) is the **Haus zum Sonneborn**, the city's registry office and a favorite spot for weddings. It is found on a little lane called Grosse Arche.

In 1808, during the French occupation, Napoleon stayed at the **Statthalteri** (Governor's Residence) on Regierung-strasse near the Anger district. It was here that he grandly entertained Alexander I of Russia and the kings of Bavaria, Saxony, Westphalia, and Württemberg. Among his guests were Goethe and his fellow poet, Christoph Martin Wieland.

Seeking the Russian tsar as an ally, Napoleon imported the Comédie Française from Paris to impress him. He surely impressed Goethe, who said he considered the emperor of France "the greatest mind the world has ever seen" and was rewarded for his admiration by being invited to Paris. In Paris, Napoleon temptingly told the then-resident of little Weimar, "You will find a larger circle for your spirit of observation . . . immense material for your poetic creations." (Goethe, however, turned him down.)

A totally different aspect of contemporary Erfurt is the permanent 250-acre Internationale Gartenbau Ausstellung (International Landscaping and Horticultural Exhibition, or IGA) at Cyriaxberg, on the southwestern outskirts of town. In the 18th century, when woad dye was replaced by indigo, the land previously planted in woad was replaced with flowers, and by the end of the 19th century the development of flower seeds had become a major industry in Erfurt. Now, in all seasons, there are floral displays at the IGA.

Staying and Dining in Erfurt

Up to now, hotel rooms have been scarce in this Thuringian capital, but a new IC Hotel, linked with the InterCity rail service, is scheduled to open next to the train station in February 1994, as well as the ▶ **Bauer Hotel Excelsior** on Bahnhofstrasse. The venerable ▶ **Erfurter Hof**, near the railway station on Willy Brandt Platz, has a certain charm and a restaurant where you can sample the sausage for which Thuringia is famous as well as *Sauerbraten mit Klössen* (marinated beef with potato dumplings). There have been recent renovations of both the hotel and the **Keller-Restaurant**, and service is helpful, with considerable English spoken. The high-rise ▶ **Hotel Kosmos** on Juri-Gagarin-Ring and the new ▶ **Hotel Ibis** on Barfüsserstrasse are also overnight possibilities. The ▶ **Hotel Cyriaksburg** on Cyriaks-strasse is a turn-of-the-century industrialist's mansion in a posh residential area that the Communist regime turned into a guest house for top party officials. It is in a green and peaceful setting, albeit a long walk from public transport. Even if you don't stay here, its dining room is worth trying.

Some of the best dining in the city is found at the **Gildehaus**, Fischmarkt 13, Tel: (361) 232-73; and at the **Museumgaststätte**, Juri-Gagarin-Ring 140a, Tel: (361) 266-41; and **Weinrestaurant Horst Kohl**, Neuwerkstrasse 31/32, Tel: (361) 642-25-61. Five minutes west of the city, the **Weinrestaurant Caponniere** on the IGA grounds is popular; Tel: (361) 264-95.

The **Café zur Krämerbrücke** offers fine coffee and cake at the foot of the Krämerbrücke, as do the **E.A. Grafik Café** at Kurschenerstrasse 8 near the Krämerbrücke, the **Angereck** at Am Angereck 61, and the **Kaffee Mühle** at the newly opened Mühlenmuseum (Mill Museum) at Schlosserstrasse 25A.

Arnstadt

In Arnstadt, 18 km (11 miles) south of Erfurt, Bach enthusiasts can visit the blue-and-white Baroque **Bonifatiuskirche** (Church of St. Boniface), just off the market square. Here, young Bach held his first job as an organist, from 1703 to 1707.

Arnstadt is a charming little town with a mauve Rathaus that boasts a gilded clock behind a statue of Bach. One turret of its 16th-century castle still stands, and arcades line its market square. A special delight in the **Stadtmuseum** (City Museum) at Schlossplatz 21 is *Mon Plaisir,* 80 Baroque and Rococo miniature settings put together in the early 18th century by Countess Augusta Dorothea von Schwarzburg-Arnstadt with the help of Arnstadt craftsmen. The settings depict, among other things, a period cooper's shop, an apothecary shop, a shoe shop, the candlelit Arnstadt market square, a wine cellar, nuns at table, billiard players, a barber, ladies at tea, and a musicale. Four hundred costumed dolls people the settings.

Bach had a light schedule in Arnstadt. Playing only for Sunday services, Monday prayers, and Thursday morning service, he was relatively free to do his own composing— and did. He wrote his first works for the organ here as well as some toccatas and chorale preludes. But he annoyed church officials by overstaying a three-month leave in Lübeck, where he studied with the master organist Dietrich Buxtehude. As the story goes, Bach, who walked the 250 miles between Arnstadt and Lübeck, hoped he would be offered the opportunity to inherit Buxtehude's position as organist at the Marienkirche. But with the job, he discovered, came Buxtehude's daughter as bride. Bach declined her on the grounds that she was too old for him, and was thus not offered the job. (Handel was also a candidate, made a similar trek from Halle, and turned down the post for the same reason.) When he returned to Arnstadt, church officials complained about the way he accompanied the choirs, and there was continual fussing over money. When Bach was offered the post of organist at the parish church of St. Blaise in Mühlhausen, he accepted.

WEIMAR

In a golden-yellow house in this town on the River Ilm, 24 km (15 miles) east of Erfurt, Goethe spent the greater part of his life writing, painting, collecting art and minerals, philosophizing, and theorizing. Here he completed his masterpiece, *Faust.* A street or two away, in another golden Baroque house, his friend Schiller busily worked on his drama *Wilhelm Tell,* which was destined to become Rossini's opera of the same name.

A statue of the two writers, side by side, stands today outside the **Deutsches Nationaltheater** (German National Theater), on the site where many of their works were performed. Here, too, in 1919, the constitution for the so-called Weimar Republic, which sought to bring democracy to Germany after World War I, was drafted. (Weimar itself was never the *capital* of the republic; Berlin was.)

For four centuries literature, music, and art had lent their glory to this tranquil ducal seat. Then, with the 20th century, the shadows fell as the Weimar Republic faltered and collapsed. Hitler, risen to power, expounded his Third Reich views from the balcony of Weimar's leading hotel, and the concentration camp of Buchenwald was established in the Weimar woods nearby.

But in the heart of the Altstadt, among Baroque and Renaissance houses, cobblestone courtyards, castle turrets, and onion-domed church towers, it is easy to forget that more recent past. Construction projects somewhat destroy the illusion, but with a little imagination they can also seem a part of the era when civic-minded Goethe, who had taken on responsibility for street building, was becoming disgruntled and disappointed with what he was able to accomplish in his post.

The modern Weimar of broad avenues, clanging trams, tree-lined streets, and 19th-century buildings surrounds the old town.

The **Altstadt** (Old City), in which both the Goethe and Schiller houses stand, is a small, easily walked area on the left bank of the river. From 1782 to 1832 Goethe lived and wrote in his house (the so-called Goethehaus) on Frauenplan, off the market square. Just up the Frauenplan, on the street that today bears his name, lived Schiller. At Schillerstrasse's other end, on Theaterplatz, was Duchess Anna Amalia's house, with the German National Theater next door. The Stadtkirche on Herder Platz, where the philosopher-theologian Johann Gott-fried von Herder preached, and the duke's palace at Burgplatz are less than a ten-minute stroll from the Goethe house.

In Weimar's pastoral river park, also within strolling dis-tance, is the rustic dwelling (now known as the Gartenhaus) where the young Goethe sowed his wild oats during his first Weimar years, as well as a Roman Renaissance house that he helped design. At the park's west entrance, on Marienstrasse, is the house where Franz Liszt summered in the late 19th century. It was across the street that the Bauhaus school of architecture and applied arts developed in the 1920s.

Goethe had arrived in the duchy of Weimar in 1775 at the invitation of teenaged Duke Karl August, who wished to fill his court with entertaining, clever people. Thanks to Goethe and his friends, the little duchy, then with a population of about 6,000, gained renown as a center of German Classi-cism. Herder, Goethe's mentor, and poet-novelist Christoph Martin Wieland were members in good standing of Weimar's Court of the Muses. Setting the tone for it all was Duchess Anna Amalia, widowed mother of the duke and niece of Frederick the Great of Prussia.

World War II bombing did considerable damage to both the Goethe and Schiller houses. Both, however, have been restored, and the **Goethehaus** is furnished with Goethe's own belongings. In his first years here, in the little garden house on the Ilm river, Goethe had virtually abandoned writing as he sought favor with the duke, joining him at social events and burdening himself with civic responsibili-ties. Goethe took charge not only of road building in the duchy but of transportation and mining as well, and he also directed the court theater. The inefficiency of the bureau-cratic system and the frivolity of court life became too much for him, however, and in the dead of night, dressed as the artist he had decided to become, he fled Weimar for Italy.

When Goethe returned to Weimar, in 1788, he was over-flowing with enthusiasm for things Italian. He replaced the Baroque staircase of the house on Frauenplan with broad stairs in the Italian Renaissance tradition. Enamored, too, of Classical art, he filled the house with plaster casts of ancient busts and statues, and designed special cabinets to display his Italian majolica plates.

Believing that colors affect one's frame of mind, Goethe painted his dining room a sunny yellow, his study a soothing green; and the reception room—in which he greeted such guests as the philosopher Johann Gottfried Fichte and the geographer Alexander von Humboldt—blue. Minerals were another of his interests, and glass-topped display cases contain part of his collection of 18,000 minerals and gemstones. Copies of Goethe's drawings of his buxom wife, Christiane, and their son, Augustus, are on exhibit here, too.

The house is large but not grand. "A surrounding of comfortable, pretty furniture paralyzes my thoughts and brings me into an easy passive condition," Goethe wrote. "Splendid rooms and elegant furniture unless we are used to them from youth are for people who have no thoughts and desire none."

Goethe was 82 when he died in his sparsely furnished little bedchamber. He and Schiller are buried together in a hilltop mausoleum in the historic **Weimar cemetery** off Poseckchen Garten. (Buried there, too, in a curious Russian-Greek chapel, is Duke Karl August's Russian daughter-in-law, Maria Pavlovna.)

The **Schillerhaus**, which stands where Frauenplan meets Schillerstrasse, reflects less of that writer's personality, furnished as it is with period—but not the writer's—pieces. It was on the attic wall here that Schiller one day tacked a map of Switzerland and immersed himself in volumes on Swiss travel and history. Drinking black coffee, pausing for meals and rest (but often falling asleep with his head on his arms), he did not stop working for six weeks until *Wilhelm Tell* was finished. In the rooms below, his wife and children led normal lives. Also in the vicinity of the Schiller house is the Renaissance **Grünes Schloss** (Green Palace), which houses the handsome Rococo **Anna Amalia Bibliothek** (Library), filled with the works of Weimar's great writers.

A short walk along Schillerstrasse leads to the elegant **Wittumspalais** (Widow's Palace), where Anna Amalia gathered her salon of artists and poets, doctors and philosophers, to discuss contemporary problems of science, metaphysics, and art. Silhouettes, popular in her day, and an extensive collection of fashion paintings decorate the walls of the dwelling, into which the duchess moved after a fire had devastated her castle. Today the reconstructed onion-domed **Residenzschloss** is a museum rich in the works of Renaissance-Reformation artist Lucas Cranach the Elder and his son, for the elder Cranach, too, was once a Weimar resident. His house, gaily decorated with mermaids, stands on the **Marktplatz.**

On the same square are the Flamboyant Gothic **Rathaus** and the 17th-century **Flamberg Hotel Elephant.** Thomas Mann (who wrote of the hotel in *The Beloved Returns*) and Adolf Hitler have been among its guests; it was from its balcony that Hitler announced delightedly—in 1944—that Germany was winning the war.

At the foot of the square, Kaufstrasse leads to the black-spired Flamboyant Gothic **Stadtkirche** (City Church), which holds one of the elder Cranach's finest paintings (completed by his son), an altarpiece depicting the Crucifixion, with likenesses of Luther, Philipp Melanchthon, and the artist himself at the foot of the Cross. Herder, by whose name the church is sometimes known, came to it as court preacher in 1776.

In the **Kirms-Krakow-Haus**, nearby at Jakobstrasse 10, a museum recalls Herder's influence on German literature, particularly his insistence on German writers expressing their own nationality in their works rather than, as was the fashion of the time, aping French masters. (For more on Herder from a modern perspective, see various works of Sir Isaiah Berlin.)

Bach lived in Weimar, too, but left in disgrace after he infuriated the duke by asking to leave his post of court conductor, and was briefly imprisoned for his ingratitude; no house he inhabited here is dedicated to his memory.

The handsomely furnished high-ceilinged **Liszthaus**, where Hungarian-born Liszt gathered young musicians around him in the late 19th century, sits at the west entrance to Ilm park. In its red-carpeted salon stands one of his pianos as well as the portable clavichord he used to keep his fingers limber when he was travelling. There, as well, are his Hungarian passport and facsimiles of letters from Felix Mendelssohn, Robert Schumann, and Johannes Brahms.

Goethe's Gartenhaus is in the park on the other side of the river. It lies across a footbridge from which, it is said, a young actress, unhappy in love, flung herself into the Ilm after reading Goethe's novel of suicide, *The Sorrows of Young Werther*. A souvenir of the Goethe Italian period is the **Römisches Haus** (Roman House), designed by the poet in the style of a Roman Renaissance house. In the park, too, is a grotto of his design memorializing the dead actress.

Across Marienstrasse from the Liszt house is a reminder of another aspect of Weimar's cultural history: The school that now stands there was, from 1919 to 1925, the **Bauhaus school**, where the modern concept of the craftsman-designer originated. Expressionists, among them the Russian Wassily Kandinsky, the Swiss Paul Klee, the American Lyonel Feininger, and the Hungarian architect and furniture designer Marcel Breuer, served on its faculty. Sleek early *Jugendstil* furniture by the Belgian Henry van de Velde may now be seen in the newly opened **Nietzsche Archive and Memorial** at Humboldtstrasse 36. It was here that the late-19th-century philosopher Friedrich Wilhelm Nietzsche spent his last years. It was Nietzsche's vision of a "superman" who would create a new morality that was misinterpreted by the Nazis to justify their ideas of racial superiority.

About 9 km (5½ miles) northwest of Weimar, at the end of a pine-lined road beyond Ernst-Thälmannstrasse, are the remains of the concentration camp of **Buchenwald**, which stood here from 1937 to 1945. Of the camp, where 65,000 victims of Nazism died, only the old SS barracks, the original gate building and detention house, the crematorium, the old canteen, roads, and a museum remain.

Originally built to hold 8,000 prisoners, 86,000 inmates were crowded into it by 1945 and forced to work in armament factories erected on the grounds. After the prisoners freed themselves in 1945, the concentration camp was used until 1950 as an internment camp for former Nazi officials.

A stone bell tower, a winding path symbolizing the prisoners' suffering, mass graves marked with eternal flames, and a monument honoring the victims have been erected at the camp entrance.

Staying and Dining in Weimar

The 205-room ► **Weimar Hilton** opened in 1992 on the Ilm, with a swimming pool and sauna as well as two restaurants.

For more than 200 years the charming ► **Flamberg Hotel Elephant**, on Marktplatz, has welcomed such notables as Bach, Liszt, and Wagner. The hotel was recently repainted and refurbished, and private baths have been added to many of the rooms. Its sweeping staircase invites climbing (there is also an elevator). English is spoken by some of the reception staff, all of whom are courteous and welcoming. The Elephant's restaurants, among the most highly regarded in the city, are big and lacking in intimacy, but the food is reasonably good in both the **Stadt Weimar** and the **Elephantenkeller**. The ► **Hotel Russischer Hof** on Goetheplatz is another overnight possibility.

Among the better restaurants outside hotels are the **Gastmahl des Meeres**, Am Herderplatz 16, Tel: (3643) 647-21; the **Grabenschänke**, which specializes in Thuringian dishes, Am Graben 8, Tel: (3643) 621-07; the **Gasthausbrauerei Felsenkeller**, Humboldtstrasse 37, Tel: (3643) 619-41 or 42, also offering Thuringian fare; the **Ratskeller**, Am Markt, Tel: (3643) 641-42; and **Sommer's Weinstube-Pilsstube**, Humboldstrasse 2, Tel: (3643) 659-19. The **Café Sperling**, Schillerstrasse 18, and the **Goethe Café**, Wielandstrasse 4, are popular for cake and coffee.

Ballet and opera as well as drama are performed at the

historic national theater, whose company Goethe once directed. Ask at your hotel about tickets. (The theater is closed in summer.)

LEIPZIG

Bach spent 27 of the most productive years of his life in Leipzig, which is northeast of Weimar and 160 km (99 miles) southwest of Berlin. Its concert hall, the **Neues Gewand-haus**, replaced the one that was demolished in World War II and is the most unusual (there is not a right angle in it) in Germany—a far cry from its origins in 1780 in a genuine *Gewandhaus,* a cloth merchant's trade hall. Its 200-member orchestra today is ranked as one of the world's finest, and its incumbent director, Kurt Masur, became director of the New York Philharmonic in 1991. Leipzig's monumental **Opern-haus** (Opera House), completed in 1960, was the first of its kind to be opened in East Germany after the war. The **Thomanerchor** (Bach came to Leipzig to be the choir's director) continues to be headquartered at the Thomas-kirche (St. Thomas' Church) and performs on Fridays, Saturdays, and Sundays. (It is best to check the schedule with the tourist office.) Leipzig was also the birthplace, in 1813, of Wagner as well as the workplace of Mendelssohn (it was he, as conductor of the Gewandhaus in the 1830s, who first established its reputation). Robert Schumann attended its university, once world famous, to study law at about the same time, but was quickly lured into its musical world instead, and eventually married his piano teacher's daughter, Clara Wieck.

With a population of 530,000, Leipzig is one of the larger cities in Germany and is accordingly lively. Goethe, who studied here in the 1760s, called it "Paris in miniature." For years to come Leipzig also will be known as the city where the revolt that brought an end to Communist rule in Germany began.

Lying at the junction of two trade routes—one running east–west between Poland and the province of Thuringia, the other north–south between North Germany and Bohemia—Leipzig has been a bustling city of fairs since the 12th century. To ensure its success as a fair city, Holy Roman Emperor Maximilian I decreed in the 16th century that no other community within a wide radius could have an annual market. Twice a year, usually the first week in September and the second week in March, Leipzig is still the site of trade fairs that bring exhibitors and visitors to its

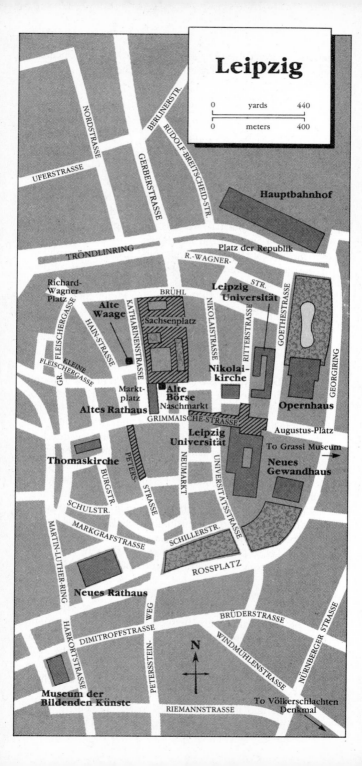

Leipzig

| 0 | yards | 440 |
| 0 | meters | 400 |

Hauptbahnhof

NORDSTRASSE

UFERSTRASSE

BERLINERSTR.

RUDOLF-BREITSCHEID-STR.

GERBERSTRASSE

TRÖNDLINRING

Platz der Republik

R.-WAGNER-

STR.

Richard-
Wagner-
Platz

BRÜHL

Leipzig
Universität

GOETHESTRASSE

GEORGIRING

Alte Waage

Sachsenplatz

NIKOLAISTRASSE

RITTERSTRASSE

FLEISCHERGASSE

HAIN-STRASSE

KATHARINENSTRASSE

KLEINE
FLEISCHERGASSE

GR.

Markt-
platz

Alte
Börse

Nikolai-
kirche

Naschmarkt

Altes Rathaus

GRIMMAISCHE STRASSE

Opernhaus

Thomaskirche

PETERS-
STRASSE

BURGSTR.

Leipzig
Universität

NEUMARKT

UNIVERSITÄTSSTRASSE

Augustus-Platz

To Grassi Museum

Neues
Gewandhaus

SCHULSTR.

MARKGRAFSTRASSE

SCHILLERSTR.

MARTIN-LUTHER-RING

ROSSPLATZ

Neues Rathaus

BRÜDERSTRASSE

HARKORTSTRASSE

DIMITROFFSTRASSE

PETERSTEIN-
WEG

WINDMÜHLENSTRASSE

NÜRNBERGER STRASSE

N

Museum der
Bildenden Künste

RIEMANNSTRASSE

To Völkerschlachten
Denkmal

more than 24 acres of pavilions and exhibition halls, where machinery, tools, books, clothes, agricultural equipment, chemicals, sporting goods, plants, and furs and skins are shown. Even though Hannover has now become united Germany's major industrial fair site, fair time in Leipzig is *not* the time for tourists to visit.

Thousands of students at its three universities, among them Leipzig university (on Augustus-Platz), founded in the 15th century by dissidents from Prague, give Leipzig a lively edge. The university lists among its past students not only Schumann and Goethe but also Wagner and the philosopher Fichte. The 34-story jagged tower of today's university (nick-named the "Broken Tooth") has become a symbol of contem-porary Leipzig. For the visitor, however, the university offers little of interest.

Relatively little of old Leipzig stands. A quarter of the city was destroyed by bombing in 1943, and the emphasis has been much more on constructing the new—square modern apartment complexes and exhibition halls, wide pedestrian streets, and big squares—than on restoring the old. But most of both the old and the new Leipzig that has appeal for visitors is concentrated in a small, easily walked area encir-cled by ring roads.

The Markt is the center of the old city; the Augustus-Platz dominates the new. Touristic sites outside this center, which can be reached by tram, are the art museum, the monument to the Battle of the Nations, the Russian memorial church, the zoo, the Grassi Museum complex, and the fairgrounds.

The Old City

At the Markt and the Naschmarkt (Snack Market) and their environs, bits of old Leipzig have been reconstructed. On the east side of the **Marktplatz**, the long gabled Renaissance **Altes Rathaus** has been rebuilt and is now the museum of the city of Leipzig, containing a history of the fairs. Originally constructed in 1556, the golden-yellow arcaded Renaissance city hall is notable for its Baroque clock tower. In its elabo-rate festival hall, which survived the war, hang life-size portraits of the electors of Saxony (the old German duchy of which Leipzig was a part). Also in the Altes Rathaus is a room of Mendelssohn memorabilia and a memorial to Bach.

Reconstructed on the north side of the square is the step-gabled Renaissance **Alte Waage** (Old Weighing House), where foreign imports to the fairs used to be weighed. Across from the Alte Waage is the 17th-century **Königshaus**, used by the rulers of Saxony on their visits to Leipzig. Later it served as a royal guest house, providing hospitality for, among others, Peter the Great of Russia and Napoleon. Today it houses a shop of expensive fashionable goods.

In the neighboring **Naschmarkt**, behind a statue of Goethe as a student, rises the blue-and-white Baroque **Alte Börse** (Old Stock Exchange, currently under construction), with sweeping stairs and stucco garlands above the windows.

To the south of the Markt, in the covered arcade of shops and restaurants that is the **Mädlerpassage,** you'll find Leipzig's most famous restaurant, **Auerbachs Keller.** The original stood here long before Goethe's student days. The poet immortalized it when he had Faust ride away from it on a wine cask with Mephistopheles. In 1912 the first Auerbachs Keller was torn down and the new one created, with statues at its door of Mephistopheles and Faust with his fellow student revelers.

Another interesting restaurant is the 17th-century **Zum Kaffeebaum** (Coffee Tree), on Kleine Fleischergasse, with a Baroque carving of a Turk under a coffee tree above its front door. Liszt, Goethe, Wagner, and Schumann all gathered here. It was a particular favorite of Schumann and his musical friends, who spent long hours in one of the downstairs rooms at work on the *New Journal for Music* that Schumann edited.

A short walk in the neighborhood of the Markt leads to the pastel Baroque burgher houses along **Katharinenstrasse** and the **Brühl.** The most famous and handsomest of these is the tawny yellow **Romanushaus,** on Katharinenstrasse where it meets the Brühl. Its 18th-century owner, Franz Conrad Romanus, is said to have stolen city funds for the construction of his impressive residence, with its 13 rows of windows, its gables and pilasters, and an oriel window at the corner, along with a statue of a flirtatious Hermes, a finger to his nose. Romanus's happy days in his house were cut short by a prison term, but he is remembered here in a more favorable light for his introduction of a sedan-chair service for theatergoers as well as for installing the city's first streetlights.

The tourist information center, where museum hours are listed and concert schedules can be obtained, is just off the Brühl on Sachsenplatz, a giant square of modern flats and fountains decorated with Christmas ornament–like balls. The Brühl itself, wide and modern, continues to be the center of the fur trade, as it has been for generations. Skins and ready-made fox, beaver, and mink garments fill its windows in the fall. In the sweeping pink-and-gray restored building across from it on Richard-Wagner-Platz is the Café am Brühl, once popular with the theater world but now, unfortunately, distinctly mediocre.

A block east of the Markt stands the 12th-century **Niko-**

laikirche (St. Nicholas' Church), where thousands of demon-
strators assembled in 1989, bearing placards and banners
demanding changes in the Communist government that led,
ultimately, to its capitulation. A block west rises the high-
pitched roof of the 1,000-year-old Gothic **Thomaskirche**, to
which Bach came at the age of 38 to be cantor and director
of the boys' choir, and director of music at the university. He
stayed in Leipzig the rest of his life. Here he did his finest
work, writing more than 300 cantatas, the *Passion According
to St. Matthew*, and the Mass in B-minor. But for all his
productivity, these were also frustrating years for him. Bach
wanted more and better singers and musicians than the city
councillors were prepared to provide. He had not been
their first choice for the post he occupied, and they never let
him forget it.

The years, however, have surely made Bach Leipzig's most
venerated citizen. A more-than-life-size statue of him stands
outside the Thomaskirche, and he is buried in its choir.
Fresh flowers are placed each day on the tablet beneath
which he lies, and he is memorialized in the 19th-century
stained-glass windows along with other luminaries, including Luther, who preached in the church in 1539 to herald the
Reformation; Luther's friend Melanchthon; various mayors of
Leipzig; and a number of electors of Saxony.

Just across the street from the church, the restored house
of a Bach family friend, the merchant Heinrich Georg Bose,
has a first-floor museum devoted to the composer's Leipzig
years, and a lovely small concert hall. Nearly 2,000 Bach
books, articles, tapes, and records are now kept in the **Bose
house**'s Bach archives.

Outside the Old City

The cultural heart of modern Leipzig is **Augustus-Platz**. The
immense, architecturally undistinguished new opera house
stands on the north side of the square; the **Neues Gewandhaus** (Bruno Walter and Wilhelm Furtwängler, in addition to
Mendelssohn, have been among the distinguished conductors of its orchestra) and Leipzig university are opposite. On
top of the Krochhaus, a 1927 version of a square-towered
Florentine building—Leipzig's first high rise—bell ringers
strike the hours.

Even more mammoth than the opera house is the cavernous 1907–1915 Hauptbahnhof (main railway station), a few
blocks north of Augustus-Platz, one of the largest train depots
in Europe, with 26 tracks inside a shell of steel and glass.
Though still in use, it is undergoing extensive renovations.

In the southwestern part of the city rises the **Neues Rathaus**. Its 13th-century turret, part of the fortress that once occupied the site, is perched anachronistically in the center of the turn-of-the-century structure. Nearby, in the monumental former supreme court building, is the **Museum der Bildenden Künste** (Fine Arts Museum). In addition to modern German works, the art museum contains paintings by such old German masters as Martin Schongauer and Lucas Cranach the Elder; Flemish masters such as Jan van Eyck, Rembrandt, and Rubens; and the Italian painters Tiepolo, Guardi, and Raphael.

On the tram line from the Hauptbahnhof, about 5 km (3 miles) southeast of the city center, on a site above a man-made lake, is the **Völkerschlachtdenkmal**, a brown stone mausoleum that commemorates the Battle of the Nations against Napoleon in 1813. Here, Russians, Prussians, Austrians, Bavarians, and Swedes roundly defeated the French emperor as he retreated from his disastrous Russian campaign. The 150,000 casualties the monument honors include Gustav Adolf, the king of Sweden, who nearsightedly ran into the enemy army in a fog. (A golden-domed Russian memorial church near the fairground commemorates the 22,000 Russians killed here.) The determined visitor can climb the 500 steps to the top of the monument, pausing to look into the Hall of Honor, and get a view of Leipzig itself in the distance (on smog-free days, which are not frequent).

Known as the City of Lions (a pet lion is said to have saved his knight-master from the Devil here in medieval times), Leipzig has a zoo that, appropriately, specializes in the breeding of lions. The zoo is ordinary, and not worth a visit unless the tourist office can verify that cubs are present.

A good collection of antique musical instruments, including those of the Bach period, are on display at the **musical instrument museum**, in the **Grassimuseum complex** east of Augustus-Platz at Täubchenweg 2.

Staying in Leipzig

Leipzig has more and better accommodations than most eastern German cities. The 474-room Japanese-built ▶ **Hotel Intercontinental Leipzig**, which opened on Gerberstrasse in 1981, is strikingly modern, with a spacious Italian marble lobby, four restaurants, and numerous bars and nightclubs (one overlooking a Japanese rock garden, complete with waterfall). Its deluxe facilities include a beauty parlor, a swimming pool, a sauna, a solarium, exercise rooms, and a bowling alley. Limousine service and sightseeing tours are available, as are massages.

The ▶ **Stadt Leipzig,** opposite the Hauptbahnhof, is sprawling, modern, and reasonably well kept, but has no special charm. It has three restaurants and a bar, a sauna, and a nightclub.

The modern ▶ **Hotel Deutschland,** in the cultural heart of the city on Augustus-Platz, lacks charm but is convenient. It offers, in addition to its 400 beds, a restaurant, bar, and nightclub.

Dining in Leipzig

By far the most popular restaurant in the city is **Auerbachs Keller,** Grimmaischestrasse 2 (Mädlerpassage), with its paintings of Dr. Johann Faust's visit to and departure from the premises with Mephistopheles, as related in *Faust.* Though the present restaurant is a modern version of the original, Auerbachs Keller has been in existence in Leipzig since the 16th century. The wine-cellar atmosphere is enjoyable, the food acceptable. *Mephistofleisch,* strips of spicy beef and pork, is the specialty. Reservations required; Tel: (341) 21-61-00.

A typical Leipzig "local" restaurant with a beer garden is **Gosenschenke Ohne Bedenken,** Menckestrasse 5; Tel: (341) 557-34 (open from 6:00 P.M.). Near the Markt, at Barfussgässchen 9, is the **Bierstube Zill's Tunnel,** a restaurant since the turn of the century that still serves such typical Thuringian dishes as *Rotkohl Roulade* (stuffed red-cabbage roll) and *Thüringer Klösse* (dumplings made with raw potatoes); Tel: (341) 20-04-46.

An interesting wine restaurant, decorated in the style of Bach's day and just opposite the Thomaskirche, is the **Bachstübl;** Tel: (341) 29-10-62 (closed Sundays).

Once upon a time, Leipzig lay in swampland and fish were plentiful. That is no longer the case, but there is still a fish restaurant here, **Gasthof das Meeres,** at Pfaffendorferstrasse 1. Reservations required; Tel: (341) 28-62-80.

For Leipzig's coffee drinkers, the **Café Concerto** at Thomaskirchhof 13 is a popular haunt. Other inviting cafés are the **Café de Saxe** on the Markt; the **Café Colonnade** at Kolonnadenstrasse 22; and the outdoor **Café am Eutritzscher Markt,** Strasse der DSF 67.

The Gewandhaus and Opernhaus are, of course, *the* places to go for an evening out in Leipzig. Ask about tickets at your hotel as soon as you arrive, or better yet make a reservation through your travel agent when you book your accommodations.

DRESDEN

On the night of February 13–14, 1945, hundreds of American and English bombers thundered over this historic city, known as the "German Florence," on the Elbe. The resulting fire-storm demolished its elegant 17th-century Baroque churches and palaces and left 80 percent of Dresden in ruins and 135,000 people dead.

Dresden had been the repository of some of the world's finest art, including Raphael's *Sistine Madonna,* Giorgione's *Sleeping Venus,* Rubens's *Bathsheba at the Well,* Greek and Etruscan sculpture, dazzling 17th-century jeweled utensils and ornaments, and incomparable porcelain. Though virtu-ally no architectural monuments remained standing after the bombing, at least Dresden's portable art had been removed for safekeeping. Today Dresden is again one of the world's great art-museum cities.

The city is divided more or less in half by the Elbe. On the south side, between the Hauptbahnhof and the river, are the major cultural attractions — the art museums, ruined and restored churches of the Altmarkt and Neumarkt, palaces, and the opera house. **Pragerstrasse**, a wide pedestrian mall lined with shops, hotels, and restaurants, and, at number 10, the city tourist office, is the main thoroughfare.

On the north side is the Neustadt, with its own Bahnhof. The **Hauptstrasse** is its main pedestrian mall. There, pretty 19th-century pink-and-gold burgher houses have been recon-structed to house shops, apartments, and restaurants. Also on the north side are a Romantic museum of the mid-19th century, a folk art museum, and an ethnological collection.

Dresden began to be a great art city in the 16th century when August I became the ruler of the electorate (later kingdom) of Saxony, wherein Dresden, about 130 km (81 miles) east of Leipzig, lies. A lover of beauty in both nature and art, August decreed that every newly married couple had to plant two fruit trees — symbolic, of course, of their union, but decorative, too, for his capital. Then he estab-lished a *Kunstkammer* (art chamber), which he filled with paintings, geological specimens, scientific instruments, and natural-history displays. But it was several generations later, during the reigns of August II (1693–1733; called "the Strong" because he is said to have been able to break a horseshoe in his bare hands and, in a fit of pique, to have dangled one of his trumpeters out a window with one hand) and his son, August III, that Dresden truly became a center of art.

Well travelled in his youth, August the Strong returned to

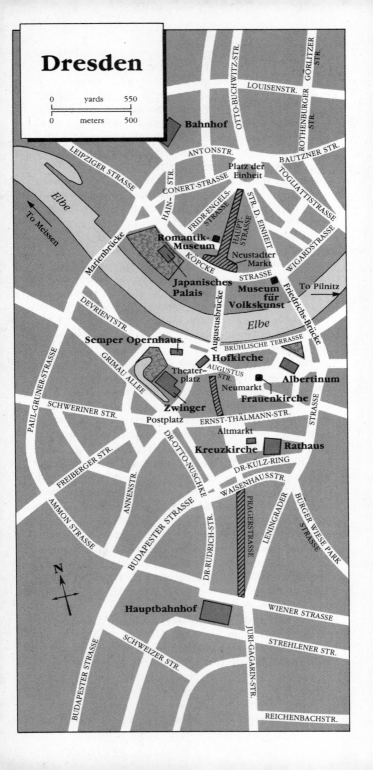

Saxony with an artistic appreciation developed in Italy and France. He soon found that his little *Kunstkammer* would hardly do for the art he was collecting. When there was no longer room for more in his castle, he decorated churches and his country residences with the work he had bought. Even the upper floor of the royal stable became an art gallery. So, wishing Dresden to be a Florence along the Elbe, with beautiful buildings on both sides of its banks, he had a splendid new palace begun on the river's south side. A fire in 1701 in the 16th-century Residenzschlass (Royal Palace) probably prompted him to realize what had long been a dream—a palace with gardens and Roman baths and promenades with porticoes and graceful fountains—a palace that would equal Versailles. It was to be built with galleries for the display of royal collections, and its gardens and promenades were to be the setting for outdoor entertainments. As architect he chose Matthäus Daniel Pöppelmann. Today's reconstructed **Zwinger**, on Theaterplatz on the river's south side, was its outer court (see below). Though the Zwinger was not completed in August's lifetime, the world-renowned Meissen porcelain that is now displayed here was a creation of his reign—albeit a forced one.

A Thuringian alchemist, John Friedrich Böttger, was the inventor of the Meissen porcelain technique. Charged in Berlin with the offense of being a magician because of his efforts to turn base metals into gold, Böttger had fled to Saxony. While he had feared imprisonment in Berlin, he actually got it in Dresden—though not for trying to produce gold. Rather, he was instructed that he *had* to produce it. He didn't, but instead, elaborating on attempts already made in Dresden to imitate Chinese porcelain, he invented the first European porcelain, as valued in the West as gold ever was. Previously, this delicate tableware was imported at great expense from the Orient.

To ensure that no one would learn the secret of Böttger's technique, August the Strong had him shut away—first in a room in the Dresden city walls below today's Albertinum museum, then in a castle at Meissen, 20 km (12½ miles) downriver. Böttger died a madman, driven insane, some say, by his solitary work.

It was during the reign of August III (1733–1763) that most of the paintings for which Dresden is now famous were amassed. Because his chief minister, Count Heinrich von Brühl, was as much an aficionado of art as August was, the king sent him off on an art-buying spree across Europe. It was during von Brühl's expedition that Raphael's *Sistine Madonna* was acquired, 40 years after August, as crown prince, had first seen it in a cloister. Other masterworks that made their way into the collection at this time included paintings by Rubens, Vermeer, Hals, Titian, Velázquez, and Andrea del Sarto. Canaletto's superlative views of Baroque Dresden, commissioned by Count von Brühl, show the magnificence of the city destroyed in World War II. A lesser work, but of interest to those who recognize it from the Baker's Chocolate package, is *The Chocolate Girl* by 18th-century Swiss painter Jean Etienne Liotard.

The Albertinum

Set on the Brühlische Terrasse, which rises above the Elbe's south bank, is the reconstructed Albertinum museum. Originally built as an armory in the 16th century, the structure was altered in the 18th to become a royal storehouse, gallery, and museum. Today it houses three of Dresden's most valued collections: of modern painting; ancient, medieval, and modern sculpture; and exquisite jeweled objects.

Its **Gemäldegalerie Neue Meister** (Gallery of Modern Masters) includes work by such 19th- and 20th-century artists as Manet, Monet, Renoir, van Gogh, Degas, Gauguin, and German Impressionists and Expressionists. In its sculpture gallery is the largest collection of Roman sculpture outside Italy. Also of interest is its numismatic collection, with thousands of coins of old Saxony.

The most dazzling display of all at the Albertinum, however, is the collection of the **Grünes Gewölbe** (Green Vault), which contains more than 3,000 jeweled objects in gold, silver, ebony, amber, glass, brass, and bronze. These were originally housed in the royal palace, or Residenzschloss, in burglar- and fireproof green-painted rooms (hence the name of these rooms in the Albertinum) whose walls were 80 inches thick. Five of these chambers, whose interior decoration is elaborate Dresden Baroque, were the only rooms in old Dresden to survive the 1945 bombing. When the reconstruction of the original Residenzschloss is completed, probably by 2006, the city's 800th anniversary, these rooms will be restored and their contents returned to them. Meanwhile, temporarily here in the Albertinum are glittering pendants of diamonds, emeralds, and rubies; Limoges ewers and bowls; a golden crucifix rising from a bed of pearls and emeralds; an elephant-shaped drinking vessel of gilded silver, mother-of-pearl, emeralds, rubies, and sapphires; and 16th- and 17th-century goblets in which rare seashells and ivory are joined with gold and silver and coral. There are gold coffee sets and ivory writing boxes and, most charming of all, the "Delhi Mogul's Birthday Party," an assemblage of miniature court figures of gold, silver, enamel, and precious stones crafted by Johann Melchior Dinglinger, Saxony's 17th-century Benvenuto Cellini. A ring with a skull on it is said to have been the property of Luther. All this and much, much more was saved from destruction by being hidden in the fortress of Königstein up the Elbe in 1942.

In the rebuilding of Dresden by the German Democratic Republic—after providing boxlike apartment complexes and pedestrian malls lined with unimaginative fountains and hotels for tourists—first attention was given to the rebuilding of the Zwinger, the masterpiece of Pöppelmann, and the Semper Oper. Now the rebuilding of other historic structures is continuing apace.

The Zwinger

Though reconstruction of the Zwinger—in Saxon sandstone as it was originally—was a priority during Communist days in Dresden, the polluted air ate away at the stone to such an extent that eventually much of the palace had to be closed to reconstruct the reconstruction. At press time, however, this work was almost completed and visitors could look down on or stroll about in the courtyard, where charming Baroque nymphs and roguish fauns gaze out from the pavilions. These figures and the onion-domed Crown Gate are from the workshop of the craftsman Balthasar Permoser, who was active in the late 17th and early 18th centuries.

Inside, the reconstructed east wing designed in Neo-Renaissance style by Gottfried Semper again houses its **Gemäldegalerie Alter Meister** (Gallery of the Old Masters). (For years the collection was on display in the Albertinum.) Here hang the Sistine Madonna, Vermeer's *Girl With a Letter,* Giorgione's *Sleeping Venus,* and Rembrandt's *Simeon's Marriage,* along with many other acquisitions of Count von Brühl.

Also now open to the public is the **Historisches Museum** (Historical Museum) of glittering chased Saxon armor and shields, 16th- to 18th-century hunting weapons, swords and daggers with jewel-encrusted scabbards, and hilts. Then there is the scientific-instrument collection, one of the earliest of its kind in the world, with compasses, telescopes, weights and scales, and terrestrial and celestial globes—some dating from the 13th century.

In the porcelain galleries are life-size bird and animal figures by the most famous 18th-century porcelain designers, Johann Joachim Kändler and Johann Friedrich Eberlein, along with delicate smaller pieces—clowns and dancing couples, musicians, flowered vases, platters, and bowls. There are red porcelain pieces (red was the first porcelain produced), white porcelain created after 1709, and porcelain painted by Johann Gregorious Heroldt. In 1720, after a careful study of Japanese and Chinese porcelain painting, Heroldt perfected German glazing. Soon Meissen china was being decorated in shimmering colors.

Old Dresden

Situated beside the Zwinger on Theaterplatz is the **Semper Oper**. Reopened in 1985, the present opera house is the second copy of the first theater erected on this site between 1837 and 1841 by Gottfried Semper. After the original burned down in 1869 it was reconstructed by Semper's son, Manfred. Built in Renaissance style and reconstructed after the 1945 bombing, it faces an equestrian statue of Saxony's scholarly 19th-century King Johannes. There is also a monument in the square to Carl Maria von Weber, who was in charge of the Dresden opera from 1816 to 1826.

Decorating the Semper façade are statues of playwrights and muses. Inside, it has been stunningly re-created to look as it did in Semper's day, with marbleized stucco and fine wood paneling. The interior fairly glows with light.

The opera, which is closed from early July to mid-August, is, of course, the place to go in the evening. Otherwise, try a Saturday Kreuzchor vespers in the **Kreuzkirche** (Church of the Holy Cross) on the Altmarkt or a Dresden Philharmonic concert at the **Kulturpalast**, also on the Altmarkt. Arrangements for tickets of any sort should be made at your hotel as soon as you arrive. Opera tickets in particular are in short supply, but there is a box office near the opera house where tickets will cost less than at the hotel—if there are any available.

Across the Theaterplatz, on Schloss-Platz, the colonnaded **Stallhof** (Royal Stables) has been restored as well. Set away from any street, and providing something of an oasis in the noisy city, the former parade ground that surrounds the stables is edged with arches decorated with the coats of arms of the towns of Saxony.

Beside it rises the onion-domed tower of the Baroque **Hofkirche**. This Catholic court church was built by the Roman architect Gaetano Chiaveri between 1739 and 1755, and though most of its roof and walls fell during the bombing, the tower stood. Most of the interior art—including a 1722 pulpit by Permoser and the 18th-century master builder Gottfried Silbermann's last and largest organ—was kept safely in a salt mine during the war. Behind the court church, reconstruction of the **Residenzschloss** is under way. A special exhibit suggests what the reconstruction will be, and it is hoped that it will be completed by Dresden's 800th anniversary in 2006.

The visitor can obtain a quick rundown of Saxon history a street away from the Hofkirche on Augustusstrasse. There, an outdoor **mosaic wall** depicts Saxony's rulers from the 12th century to the 20th. Because it was made of Meissen china, which had been prefired, the 19th-century wall withstood the intense heat of the 1945 firestorm. Astride their horses ride the electors and kings.

Across the street along the river are the 42 steps (with their statues of Morning, Noon, Evening, and Night) that lead to the **Brühlische Terrasse**, where Count von Brühl once had his palace (now the site of the Academy of Fine Arts) and where the Albertinum stands. Goethe called this walkway along the winding brown-gold Elbe "the Balcony of Europe," and although the view is no longer what it once was, it remains a lovely overlook.

Below it, behind the Albertinum in the Neumarkt, the ruins of Dresden's most famous church, the Lutheran **Frauenkirche** (Church of Our Lady), have long stood, left in their ruined state as a grim reminder of the devastation of war. The church dome was, from 1740 (when it was completed) until 1945, the landmark of this city on the Elbe. Incredibly, it survived the bombing—the only building in the Altstadt that did in its entirety. The day after the bombing, however, its mighty sandstone cupola collapsed. Now, in the new Germany, the Frauenkirche ruins are encased in scaffolding and reconstruction of it is getting under way. The façade of the new Dresden Hilton extends opposite it, while in front of it stands a statue of Luther. Another memorable site on the Neumarkt is the Renaissance **Schöne Pforte** (Beautiful Gate), which once led into the royal palace's chapel. At the neighboring Altmarkt little that is old remains—even in ruins— except the reconstructed Baroque **Kreuzkirche** (Church of the Holy Cross), the original of which was built between 1764 and 1792. The Kreuzkirche has long been notable for its boys' choir.

Across the Augustusbrücke, on the north side of the Elbe in the Neustadter Markt (New City Market), sits a golden rider—August the Strong—on a golden horse. Behind the statue stretches the tree-shaded walking street, the Hauptstrasse. Along this Neustadt riverfront, behind an extensive park, the Hotel Bellevue (see below) has been created from a 17th-century burgomaster's house. Beside it, in the 18th-century **Japanisches Palais** (Japanese Palace), which August II had built for his porcelain collection, there is now a museum of ethnography. The rooms of the **Romantik-**

Museum, also on Hauptstrasse, are filled with objects from Dresden's Romantic period of the 1840s to the 1860s. Still undergoing some interior reconstruction, but reopened as a gallery, meeting place, and church, is the **Drei Königskirche** (Church of the Three Kings), whose 19th-century tower soars above the rooftops of Neustadt. The church was designed by Poppelmann in 1732. Of particular interest inside is the pre-Reformation *Totentanz* (Dance of Death) in the back of the church.

On Meissnerstrasse, to the right, or east of Hauptstrasse, in the former hunting castle of the rulers of Saxony, is the charming **Museum für Volkskunst** (Folk Art Museum), with a collection of hand-painted furniture, textiles, costumes, and hand-painted wooden toys from the villages of the nearby Erzgebirge region.

Staying in Dresden

Dresden's most inviting hotel is the handsome golden-yellow ▶ **Maritim Hotel Bellevue**. It was a burgomaster's house until, in 1733, Pöppelmann, the Zwinger architect, redid part of it so it could be used for city administration. Now it is an elegant hostelry, with a riverfront garden, sunny corridors, and period rooms. There are nine restaurants, a swimming pool, Jacuzzi, sauna, bowling alley, solarium, jogging course, and a gift shop; English is spoken. In summer, cruises on the hotel's boat are available to the castle at neighboring Pillnitz, the hunting lodge of Moritzburg, and Meissen (see below for all of these). The ▶ **Dresden Hilton**, right on the Neumarkt, offers similar amenities but is more functional in decor.

Centrally located and offering a view of both city and river, but lacking in exterior charm, is the new high-rise ▶ **Hotel am Terrassenufer**. The deluxe 99-room ▶ **Palais Hotel Gewandhaus**, housed in a restored 18th-century building, is scheduled to open in spring 1994. Two other hotels due to open some time in 1994 or 1995 are the Solar Parkhotel and the Kempinski Taschenbergpalais, the latter being built from the ruins of the palace of Constantia von Cosel, the mistress of August the Strong.

The ▶ **Hotel Mercure Newa**, near the main railroad station, is quite a step down from these, but it has been renovated and is now operated by the French Mercure chain. It has a restaurant, café, two bars, and a sauna.

Three lesser but acceptable hotels, the ▶ **Hotel Bastei**, the ▶ **Königstein**, and the ▶ **Hotel Lilienstein**, stand near each other on Pragerstrasse. All three are now owned by the French Ibis hotel chain. English is limited.

The ▶ **Hotel Schloss Eckberg**, built as a castle estate in the last century in a parklike setting above the Elbe (the restaurant has a superlative view), is located some distance from the heart of the city. Again, English is limited.

A charming hotel in a restored old house is the ▶ **Alpha**, at Fritz-Reuter-Strasse 21 in Neustadt. And there are three hotel ships, the ▶ **Hotelschiff Florentina** and the ▶ **Hotelschiff Elbresidenz**, both on Terrassenufer, and the ▶ **Hotelschiff St. Caspar**, moored below the Brühlische Terrasse.

Dining in Dresden and Meissen

Kügelgenhaus, at Hauptstrasse 13 in the Neustadt, is what a restaurant might have been like in prewar Dresden. It is in a restored 19th-century burgher house on the north side of the river. There are engravings and woodcuts of singers and actors of the past on its walls. Reservations required; Tel: (351) 527-91.

Dresden's poshest, most dignified restaurant, and its most expensive, is **Applause**, in the Dresden Hilton. Only hotel guests are served, and reservations are essential; Tel: (351) 48-47-58. Also excellent is the hotel's Italian restaurant, **Rossini**, which is open to the public; Tel: (351) 484-17-41.

You take the Standseilbahn, a cable car, from Körnerplatz in the Loschwitz section of the city to get to the **Luisenhof**, which overlooks Dresden and the Elbe from the city outskirts. Destroyed in the war, the Luisenhof has been rebuilt in a Neo-Baroque style. There is dancing some evenings at this romantic spot, at Bergbahnstrasse 8. Reservations required; Tel. (351) 368-42 (closed Mondays).

Reached by the same cable car is the **Restaurant Erholung**, in the Weisser Hirsch district at Rissweg 39; at the turn of the century it was a health resort. It specializes in traditional Dresden fare such as Saxon Sauerbraten. Tel: (351) 37-79-93. Saxon fare is offered with a view at the **Pillnitzer Elbblick**, at Söbrigenerstrasse 2; Tel: (351) 392-86.

Try a pastry and coffee in the Bellevue's Baroque **Pöppelmann Café**, looking out on a field of flowers inspired by the Moritzburg castle garden. Some afternoons there is music to drink your coffee by. At the **Café Vis-à-Vis** at the Hilton there is outdoor seating on the terrace above the Elbe.

For students eager to meet fellow students, this university city has a number of cozy gathering places: the little **Planwirtschaft** at 20 Luisenstrasse, **Café 100** at Alaunstrasse 100, and the café and wine cellar **Tivoli** at Luisenstrasse 10.

In the cellar of the Neustadt Rathaus, the **Meissner Weinkeller**, Hauptstrasse 16, has an ambience of the past—and

good local wine and food. Tel: (351) 558-14 (the Kügelgenhaus, which will connect you). Another restaurant in Neustadt
worth trying is the **Laterne**, Bautzner Strasse 1; Tel: (351) 530-
94. On the edge of the Dresdener Heide (heath), at Bautzner
Landstrasse 83, the **Trompeter** is an historic restaurant; Tel:
(351) 361-23 (closed Sundays).

At Theaterplatz 2, the **Opernrestaurant** offers good fare
and, in season, outdoor dining beside the Zwinger lake; Tel:
(351) 484-25-00. There is also outdoor dining at the **Restaurant Elbeterrasse** at the Maritim Hotel Bellevue, Tel: (351)
566-26-45, and at the **Hubertusgarten**, Bautzner Landstrasse
89, Tel: (351) 360-74. For fish try the **Coventry**, named for
Dresden's sister city in England, at Hülssestrasse 1; Tel: (351)
274-3014. Furnished and equipped like an old train is the
Maygarten Linie 6, Schaufusstrasse 24; Tel: (351) 302-68.

The **Vincenz Richter**, An der Frauenkirche 12, is in a half-
timbered house near the Marktplatz in Meissen (see below).
If the food in this newly refurbished restaurant is as good as
it was in the old place, it is worth trying. In any case, it is
worth a visit simply to see the handsome historic structure
and have a glass of red or white Meissen wine, considered to
be the best in eastern Germany; Tel: (3521) 45-32-85; closed
October. The historic **Weinstube Rebstock**, Niederwald-
strasse 10, Tel: (3521) 353-50, is another well-established
Meissen eatery (closed Mondays and Tuesdays).

The **Parkrestaurant**, across the Elbe from Meissen town, at
Elbgasse 1, is a little square house on the river with an
inviting atmosphere and good food; Tel: (3521) 73-22-86.

After a morning of sightseeing at Meissen's Albrechtsburg
castle and the cathedral (see below), it is pleasant not to
have to go back down into town for lunch. The **Burgkeller**,
Tel: (3521) 45-31-22, and the **Domkeller**, Tel: (3521) 20-34,
are recent additions to the historic hilltop Meissen complex.

Around Dresden

Upriver in the Dresden environs, the Baroque palace of
Pillnitz, the summer dwelling of the electors and kings, is
worth a visit. It is about 11 km (7 miles) southeast of
Dresden and is easily reached in summer by Weisse Flotte
(White Fleet) steamer. Designed by Zwinger architect Pöp-
pelmann, it is a curious architectural mix of Baroque and
East Asian styles, with pagodalike roofs supported by Corin-
thian columns. Its builder, August the Strong, called it "an
Indian pleasure seat."

About 20 km (12 miles) north of Dresden there is the
sprawling yellow sandstone **Schloss Moritzburg**, a hunting
lodge set on an island among man-made ponds, first con-

structed in the 17th century and rebuilt for August by Pöppelmann. To see it, you can take the train to Meissen and continue by bus to Moritzburg, or go from Radebeul to Moritzburg on the narrow-gauge railway.

About 32 km (20 miles) farther upstream, the fortresses of **Königstein** and **Lilienstein** loom above the river, and, finally, there are the needlelike peaks of Saxony's "Little Switzerland."

Downriver 35 km (22 miles) northwest toward Wittenberg, the 15th-century fortress castle of **Albrechtsburg** and the 13th-century High Gothic **Dom** (cathedral) tower above the Elbe's left bank at **Meissen**. From 1710 to 1864 Meissen porcelain was manufactured in the castle. A short walk leads down from the castle into the half-timbered town. Today 19th-century Romantic paintings in the castle recount its history. Also in Meissen, on Talstrasse, is today's porcelain factory and museum, where visitors can see how modern Meissen is made and painted. There is also a small shop selling Meissen in the town. Meissen may be reached by steamer, rail, or by car along highway B 6.

A curiosity in Radebeul, a town adjoining Dresden, is the **Karl May Museum** of American Indian artifacts.

From the 13th to the 15th centuries, **Freiberg**, a former silver-mining town situated in the Erzgebirge (Ore Mountains) about 40 km (25 miles) southwest of Dresden on route B 173, was the richest town in Germany. The 13th-century sculptures of Old and New Testament figures on the **Goldene Pforte** (Golden Portal) of the town's Gothic **cathedral** are considered by art historians to be some of Europe's finest. Highlights within the cathedral are the porphyry **Tulpenkanzel** (Tulip Pulpit), with carvings of the master-craftsman and his angelic assistants; the **Bergmannkanzel** (Miners' Pulpit), resting on the head of a carved miner; and an 18th-century organ by Gottfried Silbermann, the master organmaker who was a native of Freiberg. You can visit the cathedral only a few times a day, however, so it is wise to check opening hours at the tourist information office, Obermarkt Rathaus; Tel: (3731) 732-65.

Freiberg's **Stadt-und-Bergbaumuseum** (City and Mining Museum) is housed in an old patrician mansion. The collections include ivory and embossed silver pickaxes, silver cups and flagons, early mining apparatus, and miniature figures of green-hatted miners. There are also hand-carved examples of the Erzgebirger toymakers' art—nutcrackers, Christmas decorations, and Noah's Arks.

You can visit the region's famed wooden-toy carvers and watch them at their traditional work in rural villages such as **Seiffen**, outside of Freiberg. The town's **Spielzeugmuseum**

(Toy Museum) is crammed with wooden toys, and more than a dozen shops offer them for sale.

GETTING AROUND

Now that there is only one Germany, connections between cities of east and west are improving all the time. For the most up-to-date information, contact one of the offices listed in the For Further Information section in Useful Facts at the front of this book. There are now regular flights on Lufthansa between Dresden and Frankfurt, Cologne/Bonn, Düsseldorf, Hamburg, Munich, and Stuttgart, and between Leipzig and Cologne/Bonn, Düsseldorf, Frankfurt, Hamburg Munich, and Stuttgart.

Rail travel in eastern Germany, generally on old tracks, continues to be slow, but trains do link most communities. Again, however, station personnel are unlikely to speak English.

A new national computer service allows you to obtain information and make reservations on all railroad and airline links; check with German National Railroads, Interflug, or Lufthansa, or with offices of the German National Tourist Board.

KD River Cruises of Europe offers trips on the Elbe from Hamburg to Dresden. Each ship has 64 double cabins and docks for the night in various German river or canal ports, offering shore excursions at cities like Dresden, Meissen, and Wittenberg. For booking information see the Around Germany section in Useful Facts at the front of the book.

Shopping

Anything you can buy in western Germany is now available in the larger cities of the east. Specialties of the east remain old books and prints, antiques, Meissen china, and—in Leipzig—furs.

Planning

Tickets for cultural events are always in demand. Whenever possible, if you are booking with a travel agent, ask him or her to reserve tickets for you. Be sure to make restaurant reservations at least a day in advance.

When planning visits to museums and churches, be flexible. Many museums and historic churches, like restaurants and hotels, are now undergoing reconstruction. Some museums close for lunch in winter. In small-city tourist offices there is often no one who speaks English. Be sure to take a dictionary.

Restaurant hours and days of opening should also be checked at hotels. Hours may not be what you expect.

Although our eastern Germany hotel information was correct as of press time, east German telephone numbers will continue to be changed in 1994. Despite considerable improvements, calling from western to eastern Germany still remains a problem. Phone lines are crowded during weekday working hours, so try calling during lunchtime (noon to 2:00 P.M.) or later in the evening. Even dialing correctly you may get a wrong number, a problem familiar to east Germans. Eastern German hotels in general are overbooked these days—packed with west German and other businesspeople trying to gain a timely commercial foothold in the former GDR. In addition, hotels now owned by the Treuhandanstalt, the government's privatization agency, are uncertain about their future—some may be closed, others sold.

ACCOMMODATIONS REFERENCE

The hotel rates listed here are 1994 projections for double-bed, double-occupancy rooms, with a range from low to high whenever possible. Prices are given in deutsche marks (DM). Basic rates are always subject to change, so please verify price when you are booking. Breakfast is usually included in the price of a room.

The international telephone country code for Germany is 49. If you are calling from within Germany, city codes must be preceded by a zero.

▶ **Alpha.** Fritz-Reuter-Strasse 21, D-01097 **Dresden.** Tel: (351) 502-24-41; Fax: (351) 57-13-90. DM 240.

▶ **Bauer Hotel Excelsior.** Bahnhofstrasse 35, D-99084 **Erfurt.** Tel: (361) 642-1307; Fax: (361) 642-2866. DM 189–269.

▶ **Christliches Hospiz Glockenhof.** Grimmelgasse 4, D-99817 **Eisenach.** Tel: (3691) 52-16; Fax: (3691) 52-17. DM 180.

▶ **Dresden Hilton.** An der Frauenkirche 5, D-01067 **Dresden.** Tel: (351) 484-10; Fax: (351) 484-17-00. DM 405–455.

▶ **Erfurter Hof.** Willy Brandt Platz 10, D-99084 **Erfurt.** Tel: (361) 53-10; Fax: (361) 646-10-21. DM 250–350.

▶ **Flamberg Hotel Elephant.** Markt 19, D-99423 **Weimar.** Tel: (3643) 614-71; Fax: (3643) 653-10. DM 240–360.

▶ **Fürstenhof.** Luisenstrasse 11, D-99817 **Eisenach.** Tel: (3691) 77-80; Fax: (3691) 20-36-82. DM 180.

▶ **Goldener Adler.** Markt 7, D-06886 **Wittenberg.** Tel: (3491) 20-53; Fax: (3491) 20-54. DM 180.

▶ **Hotel Bastei.** Pragerstrasse, D-01069 **Dresden.** Tel: (351) 485-63-85; Fax: (351) 495-40-76. DM 180–210.

▶ **Hotel Cyriaksburg.** Cyriaksstrasse 37, D-99094 **Erfurt.** Tel: (361) 249-85; Fax: (361) 643-83-73. DM 220.

► **Hotel Deutsche Eiche.** Mühlental 36, D-38855 **Werniger-ode.** Tel and Fax: (3943) 241-12. DM 60–65.

► **Hotel Deutschland.** Augustus-Platz 5/6, D-04109 **Leipzig.** Tel: (341) 214-60; Fax: (341) 28-91-65. DM 335–345.

► **Hotel Ibis.** Barfüsserstrasse 9, D-99084 **Erfurt.** Tel: (361) 664-10; Fax: (361) 66-41-10-11. DM 130–158.

► **Hotel Intercontinental Leipzig.** Gerberstrasse 15, D-04105 **Leipzig.** Tel: (341) 79-90; Fax: (341) 28-14-63. DM 290–400.

► **Hotel Kosmos.** Juri-Gagarin-Ring 126–127, D-99084 **Erfurt.** Tel: (361) 55-10; Fax: (361) 55-12-10. DM 230–320.

► **Hotel Lilienstein.** Pragerstrasse, D-01069 **Dresden.** Tel: (351) 485-60; Fax: (351) 495-25-06. DM 180–210.

► **Hotel Mercure Newa.** St. Petersburgerstrasse, D-01069 **Dresden.** Tel: (351) 481-40; Fax: (351) 495-51-37. DM 250–270.

► **Hotel Rotes Ross.** Leipzigerstrasse 76, D-06108 **Halle.** Tel: (345) 372-71; Fax: (345) 263-31. DM 198.

► **Hotel Russischer Hof.** Goetheplatz 2, D-99423 **Weimar.** Tel: (3643) 77-40; Fax: (3643) 623-37. DM 210–280.

► **Hotelschiff Elbresidenz.** Terrassenufer, D-01069 **Dresden.** Tel: (351) 459-50-03; Fax: (351) 459-51-37. DM 150–210.

► **Hotelschiff Florentina.** Terrassenufer, D-01003 **Dresden.** Tel: (351) 459-01-69; Fax: (351) 459-50-36. DM 185–215.

► **Hotelschiff St. Caspar.** Terrassenufer, D-01069 **Dresden.** Tel: (351) 459-64-72; Fax: (351) 459-50-36. DM 185–215.

► **Hotel Schloss Eckberg.** Bautznerstrasse 134, D-01099 **Dresden.** Tel: (351) 525-71; Fax: (351) 551-46. DM 260.

► **Hotel am Terrassenufer.** Terrassenufer 12, D-01069 **Dres-den.** Tel: (351) 440-9500; Fax: (351) 440-9600. DM 295–350.

► **Königstein.** Pragerstrasse, D-01069 **Dresden.** Tel: (351) 485-64-72; Fax: (351) 495-40-54. DM 180–210.

► **Maritim Hotel Bellevue.** Grosse Meissnerstrasse 15, D-01097 **Dresden.** Tel: (351) 566-20; Fax: (351) 559-97. DM 448–548.

► **Maritim Hotel Stadt Halle.** Riebeck Platz 4, D-06009 **Halle.** Tel: (345) 510-10; Fax: (345) 510-17-77. DM 298–418.

► **Mercure Hotel An der Havel.** Lange Brücke, D-14467 **Potsdam.** Tel: (331) 46-31; Fax: (331) 234-96. DM 225.

► **Palais Hotel Gewandhaus.** Ringstrasse 1, D-01067 **Dres-den.** Tel: (351) 494-90; Fax (351) 494-9100. DM 498.

► **Quedlinburger Hof.** Harzweg 1, D-06484 **Quedlinburg.** Tel and Fax: (3946) 22-76. DM 140.

► **Stadt Leipzig.** Richard-Wagner-Strasse 1–5, D-04008 **Leipzig.** Tel: (341) 214-50; Fax: (341) 214-56-00. DM 330.

► **Travel Hotel Gothisches Haus.** Am Markt 1, D-38855 **Wernigerode.** Tel: (3943) 37-50; Fax: (3943) 37-55-37. DM 245–310.

► **Travel Hotel Schloss Cecilienhof.** Neuer Garten, D-14469 **Potsdam.** Tel: (331) 370-50; Fax: (331) 224-98. DM 250–350.

► **Waldhotel Vogel.** Tonmark 10, D-06886 **Wittenberg.** Tel: (3491) 61-03-89; Fax: 61-03-92. DM 160.

► **Wartburg Hotel.** D-99817 **Eisenach-Wartburg.** Tel: (3691) 51-11; Fax: (3691) 623-33-42. DM 260.

► **Weimar Hilton.** Belvedere Allee 25, D-99425 **Weimar.** Tel: (3643) 72-20; Fax: (3643) 77-27-41. DM 355–385.

► **Weisser Hirsch.** Marktplatz 5, D-38855 **Wernigerode.** Tel: (3943) 324-34 or 35; Fax: (3943) 331-39. DM 169.

► **Zur Goldenen Sonne.** Steinweg 11, D-06484 **Quedlinburg.** Tel: (3946) 23-18. DM 140–160.

► **Zur Post.** Marktstrasse 17, D-38855 **Wernigerode.** Tel: (3945) 324-36. DM 130.

COLOGNE
(KÖLN)

By Donald S. Olson

Donald S. Olson, a freelance writer and editor, has written a guidebook to Berlin and contributed travel articles to many American magazines. The author of three novels, he also has had plays produced in New York and Europe.

Visitors to this lively metropolis on the Rhine, Germany's fourth-largest and its oldest city, are immediately struck by Cologne's audacious cheek-by-jowl juxtaposition of the very old with the very new. In Cologne, Roman ruins share space with Mercedes-Benzes and BMWs in an underground car park, the dizzyingly ornate Gothic cathedral sits beside a Late Modernist museum complex, and a humble Romanesque church is wedged in among luxury shopping emporia built in the booming eighties. On a ten-minute walk in Cologne you can traverse 2,000 years of history.

In recent years Cologne's reputation as one of Germany's most culturally vibrant cities has been steadily growing. The range of municipal museums, the buildings that house them, and the quality of their collections make Cologne one of the outstanding museum cities of Germany. And, too, the city has become *the* contemporary art capital of Germany, bursting with galleries that show the work of new and established artists from Germany and around the world. Music, whether it's a symphony concert in the fabulous new philharmonic hall, a Mozart opera at the opera house, or a boisterous outdoor concert in the Rhinepark, is likewise a vital component of life here.

Cologne is far more than a city with Germany's largest cathedral, although the cathedral is, of course, what initially draws most visitors. In addition to its substantial Roman legacy, from the time when Cologne was one of the more

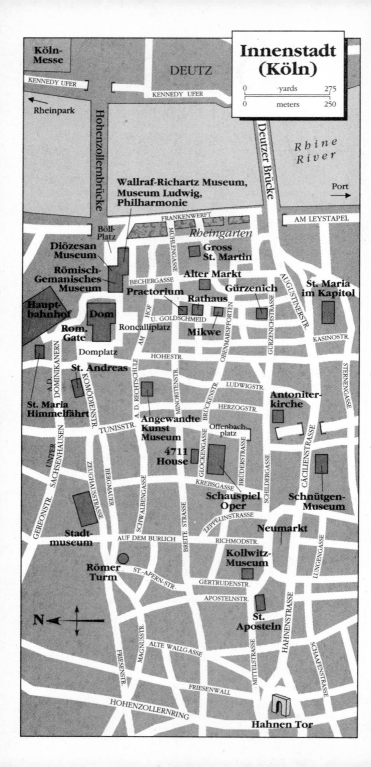

Innenstadt (Köln)

| 0 | yards | 275 |
| 0 | meters | 250 |

Köln-Messe

DEUTZ

KENNEDY UFER

KENNEDY UFER

← Rheinpark

Hohenzollernbrücke

Deutzer Brücke

Rhine River

Port →

Wallraf-Richartz Museum, Museum Ludwig, Philharmonie

AM LEYSTAPEL

FRANKENWERFT

Böll-Platz

Rheingarten

Diözesan Museum

MÜHLENGASSE

Gross St. Martin

Römisch-Germanisches Museum

BECHERGASSE

Alter Markt

Praetorium

Gürzenich

St. Maria im Kapitol

AUGUSTINERSTR.

Rathaus

GÜRZENICHSTRASSE

Haupt-bahnhof

Dom

HOF

U. GOLDSCHMEID

Mikwe

OBENMARSPFORTEN

KASINOSTR.

Rom. Gate

Roncalliplatz

AM

STERNENGASSE

Domplatz

HOHESTR.

A. D. DOMINIKANERN

St. Andreas

A. D. RECHTSCHULE

LUDWIGSTR.

Antoniter-kirche

KOMÖDIENSTR.

MINORITENSTR.

BRÜCKENSTR.

HERZOGSTR.

St. Maria Himmelfährt

TUNISSTR.

Angewandte Kunst Museum

Offenbach-platz

CÄCILIENSTRASSE

BERGMAUER

GLOCKENGASSE

BRÜDERSTRASSE

SCHILDERGASSE

UNTER SACHSENHAUSEN

ZEUGHAUSSTRASSE

4711 House

Schnütgen-Museum

GEREONSTR.

SCHWALBENGASSE

KREBSGASSE

Schauspiel Oper

Stadt-museum

BREITE STRASSE

ZEPPELINSTRASSE

Neumarkt

AUF DEM BURLICH

RICHMODSTR.

LÜNGENGASSE

Römer Turm

ST-APERN-STR.

Kollwitz-Museum

GERTRUDENSTR.

APOSTELNSTR.

N ←

MAGNUSSTR.

St. Aposteln

HAHNENSTRASSE

MITTELSTRASSE

SCHAAFENSTRASSE

FRIESENSTR.

ALTE WALLGASSE

FRIESENWALL

HOHENZOLLERNRING

Hahnen Tor

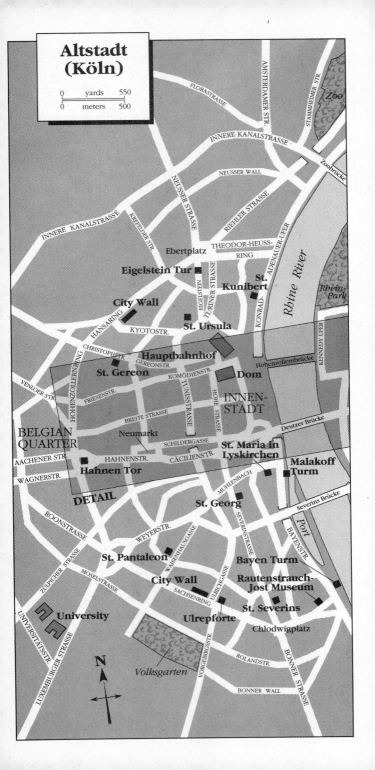

important cities of Imperial Rome, the city boasts 12 major Romanesque churches, all of which have been restored and reopened only within the last few years. These churches, older than the cathedral, drew medieval pilgrims from all over Europe to "Holy Cologne," one of the most important cities in medieval Christendom.

The Kölner themselves are extremely proud of their city but refreshingly relaxed and down-to-earth in their enjoyment of it. Every year they welcome over five million visitors, many of whom come to attend the giant international trade fairs held in the the Köln Messe. Ancient traditions are annually renewed in the city's raucous pre-Lenten Carnival, a time of masked balls, parades, and general delirium. When the weather turns warm, visitors and citizens alike stroll along Rhine promenades and flock to outdoor taverns and restaurants to enjoy the pleasures of a *Kölsch*, Cologne's unique and delicious beer (and also the name of the city's dialect), and a substantial meal of typical Rhineland cuisine.

MAJOR INTEREST
Cathedral
Römisch-Germanisches Museum
Wallraf-Richartz-Museum/Museum Ludwig
Roman ruins (the Praetorium)
Altes Rathaus
Romanesque churches
Schnütgen Museum/Käthe-Kollwitz-Museum/Museum
    für Angewandte Kunst/Museum für Ostasiatische
    Kunst
Zoo, Rhinepark, and Messe
Contemporary art galleries in the Belgian Quarter
Eating and drinking in typical Cologne tavern-
    restaurants

Cologne's prosperity stems primarily from the chemical, pharmaceutical, automotive, and banking and insurance industries that have made their headquarters here. One of Europe's largest inland ports, it is the home of the Köln-Düsseldorfer (KD) fleet of Rhine passenger steamers and a major transportation hub whose train station is the busiest on the Continent. It is also one of the media (newspapers, publishing, broadcasting) capitals of Germany. And, of course, it is the city of the original Kölnisch Wasser—known throughout the world as Eau de Cologne.

The major sights of Cologne, with a few exceptions, are located in the *Altstadt* (Old City), the restored and much-altered medieval core of the city, which spreads in a semicircle west from the Rhine to a ring road that follows the line

of the 12th-century city walls (demolished, except for three
gateways, in the 19th century). Cäcilienstrasse and Hahnenstrasse, directly west of the Deutzer Brücke, divide the area
into Altstadt-Nord (north) and Altstadt-Süd (south). The center of the Altstadt is the *Innenstadt* (Inner City), the historical heart of Cologne, where the Romans built their first
walled colony. Everything worth seeing in the Altstadt can
easily be reached on foot or on the city's efficient U-Bahn
(underground) and S-Bahn (tram) lines.

The *Neustadt,* dating from the 19th century, is girdled
between the ring road and a green belt where, in the
southwest, the university is located. Cologne's sizable student population—the first public university in Germany was
founded here in 1388—gives this ancient city a youthful
thrust and energy.

Although older citizens of Cologne still disparage Deutz,
on the Rhine's east bank, by referring to it as *Schäl Sick*
(roughly translatable as "the other—or wrong—side"), the
district is important to the life of the city. Besides providing
the best views of the cathedral-dominated Cologne skyline,
Deutz is where the Köln Messe (trade-fair grounds) and the
Rhinepark are located. It was in Deutz that the city's early
industrial plants were concentrated and where many of
them—including Ford, the city's largest employer—are still
located.

Depending on the amount of time you have and what
your interests are, there are several ways to formulate an
itinerary. The cathedral, all the major and most of the
smaller museums, the Roman Praetorium excavations, the
Rathaus and adjacent Alter Markt, and Gross St. Martin (one
of Cologne's 12 Romanesque churches) are all located in the
Innenstadt, the roughly half-square-mile area of the original
Roman colony. Although the Innenstadt is part of the larger
Altstadt, we are treating it here as a separate area to explore.
If you're selective in the museums you choose to visit (don't
try to visit all of them), the other major sites of the
Innenstadt can be seen in a day, and your visit rounded off
by an evening's stroll along the Rhine promenade in Deutz
(see The Rhine Panorama, below).

Visitors with more time can expand on this basic itinerary
by venturing into the Altstadt, either north or south of the
Innenstadt, where the bevy of Romanesque churches provides a fascinating historical and architectural garnish to the
city. Outside the Altstadt to the north is the zoo, with the
Rhinepark and Cologne Messe located directly across from it
in Deutz. An excursion to these places will take a full
morning or afternoon, as will a visit to the contemporary art
galleries of the Belgian Quarter, located just outside the

Altstadt west of Hohenzollernring. One piece of advice: Try not to visit Cologne on a Monday, when all the museums are closed.

THE INNENSTADT

The cathedral, Cologne's major landmark, demarcates the northernmost boundary of the Innenstadt, which extends to the west as far as St.-Apern-Strasse and Gertrudenstrasse and south to Hahnenstrasse and Cäcilienstrasse. Located in a busy commerical area close to the Rhine, just a few steps from the Hauptbahnhof (main train station), the cathedral is the heart and focal point of the city and can be viewed from all directions without obstruction thanks to the car-free terraces and plazas that surround it. If you are driving, you will find a parking garage beneath the cathedral.

From the train station a series of stairways built over the street leads up to the Domplatte, the cathedral's northern terrace. The busy plaza in front of the spires is the **Domplatz**, with the city's helpful Verkehrsamt (tourist information office) across the street to the west and Hohe Strasse, Cologne's major pedestrians-only shopping street, leading off to the south. The cathedral's southern façade faces Roncalliplatz, a modern piazza formed by the venerable Dom-Hotel on the west side and the city's major museums—the Römisch-Germanisches and the Wallraf-Richartz/Museum Ludwig complex—on the east. Behind the cathedral, Heinrich-Böll-Platz, named for the Nobel Laureate author who lived in Cologne, leads to a series of newly landscaped terraces and fountains that descend to the Rhine and the Hohenzollernbrücke, which spans it.

The Cathedral

Considering how much time it took to build this gigantic edifice, the largest cathedral in northern Europe, it's a wonder that it presents such a stylistically coherent Gothic façade. Over 600 years elapsed from the laying of the cornerstone in 1248 to the placement of the last finial on the south tower in 1880. (A true-to-size replica of this 28-foot-high finial can be seen on the Domplatz.) When it was finally completed, the Cologne cathedral, or **Dom**, as it's called, was the tallest building in the world, its twin filigreed spires rising to a height of 515 feet. Overwhelming is the simplest way to describe it.

The origins and siting of the present Dom date back to the earliest period of Cologne's history. A small Roman temple stood where the cathedral now stands, followed by an early Christian church built by the Franks. In the eighth century, when Cologne was raised to the status of an archbishopric, the first cathedral was built. That structure burned down in 1248, just days after a resolution had been passed to finance a new cathedral to house the relics of the Three Magi, which Frederick Barbarossa had "liberated" from Milan in 1164 and presented to the increasingly powerful archbishopric of Cologne. Cologne had been in the lucrative "relics trade" for centuries (see The Romanesque Churches below), but having the remains of the Three Wise Men gave the city a prestige that necessitated building a shrine of the first magnitude.

The new Cologne cathedral was modeled after the great French Gothic cathedral in Amiens, but it was meant to surpass Amiens—and indeed every other existing cathedral in Europe—in size and splendor. The French-style Gothic choir, called the **chevet**, with its highly decorative system of buttressing was completed by 1322, after which work began on the south aisles and the south tower. The **Portal of St. Peter,** the south (or far right) doorway as you face the spires, was executed between 1370 and 1380 and is the only portal completed in medieval times. Construction of the Dom continued until 1560, punctuated by dramatic events like the burning of Luther's 95 theses in the cathedral square. Then, suddenly, the coffers ran dry and all work on it ceased.

For 300 years the cathedral languished in its unfinished state, a rather lopsided affair with only one tower, the chevet, and a provisional roof covering the nave. When Napoleon's revolutionary troops marched into the city in 1794 they dissolved the archbishopric, closed the cathedral, and used it to store grain and incarcerate prisoners of war (who burned up all the priceless wooden furnishings in the nave and transept to keep warm).

It was in the period of German nationalism following Napoleon's defeat that plans to complete the great cathedral were finally rekindled—rather ironically, as the ruling Prussian Hohenzollerns were Protestant and Cologne had always been and remains to this day a predominantly Roman Catholic city. The archbishopric was restored and amidst great pomp and ceremony King Friedrich Wilhelm IV announced in 1842 that "in the spirit of the brotherhood of all Germans and of all faiths" the cathedral would be completed. The king and the new archbishop laid the cornerstone inaugurating reconstruction.

In the final phase of building, the cathedral's Gothic style became Neo-Gothic, but Ernst Friedrich Zwirner, then the cathedral architect, was able to adhere closely to the original plans because the medieval elevations and ground lines for the structure, lost for centuries, suddenly turned up in Darmstadt. The unity of Gothic design seen today, even though much of it dates from the 19th century, makes Cologne cathedral unique among all the cathedrals in the world. In 1880, after 632 years, the massive structure was finally finished.

But there is a saying in Cologne: "When the cathedral is completed, the world will end." There is always scaffolding on some part or another. The first damage by weathering was noted early in this century and prompted the re-establishment of a cathedral workshop called the **Dombau-hütte** (now located in a modern building and work area on the south side of the chevet). In World War II the cathedral suffered damage from bombs and had to be hastily patched up. Today the danger is one that affects all the world's monuments: destruction by air pollution, particularly sulfur dioxide. A team of over 70 stonemasons and craftsmen is employed to remove and replace damaged sections of the building with weatherproof material—prompting fears that at some future date every stone in this magnificent structure will be a copy.

As you enter the cathedral's vestibule through the central portal the sheer size and upward surge of the interior space are awe-inspiring. The **Dreikönigschrein** (Shrine of the Three Magi), housed in a glass case at the end of the choir, is the cathedral's major treasure and contains the stolen relics that prompted construction of the cathedral over 800 years ago. This giant reliquary is a masterpiece of goldsmith work dating from the end of the 12th and the beginning of the 13th century, but long gone are the days when priests would open the shrine to visitors like the British poet Algernon Charles Swinburne, who peered inside and saw "three skulls crowned and the names written in rubies."

The **choir** itself, which can be visited only on guided tours (Monday through Friday at 10:00 and 11:00 A.M. and 2:30 and 3:30 P.M., Saturdays at 10:00 and 11:00 A.M., Sundays and holidays at 2:30 P.M.), is the most important part of the cathedral. Consecrated in 1322, it contains original, richly carved oak choir stalls, choir screen paintings that mark the beginning of the Cologne school of painting, and a series of graceful, highly mannered pillar statues made in the cathedral workshop between 1270 and 1290. The famous **Three Kings windows** in the clerestory (you need binoculars to fully appreciate them) were installed sometime before 1311.

In addition to some magnificent Renaissance stained-glass windows in the north aisle, there are really only two other obligatory treasures to be seen in the cathedral. The **Gero Cross**, hanging in the Chapel of the Holy Cross on the north side of the choir, is a rare example of monumental Ottonian sculpture. Carved in Cologne in the late tenth century, it is reputedly the oldest existing large-scale crucifix in the western world. On the south side of the choir is Stephan Lochner's altarpiece, **Adoration of the Magi**, created around 1445. The painting is a masterpiece of the Cologne school—Italian in format, Flemish in the precision of its execution.

The cathedral's **Schatzkammer** (Treasury), ransacked over the centuries, is rather disappointing, and you aren't missing much if you skip it. If, on the other hand, you're in reasonably good shape, you can climb the 509 stairs of the 14th-century south tower (entry through the Portal of Saint Peter) for an inspiring view of the city and the Rhine from just below the spire. On the way up you'll pass two of the Dom's enormous bells, Speciosa and Pretiosa, hung in the mid-15th century but now mostly mute—the reverberations from their mighty peals pose a danger to the fragile structure.

From the cathedral it's only a few steps across Roncalliplatz to the Römisch-Germanisches (Roman-Germanic) Museum with its priceless cache of artifacts—many of them unearthed in Cologne—and the new Wallraf-Richartz/Museum Ludwig complex, where medieval works from the Cologne school and paintings by later European masters share space with those of the German Expressionists and American pop artists. Beneath this cultural treasure trove is the new Philharmonie (philharmonic hall).

The Römisch-Germanisches Museum

Cologne's history, and the fabric of the city today, is inextricably bound up with the history of Rome—a legacy that is brilliantly documented in the Römisch-Germanisches Museum, opened in 1974. As early as 50 B.C. Gaius Julius Caesar had extended the borders of the Roman Empire as far as the Rhine and established an alliance with the Germanic Ubii tribe on the site of present-day Cologne. Under General Agrippa, son-in-law of Augustus, the area became a military garrison whose importance was signified by the presence of an imperial shrine. It was here, in so-called Lower Germania, that Julia Agrippina, the great-granddaughter of Augustus Caesar, the daughter of Germanicus, the sister of Caligula, the mother of Nero, and the third wife of the emperor Claudius, was born in A.D. 15.

Regardless of what history tells us about Agrippina (she was, like everyone in the Roman imperial family, a relentless, power-mad schemer who ultimately murdered her husband and was herself murdered by her son), it was she who granted her birthplace the rights of a Roman city in A.D. 50, thereby initiating Cologne's first period of prosperity as Colonia Claudia Ara Agrippinensium (CCAA). A growing population of soldiers, traders, officials, merchants, retired veterans, and artisans skilled in glassware, pottery, and leather goods came to the walled port-colony (today's Innenstadt) on the left (west) bank of the Rhine. A 48-mile-long aqueduct was built to carry fresh water from the Eifel hills, and there was an efficient underground sewage and drainage system. Cologne's Roman period lasted until A.D. 401, when the Roman legions were recalled from the Rhine frontier and the city came under the rule of the Franks.

Before you enter the museum you may want to have a quick look at a section of the original **Roman city wall**, which extended for about a kilometer in each direction and enclosed this entire area. To do so, enter the parking garage through the red door across from the Cologne tourist office on Unter Fettenhennen. (Be aware, however, that the down-and-out sometimes sleep off their benders beside the ancient walls.) On the Domplatz, above the garage, a section of the **Roman North Gate** has been preserved; on the right side of the museum is **Hafenstrasse**, paved with its original stones, a street that once ran down to the Roman harbor.

The Roman-Germanic Museum was built around a magnificent mosaic floor discovered in 1941 by workers digging an air-raid shelter. The **Dionysius mosaic**, produced in a Rhineland workshop in the third century, reveals the close artistic and cultural ties between Rome and its prosperous military colony. By the time the mosaic was installed, to grace the dining hall of a sumptuous villa, Cologne had become the capital of Lower Germania and the Roman governor of the province resided down the street in the Praetorium (see below).

Towering above the in-situ Dionysius mosaic, whose mythological scenes celebrate the joys of good living, is the **tomb of Lucius Poblicius**, constructed around A.D. 40 for a Roman officer in the Fifth Legion. This, the largest antique tomb found north of the Alps, was brought to light in the 1960s by two brothers doing repair work in the basement of their parents' home in the Severin district.

The fascinating lode of exhibits in the Roman-Germanic Museum is not arranged in strict chronological order but is grouped, instead, by theme or type: religious life, trade and industry, the cult of the dead, and so on. Nor are the exhibits limited strictly to the Roman period—they extend from the Stone Age to the period of Charlemagne. If your time is limited, head for the superlative collection of glassware on the second floor. Glassworkers in Cologne developed a unique style that reached its artistic peak in the exquisite diatreta glass of the fourth century. The museum's jewelry collection, dating from the great migrations that followed the collapse of the Roman Empire, is also world-renowned. In the lowest level of the museum, devoted to the daily life of the Romans, you'll find an ancient curiosity with contemporary reverberations: a black-and-white mosaic floor covered with swastikas. Centuries before it became ominously identified with the atrocities of the Third Reich, the swastika—probably Indian in origin—was a symbol of good luck and happiness, and was known in Latin as the *crux gamata*.

If you want to have lunch before continuing on to the Wallraf-Richartz/Museum Ludwig complex and the Praetorium, the cathedral area offers plenty of choices. For a quick meal head down **Hohe Strasse**—the main thoroughfare of Roman Cologne and today one of the city's main shopping streets—where there are various streetside snack counters (the take-out herring at the Nordsee Restaurant is good). Sit-down dining is available in tavern-restaurants such as **Früh Brauhaus**, next to the cathedral, and **Alt Köln**, beside the Hotel Excelsior Ernst; these are not beer gardens, per se, but you'll still be able to mix with the locals here. If the weather is fine, you might also want to try the string of open-air restaurants located close to the Rhine, south of the cathedral: The food at most of these international tourist haunts is good, but definitely not haute cuisine (see Dining).

The Wallraf-Richartz and Museum Ludwig Complex

In contrast to the soaring verticality and dense, visually overwhelming Gothic decoration of the cathedral, the box-like Römisch-Germanisches and the brick-and-metal Wallraf-Richartz/Museum Ludwig complex beside it are simple, restrained, and deferential. The latter, built in a robust Late Modernist style, reveals the true size and complexity of its design only when viewed from behind, where the wavelike half-cylinders of its roof attempt to blend in stylistically with the restored gabled houses that form Cologne's Rhine panorama. Created by Cologne architects Peter Busmann and Godfrid Haberer and opened to a great deal of adverse criticism in 1986, the Wallraf-Richartz/Museum Ludwig complex has, thanks to the strength of its collections, become the city's most popular art museum.

Cologne's museums are unusual in that most of them

were created by the bequests of individual collectors rather than by municipal foundations. The collections in the Wallraf-Richartz and the Römisch-Germanisches museums initially belonged to Franz Ferdinand Wallraf (1748–1824), an artistically minded canon and professor with wide-ranging and eclectic tastes. Wallraf left his treasures to the city of his birth, and Johann-Heinrich Richartz (1795–1861), a wealthy merchant, provided the money to house them. The Wallraf-Richartz-Museum opened in 1861, making it one of Germany's oldest museums, and expanded its holdings over the years to include contemporary art, much of which was confiscated as "degenerate" by the Nazis in 1937. Wartime bombing destroyed the original museum building, and in 1957 a new museum building was opened (it is now the Museum für Angewandte Kunst; see below). Then, in 1976, after years of lending contemporary pieces to the Wallraf-Richartz, the ubiquitous Aachen collectors Peter and Irene Ludwig made a massive bequest of 350 modern works—on the condition that a new building be constructed to contain them. The Wallraf-Richartz/Museum Ludwig complex was thus created to join two superlative art collections under one roof. (The museums are open Tuesday through Thursday from 10:00 A.M. until 8:00 P.M., and Friday through Sunday from 10:00 A.M. until 6:00 P.M.; closed Mondays.)

The **Wallraf-Richartz-Museum** is one of Germany's greatest repositories of art from the Middle Ages to the late 19th century; you could easily spend days browsing in its myriad galleries. The floor plan that comes with an admission ticket will help guide you, but don't try to take it in all at once—you'll get dizzy trying to absorb every work on display.

On the mezzanine level there is an outstanding collection of panel paintings by the medieval Cologne school, including works by Stefan Lochner (whose *Adoration of the Magi* altarpiece is on view in the cathedral). Lochner's most famous work here is *Madonna in the Rose Bower,* dating from 1451. Many of these medieval paintings and altarpieces depict legends from the lives of martyred saints who became identified with the "Holy Cologne" of the Middle Ages—Saint Ursula in particular (see the description of the church of St. Ursula below).

Another highlight of the Wallraf-Richartz-Museum is the collection of Dutch and Flemish paintings of the 17th century, with Peter Paul Rubens's *Self-Portrait Amidst the Circle of Friends from Mantua* and an enigmatic self-portrait by Rembrandt occupying pride of place. In addition to important French and Spanish works, the museum boasts a rich collection of 19th-century paintings, with major pieces by the German Romantic painter Caspar David Friedrich, Gustave Courbet, Edvard Munch, Auguste Renoir, and Vincent van Gogh, among scores of others. There is also a graphic arts collection spanning eight centuries, a 20th-century photography section, and the **Agfa-Foto-Historama**, a museum within the museum devoted to the history of photography.

The **Museum Ludwig**, occupying floors above and below the Wallraf-Richartz-Museum, is devoted exclusively to art of the 20th century. It's impossible to list here even a portion of the works on view; nearly every major artist and art movement of the century are represented. The collection of German Expressionists is particularly fine, as is that of the Russian avant-garde. There are, in addition, outstanding surrealist paintings by Max Ernst (in particular his newly acquired *The Virgin Reprimands the Christ Child in Front of Three Witnesses*), Salvador Dali, Ernst Schwitters, and René Magritte. The Museum Ludwig has achieved international fame for its collection of American pop art, which includes pieces by Jasper Johns, Roy Lichtenstein, and the largest assemblage of Andy Warhol's work in Europe.

For another plunge into Cologne's ancient Roman past, head toward the southeastern corner of Roncalliplatz and straight on into the street called Unter Goldschmied (there are signs pointing in the direction of the Rathaus), turning left at Kleine Budengasse. The entrance to the Praetorium is at number 1, in the new Rathaus.

The Praetorium

It's rather strange that in the course of building Cologne's new Rathaus in 1953 the builders should come upon the remains of the city's administrative headquarters from some 19 centuries earlier. But so they did, and as you descend into the silent netherworld of Roman Cologne beneath the drab postwar building that sits atop it, the scurrying bustle and hubbub that once characterized these official precincts may be hard to envision—unless, of course, a group of excited schoolchildren happens to be visiting at the same time. There are two things to see below the new Rathaus: the Praetorium excavation itself, and a long walk-through section of the original Roman sewer system.

The first Praetorium was built on a Roman wall above the Rhine in about A.D. 50, soon after Agrippina had conferred her name on the military outpost and given it the right to create its own bylaws. Initially it was the official seat of the commander-in-chief of the regional army, but was enlarged, altered, and rebuilt over the ensuing centuries. It was from the Praetorium that the province of Lower Germania was administered by a Roman governor. Eventually it became an imperial palace, the so-called Regia. In A.D. 69 Vitellius was declared emperor of Rome from here, as was Trajan some 30 years later. Constantine the Great made the Praetorium his headquarters in 310 while establishing a new citadel for the protection of the empire's border on the right bank of the Rhine (in what is now Deutz). When the Romans withdrew, the Praetorium became the residence of the Merovingian kings.

Before entering, it's useful to have a look at the building plans displayed in the exhibition room—filled with Roman finds—just outside the excavation area. The large model next to the excavations, though not entirely accurate, nonetheless will give you a good idea of the size and shape of the building from which Roman Colonia and the surrounding province were governed. The most impressive feature— certainly the most recognizable—is the octagon in the center of the ruins. Take a look, too, at the photographs on the side walls, which show the bomb-ravaged area during the course of excavation.

On the other side of the exhibition room is the entrance to a section of the original Roman sewers. Although this may not sound inviting, it is fascinating to walk through and see the high degree of engineering skills the ancient Romans brought to their outpost on the Rhine. The arched tufa-and-brick tunnel is eerily quiet, and at one point a glass window allows you to peer down into the murky, illuminated depths of the Rhine flowing just below. (Open Tuesday through Sunday, 10:00 A.M. to 5:00 P.M.)

The Altes Rathaus and the Mikwe

Cologne's Altes Rathaus (Old Town Hall), located a block south of the Praetorium at Rathausplatz, was originally built in the 14th century, but it is the striking loggia, constructed by Wilhelm Vernukken between 1569 and 1573, that claims particular attention. From the upper balcony of this graceful Renaissance porch—an architectural rarity in Cologne—the city council would deliver its proclamations to the citizenry gathered in the square below. (Today it's more likely to be the triumphant members of Cologne's first-division football team, rather than any city official, greeting the crowd from the loggia.) The five-story Rathaus tower, now restored after heavy wartime damage, was built by the artisan guilds as a symbol of municipal power after they wrested independence from the archbishops and ruling patricians. Cologne, a founding member of the Hanseatic League, was elevated to the status of a Free Imperial City, with the right to mint its own coins, in 1475.

No municipal freedoms were extended to the city's Jewish population, however, which had been officially expelled from Cologne in 1424. Before this occurred, the area surrounding the Praetorium and Altes Rathaus was one of the oldest and most important Jewish communities in Germany, dating back to the fourth century. For five centuries, until it was replaced by a Christian chapel in 1426, a synagogue stood here. All that remains of this Jewish religious and cultural center is the **Mikwe**, a ritual bath enclosed by a small steel-and-glass pyramid in Rathausplatz. The actual bathing area, a basin of sandstone squares at the bottom of a deep well-shaft, is still fed by groundwater whose depth changes according to the water level of the Rhine. If you want to enter, the key can be obtained from the custodian at the Altes Rathaus (Monday through Thursday, 8:00 A.M. to 4:45 P.M.; Fridays, 8:00 A.M. to noon; Saturdays, 10:00 A.M. to 4:00 P.M.; Sundays, 11:00 A.M. to 1:00 P.M.).

Between the Altes Rathaus and the Mikwe is an excavated apse from the Praetorium's Aula. Gülichsplatz, the corner diagonally across from the Mikwe, is graced by the light-hearted **Fastnachtsbrunnen** (Carnival Fountain). Four dancing couples, presided over by a mischievous Cupid atop a stele, decorate this bronze fountain, which dates from 1913.

Several options present themselves to you at this point. A stairway next to the Altes Rathaus leads down to the **Alter Markt** (Old Market), a restored square set within an inviting warren of narrow Innenstadt streets. From the Alter Markt you can easily find your way to **Gross St. Martin**, one of Cologne's 12 Romanesque churches and the most prominent landmark (after the cathedral) along the Rhine promenade. Imposing as the exterior of Great St. Martin's is, however, the interior contains scanty evidence of its former glory. Far more interesting is St. Maria im Kapitol (a short walk south from Rathausplatz), one of no less than seven Romanesque churches to be found in Altstadt-Süd (see below).

To reach Altstadt-Süd, or to continue your tour of the Innenstadt, stroll south on Quatermarkt past the ruins of **Alt-St.-Alban**, a bombed-out church, now a war memorial, that contains a copy of a moving sculpture, *Trauerndes Elternpaar* (Grieving Parents), by Käthe Kollwitz. Cologne has honored Kollwitz by establishing a museum—one of the city's finest—of her works (see below). The church abuts the **Gürzenich**, a 15th-century festival and banqueting hall where the city council once received kings and emperors. After its destruction in the war the Gürzenich was rebuilt in the 1950s as Cologne's main concert hall (the city's Gürzenich Orchestra now plays primarily in the new Philharmonie).

Cäcilienstrasse, two blocks south of Gürzenichstrasse, marks the end of the Innenstadt and the beginning of Altstadt-Süd, where you'll find St. Maria im Kapitol and a cluster of other Romanesque churches (discussed below). If you want to forgo St. Maria and see more of the Innenstadt, head west on Gürzenichstrasse, which becomes **Schilder-gasse**, Cologne's major east–west pedestrians-only shopping street.

Set somewhat incongruously in the midst of all this consumer culture, at Schildergasse 57, is the small Gothic **Antoniterkirche** (Church of the Anthonians), consecrated in 1384. Rebuilding after the war unfortunately obliterated much of its character, but it's still worth going in to see Ernst Barlach's powerful sculpture called *Todesengel* (Angel of Death), which hangs suspended in a side chapel. The *Todesengel,* whose face is modeled on Kollwitz's, is a copy of a 1928 work that hung in Güstrow cathedral until it was destroyed by the Nazis in 1937.

Just down the street from the Antoniterkirche, at Neumarkt 18–24, is the very upscale **Neumarkt-Passage shopping arcade**, where a glass-enclosed elevator takes you to a museum devoted to the works of Kollwitz.

The Käthe Kollwitz Museum

The Käthe Kollwitz Museum is one of several smaller museums in Cologne that easily can be overlooked by travellers intent on seeing only the "big" works in the Wallraf-Richartz/ Museum Ludwig complex. It would be a shame to miss it, however, for it's one of the most beautiful museums in Germany and an eloquent testimony to the artistic powers of one of Germany's greatest artists.

Although Kollwitz's life (1867–1945) was mostly spent in Berlin and not Cologne—she made only two brief visits to the city—her presence is felt in two of Cologne's most powerful art works, both of them war memorials. The *Griev-ing Parents* in Alt-St.-Alban (see above) is a copy of the Kollwitz sculpture erected in the Roggevelde Soldiers' Cemetery in Belgium in memory of her son Peter, who died in Flanders in 1914. Kollwitz's face was used as the model for her friend Ernst Barlach's famous *Todesengel,* which hangs suspended in a chapel in the small Antoniterkirche on Schildergasse (see above). During the Third Reich the works of both Kollwitz and Barlach were banned from all German museums.

The lower rooms of this beautifully designed museum contain a superlative collection of Kollwitz's self-portraits, pen-and-ink drawings, posters, watercolors, lithographs, and bronze sculptures; the upper floor is used for temporary exhibitions. (Open Tuesday through Sunday, 10:00 A.M. to 5:00 P.M.; Thursdays the museum stays open till 8:00 P.M.)

To continue a tour of the Innenstadt from the Käthe Kollwitz Museum, head east on Schildergasse, turn left on Krebs-gasse, and right on Brüdergasse. Here you'll find Offen-bachplatz, the plaza of the **Oper der Stadt Köln** (Cologne Opera) and its adjacent Schauspielhaus (Theater). Opened in 1957, and a prime example of that postwar decade's restrained architecture, the opera house was the final proj-ect of the Cologne architect Wilhelm Riphahn, one of Ger-many's most influential exponents of the "New Objectivity" of the 1920s. The Cologne Opera, with its wide-ranging repertoire, is considered one of Germany's best.

Eau de Cologne

Directly across the street from the opera house at Glocken-gasse 4711 stands the restored 18th-century house of the Mühlens family, one of the earliest producers of Kölnisch Wasser, the scented "Cologne Water" that eventually came to be known as Eau de Cologne.

The carefully guarded secret recipe for this distinctive scent was brought to Cologne from Italy in the early 18th century, and the toilet water was first produced here by Giovanni Farina in a house near the Altes Rathaus. Originally it was sold not as a perfume but as a wondrous and ex-tremely popular cure-all for strokes, gout, coughs, and plague. When Napoleon, whose occupying troops entered the city in 1794, got a whiff of the miraculous tonic called (by the customers, not the manufacturers) Eau de Cologne, he issued an imperial decree prohibiting the advertising and sale of "secret medicines." If Eau de Cologne was so useful, the official reasoning went, the emperor would naturally want to buy the formula and make it generally available for all his subjects. Of course the last thing the makers of Kölnisch Wasser wanted was to turn their lucrative product over to the French, so they withdrew the health claims for Eau de Cologne and sold it as a toilet water instead. Any kind of toilet water is now called Eau de Cologne, or simply "cologne," but *Echt Kölnisch Wasser* (real Eau de Cologne) remains the designation of origin for the products from Cologne.

The restored **4711 House**, as it's known, is now a perfume boutique and a good place to stock up on the delightful orange-and-lavender scent of Kölnisch Wasser, available in all sizes and shapes and as soap and even premoistened towelettes. The 4711 trademark of this particular firm also originated with the French. In 1794 the French army of occupation discovered that few if any places in Cologne had street numbers (as they still don't on Hohe Strasse). A rider was dispatched to remedy the situation by writing numbers on the housefronts with a piece of chalk. The Mühlens' house on Glockengasse, the second-oldest manufactury of Kölnisch Wasser in the city, was assigned the number 4711.

The Innenstadt contains two more fine museums, although you may want to save these for another day and couple them with a tour of Cologne's earliest Romanesque church, St. Gereon's (for a description of St. Gereon's, see The Romanesque Churches, below).

To reach the **Museum für Angewandte Kunst** (Museum of Applied Arts), cross Tunisstrasse and walk north from the opera house, turning right on An der Rechtschule. The museum is housed in the former Wallraf-Richartz-Museum, designed by Rudolf Schwarz and Josef Bernhard, and was constructed between 1953 and 1957 (roughly the same period as the opera house). Spacious, elegantly redesigned galleries allow maximum enjoyment of the dazzling treasures on chronological display here: furniture, home decor, and handicrafts from the Middle Ages to the present day. The huge Art Nouveau room is particularly impressive. On the ground floor and mezzanine the exhibits are exclusively from the 20th century and include rooms and furniture by Alvar Aalto, Marcel Breuer, Ludwig Mies van der Rohe, and Charles Eames, among others. (Open Tuesday through Sunday, 10:00 A.M. to 5:00 P.M.)

The atmosphere of the nearby **Kölnisches Stadtmuseum** (Cologne City Museum) is dowdy and provincial in comparison, but that is part of its charm. Carnival, Kölnisch Wasser, Kölsch, Saint Ursula and the virgin martyrs—everything that has been connected or particularly identified with Cologne during its 2,000 years of existence has a display here. To reach the City Museum from the Museum of Applied Arts walk north on Tunisstrasse and turn left on Komödienstrasse, which almost immediately becomes Zeughausstrasse. With its bright red-and-white shutters, the City Museum, housed in the former city arsenal at Zeughausstrasse 1–3, is unmistakable.

Even if you have no particular interest in the general

history of Cologne, the museum is worth visiting for its exhibit on city life during and immediately after World War II. In no other German museum will you encounter the chilling, everyday reality of that war and its aftermath as honestly as you will here. The Nazi-era objects on exhibit include the *Judenstern* (Jewish Star) badge that Jews were required to wear, posters extolling racial purity, a student uniform with a knife inscribed *Blut und Ehre* (Blood and Honor), gas masks, and even one of the tubs that were used as toilets in the air-raid shelters. Postwar items include a CARE package, anti-Nazi posters, and the German flag that was hanging from the center portal of Cologne cathedral when American troops arrived on March 6, 1945. (Open Tuesday through Sunday, 10:00 A.M. to 5:00 P.M.; Thursdays, 10:00 A.M. to 8:00 P.M.)

At the corner of Zeughausstrasse and St.-Apern-Strasse stands a surprisingly graceful remnant of ancient Colonia— the completely preserved northwestern tower of the Roman city wall, built around A.D. 50 and known as the **Römerturm**.

THE ALTSTADT

Over the centuries, as Cologne continued to grow, it spread out in a concentric semicircle around the original walled Roman colony (the Innenstadt). A massive new wall, completed in the 12th century, was built to protect the enlarged city. The area within the medieval wall, which followed the lines of today's ring road, is Cologne's Altstadt.

With the exception of Gross St. Martin (see above), all 12 of Cologne's Romanesque churches are located in the Altstadt area that surrounds the Innenstadt. Seven of the churches—one of which, St. Cäcilien, housing the beautiful Schnütgen Museum of medieval art—are in Altstadt-Süd, the area south of Cäcilienstrasse and Hahnenstrasse; the rest are in Altstadt-Nord.

The Romanesque Churches

By the mid-13th century prosperous, ever-expanding "Holy Cologne" had become one of the greatest cities north of the Alps, and medieval pilgrims wending their way here fully expected to be dazzled by an impressive array of churches and holy sites. Though the relics trade had become big business in Cologne after Archbishop Reinald von Dassel, chancellor to Emperor Frederick Barbarossa, brought the stolen remains of the Three Wise Men from Milan in 1164, Cologne had for centuries venerated and capitalized on its own stock of Early Christian martyrs. Inspiring local legends came to be regarded as truth when there were bones to back up the stories, and of saintly body parts—found primarily in ancient Roman-Frankish cemeteries—Cologne had a seemingly inexhaustible supply. The pickings included Saint Ursula and her 11,000 virgin travelling companions, and Saint Gereon and his legion of Roman centurions, all of them allegedly martyred in Cologne.

The powerful archbishops of Cologne, who as prince-electors helped elect the Holy Roman emperor, instituted major church-building programs in the 10th and 11th centuries, as did the aristocratic founders of convents and monasteries. By 1247, one year before the cornerstone of the new cathedral was laid and the "official" style became Gothic, all 12 of the Romanesque churches in existence today were completed. The first major buildings to be erected in Cologne since antiquity, they remain an important stylistic bridge between Roman Colonia and the Cologne of the Gothic era. Taken as a whole, they represent one of the greatest periods of church building in Western Europe.

It is only fair to add, however, that because of the amount of rebuilding that was necessary after the wartime devastation, Cologne's oldest churches invariably have a "new" feeling to them; for some visitors this is a real disappointment. The smooth plaster walls look as though they've barely had time to dry, and the modern stained glass lacks the delicate mystery and patina of the old. Gone are the colorful paintings and statues that originally decorated the walls. What's left are the remarkable spaces themselves, serene and somewhat austere, with their remaining treasures carefully displayed. (Each church has its own opening times, and these can be found in the free monthly guide called *Köln Monatsvorschau,* available at the tourist office.)

It was Plectrudis, stepmother of Charles Martel, who founded the eighth-century nunnery that eventually became the church of **St. Maria im Kapitol**, located just south of Cäcilienstrasse, a few minutes' walk from Rathausplatz. The name, St. Mary in the Capitol, refers to the Roman temple of the Capitoline Trias that once occupied the site. Entering from Kasinostrasse you pass by the only remaining **cloisters** in Cologne.

Architectural history of a sort was made here in the 11th century when St. Maria im Kapitol became the first church in Cologne to have a clover-leaf choir modeled after the one in the ancient Church of the Nativity in Bethlehem. The rounded choir with apse and flanking steeples is a stylistic feature peculiar to Cologne Romanesque, and you'll see it repeated in several of the other churches. Two very different images of Plectrudis gaze out from commemorative tombstones set in the walls of the nave: in one, dating from the late 12th century, she appears as a flat and rather forbidding Byzantine icon; in the second, carved only a hundred years later, she has been considerably enlivened and humanized. The other great treasure in the church is a set of 11th-century wooden door panels with vividly carved reliefs illustrating the life of Christ.

If St. Maria im Kapitol piques your interest in the Romanesque, you may want to visit other Romanesque churches in the vicinity. The closest are no more than a ten-minute walk away: **St. Maria in Lyskirchen**, to the east along the Rhine (An Lyskirchen), and **St. Georg**, to the south (Georgsplatz). Larger and more interesting is **St. Pantaleon**, to the southwest (Am Pantaleonsberg), founded as a Benedictine abbey by Archbishop Bruno, the brother of Holy Roman Emperor Otto the Great, and consecrated in 980. The Byzantine Empress Theophanu, another important woman in Cologne's past (along with Agrippina, Ursula, and Plectrudis), extended the church and is buried here. The area around **St. Severin**, near Chlodwigplatz at the southernmost tip of Altstadt-Süd, is as close as you'll get to an old Cologne *Veedel* ("neighborhood" in the Kölsch dialect). Chlodwigplatz is dominated by the **Severinstor**, one of the three remaining gates from the medieval walls that once encircled the city.

One of Cologne's finest art collections can be found in the **Schnütgen-Museum**, housed in the former Romanesque church of **St. Cäcilien**, located due west of St. Maria im Kapitol at Cäcilienstrasse 29. Try not to miss this small, splendid sampling of sacred art from the early Middle Ages to the Baroque. The relics, reliquaries, crucifixes, and sculpture on display will give you an idea of just how artistically blessed "Holy Cologne" was. Outside, around the back, a skeleton has been spray-painted on the walled-in western portal of the church/museum. Called simply *Tod* (Death), it is an oddly engaging recent work by the Zürich graffiti artist Harald Nägele. (Open Tuesday through Sunday, 10:00 A.M. to 5:00 P.M.)

From the Schnütgen-Museum cross Cäcilienstrasse to reach majestic **St. Aposteln**, a city landmark standing unperturbed amidst the busy traffic at the western end of **Neumarkt**, where it marks the southwestern corner of the Innenstadt. The distinctive clover-leaf choir, with a so-called dwarf gallery connecting the apses, has here reached its most mature architectural expression. The area around St. Aposteln is far more concerned with expressing the commercial side of life than the spiritual, however, and from here you can stroll back into the Innenstadt along the two main pedestrians-only shopping streets of Cologne. Take Schildergasse east and turn left on Hohe Strasse, which will lead you back to the cathedral.

North of the Cathedral

In the city's lexicon of saints, the two most prominent are Saint Ursula and Saint Gereon, both of whom were said to be martyred along with their followers in Cologne. The two churches devoted to these patrons of Cologne are located north of the cathedral, and both are worth a visit.

A good starting point for a tour of Altstadt-Nord is the pink church of **St. Mariä Himmelfahrt** (Church of the Assumption), built for the Jesuits in the early 17th century. The church, on An den Dominikanern in the banking quarter a block north of the cathedral, has an unusually sumptuous interior (for Cologne, if not for the Jesuits) in which concerts are frequently held.

An den Dominikanern may seem an unlikely street name for a Jesuit church, but it in fact refers to a Romanesque church located down the street, to your left, **St. Andreas**, which came into the hands of the Dominicans after World War II. A rather ugly postwar addition mars the street façade of St. Andreas, but within you'll find the 16th-century Shrine of the Maccabees (a smaller version of the Shrine of the Three Magi in the cathedral), as well as an altar by Barthel Bruyn from the same period. The crypt contains the **tomb of Albertus Magnus** (Saint Albert the Great, 1193–1280), the famed medieval professor of theology who was canonized in 1931. Pope John Paul II paid a visit to the church on the 700th anniversary of Albertus Magnus's death in 1980.

Andreaskloster, the street just outside the church, has a Tchibo, a stand-up coffee and pastry bar, and two restaurants that cater to workers in the banking quarter: **Trattoria Pizzeria am Dom** (good for ice cream and coffee drinks if you're not interested in lunch) and the New Yorkish **Bankers**, which appeals to the business denizens of the area by offering specials with names like "Business Lunch" and "Wall Street's Finest." If you're interested in rare stamps, have a look at **Brungs**, also on Andreaskloster.

Continuing west, An den Dominikanen becomes Unter Sachsenhausen and then Gereonsstrasse, where you'll find what is perhaps the most interesting of all the Romanesque churches in Cologne.

St. Gereon

The origins of St. Gereon lay in a hazy period of late antiquity, before the Romans decamped from Cologne. Sometime in the fourth century a decagonal chapel was erected outside the Roman city wall over the presumed remains of Gereon, an early Christian centurion recruited from Egypt to serve in Roman Colonia and martyred, along with his fellow Theban legionnaires, for refusing to worship the pagan gods. The church and its "warrior saints" (a male counterpart of Ursula and the virgin martyrs) were so venerated that Archbishop Hildebold, the ninth-century builder of Cologne's first cathedral, elected to be buried in St. Gereon instead of his own church.

Over the centuries additions were made and alterations carried out, most notably in the 13th century, when the original ten-sided two-storied Roman chapel was incorporated into a magnificent Early Gothic structure with two additional stories and one of the largest ribbed vaults in Christendom. Like almost everything else in the city, it was reduced to a heap of smoking rubble during the war.

St. Gereon "feels" older than Cologne's other restored Romanesque churches. It is also rare in that it preserved traces of the 13th-century wall paintings that once covered the baptistery. In the crypt there are some remarkable 11th-century mosaics of David and Goliath and Samson and Delilah, though, unfortunately, they are poorly lit and difficult to see.

St. Ursula

Marzellenstrasse, the street west of St. Mariä Himmelfahrt, leads to Ursulaplatz and the Romanesque church of St. Ursula, a 12th-century basilica with an overlay of Early Gothic elements in the choir. The crown surmounting the Baroque crest atop the western tower is a reminder of the noble English origins of Saint Ursula and the virgin martyrs venerated here for centuries.

Unfortunately, there's no evidence that the saintly virgin who figures so prominently in Cologne's history ever existed. The story of the virgin martyrs probably originated in a third-century massacre of Christians in Cologne, but Ursula herself doesn't figure into the account until some six centuries later. No matter: Ursula and the virgin martyrs became spiritual superstars whose story brought droves of faithful pilgrims to Cologne. When the 12th-century builders of St. Ursula uncovered an ancient Roman-Frankish cemetery, the bones discovered therein were eagerly seized upon as the sacred remains of Ursula and her (by this time) 11,000 virgin companions. Eventually the story was symbolically incorporated into the city's coat of arms, which shows eleven flames—one for each thousand martyred virgins—under the three crowns of the Magi. (The number 11 seems to have an almost mystical significance in Cologne; see Carnival below.)

The appealingly carved and painted wooden busts of smiling young women (there are smiling young men, too) that fill the gilded niches of **Der Goldenen Kammer** (The Golden Chamber) in St. Ursula are, in fact, reliquaries of the sort that were subsequently made in Cologne and exported throughout Europe to spread the cult of Ursula and the virgin martyrs. There is an odd, dusty, slightly off-kilter splendor to this room with its faded pink walls, enigmatically smiling figures, and intricately arranged wall decorations made, apparently, from leftover bones. (The Golden Chamber in St. Ursula is open Mondays and Thursdays from 11:00 A.M. to noon; Wednesdays and Fridays from 3:00 to 4:00 P.M.; and Saturdays from 3:00 to 5:00 P.M.; look for the church custodian if the door is not open.)

Within the church, to the left of the choir, there is another curious reliquary, this one a copper ship with Ursula's name on the prow and the 11 symbolic flames of the virgin martyrs engraved on its billowing sail; the holy bones were stashed in the hold. The Ursula legend is portrayed in a series of nearby wall panels, the final one as grisly as a scene from a modern horror movie.

A few minutes' walk north from Ursulaplatz on Eigelstein, a busy neighborhood shopping street, brings you to the **Eigelsteintor**, one of three remaining fortified medieval gates into the city. The heavy 13th-century structure, which you pass through to reach Ebertplatz, is enlivened by a 19th-century sculpture known in Cologne dialect as *Kölscher Boor* (Boy of Cologne). There are some good restaurants close to the gate, including **Em Kölsche Boor** at number 121, serving traditional fare in a comfortable old-Cologne atmosphere, and **Trattoria Nico** at number 143, where there are outdoor tables.

A passageway under the ring road leads to Ebertplatz, a landscaped pedestrian area whose most intriguing feature, a modern fountain by Wolfgang Gödderts, resembles a ring of giant thumbtacks. The high-rise office building across the street has been dubbed "*Bleistift*" (Pencil) by locals because of its heptagonal shape.

At this point you may want to continue north, outside the Altstadt, to visit the Cologne zoo. The easiest way to reach the zoo from Ebertplatz is by U-Bahn. Two stops on line 5, 15, 16, or 18 brings you to the Zoo/Flora station.

OUTSIDE THE ALTSTADT
The Zoo

When Cologne's **Zoologischer Garten** was first opened in 1860 the animals were picturesquely incarcerated in buildings designed to look like Russian cathedrals and Moorish castles (some of these buildings still exist). Now the animals wander about—over 6,000 of them, including bears, leopards, kangaroos, elephants, and giraffes—in carefully designed natural habitats (though there's nothing "natural" about the incessant traffic noise they have to put up with).

Have a look at the tiny, wide-eyed lemurs from Madagascar peering out into the dim nocturnal atmosphere created for them in the Lemurenhaus, as well as the exotic apes from around the world swinging and scratching on perches in the new Urwaldhaus (Tropical Forest House). Buying a combination ticket also allows you to visit the modern Aquarium and Insectarium, which share quarters opposite the main zoo entrance on Riehler Strasse (where you'll notice that kennels have been thoughtfully provided for *Besucherhunde*—visiting dogs). Plants from all over the world, including a fragrant display of orchids, fill the grounds and greenhouses of the adjacent **Botanischer Garten**.

Deutz

Cologne's other great landscaped oasis, the **Rheinpark**, is located directly across from the zoo in Köln-Deutz; the best way to reach it is by the Rheinseilbahn, a cable railway that provides a fabulous view of the city and surrounding area as it floats you up over the river to the opposite shore. (In operation daily except Fridays from Easter through October.) If the Rheinseilbahn is not running, or if the very idea of swinging 130 feet above the Rhine in a small, glass-enclosed cable car causes you to break out into a cold sweat, you can easily cross over by the Zoobrücke (Zoo Bridge). There are some exceptionally beautiful plantings in the Rheinpark (at its best in the spring, when the air is thick with the smells of flowering trees and shrubs), as well as pleasant paths that skirt alongside the river under old trees. Near the southern end is the Tanzbrunnen (Dancing Fountain), a popular place for open-air concerts of all sorts (see Entertainment and Nightlife).

The Köln Messe

The slender brick tower (4711 is advertised on top of it) across the street from the Tanzbrunnen is known as the Messeturm (Fair Tower) and belongs to the original buildings of the Köln Messe, the city's important trade fair and exhibition center. Trade fairs have been held in Cologne since 1360; today they are international in scope—devoted primarily to high-tech industries, fashion, furniture, and household goods—and absolutely essential to the city's economic life and vitality, bringing in millions of visitors and making Cologne a world trading center for goods, services, and information.

The Messeturm and the low brick buildings arranged in a horseshoe shape around it, all designed in an Expressionistic style by Adolf Abel and built between 1926 and 1928, played a dark role in Cologne's history during World War II. The buildings owe their existence to Konrad Adenauer, who became mayor of Cologne in 1917 and worked indefatigably to promote expansion projects for the city. Under Adenauer the university was reopened, a new stadium was built, two new green belts were laid out, and the Cologne Fair Association was founded. He was ousted by the Nazis when they took over the city government in 1933.

Although it's true that Cologne was never particularly hospitable to Hitler, it's also true that between 1942 and 1944 the original Messe complex was turned into a concentration camp whose inmates, most of them destined for Buchenwald, were forced to build bunkers and clear up bomb rubble. According to some sources, the Messe buildings survived the war because the Allies knew of the camp's existence and wanted to spare its inmates from the air attacks that eventually destroyed 90 percent of the city. Adenauer, who returned as mayor of Cologne in 1945, became the first chancellor of the Federal Republic of Germany in 1949.

There's a great view of Cologne from the **Messeturm Restaurant** atop the 230-foot tower. The menu here doesn't offer any surprises, and the prices are slightly high, but it is a pleasant and panoramic way to enjoy a meal (Kennedy Ufer, Tel: 88-10-08; open Sunday through Friday, noon to 3:00 P.M. and 7:00 to 10:00 P.M.; Saturdays from 7:00 P.M. for dinner only). There's also a café, open from 3:00 to 6:00 P.M., Monday through Saturday.

From the southern end of the Messe you can cross back to the Altstadt on the left bank via the Hohenzollernbrücke or by ferry: The Fähre Hohenzollernbrücke–Deutzer Messe makes the Rhine crossing from Easter through October at roughly ten-minute intervals. If you want to continue your exploration of Cologne's panoramic *Schäl Sick,* or "other side," the Rhine promenade continues south to the Deutzer Brücke.

The Rhine Panorama

Cologne's stimulating atmosphere is due in large part to its location on the Rhine, that age-old artery of trade and transportation, and promenades along both banks of the river are enjoyed by walkers, joggers, and bicyclists. For the best (and quickest) panoramic view of Cologne's attractive skyline, continue south from the Messe or cross over to Deutz from the Innenstadt via the Hohenzollernbrücke behind the cathedral.

The popular riverside **beer garden** in front of the new Hyatt-Regency is a good place to stop for a bit of refreshment before continuing south along the Rhine promenade to the Deutzer Brücke, which returns you to the Altstadt. This short walk takes less than an hour, is pleasant day or night, and reveals Cologne at its most photogenic. The massive upward-thrusting Gothic cathedral dominates the scene, with the new Wallraf-Richartz/Museum Ludwig complex in front of it and the landmark spires of Gross St. Martin and the Altes Rathaus to the left. The restored gable-fronted houses of the Altstadt, painted in pastel colors, help to evoke something of Cologne's medieval past; cruise ships of the Köln-Düsseldorfer line can usually be seen docked along the bank below.

The Contemporary Art Scene

In the last decade, despite stiff competition from Berlin, Frankfurt, and nearby Düsseldorf, Cologne has become accepted as *the* contemporary art capital of Germany. With over 80 galleries here showing the work of both new and established German and international artists (many of them American), contemporary art is big business in Cologne. A major November event at the Messe is Art-Cologne, the first international art fair in the world, first held here in 1963.

Exploring the contemporary art galleries of Cologne is an exciting way to spend all or part of a day, and it opens up a fascinating side of the city most visitors never experience. Many of the galleries are located off the street in rear courtyards called *Hinterhöfe,* and thus are not immediately apparent unless you have a name and address. Advice for the serious gallery explorer: Buy a copy of *Kunst Führer Köln,* by Birgit Gatermann, which includes every gallery and has an English summary, or pick up a free copy of the bimonthly gallery exhibition guide (with map) available at the tourist office or in any of the galleries listed below. Remember, too, that galleries generally close between 1:00 and 3:00 P.M. for lunch; that most are closed on Sundays and Mondays; and that Saturday hours are generally 10:00 A.M. to 2:00 P.M.

GALLERIES IN THE BELGIAN QUARTER

The best place to begin a gallery tour is around Friesenplatz, just west of the Ring road, in the area known as the Belgisches Viertel (Belgian Quarter). Since the early 1980s this has been Cologne's "artiest" neighborhood, comparable to New York City's SoHo and just as gentrified. The number 5 U-Bahn line from the train station will take you to Friesenplatz.

To see a good international mix of art check out, in particular, **Galerie Tanja Grunert**, on the ground floor of Venloer Strasse 19; **Galerie Max Hetzler**, at Venloer Strasse 21; and **Jablonka Galerie**, upstairs in the same building. **Gallerie Frieder Keim**, Bismarckstrasse 50, occupies what was a paper factory until Paul Maenz opened it as the first contemporary gallery space in the Belgian Quarter in 1983; four exhibitions a year are held here. Next door to it is **Galerie Rudolf Kicken**, the only gallery in Cologne devoted exclusively to photography. In the same vicinity, at Bismarckstrasse 60, have a look at **Galerie Tanit**, which also has a branch in Munich, and **Gallerie Miller Nordenhake**, which opened in November 1990.

From the Belgian Quarter it's about a 20-minute walk southwest to the **Museum für Ostasiatische Kunst** (Museum for East Asian Art), or you can take the U-Bahn from Friesenplatz one stop south to Rudolfplatz and change there to the westbound number 1 or 2 line, exiting at Universitätsstrasse. The museum, located at Universitätsstrasse 100, sits in a peaceful green park beside a man-made pond called the Aachener Weihe. Designed by a pupil of Le Corbusier, it is—like the Käthe Kollwitz Museum—one of Cologne's small museum jewels. Less is more in this showcase of Japanese, Chinese, and Korean art: There are few pieces, but each one is a superb example of its kind and beautifully displayed. A lovely garden courtyard and a cafeteria that looks out over a reflecting pond are serene embellishments to the museum setting. (Open Tuesday through Sunday, 10:00 A.M. to 5:00 P.M.)

Carnival

The seasonal revelries that have been part of life in this Rhineside city since the Romans' Saturnalias and Bacchanalias continue unabated with the boisterous pre-Lenten merry-making that characterizes Cologne's Carnival. Every year Cologne blows off steam and celebrates itself by celebrating what the natives refer to as *Fasteleer* or *Fastelovend*. During Carnival—the city's "fifth season," which officially lasts from New Year's Eve to Ash Wednesday—visitors can share the tipsy fun and traditions that make this one of the most eagerly anticipated events in Germany. If you concentrate your visit during the last five days you'll experience the full delirium of Carnival fever.

A prelude to the upcoming Carnival season is held on "the eleventh of the eleventh," that is, on November 11, when a large crowd led by the Lord Mayor and representatives of the city gathers on the steps of the City Hall for a performance of a humorous play staged by a society of Carnival enthusiasts known as the "Muuzemändelchen." After speeches and songs, a procession makes its way to the Ostermannbrunnen (Ostermann Fountain) in Heumarkt, where wreaths are laid in memory of Willi Ostermann, author of many beloved Carnival songs.

At midnight on New Year's Eve the Carnival season really gets underway. In crowded halls such as the Gürzenich (see above) the "Comical Corps" parody power and militarism with marching reviews accompanied by the "Mariechen," dancing girls with flying skirts. From New Year's Eve until *Weiberfastnacht* (Women's Carnival) on the Thursday before Carnival Sunday the city buzzes with masked balls and countless *Sitzungen,* the rowdy "sessions" featuring skits, performers, and gags that local Carnival societies hold in beer halls and auditoriums. It's possible to attend these events, but the Kölsch dialect renders most of the proceedings unintelligible except to the Kölner.

Then, at exactly 11:11 A.M. on Weiberfastnacht, the festivities spill out onto the Alter Markt and Carnival moves into full public throttle. The women and girls of Cologne set the general tone by snipping off the tie of any man foolish enough to be wearing one; the pubs stay open all night; and the Lord Mayor hands over the government of the city to an official Carnival triumvirate composed of *Seiner Tollität* (His Madness), Prince Carnival; *Seiner Deftigkeit* (His Cleverness), a bawdy peasant; and *Ihre Lieblichkeit* (Her Loveliness), the Cologne Virgin (a large man in drag).

The first big "people's parade" takes place on the following Sunday and shows off Cologne's theatrical brand of local wit and satirical humor. It paves the way for the *Rosenmontag* (Rose Monday) procession, the delirious climax of Carnival festivities, viewed by as many as a million people lining the streets and watching from grandstands. The final ball of the Carnival season—during which Prince Carnival hands back his powers to the Lord Mayor—is held in the Gürzenich on the evening of Shrove Tuesday. On Ash Wednesday it's all over and the abstemious season of Lent begins.

For general Carnival information, advance sales of grandstand and reserved seats for the Rose Monday parade, and tickets for the various assemblies and costume balls, contact the Cologne Tourist Office, 19 Unter Fettenhennen, D-50667 Cologne, by mid-January.

GETTING AROUND

When to Go

Because Cologne sits on a flat plain and is directly on the river, it's often windy. Typically gray and sodden winters never deter Carnival revelers, so if you want to experience the merrymaking and watch the parades plan your trip to coincide with the last five days of Cologne's "fifth season" (the last Thursday to the Monday before Lent).

So far as weather is concerned, the city is more inviting in the late spring, when lilacs and flowering trees and shrubs spread their color and scent through the parks and promenades. In the summer the Kölner move outdoors, flocking to the outdoor beer gardens and restaurants. The misty golden haze that often cloaks the Rhineland in the fall makes September through October an appealing time to visit.

Bear in mind that finding a room during a major trade fair—they are held year-round and scheduled three years in advance—may be difficult, so book ahead.

Arriving

By car. Cologne is easily accessible by Autobahn from any direction in Germany and the rest of Europe. Aachen is about 60 km (38 miles) to the west, Frankfurt lies 200 km (124 miles) to the southeast, Düsseldorf is a mere 35 km (21 miles) to the north, and Hamburg and Berlin are located 430 km (258 miles) and 570 km (342 miles) to the northeast, respectively. If you're staying in the center of the city watch for exit signs marked Köln-Zentrum; if your destination is the Hyatt-Regency, look for Köln-Deutz. Once you're actually in the city, however, driving can be more annoying than convenient, as many streets are one-way and most of the Altstadt area is pedestrians-only.

Parking garages are scattered throughout the city, and the largest of them indicate on computerized street signs how many *Freie Plätze* (parking spots) are available. Most central, and open 24 hours a day, are the parking garages under the Dom, beside the Hauptbahnhof; at Neumarkt; and along the ring road. When in doubt, look for the word *Parkhaus* or a large P with a roof symbol above it.

By train. Cologne's Hauptbahnhof is one of Germany's busiest, with nearly 800 trains a day arriving or departing; rail connections from anywhere in Europe or Great Britain are excellent. Many hotels are within walking distance of the train station, the cathedral is directly beside it, and the Cologne tourist office (with its room reservation service and helpful information) is less than five minutes away. There is another train station on the east side of the Rhine (Bahnhof Deutz), but the major trains (ICs and ECs in particular) do not stop there.

By air. Cologne and Bonn share an international airport, located 16 km (10 miles) from the center of the city. The number 170 bus departs from the airport for Cologne (and vice versa) about every 20 minutes (beginning at 6:00 A.M.) and makes several stops en route, the last of which is the Cologne Hauptbahnhof. Cab fare from the airport to central Cologne runs about DM 30–35.

By boat. Arriving by boat on the Rhine is a wonderfully romantic way to greet the city. Cologne is the headquarters for the Köhn-Düsseldorfer German Rhine Line of excursion boats, all of which dock on the piers just below the Altstadt between the Deutzer Brücke and the Hohenzollernbrücke. Between Easter and the end of October a wide range of excursion possibilities exists for trips both up and down the river. It's possible, for instance, to take an excursion boat from Mainz, Koblenz, or Linz up to Cologne, passing all or some of the legendary Rhine sights on the way. Food and wine are served on board and fares are lower than you might expect. For a small surcharge you can exchange your train ticket for a boat ticket at any of the KD line's pickup points along the Rhine. For information contact Köln-Düsseldorfer Deutsche Rheinschiffahrt, Frankenwerft 15, D-50667 Köln; Tel: (221) 208-80; Fax: (221) 208-82-29. (See also the Around Germany section of Useful Facts at the front of this book.) The Cologne tourist office can also provide details for Rhine journeys.

Around Town

Public transportation. Central Cologne, where most of the major sights are located, is fairly compact and delightfully walkable. If your time is limited and you're going to see only the main points of interest, you probably won't need to use public transportation at all. The city does, however, have an excellent municipal transportation system made up of buses and streetcars—some of which travel the subway system (U-Bahn)—if you need it. Fares are based on the distance or number of zones travelled, and tickets must be purchased from the vending machines found at each U-Bahn stop or from the streetcar or bus driver and then machine-stamped on board. If you're unsure about the fare, a DM 2.40 ticket will get you anywhere you want to go within the city. Special unlimited-use commuter tickets are available for 24-hour (DM 7) and three-day (DM 13) periods. You can pick up a transit system map at the tourist information office.

By taxi. There are over 1,100 taxis available around the clock, and fares are reasonable (about DM 15–20 within the inner city). Don't, however, try to flag down a cab on the street because it probably won't stop. Taxi stands are found on all the major intersections and traffic junctions—including Neumarkt, Alter Markt, Philharmonie, Offenbachplatz (for operagoers), the main train station, and in front of all large hotels. You can also call 28-82 for pickup service. For the tip, round off the fare to the nearest mark and add another mark.

ACCOMMODATIONS

Thanks to the number of important trade fairs held year-round in the Cologne Messe, the city has an enormous variety of hotels in all categories to choose from—except, that is, when a major fair is actually in progress. Rooms may then be difficult to find, and prices double (the highest rate given below represents the price for a double room when a major fair is going on). Try to reserve in advance; if you have difficulties, the tourist office directly across from the Dom operates a room-reservation service.

The hotel rates listed here are 1994 projections for double-bed, double-occupancy rooms. Prices are given in deutsche marks (DM). Basic rates are always subject to change, so please verify when you are booking. Breakfast is usually included in the price of small- to mid-sized establishments but often requires an additional supplement at the luxury hotels.

The telephone city code for Cologne is 221, preceded by a zero if you are calling from elsewhere in Germany.

Located directly across from the cathedral on the east (Deutz) bank of the Rhine, the four-year-old ▶ **Hyatt Regency Cologne** tops the list for contemporary luxury, service, and the best panoramic views of the city. The lobby is a sumptuously appointed three-story glass atrium with cascading streams of water, marble floors, and dark mahogany walls. On the atrium's mezzanine level the **Glashaus** restaurant offers breakfast, afternoon coffee and cake, and evening meals or cocktails while you look out on the Rhine and Cologne's cathedral-dominated skyline. A front room with a view costs more, but all the rooms are spacious and tastefully appointed, with unusually large marble bathrooms, minibars, and TVs. The hotel's fitness club, an unusual feature for Cologne hotels, provides a full range of equipment, a heated pool with a summer outdoor terrace, and superior co-ed sauna facilities. The English-speaking staff is young, attentive, and uncommonly helpful.

The Hyatt's **Graugans** restaurant is one of Cologne's most highly rated and elegant gourmet eateries (see Dining), and its outdoor **Biergarten**, on the banks of the Rhine, is a popular warm-weather meeting place for drinks and conversation. There's a third pub-restaurant, called **Schälsick**, for more informal dining. From the Hauptbahnhof it's a ten-minute walk across the Hohenzollernbrücke to the hotel; underground parking is available. If you plan to stay in Cologne over the weekend, ask about special weekend rates.

Kennedy-Ufer 2a, D-50679 Köln. Tel: 828-12-34; Fax: 828-13-70. DM 320–695; suites DM 1,010–2,675.

Considered one of the great hotels of Europe, the venerable ► **Dom-Hotel** on the cathedral square has been operating in one form or another for 125 years, a tradition that is reflected in its detailed and elegant Old World decor. The large period-decorated rooms are fully equipped and provide a closeup view of Cologne's greatest landmark. International and regional dishes are served up in the hotel's wintergarden restaurant, **Atelier am Dom**, which opens out onto the cathedral square in warm weather. The ground floor of the hotel is occupied by luxury shops such as Hermès and Cartier, a 4711 store is within sniffing distance, and you're right at the beginning of Hohestrasse, one of Cologne's main shopping streets. Special summer rates are available in July and August.

Domkloster 2a, D-50667 Köln. Tel: 202-40; Fax: 202-42-60. DM 490–570; suites DM 660–1,200.

Situated directly across the street from the new Cologne Philharmonie and Museum Ludwig complex, the ► **Pullman Hotel Mondial** is not conspicuously opulent but it's tasteful and well-run. All rooms have a toilet and bath and double-sealed windows to keep out traffic noise. There's a bar and a beer pub for drinks, and the **Symphonie** restaurant offers special menus before philharmonic concerts.

Kurt-Hackenberg-Platz 1, D-50667 Köln. Tel: 206-30; Fax: 206-35-22. DM 225–350.

The pleasant 95-room ► **Haus Lyskirchen–Ringhotel Köln**, close to the Romanesque church of St. Maria in Lyskirchen in Altstadt-Süd, has a good restaurant on the premises, and some of the rooms are theme-decorated. If you're in the mood for a bit of ersatz German *Rustikalität* (rusticity), ask for one of the popular *Bauernzimmern* (farmhouse rooms). The price includes breakfast.

Filzengraben 26–32. D-50676 Köln. Tel: 209-70; Fax: 209-77-18. DM 198–340.

Part of a French chain of hotels, the ▶ **Hotel Arcade** manages to disguise the spareness of its design with a touch of contemporary chic. The hotel has something of a dorm-like feeling, it's a bit removed from the center (although located on a tram line), and the rooms aren't what you'd call spacious; still, if you want a larger hotel for less money, the Arcade works very well. There are often tour groups here, and that can mean a wait at the small elevators. All rooms have shower and toilet.

Neue Weyerstrasse 4, D-50676 Köln. Tel: 209-60; Fax: 209-61-99. DM 175–210.

A good centrally located choice close to the Rathaus and the Praetorium excavations in the Altstadt is the small ▶ **Hotel Krone**, whose modern rooms all have a bath/shower, toilet, and TV. A breakfast buffet is included.

Kleine Budengasse 15, D-50667 Köln. Tel: 25-76-981 or 982; Fax: 25-35-32. DM 150–220.

A real find in terms of price and atmosphere is the historic ▶ **Hotel Ahl Meerkatzen**, in the Altstadt not far from St. Maria in Lyskirchen. In the 13th century the hotel was an aristocratic court; later it became a patrician town house and then a distillery where orange bitters was made; it was completely renovated in 1983. The hotel's antique atmosphere doesn't extend much beyond the lobby, which is filled with lots of dark wood and copies of old portraits, but all 33 rooms are comfortable and have a bath/shower and toilet. Breakfast is included, and there are special weekend and off-season rates.

Mathiasstrasse 21, D-50667 Köln. Tel: 23-48-82; Fax: 23-48-85. DM 120–295.

The budget-minded looking for a special location will find the ▶ **Hotel Lindenhof** a good choice. The hotel is very small, and the rooms are very plain (not all have a bath and toilet), but the four rooms in front all have balconies opening out onto a tiny square behind Gross St. Martin church, a landmark of the city's skyline. Breakfast is included.

Lintgasse 7, D-50667 Köln. Tel: 257-77-71. DM 100.

Another possibility near the Rathaus that won't cost you an arm and a leg is the modest ▶ **Bürgerhof**, whose first floor is a *Kneipe* (pub) where guests also have their breakfast. The rooms lack color, but the afternoon carillon from the Rathaus provides a quaint charm to the ears, and you're only minutes from the cathedral area.

Bürgerstrasse 16, D-50667 Köln. Tel: 257-69-28. DM 145–250.

The rooms in ▶ **Im Stapelhäuschen**, located in a restored

historic house right on the Rhine in the busiest section of the Altstadt, are not exactly charming, but they're comfortable and the location is great. The ground floor is a wine restaurant that puts tables outside in warm weather.

Fischmarkt 1–3, D-50667 Köln. Tel: 257-78-62; Fax: 257-42-32. DM 145–250.

DINING

Although several highly rated restaurants have established themselves here in recent years, Cologne, as its citizens will tell you, is not a city particularly known for its gourmet dining. Rather, it's a place for conversation and drinking, generally over enormous portions of typical Rhineland fare in crowded restaurants that are *gemütlich* rather than elegant. In April and May the city goes mad for *Spargel* (asparagus), and asparagus soups and main courses are featured on many menus. If your tastebuds are crying out for something other than German food, the city has Asian, Bulgarian, French, Greek, Iranian, Italian, Mexican, Russian, and Turkish restaurants to choose from.

To eat and drink as the Kölner do, however, it is essential that you visit one of the city's old tavern-restaurants. First of all, ask one of the blue-aproned waiters (called a *Köbes*) for a *Kölsch,* the dry, delicious, top-fermented beer that is brewed only in Cologne. Always served in a tall, thin glass, the Kölsch will be brought to your table in a special carrier called a *Kölschkranz.*

Local dishes at these restaurants generally include *Halver Hahn* (not half a chicken as you may think, but a rye bread roll with Dutch cheese); *Tartar* (finely minced raw beef mixed with egg yolk, onions, and spices and served on bread or a roll); *Kölsch Kaviar* (smoked blood sausage served with raw onion rings); *Matjesfilet mit grünen Bohnen* (pickled white herring served with green butter beans and potatoes); *Schlachtplatte* (cured pork, bacon, blood sausage, and a small sausage or boiled pork, served on sauerkraut and potato purée); *Hämchen* (cured knuckle of pork cooked in vegetable broth); *Himmel un Äd* (apples and potatoes boiled and mashed together and served with fried blood sausage); and *Speckpfannekuchen* (pancake fried in melted, smoked bacon fat).

There are several tavern-restaurants to try. The best known are **Früh Brauhaus**, Am Hof 12–14, next to the cathedral; **Päffgen**, Friesenstrasse 64–66, close to the Römerturm and St. Gereon's; and **Brauhaus Sion**, Unter Taschenmacher 5–7, between the Philharmonie and the Rathaus. **Früh am Veedel**, in the southernmost tip of Altstadt-Süd at Chlodwigplatz 28, is a great spot for lunch and allows you to browse around the local St. Severins *Veedel* ("neighborhood" in the Kölsch dialect). Another good lunch spot is **Altstadt-Päffgen**, Heumarkt 62, close to the western end of the Deutzer Brücke. The rooms in all these places are large and smoky, and if there's a crowd you may be asked to sit with strangers. But if you're looking for the authentic Cologne, this is where you'll find it.

On the other hand, if you're out to impress a business colleague over lunch or want to enjoy an especially fine and romantic gourmet dinner for two, try **Graugans** at the Hyatt-Regency Cologne (see Accommodations, above, for address and telephone). The cooking here—a sophisticated and unusual combination of contemporary European and Far Eastern cuisine—is a world apart from the hefty fare served in most Cologne restaurants, with entrées varying from sautéed breast of wild pigeon to salmon sashimi with pink grapefruit; several kinds of fish are featured as a main course. The international wine list is as exemplary as the food and the view.

Many Kölner swear that the best fish and purest Italian cuisine in the city is to be found just around the corner from the train station at **Luciano**, Marzellenweg 68, which is why reservations are absolutely essential and necessary at least a week (preferably two) in advance; Tel: 13-54-53. From the delicious antipasti to the superb zabaione, a meal at Luciano is a memorable experience. Only Italian wines are available. There are many other good Italian restaurants in Cologne; **Trattoria Toscana** at Friesenwall 44 near Neumarkt (Tel: 31-58-47) is another top choice. Much farther down the culinary and economic ladder, but good for a hearty budget meal, is **Da Pino**, an informal pizzeria restaurant in the touristy Altstadt at Salzgasse 4–6. Their pasta is freshly made on the premises, but the various sauces for it can be disconcertingly interchangeable.

If it's French *grande cuisine* you aspire to, you can do no better than to sink into the velvety elegance of **La Poêle d'Or**, Komödienstrasse 50–52 (Tel: 13-41-00), just west of the cathedral. There's a table d'hôte lunch and dinner menu that can keep the bill down; the price of wine, however, is rather high. The service here is considered the best in town. The aptly named **Soufflé** at Hohenstaufenring 53 (Tel: 21-20-22), between Rudolfplatz and Barbarossaplatz, serves up superb versions of its namesake and other fresh, imaginative dishes; German, French, and Italian wines are available.

In a section of the train station itself is the **Alter Wartesaal**, a restored turn-of-the-century restaurant (Tel: 13-30-61) offering German cuisine and a Sunday brunch in surroundings that are chic and popular. Across the station square from the

Alter Wartesaal, and next door to the luxury Hotel Excelsior Ernst, is another popular restaurant of the brewery variety, **Alt Köln**, at Trankgasse 7–9 (Tel: 13-74-71). The atmosphere here tends toward the fake rather than the authentic, but the portions are enormous and the cooking is trustworthy if uninspired. For a good selection of *Eintopfs* (hearty meat-and-vegetable soups) in a charmingly unpretentious wine house restaurant near the old Rathaus, try **Weinkrüger** at Marsplatz 1–5 (Tel: 257-69-54). You'll find a full selection of German wines at prices that are amazingly reasonable.

In the gallery-filled Belgisches Viertel (Belgian Quarter; see Contemporary Art Scene, above), vegetarian meals are served at **Osho's Place** at Venloer Strasse 5–7 (Tel: 574-07-45), a modern, appealing café/restaurant with a rarity for German restaurants: a section for nonsmokers. Osho's is open daily from 8:00 A.M. to midnight and features a Sunday brunch buffet; artists in the district often hang out at the coffee bar in the front. The prime artists' restaurant/hangout in this area, however, is **Alcazar**, at Bismarkstrasse 39 (Tel: 51-57-33). Squeeze in for lunch between your gallery hopping (all the galleries are closed between 1:00 and 3:00 P.M. anyway) and you'll probably find yourself sharing a table with a gallery owner or a video artist.

Theatergoers can enjoy a late post-performance meal at **Theaterschänke**, hidden behind the 4711 house across from the opera at Schwertnergasse 1; the food is Greek, and the clientele is theatrically oriented. And finally, no discussion of Cologne restaurants would be complete without mentioning the revered and ever-crowded **Lommerzheim** at Siegesstrasse 18 (Tel: 81-43-92), on the right (Deutz) side of the river, about a five-minute walk from the Hyatt-Regency. You'll first notice its peeling façade: The place hasn't changed a bit since 1948—and that's why it's so popular with locals and Mercedes-driving bigwigs alike. Crowd in, at least to order a Kölsch; the portions of plain German cooking that arrive at your table can only be described as mountainous.

For those in a tasteful hurry, **Ezio-in-Biss**, a trendy upscale *Schnell-Imbiss* (fast-food snack bar) at Apostelnstrasse 50, near the Romanesque church of St. Aposteln, is a kind of German version of New York City's Dean & DeLuca. If it's just a noontime sandwich you're after, try **Merzenich**, a chain of stand-up coffee, bread, and pastry shops scattered around the city; most central is the one just around the corner from the cathedral at the beginning of Hohe Strasse.

Cafés

Afternoon *Kaffee und Kuchen* is a German tradition, and Cologne has more than its share of special cafés where you can sit and people-watch while indulging in excellent pastries or ice cream and a delicious cup of coffee. The elegant **Fassbender**, on Mittelstrasse in the Bazaar de Cologne shopping arcade, is one of the best known, as is **Eigel** at Brückenstrasse 1–3, off Hohe Strasse. The **Opernterrassen**, next to the opera house on Offenbachplatz, is a good place to stock up on calories before a performance. Delicious confections and *Printen,* a kind of spice cookie, tempt the eye and the sweet tooth at the old-fashioned **Café Printen Schmitz**, Breitestrasse 87, on a major shopping street north of the opera. On the same street, at number 50, the newly renovated **Café Cremer** offers a luscious assortment of goodies in bright, contemporary surroundings. **Café Reichard**, to one side of the cathedral and the Dom-Hotel at Unter Fettenhennen 11, is another favored establishment, although you might feel out of place if you're not properly dressed. For Kaffee und Kuchen on the run, try one of the **Merzenichs** mentioned above; the pastries are delicious and reasonably priced, and the only problem is that you can't sit down.

ENTERTAINMENT AND NIGHTLIFE

From grand opera to striptease, from chamber music and orchestra concerts to ear-shattering discos, from classical dance to avant-garde theater, the spectrum of entertainment possibilities in Cologne is unlimited. The city has a reputation for having the best live-music scene in Germany, and concerts of every description are held in locations all over the metropolitan area. For help in choosing, pick up a free copy of the monthly guide called *Monatsvorschau* at the tourist office; it has a complete listing of that month's concert, opera, theater, and exhibition schedules. If you're more interested in the contemporary music scene, the monthly *Kölner Stadtrevue,* available at most bookstores and newsstands, will fill you in on what's going on. The best place for tickets to almost everything is Ticket Köln, on Roncalliplatz next door to the Römisch-Germanisches Museum (open Monday through Friday, 9:00 A.M. to 6:30 P.M.; Saturdays, 9:00 A.M. to 2:00 P.M.; Tel: 28-01). After 5:00 P.M. on the day of a scheduled concert you may have to go directly to the theater box office for tickets.

If you're a classical music lover try to hear a concert in the new **Kölner Philharmonie** located under the Wallraf-Richartz/Museum Ludwig complex at Bischofsgarten 1. The American conductor James Conlon is currently music director of the city's two renowned orchestras: the Cologne Philharmonic and the Gürzenich Orchestra. Completed in 1986, the 2,000-seat hall is a marvel of understated elegance, with a steeply ranked auditorium and a clean, warm sound. The only problem is that philharmonic concerts tend to sell out quickly, so make a beeline for Ticket Köln or the Philharmonie box office when you arrive in the city and find out what's to be had.

The **Oper der Stadt Köln** (Cologne City Opera) at Offenbachplatz (Tel: 221-84-00) is one of Germany's best opera houses and features international casts and productions. The freshly renovated **Schauspielhaus** (theater), where classics and contemporary plays are performed, is next door (Tel: 221-84-00).

Longing to see a movie, any movie, that hasn't been dubbed into German? **Metropolis** at Ebertplatz 19, at the northernmost tip of the Altstadt, shows films in their original languages (Tel: 739-12-45). If the children are restless, take them to a performance at the famous **Hänneschen Puppet Theater** (Eisenmarkt 2, at Heumarkt). The puppet shows, performed in the Kölsch dialect, are presented at 2:30 and 5:00 P.M., Wednesday through Sunday; you may not understand a word, but it's enchanting nonetheless. And, of course, there are always the open-air **Tanzbrunnen** concerts in the Rhinepark. The performances here range from big-band concerts by Glenn Miller's orchestra to amateur nights, when anyone from an accordion player to a singer or yodeler can face the audience's cheers or boos; it's boisterous and fun.

The most popular disco at the moment is **E-Werk**, created from an old electric-power station in Mühlheim on the east bank of the Rhine above Deutz; the line to get in can sometimes stretch for what seems like a kilometer (Schanzenstrasse 37, Tel: 62-62-12). **Petit Prince**, a disco at Hohenzollernring 90 near the Belgian Quarter, has weekend DJs to spin the discs. The new "art music" scene in all its many manifestations is always in full swing at the **Stadtgartenrestaurant**, also in the Belgian Quarter, at Venloer Strasse 40 (Tel: 51-60-39); it publishes a monthly program of its events, including special film and video presentations. There's also a weekend disco at the **Alter Wartesaal** next door to the restaurant of the same name in the main train station (Tel: 13-30-61).

Tingel Tangel, Maastrichter Strasse 6–8, a very popular singles nightclub in the arty Belgian Quarter, stays open until 4:00 A.M. (Tel: 25-26-01); pop and jazz are the mainstays here, and the price of drinks is pretty steep, but it's a good place to sample *die Szene* (the scene).

SHOPS AND SHOPPING

Although the first *Fussgänger* (pedestrians-only) shopping zones in Germany originated in Cologne, until fairly recently it was said, with some justification, that if you wanted to buy anything really special or out of the ordinary you had to go to Düsseldorf. Today, confronted by Cologne's seemingly endless and interconnected conglomeration of smart shops and upscale shopping arcades where anything and everything is available, it's hard to imagine a more consumer-conscious city. A major retail building boom in the 1980s has left its mark on all of Cologne's main Altstadt shopping streets, so even if you're not interested in buying it's worthwhile to stroll through these areas to see the latest in contemporary architecture.

If you're simply in the mood for browsing, the best place to begin is right next to the cathedral. The usual Cartier, Hermès, and Georg Jensen are located on the ground floor of the Dom-Hotel. There's also an official **4711** store at Domkloster 2, where the prices for cologne and soaps are the same as at Woolworth's down the street and the atmosphere is considerably more sedate.

Hohe Strasse, the main north–south street in Roman times, is now Cologne's busiest commercial drag, jammed every day except Sunday with shoppers, punk musicians, organ grinders, snack shops, fruit sellers, and endless stores. Hohe Strasse, which begins just south of the cathedral, is where you'll find all the major international designer-clothing boutiques, stores selling silver, fine jewelry, and German Sollingen-steel utensils and silverware, pharmacies, perfumeries, the big **Kaufhalle** department store, and cheaper places like Woolworth's. **Josef Feinhals Zigarren**, at number 116, is Germany's oldest cigar shop and stocks over a thousand kinds of stogies.

Where Hohestrasse intersects with Schildergasse you'll find an enormous selection of goods, as well as cafés and a food hall, in **Kaufhof**, one of Cologne's largest department stores. The stores lining **Schildergasse** all the way to Neumarkt feature exclusive and international men's fashions, fine leather bags and purses, and French, German, and Italian designer shoes.

Schildergasse ends at **Neumarkt**, where you'll find the **Hertie** department store on your right. One interesting option here is to turn right on Zeppelinstrasse and explore one of Cologne's newest and most impressive shopping arcades, the **Olivandenhof**. The Olivandenhof's conservative façade, dating from 1913, hides an ultramodern interior of steel and glass with an oval glass cupola and decidedly futuristic escalators. There are over 40 upscale shops here, including Licht & Raumdesign for contemporary lighting fixtures and household furnishings. For coffee, beer, or a snack there's a pleasant café called **Bierchen** on the basement level.

Continuing down Neumarkt toward the Romanesque

church of St. Aposteln, you'll come to another brand-new shopping arcade, **Neumarkt-Passage**, completed in 1988. The materials—sandstone, polished pink marble, and granite—used for this complex reflect the overall tone of its shops, which sell mostly luxury items such as antique jewelry, crystal and china, and expensive writing accessories. There's also **Buchhaus Gonski**, Cologne's largest retail bookshop. (The real jewel of Neumarkt-Passage, however, is the Käthe Kollwitz Museum—see above—which you reach by glass-enclosed elevator in the rear octagonal court.)

If you continue past St. Aposteln you'll reach Mittelstrasse and the **Bazaar de Cologne**, another well-known Cologne fashion center. A right turn on Pfeilstrasse brings you to **Ehrenstrasse**, where the shops appeal to younger, hipper shoppers: Prices here are lower, fashions are punkier or at least less relentlessly chic, and there are lots of cafés and bistros. Ehrenstrasse has a preponderance of shoe stores and the latest leather fashions. If it's a *Regenschirm* (umbrella) you're looking for, check out the selection at **Schirmbusch**, Breitestrasse 104. Antique silver and pocket watches can be found at **H. H. Weiss**, Breitestrasse 159. **Walter König's Büchermarkt**, Breitestrasse 79 and Ehrenstrasse 4, provides one of the best selections of art books in the world—browsing here can easily turn into a full-time occupation.

Where Ehrenstrasse intersects Apostelnstrasse the street changes its name to **Breite Strasse**, and you re-enter the mainstream world of Cologne shopping. Ultramodern, high-fashion household goods—including china, furniture, and light fixtures—brighten the adventurous showroom of **Raumführend für Raumdesign**, Breitestrasse 155. For a large selection of art postcards and greeting cards visit **Walter König's Postkartenladen** at number 93.

Of course there are intriguing shops on streets other than the ones we have mentioned here. At **Filz Gnoss**, Apostelnstrasse 21, you'll find unusually decorated and comfortable felt slippers as well as those enormous *Überpantoffeln* you slip over your shoes and slide around in when touring German palaces; if you can get your guests at home to wear them you'll never have to polish your floors again. Antique coins, pilgrim medallions, and ancient Roman artifacts such as terra-cotta oil lamps and small glass vases line the window and shelves of **Münzhandlung Hans-Ulrich Geifert**, Unter Taschenmacher 10 (Tel: 21-14-57), close to the Alter Markt; collectors can be assured of the authenticity of the objects sold in this small but inviting shop. **Keramik Weber** at Gürzenichstrasse 16 carries Rhenish stoneware and ceramics from all over Europe.

Finally, for unusual and often surprisingly inexpensive

items don't overlook the gift shops in many of Cologne's museums. In the **Kölnisches Stadtmuseum**, for instance, you'll find some interesting stoneware glasses, prints, and glazed wall plaques. The **Römisch-Germanisches Museum** carries small terra-cotta copies of ancient deities, beautiful limited-edition glass vases faithfully copied from Roman originals, and posters. Art glass, silk scarves, and other designer items from its collection can be found in the **Museum für Angewandte Kunst**.

THE NORTHWEST

DÜSSELDORF, AACHEN, BONN, MÜNSTER, OSNABRÜCK

By John England with John Dornberg

John England, a freelance journalist, has been based in Bonn since 1972. He writes for British newspapers and magazines, and is also the author of our Mosel Valley chapter and the sections on Lübeck, Lüneburg, Bremen, and Bremerhaven in our chapter on The North.

Though the Rhine rises in the Swiss Alps, forms Germany's border with Switzerland and France for nearly 300 miles, and runs through Germany itself for a scant 200 miles before entering the Netherlands, it has left an indelible mark on Germany's history and psyche in terms of culture, art, language, and attitude, especially in the northwestern segment of the country, colloquially called "the Rhineland."

Geographically, what we call the Northwest begins around Koblenz, where the Mosel river meets the Rhine, continues northward to Emmerich, where the Rhine becomes Dutch, and includes the densely populated and highly industrialized Ruhr basin and most of Westphalia. Politically, most of this northwestern part of Germany is called Nordrhein-Westfalen (Northrhine Westphalia). The most populous (17 million) of Germany's 16 states, it is also one of the largest in area, encompassing more than 13,000 square miles, about the size of Connecticut and Massachusetts, or Wales and Northern Ireland, combined. Düsseldorf is its capital.

The Rhinelanders have a reputation for being friendly and jovial, with a lust for life that finds expression in their annual Carnival frolics, which brighten up the back end of winter for six boozy days until the arrival of Ash Wednesday. The North Rhine area cities around Cologne—Aachen, Bonn, and especially Düsseldorf—celebrate Carnival with big street parades that are worth seeing at least once.

For travellers who can visit only in the summer, these cities offer many other attractions. Ancient **Aachen**, Germany's westernmost city—situated not on the Rhine but west of Cologne near the Belgian and Dutch borders—is the town of Charlemagne and his great cathedral, bursting with history but sporting a modern international flair. **Düsseldorf**, the Rhineside big-business city north of Cologne, offers more than a touch of flashy materialism, and is also a great art center, with corners in its Altstadt (Old Town) that tell of its pre-industrial past. **Bonn**, the small, pleasant university and market town on the Rhine south of Cologne that was turned into the federal capital in 1949, has its own charming character that owes nothing to the *Politiker* (politicians). They, in any case, eventually will be leaving Bonn now that Berlin has been named the new capital of a united Germany.

Münster, a 90-minute drive northeast of Düsseldorf, in the lushly verdant Münsterland with its scores of moated castles, and **Osnabrück** are the heart of northern Westphalia and the ancient cradle of Germanic national consciousness. It was in Münster and Osnabrück that the Peace of Westphalia, ending the Thirty Years' War, was negotiated and signed in 1648. Both are cities of magnificent cathedrals and churches, colorful old quarters, important museums, and cozy inns that, after major World War II destruction, have restored their appearance so that they again resemble the powerful independent bishoprics and Hanseatic trading centers they were in the Middle Ages.

MAJOR INTEREST

Düsseldorf
Altstadt architecture and the Heine Institut
Home-brewed *Altbier*
Art collections and museums
Music and theater
Königsallee shopping, gourmet eating, and stylish nightlife
Day trips to nearby *Schlösser* (castles)

Aachen
Charlemagne's chapel/cathedral
Rathaus and Markt

Music and art museums
Thermal springs
Casino and spas
Day trips to Holland and Belgium

Bonn
Altes Rathaus and Markt
Münster (collegiate church)
Music (Beethoven Festival), opera, theater
Museums and Beethovenhaus
Old town houses, student quarter
Government quarter
Suburb of Bad Godesberg
Excursions on the Rhine
Day trips to Siebengebirge mountains and Eifel
  Massif

Münster
Dom
St. Lamberti church
Rathaus and Prinzipalmarkt
Town palaces and mansions
Old taverns and breweries
Day trips to Wasserschlösser (moated castles)

Osnabrück
Dom
Rathaus and St. Marienkirche
Old city walls
Altstadt architecture
Kulturgeschichtliches Museum for Roman artifacts
  and Felix Nussbaum collection
Erich Maria Remarque Archive

DÜSSELDORF

Düsseldorf, located on the east bank of the Rhine, the state
capital of Northrhine–Westphalia and the location of a major
international airport, is first and foremost a business and
banking city. It is sometimes called the front office of the
industrial Ruhr river area to the near north (Essen, Dort-
mund, and other cities of little interest to the traveller).
About a dozen of Germany's leading industrial corporations
have their headquarters in Düsseldorf, and many multina-
tionals have chosen it as their German and European base.
The city has 170 banking firms, including 60 foreign houses,
and 200 advertising agencies. No fewer than 3,000 foreign
companies from 50 countries operate out of Düsseldorf.

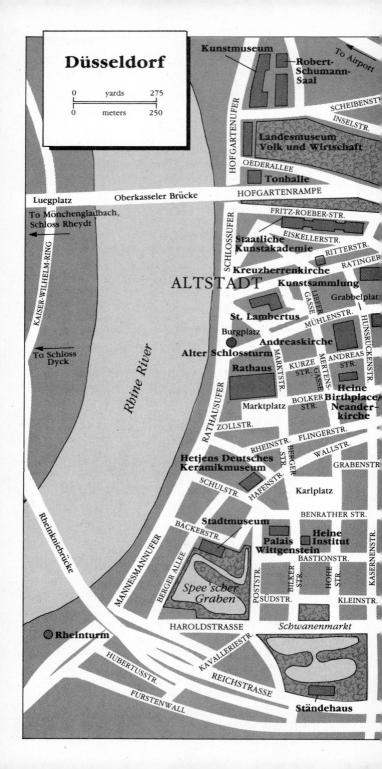

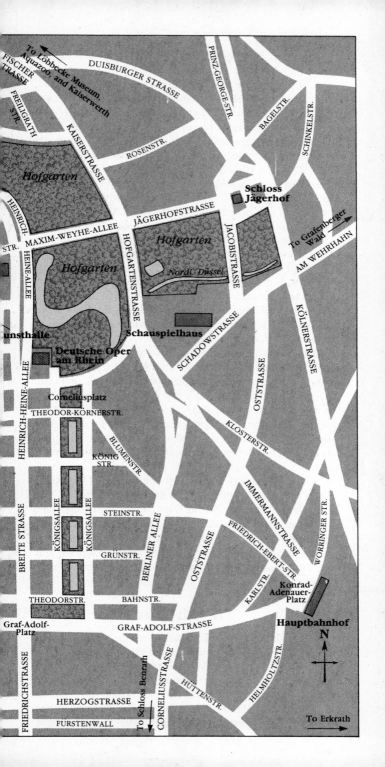

Düsseldorf handles 15 percent of Germany's foreign trade, and its stock exchange sees the country's greatest share volume, more even than Frankfurt, the nation's financial capital. It is also a major center for industrial and consumer-goods fairs. The city is therefore very much concerned with the making of money. Those who have it flaunt it, spending conspicuously in the elegant and expensive stores on Königsallee and driving the Porsches, Mercedes, and BMWs seen parked outside fashionable cafés.

So what's in Düsseldorf for nonbusiness visitors? If you like shopping you'll love Königsallee—known as the Kö. But the city has more to offer than that. Its Altstadt down by the river, although now highly commercialized (more than 200 restaurants, bars, and discos are crammed into an area about a half-mile square), still has some interesting and unspoiled historic corners. Düsseldorf is also a leading art center, with great collections to be enjoyed, and is rich in music and theater. Top wining and dining, many good hotels, a stylish nightlife, nearby castles, Rhine boat trips, and horse racing are among the entertainment opportunities the city offers.

Granted town rights in 1288, Düsseldorf (named after the small Düssel river, which runs into the Rhine) is only 700 years old, relatively young compared to Aachen or Bonn. The city blossomed around the year 1400 and became the capital of local principalities in the early 16th century. French revolutionary troops occupied the city for more than a decade; Napoleon even christened it "Little Paris," and for a while considered moving his court here from the French capital.

Düsseldorf expanded again with the coming of industrialization in the 19th century, when it was part of Prussia. The city suffered heavily in World War II; more than 30 percent of it was destroyed. In 1946 it became the capital of Northrhine–Westphalia, a British occupying-power creation constructed of two formerly independent provinces, and went on to take a leading part in Germany's postwar "economic miracle."

The Altstadt

Visitors to Düsseldorf usually make a beeline for the Altstadt, the old town quarter bounded by the Rhine to the west, the Hofgarten to the north and northeast, and Königsallee to the east. Most of it is a pedestrian zone, permitting undisturbed strolling along its narrow cobblestoned streets. Its center is the **Marktplatz** (Market Place), site of the **Rathaus** (Town Hall), the oldest part of which dates from 1573. The daily market these days is on nearby Karlsplatz, two blocks south along Marktstrasse and Bergerstrasse.

The equestrian statue in the Marktplatz is Elector Johann Wilhelm—commonly known as Jan Wellem—who ruled the city from 1679 to 1716. The small town of Düsseldorf had become the residence of the Palatine electors in 1380, when the county of Berg was elevated to a duchy. But it boomed under the energetic Jan Wellem. A friend of the arts, he took a shine to Düsseldorf and made ambitious plans to expand it. His residence was one of Europe's centers of culture, and his art collection now forms the core of Munich's Alte Pinakothek (see the Munich chapter). The elector also had an *Antikensaal* (Hall of Antiques) filled with Italian castings of all the best-known sculptures of antiquity, built Düsseldorf's first opera house, supported artists and musicians (and drank with them in the Altstadt), and collected works of artisans and craftsmen.

Under Wellem, many new and imposing buildings sprang up—including Düsseldorf's first Protestant houses of worship and its first synagogue—and its street lighting was made better than that of Paris. The elector also improved trade with other parts of Germany and neighboring European states. But his efforts to turn Düsseldorf into an industrial town were short-lived. Sadly, too, his priceless collections were lost to the city after his death in 1716. All that was left to Düsseldorf was his statue, completed in 1711 by the Flemish-born Gabriel de Grupello and considered one of the finest Baroque sculptures north of the Alps.

Burgplatz, on the Rathausufer (part of the B 1, the main north–south riverside road), a block north of the Rathaus, is an interesting square ringed by restaurants and cafés that put out tables in summer—a good place for a pleasant pause and a drink in the Altstadt's relatively quiet daytime atmosphere. There are also some small, smart shops around Burgplatz. On the southwest side is the **Alter Schlossturm**, the remains of the city's 13th-century castle, which burned down in 1872. The ruins contain a shipping museum that includes a splendid collection of models of Rhine river ships. At the north edge of the square stands **St. Lambertus**, the oldest church in the Altstadt, built in 1349 on the site of an earlier house of worship. It contains the grave of Wilhelm the Rich, a local 16th-century prince, and has Italian-Flemish Renaissance decorations and a Late Gothic tabernacle.

On **Mühlenstrasse**, off Burgplatz to the east, are some handsome 17th- and 18th-century houses and the **Andreaskirche** (St. Andrew's Church), built in 1629, a former court church with a mausoleum for the Palatine electors. The 15th-century Gothic **Kreuzherrenkirche** (Church of the Knights of the Cross), which has two naves, is one block north on Ratingerstrasse, reached via Liefergasse or Neubrückstrasse. Behind the church to the north, on Eiskellerstrasse, is the **Staatliche Kunstakademie** (National Academy of Art), which under the director Wilhelm van Schadow was the birthplace of the influential Düsseldorf school of art in the mid-19th century. Paul Klee taught here, as did the controversial Joseph Beuys, the *enfant terrible* of post–World War II German art, until he was thrown out. Beuys, known as the "Man with the Hat" because of the fedora without which he was never seen, is considered one of Germany's greatest artists: His imaginative works in such non-traditional media as felt and lard are now sought by museums around the world. The academy is open to the public only in February, when works by its students are exhibited.

Just northeast of St. Andrew's, at Grabbelplatz 5, is the **Kunstsammlung** (Art Collection), offering a fine display of 20th-century art—including almost 90 works by Paul Klee, as well as pieces by Picasso, Max Ernst, Georges Braque, Fernand Léger, Piet Mondrian, Wassily Kandinsky, Marc Chagall, Max Beckmann, Roy Lichtenstein, and Andy Warhol—housed in a building of sweeping lines clad with panels of highly polished black Swedish granite. Still, many angry taxpayers dubbed the building a "mausoleum" when it opened in 1986.

The **Städtische Kunsthalle** (City Art Gallery), across the street at Grabbelplatz 4, hosts travelling exhibitions of modern art. It is also the home of the tradition-rich *Kunstverein* (art association) for the Rhineland and Westphalia, founded in 1829 by von Schadow.

The Altstadt is also the home of the **Hetjens Deutsches Keramikmuseum** (German Ceramics Museum), in the Palais Nesselrode at Schulstrasse 4, three blocks south of the Marktplatz. The museum, one of the world's great ceramics collections, has more than 10,000 exhibits covering 8,000 years of the potter's art from the Orient and Europe.

The **Stadtmuseum** (Municipal History Museum), located in the Palais Graf Spee at Bäckerstrasse 7–9, one block south of the ceramics museum, traces Düsseldorf's history from its beginnings to the present through exhibits of paintings, graphics, sculpture, furniture, weapons, silverware, medallions, excavation finds, and much more. Special features of the museum are local art of the 1920s and contemporary works.

Bilker Strasse, an Altstadt street that runs south off Karlplatz, has many of Düsseldorf's other monuments to culture and education. Searchers after the spirit of the poet Heinrich Heine (1797–1856) should visit the **Heinrich Heine**

Institut at Bilker Strasse 12–14. A highly active center of Heine research, the institute not only contains the poet's death mask, archives, library, and various personal possessions but also stages exhibitions and discussions on his life and work. An unusual sculptural monument to Heine, a six-foot-high "death mask" lying with its skull in two pieces next to it, is in a small park on Schwanenmarkt (Swan Market), at the south end of Bilker Strasse at its junction with Haroldstrasse. The monument, which includes symbols representing various stages in Heine's life, was created by the Düsseldorf sculptor Bert Gerresheim in 1981 to mark the 125th anniversary of the poet's death. Heine was born in Düsseldorf at Bolkerstrasse 53, east of the Marktplatz, near the 1687 Neander church. The house was reconstructed in 1950.

The former **home of Robert Schumann**, who was the conductor of the city orchestra (now the Düsseldorf Philharmonic) from 1850 to 1854, is at Bilker Strasse 15, opposite the Heine Institut. Headquarters of the Robert Schumann Research Institute, the house is not open to the public, but the Heine Institut contains a Schumann collection, including letters, music, paintings, and opera glasses, as well as a dress worn by Clara Schumann. The Düsseldorf post was Schumann's last; he died in 1856 and is buried with his wife in Bonn's Alter Friedhof (Old Cemetery).

Bilker Strasse also embraces the **Palais Wittgenstein**, at number 7–9, a spacious, cream-colored, former burgher's house with an inner courtyard that was turned into an entertainment complex in the early 1980s, housing a chamber concert hall and a puppet theater. There is also a small **café** set in a re-created 19th-century butcher's shop moved from another part of Düsseldorf. Old meat hooks, a wood-paneled ceiling, and colorful enameled flower decorations provide a rustic atmosphere. The café is open only during concerts and puppet shows.

Next to the Palais Wittgenstein at number 5 is **Das Alte Haus** (The Old House), another former burgher's home; open to the public, it contains a private collection of paintings and engravings depicting Düsseldorf's history.

South of Bilker Strasse and the Heine monument, the impressive colonnaded building on an ornamental lake is the **Ständehaus**, the former seat of the Prussian provincial government and the postwar state parliament. The state assembly is now housed in a new building on the Rhine.

Eating and Drinking in the Altstadt

Düsseldorf's beer is called *Alt;* it is a pure, dark brew made with an extra dash of caramel malt and roasted malt to impart a darker hue. It contains more hops than Cologne's *Kölsch,* and is foamier. There is no lack of *Altbier* in the Altstadt (sometimes called "Germany's longest bar"), which has old pubs and tavern-restaurants galore. **Zum Schiffchen**, at Hafenstrasse 5, built in 1628, destroyed in 1944, and restored in 1963, offers good traditional eating and drinking. One of Düsseldorf's best-known pubs, **Zum Uerige**, at Bergerstrasse 1, brews its own Altbier, and has a real Altstadt atmosphere, but in summer you often have to stand in line to get in. Another "home-brew" pub, **Das Füchschen**, at Ratingerstrasse 28, is also worth a visit.

Most of the pubs serve hearty meals; **Zum Schlüssel**, Bolkerstrasse 45, also offers fresh herring snacks. For a classier fish meal, perhaps of oysters or lobster, try the French-style **Carl Maassen** restaurant at Bergerstrasse 3–7, which also serves Champagne (Veuve Clicquot) by the glass. It has its own fresh-fish shop next door. If you fancy other French food—or Italian, Chinese, Thai, Japanese, Egyptian, or Viennese—the Altstadt has it.

The quarter also has a number of small and simple, but comfortable, hotels, such as the ▶ **Rheinblick**, on Mühlenstrasse. It can be noisy, however, especially on Friday and Saturday nights.

A short distance south of the Altstadt, near the **Rheinkniebrücke** (Knee Bridge), which is named for a bend in the river at that point, is the **Rheinturm**, a telecommunications tower. At a height of 761 feet, it is Düsseldorf's tallest structure. It has a self-service restaurant, **Panorama**, at 546 feet, and a formal restaurant, **Top 180**, at 560 feet. The latter is named for its 180 window seats, which give diners a chance to enjoy a magnificent view of the city and river as the restaurant makes one rotation an hour around the tower's axis. The number 834 bus stops at the Rheinturm, and there is plenty of parking space for cars.

The Hofgarten Area

Düsseldorf has played a leading role in art and music not only within Germany but also elsewhere in Europe. The influence of the Düsseldorf school of art reached out far beyond the city. Schumann, who spent only four years in Düsseldorf, left an indelible mark on its music scene. The city today is more than ever a great center of art, music, theater, and opera. And many of Düsseldorf's cultural venues are located in the **Hofgarten**, the big, elegant swath of greenery that curves around the northern and northeastern borders of the Altstadt.

The **Ehrenhof**, Düsseldorf's riverside museum and music

center, sits at the Rhine end of the Hofgarten, immediately north of the Oberkasseler Brücke. The **Kunstmuseum** (Art Museum), located at the north end of the Ehrenhof, houses magnificent collections of paintings, sculptures, and arts and crafts from medieval days to the present, devoting much of its space to 19th-century art, especially works of the Düsseldorf school. The museum's comprehensive glass collection in its new **Glass Museum Hentrich** spans more than 2,000 years, from the development of luxury glass in pre-Roman days to the products of our times. An especially attractive feature of the collection is the exhibit of *Jugendstil* (Art Nouveau) pieces by Emile Gallé, Louis Comfort Tiffany, Karl Köpping, and the firm of Johann Lötz Witwe. The graphics collection consists of about 80,000 drawings, watercolors, and lithographs, including 14,000 Baroque sketches.

The east wing of the Kunstmuseum contains the **Kunstpalast** (Art Palace), which stages private travelling exhibitions, as well as the **Robert Schumann Saal**, a 500-seat hall where various concerts, ranging from chamber music to jazz, are given. The **Tonhalle**, at the south end of the Ehrenhof, was built in 1926 to accommodate a health and sports exhibition. Later, it was a planetarium. Rebuilt and reopened in 1978, it is now what Düsseldorf proudly claims is Germany's most beautiful concert hall after the Berlin Philharmonic. Its auditorium seats about 2,000 people, but is steep enough for all to feel close to the stage. The Tonhalle has been host to the world's leading orchestras and conductors, and presents as many as 20 concerts a month between September and June. Old and new works of art are displayed in the foyer and concert hall, and the Tonhalle also houses part of the Kunstmuseum's glass collection.

The Ehrenhof is also the home of the **Landesmuseum Volk und Wirtschaft** (State Museum of the People and Economy), on the west side of the complex, with continually updated working models, dioramas, photographs, videos, lectures, and special exhibitions on German agriculture, industry, and commerce.

If you feel like some refreshment, take a short walk north to the big riverside **Rheinterrasse Restaurant**, to the west of the Kunstmuseum, and watch the busy river traffic go by. The restaurant also operates a *Biergarten* in good summer weather. The ▶ **Hotel Germania**, a 23-room bed-and-breakfast on Freiligrathstrasse, a quiet side street only two blocks east of the Ehrenhof, across the north end of the Hofgarten, is pleasant and friendly, and conveniently located for exploring the museum quarter.

The city's other musical flagship, the **Deutsche Oper am Rhein**, run jointly since 1986 by Düsseldorf and nearby

Duisburg, is at the south end of the Hofgarten at Heinrich-Heine-Allee 16a. Its repertory includes many works by Mozart, and it is also known for its modern musical productions and good ballet company. The **Schauspielhaus** theater stands across from the opera house at Gustaf-Gründgens-Platz.

The **Goethe Museum**, in Schloss Jägerhof (Jacobistrasse 2, at the northeast corner of the Hofgarten's eastern arm), pays homage to the great man of letters, who often visited Düsseldorf. Completed in 1772, **Schloss Jägerhof** was the residence of the electors' huntmaster and parks superintendent. Since 1987 it has been the repository of the Anton and Katharina Kippenberg Foundation's superb collection of memorabilia from Goethe's time. Anton Kippenberg, who owned the Insel publishing house in Leipzig, spent 50 years putting the collection together. It includes books, pieces of music, and more than 35,000 writings, paintings, graphics, busts, medallions, and coins. Other exhibits, displayed in chronological order in 11 rooms, trace Goethe's work and life. They include vitrines containing first editions of his writings, drafts and letters, and likenesses of the poet and his friends. The museum also owns a collection of precious Meissen porcelain and 18th-century silverware.

Königsallee

Königsallee runs south of Corneliusplatz at the south end of the Hofgarten, more or less parallel to the Rhine. The Kö, as it is called, is one of the most stylish, and expensive, shopping boulevards in Europe. Along its half-mile length are more than 300 luxury stores. The Kö also has about three dozen fashionable cafés and restaurants, as well as Düsseldorf's grandest hotels, where the prices reflect their top quality and convenient central location.

The 135-room Neo-Baroque ▶ **Breidenbacher Hof**, on the corner of Heinrich-Heine-Allee and Theodor-Körner-Strasse, near the north end of the Kö, is considered by many experienced travellers the best hotel in western Germany. It has three restaurants, a beauty salon, and saunas in several suites. The ▶ **Steigenberger Parkhotel**, on Corneliusplatz, another Neo-Baroque building dating to the turn of the century, has 160 rooms. Overlooking the Hofgarten, and with the Kö at its door, it is another of the city's best addresses. Summer terrace dining at its gourmet **Menuett Restaurant** affords pleasant views of the park, and there is a bistro in the hotel lobby for quick meals. The **Etoile Bar**'s piano player provides late-night entertainment.

A posh ▶ **Holiday Inn** is on Graf-Adolf-Platz, at the south end of the Kö, with 177 luxury rooms. Its **Düsseldorfer Restaurant** offers a wide choice of German and international dishes, and its **Bistro Bar** (a nighttime *Treffpunkt*—meeting place—for the chic crowd) has draft Altbier as well as a wide range of "fantasy-inspired" cocktails. The hotel also has a heated indoor swimming pool, a sauna, and a solarium.

Chic cafés on the Kö include the **N. T.**, a "news" meeting place with ticker machines relaying news-agency reports, at Königsallee 27, on the west bank at the corner of Trinkausstrasse; and the **Café Koenig**, in the Kesting Galerie, Königsallee 36, directly opposite the N. T., which serves excellent lunches and suppers until midnight to a mixed clientele of businessmen, show-biz people, fashion models, and artists and bohemian types.

The top restaurants include the **Victorian**, an expensive French-cuisine establishment on the first floor of Königstrasse 3a, on its corner with the Kö. Reservations are recommended; Tel: (211) 32-02-22. On the ground floor is the **Victorian Bar**, another popular *Treff* for night owls, and behind the bar is the **Victorian Lounge**, a popular bistro. The **Casserole Restaurant**, Königsallee 92, at the south end near Graf-Adolf-Platz and the Holiday Inn, offers formal dining in its rotisserie as well as snacks in its bistro.

The Kö crowd's other haunts include **Bei Tino's** piano bar, Königsallee 21, where the custom is to drink Champagne while sitting around a grand piano played by visiting performers. Open until 3:00 A.M., Tino's also serves good food. **Checker's Club**, an all-night disco with food at Königsallee 28 is not for what Germans call the *Spiesser* (bourgeois-minded). It's a high-decibel Treff for the far out, but in small doses it can be fun. **Sam's West**, a nightclub at Königsallee 27, where no fewer than three doormen assess your admissibility, is considered Düsseldorf's number-one night spot. Its prices match its reputation.

The Outskirts of Düsseldorf

The **Löbbecke Museum and Aquazoo**, a scientific living nature museum, with fish, reptiles, birds, and insects, is located in the riverside **Nordpark** off Kaiserswerther Strasse, north of the Ehrenhof. Take U-Bahn (subway) line U-78 or U-79 from the main railroad station or from the Heinrich-Heine-Allee U-Bahn station (at the south end of the boulevard at its intersection with Grabenstrasse and Königstrasse) to the Nordpark stop.

Kaiserswerther Strasse runs on past the Nordpark exhibition grounds and the Rheinstadion, a sports complex that's home to the Federal League soccer club Fortuna Düsseldorf, and farther north to the village of **Kaiserswerth**, about 10 km (6 miles) from the city and easily accessible by U-Bahn line U-79. Kaiserswerth is a pleasant, quiet village worth a visit for its neat cafés, antiques shops, old houses, and the ruins of the **Barbarossapfalz**, an imperial palace enlarged in the 12th century by Emperor Barbarossa, as well as its peaceful square at the church of St. Suidbert.

The **Grafenberger Wald** (forest), about a ten-minute drive east of the city center, has a park in which deer and wild boar roam free. A *Pferderennbahn* (horse-racing track) and the Rochus tennis club are nearby. (The number 712 streetcar runs here from the city center.) On Rennbahnstrasse, next to the racetrack, stands the ► **Rolandsburg Hotel**, a modern country house opened in 1988, with 59 luxury rooms, an excellent restaurant, and a good lounge bar. In summer the hotel opens its park terrace for drinks and meals. The hotel also has an indoor pool, fitness room, sauna, solarium, and Jacuzzi.

Germans use the word *Schloss* (castle) somewhat loosely for what most foreigners would call a château. There are three *Schlösser* in the Düsseldorf area worth a day trip out of the city.

Schloss Benrath, on the southern outskirts of Düsseldorf, about 15 km (9 miles) from the city center, was built in 1755 by Elector Karl Theodor as a private summer residence and hunting lodge. Set in a beautiful, thickly wooded park that runs down to the Rhine, the castle is mirrored in a large *Spiegelweiher* (reflecting pool) on its south side. Its 80 rooms, open every day but Monday, are decorated in Rococo style. The S-Bahn (commuter train) line S-6 from Düsseldorf's main railroad station travels to the Benrath station in about ten minutes; from there the Schloss is only a five-minute walk.

A group of four buildings set in a historic park at Jüchen, 20 km (12 miles) southwest of Düsseldorf, **Schloss Dyck** was built in 1650 on the ruins of an 11th-century moated castle, parts of whose walls can still be seen. Long the residence of the van Dyck family of landowners, politicians, and churchmen, the Schloss now contains an interesting weapons museum, claimed to be Europe's most comprehensive private collection of hunting guns, dating from 1520 to 1933. Its elegant rooms are noted for their ceiling frescoes, antique furniture, and splendid hangings of hand-painted Chinese silk and gold-tooled leather. The main building, with an inner courtyard, has towers at each corner topped by Baroque domes. The informal park, with a big pond reflecting the Schloss, contains 190 different types of trees, some of them 200 years old, as well as large flower beds filled with narcissus, rhododendrons, and azaleas. Paths through the park, which is open year-round, offer pleasant walks. The museum, and a cafeteria, are open daily from April through October, except Mondays. By car from Düsseldorf, take the A 46 Autobahn southwest to the Grevenbroich exit, then take the B 59 north and follow the signs.

Schloss Rheydt, near Mönchengladbach, 24 km (15 miles) west of Düsseldorf, is a moated Renaissance château in three parts, consisting of an outer bailey, gatehouse, and manor house. It was built between 1560 and 1590 for Otto von Bylandt, a member of a noble Lower Rhine family that can be traced back to the 13th century. Its manor house has a 13-room museum displaying arts and crafts, mainly of the Renaissance and Baroque periods, including Gobelins tapestries, paintings, wood carvings, Greek and Roman pottery, furniture, glass, ceramics, handwritten books, ecclesiastical and domestic objects, maps and globes, works of gold and silver, coins, graphics, textiles, and old weapons. The outer bailey houses a museum that documents the history of Mönchengladbach from prehistoric and Roman times, and includes a weaving section with six hand looms—a reflection of the city's role as an important textile-making center since the 19th century. Schloss Rheydt is about a ten-minute drive northwest on the B 57 in the direction of Korschenbroich from Schloss Dyck, so you can visit both castles in one day.

The 50,000-year-old skeleton of a Neanderthal man was found in 1856 in a cave near **Erkrath**, in the Neander river valley, only 15 km (9 miles) southeast of Düsseldorf. Today some of his bones can be seen in the **Neandertal Museum** at the site (his skull is in the Rheinisches Landesmuseum in Bonn). A green *Wildgehege* (game reserve) surrounds the museum. The reserve is home to animals that roamed the area—aurochs, tarpane, and bison—when the Neanderthal man was alive.

To reach the museum by car from Düsseldorf, take the A 46 Autobahn in the direction of Wuppertal and get off at the Hochdahl-Haan exit. Take Haanerstrasse through Hochdahl and follow the signs to the museum. The S-Bahn line S-8 from Düsseldorf's main railroad station takes only about ten minutes to the Millrath stop at Erkrath. From there, take the well-signposted footpath through the Wildgehege for a pleasant 15-minute walk to the museum.

AACHEN

Aachen (Aix-la-Chapelle, or Aken, as its neighbors call it), Germany's main western gateway, lying directly on its frontiers with Belgium and Holland, about 65 km (40 miles) west of Cologne, is a traditional meeting place for the people of three nations. Aacheners are a cosmopolitan, friendly lot who are used to foreign visitors, and their city enjoys a pan-European identity.

Aachen has a pleasant, small-town feel about it and at the same time offers much to visitors of widely differing interests. Of major historical interest in this former imperial capital is Charlemagne's magnificent ninth-century chapel/cathedral as well as a 14th-century town hall. Charlemagne's palace court here—the palace itself is no longer extant—was the wellspring of Western Europe's first great cultural renaissance at the end of the "Dark Ages." Charlemagne, devoted to learning and the establishment of civil order, brought the scholar Alcuin from York to Aachen in 782 to educate him and his circle in grammar and other subjects. The short-term result—chronicled in Einhard's *Life of Charlemagne*—was a dramatic increase in learning throughout northern Europe. The long-term results are incalculable; Aachen is one of the great sites of Western civilization.

Aachen was badly damaged by air raids and ground fighting in World War II: Three-fifths of its dwellings were partially or fully destroyed. But by 1966 the city had largely completed its reconstruction. Coal mining was once an important industry for the city; now textiles have taken its place and Aachen produces 20 percent of Germany's woolen products. The city is also noted for its marzipan, chocolate, and gingerbread. And for the visitor there is much more: culture, museums, fountains, international riding events, a famous spa and health resort, good hotels, dining and shopping, conventions, and a noted casino.

Aachen's Innenstadt is surrounded by a ring road that traces the circle of its first *Stadtmauer* (city wall), which was built from 1171 to 1175. An outer ring road follows the course of the city's second wall, built from 1257 to 1357. Both ring roads change names in the course of their sweep around the city.

The Innenstadt

Two-thousand-year-old Aachen was settled by the Celts and Romans. Much of the city's history took place in the Innenstadt area, and many of its historic monuments can be found there.

Charlemagne, king of the Franks, chose it as his capital in 794, six years before he was crowned Holy Roman Emperor of the West. His **Dom** (Cathedral), a domed octagonal chapel or basilica modeled on churches in Rome's Eastern Empire, was inaugurated in 805, and is his greatest legacy to the city.

The cathedral, situated near the top of a steep cobbled hill at the center of the Innenstadt, with Münsterplatz (the cathedral square) on its south side, was the coronation church for no fewer than 32 German Holy Roman emperors over more than seven centuries. Its high-tiered marble throne was used until 1531; the Gothic choir hall was built between 1355 and 1414. Some of Charlemagne's bones are preserved in an exquisite golden shrine created after his canonization in 1165. The top of his skull is worked into a gold-and-silver bust-shaped reliquary held in the **Domschatzkammer** (Cathedral Treasury), one of many precious articles that make the treasury one of Germany's greatest repositories of religious relics and art. Daily tours of the cathedral start from the Domschatzkammer on Klostergasse, on the west side of the cathedral. From March through August, occasional concerts are performed on the cathedral's 1840 Zoboli organ.

A short walk uphill from the cathedral is the spacious old **Markt** (Market Square), on which sits the Gothic **Rathaus** (Town Hall), built in the early 14th century out of Charlemagne's then-dilapidated imperial palace. The **Reichssaal** (Imperial Hall) on the second floor is where newly crowned German rulers held their coronation banquets. Nowadays, every May, Europe's political leaders gather here for the presentation of the prestigious Charlemagne Prize for contributions to European unity. Winston Churchill and Henry Kissinger are on the roll of honor.

The roofs and towers of the Rathaus have been destroyed three times: in Aachen's great fire of 1656; in another blaze in 1883; and by bombs and shells during World War II. But the Rathaus was patiently restored after each disaster. Its present Baroque personality dates from the 17th and 18th centuries. There are no regular daily tours of the Rathaus; sightseeing must be arranged with the tourist information office (see below).

The tourist office offers a one-hour *Stadtbummel,* a guided walking tour of the inner city that gives a quick general overview of the area. It covers the Markt, the Rathaus, the Dom, and Münsterplatz, then drops south downhill along Hartmannstrasse to the **Elisengarten**, a park with a rotunda sheltering a public drinking fountain, the **Elisenbrunnen**, that

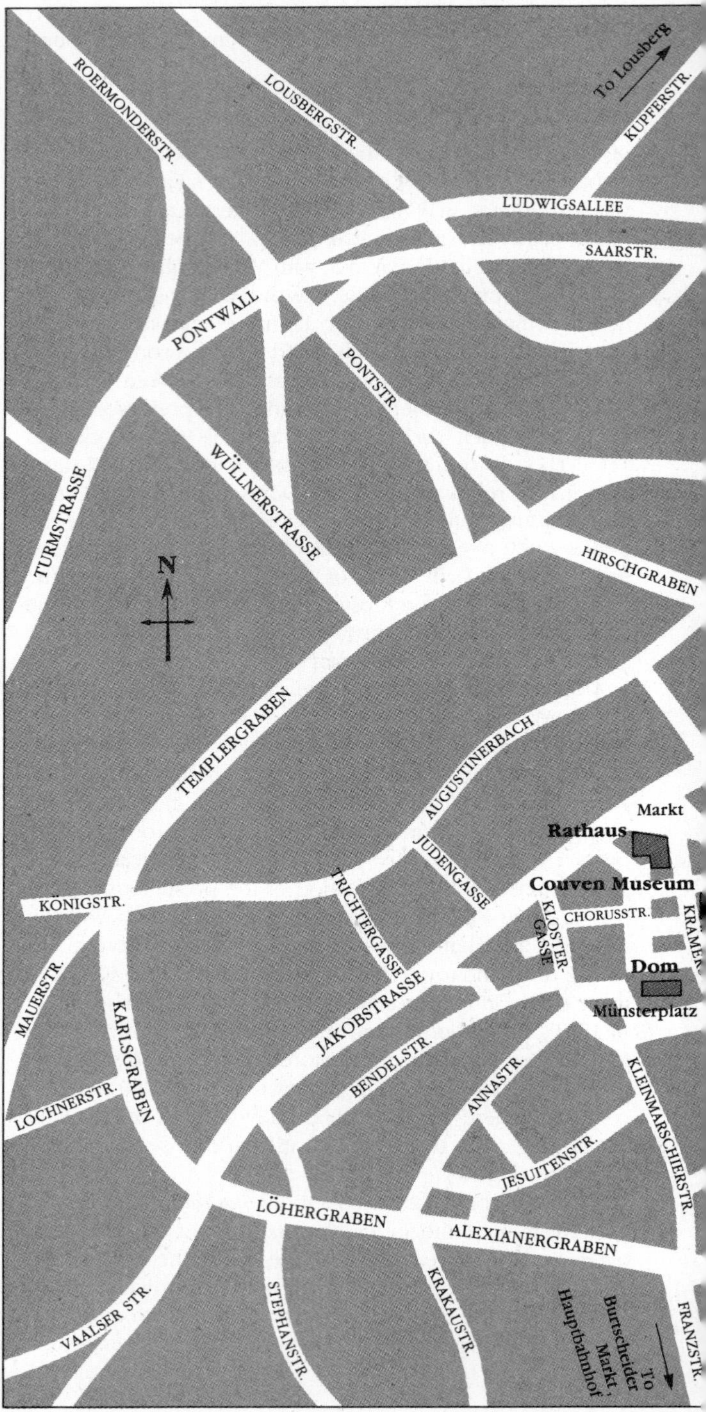

To Lousberg
KUPFERSTR.
ROERMONDERSTR.
LOUSBERGSTR.
LUDWIGSALLEE
SAARSTR.
PONTWALL
PONTSTR.
TURMSTRASSE
WÜLLNERSTRASSE
HIRSCHGRABEN
N
TEMPLERGRABEN
AUGUSTINERBACH
Markt
Rathaus
JUDENGASSE
Couven Museum
KÖNIGSTR.
TRICHTERGASSE
KLOSTER-GASSE
CHORUSSTR.
KRAMER.
Dom
Münsterplatz
MAUERSTR.
KARLSGRABEN
JAKOBSTRASSE
BENDELSTR.
ANNASTR.
KLEINMARSCHIERSTR.
LOCHNERSTR.
JESUITENSTR.
LÖHERGRABEN
ALEXIANERGRABEN
KRAKAUSTR.
STEPHANSTR.
VAALSER STR.
To Burtscheider Markt, Hauptbahnhof
FRANZSTR.

Aachen

To Soers Valley

0 yards 220
0 meters 200

Kurgarten

Eurogress Convention Center

Spielkasino

Stadtgarten

Kurbad Quellenhof

MONHEIMSALLEE

ROCHUSSTR.

SANDKAULSTR.

To Düsseldorf
To Cologne
To Ludwig Forum für
Internationale Kunst
To Europaplatz

Hansemannplatz

SEILGRABEN

ALEXANDERSTRASSE

GROSSKÖLNSTRASSE

KURHS STRASSE

KOMPHAUSBADSTR.

KLEINKÖLNSTR.

MEFFERDATISSTR.

ANTONIUSSTR.

Neue Galerie Sammlung Ludwig

NIKOLAUSSTR.

DAHMENGRABEN

PETERSTRASSE

BLONDELSTRASSE

HEINRICHSALLEE

KREMERSTRASSE

BUCHELSTR.

HOLZGRABEN

STIFTSTR.

Römerbad

Elisengarten

ADALBERTSTR.

HARTMANNSTR.

To Kornelimünster
and Monschau

Suermondt Ludwig Museum

KAPUZINERGRABEN

WIRICHSBONGARDSTR.

Theaterplatz

SCHILDSTR.

HARSCAMPSTR.

WILHEMSTRASSE

Stadttheater

THEATERSTRASSE

To Burg
Frankenburg

LOTHRINGERSTR.

splashes forth Aachen's healthy thermal spring water. The rotunda is also the location of the main tourist information office. (The office also has a bureau at the railroad station.) Directly behind the rotunda, in the center of the park, is the excellent **Restaurant Elisenbrunnen**, with a terrace for open-air dining in summer. The menu offers traditional German, international, and vegetarian dishes. From the Elisengarten the tour turns north along the pedestrians-only Holzgraben, Dahmengraben, and Grosskölnstrasse en route back to the Markt. The three streets have some of the chic boutiques for which Aachen is noted. Take a look, and a pleasing sniff, at **Pfeifen-Schneiderwind**, an old-style pipe and tobacco shop at Krämerstrasse 13–15 dating from 1846; it stocks up to 15,000 pipes.

After the tour, for a cup of real coffee and a taste of Aachen's famous *Printen* gingerbread cookies (*Printen* is Old German for "printing"—the cookies are pressed flat before baking) or rice cakes in a charming "Granny's parlor" atmosphere, go southeast from the Markt down Büchel-strasse to the corner of narrow Körbergasse and pop into the **Altes Aachener Kaffeehaus van den Daele**, founded by a Belgian 160 years ago in a house built in 1655. The house has its own bakery. The modernistic, brick-fronted, 92-room ▶ **Aquis Grana Cityhotel** is nearby at Buchkremerstrasse. The hotel has direct access by a basement passage to the spa facilities of the Römerbad (Roman Bath; see below), and is conveniently located near the cathedral and the Rathaus.

Aachen has a variety of interesting museums; several of note are in the Innenstadt. The **Couven Museum**, on Hühner-markt, southeast of the Rathaus, has a fine collection of furniture and furnishings from the Regency to Biedermeier periods (1740–1840). The **Internationales Zeitungs** (News-paper) **Museum**, Pontstrasse 13 (the street runs out of the northwest corner of the Innenstadt), has more than 120,000 newspapers in 30-some languages.

The **Suermondt Ludwig Museum**, at the old Kurhaus on Komphausbadstrasse, on the northeast edge of the Innen-stadt, exhibits 13th- to 18th-century sculptures and the works of German and Dutch masters of the 15th to 17th centuries, as well as some modern art. In 1991 Peter Ludwig, Aachen's leading chocolate manufacturer and Germany's biggest art collector, opened the **Forum für Internationale Kunst** (Fo-rum for International Art) in a former umbrella factory on the corner of Jülicher Strasse and Lombarden Strasse, four blocks beyond Monheimsallee (the outer ring road) northeast of the Markt. The Forum is based on a "living" multimedia concept of modern art, music, dance, literature, and film, with chang-ing exhibitions, performances, and discussions with artists.

Open 11:00 A.M. to 7:00 P.M.; Thursday, 11:00 A.M. to 10:00 P.M.; closed Mondays.

On fine summer evenings the **Markt** is crowded with hundreds of locals and visitors enjoying a glass of beer or wine and a meal at tables that the old tavern-restaurants set up outside at the first glimpse of sunshine. All offer good, basic German pub food, including seasonal specialties such as *Matjes* (young Dutch herring) and white asparagus beginning in June.

Underneath the Rathaus at its southeastern corner are the old **Ratskeller** restaurant and the **Postwagen Inn** (1657), with low, vaulted ceilings and rustic wooden tables and benches. On the other side of the square is the "Gold Strip," a row of old dark-wood bars and restaurants with such names as Golden Swan, Golden Unicorn, and Golden Chain. A better culinary nugget is the **Goldener Apfelbaum** (Golden Apple Tree), south of the Markt and just a short walk downhill from the town hall on Krämerstrasse. It offers a large number of traditional dishes from *Oma's Küche* (Granny's kitchen).

An informal evening's fun can be had touring the many *Studentenkneipen* (students' pubs) on and around **Pontstrasse**, northwest of the Markt. Aachen has more than 45,000 students at its technical university and technical college, and so the pubs are a lively scene.

Aachen Outside the Innenstadt

To start off your exploration of Aachen outside the Innenstadt, head for the 660-foot **Lousberg** mini-mountain for a bird's-eye view of the entire city. Located northeast of the Innenstadt outside the outer ring road, the Lousberg is a quick cab ride or about a 20-minute walk from the Markt. From the Ludwigsallee stretch of the outer ring, turn up Kupferstrasse and then follow the winding road to the top. Even if you go on foot, it's worth the effort, and from the **Belvedere** revolving restaurant at the top you can see for miles. (The restaurant is better for *Kaffee und Kuchen*—a coffee break—than for meals.)

Just off Monheimsallee, the northeast stretch of the outer ring road, in the green **Kurgarten**, is the **Eurogress convention center**. The center has two halls for concerts and plays, and is connected directly to the elegant 160-room ▶ **Steigenberger Quellenhof**, which has the public Kurbad Quellenhof spa facilities right next door, and an indoor swimming pool.

For many, a visit to Aachen would not be complete without a trip to the Neoclassical **Internationales Spielkasino**, in the former Kurhaus (spa house) next to the Eurogress. Take a turn at roulette, blackjack, or baccarat, or simply enjoy the atmosphere over a glass of *Sekt* (German sparkling wine). The **Gala**, the casino's award-winning restaurant, specializes in German cuisine and is one of the top culinary establishments in the country.

Aachen is a convention and tourist town and has many good hotels with and without thermal waters, in all categories, several convenient to the Eurogress and casino. They include the functional 117-room ▶ **Novotel Aachen**, with an outdoor pool and the good **Le Grill** restaurant offering regional and international dishes, due east of the Kurgarten on Europaplatz, the terminus of the A 4/A 544 Aachen–Cologne Autobahn at Aachen's eastern city limit; and the pricier 60-room ▶ **Best Western Hotel Regence**, southwest of the Kurgarten, with a good Japanese restaurant and a bar called the Hippo Pub. The Best Western is close to Aachen's main shopping area, centered on **Adalbertstrasse**, a pedestrian zone that runs east of the Innenstadt off the Peterstrasse stretch of the inner ring.

Aachen's symphony orchestra, founded in 1852, enjoys an international standing and has been led by many famous conductors. Renowned artists and leading orchestras visit the city often, giving concerts at the **Stadttheater**, on Theaterplatz (just outside the southeastern corner of the inner ring), where plays, operetta, and opera are also performed.

Just south of the theater is a small, friendly, family-run hotel, the 33-room ▶ **Benelux Hotel** on Franzstrasse, which runs south from the inner ring road. A short walk south of the cathedral, the Benelux is also convenient to the Innenstadt. The hotel's plain, compact bar-restaurant serves supper until midnight. Another small, but chic, accommodation handy for walking to the Innenstadt, and just north of the theater, is the 20-room ▶ **Hotel Krott**, on Wirichsbongardstrasse, a narrow street that runs east off the inner ring. The hotel has a cozy, inviting restaurant.

Southeast of the Ludwig Museum, beyond the outer ring road, is Aachen's own "hometown" museum, the **Burg Frankenburg** (Bismarckstrasse 68), which traces the city's history from the Romans through the Middle Ages.

Aachen's more than 30 curative springs, containing 19 minerals, attract many people to the city. The springs were already popular with the Romans in A.D. 100 when they built a spa for their Rhineland legions, calling it *Aquae Grani*. The municipal spa house and numerous private thermal baths and rheumatism clinics are located in and around **Burtscheider Markt**, south of the outer ring road and the Hauptbahnhof (main railroad station).

While they're on the outskirts of town, the **Römerbad** next door to the Aquis Grana hotel is much more conveniently located. It offers an indoor pool (water temperature maintained at 93°) with underwater massage jets and "quiet rooms" to relax in afterward. Bathing caps and sandals are required, and towels can be rented. (Open Monday through Friday from 7:00 A.M. to 7:00 P.M., Saturdays from 7:00 A.M. to 6:00 P.M., and Sundays 7:00 A.M. to 1:00 P.M.) An alternative to the Römerbad is the larger and somewhat more upmarket **Kurbad Quellenhof**, which offers mud-pack treatment as well as underwater massage. Free underwater gymnastic workouts are offered in both places.

Excursions from Aachen

Thanks to Aachen's frontier location, the tourist office offers (by appointment) a four-hour "three countries" bus trip that takes in Valkenberg and Maastricht in Holland as well as Tongeren, Belgium's oldest town.

The office also runs a four-hour trip into the rolling Eifel hills to **Kornelimünster**, a picturesque medieval village only 10 km (6 miles) south of the city on route 258. From there the tour continues to **Monschau**, a pretty 18th-century cloth- and mustard-making town with cobbled streets and gabled houses.

Although Aachen's excellent public transportation system—with a total of 145 bus lines running from the Bushof (depot) on Peterstrasse—also takes in Kornelimünster and Monschau (line 35), it's best to go by car and take your time. Try to avoid weekends, when visitors pack Monschau.

The world's best riders and horses gather in the Aachen area each June for the international equestrian tournament (CHIO) at the riding stadium in the Soers valley, about 5 km (3 miles) north of the Innenstadt.

BONN

The quiet university and market town that became Europe's smallest capital city in 1949 was immediately dubbed the "Bundesdorf" (Federal Village). Bonn lost its capital status to Berlin when the two Germanys united in October 1990. Following a decision by Parliament in June 1991, Bonn is also to lose that body, as well as the government, to Berlin. But their move is not expected before the year 2000 because of the huge construction program necessary to accommodate them in Berlin.

To be sure, Bonn, situated on the west bank of the Rhine some 28 km (17 miles) south of Cologne, was tiny for a

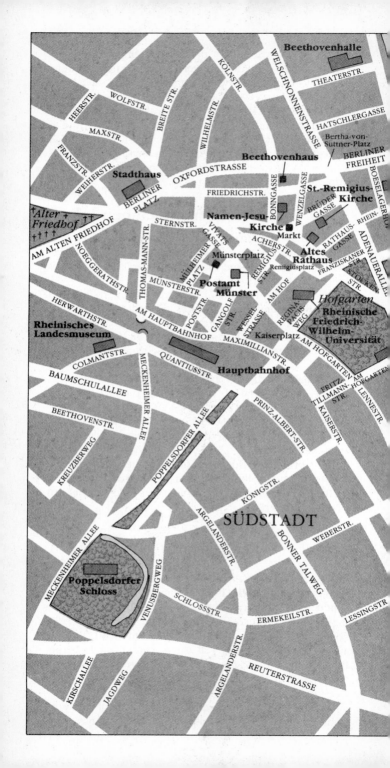

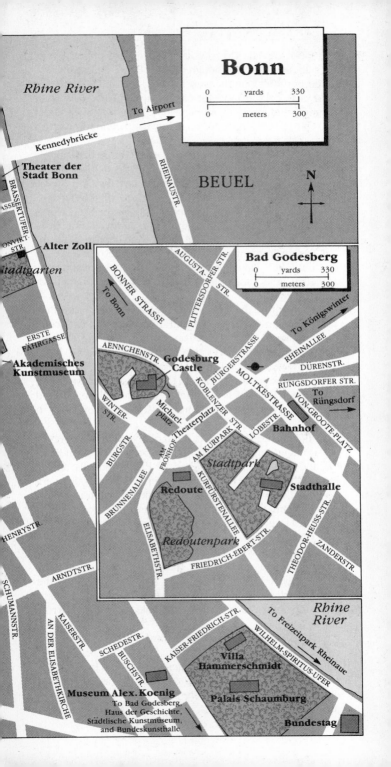

European capital. The city itself has a core population of only about 145,000, although Greater Bonn, embracing Bad Godesberg (also on the west bank, 5 km/3 miles south, see below), Beuel (opposite the city on the east bank), and other formerly independent municipalities, has a total of about 300,000. But it's a pleasant small town and definitely worth a visit.

As the city hall puts it, *"Bonn ist mehr"*: more than merely a "city of politics with those gray eminences in black limousines." And that is true, despite the fact that the 30,000 federal employees are the largest group in the 125,000-strong local work force. The federal-government quarter is located on the Rhine, but to the south and well away from the cobbled town center. The locals were shocked to learn that the government and Parliament would one day leave the city, but Old Bonn takes pride in its long pre-capital history as well as in its attractions as a relaxing and rewarding town to discover.

Settlement of the immediate area goes back more than 2,000 years, to the Celts. In fact, Bonn celebrated its second millennium in 1989, based on records showing that the Romans set up a military camp here in the years 13 to 9 B.C. The town was fortified in 1244, occupied by the French in 1794, and taken over by Prussia in 1815; its center was badly damaged in World War II. Largely reconstructed along its old lines, Bonn has retained its human scale and continues to charm.

As Beethoven's birthplace, Bonn offers much in the way of music, including the triennial International Beethoven Festival (the next one is in 1995) at the Beethovenhalle on the Rhine. There is also opera and theater at the riverside opera house, a lively summer program of open-air cultural events, and museums, ancient churches, elegant villas, good restaurants, old taverns, a student milieu—and the Rhine.

Bonn is a compact town, much of it a pedestrian zone, with shops everywhere. It takes no more than ten minutes to cross the inner town in any direction from the city ring (shaped more like a triangle). Like Aachen's ring roads, the Bonn city ring changes its name several times, and its southern and southeastern sections are little more than narrow streets.

One of Europe's greenest cities, with 1,200 gardens and parks, Bonn, in contrast to some other towns along the Rhine, also has 18 miles of promenades on both banks of the river. Pleasure boats from Bonn cruise past castles perched on top of wooded hills that are part of huge nature reserves near the city.

The Markt Area

Bonn's cobbled Markt, in the inner city, dates from the Middle Ages. The fruit-and-vegetable market, with its raucous stall holders, began in the 11th century. The foundation of the obelisk-fountain at the Markt's center was laid in 1777. In summer the Markt's cafés, restaurants, and pubs set tables outside in good weather, providing a vantage point from which to see the local action.

The pink-and-white Rococo **Altes Rathaus** (Old Town Hall) dating from 1738 stands on the site of a Gothic building destroyed by the French in 1689. The "new" building was badly damaged in an air raid in October 1944 but was restored.

The Altes Rathaus long ago became too small to house Bonn's governmental offices. In 1977 the city fathers, despite protest from their burghers, built an ugly, towering, concrete city administration center, called the Stadthaus, on Berlinerplatz, the northwestern section of the city ring. The building is totally out of scale with the rest of the town's mostly old and pleasing architecture and dominates the western skyline, especially when seen from the Markt.

The Altes Rathaus still has its moments of glory, however, especially when foreign heads of state visit Bonn. It's routine for them to sign the city's Golden Book, kept in the Altes Rathaus, and then wave to the crowds from its high, richly ornamented, double-flighted perron. General Charles de Gaulle did so in 1962, followed by John F. Kennedy a year later and former Soviet leader Mikhail Gorbachev in 1989. Queen Elizabeth II has visited the Altes Rathaus twice, in 1965 and 1978, and packed the Markt both times.

The Markt is also the setting for the *Bonner Sommer,* Bonn's summer entertainment event, featuring a musical program that ranges from classical through international folk to jazz. The plain but excellently located 79-room ▶ **Sternhotel** on the Markt overlooks it all. Near the hotel, tucked into a corner next to the Rathaus, is **Em Höttche**, a small historic tavern and restaurant serving good German pub food.

A stroll north off the Markt down Bonngasse across narrow Friedrichstrasse will lead you to the well-preserved **Beethovenhaus**, the birthplace of Ludwig van Beethoven. A private museum dedicated to the composer, it contains many of his possessions, among them stringed instruments and his last grand piano. Beethoven, who was born in December 1770, spent the first 22 years of his life in Bonn, finding important friends and teachers who helped him develop his musical genius, before moving to Vienna. It was in Bonn that the 14-year-old Ludwig played one of his own compositions to Josef Haydn—who rightly forecast a brilliant musical future for the young man.

Im Stiefel, a tavern-restaurant on Bonngasse close to the Beethovenhaus, is another good "scrubbed tables" type of old German pub. Back up Bonngasse toward the Markt is the Jesuit **Namen Jesu Kirche**, dating from 1717, with a notable Baroque façade. Also just off the Markt, to the northeast, on Brüdergasse, is **St.-Remigius-Kirche**, a Gothic basilica consecrated in 1317. Beethoven played its 18th-century Baroque organ, which was destroyed in an air raid in 1944 (its keyboard is now on display in his house).

The Münsterplatz Area

A short stroll southwest of the Markt along the narrow Marktbrücke into Remigiusstrasse brings you to Remigiusplatz, with its flower market and the traditional **Bonner Kaffeehaus** for good coffee and delicious cakes and pastries. Farther up Remigiusstrasse you enter **Münsterplatz**, the big cobbled square dominated by Bonn's premier church, the 900-year-old **Münster** (cathedral). Built over a third- to fourth-century memorial chapel to Roman martyrs, it was expanded over the centuries and saw the coronations of two German kings, in 1314 and 1356. The church has a restored 11th-century cloister and towers. Also on the Münsterplatz is a statue of Beethoven, Bonn's favorite son, in front of the 18th-century–style Postamt (post office).

Bonn's tourist information office is a short walk south of Münsterplatz by way of Poststrasse at the Cassius Bastei, Münsterstrasse 20. The office is well stocked with guides to easy strolls around the town; Tel: (228) 77-34-66.

Farther south on Poststrasse, the small Kaiser-era Hauptbahnhof (railroad station) faces the newish 34-room ▶ **Continental Hotel**, a bed-and-breakfast offering good, medium-priced comfort. Behind the station to the southwest, on Colmantstrasse, lies the **Rheinisches Landesmuseum**, with exhibits on the Rhineland's history, art, and culture from prehistoric times to the present. Its prize is the skull of Neanderthal man, dating from 50,000 B.C., which was found in the Neander valley, near Düsseldorf.

The University

Bonn's 40,000 undergraduates make up the largest student body in this part of Germany. The **Rheinische Friedrich-Wilhelm-Universität**—just south of the Markt, with its west side, Am Hof, making up part of the southeast section of the city ring—was founded in 1818 by the third Prussian king of that name, to replace another academy that was closed by the occupying French in 1798. Quartered mainly in the former elector's long, spacious Baroque palace, the university made its name early with its excellent philosophy faculty and is now also noted for law, medicine, mathematics, physics, and chemistry. Its alumni include Heinrich Heine, Karl Marx, and Prince Albert, Queen Victoria's consort. (The couple had their first "date" in Bonn during the prince's student days.)

The university's big public park, the **Hofgarten**, embraces its **Akademisches Kunstmuseum** (Academic Art Museum), which houses a fine collection of antique sculptures and Greek and Roman artifacts. East of the Hofgarten, across Adenauerallee (part of route B 9) on the river is the 135-room ▶ **Hotel Königshof**, an upscale tourist and business traveller's hotel whose noted **La Belle Epoque** restaurant offers international cuisine. The hotel has a terrace overlooking the Rhine, a pleasant spot for a coffee break in summer. Another hotel convenient to the university area is the new 144-room ▶ **Residence Hotel**, on Kaiserplatz, southeast of the Hofgarten, with three good restaurants and an indoor pool. Its informal **Kaisergarten** restaurant offers buffet breakfasts, lunches, and suppers; a wide range of German and international dishes is available in the cozily rustic **Zirbelstube**; and its cellar restaurant, opened in 1992, serves up meals in three converted wagons from an overhead railroad dating from 1901. A piano player entertains nightly in the **Wintergarten** bar next to the pool.

East and West of the Inner City

West of Bonn's inner city area, one block southwest of the overbearing Stadthaus, on the west side of Am Alten Friedhof, is the peaceful **Alter Friedhof** (Old Cemetery), where Robert and Clara Schumann are buried side by side in graves that are always decorated with flowers. Schumann spent the last two years of his life as a mental patient in a private sanatorium in Bonn (now the **Schumann Haus**, at Sebastianstrasse 182, in the southwestern suburb of Endenich, which is also the home of the **Bonn Music Library**). He died in 1856; his wife, Clara, lived for another 40 years and spent many of them in Bonn, composing her own works as well as playing on the world's stages.

Other important people buried in the cemetery include Maria Magdalena van Beethoven, the composer's mother; Friedrich Schiller's wife, Charlotte von Schiller; Adele Schopenhauer, sister of the philosopher; Elsa Reger, wife of the composer Max Reger; and the 19th-century writer-politician Ernst Moritz Arndt.

Northeast of the inner city is the **Kennedybrücke**, which you can reach via Bertha-von-Suttner-Platz and Berliner Freiheit, linking Bonn with **Beuel** on the east bank of the Rhine.

The city opera house, the **Theater der Stadt Bonn**, stands on the Rhine three blocks east of the Markt and just south of the Kennedybrücke. Five blocks north of the bridge is the riverside **Beethovenhalle**, home of the Beethoven Festival and many other events and exhibitions. It is here that the federal assembly currently elects the president.

A hotel convenient to the area is the 252-bed ▶ **Scandic Crown Hotel**, on Berliner Freiheit, at the Bonn end of the Kennedybrücke. On Sundays the hotel offers a five-course "Royal Swedish" smorgasbord in its **Rhapsody** restaurant, featuring fish dishes and exotic fare such as smoked reindeer meat and elk ham. There is also an indoor swimming pool, fitness training room, sauna, and steam bath. Open-air dining is available on the Rhein Plaza terrace until 11:00 P.M.

The Südstadt

Bonn's attractive Südstadt (South Town), southwest of the Hofgarten, is worth visiting to see the façades of the many fine old town houses built between 1860 and 1914. The tourist office has a guide to 11 of the best of them, beginning on Poppelsdorfer Allee, a beautiful wide avenue lined with chestnut trees that borders the Südstadt, and heading southwest before turning east into Königstrasse. The route zigzags through numerous narrow streets and ends back where it began.

At the end of Poppelsdorfer Allee, in the Südstadt's southwestern corner, is the **Poppelsdorfer Schloss**, the 18th-century former elector's palace, given to the university by the Prussian king who founded the school. The palace was begun by Elector Joseph Clemens in 1715 and completed by his successor, Clemens August, in 1753. The university has converted its park into a fine **botanical garden**, with ten greenhouses and many rare plants.

A daily two-and-a-half-hour city bus tour starting at the tourist office and escorted by an English-speaking guide includes the Poppelsdorfer Schloss and part of the Südstadt after covering the government quarter and Bad Godesberg. It's well worth taking for an overall introduction to the area.

Many houses in the Südstadt are honeycombed with student apartments, and the quarter has plenty of students' pubs. Some of these stay open later than those in the rest of the city, which usually close at 1:00 A.M.

If you wish to stay in the Südstadt area, try the 120-room ▶ **Hotel Bristol**, at the city end of Poppelsdorfer Allee at the corner of Prinz-Albert-Strasse. The city's finest hotel, the Bristol regularly puts up delegations of visiting VIPs.

The Government Quarter

The federal government currently carries on its business in a clutch of old and new buildings on the Rhine in the *Regierungsviertel* (Government Quarter), south of the city along Adenauerallee and the river. The **Museum Alexander Koenig**, a zoological museum on the west side of Adenauerallee, was where West Germany's founders held their first parliamentary council when they met to create a new country in 1949. They conducted their affairs of state before an audience of the museum's stuffed elephants, giraffes, and gorillas. The museum is now part of Bonn's new *Museummeile* (Museum Mile), which stretches south from here on the western side of Adenaueralle, and includes three other new museums. Three blocks south is the **Haus der Geschichte** (House of History), scheduled to open in the spring of 1994, which will trace Germany's history from the end of World War II to reunification in 1990. One block farther south is the twin-building complex of the **Städtische Kunstmuseum** (City Art Museum) and the **Bundeskunsthalle** (Federal Art Hall), which opened in 1992. The art museum includes works by August Macke (1887–1914), one of Germany's leading Expressionists, objects by Joseph Beuys among displays of German art since 1945, graphic collections, and art videos. The art hall, topped by three striking cone-shaped "lighthouses," was conceived as a "house of dialogue" between art and science, and features travelling exhibitions of art, architecture, cultural history, science, and technology.

The quarter's old (19th-century) government buildings are the most interesting. Provincial Bonn at that time was a retirement town for the idle rich, many of whom had made their money in the industrial Ruhr, which accounts for the city's many splendid villas and town houses. The **Villa Hammerschmidt**, the federal president's office and residence, is on the east side of Adenauerallee almost opposite the Alexander Koenig museum. **Palais Schaumburg**, the old chancellery next door, is interesting because its past was marked by scandal. In the late 19th century it was the home of Prince Adolf zu Schaumburg-Lippe and Princess Victoria of Prussia, a sister of Kaiser Wilhelm II, who lived here together in sin and debauchery, racking up debts by the millions. The squat brown building complex next to the Palais Schaumburg on its south side is the new chancellery. It is of no architectural merit, but its grounds include a sculpture by Henry Moore (which can just be seen through the railings). A stylized bust of Konrad Adenauer stands on the sidewalk outside the chancellery. The **Bundeshaus** (Parliament building), newly renovated for the 662 legislators at a cost of DM 280 million and reopened in October 1992, is on Görrestrasse, at the southeastern end of the chancellery grounds.

Near the government quarter, to the south, is the **Freizeit-park Rheinaue**, a highly popular park on both sides of the Rhine created in 1979 for the federal garden show. Crossed by the Konrad-Adenauer-Brücke (also known as Südbrücke, or South Bridge), the park has a boating lake, a Japanese garden donated by the Japanese Embassy, and two restaurants serving good, basic German dishes. Pop, rock, jazz, and classical concerts are given here in the summer, and a big flea market is held here every third Saturday in summer months.

The Konrad-Adenauer-Brücke also leads to the ► **Schloss-hotel Kommende Ramersdorf**, a turreted and towered former castle of the Order of Teutonic Knights that dates from 1220. Located in the southern Beuel suburb of **Ramersdorf**, not far from the Freizeitpark, the Kommende has 18 tastefully furnished rooms, a restaurant that serves Italian and international food, a museum with furnishings covering five centuries, and 20 showrooms filled with antique furniture and icons for sale. By car take the B 9 south along Adenauer-allee—which becomes Friedrich-Ebert-Allee—and take a left turn at the sign for Bonn-Beuel-Süd at the traffic light opposite the Polizeipräsidium (Police Headquarters), to pick up the A 562. Across the river take the Niederholtorf exit, turn left at its end, and drive uphill to the well-marked entrance on the left on Oberkasseler Strasse.

Bad Godesberg

Bad Godesberg, Bonn's pleasant leafy suburb, rates a special mention. An independent spa and retirement town until 1969, when Bonn annexed it, Bad Godesberg has retained its own character. It is the location of most of the capital's 136 foreign embassies, many of them housed in graceful villas, and their 1,600 diplomats. To get to Bad Godesberg by car, drive south from Bonn on route B 9. At the intersection of Bonner Strasse and Moltkestrasse, bear right into Burgstrasse and then immediately bear left onto **Koblenzer Strasse**, Bad Godesberg's narrow shop-lined one-way main street. Parking in town is tight; a more practical—and often quicker—option is the U-

Bahn (subway) line U-16 or U-3 from Bonn's main railroad station or from the University/Markt U-Bahn station on the north side of the Hofgarten. The trains take only 15–20 minutes from the main station to the Rheinallee terminus in Bad Godesberg.

Bad Godesberg is a charming little town, with a pedestrians-only center (except for Koblenzer Strasse) running four blocks north–south and four blocks east–west. **Theaterplatz**, named for Bad Godesberg's highly popular **Kammerspiele** theater, located on its southwest corner, is lined with shops selling everything from meat and groceries to electrical goods and designer clothing.

On the east side of the theater is the medium-priced, somewhat plain but centrally situated and comfortable 66-room ▶ **Insel Hotel**, with its traditional German **Café Insel** (which serves supper, but only until 8:00 P.M.) on its ground floor. Theaterplatz has a western arm that juts out and runs into another shopping area called **Am Fronhof**, dominated by a Hertie department store, which marks the western boundary of the inner town.

Immediately to the north of Theaterplatz, between it and Burgstrasse, is the so-called **Altstadt**, whose name is seen by many as a cruel joke. Bad Godesberg's real Altstadt, with its old houses and alleys, was demolished a decade ago to make way for a two-level shopping area that does nothing for the town. A bit farther to the north, across Burgstrasse, the town is overlooked by the 13th-century Godesburg castle, half destroyed by Napoleon's troops. The castle contains the comfortable medium-priced ▶ **Godesburg Hotel**, with 25 beds and panoramic views over the town and the Rhine. Its restaurant offers the same views, but the food does not match the location.

Bad Godesberg's inner town is bounded to the south by the tree-filled **Stadtpark** (Municipal Park). The **Stadthalle**, on the park, is a concert and convention hall that also has a pavilion with a spring from which you can sample the local spa water. Tucked into the middle of the park is the **Kleines Theater**, which stages productions similar to those of the Kammerspiele.

At the northwest end of the Stadtpark, across Kurfürstenallee, is the handsome **Redoute**, a late-18th-century ballroom and gaming hall that is now used for concerts and government banquets for visiting VIPs. The Redoute also has an excellent restaurant for formal wining and dining. Next to it, to the north, the gabled **Redüttchen pub** offers a cozy old inn atmosphere with plain but good food. The **Redoutenpark**, running south of the building, matches the Stadtpark as one of Bad Godesberg's finest green spaces.

Opposite the Stadtpark to the north, on Am Kurpark, is the comfortable 42-room ▶ **Hotel Eden**, whose front rooms offer a relaxing view of greenery.

The "in" restaurant in Bad Godesberg—although not so much for its food as for its clientele—is the **Maternus**, Löbestrasse 3, east of the Stadtpark off Koblenzer Strasse. It's long been a favorite haunt of politicians, and Ria Maternus, its elderly but sprightly owner, was awarded a Federal Order of Merit for her motherly services to them.

Better food in an Old World atmosphere can be found at the 74-room ▶ **Rheinhotel Dreesen**, Rheinstrasse 45–49, on the river in the suburb of Rüngsdorf, southeast of town. The hotel, built in 1893, has an elegant, formal restaurant with river views. Newly rebuilt, the hotel also has a beauty parlor and a fitness training area.

The Dreesen was Hitler's headquarters for his meetings with British prime minister Neville Chamberlain in 1938 to discuss the fate of the Sudetenland. U.S. presidents Hoover and Kennedy also stayed here. Public transport stops some way short of the hotel, so it's best reached by car or taxi.

Day Trips from Bonn

Bonn is well located for day trips up and down the Rhine and into the surrounding region. Koblenz is 52 km (32 miles) south, by way of the A 565 to the A 61, and Cologne is 27 km (17 miles) north, via the A 555. The Siebengebirge nature reserve, the resort town of Königswinter, and the Eifel Massif are all within easy reach.

A day cruise up the Rhine to Koblenz and back passes tidy riverside towns and tree-clad mountains and hills topped by castle ruins. The fast-flowing waterway is always busy with powerful barges and cruise boats flying different European flags, pushing upstream or sliding down on the strong current between Switzerland and Holland. The Rheinpfeil hydrofoil of the Köln-Düsseldorfer (KD) line, for example, stops at Koblenz, where you can spend a few enjoyable hours ashore exploring this old city at the confluence of the Rhine and Mosel rivers (see the Mosel Valley chapter, following) before continuing on to Mainz or boarding another boat for the return journey to Bonn. The line also runs *Mondfahrt* (moonlight) trips on the Rhine from Bonn on summer evenings, with dinner and dancing, and many other trips as well. Check the schedules at the KD kiosk on the Brassert Ufer, or at the Bonn tourist office.

The heavily forested **Siebengebirge** (Seven Mountains) rears up from the east bank of the Rhine opposite Bad Godesberg. The town of **Königswinter**, 10 km (6 miles) south of Bonn via the Konrad-Adenauer-Brücke and the A 59 Autobahn, is a handy point of entry to the mountain area. Königswinter can also be reached by car ferry from Bad Godesberg, by U-Bahn (lines 64 and 66), and by boats that depart frequently from Bonn.

In summer Königswinter is packed solid with German day-trippers and young families, who go there to enjoy convivial eating and drinking on the river against the backdrop of the Siebengebirge. The town is also popular with Dutch visitors, which inspired local wits to dub Königswinter the "Holländische Hauptstadt" (the Dutch capital). The **Rheinallee**, a riverside promenade lined with hotels and restaurants that put tables out in summer, is a good spot from which to watch Rhine cruise boats come and go.

If you'd like to absorb a little local history while in Königswinter, the **Heimatmuseum Siebengebirge**, with exhibits of documents, pictures, and artifacts tracing the region's social, religious, and municipal past, is in a fine old villa at Kellerstrasse 16, on the north side of the Marktplatz. The tourist office is also on the Marktplatz, at Drachenfelsstrasse 7; Tel: (2244) 88-93-25.

A pleasant excursion into the Siebengebirge is the trip to the top of the **Drachenfels**, one of the seven mountains and the legendary home of a dragon's cave. At its peak is a ruined castle, with a restaurant just below, and a 19th-century castle farther down. The mythical German hero Siegfried, immortalized by Wagner, is said to have slain the dragon that haunted the Drachenfels, then bathed in its blood to become invincible.

The Drachenfels *Zahnradbahn* (rack railway) makes the trip to the top every half hour from May to September. The station is on Drachenfelsstrasse, which runs east off Rheinallee and the south side of the Marktplatz, a short walk from the river.

The Zahnradbahn cars stop on request halfway up (or down) the mountain for those who want to visit **Schloss Drachenburg**, built for the Bonn banker Baron Stephan von Sarter between 1882 and 1884. The many-towered Gothic-style castle, which looks like a relic from the *Nibelungen* saga, is set in a park with exotic plants and a herd of deer. It was bought in 1989 by a state trust that plans to turn much of it into a center for nature protection. The castle's interior features high, vaulted ceilings and grand staircases guarded by suits of armor. Two imposing halls, the Nibelungenhalle and the Valhalla Saal, are used for classical and jazz concerts as well as travelling art exhibitions.

At the mountaintop are the ruins of the once-imposing **Schloss Drachenfels**. Completed in 1149, the castle was undermined and damaged by centuries of quarrying for stone to build Cologne's cathedral. In 1836 the Prussian government bought the castle ruins, closed the quarry, and strengthened what was left of the structure. Further preservation work was carried out after 1970, when the ruins were buttressed with cement.

The commercially run **Burg Restaurant**, just below the castle, has a great view of the Rhine valley, the Westerwald forests, and the Eifel hills—but it's best to stick to *Kaffee und Kuchen,* and enjoy the panorama.

A short walk down a well-marked path from the Zahnradbahn stop at the top is the privately owned—and exceedingly kitschy—**Nibelungenhalle**, containing pictures, sculptures, and music related to the Wagner saga, complete with a Disney-like dragon's cave, a model of the monster that Siegfried slew, and a snake and crocodile farm.

The châteaulike building perched high on a plateau of the Siebengebirge behind Königswinter, where it dominates the view of the east bank from Bad Godesberg, is the ▶ **Petersberg**, a luxury hotel that Chamberlain stayed in during his meetings with Hitler in 1938. From 1945 to 1952 the hotel was the headquarters of the Allied high commissioners who ran postwar Germany, and later it was a federal government guesthouse for visiting VIPs such as Queen Elizabeth II, Charles de Gaulle, the Shah of Iran, and Emperor Hirohito. After years of neglect, the government has rebuilt the Petersberg as its guesthouse and has made rooms available to the public as well. The prices match the rarified location of the 71-room hotel, which reopened in September 1990 under the management of the Steigenberger Hotels group. But in addition to its history it offers first-class rooms, superb panoramic views, and excellent food in its international restaurant. To get there, cross the Konrad-Adenauer-Brücke, take the A 59 Autobahn in the direction of Königswinter, and turn off at the exit for the Köln-Frankfurt Autobahn. Turn left at the first traffic light, cross the bridge over the A 59, and watch for the Petersberg direction sign on the left, a short way up the hill.

The **Eifel Massif**, with its densely forested hills, volcanic crests, and peaceful pastures, lies west and south of Bonn and stretches to Belgium and Luxembourg. **Bad Münstereifel** is a peaceful Eifel town, a one-hour drive (50 km/31 miles) southwest of Bonn, that makes for an interesting day trip. Take the B 56 due west from the Endenich traffic circle and, just before reaching Euskirchen, turn south on the B 51 for Bad Münstereifel.

Well-preserved fortifications from the 13th century, with a *Stadtmauer* (city wall) that boasts four gates and 18 defense towers, run for about a mile around the town. The narrow river Erft, crossed by ten small bridges, runs through it. **Das Rote Haus**, the red-painted town hall, housing the tourist office, dates from 1350. The town's ruined **Burg** (castle) dates from 1270, and the basilica of **St. Chrysanthus** has an 11th-century Romanesque façade. There are well-marked scenic paths in the woods surrounding Bad Münstereifel and along the town wall.

MÜNSTER

Count Fabio Chigi, later Pope Alexander VII, who spent from March 1644 to December 1649 in Münster as the Vatican's delegate to the tortuous peace conference that ended the Thirty Years' War, called the city "The Home of Rain." In a free-verse essay he moaned: "Six years it is that I have been here now, but I have never seen you except dripping in steady rain." And being an Italian who hungered not only for the sun but the cuisine to which he was accustomed in Rome, he also complained about the food: a seemingly endless diet of thick beans, cabbage, sauerkraut, smoked Westphalian ham, and the region's dark pumpernickel bread, which he described as "black stones."

Today it often seems as if almost nothing has changed since Chigi's days in Münster, which celebrated its 1,200th anniversary in 1993, and in the Münsterland.

It still rains a lot. So much, in fact, that even the Münsteraners sigh resignedly: "It is either raining or there are church bells ringing." However, considering that there are nearly a dozen churches of architectural importance within the one square kilometer of the Altstadt, each with bells ringing at a different time for Mass, and each with significant artworks to view, the precipitation problem is not as bad as its reputation.

Though this city of 275,000, located about 203 km (126 miles) northeast of Bonn and 125 km (77 miles) northeast of Düsseldorf, now has a profusion of exquisite albeit expensive restaurants, including a couple of Michelin and Gault-Millau–rated Italian ones where a Roman epicure like Count Chigi would have no complaints, local staples are still thick beans with bacon, cabbage with air-dried *Mettwurst,* smoked ham (one of Münster's and Westphalia's most sought-after export products), and that dark brown-to-black pumpernickel, all washed down with prodigious amounts of potent corn or juniper schnapps and *Altbier.* Moreover, a number of the old inns that serve such fare—Pinkus Müller, Wielers Kleiner Kiepenkerl, the Drübbelken, Höltene Sluse—have been doing so for over a hundred years.

The surrounding countryside—the actual Münsterland—still represents a settled picture of pastures, woods, scattered farms, windmills, sleepy little towns and villages, and a profusion of *Wasserburgen* and *Wasserschlösser* (moated fortresses and manor houses) that were the homes of the petty nobility and landed gentry. Many, like Burg Hülshoff, are still owned and inhabited by the aristocratic families whose forebears built them in the Middle Ages. Others, like Haus Rüschhaus, are museums. And some have been made into first-class and luxury hotels, like the 16th-century ▶ **Hotel Schloss Wilkinghege**, a mere ten-minute drive northwest from Münster's Altstadt.

Actually, what you see in Münster today is virtually all postwar reconstruction; few other German cities were so nearly completely destroyed in World War II. From October 1943 until March 1945 Münster was hit by 102 Allied air raids that left more than 90 percent of the inner city a rubble heap.

But unlike burghers and officials of many other towns, who strove to make their cities *autogerecht* (suitable for cars) by jettisoning the old and rebuilding in a generally faceless modern style with here and there an isolated reminder of past architectural splendor, Münsteraners were determined to re-create their city as closely resembling its past appearance as possible. Thus they reconstructed the cathedral and most other churches, the Gothic Rathaus and adjacent municipal Weinhaus, the step-gabled medieval merchants' houses with their arcades (to protect shoppers against the rain) along the Prinzipalmarkt, the main street, and even some of the ostentatious Renaissance and Baroque town palaces of the landed gentry, who would retreat to the city when the icy Westphalian winters made their Wasserburgen and Wasserschlösser inhospitable if not downright uninhabitable.

The result is a vibrant old quarter described by Theodor Heuss, postwar West Germany's first president, as "the most successful urban reconstruction in the country." Small wonder that local boosters today proudly describe Münster as "one of the most beautiful among Germany's beauties."

The Altstadt

Münster's *Innenstadt* (Inner City), which includes the Altstadt, is a circular area about half a mile in diameter, surrounded by the tree-lined **Promenade** that follows the city's medieval fortifications, which were razed in the 19th century. It is traversed in a southwest to northeast direction by the little Aa river. To see and explore it, you must do what the Münsteraners themselves do: walk or bike.

Münster is the *Fahrradstadt Deutschlands* ("Bicycle City of Germany"). It has more registered two-wheelers than inhabitants, and bikes are virtually the only vehicles permitted in the Altstadt between 8:00 A.M. and midnight, except for city buses, taxis with special permits, and cars of the physically handicapped (as long as they bear the appropriate sticker).

Nearly 70 percent of the locals travel to work and do their inner-city shopping by bicycle. Municipal authorities have encouraged and accommodated them by setting up a whole network of bicycle parking lots, special lanes, paths, and a traffic engineering system that gives bikes priority. Even the lord mayor pedals five miles from his home to city hall and back again each day—including all the rainy ones. Many hotels rent or lend bikes to their guests, and there are a number of bike rental outlets where you can get one for as little as DM 10 per day (see Getting Around, below).

But whether you walk, bike, or join one of the guided combination bus-and-walking tours offered by the Verkehrs-verein (city tourist office at the Rathaus, Saturdays and Sundays at 10:30 A.M., Wednesdays at 2:30 P.M.), the place to start is at and around the **Dom St. Paulus** (St. Paul's Cathedral), where Münster had its beginnings.

The Dom Area

Münster dates its official founding to A.D. 793. That was when St. Liudger, a Frisian missionary monk who had been dispatched by Charlemagne to Christianize the pagan Saxons, established a fortified monastery on the Horsteberg, a hillock on the right bank of the Aa river. Liudger named the abbey "Monasterium," which eventually got Germanized into Münster. In 804 Charlemagne appointed him bishop and spiritual head of the whole region.

Liudger began building the first cathedral, dedicated to Saint Paul, just outside the abbey walls in 805. That Carolingian structure was destroyed by fire in 1071. A second cathedral, erected virtually adjacent to it and consecrated in 1090, was also destroyed by fire. Construction of the third—and present—church began in 1225 and was completed 40 years later.

Though largely destroyed during World War II, it was faithfully reconstructed between 1946 and 1956. Except for some 14th-century exterior additions and embellishments and 16th-century interior changes in Gothic style, the Dom is one of the largest, finest, and most comprehensive examples of Late Romanesque architecture in Germany. It is striking for the harmony of its design and exterior simplicity.

Among its most important interior art works are the new **stained-glass windows** in the ambulatory of the choir, completed shortly before his death in 1990 by Cologne artist Georg Meistermann, and the **astronomical clock**. The clock, 25 feet high with a dial some 10 feet in diameter, was installed in 1540 to replace an earlier one that had been destroyed by Anabaptists in 1534, and is a masterpiece of 16th-century artisanship. The paintings and woodcarvings on it are a joy to see any time, but the real high point is at noon when the mechanical figures of the glockenspiel start making their rounds. They depict the Three Kings following the Star of Bethlehem and bringing their gifts to Mary and Jesus. The **Domkammer** (Cathedral Treasury) is a starkly modern annex leading from the north side of the cloister. Its most important object is the **St. Paul Reliquary**, an 11th-century gold-embossed bust of the apostle studded with gems and gold filigree.

The **Ludgeruskapelle** (Liudger Chapel) in the ambulatory contains the tomb of Cardinal Clemens August von Galen, Münster's bishop from 1933 until his death in 1946. Called the "Lion of Münster" because he roared so outspokenly, Count von Galen was one of the first Catholic clergymen in Germany publicly to oppose the Nazis. In pastoral letters of the 1930s he attacked the Hitler regime for its persecution of Jews and Catholics, and for the Nazis' secret euthanasia program, a precursor to the Holocaust, in which tens of thousands of mentally retarded and physically handicapped Germans, described by the Nazis as "unworthy of life," were systematically murdered. By mid-1941 von Galen was so much involved with Catholic resistance that he began preaching against the terror of the Gestapo and SS from the pulpits of the Dom and nearby St. Lambert's, where he had been parish priest before becoming Münster's bishop.

Just west of the Dom, on Pferdegasse, is the **Bischöfliches Palais** (Bishop's Palace), an early-18th-century Baroque château that counts as one of the city's most beautiful buildings. A stroll across the Domplatz, where there are lively, colorful markets every Wednesday and Saturday morning, leads to the **Westfälisches Landesmuseum für Kunst und Kulturgeschichte** (Westphalian State Museum of Art and Cultural History), Domplatz 10, open daily except Mondays from 10:00 A.M. to 6:00 P.M. It has an excellent collection of medieval panel paintings, stained glass, sculpture, and a section devoted to 17th-century Dutch masters.

On and Around the Prinzipalmarkt

Münster's *gute Stube,* its "parlor," is the **Prinzipalmarkt**, about 100 yards east of the Domplatz. Cobblestoned, lined on both sides by steeply gabled merchants' and patricians' houses that seem to sit atop vaulted and colonnaded arcades, it has been the city's main street for more than 800 years. In 1280 merchants started building elaborate residences, offices, and warehouses along it. Over the centuries they sought to outdo each other in architectural splendor. One nocturnal bombing raid in 1943 destroyed it all. But Münsteraners rebuilt the street in a remarkably faithful approximation of its original style and appearance. It is hard to believe that the houses are not as old as they look.

The grandest building of all has a stepped-gable façade with vaulted tracery windows, tracery buttresses, and slim finials topped by sculptures of angels. It resembles a church, and was undoubtedly built as an expression of burgher defiance of the prince-bishops, whose Dom it faces. But it never was and is not a church. This reconstructed 14th-century jewel, which ranks as one of the finest examples of secular Gothic architecture in Germany, is the **Rathaus** (City Hall). It was in its ornate wood-paneled 16th-century courtroom and council chamber, now called the **Friedenssaal** (Peace Chamber), that the Peace of Westphalia, ending the Thirty Years' War, was signed in 1648.

That war, which wiped out more than half the population of Germany and Central Europe, had started in 1618 in Prague as a revolt by Protestant nobles against Bohemia's Catholic King Ferdinand, a Hapsburg, who in 1619 became Holy Roman Emperor Ferdinand II. Whatever the initial religious issues, they soon evaporated and the conflict turned into a European-wide conflagration, with constantly shifting alliances and a complete loss of objectives.

The negotiations and conferences that led to the peace treaty lasted five years and took place concurrently in Münster and Osnabrück, declared neutral enclaves in 1642 and practically the only cities on German territory, the main battleground, that were spared the ravages of the war. The Spanish, Dutch, French, and German negotiators met in Münster; the representatives of Sweden and the Holy Roman Empire in Osnabrück. Count Chigi, serving as a mediator, shuttled back and forth like a commuter between Münster and Osnabrück.

As a guest observer from Padua described the scene in Münster: "Of ambassadors and delegates there are so many that you would not be able to count them in six hours and would not be able to transport them in 100 wagons. There are not enough buildings in which to house them. They fill the market squares and streets. If you stick your head out the door, there will surely be ten delegates to greet."

All lived and ensconced themselves in Münster and Osnabrück for the five years, wiling away the time between negotiating sessions by banqueting, entertaining, and bringing in amusements. The English recruited actors from London's Globe Theater to put on some Shakespeare, the French brought in a dance company from Paris to perform a "Ballet de la Paix" in the Rathaus.

The furnishings, elaborate wall paneling, and coffered wood ceiling in the Friedenssaal are all original and had been removed in 1942 before the first air raid. Except for the portraits of the conference delegates and plenipotentiaries, which were painted by Antwerp artist Janbaptist Floris in the 1650s, everything predates the peace parley. The intricately carved fireplace dates from 1621; the huge wrought-iron chandelier from 1577; the woodcarvings on the wall behind the mayor's bench are from 1540. These carvings, depicting biblical and allegorical folklore scenes, are actually doors to safes and filing and archive cabinets in which Münster's most important documents were kept. The most appropriate of all, titled "War," shows two battling beheaded men, each with a sword in one hand jointly holding one decapitated head with the other. (The Friedenssaal is open Monday through Fridays, 9:00 A.M. to 5:00 P.M.; Saturdays until 4:00 P.M.; Sundays from 10:00 A.M. to 1:00 P.M.)

A five-minute walk east of the Rathaus, along Klemensstrasse, will take you to the small family-run ▶ **Hotel Feldmann**, Klemensstrasse 23–34. For Altstadt accommodations this charming old brick house with 30 elegantly furnished guest rooms is the best. You can also lunch or dine on exquisitely prepared international cuisine.

Just across from the hotel is the **Clemenskirche** (St. Clement's Church), a Baroque masterpiece by Johann Conrad Schlaun, who designed and built it between 1745 and 1753 for Clemens August von Wittelsbach, the prince-bishop of Münster who later became archbishop and elector of Cologne. For all its exterior red-brick simplicity, the church is a splash of Baroque extravagance inside.

From the Rathaus it is a brief stroll north along the Prinzipalmarkt to its intersection with Salzstrasse and the **Lambertikirche** (St. Lambert's Church), Münster's main parish church since the 12th century. The present Late Gothic structure dates from 1375 to 1450 and occupies the site of two earlier ones. The portals are its most striking feature, especially the monumental relief of the "Tree of Jesus" over the south door. Much of the original interior decoration was lost either during the Anabaptist Terror or during World War II, but there are some fine early-17th-century stone figures of the Apostles in the choir.

What is most important about St. Lambert's is its spire. First of all there is the tradition of the *Türmer* (warder), who every night just before 10:00 P.M. climbs the 298 steps inside the tower to keep watch over the city, blowing a horn-shaped bugle every half hour until 6:00 A.M. as a signal that all is well or to alert Münsteraners of such dangers as fire or approaching enemies. It has been a custom since 1379, interrupted only for about a decade during and after World War II. The present watchman is a municipal employee. And then there are the three iron cages hanging above the clock. They contained the corpses of the Anabaptist leaders—Jan von Leiden, Bernd Knipperdolling, and Bernhard Krechting— and have been here since the three were tortured and executed on the Prinzipalmarkt in January 1536.

Though it lasted only two years, and happened more than 450 years ago, the Anabaptist tyranny was so murderous and left such an indelible imprint on Münster's history that you get the feeling the town still shudders with the memory.

Anabaptism—rebaptism of adults and a return to apostolic values—was an extremist movement that grew out of the Lutheran and Calvinist Reformation. It had its origins in Switzerland, spread more or less peacefully through Germany, Moravia, and the Netherlands in the late 1520s and early 1530s, and then erupted in revolutionary terror in Münster. It made its debut in the city through the influential pastor Bernard Rothmann, cloth merchant and city councillor Bernd Knipperdolling, and other fanatical zealots, most notably Jan von Leiden, a tailor. By early 1534 they had gotten control of the town council, declared Münster a "New Zion," and established a bizarre tyrannical theocracy that practiced communism and polygamy. Jan von Leiden proclaimed himself "King of Münster."

All those who refused rebaptism or held to the old beliefs were either driven out of the city or murdered. The churches were plundered of their art and treasures; the gold and silver melted down to produce coinage; and sculptures were used to strengthen the city's fortifications. Hundreds if not several thousand burghers were publicly tortured and massacred. "King Jan" declared Münster the "new Jerusalem" and the center of a world revolution. Anyone who opposed him was as good as dead, including one of his 16 wives. He beheaded her on the Prinzipalmarkt in a fit of anger after she dared to speak up to him. Meanwhile, Bishop von Waldeck, who had fled his cathedral redoubt for one of his country palaces and recruited an army, tried to recapture the city. Unable to break its defenses, he laid siege, trying to starve it into submission. The nightmare of terror, murder (on one day alone Knipper-dolling, who had become chief executioner, killed 53 dissidents), hunger, and disease within the walls lasted until June 24, 1535. Then the bishop's forces breached the fortifications, executed scores of Anabaptists, and took the leaders prisoner. "King Jan," Knipperdolling, and Krechting, the "chancellor of the kingdom," were paraded around the Münsterland in chains and cages for months. Finally, in January 1536, they were publicly tried in front of the Rathaus, tortured with glowing iron tongues, and executed by having red-hot spikes plunged into their hearts. Their bodies were put in cages and hoisted up St. Lambert's spire for all to see. The last of their bones, according to local lore, did not drop through the bars until around 1850.

If you need a rest from the horror story and want to see a different aspect of Münster, continue along Prinzipalmarkt, which bends westward, changing its name to Roggen-Drubbel Markt, Bogen Strasse, then Spiekerhof, and stop at the banks of the Aa and the humorous statue of the pipe-smoking **Kiepenkerl**. The *Kiepenkerle* were itinerant merchants who set out from Münster with their baskets—the *Kiepen*—full of goods, not to return until they were out of merchandise. For a break, step into the **Kleiner Kiepenkerl**, Spiekerhof 47, one of Münster's oldest and most colorful inns. The fare is as rustic as the decor, with plenty of Westphalian specialties on the lunch and dinner menus.

The Überwasser Area

Technically, *überwasser* translates as "above" and "over" water, but in this case it's "across the water," meaning the little Aa, which is more a rivulet than a river. The district is the warren of narrow streets on the Aa's west bank in the northwest corner of the Altstadt.

Where Spiekerhof makes a little bend and changes its name to Rosenstrasse is the **Überwasserkirche**, officially known as Pfarrkirche Liebfrauen-Überwasser (Church of Our Lady in Überwasser Parish). The 14th-century Gothic church, originally part of a convent, suffered comparatively little damage during World War II, but was ravaged during the Anabaptist regime. In 1535, among other desecrations, Jan von Leiden ordered its spire blown up, had cannons mounted on the stump, and used the stones and sculptures surrounding the tower to strengthen the city's defensive wall. One series of 14th-century life-size sandstone figures depicting the Madonna and the Apostles, considered among the finest examples of medieval German stone carving, was recovered by archaeologists in 1898. The figures are now in the Museum of Art and Cultural History on the Domplatz. In and outside the church be sure to see the 16th-century carved oak choir stalls and the bronze doors of the west portal, an allegorical work by the contemporary sculptor Bernhard Kleinhans, installed in 1976.

The Überwasser district is best known for its pubs and inns along Buddenstrasse and Kreuzstrasse, about 200 yards north of the church. They're especially popular with Münster's 60,000 university students. One of the favorite hangouts, open from 11:00 A.M. to 1:00 A.M. and serving everything from Westphalian smoked ham and pumpernickel on a wooden plate to rib-sticking pork steaks, is the **Drübbelken**, a reconstructed 17th-century brick-and-timber house at Buddenstrasse 14–15. Famous for its own beers, buckwheat pancakes, and *Töttchen* (a spicy veal ragout) is the **Altbierküche Pinkus Müller**, Kreuzstrasse 4–10. It has been run by the Müller family since 1816 as a brewery-tavern, and generations of guests have scratched their initials in the bare oak tables and benches.

Along Königsstrasse

Southwest of the Rathaus Prinzipalmarkt changes its name to Rothenburg. **Königsstrasse** runs due south from it. Not far from its start, at the corner of Rothenburg and Aegidiistrasse, is a small (20 rooms) modern hotel, perfectly situated as an Altstadt base, the ▶ **Central Hotel**, Aegidiistrasse 1.

In Münster's golden age Königstrasse was the avenue along which the landed gentry from the Münsterland had their winter palaces. Many of the grand town mansions that once lined both sides of the street were destroyed during the war. A few have been rebuilt and, though no longer used as private residences, can be viewed from outside. The grandest, a 16th-century Renaissance palace at Königstrasse 47, is the **Heeremannscher Hof**, now used as a courthouse. The **Beverfoerder Hof** at number 46 is a three-wing château in the style of a French *hôtel* from the early 18th century. The **Oerscher Hof**, number 42, was built around 1748 for the barons von Beverfoerde, and is the only one that survived the war without damage. In it today is Münster's most prized eatery, the Michelin-starred and Gault-Millau–rated **Kleines Restaurant im Oerschen Hof**, a very expensive spot serving nouvelle German and French cuisine; open evenings only, closed Sundays and Mondays, reservations essential; Tel:

(251) 420-61. At Königstrasse 39 is the 17th-century **Senden-scher Hof**, erstwhile home of the barons Droste zu Senden, and now used as a bank.

Directly across the street is the **Pfarrkirche St. Ludgeri** (Parish Church of St. Liudger), a three-naved Romanesque structure consecrated in 1200, with a few additions and embellishments from the 14th century. Among its art treasures are two paintings by Nikolaus tom Ring, a 16th-century Westphalian master, and an elaborately carved early-16th-century baptismal font. There is also a chapel honoring Edith Stein, the Jewish woman who converted to Catholicism in 1922, became a Carmelite nun while doing postdoctoral research in Münster in 1932, and died in the gas chambers at Auschwitz in 1942.

Outside the Altstadt

Just west of the Promenade and ring boulevard that delineate the inner city's former wall is the ornate 18th-century **Residenzschloss** (Palace Residence) of the prince-bishops. Used nowadays as the main building of Münster University, it is interesting only for its exterior and the beautiful **gardens** around it.

In the other direction you will find a hotel well worth considering as well as a restaurant of which Count Chigi certainly would have approved. The ▶ **Hotel Windsor**, Warendorfer Strasse 177, about 1½ km (1 mile) from the city center, is a turn-of-the-century half-timbered house with 30 very comfortable rooms, nearly all filled with the antiques that the proprietor collects as a hobby. Had the **Villa Medici**, Ostmarkstrasse 15 (you drive or bicycle out by way of Bohlweg) existed in the 1640s, Chigi would not even have noticed the Münster rain. In what used to be a corner tavern, proprietor Carmelo Caputo and his German chef Markus Potrafka prepare refined nouvelle Italian cuisine exquisitely. Open for lunch Wednesday through Friday, dinner Tuesday through Saturday. You must reserve; Tel: (251) 342-18.

Excursions to the Wasserschlösser

In the Middle Ages the *Wasserschlösser* and *Wasserburgen,* the moated châteaux, were a source of protection for the gentry and nobility living on the flat terrain of the Münsterland. The introduction of long-range artillery rendered these island fortresses obsolete, and the once-mighty strongholds simply became elaborate rural estates of the aristocracy. There were at one time more than 3,000 of them within a 50-mile radius of Münster. Only about 100 habitable ones remain—40 of those still owned and used by the blue-blood families whose ancestors built them.

The Verkehrsverein (municipal tourist office) has maps and brochures describing them and how to get there. It also offers five-hour bus tours to the most interesting castles every afternoon in the summer and early fall, starting at 2:00 P.M. from June through September, 1:00 P.M. in October. Departures are from the bus parking lot at the east side of the Hauptbahnhof. Prices, depending on distances and number of châteaux per tour, range from DM 35 to DM 40 per person. Space must be reserved by writing, phoning, faxing, or stopping in at the Verkehrsverein, Berliner Platz 22, D-48143 Münster; Tel: (251) 51-01-80; Fax: (251) 510-18-30.

There are two châteaux, however, intimately connected with Annette von Droste-Hülshoff, Germany's preeminent 19th-century female poet (her portrait is on DM 20 bills), that are within a few minutes by car, and less than half an hour by bike, from central Münster, both east of the city: Burg Hülshoff, in the suburb of Havixbeck, the ancestral Droste-Hülshoff home, where Annette was born in 1797, and Haus Rüschhaus, the erstwhile country home of Westphalia's most celebrated Baroque architect, Johann Conrad Schlaun, in Münster-Nienberge, where Annette lived from 1820 to 1846 and wrote most of her works.

Burg Hülshoff, first mentioned in the 11th century, and the property of the Drostes since the 15th, is a stately four-story manor house of brick and sandstone to which the last alterations were made more than 450 years ago. The Stromberg-Droste zu Hülshoff family, who own it, have made the entire ground floor of what is still their private home into a museum of the life and customs of the Münsterland nobility during the early 19th century. (Open daily, 9:30 A.M. to 6:00 P.M., mid-March through mid-December.)

Haus Rüschhaus, 2½ km (1½ miles) northeast of Burg Hülshoff, or 8 km (5 miles) north from central Münster along highway B 54, is by contrast just a country cottage that Schlaun designed for himself in 1745 on property that had belonged to the bishops. The Droste-Hülshoff family bought it in 1825 and continued to own it until 1979, when they sold it to the city of Münster and the state of Northrhine-Westphalia. Its half-dozen rooms, filled with Biedermeier furnishings, draw visitors by the tens of thousands; the graceful, manicured garden is another reflection of life in the Münsterland of old. (Open daily except Mondays, 10:00 A.M. to noon and 2:30 to 4:30 P.M., March 29 through October 31; 10:00 A.M. to noon and 2:00 to 4:00 P.M., November 1 through December 23; closed in winter.)

—John Dornberg

OSNABRÜCK

In a number of ways, Osnabrück, population 150,000, about 60 kilometers (37 miles) northeast of Münster, represents the quintessence of Germany.

As recent archaeological excavations are proving, it was just a few miles from the city where in A.D. 9 the Battle of Teutoburg Forest took place and Arminius (Hermann), leader of the Cherusci tribe, defeated Augustus Caesar's three finest legions. It marked the beginning of Germanic national awareness and so shocked the Romans that they never again attempted to extend their realm east of the Rhine.

Osnabrück was also the town where in A.D. 783 Charlemagne, then just the Frankish king, won his decisive victory over Widukind, the pagan Saxon chieftain, thus laying the foundation for what was to become the Holy Roman Empire.

Like many other German cities situated along the medieval trade routes and belonging to the Hanseatic League, Osnabrück became a prince-bishopric in which the growing classes of artisans, craftsmen, and merchants chafed at the ecclesiastical leaders' temporal powers, expressing their defiance by erecting ever grander secular buildings, such as the Rathaus, to rival the clergy's cathedral and palaces.

Like nearby Münster it was a venue for the tortuous negotiations that finally ended the Thirty Years' War. It was the Swedes who met here with the representatives of the Holy Roman emperor, the Protestant German principalities, the free imperial cities, and the municipal leagues. And like the one in Münster, Osnabrück's Rathaus has an ornate council chamber, known since 1648 as the Friedenssaal, in which the Peace of Westphalia was signed.

But there is more that relates to more recent times.

Osnabrück is the birthplace and hometown of two men— one Catholic and a writer, Erich Maria Remarque, the other Jewish and a painter, Felix Nussbaum—born just a few years apart and a few blocks from each other, who in their own ways opposed the German militarism and expansion of the early 20th century that provided the soil for Nazism and the Holocaust. Both recognized the dangers, warned against them in their pictures and novels, such as *All Quiet on the Western Front,* and were persecuted for doing so. Both fled Germany as victims of Nazi oppression and both paid dearly for their opposition: Nussbaum in the gas chamber at Auschwitz in 1944; Remarque through the 1943 execution of his sister Elfriede, to whom the chief justice of the Nazi People's

Court said: "We are sentencing you to death because we could not lay hands on your brother."

And, as in so many other cities of the German northwest, Osnabrück's historic center was almost totally destroyed by raids during World War II. But like Münsteraners, Osnabrückers set out after the war to restore and rebuild what they could, either by putting the shards and the rubble back together, preserving the façades, or re-creating in the style of the past.

The Altstadt

Osnabrück's old inner city, the Altstadt, still partially surrounded by its medieval defensive walls and some of the watchtowers and gates, is an oval-shaped warren of narrow, twisting streets and lanes, just over half a mile wide and less than two miles long. Automobile traffic is banned from much of it, so that the oldest and most interesting sights are accessible only on foot.

The most convenient, comfortable, and colorful spot to use as a base for exploring is the ▶ **Hotel Walhalla**, Bierstrasse 24. This is a restored 17th-century brick-and-half-timbered house at the western edge of the old quarter. The coziest rooms are those on the third and fourth floors, where massive 300-year-old oak beams support the ceilings and slanting walls. The hotel also has a fine restaurant serving regional Westphalian specialties as well as international dishes prepared nouvelle style. Some of the scenes in Remarque's novels *A Time to Love and a Time to Die* and *The Black Obelisk* are set here.

The Hase river, a tributary of the Ems, flows in a south-to-north direction along the eastern edge of the old quarter, and it is for this little stream, which rises in the Teutoburg forest, that Osnabrück is probably named. Historians and etymologists say that in Saxon times the river was called "Ase" or "As," and the settlement at the bridge crossing the stream was named "Asanbruggi," which evolved into "Osenbrugge." From there the linguistic transformation to Osnabrück is easy to trace.

The bridge across the Hase, probably located in the southeastern corner of the Altstadt where Schlagvorder Strasse now traverses the stream, was an important link in the eighth-century trade routes from France to Scandinavia and from the Low Countries to the Baltic Sea that crossed at Osnabrück. The crossing was also where Charlemagne defeated Widukind in 783. Some local historians claim the date of this event as the city's official founding and say that

Charlemagne designated Osnabrück as a missionary center and approved establishment of a bishop's seat here. Though there is circumstantial evidence of a diocese and the consecration of a cathedral as early as 785, the first written proof is in a charter from 803, signed by Charlemagne and kept in the archives of the Diocesan Museum at Osnabrück's Dom St. Peter.

The Dom Area

Though there is no literary or archaeological evidence of a Carolingian precursor to today's **Dom St. Peter** (St. Peter's Cathedral) at the Domhof, just west of the Hase, there must have been one: In 890 Bishop Egilmar complained to Pope Stephen V about its desecration and partial destruction by a Saxon mob.

The present sandstone structure, with its two squat, square western towers, is basically Romanesque in style and dates from the 11th century. There were some additions and alterations to it in Early Gothic style in the 12th and 13th centuries.

Though its exterior is starkly severe and almost forbidding, the cathedral is surprisingly light and airy inside, and contains some fine art objects. The most important are the 13th-century triumphal **crucifix** that hangs in the central nave, a life-size 15th-century **Pietá**, some intricately carved epitaphs and memorial tombs, and the 17th-century gilded wrought-iron gates that lead to the ambulatory of the choir. The gates are designed to give a three-dimensional illusion, as if you were walking down a long corridor. Noteworthy, too, are the finely carved 13th-century capitals on the pillars in the sacristy. Be sure to walk around the **cloister** with its Romanesque arches and columns. The nicks in some of the pillar stones are pagan Saxon marks. The stones were taken from Saxon ceremonial sites and incorporated in the cathedral and its cloister.

The poodlelike lion, or, if you prefer, lionlike poodle atop a pillar at the corner of the Domhof is called **Der Löwenpudel** and is one of Osnabrück's landmarks, not to mention a source of various legends. The official and most likely version is that he was a symbol of Saxon Duke Henry the Lion's judicial authority over the city and cathedral administration in the 12th century. But the popular story surrounding the figure relates to Charlemagne and his battle against Widukind in 783. Though he had defeated the Saxon chieftain's army, he failed to capture his foe. Angry at everyone, Charlemagne swore to kill the first living thing that crossed the bridge over the Hase. And that, so the legend goes, was his sister Gisela. What to do? Charles was in a quandary. He could neither kill his own sister nor back down on his public oath. But fate, so Osnabrückers will tell you, intervened. Suddenly Gisela's big poodle, clipped to resemble a lion, bounded across the bridge toward Charlemagne. With a swing of his great sword he felled the poor beast, thus sparing Gisela while at the same time preserving his honor.

The Neoclassical building on the Grosse Domsfreiheit, just north of the cathedral, is the **Bischöfliche Kanzlei** (Diocesan Chancellory), built between 1783 and 1785. The British coat of arms above its portal is no illusion. Osnabrück's last prince-bishop was Frederick von York, a son of King George III of England, who was also king of Hannover. George got little Freddy the job in 1764, when he was only six years old, and he reigned until 1802, when the prince-bishops lost their temporal powers.

The **Diözesanmuseum** and **Domschatzkammer** (Diocesan Museum and Cathedral Treasury) at Kleine Domsfreiheit 24, the street flanking the south side of the cathedral, exhibits some exceptional objects of ecclesiastical art, including a sixth-century bronze votive hand holding a globe and cross, an embossed-gold and gem-studded 11th-century chapter cross, and an intricately crafted gold chalice from 1468. (The museum and treasury are open daily except Mondays from 10:00 A.M. to 1:00 P.M., as well as Tuesday through Friday from 3:00 to 5:00 P.M.)

Diagonally across the street from the museum entrance is the ▶ **Dom-Hotel**, Kleine Domsfreiheit 5, a very moderately priced, conveniently located small hotel with 23 rooms, four without private bath. Continuing south along the Domhof in the direction of the central shopping district you will find the **Restaurant der Landgraf**, Domhof 9c, a dignified little restaurant offering international cuisine for lunch and dinner.

The Rathaus Area

Osnabrück developed rapidly after the establishment of its bishopric. By 889 the town that had grown around the cathedral was already so important a trade center that it was given its own market, coinage, and customs privileges. Holy Roman Emperor Frederick Barbarossa granted the city its own judicial authority in 1171. The document is preserved and on display in the treasury of the Rathaus. By the mid-13th century Osnabrück had joined Münster in the establishment of a trading and customs alliance that included several other northwestern German cities, and shortly after that it joined the Hanseatic League.

As the merchants, traders, and craftsmen gained wealth, they also sought power to protect their interests. The rivalry between burghers and bishops was expressed architecturally on the Markt (Market Square), 100 yards west of the Dom, in the splendor of the **Rathaus** (City Hall) and the Marienkirche (St. Mary's Church).

Though the cornerstone of the Rathaus was laid in 1487, and the structure was completed in 1512, it is actually the "new" Rathaus, replacing three earlier ones. The steep-roofed three-story sandstone structure, embellished by turrets and life-size statues of nine Holy Roman emperors on its façade, is used to this day as Osnabrück's city hall; the town council meets, and the mayor and other officials have their offices, on the upper floors. The original council chamber on the main floor, a vast room with a coffered oak ceiling, elaborate 16th-century wrought-iron chandelier, intricately carved oak benches along the walls, and portraits of 42 principals to the peace negotiations, is the **Friedenssaal**, the chamber in which the Peace of Westphalia was signed. Be sure also to see the **Schatzkammer,** the Rathaus treasury, just across the hall from the Friedenssaal. Among the objects on exhibit are Barbarossa's charter and the council silver, including the so-called *Kaiserpokal* (imperial goblet), a richly engraved silver and gold tankard from the 13th century whose contents—about one liter—had to be emptied in one draught by each new member of the city council upon taking office. (The Friedenssaal and Schatzkammer are open daily except Mondays from 10:00 A.M. to 5:00 P.M.)

The **Ratskeller**, Markt 30 (entry on the south side of the Rathaus), serves solid German as well as Balkan food and is open daily except Mondays for lunch and dinner.

The **Marienkirche**, virtually adjacent to the Rathaus, is a 13th-century Gothic church with Romanesque elements at the base of its spire. The massiveness of the sandstone structure, like that of the Rathaus, was an expression of the burghers' striving for independence from the prince-bishops. The church was gutted by fire during an air raid, and its interior has been reconstructed in a severe, unembellished style that highlights its Gothic architectural elements, including the powerful multiple rib pillars supporting the vault. The most important objects here are the late-13th-century triumphal **crucifix** in the central nave, a six-foot-high polychrome wood figure of the Madonna standing on a crescent moon, and the **main altar**, a richly carved work by an Antwerp master dating from 1515.

Altstadt Streets

A surprising number of Osnabrück's medieval merchant and burgher houses survived the war or have been meticulously reconstructed and restored. Among them are some fine examples of half-timbering, with elaborate decoration on the beams, and so-called *Wohntürme*—defensive living towers—whose entrances were 15 to 20 feet above the street and accessible only by rope ladders that were pulled up at night.

To see some of these, and to get a feeling for how Osnabrück looked in the Middle Ages, stroll along the quiet narrow little streets west and south of the Markt, especially Grosse Gildewart, Bierstrasse, Heger Strasse, Marienstrasse, then down Krahnstrasse as far as Nikolaiort. There you will be in the middle of the shopping district where only a few old buildings, most of those in Neoclassical style, have survived.

Just south of Nikolaiort, at Kamp 1, is the moderately priced ▶ **Hotel Nikolai**, located in a rather bizarre Postmodern structure that resembles a jumble of greenhouses piled helter-skelter atop one another. All rooms are functionally modern in decor, furnishings, and design. Proprietor Peter Zeidler also runs the nearby **Alte Posthalterei**, Hakenstrasse 4, an 18th- to 19th-century postal station converted into an inn that serves stick-to-the-ribs regional dishes for lunch and dinner in a rustic wood-paneled beam-ceilinged setting.

Diagonally across the street, at Hakenstrasse 3, was the house into which Erich Maria Remarque's parents moved in 1917, while he was already on the western front, but where he lived for some years in the early 1920s. During that period Remarque worked as an elementary school teacher and did odd jobs. He sold tombstones, like the autobiographical character in *The Black Obelisk,* and tried his hand at writing. The house, like most others along Hakenstrasse, was destroyed during World War II. The search for it plays a role in *A Time to Love and a Time to Die* when the hero of that novel, Ernst Graeber, returns to his hometown, called "Werden," in 1945 to look for his parents.

A walk south along Hakenstrasse as far as the **Katharinenkirche** (St. Catherine's Church), which has Osnabrück's tallest spire—330 feet—and then east toward Alte Münze, will bring you to the Osnabrück University Library, Alte Münze 14, which is also the home of the **Erich Maria Remarque Archive**, open Tuesdays, Wednesdays, and Thursdays from 9:00 A.M. to noon.

About 100 yards southwest of the library, along Neuer Graben, are the Fürstbischöfliches Schloss and the Ledenhof. The **Fürstbischöfliches Schloss** (Prince-Bishop's Palace), now part of the university, was commissioned by Bishop Ernst August I in 1668 and is modeled after the Palazzo Madama in Rome. The **Ledenhof**, now the municipal music library, is a complex of 16th-century Renaissance-style town houses built into part of the old town wall. The Ledenhof is a good starting point for a walk around what remains of Osnabrück's medieval wall and fortifications.

The Fortifications

Osnabrück's walls, insofar as they remain intact today, are largely those erected to protect the city in the 12th and 13th centuries. A walk west along Neuer Graben will bring you to its intersection with Heger-Tor-Wall, where you turn north and can follow along, or in some cases even walk atop, the wall. Most of the **Heger Tor**, once the city's main western gate, was razed in 1817 and replaced by a Neoclassical triumphal arch commemorating troops from Osnabrück who helped defeat Napoleon at Waterloo—which is why locals still occasionally call it the Waterloo Gate.

About 200 yards north is the **Bocksturm**, the oldest defensive tower along the wall. It frequently served as a prison, and contains gruesome reminders in the form of torture instruments used in various witches' trials, and the 10-by-10-foot **Johanniskasten**, a box of rough-hewn solid oak planks with a tiny window that served as a prison within the prison. The tower, box, and instruments can be seen on guided tours starting at 11:00 A.M. every Sunday.

The route continues north to Rissmüllerplatz, where you will find a medieval tower with the curious name **Bürgergehorsam**, which translates roughly as "burgher obedience." During the Third Reich the Hitler Youth used it as an exhibition hall for its honor flags.

From here, the route heads northeast along Hasetorwall to the **Barenturm** and the **Vitischanze**, at the northern tip of the Altstadt, right on the banks of the Hase. The 12th-century tower and fortifications played a key role in protecting the city for more than 500 years, and were breached only by the Swedes in 1633 during the Thirty Years' War. Today the whole complex has been turned into a very attractive restaurant, the **Vitischanze**, Vittihof 15, serving regional game dishes and fish from the Hase. Part of the restaurant is in the Barenturm's top floor, where you dine under the huge oak beams of that defensive tower's roof, installed in 1622. Open daily except Mondays for lunch and dinner. Reservations recommended; Tel: (541) 217-04.

The Museum of Cultural History

Osnabrück's **Kulturgeschichtliches Museum,** Heger-Tor-Wall 28/29, just across the boulevard from the Heger Gate, is a must-see for two reasons: the collection of pictures by and documents dealing with Felix Nussbaum, and the Roman objects that the museum's archaeologists have excavated since 1989 near Kalkriese, about 12 miles north of Osnabrück, documenting that this in all likelihood was the site of the Battle of Teutoburg Forest in A.D. 9.

Nussbaum, son of a well-to-do merchant family, was born in Osnabrück in 1904. He started his career as a painter in Berlin, and in 1932 won a fellowship at the German Academy in Rome's Villa Massimo. Hitler came to power in Germany while Nussbaum was there, and the painter spent the remaining years of his life in exile: first in Italy, then briefly France, and from 1935 on in Belgium. After the German invasion of Belgium in 1940 he went into hiding in Brussels, but in June 1944 he was discovered by the Gestapo and together with his Polish-born wife, Felka Platek, also an artist, was transported to Auschwitz, where he and Felka died in the gas chamber.

Until a few years ago Nussbaum was best known for his haunting *Self-Portrait With Jewish Passport,* showing him with a fedora hat, upturned coat collar revealing the yellow Star of David sewn on, holding an ID card stamped "Jew" in French and Flemish, and grim prison walls behind him. The painting, which was found by the man who had hidden Nussbaum, and acquired by the Osnabrück museum in 1975, is the most gripping picture expressing the horrors of the Holocaust. But there are many other Nussbaum paintings from the late 1930s and early 1940s documenting the torment of exile and persecution. However, until ten years or so ago Nussbaum was largely unknown and his role as one of the early German surrealists, symbolists, and then expressionists, was forgotten. Childhood friends, surviving relatives, Osnabrück burghers, and curators of the Kulturgeschichtliches Museum have banded together to change this.

Dozens of his pictures have now been acquired by or permanently loaned to the museum. The collection, in two rooms, documents that he was one of the most important German artists of the first half of the 20th century.

No less significant is the Osnabrück museum's role in excavating the Teutoburg battlefield, one of the bloodiest of antiquity and a turning point in Roman and German history. In the summer of A.D. 9 Publius Quinctilius Varus, governor of Germania Inferior, led the 17th, 18th, and 19th legions—

the pride of Augustus Caesar's army—east of the Rhine to suppress some rebellious Germanic tribes, notably the Cherusci, and to make a show of Roman strength in what is today Westphalia. Somewhere in or near the Teutoburg forest Varus and his force of 20,000 infantry and cavalry were ambushed by an alliance of German tribes, led by Arminius (also known as Hermann), chief of the Cherusci. In three days of bloody fighting the Romans were totally wiped out; Varus and his senior officers committed suicide by falling on their swords. So great was the shock in Rome that for years after the debacle Augustus would wake up at night, beat his head on a door, and cry: "Varus, Varus, give me back my legions!" For the Germans it was the beginning of their consciousness as a nation.

Until 1990, despite the huge 19th-century monument to Hermann at Detmold, no one knew where the battle was actually fought. But thanks to the Osnabrück archaeologists, and the luck of Captain Anthony Clunn, a British army officer and amateur treasure hunter stationed in Osnabrück in the late 1980s who found the first cache of Roman coins near Kalkriese hill, north of Osnabrück, the mystery has been solved.

Continuing excavations have turned up dozens of Roman military artifacts on a 250-acre site between the villages of Schwagstorf and Engter. Among the finds are a beautiful iron face mask, once covered with silver, that a Roman officer would have worn in tournaments; spear and pilum tips; slingshots; military axes; fragments of armor; toga clasps and belt buckles; remnants of legionnaires' sandals; cavalry and bridle equipment; and countless copper and silver coins, all minted before A.D. 9, and many with Varus's counter-stamp on them proving they were military pay.

The digging will continue for a number of years, but some of the finest finds are already on exhibit in the Roman-Germanic section of the Osnabrück museum. (The museum is open Tuesday through Friday from 9:00 A.M. to 5:00 P.M., Saturdays and Sundays from 10:00 A.M. to 5:00 P.M., and the first Thursday of each month until 9:30 P.M.)

—*John Dornberg*

GETTING AROUND

Düsseldorf

Düsseldorf's international airport, only 6 km (3 miles) from the city center, is a major gateway into the Northwest area. The S-Bahn local train service from the airport's underground station to the Hauptbahnhof is the fastest and cheapest way into town. The fare is DM 2.60; a cab is about DM 23.

The city has a good bus and U-Bahn (subway) system. It is also one of the towns of the Rhine-Ruhr joint transport operation, which means you need buy only one ticket for a journey involving any combination of buses, streetcars, and trains in the area.

Düsseldorf is well served by InterCity (IC) and EuroCity (EC) express trains linking it with the rest of Germany and neighboring European countries. Its central station is linked to the Frankfurt airport station by hourly InterCity trains; the Lufthansa Airport Express train, which stops at Cologne and Bonn, also travels from the station to Frankfurt airport.

Düsseldorf is also at the center of a network of north–south and east–west Autobahns. Cologne is only 47 km (29 miles) south, 35 minutes by train. All major international car-rental firms have offices in the city. For radio cabs, Tel: (211) 333-33.

The Verkehrsverein (tourist office) on Konrad-Adenauer-Platz, opposite the railroad station, runs a daily two-and-a-half-hour guided bus tour of the city, departing at 2:30 P.M. from bus stop 14 on Friedrich-Ebert-Strasse, also across from the station; Tel: (211) 17-20-20.

Düsseldorf is a main port for the KD Rhine cruises; for contact information, see Around Germany in the Useful Facts section at the front of the book.

Aachen

As a major European road and rail junction, Aachen is easily reached from all points of the compass. Its railroad station is served by almost 200 trains a day, including many InterCity and EuroCity expresses making direct links to other major German cities and numerous foreign capitals (including Paris, Moscow, Copenhagen, and Vienna).

Aachen has fast freeway links to Amsterdam, Brussels, and Paris. The A 4 Autobahn goes to Cologne and Bonn, and the A 44 to Düsseldorf. Although the city lacks an international airport, it is not far from aerial gateways at Maastricht, in Holland (35 km/21 miles west); Cologne/Bonn (85 km/53 miles east); and Düsseldorf (90 km/56 miles northeast).

Bonn

Cologne/Bonn International Airport is about 20 minutes northeast of the city via the A 59 Autobahn. Shuttle buses run every 30 minutes between the airport and the central bus depot; the fare is DM 7.60. A cab costs DM 55–60. Bonn also sits on one of the busiest rail routes in Western Europe, providing frequent express links to the rest of Germany and other countries. Hourly InterCity trains and Lufthansa's Airport Express train link Bonn with the Frankfurt airport.

Bonn's public transportation system is good, and the city radio-taxi service is efficient; Tel: (228) 55-55-55. All major international car-rental firms have offices in Bonn.

Münster

Münster and Osnabrück share an airport at Ladbergen, about 23 km (14 miles) north of the city. There are non-stop flights daily from Frankfurt, Munich, and Stuttgart. It is a major stop for almost hourly InterCity and/or EuroCity trains from Frankfurt, Cologne, Düsseldorf, Bremen, and Hamburg. Two Autobahns—the A 1 from Cologne to Bremen and Hamburg; and the A 46 and A 43 from Düsseldorf to Münster—intersect at the Münster-Süd (south) cloverleaf. From Cologne it's about 175 km (110 miles), from Düsseldorf about 125 km (77 miles).

Driving in the Altstadt is next to impossible. Bikes can be rented at the train station from the Deutsche Bundesbahn (German Federal Railways), next to the luggage check counter; at Josef Soszynski, Meesenstiege 122 in Münster-Hiltrup; and from Hansen KG, Hörsterstrasse 7. Rentals average DM 10 per day. Some hotels also provide bicycles free of charge or for a minimal fee to guests. There are well-marked bicycle routes to all moated castles within a 50-mile radius of the city. A detailed pocket-size booklet for cyclists—*Die 100 Schlösser Route*—with maps, hotel and restaurant listings, and addresses of bicycle rental outlets and shops in 75 towns and villages, is available from most hotel concierges, Münster's municipal tourist office (Berliner Platz 22), and the Informationsstand in the Rathaus, Prinzipalmarkt.

Osnabrück

The Ladbergen airport is about 25 km (15½ miles) southwest of the city. By train, there are direct IC or EC connections daily from Frankfurt, Cologne, Düsseldorf, Hamburg, and Bremen. By car, it is about 235 km (146 miles) from Cologne via the A 1, 120 km (74½ miles) from Bremen (also via the A 1), and 140 km (87 miles) from Hannover by way of the A 2 and A 30 Autobahns.

Most of the Altstadt and much of the inner city is closed to cars, so walking is best. From May through September, the city tourist office (Verkehrsamt, Markt 22–23, Tel: 541-323-44-13) offers a variety of guided walking and bus tours on Wednesday and Saturday afternoons.

ACCOMMODATIONS REFERENCE

The hotel rates listed here are 1994 projections for double-bed, double-occupancy rooms, with a range from low to high whenever possible. Prices are given in deutsche marks

*(DM). Basic rates are always subject to change, so please
verify price when you are booking. Breakfast is usually
included in the price of a room.*

*Precede all city telephone codes with a zero if you are
calling from elsewhere in Germany.*

► **Aquis Grana Cityhotel.** Büchel 32/Buchkremerstrasse,
D-52062 **Aachen**. Tel: (241) 44-30; Fax: (241) 44-31-37. DM
205.

► **Benelux Hotel.** Franzstrasse 21–23, D-52064 **Aachen**.
Tel: (241) 223-43; Fax: (241) 223-45. DM 160–210.

► **Best Western Hotel Regence.** Peterskirchof/Peterstrasse
71, D-52062 **Aachen**. Tel: (241) 478-70; Fax: (241) 390-55.
DM 240–290.

► **Breidenbacher Hof.** Heinrich-Heine-Allee 36, D-40213
Düsseldorf. Tel: (211) 130-30; Fax: (211) 130-38-30. DM 440–
610.

► **Central Hotel.** Aegidiistrasse 1, D-48143 **Munster**. Tel:
(251) 403-55; Fax: (251) 404-00. DM 175–210.

► **Continental Hotel.** Am Hauptbahnhof 1, D-53111 **Bonn**.
Tel: (228) 63-53-60; Fax: (228) 63-11-90. DM 200–260.

► **Dom-Hotel.** Kleine Domsfreiheit 5, D-49074 **Osnabrück**.
Tel: (541) 21-15-54; Fax: (541) 20-17-39. DM 110–130.

► **Godesburg Hotel.** Auf dem Godesberg 5, D-53177
Bonn. Tel: (228) 31-60-71; Fax: (228) 31-12-18. DM 170–180.

► **Holiday Inn.** Graf-Adolf-Platz 10, D-40213 **Düsseldorf**.
Tel: (211) 384-80; Fax: (211) 384-83-90. DM 295–500.

► **Hotel Bristol.** Prinz-Albert-Strasse 2, D-53115 **Bonn**. Tel:
(228) 269-80; Fax: (228) 269-82-22. DM 370–440.

► **Hotel Eden.** Am Kurpark 5a, D-53177 **Bonn**. Tel: (228)
35-60-34; Fax: (228) 36-24-94. DM 168–200.

► **Hotel Feldmann.** Klemensstrasse 23–24, D-48143 **Münster**. Tel: (251) 433-09; Fax: (251) 433-18. DM 160–210.

► **Hotel Germania.** Freiligrathstrasse 21, D-40474 **Düsseldorf**. Tel: (211) 49-40-78; Fax: (211) 498-29-14. DM 216–326.

► **Hotel Königshof.** Adenauerallee 9, D-53111 **Bonn**. Tel:
(228) 260-10; Fax: (228) 260-15-29. DM 210–260.

► **Hotel Krott.** Wirichsbongardstrasse 16, D-52062 **Aachen**. Tel: (241) 483-73; Fax: (241) 40-38-92. DM 170–220.

► **Hotel Nikolai.** Kamp 1–Nikolaiort, D-49074 **Osnabrück**.
Tel: (541) 33-13-00; Fax: (541) 331-30-88. DM 160–190.

► **Hotel Schloss Wilkinghege.** Steinfurter Strasse 374, D-
48159 **Münster**. Tel: (251) 21-30-45; Fax: (251) 21-28-98. DM
220–280.

► **Hotel Walhalla.** Bierstrasse 24, D-49074 **Osnabrück**. Tel:
(541) 272-06; Fax: (541) 237-51. DM 160–200.

► **Hotel Windsor.** Warendorfer Strasse 177, D-48145 **Münster**. Tel: (251) 303-28; Fax: (251) 39-16-10. DM 145–190.

▶ **Insel Hotel.** Theaterplatz 5–7, D-53177 **Bonn.** Tel: (228) 36-40-82; Fax: (228) 35-28-78. DM 177–207.

▶ **Novotel Aachen.** Europaplatz, Joseph-von-Görres-Strasse, D-52068 **Aachen.** Tel: (241) 168-70; Fax: (241) 16-39-11. DM 208.

▶ **Petersberg.** D-53639 **Königswinter/Petersberg.** Tel: (2223) 744-02; Fax: (2223) 744-43. DM 420–520.

▶ **Residence Hotel.** Kaiserplatz 11, D-53113 **Bonn.** Tel: (228) 269-70; Fax: (228) 269-77-77. DM 260–326.

▶ **Rheinblick.** Mühlenstrasse 15, D-40213 **Düsseldorf.** Tel: (211) 32-53-16; Fax: (211) 32-53-56. DM 130.

▶ **Rheinhotel Dreesen.** Rheinstrasse 45–49, D-53179 **Bonn.** Tel: (228) 820-20; Fax: (228) 820-21-53. DM 226–406.

▶ **Rolandsburg Hotel.** Rennbahnstrasse 2, D-40629 **Düsseldorf.** Tel: (211) 61-00-90; Fax: (211) 610-09-43. DM 350–490.

▶ **Scandic Crown Hotel.** Berliner Freiheit 2, D-53111 **Bonn.** Tel: (228) 726-90; Fax: (228) 726-97-00. DM 275–305.

▶ **Schlosshotel Kommende Ramersdorf.** Oberkasseler Strasse 10, D-53227 **Bonn.** Tel: (228) 44-07-34; Fax: (228) 44-44-00. DM 150–170.

▶ **Steigenberger Parkhotel.** Corneliusplatz 1, D-40213 **Düsseldorf.** Tel: (211) 138-15-91; Fax: (211) 138-15-92. DM 440–570.

▶ **Steigenberger Quellenhof.** Mohnheimsallee 52, D-52062 **Aachen.** Tel: (241) 15-20-81; Fax: (241) 15-45-04. DM 290–420.

▶ **Sternhotel.** Markt 8, D-53111 **Bonn.** Tel: (228) 726-70; Fax: (228) 726-71-25. DM 155–225.

THE MOSEL VALLEY

By John England

Winding and looping from the southwest to the north-east, through the steep hills of the volcanic Eifel and Hunsrück regions, the Mosel valley follows the course of the Mosel river for more than 100 miles. A journey in this region takes you from the ancient city of Trier, in the southwest near the city of Luxembourg, to Koblenz in the northeast, where the Mosel river joins the mighty Rhine. The valley encompasses thousands of acres of vineyards—10 percent of the national total. Its beautiful scenery, fine wines, Roman ruins, medieval castles, and riverside towns with cobbled streets and half-timbered houses merit a leisurely visit.

Thanks to its favorable climate and ideal soil, the Mosel valley is wine country, and vineyards are found practically along the entire length of the valley. The Romans began producing wine here more than 2,000 years ago when they imported vines from France. The white Mosel wines are now known around the world, but the valley also produces some fine—if lesser-known—reds. Riesling grapes once domi-nated, producing white wines with a piquant, fruity taste; in recent years, Riesling production has dropped as the drier Müller-Thurgau vintages have gained ascendancy. There are many fine wines produced in the area, but the most famous is the "Doktor" of Bernkastel-Kues, 61 km (38 miles) down-river from Trier.

The area is also rich in history; even a cursory study of the Mosel valley's past will take you from Roman times through the Middle Ages, the Renaissance, and the rampages of Napoleon's soldiers. Castles are perched protectively on the heights above riverside towns; around the perimeters of cities and towns stand walls built by the Romans to keep out

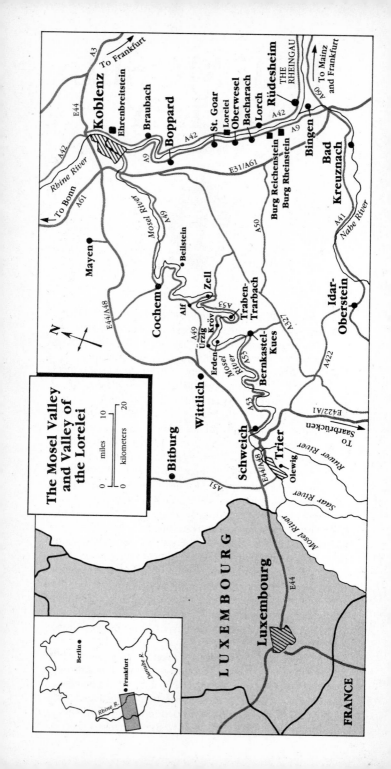

The Mosel Valley and Valley of the Lorelei

their enemies. Within those walls are the remains of Roman baths and theaters; hard by are medieval houses lining narrow streets. Everywhere, there are wine cellars and vintners, all part of the trade that has been this valley's constant through 2,000 years of turbulence.

MAJOR INTEREST

River cruises
Vineyards and wine tasting
Roman ruins, medieval castles, and wine villages

Trier
Ancient Roman gate of Porta Nigra
Early Gothic cathedral and treasury
Aula Palatina, former Roman imperial throne room
Rheinisches Landesmuseum
Kaiserthermen, fourth-century imperial palace and baths
Day excursions to Mosel valley wine villages

Bernkastel-Kues
Medieval market square surrounded by half-timbered houses
Ruin of Burg Landshut
Church tower of St. Michael
River cruises

Cochem
Reichsburg castle
Altstadt's cobbled streets and half-timbered houses
Chairlift to Pinnerkreuz peak

Koblenz
Deutsches Eck, confluence of Mosel and Rhine rivers
Altstadt
Florinskirche
Chair lift to Ehrenbreitstein fortress
Mosel and Rhine riverboat cruises

TRIER

The people of Trier, Germany's oldest city, say that if you dig down a few feet anywhere in their town there is a good chance you'll unearth a bit of Roman history. Certainly, the place has an ancient heritage—its bimillennial was celebrated in 1984. Trier may be even older than that: Legend says the city was founded in 2000 B.C. by Trebeta, son-in-law of Queen Semiramis of Assyria.

The city's history continues to reveal itself in unexpected ways. In 1987, construction workers excavating the old **Viehmarkt** (Cattle Market) for an underground garage unearthed the walls of a monastery built in 1617; beneath the walls were the remains of Roman baths dating from the first to the fourth century A.D.

The bulldozers were halted as archaeologists stepped in to clear the rest of the site, while civic planners went back to the drawing board with their plans for the much-needed garage. At last report, it was to be built underneath the Roman ruins, which were to be encased in glass.

The **Lenz Weinstuben**, on the east side of the Viehmarkt square opposite the latest Roman excavations, is one of Trier's many good wine restaurants and well worth a visit. Its several rooms, paneled in dark wood, are frequented at lunchtime by executives, and in the evenings by a mix of local people and tourists. The menu is limited but good, and you can choose from several hundred wines.

On the south side of the Viehmarkt next to the big Europahalle convention center is the ▶ **Ramada Hotel**, on Kaiserstrasse; a modern 130-room hotel, the Ramada has a pleasant breakfast room, restaurant, and a covered terrace for open-air dining in summer.

On the west side of the Viehmarkt at Am Augustinerhof opposite the Rathaus is the **Stadttheater**, where opera, operetta, musicals, and plays are staged from the end of September through the beginning of July.

Although the people of Trier are proud of the Roman link in their history, the city is not fossilized in its Roman past. It is a lively, bustling regional capital and an important communications center of 100,000 inhabitants, with a population of 13,000 university students thrown in to keep it young. It is located only 10 km (6 miles) from the Luxembourg border and 48 km (30 miles) from France.

But history practically oozes out of its pores, not all of it Roman history—for Trier was not only the home of the Roman emperor Constantine, but also of Karl Marx. Located at the intersection of two main trade routes (north–south and east–west), Trier has always been an important strategic base. As a consequence, the city's history includes many bloody episodes. Trier suffered occupation and destruction by the Franks in the second and fifth centuries, the Normans in the ninth century, slaughter during the Thirty Years' War (1618–1648), and capture by French revolutionary troops in 1794 and by Prussian forces in 1814. In our own century, about 60 percent of Trier was badly damaged or destroyed in 1944–1945.

The best way to get a feel for Trier's past is to take the city tourist information office's excellent two-hour, guided walking tour ("2,000 steps through 2,000 years of history"), which is offered in German and in English. It starts at 2:00 P.M. daily, May through October, at the tourist office in the same building as the Simeonstift (Municipal Museum) next to the Porta Nigra, the huge north gate built by the Romans. The tour winds through the streets of Trier past Roman, medieval, Baroque, and Rococo landmarks that attest to the area's rich heritage.

Whether you take the guided tour or not, a good place to start your exploration of Trier is the **Simeonstift**, housed in the monastery of Saint Simeon. The collections of art and cultural artifacts reflect Trier's more recent history into the 20th century. Exhibits include Gothic sculpture, paintings and graphics, furniture, handicrafts, and folklore. The monastery also houses the **Brunnenhof**, a restaurant featuring local wines. The restaurant's courtyard is the setting for the *Sommertreff,* an open-air program of concerts, plays, and dancing staged every weekend from June to August.

A few steps away is the **Porta Nigra**, built when Trier was known as Colonia Augusta Treverorum—named after its founder, Augustus Caesar. The city served as the supply base for Roman troops manning the Rhenish Limes, the boundary marking the limits of the empire. On the other side of the Limes were the fierce and feared Germanic tribes.

The double-gated building, believed to have been constructed between A.D. 175 and 200, is an architectural masterpiece. It is built of rough-hewn sandstones laid one on top of another in a staggered pattern, totaling 52 layers. The Romans used no mortar to bind the stones, employing iron clamps instead. The building has an inner courtyard intended to lay a deadly trap for any attackers who breached the outer gate, because once they were inside the defenders could hurl missiles at them from the galleries above. But the great gate failed to save the citizens of Trier from capture by the Franks in the fifth century after Roman troops withdrew from the boundaries of their empire and the remaining civilians could not hold the city's fortifications.

The Porta Nigra was abandoned for about 600 years until the 11th century, when it became a church, and a tower with a tall spire was added to the gate's western side. In 1800, Napoleon, whose troops had occupied the city, ordered the church to be secularized and four years later decreed that the Porta Nigra should be preserved as a Roman monument and cleared of all its later architectural additions. Restored to its original form, the gate is now a pedestrian entrance to the city. You can go inside the building for a look at the defense galleries.

Two good hotels near the ancient gate are the 52-room bed-and-breakfast ▶ **Altstadt-Hotel** and the modern 106-room ▶ **Dorint-Hotel Trier**, both of which are on Porta-Nigra-Platz. The Altstadt, which opened in 1987, is a former patrician house (and a listed historical monument) with an attractive gabled and turreted façade and a slate roof with dormer windows. All rooms are well-equipped, and the hotel is handy to the inner-city pedestrian zone. The Dorint, by contrast, is built like a box. But, located opposite the Porta Nigra on its north side, it offers great views of the old gate from its front-facing rooms as well as from its gourmet **Restaurant Porta**, one of four dining options in the hotel. The others are the **Café Latinum**, serving business lunches with a hot and cold buffet; the **Atrium**, an Italian bistro; and the **Espresso Romano**, where you can have light snacks. If you just want a beer in cozy surroundings, you can pop into the **Salong**, a pub on the ground floor.

The Hauptmarkt

From the Porta Nigra, head south along Simeonstrasse, the old Roman main street (now a pedestrian shopping area), past the 13th-century **Drei Königshaus** (Three Kings' House), one of Trier's oldest residences, to the Hauptmarkt (Main Market). The stone cross at the center of the large square was erected in 958 when Trier was granted the right to have a market. (On weekdays the market still flourishes here.) The delightful gabled and half-timbered buildings around the Hauptmarkt—many with shops or restaurants on the ground floor—are representative of the city's post-Roman history, from the Middle Ages through the Baroque and Rococo eras. They include the **Ratskeller zur Steipe**, a 15th-century municipal wine and festival house; and the Early Baroque **Rotes Haus**, next door, which bears the inscription "Trier lived for 1,300 years before Rome." The Rotes Haus has a café on the ground floor.

At the Hauptmarkt's center is a 1595 fountain topped by a statue of Saint Peter that tests the mayor's head for heights on Saint's Day (June 29), when he is obliged to place a bunch of flowers in the saint's arms (a fire department ladder-truck now provides the necessary elevation). On Sternstrasse—a narrow little street off the east side of the Hauptmarkt, in the direction of the Dom—is **Palais Walder-dorff**, a Rococo palace built in 1765 by an electoral prince of that name. Now housing municipal offices, the palace occupies the site of a medieval mint whose coins are still turning up in Trier's soil.

If you would like to buy some genuine ancient coins,

drop into **Antiken Haubrich**, a small and friendly antiques store at Palaststrasse 15. (The narrow street, southeast of the Hauptmarkt, is given over to foot traffic.) Antiken Haubrich also offers a large collection of Roman pottery and earthenware oil lamps, as well as Victorian dolls, miniatures, and thimbles, and is one of the few really interesting stores in Trier (despite the city's pride in its merchants). There is also an abundance of shops on the many pedestrian streets in the neighborhood.

After shopping for Roman artifacts, you could walk back the few yards to the Hauptmarkt and dine in a cozy Roman atmosphere at the informal **Romischer Weinkeller** (Roman Wine Cellar), in the basement of the Zum Domstein restaurant on the east side of the Hauptmarkt. It's not exactly the food Augustus Caesar might have enjoyed, but you'll find good, basic German food, a wide selection of wines, and an interesting array of Roman pottery in glass cases.

Two blocks south of the Hauptmarkt, at Nagelstrasse 4–5, is the delightful **Spielzeug Museum** (Toy Museum), which has a collection of more than 5,000 toys—from dolls and stuffed animals to a miniature railroad and steam engines.

The Cathedral

The huge Trier Dom, which looms a short distance from the market, is the oldest cathedral on German soil. It is an unusual conglomeration of architectural styles of different periods, from the central fourth-century Roman structure to the 1901 vestry. Trier was the residence of Constantine the Great, who in the early fourth century made Christianity the official religion of the Roman Empire; he built the Dom on the site where his mother, Helena, had had her palace.

In the **Domschatzkammer** (Treasury), built about 1470, are a great many relics, a number of them attributed to Saint Helena, who made several pilgrimages to the Holy Land. (She was canonized after her death.) Among the relics and treasures are her amethyst drinking vessel; a golden case purportedly bearing a nail from the Cross; a foot of Saint Andrew, whose portable altar is also here; and a large ivory tablet from the fifth century depicting the transfer of a relic to Constantinople. But the Dom's most important relic, shown to the public only once every two or three decades, is the Holy Coat, which is said to have been worn by Christ on his way to the Crucifixion. Nowadays the Dom is host to an international organ festival held on Wednesdays during May and June.

The nearby **Bischöfliches** (Episcopal) **Museum**, Windstrasse 6–7, exhibits Early Christian finds from excavations at the Dom and cemeteries on the edge of the city, as well as religious art from the time of Constantine.

Next to the Dom, across a peaceful Gothic cloister, is the 13th-century **Liebfrauenkirche** (Church of Our Lady), built in the form of a Greek cross. Completed in 1260, it is the second-oldest Early Gothic church in Germany, after St. Elisabeth's in Marburg.

If you are ready for a meal after touring the Dom and the Liebfrauenkirche, head for the most elegant restaurant in Trier, the **Palais Kesselstatt**, just a few steps from the Liebfrauenkirche at Liebfrauenstrasse 10. The Baroque (1740–1745) palace has terrific atmosphere, international cuisine, and fine wines. Reservations are recommended; Tel: (651) 402-04; closed Sundays and Mondays.

Elsewhere in Trier

A short walk south along Liebfrauenstrasse and east across to Konstantinplatz leads to the **Aula Palatina**, the lofty and once richly decorated former Roman imperial throne room, believed to have been constructed by Constantine in about 310; now it is the simply furnished Protestant church of Our Savior. Built to awe common folk turning up with petitions to the emperor, the massive hall is more than 220 feet long, with a ceiling almost 100 feet high. The ever-efficient Romans heated the vast space with cellar furnaces, some of which can still be seen. Today the basilica hosts a series of organ concerts on Wednesdays in July and August.

A few steps from the Aula Palatina is the attractive pink-and-white **Kurfürstlicher Palais** (Elector's Palace), with its formal gardens just around the corner. The palace's east and north wings, known as the Red Tower and St. Peter's Portal, were built in Renaissance style in the 17th century; the Baroque south wing was added in the 18th century. Today the palace is the seat of the district government. Walk southeast through the gardens and down tree-shaded Ostallee to the city's largest museum, the **Rheinisches Landesmuseum**, at number 44. Extensive collections of prehistoric, Roman, Early Christian, Frankish, and medieval art and artifacts, including burial monuments, floor mosaics, glassware, terracotta and bronze figurines, gold discs, metal harnesses, and about 40,000 coins minted in Trier, are among the high points of this museum.

Opposite the Landesmuseum, to the east across the palace gardens at Weberbachstrasse 25, is the **Schatzkammer der Stadtbibliothek** (Treasury of the City Library). It contains manuscripts, documents, and prints from as early as 895, including a 42-line Gutenberg Bible and letters from Goethe and Karl Marx.

A short distance south of the Landesmuseum is the massive **Kaiserthermen**, ruins of a fourth-century imperial palace and baths. The baths, which may be explored, are included in the tourist office's walking tour of Trier.

A few minutes' stroll southeast along Olewiger Strasse are the ruins of the **Roman amphitheater**, an arena built about A.D. 100, where up to 20,000 bloodthirsty spectators could watch gladiators battling with wild animals.

If by now you have not had enough of the Roman era, return to and pass the Kaiserthermen and walk west down Südallee toward the Mosel river to the **Barbarathermen**, Roman baths dating from the second century. Then go the short distance to the riverbank and turn right on St.-Barbara-Ufer to the **Römerbrücke** (Roman Bridge), which has pillars from the second century and arches dating to 1717–1718. Farther along the river, on Johanniterufer and Krahnenufer, are two old river-freight cranes dating from 1713 and 1774.

A short walk north from the cranes along Krahnenufer brings you to the Kaiser-Wilhelm-Brücke and the city harbor on Zurlaubener Ufer—a busy scene, full of pleasure boats and tourists. The **Pfeffermühle Restaurant** here (Zurlaubener Ufer 76) comes close to the Palais Kesselstatt for elegance and fine food. Open for dinner only; closed Sundays and Mondays. Reservations are recommended; Tel: (651) 261-33.

The large (216-room) and rather formal ▶ **Scandic Crown Hotel**, part of a Swedish chain, is on Zurmaiener Strasse, which heads northeast from the city end of Kaiser-Wilhelm-Brücke. The hotel has a pool, sauna, and solarium, as well as two restaurants—one of which, **La Brochette**, is highly recommended (closed Sundays). The Lobby Bar is a favored rendezvous at cocktail time. Like the Scandic Crown in Bonn and Koblenz, the hotel offers a "Royal Swedish" smorgasbord in its **Rhapsody** restaurant on Sundays.

Wine Tasting and
Side Trips from Trier

After so much history, a glass of wine might be refreshing—and there is no lack of refreshment in Trier, Germany's oldest wine-producing city, with more than three million vines. The many winery cellars near the city (open for tastings daily year-round, 10:00 A.M. to 6:00 P.M., except for the Christmas holidays) are great places to relax on a hot day and sample the local vintages in a cool, subterranean atmosphere. (You can try four wines for DM 6, six wines for DM 10, or eight for DM 12.) Tastings must be booked, and schedules rotate weekly, so ask at the tourist information office for the program, or do some wine tasting downtown at any of the *Weinstuben* and restaurants mentioned above. Also highly recommended are **Das Weinlädchen**, Weinhaus Haag, on Stockplatz, one block northwest of the Hauptmarkt; and the **Weingut Friedrich-Wilhelm-Gymnasium**, at Weberbach 75, a block west of the Kurfürstlicher Palais garden. You can also taste wine at the wine information center on Konstantinplatz (six glasses for an average price of DM 9). The ▶ **Weinhaus Haag** is a comfortable 16-room bed-and-breakfast, and the owner also sells bottles of good local wine for under DM 5.

For really keen oenophiles, Trier has a three-kilometer-long wine tour with 35 points of interest covering everything from the cultivation and life cycle of the vine to grape varieties and soil formations. Tours end with a visit to a winery cellar and a tasting. The tourist office has a brochure in English giving all the details of the tour, which begins at 11:00 A.M. daily, May through September.

Equestrians can take advantage of the indoor riding facilities at the **Trimmelter Hof**, in the Olewig wine village, a short walk east of the amphitheater on Olewiger Strasse.

The Trier tourist office provides information regarding the bus trips that run several times a week during the summer months to the city of Luxembourg, only 47 km (29 miles) to the west, as well as into the Trier countryside (a third of the area is forests and parks) and the Eifel hills (across the Mosel and the Hunsrück hills on the Trier side of the river). There are also day excursions to wine villages along the Mosel and the nearby Saar and Ruwer rivers (two other noted wine-growing areas).

The Trier area has a lot to offer visitors besides wine and history. Take the cable car from Zurlaubener Ufer, on the north side of the Kaiser-Wilhelm-Brücke, up to the Weisshaus terrace for a great view of the city and easy access to the **Wildfreigehege** (Animal Park). There are more than 144 km (89 miles) of marked hiking trails on both sides of the Mosel, and sailing, waterskiing, boat trips from Zurlaubener Ufer, and fishing (ask the tourist office about a license) on the river.

ALONG THE VALLEY

The Mosel river is at its picture-book best as it meanders through the Rhineland-Palatinate between Trier and Koblenz before flowing into the Rhine. It is worth taking at least a couple of days to explore the valley between the two cities, making overnight stops at Bernkastel-Kues and Cochem, two of the Mosel's most delightful medieval wine towns, before continuing on to Koblenz and the Rhine.

To get to Bernkastel-Kues, the next major stop on the Mosel, take the A 602 expressway from Trier to the A 48 Autobahn and then head north toward Koblenz, crossing the Mosel, and shortly afterward taking the exit to Schweich, an old bridge town on route B 53. That road, called the **Römerweinstrasse** (Roman Wine Road) and later the **Moselweinstrasse**, runs alongside the river, crossing and recrossing its serpentine course all the way to Koblenz. (Its number changes to route B 49 at Alf, a wine village about halfway down the valley.) The road runs into the Gestade, Bernkastel's riverfront road, where it is best to park before exploring the town on foot. As throughout most of the valley, charming wine villages along the 60-km (37-mile) stretch between Trier and Bernkastel-Kues present plenty of temptations to stop. Village wine cellars offer free samples, and the growers sell their products at a discount.

Bernkastel-Kues

Bernkastel and Kues are 700-year-old "twin" towns lying on opposite sides of the river. Apart from its fine dry Rieslings (more on those later), the area's main attractions are Bernkastel's intact medieval townscape and its romantic quarters, Andel and Wehlen.

Bernkastel, granted municipal rights in 1291, was put on the map in 1017 with the building of a castle above the town. That castle was replaced by another in 1280, which burned down in 1693 and has been a ruin ever since. **Burg Landshut**, as it is known, dominates the town and offers a magnificent panorama of Bernkastel-Kues and the Mosel valley, worth the steep but well signposted two-mile hike that starts on Karlstrasse, off the Bernkastel Markt. For the less energetic, a bus (**Burg Landshut Express**) runs from the Bernkastel Gestade every hour on the hour from April through October.

The Romans grew wine grapes in the Bernkastel-Kues area, and viticulture has shaped and influenced the region and its people ever since. One famous wine of the area is the Bernkasteler Doktor Riesling, which is said to have been named in the late 13th century by an archbishop who, having fallen mortally ill, drank it and was cured. Other renowned vintages are the Kueser Kardinalsberg and Wehlener Sonnenuhr. With so much wine around, the twin towns naturally have plenty of taverns, cellars, and stores to choose from. They also hold a lively (and crowded) wine festival with fireworks the first weekend in September.

The small cobbled **Markt**, two blocks east of the Gestade in Bernkastel, seems like a holdover from the Renaissance. The square is surrounded by 400-year-old half-timbered houses and has a fountain dating from 1606 and a Rathaus built in 1608. Radiating from the marketplace are streets no wider than alleys. Just around the corner on Karlstrasse, leaning almost drunkenly over the narrow street, is a quaint, slim house with a sharply peaked roof. Known as the **Spitz-häuschen**, it dates from 1583. It is a private house, but there is a public wine bar in the cellar.

Another architectural landmark in Bernkastel is the huge 600-year-old tower of the parish church of **St. Michael**, which houses many art treasures. Across the river in **Kues** is the 500-year-old **St.-Nikolaus-Hospital**, whose vineyards still produce enough grapes to provide a healthy income. The hospice was founded for the needy by Nikolaus Cusanus, Kues' most famous son. Born in 1401, the son of a river boatman, Cusanus became a scholar, scientist, philosopher, and cardinal. The hospital's library contains more than 300 manuscripts dating from the ninth to 15th centuries.

The noted **Moselwein-Museum** at Cusanusstrasse 2 in Kues is worth a visit. Local winegrowers also welcome visitors to their vineyards at various times. Check with the tourist information office at Gestade 5, on the riverfront.

To make the most of Bernkastel's medieval atmosphere, book a room at the ▶ **Hotel Binz** on the marketplace. The hotel's modern facilities and restaurants are well run but lack romance; the location, however, is superb. The old **Ratskeller** and the **Cusanus Weinstuben** are right on the market for cozy wining and dining. The **Gildenhaus Wein-stube** is just around the corner at Moselstrasse 6, and the **Weinstube Schmitz**, at Karlstrasse 13, and the **Zum Lands-knecht** wine tavern and restaurant, at Römerstrasse 36, are also nearby. All are local favorites as well as tourist hangouts.

The **Gestade**—the river road that runs through Bernkastel past the bridge to Kues—is lined with several of Bernkastel's family-run restaurants and hotels. Park at the north end of the Gestade and walk south a short distance to the **Altes Brauhaus** (Gestade 4), a restaurant in a building that was once a brewery, with a terrace overlooking the busy riverboat dock. The huge lid of an old copper beer vat mounted on the main restaurant wall testifies to its past. The food, which is mostly *rustikal* (rustic)—consisting of plain but tasty meat or fish dishes, served up in generous portions—is typical of Bern-kastel's restaurants. Mosel eel is the specialty of the region.

The Altes Brauhaus family also owns the informal and comfortable ► **Hotel Behrens** on Schanzstrasse, a terrace near the town park, a few blocks south of the Markt overlooking the Mosel. Other noteworthy restaurants and wine taverns on the Gestade include the **Alte Kanzlei** and the **Bacchuskeller**. Informal hotels on the Gestade with good views of the river include the 30-room ► **Burg Landshut**, named for the castle. A family-run business for more than a century, it has a *Tanzkeller* (dance cellar) and a Hofgarten Terrasse for open-air dining in summer. The home-style cooking is good and the wine list is extensive.

The ► **Römischer Kaiser Hotel**, only 30 yards from the marketplace, is next door to the Burg Landshut. It offers comfortable rooms, a stylish restaurant with good food, a sizable wine list, and a cozy "Kaiser Keller" cellar bar with a two-man band playing dance music nightly. Also on the Gestade is the traditional ► **Hotel zur Post**, which dates from 1827 and was enlarged in 1985. Run by the Rössling family, it has an inviting wood-beamed and paneled breakfast room and an equally attractive restaurant serving local and international food. It offers more than 100 Mosel wines and has a "Poststube" (Coach Bar) and a terrace for outdoor drinking.

The Gestade north of the bridge is also the depot for regular bus lines running up and down the Mosel and into the surrounding countryside; river cruise boats dock alongside it.

Cochem

Cochem, probably the prettiest town on the Mosel, is dominated by the medieval-style Reichsburg castle overlooking it from the top of a steep hill. It is certainly the most popular excursion and vacation resort on the river, attracting many German and foreign visitors. It is a good idea to visit midweek if possible, even though the compact, hilly town is well equipped to handle mass tourism and manages to absorb the milling summer weekend crowds. From Bernkastel-Kues drive north on B 53 through the wine villages of Ürzig, Erden, and Kröv and the towns of Traben-Trarbach, Zell, and Alf— where B 53 becomes B 49—until Cochem's turreted and towered castle comes into sight on its high perch. The road then runs along Cochem's **Moselpromenade**, which is faced with a long battery of hotels and restaurants. There are parking lots the length of the promenade.

The town's history in Celtic and Roman times and the early Middle Ages is not well documented. But swords from the Bronze Age, Roman foundations, and graves from the time of Charlemagne long ago confirmed the fact that Cochem occupies the site of one of the valley's earliest settlements.

Reichsburg, the castle that dominates Cochem physically and historically, has seen some turbulent times. It was seized by Holy Roman Emperor Konrad III in 1151, pawned to the archbishop of Trier by another German ruler, Adolf von Nassau, in 1294 (it stayed in hock for another 500 years), and totally destroyed by French soldiers in 1689. The castle remained a ruin for 200 years, until it was bought by a wealthy Berlin merchant and reconstructed according to old plans. The Reichsburg is therefore not genuinely medieval, though its lower part was built around 1000. Its furnishings are largely those of a 19th-century château, with a mix of styles that can be a little jarring.

Schlossstrasse (southwest of the Markt, off Herrenstrasse) leads up to the Reichsburg, where there are regular 40-minute tours of the castle. English-language tours must be booked in advance at the tourist office on Endertplatz near the river; Tel: (2671) 39-71. The castle has a souvenir shop that sells replicas of medieval weapons, as well as a restaurant with a small terrace affording sweeping views of Cochem and the valley. The **Pinnerkreuz** peak, on the northeastern outskirts of town, is reached by chair lift from Endertstrasse, a continuation of the bridge road. The peak is also an excellent lookout point.

After visiting the castle, a trip to the **Altstadt** (Old Town)—with its cobbled streets and half-timbered and gabled houses—is called for. Start at the Markt, which has a fountain at its center, and the Rathaus, which dates from 1739. Nearby, at Brückenstrasse 3, is the picturesque 36-room ▶ **Hotel Alte Thorschenke**. Built in 1332 into part of the old city wall at the Enderttor (one of the three still-intact gates), it was originally a guardhouse and town prison. The Alte Thorschenke offers the most elegant atmosphere, and probably the best food, in town. A suit of armor stands guard in the lobby, and the restaurant, comprised of several low-ceilinged rooms, is tastefully decorated with antique furniture.

Other antiquities worth seeing are a former Capuchin monastery dating from 1623 on the Klosterberg (a block north of the Markt, up the steps of an alleyway called Hinter Kempeln); the defense tower at the Balduin gate, at the end of Obergasse, northwest of the Markt; and defense galleries or walkways at the Burgfrieden gate, on the Moselpromenade at the western, or upriver, end of town. Across the Mosel is **Cond**, Cochem's oldest district; dating from 694, it sits at the foot of lush vineyards.

Cochem has a lot to offer beyond its fascinating history—most visitors revel in its beautiful scenery and its many informal wine taverns and restaurants. Several winery cellars, such as the **Weinstube Schlossbergkeller** at Schlossstrasse 15, offer wine tasting by candlelight with hearty snacks and crusty, oven-fresh, whole-wheat bread. The Schlossberg wines, as well as the Herrenberg and Pinnerkreuzberg labels, are among the best produced by Cochem's vineyards.

Another attraction in Cochem is the busy riverfront; here the cruise boats of three operators (Kolb, Undine, and Köln-Düsseldorfer; all have ticket kiosks on the Moselpromenade) come and go on the scenic Mosel. It is also pleasant on summer evenings to indulge in a popular local spectator sport—sitting on the terrace of a hotel or restaurant overlooking the Moselpromenade, enjoying a meal and a bottle of wine, and watching other people go by.

Hotels on the Moselpromenade are informal and comfortable, if lacking the elegant character of the Alte Thorschenke. The ▶ **Burg Hotel**, with about 50 rooms, has several dining rooms, some decorated with suits of armor, fine porcelain, and antique paintings; here, if you are in the mood for romantic accommodations, you may ask for a room with an old-fashioned four-poster bed. The hotel also has a pool, sauna, and solarium. The ▶ **Hotel-Pension Weinhof**, with 35 beds, offers jolly "Mosel Evenings," with dancing and dining by candlelight. On these occasions, strangers link arms and sing and sway together to the strains of local music.

Around Cochem

The tourist bus operators Knieper (at Endertstrasse 30) and Dä Schmandelecker (Bahnhofsvorplatz 3, at the railroad station, six blocks northeast of the Markt) run half-day and full-day trips to places outside Cochem, including **Burg Eltz** (a medieval castle); **Idar-Oberstein** and its precious-stones museum; the **Vulkan Eifel**, hills showing traces of their volcanic origin; Koblenz and the Ehrenbreitstein fortress; and the famous Nürburgring auto-racing circuit.

A boat trip to the wine village of **Beilstein**, a few miles upriver on the opposite bank and known locally as the Sleeping Beauty, is highly recommended. Its medieval marketplace, half-timbered houses, and dreamy, peaceful atmosphere are watched over by no fewer than four castles. The local Beilsteiner Schlossberg wine is quite good.

KOBLENZ

Koblenz, an ancient but lively city of about 110,000 people, is situated at the confluence of the Mosel and Rhine rivers. Two thousand years ago the Romans called it Confluentes. This highly popular tourist town has something for all tastes. Wine lovers can enjoy the great vintages that grow along the banks of the two rivers. History buffs can explore the Altstadt, the castles and palaces dating from the Middle Ages through the 18th century, and the Ehrenbreitstein fortress across the Rhine.

There are 20 miles of scenic paths for rambling along the banks of the Rhine, and drinking and dancing at the Weindorf, a replica of a wine village with its own vineyard that is a favorite summer evening haunt for locals and visitors alike (see below). An important hub of road, rail, and river traffic, Koblenz is also an ideal base for trips up and down the Mosel and the Rhine as well as into the countryside around both rivers.

The best way to explore historic Koblenz is on foot. The tourist office opposite the Hauptbahnhof and its Rhineside kiosk on Konrad-Adenauer-Ufer offer guidebooks and maps of the city. Begin your tour at the **Deutsches Eck** (German Corner), at the confluence of the Mosel and the Rhine, where the Order of Teutonic Knights founded a settlement in 1216. A massive equestrian statue of Kaiser Wilhelm I was erected here in 1897, but the Allies blew him out of his saddle in 1945. A new statue was completed in 1992, but a local political argument prevented it from being raised and its fate remains uncertain. The monument's base provides a platform for all-round views of the city, the two rivers, and Ehrenbreitstein fortress.

Next to it is the **Deutschherrenhaus** (with its Blumenhof, or flower court), a former administrative building built by the Teutonic Knights and now the **Ludwig Museum für Gegenwartskunst** (contemporary art). Sponsored by the art collector Peter Ludwig, who was born in Koblenz, the museum includes works by Jean Tinguely and Louis Cane. (Open Tuesday through Sunday, 11:00 A.M. to 7:00 P.M.)

The Romanesque church of **St. Castor**, next door, was consecrated in 836 and completed in the 12th century; its more modern fountain is meant to symbolize the rise and fall of Napoleon. The garden is open to the public. A short walk along Peter-Altmeier-Ufer, past the dock for international river cruise boats on the Mosel, brings you to the **Deutscher Kaiser**, an early-16th-century residential tower with battlements (and a wine tavern underneath them).

From here, a left turn on Kornpfortstrasse leads to the bay-windowed Dreikönigenhaus (Three Kings' House) of 1701 (now the Stadtbibliothek, or city library), then the Franconian royal palace, an early-18th-century Baroque building with rear towers belonging to the fourth-century Roman **town wall**. The ► **Hotel Kornpforte** on Kornpfortstrasse, a 16-room bed-and-breakfast, is handy to them and to the Florinsmarkt, a compact cobbled square and former market a few steps away along Auf der Danne, in the Altstadt. The hotel has a wine parlor for pleasant evening sampling; light snacks are also served.

The Altstadt

The **Florinsmarkt** is dominated by the Romanesque **Florins-kirche** (Church of St. Florin), dating from the 11th and 12th centuries, with a 14th-century Gothic chancel. Next to it on the square is the **Mittelrhein Museum** in the Altes Kaufhaus, Koblenz's oldest residential house, built in 1419, and next to it the Schöffenhaus (Old Courthouse), dating from 1530.

Taverns on the Florinsmarkt offer good wine and simple but tasty food. Try the gabled **Alte Weinstube zum Hubertus**, built in 1695. Then take a short walk toward the end of Burgstrasse, off the Florinsmarkt, to its junction with the Balduinbrücke, begun in 1337, to see the **Alte Burg**, a 13th-century castle built by an elector of Trier to dissuade the people of Koblenz from thoughts of secession. The castle now houses the Stadtarchiv (City Archives); only the impressive spiral staircase, decorated with ancient coats of arms, is open to the public.

Along Gemüsegasse from the Florinsmarkt is the **Lieb-frauenkirche** (Church of Our Lady), begun in the late 12th century and completed in the mid-13th. You are now in the Altstadt center near **Münzplatz**, a small, charming market-place. The mint master's house, built in 1763, is still standing.

Also on Münzplatz is the medieval **Haus Metternich**, birthplace in 1773 of the Austrian chancellor Prince Metternich; the first and second floors are used for travelling exhibitions of modern art. The comfortable family-run 43-room ► **Cityhotel Metropol**, also on the square, serves up good German food in a pub-style restaurant. A short way down Marktstrasse (which together with its continuation, Löhrstrasse, forms the city's main pedestrian shopping zone), is the **Plan**—a large square and popular meeting place on the edge of the Altstadt. Its **Ratskeller** and the neighboring **Ratsstuben**, both wine restaurants, are worth a visit. Where Marktstrasse becomes Löhrstrasse are four turreted houses built in 1689–91.

There is much more of historical interest in Koblenz, especially the Neoclassical **Residence Schloss** (Elector's Palace; 1777–1786), on the Rhineside Augusta Anlagen. The upmarket ▶ **Scandic Crown Hotel** is located opposite the Elector's Palace, on the south side of Pfaffendorfer Brücke, the city's northern bridge. The hotel provides luxurious accommodations and two restaurants, the **Rhapsody** and **Rotisserie**; in the **Lounge Bar** on the tenth floor you can enjoy panoramic views of Koblenz and the mighty Rhine.

Other attractions include the Neoclassical **Stadttheater**, built in 1787 on Deinhardplatz, and offering a rich program of plays, ballet, and operetta; **Schloss Stolzenfels**, a 13th-century castle rebuilt by the king of Prussia between 1836 and 1842 on a hill in the Stolzenfels district at the south end of the city; and the commanding **Ehrenbreitstein fortress** across the Rhine, the site of a tenth-century citadel destroyed by the French in 1799 and rebuilt by the Prussians between 1817 and 1828.

To get to the fortress, cross the Rhine by ferry from Konrad-Adenauer-Ufer, or, by car, take the Pfaffendorfer Brücke on route B 49, and then turn left on route B 42 and follow the signs to the base of the fortress. You can drive up to the top, walk, or take the chair lift. Whichever way you go, the tour and the views from the battlements are worth the trip. The fortress, as well as Schloss Stolzenfels, are great vantage points for the "Rhine in Flames" fireworks spectacular staged every year on the second Saturday in August.

Other Eating and Drinking in Koblenz

Koblenz has many agreeable wine taverns and restaurants outside the Altstadt. There is a row of restaurants on the **Rheinzollstrasse**, a terrace above Konrad-Adenauer-Ufer with good views of the Rhine and Ehrenbreitstein fortress. Try the **Wacht am Rhein**, the **Stresemann**, or the **Rheinzollstube**. For a fun night out, go to the **Weindorf** on Rheinallee next to the Pfaffendorfer Brücke. Built in 1925, it is an exact replica of a wine village with a square enclosed by a vineyard and four half-timbered taverns. There is seating for 700 inside and 1,300 in the square.

There is music, dancing, and entertainment here every night from Easter through October. Of course, it's a crowd scene.

Excursions from Koblenz

Tour bus services offer day trips from Koblenz to such favorite spots as the Rhine wine town of **Rüdesheim** (75 km/ 47 miles south of Koblenz); the Eifel and Hunsrück hills along the Mosel; and into the **Westerwald** (forest) on the east bank of the Rhine. Check with the tourist office opposite the main railroad station for details. On the west bank of the Rhine just south of Koblenz is Boppard and the beginning of the Lorelei Valley/Rheingau wine area; see the Rhine Around Frankfurt chapter.

GETTING AROUND

Koblenz is the major gateway from the rest of Germany into the Mosel valley. Cologne/Bonn and Frankfurt are the nearest airports.

The A 61 Autobahn links Koblenz with Bonn (52 km/32½ miles to the northwest) and Cologne (90 km/56 miles, also to the northwest). The fastest way to Frankfurt (126 km/78½ miles east) is to take route B 9 north to the Koblenzer Kreuz Autobahn junction, take the A 48 across the river, and join the A 3 to Frankfurt. A slower but prettier route along the Rhine takes you across the river by the Koblenz city bridge, south on route B 42 to Rüdesheim and Wiesbaden, and then into Frankfurt on the A 66.

Koblenz is well served by rail to and from the rest of Germany and neighboring European countries, with hundreds of passenger trains, including InterCity and EuroCity expresses, daily.

The freeway parallel to the Mosel valley is the A 48 Autobahn, which runs between Koblenz and Trier. Although the **Mosel Express** trains, which run from Koblenz to Luxembourg via Trier, stop at several towns along the way, including Cochem, they no longer stop at Bernkastel (there is no rail traffic to Bernkastel). There is also bus service between Koblenz and Trier, which makes local stops along the way.

Trier is an important junction for road and rail traffic to and from nearby Luxembourg and the rest of Germany. The local A 602 expressway links Trier with Koblenz (124 km/77½ miles northeast) via the A 48 Autobahn (which also runs a short distance into Luxembourg). Saarbrücken is 94 km (59 miles) to the south via the A 1 Autobahn.

Trier has a small airport for sport and small passenger aircraft. The nearest full-service airports are Luxembourg, Saarbrücken, Cologne/Bonn, and Frankfurt.

Trier itself has reliable public transportation, with 11 bus lines serving the city and surrounding areas. Visitors can buy a 24-hour ticket for rides on the entire urban network. Koblenz's location on the Rhine and Mosel rivers makes it a major base for the "great white fleet" of the Köln–Düsseldorfer (KD) line (Tel: 261-310-30), as well as such smaller operators as Holzenbein (Tel: 261-377-44). Boats leave from Konrad-Adenauer-Ufer starting at 9:00 A.M. daily.

Excursions range from a few hours to several days, going as far as Trier on the Mosel and Cologne on the Rhine and even to Frankfurt-am-Main.

The Kolb passenger line, based at Briedern/Mosel, offers daily boat trips from mid-May to mid-October from the Zurlauberufer dock in Trier; Tel: (2673) 15-15. There are one-hour tours of the local shoreline as well as longer excursions to places like Bernkastel. On Mondays and Wednesdays, from May to October, the big modern passenger ships of the Köln–Düsseldorfer line make excursions from Trier to Koblenz and Cologne on the Rhine. The KD agency in Trier is at Georg-Schmitt-Platz 2; Tel: (651) 72-66-66.

Most other towns along the Mosel offer tours by boat as well. Check with local tourist bureaus for information.

ACCOMMODATIONS REFERENCE

The hotel rates listed here are 1994 projections for double-bed, double-occupancy rooms, with a range from low to high whenever possible. Prices are given in deutsche marks (DM). Basic rates are always subject to change, so please verify price when you are booking. Breakfast is usually included in the price of a room.

City telephone codes must be preceded by a zero if you are calling from elsewhere within Germany.

► **Altstadt-Hotel.** Porta-Nigra-Platz, D-54290 **Trier**. Tel: (651) 480-41; Fax: (651) 412-93. DM 180–220.

► **Burg Hotel.** Moselpromenade 23, D-56812 **Cochem**. Tel: (2671) 71-17; Fax: (2671) 83-36. DM 90–220.

► **Burg Landshut.** Gestade 11, D-54470 **Bernkastel-Kues**. Tel: (6531) 30-19; Fax: (6531) 73-87. DM 100–290.

► **Cityhotel Metropol.** Münzplatz, D-56068 **Koblenz**. Tel: (261) 350-60; Fax: (261) 16-03-66. DM 150–250.

► **Dorint-Hotel Trier.** Porta-Nigra-Platz 1, D-54292 **Trier**. Tel: (651) 270-10; Fax: (651) 270-11-70. DM 255.

► **Hotel Alte Thorschenke.** Brückenstrasse 2, D-56812 **Cochem**. Tel: (2671) 70-59; Fax: (2671) 42-02. DM 165–225.

► **Hotel Behrens.** Schanzstrasse 9, D-54470 **Bernkastel-Kues**. Tel: (6531) 60-88; Fax: (6531) 60-89. DM 96–170.

► **Hotel Binz.** Markt 1, D-54570 **Bernkastel-Kues**. Tel: (6531) 22-25; Fax: (6531) 71-03. DM 90–120.

► **Hotel Kornpforte.** Kornpfortstrasse 11, D-56068 **Koblenz**. Tel: (261) 311-74. DM 95–120.

► **Hotel-Pension Weinhof.** Moselpromenade 27, D-54282 **Cochem**. Tel: (2671) 74-44; Fax: (2671) 74-45. DM 60–100.

► **Hotel zur Post.** Gestade 17, D-54463 **Bernkastel-Kues**. Tel: (6531) 20-22; Fax: (6531) 29-27. DM 150–185.

► **Ramada Hotel.** Kaiserstrasse 29, D-54290 **Trier.** Tel: (651) 949-50; Fax: (651) 949-56-66. DM 246–266.

► **Römischer Kaiser Hotel.** Markt 29, D-54470 **Bernkastel-Kues.** Tel: (6531) 30-38; Fax: (6531) 76-72. DM 100–160.

► **Scandic Crown Hotel.** Julius Wegeler Strasse 2, D-56068 **Koblenz.** Tel: (261) 13-60; Fax: (261) 136-11-99. DM 255–295.

► **Scandic Crown Hotel.** Zurmaiener Strasse 164, D-54292 **Trier.** Tel: (651) 14-30; Fax: (651) 143-20-00. DM 260–350.

► **Weinhaus Haag.** Stockplatz 1, D-54290 **Trier.** Tel: (651) 723-66. DM 80–145.

FRANKFURT-AM-MAIN

By Thomas C. Lucey

Thomas Lucey, a resident of Frankfurt for more than 25 years, is a freelance journalist. He has also been a newspaper and magazine editor, and has contributed to two other travel guides.

Johann Wolfgang von Goethe believed Frankfurt-am-Main, his hometown, to be the nation's secret capital. Actually, Frankfurt has traditionally been associated with business and finance more than politics. It is true that after World War II this badly bombed city wanted to become the capital of the new Federal Republic and even rebuilt the bombed Paulskirche as a new house of parliament in anticipation. But the national nod went to Bonn, a small town on the Rhine; Frankfurt's would-be parliamentary building now houses meeting and exhibition halls.

Instead, Frankfurt has become Germany's financial capital. Even though unification has made Berlin the national capital again, Frankfurt will remain the financial capital. The Bundesbank (Federal Central Bank) and leading commercial banks, as well as the country's principal stock exchange, are headquartered here, and Frankfurt has bid to become the location of the new European Central Bank. A 63-story office building, Europe's tallest, opened here in 1990 next to the Frankfurter *Messe* (Frankfurt Trade Fair); its pyramid top, illuminated at night, can be seen from all over town. The Messe, an institution that dates to the Middle Ages, makes the city a major stop on the international exhibition circuit.

Ironically, this city of finance and commerce was also the birthplace of the Frankfurt School, which pioneered neo-Marxist studies. The School originated in the university-affiliated Institute for Social Research that was started in the 1920s. Opposed to both Hitler and Stalin, its staff fled Nazi Germany for the United States. Two of the School's academics went on to become American celebrities: Herbert Marcuse, a leading influence on the 1960s counterculture, and Erich Fromm, a psychoanalyst and popular writer. Jürgen Habermas, who teaches philosophy in Frankfurt, is the school's best-known heir.

The Middle Ages are still evident in this city, especially in the Altstadt's coronation cathedral of the Holy Roman Empire. Also, as part of a municipally financed campaign to show that Frankfurt knows there is life beyond business, the Museumsufer—a long outdoor showcase for the fine and decorative arts, and for movies—has been created. The city is designed for walking, with wide, often tree-lined *Fussgängerzonen* (pedestrian zones) in the downtown area. Frankfurt is the home, of course, of the genuine Frankfurter sausage, as well as a tangy apple cider called *Ebbelwei*. Since Ebbelwei (or *Apfelwein*) doesn't travel well, or at least not very far, people must travel here to drink it.

And they do. Frankfurt is one of the most visited cities in Germany. The Messe deserves a good part of the credit, drawing thousands of visitors to its chemical, book, textile, car, antiques, and modern-art fairs. Therein lies a warning: If you are not coming to Frankfurt for a fair, you should avoid the biggest crowd-drawers, particularly on weekends. There is a lot to see in Frankfurt, and you don't want your view blocked.

MAJOR INTEREST

The Dom and Römerberg
Museumsufer (The Museum Embankment)
Sachsenhausen and its Apfelwein taverns
The Alte Oper
Goethehaus
The Zoo
Day trips to Bad Homburg and the Roman camp at
  Saalburg

The Dom and Römerberg

Voltaire was partly right when he remarked that the Holy Roman Empire was "neither holy, nor Roman, nor an empire." It certainly did have longevity, however: Created by Charlemagne and dissolved by Napoleon, it lasted from the ninth century to the 19th. Frankfurt was a Free Imperial City within the empire; for centuries, it was also the city in which

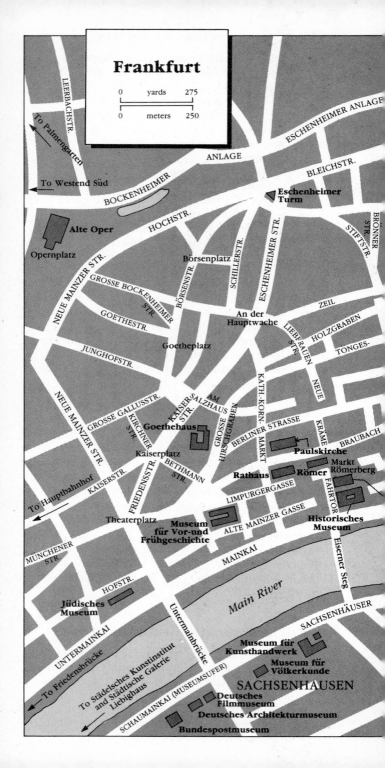

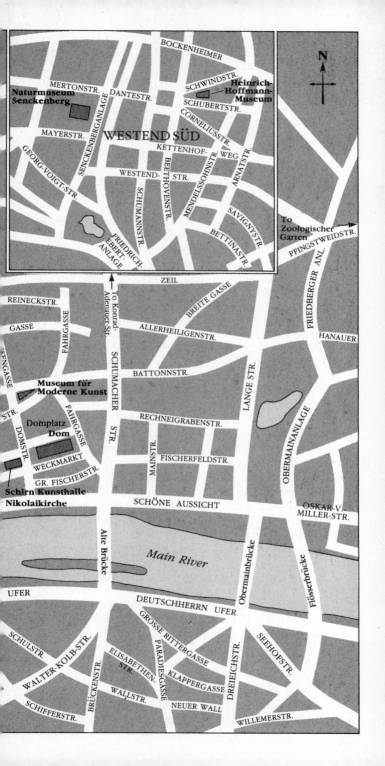

the emperor was elected (from 1356 on) and crowned (from 1562 to 1792).

The coronations took place in the **Dom** (Cathedral), which celebrated its 750th anniversary in 1988. The Dom does not have a massive presence; its spiky Gothic tower dominates the skyline of Frankfurt's **Altstadt** (Old City) only because high-rise buildings are banned in the area. In truth, this red-sandstone church is not even a cathedral, and never was. The Roman Catholic cathedral for this diocese is in the town of Limburg, and Frankfurt's Dom is actually a collegiate church named after Saint Bartholomew. But because ten Holy Roman emperors acquired their crowns here, the church of Saint Bartholomew has gone down in history as the Kaiserdom (Emperor's Cathedral), or simply the Dom, as it is called by everyone in Frankfurt.

Its lack of colossal proportions—and of streams of organized sightseeing groups—makes the Dom approachable. It contains a few outstanding artworks. The *Kreuzigungsgruppe* (Crucifixion Group) was made in 1509 for the cathedral cemetery. The recently restored *Bartholomäus Fries,* designed in 1427, wraps around finely carved choir stalls that date to 1352. The *Maria-Schlaff-Altar,* completed in 1434, depicts the death of the Virgin. The Wahlkapelle (Election Chapel), behind the choir, is the chapel where the Holy Roman emperors were elected.

The Dom was badly damaged in World War II, but it was one of the few structures to survive the March 1944 raid that destroyed the surrounding complex of wooden houses and alleylike streets that had been Germany's largest surviving medieval Altstadt. (A model of the Altstadt can be seen in the nearby Historisches Museum; see below.)

The cathedral's treasures had been doubly protected behind brick walls, and in 1987 a small museum was opened in the Dom's *Kreuzgang* (cloister). On display are Catholic liturgical vestments, pictures, and statues, including one of Saint Bartholomew, as well as models of two earlier versions of the Dom.

In preparation for the city's 1,200th anniversary in 1994 the Dom has been undergoing major, very costly interior renovation, including restoration of almost 60 artworks. Most of the work is scheduled to be completed by early 1994. Meanwhile, the tower and museum will remain open and tours, starting at the museum entrance, will be conducted. The museum is open Tuesday through Friday, 10:00 A.M. to 5:00 P.M., and weekends from 11:00 A.M. to 5:00 P.M.

After his coronation at the Dom, a new emperor and his entourage would parade to the **Römer**, now the city hall, a route you should follow, too. While this area had settlers as early as the Stone Age, the small cluster of ruins near the Dom dates from the Roman and Charlemagne periods. The Romans settled this piece of high ground, which is still called the **Römerberg** (Roman Hill), and also constructed a bridge across the river Main. But to the Romans, Frankfurt was very much an outpost. The northernmost frontier of the Roman Empire, the Saalburg camp, is only a few miles to the north (see Day Trips, below). After the Germanic tribes defeated the Romans, the settlement fell into ruins and was forgotten until 20th-century construction workers stumbled across its remains. The Römerberg was also the site of **Villa Franconofurd**, one of the residences of Charlemagne. A document dating to 794 contains the first written reference to anything resembling the word "Frankfurt," and is the historical basis for the 1,200th anniversary celebrations to be held in 1994. The origin of the city's name may have been Charlemagne's way of commemorating the Frankish conquest of this crucial north–south river crossing in a war some 300 years earlier. The vanquished in that battle were the Alemanni, the same Germanic tribe that had driven out the Romans.

The area between the Dom and the Römer has been built up in recent years. Near the Dom, at Am Römerberg 6a, is the **Schirn Kunsthalle**, where major art exhibitions are held. If there is an exhibition at the Schirn while you are in Frankfurt, it is probably worth seeing. You can rest your feet at the airy Kunsthalle café outside the entrance. (Open during exhibitions only, 2:00 to 6:00 P.M. on Mondays, 10:00 A.M. to 10:00 P.M. Tuesday through Friday, and 10:00 A.M. to 7:00 P.M. on weekends.)

The fresh-looking half-timbered houses facing the city hall are quite new. Purists were shocked when the city built them, but they provide a picture of the long-gone Altstadt while brightening a once drab area. Even when fairs, complete with merry-go-rounds, are not being held here, this square (Römerberg) and the surrounding cafés, ice-cream parlors, and restaurants fill up on sunny Sundays. Crowds have been drawn here for many years. Medieval city officials and their families watched plays and tournaments from a specially built gallery on the **Nikolaikirche** (St. Nicholas Church), the small chapel in front of the city hall. The chapel itself has a rare 35-bell carillon that plays daily at 9:05 A.M., 12:05 P.M., and 5:05 P.M.; Saturdays it is played by hand from 12:05–12:30 P.M.

The large corner building with the drab appearance, another architectural provocation of some years ago, houses the **Historisches Museum**. The history here is Frankfurt's for the most part, and the exhibits provide fascinating glimpses of yesterday's quotidian life, with whole rooms of furniture, pictures, and posters. On the museum's ground floor is a historic-looking café-restaurant with a small Apfelwein Museum. (Open Tuesday through Sunday from 10:00 A.M. to 5:00 P.M., and Wednesdays until 8:00 P.M.; special collections open 10:00 A.M. to 1:00 P.M. Tuesday through Thursday.)

Haus Wertheym, the half-timbered corner house across the square from the museum's entrance, is one of Frankfurt's few original structures to have survived World War II. An important part of Frankfurt's—and Germany's—history is the **Paulskirche** (St. Paul's Church), which is just across the street from the city hall, toward Berliner Strasse. This is where Germany's first, short-lived democratic parliament met in the heady days of the 1848 revolution. The present structure, rebuilt from the ruins of the original destroyed in the 1944 bombing, is used for ceremonies and exhibitions.

Limpurgergasse, a small street between the Historisches Museum and Haus Wertheym, leads to the river Main. Excursion ships dock here, including some that cruise the Rhine. Schedules and tickets are available near the dock. The wide iron footbridge nearby, the **Eiserner Steg**, is the subject of a 1922 painting by Max Beckmann. The bridge crosses to the south bank, with its new Museumsufer (Museum Embankment), and the Sachsenhausen district.

Savor the view of the Museumsufer from the Eiserner Steg, then cross to the south bank and admire the top of the Dom, the three centuries of architectural styles that make up the Historisches Museum (including a 15th-century corner tower that was part of the city's defenses), and the white excursion boats docked next to the Eiserner Steg in spring and summer. These are two of the best views in town.

The Museumsufer

There are seven museums on the half-mile-long museum embankment, where architects have expanded 18th- and 19th-century patrician houses and in some cases combined them with structures of a contemporary style to create some of Germany's best museums. All museums on the embankment are open Tuesday through Sunday from 10:00 A.M. to 5:00 P.M., and Wednesdays to 8:00 P.M.

To the right as you step off the footbridge is the **Museum für Kunsthandwerk** (Museum of Applied Arts), at Schaumainkai 15–17. Inside is one of those collections that got out of hand. Begun at another site in 1877 with only 50 articles, the collection was generously endowed by local benefactors until it became internationally known in the field of decorative arts. Unfortunately, until this structure was expanded in 1985, the collection did not have sufficient display space; even now, only two-thirds of the 300,000 objects in the collection can be shown (the rest is in storage). Items on display include rare examples of German furniture and woodwork, porcelain, rugs, glassware, tapestries, and bronze and gold works, as well as decorative art from other European countries and the Near and Far East. There is also a special collection of books and calligraphy. The European furniture collection is the best of its kind in Germany.

The building itself attracts visitors. The original villa, which the museum occupied in 1967, was far too small to house the collection. Richard Meier, the New York architect who is renovating the Getty Museum in Malibu, California, designed the airy addition. The Café im Museumpark provides outside tables in summer.

More than 200 Russian icons dating from the 17th through the 19th centuries can be seen in the new **Ikonen Museum**, a nearby annex in part of the medieval Teutonic Order monastery at Brückenstrasse 3–7 (at the corner of Elisabethenstrasse).

Next in line is the **Museum für Völkerkunde** (Museum of Ethnography), which is at Schaumainkai 29, in the direction of the Untermainbrücke. The original museum was destroyed by bombs in World War II; this new building is not nearly large enough. Only 300 of the collection's over 65,000 articles are on display, consisting mostly of artifacts from South Pacific, African, and South American cultures that are dying out. The museum seeks to use its display space to give visitors an appreciation of those cultures. Exhibitions are regularly held on various aspects of the contemporary Third World as well.

The museum is increasing display space by moving the education section to the former police station at Schaumainkai 37, where Third World art shows can also be held. Another building, also designed by Richard Meier, is scheduled for completion in 1995, making the Völkerkunde Frankfurt's third-largest museum.

On the intersection at the Untermainbrücke, Schaumainkai 41, is the five-story house that contains the **Deutsches Filmmuseum**, which opened in 1984, the first of the new museums on the embankment to open and the most popular. Exhibitions on King Kong, special effects, and cartoon characters, along with a permanent display of historic movie equipment, draw a quarter of a million visitors annually. A movie theater shows classic and foreign films; in summer, a large outdoor screen is erected next to the river. Visitors can also use the museum's extensive research library.

The Deutsches Filmmuseum was a pet project of Hilmar Hoffmann, who headed Frankfurt's Culture and Leisure Department for 20 years, until his retirement in 1990. Hoffmann was the driving force behind Frankfurt's cultural makeover and has worked hard to create the museum embankment. He is also an author and lecturer on motion pictures, especially those of the Nazi era.

The **Deutsches Architekturmuseum** (German Architectural Museum) is next door at Schaumainkai 43. It, too, offers special exhibits, which have covered subjects as varied as the Postmodern movement and the New York architectural boom of the past two decades. Only 20th-century architecture is on display. The collection includes more than 10,000 plans and drawings by German and foreign architects and 700 models of architectural projects.

Your next stop is a few steps away at the **Bundespostmuseum** (Federal Post Office Museum), Schaumainkai 53. This collection of historic post-office signs, uniforms, telephone and telegraph equipment, mail coaches, and special stamp exhibitions reopened after renovation in 1990.

The nearby **Städelsches Kunstinstitut und Städtische Galerie** (Städel Art Institute and City Gallery), at Schaumainkai 63, occupies the only building on the museum embankment that was actually intended from the start to be a museum. The Städel, as it is called, has its own art school and park, and occupies a full block. The museum, the city's first, set a pattern that Frankfurt's museums have followed until recently: They are started by private foundations and supported by private wealth. The Städel is named for Johann Friedrich Städel, a banker and art collector who lived on the Rossmarkt, near the Goethe family. He bequeathed his collection of 500 paintings to a museum upon his death, in 1816, at the age of 88. Still organized to fulfill Städel's goal of showing European paintings since the 14th century, the museum is one of the best of its kind in Germany. Although the period it covers is vast, only outstanding works from each period and school are on display. Visitors can see works by Botticelli, Rembrandt, and Rubens, along with the German masters Albrecht Altdorfer, Lucas Cranach, Adam Elsheimer, Matthias Grünewald, Hans Holbein the Younger (notably his altar from the local Dominican church), Max Beckmann (who lived nearby and taught at the Städel's art school), Ernst Nolte, and Ernst Ludwig Kirchner, whose graphics make up part of the **Kupferstichkabinett** collection of prints, drawings, and engravings. The museum suffered a blow in 1937 when the Nazis confiscated "decadent" works by Picasso, Oskar Kokoschka, Beckmann (who had left Frankfurt in 1933), and others. Exact figures on the number of artworks taken by the Nazis probably will never be known, but a 1991 museum catalogue estimated the total at 672, including 77 paintings, 23 sculptures, and 572 drawings and other graphics. Only six paintings were recovered after the war. The building itself was badly damaged by wartime bombing and wasn't restored until the 1960s.

While the Städel has some sculpture, that form of art is really the domain of the **Städtische Galerie Liebighaus**, at Schaumainkai 71, in the direction of the **Friedensbrücke** (Peace Bridge). (Note that the Liebighaus is not on the Liebigstrasse, which is in another part of town.) The museum was installed in the house of Baron von Liebig in 1909, and gradually acquired the house's name, the house itself, and its parks, planted with locally rare trees. The collection spans 5,000 years and includes sculpture from the Egyptian, Greek, and Roman eras; the Far East; and medieval and Renaissance Germany, France, and Italy. The exhibits have been carefully selected so that they fit in the old building without crowding. To accommodate the collection, the Liebighaus has been expanded, and works that have never been on display have been brought out of its basement storerooms. The gem of the collection, the *Frankfurter Athena,* a first-century Roman copy in marble of a lost Greek bronze, is shown in a new light—in a glass-roofed tower that does justice to the armless goddess.

From here, you can stay on this side of the Main river and begin to explore Sachsenhausen. A new footbridge over the river, Holbein Steg, connects Schaumainkai, in front of the Städel, to Untermainkai, near the Frankfurt Intercontinental. (Although the Friedensbrücke will be closed for repairs through 1995, all traffic is being handled by a small temporary bridge.)

Sachsenhausen

When people in Frankfurt refer to *"dribb der Bach,"* they mean the area "across the stream," Sachsenhausen. This district south of the river Main has long enjoyed the reputation of being the place to go for fun. The mood in its many taverns is informal. Everyone sits together at long plain wooden tables, and as the night goes on the singing starts and newfound friends link arms and sway in rhythm, more or less. Here, the drink is not beer or wine but the dry apple cider called Apfelwein, or "Ebbelwei," as it is pronounced in the local dialect. Ebbelwei is the drink of Frankfurt. It is poured from a gray-and-blue stoneware jug, called a *Bembel,* into glasses decorated with an embossed diamond-shaped pattern. The first sip of this *Stöffche* (little stuff) may pucker your whole body and convince you that the waiter or waitress brought you some kind of vinegar. If so, try a *Gespritzte,* a mixture of

Apfelwein and plain mineral water (*Sauergespritzt*), or a lemonade-flavored mineral water (*Süssgespritzt*). Many local people drink the tangy cider this way. Apfelwein has an alcoholic content of about 10 to 12 proof.

While Apfelwein is available year-round, it also comes in different versions, depending on the season. *Süsser* (sweet), a dark, cloudy product of the freshly pressed apple harvest, is sold in the autumn. When Süsser starts to ferment, it is called *Rauscher*, a darker, slightly more acidic drink. Thanks to an ancient magic formula, the third glass of Rauscher has special properties that will clear the digestive tract. Süsser and Rauscher are meant to be taken straight, not mixed with mineral water. Apfelwein is drunk with meals, but Süsser and Rauscher are probably too strongly flavored to go well with most dishes. Apfelwein mixed with hot water, cinnamon, and cloves makes a nice toddy.

Sachsenhausen's Apfelwein taverns, which display a pine wreath outside when a new barrel has arrived, tend to serve traditional food such as *Rippchen mit Kraut* (pickled pork chops with sauerkraut), *Haspel* (pigs' knuckles), and *Handkäs mit Musik* (strong tasting—and smelling—cheese with vinegar, oil, and chopped onions). A dish that you will not find outside Frankfurt is *grüne Sosse*, a green sauce made from seven herbs and other seasonings, chopped hard-boiled eggs, and sour cream, usually served with boiled eggs, boiled beef, or poached fish. In Sachsenhausen you are likely to find real Frankfurters made from pork, flavored with spices, and then smoked. The sausage originated in the traditional butchers' area between the Dom and the Römer, in the Middle Ages; the oldest known recipe dates from 1487. The local product has been labeled "genuine Frankfurt sausage" since about 1900 in order to distinguish it from its New World upstart, the American hot dog, which is now for sale in Frankfurt under that name. Unlike the hot dog, Frankfurters are always served in pairs.

For nibbling, there are usually hard rolls, salted bread sticks, and *Brezeln* (pretzels) on the tables. What you eat goes on your tab.

The taverns in Sachsenhausen are especially popular during the summer, when tables are set up outdoors. But getting a seat can be difficult any time of the year, especially on weekends. One trick is to get in just before the "shifts" change from the lunch crowd to the afternoon drinkers to the supper shift. Hot meals are usually not available after 10:00 P.M., and closing time is midnight or 1:00 A.M. While there are no class or age barriers in Apfelwein taverns, patrons who appear to be slumming probably are; it has become fashionable for the local *Schickeria* (chic set) to drop by.

Unfortunately, the traditional Apfelwein *Lokal* has been losing ground in Sachsenhausen to fast-food places, discos and bistros, and trendy restaurants. Nonetheless, establishments that serve the "national beverage" on plain wooden tables are holding their own, and the narrow tavern-lined streets between Paradiesgasse and Grosse Rittergasse have been turned into a pedestrian zone. On sunny days this area seems to be one vast outdoor café. Here you'll have a good chance of meeting folks from back home. (For a list of some of the best Apfelwein *Lokale,* see the Dining section below under Sachsenhausen.)

If you wish to take in a very wide view of the district, visit the **Henninger Turm** (tower), atop the Henninger brewery's storage silo at Hainer Weg 60. An observation platform here provides a vista of the city and surrounding countryside. The same view is available from the tower's revolving restaurant.

Alte Oper

Frankfurt's network of pedestrian zones makes a stroll through the downtown area very enjoyable. You can combine shopping with stops at several interesting and historic buildings. One is the Alte Oper (Old Opera House), which opened in 1880 and was a copy of the lavish Paris Opéra. Kaiser Wilhelm I was so impressed with the opera house that when he arrived for the first performance he exclaimed, "Only the city of Frankfurt could afford such splendor!" The building was bombed in World War II and then restored, at great cost, during the urban renewal of the late 1970s. The opera house now serves as a grand setting for concerts, musicals, conventions, and other festive events. You can see the elaborate entrance, lobby, and Belle Epoque café (upstairs) whenever the main doors are unlocked. The broad **Opernplatz** (Opera Square), with its large fountain and Paris-style streetlights, makes this a pleasant place indeed.

Goethehaus

Germany's greatest writer lived in Frankfurt until 1765, when he was in his mid-twenties. The Goethehaus actually consists of two houses that were joined by Goethe's father, and they have been in foundation hands since 1863. They were restored to their 18th-century appearance in 1900 and again after being bombed in World War II. The **Goethehaus und Museum**, near but not on Goetheplatz or Goethestrasse, is located at Grosser Hirschgraben 23 and can be visited conveniently while you are sightseeing or shopping downtown. (Open 9:00 A.M. to 6:00 P.M. Monday through Saturday, and Sundays from 10:00 A.M. to 1:00 P.M.; from October to March, 9:00 A.M. to 4:00 P.M. Monday through Saturday.)

Palmengarten

Not far from the university and next to the American Consulate-General is an oasis called the Palmengarten, a botanical garden with tropical, subtropical, and domestic plants. Some grow in a hangar-sized greenhouse, others in the well-kept park, which also has a restaurant and café where old-fashioned outdoor concerts are held in summer. The Palmengarten tends to be crowded on Sundays and holidays. You can enter at Siesmayerstrasse and Grüneburgweg, a half-block from the American Consulate-General, or from Palmengartenstrasse, a small street off Bockenheimer Landstrasse. The number 36 bus, which stops on Siesmayerstrasse, continues on to Sachsenhausen. There is also a subway station a few blocks away. (Open daily, 9:00 A.M. to 4:00 P.M. in winter, and until 6:00 P.M. in summer; buildings close one hour earlier.)

The Zoo

The late Professor Bernhard Grzimek made Frankfurt's **Zoologischer Garten** internationally known through his books, his encyclopedia of animals, and, most of all, through his films and television series. The zoo has some 3,500 animals in all. Be sure to visit the **Exotarium** (open until 9:00 P.M.), where you'll find especially exotic creatures, and the **Grzimekhaus**, named after the former director, where you can observe nocturnal animals during the day as if it were night. Both are in the middle of the zoo, behind the large lake near the entrance; both also require an additional admission charge. There is also a small extra fee to take pictures. The zoo is easy to reach by U-Bahn (subway), with its own station outside the entrance. It is best, however, to avoid the zoo on Sundays and holidays, as it is one of the most popular places in Frankfurt. (Open daily, 8:00 A.M. to 5:00 P.M.)

Other Museums

The Rothschild family originally came from Frankfurt, and Anne Frank, the author of *The Diary of a Young Girl,* was born here, too. Anne Frank died in the Bergen-Belsen concentration camp in 1945, near the end of the war; a Frankfurt school has been named after her. These are only two examples from the city's long Jewish history.

On November 9, 1988, the fiftieth anniversary of *Kristallnacht,* when hundreds of synagogues were set afire, Jewish-owned shops destroyed, and 30,000 Jewish men incarcerated and tortured in concentration camps as part of a nationwide Nazi pogrom, Germany's first **Jüdisches Museum** (Jewish Museum) was opened in the Rothschild Palais, the former home of the Rothschilds. The building, which dates to 1821, is at Untermainkai 14–15.

The museum explores the history of Frankfurt's Jewish community. On the second floor is a large, plain wooden model of Frankfurt's medieval ghetto, which consisted of small houses tightly packed along Judengasse (Jews' Lane), extending from Konstablerwache, the large square along the Zeil shopping area, to Börneplatz, a long block to the south. Mayer-Amschel Rothschild, the founder of the Rothschild dynasty, was born here in 1744.

The ghetto was torn down in the second half of the 19th century and wasn't seen again until construction workers uncovered the remains of houses on Börneplatz a few years ago. Some ruins have been preserved for the small **Museum Judengasse**, which opened in 1993 on the ground floor of the Stadtwerke building, Kurt-Schumacher-Strasse/Börneplatz.

To reach the Jüdisches Museum from the Theaterplatz U-Bahn station, follow Neue Mainzer Strasse to the river and turn right on Untermainkai. The museum is open Tuesday through Sunday, 10:00 A.M. to 5:00 P.M., and Wednesdays until 8:00 P.M.

The **Museum für Moderne Kunst** (Museum of Modern Art), on Berliner Strasse, opened in 1991. Showing only works created after 1945, the museum displays pop and minimal art from the Ströher collection, sold to the city by the heirs of the Wella hair-care products and cosmetics fortune. A highlight is Joseph Beuys's *Blitzschlag mit Lichtschein auf Hirsch* (Lightning Bolt with Glow of Light on Stag), an environment consisting of 39 pieces of bronze and aluminum. While there are many American artists, from Andy Warhol to Bruce Nauman, represented in the museum, you'll also find works by Japan's On Kawara and Germany's Gerhard Richter. Also of interest is the pink-and-white Postmodern building itself, nicknamed *Tortenstück* (piece of cake) and designed by Vienna's avant-garde architect Hans Hollein. Open Tuesdays, Thursdays, Fridays, and Sundays, 10:00 A.M. to 5:00 P.M.; Wednesdays until 8:00 P.M.; Saturdays, noon to 7:00 P.M. Entrance at Domstrasse 10. Admission free on Saturdays.

If you are interested in natural history, don't miss Frankfurt's largest museum, the **Naturmuseum Senckenberg**. Housed in an imitation Baroque palace built at the beginning of this century, the Senckenberg contains the usual fossils and dinosaurs plus extensive collections in the fields of zoology, geology, paleontology, and botany. The founder, Johann Christian Senckenberg, an 18th-century physician, originally created a foundation to support a hospital. Goethe, a genius for all occasions, urged that it support the study of nature instead. Today the Senckenberg research society has more than 3,000 members worldwide and is actively engaged in numerous projects. Located at Senckenberganlage 25, two blocks north of the Messe in the university area, the Senckenberg keeps its own hours: Mondays (when the museum embankment is closed), Tuesdays, Thursdays, and Fridays, 9:00 A.M. to 5:00 P.M.; Wednesdays, 9:00 A.M. to 8:00 P.M.; and weekends, 9:00 A.M. to 6:00 P.M. Free guided tours are offered on Wednesdays at 6:00 P.M. and Sundays at 10:30 A.M.

Struwwelpeter, the dirty little boy who wouldn't cut his hair or fingernails, was "born" in Frankfurt, the creation of Heinrich Hoffmann, a humanitarian, psychiatrist, and children's book author. Two museums are dedicated to their memory. The **Struwwelpeter Museum**, opened in 1982, displays sketches and manuscripts by the author, various editions and parodies of the original book, and other items on loan from Hoffmann's heirs. The museum moved from its location at Hochstrasse 45–47, where the author lived from 1851 to 1859, to the Schirn Kunsthalle, entrance on the Dom side; it is open Tuesday through Sunday, 11:00 A.M. to 5:00 P.M., and Wednesdays until 8:00 P.M. The **Heinrich Hoffmann Museum** at Schubertstrasse 20, a block from the Senckenberg, collects works about the author and puts on special exhibitions. The small museum is open daily except Mondays from 10:00 A.M. to 5:00 P.M.

The remains of a Roman garrison and the contents of the graves of an early Iron Age warrior and Frankish settlers from the fourth to eighth centuries—all found in Frankfurt—can be seen in the **Museum für Vor- und Frühgeschichte** (Museum of Pre- and Early History). Exhibits also span the period from the Stone Age to the Dark Ages and include primitive tools, ceramics, jewelry, cult figures from the Mediterranean and Near East, and Persian bronze works. The museum is housed in a new building, a virtually windowless candy-striped "wall" wrapped around the Late Gothic Karmeliter-kloster (Carmelite Monastery), whose frescoes have been painstakingly restored. (Putting the two together displayed a "crude lack of taste," complained the prestigious local newspaper, the *Frankfurter Allgemeine*.) The monastery-museum is

near the Goethehaus, at the beginning of the broad and busy
Berliner Strasse behind the Hotel Frankfurter Hof; it is open
Tuesday through Sunday, 10:00 A.M. to 5:00 P.M., and Wednes-
days until 8:00 P.M.

Day Trips from Frankfurt

Frankfurt's central location, which has contributed to its
prosperity since the Middle Ages, also makes it a good base
for day trips. (Many of the places within easy travelling
distance from Frankfurt are covered in the next chapter, The
Rhine Around Frankfurt.) **Heidelberg** is only an hour away
by InterCity (IC), EuroCity (EC), and InterCity Express (ICE)
trains, and can be reached via the Autobahn in about the
same amount of time.

Wiesbaden and **Mainz**, both on the Rhine near charming
wine districts, are easily reached by S-Bahn (interurban) and
regular Bundesbahn trains. The S-Bahn starts at the Kon-
stabler Wache subway (U-Bahn) station and runs underground to the Hauptbahnhof (main railway station). Bundesbahn trains depart from the Hauptbahnhof. The trips take
about half an hour; the quickest S-Bahn does not go via the
airport. The Baroque wine-growing city of **Würzburg** in
northern Bavaria is only an hour and 20 minutes distant by
IC, ICE, or EC (see The Romantic Road chapter). Wiesbaden,
Mainz, and Würzburg can also be reached by Autobahn.

Bad Homburg is a famous spa with a traditional casino
where gamblers in dark suits and even black tie (there is a
dress code) sedately play roulette and blackjack (but not slot
machines). The **Spielkasino**, which opened in 1841, was the
world's first and served as the model for the casino in Monte
Carlo. The town preserves its turn-of-the-century atmosphere, especially in and around the Kurpark (Spa Park);
elsewhere, the modern office buildings and fast-food shops
can be ignored. The homburg hat was created here and is
commemorated by a hat section in the **Heimatmuseum**.
Originally a hunting hat, the homburg was popularized for
street wear by Edward VII of Great Britain, who was a
frequent visitor to Bad Homburg and the casino. Located just
22 km (14 miles) from Frankfurt, Bad Homburg is easily
reached by car, S-Bahn, and the casino's courtesy bus.

Bad Homburg is linked by local transportation to the
Saalburg. This reconstruction of a Roman fort on the Limes,
the northern wall of the Roman Empire, effectively conveys
the feeling of a place where 600 legionnaires were stationed almost 2,000 years ago, although to purists it may
look too tidy.

A tip for day-trippers: About half the people who work in

Frankfurt commute by train (especially via the Hauptbahn-hof) or car. Avoid rush hours (7:00 A.M. to about 8:30 A.M., 4:30 P.M. to about 6:30 P.M., and Friday afternoons). Motorists should avoid the Messe area during large fairs.

GETTING AROUND
Frankfurter Flughafen, once the home port of Germany's zeppelin fleet, has become one of Europe's busiest airports. With scores of international direct flights every day (about 40 to and from New York alone), this airport is likely to be your gateway to Germany.

Ground transportation to and from the Flughafen, including quick and easy access to downtown Frankfurt, runs smoothly. Taxis always seem to be available, even late at night. The fare to downtown Frankfurt is about DM 40. At the train station, on the level below the airport's arrival area, an S-Bahn departs every 20 minutes for the Hauptbahnhof in the city, a 12-minute journey. S-Bahn tickets for Frankfurt can be bought at the blue machines just before going down to the platform. Never get on a German subway or bus without a ticket. Inspectors make periodic checks, and the fine for *Schwarzfahren* (travelling black) is DM 60, payable on the spot.

Airport trains run to and from the Hauptbahnhof via the Bundesbahn (federal railway) tracks on the main floor; the S-14 train, which serves the airport and Mainz and Wiesbaden, runs on subway tracks through downtown (via the Hauptwache and Konstablerwache) and Sachsenhausen (last stop, Südbahnhof). Airport trains, marked with the figure of an airplane, are announced in English as well as German. The fare is DM 5 during rush hour; at other times it is DM 3.70. The fare is slightly higher in outlying parts of the city and the surrounding area.

Some long-distance Bundesbahn trains also stop at the Flughafen. Information and tickets are available in the arrivals area.

Since you don't need a car for local sightseeing and driving downtown is best left to others, the clean and efficient S-Bahn/U-Bahn system is the best way to travel. Many visitors complain that they find it confusing. It isn't if, instead of trying to grasp all the fine points, you just concentrate on what you need to know. A ticket (DM 1.90; rush hours, DM 2.60) is good for one ride in one direction to any stop in the same color-coded area. The trip may include transfers to other S-Bahn and U-Bahn trains and city buses, and may not last longer than one hour. (Some bus stops have ticket machines; otherwise the bus driver sells tickets.)

Trains are identified by S or U and a route number (the

letter is important because there are S and U routes with the same number). The direction is indicated by the name of the last stop. On trains, number and last stop appear on the front of the first car and on electric platform signs. On buses, they are on the front, and all the stops are listed on a schedule displayed at each stop. The same route numbers and destinations mark stairways at entrances and transfer points, with a large white U on a blue background or an S against green posted at station entrances.

The S-Bahn, mostly above ground, links the center of the city with the suburbs as far as Wiesbaden and Mainz, Hanau, and Friedberg (where Elvis Presley was stationed as a GI in the 1950s). The U-Bahn, which serves Frankfurt proper, covers the points of most interest to visitors, with stations at the Alte Oper, Hauptwache, Römer, the zoo, and Schweizer Platz (for Sachsenhausen and the museum embankment). Buses complement the U-Bahn routes.

The streetcar lines are part of the city system, and use the same tickets as the buses and trains.

If you want to go only a few stops, it is best to purchase a cheaper *Kurzstrecke* (short-route) ticket. A Kurzstrecke ticket costs DM 1.40 (DM 2.10 during rush hours, Monday through Friday, 6:30 to 8:30 A.M. and 4:00 to 6:30 P.M.). The best bet for visitors is a DM 5 *Tageskarte* (all-day ticket) for one zone (the yellow zone includes almost all of the city, Sachsenhausen, and the airport). A three-day ticket costs DM 12.

No matter what kind of ticket you buy, the ticket machine shows the price when you press the color-coded destination button. Train service phases out at about midnight or 1:00 A.M. and resumes at 5:00 A.M.

You should take advantage of the network of *Fussgänger-zonen* (pedestrian streets) for shopping and sightseeing. Start at the Alte Oper, stroll along Grosse Bockenheimer Strasse (better known as Fressgass', or Gluttony Lane, because it is lined with food stores and restaurants), and continue to the Hauptwache square. A block to the left, at the end of Schillerstrasse, stands the **Eschenheimer Turm** (the Eschen-heimer Tor station on the U-Bahn), a restored medieval tower and gateway that most photographers can't resist. The Hauptwache is at the beginning of the broad **Zeil**, which claims to do more business than any other shopping street in Germany. To the right, via Liebfrauenstrasse and Neue Kräme, are the Römer and the Dom. A footbridge leads to the Muse-umsufer. This route crosses only five streets open to cars.

The Hauptbahnhof, its subterranean passage, and the rough honky-tonk area around it are not safe for evening strolls.

The city operates tourist information offices opposite

track 23 in the Hauptbahnhof and at the northern corner of
the Römer. In addition to stocking city maps, calendars, and
brochures, these offices sell tickets for the city-run bus tours
(there are three a day). At the train station office helpful
staffers will also find hotel rooms for visitors; Tel: (69) 212-
388-49 or 51. Hours: Hauptbahnhof, 8:00 A.M. to 9:00 P.M.
(April to October until 10:00 P.M.), Sundays and holidays,
9:30 A.M. to 8:00 P.M.; Römer, 9:00 A.M. to 7:00 P.M. weekdays;
9:30 A.M. to 6:00 P.M. weekends and holidays.

On weekends, the **Ebbelwei Express**, a brightly painted
streetcar, runs every 40 minutes from 1:32 P.M. to 5:32 P.M.
from Bornheim (a north Frankfurt area) via the zoo and
Theaterplatz to Sachsenhausen. There is piped-in music, and
Apfelwein and pretzels are served. You can board anywhere
en route; the price is DM 3.

Major car rental agencies are at the Flughafen, with offices
at the leading hotels; in smaller hotels the desk can make
arrangements. The agency will bring the car to you. Frankfurt has wide streets feeding into the various north–south
and east–west Autobahns that twist around and through the
city. It is considerably easier to drive in and out of Frankfurt
than within it. Autobahns run along three sides of the
Flughafen. The nearby clover-leaf intersection, Frankfurter
Kreuz, will point you toward Hannover, Cologne, Mannheim, or Nürnberg.

ACCOMMODATIONS

First, a warning: Major trade fairs overburden hotels and
pensions in and around the city, including the large river
excursion boat/hotels docked along the Main. Prudent businesspeople attending the fairs make reservations a year in
advance. Room prices are also higher during fairs, so if
possible, time your visit to avoid a large Messe. (The international Frankfurt Book Fair, one of the largest trade fairs in
the world, is held here each October, for example.)

The hotel rates listed here are 1994 projections for
double-bed, double-occupancy rooms, with a range from
low to high whenever possible. Prices are given in deutsche
marks (DM). Basic rates are always subject to change, so
please verify price when you are booking. Large hotels now
tend to charge for breakfast, which can add up to DM 30 per
day and per person to your bill.

The telephone area code for Frankfurt is 69 preceded by a
zero if you are calling from elsewhere in Germany.

Downtown
The ► **Arabella Grand Hotel**, which opened in 1988, targets
business travellers with a VIP floor, conference rooms, and a

fitness center, plus restaurants (see Dining, Luxury Gourmet, below) and bars. It is in the shopping area, just half a block from the Konstablerwache station, where you can catch the train to the plane.

Konrad-Adenauer-Strasse 7, D-60313 Frankfurt. Tel: 298-10; Fax: 298-18-10. DM 465–615.

▶ **Frankfurter Hof**, the flagship of Germany's Steigenberger group, is a 19th-century grand hotel that offers guests an atmosphere of hushed elegance in a central location.

Bethmannstrasse 33, D-60311 Frankfurt. Tel: 215-02; Fax: 21-59-00. DM 360–510.

▶ **Hessischer Hof**, opposite the Messe, is similar to the Frankfurter but smaller. Both it and the Marriott (below) are popular with trade-fair guests.

Friedrich-Ebert-Anlage 40, D-60325 Frankfurt. Tel: 754-00; Fax 754-09-24. DM 585.

The ▶ **Frankfurt Intercontinental** stands on the Main, two blocks from the Hauptbahnhof. Its upper floors offer panoramic views of the city.

Wilhelm-Leuschner-Strasse 43, D-60322 Frankfurt. Tel: 260-50; Fax: 25-24-67. DM 310–510.

The ▶ **Mozart** is a small, modern hotel tucked away in the gentrified Westend. It is quiet, and only breakfast is served.

Parkstrasse 17, D-60322 Frankfurt. Tel: 55-08-31; Fax: 596-45-59. DM 210.

The ▶ **Mövenpick Parkhotel Frankfurt**, owned by a Swiss company, calls itself "a small grand hotel." It is also a convenient pied-à-terre across from the Hauptbahnhof.

Wiesenhüttenplatz 28, D-60329 Frankfurt. Tel: 269-70; Fax: 269-78-84. DM 346–578.

Marriott bought the Plaza from Canadian Pacific in 1989 and carried out a complete renovation. Renamed the ▶ **Frankfurt Marriott Hotel**, it is located in the upper stories of a high rise across from the Messe's main entrance. The entrance is through a ground-floor lobby.

Hamburger Allee 2, D-60486 Frankfurt. Tel: 795-50; Fax: 79-55-24-32. DM 415–620.

The ▶ **Scandic Crown Hotel** (formerly the Savoy) is a modern hotel across from the Hauptbahnhof.

Wiesenhüttenstrasse 42, D-60329 Frankfurt. Tel: 27-39-60; Fax: 27-39-67-95. DM 275–380.

▶ **Schwille**, a small hotel next to the popular café of the same name, is in the Fressgass' section of the *Fussgängerzone,* near the Alte Oper.

Grosse Bockenheimer Strasse 50, D-60313 Frankfurt. Tel: 92-01-00; Fax: 92-01-09-99. DM 190–270.

The ▶ **Turm**, new, efficient, and expanding, is a medium-

size hotel on a wide, busy street near the Eschenheimer
Turm.

Eschenheimer Landstrasse 20, D-60322 Frankfurt. Tel: 15-
40-50; Fax: 55-35-78. DM 190–230.

The ▶ **Pension Uebe**, in a corner house half a block from
the Turm, is an institution to which many faithful guests
return year after year. Only breakfast is served.

Grüneburgweg 3, D-60322 Frankfurt. Tel: 59-12-09. DM
95–130.

Sachsenhausen

The ▶ **Holiday Inn** is a long uphill walk (or three stops on
the number 30 or 36 bus) from Apfelwein territory. This top-
of-the-line Crowne Plaza hotel has special meeting facilities
for business travellers and is the only large modern hotel in
Sachsenhausen.

Mailänder Strasse 1, D-60598 Frankfurt. Tel: 680-20; Fax:
680-23-33. DM 450.

Out of Town

The ▶ **Gravenbruch-Kempinski-Frankfurt** provides a posh
country-resort atmosphere within a short drive of the city
and the airport. However, the avid sightseer may find it
remote. Top executives, who can hold large and small meetings here with breaks for tennis, love it.

Gravenbruch Ring, D-63263 **Neu-Isenburg**. Tel: (6102) 50-
50; Fax: (6102) 50-54-45. DM 460–520.

The ▶ **Schloss-Hotel Kronberg**, built in the 19th century
for Kaiser Friedrich's young widow, Victoria (daughter of
Britain's Queen Victoria), is furnished with antiques and has
an Old World atmosphere. This is a place to relax in old-
fashioned elegance.

Hainstrasse 25, D-61476 **Kronberg im Taunus**. Tel: (6173)
701-01; Fax: (6173) 70-12-67. DM 395–655.

Easily reached by pedestrian bridges from the airport
passenger terminal, the ▶ **Sheraton** provides meeting facilities, including an adjoining convention hall, for business
travellers, as well as R & R for transient passengers. This is
the second-largest hotel in Europe.

Hugo-Eckener-Ring 15, D-60549 Frankfurt. Tel: 697-70;
Fax: 69-77-22-09. DM 380–595.

Nearby is the ▶ **Steigenberger Avance Frankfurt Airport**,
which recently added an executive tower with a tenth-floor
VIP lounge where breakfast as well as evening cocktails are
served. Although it overlooks an Autobahn, the hotel is
surrounded by woods and is actually quite peaceful. It
provides frequent courtesy bus service to and from the
passenger terminal.

Unterschweinstiege 16, D-60549 Frankfurt. Tel: 697-50; Fax: 69-75-25-05. DM 400–500.

Each of these hotels has a fine restaurant.

DINING

Luxury Gourmet

Weinhaus Brückenkeller, a 300-year-old wine cellar with vaulted ceilings and wandering musicians, had long been popular with visitors to Frankfurt. In 1988 Michelin awarded it a star, and Frankfurters rediscovered it. Another star was added under chef Alfred Friedrich. The menu is small and changes daily; the wine list is extensive and pricey. Schützenstrasse 6; Tel: 28-42-38 and 28-50-92. Evenings only, from 7:00 P.M. Closed Sundays.

Restaurant Français, which occupies a comfortably small room in the Frankfurter Hof hotel, feels old-fashionedly French; that is, formal, elegant, and Michelin-starred. The menu, however, is not limited to French dishes. Tel: 21-58-06. Closed Sundays and Mondays, and for four weeks during July and August.

Premiere is the showcase restaurant of the Arabella Grand Hotel, and is decorated in the same Art Deco style. With frequently changing inventive dishes, Premiere has established itself in recent years among local diners as well as hotel guests. French and German wines dominate the wine list; after-dinner drinks can be very expensive. Open evenings only. Konrad-Adenauer-Strasse 7; Tel: 298-10.

Finally, bear in mind the **Gourmet Restaurant** in the Gravenbruch-Kempinski-Frankfurt and the restaurant in the **Schloss-Hotel Kronberg** (see Accommodations, Out of Town). Reservations are required for all the restaurants mentioned above.

Moderate

Bistrot 77 would be in the preceding category if it did not offer a four-course business meal for DM 80 as well as a splurge on a nine-course feast for DM 145 (plus pricey French wine). This is not a bistro but a gourmet restaurant (with a Michelin star) located deep in Sachsenhausen's Apfelwein district. Bistrot 77 is the achievement of the brothers Mosbach, Guy and Dominique, sons of an Alsatian wine grower whose products can be sampled here. Ziegelhüttenweg 1–3. Tel: 61-40-40. Open for lunch and dinner weekdays, dinner only on Saturdays (from 7:00 P.M.); closed Sundays. Reservations required.

A Frankfurt restaurant critic noted recently that traditional German dishes have become "almost exotic" here. And indeed, you'll have no trouble finding Italian, Yugoslav, Chinese, and Indian restaurants. But what of the German restaurants? In addition to those in Sachsenhausen (see below), you might try:

Dippegucker for its rustic decor, good beer, affordable wine, and hearty meals. It can be found at two locations: Eschenheimer Anlage 40, facing the Eschenheimer Turm, Tel: 55-19-65 or 66; and Münchner Strasse, facing the Hauptbahnhof, Tel: 23-49-47 or 48. The former opens for lunch and then from 5:00 P.M.; the latter is open all day until midnight.

Gutsschänke Neuhof is in a class by itself: a 500-year-old half-timbered farmhouse in a setting complete with pond, ducks, and swans. There is outdoor dining in good weather, and the large menu includes homemade *Wurst* and *Schinken* (ham), both also sold to go. It is in Dreieich-Götzenhain, between Götzenhain and Neu-Isenburg; Tel: (6102) 300-00. Open every day from 10:00 A.M. to midnight; hot meals are served from noon to 2:30, and 6:00 to 9:30 P.M. Coffee and cake are served from 3:00 P.M. on. The place tends to be mobbed on Sundays.

Apfelwein Klaus is at Meisengasse 10, just off Grosse Bockenheimer Strasse (Fressgass'). Everything here is genuine—the long tables, the blackboard menu, and, of course, the Ebbelwei. Open 11:00 A.M. to 11:00 P.M. Tel: 28-28-64.

Sachsenhausen

Picking an Apfelwein place here is a matter of personal preference and available seats. Some of the most traditional and popular establishments include:

Zum Eichkatzerl, at Dreieichstrasse 29; open from 3:00 P.M. to midnight, closed Wednesdays and the first Thursday of every month. Tel: 61-74-80.

Fichtekränzi, at Wallstrasse 5; open 5:00 P.M. to midnight, closed Sundays and holidays. Tel: 61-27-78.

Zum Gemalten Haus, at Schweizer Strasse 67; open 10:00 A.M. to midnight, closed Mondays and Tuesdays, and mid-June to the end of July. Tel: 61-45-59.

Germania, at Textorstrasse 16; open from 4:00 P.M. to midnight, Tuesday through Thursday; from 11:00 A.M., Friday through Sunday; closed Mondays. Tel: 61-33-36.

Adolf Wagner, at Schweizer Strasse 71; open 11:00 A.M. to midnight. Tel: 61-25-65.

All of the above are *Gartenlokale;* that is, they move their tables out under the trees in nice weather.

Cafés

Germany's rich cakes and strong coffee are served not as desserts but as late-afternoon fare at 4:00 P.M. The Frankfurt specialties are *Frankfurter Kranz,* a ring-shaped cream cake with vanilla flavoring, and *Bethmännchen,* almond and marzipan cookies named after the Bethmann banking family. A good place to sample them and other Konditorei goodies is **Altes Café Schneider**, Kaiserstrasse 12 (near the Frankfurter Hof), closed Sundays in summer; and **Café Schwille**, on Fressgass', Grosse Bockenheimer Strasse 50. The **Café Boulevard le Opera**, in the Mövenpick restaurant complex on Opernplatz, facing the Alte Oper, has even richer, Swiss-style cakes.

SHOPS AND SHOPPING

Hauptbahnhof-Kaiserstrasse

Etienne Aigner, Kaiserstrasse 9, stocks fashions and leather goods by the Munich-based designers. **Behagel**, Kaiserstrasse 3, is a long-established shop for porcelain, including Meissen, and crystal. **Friedrich**, Kaiserstrasse 17, sells antique and modern jewelry and silver, including their own award-winning designs. **Türpitz**, Liebfrauenberg 26 (near the Hauptwache) is a leading fur shop. **Gold-Pfeil**, Kaiserstrasse 22, carries its own leather goods, made in nearby Offenbach. **J. A. Henckels Zwillingswerke**, Kaiserstrasse 20 and Rossmarkt 11, sells scissors and knives made of Solingen steel. **John Montag**, Kaiserstrasse 41, deals in porcelain, and has a permanent Meissen exhibition. **Rosenthal Studio Haus**, Kaiserstrasse 38, stocks everything Rosenthal, including avant-garde china patterns.

Goethestrasse

Annabel of Königstein, number 9, carries a wide selection of Armani and Ungaro fashions. **Bogner Sportmoden**, number 21, sells fashions and sportswear by that well-known skiing family. **Christofle-Pavillon**, number 29, stocks French silverware and gold and silver jewelry. **Escada**, number 13, is an outlet for another famous Munich fashion name. **MCM**, number 1, has leather goods and men's and women's sportswear. **Spangenberg**, number 29, sells furs, many custom made. **Vonderbank**, number 11, one of Frankfurt's oldest art galleries, deals in paintings, prints, and graphics.

The Hauptwache

Frankfurter Kunstkabinett, Börsenplatz 13–15, is a leading traditional art gallery. **Lorey**, with entrances at Schillerstrasse 16 and Grosse Eschenheimer Strasse 11, is a small, upscale department store that stocks porcelain, glass, handicrafts, and other luxury goods. **Prange**, at Hauptwache 2, carries Bally and other well-known shoe brands. **Wempe**, at Hauptwache 7, sells watches and clocks by that Hamburg concern, as well as top international brands.

Near the Dom/Römer
Wilhelm Döbritz, Braubachstrasse 10–12, deals in 17th- to 19th-century paintings, antique furniture, silver, porcelain, and pewter. **Joseph Fach**, Fahrgasse 8, sells antiques. **Pia Forner, Kunst um 1900**, Fahrgasse 1, carries turn-of-the-century artworks. **Galerie Prestel**, Braubachstrasse 30 (opens at 11:00 A.M.), is a prestigious art gallery. **Thomas Poller**, Kirchnerstrasse 1–3, sells antiques. **H. Stör**, Fahrgasse 9, sells antique dolls and toys.

Flea Market
The Saturday-morning flea market, with 700 vendors and 150 stands for children, is located on the south bank of the Main river, along the museum embankment. The **Flohmarkt** is not noted for gems; it deals in used household goods and bric-a-brac. Open from 9:00 A.M. until 2:00 P.M.

THE RHINE REGION AROUND FRANKFURT

By James A. Clark

James Clark, who has contributed to The New York Times, *teaches at a university in Heidelberg.*

The Rhine region south and immediately west of Frankfurt delights in Germany's warmest and driest climate. Thomas Mann, speaking as confidence man Felix Krull, says: "The Rhine valley brought me forth—that region favored of heaven, mild and without ruggedness either in its climate or in the nature of its soil, abounding in cities and villages peopled by a blithe and laughter-loving folk—truly of all the regions of the earth it must be one of the sweetest." In this case, Krull is trustworthy. The **Rhine valley** from Koblenz south to Alsace, with its almond, cherry, fig, and other fruit trees and its sheltered sunny slopes covered as far as the eye can see with vineyards, has often been described as a sort of northern annex to Italy—as in fact it was under the Romans. Though wine grapes were indigenous here, it was the Romans who taught the Rhinelanders how to make the best of their grapes, skills later encouraged by Charlemagne, who spread viticulture as assiduously as he did Christianity. This part of the Rhineland not only turns out fine wines, it has been fundamentally formed by the culture of wine, as reflected in its economy, traditions, festivals, and innate magic. That very Mediterranean deity, Dionysus, holds sway over

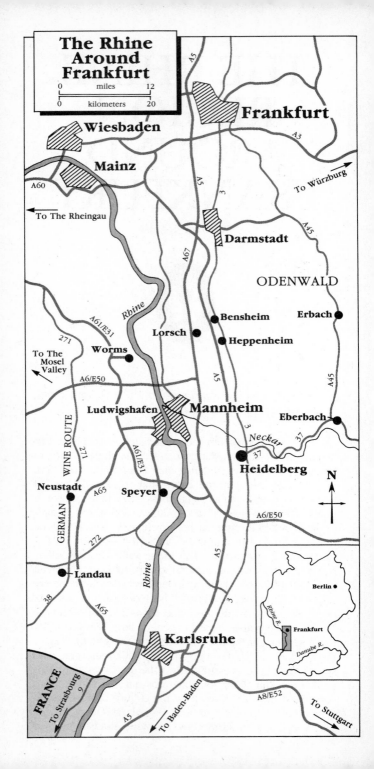

The Rhine Around Frankfurt

miles 0–12
kilometers 0–20

Frankfurt
Wiesbaden
Mainz
A60
To The Rheingau
A3
To Würzburg
A5
A45
Darmstadt
A67
Rhine
ODENWALD
A61/E31
271
Bensheim
Erbach
Lorsch
Heppenheim
To The Mosel Valley
Worms
A6/E50
A5
A45
Ludwigshafen
Mannheim
Eberbach
271
A61/E31
Neckar
37
Neustadt
A65
Speyer
Heidelberg
37
N
272
A6/E50
GERMAN WINE ROUTE
Landau
Rhine
38
A65
3
A5
Karlsruhe
FRANCE
To Strasbourg
9
45
To Baden-Baden
A8/E52
To Stuttgart

Berlin
Rhine R.
Frankfurt
Danube R.

the northern gods as far down the Rhine as Boppard, near Koblenz and the mouth of the Mosel.

To the beneficent climate and the congenial customs of this middle Rhine landscape add its varied, pervasive beauty, and you have a guaranteed formula for attracting vacationers. The charms of the area are diverse. If the stately progression of the Rhine from Wiesbaden west to Rüdesheim is too slow for you, head south of Frankfurt to the **Odenwald**, where every bend in the road—and roads here consist mostly of bends—brings a surprise: a hidden valley, an unsuspected village, a Renaissance palace in a little market town. The steep wooded banks of the **Neckar**, itself a wine-producing area, with its medieval castles brooding unassailably over the silent river, are only an hour away from the Weinstrasse's hearty, convivial welcome: There is a festival practically every day somewhere here on the west bank of the Rhine south of Mainz.

Fortunately for the millions of visitors attracted by all this atmosphere, cultural wealth, and fine wine, the well-known German efficiency and industry are also steadfast in the area. Its hotels and restaurants are impeccably managed; trains, buses, and trams run everywhere and on time; the roads are superb (and so are the maps, luckily, because German road signs tend to be useful principally to natives). Despite some lapses, on the whole this region's historical riches and romantic associations have been preserved and made accessible rather than immoderately exploited. The region is superb for walking, which brings blessings denied those who rely on wheels. The Rheingau and the Weinstrasse (Wine Route) have instructive, well-marked trails of all lengths through their famous vineyards; in the Odenwald and around Heidelberg you are never more than a few moments from a solitude enriched by traces of the past and drenched in the natural beauty of the land.

This chapter, setting out westward from Frankfurt, begins with visits to ancient Mainz and the spa city of Wiesbaden before following the Rhine downstream (west and north) from Frankfurt through the Rheingau and the **valley of the Lorelei**. We then move south of Frankfurt, upstream, to Darmstadt, and from there plunge south into the Odenwald, traversing it to see a selection of its historic towns.

Farther south, we pick up the river Neckar at Bad Wimpfen and follow the river north and west to **Heidelberg**, with excursions to the cathedral cities of Speyer and Worms on the Rhine. Finally, west of the Rhine, we trace the Deutsche Weinstrasse (German Wine Route) south through the Pfalz (Palatinate), from Grünstadt down to Schweigen on the French border.

MAJOR INTEREST

Mainz
Cathedral
Gutenberg Museum
Altstadt

Wiesbaden
Thermal springs
Altstadt
Bath district (casino, parks)
Shopping, theater, cultural events

The Rheingau
Landscape (vineyards, Rhine)
Strausswirtschaften (vineyard taverns)
Historic towns
Eberbach Monastery
Johannisberg (Spätlese wine)
Brömserburg wine museum

Valley of the Lorelei
Bingen (Burg Klopp)
Rhine castles (Mäuseturm, Rheinstein, Reichenstein)
Lorch (picturesque village)
Bacharach (old-city houses)
Oberwesel (Schönburg castle, city walls)
The Lorelei and St. Goar (Rheinfels castle)
Boppard (Roman walls, Altstadt, Rheinallee)

The Odenwald
Nibelungenstrasse (legends, landscape)
Half-timbered medieval villages
Handicrafts (pottery, beekeeping)
Darmstadt (Art Nouveau)
Lorsch (Königshalle)
Michelstadt (Rathaus, Fürstenau castle)
Amorbach (abbey)
Miltenberg (half-timbered houses)

Castles on the Neckar
Landscape
Bad Wimpfen
Burg Guttenberg (falconry, museum)
Burg Hornberg (Götz von Berlichingen)
Schloss Zwingenberg
Hirschhorn
Dilsberg (walled village)

Heidelberg
Romantic associations

Altstadt
University
Castle
River Neckar (Old Bridge, Philosophers' Walk)

Speyer and Worms
Cathedrals
History
Pfälzer wines and food

The German Wine Route
Haardt foothills landscape
Wine tasting
Deidesheim's Marktplatz
Rhodt's Weinhöfe
Dörrenbach's Rathaus

MAINZ

The capital city of the state of Rheinland-Pfalz, Mainz is on
the west bank of the Rhine, opposite Wiesbaden and the
mouth of the Main, a convenient 20-minute drive west of
Frankfurt's international airport on the A 60. Most of Mainz's
points of interest lie in a compact area within or immediately adjacent to the Altstadt (Old City), between the Rhine
and the low hills to the west. Although Allied bombing
obliterated 80 percent of the city in 1945, the Mainzers have
succeeded in preserving many remnants of a history that
began with the Romans in 38 B.C., saw the construction of
one of Germany's great cathedrals and the invention of the
printing press, and culminated with Mainz's emergence as
an important modern commercial and cultural center.

Like other Rhineland cities, Mainz has lubricated the passage of the centuries generously with wine; in fact, it has a
larger expanse of vineyards (1,111 acres) than any other
large German city, enough wine taverns to consume most of
its own output, and a citizenry known for its willingness to
try. Mainz's reputation for riotous merrymaking is renewed
each winter when German TV brings the costumes and
buffoonery of the city's traditional winter carnival festivities
(the Mainzer *Fastnacht*) to viewers across the country.

The Cathedral

Behind the zany makeup and clownish humor it adopts in
February, Mainz has historically had another visage: a stony-
featured ecclesiastical power that for a thousand years stood
eye to eye with electors and emperors, princes and popes.

The strong-willed prince-archbishops of Mainz rarely blinked first.

Ceremoniously robed, mitred, and bearing their episcopal croziers, a procession six centuries long of these imperious and acquisitive prelates glares down at you from the columns and walls within the Mainzer **Dom** (in the center of the Altstadt), one of the three great imperial cathedrals of the land (with those of Speyer and Worms). The archbishop of Mainz, as one of the seven electors of the Holy Roman German emperor, held enormous temporal power. He accumulated domains, fortresses, and rights of taxation from the monarchs his vote helped enthrone, thus increasing the worldly riches and might of the archbishopric.

The original seat of the archdiocese was an eighth-century church built over a pre-Christian temple site where the Protestant church of St. John now stands, west of the Dom across the Leichhof square. This edifice, however, was too modest to support such magnificence. So, in about 978, shortly after becoming archbishop of Mainz, Willigis, the emperor's chancellor, began building the present cathedral. Now the chief landmark and focus of the Altstadt, the Dom is an enormous structure whose exterior is best seen from some distance: Though its six towers are impressive, it lacks the soaring spires that make some other cathedrals, such as Cologne's, awe inspiring, even viewed from directly below. A thousand years of building, destroying, and rebuilding have given the Dom a somewhat heterogeneous character, but recent restorations have shaded its mixture of Romanesque, Gothic, and Baroque elements a uniform ochre that emphasizes their essential harmony.

The great **bronze doors** at the north entrance (facing the Marktplatz, past the Dom information office), the gift of Willigis himself, are the second oldest in Germany (Aachen's are older). Within, on the left, flanking the steps to the east apse, you will find the earliest grave markers, beginning (to the right) with that of Siegfried III, who died in 1249. A walk down the nave and aisles takes you through 600 years of German funerary art, from the Romanesque period into the 19th century. Through the door at the southeast corner, past the tranquil cloister, the Dom **museum**, recently renovated, displays fragments of a rood screen sculpted by the anonymous Master of Naumburg, whose expressive powers, seen here in his powerful carved heads, remained unequaled for centuries.

Facing the Dom, across the Marktplatz to the north, is a row of 18th-century houses. The **Café Korfman** (Markt 11–13) occupies one of these houses, whose ornate and flowery façades are confections as delightful as the café's house specialty, homemade *Apfelstrudel* with ice cream. A table in front of the café makes a good vantage point from which to watch the spectacle of a German market (every Tuesday, Friday, and Saturday) unfold against the backdrop of the venerable Dom.

The Gutenberg Museum

On the east side of the Marktplatz, the **Marktbrunnen**, with its colorful saints and cherubs, was erected in 1526 to celebrate Emperor Charles V's victory over the French at Pavia. Beyond this fountain, across Liebfrauenplatz east of the Dom, you will find a fascinating museum: the World Museum of Printing, better known as the Gutenberg Museum, established in 1900. With the invention of a hand printing press using movable cast type, Johannes Gutenberg, a native Mainzer, opened the floodgates to the sea of information that inundates us today. About Gutenberg himself we know almost nothing, other than that he was rarely out of debt. The numerous portraits adorning the museum are fanciful, as no artist portrayed the legendary inventor in his own lifetime. The museum houses a complete reconstruction of his workshop; judging by the amount of muscle required to work the printing press, Gutenberg must have had shoulders like a football player or else had very burly assistants (he employed as many as 20 craftsmen). The museum's proudest possession is the B 42, one of the few remaining copies of the original Bible Gutenberg printed between 1452 and 1455. Housed in a barred vault among other precious volumes, it is displayed under controlled light and temperature conditions to prevent fading and deterioration of the paper.

Set aside an hour and a half or so to wander through the whole of this attractive well-lit compendium of printing history. Tours in English can be arranged for groups. (Closed Mondays.) The shop in the entrance hall offers a rich choice of mementos and gifts, including facsimile manuscripts, printing devices, and books.

In the Altstadt and Environs

To the right as you leave the Gutenberg Museum, Mailandsgasse takes you east toward the Rhine (streets leading down to the river have red signs; streets parallel to the Rhine have blue signs). Just behind the museum you come to the restaurant **Heilig Geist** (Rentengasse 2), a convenient and atmospheric setting for a hearty Mainzer meal under the vaults of a 13th-century hospital. Two blocks north along

Rheinstrasse, past Mainz's rakishly modern **Rathaus** and convention center complex, the Rheingoldhalle, is the adjoining ▶ **Hilton International Mainz**. Equipped with minibars, color television, and lavish furniture, this expensive hotel is more than comfortable, it is almost overpowering. For a Rhine view, you should specify quarters in the older of its two sections; a glassed-in walkway above the street leads west, away from the river, to the 1982 addition, containing sauna, fitness center, solarium, and other facilities. The hotel's fashionable **Rheingrill**, recently enlarged and under new management, now ranks as one of the better restaurants in Mainz, with many appetizing seafood dishes; open evenings only, closed Mondays and Tuesdays; Tel: (6131) 24-50.

Starting from the Dom, explore the wine bars, shops, and cafés of the Altstadt neighborhoods just south and west of the Dom, clustered on Augustinerstrasse, Kirschgarten, and nearby streets. Half-timbered façades and steep slate roofs with ornate gables, elaborate moldings, and colorful trim give the area its architectural flavor, but it is the Mainzer's fondness for a good time that gives the Altstadt its character. You'll find *Weinstuben* everywhere; featuring wide selections of Rheingau and other local wines, they usually do not open until late afternoon. At Rotekopfgasse 3 (immediately behind the Gutenberg Museum), for example, is the Weinstube **Rote Kopf**, whose warm wood paneling, Art Deco lamps, and friendly service appeal to locals as well as visitors. **Kartäuser Hof** (Kartäuserstrasse 14, off Augustinerstrasse a few streets south of the Dom; open for lunch) claims the honor of being Mainz's oldest inn (the first records of it date from 1171); it has a cozy vaulted cellar with many authentic Old German details. Across the street, the **Klosterschänke**, also open for lunch, boasts a terrace shaded by two enormous chestnut trees whose roots are said to reach all the way down to the Rhine.

Mainzer nightlife reaches a crescendo at Carnival time— from New Year's Day to Ash Wednesday—when Mainzers greet one another with an exuberant *"Helau!"* Mock ceremonies lampooning German pomp and bureaucratic ritual, and parades, masked balls, and street parties are the order of the day. Mainz welcomes summer around June 24 with the three-day festival of Saint John, Gutenberg's name day. Highlights are the hilarious reenactments (on Gutenbergplatz, west of the Dom) of medieval initiations undergone by printers' apprentices and the jousting matches between boats on the Rhine. In late August and early September, the Mainzer *Weinmarkt* marks harvest time with the appropriate consumption of wine on a grand scale and a fireworks display over the river.

Above the merrymaking in the Altstadt is the **Stefanskirche** (St. Stephan's Church). From Gutenbergplatz, follow Ludwigstrasse west to Schillerplatz, then take Gaustrasse southwest one block to Ölgasse, which leads directly up to the church. Behind its plain exterior St. Stephan's shelters a set of remarkable stained-glass windows on Old Testament themes by Marc Chagall, executed between 1976 and 1979. One hundred thousand visitors annually lose themselves in the meditation-inducing blue of Chagall's windows, but many overlook the magnificent Late Gothic **cloister** adjoining the south wall of the church, considered the finest of its kind in the Rheinland-Pfalz.

Not far from the church (two blocks east down Stefansbergstrasse and then left into Ballplatz) is the moderately expensive **Drei Lilien**, the best-known French restaurant in a city not distinguished by haute cuisine. Chef Hans-Joachim Stuhlmiller's creative use of fresh local ingredients draws a mix of business and academic folk as well as out-of-towners. Tel: (6131) 22-50-68; closed Sundays and Mondays.

Southwest of the Altstadt, a few streets beyond St. Stephan's, the heights on which the Romans once built their fortifications are crowned with strips of parkland where a stroll offers a panorama of the city and the Rhine. In the southern section of the park, directly above Weisenauerstrasse (about a mile south of the Dom, with a convenient streetcar line a block away), is the ▶ **Favorite Parkhotel**. It offers modern accommodations in exceptionally pleasant surroundings, with views of the river and the park in which the hotel lies. In good weather, the large terrace is particularly appealing, and the hotel has all the facilities one expects in its higher price range.

A friendly family atmosphere and suburban setting make the ▶ **Hotel Kurmainz** an oasis of calm after a day's sightseeing in the city. The Kurmainz is on streetcar lines 10 and 11, 7 km (4 miles) west of the Rhine, among the vineyards and orchards of Finthen.

In Mainz, take the Rheinallee north to the A 643 and follow signs across the river to Wiesbaden. The number 9 bus takes you from the Mainz Hauptbahnhof to Wiesbaden, as do frequent trains.

WIESBADEN

A city of elegance and charm, Wiesbaden, west of Frankfurt right across the Rhine from Mainz, invites you to indulge your senses: to bathe in a splendid Art Nouveau setting; to taste Rheingau food and wines at their best; to enjoy music or theater in Baroque palaces; to savor a little risk at the casino or a little self-indulgence in its fashionable shops. Though it's easy to spend money here, some of Wiesbaden's most characteristic pleasures, such as strolling in the many parks or exploring the city's fanciful and extravagant architecture in the Villa Quarter in the hills just north of central Wiesbaden, are free.

Wiesbaden's center lies at the foot of the Villa Quarter, about half a mile north of the Hauptbahnhof (main train station) up Wilhelmstrasse, which bisects the city. West of the boulevard the Altstadt clusters around Marktplatz (Market Square), while the Bath District, including the Kurpark, extends eastward. Turning west from the top of Wilhelmstrasse into Taunusstrasse you will find a small park (Kranzplatz) centered around a fountain immediately on your left. People have been using the hot springs here since 3000 B.C. Those indefatigable bathers, the Romans, built their baths where today the **Kochbrunnen** fountain steams to the surface. The Romans called the baths *Aquae Mattiacorum,* "the waters of the Mattiaci" (the local Germanic tribe); in these waters many a pensioned legionnaire soothed the soreness acquired in long night watches at this outpost of the empire. Some 400 years after the Romans decamped (A.D. 400), Charlemagne's biographer Einhard was the first to record, as Wisibada, the city's present name, meaning "baths in the meadows."

The baths remained Wiesbaden's focus and source of prosperity as it attained the title of imperial city (1215). The last of the great Hohenstaufen emperors, Friedrich II, attended Mass here in 1236, having just issued the imperial decree at the Diet of Mainz by which he hoped to establish lasting peace; instead, his proclamation marked the beginning of the end of the Holy Roman Empire. Barely six years later, the archbishop of Mainz conquered and destroyed the city. When Wiesbaden emerged again it was as the ruling seat of the counts of Nassau, the family whose history was to be Wiesbaden's for the next 600 years.

Wiesbaden's 26 thermal springs produce 528,000 gallons of hot water daily. Rainwater seeping into mountain fissures heats up in the volcanic depths and bubbles out under pressure at 150 degrees Fahrenheit. The Kochbrunnen alone supplies 132,000 gallons daily to curative baths in nearby hotels and the Aukamm district, site of the largest clinics. Wiesbadeners often pause for a sip of the bitter waters that flow from the spigots under the cupola near the fountain. The second-largest spring, the Adlerquelle, rises in the **Kaiser-Friedrich-Bad**, a public bath and sanitarium a block south of the Kochbrunnen. If one of your motives for travelling is simple curiosity about people, this is your chance to encounter the Germans *hautnah* (skin-close) by joining them in their cherished ritual of steambaths and cold showers. As you enter the front hall, vibrant Art Nouveau frescoes, decorative windows, and a massive carved oaken staircase hint at luxuries to come. Within, the **Römisch-Irisches Bad** (Roman-Irish baths), opulent with marble columns and arches, majolica tiles, and bubbling basins, fulfill this promise. A ticket from the cashier entitles you to three hours of soaking, steaming, and swimming; for a few marks more, you get a private dressing room (advisable, as public ones are cramped). Towels and other accessories are available. Check the schedule posted at the entrance for times reserved for men, women, and (most popular) mixed sauna.

The Altstadt

In the narrow lanes of the Altstadt below the Kaiser-Friedrich-Bad you can browse among antiques stores and secondhand shops in the quarter called **Schiffchen** ("shuttle," as in loom), washing down the dust with a glass of cold Riesling in one of the taverns you'll find here. The crooked streets, whose names evoke the district's medieval past (Gold Lane, Ditch Street, Weaver Lane), converge on the **Marktplatz**, the focal point of the Altstadt. On Wednesdays and Saturdays the Marktplatz becomes a cheerful jumble of vendors' stands where you can haggle over homemade sausages, fresh fruit, vegetables, and flowers.

Since 1946, Wiesbaden has been capital of the state of Hesse, and the Hessian *Landtag* (parliament) meets in the Neoclassical **Schloss** (palace) bordering the Marktplatz to the northwest. The Schloss was built for Duke Wilhelm of Nassau in 1842, though he didn't live to occupy it; it sits where the castle of his ancestors probably stood in the 17th century, surrounded by fortifications of which no trace remains. Just a stone's throw across from the Schloss stands the one visible relic of that time, the **Altes Rathaus** (Old Town Hall), but restorations have left only the bare outlines of its former Renaissance glory.

The Gothic Revival **Marktkirche** (Market Church) dominates the square, its five sandstone steeples (the tallest is 290 feet) the most notable feature of Wiesbaden's skyline. Builder Carl Boos succeeded in imparting an improbable lightness to this red-brick basilica, whose lofty lines draw the eye upward. Don't miss the weekend organ concerts played on the church's two organs.

The Bath District

When the house of Nassau gained ascendancy in 1750, the city prospered, but despite half a century of recovery and growth, the Altstadt's grim history of war, plague, fire, and famine remained. In 1820 Christian Zais, the duke of Nassau's construction chief, set out to remake Wiesbaden. He cordoned off the Altstadt's bad memories in a pentangle of five broad boulevards. Then, to the east, he made a fresh start, envisioning a resort for the wealthy and titled elite who might wish "to enjoy and experience a heightened Life and a better Existence, and not to be introduced to common Scenes." When he completed his first *Kurhaus* (literally, "cure house") in 1810—far from any actual thermal springs—Wiesbaden's glory days began. When Goethe first took the cure in 1814, the city had about 4,000 inhabitants; less than a century later there were more than 100,000, of whom more than 200 were millionaires, more per capita than any other German city.

The present-day **Kurviertel** (Bath District) includes the Kurpark, a vast expanse of lawn flanked by rows of plane trees and two Neoclassical colonnades. At their far end, facing Wilhelmstrasse, is the ponderous sandstone front of the present **Kurhaus**, which has engulfed Zais's original structure. The gaming room incorporates a reconstruction of the old *Kursaal;* even if you don't try your luck at roulette or blackjack, you can enjoy a concert or a casual meal at **Käfer's Bistro**, suavely served in fin-de-siècle surroundings; Tel: (611) 53-62-00. Wilhelm exemplified Hohenzollern aesthetics in his praise of the Kurhaus as "the most beautiful in the world"; but echoes of the old Hohenzollern puritanism could be heard in his objections to some of the Art Nouveau frescoes. In fact, there was no gambling in the present Kurhaus when Kaiser Wilhelm II inaugurated it in 1907, for the Prussians had long since forbidden games of chance.

Another of the kaiser's enthusiasms was the **Hessisches Staatstheater** (Hessian State Theater), south of the Kurhaus: a private entrance for his coach allowed him to be driven through the cellars directly to his box. An opera, ballet, or play should be part of any visit to Wiesbaden. Especially during the May Festival (book well in advance), artists of international repute appear in the Staatstheater's splendidly Baroque **Grosses Haus**. For current program information and bookings, contact the Hessisches Staatstheater, Tel: (611) 13-21, or Wiesbaden tourist information, Tel: (611) 172-97-80; Fax: (611) 172-97-99.

North of the Kurhaus, across Sonnenbergerstrasse, you can

take a winding path up to the **Schöne Aussicht** (Beautiful View) district, from which the city's finest villas look out over the Kurpark. In the past century and a half Wiesbaden's growing wealth has manifested itself here in a profusion of showpieces, each house outdoing the next in grandeur. Somehow the mélange of striking details from the Baroque, Neoclassical, Gothic Revival, Renaissance, and turn-of-the-century *Jugendstil* (Art Nouveau) styles manages to form a harmonious whole. Zais, whose inspiration this Villa Quarter was, would have been pleased.

Staying, Dining, and Shopping in Wiesbaden

Wiesbaden's oldest hostelry, the ► **Schwarzer Bock** (Kranzplatz 12), has been looking out on the Kochbrunnen for 500 years, a tradition reflected in its opulent furnishings. The place has a rich history, abounding with such tales as that of Dostoyevski, who managed to stay away from the roulette wheel long enough (26 days) to write *The Gambler* here—and earn enough thereby to pay his hotel bill. The rooms are spacious and luxurious: Try for one on the courtyard with a tanning terrace. The Bock's **Bock Schänke**, a superb *Weinstube* paneled and ceilinged in oak and walnut with 16th-century carvings, is the proper place for wine and stylish company.

Back to back with the Bock, at Kaiser-Friedrich-Platz 3–4, is the more modern ► **Nassauer Hof**, a luxury hotel with a rooftop thermal pool and sun terrace; many of its rooms have fine views of the Kurpark. It also has the distinction of housing two prime eating places: the **Orangerie**, a sunny pavilion looking out on the square and featuring homey dishes served with urbane grace, Tel: (611) 13-36-33; and **Die Ente vom Lehel**, whose guiding spirit, Hans-Peter Wodarz, has been called Germany's answer to Paul Bocuse. At Die Ente (The Duck)—if you're fortunate enough to get a table—you can marvel at the spectacular presentations for which Wodarz is famous—at corresponding prices. Try his breast of quail in goose-liver gravy, or a filet steak garnished with horseradish-ginger sauce. Tel: (611) 13-36-66.

At about half the price, the ► **Klee am Park** has comfortable up-to-date accommodations in a convenient but quiet location overlooking the Kurpark, just behind the Staatstheater. Amenities include a bar, café, and restaurant, and each room has a private balcony. Unpretentious, but distinguished by its friendly, familiar atmosphere, is the ► **Hotel de France**, two blocks north of Kranzplatz on Taunusstrasse. Its loyal clientele appreciates the personal touch Frau Petra Stender-Wentz gives her hospitality.

One of Wiesbaden's chief shopping joys is a stroll up **Taunusstrasse**, which crowds enough antiques, curios, and collectibles into a few blocks to rank it alongside London's Portobello Road. From Taunusstrasse, turn south down Wilhelmstrasse for a series of ultra-chic stores on the west side of this flaglined boulevard, across from the Warner Damm park. Known as **the Rue** to Wiesbadeners, and commemorating Duke Wilhelm of Nassau, Wilhelmstrasse is where you'll find purveyors of furnishings, fashions, jewelry, and art, as well as glassed-in shopping arcades screened by hanging plants. If you need time to think carefully about an expensive purchase over a coffee, try **Café Blum** (Wilhelmstrasse 44), which has a century's experience in making Wiesbaden's favorite confection, *Nusstörtchen,* a tart with walnut-cream filling.

Outside the City

For more than a century the princes and dukes of Nassau resided not in Wiesbaden but on the Rhine just to the south, in the majestic Baroque palace in **Biebrich**. Napoleon came here in 1804 to persuade Prince Friedrich August to join his Rhine Alliance, a pact that in 1806 formally killed off the long-moribund Holy Roman Empire. Napoleon rewarded Friedrich with a dukedom, and it was as the duke of Nassau's guest that Goethe, in 1815, heard the news of Napoleon's defeat at Waterloo. A tour of **Schloss Biebrich** ends in the *Festsaal,* with its beautiful inlaid parquetry, marble columns, and frescoed cupola depicting the Olympian deities; this is where Goethe and the duke were dining when they heard the news.

Approached from Wiesbaden along Biebricherallee, which is lined with chestnuts and silver beeches, the Schloss lies at the southern end of a mile-long park in which the International Horse Show is one of the spring's splendid social events.

The best view of Wiesbaden is from the observation platform built atop the iron lampposts that once illuminated Wilhelmstrasse. The platform is atop the **Neroberg**; you can get there most scenically on the Victorian cable car. Counterweighted with 1,850 gallons of water, it trundles from the top of Taunusstrasse to the peak (altitude 800 feet). The car takes you over the vineyards that furnish Wiesbaden's prized (and pricey) Neroberger, a light, fragrant Riesling.

Five minutes from the observation platform (directional

signs mark the path) is the small, delicately domed **Russian Orthodox Chapel** (called the Greek Church) that has become a symbol of Wiesbaden. The church is the burial place of the last duke of Nassau's first duchess, Elizabeth Michalovna, niece of the tsar and a Russian princess. Beneath impressive frescoes by Hopfgartner and Jacobi, the sculptured likeness of the 18-year-old, who died in childbirth, lies atop her tomb.

From the Neroberg you can see another high point rising to the west of Wiesbaden: **Schloss Frauenstein**, about a 30-minute drive westward. From the south end of Wilhelmstrasse, take Rheinstrasse west to the Ringkirche and continue west on Dotzheimerstrasse, following the signs for Frauenstein. Entering Frauenstein village, take the first left (sign for Nürnberger Hof). A short walk north of the parking area at the road's end brings you to a curious rough stone obelisk commemorating Goethe's 1814–1815 visit. Should you come in May, the surrounding hillsides will be a white blanket of cherry blossoms, and at any season the views of the Rhine and the vineyards falling away toward it are rewarding. A one-lane farm road descends through the Herrnberg vineyards from the Nürnberger Hof to the village of **Frauenstein** below.

Here the knights of "Frowensteyn" built their Burg (fortified citadel) in the 13th century. A railed walk leads up its ruined ramparts to an overall view of the town. In its protective shadow stand a number of handsome half-timbered houses. The one directly across from the early-16th-century church may be as old as the Burg itself, but Frauenstein's oldest citizen is the gnarled linden tree in the churchyard, estimated to be 700 to 1,000 years old.

The place to eat in Frauenstein is the **Weinhaus Sinz**, where game, meat, and vegetables fresh from the area are featured and the wine is exclusively the local vintage. Try the Grorother Spätburgunder red wine if you can persuade Herr Sinz to part with some from his special stock. It is lighter and less sweet than its French counterpart, Burgundy; Frauenstein shares with Assmannshausen (see below) the distinction of being the sole producers of this wine in the Rheingau. Tel: (611) 42-13-65.

THE RHEINGAU

Sharing the same latitude as Winnipeg and northern Mongolia, the world-renowned Rheingau wine district ought to be too far north for wine growing. Yet nowhere in Germany is the climate milder than along this 45-km (27-mile) jog to the

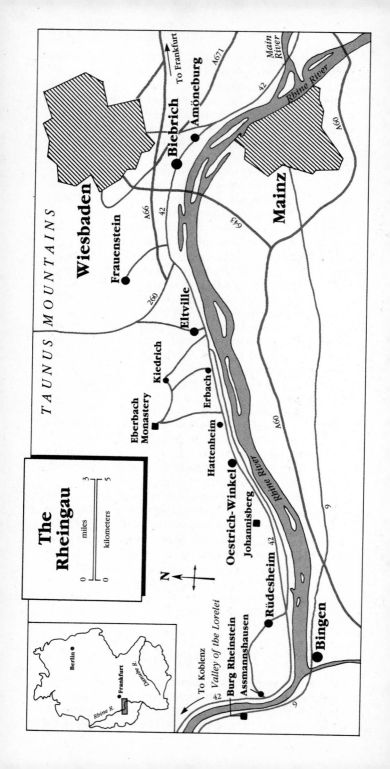

west (at Mainz and Wiesbaden) in the Rhine's generally north-ward course. The wind-sheltered southern slopes of the Taunus range, on the river's right—in this case, northern—bank, get plenty of sunshine and comparatively little rain. The Romans recognized these conditions, together with the fertile soil, as ideal for vineyards; the Roman influence on Rheingau wine is commemorated still in the distinctive glass, the *Römer,* from which it is traditionally drunk.

For centuries monks and peasants cleared and terraced the ground and planted the vineyards. Today one Rhein-gauer out of three lives, directly or indirectly, from the wine trade. The Rheingau wine grapes, not as sweet as most, produce a delicately fruity wine, full in aroma and capable of aging superbly. Eighty percent of this wine comes from the Riesling grape, and Rheingau Rieslings are considered to be among the best white wines made anywhere.

The area has more than wine, though. It contains so much of historic and scenic interest that you should plan at least two days here, and more if possible. Like its Rieslings, the Rheingau should be sipped, not gulped. Its essence is in its deliberate tempo: the quiet flow of the river, the slowly ripening grapes, the vintner's patient watch over his matur-ing wine, the centuries of weathering that have given the monasteries and castles their fabled *Romantik.*

Eltville

Of Eltville, the Rheingau's unofficial capital, right outside Wiesbaden on the Rhine's right bank (accessible by the B 42 along the Rhine or by train), Goethe wrote: "Everyone has a peaceful, by no means hurried, appearance." Thomas Mann chose Eltville as an appropriate birthplace for his charming swindler, Krull, and said of it: "Everywhere nature smiled." All this relaxed good humor may stem, in part, from the tranquil-lity of the town's historic center, directly on the river. Here, undisturbed by the highways and rail tracks that crowd the Rhine's banks farther downstream, you can stroll under plane trees along what was once a tow path as the barges chug by. The sun terrace of the **Café zur Rheinhalle** is a good place from which to watch the gulls circle the turreted tower of Eltville's landmark, its 14th-century **Burg** (castle).

For a century and a half following the tower's completion in 1348, successive archbishops of Mainz cast an acquisitive eye from its windows on the Free Imperial City of Mainz across the Rhine. Finally, in 1462, Archbishop Adolph II of Nassau conquered the prize, but the ensuing street fighting drove many of the Mainzer patricians from the city. One of those displaced was Gutenberg. Generous in victory, the mighty archbishop took the aging and impoverished inventor into Eltville castle and later made him a noble of his court, with an annual pension of one ton of grain and 2,000 liters of wine. Gutenberg in turn brought Eltville the distinction of being one of the earliest centers of printing; here he and his relatives set up a small press beside the castle. In the Gutenberg room in the castle you can see pages from a dictionary printed on this press.

The **Bechtmünzer Hof**, site of the press, is one of several imposing noble-family residences near the castle. Here, as in the neighboring complex of Baron Langwerth von Zimmern (just behind the castle, on Kirchgasse), you can visit the wine cellars for a tasting. If you prefer, like the Eltvillers, to savor their Sonnenberger Riesling on the banks of the Rhine, go to the **Gelbes Haus**, on Burgplatz, where you also get a substantial meal in the garden terrace with a river view. For help in arranging wine tastings go to the Verkehrsamt (tourist office), Schmittstrasse 2; Tel: (6123) 69-70.

In Rosengasse, among a section of pretty half-timbered houses, the 14th- to 15-century **Pfarrkirche** (Parish Church) harbors a wonderfully expressive Gothic fresco of the Last Judgment as well as a pensive Madonna, the *Madonna of the Half Moon,* the work of a 16th-century master.

The ▶ **Sonnenberg**, a small, comfortable hotel, occupies a quiet corner at the foot of the Sonnenberg vineyards at Friedrichstrasse 65.

To try the Rheingau's celebrated wines, seek out a *Strausswirtschaft*—a wine tavern run by proprietors of small vineyards on their own premises. There are numerous *Strausswirtschaften* in the area, but they are open only seasonally. This institution dates back to Charlemagne, who ordered the *Strauss* (wreath) of fir boughs to be hung out as a sign of hospitality. To protect the trade, no vintner could hang out his Strauss for more than four months a year, and each was restricted to serving his homegrown wine only. In these informal family-run establishments there is nearly always someone among the regular local customers who speaks enough English to advise you about wine, a subject that melts the reserve of even the shyest Eltviller. The proper accompaniment to the wines you will be offered are homemade delicacies such as *Handkäse mit Musik* (strong farmer's cheese with raw onion), *Spundekäs* (a soft cheese mixture), or *Hausmacher Wurst* (home-cured sausage). Strausswirtschaften are found everywhere in the Rheingau, but do not open before 5:00 P.M. Charlemagne's taste for wine was equaled by his distaste for drunkenness, and he forbade any drinking before the sounding of the wine bell at day's end or the end of Mass on Sunday.

Larger wine estates may qualify as *Gutsausschänken* (wine restaurants), operating all year and offering a wider range of food, often in a centuries-old private residence the likes of which you couldn't otherwise see. Immediately north of Eltville (going toward Kiedrich, turn right just before the Autobahn underpass and follow the "Klostermühle" signs), the historic **Klostermühle** (Eltvillerstrasse 2) is an appropriate venue to sample local Rieslings. The one-time monastery mill, with its walnut-shaded courtyard and half-timbered house, has for two hundred years been in the family of witty host Helmut Witte. The homemade appetizers he lays out on a millwheel table include a potent Handkäse called *Klosterduft,* "a whiff of the cloister." Tel: (6123) 40-21.

Kiedrich

Three kilometers (2 miles) northwest of Eltville, Kiedrich nests in the shadow of the ruined **fortress of Scharfenstein**, once a stronghold of the archbishops of Mainz. Kiedrichers are hill folk, less open and friendly than their Rhineside neighbors, with a reputation for shrewd bargaining and tight-fistedness. They keep their showpiece Gothic church, **St. Valentine's**, locked tight when there is no service. If you come on a Sunday, however, you'll hear inside this little treasure box of carved wood furnishings and tracery windows two matchless sounds: the authentic 15th-century notes of Germany's oldest playable organ, and Gregorian plainsong rendered by the Kiedrich men's choir in the Gothic-Germanic idiom now heard only here. For both of these medieval treats, and for much else that he restored and preserved in the village, Kiedrich has to thank an Englishman, Baron John Sutton; he adopted the village in the mid-19th century, and the street that leads to its famed Gothic square and St. Valentine's is named for him. In German, the first syllable of Valentine sounds like "fall"; for centuries the church was the goal of pilgrims wishing to cure the "falling sickness," epilepsy. The artistic riches of the church, which Sutton rescued after years of neglect (the chapel of St. Michael was about to be demolished and its stones used to pave the road to Eltville), stem from the gifts of the grateful healed.

A block north of the church up Suttonstrasse, turn left on Oberstrasse to find the **Gutsausschänke Schloss Groenesteyn**. A nine-generation tradition of noblesse oblige graces the hospitality offered here by your hosts, Baroness Malisa and Baron Heinrich von Ritter zu Groenesteyn, in the former bakery they have lovingly restored. The fine Rieslings they set before you come from vineyards in their family since 1640, and the warmth of furnishings hand-made from old wood matches the hearty flavor of such dishes as a Rheingauer *Winzerspiess* (vintner's kebab); Tel: (6123) 15-33.

Eberbach Monastery

Across the valley a few kilometers west of Kiedrich, **Kloster Eberbach** (Eberbach Monastery) was built up between the 12th and 14th centuries by Cistercian reformers, who were not only religious purists but also industrious wine makers. Following their ascetic rule *"Ora et Labora"* ("pray and work"), they worked so hard that the monastery, at its peak, possessed Europe's largest vineyards and its own fleet to take the wine down to Cologne for sale. Eberbach's wealth and power ultimately led to slackness, corruption, and internal dissent, and the declining monastery was practically wiped out in the Thirty Years' War. Following secularization in 1803, Eberbach passed to the dukes of Nassau; they seized choice bits to ornament their palace grounds in Biebrich and converted the dormitorium into an asylum. Since 1945 the Hessian State Wine Authority has administered Eberbach and its vineyards (still Germany's most extensive), staging artistic events and wine seminars in the restored splendor of the medieval buildings, which also provided authentic backgrounds for the film version of Umberto Eco's book *The Name of the Rose*.

The mighty Romanesque basilica, a monument of cold serenity, becomes a magnificent setting for the festivities when Rheingau vintners celebrate their Thanksgiving—on the first Sunday in December. In the apse of the church, the tombs of two Nassau archbishops are adorned by a remarkable *Resurrection,* a masterpiece of the late 14th century. The vaulted ceiling of the adjacent chapter hall is of the same era. Beneath the dormitorium, whose echoing length is matched by few Gothic halls, is the cabinet cellar; here you can taste the product of eight centuries of refinement: Eberbach's pride, the Steinberger Cabinet Riesling. For information on a week-long English-language wine seminar, including room and festive dinners in the monastery, contact the German Wine Academy, Reisebüro Bartholomae, Wilhelmstrasse 8, D-65185 Wiesbaden; Tel: (611) 13-41-01; Fax: (611) 13-41-04.

Oestrich-Winkel

Between Eltville and Oestrich-Winkel farther west along the river, the Rhine highway passes through Erbach and Hattenheim, two pretty and prosperous wine centers. **Erbach** has the famous Marcobrunner vineyard, of whose robust, full-bodied wine Prussian novelist Theodore Fontane wrote: "It's wonderful how many buffets the heart can endure if you can fend them off with a bottle of Marcobrunner." **Pan zu Erbach** is a small but elegant outpost of haute cuisine concealed in Erbach's outskirts (Eberbacherstrasse 44; Tel: 6123-635-38): For starters, have a glass of Riesling Sekt (a sparkling wine) from the restaurant's own vineyard. Stately and rather severe, as befits a Prussian palace, ▶ **Schloss Rheinhartshausen**, on the Rhine highway leaving Erbach to the west, was reopened in 1991 by Prince Friedrich of Prussia as a luxury hotel. Lavishly refitted, its three restaurants and 50 elegant guest rooms overlook a formal park toward the Rhine islet of Mariannenau, the hotel's private nature park and vineyard.

As you approach Oestrich, you'll see on the Rhine side of the road a curious squat tower with a conical roof, topped by a crane that projects over the river. For centuries, starting in the early 1500s, the **Oestricher Kran** has hoisted casks of Rheingau wine into moored barges. The crane machinery was operated by an ingenious wooden treadmill. The present structure was built in 1745. Another Oestrich landmark, the ▶ **Schwan** (Rheinallee 5–7), is the best place to stay in the area, and its riverside terrace is the best place to watch the Rhine flow past the Kran or arrange to take a cruise in one of the excursion boats that dock here. You can taste the hotel's own vintages by candlelight in its wine cellar; taste moderately, however, before mounting the winding 17th-century wooden stairway (only one flight) to your room. Just behind the Schwan's homey Renaissance horizontals rise the severe Gothic verticals of **St. Martin's**. This handsome but heavily restored church contains several interesting works, including a Late Gothic Holy Sepulcher in which three virgins in low relief seem to look askance at three drunken knaves in medieval armor.

Oestrich's twin is **Winkel**, and the two towns, with Mittelheim in the middle (naturally), form a single community "so long-drawn-out as to make those driving through impatient," Goethe commented. The 65-year-old poet had first been lured to the Rheingau by young Bettina von Brentano's seductive letters describing it. In the **Brentano-haus** (89 Hauptstrasse), Goethe's study is preserved as it was when he visited in 1814–1815. Other visitors—Beethoven, the brothers Grimm, Bettina's brother Clemens—made Winkel a focus of Rhine *Romantik* and the associated nationalism that followed Napoleon's defeat and the expulsion of the French from the area. Winkel has a culinary focus, too; the **Graues Haus** (Graugasse 10), the oldest stone-built house in Germany, is one of the Rheinland's best restaurants. Within its ivy-clad ninth-century walls, Chef Egbert Engelhardt, using fresh ingredients largely from the restaurant's own gardens, transforms sturdy Rhenish recipes into delicate fare for the discerning palate, to match the accompanying Riesling wines. These are selected by a committee of oenologists to represent the region's finest—meaning the best in the world. Dining here, you tap German wine culture's deepest sources, for the owner, Count Matuschka-Greiffenclau, descends from the oldest vintner family in Germany, with eight centuries of wine-making experience. Tel: (6723) 26-19.

For a fitting daytime prelude to an epicurean evening at the Graues Haus, visit **Schloss Vollrads**, residence of the Matuschka-Greiffenclaus, on the heights above Winkel (follow the signs from the Graues Haus). In an idyllic setting, the castle's terrace restaurant serves aristocratic Rieslings from the surrounding slopes, with piquant specialties such as jellied venison or Rheingau baker's cheese. The Rheingau has no prettier sight than the castle's moated 14th-century tower keep with its Baroque cupola, all surrounded by a stately garden. Tel: (6723) 52-70.

Johannisberg

In about 1100, the Benedictine brothers established the Rheingau's first monastery at Johannisberg, between Winkel and, to the west, Rüdesheim. Unfortunately, these monks met with less success than their Cistercian colleagues at Eberbach. Despite its excellent wines, the monastery, battered by wars and deep in debt, was dissolved in the 16th century. The abbots of Fulda (see The Center chapter) built a Baroque castle over the monastery's cellars in the 18th century, but that was bombed out in 1942, and today's Schloss is a postwar reconstruction. But one of history's happier accidents also happened here. In the fall of 1775, a mounted messenger was sent to bring the abbot of Fulda's permission for the start of the grape harvest; but the messenger was delayed, and by the time the grapes were picked they were overripe and covered with fungus. Then came the historic discovery: Instead of ruining the wine, this *Spätlese* (late harvest) actually improved it by intensifying the sugar content. Highly prized today, Spätlese wines are also high priced, because late picking reduces the wine's volume.

Goethe's best-loved stroll from the Brentano house was into the vineyards below Johannisberg, and the Brentano housekeeper was shocked at the amount of Schloss Johannisberg 1811 the great man could put away. Heinrich Heine later exclaimed: "*Mon Dieu!* If only I had the faith to move mountains [*Berge*]! The Johannisberg would be the *Berg* I'd summon, wherever I was!"

Schloss Johannisberg has been a possession of the house of Hapsburg ever since the Austrian emperor presented it in 1816 to the wily chancellor Metternich, who retired here to scheme out a new Europe after the Congress of Vienna and who asserted of his feeling for the Rheingau, "The Rhine flows in my veins." Visit the 900-year-old cellars for a taste of the wine that inspired poets and statesmen, and visit the Schloss for its unmatched views.

Rüdesheim

Like a lot of travellers, the tranquil Rhine loses its composure at Rüdesheim, where it plunges into the turbulent Bingen gorge. Though a canal was blasted out here in 1935, Rhine captains still take a pilot through the gorge, whose once-wild waters prompted many a medieval merchant to leave his ship at Rüdesheim and go overland to Lorch (or vice versa). The city prospered as a Rhine harbor. Now it is tour buses that harbor here; Rüdesheim (on the B 42, 6 km/ 3½ miles from Johannisberg) embodies Rhine *Romantik* for three million visitors a year, and its hotels and taverns thrive.

Rüdesheim has always been someone's gold mine. In the 13th century the archbishops of Mainz squeezed river tolls out of Rhine ships from a former Frankish castle. Today known as the **Brömserburg**, the castle houses a fascinating museum of wine making. The display of more than 1,500 drinking vessels reminds visitors that wine has also, since Roman times, brought riches to Rüdesheim. Later, the archbishops moved a mile or so downstream for an even tighter grip on the Rhine's gorge from **Schloss Ehrenfels**. Their toll booth was the **Mäuseturm** (Mouse Tower), a fortification on a rocky islet below Ehrenfels. Legend has it that the cruel and miserly Archbishop Hatto, whose granaries bulged while the peasants were starving, was devoured in the tower by mice from one of his own grain stores. The tale reflects the commoners' view of the extortionate prelates from Mainz—but in fact the word *Mäuseturm* derives from *Maut* (toll). Now the restored tower is a navigational aid and, like the ruins of Ehrenfels, a romantic milestone along the Rhine.

Little remains of three other castles, besides the Brömserburg, that once guarded Rüdesheim, but town houses built by lords still ornament the city's center with their Gothic slate roofs, bay windows, and half-timbering. The best known is the **Brömserhof** on Oberstrasse (at the head of Drosselgasse), a picture-book example of Late Gothic residential architecture; it now houses a display of automated musical instruments.

If a stroll down Rheinstrasse reminds you of a seaside

boardwalk minus the beach, a turn up **Drosselgasse** places you firmly back in Romantic Germany; you can't mistake the aromas of sizzling bratwurst and wine and the thumping rhythm of drinking songs coming from the many taverns packed into its 158-yard length. Right in the middle of it all, the ▶ **Lindenwirt**, with its vaulted cellars, bedrooms tricked out to look like wine casks, and a talking suit of armor named Kunibert, offers concentrated doses of extroverted *Romantik.* The quiet ▶ **Central Hotel** (Kirschstrasse 6), directly opposite St. Jakob's church, is a pleasant family-style hotel with quite a good restaurant.

Niederwald and Assmannshausen

Atop the grandiose **Niederwald-Denkmal** (monument) over Rüdesheim a 32-ton bronze lady called Germania reminds us that Rhine *Romantik* is tied historically to the German long-ing for a national identity. The tide of nationalism rose through the 19th century to flood proportions following Germany's victory over France in 1871, and on that tide Bismarck launched the Second German Reich. "The Rhine is Germany's river, not its boundary," proclaimed Romantic poet E. M. Arndt in 1813; 60 years later, Germania raised the imperial crown above the river, representing an attempt to recapture the glories of the past. The effort was doomed; the near-assassination of Kaiser Wilhelm I at the monument's inauguration was a portent of the Second Reich's eventual fate. Take the cable car from Oberstrasse at the head of Drosselgasse, or drive east on Oberstrasse to Grabenstrasse: Follow signs up to Niederwald-Denkmal.

The hotel ▶ **Jagdschloss Niederwald**, where in 1948 Kon-rad Adenauer presided over the meeting of leaders that produced the *Grundgesetz,* the Federal Republic's equivalent of a constitution, is a 20-minute walk through the woods west of the Niederwald monument. The state of Hesse modernized the hotel, formerly a hunting lodge, in the 1960s, without sacrificing its pleasantly old-fashioned charm. Rooms are large and the setting lovely.

Assmannshausen, a short, scenic cable-car ride away from the Niederwald-Denkmal, is a smaller and quieter version of Rüdesheim. You can relish its main attractions simulta-neously: a glass of fine Spätburgunder, sipped on the Rhineside terrace of the hotel ▶ **Krone Assmannshausen** at the foot of the Hollenberg vineyard from which the wine comes. Although it has been in existence since 1541, the Krone most vividly evokes the Romantics of the early 19th century. The Freiligrath room commemorates the fiery poet Ferdinand Freiligrath, who completed his revolutionary

Glaubensbekenntnis (credo) here in 1844, following which he lost his government pension and had to flee to England. Manuscripts and autographs of other Romantic figures are also on view. The Rhine is your companion in the Krone's spacious dining room, where you can dine in style on the freshest fish and game. The Krone's new management has spent freely to equip its spacious, splendidly furnished rooms with every imaginable luxury (suites even have their own sauna). It's no secret that a stay here can be the high point of any visit to the Rheingau, so book well in advance. Try for a room in one of the corner bays, with views of the river and the famed vineyards.

VALLEY OF THE LORELEI

Beyond Rüdesheim, the Rhine races through the Binger Loch (gorge) and resumes its mostly northward course toward the sea. From Bingen (on the Rhine's west bank opposite Rüdesheim) you follow the river for 60 km (37 miles) north to Koblenz on the B 9, through the valley of the Lorelei, where the swift current has gouged a sinuous bed between terraced, forested cliffs of slate towering hundreds of feet above you. With its dramatic scenery, its legends, its wine, its pretty towns graced by medieval churches and lofty fortresses, the valley of the Lorelei is still seductively veiled in the mists and clouds of German Romanticism. (See the map of the Mosel Valley, in the chapter of the same name, for a map of the valley of the Lorelei.)

From her perch on the sheerest of these precipices (on the east bank near St. Goarshausen), the Lorelei, a legendary siren, is supposed to have lured voyagers to their destruction on reefs still visible today. Clemens von Brentano based his first novel, *Godwi,* on the legend, and in 1827 Heine immortalized the golden-haired temptress in his poem *"Die Lorelei."*

For most of its history, the Rhine gorge between Bingen and Koblenz hindered and frightened more travellers than it enchanted. The place is also the setting for a body of grimly fascinating Rhine legends, such as those of the Nibelungen, the warrior dwarfs who guarded a fabulous treasure—the Rheingold—in the cliffs of the gorge. Merchants and pilgrims on the Rhine avoided this stretch of the river or, if necessary, made a white-knuckled, prayerful passage through its narrows and rapids. Those who escaped the dwarfs and the reefs still had to cast an apprehensive glance at the looming Gothic castles, from which parties of armed toll collectors were all too likely to descend.

With Germany's reconquest of the Rhineland from France in 1814, a wave of Romantic enthusiasm brought the first travellers who came to see the valley of the Lorelei, rather than merely to survive it. Many of them were English, inspired by the adventures of Byron's gloomy wanderer Childe Harold, whose creator toured the Rhine in 1816—even before the first steamboat braved the river as far up (south) as Koblenz. By the mid-1820s boatloads of diligent English tourists were careening past the Lorelei, prepared to exchange their sterling for improvised lodgings, leftover wine, and souvenir etchings of dubious quality. Hardship and danger were all part of the romantic thrill of a Rhine cruise in the 19th century.

Though the hardships are fewer nowadays, the valley of the Lorelei still offers most of the scenic charms of the past century. Foremost among them is the dramatic beauty of the Rhine gorge itself, through which the river prowls past rocky cliffs and deep, vineyard-clad side valleys that appear by turns starkly shadowed or blindingly sunny. You can join a boat cruise at any of the riverside towns, and many of these outings feature wine-tasting and sightseeing stops along the way. Historic structures such as churches, city walls, and towers ornament the communities, as do some grim and grand castles. Some of the latter offer accommodations at costs surprisingly low in view of their amenities (saunas, swimming pools, and effectively restored medieval surroundings—not to mention memorable views). It is possible to see a good sampling of both sides of the Rhine in one very busy day, but two to three days allow you more leisure to attune your hearing to the Lorelei's siren song.

Bingen

Directly across the Rhine from Rüdesheim (see The Rheingau, above), and reached by car ferry, Bingen grew up around a Roman fort guarding the heights between the Rhine and the mouth of the river Nahe, which itself drains a well-regarded wine-growing region and flows into the larger river here. Drusus Germanicus, the younger brother of Emperor Tiberius, made his name—literally—by keeping the German tribes down; he may have built the original wooden bridge across the Nahe, around 10 B.C. A thousand years later Archbishop Willigis of Mainz constructed the present **Drususbrücke**, probably the oldest surviving stone bridge in Germany, on the original Roman foundations about half a mile south of the Rhine.

Crowning Bingen's central hill on the site of the Roman fort, **Burg Klopp** houses the city's administrative offices in a handsome stone palace, a 19th-century reconstruction in the gabled Late Gothic style. Parkland and vineyards surround the Burg, which you can reach from the Rhine side by a steep stairway leading up the hill from Bürgermeister-Frans-Neff-Platz, or by car from the east over a bridged moat by way of Mariahilfstrasse (there is a parking area just outside the moat). From the Burg's pleasantly shady grounds, an airy view across the Rhine of Rüdesheim, Ehrenfels castle, and the Niederwald monument rewards your efforts.

From Burg Klopp, follow Rochusallee (from the east end of Mariahilfstrasse) 2 km (1½ miles) up to the church of St. **Rochus**, perched on vineyard-clothed heights looking out over the Rhine. Pilgrims flocked to the original 17th-century chapel to appeal for St. Rochus's help against the Black Death. Destroyed by German artillery during the French occupation in 1795, the church was hastily reconstructed in 1813, when St. Rochus's intervention was again urgently needed: Napoleon's armies, now in headlong retreat from their defeat at Leipzig, had brought typhus to Bingen. Goethe describes the St. Rochus festival of August 1814, following the consecration of the rebuilt church, and its processions, feasting, and much wine. The surrounding Rochusberg park has inviting footpaths.

Back in town, between the Rhine and Burg Klopp, a lively pedestrian zone leads you from the foot of the Burg down Basilikastrasse west to the Nahe and Bingen's stately Gothic basilica of St. **Martin**. (Don't panic when all roads seem to lead back to the water: Remember, two rivers come together here.) An 11th-century crypt, in which some remains of a Roman temple have been found, is the oldest surviving part of the church, which went up in flames along with most of Bingen in the great fire of 1403 and has been rebuilt and restored frequently since then. One work of art survived the fire—an enthroned Madonna and Child from about 1320 (northeast corner of the church, near the crypt)—but the finest pieces are the lovely early-15th-century figures of Saint Catherine and Saint Barbara gracing their respective altars to the left and right of the nave.

A few blocks north and east of St. Martin's, you can stroll through Bingen's gracious park along the Rhine, past the docks of the various cruise boats plying the river; you can also cross over to Rüdesheim in a car ferry from here. Facing the river (and, unfortunately, the busy railway tracks) is a whole row of hotels on the Rheinkai, across the tracks from the park; the chief virtue of their rooms and restaurants is the view. Most put out tables on the street in good weather, and conviviality reaches its height here during the first two weekends of September, during the Bingen wine festival.

Castles on the Rhine

Leaving Bingen by rail or car (via the B 9) toward the west, you cross the Nahe and pass Bingerbrück, an important rail junction. Just off the west bank, the **Mäuseturm** appears on its islet in the Rhine. This was once the toll station of the archbishop of Mainz (see the section on Rüdesheim, above). A chain anchored at the foot of the tower spanned the river to Ehrenfels castle on the opposite bank, blocking passage until long-suffering Rhine skippers crossed the palms of the archbishop's toll collectors with sufficient silver. A ruin in the 18th century, the Mäuseturm was restored in its present late Gothic picturebook style by Prussia's king, Friedrich Wilhelm IV in 1855 for the more benevolent purpose of aiding navigation.

Directly above the road, 3 km (2 miles) beyond the Mäuseturm, **Burg Rheinstein** clings to its cliff as naturally as if it had been growing there for millennia. In fact, Rheinstein castle in its present form dates back only to the 19th century. In 1825 Prince Friedrich Ludwig, a cousin of Friedrich Wilhelm IV, employed Karl Friedrich Schinkel, virtuoso of the Gothic Revival, to rebuild what was then the ruin of Schloss Vogtsburg, as it had been known for 600 years. Dubbing it Rheinstein, the prince turned his 13th-century rubble heap into a romantic fantasy with Gothic battlements and turrets where the Prussian aristocracy, dressed up in "authentic" costumes, could play at Middle Ages. Leave your transportation at the parking lot and walk up the winding path (15 minutes) to the castle for the short tour, offered daily in season. It features delicate frescoes by Ludwig Pose and some lovely cast-iron staircases among other period details, with fine views of the Rhine and Assmannshausen from the castle's terraces.

Linked to Burg Rheinstein by legend as well as history, **Burg Reichenstein** is about 1½ km (1 mile) farther north on the B 9 (in the village of Trechtingshausen, turn left at a sharp angle off the B 9 at the sign for Burg Reichenstein). Legend has it that the handsome Kuno von Reichenstein loved the lady of Rheinstein (or Vogtsburg, as it was then), but her family had pledged her to marry a rich old knight. Luckily, as the wedding procession set out from Rheinstein, a horsefly stung the bride's mount, and the runaway steed took her straight to the arms of her lover in Burg Reichenstein. History tells the less-romantic tale of Philip von Hohenfels and his son Dietrich, the robber knights of Burg Reichenstein, who so assiduously "robbed the ladies, imprisoned the clergy, mistreated their vassals and plundered merchants," according to one complaint, that in 1253 the

League of Rhenish Cities razed the fortress. The indefatigable von Hohenfels family rebuilt it, and it had to be pulled down once and for all by King Rudolf of Hapsburg (see the section on Speyer, below) in 1282. Rudolf put an end to the robber knights by the simple expedient of beheading them; the executions took place at the Early Gothic **Clemenskirche** (Church of St. Clemens), one of the oldest and prettiest churches on the Rhine (from Trechtingshausen, follow the camping signs across the railway and up the Rhine through orchards and gardens about 1 km/½ mile to the church in its riverside cemetery; not open to visitors). For centuries largely a ruin, in 1899 Reichenstein came into the busy hands of Baron Nikolaus Kirsch-Puricelli, whose family manufactured cast-iron stoves. He restored the Burg in grandiose Romantic style. You can visit its salons, bedrooms, library (complete with concealed staircase), business office, chapel, and battlements, all in one entertaining (if somewhat chronologically confusing) tour. The Burghotel, just north of the castle gate, is small and in need of repair; but the grounds and view are still delightfully unspoiled.

Four kilometers (2½ miles) north of Trechtingshausen on the B 9 lies Niederheimbach, the western terminal of a car-ferry service to Lorch on the east bank.

Lorch

Besides making a pleasant excursion across the winding Rhine, a side trip to Lorch allows a stroll (plentiful parking in the riverside park in front of the city gates) through a quiet, picturesque Rhine village that played an important role in history. Medieval merchants who dreaded the swift whirl of current at Bingen could unload the goods they had brought by ship this far up the Rhine and pack them through the Taunus hills south to Rüdesheim or Geisenheim in the placid Rheingau. Lorch grew up on the mouth of the river Wisper, thriving on the wood and wine trade as well as on the skills of its weavers. The finest extant example of this prosperity is the **Hilchenhaus**, whose noble façade rises above the Rhine in Renaissance step gables crowned with mussel-shell ornamentation. The city honors its builder, Johann Hilchen, a 16th-century imperial field marshal, with an annual wine festival celebrated in Renaissance dress. Just north of the Hilchen house, a steep cobbled lane leads to the church of **St. Martin**, where Hilchen's gravestone, bearing his coat of arms, can be seen. A magnificent 15th-century carved altarpiece, one of the finest in the Middle Rhine, depicts Saint Martin, patron of wine makers, and the Virgin. At her feet kneel the master carvers who created this work.

Bacharach

Returning to the west bank of the river, 4 km (2½ miles) beyond Niederheimbach, you enter Bacharach. Here, cut off from the Rhine by the railway and the B 9, half-timbered houses with steep Gothic slate roofs line the bank and a narrow valley. For Victor Hugo, who visited here in 1838, Bacharach was a "fairytale village, drenched in saga and legend." Hugo describes the Ara Bacchi (Altar of Bacchus), a rocky outcrop in the Rhine just downstream from Bacharach, where according to legend burnt offerings to the Roman wine god ensured a good vintage. The legendary rock didn't long survive the romantic French novelist's visit; unromantic German engineers considered it a navigational hazard and blasted it out of the water around 1850. Nor is it any longer thought that Bacharach's name derives from that of the vinous deity; instead, it has been traced to the Celtic *Baccaracum* (settlement).

Nevertheless, for centuries Bacharach and wine were practically synonymous. Until the Thirty Years' War, all wine shipped down the Rhine was indiscriminately called "*Bacharacher*." The wine that had come through the perilous Binger Loch—on craft small enough to navigate the narrows—was stored, traded, taxed, and reshipped from Bacharach.

A stroll along the 14th-century **city walls** from one medieval tower gate to the next affords views of the Rhine on one side and the village on the other. From the market square, almost everything worth seeing can be encompassed in a glance: the handsome Gothic Peterskirche, the Alter Posthof with its half-timbered gables and courtyard, and the well-known **Altes Haus**.

Built in 1568, the Altes Haus is one of the few structures that survived the manifold occupations and destructions that beset Bacharach in the 17th century. Behind its charmingly crooked, steep-roofed façade, crowded with flower boxes and tracery windows, you can partake of ponderous Rhineland fare in one of several beamed and paneled rooms heavy with atmosphere. (Take home a souvenir brochure bearing a sketch of the Altes Haus by Hugo himself.) Around the corner, at Rosenstrasse 16, is the **Jost Beerstein Factory Outlet**; even if you don't find the array of German crafts to your taste, it's an economical place to buy the sort of gifts people expect you to bring back from the Rhine. Though there are no hotels of distinction in Bacharach, adequate rooms simply furnished can be found at the ► **Altkölnischer Hof** (two doors south of the Altes Haus) and at ► **Zur Post**, Oberstrasse 35, near the market square. Both have beautiful *Fachwerk* (half-timbered) exteriors and atmospheric dining rooms. (For more on *Fachwerk* see the Odenwald section, below.)

Directly south of the Peterskirche on Oberstrasse, a flight of one hundred steps leads to the famed **Wernerskapelle** (Chapel of St. Werner). Built at the end of the 13th century to commemorate a youth who purportedly was the victim of ritual murder by Jews (a tale refuted by modern scholars), the chapel was not completed for 140 years; then it was destroyed in the 17th century. By the beginning of the 19th century the ivy-covered roofless ruin was one of Bacharach's romantic sights, and its legend was echoed by Heine in "The Rabbi of Bacharach." (Don't climb all those steps unless you want exercise—the chapel is boarded up for repairs.)

The finest view of Bacharach is from its medieval fortress, **Burg Stahleck**. Most of its present inhabitants don't mind the steep 15-minute climb from Blücherstrasse above the market square—since 1926, when it was restored, the Burg has been a youth hostel. From the medieval gate tower at the end of Blücherstrasse you can drive to the Burg, by way of Steeg, between steep vineyards; from Steeg, keep left through the forest up to the Burg. Begun in the 11th century, the Burg served as a Hohenstaufen stronghold until the interregnum of the 13th century; it then became the site of the hotly disputed 1314 election, which finally named Ludwig IV of Bavaria as Holy Roman Emperor. The Burg's massive walls also looked down on the festivities when Emperor Charles IV consolidated his iron grip on the Rhine by marrying Anna, daughter of the prince elector of the Pfalz, in 1349.

The Pfalzgrafenstein and Kaub

About 4 km (2½ miles) downstream from Bacharach, rounding a river bend on the B 9, you catch your first glimpse of one of the most remarkable of the Rhine's castles, the **Pfalzgrafenstein**. Rising out of an islet in the center of the stream, the Baroque-turreted Pfalz looks like a red-and-white fortified steamer plowing up the Rhine. Take the Engelsburg auto ferry over to Kaub on the opposite bank; from Kaub you can visit the castle via a second ferry (time for transit and tour is about one hour). The Pfalz was first built in 1327 by Emperor Ludwig IV in order, as his political opponent Pope John XXII complained, "to squeeze out even more harshly . . . his cursed taxes and tolls." Increasingly heavily fortified, the Pfalz carried on despite the pope's excommunication of Ludwig. Its toll collectors, sounding trumpets to halt passing ships, boarded and searched them mercilessly for contraband. Always vulnerable to high water, the Pfalz is entered through a gateway in the third story that is defended by a portcullis and surmounted by the quarters of the commandant.

Kaub, known since the 14th century for its slate quarries from which came much of the Rhineland's roofing material, also benefited from the toll station; sailors and passengers had to come ashore for food and accommodations while fees were being settled. The best known of the inns that catered to this trade was the 18th-century **Stadt Mannheim**, from which Field Marshal Blücher directed on New Year's Eve 1813 the monumental Rhine crossing of 83,000 Prussian and Russian troops on their way to Paris in pursuit of Napoleon's armies. Today the Stadt Mannheim has been converted into the **Blücher Museum** (Metzgergasse 6), exhibiting documents, weapons, and portraits associated with Blücher and the Napoleonic Wars. **Burg Gutenfels**, high above the town, dates from 1200. Until recently this scenic oft-restored fortress served as a popular city-run hotel; now, however, it is privately owned, and its massive gates open only for a select clientele. Its bulwarks have reverted to their medieval function of keeping the common folk out.

Oberwesel

About 3 km (2 miles) below the Engelsburg ferry (again on the west bank), visitors get a hearty welcome at the delightfully romantic ▶ **Burghotel Auf Schönburg**. High above the village of Oberwesel is perched the handsome 12th-century **Schönburg castle**, which for more than 500 years was the property of the Schönburg family and is now the hotel. The castle was burned and pillaged by Louis XIV's rampaging troops in 1689, and the Schönburg clan died out a few decades later. This tragedy is not surprising, in view of the stubborn virginity attributed to the seven lovely and legendary Schönburg sisters, who were driven out of their home and across the Rhine by a sudden onslaught of frustrated suitors one misty morning. Father Rhine is said to have commemorated the proud ladies and their stony virtue in the form of seven man-killing reefs that plagued rivermen passing Oberwesel until the mid-19th century, when dynamite finally forced the maidenly barriers. In 1885 an American industrialist (with the unlikely but appropriate name of T. I. Oakley Rhinelander) purchased and began restoring the dilapidated Schönburg castle, a labor of love that ended only with his death more than 60 years later. The **Restaurant auf Schönburg**, occupying the proud towers and medieval chambers of the restored castle, combines the charm and atmosphere of a romantic past with modern service and comfort, as does the hotel. Reserve a table or accommodations as far in advance as you can, particularly for weekends; Tel: (6744) 70-27. In view of what it offers, the hotel is still very reasonably priced.

Despite some ill-advised 19th-century planning for railways and highways, Oberwesel is distinguished by its unusually well-preserved **city walls** and fortified towers. Back in the 1850s, when the railroad was still a novelty, enterprising Oberweselers vied to have the tracks laid as close as possible to their inns, so that guests could enjoy watching the trains pass. Today the most prominent fortified tower, the 14th-century **Ochsenturm**, trembles as the trains brush past its inland side, while the B 9 traffic whizzes by on the Rhine side. Serene above the turbulence of modern life, however, stands Oberwesel's great treasure, the Gothic **Liebfrauenkirche** (Church of Our Lady), often referred to by locals as the "red church" because of its red plaster exterior (closed for restoration until mid-1993). The high altar, constructed in 1331, is one of the oldest and most beautiful of its kind. With a double row of expressively carved saints and apostles, it depicts events in Christ's redemption of man, centered on the crowning of the Virgin. All but three of the figures that were lost in a sensational 1975 robbery have been recovered, but access to the high altar is understandably restricted. (Apply at the Verkehrsverein across from the Rathaus to arrange to see the altar close up, or for information about organ concerts.) Fine side altars in the north and south choirs are devoted, respectively, to Saint Nicholas, patron of sailors, and Christ and the Apostles with Mary and Martha. Both were donated around 1500 by Canon Peter Lutern, whose memorial stone carved by the famous master Hans Backoffen graces the west side of the south aisle. Carved memorials of the Schönburg clan, vivid 16th-century frescoes, and many other details make a visit to this church fascinating.

Apply at Bäckerei Heinrich, at Rathausstrasse 14, for admission to the Oberwesel **Bakery Museum**, whose four-century-old oven still produces incomparable German bread. Oberweselers join visitors in praising the food at the gabled, half-timbered ▶ **Weinhaus Weiler**, directly behind the Rathaus. Chef Klaus Weiler livens up typical Rhineland cuisine with such ingenious surprises as a spinach-strawberry salad in lime dressing or cream of fennel soup with a dash of Pernod. This unassuming but well-managed family concern makes guests feel at home with smiling service and a pleasant traditional atmosphere in tastefully rustic rooms.

The Lorelei and St. Goar

Below Oberwesel, the Rhine foams through a narrowing channel between steeper and steeper cliffs until it reaches the fabled Lorelei. Here the river passes a rock face on the east bank towering 433 feet above it. For ages rivermen feared this passage and wove stories around the echo that followed them through it: In the cliff's caves lived a tribe of dwarfs, warrior guardians of the golden treasure of the Nibelungen. Today the roar of auto and train traffic on both banks has drowned out the echo, but the somber cliff looming over the Rhine has lost none of its fascination. In 1801, in his first novel, *Godwi,* Clemens von Brentano invented the legend of a golden-haired temptress calling to passing ships from the heights; 22 years later Heine immortalized Brentano's siren in the poem *"Die Lorelei,"* which begins *"Ich weiss nicht, was soll es bedeuten, dass ich so traurig bin"* ("I know not what this sorrow of mine may mean"). You too will be sorry—if you join the masses who drive to the top of the Lorelei, unaccountably compelled to visit the only spot in the area from which its chief attraction is not visible.

Seven kilometers (4 miles) downstream from Oberwesel, the lively, colorful town of **St. Goar** has since the sixth century been the home of the Rhine pilots who guide river traffic through the Lorelei narrows. But the relation between town and Rhine shipping has not always been friendly. St. Goar's redoubtable fortress, **Burg Rheinfels**, was built on the heights above the town in 1245 by Count Diether III of Katzeneln-bogen, one of the toll-collecting lords who preyed on passing ships. Only a decade after the construction of Rheinfels, 26 cities of the Rhine Alliance, fed up with the count's extortionate rates, unsuccessfully besieged his castle for more than a year—the first of many sieges the mighty fortress withstood. Finally, at the end of the 18th century, the French brought down its walls for good. Today the ▶ **Schloss Hotel auf Burg Rheinfels** (at the top of Schlossbergstrasse) once more stands for a warm welcome to travellers, who can enjoy views of the Rhine from its newly renovated, modern rooms. The present-day tariff, though still higher than average, is justified by the amenities offered, which include indoor swimming pool, sauna, and fitness center. The hotel occupies the restored part of the ruined castle, and you can take a tour of the medieval battlements followed by a quick swim or dinner on the outdoor terrace.

Below, in town, the Protestant **Stiftskirche** (Collegiate Church), on the Marktplatz just east of the railway station, dominates St. Goar with its Gothic tower. Built on the foundations of an earlier Romanesque church by the counts of Katzenelnbogen in about 1469, the Stiftskirche is dedicated to St. Goar, whose image appears repeatedly among the church's delicate, pastel-toned Late Gothic **frescoes**. The saint himself came to the Rhine from Aquitaine in the sixth century, and tales of miracles wrought at his grave made the town's fortune as a place of pilgrimage until the Reformation lowered the stock of saints.

St. Goar is further blessed with several agreeable middle-priced hotels and a very good place to eat, all on the same street. Next to the Stiftskirche at the south end of Heerstrasse, the ▶ **Hotel am Markt** is convenient, quiet, and friendly, with views of the Rhine. A few steps down the street, Sebastian Burch not only offers clean, comfortable rooms at the family hotel ▶ **Zur Lorelei**, but has also built a local reputation for the best food in town. Try Burch's Lorelei steak, which comes to your table sizzling on a hot slate slab.

On the east bank, across the Rhine from St. Goar and linked to it by a convenient ferry, **St. Goarshausen** is a small community watched over by Wilhelm II of Katzenelnbogen's 14th-century Gothic castle, usually referred to as **Burg Katz**. Count Wilhelm's "Katz" was his response to the construction by his rival, the archbishop of Trier, of **Burg Maus**, a similar fortress at Wellmilch, 2 km (1¼ miles) down the Rhine. Though Burg Katz was destroyed by Napoleon in 1806, the restored fortress of the robber knights served in modern times to house retired officers of the German federal revenue service, a turn of events that draws ironical smiles from local taxpayers. Burg Maus has also undergone extensive restoration and today is the setting for three falconry exhibitions daily (in season, at 11:00 A.M., 2:30 P.M., and 4:30 P.M.; Tel: 6771-76-69 for information).

Boppard

Tucked into an elbow of the Rhine 12 km (7½ miles) north of St. Goar and just south of Koblenz at the mouth of the Mosel, Boppard is a compendium of Rhineland attractions: Roman walls and medieval fortress, Gothic churches, Renaissance half-timbered houses, Rhine wines, and Rhineside hotels. Entering the town from the south on the B 9, follow the parking signs to the Marktplatz in the center of town. Unlike most Lorelei valley towns, Boppard has not allowed the highway and the railroad to sever it from the Rhine. The city's tenacious hold on the river dates back to the middle of the fourth century A.D., when the Roman emperor Julian ("the Apostate") anchored the Roman Limes (fortified boundary) here with a fort called "Bodobrica." Parts of the massive **Roman foundations** can still be seen (south of the Marktplatz at the top of Kirchgasse, for example), and elaborate baths have been found under the Marktplatz itself.

A century later the Roman baths became baptismal basins after early Christians turned the bathhouse into a church. The fifth-century church was succeeded by the Romanesque **St. Severus**, which today dominates the Marktplatz; on the floor of St. Severus you can still trace the outlines of the earlier building. As you enter from Kirchgasse, notice inside on the righthand wall a stone with two stylized birds; this is a memorial, dating back to A.D. 500, to one Besontio, a deacon of the earlier church. St. Severus, completed around 1234, boasts an early Gothic masterpiece: the great crucifix over the high altar, considered one of the finest examples of its period.

Boppard enjoyed the power and privileges of a Free Imperial City until 1312, when Emperor Heinrich VII presented both Boppard and Oberwesel to his brother Baldwin, archbishop of Trier, to whom the townspeople were required to swear oaths of fealty. The resentful citizens of the proud Rhine city balked, and eventually Baldwin had to besiege and storm Boppard. Baldwin then built, just east of the Roman walls (one block north down Burgstrasse from the Marktplatz), the 1327 fortress known as the **Alte Burg** (Old Fortress), of which only the original tower remains. In it (and in the newer, 18th-century parts of the Burg) Boppard's **Städtisches Heimatmuseum** (Civic Museum) invites you to visit a cabinetmaker's workshop, a forestry museum, and displays from Roman and prehistoric times. But the proudest exhibit is a gallery of lovely bentwood furniture created by Boppard's best-known native son, Michael Thonet, the founder of the firm that furnished the cafés of Vienna, Paris, and the world with the familiar bentwood chair. It is doubtful whether Baldwin's own seat in this fortress on the Rhine was ever so comfortable.

As the wine and shipping trade grew and Boppard flourished, its noble families dwelt in increasing luxury. Two blocks east of the Alte Burg along the Rheinallee you come to a fine example, the meticulously restored Late Gothic **Ritter-Schwalbach Haus**. Stroll back down the Rheinallee past other imposing façades to find the 14th-century **Karmeliterkirche** (Church of the Carmelites), where the Ritter (Knight) Siegfried von Schwalbach himself stares combatively out from under his helm on a memorial stone. It depicts with appropriate ferocity the man who died in 1497 leading Boppard's unsuccessful resistance to the elector of

Trier's conquering forces. The church's rich collection of Late Gothic art is one of Boppard's gems.

Boppard's 3-km- (2-mile-) long **Rheinallee** is a busy and colorful riverside promenade lined with hotels, cafés, and boat landings, all competing for your attention. Queen of the lot is the luxurious ▶ **Bellevue Rheinhotel**, near the Alte Burg. Relatively expensive, the Bellevue is a fine old *Jugend-stil* (Art Nouveau) dame with her turn-of-the-century airs and graces still intact, despite the thoroughly modern facilities (sauna, steambath, pool, and tennis). Rooms 412 to 416 have terraces on the Rhine; the rooms in general are spacious and handsomely furnished. Have a festive dinner in the hotel's **Pfeffermühle** dining room, where you can have, for example, a Belle Rose mystery aperitif followed by a Swabian snail plate and medallions of wild boar stuffed with mushrooms in red-wine sauce.

A few blocks up the Rheinallee, the ▶ **Rheinlust**'s moderately priced rooms also overlook the river. Service here is professional but cordial, and the wines decanted in the hotel's two good restaurants come from the famous **Bopparder Hamm**. This slate-covered slope, situated downstream and around the bend of the Rhine north of Boppard, rises at such a steep angle that wine growers practically have to rope up to tend their vines. Don't miss the truly spectacular view of the Hamm and Boppard from the **Vierseenblick**, high above the "bendiest bend" in the Rhine. From the east end of the Rheinallee, cross the B 9 and go under the railway bridge, following the "Sesselbahn" signs. A thrilling 20-minute chair-lift ride and a brief walk bring you to the clifftop café and lookout point: a surefire photo opportunity.

Take the ferry across the Rhine from Boppard to the B 42 on the east bank and drive downstream for an almost equally dramatic view of these vertical vineyards from the road between Filsen, where there are some fine *Fachwerk* houses, and Osterspai. In about 8 km (5 miles) you'll reach **Braubach**, the northern terminus of our Lorelei valley route, triumphantly crowned by the **Burg Marksburg**. Never successfully besieged, this regal 13th-century fortress is the only castle on the Rhine that has withstood the centuries intact. The counts of Katzenelnbogen were responsible for its construction around 1283 on an older foundation, insuring their grasp on Braubach's profitable lead and silver mines. Though never taken by storm, the Marksburg suffered from neglect over the centuries as it lost its strategic significance. Following its acquisition by the German Castle Society in 1900 it was painstakingly restored by Bodo Ebhardt to serve as the society's headquarters. Today a tour of the castle (open daily) with its authentic and reconstructed furnishings and collections of medieval weapons makes a fitting climax to a trip through the valley of the Lorelei.

THE ODENWALD

Coming south from Wiesbaden on the eastern side of the Rhine, the A 5 at Darmstadt (29 km/18 miles due south of Frankfurt) begins to parallel a line of steep castle-crowned hills overlooking the Rhine valley. These heights are the western edge of the Odenwald (Oden Forest) upland, whose ancient woodlands and narrow winding river valleys are rich in medieval legend. Medieval, too, seem its towns, with their half-timbered buildings clustered around market squares, carved stone fountains, and arched bridges. The Odenwälders themselves keep old-fashioned trades alive—farming, ivory carving, beekeeping, and innkeeping—but they live very consciously in the 20th century. Many commute to work in the industrial centers beyond the Neckar, which bounds the Odenwald to the south near Heidelberg. Others take advantage of the Odenwald's own industry, the tourist and health-resort trade. Fresh mountain air, spring water, and a judicious use of Frankfurt ad agencies keep their ubiquitous little pensions and hotels full of German vacationers as well as foreign guests, so advance bookings are advisable.

Measuring some 50 miles long (between the Main and the Neckar) by about 40 miles wide, the Odenwald is compact enough to "do" in a day or so, but its storybook scenery, hearty food, and mild, sunny climate often cast their delaying spell; three or four days are none too many.

Darmstadt

The bombs of 1944 left intact little of the former capital of the grand duchy of Hesse-Darmstadt (population today, 140,000), and the postwar economic success has overwhelmed what remained in cement waves of modern construction. The most significant survivor is the Jugendstil artists' colony on **Mathildenhöhe**, the eastern heights of the city. At the turn of the century, the last grand duke of Hesse, who was himself only 21, brought together a group of young German-speaking artists whose goal was not just to produce art, but to live it. On the Mathildenhöhe they built homes, studios, and exhibition areas based on their own design philosophy, and in 1901 they staged their first and most original exhibition, A Document of German Art. A walk

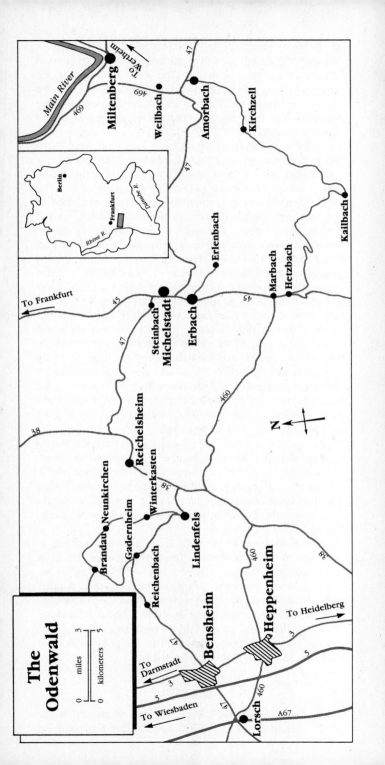

through the area today will recall some of the freshness and daring of that artistic vision. The stark boldness of the **Hochzeitsturm** (Wedding Tower), in particular, will surprise those for whom Art Nouveau has come to mean flowery trivia; it was built on the occasion of the grand duke's marriage in 1907.

From Mathildenhöhe, less than a kilometer west down Dieburgerstrasse, you come to the historic center of the city and Darmstadt's **Schloss**, immediately north of the Markt-platz, which is a busy pedestrian shopping zone. The Schloss, a charming accumulation of seven centuries of German architecture, is worth visiting for its furnishings and collections. Its finest possession is the *Madonna of Burgo-meister Meyer,* a masterpiece of Renaisssance character por-trayal painted in 1526 by Hans Holbein the Younger. Also among its respectable collection of Old Masters is Pieter Brueghel's last work, *Magpie in the Gallows* (1568). The Schloss looks north across Friedensplatz to the Neoclassical façade of the **Hessisches Landesmuseum** (Hessian State Mu-seum), built in 1902 to house the collections of the grand duke. The museum's attempt to display objects in an authen-tic environment reflects the influence of Art Nouveau ideas: Roman finds are displayed in an atrium, Gothic religious art in a Gothic chapel. One flight down from the Roman exhibit you pass through a beautiful display of Art Nouveau objets d'art, jewelry, and furniture to a wonderland of stained-glass windows glowing in a dimly lit hall.

Beyond the museum, the former Schloss park, the **Herrn-garten**, stretches north in a refreshing expanse of lawns, paths, and trees. On its northeast corner, in the Prinz-Georg-Garten, the Rococo **Prinz-Georg-Palais**, often called the **Porzellanschlösschen**, harbors the grand-ducal porce-lain collection, including pieces of Sèvres, Meissen, Wedg-wood, and Kelsterbach.

The ▶ **Weinmichel** is ideally located across the street to the west of the museum at Schleiermacherstrasse 10–12. It has recently undergone discreet renovation and offers ac-commodations moderate in price. The restaurant, popular with locals, has an excellent wine list. Near the Hauptbahn-hof, west of the center, is the ▶ **Maritim Rhein-Main Hotel** (Am Kavalleriesand 6): Behind its plate-glass exterior, 115 rooms are equally contemporary. This is a popular stop for business folk from Frankfurt and Mainz.

Lorsch

Today an unremarkable village of small shops and farms, Lorsch, about 25 km (15 miles) due south of Darmstadt on the A 5, A 67, or B 3, was once a spiritual and political power center of Charlemagne's empire. The slight elevation that kept it dry during the Rhine's periodic floods made Lorsch a north–south crossroads and a gateway to the Odenwald. Here the Romans erected a temple to Mithras, and here in 767 an abbey was founded that, under imperial patronage, was to achieve immense influence and wealth. A beautifully preserved remnant of that glory is the **Königshalle**, the triumphal gateway through which Charlemagne paraded into the abbey of Lorsch in 774 to dedicate its new church. The emperor made the Lorsch abbots independent princes, answerable only to Rome and to himself; many were imperial relatives. During the next two centuries the abbey acquired enormous holdings through patronage; in turn, it bolstered the emperor against rebels and spread Christianity through the pagan darkness of the Odenwald, founding many churches and monasteries. Today the Königshalle is the only intact edifice of the Carolingian Renaissance remaining in Germany. Emblematic of Lorsch's importance as a cultural crossroads, its steep-pitched Germanic royal hall (with festive Gothic frescoes) rests on the classical arches and pillars of a Roman triumphal gate.

The interior of the Königshalle is expected to remain closed to visitors through 1993 while its frescoes are being restored. However, a brand-new museum is scheduled to open late in 1993, directly across Nibelungenstrasse from the Königshalle. The **Lorsch Museum Center** will focus on the history of the monastery but will also display Hessian folk art (previously housed in Darmstadt's Landesmuseum) and the contents of the tobacco museum originally in Lorsch's handsome Rathaus.

You can admire the turrets and gables of the Rathaus while cooling off with Frau Dreyss's homemade ice cream at the **Café am Kloster** on the square between the Rathaus and the Königshalle. For the serious appetite, head for the popular restaurant **Zum Schwanen**, down Nibelungenstrasse. Antique curios occupy the space here not filled with diners intent on Heinz Metz's French-accented New German cuisine. Reserve in advance, or come very early; Nibelungenstrasse 52; Tel: (6251) 522-53.

About Fachwerk

With its mild winters, plentiful wood, and skilled native craftsmen, no region met the necessary conditions for the building of *Fachwerk* (half-timbered) houses better than the Odenwald. The frames of heavy squared timbers were assembled on the ground according to coded marks, then hauled upright with block and tackle or windlasses manned by chanting villagers. Wooden pegs or large iron nails held the frames in place, while spaces between the beams were filled with the most convenient and economical materials at hand: wattle and daub, stone, brick, timbers, or plaster. Fachwerk's endlessly varying patterns give the Odenwald villages much of their charm, and you could hardly find a more delightful introduction to the technique than the village of **Heppenheim,** 5 km (3 miles) east of Lorsch and once its possession. Coming into Heppenheim on Lorscher Strasse, continue east to Grabenstrasse (where parking is available) and walk one block up to the market square. Its central fountain is a good vantage point from which to take in the surrounding 16th-century façades, each prettier than the next.

The Nibelungenstrasse

East from Lorsch you can explore the Odenwald along the Siegfriedstrasse, by way of Heppenheim, or the Nibelungenstrasse, which begins at Bensheim, a few kilometers north. From Bensheim, follow the B 47 northeast through the Lauter valley to the foot of the Neunkirchener heights, then southeast to Lindenfels and generally eastward to Michelstadt and Amorbach, where the Nibelungenstrasse follows B 469 north to Miltenberg on the Main. Conjecture makes one of the abbots of Lorsch the author of the *Nibelungenlied,* that grim and vengeful epic of the winning of the warrior maid Brunhilde through Siegfried's magical prowess, and his death by Hagen's dagger beside a forest spring. The Odenwald, hunting ground of the Nibelungen, is dotted with enough "Siegfried's Springs" to backdrop half-a-dozen Wagnerian arias. About 8 km (5 miles) along the Nibelungenstrasse beyond Bensheim, turn left (north) at Reichenbach on the Lauter to see the first of these springs. In this case, though, the fatal spring, which is about 1 km (½ mile) from Reichenbach, is only incidental to the main event, the **Felsenmeer** (Sea of Boulders). Produced perhaps by a legendary battle of Titans, or perhaps as the result of granitic erosion, these photogenic rock cascades (some bearing the marks of Roman quarriers) tumble down from a ridge that commands a fine view of the forested valley. (A trip to the Felsenmeer makes a nice weekday hike; it gets crowded on weekends, however.)

Neunkirchen and Lindenfels

At the Brandau junction, 11 km (7 miles) east of Bensheim, just before Gadernheim, turn left off the B 47 and follow the winding secondary road 3 km (2 miles) north to Brandau, and then 4 km (2½ miles) east to Neunkirchen. The German passion for unsullied mountain air and long walks has made Neunkirchen, the highest village in the Hessian Odenwald, a popular health resort. Founded by the abbey of Lorsch in the 13th century, the village church occupies the site of an earlier chapel dedicated to the twin saints of healing, Cosmos and Damian.

Neunkirchen's true patron spirit is no saint, but a tormented ghost. The lords of **Schloss Rodenstein**, whose ruins lie a mile east of Neunkirchen, held the village and its environs from the Middle Ages until the last one died of plague in 1671. The tale is told of the 14th-century knight Hans von Rodenstein, who won a beautiful lady in a tourney in Heidelberg, then basely deserted her. Dying in battle, the unchivalrous knight was doomed to be hunted ever after by the hounds of hell, who chased him across the lonely peaks of the Odenwald. Through the ages, Odenwälders have heard—but not seen—repeated passages of the knight's spirit, a droning, wordless wail suddenly traversing a cloudless sky, presaging fire and war if it comes to the ruined castle, but a good omen if it flies north.

From Neunkirchen it is a scenic 8 km (5 miles) due south back to the B 47 (Nibelungenstrasse) at Lindenfels (by way of Winterkasten). Like Neunkirchen, **Lindenfels** lives on air. Perched on a high ridge from which five river valleys fall away into the blue distance, it offers pine-scented breezes to refugees from urban smog. Fill your lungs well before mounting to the **castle** ruins: The ascent is short, but the view from the remaining ramparts is breathtaking. Erected in 1123 by the first Hohenstaufen emperor, Conrad, the castle survived countless assaults and sieges, mostly while it was in the possession of the electors of the Palatinate, only to be ignominiously sold and pulled down for building materials at the end of the 18th century. On your left as you descend from the castle along Burgstrasse, the city museum, housed in the medieval **tax house**, has four floors of ingenious displays recreating the daily life of an Odenwald village since medieval times (open Sunday and holidays, 9:00 A.M. to 4:00 P.M.).

"The Pearl of the Odenwald," as Lindenfels likes to be called, is a good base for exploring the surrounding hill country. Pick up a *Wanderkarte* (hiking map), as the forest is laced with trails of every imaginable length and degree of difficulty. You won't soon forget the tranquil beauty of the landscape through which they take you.

Lindenfels has many pensions and hotels. Especially central is the well-reputed ► **Hessisches Haus**, which faces the castle and the lion's head fountain. Directly across Burgstrasse from the hotel, the **Altes Rauch'sches Haus** has home-made confections and good, solid Odenwald food. Both of these establishments are at the heart of the festivities on the first August weekend when Lindenfels celebrates its Castle and Costume Week with folk dancing, singing, and parades.

Michelstadt and Erbach

Every German community believes that its Rathaus is the fairest in the land. Surely the most photographed is the one in Michelstadt, on the eastern side of the Odenwald, 25 km (15 miles) east of Lindenfels on the Nibelungenstrasse (and also on route B 45, which runs south from Frankfurt). Framed between the flower-decked fountain and the Gothic steeple of the church behind it, the Michelstadt **Rathaus** adorns countless brochures and guides. Go a long block up the main street and turn right into Erbacherstrasse to find Chef Günter Steinbach's **Brasserie**. The specialty here is local fish and game freshly procured and served according to regional recipes; Tel: (6061) 33-63. Around the corner from the Rathaus, at Grossegasse 17, the ▶ **Grüner Baum** claims a 300-year history, which the photogenic building reflects (perhaps too abundantly) inside and out. The rooms are small, tidy, and laden with tradition.

After Charlemagne died in 814, his son Louis presented Michelstadt to the emperor's courtier and friend Einhard, who retired here to begin his *Vita Caroli*. The pious biographer, who was also an abbot, built a church in Steinbach (the town through which the Nibelungenstrasse enters Michelstadt) and stocked it with the requisite relics, which he had sent his secretary to filch from the graves of Christian martyrs in Rome. Not much remains of the **Einhardsbasilika**—what you see is largely restored—but just down the path, on the wooded bank of the river Mümling, is the lovely Renaissance **Schloss Fürstenau**. Originally a moated 13th-century stronghold of the archbishops of Mainz, the castle was rebuilt later by the counts of Erbach, who added its graceful and distinctive arched gateway. (Open to visitors weekends and holidays, 9:00 A.M. to 4:00 P.M.)

The elegant Baroque façade of **Schloss Erbach**, since 1736 the residence of the counts of Erbach, forms the west side of the market square in **Erbach**. Behind it, the stern cylinder of the castle keep, a remnant of the original 13th-century fortress, looms above an array of Renaissance and 18th-century buildings. The castle's several museums are as worthwhile for their vaulted Gothic interiors, stained-glass windows, and parquet floors as for Count Franz I's collections of armor and weapons, Roman artifacts, stuffed animals, and objets de vertu. On the square, a colorful farmers' market is held on Saturdays against the festive backdrop of the castle, the Mümling and its bridges, and the half-timbered buildings of the **Städel**, Erbach's medieval mini-village. You can watch the action on the square from the terrace of the riverside **Brauerei Ausschank**, across from the castle. This one-time brewery in an 18th-century building serves locally brewed beer and plain regional dishes in a pleasant atmosphere; Tel: (6062) 57-32.

Ivory carving, brought to the Odenwald from Africa by Franz I in 1783, still thrives despite restrictions on the elephant ivory trade. Local craftsmen are switching to mammoth tusks, preserved for 10,000 years in Siberian icefields. Although the town's plethora of ivory shops is unlikely to escape your notice, for the best introduction to the carver and his work visit the **Deutsches Elfenbeinmuseum** (German Ivory Museum), whose informative and exhaustive ivory exhibit is open daily (the carving workshop is closed Mondays). Entering Erbach from the north on the B 45, turn left on Obere Marktstrasse and left again at the first parking area you reach.

At Bahnhof Strasse 21, just south of the square, you can watch master potter Hermann Dönig and his son Bernd at their potter's wheel, continuing a 350-year family tradition of Odenwald ceramics as they turn out dishes, bowls, pitchers, and a thousand other forms; their patterns are naïve folk motifs in red and beige, blue and green. Beekeeping, another ancient tradition, is practiced by Hermann Gabel in nearby Erlenbach. He welcomes English-speaking visitors, and you can call to arrange a visit to his *Imkerei* (apiary); Tel: (6062) 48-46 or 25-37. Candles, candy, and cosmetics, all made of honey, are for sale.

Amorbach

The **abbey church** in Amorbach, 25 km (15 miles) east of Erbach on the Nibelungenstrasse, is a particularly beautiful example of Late Baroque architecture. Starting in the eighth century, the abbey was the nucleus around which Amorbach grew. As it celebrated its first millennium in 1734, it was in the hands of the archbishops of Mainz, under whom Mainz was experiencing its Baroque flowering. Shortly before the French Revolution put an end to the power and glory of the Church's earthly dominion, church architecture had reached its peak of opulence. Amorbach's church was one of many Romanesque and Gothic churches transformed by Baroque builders such as Maximilian von Welsch, court architect to the archbishop. Von Welsch retained the church's twin Romanesque towers as he conceived the restrained and harmonious sandstone façade above which they now rise. Within, outstanding stuccowork by Bavarian masters Uebelherr and Feichtmayer magically blends with Matthäus Günther's fascinating trompe l'oeil effects. Come on Wednesdays, Fridays, or Saturdays at 1:00 P.M., or 11:00 A.M. on Saturdays, from May to October, to enjoy an afternoon concert on the famous organ, which has 3,000 pipes and is one of Europe's largest Baroque instruments. The abbey tour includes another Late Baroque gem, the **library**, housing 30,000 volumes collected by the prince of Leiningen, now proprietor of the abbey.

Amorbach boasts two hotels with a storied past. The ► **Post** (Schmiedstrasse 2) traces its lineage to 1546 and was once a post station; its rooms, in a modern addition behind the restaurant, are quiet and comfortable. The homier, more picturesque ► **Badischer Hof** (Am Stadttor 4) groups its rooms around the former farmyard, which now serves as a garden café. The hotel's Biedermeier charm brought physicist Max Planck back year after year. Both hotels have good restaurants.

Miltenberg

In a deep bend of the river Main, 10 km (6 miles) north of Amorbach on the B 469, the wealthy merchants of Miltenberg lined both sides of their long Hauptstrasse with imposing medieval and Renaissance houses, Fachwerk abutting Fachwerk all the way from the foot of the Burg (fortress) to the massive city gate on the Main bridge. Midway down this parade of patrician pomp is ► **Zum Riesen**, which claims to be the oldest hostelry in Germany—its first guest having been Emperor Frederick Barbarossa in 1158. Other guests in its annals are Martin Luther, Albrecht Dürer, Richard Strauss, Franz-Josef Strauss, and an endless list of kings, generals, and notables. Accommodations in its undeniably atmospheric precincts range from regal to merely comfortable, and a tiny elevator supplements the spiral staircase. In the adjoining restaurant you can dine on such favorite medieval delicacies as bear chops, stuffed partridge, veal with smoked oysters, and shredded ox marinated for two weeks and flavored with 22 herbs, washed down with quince wine.

Miltenberg began as a Roman fort on the Main where the Limes (fortified imperial boundary) emerged from the Odenwald to run north along the river. The archbishops of Mainz, their eyes fixed firmly on potential income from river traffic, built the Burg about 1200, and the merchant community prospered in its protective shadow, as evidenced by the Gothic grandeur of the **Altes Rathaus**, now called the Merchants' Hall, on Hauptstrasse. Here goods were stored and traded, and duties were levied.

Miltenberg's prettiest corner is its **Marktplatz**, from which a low gateway leads through the Schnatterloch tower (where witches are said to have been burned) up to the Burg. The ► **Weinhaus am Alten Markt** has attractive, moderately priced rooms, many with views over the square (request a room with a bay window). A few steps away on Hauptstrasse—and farther up the price scale—the ► **Altes Bannhaus** offers uncluttered, quiet rooms. In the medieval cellars of the Bannhaus, once a prison, such specialties as venison liver grilled with sesame, partridge terrine with homemade quince jelly, and dove stuffed with chanterelles and garnished with Port sauce are served with unobtrusive attentiveness; Tel: (9371) 30-61.

The Nibelungenstrasse continues northeast (upstream) along the Main toward Wertheim, in the direction of Würzburg; or you can return to Amorbach to pick up the **Siegfriedstrasse**. The latter runs southwest from Amorbach through Kirchzell to Kailbach, then swings northwest to join the B 45 at Hetzbach. From there it runs north to Marbach and follows the B 460 back to Heppenheim—yet another route through the endlessly scenic Odenwald. Contact the German National Tourist Office for detailed information on the Siegfriedstrasse and the Burgenstrasse (see below).

CASTLES ON THE NECKAR

From Heilbronn, a medium-size town north of Stuttgart, the river Neckar winds north and west across the southern flank of the Odenwald and past Heidelberg toward its rendezvous with the Rhine at Mannheim. You can follow the river down the **Burgenstrasse** (Castle Road), which begins to the southwest in Nürnberg and of which this section, along B 27 and B 37, is the northwestern end. A gentle landscape of vineyards, fields, and orchards alternates with the somber beauty of wooded hills, which predominate as the river nears Heidelberg. For centuries a trade artery carrying wine, wool, wood, salt, and iron, the Neckar provided natural sites for fortified castles, protecting their approaches while offering their lords transportation—and often booty. Now highways and railroads flank the Neckar, but its valley is still as beautiful as in 1878, when Mark Twain wrote in *A Tramp Abroad,* "There is no pleasanter place . . . than a raft gliding down the winding Neckar, past green meadows and wooded hills and

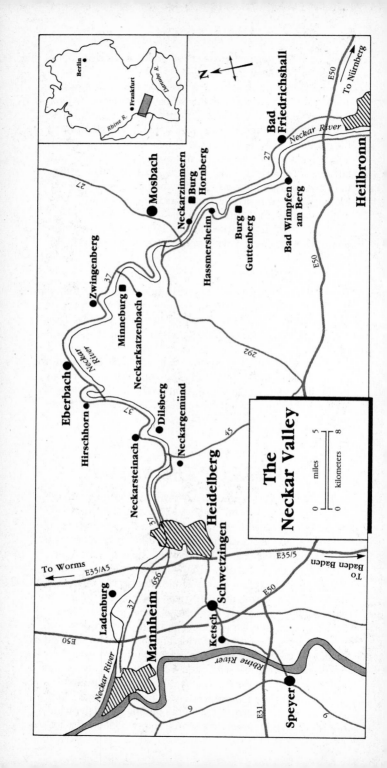

The Neckar Valley

miles 0 — 5
kilometers 0 — 8

slumbering villages, and craggy heights graced with crumbling towers and battlements."

Bad Wimpfen

Twain's famous raft trip down the Neckar was imaginary, but he did tour the river area by boat, carriage, and train. He spent his first night at Bad Wimpfen, describing it as "very picturesque and tumble-down, and dirty and interesting." **Bad Wimpfen am Berg**, high above the Neckar northwest of Heilbronn, is an acropolis-like walled city whose fortifications Barbarossa laid out in the 12th century. The best time to visit here is early in the morning, before the tourist buses arrive, when the cobbled streets lined with half-timbered, window-boxed medieval houses are still slippery with dew.

A short walk up to the highest part of the **Altstadt** (Old City) and along the Burgviertel brings you to a courtyard on the left at number 19. Here, from the arcade of Barbarossa's **Pfalz** (imperial palace), you can watch the mists rising from the river. The arcade's graceful columns framed the same view for Barbarossa's successors as they strolled through the great hall of the palace (of which the arcade is the only remnant) on their way to the chapel at its west end. Today the restored chapel serves as the town's **church museum**, open daily except Fridays from March to mid-October.

From the chapel, a passage at the back of the imperial gallery provided an escape route to the nearby Roter Turm in case of attack. Walk along the rebuilt ramparts leading to the **Roter Turm** (Red Tower) to appreciate medieval siege mentality. Scenic as they usually are, the Burg sites were chosen for defensibility, not for the view. Several lines of defense barred the besiegers' way: first, a difficult approach, such as a moat; then a battlemented wall with massive iron-reinforced gates and corner towers from which the wall could be swept by defensive missiles. Once through the outer wall the attacker faced a walled inner courtyard, containing the actual palace and dominated by the *Bergfried* (keep). Bad Wimpfen's Roter Turm served the lords of the Burg as a last refuge under siege; it had living quarters, a hearth, arched niches, and even a WC (at the end of a long, zigzagging passage, to discourage odors). A secret tunnel connected the keep's basement with the outside world.

The town's landmark is the Gothic turreted and spired **Blauer Turm** (Blue Tower), whose top, 196 steps up, offers a fine vantage point overlooking Bad Wimpfen's medieval core. Here—where watchmen kept their vigil for fire or an approaching enemy—at noon on Sundays you can hear the fanfares and alarums of the tower trumpeters. The hotel adjacent to the tower, the ▶ **Blauer Turm**, offers panoramic views from its rooms and a breezy terrace where you can have *Maultaschen* (meat pies) high above the Neckar. Nearby is the **Steinhaus,** once the queen's dwelling and one of the largest surviving secular Romanesque buildings. Now a museum, it houses displays of medieval armor, weapons, furnishings, tools, and art, as well as artifacts from the salt industry, long a major source of income for Bad Wimpfen.

The town's prosperity reached its acme in the 15th century when, as a Free City, it joined the influential Swabian League, but the terrible 17th century saw it twice occupied, pillaged, and burned to the ground. Few of the Fachwerk houses along Klostergasse and Hauptstrasse predate the Thirty Years' War, and those, handsome as they are, represent but a shadow of the town's former riches.

As an official *Kurort* (health resort), Bad Wimpfen has plenty of accommodations. The ▶ **Sonne**, in two 16th-century half-timbered houses, combines a cheerful, homey atmosphere and central location (where it has been for four centuries) with moderate prices. If tramping the battlements has given you a hearty appetite, try the **Gasthaus Barbarossa** on the shady Marktplatz for roast pork with fine herbs and *Spätzle* or their special *Wimpfenertopf* (stew).

Down on the edge of the river below, **Bad Wimpfen im Tal** was known as Cornelia in the days when Roman sentries sent up smoke signals from their wooden watchtowers. This was one of the strongest anchor points of the Limes, the 300-mile-long fortified road that was the empire's northeast frontier from the Danube to the Rhine. On the foundations of the Roman fort stands the church of Sts. Peter and Paul, now part of a Benedictine abbey. Its notable **cloisters** illustrate the decline of the Gothic from 13th-century opulence to 15th-century austerity.

Burg Guttenberg

On the west bank of the Neckar, continue north from Bad Wimpfen (follow signs for Heinsheim) through an exceptionally lovely stretch of wooded hills. Seven km (4 miles) along, on a high ridge between the Neckar and Mühlbach valleys, Burg Guttenberg may forever form your image of the complete medieval castle. Its preservation has been in the capable hands of the Gemmingen family since 1449, when Hans von Gemmingen paid 6,000 guldens for it. Its uncompromisingly square Hohenstaufen tower keep betrays its 12th-century origins, when vassals of the emperor held Guttenberg. During the Reformation it became a refuge for hunted Lutherans, but the Gemmingen family, though staunch Protestants, were clever enough to play one side against the other during the Thirty Years' War and so preserve Guttenberg from the reduction to rubble suffered by many such castles.

By turns amusing, fascinating, and horrifying, the six-tiered **Burgmuseum** takes you through the castle's past. Tin soldiers fight out the battle of Wimpfen (1622) on a dusty plaster plain; an ivory ladies' flea-catcher reminds you of the casual approach to hygiene that prevailed; and instruments of torture bear witness to the right of high justice exercised by the lords of Guttenberg for 400 years. Most memorable of all is the twice-daily (March to November) display of falconry staged on the castle's Neckar valley terrace. Claus Fentzloff keeps and trains more than 100 birds of prey at Guttenberg, helping replenish threatened species by periodically releasing young eagles, falcons, hawks, and owls bred in his aviary. The beauty and the savagery of the Middle Ages are both manifest in a falcon's deadly swoop on the bait. After the show, have a hot *Würstchen* and a cold beer in the **Burgschenke**, adjoining the Burg.

The Hornberg and the Minneburg

Below Burg Guttenberg, follow signs for Gundelsheim across the Neckar bridge and north along the east bank on B 27 to the next town, Neckarzimmern. As you enter it, follow the sign pointing the way up to ▶ **Burg Hornberg**. At the surprisingly luxurious hotel of the same name right in the castle precincts, balconied rooms open on views of the forest or (more expensive) the Neckar; the view is an attraction they share with the rather pricey restaurant specializing in local fish and game. Tel: (6261) 40-64.

The dominant figure at Burg Hornberg had an iron fist; since he bought the castle in 1516 with the ransom wrung from a hapless captive, the one-handed robber-knight Götz von Berlichingen has been identified with Hornberg. Twain reports: "In an assault upon a stronghold in Bavaria, his right hand was shot away, but he was so interested in the fight that he did not observe it for a while." Goethe made Götz a romantic hero in the eponymous play, idealizing him considerably, but it is historically accurate that he led a band of rebels against the oppressions of the feudal lords—his own class—during the Peasants' Revolt in 1525. The castle, from which Götz conducted raids on Neckar shippers to finance his campaigns, is as satisfyingly picturesque a ruin as the old rascal himself must have been before expiring at the unusually ripe age of 82.

The B 27 turns east, away from the Neckar, at mostly modern Mosbach (3 km/2 miles beyond Hornberg), whose

Marktplatz is a lovely oasis of medieval houses. Outstanding in the richness and variety of its Fachwerk is the **Palm'sches Haus** (1610), across from the 16th-century Rathaus.

Downstream from Mosbach, now along the B 37, the Neckar valley narrows and deepens, edged by steep, forested slopes. As you go north along the east bank, the ruined towers of the **Minneburg** loom above the trees on a bluff across the river. Cross the bridge here, at Neckargerach, and continue about 5 km (3 miles) inland to Neckarkatzenbach, where a right turn at the fountain before the village takes you another mile to a parking place on the Schlossberg. From here, a pleasant 45-minute stroll along a broad level path leads to the castle of Minneburg, whose mossy remains date largely from the 16th century. The Minneburg can only be reached on foot, and the quiet beauty of its surroundings remains undisturbed except for the occasional picnicker.

Schloss Zwingenberg

Six hundred and fifty feet above the Neckar, beyond the village of Zwingenberg farther down route B 37, Schloss Zwingenberg is not only not a ruin, it is the handsomely preserved residence of the margravine of Baden. Tours are conducted from 2:00 to 5:00 P.M. on Tuesdays, Fridays, and Sundays, and you should not miss this chance to see a particularly fine castle (tours are in German, but the guide speaks some English). If you leave your car in the parking lot of the last restaurant downstream, you can walk (15 minutes) up the **Wolfschlucht**, a heavily wooded, idyllic gorge. The path circles behind the Schloss to its entrance. The tour gives you fascinating glimpses of the stronghold from which the 14th-century nobles of Zwingenberg preyed on river traffic; so merciless were they that in 1364 the Palatinate and Württemberg sent a combined force to seize and raze the castle. The Schloss was closed in 1992 for renovation but is expected to open again in 1993. Beyond the Schloss, the Wolfschlucht path goes on up past Gothic crags and waterfalls through the romantic scenery in which Carl Maria von Weber set his opera *Der Freischütz* in 1820. A milestone of German Romanticism, the opera is performed annually in late August in the open courtyard of Schloss Zwingenberg.

Eberbach to Neckarsteinach

Staying at the ▶ Hotel **Krone-Post** in Eberbach, 9 km (5 miles) west down the Neckar from Zwingenberg, may be as close as you can get to the sort of raft cruise Twain fantasized.

Your room has a window over the Neckar, and you dine on a grape arbor–shaded terrace overlooking the river. On Eberbach's historic market square, a few paces inland, facing the 15th-century Rathaus, is another hotel, the ▶ **Karpfen**; you can't miss its façade, which is covered with frescoes depicting the city's prominent figures and events. The service is friendly and personal, and the food consistently good. At the **Altes Badhaus** restaurant on Lindenplatz, a few blocks west of Marktplatz, chef Uwe Zöller prepares fish and game specialties with an original touch. A sure instinct for public relations has helped the Badhaus's gourmet fare win recognition throughout southwest Germany; Tel: (6271) 710-57. For an informal meal from the same kitchen go downstairs to the **Badstube**; try the *Kaninchen* (rabbit) ragout with marjoram sauce and *Bubespitzele*.

The Neckar nearly ties itself in a knot at **Hirschhorn**, 9 km (5 miles) below Eberbach. Dominated by its 12th-century **castle** (much of it later rebuilt), Hirschhorn's medieval houses cluster around the 15th-century **Carmelite abbey church**. Here you can see some interesting, though over-restored, 16th-century frescoes. Up on the Burg, a café terrace looks out across the river's hairpin bend and beyond into the lush Odenwald. Twain, who described Hirschhorn's "packed and dirty tenements," would delight in today's tidy and conscientiously restored village, whose 17th-century half-timbered façades invite you to explore its lanes; especially noteworthy are the riverfront houses built next to or on the old city wall. At number 25 on Hauptstrasse, which parallels the Neckar, the **Weinstube zum Hirsch**, in a building that dates in part to 1621, features such delicacies as home-smoked salmon created from an old Norwegian recipe.

Downstream 9 km (5½ miles) from Hirschhorn, just past Neckarsteinach, a path leads from the roadside parking area, on the right, up the hillside past three of the town's four castles. Persevere until you reach the **Schwalbennest**, highest and prettiest of the four, about half an hour's hike from the road. The restored watchtowers of this early-13th-century ruin afford a fine view of Neckarsteinach, the river, and the fortified village of **Dilsberg** on the opposite bank. The B 37 crosses the Neckar at Neckargemünd a few kilometers downstream. Coming off the bridge, turn left onto Hauptstrasse and head back upstream toward the village. Imagine, Twain suggested, "a comely, shapely hill, rising abruptly out of the dead level of the surrounding green plains ... and with just exactly room on the top of its head for its steepled and turreted and roof-clustered cap of architecture," and you have Dilsberg as it still looks today. The prince-elector took refuge here when the French overran

Heidelberg castle, and Dilsberg's walls held General Tilly at bay in 1622 and 1629, during the Thirty Years' War. Not until 1827 was the central fortress dismantled. From the 52-foot-high defensive wall you can look deep into the Neckar valley across grazing lands and forest toward Heidelberg. Below the fortress wall, the restaurant **Zum Deutschen Kaiser** offers homemade sausages and pastries, and a terrace with a view; Tel: (6223) 21-86.

Back in Neckargemünd, the colorful, tradition-rich ▶ **Hotel Zum Ritter** has many rooms overlooking the river and the dock used by cruise boats. The river traffic serves as a background to meals in the glassed-in terrace, one of the Heidelberg region's most popular dining spots.

HEIDELBERG

Like most European cities, Heidelberg has a modern and a historic face. Unlike most, however, its Altstadt is not its center but its eastern extremity: a long wedge of slate-roofed sandstone buildings jostling for space along the narrow south bank of the Neckar. The Altstadt began upstream under the protective ramparts of the elector's hillside castle; through the centuries it edged westward down the river, squeezed between the last heights of the Odenwald. Reaching the Rhine plain, Heidelberg at last expanded into the Weststadt, whose research towers, high-tech industries, and chain hotels form most visitors' first, rather disappointing, impression of "romantic" old Heidelberg.

From Bismarckplatz, Heidelberg's present-day center, a walk east along **Hauptstrasse** into the Altstadt takes you progressively back in time. Hauptstrasse is now a broad and busy pedestrian mall, but narrow medieval lanes on both sides frame glimpses of looming green hills, including, to the south, the Königstuhl (Throne), and to the north, the Heiligenberg (Holy Mount), omnipresent representatives of State and Church.

The **Kurpfälziches Museum**, at Hauptstrasse 97, about halfway to the castle, is prettily housed in an early-18th-century *palais* with a courtyard café. The museum's masterpiece is Tilman Riemenschneider's 1509 altarpiece of Christ and the Apostles, their realistically carved faces gaunt with pathos. Anthropology buffs will seek out the cast of the 300,000-year-old lower jaw of *Homo heidelbergensis,* discovered in the vicinity 80 years ago. Not far from the museum, the restaurant **Zum Güldenen Schaf**, at Hauptstrasse 115, has an herb garden for open-air luncheons and an atmospheric interior; the proprietor has created a droll museum of the city's history in a back room. You can arrange a medieval dinner or special show in advance; Tel: (6221) 208-79.

Heidelberg University

The key event in Heidelberg's history was the founding, in 1386, of the first university in Germany; it was the brainchild of Elector Ruprecht I of the Palatinate. Ruprecht's university got off to a roaring start when the German emperor backed the Italian candidate for the papacy during the Great Schism rather than the French; part of the fallout from this political event was the exodus of German intellectuals from the Sorbonne. The professors of Heidelberg's four faculties, modeled on the Sorbonne, were partly paid by Ruprecht but depended mostly on benefices granted by Pope Urban VI, who also issued the bull authorizing the university.

When the university's rapid growth caused a space problem, Ruprecht II had a simple solution: He drove the city's Jews from their homes and synagogues and converted those to faculty housing for the university's clerical professors. But the university grew up outside the walls of the original city, whose limits the **Universitätsplatz** marks. Here, where the building known as the **Alte Universität** (Old University) now stands, Luther stood in 1518 to dispute with a faculty still loyal to their benefactor in Rome. Only 45 years later its members, reflecting the Calvinist convictions of Elector Friedrich III (the Pious), composed the Heidelberg Catechism, the definitive statement of reformed Christian faith.

If the Baroque façade of the Alte Universität does not match your conception of a medieval university, it is because the Wars of the Orléans Succession at the end of the 17th century more or less erased Heidelberg and the then-existing university from the map. Built in 1728, the Old University has its own considerable tradition; among more recent lecturers have been Karl Jaspers, Martin Heidegger, Arnold Toynbee, and Somerset Maugham. A few steps past it and up Augustinerstrasse, visit the best-known relic of Twain's and Sigmund Romberg's Heidelberg: the **Studentenkarzer** (student prison). Generations of unrepentant scapegraces confined to its cramped second-floor rooms for minor offences have scribbled with candle smoke and chalk on the walls, immortalizing their plaints and witticisms.

Universitätsplatz is usually alive with students perched on the central fountain, draped on the Old University's steps, and flowing in tidal rhythms through the portals of the New University and the library. The New University, built in the 1930s with funds collected by a former American ambassador, is on the south side of the square. The library, the

Bibliotheca Palatina, is worth seeing, not only for its wonderfully exuberant entrance on Seminarstrasse but also for its exhibit of medieval manuscripts. The most significant is the Codex Manesse, a beautifully illuminated 14th-century collocation of earlier courtly love lyrics (facsimile display). The oldest church in Heidelberg, the 12th-century **Peterskirche** (St. Peter's Church), stands opposite the library; within are the gravestones of three centuries' worth of university professors and Palatine courtiers.

Heilig-Geist-Kirche

In 1400, Elector Ruprecht III celebrated his ascension to the imperial throne (as Ruprecht I) by building a new church on the Marktplatz, a few blocks east of Universitätsplatz. Though his reign lasted only one inglorious decade, Ruprecht's Heilig-Geist-Kirche (Holy Ghost Church) has raised its Gothic flanks over the attached merchants' stalls for almost 600 years. The tombs of more than 50 prince-electors ornamented the church until 1693, when French troops smashed them and scattered the bones of the dead; oddly, the only surviving gravestones are those of Ruprecht himself and his wife, Elizabeth, who still smile naïvely up at you from their place in the north aisle.

If you attend—and you should—one of the frequent concerts in the Heilig-Geist-Kirche, be sure to sit in the gallery, opposite the performers. These galleries were specially built in 1440 to house the library the prince-electors had begun with manuscripts commandeered from the abbey of Lorsch. By the end of the 16th century the Bibliotheca Palatina was one of Europe's most important. Though Heidelbergers still grind their teeth over the story, its seizure in 1622 and presentation to the Vatican by General Tilly no doubt saved its 5,000 books and 3,500 manuscripts from destruction.

Across from the church, the ▶ **Romantik-Hotel zum Ritter St. Georg** is another treasure that survived the holocaust of 1693. Built by a cloth merchant in 1592, its richly ornamented gables and bays reflect the growing self-confidence of the rising middle class. Its historic rooms are small and the range of services limited, but the hotel's colorful and busy restaurant is a local favorite, its location unbeatable.

The Castle

For six centuries the Heidelberg **Schloss**, seat of the princes and electors of the Palatinate, watched over the city; but in

1774, a fire completed the destruction begun by the French 80 years earlier. Ironically, now that the invading hordes are composed of tourists, the castle has done Heidelberg more good as a ruin than it ever did intact as a fortress. Among the first waves of seekers of the *Romantik* to come down the Rhine was a French nobleman, Charles de Graimberg. Falling in love with the castle—which was being carted away stone by stone for building material—he battled for 50 years to save and restore what his countrymen had almost obliterated. The result, Europe's quintessential romantic ruin, is worth the 15-minute climb (from the Marktplatz, cross Kornmarkt and take Burgweg; a cable car also ascends from this point; from Friday through Sunday, cars and buses are barred from the castle area). The green terraces surrounding the castle were once Renaissance gardens whose ornamental hedges, trees, and fountains were considered a wonder of the early 17th century. Join one of the English-language tours that form hourly in the castle courtyard for an entertaining and comprehensive history of the ruin. Its finest points are evident at first glance, though: the Renaissance beauty of the northern and eastern walls, the latter now only a façade, but with a wealth of ornament. The **Apothekenmuseum** (Pharmaceutical Museum) in the Otto Heinrich wing documents the history of German pharmacies and medicaments (open daily, 10:00 A.M. to 5:00 P.M.).

Originally a formidable stronghold securing the Neckar ford and ferry, the castle was gradually converted by the prince-electors into a palace, an increasingly vulnerable stage-setting for their own family dramas, one of which proved disastrous. In 1671 the young Princess Elizabeth-Charlotte was commanded by her father, the elector, to marry the epicene duke of Orléans, brother of Louis XIV. Over the ensuing 50 years "Liselotte," who had been born in the Heidelberg castle, wrote 4,000 homesick letters about her existence as a "royal slave" in Paris. When her brother died without an heir, the Sun King used her supposed claim to the Palatinate as a pretext for invading it. Heidelberg fell without resistance in 1688, and French troops later razed the city and demolished the castle.

Along the Neckar

The Neckar crossing that the castle had been built to guard was first bridged in 1310, but in the next four centuries fire, ice, and flood destroyed four successive wooden bridges between the Altstadt on the south bank and Neuenheim on the north. The last elector to live in the castle, Karl-Theodor, left a more enduring stone bridge as a memorial to his tranquil 57-year reign (legend has it that he also left 200 children, by as many different mothers). The twin towers at the south end of the **Karl-Theodor Brücke** (or, simply, the Alte Brücke—Old Bridge) were the medieval city's main gate. Today, crowned with Baroque helms and graced with a classical arch, the gate and bridge have become Heidelberg's symbol. Friedrich Hölderlin, in his "Ode to Heidelberg" (1799), likened the bridge to the graceful arc of a bird in flight, and Goethe called it one of the world's wonders. Germany's greatest poet visited Heidelberg eight times and, like so many others, lost his heart here (to Marianne von Willemer, another poet's wife). In 1795 Goethe *almost* stayed at the **Goldener Hecht**, facing the Old Bridge across the square, according to a plaque the hotel now proudly displays. The Hecht's popular restaurant is crowded every evening with young locals who enjoy its plain fare under fanciful wall frescoes highlighting its history.

From the Old Bridge up to the Heilig-Geist-Kirche, **Steingasse**, Heidelberg's oldest paved street, has some of the city's best antiques and curio shops. Nearby, at Haspelgasse 18, the quiet **Weinstube zum Backofen** serves traditional Heidelberg dishes; try the *Leberknöpfle* (liver dumplings) with *Specksalat* (bacon salad) and a Schwarzer Riesling wine. Another good place to eat is the **Schnookeloch** (Haspelgasse 8), filled with mementos of student life; more staid, but even richer in student atmosphere, is the **Café Knösel** (Haspelgasse 20), a favorite in the Altstadt since 1863. Frau Knösel invented the *Heidelberger Studentenkuss* (Student's Kiss), a bittersweet chocolate confection filled with nougat and praline.

Cross the Old Bridge and climb Schlangenweg, zigzagging steeply through vineyards and orchards (20 minutes) up to **Philosophenweg**. No visitor to Heidelberg should pass up this view of the bridge, Altstadt, and castle. For six centuries university students and teachers have, like Aristotle, done their best thinking on their feet—to what effect may be judged by the eight Nobel prizes they have won, most recently in 1991.

From the middle of Philosophenweg, high above the Neckar and paralleling it for about half a mile, follow the signposted paths leading even higher up the Heiligenberg to its peak (another hour of easy walking). At the top (1,562 feet) the ruined **Michaelskloster** (Monastery of St. Michael), founded in 870 by the abbey of Lorsch, stands in a grove that has been a place of worship since Celtic times. The ruins here recently have been tidied up and fenced in, but the scene still evokes the pure religious ardor of the Carolingian founders.

If you prefer an easier walk, follow Philosophenweg east (and gradually downhill) to its juncture with Hirschgasse, which will take you down to the Neckar. Twain came to the Hirschgasse to observe the bloody ritual duels fought by student fraternities "in a two-story public house": the ▶ Hirschgasse, at Hirschgasse 3, where an inn has stood since 1490. The hotel enjoys an unequaled location directly across the Neckar from the castle and features Laura Ashley–style suites, a restaurant aspiring to the gourmet level, and an eager, friendly young staff. The ▶ Prinz-Hotel Heidelberg, at Neuenheimer Landstrasse 5, overlooks the river from the other (western) end of Philosophenweg in Neuenheim, with such extras as an oversized thermal whirlpool, steam sauna, and waterfall shower. At the hotel's new California-style restaurant, Stars, you can watch the barges glide down the Neckar while enjoying a shrimp jambalaya (try the white chocolate cheesecake for dessert).

From Neuenheim, the Theodor-Heuss bridge leads back to Bismarckplatz, hub of Heidelberg's excellent streetcar and bus network. Two blocks south is the city's premier hotel, the ▶ Europäischer Hof–Hotel Europa. Generously proportioned in 19th-century grand-hotel style, the hotel has a new wing overlooking a quiet garden courtyard. Rooms in the older section are more spacious, but all are comfortable.

Diagonally across the park to the west, the ▶ Holiday Inn Crowne Plaza Heidelberg has taken over another old-timer, the Schrieder Hotel, renovating it within municipally imposed limits and adding no-smoking rooms and a basement pool and sauna. You can, of course, dine sumptuously at both hotels, but epicures should read further.

The gourmet restaurant Simplicissimus, at Ingrimstrasse 16, strikes a French note in the middle of the Altstadt. The decor is classic Parisian café style, the food light, delicate, and fresh; Tel: (6221) 18-33-36. The Old City abounds in Greek, Turkish, and especially Italian restaurants to which Heidelbergers flock: Piccolo Mondo, at Klingenteich Strasse 6, grills its fresh fish and meat specialties with finesse and serves them with humor; Tel: (6221) 129-99.

If you should notice that Heidelberg streetcars are flying the city's colors on little flags during your visit, head for Philosophenweg or the Theodor-Heuss bridge, two good vantage points for an evening fireworks display over the castle. The Schloss is artfully lit to simulate its siege and destruction, and the climactic blaze of pyrotechnics over the Neckar is a heart stopper.

Outside Heidelberg

Less than 10 km (6 miles) down the Neckar, **Ladenburg** gives the impression of having been touched up with fresh paint just before your visit. The village's original Celtic name, Lokwodunon (Swamp Fortress), indicates how muddy things could get here before the Rhine and the Neckar were tamed. Now you can explore with dry feet the city walls and gates as well as the network of curving lanes lined with immaculate half-timbered houses, many bearing their 15th- and 16th-century dates in Gothic flourishes. Proud of their 2,500-year history, Ladenburgers have marked the courses of Roman roads on Kirchenstrasse near the pretty 14th-century church of **St. Gallus**, built over the Roman forum. Stone images of the Roman sun god and Mithras, the warriors' god, brood in the **Lobdengaumuseum**, which occupies the 17th-century Bischofshof, once the resort of the bishops of Worms. The most notable bishop, Johann von Dalberg, privy councillor to Elector Philipp I, brought humanist scholars and teachers to Heidelberg during the university's late-15th-century flowering. The showpiece of the museum's medieval collection, a benign Late Gothic carved Madonna (*Rathausmadonna*), probably dates from von Dalberg's time.

It is almost impossible to avoid eating asparagus in the Rhine area between April and June, when every café and restaurant displays a banner proudly proclaiming *Spargelzeit* (asparagus time). Though you don't have to go to **Schwetzingen**, 10 km (6 miles) west of Heidelberg, to eat that delicacy, Schwetzingen's plump white asparagus is thought by connoisseurs to be the best. Have a helping of it covered with hollandaise (or in some 50 other forms) at the restaurant **Löwen**, Schloss Strasse 4–6, across from the castle; if you have a place to cook, buy it fresh by the kilo at the Spargelmarkt.

Schwetzingen's **Schlossgarten** is not only one of the prime examples of formal landscape gardening in 18th-century Europe, it is also a delightful place to spend a day. The park combines Baroque opulence with romantic lavishness, reflecting the sequence of architects employed by Elector Karl Theodor, whose summer residence this was, and for whose delectation they created fountains, lakes, a mosque, a ruined aqueduct, and a "Roman" fortress.

SPEYER

About 25 km (15 miles) southwest of Heidelberg on the far side of the Rhine, Speyer is most easily reached by car by way of Schwetzingen (the train trip from Heidelberg to Speyer, because it requires several transfers, takes an hour to an hour and a half). Originally a Roman fortification, Speyer became a bishopric in the seventh century, and first assumed importance as a town in the 11th century with the construction of its **Dom** (Cathedral), the most enormous building project of the day. As you approach the Rhine bridge from the east, the Dom rules the town's skyline and is its main attraction for visitors.

Emperor Conrad II began construction of the Dom in 1030, ushering in a new, monumental phase in European religious architecture. One of the most important Romanesque structures in Germany, it was also the land's largest church until it was eventually surpassed by the Cologne cathedral. Whether you approach it from the Rhine through the shady park on whose west edge it stands or through town along Maximilianstrasse, the cathedral's red-sandstone bulk with its massive Romanesque domes and towers confronts you majestically. From its steps on St. John's Day in 1146 Bernard of Clairvaux, acting as God's messenger, ("O Man . . . I have raised you to the heights of royalty. And you, what have you done for me?") summoned Conrad III to set off on the disastrous Second Crusade. Here in the Dom the second Diet of Speyer in 1529 annulled religious freedoms previously granted, provoking the protests of six princes and 14 cities, all followers of Luther—who were from that time on known as "protestants."

Entering the Dom from the west, you cross the lofty nave, whose bare sandstone walls and massive columns emphasize its airy proportions. To the right, at the end of the south aisle, a flight of stairs leads down into the **crypt**. Begun in 1025, the crypt, the largest north of the Alps, is considered one of the world's most beautiful. Four emperors, three empresses, and four German kings rest here in stone sarcophagi (with modern covers). "Nothing is more magnificent, nothing nobler, nothing in Germany and Europe holier than these Imperial tombs," Hugo wrote.

When the French razed Speyer in 1689, Louis XIV's soldiers played football with the heads of royalty from the pillaged crypt—but they found only the top level of graves. Not until 1900 did excavations reveal the graves of the Salian emperors, Conrad II and his descendants Heinrich III, IV, and V, identified by their wooden orbs and copper crowns.

At the base of the vault where they now lie, the image of Rudolph of Hapsburg, the first of a great dynasty, is sculpted upon his gravestone holding the orb and scepter. His furrowed brow and tense mouth give the impression of a conscientious, somewhat harried man doing his best in a difficult position.

A few steps south of the Dom the towered and turreted 19th-century **Historisches Museum der Pfalz** is not expected to reopen, following major reconstruction, until early in 1994. Its extensive display of wine technology through the ages is worth waiting for, however. The museum's best-known exhibit is the so-called **Golden Hat**, a Bronze Age cult object (circa 12th century B.C.) of pure gold.

Behind the Dom and the museum, a wooded park full of benches and paths stretches down to the Rhine. You can stroll along the river or take a two-hour cruise on the little steamer that docks here. (On a rainy day or for a change of pace, walk up the river under the bridge and turn left past the pond; Geib Strasse takes you to the **Technik-Museum**. Vintage cars, flying machines, locomotives, and other low-tech curios are attractively displayed in a huge turn-of-the-century airplane factory built in France and brought piece by piece from Lille to Speyer during World War I.)

Speyer's main street, Maximilianstrasse, once the triumphal way by which monarchs and princes of the church proceeded ceremoniously to the Dom, is now a pedestrian mall leading west to the Altpörtel, Speyer's best-known landmark after the cathedral. About midway between the two, just off Maximilianstrasse at the head of Korngasse, you'll find, in a carefully renovated Fachwerk structure, the restaurant **Zur Alten Münze**. Here moderately priced Pfälzer cooking is tastefully dished up in the wood-beamed interior or, in good weather, at tables on the square in view of the cathedral; Tel: (6232) 797-03.

The **Altpörtel**, one of the few structures that survived the conflagration of 1689, is Speyer's only remaining medieval gate. The **Altpörtel Café**, with its pretty Baroque façade, makes an excellent vantage point from which to admire the ponderous portal—actually a tower—of which the base is 13th century, the top story with its Gothic arched arcade 16th century, and the steep slate roof 18th century. Just a few steps south down the Karmeliter Strasse at number 11–13, the **Backmulde** is a cozy (but not cheap) restaurant featuring specialties from the Pfalz and a fine selection of French and Pfälzer wines. Try the *Lammrücken am Knochen gebraten in Kohlrabi* (roast lamb on turnip cabbage) with spinach and potatoes au gratin in a leek-cream sauce. The Backmulde is small enough for owner-chef Gunter Schmidt to personally advise his guests, so be sure to reserve a table; Tel: (6232) 715-77.

WORMS

Worms lies on the Rhine's west bank about 30 km (18 miles) northwest of Heidelberg (follow the A 5 to Bensheim, then go 20 km/12 miles west of Bensheim on route B 47, the Nibelungenstrasse). Between June and September, boat excursions leave on Wednesdays and Sundays for Worms from Heidelberg's main boat landing (below the **Stadthalle** on the Neckar) for a pleasant day trip, including three hours in Worms.

Larger than Speyer, Worms too is dominated by its mighty Romanesque **Dom**, practically the sole memorial to Worms's century-long status as one of the the leading imperial cities of the Holy Roman Empire. Whether you arrive by car, train, or boat, you will have no difficulty finding the Dom in its park on the highest hilltop of the Altstadt. Here, safely above high water, the Romans built the forum of their Civitas Vangonium, one of Rome's earliest bases on the Rhine, at a trade-routes crossroads settlement the Celts had called Borbetomagus. Later the Frankish kings held court where the forum had been; on this historic hill, Charlemagne celebrated two of his five weddings and received the homage of the defeated Tassilo, duke of Bavaria.

The Dom, graced by Romanesque round towers and arches, and enlivened by many grotesque and fanciful exterior carvings intended to drive off evil spirits, was largely constructed between 1130 and 1200. The main entrance (on the south side) is through a soaring Gothic arch flanked by lively early-14th-century sculptures of biblical scenes. Cross the nave and go left down the north aisle past a series of intricate and expressive Late Gothic sandstone reliefs commissioned by the great humanist bishop of Worms, Johann von Dalberg. Standing in the characteristically pentagonal west chancel under three Gothic rose windows, you look down the years to the ornate Baroque high altar in the east chancel.

Though the Dom's crypt (entrance at the head of the south aisle) shelters no imperial graves, it does hold the ancestors of the Salian emperors, particularly the tomb of Conrad the Red, father of Emperor Conrad II and founder of the Salian line. Worms remained a steadfast rock for the Holy Roman emperors in a stormy sea of rivalry through the centuries, and was the scene of many historic imperial meetings. The Concordat of Worms in 1122 ended the struggle between church and state over investiture (the power to invest bishops and abbots); the agreement provided that this privilege resided solely with the papacy, but granted the state a certain amount of veto power in the decision. Not long after completion of the Dom, Frederick Barbarossa made Worms a Free Imperial City, recording his action on a bronze tablet over the cathedral's north portal (a replica can be seen there today).

This north entrance, the Kaiserportal, was once the ceremonial portal of the emperors and bishops, whose courts were situated in the present **Schlossplatz** north of the Dom. Here, where the Romans had met in their forum, where the Nibelungen and the Franks had held court, Luther faced Emperor Charles V on a spring day in 1521 and refused to retract his criticisms of the Catholic Church. The Diet of Worms had taken up the question of Luther; the Edict of Worms declared him an outlaw. With his words, "Here I stand. I can do no other. God help me. Amen," Luther provoked his own excommunication and laid the foundation of the Reformation. A simple stone in the pretty Schlosspark marks the spot. A few steps up Stephansgasse to the north is a park where a 19th-century memorial to that historic day centers on the robed and adamant figure of Luther towering over other great reformers such as Wycliff, Hus, and Savonarola. Just off the Schlossplatz at Hofgasse 2, on a quiet lane between the Dom and the Dreifältigkeitskirche, the ▶ **Kriemhilde** has tidy rooms facing the Dom. The hotel's flowery terrace is a good place for lunch.

In Charles V, Worms had a champion of Catholicism; in Luther, the founder of Protestantism; and in Rabbi Salomon Ben Isaak—called Raschi—Worms had, from 1055 to 1056, the definitive medieval Talmudic scholar. Walk north from the Luther memorial to the handsome 13th-century church of **St. Martin**. From here, follow Martinsgasse to St. Martin's Gate in the former city walls. Across the Friedrichstrasse, enter **Judengasse**, and turn right into Synagogenplatz to find, at the center of what used to be one of Germany's oldest and most important Jewish communities, the Men's Synagogue. First built in 1174, the synagogue was destroyed and rebuilt several times during outbreaks of racial persecution (most recently in 1938). As the Talmudic scholar's memorial, the **Raschi Judaic Museum** was set up here in 1982 in a modern building on Renaissance foundations, with a valuable collection of documents, pictures, and religious objects, many from Worms's silversmith workshops. Nearby, in the synagogue garden, a stairway leads down into the ritual **Mikwe** (women's bath), which also dates to the 12th century. A block southwest of the

Dom, on busy Andreasring, Germany's oldest **Jewish cemetery** is an overgrown jumble of 2,000 gravestones, many ancient and illegible, the oldest dating back to the 11th century.

Follow Andreasring east one block to the Andreaspforte
(gate), through which, to the right, you'll find the 12th-
century cloister of the **Andreaskirche** (St. Andrew's Church),
which since 1928 has housed the city's archaeological and
historical museum. Don't miss its fascinating display of Roman artifacts, especially the glass. The Romanesque abbey
church now houses a display of medieval and later sacred
objects.

Though nothing tangible remains of Worms's fifth and
sixth-century Burgundian royal courts, the resounding names
of mythological Nibelungen heroes, derived from Burgundian times, still adorn the city's streets, parks, and squares.
Siegfried came to Worms to woo Kriemhilde, sister of Burgundian king Gunther; before he could attain his own heart's
desire, Siegfried had to win the Valkyrie Brünhilde for Gunther. Blood oaths, treachery, magic, and revenge characterize
the story, best known to us from Wagner's operatic cycle, *Der
Ring des Nibelungen*. The story ends with Hagen's murder of
Siegfried and his casting of the Nibelungen gold into the
Rhine. No visit to Worms is complete without a pilgrimage to
the Hagen statue in the Rhineside park, just north of the
bridge, where the old warrior is immortalized in the act of
disposing of the troublesome treasure.

THE GERMAN WINE ROUTE

West of Heidelberg and Mannheim, the broad Rhine valley
stretches 35 km (22 miles) to the foot of the Haardt massif
overlooking the left (west) bank. On that bank, below the
heights, lies the **Deutsche Weinstrasse** (German Wine
Route). The northern section stretches from Grünstadt (20
km/12 miles southwest of Worms) south on the B 271
through Kallstadt, Bad Dürkheim, Wachenheim, and Deidesheim to Neustadt, the Weinstrasse's unofficial capital. From
Neustadt, the southern section of the Weinstrasse continues
on the B 38 south to Maikammer, St. Martin, Edenkoben,
Rhodt, Landau, Bad Bergzabern, and Schweigen on the
French border, 80 km (50 miles) of gentle, sunny landscape. Almond, apple, and cherry trees bloom along the
Weinstrasse's fertile slopes, and the charm of its villages,
with their half-timbered houses and distinctive high-arched
gateways, produces an abundant annual harvest of tourists.
Most important, this is the finest wine-growing country of
the Rheinpfalz (Rhineland-Palatinate). The Pfälzers maintain

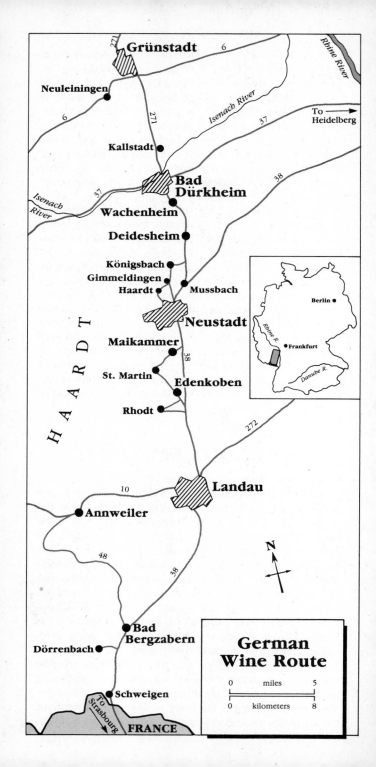

German Wine Route

that their best Rieslings will stand comparison with the Rheingau's most aristocratic vintages. Certainly white Riesling from the Pfalz—usually dry to semi-dry, with a subtle, refreshing, rather fruity flavor—makes an excellent accompaniment to any meal. The Pfalz now produces only slightly more than half as many Riesling grapes as it does Müller-Thurgau, a hybrid developed in the Rheingau at the end of the last century. A heartier wine with a fruity bouquet, Müller-Thurgau is a good choice for the novice wine taster and goes well with the sort of spicy, flavorful dishes for which Pfälzer home cooking is noted. A light wine known in Germany for over 300 years, Sylvaner is still popular with snacks, while the Kerner, a new hybrid, modifies Riesling with a touch of Trollinger red.

The word *Pfalz* comes from the Latin *palatium* (palace). The Pfälzers, as distinct a breed as their wines, pronounce it "Palz," and refer to themselves as "Pelzer" or even "Belzer." Other Germans find the Pfälzer dialect funny but admire their initiative and success: Pfälzer emigrants have made good the world over (in Pennsylvania, for example); German Chancellor Helmut Kohl is a Pfälzer. As you drink with the Pfälzers, their humor, openness, and hospitality bloom. A joke here may not be wittier than elsewhere, but it is certainly louder, and a significant custom is the handing around of their oversize (one-pint) wineglasses for everyone to drink from. (It's bad form to reach for the glass, though; wait for it to be handed to you.) The glass, or *Schoppen,* may be dimpled to give greasy fingertips a better grip, for some delicacy—a slice of *Saumagen* or hunk of fragrant *Handkäse*—invariably accompanies and sets off a good wine here.

The Northern Wine Route

Visitors have sometimes compared the land around the Weinstrasse to Tuscany, and nothing in Germany could be more Tuscan than the little fortified town of **Neuleiningen,** near Grünstadt, with its cliffside houses overshadowed by the ruined 13th-century castle of the Leiningen counts. (From Grünstadt, take the Weinstrasse, B 271, 1 km/½ mile to Kirchheim, and follow the signs from Kirchheim 3 km/2 miles west to Neuleiningen.) Here, in 1525, the Countess Eva is supposed to have quelled a peasant uprising by stuffing the rebels with good food until they forgot their grievances. The restaurant **Burgschänke**, at the base of the castle, still sends its patrons away in the same happy condition; its specialty is thick beefsteaks. At the bend in the road approaching the village, **Liz's Stuben** (Am Goldberg 2) is tiny, intimate, and friendly, offering whatever Frau Gissel feels like cooking that day—the menu is light and Italianate. Reservations essential; Tel: (6359) 53-41. Directly above the village (north through the Autobahn underpass), the sunny terrace of the ▶ **Haus Sonnenberg** commands a sweeping view across the Rhine plain, as do its airy, modern rooms. The Nippgen family, your hosts, are proud of the wines they glean from the Sonnenberg's slopes, and especially recommend their 1989 Neuleininger Sonnenberg Schwarzriesling Spätlese. You can work off a rich repast in the hotel restaurant with a few laps in the pool or a snooze in the sauna.

Ten kilometers (6 miles) south of Neuleiningen, **Kallstadt** calls its best vineyard the *Saumagen,* after the Pfälzer national dish: a spicy, haggislike pork-and-potato compound that goes particularly well with the rich, aromatic wines produced hereabouts. A prime place to test this observation is the ▶ **Weinkastell zum Weissen Ross** in central Kallstadt (Weinstrasse 80–82). Jutta and Norbert Kohnke preside over the historic hostel's charmingly traditional guest rooms and cozy vaulted restaurant. In the latter, the Kohnkes dish up *Saumagen* prepared according to ancient recipes and simmered for hours in a sewn-up pig stomach. Jutta Kohnke's family, the Philippi, make wine as they have for generations, in oaken casks; try their prizewinning 1989 Saumagen Riesling Spätlese.

About 4 km (2½ miles) south on the B 271, **Bad Dürkheim** rises like an amphitheater up the lower slopes of the Isenach valley. On the second and third weekends of September the town stages a Rabelaisian spectacle, the Dürkheimer Wurstmarkt, which Dürkheimers claim is the world's largest wine festival. Shaded by gigantic tents from the late-summer sun, half a million celebrants consume a quarter of a million liters of wine. A gargantuan wine cask, the Dürkheimer *Fass,* contains not the wine but the drinkers—450 people can crowd into its two levels. Lurching in unison from side to side in time with traditional drinking songs, the merry Pfälzers pass around their giant wine tumblers in a scene worthy of Brueghel, from whose brush could have come the procession of vintners wheeling in wine kegs on medieval-style wheelbarrows. The custom recalls the original 15th-century Wurstmarkt: Pilgrims came in such numbers to the chapel of St. Michael on the hill above Dürkheim that the local merchants trundled their wares, including sausage and wine, up the Michelsberg in barrows.

Known also for its Michelsberger Riesling, Bad Dürkheim has become equally famous for its water, with many pilgrims today coming to be cured by immersion or inhalation rather than by prayer.

► **Haus Boller,** a small hotel near the spa, offers the refined and genteel ambience of a 19th-century resort. Many of the primly decorous rooms have sun terraces, and you can dine staidly but well here on an elevated version of Pfälzer fare.

Overlooking Bad Dürkheim about 5 km/3 miles to the west, the 11th-century **abbey of Limburg,** once the repository of the symbols of imperial power (crown, orb, scepter, and sword), was destroyed in 1404. Today its roofless abbey church, with two rows of plane trees replacing its monolithic sandstone columns, is part of an impressive ruin in which the city often stages concerts.

According to tradition, it was Boniface, an abbot of Limburg, who lost a drinking contest to the *Bürgermeister* of **Wachenheim,** south of Bad Dürkheim (now on the B 271), and had to forfeit the tax paid to the abbey by the Wachenheimers. It is easy to see that Wachenheim has always prospered from its wine by its numerous handsome *Höfe* (estates) belonging to prosperous wine proprietors. One of the most interesting is that of Dr. Bürcklin-Wolf in the **Kolb'schen Hof,** at Weinstrasse 65. Its vaulted cellars, where Boniface is said to have lost his wager, can hold 1.4 million liters of wine. Tours of the cellars, in which modern winemaking technology has not done away with the use of traditional wooden casks, are conducted with characteristic Pfälzer gusto and spontaneity; you can take home such fine vintages as a 1990 Wachenheimer Mandelgarten Scheureben to conjure up memories. Right around the corner, the wine restaurant **Alte Münz** (Langgasse 2) would remind you that Wachenheim was the 15th-century *Münze* (mint) for the dukes of Zweibrücken—if you weren't preoccupied with your *Münzplatte,* a platter of solid Pfälzer *Wurst* specialties, and your choice of 14 different wines. Tel: (6322) 652-19.

Like Wachenheim, **Deidesheim,** to the south via the B 271, conceals an underground labyrinth of wine cellars. Deidesheim's great wine estate is **Bassermann-Jordan,** whose Forster Kirchenstück vineyard received the formal military salute, complete with flourished saber and drumroll, of the withdrawing Spanish army of occupation following the Thirty Years' War. Known for its traditional wine-making methods, Bassermann-Jordan stores its wines only in oaken casks. Go to the tourist office, across from the railway station and post office, to arrange for a tour and tasting at a Deidesheim winery; Tel: (6326) 50-21 or 22.

An excellent complement to your visit to a working winery is a tour of the **cultural wine museum** next to the church. Among many other displays are wine labels and bottles, wineglasses from Roman times to Jugendstil, a cooper's shop, and the grandly furnished city council chambers—and the museum is still expanding. It is housed in Deidesheim's pretty Baroque Rathaus, from whose steps on the first Tuesday after Pentecost, between 5:45 and 6:00 P.M., a billy goat is auctioned off with great ceremony, the final bid coinciding with the six o'clock bell. The goat, which is paid to Deidesheim as a "grazing fee" by the hill town of Lambrecht, is presented by Lambrecht's most recently married couple; the offering must be "well-horned and potent," leaving the ceremony's significance in little doubt. You can watch the billy-goat auction from your window if you get a front room facing the square at the ▶ **Deidesheimer Hof**, one of the best hotels on the Weinstrasse. The Hof owes its growing reputation to its first-class accommodations and first-class chef, Manfred Schwarz (the hotel's **Schwarzer Hahn** restaurant joins his name to that of owner Anita Hahn). Schwarz's gourmet creations, served with élan in a sumptuously furnished vaulted cellar, draw cognoscenti from all over the world to vie for only 35 seats—so book well in advance. Chancellor Helmut Kohl entertained Mikhail Gorbachev here in November 1990. Tel: (6326) 18-11/12.

Just south of the Marktplatz, at Weinstrasse 31, the restaurant **Zur Kanne** offers a 700-year tradition, elegantly rustic decor, and refined Pfälzer cooking: for instance, a hearty saddle of venison, a delicate *carpaccio* with green beans, and foie gras on sliced apples with truffle sauce. The white wines come from Bürcklin-Wolf, and are complemented by some good reds from France.

At Mussbach, 3½ km (2 miles) south of Deidesheim, the Weinstrasse continues southwest on the B 38 toward Neustadt. Less than a mile beyond Mussbach, turn right and follow Haardterstrasse to the top of the road in Haardt. Here, at Mandelring 11, the ▶ **Wirtshaus Mandelhof** has small but delightful rooms, and owner-chef Roland Starmans, a graduate of the Cornell School of Hotel Management, has one of the Neustadt area's most (deservedly) popular dining places.

Neustadt an der Weinstrasse is a bustling, cheerful market town with an exemplarily restored **Altstadt** that seeks to harmonize recent construction with older buildings. The Gothic church contains the tomb of Elector Ruprecht I, founder of Heidelberg University, and boasts the world's largest cast-iron bell, capable of loosening roof tiles with its thunder. In the Marktplatz in front of the church, the queen of the wine harvest is chosen every October, the climax of a week of festivities. Ever ready for a party, the Neustädters are a friendly, gossipy lot, with the trick of making a guest feel at home. The prettiest *Weinstube* in the Altstadt is the sunny **Liebstöck'l**, at Mittelgasse 22, in a gabled 18th-century building facing the huge linden tree that shades its garden. Try chef Karen Glaser's *Ochsenfetzen* in a garlic-bacon sauce with a salad and homemade *Spätzle;* she will advise you about wine; Tel: (6321) 331-61. Equally delighted to discuss his food and wine, Jürgen Reis runs the **Altstadtkeller** at Kunigunden-strasse 2, one street south of the Marktplatz. He brings you the day's menu, chalked on a large slate, usually featuring thick steaks or a veal filet—hearty food suited to the Keller's vaulted stone interior and backed by 18 open Pfälzer wines. Tel: (6321) 323-20.

The Southern Wine Route

The southern Weinstrasse begins at Maikammer, 6 km (3½ miles) south of Neustadt on route B 38, and winds through rich vineyards down toward Alsace, where the wines of the southern Pfalz have won increasing acceptance of late. Less than a mile west of Maikammer is **St. Martin**, Germany's only wine village bearing the name of the vintners' patron saint. Mounted on his war horse, armored and with sword drawn, the image of St. Martin, a fourth-century bishop of Tours and former Roman officer, heads an annual (November 11) procession of costumed vintners through the village to the winery, chosen by lot, whose guest he will be for the next year. You can judge whether his presence benefits the wines by visiting the **Altes Schlösschen** (Maikammerstrasse 7), where a small 16th-century castle snugly houses the Schneider winery. Here you can sample the silky texture of a 1989 Spätburgunder Weissherbst Spätlese while surrounded by the carved portals, oriel windows, and Renaissance gables that make St. Martin famous throughout Germany.

Should you choose, as Martin of Tours did, to linger in this eminently *gemütlich* village, just walk through the high-arched gate of the ▶ **St. Martiner Kastell** directly across from the Schlösschen (having booked a room well in advance). Recently rebuilt in half-timbered Renaissance style, the Castell has an abundance of carved wood and tracery windows; the snug guest rooms lie off a central stairway that winds around a wrought-iron grapevine three stories high. You dine well here, too, on game in season and specialties such as Barbary duck; the wines come from the Altes Schlösschen.

From St. Martin, continue southwest for 3 km (2 miles) to Edenkoben and follow the road signs from there for another 2 km (1½ miles) to the village of **Rhodt**, one of the Weinstrasse's treasures. A stroll down its Theresienstrasse under a line of venerable chestnut trees takes you past one imposing example after another of the distinctive Pfälzer

Höfe (courtyards) from the 17th and 18th centuries; most have high-arched stone carriage gates, elaborately carved and set off with fig trees, flowers, and vines.

Rhodt's real treasure is its Traminer vineyards, which produce a wine so prized during the Renaissance that in 1603 the margrave of Baden-Durlach traded the duke of Württemberg *two* of his villages for Rhodt. As part of Baden-Durlach, Rhodt escaped the general destruction that Louis XIV visited upon the Pfalz in 1693, so the wine not only built Rhodt's proud *Weinhöfe,* it also rescued them. Some of these Traminer vines, in the Rosengarten vineyard at the village's edge, are thought to have been producing fruit since the 17th century—which, if true, would make them the oldest bearing grapevines in Germany, and possibly anywhere in the world.

For a look behind the village's massive gates, which are kept protectively closed on its liquid gold, visit a *Weinstube* established in a *Hof.* A good choice is the ► **Weinstube Waldkirch**, at Weinstrasse 53. At tables set out in the cobbled courtyard, Frau Dorothea Waldkirch offers you a tray of wine-taster's glasses from which to select your wine and a list of some two dozen local specialties from which to select your dinner. (Insiders go for the simple, homemade *Bratwurst* with fried potatoes and *Kraut.*) Frau Waldkirch has picturesquely converted a part of her *Hof* into comfortable rooms away from the street.

In a landscape as dramatic as its history, one of the grimmest fortified castles in Germany, **Burg Trifels**, rises from the limestone precipices above **Annweiler**, 15 km (10 miles) beyond Edenkoben west of route B 38 on route B 10. Here the Salian emperors kept the symbols of imperial majesty—crown, orb, and scepter—for 150 years, and it was to Burg Trifels that Emperor Heinrich VI, son of Frederick Barbarossa, returned in 1196 from his savage conquest of Sicily with 150 pack mules laden with treasure. Heinrich pursued his vision of a Hohenstaufen world empire with ruthless single-mindedness. When he captured Richard the Lion-Hearted of England, Heinrich not only held him for ransom for a year at Trifels, but also forced the English king to acknowledge him as his feudal overlord. Malaria struck Heinrich down in Sicily before he could realize his dream of conquest. His castle, destroyed by lightning in the 17th century, was restored and enlarged by his spiritual successors from 1937 to 1942. The view from Burg Trifels' parapets west across the rugged Wasgau compensates you for the 20-minute hike from the parking area. In Annweiler, stroll from the Rathaus square down to the Queich, a mountain brook that flows through the prettiest part of town. Some of the half-timbered houses appear to have been here since Friedrich II granted Annweiler free imperial status in 1219, but in fact everything was bombed flat in 1944 and has been lovingly restored. Thanks to a typically ingenious Pfälzer scheme, the venerable machinery of a medieval water mill on the Queich now grinds out 12 kilowatts of electricity instead of flour and, in its snazzy new (1986) glass housing, serves as a tourist attraction too. Try the *Flammkuchen,* a kind of Pfälzer pizza, fresh out of the cast-iron oven at the **Weinstube S'Reiwerle** (Flitschberg 7) on Wednesday or Friday evenings, or the good wine selection any time; Tel: (6346) 88-71.

In **Bad Bergzabern**, south down either route B 48 from Annweiler or route B 38 down from Edenkoben and Landau, you are just 5 km (3 miles) from the wine gateway that marks the southern end of the Weinstrasse. The ▶ **Kurhotel Petronella**, directly behind Bad Bergzabern's Kurpark, is in the middle of this spa-resort's prettiest scenery; every large, airy room has its own balcony overlooking the park. Although the management speaks good English, the hotel's **La Casserole**, a small but aspiring gourmet haven, has a distinct French accent. Try the quiche Lorraine. Bad Bergzabern's Altstadt is rich in historic buildings, most built by the counts and dukes of Zweibrücken. The oldest and finest is the **Gasthaus zum Engel**; with its ornate gables and bays, it is the Pfalz's most notable Renaissance construction.

At the head of a valley just southwest of Bad Bergzabern (leaving Bad Bergzabern on the Weinstrasse, take the first turnoff to the right), shaded by chestnut and fir trees and accented by roses, **Dörrenbach** celebrated its millennium in 1992. Plan to get here early in the day to make the best of this gemlike village's genuinely medieval atmosphere. Everything is concentrated in the space around the Renaissance Rathaus, across from the Late Gothic defensive towers of the fortified churchyard. Standing between them is like being caught in a time warp. Don't linger too late; by the time the tourist buses are pulling in down at the square, you can already be tucking into your lunch at the **Altdeutsche Weinstube**, at Hauptstrasse 14. A suitable medieval dish here would be the *Kunsthammelfleisch* (mutton roast), marinated for three days in red wine and spices and served with a garlic cream sauce. And by now you'll know which Pfälzer wine to order. Tel: (6343) 15-05.

GETTING AROUND

Frankfurt International Airport is the main gateway to the region. Rail service from the airport itself to Frankfurt and from there to Wiesbaden, Darmstadt, and Heidelberg is frequent and fast (see the Getting Around section in the Frankfurt-am-Main chapter).

From Wiesbaden you can visit the Rheingau by train, supplemented by bus: For example, a bus takes you from Eltville to Kiedrich and Eberbach abbey. From Mainz, trains running down the valley of the Lorelei stop at Bingerbrück (across the river Nahe from Bingen) before racing on to Koblenz; plenty of local trains also stop at all the villages along the west bank of the Rhine.

From Darmstadt you can reach the central Odenwald by train, traveling down to Eberbach on the Neckar by way of Michelstadt and Erbach. Buses link the towns and villages of the Odenwald with a reliable, though not necessarily frequent, service. The Neckar valley is accessible by rail from Heidelberg all the way up to Stuttgart, a scenic trip of a few hours. East–west rail connections in the area, on the other hand, are rather complicated, when they exist at all; it is difficult, for example, to get from Heidelberg to the Weinstrasse. Once you reach Grünstadt, however, the rest of the Weinstrasse can be explored by the rail-bus combination.

Though river cruises allow little latitude for independent exploration, they are scenic and relaxing. Short-distance cruises with local lines operate out of most Rhine and Neckar towns, often featuring shoreside wine-tasting and sightseeing arrangements. The cruise ships of the well-known KD German Rhine Line White Fleet, based in Cologne, are floating hotels complete with swimming pools, bars, glassed-in observation decks, and English-speaking crews. You can see the Rhine between Frankfurt and Cologne on a two-day cruise, with stops at Mainz, Rüdesheim, Bacharach, Boppard, and Braubach (Marksburg castle). Other cruises go up the Rhine to Worms, Heidelberg, Speyer, and beyond. It is possible to join KD Line cruises in progress for short stretches as well, provided there is space available, and you can (for an extra charge) also convert your railway ticket to a boat ticket (or vice versa) at any KD dock. The KD line also offers daily Rhine service between late March and October 27 to all points of interest between Cologne and Frankfurt, including Boppard, St. Goar, Oberwesel, Kaub, Bacharach, Lorch, Bingen, Rüdesheim, Eltville, Wiesbaden-Biebrich, and Mainz. Normal crusing time from Boppard to Mainz is eight hours, but you can do it by KD hydrofoil in less than two. Local tourist information offices can furnish current schedules and help with bookings; see also "Around Germany" in the Useful Facts section at the front of the book.

By far the most flexible and convenient way to get around the area is by car. The major rental agencies have offices in all the larger towns. But your aim should be to get rid of your car as soon as you reach your destination because everything described in this chapter is best seen on foot. (The local Hauptbahnhof—train station—is often the best place to park.) Heidelberg, for example, which is an exasperating city for drivers, has an excellent bus-streetcar system with special daily and weekend rates for sightseers. All the major towns and cities in this region have pedestrian zones embracing their most interesting districts, and so do most of the smaller ones. By all means get a hiker's map from the tourist office and explore the outlying areas. The trails are well maintained and much used.

ACCOMMODATIONS REFERENCE
The hotel rates listed here are 1994 projections for double-bed, double-occupancy rooms, with a range from low to high whenever possible. Prices are given in deutsche marks (DM). Basic rates are always subject to change, so please verify price when you are booking. Breakfast is usually included in the price of a room.

City telephone codes must be preceded by a zero if you are calling from elsewhere in Germany.

▶ **Altes Bannhaus**. Hauptstrasse 211, D-63897 **Miltenberg**. Tel: (9371) 30-61; Fax: (9371) 687-54. DM 145–164.

▶ **Altkölnischer Hof**. Blücherstrasse 2, D-55422 **Bacharach am Rhein**. Tel: (6743) 13-39; Fax: (6743) 27-93. DM 95–180.

▶ **Badischer Hof**. Am Stadttor 4, D-63916 **Amorbach/ Odenwald**. Tel: (9373) 12-08. DM 100–135.

▶ **Bellevue Rheinhotel**. Rheinallee 41–42, P.O. Box 126, D-56139 **Boppard am Rhein**. Tel: (6742) 10-20; Fax: (6742) 10-26-02. DM 175–245.

▶ **Blauer Turm**. D-74206 **Bad Wimpfen**. Tel: (7063) 78-84 or 225; Fax: (7063) 67-01. DM 90–140.

▶ **Burg Hornberg**. D-74865 **Neckarzimmern**. Tel: (6261) 40-64; Fax: (6261) 188-64. DM 170–270.

▶ **Burghotel Auf Schönburg**. D-55430 **Oberwesel am Rhein**. Tel: (6744) 70-27; Fax: (6744) 16-13. DM 215–310.

▶ **Central Hotel**. Kirschstrasse 6, D-65385 **Rüdesheim**. Tel: (6722) 30-36; Fax: (6722) 28-07. DM 162–210.

▶ **Deidesheimer Hof**. Am Marktplatz, D-67146 **Deidesheim**. Tel: (6326) 18-11; Fax: (6326) 76-85. DM 180–420.

▶ **Europäischer Hof–Hotel Europa**. Friedrich-Ebert-Anlage 1, D-69117 **Heidelberg**. Tel: (6221) 51-50; Fax: (6221) 51-55-55. DM 405–495.

▶ **Favorite Parkhotel**. Karl-Weiser-Strasse 1, D-55131 **Mainz**. Tel: (6131) 820-91; Fax: (6131) 83-10-25. DM 265.

▶ **Grüner Baum**. Grossegasse 17, D-64720 **Michelstadt/ Odenwald**. Tel: (6061) 24-09; Fax: (6061) 732-81. DM 80.

▶ **Haus Boller.** Kurgartenstrasse 19, D-67098 **Bad Dürkheim.** Tel: (6322) 14-28. DM 95–150.

▶ **Haus Sonnenberg.** D-67271 **Neuleiningen.** Tel: (6359) 826-60. DM 110.

▶ **Hessisches Haus.** Burgstrasse 32, D-64678 **Lindenfels.** Tel: (6255) 24-05. DM 95.

▶ **Hilton International Mainz.** Rheinstrasse 68, D-55116 **Mainz.** Tel: (6131) 24-50; Fax: (6131) 24-55-89. DM 375–470.

▶ **Hirschgasse.** Hirschgasse 3, D-69120 **Heidelberg.** Tel: (6221) 403-21-60; Fax: (6221) 403-21-96. DM 295–550.

▶ **Holiday Inn Crowne Plaza Heidelberg.** Kufürsten-Anlage 1, D-69115 **Heidelberg.** Tel: (6221) 91-70; Fax: (6221) 210-07; in U.S., Tel: (800) 465-4329. DM 300–340.

▶ **Hotel de France.** Taunusstrasse 49, D-65183 **Wiesbaden.** Tel: (611) 52-00-61; Fax: (611) 52-81-74. DM 190–205.

▶ **Hotel Krone-Post.** D-69412 **Eberbach am Neckar.** Tel: (6271) 20-13 or 14. DM 118–195.

▶ **Hotel Kurmainz.** Flugplatzstrasse 44, D-55126 **Mainz-Finthen.** Tel: (6131) 49-10; Fax: (6131) 49-11-28. DM 205–305.

▶ **Hotel am Markt.** Markt 1, D-56329 **St. Goar.** Tel: (6741) 16-89; Fax: (6741) 17-21. DM 105.

▶ **Hotel Zum Ritter.** Neckarstrasse 40, D-69151 **Neckargemünd.** Tel: (6223) 70-35 or 37; Fax: (6223) 733-39. DM 125–220.

▶ **Jagdschloss Niederwald.** D-65385 **Rüdesheim.** Tel: (6722) 10-04; Fax: (6722) 479-70. DM 260–285.

▶ **Karpfen.** Am Alten Markt 1, D-69412 **Eberbach am Neckar.** Tel: (6271) 710-15; Fax: (6271) 710-10. DM 100–180.

▶ **Klee am Park.** Parkstrasse 4, D-65189 **Wiesbaden.** Tel: (611) 30-50-61; Fax: (611) 30-40-48. DM 220–300.

▶ **Kriemhilde.** Hofgasse 2, D-67550 **Worms.** Tel: (6241) 62-78; Fax: (6241) 62-77. DM 110–130.

▶ **Krone Assmannshausen.** Rheinuferstrasse 10, D-65385 **Rüdesheim-Assmannshausen.** Tel: (6722) 40-30; Fax: (6722) 30-49. DM 250–295.

▶ **Kurhotel Petronella.** Kurtalstrasse 47, D-76887 **Bad Bergzabern.** Tel: (6343) 10-75; Fax: (6343) 53-13. DM 145–185.

▶ **Lindenwirt.** Drosselgasse, D-65385 **Rüdesheim.** Tel: (6722) 10-31 or 32; Fax: (6722) 475-85. DM 150–220.

▶ **Maritim Rhein-Main Hotel.** Am Kavalleriesand 6, D-64295 **Darmstadt.** Tel: (6151) 30-30; Fax: (6151) 30-31-11. DM 310–525.

▶ **Nassauer Hof.** Kaiser-Friedrich-Platz 3–4, D-65183 **Wiesbaden.** Tel: (611) 13-30; Fax: (611) 13-36-32. DM 415–480.

▶ **Post.** Schmiedstrasse 2, D-63916 **Amorbach/Odenwald.** Tel: (9373) 14-10; Fax: (9373) 14-56. DM 100–134.

▶ **Prinz-Hotel Heidelberg.** Neuenheimer Landstrasse 5, D-

69120 **Heidelberg**. Tel: (6221) 403-20; Fax: (6221) 493-01-96. DM 195–295.

▶ **Rheinlust**. Rheinallee 27–30, D-56139 **Boppard**. Tel: (6742) 300-13; Fax: (6742) 30-04. DM 120–170.

▶ **Romantik-Hotel zum Ritter St. Georg**. Hauptstrasse 178, D-69117 **Heidelberg**. Tel: (6221) 242-72; Fax: (6221) 126-83. DM 240–320.

▶ **St. Martiner Kastell**. Maikammerer Strasse 2, D-67487 **St. Martin**. Tel: (6323) 20-98. DM 136.

▶ **Schloss Hotel auf Burg Rheinfels**. D-56326 **St. Goar**. Tel: (6741) 80-20; Fax: (6741) 76-52. DM 195–240.

▶ **Schloss Rheinhartshausen**. Erbach im Rheingau, D-65346 **Eltville**. Tel: (6123) 67-60; Fax: (6123) 67-64-00. DM 380.

▶ **Schwan**. Rheinallee 5–7, D-65375 **Oestrich/Rheingau**. Tel: (6723) 80-90; Fax: (6723) 78-20. DM 185–260.

▶ **Schwarzer Bock**. Kranzplatz 12, D-65183 **Wiesbaden**. Tel: (611) 15-50; Fax: (611) 15-51-11. DM 465–525.

▶ **Sonne**. Hauptstrasse 87, D-74206 **Bad Wimpfen**. Tel: (7063) 245; Fax: (7063) 65-91. DM 150.

▶ **Sonnenberg**. Friedrichstrasse 65, D-65333 **Eltville/Rheingau**. Tel: (6123) 30-81 or 83; Fax: (6123) 618-29. DM 140–160.

▶ **Weinhaus am Alten Markt**. Marktplatz 185, D-63897 **Miltenberg**. Tel: (9371) 55-00. DM 95–148.

▶ **Weinhaus Weiler**. Marktplatz 4, D-55430 **Oberwesel am Rhein**. Tel: (6744) 70-03; Fax: (6744) 73-03. DM 85–110.

▶ **Weinkastell zum Weissen Ross**. Weinstrasse 80–82, D-67169 **Kallstadt**. Tel: (6322) 50-33; Fax: (6322) 86-40. DM 145–185.

▶ **Weinmichel**. Schleiermacherstrasse 10–12, D-64283 **Darmstadt**. Tel: (6151) 290-80; Fax: (6151) 235-92. DM 228.

▶ **Weinstube Waldkirch**. Weinstrasse 53, D-76835 **Rhodt/Weinstrasse**. Tel: (6323) 58-25; Fax: (6323) 811-37. DM 100–120.

▶ **Wirtshaus Mandelhof**. Mandelring 11, D-67433 **Neustadt/Weinstrasse-Haardt**. Tel: (6321) 882-20; Fax: (6321) 333-42. DM 145.

▶ **Zur Lorelei**. Heerstrasse 87, D-56329 **St. Goar**. Tel: (6741) 16-14; Fax: (6741) 25-50. DM 90–110.

▶ **Zur Post**. Oberstrasse 35, D-55420 **Bacharach am Rhein**. Tel: (6743) 12-77; Fax: (6743) 12-77. DM 75–100.

▶ **Zum Riesen**. Hauptstrasse 97, D-63897 **Miltenberg**. Tel: (9371) 25-82. DM 108–178.

NORTHERN BAVARIA
THE DANUBE AND FRANCONIA

By John Dornberg

Bavaria is Germany's largest state; at more than 27,000 square miles it is a substantial chunk of territory, and not only by European standards. You could fit Belgium, Holland, and Luxembourg into it with room to spare, or Massachusetts, New Hampshire, and Vermont. Moreover, none of the other German *Länder,* as the 16 German states are called, has so completely preserved its 19th-century territorial integrity as this proud one-time kingdom, which calls itself a *Freistaat* (Free State).

Bavaria is bordered on the south by Austria; on the east by the Czech Republic; on the northeast and north by Saxony and Thuringia, whose capitals are Dresden and Erfurt; and along its western boundaries by the states of Hesse, whose principal city is Frankfurt-am-Main, and Baden-Württemberg, whose capital is Stuttgart. It is traversed from west to east by the Danube river, which enters Bavaria from Baden-Württemberg as it passes between the twin cities of Ulm and Neu-Ulm, and leaves at Passau, to the east, where it enters Austria, from there continuing past Vienna, Budapest, and Belgrade before eventually reaching the Black Sea. The Danube divides Bavaria—which is named after the Germanic Baiuoarii tribe, which inhabited the area during the so-called Dark Ages and was subsequently conquered by the Franks—into northern and southern halves, in what is more than just a geographical division: There are significant topographical and climatological differences between the two halves, as well as cultural and linguistic ones.

In this chapter we first follow the Danube from west (Ulm) to east (Passau), with occasional side trips into the Bayerischer Wald (Bavarian Woods) to the north, as well as to special places in Niederbayern (Lower Bavaria) to the south. Then we discuss the half of Bavaria *north* of the river, a region that is centered on Nürnberg and known historically and geographically, as well as politically, as Franconia (Land of the Franks—the Franks being the same general Germanic group that later produced the Merovingians and Carolingians).

(The *southern* half of the state—alpine Oberbayern, or Upper Bavaria, upper meaning higher in altitude—is covered in a separate chapter following that on Munich. The chapter immediately after this one covers a band—the so-called Romantic Road—that stretches down the *western* side of Bavaria, from Würzburg in the north to Füssen, on the Austrian border, in the Alps. The *Romantische Strasse,* as it is called in German, intersects the route we cover here as it crosses the Danube at Donauwörth.)

Northern Bavaria is agreeable country, largely bottomland and gently rolling hills covered with dense forests around the Danube basin, becoming somewhat more mountainous as you travel farther north into Franconia. In the towns of the region, the Middle Ages lie spread out before you, and every hill seems to be crowned by a castle or a fortress—though the sounds you'll hear will most likely be those of a tractor in a nearby field. Still, as you travel the region's smooth roads, with good hotels and picture-book inns awaiting you at every turn, you will feel as if you have been transported into the past.

Some of the most breathtakingly beautiful Gothic, Renaissance, and Baroque architecture in Europe dots this peaceful, modest landscape. In the course of your tour you will encounter the magical work of Cosmas Damian and Egid Quirin Asam, brothers who in their day were the most celebrated masters of Bavarian Baroque architecture and stuccowork; the deeply moving wood carving and sculpture of Tilman Riemenschneider and Veit Stoss; and the painting of Lucas Cranach and Albrecht Dürer. You will see splendid palaces built by prince-bishops, the powerful ecclesiastical and temporal rulers of once-sovereign states. And you will stay in rustic country inns that have been in business for centuries. The air is clean here, and if you keep off the Autobahn and avoid following signs that point the way to a town's *Industrieviertel* (industrial district), you will never realize that Bavaria, in addition to being Germany's second most populous state, has also become the country's high-tech "sunbelt."

MAJOR INTEREST

Along the Danube
Ulm and the world's tallest church spire
Ingolstadt's fortified medieval Altstadt
Well-preserved Regensburg and its Roman ruins
Straubing's Baroque architecture
Frauenau and Zwiesel, centers of glassblowing
Passau and the convergence of the Danube, Inn, and
   Ilz rivers
Naturpark Bayerischer Wald; Metten; Grafenau

Franconia
Nürnberg, city of the Meistersinger
Bayreuth and the Wagner festival theater
Kulmbach (beer)
Coburg, ancestral home of Prince Albert
Baroque churches of Banz and Vierzehnheiligen
Bamberg, jewel of Romanesque, Gothic, Renaissance,
   and Baroque architecture

The Food of Northern Bavaria

Northern Bavarian food is hearty and should be approached
with gusto. It is influenced by the cooking of neighboring
Austria, Czech Bohemia, and Swabian Württemberg, and
encompasses a variety of local traditions. In villages and
small towns the noon meal is the main one, and always starts
with a soup that usually has something substantial floating in
it—a farina or liver dumpling, or sometimes a soft, thin
pancake cut into noodlelike strips and eaten with a happy
slurp. If the soup is thick, like lentil soup, it will contain
slices of wurst. From there the meal usually moves on to a
meat dish with gravy, accompanied by potatoes or a baseball-
size dumpling, cabbage, or sauerkraut. Dessert is rarely
served, though when it is, it is usually compote or custard.

Brotzeit (literally, "bread time") is the evening meal in
more tradition-bound homes and small towns. The bread is
dark, usually rye, with a crisp crust, and there are countless
variations on the basic theme. Sausages of all kinds, and
cured and smoked meats (especially hams of infinite variety)
are the standard accompaniment.

Michelin stars and Gault-Millau toques are rare in this part
of Germany. Nürnberg is a bit more rewarding for the
discriminating gourmet, as is northern Franconia, where you
will find top-rated restaurants in and around Bayreuth,
Coburg, and Bamberg. Still, you'll be able to eat well
(though the portions may seem formidable).

In Franconia, there are some distinctive regional specialties you should try. Though pork seems omnipresent, veal is also a popular entrée; one particularly delicious dish is *Kalbshaxe Blau,* which translates as "blue leg of veal," though it isn't blue at all. The meat is first browned in butter, then simmered in vinegar with a variety of vegetables. Nürnberger *Bratwürste* are different from other bratwurst you may have tried, especially in terms of their size—about equal to a little finger in both thickness and length. Six of them are considered a snack, a dozen a light meal. Although those from Regensburg look like their twins, they are in fact just cousins (the ingredients and spices are somewhat different). Both kinds are usually accompanied by sauerkraut, however. Up in Coburg try *Taschnudeln,* which, in effect, are potato noodles, buttered and baked. *Pfifferlinge* (chanterelles) abound in Franconia as well as in the Bayerische Wald. Sautéed, they make a wonderful side dish, and don't pass them up when offered in a soup such as *Pfifferlingsuppe.*

Of course, sweets and pastries abound in this part of Germany. A *Fränkischer Käsekuchen* is a cheesecake with apples baked across it; *Zwetchgenblootz* is plum cake buried under almonds and crumbs. *Honigkuchen* is made with half a pound of clover honey and a cup of walnuts, and traditionally is sliced extremely thin—mercifully, because of its richness. *Coburger Makronen* are different from other macaroons in that they are made of equal amounts of almonds and hazelnuts. Last but by no means least are *Nürnberger Lebkuchen,* the Christmas specialty that is exported around the world and to which the loosely translated term "gingerbread cookies" does not do justice (in part because they do not contain any ginger).

Beer is as available as water in Northern Bavaria—it seems every town has a brewery whose suds the locals praise as the best in the world. Indeed, of Bavaria's remaining 1,500 independent breweries (there used to be more than 6,000, but mergers and takeovers have swallowed many), two-thirds are in the northern part of the state and some of the most famous brands and varieties are brewed in Franconian Kulmbach and Bamberg.

Elsewhere in Franconia *the* beverage is wine, with the *Frankenweine* (Franconian wines) grown along the Main river and its numerous tributaries, especially in the area around Würzburg, among the most prized in Germany. Generally fuller-bodied and drier than those from other German regions, *Frankenweine* are also known to be earthier and less aromatic. What distinguishes all of them is the flat, dark-green *Bocksbeutel* (literally, "goat's scrotum," referring to the shape) in which they are sold.

ALONG THE DANUBE

The Danube, which meanders its way for 1,725 miles through eight countries to its estuary at the Black Sea, making it Central Europe's longest river, is also its most celebrated—in story, song, poetry, and legend. No other river in Europe is as scenically varied, and none has been witness to as turbulent a history—from the first-known settlement of Celts along its banks around 800 B.C. right through the extraordinary political changes of the past few years.

Yet, when you mention the Danube, most people think of Vienna, Budapest, Belgrade, and the Balkans. That its origins are actually in Germany's Black Forest, and that 400 of its more than 1,700 miles pass through German territory, is both a little-known and oft-forgotten fact. However, it is along this section, as the river passes by and through pictur-esque villages and towns, old moated castles, frowning for-tresses, and majestic medieval cities such as Ulm, Ingolstadt, Regensburg, Straubing, and Passau, that the Danube valley is frequently at its loveliest.

ULM

Ulm, the first stop on our itinerary, is 90 km (56 miles) southeast of Stuttgart by way of the Stuttgart–Munich (A 8) Autobahn. Legally, this city of 110,000 is part of the state of Baden-Württemberg, thanks to the way Napoleon carved up the region in 1810, a rather arbitrary process that caused the Bavarians to create a new city—Neu-Ulm, current popula-tion about 50,000—on the east bank of the river. All the important sites and attractions are in "old" Ulm.

And old it certainly is, having started as an Alemannic settlement in the seventh century. It obtained a municipal charter in 1164, and 110 years later became a *Freie Reichs-stadt,* that is, a free city of the imperial realm, with its own coinage rights and judicial jurisdiction, and answerable only to the Holy Roman emperor. The weaving of fustian (a blend of linen and cotton), trade, and shipping accounted for much of its prosperity in the Middle Ages. In fact, it is in Ulm where the Danube first becomes navigable for small craft—flat-bottomed boats called *Ulmer Schachteln* (Ulm boxes). Long before a string of locks interrupted the river's flow from here to Vienna, Ulm's quays bustled with these

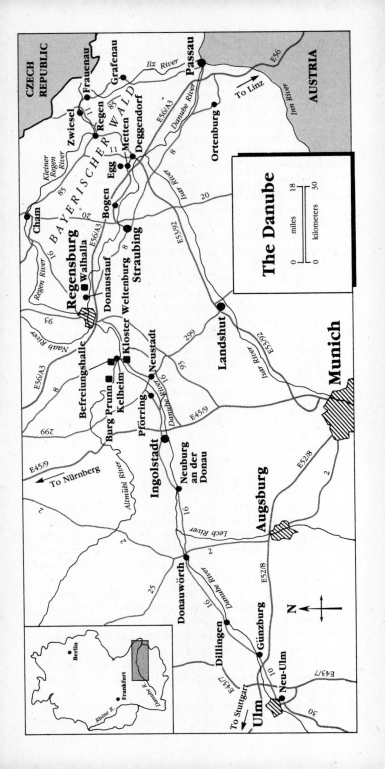

fragile vessels as they prepared to navigate what were then very treacherous waters. Powered by strong men wielding massive oars, they carried their cargo (and sometimes passengers) as far downstream as Belgrade.

Ulm's two most famous natives are Albert Einstein, son of a local merchant (who moved the whole family to Munich when Albert was a little boy), and Albrecht Ludwig Berblinger, known as the "Flying Tailor of Ulm," reputedly the first human being after Icarus to attempt flight. He actually had mastered it quite successfully until an embarrassing mishap in 1811. In honor of a visit to Ulm by King Friedrich I of Württemberg, Berblinger decided to demonstrate his flying machine publicly. Before some 10,000 onlookers, he leaped from the town wall flapping his weird wings and proceeded to plummet like a stone into the Danube.

The wall from which the tailor attempted his flight is Ulm's oldest, dating well back into the 12th century. An outer ring of defenses was built in the 14th century, enclosing an area so large that the town did not outgrow it until 500 years later. Both sets of walls were so formidable that Ulm was able to withstand all the furious conflicts of the Middle Ages, including the Thirty Years' War, unvanquished. In fact, it took the Allied air forces to destroy the city— more than 65 percent of which was leveled by air raids in 1944 and 1945. Miraculously its two most famous landmarks, the brightly frescoed Rathaus (City Hall), with its fanciful clock, and the Münster (Minster), with its 528-foot-spire, the highest church tower in the world, were both spared.

The Münster

The Münster, visible from miles away, dominates Münsterplatz, the center of the city. One of the largest cathedrals in the world, its vaulted ceiling soars 137 feet above the central nave. It is also one of the finest examples of Gothic craftsmanship in Europe, as well as one of the richest in terms of interior decoration.

The foundation stone was laid in 1377. According to local lore the mayor and townspeople covered it with gold coins and jewels, all of which have long since been encased in mortar. Ulmers continued to build and add to the church over the next five centuries, and though most of the work was done by the early 16th century, the two eastern towers and the tall western steeple, Ulm's landmark, weren't completed until 1890.

Not surprisingly, given its grand scale, the construction of the cathedral attracted some of the greatest architects, sculptors, and painters of medieval Germany—each of whom seemed bent on outdoing the others. Among the main interior features are the magnificent 15th-century choir windows, striking for their size and coloring; the beautifully carved choir stalls, which were created by Jörg Syrlin the Elder between 1469 and 1471; the 1471 fresco of the Last Judgment, considered one of the most important examples of Gothic wall painting; and Syrlin's 85-foot-high limestone-and-sandstone tabernacle.

Atop the roof of the central nave is a carved stone figure of a sparrow with a blade of grass in its beak—the *Ulmer Spatz*—the town's mascot. According to legend, a group of (apparently dim-witted) laborers had unsuccessfully tried to bring a long log through one of the city's gates. Finally, they noticed a nest-building sparrow carrying a blade of grass that had to be negotiated through a small hole before it could be added to the nest. The observant laborers watched as the clever bird turned the blade lengthwise and brought it easily through the hole. Their lesson learned, they then put their shoulders to the task and got the log into town.

"Ulm Sparrows"—in porcelain, ceramic, plastic, tin, chocolate, and marzipan—are sold all over town. And if you wish to completely immerse yourself in the legend, you'll find the ▶ **Hotel Ulmer Spatz**, Münsterplatz 27, right in the shadow of the church, a moderately priced place to eat and stay. The hotel also has a wine tavern and garden restaurant.

Around in Ulm

Ulm's **Rathaus**, just south of the Münster on Rathausplatz, dates back to 1360 and has presented the same façade to the town since 1420. The statues that grace the upper story, depicting various electors and emperors of the Holy Roman Empire, have been there since 1427. The astronomical clock, with its zodiac signs, positions of the moon and planets, and countless other bits of incidental information, was added to the façade in 1520, but the one you see nowadays—in perfect working order—is a 1580 replacement. The Renaissance-style Neuer Bau (New Wing) was incorporated into the original structure in the late 16th century, and looked so palatial when completed in 1593 that Ulm's burgomaster and town councillors moved right in, figuring they could make better use of it than the grain merchants for whom it had been built.

The **Ulmer Museum**, just east of the Rathaus, with its entrance at Neue Strasse 92, has a fine collection of Gothic and applied art, as well as a substantial collection of modern regional painting and sculpture.

A short stroll south from the museum, along Marktplatz,

brings you to the **Metzger Turm** (Butcher's Tower), which is part of Ulm's medieval wall. This "leaning tower of Ulm" has been listing more than six feet in a northwesterly direction for well over six centuries. The nearby Adlerbastei (Eagle's Bastion) is the section of the wall from which Berblinger made his leap into the Danube.

If you walk west along the fortifications you'll come to the idyllic **Fischer-und-Gerberviertel** (Fishermen's and Tanners' Quarter), which is laced by canals and outlets of the Blau river, a small tributary of the Danube. Dubbed "Little Venice," the quarter is one of the city's loveliest. It is also a perfect spot to stop for lunch, and you won't find a more delightful or historic choice than the **Restaurant zur Forelle**, Fischergasse 25, an elegantly rustic 16th-century inn specializing in fish dishes—notably trout—that have won it recognition throughout Europe.

About 2 km (1 mile) upstream along the Danube is the **Deutsches Brotmuseum** (German Bread Museum), Fürsteneckerstrasse 17. Germany has more odd and specialized museums than any other country in Europe; this one is devoted entirely to the cultural history of bread. Among the exhibits are a 5,000-year-old Mesopotamian bas-relief illustrating the bread-baking process, medieval bakers' utensils, and documents and paintings dealing with the role of bread in religion.

Most of Ulm's hotels are located northeast of the Münster and within walking distance of the railway station. The most functional, and a member of the French chain, is the ► **Ibis Hotel**, Neutorstrasse 12. If you prefer a more personalized atmosphere, try the ► **Hotel Neuthor**, Neuer Graben 23, about a ten-minute walk from Münsterplatz.

Between Ulm and Ingolstadt

To continue your exploration of the Danube valley, cross the river to Neu-Ulm and follow the signs and B 10 out of town in the direction of **Günzburg**, a drive of about 16 km (10 miles). If you're not in a hurry, stop off in the center of town for a look at the **Frauenkirche** (Church of Our Lady), a fine example of Baroque architecture by the Swabian-Bavarian stucco master Dominikus Zimmermann completed in 1741.

Close to the church is a major road junction. Instead of continuing on B 10, you'll want to bear left (north) onto B 16 for the 51-km (32-mile) drive to Donauwörth.

The road, which follows the left (north) bank of the Danube, passes through the town of **Dillingen**, exuberantly rich in Baroque churches and monasteries, and also the location of a magnificent palace. The **Schloss** (palace), on Schlossstrasse, served as the residence of the bishops of Augsburg after the burghers in that city rebelled against the bishops' temporal rule in the 15th century. The Augsburg bishops soon turned Dillingen into a major ecclesiastical center, complete with a **university**, whose 17th- and 18th-century buildings you will find on Kardinal-von-Waldburg-Strasse. The **Maria Himmelfahrtkirche** (Church of the Assumption), completed in 1617 and renovated in Rococo style in 1768, is part of the complex. The church's rich decoration is equaled only by that of **St. Peter**'s, a former parish church elevated to the rank of a papal basilica in 1979, on Klosterstrasse, adjacent to Dillingen's Franciscan monastery. In both you will find sculptures and stuccowork by Johann Michael Zimmermann and Johann Georg Fischer, two of 18th-century Bavaria's finest and most prolific architect-artists.

Donauwörth, our next destination, is where the **Romantic Road** crosses the Danube; you will find a description of it in the following chapter. Highway B 16 then continues east from Donauwörth along the Danube's right bank for 32 km (20 miles) to Neuburg.

Neuburg an der Donau, population 25,000, has its roots in Roman times and, thanks to its strategic location, became a major stronghold and customs station of Bavaria's Wittelsbach dynasty as early as the eighth century. The foundations for its **Schloss** (castle) were laid in 788, though most of the huge complex that now rises above the river was built between 1530 and 1545 by Count Ottheinrich of the Wittelsbach family's Palatinate line, one of the most prolific builders of the German Renaissance period.

Besides the castle, be sure to see the **Frauenkirche** (Church of Our Lady) on Karlsplatz, completed in 1618 and regarded as a perfect blend of Late Gothic design and Renaissance interior ornamentation. Italian stucco artists did much of the work. Worth seeing, too, are the 17th-century **Rathaus** and the **Church of the Holy Cross**, an 18th-century structure with a high altar by Fischer.

Neuburg is ideal for strolling and soaking up medieval atmosphere. And just 2 km (1 mile) northwest of the city, in Neuburg-Bittenbrunn at Monheimer Strasse 119, you will find the ▶ **Kirchbaur-Hof**, a rustic country inn with moderately priced rooms and a prodigious kitchen that specializes in fish dishes, especially trout, pike, carp, and perch. Even if you don't spend the night or stop for lunch, consider the Kirchbaur for an afternoon coffee and slice of cake; its apple strudel is some of the best to be found along the Danube. Tel: (8431) 25-32.

Highway B 16 crosses the Danube again at Neuburg and continues along the north bank in an easterly direction for another 23 km (14 miles) to Ingolstadt.

INGOLSTADT

Though better known today as both the center of Bavaria's oil-refining industry and the home of Audi cars, Ingolstadt (current population 100,000) has roots that go back 2,500 years. But while it began to burgeon as a powerful Danubian citadel as early as the sixth century A.D., its golden age didn't begin until 1255, when Bavaria's Duke Ludwig the Severe built a fortress here, now known as the Altes Schloss. Two centuries later another Bavarian ruler, Ludwig the Rich, founded the duchy's first university here, putting the city on the map as a center of learning, science, and culture. Thanks to a massive defensive system comprised of three walls completed in 1430, it was also one of the best-fortified towns in southern Germany—so well protected, in fact, that it withstood several onslaughts by the armies of Sweden's King Gustav Adolf during the Thirty Years' War.

The crafts played a key role in the life of the town during the Middle Ages, and because of its advantageous position on the Danube Ingolstadt retained its industrial importance well into the 17th century. It really began to boom after World War II, however, and now is not only a major car-manufacturing center and the terminus for three transcontinental oil pipelines but also has four oil refineries. Fortunately, all of this heavy industry lies well to the east of the historic old city, which, snuggled safely within its ancient walls, looks much as it did in the Middle Ages.

The old city is a semicircular maze of narrow streets, many of them cobblestone, lined by gabled houses, and measures a little more than half a mile in diameter. You can, if you wish, still walk around the wall, which was reinforced at strategic spots by formidable towers, all of which have survived. Of the main gates, however, only one remains—the **Kreuztor**, at the western end of Kreuzstrasse.

Just a few steps from the latter is the **Liebfrauenmünster** (Basilica of Our Lady), one of the finest examples of brick Gothic architecture in Bavaria. Though commissioned in 1425 by Duke Ludwig the Bearded, it wasn't completed until more than a century later. Its high altar, dating back to 1572, is made up of 91 painted panels depicting bearded learned men of the time. Be sure also to see the richly carved 16th-century pulpit and choir stalls.

Continuing along Kreuzstrasse, which changes its name to

Ludwigstrasse and becomes a pedestrian mall, you will eventually come to the center of the city and its other architectural treasures.

The **Stadtpfarrkirche** (City Parish Church) **St. Moritz**, Moritzstrasse 4, a late Romanesque structure that was consecrated in 1234, was expanded in the 14th century with Gothic additions. The Baroque stuccowork inside the church was done by Johann Baptist Zimmermann in the 18th century. The **Minorite Church**, on Harderstrasse, is a 13th-century basilica, noteworthy for its finely carved stone epitaphs. Munich's Asam brothers left their magnificent imprint on the small church of **Maria Viktoria**, Neubaustrasse 1, which was begun in 1732 as the prayer hall of the Marian student congregation. The enormous ceiling fresco, a masterpiece, is unusual for its brilliant colors, and was probably a collaboration between the two brothers. The high altar is the work of Fischer.

Ludwig the Severe's original castle in Ingolstadt, the **Altes Schloss**, on Hallstrasse, is also known as the *Herzogskasten* (Duke's Box), and served the Wittelsbach rulers for almost two centuries. After that the Duke's Box was turned into a grain warehouse, which is fitting enough, for that is what it looks like. (Today it's the municipal library.) The **Neues Schloss** (New Castle), Paradeplatz 4, which looks a bit more like a ducal palace, was commissioned by Ludwig the Bearded and built between 1418 and 1432, then expanded in the 16th century. Today it houses the **Bayerisches Armeemuseum** (Bavarian Army Museum), a collection of weapons and military paraphernalia that will tell you anything you want to know about soldiering.

For lunch or dinner consider stopping at the **Restaurant im Stadttheater**, Schlosslände 1, almost adjacent to the Neues Schloss and Army Museum, and with a terrace overlooking the Danube. The menu is rather international, although the sole garnished with crab, asparagus, olives, and mushrooms stands out.

The best spot to spend the night in the old city is the ▶ **Hotel Rappensberger**, Harderstrasse 3, near the Minorite Church. The rooms are clean and comfortable, and you sense instantly that it is family run.

Between Ingolstadt and Regensburg

Highway B 16, which brought you into Ingolstadt, will also take you out of town. If you want to continue driving along the Danube, however, take a left turn at the fork in the road about 12 km (7 miles) outside of Ingolstadt and follow the unnumbered county road, which hugs the north bank of the river, as far as the town of Pförring; signs will point the way.

Just beyond Pförring the road intersects with a wider one that will take you into Neustadt. In Neustadt, make a left turn onto the river road, and follow the directions to Bad Gögging, Weltenburg, and Kelheim. Going this way, it will be about a 35-km (22-mile) drive along the river from Ingolstadt to the next stop on our itinerary, Weltenburg.

Kloster Weltenburg, located on the Danube's south bank at a sharp bend in the river, is Bavaria's oldest monastic community. It is also almost impossible to find. From Kelheim (see below) it is best reached by boat. Coming from Ingolstadt, your best bet is to leave your car at the parking lot upriver, even if the attendant on duty does little to encourage you. Your persistence will be well rewarded, however, for the monastery church of **St. Georg and St. Martin** is one of the most vibrant masterpieces of the Baroque, not to mention one of the finest works ever created by the Asam brothers.

Despite its remoteness, Weltenburg was thoroughly plundered by iconoclasts in 1546, and the abbot was subsequently forced to sell what remained of the monastery's library to pay for minimal repairs. For more than a century and a half the place gradually declined. Then, in 1716, the Asams were called in to do some badly needed restoration. Cosmas Damian was then 29, his brother Egid Quirin, 23. Both had only recently returned from their studies in Rome. What they brought back to Bavaria—and to Weltenburg—was an artistic vigor and brilliance unmatched in a period that was characterized by its artistic exuberance. The elder Asam, who was responsible for most of the architectural work, also painted the ceiling fresco (in which he portrayed his younger brother as an angel). The finest feature of the church, however, is its high altar, on which the brothers collaborated, and which portrays the struggle of Saint George against the dragon.

Kelheim, 8 km (5 miles) downstream from Weltenburg, is where the Altmühl river meets the Danube, and is also the start of the Rhine-Main-Danube canal, which opened in September 1992. The waterway, a dream since the days of Charlemagne, and under construction for almost 70 years, enables freight barges to operate between the North and Black seas.

A Celtic settlement for almost 500 years before the Romans came along and turned it into a military base, Kelheim owes its present appearance to Duke Ludwig the Severe, who commissioned its construction as a totally planned city in 1206. Unlike other medieval towns, with their narrow, twisting streets, Kelheim was laid out as an orderly grid and is surrounded by a protective wall that bends at right angles. While you're here, be sure to see the 15th-century parish church of the Assumption on the Marktplatz as well as the 13th-century hospital church of St. John.

The main reason for stopping off in Kelheim, however, is to visit the Brobdingnagian **Befreiungshalle** (Liberation Hall; open daily) on the Michelsberg, a lush green mountain that rises above the town. The last of the many Greco-Roman–style monuments commissioned by Bavaria's flamboyant King Ludwig I, the Befreiungshalle commemorates the so-called Wars of Liberation waged by other European powers against Napoleon from 1813 to 1815.

With Friedrich von Gärtner, one of Ludwig's favorite Munich architects, in charge of the project, the cornerstone was laid in 1842. By 1847, only the huge circular terrace had been completed. Then Gärtner died of a heart attack, at which point Ludwig turned to an even greater favorite, Leo von Klenze. Klenze accepted the assignment on condition that Ludwig allow him to scrap Gärtner's somewhat eclectic plans and proceed with an "Antique Roman" monument. Ludwig agreed to the change, but a year later, after he was forced to abdicate because of his scandalous affair with the dancer Lola Montez, work on the project was halted.

Construction resumed in 1849, with Ludwig paying for much of it out of his own pocket, but it proceeded at a much slower pace and with considerable cost cutting, including the use of brick instead of limestone blocks for the shell. The monument was finished and dedicated in 1863, on the 50th anniversary of the "Battle of the Nations" at Leipzig, in which Napoleon suffered his first decisive defeat in Western Europe. The ex-king and Klenze, both 79 years old by then, were in attendance.

The rotunda Klenze wrought atop the Michelsberg is certainly vast—more than 160 feet in diameter and almost 200 feet high. Set in a circle around its perimeter, and holding hands as if they were playing "ring-around-the-rosy," are 34 twice-life-size marble figures of Winged Victory, each representing one of the then-independent German kingdoms, principalities, duchies, and city-states. Between these 34 monumental statutes are 17 bronze shields inscribed with the names of the principal battles waged against Bonaparte, and above them 17 plaques inscribed with the names of the most important German and Austrian field marshals and generals.

Bombastic as the Liberation Hall may be, however, it pales in comparison to Ludwig's other great monument on the Danube, Walhalla, some 34 km (21 miles) farther downstream (northeast). But before driving that far, plan on spending a day or two in Regensburg, the greatest of the cities on our Danube route, just 24 km (15 miles) to the east.

REGENSBURG

The city has had many names. To the Celts, who founded it around 500 B.C., it was Radaspona. To the Romans, who made it an impregnable fortress during the reign of Marcus Aurelius in the second century A.D., it was Castra Regina, meaning "camp on the Regen," a reference to the tributary that meets the Danube here. Then, four centuries later, came the Germanic Baiuoarii, ancestors of today's Bavarians, who called it Regenespurc, which seems close enough to its contemporary German name.

Its many names—there have been 75 others as well, including the seven coined by Goethe's Mephistopheles as he was flying toward it on his magic cloak with Dr. Faustus— speak volumes. The age of Germany's cities is frequently in dispute and often the source of considerable rivalry between them, but Regensburg regards itself above such petty competition. By virtue of its documented past, most of the others are upstarts. Its past, moreover, has been remarkably well preserved.

Regensburg is how all German cities are expected to look—like a travel poster. Left virtually untouched during World War II, it is, with a population of 130,000, the largest and most perfectly preserved medieval city in western Germany. Known for centuries as the German gateway to the Balkans and the Orient, it is an urban gem—a town for strolling, exploring, and soaking up history; for admiring the art and craftsmanship of past epochs; a city of narrow lanes, cobblestone streets, secluded courtyards, gabled burgher houses, imposing defensive walls and towers, splendid palaces, and majestic Romanesque and Gothic churches.

It is a city, morever, where the living past is treated with lighthearted humor. Amble through the town—and walking is not only the best but virtually the only way to master the mile-by-half-mile historic center that hugs the Danube's south bank—and you will come upon streets with such charming names as the Fröhliche-Türken-Strasse (Cheerful Turks Street), Zur Schönen Gelegenheit (Good Opportunity Corner), the Entengang (Ducks' Way), the Gässchen Ohne End (Alley Without End), or the Hundsumkehr (Dogs' Turn-around Lane). Human foibles are as much the theme of the murals and bas-reliefs that grace the city's ancient buildings as are great deeds.

Regensburg's Roman military contingent numbered 6,000, and with the usual codicil of families, camp followers, merchants, and other hangers-on, it was a fortified town of 12,000, replete with forum, temples, pottery workshops, and a mint, which struck the last Roman coin in A.D. 408. The wall surrounding old Regensburg, more than a mile long and 23 feet high, was built of huge limestone blocks fitted so exactly without mortar that even today a razor blade cannot be squeezed between them. Massive gateways to the fortress, such as the **Porta Praetoria**, guard towers, and other sections of the wall remain visible today, integrated into churches, hotels, shops, and a parking garage. In Regensburg, Germany's Roman heritage is very much alive.

Unlike other frontier towns of the Roman Empire, Regensburg was not abandoned when Rome itself collapsed and the Baiuoarii invaded in the fifth and sixth centuries. Somehow, it just absorbed them, turning those proto-Bavarians into Christians long before Christianity took root elsewhere in Germany. In fact, the oldest Christian tombstones found in the city date from the late fourth and early fifth centuries; its first abbey was founded 1,300 years ago; and by the time Saint Boniface, the Irish missionary known as the Apostle of the Germans, arrived in 739, Regensburg was, by the standards of the time, a surprisingly civilized place. Charlemagne then made it the most important town in southern Germany, and from the tenth through the 18th centuries it ranked as one of the great centers of the German Holy Roman Empire.

The Rathaus Area

Within the empire Regensburg enjoyed a privileged position, not only as an independent city-state but as the seat of the *Reichstag* (Imperial Diet). Throughout the Middle Ages this parliament of nobles met periodically in the ornate chambers and council halls of Regensburg's beautifully preserved 14th-century **Rathaus** (City Hall), on Rathausplatz, and had its permanent home there from 1663 until 1806, when Napoleon disbanded the diet and abolished the Holy Roman Empire. There are numerous daily guided tours of the building (in which the mayor still has his office); these include its lavishly appointed Reichssaal (Imperial Hall), the Kurfürstenkollegium (Electors' Chamber), the Fürstenkollegium (Princes' Chamber), and the bloodcurdling Fragstatt (torture dungeon). Regensburg's Verkehrsamt (tourist office) is on the ground floor of the Rathaus.

Be sure, before or after your tour of the city hall, to have coffee and pastry at the **Café Prinzess**, Rathausplatz 2, which has been open for business since 1686, making it Germany's oldest coffeehouse.

For all of Regensburg's historic role as a political center, its real power and influence derived from its advantageous location on the Danube as well as from its famous **Steinerne Brücke** (Stone Bridge) across the river, unaltered in appearance and still very much in use today. Completed in 1146 after only 11 years of construction, it was one of the engineering marvels of the Middle Ages, and for hundreds of years virtually the only bridge across Europe's chief transportation artery. So large did it loom in the affairs of its day, in fact, that two Crusades—the second, led by Holy Roman Emperor Conrad III in 1147, and the third, begun by Emperor Frederick Barbarossa in 1189—set out from this bridge in Regensburg.

At its southern end, right on the Danube embankment, is the **Alte Wurstküche** (Old Sausage Kitchen), Thundorferstrasse 3, famed precisely for what its name suggests: sausages. They are pork, four inches long, half an inch in diameter, and charcoal broiled; come in portions of four, six, eight, or twelve; and are accompanied by sauerkraut. Other than potato soup, there is little else on the menu. The Wurstküche has only a half-dozen plain wooden tables, but what it lacks in elegance is more than compensated for by venerability: It has been in business continuously for more than 800 years, having been started in the late 1130s as a canteen serving the masons and construction workers who built the Stone Bridge. (Right in front of the building is the landing for the excursion steamers that take travellers to Regensburg's barge harbor, through the locks of the Rhine-Main-Danube canal, and on longer trips on the river.) Diagonally across the river from the Würstküche, on the Danube's opposite bank, is the 70-year-old side-wheel steamship **"Ruthof-Ersekcsanad,"** which serves as a museum devoted to the Danube's shipping history.

The Stone Bridge bolstered Regensburg's position as the principal trade crossroads between southern Europe and Scandinavia, as well as between the Orient and Middle East and France and the Netherlands. In time, the city's merchants amassed fabulous wealth, and Regensburg's coinage was considered so solid that it was accepted as legal tender throughout Europe. For centuries its only serious commercial rival was Venice, and some Regensburg merchants were even entrenched in that fair city. Its ties to other Italian city-states—Florence and Siena—were close as well, and it was from these that rich Regensburgers imported an architectural style that became peculiar to the city: fortresslike tower houses, some 12 stories high. The higher the house, the richer its owner was presumed to be. While 60 of these medieval skyscrapers once punctuated the city's skyline, making Regensburg a kind of Manhattan of the Middle Ages, only 20 survive today, most of them as studio-apartment houses much sought-after by local university students and artists. The best preserved, both dating to the 13th century, are the **Baumburger Turm**, on the Watmarkt, seven stories and 92 feet tall, and the **Goldener Turm**, also called *Haymohaus,* Wahlenstrasse 16, which is nearly 139 feet high.

Equally impressive is the **Goldenes Kreuz** (Golden Cross), at Haidplatz 7. From the 16th through the 19th centuries the Goldenes Kreuz served as Regensburg's imperial inn, a sort of grand hotel for visiting emperors, kings, electors, princes, foreign emissaries, and other potentates. And, like any hotel, it had its share of scandal and hanky-panky in the bedrooms. Perhaps the most famous affair was the 1546 tryst between Emperor Charles V (grandson of Spain's Ferdinand and Isabella) and 18-year-old Barbara Blomberg, a Regensburg saddlemaker's daughter 28 years his junior. The young lady, famous for her beauty, bore the emperor a son on February 24, 1547, Charles's own birthday, in the 13th-century Weinstube zur Stritzelbäckerin, now called **Historisches Eck**, Watmarkt 6, near the Baumburger Turm, renowned then and now thanks to its wine cellar, superb food, and salty rolls known as *Stritzel.* Indeed, proprietor-chef Rüdiger Forst has made it into Regensburg's most highly rated eatery, earning a Michelin star and two Gault-Millau toques in the process; Tel: (941) 589-20.

The emperor's illegitimate offspring, Don Juan de Austria, became an important figure in his own right. As admiral of the Holy League's fleet, he was said to have saved Christian Europe and the Occident from conquest by the Ottoman Turks in 1571 by winning the murderous Battle of Lepanto against Uluc Ali Pasha. Shortly after the victory, the grateful citizens of Sicily, which had provided a good part of Don Juan's fleet, erected a bronze monument to him in Messina. In 1971, some 400 years later, a copy of it was cast and brought to Regensburg, where it now stands on Zieroldsplatz, a tiny square near the Rathaus. The tale of the emperor's liaison with Blomberg is told in a mural that graces the façade of the house. Another reminder of the tantalizing affair are the delectable chocolate pralines, called "Barbara's Kisses," made by the Café Prinzess.

One of the city's newest hotels, the ▶ **Altstadthotel Arch**, is one of its oldest buildings—a totally renovated 18th-century patrician house at Am Haidplatz 4. For elegant dining with a French touch in a beautifully restored medieval house, there is the **Restaurant zum Krebs**, Krebsgasse 6, at the corner of the Haidplatz near the Goldenes Kreuz; Tel: (941) 558-03.

South and North of the Rathaus

Don Juan was by no means Regensburg's only famous native son. Albertus Magnus, the "universal doctor," also known as Saint Albert the Great, taught in the city from 1236 to 1240, and was its bishop from 1260 to 1262. Albrecht Altdorfer, the first German landscape painter and founder of the Danubian school, was born in Regensburg in 1480 and died here in 1538. For a while he was the city's chief architect, served two terms as a town councillor, and was even nominated for mayor, an honor he rejected because he feared it would take too much time from his art. The house in which he lived and worked from 1513 to 1538 is at Obere-Bach-Gasse 7, about a ten-minute walk due south of the Rathaus. Though Altdorfer's most prized paintings are in galleries elsewhere, the **Museum der Stadt Regensburg** (Regensburg Municipal Museum), Dachauplatz 2-4, exhibits a number of his important pictures.

Johannes Kepler, the mathematician and astronomer whose description of the elliptical movement of the planets is still the basis of modern astronomical studies, had numerous ties to Regensburg. His first long stay in town began in 1613, and he was often a guest at the **Walderbacher Hof**, an inn at Georgenplatz 6, now a tavern oddly called the Old Vienna. While some of his visits were to see friends and relatives, others were strictly business—to collect the 12,000 guilders in back pay that a succession of Holy Roman emperors, his nominal employers, owed him. In the late 1620s Kepler used the city as a base for travelling to other centers of science, leaving his wife and children in a rented house at what is today Keplerstrasse 2, a picturesque street running parallel to the Danube just two blocks north of the Rathaus. He died, in 1630, in the building across the street, Keplerstrasse 5. The latter, today, is the **Kepler Gedächtnishaus** (Kepler Memorial House), a museum containing many of his original scientific instruments and manuscripts; guided tours four times daily, and two on Sundays.

Conveniently located across from the Kepler house is the rustic **Restaurant Gänsbauer**, Keplerstrasse 10, specializing in good regional cuisine prepared in a nouvelle style. Open for dinner only; reservations recommended; Tel: (941) 578-58.

The St. Peter's Area

Regensburg's wealth was directly responsible for its profusion of magnificent Romanesque and Gothic churches—26 in all—of which the **Dom St. Peter** (St. Peter's Cathedral), on the Domplatz, about a ten-minute walk east of the Rathaus, is actually the newest, not having been completed (despite the fact that it was begun in 1250) until 1525. It is one of Europe's most impressive and harmonious Gothic cathedrals, ranking with those of Chartres, Cologne, Reims, Strasbourg, and Ulm in sheer size and splendor. It's impressive for its exterior stonework and sculpture, especially the west portal, and you'll want to go inside to see its stained-glass windows and fine altars from the 13th and 14th centuries. The cathedral is part of a larger complex called the *Domstadt* (Cathedral City), much of it considerably older than the Dom itself, and which includes the 12th-century **Allerheiligenkapelle** (All Saints' Chapel) and the adjacent **St.-Ulrich-Kirche** (St. Ulrich's Church), built between 1230 and 1250.

One of the cathedral's greatest "treasures" is more audible than visible, and best heard not in the Dom itself but in the 12th-century **Niedermünster**, adjacent to the bishop's palace, about 300 feet east of St. Peter's: The **Regensburger Domspatzen** (Cathedral Sparrows), a 60-member boys' choir, has been getting rave reviews for more than 1,000 years. Founded by Bishop Wolfgang in 975, the choir is part of the cathedral school. Although the performance of liturgical music remains the choir's primary charge, over the centuries it has turned its attention increasingly to secular works. The proceeds from these concerts, as well as radio and television performances and commercial recordings, go toward the running of the school. The Domspatzen can be heard most Sundays and holidays at the 9:00 A.M. Mass; their performances of secular music take place throughout the concert season.

The **Domschatzmuseum** (Cathedral Treasury Museum), entrance via the cathedral garden, is a stunning collection of ecclesiastical art from the Middle Ages and the Renaissance, including a 13th-century gem-and-pearl-studded crucifix that belonged to Bohemia's King Ottokar III.

The Domplatz and Domstadt are convenient to some of Regensburg's more commendable "old city" hotels. The ▶ **Hotel Bischofshof**, Krauterermarkt 3, tucked into a section of the Roman wall and the Porta Praetoria, offers all the modern comforts in a centuries-old environment. Run by Monika and Herbert Schmalhofer, the hotel also has a fine restaurant. The ▶ **Hotel Karmeliten**, Dachauplatz 1, about a quarter-mile southeast of the Domplatz, across from the Regensburg city museum, is located in a 150-year-old house that sits on Roman foundations (which proprietor Emil Seidl eagerly shows to guests), and is moderately priced.

The old city's most fashionable inn is the ▶ **Parkhotel Maximilian**, Maximilianstrasse 28. A grand 19th-century Neo-

Baroque hotel that was completely renovated in 1985, the Maximilian offers touches of luxury and elegance at reasonable prices.

St. Emmeram's

From the Maximilian it is a 10- to 15-minute walk west along Sankt-Peters-Weg to the most remarkable of Regensburg's churches, **St. Emmeramskirche**, as well as the Thurn-und-Taxis palace.

St. Emmeram's is the oldest center of Christianity in Regensburg, having been founded in the fifth century by Christianized Romans and Baiuoarii. It is named for a missionary monk, Saint Emmeram, who was martyred in southern Bavaria and entombed in the church in 685. A Benedictine abbey was built adjacent to the church soon after, and by the tenth century it was known as one of the greatest centers of learning in Europe. The abbey **library**, with more than 200,000 books, includes numerous illuminated manuscripts. A number of the sculptures and tombs in the church itself, some dating to the ninth and tenth centuries, are of inestimable value to art historians. Also of interest are the **cloisters**, among the largest and most beautiful in Germany, and the Romanesque nave of the **church**, which was redecorated with a dazzling splash of stucco, trompe l'oeil frescoes, and magnificent sculptures by the Asams in the 18th century.

The immense monastery is now the gaudy Neo-Renaissance-style **Thurn-und-Taxis Schloss**, the 500-room palace of the Thurn-und-Taxis family, who acquired the abbey in 1812. The family traces its origins to northern Italy and the southern Tyrol, where the ancestral name was Daxis, to which they later added the "de la Torre" that became today's "Thurn." Their business in the Middle Ages was robber barony, or, to be more precise, piracy. Then, in the 15th century, the Daxis barons became mailmen. That is, they invented—and eventually gained a Europe-wide monopoly on—postal services. By the 17th century their network of stagecoaches, dispatch riders, and postal relay stations spanned the Continent. Legend has it that, in addition to delivering the mail, they also read it. This made their services doubly valuable to scheming dukes, kings, emperors, and popes, all of whom rewarded—or in some cases paid off—these clever postmen. The "postage," in many cases, amounted to titles of nobility as well as land—lots of land. The latter is one reason why the family (reigning Prince Johannes died at age 64 in December 1990, his heir—Inheritor Prince Albert—is only 10 years old, and his widow, Gloria, 34, once known as the "Punk Princess," is running matters after a crash course in business administration), with assets conservatively estimated at $3 billion, rates as one of the richest in Germany.

The Thurn-und-Taxis clan moved to Regensburg in 1790, and when St. Emmeram's was secularized by an edict of Napoleon they bought the monastery and turned it into their palatial digs. Today the family lives in a resplendent third-floor "apartment" surrounded by servants who, on formal occasions, wear 18th-century livery. When they do not need them—and with seven other castles and palaces to call home, they often don't—the lavishly decorated formal rooms of the palace, all crammed with priceless art, are open to the public. So are the cloisters of St. Emmeram's, which connect the church to the abbey/palace, and the **Marstall** (Stables) **Museum**, with its scores of 19th-century coaches and carriages, silver and gold harnesses, and equestrian paintings.

Across the square from the church and the entrance to the palace is another worthwhile museum, the **Diözesan** (Diocesan) **Museum**, Emmeramsplatz 1, with a fine collection of ecclesiastical art spanning a period of some ten centuries.

On your way back toward the river and the area around the Rathaus and Dom, you may want to stop for a look at two other interesting churches. The **Dominikanerkirche** (Dominican Church), on Beraiterweg, was consecrated in 1300, and is one of the earliest Gothic structures in Germany. **St. Jakob** (St. James), on Jakobstrasse, off Bismarckplatz, was completed in 1195, and was once the chapel of an Irish-Scottish missionary monastery, which is why it is also called the *Schottenkirche* (Scottish Church). Its most remarkable feature is its main portal, a dazzling example of Romanesque sculpture and stonework that blends Roman and Celto-German influences with Christian symbols and imagery.

Even if you decide not to continue along our Danube route, choosing, instead, to drive northwest 90 km (56 miles) to Nürnberg, no visit to Regensburg would be complete without stopping at Donaustauf and the Walhalla, 10 km (6 miles) downstream.

WALHALLA

Walhalla is an almost perfect replica of the Parthenon, and has virtually the same dimensions. But instead of being sited on the Acropolis, it rises from a nondescript mound called the Breuberg, near the bucolic village of **Donaustauf** on the north bank of the Danube, where it has stood for a century and a half—a temple to Germanic greatness as well as a symbol of imperial dreams gone awry.

This huge edifice is quite literally a "hall of fame" containing busts of and memorial plaques to more than 200 German luminaries. That not all enshrined here were Germans in the strictest sense, and that some defy the dogged efforts of historians and encyclopaedists to attribute to them even a modicum of greatness, hardly seems to matter to the almost one million people who visit the monument annually.

The idea for Walhalla began to germinate in the future King Ludwig I's head in 1807, when, as Bavaria's 21-year-old crown prince, he was dispatched to Berlin to attend Napoleon's galling celebration of victory over Prussia at the tomb of Frederick the Great. Young Ludwig, who had been less than enthusiastic about Bavaria's alliance with France, became even more disenchanted as he witnessed Bonaparte's triumphant prancing in Berlin. On his return to Munich he decided he would avenge the Corsican's performance by building a monument to Frederick and other great Germans once he was king.

Ludwig's day was a while in coming. In fact, his father Maximilian I remained on the throne for another 18 years. In the meantime, Ludwig began ordering busts. He also began to search for an appropriate site, finally persuading Regensburg's Prince von Thurn-und-Taxis to donate a portion of his vineyards on the Breuberg slope near Donaustauf. Within a year of becoming king, Ludwig commissioned his then-favorite architect, Klenze, to start drawing up plans for the pantheon, telling him, "I want it to be great, not just colossal in size, but great in concept and design."

Klenze, who was deeply involved in turning Munich, Ludwig's capital, into a "new Athens," drew up his plans and began ordering marble for the project: 6,000 blocks of the finest available from Italy, hauled over the Alps by ox-drawn wagons. The ceiling was to be made of plates of bronze, gilded with gold leaf and inset with stars of platinum. The iron portals were designed to be—and are—28 feet high and weigh two tons each.

The cornerstone was laid in 1830; the monument opened officially 12 years later. To avoid antagonizing Bavaria's parliament, Ludwig financed virtually all his building projects from his civil list of four million guilders annually.

The placement of people along the walls of Walhalla always was, and remains, a puzzle. Thus the watchmaker Henlein has a niche above Charlemagne; Erasmus of Holland sits next to Philippus Paracelsus, whose next-door neighbor is Copernicus (considered a Pole in Poland). The Holy Roman emperor Charles V is in a row with a barely known duke of Württemberg, who shares his billing with Goethe and Austria's Count Joseph Radetzky (in whose honor Vienna's Johann Strauss composed the famous "Radetzky March"). Strauss himself has yet to make it into Walhalla, though his Munich-born namesake and fellow composer Richard is duly enshrined. Painter Hans Holbein the Younger is here, his father is not. Likewise, the composer Anton Bruckner is represented, but not Johannes Brahms.

If you're not ready to turn back to Nürnberg and Franconia after your visit to Walhalla, continue along the Danube (B 8) for approximately 40 km (25 miles) to Straubing.

STRAUBING

Straubing, like Regensburg, can trace its origins to Roman times, when it was a military camp called Sorviodurum, out of which the sixth-century Baiuoarii came up with "Strupinga." Although it is mentioned as early as A.D. 900, the town you see today began as a planned city of the early 13th century, and its medieval character has been almost perfectly preserved. Indeed, a 16th-century model of the town, made by a local carpenter and on permanent exhibit at the Bavarian National Museum in Munich, shows Straubing 400 years ago pretty much as it appears today.

The most striking feature of the town is its main street, a vast half-mile-long market square—which, in fact, is exactly what it was; Straubing has been the principal market town of Bavaria's richest agricultural region for centuries. No less striking is the 14th-century **Rathaus**, standing right in the center of this elongated plaza, one end of which is now called Ludwigsplatz, the other Theresienplatz (in honor of Bavaria's King Ludwig I and his Queen Theresa). The building's square tower, one of the tallest of the many in town, is unusual for the four oriels on its corners—medieval lookout posts for vigilant watchmen.

The Asam brothers twice left their characteristically exuberant mark on Straubing: with a side altar in the **Stifts und Pfarrkirche St. Jakob** (Collegiate and Parish Church of St. James), Pfarrplatz 7, a 15th-century basilica whose red-brick Gothic exterior has been preserved despite the Baroque restyling of its interior; and with the 18th-century **Ursulinenkirche**, the convent church of the Ursuline Order, at Burggasse 9. One of their chief rivals, Johann Wolfgang Dientzenhofer, was the architect and master builder who contributed the Baroque interiors to the 14th-century **Karmelitenkirche** (Carmelite Church), Albrechtgasse 20. You can get a welcome break from all this Baroque extravagance at the **Pfarrkirche St. Peter** (Parish Church of St. Peter), a refreshingly simple triple-naved Romanesque basilica on Petersgasse that was completed in 1200.

In the little cemetery surrounding St. Peter's you'll find the tomb of Agnes Bernauer, Bavaria's best-loved tragic folk heroine. Agnes was the daughter of a bathhouse proprietor in Augsburg, where, during the 1428 Carnival season, Albrecht III, heir apparent to the Bavarian throne and son of Duke Ernst, first met her. Only 16 at the time, Agnes was considered one of the great beauties of the age, and the young nobleman fell in love with her after their first bath together—a not uncommon practice in those days. It was the beginning of a torrid love affair. In 1432 the two were secretly married in a village church, and a year later Agnes bore the future duke of Bavaria a daughter. Her Cinderella story might have had a happy ending had it not been for all the gossip and Papa Ernst's indignation. The duke had Agnes arrested, imprisoned in the ducal castle at Straubing, and put on trial as a witch. The trial consisted of tying her hands and feet and tossing her into the Danube; her guilt would be proven if she floated, her innocence if she drowned. Alas, poor Agnes was innocent. Her tragic story is re-enacted every four years in the courtyard of Straubing's castle during the quadrennial Agnes Bernauer Festival, which will next be held in July of 1993.

The best and most historic place to stay, or to have lunch or dinner in town, is the 500-year-old ▶ **Hotel Seethaler**, Theresienplatz 25.

DEGGENDORF AND THE BAYERISCHER WALD

Deggendorf, on the opposite bank of the river, some 28 km (17 miles) downstream from Straubing by way of country roads, is not only a charming little city worth exploring but also the gateway to the Bayerischer Wald (Bavarian Forest).

Somewhat smaller than Straubing, Deggendorf has been an important transfer point of Danube shipping for some 1,000 years. It was fortified in 1242 when it became Bavarian ducal property, and today boasts one of the area's most beautiful city squares—the **Marktplatz**—in the middle of which stands a Gothic **Rathaus**.

Metten

Five kilometers (3 miles) west and back upstream from Deggendorf's Marktplatz is the village of Metten, site of the Benedictine monastery church of **Saint Michael**, one of the "musts" on our Danube route. The church, which was completed in 1720, has a high altar with Cosmas Damian Asam's painting of *Lucifer Destroyed by St. Michael*. Even more important are the 17th-century monastery buildings, and most important of all is the **Klosterbibliothek** (Monastery Library), built and stocked between 1706 and 1720. Wherever there's a spare inch inside the library there is Rococo stuccowork, and where there's a surface, there is an elaborately decorated panel—which means there's not much space for books. The ten carved figures that surround the columns supporting the library's gallery depict the trades involved in producing and publishing books. Perhaps not surprisingly, the critic fares the worst, here being pinched on the nose by a crane.

From Deggendorf two scenic highways—B 11 and an unnumbered state road—both lead north into the Bayerischer Wald.

The Bayerischer Wald

This mountainous, densely wooded region stretches in a broad band some 50 km (31 miles) wide and nearly 150 km (93 miles) long from the German-Austrian-Czech border north and west along the frontier with the Czech Republic. Within its confines are two nature preserves and a national park.

Settlement of the region goes back to the Stone and Bronze ages: Its first known inhabitants were Celts and Marcovinians, who were displaced by Slavic tribes in the fifth century. The Slavs in turn were overrun in the sixth century by the Baiuoarii. Measurable settlement did not really begin until the 13th century, with small villages slowly growing up around monasteries and churches. As a result of this pattern, the entire region remains one of the least populated and least industrialized in southern Germany. Even modern mass tourism remains in its infancy here, which is perhaps a blessing, although the potential for summer recreation and winter sports is great. Only a few isolated spots have been turned into ski resorts, and they are mostly of the cross-country variety. Resorts that draw summer visitors emphasize the clean air, the pristine environment, and the wonders of nature.

It is possible to drive for miles in the Bayerischer Wald without seeing signs of human habitation. In the minds of most Germans, however, the region has an aura of hokey backwoodsiness about it, no doubt reinforced by sensational media stories in the 1960s and 1970s about local village women who were ostracized by their neighbors for practicing witchcraft.

Although a number of clean high-tech industries have struck roots in some of the larger towns in recent years, crafts and cottage industries such as wood carving, glassblowing, and the production of snuff jars called *Schmalzler* remain the most important components of the local economy. And so it is to two of the glassblowing centers—Frauenau and Zwiesel— that we want to direct you in particular.

The glassblowing tradition in the forest is some 650 years old, and no doubt owes its origins to the abundance of quartz in the region. The original *Glashütten* (glass smelters and factories) were small family-run enterprises—many of which have become fairly large operations. A specialty—actually an art—developed through the centuries was the blowing of the so-called *Schmalzlerglas*, the clear-glass stoppered flagons bearing tantalizing spiral decorations, swirls of color, and even lettering. They were, and are, used for snuff, which is popular in Bavaria. To prevent the glassblowing art from dying out, a number of communities have started trade schools to teach their youngsters the craft.

Zwiesel, 35 km (22 miles) northeast of Deggendorf by way of the unnumbered road that takes you through the town of Regen, has been a glassblowing center since the 14th century. A town of 10,000 inhabitants, it has a state-run school for apprentice glassmakers and a very fine **Glasmuseum** located right behind the city hall on the Stadtplatz, the main square. The town is also a summer hiking and winter ski resort, and has a number of commendable hotels, inns, and restaurants. The best is the ▶ **Kurhotel Sonnenberg**, Augustinerstrasse 9.

Frauenau, just 6 km (4 miles) south of Zwiesel via the scenic road that leads into the Nationalpark Bayerischer Wald and then on to Passau, also has a fine **Glasmuseum** located right on its Rathausplatz; it's also the best place to pick up information on glass factories open to the public.

Though only a third the size of Zwiesel, Frauenau also banks on summer recreation and winter sports, including downhill skiing on the 4,790-foot-high Rachel peak that looms above the town. There is a range of accommodations in moderately priced country inns as well; the coziest, right in the center of town, is the ▶ **Gasthaus Eibl-Brunner**, Hauptstrasse 18.

From Frauenau you have a choice of two routes to Passau, our last destination on the Danube. If you'd like to stay close to the river, return to Deggendorf the way you came (by way of Zwiesel and Regen), and then follow it downstream for another 65 km (41 miles). The alternative is to drive south for about 60 km (37 miles) through the national park and the southeastern corner of the Bayerischer Wald. This route will take you first to the town of **Grafenau**, where there is an especially fine and renowned restaurant (which we recommend as a gastronomic side trip from Passau in our discussion of that city). From Grafenau, B 85 takes you directly into Passau.

PASSAU

The Celts had a sense of location that was uncanny, in terms of both defense and aesthetic appeal. They outdid even themselves when they chose to settle on the site of what is now Passau, population 50,000, some 2,500 years ago.

The little city is situated on a tongue of land at the confluence of two rivers, the Inn and the Ilz, with the Danube. The Inn flows into the Danube after its long, twisting course from the Alps through Switzerland, Austria, and southern Bavaria. The Ilz arrives after a short but turbulent journey through the Bayerischer Wald, where it rises. In addition to the almost impregnable natural barrier it poses for would-be attackers, the meeting of the three rivers creates one of the most memorable spectacles of nature, which you can observe from a cliff towering high above the bank of the Danube: The Inn is a chalky green on arrival, the Ilz almost turquoise, and the Danube, contrary to song and legend, a rather muddy brown; spread out beneath you on nature's canvas, the colors are blended magically.

The Celts called their settlement Boiodurum; the Romans, who, here as elsewhere along the Danube, built one of their forts, named it Castra Batava, or just Batavis, for the ninth Batavian Cohort, which was stationed here. Then, in the fifth century, came the Baiuoarii, who called it Bazzawa, which eventually became Passau. Some 1,400 years later the German naturalist Alexander von Humboldt arrived, took one look, and declared Passau "one of the seven most beautiful cities in the world."

It was Saint Boniface who established Passau as a bishopric in 739 (though there is evidence that the first Christian church here was built as early as 460). The bishops of the day were also temporal rulers, and they turned Passau into one of the most powerful church city-states of southern Germany. Among them were many learned men, and one of the most learned was Bishop Pilgrim, who during his rule (970–991) had the *Nibelungenlied* (Song of the Nibelungs), one of the old Germanic sagas, set down on parchment in Middle-High German. Elsewhere in town, a large-scale mural in the great hall of the 17th-century **Rathaus**, on the right bank of the Danube, depicts the arrival of the Nibelungs in Passau. Of course, it was left to Richard Wagner, in the 19th century, to move the Nibelung legend from the Danube to the Rhine, turning what must have been originally "Danube maidens" into Rhine maidens.

The Stephansdom Area

Passau is dominated by the **Stephansdom** (St. Stephan's Cathedral), its immense octagonal dome a familiar landmark visible for miles around. Begun in Late Gothic style in 1407, the cathedral wasn't completed until 1530, by which time a number of Renaissance elements had been added. Then, in the late 17th century, after a devastating fire, some of the restoration work was done in Italian Baroque style. The result is a church that is overwhelming both in its size and in the richness of its decoration. It is also downright overpowering acoustically, for it contains the world's largest organ. The instrument, with 17,388 pipes and 231 registers, is played at noon every day of summer; an additional recital is added at 6:00 P.M. during July and August.

The bishops of Passau commissioned several palaces in and around town. Adjacent to the cathedral, on Residenzplatz, are the **Alte Residenz** (Old Residence) and the **Neue Residenz** (New Residence), the former a largely Renaissance creation, the latter Baroque. More important are the **Veste Oberhaus** (Upper Citadel) and **Veste Niederhaus** (Lower Citadel) on the north bank, where an escarpment is all that stands between the Danube and the Ilz. Built in the 13th century (though added on to for the next few centuries), the Veste Oberhaus was designed to keep the bishops in firm control of Passau's burghers. The Veste Niederhaus, which dates to the 14th century, had pretty much the same purpose. The complex, which is reached by crossing the Luitpold bridge across the Danube, today houses three museums, including the **Historisches Stadtmuseum** (City Historical Museum) and a branch of the **Bayerische Staatsgemäldesammlungen** (Bavarian State Pictures Collection).

Other worthwhile museums in Passau are the **Spielzeugmuseum** (Toy Museum), on Residenzplatz, and the **Passau**

Glasmuseum (Glass Museum), with a fine collection of the Bavarian, Bohemian, and Austrian glassblowers' art, on Rathausplatz.

Exploring Passau

Above all, Passau is a town for strolling, and a day of window shopping along its cobblestone streets will barely do it justice. Like Deggendorf, the city is also a gateway to the Bavarian Forest, as well as to neighboring Austria and the Czech Republic. Last but certainly not least, Passau is the chief passenger port for Danube cruises, its main quay lined end to end during the summer months with German, Austrian, Hungarian, Romanian, Russian, and Ukrainian river steamers about to embark on their week-long trips to the Black Sea.

The most romantic and historic place in town to have lunch is the **Heilig-Geist-Stift-Schenke**, Heiliggeistgasse 4, less than half a mile east of St. Stephan's Cathedral. Its vaulted cellar tavern has been in operation since 1358, and the wines served are from the Holy Ghost Monastery's own vineyards in Austria's Wachau district. For a special treat, order one of the meat dishes, which here are skewered and grilled over the open hearth.

Passau's two most highly rated restaurants are in the ▶ **Hotel Wilder Mann**, Schrottgasse 2, and the ▶ **Hotel Passauer Wolf**, Rindermarkt 6. Both serve nouvelle cuisine as well as regional specialties. Both hotels are also ideal for spending a night or two in Passau. The Wilder Mann, with 60 rooms, is a modernized patrician's house, and has entertained such notables as Goethe, Napoleon, Tolstoy, and Austria's Empress Elizabeth. The Hotel Passauer Wolf, with 40 rooms, is located in an elaborate Baroque building.

For the ultimate in dining pleasure along the Danube, make a special trip back north into the Bayerischer Wald to **Grafenau** for dinner or lunch (lunch on Fridays, Saturdays, and Sundays only) at the ▶ **Säumerhof**, Steinberg 32; Tel: (8852) 24-01. Proprietor-chef Gebhard Endl, ably assisted by his wife, Renate, who acts as hostess, was an understudy of Munich's Eckart Witzigmann, Germany's greatest chef, before opening the Säumerhof some years ago. On his own now, he approaches regional Bavarian and Austrian specialties with an adept touch. Every meal here is a celebration of food and the culinary art, and well worth the 37-km (23-mile) drive each way. The chalet-style inn also has 11 rooms.

From Passau, you can wind your way in a northwesterly direction through the Bayerischer Wald and its extensions to reach the heart of Franconia, the focus of our next section. But if you really want to understand Franconia, you should start your tour of the region by visiting its capital, Nürnberg. The quickest way to do that is to take the A 3 Autobahn directly from Passau. The distance to Nürnberg is 220 km (136 miles), about a two-and-a-half-hour drive.

FRANCONIA

Our proposed Franconia route loops around the northeast-ern corner of Northern Bavaria in a counterclockwise direc-tion from Nürnberg to Bayreuth to Coburg to Bamberg. It is a restful and relaxing itinerary, and at the same time a stimulating one. It includes the **Bier und Burgenstrasse** (Beer and Castle Road) in the Fränkischer Wald (Franconian Forest), with stops at some of the remarkable castles in the area, as well as a taste of Kulmbach's and Bamberg's strong and excellent beer. From there it is on to the **Porzellan-strasse** (Porcelain Road), along which some of Germany's best-known chinaware factories are located, and where Rich-ard Wagner came to build his opera house. And, finally, it is the land that sent Albert, Prince of Saches-Coburg-Gotha, to marry his cousin Victoria in London.

Franconia is a land rich in churches and cathedrals, in castles, and in palaces and residences built by powerful prince-bishops, who ruled the region from the Middle Ages until the great secularization imposed by Napoleon. But in spite of all its man-made splendors and riches, the landscape itself is unpretentious, the towns, half-timbered houses, and well-tended fields endearing. There is a toylike quality to its villages, and a naïveté and sweetness in the scenery.

Whichever way you decide to do the loop, ending at Bamberg, as we suggest, or ending at Nürnberg, the route to Würzburg, which is at the beginning of the Romantic Road and the start of our next chapter, is short and direct.

NÜRNBERG

Glowing testimonials to Nürnberg abound, but so do the harshest judgments. Martin Luther said it "shone forth

throughout Germany like a sun among the moon and stars."
Goethe lavished praise on it. Hans Christian Andersen, who
visited Nürnberg in the 19th century, spoke of its "royal
dignity" and saw it as the "quintessence of medieval culture."
Mozart, on the other hand, was deeply depressed by its
Gothic severity. "An ugly city," he wrote tersely in 1790 in a
letter to a friend.

Nürnberg, with a population of 500,000, making it the
second-largest city in Bavaria after Munich, evokes mixed
emotions precisely because it embodies like almost no
other city in Germany the contradictions of the German
soul: the spirit of both Christmas and the Holocaust; the
artistic achievements of medieval craftsmen as well as the
architectural braggadocio of a murderously criminal regime;
the forces of light and darkness locked in perpetual conflict
but also in perennial symbiosis.

It is the city of Dürer, Veit Stoss, Peter Vischer, and Adam
Kraft, artists whose inimitable legacy endures, but also of
Albert Speer, whose bombastic temples to Nazism have
doggedly defied the demolition teams. It is the city of Hans
Sachs, the master cobbler turned mastersinger of thousands
of poems and fables, but also of Julius Streicher, the sadistic
anti-Semite whose vicious rag *Der Stürmer* became the ga-
zette of the Third Reich. It is the city where Martin Behaim
made the first terrestrial globe, and where a local astronomer, Regiomontanus, drew the navigational charts that Co-
lumbus carried with him on his voyage to America in 1492.
But it is also the city where Hitler promulgated the racial
laws that unleashed the "final solution," as well as of the
historic war-crimes trials that closed the era of a Reich that
was to have lasted a thousand years.

What Nürnberg was, and once represented, collapsed in a
storm of fire on the night of January 2, 1945, during the most
destructive of many air raids that were targeted on the city.
That raid, which lasted a mere 53 minutes, left a fourth of the
population homeless and turned the historic medieval part
of Nürnberg into a rubble heap. No other city, with the
exception of Dresden six weeks later, was so totally devastated in a single raid.

Nürnberg has since been completely and splendidly rebuilt. Proposals for an entirely new city were rejected in
favor of a plan that called for patching up as many of its
historic monuments, majestic Gothic churches, and elegant
patrician houses as could be salvaged from the wreckage. At
the same time, the rest of the Old Town was reconstructed in
an updated version of the original style, using the materials
that had characterized Nürnberg for centuries, especially
red sandstone. Wherever walls, towers, fountains, bridges,

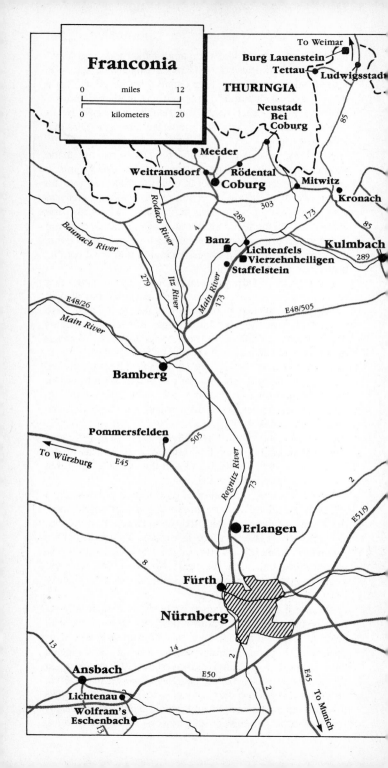

Franconia

| 0 | miles | 12 |

| 0 | kilometers | 20 |

To Weimar

Burg Lauenstein
Tettau **Ludwigsstadt**

THURINGIA

85

Neustadt
Bei
Coburg

● **Meeder**

Weitramsdorf ● **Rödental** **Mitwitz**
● **Coburg**

Kronach

Baunach River

Rodach River

303 289 173 85

4

Iz River

Banz ■ **Lichtenfels** **Kulmbach**
● **Vierzehnheiligen**
Staffelstein

279 *Main River* 173 289

E48/26

Main River E48/505

Bamberg ●

Pommersfelden ● 505

← To Würzburg E45

Regnitz River 73

2

● **Erlangen** E51/9

8 **Fürth** ●

Nürnberg

13 14 2

Ansbach ● E50

Lichtenau ● 2

Wolfram's E45
Eschenbach ●
3 To Munich ↓

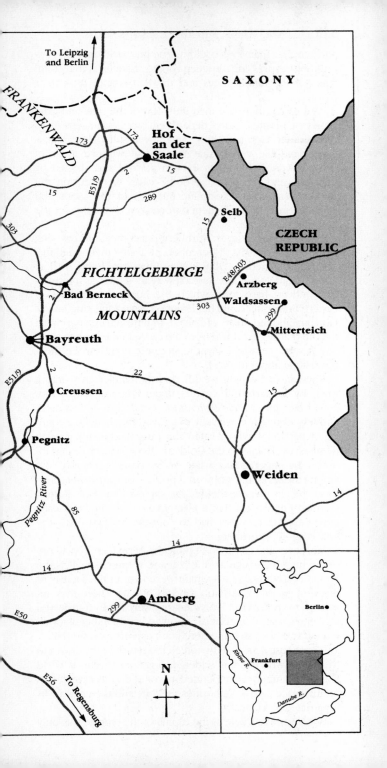

and burgher mansions could not be put back together, new buildings expressing the steep-roofed, turreted architectural spirit of the Middle Ages and the Renaissance took their place.

As a result, there are mercifully few of the steel-and-glass boxes or plastic-façaded department stores one sees in so many other German cities. And fewer still of the cutesy Disneyland-like copies that mar the downtown areas of some towns. Neither has it been scarred and slashed by thruways and turnpikes, as some cities were during the *Wirtschaftswunder* (Economic Miracle) of the 1950s and 1960s in order to make them *autogerecht,* or suitable for the new automotive age.

By German standards, Nürnberg is a comparatively young city. In the year 1050, "Nourenberc" was first mentioned in a document signed by Holy Roman Emperor Heinrich III. It had probably gotten its start a few years earlier as a fortress and military base from which the imperial territories of eastern Franconia could be defended against the kingdom of Hungary and the duchy of Poland. In time, a hamlet grew on the hill that sloped down from the castle to the Pegnitz river, and it soon became a favorite stopping point for the then-peripatetic imperial court.

Royal favor brought wealth, and the hamlet grew into a town. By the early 13th century, under Emperor Barbarossa, it had become a *Freie Reichsstadt,* entitled to collect taxes and levy duties, and virtually self-governing through a council of patricians who rotated the burgomastership among themselves. Thanks to the Golden Bull of 1356, which established the imperial succession on the basis of majority vote among the seven most powerful princes, or *Kurfürsten* (electors), the city became the de facto capital of the Holy Roman German Empire, for that document also specified that each newly elected emperor had to convoke his first diet—the *Reichstag*—in Nürnberg.

Moreover, the city soon became the permanent repository of the imperial insignia—the ball and scepter as well as the crown of Charlemagne—which were kept in the sacristy of the Heiliggeistkirche (Holy Ghost Church). There they remained from 1424 to 1796, when they were finally transferred to Vienna, seat of the Hapsburgs, who had long been, for all intents and purposes, the hereditary emperors. (After Hitler annexed Austria in 1938 he forced the return of the crown to Nürnberg, where it was hidden during the last year of World War II. The American-appointed mayor of the city revealed its hiding place to U.S. authorities in 1945, and the crown was repatriated to Vienna.)

But Nürnberg's role as the capital of the empire was only

one factor in its rise to fame, wealth, and power. Far more important were the industriousness of its burghers, who benefited greatly from its fortuitous location at the crossroads of four major European trade routes: from the Orient and Balkans to the Low Countries; from Venice to Hamburg; from Strasbourg to Prague; and from Switzerland to Poland. Together, they combined to make the city one of the principal commercial and manufacturing centers of the Middle Ages and early Renaissance.

Ironically, it was Nürnburg's contribution to the science of navigation that precipitated its decline, for the discovery of the New World and sea passages to Asia soon led to the overshadowing of the old overland trade routes that passed through the city. The Thirty Years' War and the decline of the old German empire accomplished the rest. By 1806, when Napoleon elevated the duchy of Bavaria to a kingdom and gave it Nürnberg with surrounding Franconia as a colonial prize, the city was a sleepy provincial backwater with 25,000 inhabitants—about half the number it had had 300 years earlier. The Bavarians and their kings treated it as such, though in 1835, under the aegis of Ludwig I, they built Europe's first railroad line between Nürnberg and nearby Fürth. Nürnberg did not regain its importance until the end of the 19th century, and, much to the chagrin of Nürnbergers, it was only because of Hitler that it again made its mark on history.

To Hitler, Nürnberg's architecture, appearance, and role in the Holy Roman Empire represented the quintessence of everything German, and of the Third Reich he envisioned in particular. To that one must add the special role of Streicher, the virulently anti-Semitic Franconian Nazi party leader to whom Hitler owed much as a result of the key role that Streicher had played as agitator and propagandist during the abortive 1923 "beerhall putsch" in Munich.

Hitler's cult in Nürnberg had actually begun a couple of months before the putsch when his National Socialists and other radical rightist organizations staged a so-called "German Day" in the city, the high point of which was a review of their private armies on the picturesque Hauptmarkt, the market square. In 1927 and 1929 the Nazis held their party conventions in Nürnberg, and after taking power in 1933 Hitler made the city the party's permanent convention and rally site. It was during the 1935 convention that he also convened a special session of the Reichstag to enact the so-called "Nürnberg Racial Laws," which foreshadowed the Holocaust.

It was to stage these frightening displays of political power and hysteria that Hitler commissioned Speer to build the various temples to Nazism on a 1,500-acre plot at the southeastern edge of the city. The plans were megalomaniacal: a congress hall that would accommodate 50,000 people; a stadium with a seating capacity of 400,000; marching and rally arenas where hundreds of thousands of storm troopers could goosestep in review. Only some of these monstrosities were completed by 1939, at which point the invasion of Poland and the subsequent demands of the war put an end to the annual rallies and construction effort.

How Nürnbergers feel today about the Nazi past is perhaps best reflected by what has happened to Speer's concrete mecca. Most of the huge parcel of land has been turned into a park dotted by ponds and wooded glens. Apartment blocks, the ultramodern Meistersingerhalle (a concert hall and convention center), and the Messe, Nürnberg's trade fair grounds, occupy another chunk of it. Speer's horseshoe-shaped Kongresshalle, larger than Rome's Colosseum, and completed except for its central auditorium roof, now serves as a warehouse for a mail-order company and as the recording studio for the Nürnberg Philharmonic orchestra. The grand avenue, a mile and a half long and 200 feet wide, has been turned into a gigantic parking lot. The Zeppelinfeld arena, in which half a million jack-booted SA and SS troopers used to stand hoarsely shouting allegiance to their Führer, does double duty: as a site for rock and pop festivals and as an athletic field for U.S. Army units still stationed in Nürnberg. For those with an inclination for the macabre, the Nazi relics are here to ogle. Fortunately, Nürnberg has more and better things to offer.

Exploring the Altstadt

Nürnberg is a city that must be walked; no tour on wheels will do it justice. Moreover, much of it has been turned into a pedestrian mall. But because of the size of its medieval center, strong legs and sturdy shoes are a must. The defensive **wall** alone is three miles long. With 120 sentry towers, 12 fortified gates, numerous bastions, and a 60-foot moat, the wall is also the perfect place from which to get your bearings and a feeling for the geographical layout of the city.

Huddled inside the wall at the Königstor (King's Gate), near the southern periphery of the Old Town and the railway station, is the **Handwerker Hof** (Crafts Court), an enclave of half-timbered shops and stalls that conjures up images of life in the Middle Ages. The wares made and sold here range from wooden toys and stained glass to *Nürnberger Bratwürste* and *Lebkuchen,* the city's most renowned comestibles. Although it may be too early in the day to think about eating, their mention in connection with the Handwerker Hof is reason enough to pause and talk briefly about Bratwürste and Lebkuchen.

Finger-size Nürnberger Bratwürste are made of pork and various spices, and are charcoal broiled on grills in open booths like the ones in the Handwerker Hof. The sausage man stands high above the action shouting, "One, two, three, four . . ." and so on. You'll feel as if you're at an auction, until you realize you are expected to shout back the number of sausages you want. Less than six makes a snack, 14 will do for lunch. You also have the option of consuming them with sauerkraut or a slab of rye bread. The mustard is very hot.

Lebkuchen, which are sometimes called gingerbread cookies, though traditional recipes do not call for ginger, is to Nürnberg what marzipan is to Lübeck: The city is the Lebkuchen capital of the world, and has been since at least 1409, when the baking of the sweet little confections was first mentioned in municipal records as an independent craft, subject to taxation. Each year, 50 million pounds of Lebkuchen are produced by Nürnberg's bakeries. The oldest Lebkuchen maker has been in business since 1598.

Though these honey-and-spice cakes have been considered delicacies for almost 4,000 years, having originated in ancient Persia, there seems to be no disputing the fact that it was really in medieval Nürnberg where they evolved their classical form—round, generally four to five inches in diameter, a half-inch thick, and stuck on a wafer-thin sheet of unleavened and unsweetened dough that is somewhat reminiscent—in taste, consistency, and appearance—to parchment paper. Today, Lebkuchen can be made oblong, square, bite-sized, or heart-shaped. They can come sugar-coated, chocolate-coated, sugar-glazed, or plain. In fact, there are probably as many recipes as there are commercial bakers, and each is a closely guarded secret. The crème de la crème, however, is the *Elisen*-Lebkuchen, so named, legend has it, for Franconia's Countess Elisa, whose husband became one of the margraves of Brandenburg.

Whether or not you've fortified yourself with Bratwürste and Lebkuchen, you will find food for the eyes and intellect about two blocks west of the Handwerker Hof at the **Germanisches Nationalmuseum** (Germanic National Museum), Kornmarkt 1. Founded by a Franconian baron in 1852 amid the prevailing Romantic-era enthusiasm for things old and German, this huge complex, which includes a 600-year-old Carthusian monastery, is dedicated to exhibiting and preserving the art, culture, handicrafts, and technology of the Germanic lands and tribes, from the earliest times through the 19th century. Its art collection includes some of the finest paintings by Altdorfer, Hans Baldung-Grien, Hans Burgk-mair, the Cranachs, Dürer, and the Holbeins, as well as sculptures by Adam Kraft, Tilman Riemenschneider, Veit Stoss, and Peter Vischer. There are, in addition, more than 1,000 antique musical instruments, countless pieces of medi-eval armor, the original score of Wagner's *Die Meistersinger,* and Behaim's famous globe.

The **Verkehrsmuseum** (Transport and Communications Museum), Lessingstrasse 6, two blocks south of the Na-tionalmuseum, and just outside the wall, is equally over-whelming. Here, among many other exhibits, you'll find one of the world's largest postage stamp collections, antique coaches, early railroad cars, and a working replica of the "Adler," the 1835 train that ran between Nürnberg and Fürth.

To reach the main sights of the inner city, walk north from the Handwerker Hof along Königstrasse. At the corner of Königstrasse and Lorenzerplatz stands the **Pfarrkirche St. Lorenz** (Parish Church of St. Laurence). Begun in the 13th century and completed in the 15th, this twin-spired church is generally regarded as the most beautiful in the city, and contains three prized works of art: a magnificent stained-glass rosette window above the organ at the west end of the nave; the "Angelic Salutation," an intricate wood carving by Veit Stoss that is suspended from the cross-vaulted ceiling over the entrance to the choir; and Adam Kraft's remarkable tabernacle, chiseled from stone and supported by a kneeling self-portrait of the sculptor and likenesses of two of his apprentices.

Farther up Königstrasse is the Pegnitz river, which bisects the inner city on an east–west axis. To call it a river, however, is being generous: "creek" would be a more appropriate term, for nowhere is it more than 50 feet wide. Still, it gives Nürnberg a verdant and picturesque charm, and a walk along its banks is like strolling into a fairy-tale world. The most memorable views are of the **Heiliggeistspital** (Holy Ghost Hospital), Spitalgasse 12, whose foundations spill into the streambed, and which now serves as a moderately priced restaurant; the half-timbered **Weinstadel**, a 15th-century wine warehouse; and the **Henkersteg** (Hangman's Bridge), which is surrounded, fittingly, by weeping willows.

The Hauptmarkt

Nürnberg's heart—geographically as well as figuratively—is the cobblestone Hauptmarkt, the main market square, just north of the river at the northern end of Königstrasse. Eleven months of the year it teems with flower, fruit, and vegetable sellers hawking their produce, but during the four weeks from Advent Sunday until December 24 it is transformed into a small town of wood-and-cloth stalls and the scene of one of the city's most popular and colorful attractions—the *Christkindlmarkt* (Christ Child Market).

In addition to being the world's oldest Christmas fair, having been held on the same spot for more than 400 years now, it is by far the most dazzling—a kaleidoscope of stands selling toys, tree ornaments, tinsel, handicrafts, candles, candy, Lebkuchen, fruitcakes, and *Glühwein* (hot red wine spiced with cinnamon and cloves). There are daily carol and trombone concerts, as well as performances by theater, dance, and puppet groups. The setting for all this is as spectacular as the month-long event itself, for the Haupt-markt is squeezed between the Rathaus, with its filigreelike façade, the red-sandstone front of the Frauenkirche, and the Schöner Brunnen, a gilded 60-foot spirelike Gothic fountain. The best time to visit the Christkindlmarkt is at night, when everything is floodlit and the square is suffused with the magic that is so much a part of Christmas here.

The **Frauenkirche** (Church of Our Lady), on the eastern edge of the Hauptmarkt, is situated on the site of a Jewish synagogue that was destroyed, along with the entire Jewish quarter, in an early-14th-century pogrom. The gilded 16th-century mechanical clock on the façade depicts the pageant of the seven electors of the Holy Roman Empire paying homage to the emperor. The **Altes Rathaus**, on Rathausplatz, just off the market square, combines Late Gothic and early Renais-sance elements in its design. The **Schöner Brunnen** (Beautiful Fountain), on the northwest corner of the Hauptmarkt, was completed in 1396, and is the finest example of Gothic fountain architecture anywhere. Unfortunately, the many fig-ures on it are copies. (Fragments of the originals are on exhibit at the Germanisches Nationalmuseum.)

Wherever you walk in Nürnberg, the **Kaiserburg** (Imperial Castle) is in view, but the view is most beckoning from the Hauptmarkt, so start your climb up the steep narrow cobble-stone streets from there. The Kaiserburg was one of Eu-rope's largest fortified castles, though unique in the sense that it was never really any sovereign's permanent home but rather a kind of hotel in which the emperor, the electors, princes, and dukes lived when the Reichstag was in session. There are guided tours of its knights' hall, chapel, apart-ments, and council chambers.

Heading back downhill after your tour of the castle, stop first on the picturesque little square below the Kaiserburg's western bastion for a visit to the **Albrecht Dürer Haus**, Albrecht-Dürer-Strasse 39. Dürer bought this magnificent burgher house in 1509 and used it as his home and studio until his death in 1528. It contains period furnishings and interiors, as well as originals and copies of his work.

Three steep blocks downhill from Dürer's house is the **Stadtpfarrkirche St. Sebaldus** (Parish Church of St. Sebald), Winklerstrasse 26. Named for Nürnberg's patron saint, it was built in the 13th century and represents the stylistic transition from late Romanesque to early Gothic. It is also filled with works by Nürnberg artists, including Stoss and Kraft. Its greatest masterpiece, however, is the elaborate bronze tomb created by Peter Vischer in 1519 for St. Sebald's remains. One of the newest additions to the church, which was heavily damaged during the war, is its organ, a magnificent instrument with 84 registers that was completed by a Nürnberg craftsman in 1975.

From St. Sebald's it is a two-minute stroll to the charming **Spielzeugmuseum** (Toy Museum), Karlstrasse 13, a dazzling collection of dolls, dollhouses, miniature trains, tin figures, and children's books from medieval times to the present.

Returning to the Hauptmarkt, take another stroll down Königstrasse and stop in briefly at the little church of **St. Martha**, Königstrasse 77, which is noted both for its stained-glass windows and for the fact that it's where the Meistersingers had their school in the 16th and 17th centuries.

Dining and Staying in Nürnberg

You will, of course, find more to eat in Nürnberg than Bratwürste and Lebkuchen, though, alas, the few culinary stars that once shone in the center of town flickered out a number of years ago. Nonetheless, you will eat well at the **Goldenes Posthorn**, Glöckleingasse 2, just north of St. Sebald's. One of Nürnberg's oldest restaurants, the Posthorn has a dining room filled with historic artifacts, and emphasizes the nouvelle approach to Franconian specialties. Reservations are recommended; Tel: (911) 22-51-53. At **Essigbrätlein**, Weinmarkt 3, Nürnberg's oldest extant inn, Andree Köthe, a 28-year-old chef, prepares exquisite nouvelle cuisine that has gained him three Gault-Millau toques. Reservations for dinner are essential; Tel: (911) 22-51-31. **Böhm's Herrenkeller**, Theatergasse 19, just off Königstrasse, has a pedigree that goes back to 1499, and is recommended by Nürnbergers for its excellent selection of Franconian wines; Tel: (911) 22-44-65. The **Zum Sudhaus**, Bergstrasse 20, just below the Kaiserburg, is an old tavern that serves Franconian dishes prepared nouvelle style. Open evenings only; Tel: (911) 20-96-66.

When it comes to hotels, the choice is complicated by the necessity of making a decision on whether to try for a spot within the Altstadt, where establishments are generally less expensive and sometimes hard to reach because of the pedestrians-only areas, or settle for the posher spots outside the wall. Of the latter, the ultramodern ▶ **Hotel Maritim**, Frauentorgraben 11, ranks highest and is the most expensive, despite the fact it is part of a chain operation and rather faceless. Not so the ▶ **Grand Hotel**, Bahnhofstrasse 1, directly across the square from the railway station and virtually adjacent to the Königstor gate. Every room at this truly grand establishment is decorated differently.

Within the wall there are some interesting and appealing choices. The ▶ **Dürer Hotel**, Neutormauer 32, is a modern bed-and-breakfast establishment located just below the Kaiserburg and around the corner from the Dürer House. The most picturesquely located establishment in the same little neighborhood is the ▶ **Burghotel-Grosses Haus**, Lammsgasse 3, at the corner of Albrecht-Dürer-Strasse. It has a *dependence,* the ▶ **Burghotel-Kleines Haus**, about a block away at Schildgasse 16. In either one you can ask for a room looking out on the cobblestone streets, which may get a bit noisy but give you the feeling of being back in the Middle Ages. The ▶ **Merrian Hotel**, Unschlittplatz 7, a 400-year-old house with a charming fountain and linden trees in front, has only 21 rooms, each individually furnished with antiques; the hotel is virtually on the banks of the Pegnitz. The ▶ **Romantik Hotel am Josephsplatz**, Josephsplatz 30–32, has a pedigree going back 150 years.

NORTH TO BAYREUTH

To head north from Nürnberg, you can of course take the Nürnberg-to-Berlin Autobahn (A 9), which, since German reunification, has become a nightmare of traffic and mile-long tie-ups. It is more interesting, instead, to take the B 2 (follow the signs to the Nürnberg airport to get out of the city), which runs through picturesque Franconian villages to Pegnitz, Creussen, and Bayreuth, our next three destinations.

Pegnitz, 60 km (37 miles) northeast of Nürnberg, is on our route not for its cultural attractions, of which there really are none, but for its earthly pleasures, especially the marvelously memorable ▶ **Pflaum's Posthotel**, Nürnberger Strasse 14.

This luxury establishment, with its outstanding restaurant and rooms appointed by leading German designers and interior architects, has been a country inn, brewery, and postal relay station belonging to the Pflaum family for more than 280 years. Two Pflaum brothers, educated and trained in New York, Paris, and London, have been operating it as a resort hotel and restaurant catering to the silk-stocking Bayreuth Festival crowd since the early 1970s. Andreas, the younger of the two, is the manager; Hermann is the chef— and he cooks sublimely. Using local produce and livestock, as well as the freshest local fish, and accompanying his creations with the finest wines Franconia has to offer, he has managed to synthesize the best of gourmet and local peasant cuisine. Try, for example, the brook trout soufflé with wine sauce and sorrel, the fresh spinach soup, the roast quail in morel sauce, and the pear sherbet as dessert. The Pflaums also run a bus to and from Bayreuth for performances during the festival season.

Creussen

You will pass through this charming hamlet, 14 km (8½ miles) north of Pegnitz, on your way to Bayreuth; be sure to stop. The town grew up around a fortress that dates back to the year 1000, and still has a well-preserved (in parts) 15th-century defensive **wall**. Be sure also to visit the **Städtisches Krügemuseum** (Municipal Stoneware Museum), Rennsteig 36, with its fine collection of Creussen's best-known pro-ducts—stoneware jugs and beer steins—as well as a good collection of Bayreuth faïence. No less interesting is the 16th-century **church** in the town district of **Lindenhardt**, which features an altar painting by Matthias Grünewald.

From Creussen it is a leisurely 12 km (7½ miles) to Bayreuth.

BAYREUTH

This city of 72,000 owes its international fame in part to two extreme personalities and two opera houses. Initially, there was, and still is, the **Markgräfliches Opernhaus**, built from 1745 to 1748 for the Margravine Wilhelmine, a Prussian princess who was the older sister of Frederick the Great. Inside, it is a riot of wreathed columns, gilded cupids, and Rococo shells. The second theater, Wagner's Festspielhaus, completed in 1876, represents the opposite extreme, in which nothing architectural or ornamental was, or is, al-lowed to distract from the stage or Wagner's music.

The earliest documents referring to Bayreuth date back to 1194. In the 13th century it became the property of the margraves of Kulmbach, cousins of the Hohenzollerns, who became the rulers of Brandenburg, Prussia, and eventually all of Germany. The margraves first ruled their little fief from the mighty Plassenburg fortress in Kulmbach, north of Bayreuth (see below), but in 1542 it was decided that the latter would make a far nicer capital. So the margraves built a little palace, the Altes Schloss, to which they kept adding. In the 18th century Margrave Frederick and his wife Wilhelmine built an even more splendid château, the Neues Schloss. In time, Wilhelmine, envious of what her brother Frederick, the king of Prussia, was doing in Berlin and Potsdam, decided that she, too, needed an opera house, and so had the Markgräfliches Opernhaus built, with the result that by 1750 little Bayreuth was one of the most splendid residence cities in Germany. Its golden age came to a rather sudden end in 1806 when Napoleon invaded, occupied the town, dissolved the independent and sovereign margraviate of Kulmbach, and then, four years later, sold it and the principality to his ally, Bavaria's King Maximilian I.

Enter, some 60 years later, Richard Wagner and his bride Cosima, daughter of the composer Franz Liszt and for 13 years wife of the Munich opera conductor Hans von Bülow, from whom Wagner had stolen her in one of the most scandalous affairs of the 19th century. By 1848, when he participated in the anti-monarchist nationalist revolution, Wagner was one of the most celebrated personalities in the European music world. Because of his role in the abortive revolution, however, he was forced to flee to Switzerland. There followed a number of peripatetic and impecunious years, including a season as the conductor of the London Philharmonic. Then, in 1864, Bavaria's 18-year-old "Dream King," Ludwig II, a gushing fan, invited him to settle in Munich.

Wagner's stay in Munich certainly started out promisingly enough. *Tristan und Isolde* premiered (with von Bülow conducting), and Wagner, having finished *Die Meistersinger von Nürnberg,* resumed his work on *Siegfried* and *Götterdämmerung,* the last two operas of "The Ring" cycle, and began *Parsifal.* But his affair with Cosima, whom he had known as a child, and Ludwig II's outlay of public funds for the composer's productions and to support his lavish lifestyle, soon won Wagner more enemies than friends in the Bavarian capital. In 1867 he was asked to leave town. Together with Cosima, who was still legally married to von Bülow, he returned to Switzerland and settled at Triebschen near Lucerne. Restless and ambitious as ever, he began to look for an opera house in which to stage "The Ring"—a dream that was fulfilled by Bayreuth in 1871.

The city offered Wagner Margravine Wilhelmine's Baroque theater. After he and Cosima visited Bayreuth, however, Wagner turned down the offer on the grounds that the margravine's opera house was too small for "The Ring."

Turning to his erstwhile sponsor, Ludwig II, Wagner proposed building a new festival opera house in Bayreuth, and asked for money. Ludwig, no doubt figuring that the cost of an opera house would be piddling compared to what he was already spending on his fairy-tale castles in the Bavarian Alps, coughed up the needed funds. The cornerstone for the **Festspielhaus**, which was to rise on a hill at the northern end of Bayreuth at the end of a mile-long boulevard now called Nibelungenstrasse, was laid on May 22, 1872. Designed by Gottfried Semper, who had also built the Dresden opera house, the Festspielhaus opened with the first complete performance of "The Ring" four years later.

The Wagner **Bayreuth Festival** usually takes place from the last week of July through the last week of August. Tickets are very hard to get in Germany, so it's best to order them through your travel agent at home. The ticket office in Bayreuth is Kartenbüro, Festspielleitung Bayreuth, Postfach 100262, D(W)-8580 Bayreuth 1, Germany. The Festspielhaus should be seen even if it is empty, however.

For festival-goers, elaborate and mysterious dinner arrangements at hotels and restaurants in and around Bayreuth—whereby you leave your soup after the first intermission and find your place at the same table in the second intermission, with your next course ready and waiting—seem to be the rule. In addition, the audience is always summoned back to the auditorium by a fanfare of trumpets that ties in with the leitmotif of the next act. Though Bayreuthers are perfectly normal people living in a normal city, during the Wagner Festspiel they go quite mad. Many of them dress in costumes to match the work being performed. And there is usually one elderly couple in lace shawl and black velvet tam-o'-shanter playing the part of Richard and Cosima.

Another important Bayreuth sight is the composer's mansion, **Villa Wahnfried**, the large Neoclassical cube at Richard-Wagner-Strasse 48. The giant bronze head that rests on a polished marble pedestal in front of the house is King Ludwig II as he looked in the 1860s. There is a Wagner kitsch show put on in the villa.

Though it is Wagner who occupies center stage in Bayreuth, he does not totally monopolize it. The Margravial opera house, on Opernstrasse, is still very much used during the annual Franconian Rococo festival (Musica Bayreuth; the first two weeks of May), as well as for concerts. Stop in at the **Café Zellinger**, in the corner of the building, for coffee and pastry while waiting for a guided tour of the theater. All Bayreuthers and most visitors seem to congregate there sooner or later for a second breakfast, afternoon coffee, or assorted delicacies at intermission.

The **Altes Schloss** (Old Palace), on Maximilianstrasse, just a few steps west of the opera house, should be seen, as should the **Schlosskirche** (Palace Church), which was added to the complex in the 1750s.

The **Neues Schloss** (New Palace), at Ludwigstrasse 21, commissioned by Wilhelmine and built from 1753 to 1754, expresses her fondness for nature and East Asian motifs. The New Palace is now a museum, rich in artifacts from Bavaria's past, and also has a branch of the **Bayerische Staatsgemäldesammlungen** (Bavarian State Pictures Collection).

Wagner fans who also appreciate fine food have long complained about the lack of it in Bayreuth. That changed when Wolfgang Hauenstein opened his 30-seat **Restaurant Cuvee** at Markgrafenallee 15, east of the railway station. His nouvelle German cuisine earns him a Michelin star. Dinner only, so be sure to reserve; Tel: (921) 79-99-70.

For in-town dining in rustic country-style surroundings, try the ▶ **Hotel Gasthof zur Lohmühle**, Badstrasse 37, near the Margravial opera house. The emphasis here is on fish dishes from the region and game in season. The inn also has 12 comfortable, moderately priced rooms. For dinner, reservations are recommended; Tel: (921) 530-60.

Bayreuth's three other major hotels are all close to the railway station, about halfway between the Festival Theater and the Old Palace. The ▶ **Hotel Bayerischer Hof**, Bahnhofstrasse 14, has 62 pricey rooms, all decorated in Neo-Baroque style, and has had as guests Konrad Adenauer and boxing champion Floyd Patterson. The ▶ **Hotel Königshof**, Bahnhofstrasse 23, also in the first-class category, has 44 rooms and was totally renovated and redecorated in 1980. The somewhat more moderately priced ▶ **Hotel Goldener Hirsch**, Bahnhofstrasse 13, has a pedigree as an inn going back 300 years.

Outside Bayreuth

The **Eremitage**, 4 km (2½ miles) east of the city on B 22, offers a glimpse of how 16th- and 17th-century royalty escaped the responsibilities of their position. At the Hermitage outside of Bayreuth the margraviate court would come dressed as shepherds and shepherdesses to lead the simple life, with the margrave himself dressed in religious habit and acting as a kind of abbot. The era was also one of preoccupation with landscaping, and so, not surprisingly, there is a fine park around the Hermitage. In it, you will find a Sun Temple, considered one of the finest rotunda structures of the late Rococo period, as well as a Dragon's Den, a Hermit Chapel, fountains, cascades, and the tomb of Margravine Wilhelmine's dog Folichon, which was built to resemble an ancient ruin.

Just 6 km (3½ miles) south of Bayreuth, in the suburb of Thiergarten back toward Creussen on B 2, is Schloss Thiergarten, built in 1753 by Wilhelmine's son, Margrave Georg Wilhelm, as a hunting château. An armchair sportsman if ever there was one, Wilhelm was the envy of crowned and coroneted Europe for his hunting lodge. It had one room so large that servants could drive deer through it while the royal hunters, seated on balconies along the wall, shot the bewildered animals without sacrificing their comfort. The château is now the ► Schlosshotel Thiergarten (12 rooms), with a very expensive restaurant serving nouvelle cuisine and Franconian dishes.

NORTHWEST TOWARD COBURG

Though the next destination, Kulmbach, is only 20 km (12 miles) northwest of Bayreuth by way of the B 85, you might consider using either Bayreuth or Kulmbach as a base for travelling eastward toward the border with the Czech Republic and into the **Fichtelgebirge** (Fichtel Mountains), or for a drive along the **Porzellanstrasse** (Porcelain Road), with stops in such porcelain manufacturing towns as **Arzberg** or **Selb**. The best way to do the latter is to leave Bayreuth via the B 2, heading north by way of the airport to the resort town of Bad Berneck, and then continuing on B 303 some 33 km (20 miles) east to its junction with B 15. The latter is the so-called Porcelain Road. Selb is 20 km (12 miles) north of the intersection, right on the highway. To get to Arzberg, continue east on B 303 for another 9 km (5½ miles). (For more information on the Porcelain Road contact the German National Tourist Office.)

Kulmbach

The picturesque smallish town of Kulmbach, 20 km (12 miles) northwest of Bayreuth, is famous for three things: its beer, Plassenburg Fortress, and the German Tin Figures Museum.

Start with the beer, the richest and strongest in the world, called *Kulmbacher Eisbock* (ice bock), which came into being a child of coincidence. According to local legend, on a bitterly cold winter afternoon in the year 1890 a worker at the **Reichelbräu**, one of two breweries in Kulmbach, was told to move several barrels of regular bock beer from the courtyard into the cellar. However, it was late in the day, and he was tired and wanted to go home—which he did, leaving the beer to stand outside overnight. The next morning the barrels of beer were frozen solid, their staves and hoops burst, but in the middle of each block of ice was a core of concentrated beer. Naturally, the brewmaster was furious and, to punish the worker, ordered him to drink the liquid. The young employee did as told, fully expecting to get sick. But after just one sip, he smiled. Never before, he exclaimed, had he tasted anything as delicious. Somewhat reluctantly, his boss tried it too, and agreed. The two hurried off to get the brewery director, who, after having a taste, decided on the spot to call it Eisbock and to mass produce and market it. To this day both the Reichelbräu and its chief competitor, Erste Kulmbacher Actien Exportbierbrauerei (EKU), produce Eisbock and sell it all over Germany. EKU's is even stronger than Reichel's—a syrupy honey-blond concoction with an alcohol content of 8 to 9 percent. To try it, stop in at the **EKU-Inn**, the brewery's tavern at Klostergasse 7, right in the center of town at the foot of the Buchsberg, the hill crowned by the Plassenburg.

Veste Plassenburg, visible for miles, is one of the largest, most elaborate, and most impressive Renaissance castle-fortresses in Germany, an impregnable walled city sitting atop the Buchsberg. The first references to it date back to the early 12th century. To visit it, head up the steep incline from the center of Kulmbach to the Kommandantenhaus (Commandant's House), and go on through the main gate and into the **Schöner Hof** (Beautiful Courtyard).

The mammoth structure was designed by Caspar Vischer, who knew all there was to know about making walls impregnable. But the Plassenburg's builders also took pains to beautify the castle, especially its inner courtyard, which blooms with more than a hundred carved portrait medallions, *putti* and monsters, wreaths and delicate tracery, birds and flowers, and every now and then an intricate interweaving of mermaids and garlands.

Today the Plassenburg **apartments** are open to the public as a museum containing rare collections of arms and silver, furniture and paintings. But within the huge complex is another museum, the **Deutsches Zinnfigurenmuseum** (German Tin Figures Museum), the largest museum of tin soldiers and tiny metal figures in the world. For the sheer beauty, diversity, and artistic perfection of its figures it is also, by far, the most spectacular and impressive collection in the world.

Every two years in August, Kulmbach and the Plassenburg are the scene of the **International Tin Figures Bourse**, a trade fair that attracts collectors and dealers from nearly three dozen countries. (The next fair will be in 1995.)

Hotels, however, are few. The most attractive is the ▶ **Hansa-Hotel**, Weltrichstrasse 2a, at the southwestern end of town. Its rooms and interior were recently redecorated by award-winning designer Dirk Obliers, who also did the futuristic suites of Pflaum's Posthotel in Pegnitz.

Kulmbach also marks the start of the **Bier und Burgenstrasse** (Beer and Castle Road), a promotional term for B 85, along which it is a mere 19 km (12 miles) northwest to Kronach and its fortress castle, Veste Rosenberg.

Kronach

Though there is not much evidence of it besides a plaque, the painter Lucas Cranach the Elder was born in Kronach, and locals still dispute whether it was in the house at Zum Marktplatz 1, or at the Haus zum Scharfen Eck. Either way, Cranach, intimately connected with Martin Luther and the Reformation, was one of the greatest German artists of the late 15th and early 16th centuries, and his hometown is justly proud of him.

The artist was actually born Lucas Sunder in 1472, but subsequently adopted the town's name and changed the spelling on numerous occasions in his long career. Eventually he became court painter to the Elector Friedrich the Wise, duke of Saxony, who was the chief protector of Luther and founder of the university of Wittenberg, where Luther taught and first posted the theses that triggered the Reformation. Cranach did much of his best work in Wittenberg, including portraits of the various leaders of the Reformation and of most of the university's faculty members. His son, Lucas Cranach the Younger, was almost his equal, and you will find some fine paintings of his in Veste Rosenberg, the mighty fortress that sits high above Kronach.

Veste Rosenberg was built in the early 12th century by a prince-bishop of Bamberg. Enlarged several times in the Middle Ages, it became a residence of the Bamberg prince-bishops in the 16th century, and played a key role in the Thirty Years' War. In 1730 Balthasar Neumann, one of Germany's greatest and most imaginative Baroque architects (now immortalized on DM 50 bills), redesigned it to its present appearance. It now serves as a youth hostel as well as the home of the **Frankenwald Museum**, which has Cranach the Younger paintings in its collection.

For a look at an even more impressive castle, drive 35 km (22 miles) north along B 85, the Beer and Fortress Road, to Ludwigsstadt and Burg Lauenstein.

The trip takes you through hilly, wooded countryside, the **Naturpark Frankenwald** (Franconian Forest Nature Preserve), which, because of the abundance of blue-black slate, takes on a somewhat mysterious character. In the towns and villages along the way nearly all the buildings are covered with small slate shingles, walls as well as roofs. In sunlight they reflect a striking sea-blue color; in shade they appear almost black. In contrast, window frames are always a gleaming white, and foundations and ground floors painted a pale yellow or white.

Ludwigsstadt, near the end of the route, is a small town that saw better times during its mining days, and has now become a health resort. Its chief attractions are a 12th-century Romanesque church and nearby Lauenstein fortress.

Burg Lauenstein has, since the 14th century, stood on a rock looking out across pine-wooded hills and a wild landscape that matches its blue-green slate roofs and turrets. As a castle site it dates back to the year 915, when the Holy Roman emperor Conrad I had Lauenstein built as an outpost, but it was frequently rebuilt and enlarged, and just as frequently changed hands. The castle now belongs to the state of Bavaria, which financed its restoration in the 1960s and 1970s.

Inside, it is beautifully furnished, and contains many interesting and curious collections, among them one of rare locks and door hardware, another of lighting fixtures. In fact, it lacks nothing that a medieval castle should have, not even a ghost. The "white lady" is condemned forever to walk the ramparts of Lauenstein because of a fatal misunderstanding. Legend has it she was a widowed countess of Orlamünde who desperately wanted to marry Albrecht the Handsome of Nürnberg. He turned her down on the grounds that there were "four eyes in the way." She misunderstood this to mean her two children and, tragically, killed them. (Albrecht had actually meant his own aged parents.)

You can spend a night like a knight right in Lauenstein. The ► **Burghotel Lauenstein** here has 22 rooms at moderate prices, and its rustic restaurant is justly famous for stick-to-the-ribs Franconian dishes; Tel: (9263) 256.

From the castle you can drive some 70 km (44 miles) north on B 85 to Weimar in Thuringia (see our Bach and Luther Country chapter), or head south as far as Kronach, then west on B 303 to Coburg, a total of 62 km (39 miles).

COBURG

For nearly 400 years this little city of 45,000 inhabitants just south of the state of Thuringia was the residence and capital of the dukes of Sachse-Coburg-Gotha, a dynasty whose major impact on world history lies in the fact that one of its scions, Prince Albert, married his first cousin, Queen Victoria of England, in 1840.

The town is idyllically situated astride the little Itz river, a tributary of the Main, amid the rolling foothills of the Thüringer Wald (Thuringian Forest). Among its most important sights and attractions are the Veste Coburg, the huge fortress that towers over the city; Ehrenburg Palace; the 16th-century Rathaus; and a market square lined by beautiful burgher houses.

Veste Coburg (Coburg Fortress), the "Crown of Franconia," literally dominates the town, an enormous, intimidating complex that had become impractical and virtually uninhabitable long before the ruling dukes moved out in the 16th century. The fortress commands sweeping views over much of Franconia and parts of Thuringia to the north (on a clear day, it can itself be seen for miles around), and three sides of it overhang the practically unscalable rocks on which it sits (the fourth—or southern—side was protected by two drawbridges and entry courtyards). It wasn't until our own century, in fact, that the advent of new weapons and aircraft made the castle vulnerable.

This stupendous stronghold was begun in the 11th century, and expanded and strengthened over the next 200 years. The ruling family of Sachse-Coburg-Gotha inhabited it continuously from 1056 until 1547, when its discomforts persuaded the then-reigning duke, Johann Ernst, to move his family and entourage into the relative comfort of Ehrenburg Palace, in the center of town. (Only the rats, they say, were comfortable in the fortress.)

Yet it is well worth a visit. Among the famous people who have stayed in it were the elder Lucas Cranach, Goethe (who allegedly could bear it for only three days), Queen Victoria, and Martin Luther, who, rather involuntarily, remained here for five months in 1530 while awaiting an opportunity to present his arguments to a papal emissary in Augsburg. During that time he continued to work on his translation of the Bible into German. The **Luther room** in the fortress still holds the table at which he wrote. Among the castle's other treasures are a fine selection of Cranach paintings, a library of 450,000 volumes, medieval coins, engravings and etchings, a glass collection, and Germany's largest trove of antique firearms and hunting weapons.

Given the disadvantages of living in the fortress, it is small wonder that Johann Ernst moved into the more comfortable and elegant environs of **Schloss Ehrenburg**, a former Franciscan monastery on Coburg's Schlossstrasse. Its curious name—it means "Honor Castle" in German—is owed to the honor of a visit paid it in 1547 by Holy Roman Emperor Charles V. The palace in its present form is an extensive 17th- and 18th-century renovation of the Renaissance original. Most of it is now a museum, which makes it possible to see the Giants' Hall, so named for its 28 stucco figures of giants; the ornately decorated Gobelin Room; and the lavish Throne Room, which is very properly decked out in red velvet, crystal, and gold. The room is unusual, however, in that it does not contain a throne at all; instead, there is a long cushioned sofa from which the dukes of Sachse-Coburg-Gotha apparently ruled in a kind of semi-reclining position. The museum also includes the bedroom that Victoria and Albert used on their various visits to his family in Coburg. In the left back corner of the bed-niche, partly hidden by a curtain, is what appears to be a telephone booth. In its day it actually was an unprecedented sensation and the first of its kind in the region: an English water closet.

Albert's early death left Victoria bereft the rest of her life. It was she who gave Coburg the tall statue of Prince Albert that stands in the center of the Marktplatz amid the people and activities of the city he loved. He is portrayed as wonderfully handsome, in the full regalia of his office, extending a shapely leg adorned with the Order of the Garter.

Traffic, which ill suits the magnificently orieled and gabled medieval **Rathaus** and the half-timbered burgher houses lining the Marktplatz, moves slowly around the statue of Prince Albert, while pigeons flutter about his head and market women screech at his feet. Coburg's characteristic olfactory sensation, the scent of Bratwürste broiling over charcoal fires, drifts across the square and rouses hundreds of Coburgers to their accustomed morning snack. Be advised, however, that Coburg Bratwürste are unlike those you may have tasted in Nürnberg and Regensburg. None of that finger-long, finger-thick stuff here. A Coburg sausage is precisely 31 centimeters (about 12 inches) long—a measure determined by the length of the marshal's staff in the hand of Coburg's patron saint, Mauritius, who stands high atop the Rathaus gable—thumb-thick, and is consumed between the halves of a small crisply crusted roll.

Dining and Staying
in Coburg

For more substantial lunching or dining, saunter a block west of the Marktplatz to the ▶ **Hotel Goldene Traube**, Am Viktoriabrunnen 2, where the menu lists a variety of international dishes as well as Franconian specialties, not to mention a fine selection of Franconian wines. The hotel has 88 rooms in the moderate-price category. For the ultimate in fine dining and accommodations in Coburg, you will have to travel a little beyond the confines of the picturesque Old City, about half a mile south of the Marktplatz along Ketschendorfer Strasse, to the **Restaurant Schaller** in the ▶ **Hotel Coburger Tor**, Ketschendorfer Strasse 22. Proprietor-chef Ulrich Schaller deserves the recognition he has won, including a Michelin star and two Gault-Millau toques, since turning the dining room of this small (15 rooms) moderately priced hotel into Coburg's most elegant and dignified eatery. The decor is subdued, the cuisine memorable. The menu changes daily according to season and the availability of the best and freshest products. Schaller is a master at putting a light, nouvelle touch to regional specialties such as quenelles of Main river pike or wild duck in a morel sauce. Reservations are recommended, as there is seating for only 50; Tel: (9561) 250-74. No credit cards are accepted, which also goes for the hotel. The restaurant is open evenings only; closed Sundays, holidays, and part of July.

BETWEEN COBURG
AND BAMBERG

From Coburg our route heads south again, toward Bamberg, by way of two of Franconia's most stunning Baroque churches—Banz Monastery and Vierzehnheiligen church—situated on opposite sides of the road just south of the basket-weaving town of **Lichtenfels**. The best way to get there is to take B 4 south out of Coburg for 9 km (5½ miles) to its junction with B 289. Follow B 289 for another 10 km (6 miles) to Lichtenfels. Just past Lichtenfels, you'll come to its junction with B 173. Take it south (follow the signs to Bamberg), and you will see Banz and Vierzehnheiligen after about half a mile. The highway follows the south bank of the Main river.

Banz and Vierzehnheiligen

These two churches are breathtaking examples of Baroque architecture and craftsmanship. Here, rising unexpectedly against wooded hills on opposite banks of the Main river, they are exalting. As you approach them from the north, you'll see Vierzehnheiligen towering on the hill to your left, Banz across the valley to your right.

Banz began as a fortress castle belonging to Countess Alberada of Schweinfurt, who, in 1065, donated her property to the Benedictine order for conversion into a monastery. In 1071 the abbey came under the supervision of the prince-bishop of Bamberg. An abbey church, consecrated in 1114, was destroyed during the Thirty Years' War. Nearly half a century later, the architect Johann Leonhard Dientzenhofer drew up plans for a new church. Work, largely by lay brothers, began in 1695 and continued through the first half of the 18th century, with other members of the Dientzenhofer family as well as Balthasar Neumann contributing not only to the church itself but to the reconstruction of the entire monastery complex.

The result was two long structures, each with 27 bays, running parallel to the mountain and overlooking the Main river. These structures, connected by wings, contained an enormous library, a number of schools, and the friars' quarters. But the most important part of the complex was the church dedicated to St. Dionysius, with its magnificent ceiling frescoes, choir stalls, high altar, and pulpit. The abbey was secularized in 1806, and is used today as an old people's home, but the church, the abbot's chapel, and the Kaisersaal (Imperial Hall) are open to visitors.

Vierzehnheiligen (Church of the Fourteen Saints of the Intercession) is a pilgrimage church that owes its origins to a 15th-century vision. According to legend, a shepherd boy, Hermann Leicht, saw a vision of the Christ child and the 14 Auxiliary Saints on several occasions between 1445 and 1446 and told the abbot of Banz about the appearances; eventually, the abbot ordered the construction of a small chapel on the spot. The chapel became the object of many pilgrimages, and by the early 18th century was clearly too small to accommodate all its visitors. Eventually, Balthasar Neumann was commissioned to build a new church. Work began in 1743 and continued through 1772. Some of the greatest artists of the time—Johann Michael Küchel, Franz Xavier Feuchtmayer, and the Italian fresco painter J. I. Appiani—contributed to the project. The result is one of the most harmonious and dazzling examples of Baroque artisanship, a beautiful blend of marble and stucco, painting, and elegant—albeit exuberant—interior design.

Should you be ready for a lunch break after seeing Vierzehnheiligen and Banz, drive 5 km (3 miles) south to the charming town of Staffelstein and turn in at the **Gasthaus Rödiger**, Zur Hergottsmühle 2, where the cooking is unpretentiously Franconian. The restaurant is closed on Fridays and during the month of August. From here it is another 26 km (16 miles) south along B 173 and west on E 48 to Bamberg.

BAMBERG

Nestled in the rolling hill country of Franconia, at the confluence of the Regnitz and Itz rivers with the Main, this town of 70,000 is billed as "the gift of a thousand years," which is how long it has been making its mark on history. Probably no other city in Germany evokes the essence of the country more effectively, and many Germans simply say, "We may not have Florence or Venice, but we do have Bamberg, which is even greater."

To be sure, Germany has numerous other picturesque and historic spots—but most of them are either living museums of the past or situated so squarely on well-trodden tourist trails that visitors to them invariably photograph each other. Bamberg is a refreshing exception to the clichés. Although it welcomes, and gets, plenty of tourists, it does not depend on them. And although its architectural masterpieces are in mint condition, it is neither frozen in time nor mired in its once-great past. As one of its burgomasters once put it, "Our city is the house in which we live, but because it is so unique and beautiful, we live like the gods."

Bamberg is a radiant assemblage of Europe's greatest architectural styles—Romanesque, Gothic, Renaissance, and Baroque—as well as a treasure trove of some of Germany's finest art. It abounds with majestic churches, lavish palaces, and dazzlingly ornate mansions. The town itself is an engaging maze of narrow, winding cobblestone streets and an oasis of sparkling little streams, dreamy canals, old bridges, and vibrant colorful market squares.

For 800 of its 1,000 years Bamberg was the capital of an independent prince-bishopric whose properties included substantial chunks of real estate as far afield as present-day Austria, Italy, and Switzerland, and whose affluent art-loving rulers, usually more princely than pious, exercised both secular and ecclesiastical powers. That is why there are actually two towns—the **Bischofstadt** (Bishops' City) and the **Bürgerstadt** (Burghers' City)—each strikingly different.

They are separated by the Regnitz river, in the middle of which sits Bamberg's most photogenic edifice, the ornately embellished and fresco-painted **Altes Rathaus**. Built on an artificial island in 1450 as a compromise between the bishop and the burgomaster, each of whom wanted the city hall on his side of the Regnitz, it was redecorated in its present Baroque style in the 1750s. The medieval **Obere Brücke** (Upper Bridge) links it to either bank of the river.

There is also a **Neues Rathaus** (New City Hall) about half a kilometer north on Maximiliansplatz, in the Bürgerstadt, designed in 1732 by Balthasar Neumann.

The officially celebrated date of Bamberg's founding is 973, when it became the property of Heinrich the Squabbler, a litigious and cantankerous duke of Bavaria. His son, Holy Roman Emperor Heinrich (Henry) II, briefly made Bamberg the capital of the German Holy Roman Empire, which in those days stretched from the North Sea and Baltic to the Mediterranean and Adriatic.

The Cathedral Area

Like Rome, Bamberg is built on seven hills, and the only practical way to explore it is on foot. Almost every hill is crowned by a church, of which the **Dom** (cathedral), commissioned by Heinrich II in 1004 and completed in its present form in 1237, ranks as one of the finest and most harmonious examples of Late Romanesque and Early Gothic architecture in Europe. With its four massive spires, it towers above the city and is visible from miles away. (As the crow flies, it is no more than 500 yards southeast of the Altes Rathaus, but because the way up follows steep, winding streets, figure on a 15-minute climb.)

On your way to the Dom, consider checking in at the ► **Barock-Hotel am Dom**, Vorderer Bach 4, a small (19 rooms), charming, moderately priced hotel tucked into an 18th-century town house. Breakfast is served in its cross-vaulted cellar.

Although the Dom's exterior is surprisingly austere (the main embellishment being a few gargoyles and a vividly sculpted scene of the Last Judgment in the tympanum of the Prince's Portal), the cathedral is crammed with art treasures. The most famous is the **Bamberger Reiter** (Bamberg Rider), which was sculpted in 1235. The identity of the rider is as anonymous as that of the artist. A number of other statutes in the cathedral, as well as the Tomb of Clement II, the only pope buried north of the Alps, are believed to be works by the same unknown master.

There is no mystery, on the other hand, about the **sarcophagus of Heinrich II and Kunigunde** (his wife), which was sculpted out of Italian marble by the Würzburg master Tilman Riemenschneider in 1513, or the **Nativity Altar**, carved from linden wood in 1523 by Veit Stoss. The tomb of Heinrich and Kunigunde depicts many of the legends surrounding their lives, including the one in which she walked barefoot, without suffering so much as a blister, over red-hot plowshares in order to prove she had remained faithful to her husband during one of his sojourns through the empire. Both were canonized for their piety and good works.

North of and adjacent to the Dom is the soaring Renaissance façade of the **Kanzleibau** (Episcopal Chancellery), which leads to the **Alte Hofhaltung** (Old Court), a large, gabled, half-timbered Gothic palace that served emperors and, later, the prince-bishops as a palace and residence until the bishops, in 1703, moved into the Neue Residenz diagonally across the square from the cathedral.

In the minds of many people there are striking similarities between Bamberg and Prague, in part because the layout of both cities encourages that impression. But there are also very tangible links, and one is the **Neue Residenz** (New Residence), designed in 1697 by Johann Dientzenhofer. The Dientzenhofers were to Baroque architecture what the Bachs were to music: an entire family—five brothers plus a nephew—who devoted their lives to building churches, monasteries, palaces, and mansions throughout northern Bavaria, Franconia, and neighboring Bohemia. In fact, half the Baroque buildings in Prague, and nearly all those in Bamberg, are their work.

Today the Neue Residenz, crammed with works by the Cranachs, Hans Baldung Grien, and other German Old Masters, serves as Bamberg's main art gallery. Its richly decorated imperial hall is also used for chamber concerts by members of the Bamberger Symphoniker. This internationally acclaimed orchestra, established in 1946, is another link to Prague: All its founding musicians were members of the Prague German Philharmonic who fled Czechoslovakia in May 1945 and settled in Bamberg and the surrounding region.

Exploring Bamberg

Bamberg is a music center thanks also to E. T. A. Hoffmann, the early-19th-century novelist, illustrator, and composer (though a lawyer and judge by profession), who spent the five most productive years of his life as director and conductor of Bamberg's municipal theater. Hoffmann was not only a highly talented musician, greatly influenced by Robert Schumann and Johannes Brahms, but also a master teller of stories of madness and horror (many of which reputedly were written in an alcoholic delirium). At night the winding streets that climb the hill between the cathedral and the Regnitz evoke visions of his "Devil's Elixir," "Educated Cat," and the grotesque tales that composer Jacques Offenbach later turned into the opera *The Tales of Hoffmann*. The modest house in which Hoffman lived, the **E. T. A. Hoffmann-Haus**, at Schillerplatz 26, across the street from the theater that bears his name (and around the corner from the taverns where he drank to fatal excess), is now a museum devoted to him.

For all of Bamberg's fine examples of various architectural styles, however, its showiest style is Baroque, and the most ostentatious display of it is the **Böttingerhaus**, Judenstrasse 14, tucked into a narrow street on the left bank of the Regnitz. A cornucopia of stone and stucco cupids, gods, goddesses, mythical fauna, and swirls of flora, it was built between 1706 and 1713 as a private mansion for Johann Ignaz Tobias Böttinger, a commoner who became one of 18th-century Germany's richest men by playing at politics.

The Regnitz was dotted with mills in the days when it was Bamberg's chief source of energy, and in one of these, now the 35-room ▶ **Hotel St. Nepomuk**, just a block northeast of the Böttingerhaus, you will find the pleasant, moderately priced **St. Nepomuk** eatery, Obere Mühlbrücke 9, Tel: (951) 251-83, whose windows offer breathtaking views of the Altes Rathaus and the old fishermen's district, **Klein Venedig** (Little Venice). (You can also get a good view of Klein Venedig from the Untere Brücke, which is just downstream from the Altes Rathaus.)

Though Bamberg is just a few miles east of the Franconian wine region, *the* Bamberg beverage is beer, of which more is consumed here than anywhere else in Germany. The city's 11 independent breweries—actually a drop in the keg compared to the 1,500 that operated in the 16th century—all produce a unique local specialty: *Rauchbier* (smoked beer), which is made by drying barley malt over logs of smoldering beech wood. Rauchbier dates from the Middle Ages when, so the story goes, a fire broke out in one of the abbey breweries. The monks liked the resulting beverage so much that they began to duplicate the process, although less pyrotechnically. Dark, somewhat bitter and tangy, and not as strong as most German beer, it takes some getting used to. It's especially good when used to wash down regional specialties such as baked carp, sauerbraten, bratwurst, and an aspic of sausage meats called *Wurstsülze*.

In the warm months Rauchbier is best in any of the dozens of beer gardens that dot Bamberg's seven hills; during the rest of the year you'll find it in the many taverns operated by the breweries, of which the **Schenkerla**, Dominikanerstrasse 6, is the most famous. Located in the vaulted halls of a 13th-century Dominican monastery, it has been in operation since 1678. Though you can also order a hearty meal here, the Schenkerla is unique in that, except between noon and 2:00 P.M., you can bring your own food and will be given a plate and cutlery with which to eat it, provided you order a glass of beer.

Those who seek more elegant dining than the rustic fare served up by the Schenkerla and other beer halls, with their cavernous rooms and bare wood tables, will find a number of restaurants in Bamberg in a category just a notch below a Michelin star or a Gault-Millau toque. The **Würzburger Weinstuben**, Zinkenwörthstrasse 6, was one of E. T. A. Hoffmann's favorite watering places, and is just around the corner from his house on Schillerplatz. Though it looks like a pizzeria from the outside, **Il Bassanese**, Obere Sandstrasse 32, close to the Altes Rathaus, has an elegant interior and serves up superb French-Italian cuisine. There is no menu. Instead, tell proprietor Gabriele Tonin how many courses you'd like and whether you prefer fish, meat, or poultry as a main course. She'll make a number of suggestions, and when an agreement has been reached will pass the order to the kitchen, where everything is prepared with the finest, freshest ingredients; Tel: (951) 575-51.

The most elegant accommodations in town are found at the ▶ **Hotel Residenzschloss**, Untere Sandstrasse 32, a Baroque palace that was completely renovated and restored in 1991. The best rooms overlook Klein Venedig and the Regnitz river. The ▶ **Hotel Bamberger Hof-Bellevue**, Schönleinsplatz 4, is a first-class establishment in a Neo-Baroque mansion. Bamberg's most historic eatery is the **Weinhaus Messerschmitt** in the ▶ **Romantik Hotel Messerschmitt**, Lange Strasse 41, just a few steps from Schönleinsplatz. Run by the same family since 1832, it is a jewelbox of antique furnishings and bric-a-brac amassed by six generations. The hotel itself has 14 rooms.

Just 21 km (13 miles) south of Bamberg, along B 505 near its junction with the Autobahn heading south to Nürnberg or west to Würzburg, is the last destination on our route, the hamlet of Pommersfelden, worth a detour if not a special trip for its magnificent Baroque palace.

POMMERSFELDEN

Although you may think you have seen Baroque splendor, you really haven't until you see **Schloss Weissenstein** in Pommersfelden. In 1711 Lothar Franz von Schönborn, ecclesiastic and temporal ruler of Würzburg, and also archchancellor of the Holy Roman Empire, commissioned three of Europe's leading architects to build these palatial digs: Balthasar Neumann, Maximilian von Welsch, and Lukas von Hildebrandt, court architect to the Hapsburgs in Vienna. Legend has it, however, that Schönborn, a hands-on ruler born with a draftsman's compass in his hand, acted as foreman throughout.

Schönborn placed Schloss Weissenstein on open ground in a vast park southeast of Pommersfelden so that it could be seen from all directions—and so that it could grow in all directions as well. The central building was flanked by two projecting side wings, an arrangement that created the huge courtyard called the *Ehrenhof.* Opposite this "court of honor" was—and is—the *Marstall* (stable) building, which housed equipages, carriages, coaches, and sleighs.

Oddly enough, the exterior of the palace has none of the lavish ornamentation or joyfulness that one finds in other Baroque buildings. It might, instead, better be called German Renaissance. The interior, on the other hand, is an eye-popper.

Weissenstein is still the private property of the Schönborn family, who live in it part of the year, keep it in mint condition, and allow it to be used for summer musicals and chamber concerts. As a result, it is not the sort of place where visitors can just roam. In fact, guided tours are taken through in rather quick succession. Still, it's the first look through the main door that impresses most. An arched passageway under the grand staircase leads to the oval **Grottensaal** (Grotto Hall), which opens, in turn, onto the garden beyond. The grotto is lined with stucco seashells, leaves, and sea creatures. The tour also takes you through the five-story-high **Hauptsaal** (Main or Marble Hall), an audience room, a great gallery where some of the Schönborn art treasures are on exhibit, and a lavishly ornamented dining room done all in pink.

Pommersfelden is one of the grand monuments to Europe's, and especially northern Bavaria's, past. If you wish to relive a bit of that past, you will find the **Schloss Restaurant** in the palace itself, and the moderately priced ▶ **Schlosshotel Pommersfelden** in a guest house just across the way.

Pommersfelden is only 40 km (25 miles) northwest of Nürnberg, where our tour of Franconia began, and 75 km (47 miles) east (by way of the Nürnberg–Frankfurt Autobahn, A 3) of Würzburg, the beginning of the Romantic Road and the next chapter.

GETTING AROUND

Major airline gateways to the Danube region are Stuttgart and Munich; for Franconia they are Nürnberg, Frankfurt, Munich, and Berlin. Major car rental agencies are represented at all these airports.

From Stuttgart to Ulm there are more than 60 trains daily, 18 of them InterCity (IC) or EuroCity (EC), which make the trip from Stuttgart to the Ulm main station in a little under an hour. The 14 Inter Regio (IR) make the same trip in 62 minutes, and the 15 InterCity Express (ICE) get you there in 54 minutes. Figure about an hour, depending on traffic conditions, from Stuttgart airport to Ulm by car, using the Stuttgart-to-Munich (A 8) Autobahn route. From Munich to Ulm there are 45 trains daily, 16 of them either IC or EC, 8 IRs, and 16 ICEs, which take 70 minutes. By car it is approximately 90 minutes on the Munich-to-Stuttgart Autobahn.

Nürnberg is the start of the Franconia route. From Frankfurt to Nürnberg there are 20 trains daily, including 16 IC expresses, all of which can be boarded directly at Frankfurt airport. The trip from the Frankfurt station takes 2 hours and 19 minutes; from the Frankfurt airport it's 2 hours and 50 minutes. By car it's 2½ to 3 hours, depending on traffic, from the Frankfurt airport to the center of Nürnberg, using the Frankfurt–Nürnberg (A 3) Autobahn.

From Munich to Nürnberg there are 35 trains daily, including 15 IC expresses. The trip takes 1 hour and 45 minutes. Depending on traffic, it may take you 1 to 1½ hours by car from the Munich airport to the center of Nürnberg, using the A 9 Autobahn.

Train connections from Berlin to Nürnberg are few, 15 per day, and nearly all require one or two changeovers; the trip takes 6½ to 7 hours. Until service is improved, the best way to get from Berlin to Nürnberg is to drive, using the A 9 Autobahn. The total distance is about 400 km (248 miles), and you should allow 5 to 6 hours for the trip, depending on traffic. There is a posted speed limit of 100 km (62 mph) almost all the way from Berlin to Nürnberg.

There are train connections between all the towns described on both the Danube and Franconia routes, though service between smaller communities is infrequent and slow. The only fast train connection on the Danube route is between Ulm and Regensburg, with 28 trains daily, 11 of which require transfer at Munich, making it a 3-hour trip. Should you stick with the trains, there are also good connections between Regensburg and Nürnberg, and vice versa, with 30 trains daily in both directions, eight of them ICs or ECs. The trip takes about an hour. There are also regular train connections between Regensburg and Munich, with 26 trains daily in both directions, none of them express. It's a 90-minute journey.

Though bus service does exist between towns and cities on both routes, it is infrequent (at best) and slow.

The best way of getting around and seeing the sights described above is to drive, and our itinerary is designed accordingly. We have intentionally given directions that will keep travellers off the Autobahns and, in the case of the Danube, as close to the river as possible (using unnumbered country roads where necessary). Do, however, carry along a detailed map or road atlas (the *Shell Atlas,* available in bookstores as well as Shell gas stations, is used by most Germans, though there are other good ones such as the *Aral Atlas* and the *V.A.G. Atlas*). You may also want to purchase the appropriate *H-B Bild Atlas* for these regions. Though they are published only in German, you will find the maps in them very detailed and useful. For the Danube route and the Bayerischer Wald, the two you'll want are number 36, "Niederbayern"; and number 6, "Bayerischer Wald." For Franconia, number 50, "Mainfranken," covers part of our route.

ACCOMMODATIONS REFERENCE

The hotel rates listed here are 1994 projections for double-bed, double-occupancy rooms, with a range from low to high whenever possible. Prices are given in deutsche marks (DM). Basic rates are always subject to change, so please verify price when you are booking. Breakfast is usually included in the price of a room.

City telephone codes must be preceded by a zero if you are calling from elsewhere in Germany.

Along the Danube
▶ **Altstadthotel Arch**. Am Haidplatz 4, D-93047 **Regensburg**. Tel: (941) 50-20-60; Fax: (941) 50-20-61-68. DM 215.

▶ **Gasthaus Eibl-Brunner**. Hauptstrasse 18, D-94258 **Frauenau**. Tel: (9926) 316; Fax: (9926) 726. DM 96–156.

▶ **Hotel Bischofshof**. Krauterermarkt 3, D-93047 **Regensburg**. Tel: (941) 590-86; Fax: (941) 535-08. DM 185–295.

▶ **Hotel Karmeliten**. Dachauplatz 1, D-93047 **Regensburg**. Tel: (941) 543-08; Fax: (941) 56-17-51. DM 165–220.

► **Hotel Neuthor.** Neuer Graben 23, D-89073 **Ulm**. Tel: (731) 151-60; Fax: (731) 151-65-13. DM 180–190.

► **Hotel Passauer Wolf.** Rindermarkt 6, D-94032 **Passau**. Tel: (851) 340-46; Fax: (851) 367-57. DM 170–240.

► **Hotel Rappensberger.** Harderstrasse 3, D-85049 **Ingolstadt**. Tel: (841) 31-40; Fax: (841) 31-42-00. DM 175–195.

► **Hotel Seethaler.** Theresienplatz 25, D-94315 **Straubing**. Tel: (9421) 120-22; Fax: (9421) 233-90. DM 150–160.

► **Hotel Ulmer Spatz.** Münsterplatz 27, D-89073 **Ulm**. Tel: (731) 680-81; Fax: (731) 602-19-25. DM 150.

► **Hotel Wilder Mann.** Schrottgasse 2, D-94032 **Passau**. Tel: (851) 350-71; Fax: (851) 317-12. DM 130–230.

► **Ibis Hotel.** Neutorstrasse 12, D-89073 **Ulm**. Tel: (731) 61-90-01; Fax: (731) 631-03. DM 168.

► **Kirchbaur-Hof.** Monheimer Strasse 119, D-86633 **Neuburg-Bittenbrunn**. Tel: (8431) 25-32; Fax: (8431) 411-22. DM 130–140.

► **Kurhotel Sonnenberg.** Augustinerstrasse 9, D-94227 **Zwiesel**. Tel: (9922) 20-31; Fax: (9922) 29-13. DM 105–140.

► **Parkhotel Maximilian.** Maximilianstrasse 28, D-93047 **Regensburg**. Tel: (941) 510-42; Fax: (941) 529-42. DM 268–288.

► **Säumerhof.** Steinberg 32, D-94481 **Grafenau**. Tel: (8552) 24-01; Fax: (8552) 53-43. DM 170.

Franconia

► **Barock-Hotel am Dom.** Vorderer Bach 4, D-96049 **Bamberg**. Tel: (951) 540-31; Fax: (951) 540-21. DM 145–155.

► **Burghotel-Grosses Haus.** Lammsgasse 3, D-90403 **Nürnberg**. Tel: (911) 20-44-14; Fax: (911) 22-38-82. DM 175–190.

► **Burghotel-Kleines Haus.** Schildgasse 16, D-90403 **Nürnberg**. Tel: (911) 20-44-14; Fax: (911) 22-38-82. DM 175–190.

► **Burghotel Lauenstein.** Burgstrasse 4, D-69337 **Ludwigsstadt-Lauenstein**. Tel: (9263) 256; Fax: (9263) 71-67. DM 100–130.

► **Dürer Hotel.** Neutormauer 32, D-90403 **Nürnberg**. Tel: (911) 20-80-91; Fax: (911) 22-34-58. DM 215–275.

► **Grand Hotel.** Bahnhofstrasse 1, D-90402 **Nürnberg**. Tel: (911) 232-20; Fax: (911) 232-24-44. DM 255–350.

► **Hansa-Hotel.** Weltrichstrasse 2a, D-95326 **Kulmbach**. Tel: (9221) 79-95; Fax: (9221) 668-87. DM 175–210.

► **Hotel Bamberger Hof-Bellevue.** Schönleinsplatz 4, D-96047 **Bamberg**. Tel: (951) 985-50; Fax: (951) 98-55-62. DM 220–380.

► **Hotel Bayerischer Hof.** Bahnhofstrasse 14, D-95444 **Bayreuth**. Tel: (921) 220-81; Fax: (921) 220-85. DM 180–250.

► **Hotel Coburger Tor.** Ketschendorfer Strasse 22, D-

96450 **Coburg**. Tel: (9561) 250-74; Fax: (9651) 288-74. DM 155–210.

▶ **Hotel Gasthof zur Lohmühle**. Badstrasse 37, D-95444 **Bayreuth**. Tel: (921) 530-60; Fax: (921) 582-86. DM 190–210.

▶ **Hotel Goldener Hirsch**. Bahnhofstrasse 13, D-95444 **Bayreuth**. Tel: (921) 230-46; Fax: (921) 224-83. DM 135–200.

▶ **Hotel Goldene Traube**. Am Viktoriabrunnen 2, D-96450 **Coburg**. Tel: (9561) 87-60; Fax: (9561) 87-62-22. DM 160–195.

▶ **Hotel Königshof**. Bahnhofstrasse 23, D-95444 **Bayreuth**. Tel: (921) 240-94; Fax: (921) 122-64. DM 200–260.

▶ **Hotel Maritim**. Frauentorgraben 11, D-90443 **Nürnberg**. Tel: (911) 236-30; Fax: (911) 236-38-36. DM 296–452.

▶ **Hotel Residenzschloss**. Untere Sandstrasse 32, D-96049 **Bamberg**. Tel: (951) 609-10; Fax: (951) 609-17-01. DM 255–295.

▶ **Hotel St. Nepomuk**. Obere Mühlbrücke 9, D-96049 **Bamberg**. Tel: (951) 251-83; Fax: (951) 266-51. DM 170–280.

▶ **Merrian Hotel**. Unschlittplatz 7, D-90403 **Nürnberg**. Tel: (911) 20-41-94; Fax: (911) 22-12-74. DM 180.

▶ **Pflaum's Posthotel**. Nürnberger Strasse 12–16, D-91257 **Pegnitz**. Tel: (9241) 72-50; Fax: (9241) 804-04. DM 195–690.

▶ **Romantik Hotel am Josephsplatz**. Josephsplatz 30–32, D-90403 **Nürnberg**. Tel: (911) 24-11-56; Fax: (911) 24-31-65. DM 200.

▶ **Romantik Hotel Messerschmitt**. Lange Strasse 41, D-96049 **Bamburg**. Tel: (951) 278-66; Fax: (951) 261-41. DM 185–220.

▶ **Schlosshotel Pommersfelden**. Im Schloss Weissenstein, D-96178 **Pommersfelden**. Tel: (9548) 680; Fax: (9548) 681-00. DM 76–156.

▶ **Schlosshotel Thiergarten**. Oberthiergärtner Strasse 36, D-95448 **Bayreuth-Thiergarten**. Tel: (9209) 13-14; Fax: (9209) 18-29. DM 220–260.

THE ROMANTIC ROAD

WÜRZBURG, ROTHENBURG, AUGSBURG, NEUSCHWANSTEIN CASTLE

By John Dornberg

The Romantic Road—*Die Romantische Strasse*—is purely an invention, the promotional brainchild of some wordsmith at the German National Tourist Board. It was coined in 1949, when the automobile age in West Germany was just dawning. Although the Romans used a part of it, calling it the Via Claudia, it is a route rather than a road, which, being a mere 220 miles long, you could drive in four to five hours, assuming you were in a hurry. But what a shame if you did, for the Romantic Road—from Würzburg on the Main river south across the Danube, through Augsburg in Bavaria to Füssen in Bavaria's Allgäu Alps—is a trail through Germany incarnate, a splendid pathway to the past, a glittering chain of majestic cities, storybook towns, and picture-postcard villages studded with gems of art and architecture that span more than two millennia of human creativity and history.

From the meandering, twisting Main river south to the Alpine border with Austria, the Romantische Strasse is a route through Germany at its most picturesque, a living travelogue of wooded hillocks, placid valleys, dark forests, formidably walled medieval towns, graceful Gothic churches, elegant Renaissance town halls, dazzling Baroque palaces, and fanci-

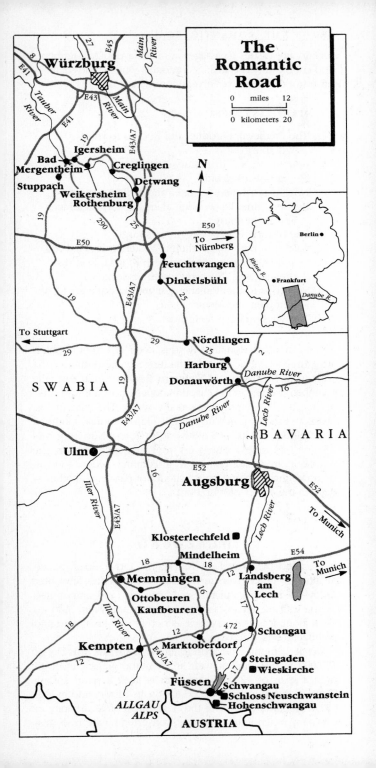

The Romantic Road

| 0 | miles | 12 |
| 0 | kilometers | 20 |

N

Würzburg

Main River
Main River
E45
27
8
E41
E43
E41
Tauber River
19
E43/A7

Igersheim
Bad Mergentheim
Stuppach
Weikersheim
Rothenburg
Creglingen
Detwang

19
200
25
E50

E50
E43/A7
19

To Nürnberg
E50

Feuchtwangen
Dinkelsbühl
25

To Stuttgart

29
29
Nördlingen
25
2
Harburg
Donauwörth
Danube River
16

SWABIA
19
E43/A7
16
Danube River
2
BAVARIA

Ulm
16
E52

Augsburg
Lech River
E52
To Munich

Klosterlechfeld
E54

Mindelheim
18
18
12
Landsberg am Lech
To Munich

Memmingen
16
Ottobeuren
Kaufbeuren
12
17

Iller River
12
472
Schongau

Kempten
Marktoberdorf
E43/A7
16
Steingaden
Wieskirche
17

18
Iller River

Füssen
Schwangau
Schloss Neuschwanstein
Hohenschwangau

ALLGÄU ALPS

AUSTRIA

Berlin
Frankfurt
Rhine R.
Danube R.

ful fairy-tale castles: a passageway to enclaves of half-timbered
and cobblestoned charm, to redoubts where time seems to
have stood still and yesteryear comes alive.

MAJOR INTEREST

The medieval, Baroque, and Rococo town of
    Würzburg
Rothenburg's 17th-century Altstadt
Medieval Dinkelsbühl
Nördlingen's meteor crater and walled Altstadt
Riemenschneider wooden altarpieces in Creglingen
    and Rothenburg
The historic Fugger city of Augsburg
Castles in Bad Mergentheim, Weikersheim, Harburg,
    and Hohenschwangau (where King Ludwig II's
    dream castle, Neuschwanstein, is located)
Side trips to the Romanesque and Baroque towns of
    Kempten and Memmingen
The Wieskirche at Steingaden

The north–south Romantic Road is, in effect—as our book is
structured—a vertical band separating Stuttgart/Swabia to the
west from Northern and Southern Bavaria to the east (the
Danube coverage in the chapter about Northern Bavaria cuts
across this band from Ulm in the west). The start of this
chapter's journey is in Würzburg, 121 km (75 miles) southeast
of Frankfurt, 110 km (68 miles) northwest of Nürnberg, and
75 km (47 miles) due west of Pommersfelden on the
Autobahn. If you are coming from Pommersfelden, you will
be travelling from one great Schönborn palace to another—
right in the center of Würzburg.

WÜRZBURG

It is called the "Jewel on the Main," and it does indeed
gleam. Few other rivers in Germany are as gentle, few other
valleys as romantic, picturesque, pastoral, and untrampled
by the touring masses as the Main river and valley. And no
town along it is as majestic or as rich in treasures of art and
architecture as Würzburg.

Nestled among vineyards along the riverbank, this city of
125,000 is resplendent with architectural gems conceived
over a span of 12 centuries, and is itself a jewel among
German Baroque and Rococo towns. Its history and monuments in stone date from the beginnings of Christianity in
Germany, when Frankish dukes, converted by the Irish mis-

sionary monk Saint Kilian, settled on the site of the present town and built the massive Marienberg fortress on the crest of the highest of Würzburg's many terraced and vine-covered hills. One of the oldest churches in the country, the **Marienkirche** (Church of St. Mary), built in 706, stands almost pristine in the citadel's courtyard.

Although it is the site of a 400-year-old university, Würz-burg today is merely a provincial capital, best known for its palaces and churches and white Franconian wines, inimita-ble in taste and distinctive for their *Bocksbeutel* bottles. But from the eighth century until 1806, when Napoleon re-shaped the map of Europe, imposed secularization, and ceded the town to the newly created kingdom of Bavaria, it was an independent and influential prince-bishopric. Its rulers, who enjoyed both ecclesiastical and temporal pow-ers, were nearly all great patrons of the arts. They attracted the services of some of the greatest masters of their times, and left an incomparable legacy.

It was in Würzburg that the painter Matthias Grünewald was born, in 1475, and did much of his work, and it was under Prince Bishop Rudolf von Scherenberg that Tilman Riemenschneider, arguably the greatest of the medieval wood sculptors, came to the city and settled in 1483, ulti-mately becoming Würzburg's burgomaster. His work is richly represented in some of the city's churches as well as those of villages nearby. It was Prince Bishop Johann Philipp Franz von Schönborn who commissioned the Residenz, an ornate 300-room château.

Much of Würzburg's Romanesque, Gothic, Renaissance, Baroque, and Rococo heritage was blasted to rubble during a single air raid in March 1945, with the result that nearly all its beautiful churches, magnificent bridges, patrician houses, and splendid hospices are reconstructions—stone by stone, gargoyle by gargoyle, cupid by cupid. Amazingly, the Re-sidenz escaped with relatively little damage.

Besides all the art and architecture, the town is the epit-ome of romantic ambience and Old World charm. The two largest hospices, the Bürgerspital and the Juliusspital, are famed for their wine taverns, and serve vintages from their own vineyards.

Marienberg Citadel

This former fortified residence of the prince-bishops, now the home of the Mainfränkisches Museum, is Würzburg's distinctive landmark, visible from miles away. The citadel's threatening appearance is softened by the vineyards on the hill it crowns. Situated on the west bank of the Main, it is the ideal place to start your tour—the magnificent view from its ramparts will help orient you, and the citadel itself provides a splendid introduction to the city's history.

The oldest walls and buildings of the complex date from the early 13th century; the Marienkirche, part of the fortress, has sections going back to its consecration in 706.

The **Mainfränkisches Museum** contains the world's most complete collection of Riemenschneider sculptures and wood carvings. These are the originals of copies you will find in churches elsewhere in Würzburg and Franconia. One of its greatest treasures is Tiepolo's canvas *The Appointment of Cincinnatus,* and there are some fine paintings by both Cranachs (Elder and Younger). The collection also includes a complete 18th-century apothecary shop, some excellent Bayreuth faïence, old toys, a great many 16th- through 18th-century wine presses, and a huge lode of local and regional applied art.

The Old City

A walk downhill and north of the Marienberg will lead you to one of Würzburg's oldest inns, the **Wein und Fischhaus Schiffbäuerin**, Katzengasse 7, where you may want to stop for lunch after exploring the citadel. The *Schiffbäuerinnen* (ship peasant women) were two women who presided over a lovely half-timbered house to which the Main fishermen brought their choicest catch straight from the river—as they still do today.

The nearby **Alte Mainbrücke** leads you into the center of the Altstadt. The bridge was completed in its present form in 1543, after 70 years of construction work, and ranked as one of the engineering marvels of its time. The 12 statues of mitered, sword-bearing, and rather belligerent-looking bishops that adorn it are additions of the Baroque period.

Just north of the bridge, on the river's east bank, is the **Alter Kranen**, a Würzburg landmark constructed in 1773 by the son of the great Baroque architect Balthasar Neumann. Once essential to the city's river port, the old loading crane bears a Latin inscription that translates: "I receive transport and dispatch anything you like."

The **Marktplatz**, Würzburg's main square, is a couple of blocks farther east. On your way you will pass the **Rathaus**, much of it dating from around 1200, with upper stories added in the 15th and 16th centuries, making it a fine example of Renaissance architecture. Just west of the square, at Gressengasse 1, is Würzburg's oldest wine tavern, the **Weinhaus zum Stachel**. Dating from the 15th century, it's where the Peasant Wars' conspirators used to meet.

At the Weinhaus you may find one of Würzburg's local specialties—*Meefischli*. *Mee* is local dialect for the Main, and *fischli* are small fish—in fact, they're about the length of your little finger, no thicker than your thumb, and are plunged into deep hot fat without being drawn. Würzburgers say they swim three times: once in the Main, once in deep fat, and once in golden Franconian wine, which is the perfect beverage to accompany them. Your concierge will be able to tell you which restaurant has the best catch that particular day. The real secret of Meefischli is to add a pinch of cinnamon to the flour in which they are dredged. A meal-size portion can be up to a dozen, served with lemon wedges and potato salad.

The **Marienkapelle** (St. Mary's Chapel) on the Marktplatz was built on the site of a synagogue destroyed in a 14th-century pogrom. Construction began in 1377 and continued for almost 100 years. A number of the exterior statues are copies of works by Riemenschneider, who was as skilled a carver in stone as he was in wood. The originals are in the Mainfränkisches Museum. Though reconstructed, and much changed after the war, the **Falkenhof**, right behind the Marienkapelle, is still one of Würzburg's loveliest Rococo buildings. It houses the city library.

The **Neumünster**, on St.-Kilians-Platz, just a little east of the market square, was the original bishops' church, built in the eighth century on the spot where Saint Kilian and his brother missionaries were murdered by heathen Franks in 689. Though redesigned in Baroque style in the 18th century, the present church actually dates from the 13th century. The exterior is a meticulous reconstruction done after the 1945 air raid, but the interior is disappointing.

From the outside, Würzburg's **Dom** (Cathedral), on the Domplatz just south of St.-Kilians-Platz, is a classic example of Romanesque style; its interior, on the other hand, was transformed into Baroque decor with stuccowork in the 18th century. Construction of this cruciform pillared basilica began in 1050 and was completed about a century later. There were some major additions, including the east tower, in the 13th century. Among its most important works of art are the numerous tombstones, covering 700 years of stylistic development, placed between the pillars of the nave. Two of them, depicting prince-bishops Rudolf von Scherenberg and Lorenz von Bibra, are magnificent original works by Riemenschneider. The Dom is also a kind of pantheon, harboring the tombs of some of Würzburg's most famous burghers, among them Matthias Grünewald, Wilhelm Conrad Röntgen, the Nobel Prize–winning physicist who discovered the X ray and who taught for many years at Würzburg University, and not least, Riemenschneider himself, who was tortured and slain because of his participation in the 1526 Peasants' War.

A stroll back north along **Schönbornstrasse**, Würzburg's main pedestrian and shopping mall, will take you to the **Juliusspital**, at Juliuspromenade 19. The hospital and the vineyard that supported it date back to 1586 and were founded by Prince-Bishop Julius Echter, from whom it draws its name. The original hospital complex was often modified over the centuries, then almost completely destroyed in World War II. Among the buildings restored is the central **Fürstenpavillon** (Prince's Pavilion), which includes a magnificent 18th-century pharmacy. Beneath the building are cavernous wine cellars with huge oak casks where the premium vintages from the Julius Echter Berg and other hospital-owned vineyards are matured before being sold to the public—by the glass, by the carafe, and by the *Bocksbeutel*. Go there for a *Frühschoppen* (an early glass), served before noon and imbibed with a small snack of Franconian cold cuts.

The Juliusspital's principal competition for Würzburg and Franconian wine is the **Bürgerspital**, Theaterstrasse 19, at the corner of Semmelstrasse, about 500 feet south of the Juliusspital. Founded in 1371 and endowed by a bourgeois family, this infirmary was also supported by the sale of wine from its own vineyards. More than 30 of its wines are dispensed by leather-aproned cellar masters who dart among the scores of tables in ten different rooms.

From the Bürgerspital, continue south for another 1,000 feet along Theaterstrasse to Residenzplatz and the Residenz, Würzburg's most magnificent Baroque jewel.

The Residenz

Johann Philipp Franz von Schönborn was the first prince-bishop of Würzburg who wanted to move from the medieval digs in Marienberg fortress down into the city, right after being elected Würzburg's ruler in 1719. He found the available city palace inadequate, so plans for a new one were drawn up. Schönborn finally approved a château with about 300 rooms—plus large reception and official state halls, a court church, gardens, parade halls, a gallery for his paintings, and a magnificent *Treppenhaus* (stairwell), all shielded from the rest of Würzburg by a huge square, the Residenzplatz. It was said at the time that the Schönborns built their palace behind the plaza to avoid contact with commoners. This exclusivity is now seen as a blessing, as it provides the tourist throngs with an enormous parking lot. Be that as it may, the Residenz is today one of the largest, most grandiose—and harmonious—Baroque palaces in Central Europe.

Schönborn retained his favorite builder, Balthasar Neumann, who was soon joined on the project by Vienna's Lucas von Hildebrandt and Maximilian von Welsch, who had done most of Schönborn's work in the bishopric city of Mainz. The joint project went well, although there were disagreements. Hildebrandt did not believe that Neumann's unsupported ceiling over the stairwell would hold. Neumann offered, at his own expense, to bring in heavy artillery to create vibrations and prove that it could. He was again proven right in 1945 when the bombs that destroyed 85 percent of Würzburg and took the lives of 5,000 people left the staircase intact.

Schönborn could hardly wait to move into his Residenz, and drove his artists and workmen mercilessly. But he didn't live to see moving day: He died (so suddenly that poison was suspected) while out hunting one morning. His family and successors carried on, and in December 1744, 24 years after the cornerstone had been laid, the main building was completed.

As was common in Baroque architecture, the grand central staircase forms the centerpiece of the palace. This was not only where the stucco masters and sculptors were supposed to do their greatest and most representational work, but where the ceiling space was meant to dazzle. The responsibility for the latter fell to none other than the Venetian painter Giovanni Battista Tiepolo, assisted by his sons, Domenico and Lorenzo.

The Tiepolos stayed in Würzburg for more than three years, as the job eventually entailed far more than the banquet hall (nowadays the scene of Würzburg's annual Mozart Festival). The **stairwell ceiling**, allegorically depicting the then-known four continents, was not only Tiepolo's crowning work but so monumental that in size alone it is unique in the history of art. Visitors are likely to be amazed by its exuberance, as well as amused by the self-portrait of the master, with his dog, near the top. One of Tiepolo's original sketches for the ceiling fresco is at the Metropolitan Museum of Art in New York; an original sketch for the Kaisersaal (the banquet hall) ceiling is in the Mainfränkisches Museum.

The central building of the palace complex is situated atop the prince-bishops' wine cellars, with storage space for 1.4 million bottles. Also not to be missed are the Hofkirche (Court Church); the Gartensaal (a banquet hall facing the court garden); and the geometrical, meticulously manicured Hofgarten itself, where the highlights are the splendid wrought-iron gates designed by Neumann and sculptures by

Martin von Wagner. The south wing of the Residenz houses the **Martin von Wagner Museum**, an exquisite collection of Greek vases, Roman sculptures, and European and German paintings from the 14th through the 19th century.

A two-minute walk southwest from the Residenz, along Balthasar-Neumann-Promenade, will take you to the **University**, founded in 1582 by Prince-Bishop Julius Echter (of Juliusspital fame). Be sure to take in the courtyard side of this extensive Renaissance complex. **St. Peter's**, on the nearby Petersplatz, is a Romanesque basilica, rebuilt in the 18th century in Baroque style. Its western towers, however, remain unchanged.

Staying and Dining in Würzburg

From Petersplatz it is just a few steps north along Münz-strasse to the ▶ **Hotel Rebstock**, at Neubaustrasse 7. An inn since 1408, it is as notable for its comfortable rooms as for its magnificent Rococo façade, dating from 1737. The inn's **Weinstube** is good for unpretentious dining. The main dining room offers a six-course gourmet menu that changes daily as well as a vast array of Franconian specialties, prepared nouvelle style, as à la carte selections.

For a more modern hotel consider the ▶ **Maritim Hotel Würzburg**, at Pleichtorstrasse 5, near the northern tip of the Altstadt. A swimming pool is among the amenities. Its **Palais Grill** is another first-rate restaurant. The ▶ **Hotel Walfisch**, at Am Pleidenturm 5, has rooms with views of Marienberg fortress and is somewhat more moderately priced.

The best accommodations out of town are at the ▶ **Wittelsbacher Höh**, Hexenbruchweg 10, in Würzburg-Zellerau, 2 km (1¼ miles) northwest of the city center on the Marienberg side of the river. A Victorian-style inn with a modern annex, it includes a restaurant offering rustic Franconian decor, solid regional fare, and a wide selection of local Franconian wines.

To reach Bad Mergentheim, the next destination on the Romantic Road, pick up the B 19 on the Marienberg side of the river and drive 45 km (28 miles) south.

BAD MERGENTHEIM

Nearly 200 German towns are legally permitted to precede their names with the word *Bad* (bath). They are spas—and the definition of a bath is rather flexible. In some you can actually bathe in various healing mineral waters, guaranteed to cure whatever you think ails you, or in various kinds of mud; in others you merely drink the water; and in still others (where there is no mineral water at all) you breathe the air until you are dizzy. Germans call this kind of activity a *Kur,* and for millions of them it is a way of life.

Bad Mergentheim has been part of the cure circuit since 1826, when healing bitter salt springs were discovered and doctors began sending patients here to take the waters. The town was then some 600 years old and already rather famous.

Its fame derived from its role as the residence, or capital, of the *Deutschordens-Ritter* (Order of Teutonic Knights). Founded in 1190, during the Third Crusade, this German military religious order of nobles was dedicated to poverty, chastity, and obedience, but it played a key role in German expansion into Eastern Europe and eventually colonization of vast areas of Poland, today's Baltic republics, and Russia itself. Wherever the Teutonic Knights went and conquered, German-speaking peoples soon followed as settlers. (In 1263 the pope allowed the knights to engage in trade, a privilege they increasingly abused.) The knights' heyday lasted from the mid-13th through the early 16th century, until the Protestant Reformation broke their power, a demise effected in part when their own grand master, Albrecht of Brandenburg, accepted the Reformation in 1525. After that the order's influence was confined to predominantly Catholic southern and western Germany, which is how Bad Mergentheim entered the history of the Teutonic Knights. It was in the town's moated castle that the order's grand masters (who remained Catholic and loyal to the pope) established their residence in 1527.

The **Deutschordens Schloss** (Castle of the Teutonic Order) had been the property of the knights since the 13th century, but owes its present appearance to extensive enlargement and modification in the years 1565 to 1570, after it had become the grand master's palace. Most of the various Renaissance-style towers were added about 50 years later. The **Deutschordens Museum** and a museum of local history and handicrafts now occupy most of the rooms in the large complex. The **Schlosskirche** (Castle Church), nowadays Protestant, is a collaboration between two of Europe's greatest Baroque architects: Balthasar Neumann and the French Walloon François de Cuvilliés, who made his mark originally in Munich.

St. Johanneskirche (St. John's Church), on Kirchstrasse, built from 1250 to 1270 by the Knights of St. John of Jerusalem and taken over by the Teutonic Order in 1554, is a fine example of Gothic style with Renaissance additions. Neo-Gothic restoration in the late 19th century unfortunately reduced the appeal of the Dominican **Marienkirche** (St. Mary's Church) on Hans-Heinrich-Ehrler-Platz, though the building itself was completed in 1388. Be sure, however, to see the bronze epitaph of Walther von Cronberg, a Teutonic Order grand master; it is the creation of the Nürnberg bronze caster Hans Vischer. Mergentheim's **Marktplatz**, with its 16th-century Rathaus, is an almost perfect ensemble of Renaissance buildings.

Like all spa towns, Bad Mergentheim has a profusion of comfortable hotels. The ▶ **Hotel Victoria**, Poststrasse 2, has its own mineral baths and massage department, a pool, and a sauna, and even rents bicycles. The wood-paneled dining room is distinguished and has a prodigious wine cellar. Wines in carafes and by the glass are all from the Tauber river valley, one of Germany's smallest growing areas—so small that most of its excellent wine is consumed by locals. If you're looking for something super-modern in accommodations, consider the ▶ **Parkhotel Maritim**, Lothar-Daiker-Strasse 6. Many of the rooms have glass-enclosed loggias with views of the lovely Tauber valley. The hotel also has a medicinal bath, an in-house spa doctor, a swimming pool, and a beauty farm, and you can rent bikes for the duration of your stay.

No visit to Bad Mergentheim would be complete without making the short, 6-km (3½-mile) trip south on B 19 to the village of **Stuppach** to visit its **Pfarrkirche** (Parish Church), the repository of Matthias Grünewald's 1517–1519 painting of the Virgin Mary, one of the greatest masterpieces of Old German painting.

To continue on the Romantic Road, head back north through Bad Mergentheim on B 19, and drive on another 4 km (2½ miles) to the intersection just past the village of Igersheim. There, take a right turn and follow the signs to Weikersheim, your next destination. You will be driving on an unnumbered road that follows the east bank of the Tauber upstream for about 6 km (3½ miles).

SOUTHEAST TO ROTHENBURG
Weikersheim

Called "The Heart of the Tauber Valley," this town of 6,500 should be visited if for no other reason than to see **Hohenlohe Castle** and its stupendous **Rittersaal** (Knights' Hall), a former residence of the princes of Hohenlohe rich in untouched Renaissance, Baroque, and Rococo interiors. The Hohenlohes, a German dynasty dating back to the 12th century, once owned so many castles and châteaux here that the area around Weikersheim is called the Hohenlohe Land. In its heyday it was an independent and sovereign state.

The dimensions of the castle are overwhelming, for when Count Wolfgang von Hohenlohe built it in the waning years of the 16th century he wanted his residence to be second to none. The Knights' Hall is an overwhelming 115 feet by 39 feet and a cavernous three stories from floor to ceiling. Its fireplace, too, is three stories tall. Life-size carved animals, including an elephant, project from the upper walls among the antlered heads of hunting trophies. Family portraits are hung at an angle outward from the walls, the better to see them. One of Europe's deepest coffered ceilings crowns the whole thing. It has been said that knights rode their mounts up the wide, shallow stairs leading to the hall, and there is no question that a few horses would be inconspicuous in such a space.

Other rooms in the castle are on a slightly more normal scale, although one contains a bed that called for a ladder to scale the carved enclosure and reach the top of the mattresses. There are angels at its corners, a ceiling-high headboard, and a baldachin that would, if it collapsed, wipe out the bed's occupants.

The beautifully laid-out castle gardens face south and end in an architectural composition of obelisks, statuary, and an amusing dwarf's gallery. The castle is entered from town at the bottom of the fountained Marktplatz, through an arcade, a gate, and a second courtyard; keep your eye on the castle tower ahead and you'll find it.

In keeping with such stupendous digs in Weikersheim, a luxury hotel with a fabulous restaurant might be welcome, but the best in town is only a (very) comfortable inn, the ▶ **Laurentius,** Marktplatz 5. Its restaurant, presided over by proprietor-chef Heinrich Koch, offers exquisitely prepared nouvelle German dishes.

An 18-km (11-mile) drive farther east will take you to Creglingen.

Creglingen

It is said that two miracles happened in this town of 5,000. The first was on August 10, 1384, on the eve of the feast of Saint Laurentius, when a local peasant found the Sacred Host in a newly plowed furrow in his field. Numerous healings ensued; prayers were answered. Finally a small chapel was built over the sacred spot. With time, the chapel proved too small to accommodate the pilgrims who came to Creglingen, and the **Herrgottskirche** (Church of Our Lord) was built. It was completed in 1505 and is situated on land donated by the brothers Konrad and Gottfried Hohenlohe-Brauneck a bit south of Creglingen's center.

The two noblemen commissioned Tilman Riemenschneider to create an altar, dedicated to the life of Mary, to stand in the center of the small church right over the spot where the Host had been found. It is one of Riemenschneider's most sensitive and elaborate pieces of wood carving. The doors to the altar, however, remained uncarved because Creglingers could not afford to pay for more work, with the result that when the altar was closed, it looked like a plain wooden box. With passing time, according to custom, funeral wreaths were hung against it, and, as they dried, others were hung over them, creating a pyramid of dried wreaths in the center of the church. For nearly 300 years no one ever asked what was under them. Then, in 1832, Creglingen experienced its second miracle. Curious parishioners opened the doors to the altar and discovered one of Germany's most important missing works of art.

Continue upstream (south) along the Tauber for another 14 km (8½ miles) to Detwang, our next destination.

Detwang

This is probably the smallest and most bucolic village on the Romantic Road, and rates a stop for its carefully guarded masterpiece: Riemenschneider's magnificent 1510 **Holy Cross Altar**, installed in the tenth-century Romanesque **Peter-und-Paul-Kirche**.

There is room for two cars in the space in front of the church, and as soon as you drive into one of them, the guardian pops up, as if by magic, to sell you a ticket and unlock the door. Given the vast amount of ecclesiastical art that has been stolen in Germany during the past three decades, including some fine Riemenschneider carvings from village churches near Würzburg, the security is hardly excessive. The crucifixion scene, exquisitely carved in light blond lindenwood, was, unfortunately, stained a dark walnut in the 19th century.

From Detwang it is a mere 3 km (2 miles) farther south along the river to Rothenburg-ob-der-Tauber, the very embodiment of what is called "Romantic Germany," and one of the most visited spots on the Romantische Strasse.

ROTHENBURG

Rothenburg is a child's dream of knighthood, shining armor, and medieval chivalry come true: a walled and gate-towered city that stands today exactly as it stood in the 11th century, with steeply roofed step-gabled houses, soaring spires, narrow cobblestone streets, and fortified ramparts. No one has ever put up a neon sign or taken down an old street lantern here. Its visitors (and on weekends and public holidays it is crowded to bursting) are more like pilgrims who come to see a relic of the Middle Ages than conventional sightseers. It has been one of Germany's major attractions since mass tourism began in the second half of the 19th century. It is also the incarnation of romanticism: Thousands are the middle-aged to elderly German couples who will tell you with a blush that they honeymooned in Rothenburg, adding, "So did our parents and grandparents." Rothenburgers themselves—of whom 8,000 live within the old walls, 12,000 in newer districts around the historic quarter—all seem to be engaged in preserving its image. Odd vicissitudes of history helped to create the medieval appearance, and to maintain it.

Though mentions of Rothenburg go back to the year 700, it was not until the 11th century, when it became the property of the Hohenstaufen dynasty and Holy Roman Emperor Conrad began enlarging the tenth-century castle on the hill overlooking the Tauber, that it began to flourish. The town became a *Freie Reichsstadt* (Free Imperial City) in 1274 by decree of Emperor Rudolf, the first Hapsburg on the Holy Roman throne. What this meant was that Rothenburg was not subordinate to any baron, count, prince, or duke, but only to the emperor himself. It had its own judicial jurisdiction and the right of coinage, paid taxes only to the emperor, and needed to grease his palm and no one else's to obtain the trade and crafts privileges that were the keys to medieval prosperity and wealth.

By the mid-14th century, thanks to its location at the junction of major south–north and west–east trade routes; to its milling and textile production; and to the energetic promotional activities of its then mayor, Heinrich Toppler, Rothenburg had become one of the most prosperous free cities in the empire. That wealth is evident in its richly furnished and endowed churches, magnificent public buildings, and great burgher houses.

But weren't there many such towns in the German realm? Why and how was Rothenburg preserved? The answer is "two miracles"—and commercial decline.

The first miracle occurred in October 1631 during the Thirty Years' War when, after bitter, stubborn resistance, the town was conquered by the troops of Count Johannes von Tilly, the imperial field marshal. Tilly was so angry about the staunch defense that Rothenburg's militia had put up that he

announced he would immediately execute the four councillors who had ordered the resistance and then destroy the
town. The niece of one of the councillors, accompanied by
two other small children, implored Tilly to spare the men's
lives. The general refused. Then the daughter of the town's
cellar master arrived, offering refreshments while everyone
waited for the executioner, and praised Rothenburg's fine
Tauber valley wine. Tilly, so the story goes, agreed to try the
wine, which was brought to him in a huge three-quart
tankard. He tasted it, and humorously suggested, because
the goblet was so enormous, that he would pardon the four
councillors and spare the town if one of Rothenburg's men
could empty the tankard in one swallow. Hastily, a former
mayor, Herr Nusch, known more for his drinking prowess
than governing skills, was brought to the square, where he
drank off the wine in one draught without so much as taking
a breath. Tilly, amazed, kept his word, and Rothenburg as
well as its councillors were saved. Nusch himself, after
sleeping straight through for three days, also survived and
lived to tell the tale for another 37 years. The *Meistertrunk*
(master draught) is reenacted in a folk play by Rothenburgers wearing 17th-century costume every Whitsuntide weekend and the second Sunday in July. The pageant draws
visitors by the tens of thousands.

The second "miracle" is of more recent origin—April 15,
1945. Credit for it goes to the late John J. McCloy, then the
U.S. assistant secretary of war, later the American high com-
missioner for occupied Germany. Rothenburg was about to
be subjected to a U.S. Army artillery barrage when McCloy
flew to the front near the town and dispatched an armistice
commission promising that no shot would be fired if the
German defenders surrendered unconditionally. They did.

Through an ironic twist of history, there probably would
have been little of medieval Rothenburg to spare in 1945
had not the town suffered a prolonged economic decline
during the 17th, 18th, and 19th centuries, due to the shift of
commerce and trade routes elsewhere. Lack of money hindered Rothenburgers from modernizing as many other communities did, forcing them to preserve the old town to a
degree found nowhere else in Germany.

The town is situated on the flat top of a hill some 180 feet
above a 14th-century viaduct over the Tauber. Its full name,
Rothenburg-ob-der-Tauber, means "Red Fortress over the
Tauber." While nothing of that original tenth-century castle
remains, there is so much else to see and do that you could
easily spend a couple of days here and still not scratch the
surface. The best initiation to the town's delights is to start
with a walk around the wall and ramparts.

The Wall

The fortifying of Rothenburg began in the 12th century. As the town grew and expanded through the 15th century, the wall assumed an ever-greater circumference. You can still circle most of the city on the roofed-over ramparts from which burgher militiamen shot their arrows and poured boiling oil on attackers. It is a walk of about 3 km (2 miles) that includes 16 towers, five of them with gates to the city. While all the gates and towers are worth seeing, you would soon wear yourself out if you tried to climb all of them. The **Klingenturm**, which protected Rothenburg from the north, has an especially fine view of the city and the valley.

In the Town

Rothenburg's most important ecclesiastical structure, the **Jakobskirche** (Church of St. James), on Kirchplatz, was begun in 1300 and consecrated in 1448. Though it is somewhat austere on the outside, its interior is a splendid example of Gothic design and appointment. The greatest treasure here is the **Heiliges-Blut-Altar** (Altar of the Holy Blood), one of Riemenschneider's finest works. Another of his pieces is the Altar of St. Francis. Be sure also to see the Altar of the Twelve Apostles, with its paintings by Nördlingen artist Friedrich Herlin. On one of the panels, completed in 1466, he depicted Rothenburg's market square and Rathaus almost as they look today. The stained glass in the three choir windows dates from the late-14th through the mid-15th century.

The **Marktplatz**, with its magnificent **Rathaus**, is just a block south of the Jakobskirche. The town hall was built in two stages. The older section, dating from the 13th century, is graced by a tall, slender belfry that in the Middle Ages also served as a watchtower. The newer portion, though refaced later with Renaissance elements, was completed in the 15th century. Compare what you see with Herlin's altar painting in the Jakobskirche and you will notice the exterior changes made about a century after the whole complex was completed.

Adjacent to the Rathaus is the **Ratsherrntrinkstube** (Councillors' Tavern). On its gable are three clocks. The bottom one gives the correct time, the middle instrument is a calendar clock, and above it is a sundial, which is accurate when there is sun and daylight saving time is not in effect. Seven times daily the two little windows on either side of the the lower clocks open to reveal figures of Tilly and Nusch reenacting the Meistertrunk.

The original tankard, made of pewter and dated 1616, is

on exhibit in the **Reichsstadtmuseum** (City Museum), which is housed in Rothenburg's 700-year-old Dominican convent, at Klosterhof 5, just north of the Jakobskirche. The structure ranks, together with St. James's and the Rathaus, as one of the town's oldest and most important architectural sights. The original convent kitchen is still intact, even to its utensils. Besides the huge pewter tankard, the collection includes craftsmen's tools, furnishings, and artifacts reflecting daily life and the decorative arts in Rothenburg over a period of nearly a millennium.

You will also find a **Puppen und Spielzeugmuseum** (Doll and Toy Museum) at Hofbrunnengasse 5, and—a bit on the macabre side—the **Mittelalterliches Kriminalmuseum** (Medieval Crime Museum) at Burggasse 3, the latter illustrating a thousand years of the history of crime and punishment. Among the instruments of torture on exhibit are a spiked cane chair, an iron maiden, and a dipping basket.

The chief experience in Rothenburg, however, is simply walking the town's ancient streets, admiring the beautiful old patrician and burgher houses on **Herrengasse**, and soaking up the atmosphere of being in one of Europe's best-preserved medieval cities—a city, moreover, that is very much alive. Interrupt your walking with a Rothenburg specialty—*Schneeballen* (snowballs), crisp round pastries powdered with sugar and sold in most of its bakeries and pastry shops. And after looking at the Middle Ages, move *into* them at the Hotel Eisenhut.

Staying and Dining in Rothenburg

The ► **Hotel Eisenhut**, Herrengasse 3–7, located in four 15th- and 16th-century patrician houses, is as famous as Rothenburg itself. It belongs to Frau Georg Pirner, née Eisenhut. *Eisenhut* means an "iron, armored hat," or casque, and a large one hangs over the hotel's entrance. Guests here find living in the Middle Ages both fascinating and comfortable. The Eisenhut combines old walls, beautiful antique furnishings, impeccable service, modern amenities, and a master chef to create near perfection.

For comfortable accommodations behind even older walls, consider the ► **Goldener Hirsch**, at Untere Schmiedgasse 16, located in two adjacent 500-year-old houses. The interior decor may at first seem a bit incongruous—Chippendale cheek by jowl with Germanic wrought iron—but the incongruity is more than compensated for by the hotel's location adjacent to the fortification wall and the view of the romantic Tauber valley from the terrace restaurant.

The ► **Romantik-Hotel Markusturm**, Rödergasse 1, almost next to the Rödertor, the city's eastern gate, is a family hotel popular with honeymooners and tourists alike. It is run by Marianne Berger and her schoolmaster husband, who lends a helping hand when not busy with his pupils. Specialties of the hotel's kitchen are trout fresh from the Tauber, chanterelles from the nearby forests during August, September, and October, and game dishes from November through January.

The ▶ **Hotel Bären**, Hofbronnengasse 9, near the Kriminalmuseum, has existed since 1577. Proprietors Fritz and Elizabeth Müller treat their guests like family and have made the dining room a favorite of gourmets. Two other establishments that combine medieval ambience with modern comforts and amenities are the ▶ **Tilman Riemenschneider**, Georgengasse 11, and the ▶ **Prinzhotel Rothenburg**, An der Hofstatt 3.

The best eating in town is in the hotels, all of whose dining rooms (except the Prinzhotel's) are open to the public.

In planning your trip along the Romantic Road, Rothenburg is a perfect base. Bad Mergentheim is only 45 km (28 miles) to the north, and your next destination, Feuchtwangen, is a mere 32 km (20 miles) farther south. Highway B 25 will take you there.

Feuchtwangen

This picturesque town of 10,000 developed around its eighth-century Benedictine monastery, and one of its main attractions is the 13th-century **Stiftskirche** (Collegiate Church) on the Marktplatz, where the friars once prayed. Major works of art in the church are the high altar, completed in 1483 by a Nürnberg master, and the early-16th-century choir stalls.

The Stiftskirche's 800-year-old **Kreuzgang** (cloister) is the site of a repertory theater festival in June and July. The cast is good, the seats are comfortable, but the performances are in German (and Shakespeare can be hard to sit through if you don't understand the language).

Your time in Feuchtwangen can be happily spent in the Stiftskirche and its cloister without going to the theater, because the secularized complex now houses half a dozen perfectly reproduced crafts shops where artisans work at weaving, cobbling, pewter smithing, pottery making, and baking. There is also an excellent café, bakery, and pastry shop in the corner of the building.

The nearby **Fränkisches Museum** houses a fine collection of Franconian folk and applied art.

No less an attraction in town, and almost as old as the Stiftskirche, is the ▶ **Romantik-Hotel Greifen-Post**, Marktplatz 8. At one time actually two rival adjacent inns, both in business for more than 500 years, the Post is the older, dating from 1369. The register over the centuries has recorded such notables as Holy Roman Emperor Maximilian I and Lola Montez, the Irish dancer with the Spanish stage name whose torrid liaison with Bavaria's King Ludwig I led to his abdication. You can rent bicycles here to explore Feuchtwangen and the surrounding countryside. Among the other amenities are rooms with Biedermeier furnishings and one suite where you can slumber peacefully in a baldachin bed with eiderdown covers. The hotel has been maintained by the family of Eduard and Brigitte Lorentz for four generations. Its restaurant, one of the best along the Romantische Strasse, emphasizes a nouvelle approach to regional dishes. Like Rothenburg, Feuchtwangen is a good base for a day or two if you want to explore the Romantic Road without hotel hopping, and the Greifen-Post will make you feel at home.

Your next destination, Dinkelsbühl, is a mere 12 km (7½ miles) farther south on highway B 25.

DINKELSBÜHL

What distinguishes Dinkelsbühl from Rothenburg, according to the early-20th-century German novelist and essayist Kasimir Edschmid, is that it "does not have the sound of trumpets in the air, nor the bloody drama, nor the ghosts of history." That may well be to its advantage, for although the town of 11,000 is just as well preserved in its medieval appearance, it does not attract quite the crush of visitors.

Driving south from Feuchtwangen, you will see two of Dinkelsbühl's 20 gate and church towers rising out of the woods to your right. They mark the turnoff that leads you through the Wörnitztor and on to the **Alt-Rathaus-Platz** (Old Town Hall Square), where everything happens.

From late June until August, for example, the Alt-Rathaus-Platz is the stage for an open-air theater festival with special weekend performances for children. Children were as heroic to Dinkelsbühl as Nusch was to Rothenburg, with the important difference that this time the villains were the anti-Imperial and Protestant Swedes. It happened in 1632, and the Swedish siege was one of eight to which this medieval trade junction and weaving center was subjected during the Thirty Years' War.

According to legend, Dinkelsbühl's ill-equipped, undernourished citizens' militia held out long and valiantly against a division of King Gustav Adolph's army, commanded by

Colonel Sperrent. The townsfolk hoped in vain for relief from General Albrecht von Wallenstein, Tilly's successor as supreme commander of the Imperial armies. When Sperrent threatened to level the entire town, its councillors threw open the city gates and the mayor humbly presented Sperrent with the keys to the arsenal and warehouses. But the Swedish commander seemed bent on revenge.

Suddenly the town's children, led by Lore, the gatekeeper's daughter, approached Sperrent singing and praying. Falling on their knees, they implored the colonel to spare their beloved town. Sperrent, so a slightly embellished history tells it, had recently lost his only son, and wept when a little boy his child's age was handed up to him. For the children's sake, he decreed that Dinkelsbühl should be spared.

On and around the third Monday of July, Dinkelsbühl stages its annual *Kinderzeche* festival for children. The highlight is a colorful pageant parade in which youngsters and town fathers wearing 17th-century costumes reenact the event. All of it takes place on and around the Old Town Hall Square, and not a room or even a window looking down on the plaza can be had.

Though the date of Dinkelsbühl's actual founding is uncertain, the town's name first appeared in documents as long ago as the year 928. The origin of the name is in dispute. One version holds that an Alemannic settler called *der Dinkelbauer* led his herds to the banks of the Wörnitz river (a Danube tributary that flows through the town) about 1,500 years ago, and there planted seeds of *Dinkel* (spelt wheat). He later offered hospitality to a group of wandering monks, who established a monastery on a hill—a *Bühl,* in southern and Alemannic German dialect—and eventually people began settling around it. Ergo, Dinkelsbühl. Another version has the name deriving from *Ding,* Old German for "court" or "assembly."

The point on which everyone agrees is that its location at the intersection of major medieval trade routes was vital to the town's growth in the Middle Ages. Walls to protect it were first built in the tenth century, but as the town grew in population and importance the defensive perimeter was enlarged, with new walls going up in the 12th and 14th centuries.

Spared in the Thirty Years' War and, much later, in World War II, Dinkelsbühl today looks much as it did in the Middle Ages. Its ramparts and fortifications are still intact, including 16 wall and gate towers, of which the 13th-century **Wörnitztor** and the 14th-century **Rothenburger Tor** are the oldest.

Within the wall every street offers flower-decked, steeply

gabled burgher houses, many of which now contain attractive shops. The most famous half-timbered house in Dinkelsbühl (perhaps in all southern Germany) is the ► **Deutsches Haus**, Weinmarkt 3, just opposite the Marktplatz. Built in 1440, it was originally the town house of the counts of Drechsel-Deufstetten, and today presents a flower-boxed seven-story façade that outshines all others. The Deutsches Haus is also a hotel, and serves lunch and dinner in its **Altdeutsches Restaurant**. Because it has only 11 rooms for overnight guests, a spur-of-the-moment decision to stay here might backfire. An alternative is the 12-room ► **Hotel Eisenkrug**, Martin-Luther-Strasse 1, whose proprietor-chef Martin Scharff, one of Germany's Michelin-starred cooks, has made its historic restaurant, called **"Zum Kleinen Obristen"** (The Little Colonel), one of the finest along the Romantische Strasse. The ► **Hotel Blauer Hecht**, at Schweinemarkt 1, with 30 rooms, is another establishment in the moderately priced category.

Be sure to visit the **Stadtpfarrkirche St. Georg** (Parish Church of St. George) on the Marktplatz. The 15th-century Gothic church contains a number of objects from the time of its construction, including the tabernacle, pulpit, and a baptismal font. The **Historisches Museum**, Martin-Luther-Strasse 6, across the street from the Hotel Eisenkrug, has a collection of exhibits devoted to the town's history and local arts and crafts.

Change has come slowly to Dinkelsbühl, and in some respects has not come at all. It is one of Germany's few towns that still has a salaried lantern-carrying town crier, who makes his rounds every night calling out "All is well!"

From Dinkelsbühl continue south on B 25 for 31 km (19 miles) to Nördlingen, the Romantic Road's third pristinely walled medieval town. But be prepared for a change of pace, for this town of 20,000 is a former Roman settlement, and the center of a great deal of old culture and architecture and also of a natural wonder that literally shook the world nearly 15 million years ago.

SOUTH TO THE DANUBE
Nördlingen

One way to appreciate what Nördlingen is all about is to climb the 350 steps to the top of the Daniel, as the belfry tower of its 15th-century Stadtpfarrkirche St. Georg (Parish Church of St. George), on the Marktplatz, is called. First you will see how perfectly this medieval town, with its maze of cobblestone streets and steeply roofed houses, has been preserved, as well as how it is totally enclosed by its massive 16th-century fortification wall. And on a clear day you will see that Nördlingen is surrounded by yet another, far more distant ring, the Ries, made up of sparsely wooded hills that vaguely resemble the raised edge of a dinner plate.

The "plate," some 25 km (16 miles) in diameter, is dotted by nearly 100 small villages, and until as recently as 1960 was one of the great unsolved mysteries of geologic science. Two Americans—Dr. Eugene C. Shoemaker and Dr. Edward T. C. Chao, of the U.S. Geological Survey—finally solved it. The "plate" and the hilly "ring" surrounding it are what remain of a crater caused by one of the largest meteorites to strike our planet in recent times ("recent" being 14.8 million years ago).

Knowledge that the Nördlinger Ries was a crater formation goes back to at least the mid-18th century, but for more than 200 years scientists speculated that it had been caused by something else: a now-extinct volcano or, according to another theory, a massive underground explosion of water vapor or subterranean gases like the one that blew up most of the Indonesian island of Krakatoa in 1883. Neither theory accounted for the strange deposits of crushed rock, called suevite, found all around Nördlingen (of which St. Georg's parish church is built) or the odd fact that the rock formations in the area look as if some huge Brobdingnagian hand had grabbed a fistful of earth and let it fall again, leaving much older stone piled atop much younger strata. Not until Shoemaker and Chao found the telltale signs of meteor impact, of a type that they had already discovered at Meteor Crater in Arizona, was the "Ries Mystery" solved.

It was an asteroid from the belt between Mars and Jupiter that struck here so long ago. The missile from space had a diameter of half a mile and crashed with the force of 250,000 Hiroshima-type atomic bombs. As it bored into the ground it totally vaporized five cubic kilometers of stone into steam, melted and pulverized another 250 billion tons of rock, and created a mushroom cloud of gas and dust at least 12 miles high. Pellets of melted stone-turned-into-glass jetted 250 miles eastward, as far as Brno in today's Czechoslovakia. Huge boulders of Jurassic and crystalline bedrock from the earth's crust were catapulted up to 37 miles away. All life within a radius of 310 miles was killed, and there may have been a kind of "nuclear winter" that lasted for decades. And it all happened within seconds.

Ever since Shoemaker and Chao proved their theory 30 years ago, Nördlingen has been the center of some of the world's most important astrogeological research. Thousands of scientific papers have been written about the Ries. In 1970

U.S. astronauts spent several weeks in Nördlingen to learn the kinds of rocks they should be looking for when their Apollo capsules landed on the moon.

Much of the story is told at the **Ries Crater Museum**, Vordere Gerbergasse 1, located in a 16th-century warehouse in the center of this picturesque medieval town. The centerpiece of the many scientific and geological exhibits devoted to meteorite, crater, impact, and solar system phenomena is a 5.5-ounce piece of moon rock, on permanent loan from the U.S. National Aeronautics and Space Administration.

Nördlingen grew originally from a Roman settlement, became a king's court under the Carolingian Stauffens, and waxed prosperous in the 12th century. You can walk around the completely preserved **Wehrgang** (covered ramparts) of the fortification wall and see the city from every angle. Visible from every angle, too, is St. Georg's 297-foot-tall Daniel tower.

St. Georg's, begun in 1444 and completed in 1508, with nine different architects in charge at various times, has a high altar with some fine 15th-century wood carvings depicting the crucified Christ between the mourning figures of Mary, John the Baptist, Mary Magdalene, and Saint George.

St. Salvator, Salvatorgasse 15, was the church of a Carmelite convent and is noteworthy for its well-preserved 15th-century wall frescoes and a high altar attributed to the Bamberg master Hans Nussbaum.

The **Rathaus**, on the Marktplatz, was built in the 14th century and, except for the early-17th-century Renaissance-style open-air staircase on its façade, exhibits classic Gothic design and decoration. There are numerous fine old public and burgher houses on the Marktplatz, on the Weinmarkt, and along Rübenmarkt, Nonnengasse, and Kämpelgasse.

The **Stadtmuseum** (City Museum), just across the street from the Ries Crater Museum, has a fine collection of Roman, Carolingian, and medieval artifacts and applied art.

Indeed, the only thing missing in this otherwise captivating and charming town is a suitable hotel. So either overnight in Dinkelsbühl or head on to our next destinations: Harburg and Donauwörth.

Harburg

Just 16 km (10 miles) southeast of Nördlingen on B 25, Harburg is notable primarily for its huge fortress-castle, visible from miles away, which guards the highway, once an old trade route, between Nördlingen and Donauwörth.

No one knows for sure when the **Felsenburg** was built, but it was already around in 1150 when Emperor Conrad

III, first of the Hohenstaufen dynasty and uncle of Barbarossa, had title to it. In 1295 it became the property of the counts of Oettingen, whose descendants still own it. It was never conquered, and remains one of the best-preserved castle complexes in western Germany. Among its highlights are the **Schlosskirche St. Michael**, the castle church dedicated to Saint Michael. Although the church was enlarged in the 14th century and then reworked with Baroque stucco elements in the 18th, its earliest parts are austerely and quietly Romanesque.

The castle's **Fürstenbau** (Prince's Building) contains the Oettingen clan's prodigious art collection, including the side wings of a Tilman Riemenschneider altar and an exquisite 12th-century ivory crucifix.

If you want to spend a night like a prince right within the fortress complex, then opt for one of the nine rooms in the ► **Fürstliche Burgschenke**, the castle tavern, which provides not only accommodations but a magnificent view, and serves a good lunch.

From Harburg it is 12 km (7 miles) along B 25 to Donauwörth, the last stop on the northern half of the Romantic Road, where you have to make an important choice: Either continue south on this route or follow our Danube river itinerary, heading west to Ulm or east to Passau, the last Danube river port in Germany.

DONAUWÖRTH

Donau is the German term for Danube, and Donauwörth, as the name indicates, is situated on the Danube at its confluence with the little Wörnitz river. It is not a very dramatic meeting of rivers in the geological-geographic sense, but in historical terms, this is where medieval river routes intersected and where the Reichsstrasse, the old imperial trade route between Nürnberg and Augsburg, crossed the most important commercial artery between Füssen in the Alps and Würzburg, where the road continued into northern Germany.

Considering Donauwörth's advantageous location on this crossroads, its nearly 18,000 inhabitants, and the fact that the Danube is still quite navigable this far upstream, it is surprising that it has neither a starred restaurant nor a luxury hotel. But never mind; it does have the pleasant, 300-year-old ► **Posthotel Traube**, with some 40 rooms, at Kapellstrasse 14.

More sumptuous, though a bit out of the center, is the ► **Parkhotel**, Sternschanzenstrasse 1, in the district of Donauwörth-Parkstadt. The best dining right in town is at the **Tanzhaus**, Reichsstrasse 34, on the second floor of a building that has stood here since 1400.

Visible from everywhere in the little city thanks to its massive spire is the **Pfarrkirche Maria Himmelfahrt** (Parish Church of the Assumption), on Reichsstrasse, built between 1444 and 1461. Among its rich furnishings and appointments are 15th-century frescoes and stained-glass windows, a tabernacle from the year 1500 ascribed to Augsburg stonemasons, and 16th-century paintings. The **Heilig-Kreuz-Kirche** (Church of the Holy Cross), on Heilig-Kreuz-Strasse, is a Baroque edifice, part of a former Benedictine monastery, built between 1717 and 1720 on the site of a 12th-century church, of which the lower stories of the tower remain.

The **Fuggerhaus**, also on Reichsstrasse (not far from the Church of the Assumption and the Tanzhaus restaurant), was built in 1543 by the fabulously wealthy Fugger family of Augsburg. A stunning Renaissance building, it served as a guest house for nobility for nearly two centuries after its construction and well after the Fuggers themselves had lost their position as Europe's richest commercial and banking dynasty. Sweden's King Gustav Adolph used it as his headquarters and temporary residence in 1632 during the Thirty Years' War.

The 15th-century half-timbered **Gerberhaus** (Tanners' House), Im Ried 103, is now the home of the **Heimatmuseum** (Local History Museum), with an interesting collection of folk and applied art, including votive tablets and *Hinterglas*—behind-glass—paintings, a southern German and Alpine art that entails building up the picture in reverse order (the last touches first) directly on a sheet of glass.

Portions of Donauwörth's fortification wall remain to be seen, as do two of the old town gates.

Across the Danube

After Donauwörth, and across the Danube, the Romantic Road follows B 2 south along the Lech river, a Danube tributary, for 34 km (21 miles) to Germany's second-oldest, and Bavaria's third-largest, city, Augsburg (population 250,000).

AUGSBURG

The official reading is that Augsburg, set astride what used to be known as the Claudian Road, the trade artery linking the Adriatic with the North Sea, was founded in 15 B.C. as a fortified encampment by two famous Roman generals, Drusus and Tiberius, both stepsons of Augustus Caesar. They called it Augusta Vindelicorum—the citadel of Augustus in the land of the Vindelicians (the Celtic tribe they had subjugated). A heroic statue of Augustus, cast in 1594, tops the elaborate fountain—one of more than a hundred in town—in front of the Rathaus. In A.D. 98 Tacitus referred to this "City of Augustus" as "exceedingly splendid," and since then there has been no dearth of other testimonials.

Holy Roman Emperor Maximilian I was so fond of the town and spent so much time within its walls in the late 15th and early 16th centuries that he was known, among other titles and honors, as "Augsburg's other burgomaster." Maximilianstrasse, one of the grandest boulevards of the Renaissance, is named for him.

In 1761 the Chevalier de Seingalt, better known as Casanova, spent six months carousing and shocking the local burghers as Portugal's delegate to the peace parley that ended the Seven Years' War between Austria and Prussia. He had intended to reside in what is now the ▶ **Steigenberger Drei Mohren**, a splendid Renaissance hostelry, but the French ambassador had already booked the entire establishment for his own entourage. An accommodating banker provided Casanova with a nicely furnished private villa. Alas, neither that house nor the original Drei Mohren survived a 1944 air raid, but the hotel, although a modern postwar shadow of its erstwhile splendor, is still Augsburg's best.

Fifteen-year-old Marie Antoinette, on her sojourn from Vienna to Paris in 1770 to marry the French dauphin who was to became Louis XVI, was so enamored with Augsburg and stayed so long that the groom sent a courier with an urgent note asking her to stop dallying. During her visit she inaugurated the magnificent **Schaezler Palais** on Maximilianstrasse—a banker's mansion that now houses the Municipal Art Museum, the Baroque Gallery, and the State Gallery—by dancing all night in its opulent gilded banquet hall (where candlelit Mozart concerts are now held in the summer months).

Augsburg lore abounds with such anecdotes, as it does with tales of famous native sons. Among them are the master painters Hans Burgkmair and both Holbeins (Elder and Younger); Elias Holl, Germany's leading Renaissance architect, who created most of the city's splendid buildings; Mozart's father, Leopold, who got his musical training at St. Salvator Gymnasium and remained an Augsburg citizen all his life despite moving to Salzburg in 1737; Rudolf Diesel, inventor of the engine that bears his name; Willi Messerschmitt, the aircraft designer and builder; and the playwright

Bertolt Brecht, whose sharp-tongued irreverence and Marxist proclivities Augsburg citizens did not really forgive until early 1985, when his birth house, at Auf der Rain 7, bought and renovated by the city, was opened as a museum.

Though their town is only 60 km (37½ miles) northwest of Munich (a half-hour train ride) and administratively part of Bavaria, Augsburgers emphasize that they are Swabians, not Bavarians—with important differences in dialect, cuisine, architecture, customs, and costume. In fact, it was not until 1806, by decree of Napoleon, whose armies were occupying that area of Germany, that Augsburg and the southeastern Swabian lands were ceded to Bavaria. Augsburgers are quick to point out there might never have been a Munich had it not been for a conference in 1158 in Augsburg between Emperor Frederick Barbarossa and his cousin Henry the Lion, duke of Saxony and Bavaria, at which Barbarossa chartered Munich, where Henry had built a bridge to levy duty on the salt trade.

Little remains of Augsburg's role in Roman times except for a substantial collection of artifacts, tools, coins, statues, sarcophagi, tombstones, and other archaeological finds, most of which are on exhibit at the Roman Museum, located in a former Dominican monastery church at Dominikanergasse 15 (see below).

Christianity had a comparatively early impact here. The city's patron saint, Afra, was a local maiden martyred in 304 during the persecution ordered by the Roman co-emperors Diocletian and Maximinian. The town was already a bishopric in 400, and the names of all its bishops, who were both spiritual and temporal rulers, are known since 596. Their portraits hang on a wall of the Dom, construction of which began in 944 by incorporating foundations and elements of a sixth-century church.

By the tenth century Augsburg was already one of Europe's most important cities. A scant century later it was given its own coinage privileges, and in 1156 Barbarossa confirmed its status as a *Freie Reichsstadt* (Free Imperial City).

But its golden age was undeniably the 15th through the 17th centuries, when it was one of the richest and most prosperous towns on the Continent, due to its role as a center of weaving and gold- and silver-smithing, and thanks to its two leading families, the Fuggers and the Welsers. In 1500 Augsburg had 50,000 inhabitants (more than Paris or London), 2,500 weaving shops, and was exporting a staggering quantity of linen and fustian annually.

The Fuggers are still one of Germany's richest families, with vast real-estate and forestry holdings. The Fugger and

Welser legacy is architecturally omnipresent in Augsburg as well. It begins with the huge Fugger palace at Maximilianstrasse 36, which houses the Fuggerkeller restaurant and a branch of the Fugger Bank; continues with a whole array of Fugger and Welser mansions dotted around town; and culminates with the picturesque Fuggerei, the world's oldest welfare housing project, where an indigent family can still live in dignity for the equivalent of one dollar a year.

Of the many famous visitors to Augsburg during its 20 centuries, one of the most renowned was Martin Luther, summoned here in 1518 to recant his 95 theses before the papal legate, Cardinal Thomas de Vio. Luther stayed in the Carmelite monastery of **St. Anne** on **Annagasse**, now the city's main shopping street. St. Anne's became Protestant a mere seven years after his visit. His book-lined cell on the second floor of the cloister is one of its treasures, along with portraits of him and Saxon Duke Friedrich the Wise by Lucas Cranach the Elder. The church, which is a five-minute walk northeast of the railway station, also contains the private burial chapel of the Fuggers. Two of the reliefs on their sepulcher were designed by Albrecht Dürer.

The city played a key role in the Reformation. There was the Augsburg Confession of 1530, the official statement of creed by the Lutheran churches. The 1555 Peace of Augsburg, a temporary settlement of the religious conflict in the Holy Roman Empire, was shattered in 1618 by the outbreak of the Thirty Years' War. Miraculously, the city escaped that murderous conflict virtually unscathed. It was less fortunate in World War II. The big February 1944 air raid, aimed at the Messerschmitt plant and at Maschinenfabrik-Augsburg-Nürnberg (M-A-N), where Rudolf Diesel had developed his engine, left some ugly rents in the historic fabric. A few remain and others have been mended with patches of challengeable aesthetic value. Nonetheless, few other large German cities have as much to offer visitors in terms of architectural splendor, art treasures, living history, or medieval and Renaissance patina. The best way to see them is to walk. Sturdy shoes are recommended because most of the historic streets are paved with cobblestones, over which, legend has it, Napoleon tripped on visits in 1805 and 1809.

Rathaus and Rathausplatz

Augsburg's epicenter is the Rathausplatz, with its 16th-century fountain and statue of Augustus Caesar. The greatest showpiece here is the Rathaus, built between 1615 and 1620 by Elias Holl to replace a Gothic town hall that had stood for 300 years. A palatial eight-story structure that towers over the square, it is the most dazzling example of secular Renaissance architecture north of the Alps. Next to it stands the **Perlachturm**, once an 11th-century watchman's turret, then a church belfry, and now a largely decorative campanile raised to its present height of 230 feet strictly for its aesthetic appeal in 1616. The 35-bell carillon chimes every day at noon.

The air raid left the Rathaus a gutted shell, the greatest interior loss being that of its magnificent **Goldener Saal** (Golden Hall), a 6,000-square-foot, three-story reception hall with painted cedarwood ceiling, frescoes, intricately carved paneling, and lavish gold-leaf decor. The building was patched up hurriedly by 1947, but it was not until 1980 that Augsburgers set out in earnest to raise the money and restore the Golden Hall to its former splendor. It reopened in 1985, the city's 2,000th anniversary.

Die Ecke, just behind the Rathaus at Elias-Holl-Platz 2, began as a tavern in 1492 and claims such local luminaries as Hans Holbein the Elder, Hans Burgkmair, Leopold and Wolfgang Amadeus Mozart, Diesel, and Brecht among its former customers. It is now one of Augsburg's better eateries, especially for game dishes.

The Dom and the Mozart Museum

A walk north from the Rathaus along Karolinenstrasse, which changes its name to Hoher Weg, leads to the **Dom St. Maria** (St. Mary's Cathedral) and the former bishops' palace, a complex of Baroque buildings that now accommodates various government offices. The tree-shaded square in front of the cathedral, the **Fronhof**, was the Roman forum. The five-naved church, much of it Romanesque with Gothic additions, is a treasure trove of masterworks, including four altarpieces by Holbein the Elder and five 12th-century windows, the world's oldest examples of stained glass. The huge bronze portal, with scenes from the Old Testament, was cast in the 11th century.

Mozart buffs will find Papa Leopold's birth house just north of the cathedral at Frauentorstrasse 30. The austere magenta-colored building is now the **Mozart Museum**, devoted to the family's history. Among the furnishings and various artifacts is a 1785 pianoforte made by Johann Andreas Stein, an Augsburg organ and piano builder whose instruments were favored by Mozart and Beethoven. It is still used for recitals in the house. Besides documents dealing with Leopold's own career as a composer, conductor, and virtuoso violinist, the collection also includes some of 21-year-old Wolfgang's pornographic letters to his young Augsburg cousin Maria, with whom he once had a torrid affair. But the most interesting exhibits are those tracing the origins of the family name, which is linked to a village 19 miles west of Augsburg that in 13th-century Middle High German was called Mothardishouen. Historians and philologists believe that Mutzharts, Mutzerts, Motzets, and Motzardts came from there, and that some of the latter eventually simplified the spelling to Mozart. Suffice it to say that by 1597 there were 19 Mozarts registered in Augsburg, and the current phone book still lists eight.

Jesuitengasse, a street that intersects with Frauentorstrasse near the Mozart Museum, leads past the Jesuit school where Leopold got his primary and high school education and ends at the **Heilig-Kreuz-Kirche** (Holy Cross Church), where he sang in the choir and played the organ. An altar picture, *The Assumption of Mary* by Peter Paul Rubens, is one of its treasures.

The ▶ **Hotel Fischertor**, Pfärrle 16, just north of the Mozart house on Frauentorstrasse, then around the corner, is a pleasant, moderately priced inn in quiet, historic surroundings. The adjacent **Zum Alten Fischertor** restaurant, Pfärrle 14, while hardly moderate in price, is Augsburg's temple of haute cuisine. A local scribe not long ago declared its Michelin-starred owner Albert Oblinger to be the "Boris Becker of German nouvelle chefs."

Maximilianstrasse

Augsburg's grand boulevard, Maximilianstrasse, runs uphill and south from the town hall and the Rathausplatz. The cobblestone avenue, nearly a mile long and as broad as a market square, is interrupted in its path only by two magnificent Renaissance fountains. Many historians maintain that it follows the axis of the Roman Via Claudia. Be that as it may, it was a road travelled by some of the most illustrious figures of European history and is lined on both sides by the palaces of rich Renaissance merchants and bankers.

The **Fugger Palais**, at number 36, is actually a whole complex of adjoining houses and wings, connected by four Italianate courtyards. The best preserved of these, the Damenhof, is where the Fugger ladies entertained guests and played badminton in summer. A bit of exploration through the courtyards will take you to the back of the building and Zeughausplatz, where Elias Holls's first civic structure, the **Zeughaus** (Armory), stands. Long neglected after being damaged in World War II, it has been rebuilt and now serves as a community center, adult education facility, and gallery for visiting art exhibits.

The **Fugger Keller**, at number 38, in the cellar of the palace, serves solid Swabian and Bavarian food in rustic beer-hall surroundings.

The **Schaezler Palais**, at number 46, where Marie Antoinette danced the night away on April 28–29, 1770, was built as a 60-room mansion for an Augsburg banker, Benedikt von Liebert, whose descendants willed it to the city after World War II. Today it houses the **Städtische** (Municipal) **Galerie** and the **Deutsche Barockgalerie** (German Baroque Gallery), which include works by German masters as well as by Rubens, Van Dyck, Rembrandt, Veronese, and Tiepolo. A passageway from the extravagant, richly ornamented festival chamber on the mansion's second floor leads directly to an adjacent former convent, secularized in 1807, that now holds a stunning collection of Old German masters belonging to the **Staatsgalerie** (Bavarian State Gallery), including works by Holbein the Elder, Burgkmair, Cranach the Elder, and Dürer.

Brass plaques on the houses along Maximilianstrasse briefly tell the histories of the most important edifices. More often than not, the courtyards and interiors are as interesting as the façades. Among these are the arcaded courts of numbers 48 and 58 (which was the home of Philipp Fugger), or the beautifully frescoed staircase at number 51.

Augsburg's most colorful and unusual gustatory pleasure is offered at the **Welser Kuche**, Maximilianstrasse 83, a medieval cellar where you dine as Augsburgers did 450 years ago—at large wooden tables using only a dagger and your fingers as utensils. The gargantuan, eight-course meals are served by "knaves" and "wenches" in 16th-century costumes. Unlike similar establishments elsewhere in Europe, this one is more than just a show. The food is as genuine as the ambience, and is strictly prepared according to the recipes of Philippine Welser (1527–1580), who was married to Hapsburg Archduke Ferdinand. A typical repast consists of a pre-dinner drink of mead served in a bull's-horn cup, dark flatbread with lard, pike fritters with a saffron sauce, lamb broth, capon pie with plum sauce, roast ribs of beef, air-cured cheese from the Allgäu, sage cake, and apple fritters. For those who cannot decipher the menu printed in Old German, or the accompanying ceremony in 16th-century Swabian dialect, a translation in impeccable Shakespearean English is furnished. Best to reserve; Tel: (821) 339-30.

Maximilianstrasse culminates in what is Augsburg's largest and most impressive basilica, visible from miles around and even more impressive than the cathedral: the **St. Ulrich- und St.-Afra-Kirche**, named after the Augsburg bishop who helped Holy Roman Emperor Otto I defeat the Magyars at the Battle of Lechfeld in 955, and the Roman girl killed for refusing to recant her Christian faith. Built between 1476 and 1500 on the site of a Roman temple, the basilica holds the remains of both saints. The sepulcher of Ulrich is a masterpiece of Rococo sculpture. Of the many art treasures, one of the finest is the intricate wrought-iron fence that separates the nave from the vestibule. Cast in 1712, this trelliswork uses optical tricks to create a three-dimensional illusion.

The smaller church in front of the basilica, also named for St. Ulrich, is Protestant, a testimony to the coexistence of both faiths in the city. In the 14th century it was a market hall (it did not become a house of worship until 1457). Its present interior, a dazzling example of stuccowork, dates from the 18th century.

The Lower Town

The narrow, hilly streets sloping down from Maximilian-strasse lead to the **Untere Stadt**, Augsburg's lower town, where the weavers, goldsmiths, and craftsmen had their shops, where the first textile and calico printing plants were started, and where the artisans, workers, and artists lived. Here you will find the **Holbeinhaus**, the home of both Holbeins, at Vorderer Lech 20, rebuilt after World War II damage and now a gallery of changing contemporary art exhibitions; the **Brechthaus**, Auf der Rain 7, with documents and photographs pertaining to Brecht's life in Augsburg; and the **Römisches Museum**, Dominikanergasse 15, with exhibits of prehistoric, Roman, and early Germanic artifacts, art, sculpture, jewelry, coins, glass, and pottery.

The Untere Stadt is a quarter of small medieval buildings, narrow lanes, cobblestone alleys, dimly lit courtyards, and a labyrinthine network of little canals and offshoots of the Lech. Their names are often as colorful as the streets: Bauerntanz-gasse, Findelgasse, Waisengasse, Katzhof, and Im Sack, which translate as Peasant Dance Alley, Foundlings' Alley, Orphans' Lane, Cat's Court, and In-the-Sack. Recently gentrified and now filled with boutiques and antiques shops, this is a district for strolling, exploring, and soaking up atmosphere.

The Fuggerei

From the Untere Stadt it is just a couple of blocks eastward to the Fuggerei section, founded in 1519 by Jakob Fugger (Jakob the Rich), the wealthiest and most flamboyant of the Fuggers. According to popular local legend, his immense wealth caused this Croesus pangs of conscience. To soothe them, he decided on a grand philanthropic act: building the world's first low-rent housing project. Historians who are not as convinced of Jakob's generosity and altruism tell a different version: According to them, the Fuggerei was a Renaissance tax shelter. The most disrespectful chroniclers even describe it as a kind of "laundry" for money that Fugger had earned by violating, or at least ignoring, the antitrust laws of his day.

Whatever Jakob's motives, the Fuggerei was a revolutionary concept and represented a unique approach to 16th-century social problems: a refuge for Augsburgers who had become impoverished through no fault of their own. Unlike the simple hospices and almshouses that then existed elsewhere in Europe, it was built as a town-within-a-town, consisting of 106 gabled cottages lining ruler-straight streets. It did not just dispense charity and welfare, but was based on the principles of self-help, human dignity, and thrift.

Each little house has a ground-level shop for indigent craftsmen, with dwelling space for their families on the second floor. Tenants had to pay a nominal annual rent of one guilder: a pittance, but enough to give them a sense of self-reliance and self-worth. The compound had a resident nurse and was visited by a doctor once a week. Walled and protected against thieves and marauders, the settlement included a chapel and church and a small hospital, and was granted some self-management.

Among its residents over the centuries were many a former petit bourgeois Augsburger who had fallen on hard times, including a once-respected master mason named Franz Mozart, Wolfgang's great-grandfather, who lived at Mittlere Gasse 14 from 1681 until his death in 1683. The house at **Mittlere Gasse 13** is a museum. Its rough-hewn 16th- and 17th-century furnishings, utensils, and artifacts are original. Its wood-paneled walls and ceilings, the cast-iron heating stove, and the objects in the rooms give some idea of what life was like four centuries ago. It is open daily from 9:00 A.M. until 6:00 P.M., March 1 through October 31.

The Fuggerei and its lifestyle have remained remarkably untouched by time. An oasis of six quiet and impeccably clean streets within the city, its gates are closed at 10:00 P.M. each day and reopen at 5:00 A.M. It is still owned and operated by the Fugger family and is financed from the family foundation's private forest holdings. Moreover, it operates on the same principles set down more than 470 years ago. Even the symbolic rent remains unchanged—one Rhineland guilder per year, which the Fugger foundation equates at DM 1.72 (though today's residents do pay a DM 25 annual surcharge for such modern public services as refuse disposal, sewage, running water, and street cleaning). It is a compact little world largely made up of old-age pensioners and cheerful grandmothers. But it is also a little world with strict regulations and tough entry requirements. Occupants must be Catholic and either natives or longtime residents of Augsburg. They must be "poor but industrious." Cleanliness and a pious and honorable lifestyle rank at the top of the community's regulations.

A pamphlet in the museum says: "What you see here is not intended for your amusement but to convey an impression of the life of the poor centuries ago." Thanks to the Fugger family, it was at least a life with some comfort and dignity.

SOUTH OF AUGSBURG
Klosterlechfeld

After Augsburg you continue on the Romantic Road south along the Lech by following B 17 out of the city. The first point of interest is in Klosterlechfeld, 22 km (14 miles) south of Augsburg, the site of the Battle of the Lechfeld, the bloody conflict in 955 in which Holy Roman Emperor Otto I defeated the Magyars, forebears of today's Hungarians.

Historians really aren't sure where the famous battle took place. According to some it was on a plain north of Augsburg, according to others, south of the city. But this did not deter Regina Imhoff, the widow of a wealthy Augsburg patrician, from commissioning Elias Holl some six centuries later to build the pilgrimage and monastery church of **Maria Hilf** on what she believed was the right spot. Holl based the cylindrical design and the half-dome on the Pantheon in Rome, and completed his work in 1603. A nave was added in 1656–1659, and two little chapels in 1691. All the towers have onion domes. Franciscans built a monastery adjacent to the church in the late 1660s. While there are no signs of the famous battle, the whole complex is worth a short visit, especially for a view of the ornate stucco-and-gilt Rococo interior of the church.

From here it is another 16 km (10 miles) south along the Lech valley, which narrows and becomes more verdant, to Landsberg.

Landsberg am Lech

This town of 20,000, one of the most picturesque and idyllically situated on the Romantic Road, looks like the stage set for a fairy tale, though its name also evokes a more recent history: It was in the **Festung**, the fortress prison here, that Adolf Hitler was incarcerated after his abortive 1923 "Beerhall Putsch" and wrote *Mein Kampf,* his blueprint for world conquest and genocide. Ironically, after World War II the jail was taken over by the U.S. Army, and scores of convicted Nazi criminals were interned and executed here. The prison still stands, serving its intended purpose as a Bavarian state penitentiary.

Situated on the old tribal boundary line dividing Bavarians and Swabians, Landsberg owes its origins to Henry the Lion, who, in 1160, four years after Emperor Frederick Barbarossa had deeded him the duchy of Bavaria, built a fortress castle on the hill above the swiftly flowing Lech from which his customs agents levied duty on the east–west salt trade. A market community soon sprouted around the castle, and grew so fast that by 1260 it was a little city with municipal rights.

To this day Landsberg is partially surrounded by a 13th- to 15th-century defensive wall with mighty towers and fortified gates. Although the town grew so rapidly in the Middle Ages that its fortifications had to be expanded several times, its eastern **Bayertor** (Bavarian Gate), constructed in 1425, is one of the best preserved in all Germany; with its carved and painted coats of arms and a crucifixion scene, it is also one of the most photogenic.

Landsberg's market square, lined by colorfully painted and stuccoed Renaissance and Baroque town houses, is among the most beautiful in the country. It is dominated by the late 17th- to early-18th-century **Rathaus**, whose exterior and interior stuccowork was executed by Dominikus Zimmermann. Zimmermann, one of the great master architects of the Baroque and Rococo periods in southern Germany, served as the mayor of Landsberg from 1759 to 1764. He also designed the **St. Johannes Kirche** (St. John's Church) on the Vorderanger and did the stuccowork in the sacristy of the **Heilig Kreuzkirche** (Church of the Holy Cross) on Helfsteingasse, which is almost undecorated on the outside but resplendent with embellishment inside. The most impressive building in town is the **Pfarrkirche Maria Himmelfahrt** (Parish Church of the Assumption), a 15th-century basilica on Georg-Hellmair-Platz that has been *"barockiziert"*—baroquized—with blinding splendor.

The traditional spot to stay is the ▶ **Hotel Goggl**. The original 17th-century building was razed some time ago, but its replacement successfully maintains its traditions.

Landsberg is the departure point for a side trip due west to Memmingen and then south from Memmingen to Kempten. The highway heading west out of Landsberg combines B 12 and B 18 and is in fact an Autobahn (A 96) still under construction. About 20 km (12½ miles) out of town it divides, with the B 18 continuing straight for about 50 km (31 miles) via Mindelheim to Memmingen. The B 12 fork runs generally southwest for about 60 km (37½ miles) by way of Kaufbeuren to Kempten. Memmingen and Kempten in turn are linked by a 38-km (24-mile) stretch of north–south Autobahn (the A 7).

Memmingen

Founded in 1160, Memmingen (population 38,000) has been a prosperous trading town for some eight centuries—a fact revealed by its public buildings and richly appointed churches. Of the latter the most interesting are the 15th-century **Martinskirche** (St. Martin's Church) on Martin-Luther-Platz and the **Frauenkirche** (Church of Our Lady) on Frauenkirchplatz, which is famous for a series of 15th-century frescoes that had been painted over only to be rediscovered during restoration work in the 1890s. The town's secular landmark is the half-timbered **Siebendächerhaus**, a house with seven roofs—four on one side, three on the other—each overlapping the next. Dating from 1601, it was the tanners' guild hall, and the roofs had a very practical purpose: Skins were hung to dry on them, so that more roofs meant more drying space. The **Rathaus**, on the Marktplatz, is a classic South German Renaissance structure of the late 16th century whose 18th-century façade is a fine example of Rococo stuccowork. The nearby ► **Hotel Falken**, Am Rossmarkt 3–5, has moderately priced and comfortably appointed rooms but serves breakfast only. Nouvelle-style Swabian food is prepared and served elegantly in the 35-seat **Die Traube**, Kramerstrasse 8.

From the center of Memmingen it is 11 km (7 miles) southeast by unnumbered country road to **Ottobeuren**, site of one of Germany's most magnificent Baroque monasteries and monastery churches. The Benedictine abbey with its **Klosterkirche zur Heiligen Dreifältigkeit** (Trinity Church) was founded in 764. Various buildings dating from the 11th through 16th centuries burned down before work on the present complex began in the early 1700s. The most noted architects and artists of the time, including Zimmermann, competed for the commission, with the nod finally going to Johann-Michael Fischer, who is responsible for church buildings all over Bavaria and Swabia. The 290-foot nave is an incomparable splash of stucco and gilded Baroque decoration, with gloriously colorful ceiling frescoes. A bit more subdued, though no less interesting, are the monastery's chapterhouse, library, and theater.

Kempten

A journey to this architecturally rich little city of 58,000 astride the swift, chalky Iller river will take you to the verdant doorstep of the Allgäu Alps, Germany's largest cheese-producing region, as well as back in history to Roman times. Exactly when the Oppidum Cambodunum was founded as a military camp by Roman legionnaires is unknown, but it must already have been a substantial town when first mentioned in A.D. 18. Excavations have uncovered a basilica, baths, a forum, and countless artifacts that are on exhibit at the **Römische Sammlung** (Roman Collection), on Residenzplatz.

In the Middle Ages Kempten began a kind of two-track, split-personality existence that continued into modern times. On the one hand, in 752, it became the site of a Benedictine monastery whose abbots were also temporal rulers. On the west bank of the Iller a trading town developed that by the year 1289 was already a Free Imperial City. During the Reformation the city turned Protestant, but the area around the abbey remained Catholic, and the division has, in a sense, never ended. When the first railroad line reached the town around 1850, local burghers thought seriously of erecting two stations: one Catholic, the other Protestant.

During the Thirty Years' War the Swedes, supported by Protestant burghers, destroyed most of the monastery and surrounding area. The Catholic imperial troops responded in kind by demolishing the Protestant city. As a result, nearly everything you see in Kempten today is a reconstruction dating from the middle of the 17th century. That includes both the **Stiftskirche St. Lorenz** (Collegiate Church of St. Lawrence) on Stiftsplatz, and the former **Prince-Abbot's Residence**, on Residenzplatz.

The Stiftskirche St. Lorenz was the first large ecclesiastical construction of any kind in Germany after the Thirty Years' War. Begun in 1651 and completed in 1654, it is in North Italian style. The interior stucco decoration was the work of Giovanni Zucalli, a Swiss architect and plasterer whose uncle, Enrico, was busy in a similar role, and working in a similarly grand manner, at about the same time in Munich. Work on a new palace for the prince-bishop also began in 1651, but as it took longer and extended into the Rococo era, the Residenz, with its ostentatious state and guest rooms, is even richer. Its architects borrowed many ideas from the French master Cuvilliés, then working in Munich, as well as from the brothers Dominikus and Johann-Baptist Zimmermann, who were among the most flamboyant builders of their era.

There is much else to see in town, especially on and around the Rathausplatz, including the **Rathaus** itself, one of the few survivors of the Thirty Years' War, though reconstructed afterward; the **Weberzunfthaus** (Guild House of the Weavers); and numerous patrician mansions such as the Ponikauhaus and the Londoner Hof, where foreign merchants stayed.

If you wish to spend the night in Kempten, the best address is the ▶ Fürstenhof, on the Rathausplatz. Most of the rooms and suites are paneled with inlay root wood.

To return to the Romantic Road without retracing your steps, follow B 12 east out of Kempten for 25 km (16 miles) almost to the town of Marktoberdorf, and there get on the B 472 for the very scenic 29-km (18-mile) drive east to Schongau. Here the road intersects with the B 17, the Romantic Road, for the next leg southward, 12 km (7½ miles) to Steingaden and the Wieskirche, the Church in the Meadow.

Steingaden

This region is called the *Pfaffenwinkel* (Parsons' Corner), an allusion to its profusion of Baroque chapels, churches, and monasteries whose spires are capped by those distinctive onion domes that make you wonder whether you are in Bavaria or Russia. It is an area of gloriously stunning ecclesiastical architecture and art, the most elaborate examples of which are found in and around the village of Steingaden. Its 12th-century minster, **St. Johann Baptist,** has changed little on the outside during the past 800 years, but its interior is a breathtaking splash of gilded Rococo sculpture and stuccowork. Even more spectacular, about 6 km (3½ miles) southeast, is the **Wieskirche,** known as the "Miracle in the Meadow church." Considered the most beautiful Rococo church in the world, it was built between 1746 and 1754 by Dominikus Zimmermann, the Landsberg master who also designed the Steingaden minster.

What is such a building doing by itself in the middle of a meadow? The carved figure showing the scourging of Christ in the Wieskirche's high altar was the impetus. The wayside carving belonged to a local farmer, who reported one day in 1730 that it suddenly had begun to shed tears. He persuaded the abbot of Steingaden to build a chapel for it in the meadow where he had observed the miracle. In time it became the object of pilgrimages, so that a larger church had to be built, and Zimmermann was given the commission.

The Wieskirche was his crowning achievement. He led a team of the best artists of his time to create the interior decoration, stressing the concept of harmony between architectural shape and color. His brother was responsible for most of the fresco and stuccowork. There is probably no other building with such unity of Rococo style.

The Wieskirche was closed for repair and renovation in 1986, after its magnificent ceiling showed structural cracks. The cause: vibrations from low-flying supersonic German air force jets stationed at Memmingen. To be sure, the church had been renovated before, most recently in 1903, 1950, and 1970. But never had so much work been necessary or the cost so high—about DM 7 million—and never was the danger to the church as great. A team of 30 architects, restorers, and stucco masters worked on it for nearly five years.

Steingaden and the Wieskirche will occupy you for at most an hour or two each. Consider Füssen and Schwangau, the southern terminus of the Romantic Road, as destinations in themselves. From Steingaden it is about 20 km (12 miles) southwest along highway B 17 through steadily rising countryside to the base of the jagged, snow-capped Allgäu Alpine range, the medieval town of Füssen, and what is surely the gaudiest example of Romanticism on the Romantic Road: King Ludwig II's fairy-tale castle, Neuschwanstein.

SCHWANGAU AND FÜSSEN

Bavaria was a full-fledged kingdom for only 112 of its 1,100 years of recorded history, from 1806 until 1918, when the monarchy was replaced by a republic. Brief as it was, Bavarians regard the era as their greatest and grandest, and many still yearn for it. But when they speak wistfully and longingly about "the king," they mean only one: Ludwig II, the lonely "dream king" and patron of Wagner.

His reign and indeed his life were short. He ascended the throne at age 19 in 1864, was deposed on charges of mental incompetence on June 9, 1886, and four days later drowned mysteriously, together with the psychiatrist who had ruled him insane, in Starnberg lake south of Munich. He was a legend in his lifetime, and has remained one since. No monarch since Louis XIV of France—whom he idolized and tried to emulate—captured the imagination of Europe more thoroughly than this Louis of Bavaria, the "Sun King of the 19th century." Paul Verlaine called him "a poet, a soldier, the only real king of this century of impotent kings." Wagner described him as "outstandingly talented, a ruler of prodigious capabilities." More than 200 biographies have been written about him, and five full-length feature films have been made about his enigmatic life.

A magnificent figure—six feet four, blue-eyed, with carefully coiffed brunet locks—he was the idol of his time and the quarry of artful women and scheming mothers who haunted Munich's Residenz, the royal palace, with but a single thought: to meet him alone—just once. But with the notable exception of his first cousin, Sissy, who became Empress Elizabeth of Austria and met a fate as tragic as his own, Ludwig had little, indeed no, interest in women. Nor did he have much interest in governing his country; instead, he found escape in fantasy.

Ludwig had many eccentricities—all of them expensive. On the roof of the royal palace in Munich he built a winter garden with exotic trees, a painted Himalayan backdrop, and an artificial lake into which servants poured gallons of copper sulfate each day to make it look marine blue. He spent hours, dressed as Lohengrin, riding in a swan-shaped boat in the Venus Grotto he had installed behind one of his mansions. But of all his eccentricities, the greatest was undoubtedly his mania for building castles. They were also his undoing, for they put him 20 million gold marks into debt. Bismarck helped him out with a loan, in exchange for which Ludwig agreed in 1871 to the creation of the Second German Reich, with Prussia's King Wilhelm I as the first kaiser.

On an island in the Chiemsee in southeastern Bavaria he created a replica of Versailles; on the steep slope of a craggy alp he put up a hunting lodge in Moorish style; at Linderhof, deep in rugged mountain country, he created a gaudy, ostentatious imitation of a Baroque French château. And at the time of his death he was planning a full-scale copy of Beijing's Forbidden City. His most outlandish concoction of all, however, was Neuschwanstein, a romantic 19th-century fantasy adumbration of Disneyland, perched dizzily on a peak overlooking the village of **Schwangau**.

Before walking or taking a carriage ride up to it, a visit to **Hohenschwangau**, another castle in this hamlet, may give you some insights into the reclusive, enigmatic character of Ludwig II.

Like five other castles on peaks around Füssen, all once owned by the lords of Schwangau (a family that died out in the 16th century), Hohenschwangau was a ruin when Ludwig's father, Maximilian II, then Bavaria's crown prince, bought it in 1832. On the ruins he built a Neo-Gothic palace that he used as a summer holiday residence. Completed in 1837 (and now open to the public from 9:00 A.M. to 5:00 P.M. daily), it was where Maximilian took his family on vacation every year and where Ludwig II spent a good deal of his joyless childhood. Maximilian was as straitlaced as his own father, Ludwig I, was flamboyant. He used to say that had he not been king he would have become a university professor. He had a love of Germanic legends, and had them painted on the walls of Hohenschwangau: the tale of the Holy Grail, of the Minnesinger (lyrical poet) Tannhäuser, and of Lohengrin, who, according to 19th-century lore, once lived in the old Hohenschwangau fortress. It was in this summer residence, and through the one and only frivolous passion of his father, that Ludwig II acquired his own love for the myths and solitude of the Bavarian Alps.

Hohenschwangau was the capital of the *Schwangau* (Swan Country). There were swans everywhere: on lakes such as the Forggensee, Alpsee, and Schwansee; painted on the walls of the royal apartments; carved in the form of knickknacks. The swans fascinated father and son, and for the son they later became nearly an obsession.

A couple of years after his coronation, Ludwig II again spent part of a summer at Hohenschwangau and decided to buy property almost adjacent to it: the castle ruin of Vorderhohenschwangau, perched precipitously at the edge of a gorge with a waterfall. In May 1868 he wrote Wagner of his plans to build a castle on the ruins "in the style of the old German knights' castles." A year before, he happened to have visited the Wartburg above Eisenach (see the Bach and Luther Country chapter), scene of the Tannhäuser legend and of medieval minstrel competitions, and it was a romanticized version of that fortress he wanted. Thus **Schloss Neuschwanstein** was born.

The court architect, Eduard Riedel, and Christian Jank, the chief set designer of the Bavarian State Opera, drew up the plans, which looked like stage sets for *Tannhäuser.* Work began in 1869 and was not even quite finished when, 17 years later, on June 10, 1886, a day after he had been declared incompetent by a royal commission of doctors, Ludwig II was arrested in his dream castle and taken to Schloss Berg, on the shore of the Starnbergersee, where he was interned.

To describe Neuschwanstein's appearance and its interior decoration as opulent and like a fairy tale is probably the all-time understatement. The rich ornamentation had an influence on the later *Jugendstil,* the German form of Art Nouveau. The most important chambers in the castle are the Throne Room (without throne), which is patterned on a Romanesque basilica, and the Sängerhalle (Singers' Hall), its dark, heavy, wooden ceiling and murals depicting the Parsifal saga. The king's study, with pictures of the Tannhäuser legend, adjoins an artificial grotto complete with artificial waterfall and electric light effects.

Neuschwanstein was the least expensive of Ludwig II's castles (costing only 6.2 million gold marks to build, compared to 8.5 million for Linderhof and 16.6 million for Herrenchiemsee), yet it is not only the most visited—on average about 950,000 people a year—but also the most photographed building in all Germany. Ironically, although Ludwig II was deposed for spending so recklessly on his palaces, admissions revenues from them alone pay for nearly the entire upkeep and maintenance of *all* the old Wittelsbach family castles now owned and administered by the state of Bavaria. (Hours at Neuschwanstein are 9:00 A.M. to 5:30 P.M. daily, April through October; 10:00 A.M. to 4:00 P.M., November through March.)

Although the town of Füssen is only 7 km (4 miles) from the Hohenschwangau and Neuschwanstein castles—a five-minute drive or a 15-minute walk by a back road—you may want to spend the night in Schwangau itself. The ► Hotel Lisl-Jägerhaus, built in the style of a hunting château, has 62 rooms and a dining room featuring trout from the lakes in and around Schwangau. The ► Hotel König Ludwig, on a quiet side street just 300 yards from the Forggensee, largest of the area's lakes, is built and decorated in Alpine chalet style, with lots of natural pine paneling and furniture.

Füssen

Nearby Füssen, romantically divided by the Lech river and just 4 km (2½ miles) from the Austrian border, is a dramatic change of pace from the 19th-century artificiality of Maximilian's and Ludwig's castles. This town of 16,000, at an altitude of more than 2,600 feet, is genuine, as picturesquely medieval as can be. More than medieval, in fact, for like other spots along the Via Claudia, it goes back to Roman times, when it was known as Foetibus.

Of course there's a castle. The **Hohes Schloss**, on Magnusplatz, dates back to the early 14th century, when Bavaria's Duke Ludwig built it as a fortress and occasional residence, though most of the structure was completed a century later. The interior, containing a division of the Bavarian State Pictures Collection, is largely 17th century.

Post-Roman Füssen owes its origins to an Irish missionary monk, Saint Magnus, known as the "Apostle of the Allgäu," who established a chapel here in the eighth century. A Benedictine abbey was built adjacent to it some years later, and enlarged in Romanesque style in the 12th century. Little of that remains, for in the early 18th century a local architect, Johann-Jakob Herkomer, who had studied in Venice, got a commission to build a new monastery and church around the old tower. What he created is a perfect Baroque gem exhibiting a strong Venetian influence.

Above all, Füssen, tucked into the Lech valley and surrounded by 6,000- to 7,000-foot peaks, is perfect for strolling along its narrow, atmospheric, cobblestone streets. At the **Gasthof zum Schwanen**, Brotmarkt 4, a colorful old inn in a Gothic town house, you can sample Bavarian dishes such as pork roast with potato dumplings, or Allgäu-Swabian cuisine, including such specialties as *Maultaschen,* a kind of ravioli, and *Spätzle.* The area around Füssen is a popular summer and winter holiday resort and abounds with inns and hotels, all of them modern. For Altstadt atmosphere at moderate prices right in Füssen, the best accommodation is the ▶ **Hotel Hirsch.**

GETTING AROUND

To drive the entire Romantische Strasse from Würzburg to Füssen, leave Würzburg heading south on B 19 to Bad Mergentheim. At Mergentheim double back 4 km (2½ miles) on B 19 to the village of Igersheim, where, just north of the town limit, you will find an unnumbered road to the right (east) leading to Weikersheim, Creglingen, Detwang, and finally Rothenburg-ob-der-Tauber. This unnumbered country road follows the Tauber river valley all the way, making it almost impossible to become lost.

To continue from Rothenburg, take B 25 south to Feuchtwangen, Dinkelsbühl, Nördlingen, Harburg, and finally Donauwörth. On the German Shell map or atlas, the B 25 is colored yellow from Rothenburg to Nördlingen, and red from Nördlingen to Donauwörth. Don't let it confuse you. It is the same Bundesstrasse. The yellow marking indicates it is narrower and perhaps not in as good condition as the southern portion.

From Donauwörth follow B 2 to Augsburg. From Augsburg the Romantic Road heads south along B 17, which terminates in Füssen.

To make the detour to Memmingen, Ottobeuren, and Kempten from Landsberg am Lech, leave Landsberg on B 12/B 18, which is being widened into the A 96 Autobahn. About 20 km (12 miles) out of town there is a divide. The B 18 takes you to Memmingen, while the B 12 goes southwest to Kempten. In Memmingen an unnumbered road heading southeast (there will be directional signs) takes you to Ottobeuren. From Ottobeuren it is best to retrace your route back north until you find a blue Autobahn sign, then take the A 7 south to Kempten. To return to the Romantische Strasse from Kempten, take B 12 almost to Marktoberdorf, where it joins B 472, which you follow east to where it intersects the B 17 at Schongau, and then continue south on the Romantic Road.

Steingaden is just off the B 17. To get to the Wieskirche (it is well marked), follow the unnumbered country road east for 3 km (2 miles), then another 3 km (2 miles) south. The only way to return to the B 17 is by doubling back.

In Schwangau there is a marked but unnumbered cutoff to Hohenschwangau and Neuschwanstein.

If you do not want to drive into Füssen, where parking is sometimes difficult, there is a footpath from Hohenschwangau into the center, a distance of less than a mile.

ACCOMMODATIONS REFERENCE

The hotel rates listed here are 1994 projections for double-bed, double-occupancy rooms, with a range from low to high whenever possible. Prices are given in deutsche marks (DM). Basic rates are always subject to change, so please verify price when you are booking. Breakfast is usually included in the price of a room.

City telephone codes must be preceded by a zero if you are calling from elsewhere in Germany.

▶ **Deutsches Haus.** Weinmarkt 3, D-91550 **Dinkelsbühl.** Tel: (9851) 60-58; Fax: (9851) 79-11. DM 220–260.

▶ **Fürstenhof.** Rathausplatz 8, D-87435 **Kempten.** Tel: (831) 253-60; Fax: (831) 253-61-20. DM 190–225.

▶ **Fürstliche Burgschenke.** Auf Schloss Harburg, D-86655 **Harburg.** Tel: (9003) 15-04. DM 100–140.

▶ **Goldener Hirsch.** Untere Schmiedgasse 16, D-91534 **Rothenburg.** Tel: (9861) 70-80; Fax: (9861) 70-81-00. DM 190–320.

▶ **Hotel Bären.** Hofbronnengasse 9, D-91541 **Rothenburg.** Tel: (9861) 60-33; Fax: (9861) 48-75. DM 250–320.

▶ **Hotel Blauer Hecht.** Schweinemarkt 1, D-91550 **Dinkelsbühl.** Tel: (9851) 811; Fax: (9851) 814. DM 134–162.

▶ **Hotel Eisenhut.** Herrengasse 3–7, D-91541 **Rothenburg.** Tel: (9861) 70-50; Fax: (9861) 705-45. DM 285–380.

▶ **Hotel Eisenkrug.** Martin-Luther-Strasse 1, D-91550 **Dinkelsbühl.** Tel: (9851) 60-17; Fax: (9851) 60-20. DM 130–165.

▶ **Hotel Falken.** Am Rossmarkt 3–5, D-87700 **Memmingen.** Tel: (8331) 470-81; Fax: (8331) 470-86. DM 145–170.

▶ **Hotel Fischertor.** Pfärrle 16, D-86152 **Augsburg.** Tel: (821) 15-60-51; Fax: (821) 307-02. DM 138–168.

▶ **Hotel Goggl.** Herkomerstrasse 19, D-86899 **Landsberg.** Tel: (8191) 32-40; Fax: (8191) 32-41-00. DM 145–225.

► **Hotel Hirsch.** Kaiser Maximilianplatz 7, D-87629 **Füssen.** Tel: (8362) 50-80; Fax: (8362) 50-81-13. DM 165–195.

► **Hotel König Ludwig.** Kreuzweg 11/13, D-87645 **Schwangau.** Tel: (8362) 88-90; Fax: (8362) 817-79. DM 190–250 (no credit cards).

► **Hotel Lisl-Jägerhaus.** Neuschwansteiner Strasse 1, D-87643 **Schwangau.** Tel: (8362) 88-70; Fax: (8362) 811-07. DM 142–242.

► **Hotel Rebstock.** Neubaustrasse 7, D-97070 **Würzburg.** Tel: (931) 309-30; Fax: (931) 309-31-00. DM 280–350.

► **Hotel Victoria.** Poststrasse 2, D-97980 **Bad Mergentheim.** Tel: (7931) 59-30; Fax: (7931) 59-35-00. DM 210–310.

► **Hotel Walfisch.** Am Pleidenturm 5, D-97070 **Würzburg.** Tel: (931) 500-55; Fax: (931) 516-90. DM 200–280.

► **Laurentius.** Marktplatz 5, D-97990 **Weikersheim.** Tel: (7934) 70-07; Fax: (7934) 70-77. DM 125–150.

► **Maritim Hotel Würzburg.** Bleichertorstrasse 5, D-97070 **Würzburg.** Tel: (931) 305-30; Fax: (931) 186-82. DM 288–398.

► **Parkhotel.** Sternschanzenstrasse 1, D-86609 **Donauwörth-Parkstadt.** Tel: (906) 60-37; Fax: (906) 232-83. DM 140–170.

► **Parkhotel Maritim.** Lothar-Daiker-Strasse 6, D-97980 **Bad Mergentheim.** Tel: (7931) 53-90; Fax: (7931) 53-91-00. DM 250–330.

► **Posthotel Traube.** Kapellstrasse 14, D-86609 **Donauwörth.** Tel: (906) 6096; Fax: (906) 233-90. DM 130–180.

► **Prinzhotel Rothenburg.** An der Hofstatt 3, D-91541 **Rothenburg.** Tel: (9861) 60-51; Fax: (9861) 60-52. DM 150–220.

► **Romantik-Hotel Greifen-Post.** Marktplatz 8, D-91555 **Feuchtwangen.** Tel: (9852) 20-02; Fax: (9852) 48-41. DM 255–275.

► **Romantik-Hotel Markusturm.** Rödergasse 1, D-91541 **Rothenburg.** Tel: (9861) 20-98; Fax: (9861) 26-92. DM 180–350.

► **Steigenberger Drei Mohren.** Maximilianstrasse 40, D-86150 **Augsburg.** Tel: (821) 503-60; Fax: (821) 15-78-64. DM 270–340.

► **Tilman Riemenschneider.** Georgengasse 11, D-91541 **Rothenburg.** Tel: (9861) 20-86; Fax: (9861) 29-79. DM 180–240.

► **Wittelsbacher Höh.** Hexenbruchweg 10, D-97082 **Würzburg-Zellerau.** Tel: (931) 420-85; Fax: (931) 41-54-58. DM 160–240.

MUNICH
(MÜNCHEN)

By John Dornberg

Thomas Mann, who spent 40 of the most productive years of his life in Munich, wrote a singular tribute to it in his *Gladius Dei*: "Munich shines forth, a heaven of blue silk radiates over her festive squares and columned white temples, her Neoclassical monuments and Baroque churches, her playing fountains, her palaces and her parks. Art blooms, art reigns, art stretches her rose-clad scepter over this city and smiles." Henrik Ibsen, who wrote some of his greatest plays during the 15 years he resided here, declared shortly after arriving in 1874: "There are but two cities in which one can really live—Rome and Munich. But in Munich even reality is beautiful."

No other German city has contributed as much to the arts, literature, or music as this former capital of a former kingdom. Though today merely the capital of one of the German Federal Republic's 16 states, Munich is Germany's "secret capital," the city where most Germans would live if they could, and on which 1.8 million of them—and an additional 1.4 million foreigners—converge as visitors each year, including more than 200,000 Americans.

Munich is a city of superlatives, offering *more* of just about everything. It is, for example, the most expensive city in Germany in which to live. It has more glitter, fashion, chic, and conspicuous consumption; more restaurants (one per 240 inhabitants), as well as more with Michelin stars; more fine-food shops and open-air markets; and also more privately owned Rolls-Royces, Jaguars, Lamborghinis, Ferraris, and Maserattis than any other city in Germany. (BMWs do not really count, because they are made here.) It also counts more movie stars and filmmakers, thanks to having Europe's

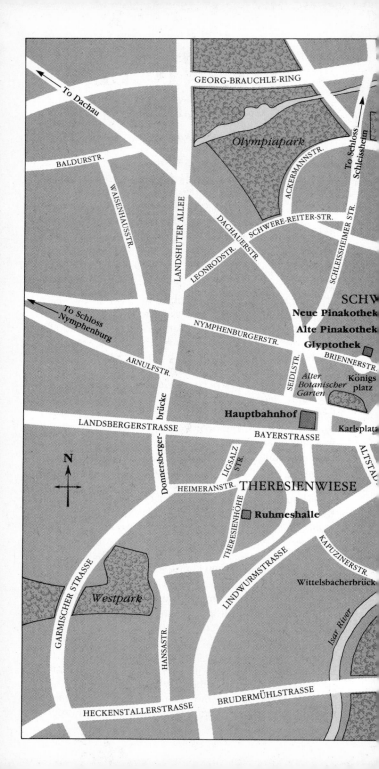

Munich
(München)

| 0 | yards | 1,100 |
| 0 | meters | 1,000 |

PETUELRING

LEOPOLDSTRASSE

Luitpoldpark

KARL-THEODOR-STR.

JOHANN-FICHTE-STR.

UNGERERSTRASSE

Isar River

BELGRADSTR.

LEOPOLDSTRASSE

ISARRING

OBERFÖHRINGERSTR.

SABETH STR.

Englischer Garten

IFFLANDSTR.

R.-STRAUSS-STRASSE

BING

BARERSTR.

Universität

Max-Joseph-Brücke

MONTGELASSTR.

ISMANINGER STR.

RING-VON-DER-TANN-STR.

Bayerisches Nationalmuseum

BOGENHAUSEN

arolinenplatz

Prinzregenten-brücke

Friedensengel

Prinzregenten-platz

HOFGARTEN STR.

THEATINER-STR.

DIENERSTR.

EINSTR.

PRINZREGENTENSTRASSE

Villa Stuck

TROGER STR.

Prinzregententheater

UFINGER STR.

Residenz

WIDENMAYER STR.

ERANGER STR.

Marienplatz

MAXIMILIANSTR.

EINSTEINSTRASSE

NNENSTADT

Maximilians-brücke

INNERE-WIENER-STR.

Maximilianeum

KIRCHENSTR.

GRILLPARZER STR.

ZWEIBRÜCKENSTR.

Zweibrücke

PREYSINGSTR.

ING

Deutsches Museum

ANS SACHS-STR.

FRAUNHOFERSTR.

Gasteig Philharmonie

HAIDHAUSEN

INNSBRUCKER RING

ITTELSBACHER STR.

Reichenbach-brücke

HOCHSTR.

ROSENHEIMER STR.

HUMBOLDTSTR.

WELFENSTR.

LANDSTR.

WERINHERSTR.

GIESING

CHIEMGAUSTRASSE

largest studio and Germany's greatest number of production houses.

Munich also has more art, music, and culture than any other German city with the exception of Berlin, in the form of 32 museums, 230 commercial galleries, 42 repertory theaters, two opera houses, five concert halls, and four symphony orchestras; more students—96,000—attending Germany's two largest universities; more scientific institutes and high-tech industries; and more trade fairs, congresses, and conventions. The city boasts the world's oldest and largest public park; Europe's biggest and bawdiest folk festival, the Oktoberfest; the Continent's cleanest, safest, and most efficient public-transit system (but also Germany's densest motor traffic); and the country's best soccer team, FC Bayern.

We begin our coverage of Munich in the compact *Innenstadt* (Inner City). The area around Marienplatz, the city's historical hub, contains Munich's major churches, monuments, the enormous Residenzmuseum, the Nationaltheater, and the famous Hofbräuhaus—in other words, enough to keep you busy for at least one full day and probably two or three. From here we head north, beyond the Altstadtring that encircles the Innenstadt, to Ludwigstrasse—one of Munich's grand boulevards—and west to Schwabing, a neighborhood rich in cultural (and counter-cultural) history where Munich's universities and several more great museums are located. From Schwabing we turn eastward to the Englischer Garten, museum-studded Prinzregentenstrasse, and south to Haidhausen, site of the acclaimed Deutsches Museum of science and technology. We end our coverage of this inexhaustibly rich city in the outskirts of Theresienwiese, where the annual Oktoberfest is held. Visitors with more time can go on to explore the major sites in Munich's environs: Schloss Nymphenburg, the royal summer palace to the west of the city; Olympiapark, site of the 1972 Olympic Games; Dachau, that grim reminder of the Nazi era; and the palaces of Schleissheim.

MAJOR INTEREST

Innenstadt
Marienplatz
Glockenspiel in Neues Rathaus
Peterskirche
Viktualienmarkt (Food Market)
Frauenkirche, Michaelskirche, Asamkirche,
   Theatinerkirche
Hofbräuhaus

Maximilianstrasse (theaters, shopping)
Nationaltheater (Bavarian State Opera)
Residenzmuseum (palace museum)

Outside the Altstadtring
Ludwigstrasse
Schwabing (neighborhood)
Königsplatz
Glyptothek (Greek and Roman sculpture)
Antikensammlung (Celtic, Greek, Etruscan, Roman
    applied art)
Alte and Neue Pinakotheken (Old Masters and 19th-
    century art)
Städtische Galerie im Lenbachhaus (modern art)
Englischer Garten
Prinzregentenstrasse (Belle Epoque and Art Nouveau
    architecture)
Haus der Kunst (modern and contemporary art)
Staatsgalerie Moderner Kunst (20th-century art)
Bayerisches Nationalmuseum (8th- through 19th-
    century Bavarian and applied art)
Villa Stuck
Haidhausen (neighborhood)
Deutsches Museum (science and technology)

The Outskirts
Theresienwiese (site of Oktoberfest)
Ruhmeshalle (Hall of Fame) and statue of Bavaria
Schloss Nymphenburg
Nymphenburger Porzellanmanufaktur (porcelain
    factory and sales rooms)
Olympiapark

Environs
Schloss Dachau
KZ-Gedenkstätte Dachau (Nazi concentration camp
    memorial)
Palaces in Schleissheim

By German standards Munich is not old. It was founded
officially on June 14, 1158, by decree of Frederick Barbarossa, the Hohenstaufen emperor, under duress from his
cousin Henry the Lion, the Guelph duke of Saxony, to whom
two years earlier Frederick had given the duchy of Bavaria.
The city's beginnings lay in a crude act of extortion. Henry
wanted to get the most out of his new Bavarian properties,
including the lucrative customs revenues on the salt trade
between the Bavarian Alps and the rest of the empire that
Bishop Adalbert of Freising was collecting at the only bridge

over the Isar river, located in the village of Föhring. Henry and a force of knights destroyed the bishop's bridge, then built a new one three and a half miles upstream at a tiny settlement called Zu den Munichen—"At the Monks"—which surrounded the church of a few mendicant friars. Of course, he made his bridge, which connected the banks of the Isar via an island (now the site of the Deutsches Museum), into a major toll station.

Bishop Adalbert, who also happened to be the emperor's uncle, was furious, and pressured his nephew to do something about Henry's act of piracy. Barbarossa, who probably considered the whole matter a storm in a schnapps glass, was powerless to act, however, counting as he was on Henry's military aid in the next invasion of Italy. On June 14, 1158, during a session of the Reichstag in Augsburg, Barbarossa proposed the compromise that led to the official birth of Munich: Henry could keep his bridge and levy duty, provided he paid the bishop of Freising a third of the customs revenues he collected.

The new town prospered. Henry was less fortunate. In 1176 he and his cousin Barbarossa went to war against each other. Henry lost, was stripped not only of his Saxon but also his Bavarian holdings, and then was exiled to England. After a period of penance, he returned to German soil as ruler of the insignificant, pocket-size duchy of Braunschweig. In 1180, Barbarossa deeded Bavaria to Count Otto von Wittelsbach, a minor nobleman, whose descendants were to rule it as dukes, electors, and finally kings for more than 700 years. Munich became their capital in 1255.

To be sure, the Wittelsbachs quarreled a great deal among themselves. But no other dynasty in Europe ruled as long, gave its realm as great a sense of identity, or left as indelible an imprint on its capital. Granted, some of them were downright eccentric, and all were unusual in one sense: Unlike the Hapsburgs of Austria or the Hohenzollerns of Prussia, the Wittelsbachs were more drawn to the fine arts than the art of war. It was they who laid the foundations of Munich's magnificent art collections; they who patronized musicians from Orlando di Lasso to Richard Wagner; and they who created the city's splendid parks, subsidized its great libraries and educational institutions, and created a fertile environment for writers, thinkers, and scientists.

At the same time, nearly all the Wittelsbachs were dogged builders who left monuments and boulevards, theaters and museums, and castles and palaces. Among the latter are the Residenz, the "winter palace," in the center of the city; Schloss Nymphenburg, one of Germany's most dazzling Baroque-Rococo digs; and the Alte and Neue Schlösser at

Schleissheim, built as additional summer retreats in the 17th and 18th centuries respectively. The greatest builder of them all—if you exclude his grandson King Ludwig II, who put up all those fairy-tale castles in the Alps south of Munich—was Ludwig I.

Ludwig reigned from 1825 to 1848, when, at the age of 62, he was forced to abdicate in favor of his son, Maximilian II, because of his scandalous love affair with the Irish dancer Lola Montez. Ludwig was both a Germanophile (at a time when a united Germany was but a distant dream) and a Grecophile (at a time when Greece was still under the yoke of the Ottoman Turks). Well before ascending to the throne he had vowed to make Munich a stately metropolis that would "do honor to all Germany" and become a "new Athens, a center of learning and culture." In order to carry out his vow he retained the services of two of the greatest architects of his time, Leo von Klenze and Friedrich von Gärtner, as well as the sculptor Ludwig Schwanthaler and the Nazarene painter Peter Cornelius. Subsequent Wittelsbachs also contributed lavishly to this dream, especially Maximilian II and a nephew, Prince Regent Luitpold, who reigned from 1886 to 1912.

THE INNENSTADT

What Müncheners call the Innenstadt (Inner City) is an oval-shaped district about a mile by half a mile on the left (west) bank of the Isar river, which flows into the Danube near Deggendorf. It is belted by a piece of postwar madness called the *Altstadtring*, a four- to six-lane thruway on which traffic is usually choked to a standstill. The ring more or less follows the city's medieval fortifications, all of which, with the exception of three town gates—the Isartor, Sendlinger Tor, and Karlstor—were razed in the late 18th and early 19th centuries. The Innenstadt can easily be explored on foot. In fact, there is no other option, as most of the area has been turned into a pedestrian zone.

Marienplatz is the Innenstadt's—and Munich's—epicenter.

Marienplatz

Marienplatz means "St. Mary's Square"—a name that this plaza, which has been the political, social, and commercial heart of Munich since the 13th century, has borne only since 1854. The renaming of the square was a belated tribute to the gilded bronze figure of Mary, Bavaria's patron saint, which had stood atop a red marble Corinthian column in the middle

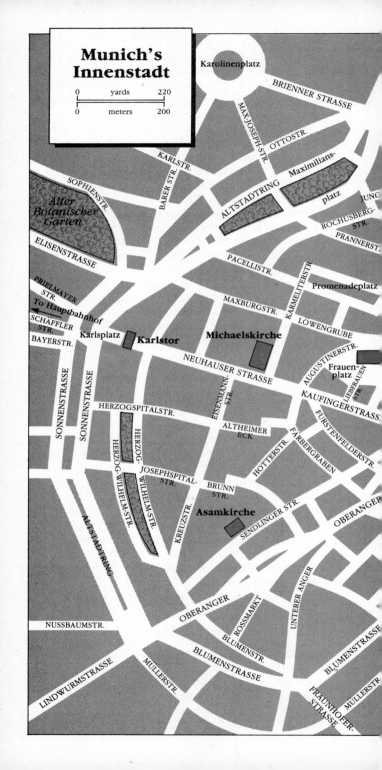

Munich's Innenstadt

```
0        yards        220
|---------------------------|
0        meters        200
```

Karolinenplatz

BRIENNER STRASSE

MAX-JOSEPH-STR.

OTTOSTR.

KARLSTR.

BARER STR.

ALTSTADTRING

Maximilians-platz

JUNG

ROCHUSBERG-STR.

SOPHIENSTR.

Alter Botanischer Garten

ELISENSTRASSE

PRANNERST.

PACELLISTR.

KARMELITERSTR.

Promenadeplatz

PRIELMAYER STR.

To Hauptbahnhof

MAXBURGSTR.

LÖWENGRUBE

SCHÄFFLER STR.

BAYERSTR.

Karlsplatz

Karlstor

Michaelskirche

AUGUSTINERSTR.

Frauen-platz

SONNENSTRASSE

SONNENSTRASSE

NEUHAUSER STRASSE

EISENMANN-STR.

LIEBFRAUEN

KAUFINGERSTRASS.

HERZOGSPITALSTR.

HERZOG-

HERZOG-WILHELM-STR.

ALTHEIMER ECK

FÜRSTENFELDERSTR.

FÄRBERGRABEN

JOSEPHSPITAL-STR.

WILHELM-STR.

KREUZSTR.

BRUNN STR.

HOTTERSTR.

ALTSTADTRING

Asamkirche

SENDLINGER STR.

OBERANGER

NUSSBAUMSTR.

OBERANGER

UNTERER ANGER

ROSSMARKT

BLUMENSTR.

BLUMENSTRASSE

BLUMENSTRASSE

LINDWURMSTRASSE

MÜLLERSTR.

FRAUNHOFER-STRASSE

MÜLLERSTR.

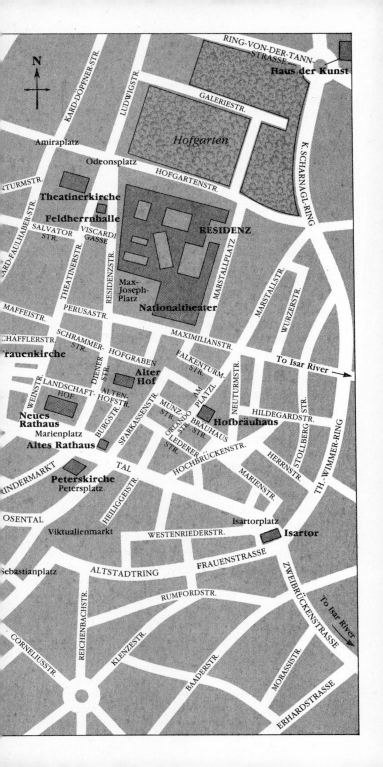

of the square since 1638—and was also a public prayer that the city fathers hoped would spare Munich from a cholera epidemic. (Before that it had been called Schrannenplatz— Grain Market Square.)

Over the centuries the square has been the site of festivals, imperial receptions, ducal weddings, political rallies, public executions, riots, rebellions, revolutions, and mayhem.

The biggest bash on the Marienplatz was the eight-day celebration of the marriage of Duke Wilhelm V to Renate of Lorraine in 1586, a party that cost millions and that brought the crowned heads of Europe to Munich as wedding guests. In 1683, as a gesture of gratitude for the end of the plague, the plaza was the scene of the first *Schäfflertanz* (Dance of the Coopers), a colorful folk ritual that the members of the barrelmakers' guild continue to stage every seven years (the next one will be in 1997) in accordance with their 300-year-old pledge.

And then there was the "invention" of the *Weisswurst,* a deed ascribed to Sepp Moser, butcher and then keeper of a Marienplatz inn called the Tavern to the Eternal Light, now the **Gaststätte Peterhof.** On the morning of February 22, 1857, so the story goes, Moser went into his kitchen to make the day's usual batch of *Bratwürste.* He proceeded to reach for the wrong spice containers, ground up more veal than pork, miscalculated a few other ingredients, and overcooked the whole forcemeat mixture, thus accidentally coming up with a new sausage concoction. When he realized what he had done, Moser was horrified. Fearing the sausages would taste terrible, he decided to steam them in a tureen rather than broil them over charcoal. His guests were delighted, and news of the new delicacy spread through town within hours, winning Moser the eternal gratitude of sausage lovers everywhere. Today, though hundreds of Munich inns, restaurants, and butcher shops serve and sell *Weisswürste,* those at the Peterhof are still the best.

Marienplatz is still where everything happens. When cars were banned and the maze of streetcar tracks removed from the inner city in 1971, the square became the underground transportation hub of Munich, with two subway and seven interurban rapid train lines intersecting on three subterranean levels. Above ground it is the focal point of the city's shopping district, with a dizzying rush of humanity hurrying into stores and dashing into the streets that radiate from it.

The scene changes with the seasons. In balmy weather street musicians perform, agitators orate, Müncheners quaff beer and wolf down Weisswürste or creamy pastries at the many sidewalk restaurants and cafés, and foot-weary shoppers relax on chairs scattered among the planter boxes.

From late November through December the plaza overflows with Christmas Market stalls selling handicrafts, toys, tree ornaments, and a cornucopia of traditional snacks and sweets, including sugar-coated toasted almonds, fruitcakes, gingerbread cookies, smoked meats and hams, and *Glüh-wein,* a spiced red wine served piping hot.

Marienplatz is also the political and administrative heart of Munich, where election campaigns climax, demonstrations are staged, and the burgomaster and city councillors preside. The latter conduct business in the **Neues Rathaus** (New City Hall), the largest building on the square. It looks old, but don't let the gargoyles and stone demons, statues of Guelph and Wittelsbach rulers, and filigreed façade fool you: This is a Neo-Gothic structure, built in three stages between 1867 and 1909 after the Altes Rathaus (Old City Hall), off to the right at the plaza's eastern end, had become too small. The **Altes Rathaus**, which was built in the 15th century, was almost totally destroyed during World War II. The building, with its elaborate Gothic council chamber, was reconstructed in the 1950s. The adjacent tower is a 1974 replica of the late-15th-century original, which had to be razed after the air raids for safety reasons.

If all those shops along the ground-floor façade of the Neues Rathaus, including the city's oldest and priciest sporting-goods store at the corner, seem oddly out of place, chalk it up to Henry the Lion, who initiated the symbiosis of politics and commerce in Munich.

The best show on Marienplatz—11:00 A.M. and 9:00 P.M. daily, as well as noon and 5:00 P.M. during the high season and pre-Christmas month—is the 43-bell glockenspiel on the 280-foot central spire of the Neues Rathaus. The brightly painted mechanical figures re-enact two of the most famous pageants from Munich history: the knights' tournament during the 1586 wedding feast of Wilhelm V and Renate of Lorraine and, on the level below, the Coopers' Dance. An elevator will take you to the spire's first balustrade, above the carillon, and stairs lead to the second and third tiers over that. From each tier the view of central Munich can be spectacular.

For an even loftier view—303 feet high—try the Alter Peter, the spire of the **Peterskirche**, which rises just south of Marienplatz. St. Peter's is Munich's oldest church, older indeed than the city itself. Excavations during its postwar reconstruction—like everything else in the Innenstadt it was then a bomb-gutted ruin—turned up the foundations of an 11th-century Romanesque basilica that was probably the monastery church of the Benedictines for whose abbey the original settlement was named. That church was replaced in the late 13th century by a Gothic building, which was, in turn, destroyed by fire in 1327 and reconsecrated in its present, larger form in 1368. The spire is just as old. Virtually all the leading artists and artisans who worked in Munich from the 15th through 18th centuries contributed to the interior furnishing and decoration of St. Peter's, among them the wood carver Erasmus Grasser, the painter Jan Polack, the sculptor and stucco master Egid Quirin Asam, the architect Andreas Faistenberger, and the muralist Johann Baptist Zimmermann.

A stroll down either side of Petersplatz, the square on which St. Peter's is situated, will lead you directly from the heart of Munich to its belly, the Viktualienmarkt.

The Viktualienmarkt

For Thomas Wolfe, Munich was a kind of German heaven, "an enchanted land where one ate and drank forever . . . a city fairly groaning with little fat, luxurious food, pastry or sweet shops." It still is, and the best groaning is in the Viktualienmarkt (Food Market).

Located on the square of the same name, the Viktualienmarkt has been serving Müncheners for more than 180 years. Picture two dozen butcher shops, five cheese sellers (including one who offers a choice of 350 varieties), a whole section of bakeries (each stocked with dozens of kinds of Bavarian breads and rolls made fresh several times a day), fishmongers, wine merchants, and a virtual sea of produce stalls—each more tempting and colorful than the next and all of it squeezed into an area the size of a city block. Farmers come in very early with produce, poultry, eggs, and flowers, and most of the permanent stands open for business at 6:00 A.M. (which is also when the chefs of Munich's finest restaurants arrive to do their shopping) and stay open until 6:00 P.M. weekdays, 1:00 P.M. Saturdays. The vegetables here are always the best in town, and several stalls feature only herbs. One sells only potatoes—dozens of different kinds. Another features honeys from all over the world.

While you need facility in neither German nor Bavarian to enjoy the Viktualienmarkt, it helps to remember two things. Don't touch the merchandise until it's yours. Feeling tomatoes for ripeness or lettuce for firmness is a mortal insult as well as a violation of German food laws. Moreover, unlike other open-air markets, the Viktualienmarkt is not the place to try out your bargaining skills. On the contrary, prices are usually even higher than those at the finest gourmet emporiums. Quality is what counts here, and you'll pay accordingly.

A belly laugh after the food market can be found just

north of it at Westenrieder Strasse 26 at ZAM—the **Zentrum für Aussergewöhnliche Museen**, which translates as the Center for Unusual Museums. Unusual they certainly are: the world's first "Pedal Car," "Night Pot," "Bourdalou," "Corkscrew," and "Easter Bunny" museums are among the seven under one roof here, covering 6,000 square feet of exhibit space. The complex is open daily from 10:00 A.M. to 6:00 P.M.

Munich's Major Churches

In addition to St. Peter's, Munich's four other major churches—the Frauenkirche, Michaelskirche, Asamkirche, and Theatinerkirche—are all within a few minutes' walk of Marienplatz.

From the square it is about 250 yards down **Kaufingerstrasse**, the main shopping mall, to Liebfrauenstrasse and Munich's cathedral, the **Frauenkirche**, officially known as Domkirche zu Unserer Lieben Frau (Cathedral Church of Our Lady). Its 325-foot twin towers, each topped with an onion dome, are *the* landmark of the city.

This huge 15th-century Gothic structure, more than 300 feet long and 132 feet wide, is austere on the outside—a striking contrast to the rich façades of downtown Munich. Despite losses and thefts over the centuries the interior furnishings still include some major art treasures, among them the 15th- to 16th-century stained-glass windows of the chancel, the carved figures of Erasmus Grasser on the choir stalls, and the tomb of Ludwig the Bavarian, one of two Wittelsbachs elected Holy Roman Emperor.

From Liebfrauenstrasse it is a couple hundred yards more along Kaufingerstrasse to Neuhauser Strasse and the **Michaelskirche**, the Jesuit Church of St. Michael, built in the late 16th century as a spiritual center of the Counter-Reformation by Duke Wilhelm V of wedding feast and glockenspiel fame. Like most of the Wittelsbachs, he thought in grand terms and was a builder on an even grander scale.

For St. Michael's, which Wilhelm V commissioned in the 1580s, he hired architects, artisans, and artists from Italy and the Netherlands. When a tower collapsed during the work in 1590, damaging much of the building and destroying the finished choir area, he saw it as a sign from the Archangel Michael to expand the project and build an even larger tower, which was completed in 1597. Wilhelm V's building boom took its toll on Bavaria's treasury, however, and brought the duchy to the brink of bankruptcy, forcing the duke to abdicate in favor of his son. Undeterred, the deposed duke paid for completion of the Michaelskirche out of his own pocket.

Lavish in its exterior embellishment and interior furnishings, St. Michael's ranks as the prototype of Renaissance ecclesiastical architecture in southern Germany. It is also one of the churches where the Wittelsbachs are buried. The elaborate tombs and sarcophagi of 30 Bavarian rulers (Wilhelm V included) are in the **Fürstengruft** (Princes' Crypt) under the choir. Moreover, St. Michael's was the parish church of one of Germany's most outspokenly anti-Nazi priests, Rupert Mayer, who began preaching against Hitler and the Nazis from its pulpit as early as 1920, shortly after Hitler made his political debut in Munich, and continued to do so through 1937, when he was arrested and incarcerated at Sachsenhausen concentration camp, from which he was liberated by U.S. troops in 1945. Mayer died several months later and is buried in a crypt at the **Bürgersaal** church, 200 yards farther along Kaufingerstrasse. Pope John Paul II presided at the beatification ceremony for Mayer there in 1987.

From Marienplatz, another busy shopping street, **Sendlingerstrasse**, leads to the **Asamkirche**. Its official name is Kirche St. Johann Nepomuk—Church of St. John of Nepomuk, the patron saint of Bohemia, who was tortured and drowned in Prague in 1393 on orders of King Wenceslaus IV, allegedly for refusing to disclose the queen's confessional secrets. But Asamkirche is the Munich name, and it will do, because the brothers Egid Quirin and Cosmas Damian Asam built it for themselves.

Born in the latter half of the 17th century, the Asams were multitalented men who left their imprint—churches, chapels, monasteries, palaces, mansions—all over Bavaria, as well as Bohemia, Swabia, Switzerland, and the Tyrol. Cosmas, the elder of the two, was a painter and muralist; Egid was a sculptor and stucco master. Both were also architects. After studying in Rome, where they were much influenced by Bernini, they were instrumental in bringing the Italian Late Baroque style north of the Alps, developing it into a decorative trademark that was opulent in its use of color, and perfect in its structural harmony.

In 1733 the brothers bought two adjacent lots on Sendlingerstrasse. On one they built a town house (the Asamhaus) to serve as a studio and workshop, and on the other the small church dedicated to St. John of Nepomuk. They paid for the latter themselves in order to implement their artistic and architectural concepts unhampered by the wishes or strictures of a patron. Cosmas died in 1739, seven years before the church was finished, so Egid gets most of the credit. The Asamkirche is a dazzle of ecclesiastical theater, with silky blue-and-gold draperies of stucco, walls with red stucco marble, and a profusion of medallions, cupids, elaborate columns, and porticoes.

The Theatinerkirche lies in the opposite direction, north of Marienplatz via Weinstrasse, which changes its name to Theatinerstrasse. As you stroll along these two streets—now pedestrian zones lined by pricey stores—you may want to visit a current exhibition at the **Hypo-Kunsthalle** on Theatinerstrasse, the newest addition to Munich's vibrant art scene. Sponsored by a bank, it hosts a variety of visiting exhibitions and retrospectives.

The saffron-yellow **Theatinerkirche**—its official name is St. Cajetan's—is visible from miles around thanks to its two elegant towers and immense central dome. To call it Italianate is an understatement: Not only was it commissioned by an Italian princess, who donated it to the Theatines (a community of priests founded by the Italian churchman and reformer Saint Cajetan), it is also the work of Italian architects, artisans, and artists.

Its story begins with the marriage in 1650 of Duke Ferdinand Maria, grandson of Wilhelm V and the second Wittelsbach to hold the title of elector of the Holy Roman Empire, to Princess Henrietta Adelaide of Savoy. When, in 1662, Adelaide fulfilled the duke's most fervent hope, providing him with an heir, the happy couple gave thanks by commissioning the church.

Adelaide hired the Bolognese architect Agostino Barelli for the church and Nicolo Petri of Como to build the adjacent Theatine abbey (which has served as a Dominican monastery since its postwar reconstruction). Barelli designed a building reminiscent of Rome's San Andrea della Valle, the mother church of the Theatine order, and construction began in 1663. He and the impetuous duchess had a falling out, however, and in 1669 he was replaced by Enrico Zucalli, a Swiss from the Grissons, who changed the plans by adding the 230-foot central dome and the two spires that emulate those of the church of Santa Maria della Salute in Venice. By 1688—twelve years after Adelaide's death and nine years after Ferdinand Maria's—St. Cajetan's was more or less completed—"more or less" because the façades were still bare and just roughly plastered over. It took another foreigner, François Cuvilliés, and some 80 years to solve that problem; the Frenchman added the Rococo embellishments and structural elements that you see today. Despite the various architects who had a hand, the Theatinerkirche is enticingly harmonious, and one of the city's architectural jewels.

Like St. Michael's, it is also a burial church for the Wittelsbachs. Among those interred in its royal crypt are Adelaide and Ferdinand Maria and their son Maximilian Emmanuel.

The Hofbräuhaus

No foreigner was a more literate connoisseur of Munich beer than Thomas Wolfe. In fact, the American glowingly wrote that "the best beer in Germany, in the world, is made in Munich"—despite getting clobbered with a one-liter stein during a brawl at the 1925 Oktoberfest.

Today, the most renowned beer cellar in Munich is the Hofbräuhaus (Court Brewery), located on a little square called Am Platzl, only three minutes' walk northeast of Marienplatz. The Hofbräuhaus is more than just a beer hall, however. It is an institution—and one that is immortalized in history, legend, and raucous drinking songs. Again it is Duke Wilhelm V who gets the credit. In 1589 he decided to build *ein aigen Preuhaus* (a personal brewing house) in order to halt expensive imports of "foreign" beer, meaning from Einbeck, 400 miles north of Munich (see our chapter on The Center). Though it took until 1613 for Munich brewmasters to get the knack of making the light, golden Einbeck suds (from which, incidentally, the name "bock beer" derives), the original Hofbräuhaus started operating in 1592.

The present building, in place since 1644, was extensively reconstructed in 1896. Beer has not actually been produced on the premises since 1890, when a huge new brewery opened on the east bank of the Isar in the Haidhausen district. But otherwise little has changed, especially the fact that Müncheners still regard beer as a food, not a beverage, and that it must be made in strict accordance with the pure-food laws promulgated in 1516 by Wilhelm V's grandfather, Duke Wilhelm IV.

History has been written here as well. It was in the Hofbräuhaus, in 1844, that King Ludwig I first encountered the public disenchantment with his reign, a sentiment that culminated in his abdication four years later, after he had raised the price of a *Mass*—a liter of beer—from 6 to 6½ kroner. And it was in the *Festsaal* (ballroom), on February 24, 1920, that Adolf Hitler, then a little-known political agitator who only a few months earlier had joined an obscure radical party, delivered his first speech to a large audience. Political speeches and rallies are still held in the Hofbräuhaus, as they are in the ballrooms of Munich's other big brewery-connected beer halls, such as the Löwenbräukeller on Stiglmaierplatz.

Although the Hofbräuhaus has various side rooms and upstairs dining chambers where solid Bavarian food at moderate prices is dished out in relatively quiet, rustic surroundings, the real action and local color are concentrated in the cavernous street-level *Schwemme* (Trough), with its rows of long wooden tables, rough benches, oompah-pah band, and assemblage of bearded lederhosen-garbed regulars who arrive for their breakfast suds when the place opens at 9:00 A.M. and often remain all day. The noise is usually deafening—never more so than when imbibers, many of whom seem to be non-Bavarians and non-Müncheners, rise up to belt out drinking songs. The liter-size steins—a *Mass* actually means a "measure"—seem at first awesomely daunting, but rare is the first-time visitor who doesn't down one to the last drop.

Maximilianstrasse

Given their proclivity for seeking immortality in stone, it should come as no surprise that the Wittelsbachs commissioned entire avenues and boulevards. Thus there is Ludwig I's Ludwigstrasse and Prince Regent Luitpold's Prinzregentenstrasse. King Maximilian II, Ludwig I's son, who reigned from 1848 to 1864, is commemorated by Maximilianstrasse, which starts two blocks north of Marienplatz and runs in a straight line east for nearly 2 km (1¼ miles), crossing the Isar by way of the graceful Maximiliansbrücke and continuing up the verdant hill of the river's right bank to the Maximilianeum, a Neo-Renaissance structure originally built as a picture gallery and boarding school for gifted offspring of the nobility, and now the Bavarian state parliament building.

Maximilian II began making plans for the street as early as 1832, when he was merely the 21-year-old crown prince. A romanticist of the first order, he envisioned a boulevard lined by a mix of government buildings, private homes, hotels, and shops that would connect the inner city and the Residenz (the Royal Palace) with Munich's outlying districts on the Isar's right bank. The resulting style combines elements of English and Flemish Gothic Revival with Italian Late Renaissance and the odd bit of eclecticism. Whatever its provenance, however, it would be hard to find another avenue of comparable length anywhere in Europe with such stylistic unity. Undoubtedly, this unity owes much to the brevity of its construction period, which began in 1854 and was more or less over by 1875. (Though there were some later additions, all are reasonably faithful to the original concept.)

In fact, the only blemish on this masterpiece of 19th-century urban planning was a postwar abomination—the six-lane Altstadtring, which intersects the avenue at midpoint and destroyed the original "Roman Forum" arrangement there. Müncheners began howling about this disruption of Maximilianstrasse's architectural unity as soon as the deed was done in 1969, and finally won a small victory by getting the highway reduced to four lanes in 1984.

As soon as the street had begun taking shape in the 1850s it became popular among actors, artists, and authors. Ibsen had an apartment at Maximilianstrasse 32, and was seen every afternoon at the Café Maximilian, meeting place of Munich's literati, where he had a permanently reserved marble table on which a stein of beer and a glass of cognac awaited him as he entered.

From early on it was also a street of playhouses (*Hedda Gabler* had its world premiere at the Residenztheater in January of 1891), and still is: the Kammerspiele, Kleine Komödie am Max II Denkmal, and Theater Kleine Freiheit make it a kind of off-off-Broadway. Museums, too, are part of the scene: the **Museum für Völkerkunde** (Ethnology Museum) at Maximilianstrasse 42 (but closed for renovation until late 1995), and the privately run **Jüdisches Museum** (Jewish Museum), at Maximilianstrasse 36 (open Tuesdays and Wednesdays, 2:00 to 6:00 P.M., Thursdays from 2:00 to 8:00 P.M.).

Ever since the 1857 opening of the luxurious Hotel Vier Jahreszeiten (now the ▶ **Vier Jahreszeiten Kempinski**; see Accommodations, below) at number 17, Maximilianstrasse has also been a boulevard favored by the rich and powerful. Over the nearly 140 years that the "Four Seasons" has been Munich's classiest address, this often renovated and enlarged grand hotel has been a home away from home for hundreds of globe-trotting VIPs and royalty, among them the king of Siam, who arrived in July of 1934 with 1,320 pieces of luggage. Henry Kissinger, who stayed here as secretary of state in 1976, was guarded by a platoon of troopers armed with bazookas pointing out the windows. Mikhail Gorbachev was a guest in 1992.

Maximilianstrasse is a kind of "miracle mile," lined with the top names in fashion, jewelry, leather goods, footwear, and furnishings, all of it further proof that Munich has more money looking to be spent—and places to spend it—than any other city in Germany. It is also the home of more than two dozen commercial galleries, most of them dealing in modern and contemporary art.

The Nationaltheater

Maximilian I, the first Wittelsbach king, was a Francophile who allied himself with Napoleon, who in turn elevated the duchy of Bavaria to a kingdom. Though their partnership resulted in a doubling of Bavaria's size, it also cost Bavaria the lives of 30,000 of its finest men in Napoleon's ill-fated Russian campaign. Shortly before that disaster Maximilian I had visited Paris and been greatly impressed with the Thé- âtre de l'Odéon, and he returned home eager to have a similar drama and opera house in Munich.

As the site for what is today called the Nationaltheater, the home of the **Bayerische Staatsoper** (Bavarian State Opera), he selected a plot adjacent to the royal Residenz (see below) at what is now the beginning of Maximilianstrasse. Work on this huge Neoclassical temple of the performing arts began in 1811 and was completed in 1818. Twice destroyed—by a fire in 1823 and an air raid in 1943—and each time rebuilt exactly as before, it was and still is one of the largest opera houses in Europe. It was here, for example, that Richard Wagner, lavishly subsidized by Ludwig II, staged the world premieres of *Tristan und Isolde, Die Meistersinger von Nürnberg, Das Rheingold,* and *Die Walküre.* Some of the greatest conductors of the 20th century have performed here as well, among them Bruno Walter, Hans Knappertsbusch, Joseph Keilberth, Sir Georg Solti, Karl Böhm, and Wolfgang Sawallisch.

A night at the opera is a must: not just for the performance or a glimpse of the ornate marble foyers and the red-and-gold auditorium with its statuary and Corinthian columns, but also for eyeing the audience, who arrive in anything from white and black tie to lederhosen. The season is year-round except for a six-week break in August and September. Tickets are always hard to obtain, however. For performances several days ahead they can be purchased at the Vorverkauf office, Maximilianstrasse 11 (Tel: 22-13-16); open weekdays, 10:00 A.M. to 1:00 P.M. and 3:30 to 5:30 P.M.; Saturdays from 10:00 A.M. to 12:30 P.M.

The Residenz

Though you wouldn't notice it today, given all its Renaissance, Baroque, Rococo, and Neoclassical additions, the Residenz, Munich's sprawling royal palace just north of Max-Joseph-Platz, was actually begun in 1385 as a Gothic-style castle called the Neuveste (New Fortress). Until then the dukes had resided closer to Marienplatz in the Alte Hof (Old Court), a medieval structure of which little remains.

The reason for the 14th-century exodus from the Alte Hof

was an uprising on Marienplatz that culminated in the beheading of Hans Impler, a cloth merchant who was a friend
of the ducal family and whom angry Müncheners wrongly
accused of fraud. Figuring that the old digs were no longer
safe for nobility, Duke Stephan III started construction of the
Neuveste, a fortified palace located a full third of a mile—
quite a distance in the Middle Ages—from the town's unruly
burghers.

By the mid-16th century the Neuveste was a walled and
moated castle with practically impregnable defense towers,
a ducal chapel, a knights' hall, residential apartments, servants' quarters, an apothecary, an alchemist's laboratory,
stables, and a central keep to which everyone could retreat.
Then various Wittelsbachs began to commission additions to
the castle in Renaissance style—a ballroom tract here, an
Antiquarium to display Greek and Roman sculptures there, a
palace for the crown prince, a mansion for ducal widows—
and they continued adding on in various architectural styles
until the entire complex had become the vast maze that it is
today. One of the last additions was a huge winter garden,
with a menagerie of parrots and peacocks, stuffed lions and
carved marble elephants, Moorish fountains, opera-house
sets, and artificial lake—all of which King Ludwig II had
installed on the roof of one of the buildings in 1865. The
Neuveste itself, meanwhile, dwarfed and surrounded by the
other structures and wings, fell victim to a fire in 1750 (and
Ludwig's gaudy winter garden was destroyed by a bomb
during World War II).

The Wittelsbachs did more than enlarge and embellish
the palace, however; with the exception of Ludwig II, who
preferred his fairy-tale castles in the Alps, all of them resided
in and governed from the Residenz until November 7, 1918.

That was the day when thousands of Müncheners rallied
on Theresienwiese, site of the annual Oktoberfest, to demonstrate for peace and an end to World War I. The main
speaker was Kurt Eisner, leader of the Independent Socialist
Party. The demonstration was just about to culminate in a
silent march through the city when one of Eisner's followers, brandishing a red flag, leaped on the platform and
shouted, "Long live the Revolution!" Within a few hours
Eisner's group had occupied the military and police barracks, the government ministries, and the Bavarian parliament building. There Eisner was proclaimed head of a
workers' and soldiers' soviet and named himself provisional
president and prime minister of the People's Republic of
Bavaria. A few hours later, under cover of darkness, and
without formally abdicating, 73-year-old Ludwig III, Bavaria's

last king, fled the Residenz through a side entrance and headed, by car, into exile at his Berchtesgaden castle.

Ever since that revolution, the Residenz has harbored a potpourri of government offices, scientific institutions, theaters, concert halls, and museums. It was also here that the leaders of the world's seven richest industrial countries, including George Bush, John Major, and Brian Mulroney, held their annual "economic" summit meeting in July 1992. The museums require sturdy legs, comfortable shoes, and a strategy.

The **Residenzmuseum** itself comprises more or less the entire palace. Only portions of it are open at specific times: some sections in the morning, some in the afternoon, still others morning *and* afternoon. There are two tours daily (except Mondays), one in the morning (10:00 A.M. to 12:30 P.M.), the other in the afternoon (12:30 to 4:30 P.M.). Doing them both is a marathon that will take you through more than 120 richly appointed rooms, chambers, and halls spread over a dozen buildings and wings. The morning tour includes the **Antiquarium**, the largest secular Renaissance building north of the Alps, and one that is not only crammed with ancient sculpture but is still used for formal state occasions like the banquet for the 1992 summiteers; the **Porzellankammer** (Porcelain Chamber), which is filled with East Asian and 19th-century European china; and the opulent **Ahnengalerie** (Ancestors' Gallery), a collection of dozens of amusing portraits and Wittelsbach family trees framed by an overwhelming splash of gilded Rococo stuccowork. Among the sights on the afternoon tour are the throne room and the spectacular apartments of Ludwig I and his queen, as well as more than a dozen chambers filled with 18th-century porcelain.

The **Schatzkammer** (Treasury) is a separate museum within the Residenz (open 10:00 A.M. to 4:30 P.M., daily except Mondays). Its ten rooms harbor the dazzling collection of jewelry, gold and silver artifacts, and other bibelots amassed by the Wittelsbachs over a period of a thousand years, including the royal insignia and crown jewels. The standouts in this collection are a miniature golden ciborium made around 890 for the Frankish King Arnulf, an 11th-century gold crucifix, the 11th-century crown of the Holy Roman empress Kunigunde, and a 16th-century reliquary on which a bejeweled Saint George slays a ruby-encrusted dragon.

The **Staatliche Münzsammlung** (State Numismatic Collection), to which the entrance is not from Max-Joseph-Platz but at Residenzstrasse 1, is open daily except Mondays from

10:00 A.M. to 4:30 P.M. The collection, begun by Duke Albrecht V, the father of Wilhelm V and builder of the Antiquarium, contains more than 250,000 coins and medallions dating from Roman times to the present.

The **Altes Residenztheater**, popularly called the Cuvilliés-Theater (open Monday through Saturday, 2:00 to 5:00 P.M.; Sundays, 10:00 A.M. to 5:00 P.M.; entrance by way of the Residenzstrasse 1 portal), is not truly a museum, as it is used regularly for concerts, plays, and chamber opera performances. But don't let a semantic technicality deter you. Designed by François de Cuvilliés in 1750 and opened in 1753, it is the epitome of the floriated, gilded, cupid-rich Rococo style. Seeing it is one thing, but nothing equals sitting in it for an evening performance of, say, Mozart's *Marriage of Figaro*.

The **Staatliche Sammlung Egyptischer Kunst** (State Collection of Egyptian Art) is accessible from the Hofgarten (Palace Garden) side of the Residenz at Hofgartenstrasse 1 (open Tuesday through Friday, 9:00 A.M. to 4:00 P.M., Tuesday evenings from 7:00 to 9:00 P.M.; Saturdays and Sundays from 10:00 A.M. to 5:00 P.M.). It contains a rich yield from the tombs of the pharaohs as well as some gems of Assyrian and Egyptian craftsmanship, covering the spectrum from ship-building to weaving.

OUTSIDE THE ALTSTADTRING

Vexing as the Altstadtring may be, it has the advantage of compartmentalizing the inner city, making it easy to explore. But what lies beyond it in all directions is of no less importance to appreciating Munich.

Ludwigstrasse

Ludwig I's dream of making Munich a world capital and the "new Athens" is expressed in the grand boulevard that bears his name and connects the Innenstadt with the former suburb of Schwabing to the north. Straight as a ruler, exactly one kilometer long, and grandiosely wide, it begins with the Feldherrnhalle on Odeonsplatz, at the northwestern corner of the Residenz, and culminates in the triumphal arch of the Siegestor. Construction began in 1817 under the supervision of Ludwig I's then-favorite architect, Leo von Klenze, and was completed by Klenze's rival and successor, Friedrich von Gärtner, in 1850.

When Ludwig and Klenze first started planning the boulevard in 1816 they were of one mind. Both were Greco-Roman buffs and envisioned an avenue in Neoclassical style. By the late 1820s and early 1830s, however, Ludwig had become enamored of the Neo-Romanesque, Neo-Renaissance, and Italianate fashions sweeping Europe—styles Klenze abhorred. As a result, Ludwig turned more and more to Gärtner, who in turn imparted the cold and haunting look that the upper end of Ludwigstrasse has to this day.

The most obvious monument between the Residenz and the Theatinerkirche, right where Residenzstrasse and Theatinerstrasse merge to become Odeonsplatz, is the **Feldherrnhalle** (Hall of the Field Marshals). Begun in 1841, the Feldherrnhalle was completed in 1844.

The bronze field marshals who stand in it are Count Johannes von Tilly, the bloodthirsty but luckless Bavarian hero of the Thirty Years' War, and Karl Philipp von Wrede, the general who led the Bavarian corps that aided Napoleon's victory at Wagram in 1809 and later accompanied Bonaparte's Grande Armée into Russia but who, just before the 1813 "Battle of the Nations" at Leipzig, turned against Napoleon and joined the allies. The bronze memorial between and behind the two is supposed to honor the Bavarian army for its role—actually small—during the Franco-Prussian War of 1870–71.

The Feldherrnhalle was also where Hitler's "Beerhall Putsch," his first grab for power, ended in a bloodbath on November 9, 1923. The previous evening he and his armed followers had attempted, and failed, to topple the Bavarian government by taking hostage key officials who were attending a political rally at the Bürgerbräukeller, a beer hall in Haidhausen on the Isar's east bank. Shortly before noon the next day, Hitler and his closest aides led their ragtag army of 3,000 storm troopers on a demonstration march through the Innenstadt. When they reached the Feldherrnhalle and Odeonsplatz they were stopped by a company of state police. After a wild, one-minute gunfight, 14 Nazis and four policemen lay dead or dying on the square, and scores of others were critically wounded. Hitler was subsequently imprisoned at Landsberg fortress, where he wrote his blueprint for world conquest, *Mein Kampf.*

During the 12 years of the Third Reich the Nazis annually reenacted the march, and the Feldherrnhalle became a temple to Nazi martyrdom. A bronze plaque on its Residenzstrasse side, guarded round the clock by two black-uniformed SS men, commemorated the putsch, and everyone who passed by had to stop and salute. Those Müncheners who

opposed the Führer would make a detour behind the Feldherrnhalle by dashing from Residenzstrasse to Theatinerstrasse via narrow little Viscardigasse, which soon became
known as Drückebergergasse—"Bugout Alley."

One of Munich's newest and most unusual museums, the
Museum für Erotische Kunst, has opened right on Odeonsplatz. It is a collection of erotic art—paintings, prints, books,
sculptures, and bric-a-brac—from Asia, Europe, Africa, and
Polynesia covering nearly a millennium of the human species' preoccupation with sex. Manfred Schilling, the owner
of this offbeat lode, is a former high school teacher who now
serves as his own museum director and curator. It's at
Odeonsplatz 8, open daily except Mondays, 11:00 A.M. to
7:00 P.M.

The vicissitudes of history are also embodied in the monument at Ludwigstrasse's northern end, the **Siegestor** (Victory
Gate). A triumphal arch, it was begun in 1843 to honor the
Bavarian army's role during the "Wars of Liberation" against
Napoleon. Badly damaged during World War II but rebuilt,
the inscription on it now reads: *Dem Sieg geweiht, im Krieg
zerstört, zum Frieden mahnend*—"Dedicated to victory, destroyed in war, an admonishment to peace."

Ludwig's avenue of government, learning, and banking is
still evident between the two monuments. Since Bavaria no
longer has its own army, the former war ministry building at
Ludwigstrasse 14 is now the Bavarian state archives. The ministry of agriculture occupies the building at number 2, and on
Odeonsplatz are the ministries of interior (number 3) and
finance (number 4). Gärtner's **Bayerische Staatsbibliothek**
(Bavarian State Library), one of the world's largest with 5.5
million volumes, is at number 16. The four seated figures on
the library's steps are Aristotle, Hippocrates, Homer, and
Thucydides. The **Ludwigskirche** (Church of St. Louis), at
number 20, an eclectic Romantic-Christian-Italian–style building that was Gärtner's first effort on the boulevard, was begun
in 1829 and completed in 1844. His contributions to **Munich
Universität**, formally called Ludwig-Maximilian-Universität,
Germany's largest with 65,000 students, flank both sides of the
street. The forumlike circle between them is now called
Geschwister-Scholl-Platz, in honor of Hans and Sophie
Scholl, the brother and sister who, as students in 1943,
launched the anti-Nazi resistance group called the "White
Rose." (They were later executed by the Nazis at Munich's
Stadelheim prison.) Imbedded in the stones at the university
entrance are ceramic replicas of the leaflets and calls to
resistance the Scholls and their collaborators distributed clan-
destinely all over Germany.

Schwabing

Schwabing once was a nondescript village northwest of Munich's great public park, the Englischer Garten. After Ludwig I built Ludwigstrasse it became an integrated district of Munich. Today it comprises, more or less, the entire area west of the Englischer Garten to Luisenstrasse, on which the Lenbachhaus is located, and from just beyond Odeonsplatz and Briennerstrasse in the south to the area in the north where Munich begins to fray into industrial sites and high-rise residential blocks. Five major museums are located in Schwabing (see Königsplatz and the Museums, below).

But to describe Schwabing geographically misses the point. It is not so much a neighborhood as a state of mind—*the* state of mind, in fact, that made Munich the intellectual and cultural center of Germany from the time Wagner arrived in 1867, at Ludwig II's invitation, until 1919, when the title passed, for the 14 years of the Weimar Republic, to Berlin. Schwabing was to Munich what the Latin Quarter is to Paris or Greenwich Village once was to New York City, an enclave of artists, musicians, writers, thinkers, and revolutionaries.

Not only was (and is) Schwabing the site of Ludwig-Maximilian University as well as Munich's Technical University and the Academy of Art, it was also inexpensive. As a result, it attracted struggling students as well as impecunious poets, writers, musicians, artists, intellectuals, and low-budget publishers. It was the perfect soil for a counterculture that, given the unique Bavarian climate, rejected all things Prussian, including the new Wilhelminian era with its adoration of powerful captains of industry, swaggering militarists, and heraldic decor.

In Schwabing were found not only a mixture of scholarliness and skepticism, thanks to the universities and academies, but also the traditional Munich *Gemütlichkeit* (friendliness) of beer cellars, coffeehouses, and taverns. To list those who at one time or another lived and worked here is tantamount to name-dropping: three chemistry and physics Nobel laureates, Adolph von Baeyer, Walter Wien, and Werner Heisenberg; writers, poets, and dramatists such as Bertolt Brecht, Oskar Maria Graf, Stefan George, Ibsen, Thomas and Heinrich Mann, Rainer Maria Rilke, and Frank Wedekind; all the Munich Secession and Blue Rider artists; and historians and philosophers such as Oswald Spengler, who wrote and published his *Decline of the West* during the 25 years he lived in the district.

Schwabing bubbled with the enthusiasm of young talent and crackled with the tension of new ideas. Lenin, who lived here for two years at various addresses—Kaiserstrasse 53,

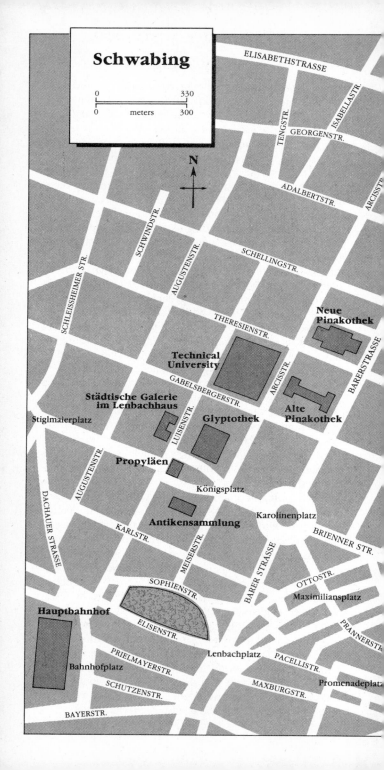

Schwabing

```
0                          330
|----|----|----|----|----|
0          meters          300
```

N

ELISABETHSTRASSE

TENGSTR.

GEORGENSTR.

ISABELLASTR.

ADALBERTSTR.

ARCISSTR.

SCHWINDSTR.

AUGUSTENSTR.

SCHELLINGSTR.

SCHLEISSHEIMER STR.

THERESIENSTR.

Neue Pinakothek

BARERSTRASSE

Technical University

GABELSBERGERSTR.

ARCISSTR.

Städtische Galerie im Lenbachhaus

Stiglmaierplatz

LUISENSTR.

Glyptothek

Alte Pinakothek

Propyläen

Königsplatz

Karolinenplatz

Antikensammlung

BRIENNER STR.

AUGUSTENSTR.

KARLSTR.

MEISERSTR.

BARER STRASSE

DACHAUER STRASSE

SOPHIENSTR.

OTTOSTR.

Maximiliansplatz

Hauptbahnhof

ELISENSTR.

PRANNERSTR

PRIELMAYERSTR.

Lenbachplatz

PACELLISTR.

Bahnhofplatz

SCHUTZENSTR.

MAXBURGSTR.

Promenadeplatz

BAYERSTR.

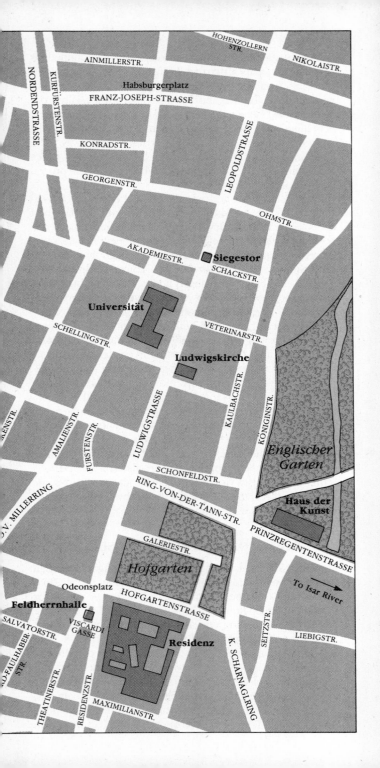

Schleissheimerstrasse 106, Siegfriedstrasse 14—founded his revolutionary paper *Iskra* while living in Schwabing. Hitler lived in Schwabing only briefly before World War I, but was an habitué of the neighborhood afterward, especially from 1925 to 1931, when the Nazi party had its headquarters at Schellingstrasse 50. (An eagle with its head and swastika chiseled away remains carved over the entranceway.) The **Schelling Salon**, a popular café with billiard and card tables at Schellingstrasse 56, was one of his haunts until the proprietor cut off his credit.

Today old-timers and nostalgic Müncheners say Schwabing isn't what it used to be. They bemoan the fast-food spots, pizzerias, pseudo-ethnic restaurants, heavy-metal discos, *schicki-micki* (jet-set) cafés, beautiful-people bars, overpriced boutiques, and usurious interior design shops. Schwabing, they say, has been *vermarktet*—commercialized.

Yes, Schwabing has changed and is changing, but not as fast as some of the critics would have you believe. Leopoldstrasse (the northern continuation of Ludwigstrasse after the Siegestor), its main boulevard, continues to shine as Munich's liveliest avenue, lined with sidewalk cafés, terrace restaurants, and, on balmy summer evenings, the stalls of artisans hawking their wares. Since neither the two universities nor the art academy have moved, it is more a student quarter than ever before. Schellingstrasse and Amalienstrasse are still lined with book shops. Artists continue to opt for studios in Schwabing, and for writers and publishers a Schwabing address continues to look good on business cards. Traditional hangouts like **Alter Simpl**, Türkenstrasse 57, or **Atzinger**, Schellingstrasse 9, are also still around.

In other words, a visit to Munich without soaking up some daytime and nighttime atmosphere in Schwabing is missing what the city was and is about.

Königsplatz and the Museums

Munich's Königsplatz (King's Plaza), a mile-long walk straight down Briennerstrasse northwest from Odeonsplatz into Schwabing, is the finest example of Leo von Klenze's talent for translating Greco-Roman dreams into reality.

The idea of creating a Bavarian Acropolis on what in those days was a virtual wasteland was germinated in 1808. Construction began in 1816 with the laying of the cornerstone for the templelike Glyptothek, which was intended to house the collection of Greek and Roman sculpture that Ludwig I was amassing. That marble building, with its Ionic columns, was completed in 1830, and was merely the beginning. Across from it Ludwig wanted an exhibition hall in Roman style with Corinthian columns, which now houses the Staatliche Antikensammlung (State Collection of Antiquities). Then Klenze proposed closing off the area at its far end with a huge Propylaeum. In all, work on the complex went on for more than 45 years. When it was completed, Ludwig I had one more brilliant thought: With the exception of a cobblestone main street through the plaza, the rest of the area would remain covered with grass in order to create an urban version of the Elysian Fields.

So it was until 1934, when Hitler decided that Königsplatz was an ideal site for Nazi rallies. Out went the grass and in came slabs of stone, which gave the jackboots of marching storm troopers just the right resonance. One might have expected Müncheners to get rid of those stones as soon as they were rid of Hitler. But in the postwar years Königsplatz was turned into Munich's largest parking lot. Given that no other German city has so many cars, resistance to relinquishing so convenient an area was great. Only in 1988 did traditionalists on the city council triumph, with the happy result that Königsplatz, replete with replicas of 19th-century streetlamps, now looks almost as grassy as it did in the days of Ludwig I and Klenze.

It is unlikely, however, that two other nearby architectural relics of the Third Reich will ever disappear: Albert Speer's massively grim Führerbauten, the headquarters and administrative buildings of the Nazi party. While Speer, Hitler's architect and minister of armaments, built them to last the 1,000 years that the Führer envisioned for his new Reich, they now serve a useful, peaceful, and democratic purpose: The one on Arcisstrasse is the state music conservatory; its horrid twin on Meiserstrasse houses various institutes of the academy of art and departments of the ministry of culture.

Königsplatz (the foot-weary will be happy to know there's a glossy U-Bahn station of the U-2 line right underneath it) is more than just a remarkable architectural ensemble. It is also the gateway to Munich's most rewarding museum area.

The **Glyptothek** (open Tuesdays and Wednesdays, and Friday through Sunday, 10:00 A.M. to 4:30 P.M.; Thursdays, noon to 8:30 P.M.) contains the Greek and Roman sculpture that Ludwig I collected on his many buying sprees, plus much more that has been added since.

The **Antikensammlung**, across the square at Königsplatz 1 (open Tuesdays and Thursday through Sunday, 10:00 A.M. to 4:30 P.M.; Wednesdays, noon to 8:30 P.M.), contains a wonderful collection of classical craftsmanship: Greek vases and pottery; Greek, Celtic, Etruscan, and Roman jewelry; glass, miniature sculptures, and applied art.

From Königsplatz a walk of two blocks up Arcisstrasse will take you to the Alte and Neue Pinakotheken.

The **Alte Pinakothek** (Old Picture Gallery), Barerstrasse 27 (open Tuesday through Sunday, 9:15 A.M. to 4:30 P.M.; Tuesdays and Thursdays, 7:00 to 9:00 P.M.), was designed by Klenze and opened in 1836. In addition to later purchases, donations, and permanent loans, it houses the entire collection of paintings amassed by various branches of the Wittelsbach family, starting with Duke Wilhelm IV, who began to collect in 1530.

Owing to the building's comparatively small size, only a fraction of the collection can be shown at any one time. Still, on display are hundreds of paintings by the likes of Rubens, Brueghel, van Dyck, Rembrandt, Dürer, Tintoretto, and Titian. While the Alte Pinakothek's reputation is based to a considerable extent on its early German masters, it is also a stunning repository of Flemish, Dutch, Italian, Spanish, and French painting. Moreover, if there was ever a museum where you can be sure of authenticity, this is it. Virtually every painting has an unbroken pedigree of ownership— the Wittelsbachs. The Alte Pinakothek is closed for total renovation until Easter 1994, and some 200 works will be rehung in the Neue Pinakothek.

The **Neue Pinakothek** (New Picture Gallery), directly across the street at Barerstrasse 29 (open Tuesday through Sunday, 9:15 A.M. to 4:30 P.M.; Tuesday evenings, 7:00 to 9:00 P.M.) is so named because of what Ludwig I intended it to be: a gallery of "new" painting from his own era, the 19th century. The building, designed by Gärtner, was so badly damaged during World War II that it was razed in 1949. The collection (which begins with Goya and Jacques-Louis David) was placed in storage and shown in part elsewhere around town while a debate raged for decades over whether to build another Neue Pinakothek. The debate was finally settled in 1975 when ground was broken on the site of the old Neue Pinakothek and work began on the present building.

The collection includes works by major French Impressionists, including Manet's *Breakfast in the Studio,* Monet's *The Bridge,* and Degas's *Laundry Girl,* as well as canvases by Daumier, Courbet, van Gogh, Goya, and Turner, and sculptures by Maillol and Rodin. The main body of the collection, however, is German, in particular work by Bavarian and Munich artists, including Arnold Böcklin and Franz von Lenbach, whose luxurious villa (site of the next museum) is just three blocks away, virtually adjacent to Königsplatz.

The **Städtische Galerie im Lenbachhaus** (Municipal Gallery in the Lenbach House), Luisenstrasse 33 (open Tuesday through Saturday, 10:00 A.M. to 6:00 P.M., Thursdays until 8:00

P.M.), is what its name implies: a city-owned museum and collection. (All the other collections are owned and maintained by the Free State of Bavaria, legal heir to the Wittelsbach riches.) The sprawling Italian Renaissance–style villa was built by Franz von Lenbach in the late 1880s when he was at the height of his fame as the portrait painter of everybody who was anybody in imperial Germany, and at the zenith of his power as the virtual dictator of art in Munich. In effect, the "Lenbach Circle" determined not only what was painted but how it was painted until the "Munich Secession," led by another "painter-prince," Franz von Stuck, the self-anointed prophet of *Jugendstil,* the Austro-German form of Art Nouveau, came along. The city of Munich acquired the Lenbach mansion and private collection in 1929, 25 years after his death, and turned it into a museum.

The collection as a whole covers Munich and other German art from the 15th century to the present. Its high point is the huge lode of works by Wassily Kandinsky, Paul Klee, Franz Marc, August Macke, Alexej Jawlensky, Marianne von Werefkin, Alfred Kubin, and Gabriele Münter. Nearly all of these works were donated by Münter, Kandinsky's mistress and collaborator for most of the 20 years (1894–1914) that he lived and worked in Munich and the nearby mountain town of Murnau (see the Southern Bavaria chapter). In a striking departure from standard museum policy, the rooms in which they are shown were painted in bright reds, yellows, and blues in 1992.

Munich was where Kandinsky began painting in the abstract, and where in 1910 he, Münter, Marc, Jawlensky, Werefkin, Klee, and Kubin founded the Neue Künstlervereinigung (New Artists' Association), which soon broke with genre painting and Jugendstil, and launched the almanac *Der Blaue Reiter* (The Blue Rider), heralding an entirely new international art movement and style. In 1957, Gabriele Münter donated 90 Kandinsky oils, 300 of his watercolors and drawings, 29 sketchbooks, and numerous other works of the Blaue Reiter circle, including her own, to the Lenbachhaus.

For an even more vivid and concrete view of modern art—and what the Nazis thought of it—visit the Haus der Kunst on Prinzregentenstrasse, at the southwestern tip of the Englischer Garten.

The Englischer Garten

The Englischer Garten, east of Ludwigstrasse and north of Prinzregentenstrasse, is not only the oldest—200 years—and largest—922 acres—public park in the world, it is also one of the oddest. The brainchild of an American, it was started in 1789, the year of the French Revolution, and is a natural garden, deliberately asymmetrical and unmanicured in the English style. It is dotted with a grab bag of seemingly displaced structures, among them a Chinese pagoda, a Japanese teahouse, a Greek temple, Roman-style statuary, and a Neoclassical château, and on any balmy summer day it is populated with hundreds of sunbathing nudists.

From Prinzregentenstrasse the park runs for more than three miles along the west bank of the Isar to the northern edges of the city. In places it is more than a mile wide—a mosaic of lawns, densely wooded glens, lakes, ponds, rippling brooks, waterfalls, recreational facilities, beer gardens, restaurants, and 45 miles of bridle paths, walkways, and trails. Its praises have been sung by some of Germany's greatest literary figures, from Bettina von Arnim to Arnold Zweig, and it even gave birth to a school of art—early-19th-century German Romantic landscape painting.

Credit for this vast green repose goes to Benjamin Thompson (1753–1814), commemorated by a stone monument just off Prinzregentenstrasse between the Haus der Kunst and the Nationalmuseum. Franklin D. Roosevelt once put Thompson on a par with Benjamin Franklin and Thomas Jefferson as "the three greatest intellects America ever brought forth."

The Massachusetts-born Thompson was an international adventurer who ultimately became Bavaria's minister of war and police under the patronage of Elector Karl Theodore, uncle of the future king, Maximilian I. Thompson proposed the idea of the Englischer Garden to Karl Theodor shortly after the storming of the Bastille in Paris, arguing that a people free to stroll, relax, and enjoy themselves in a public park would be disinclined to storm their monarch's palace. Thompson personally selected the site, a vast marshland along the Isar; commanded the regiments of soldiers who drained and turned it into a garden; drew the plans; hired the landscape architect who implemented them; and provided most of the ideas for its bridges, monuments, and amusement facilities.

The transformation was close to miraculous. Thousands of nearly full-grown trees were planted; coach roads, bridle paths, and footpaths were laid out; and 11 charming stone and wrought-iron bridges were built across brooks. There was a little wooden Apollo temple, precursor to today's Monopteros. A veterinary school in the park, now an institute of Munich University, opened its doors to 30 students and two professors.

The high point of Thompson's work in the Englischer

Garten was the Chinesischer Turm, a Chinese pagoda modeled on a similar one in London's Kew Gardens. Two centuries later the **Chinesischer Turm** is still the high point of a visit to the park, all the more so because it is surrounded by one of Munich's largest and most popular beer gardens, with seating for 7,000. Today's tower is an exact replica of the original pagoda, which burned to the ground in a World War II bombing raid.

Prinzregentenstrasse

Prinzregentenstrasse (Prince Regent Street), at the southern end of the Englischer Garten, is the newest of Munich's grand avenues. Begun in 1891 and completed in 1907, it was named for Luitpold, who ruled Bavaria as prince regent from 1886 to 1912, between the reigns of his nephew, Ludwig II, and his son, Ludwig III. A wide tree-shaded boulevard that runs east for nearly one and a half miles from the edge of the Hofgarten to the Bogenhausen district, it is one of the city's many examples of Belle Epoque and Jugendstil architecture.

Its starting point is the Neoclassical **Prinz Carl Palais**, which since 1807 has served variously as the home of Wittelsbach scions, the Austrian embassy, a Third Reich guest house, and, since 1972, as the official seat of Bavaria's prime minister.

Diagonally across from it is the **Haus der Kunst**. This colonnaded gray stone building at the southern end of the Englischer Garten is the first of various architectural monstrosities Hitler bequeathed to Munich. Designed by Paul Ludwig Troost in what was then called Germanic Tectonic (now known as Third Reich bombastic) style, it opened on July 18, 1937, as the Haus der Deutschen Kunst (House of German Art)—a pantheon for the propagandizing kitsch the Nazis endorsed. That inaugural show coincided with one in the nearby Hofgarten gallery called *Entartete Kunst* (Degenerate Art): an exhibition of 600 masterworks of Expressionism, Cubism, Abstractionism, and Surrealism (of the thousands that had just been confiscated from museums and private collections all over Germany) mounted with the object of deriding them.

Nowadays the west wing of the Haus der Kunst is the temporary home of the **Staatsgalerie Moderner Kunst** (State Gallery of Modern Art), which shows paintings and sculptures by 20th-century artists the Nazis hounded or banned, including Max Beckmann, Max Ernst, Paul Klee, and Oskar Schlemmer. A new museum of modern and contemporary art is planned on a site near the two Pinakotheken, with completion expected around the year 2000. The building also houses the city's hottest, most fashionable discothèque, **P-1**, located in the basement of the east wing, and open until 4:00 A.M. daily except Mondays.

The **Bayerisches Nationalmuseum**, Prinzregentenstrasse 3 (open Tuesday through Sunday, 9:30 A.M. to 5:00 P.M.), is an architectural Disneyland: The east wing is Romanesque, the west wing Rococo, the façade Renaissance, the central tower Baroque—and all of that "neo." Müncheners call it "Bavaria's Attic," and you're never sure whether they mean it benignly or scornfully. But what an attic! The vast collection of 5th- through 19th-century painting, sculpture, wood carving, stained glass, porcelain, ceramics, tapestries, jewelry, goldsmithing, furniture, armor, ecclesiastical art, and folk handicrafts covers 140,000 square feet of exhibit space spread over three floors. Among its highlights are the chamber with medieval ivory carvings, the gallery with works by Erasmus Grasser, the room with Tilman Riemenschneider wood sculptures, and the section of porcelain figures designed by Franz Anton Bustelli. A separate wing houses the **Neue Sammlung** (New Collection), a museum of applied art and design. In fact, with more than 36,000 objects, it is the largest and most comprehensive design collection in the world. But for lack of space to show them, the Neue Sammlung is open only for special, rotating exhibitions. It will move, along with the Staatsgalerie Moderner Kunst, to the aforementioned new museum of modern art when that building is completed.

The **Schackgalerie**, Prinzregentenstrasse 9 (open daily except Tuesdays, 9:15 A.M. to 4:30 P.M.), located in what used to be the Prussian embassy, is a small but well-appointed gallery of 19th-century German Romantic and genre painting.

If your feet haven't given out at this point, continue east across the Isar by way of the Prinzregentenbrücke, around the Friedensengel (Angel of Peace) monument, to the silk-stocking and carriage-trade section of Prinzregentenstrasse in **Bogenhausen**.

The four reclining figures on the bridge, a gift to Luitpold on his 70th birthday in 1891, represent the tribal areas of the Wittelsbach realm when it stretched across southern Germany from the Rhine to Bohemia. The Angel of Peace ensemble, with its gilded figure of Winged Victory atop a Corinthian column, fountain, graceful steps, terrace, and loggias where lovers tryst on balmy evenings, is a contradiction in terms: Its cornerstone was laid in 1896 to mark the

25th anniversary of Germany's triumph in the Franco-Prussian War, and its bas-relief portraits of various generals, the three kaisers, Otto von Bismarck, and, naturally, Luitpold, do little to convey a message of peace. But as a Munich landmark and an example of iconographic 19th-century architecture, it's a joy.

The **Villa Stuck**, Prinzregentenstrasse 60 (open daily except Mondays, 10:00 A.M. to 5:00 P.M., Thursday evenings until 9:00), is proof that artistic rebellion pays. Franz von Stuck, the leader of the Munich Secession, was soon so successful that he could afford to build a house with a studio every bit as grand as Franz von Lenbach's, *and* on a hill above the Isar from where he could look down on his rival. This Roman-style villa, with its exterior motifs borrowed from antiquity and its interior blend of Classical, Baroque, and Pre-Raphaelite decor, is a perfect example of Jugendstil. The Stuck villa is also used for rotating exhibitions of Jugendstil, Classical Modern, and contemporary art. The **Tai Tung** in the courtyard is one of Munich's five dozen Chinese restaurants.

You will find a symbol of what late-20th-century Munich is about—money and conspicuous consumption—at Prinzregentenstrasse 73, the home of **Käfer's**, a resplendent fine-food emporium boasting more than 15,000 of the best and most expensive comestibles, as well as its own restaurant. The ornate Art Nouveau building, brightly illuminated at night, is one of the avenue's architectural gems.

Another gem is the **Prinzregententheater**, Prinzregentenstrasse 82. A virtual copy of the Wagner Festival theater in Bayreuth, it was built for festival purposes in 1901 despite strong protests by the composer's widow, Cosima, who was still angry at Munich for having snubbed her Richard following their scandalous liaison. Because the Nationaltheater on Maximilianstrasse was a bombed-out ruin at the end of World War II, the Bavarian State Opera used the undamaged Prinzregententheater until 1963. After the reopening of the Staatsoper it was shut and became a warehouse for stage sets. In 1988, more splendid than ever, it reopened as a repertory drama theater and concert hall. The restoration uncovered the dazzling Art Nouveau interior frescoes and stucco reliefs that had been painted over and covered with panels on Hitler's orders in the 1930s because they depicted scenes of bacchanalian debauchery. During the Nationaltheater's stage renovation it will be used for opera performances again.

Just as the Prinzregentenstrasse starts with a Hitler legacy, so in a sense it ends with one, for his erstwhile home stands where the avenue intersects with Grillparzerstrasse and widens and changes its name to Prinzregentenplatz. In 1929, flush with royalties from *Mein Kampf,* Hitler rented a vast nine-room apartment on the third floor of the gray Jugendstil building at Prinzregentenplatz 16, retaining it as his legal residence until he committed suicide in his Berlin bunker on April 30, 1945. There he also lived in incestuous sin with his half-niece, Geli Raubal. On September 18, 1931, they had a lovers' quarrel that culminated in a shouting match—Geli standing on the third-floor corner balcony screeching down at Hitler, who was getting into an open-roof car on the street. After he drove off, she went to her room—so the official version goes—and shot herself. But according to rumors that still percolate, she may have been murdered by his henchmen. The apartment house today is an office building.

From Prinzregentenplatz a convenient subway connection on the U-4 line provides a short ride back to Odeonsplatz or Haidhausen's Max-Weber-Platz station; from both it is a 15-minute walk to the Museumsinsel.

Museumsinsel and Haidhausen

The Museumsinsel (Museum Island) is the site of the **Deutsches Museum** (open daily, 9:00 A.M. to 5:00 P.M.), the world's largest, most unusual museum of science and technology and, with some two million visitors annually, one of the most popular. It was founded in 1906 by Oskar von Miller, a civil engineer and businessman who built the world's first long-distance high-voltage line.

Miller, born in Munich in 1855, was by avocation a kind of collecting Boswell to the towering figures of technical ingenuity and mechanical innovation. He created this museum to honor the great scientists and inventors by displaying originals, replicas, and models of their achievements. It is a huge institution, with some 80,000 objects plus a library, also open daily, containing nearly a million volumes on science and technology, manuscripts, letters and diaries by great inventors, and original sketches, drawings, and blueprints. The Deutsches Museum owns such treasures as an original 1895 Otto Lilienthal glider, the monoplane with which Bleriot crossed the English Channel in 1905, an 1839 camera of Louis Daguerre, a glass harmonica designed by Benjamin Franklin, and the laboratory table on which Otto Hahn and Lise Meitner split the uranium atom in 1938.

But Miller's aim was also to familiarize as many people as possible with the laws and phenomena of science, the methods and tools of technology, their historical development, and their practical uses. He built a museum that would unravel the secrets of science and technology for lay visitors, especially the young, by means of simple explanations, working models, and demonstrations. Wherever you go in the Deutsches Museum, things snap, crackle, and pop. An old James Watt steam engine still works. A turn of the crank would start the world's first motorcar, built by Carl Benz. An early Wright airplane remains flyable. A scaled-down model of the Montgolfier brothers' 1784 hot-air balloon takes off from its pad. A 1.1-million-volt generator sends lightning bolts into a group of doll-size houses to show the benefits of proper grounding. It is a museum that comes alive at the touch of a button, and there are hundreds of buttons that visitors are encouraged to press.

Miller wanted people to go through his museum the way they go "to the sideshows at the Oktoberfest." While just as much fun, and far more enlightening, it could take you even longer. There are more than 13 miles of exhibit rooms and halls spread over five floors and several wings. It would take three to four hours just to walk through, without stopping to look at anything.

Haidhausen, the rapidly gentrifying neighborhood that begins on the hill of the Isar's east bank just beyond the Deutsches Museum, is touted as the "new Schwabing." That is premature, but it is worth a visit nonetheless for two things: the **Gasteig Philharmonie** (Philharmonic Hall) and the **Kulturzentrum** (Cultural Center), just a block from the Deutsches Museum, and the so-called *Franzosenviertel* (French Quarter), a planned neighborhood of the 1870s to 1890s.

The fortresslike Gasteig complex, incorporating the Philharmonie, a smaller concert hall, the public library, and the Volkshochschule, an adult-education facility, was completed in 1986. While Müncheners are gradually getting accustomed to the architecture, musicians remain up in arms over the hall's fickle acoustics—so fickle, in fact, that after conducting the Munich Philharmonic in it for the first time the late Leonard Bernstein had only one comment: "Burn it!"

Haidhausen's **Franzosenviertel** is interesting not only for all the boutiques, fancy restaurants, art galleries, and artists' studios (such as the **Künstlerwerkstatt**, Lothringer-Strasse 13, a former factory with studios and exhibition spaces, open daily from 1:00 to 7:00 P.M.), but also for the French Neo-Baroque façades of the rows of 19th-century apartment houses and the names of its streets—Orléans, Metz, Bordeaux, Paris, and others—that serve as reminders of the victory over France in 1871, when construction of the district began.

THE OUTSKIRTS
Theresienwiese

Theresienwiese (Theresa's Meadow), west of the Innenstadt, easily reached by taking the U-4 or U-5 subway line to the stop of the same name, is the site of the annual Oktoberfest, first staged in 1810 as part of the celebration for Ludwig I's wedding to Princess Thérèse. A meadow is all it is except during Oktoberfest time. A different matter is the Neo-Greek temple with the huge statue of Bavaria on the hill, called Theresienhöhe, overlooking the field—two more of Ludwig I's legacies.

The building, designed by Leo von Klenze, is the **Ruhmeshalle** (Hall of Fame), and it contains the busts of famous Bavarians. **Bavaria** is a lady weighing 171,600 pounds and standing 60 feet tall. She is made of cast bronze, and inside her head, to which some 50,000 people climb annually for a good view of Munich, there is room for 30 adults. To build her was a herculean artistic and technological achievement. Ludwig commissioned the monument in 1833 and chose Klenze, who did the initial sketches of a majestic woman with helmet, lance, and shield looking remarkably like Athena. Details for creating the figure were left to Ludwig von Schwanthaler, then Munich's most prominent sculptor, who ultimately came up with something quite different: a very Germanic woman in a shirtlike garment, partly covered by a bearskin, a wreath of oak leaves in her left hand, a short sword in the right, and the Lion of Bavaria at her feet. It was a far cry from Greece, but King Ludwig nonetheless gave his approval.

Nymphenburg

Schloss Nymphenburg, the "summer palace" in the west end of Munich (open daily except Mondays, 9:00 A.M. to 12:30 P.M. and 1:30 to 4:00 P.M.), reachable by tramway number 12, is how a royal palace should look. Its origins take you back to Duke Ferdinand Maria and his flamboyant Italian wife, Princess Henrietta Adelaide of Savoy on the occasion of the birth of their son Max Emmanuel in 1662. Ferdinand Maria ordered Nymphenburg as a little present for Henrietta Adelaide. When Henrietta Adelaide died, Ferdinand Maria lost interest in the château, but Max Emmanuel expanded it into a real summer palace in the early 18th century, adding courtiers' buildings and pavilions in its expansive park. His son and grandson contributed even more. By 1760 it was one of the largest and loveliest Baroque-Rococo palace complexes in Europe. It still is, and to see the parts open to the public (Wittelsbach duke Albrecht von Bayern, titular head of the royal family, still resides in one wing) takes the better part of a day.

High points are the lavishly furnished and ornately decorated representational rooms and apartments in the main building; the **Marstall** (Stable) **Museum**, with its grand collection of richly carved and gilded royal coaches, carriages, sleighs, and silver equestrian equipment; the **Badenburg**, built as a little "bathing château" for Max Emmanuel; the **Pagodenburg**, designed for him as a "pleasure palace"; the **Magdalenenklause**, Max Emmanuel's "hermitage" in the form of an artificial medieval castle ruin; and the enchanting **Amalienburg**, designed by Cuvilliés as a hunting château for Elector Karl Albrecht's wife, Maria Amalia. The Badenburg, Pagodenburg, Magdalenenklause, and Amalienburg are all located in the 500-acre park, where you will also encounter fountains, cascades, artificial lakes, little temples, flower gardens, and numerous sculptures of Greek gods, goddesses, and mythological figures.

During the lunch break, when the palaces and museum are closed, you may want to retire to the nearby **Königlicher Hirschgarten** (Royal Deer Park), Munich's largest beer garden (seating for 10,000).

Like many other German and European rulers, the Wittelsbachs also had their own china and porcelain manufactory here at Nymphenburg. The workshop was in one of the Rondel buildings, the semicircle that faces the front of the palace. **Nymphenburger Porzellanmanufaktur**, now owned by the Free State of Bavaria, is still very much in business, making not only modern and traditional chinaware but also copies of Bustelli porcelain figurines. There is a sales and showroom in the same 18th-century building that housed the original factory.

Olympiapark

Olympiapark (final stop for the U-2 and U-3 subway lines northwest of the Innenstadt), site of the 1972 Olympic Games, is one of Munich's splashiest examples of modern architecture. It is also of interest to modern history buffs. Called the Oberwiesenfeld until construction started for the stadium and other sports facilities, this was, before 1939, Munich's airfield, and where Neville Chamberlain arrived to sign the Munich Accord with Hitler, sealing the fate of Czechoslovakia and setting the stage for World War II. The 200-foot-high mountain in the park is artificial, constructed of the rubble of Munich buildings bombed during World War II.

The things to see here are the Olympiastadion (Olympic Stadium), the Schwimmhalle (Swim Hall), and the Olympiahalle (Olympic Hall), all accommodated under the 82,000 square yards of a "tent" roof made of mesh steel netting covered with translucent acrylic panels.

Not part of the park is the spectacular "four-cylinder" 20-story headquarters building of Bavarian Motor Works, with the adjacent silvery-gray **BMW Museum**, which looks like a flying saucer. BMW, which started as a manufacturer of aircraft engines and planes long before it got into the motorcycle and automobile business, has been at this location since 1916. The museum is a retrospective of aero-engine and motor vehicle manufacturing, with plenty of exhibits and multilingual video presentations.

The 963-foot **Fernsehturm** (Television Tower) is not only Munich's tallest structure, but also, thanks to its observation platforms and rotating restaurant, the highest point from which to get a view of the entire city and the Alps beyond. From its platforms on a clear day you can see the Italian Dolomites and Switzerland's Bernese Oberland.

MUNICH'S ENVIRONS
Dachau

Dachau, only nine S-Bahn stops northwest of Marienplatz on the S-2 line, is not only a separate city of 35,000 people but also considerably older than Munich itself. It was first mentioned in documents in 805. A branch of the Wittelsbach family built a fortified castle here in the 11th century, which fell into disuse a century later. In 1546 Duke Wilhelm IV began building a "country palace" on the ruins, to which his various descendants and successors, right through Max Emmanuel, kept adding.

The high points of **Schloss Dachau** are the *Festsaal* (Festival Hall), with its magnificent coffered ceiling, and the stately early-18th-century staircase leading up to it.

But Dachau is no longer known for its castle, of course. Instead, it is infamous as the site of the Nazis' first concentration camp, now a memorial. The **KZ-Gedenkstätte Dachau** is open daily except Mondays, 9:00 A.M. to 5:00 P.M. The central administration building, with photographic exhibits and twice-daily (11:30 A.M. and 3:30 P.M.) showings of a documentary film in English, has been preserved, as have two of the original barracks. The foundation outlines of the other barracks remain as well, as do guard towers and barbed-wire fences, to give visitors a feeling for the grim place where, between 1933 and 1945, more than 206,000 people were incarcerated and tortured, and nearly 32,000 murdered.

Schleissheim

Though Müncheners generally speak of **Schloss Schleissheim**, in the suburb of Oberschleissheim (nine station stops north of Marienplatz on the S-1 line), as one palace, there are actually three, and each can keep a visitor busy.

The classically Renaissance **Altes Schloss** (Old Palace) was built as a country retreat for Duke Wilhelm V. Work started in 1597, the year of his abdication, after Bavaria was declared bankrupt, and completed in 1616. Today the Altes Schloss houses a collection of religious folk art (open daily except Mondays from 10:00 A.M. to 5:00 P.M.).

The **Neues Schloss** (New Palace), commissioned by Max Emmanuel, was never completed, though you would hardly notice. Problems first arose after the laying of the cornerstone: The entrance hall collapsed because Zucalli, the chief architect, apparently had made some miscalculations regarding the foundations. The problem was solved by reinforcement with earth, but this affected the proportions, making the palace look a bit sunken. When Max Emmanuel was forced into exile after the War of the Spanish Succession, work on the building came to a complete halt. Construction resumed in 1719 after Max Emmanuel's return, and what the artists and artisans eventually achieved is one of the finest works of German Baroque, in no small measure because some of the finest masters did the job. Cosmas Damian Asam did the fresco painting, Johann Baptist Zimmermann the stuccowork. The frescoes depict mythological scenes alluding to Max Emmanuel's successful campaign against the Turks at Belgrade. Few palaces are as lavish. While you can visit the Neues Schloss daily except Mondays from 10:00 A.M. to 12:30 P.M. and 1:30 to 4:00 P.M., it is at its most impressive during the July and August music festivals here.

Schloss Lustheim, across the neatly manicured park from the Neues Schloss, was built as a hermitage for Max Emmanuel in 1687. Zucalli, who made no mistakes on this one, modeled it on Italian Baroque châteaux and created a jewel. Its great hall is vaulted with mirrors, decorated with frescoes, and supported by painted atlantes. Lustheim, open the same hours as the Neues Schloss, houses a vast collection of Meissen china.

GETTING AROUND

Because of Munich's proximity to the Alps, its weather is unpredictable. A week of uninterrupted downpour can be followed by two weeks of glorious sunshine. There can be blizzards as late as mid-May and as early as mid-October. One real freeze, well below zero Fahrenheit, is guaranteed for a week to ten days in winter, as is a scorcher in the low 90°s for an equal duration once each summer.

Generally speaking, the weather from May through October is best. But there are 15 to 18 major trade fairs each year, during which accommodations are at a premium, so booking well in advance is advisable. The most difficult period is during the two-week Oktoberfest, from late September through the first week of October, which is followed by the German Art and Antiques fair.

Arrival

Munich's new Franz-Joseph-Strauss Airport, inaugurated in May 1992 after 30 years of planning, is Germany's second largest (after Frankfurt). In addition to Lufthansa, a number of American carriers (American, Continental, Delta, TWA, and United) offer service from various cities in the U.S. to Munich. Others flying there include: Air Canada from Toronto; British Airways, British Midland, and Dan Air from London, Birmingham, Glasgow, and Manchester; Air France from Paris, Marseilles, and Nice; Swissair from Zürich; Austrian Airlines from Vienna; SAS from Copenhagen, Oslo, and Stockholm; Sabena from Brussels; KLM from Amsterdam; and Alitalia from Rome and Milan.

The airport is 35 km (22 miles) from the city, and the best way to get into town and back again is by S-Bahn, the rapid suburban train system, whose number S-8 line (also called the "Munich Airport Line") operates between the lower level of the airport terminal building and all stations in the inner city. Trains into town run every 20 minutes starting at 3:55 A.M. until 12:55 A.M., and between 3:22 A.M. and 12:42 A.M. from the Hauptbahnhof (main railway station) back to the airport. The trip between the airport and Hauptbahnhof takes 40 minutes. The price is DM 10 one-way, and you must obtain a ticket from a dispensing machine and cancel it in the meter on the platform before boarding.

There is also a "Munich Airport–City Bus" that operates at 20-minute intervals from 3:10 A.M. and midnight between the terminal building and the Hauptbahnhof. The trip takes 45 to 60 minutes depending on traffic, and costs DM 12 one-way, DM 20 round trip.

A taxicab between the airport and downtown Munich costs between DM 90–100.

If you have reserved a rental car at the airport, count on an hour to get into the center, possibly longer during morning rush hour (when most flights from the U.S. arrive), as well as for driving back out during the afternoon rush hour. Your route from the airport to the city is westward on Autobahn A 922 to the junction with A 9, the Berlin–Nürnberg–Munich route.

The Hauptbahnhof, about a 15-minute walk from Marienplatz and just outside the Altstadtring to the west, is served by InterCity (IC), EuroCity (EC), and InterCity Express (ICE) trains operating on an hourly schedule from every major German city north of Munich. Connections from Austria, Italy, Switzerland, and France are far less frequent, however. Four U-Bahn (U-1, U-2, U-4, U-5) and all seven S-Bahn lines (discussed below) intersect on several underground levels of the Hauptbahnhof, with access to them from the main concourse. The tourist office has an information center (open Monday through Saturday, 8:00 A.M. to 10:00 P.M., and 11:00 A.M. to 7:00 P.M. on Sundays) on the main platform area near the Bayerstrasse exit across from the end of tracks 11–14.

Three Autobahn routes—from Stuttgart, Nürnberg, and Salzburg—converge on Munich and end at the city limits. On the Stuttgart and Salzburg routes there are information kiosks just before the last exit. At both there is also a *Lotsendienst* (pilot service), whose guides will either give you directions or lead you in another car to your destination.

In the City

A car is not merely a burden in Munich but a curse. Much of the inner city is a pedestrian zone, and where you are permitted to drive either the traffic is choking or parking is impossible. Fortunately, most of Munich is easily walked, and the transit system is superb.

The whole network—U-Bahn (subway), S-Bahn (interurban trains), Strassenbahn (tramway), and buses—interconnects, with subways, trams, and buses running at ten-minute intervals most of the day and twice as frequently during morning and afternoon rush hours. A single ticket allows you to ride all conveyances as well as transfer among them. It operates on the honor system, backed by spot inspections, with a DM 60 fine if you violate it. You buy a ticket from the vending machines found at U-Bahn, S-Bahn, and tramway stops, or from hotel concierges, and validate it in the meters at the platform entrances or aboard trams and buses. Bus drivers also sell tickets. Five-ride tickets, which require validating two strips for travel within the city limits (more on a zonal basis if you ride the S-Bahn to Dachau and Schleissheim), are cheaper per ride than single-ride tickets, and the best deal is a *Tageskarte* (one-day pass), good for unlimited rides within the city limits and transfers from the time you validate it until 4:00 A.M. the next day.

Taxis, all cream colored, are usually plentiful and expensive. They also get stuck in traffic. There are plenty of taxicab stands around the city, and cabs can also be hailed on the street if the rooftop sign is illuminated, or called (Tel: 216-10 and 194-10).

One of the best and fastest ways of getting about is by bicycle. There are 750 miles of marked bike lanes, many with their own traffic signals, to accommodate the 800,000 bicycle owners (out of a total population of 1.3 million). Recently a reporter for the biggest Munich daily newspaper tested getting to his office by car, subway, and bicycle: It took him 27 minutes, 35 minutes, and 23 minutes, respectively. A booklet (in German) with proposed bicycle sightseeing tours and maps is available from the tourist office information centers at the airport and in the main railway station. Bikes can be rented by the day or week year-round at **Lothar Borucki**, Hans-Sachs-Strasse 7 (Tel: 26-65-06); **Radl Gipp**, Kirchenstrasse 23 (Tel: 47-98-46); and, from May through mid-October, from **Radius Touristik**, opposite Track 31 in the railway station (Arnulfstrasse exit); Tel: 59-61-13; Fax: 59-47-14.

ACCOMMODATIONS

Given that 3.2 million visitors converge on Munich annually, rooms are always scarce here and, regardless of category, more expensive than elsewhere in Germany. But the squeeze is easing gradually, thanks to the opening in recent years of a number of new hotels in the first-class and moderate categories.

All the major chains—Hilton, Holiday Inn, Marriott, Novotel, Ramada, Sheraton—are represented, and standardized in their service and decor, though not one of them has a hotel in the Innenstadt or the railway station area.

The hotel rates listed here are 1994 projections for double-bed, double-occupancy rooms, with a range from low to high whenever possible. Prices are given in deutsche marks (DM). Basic rates are always subject to change, so please verify price when you are booking. Breakfast is usually included in the price of a room.

The telephone area code for Munich is 89, which must be preceded by a zero if you are calling from elsewhere in Germany.

Innenstadt and Station Area

A list of the crowned heads, presidents, prime ministers, famous writers, opera singers, musicians, and stars of stage and screen who have called the ▶ **Vier Jahreszeiten Kempinski** a home away from home since it opened in 1858 would fill another book. Neither wartime destruction nor a 1970 expansion and renovation deprived this *"beste Adresse Münchens"* of its genteel, mahogany-paneled elegance, and its appeal to an upscale clientele remains undiminished. What enhances the attraction is its location on Munich's most expensive street as well as its proximity to everything, especially the opera.

Maximilianstrasse 17, D-80539 München. Tel: 23-03-90; Fax: 23-03-96-93. DM 465–730.

Competition in the luxury class opened nearby in 1989 in the form of the ▶ **Hotel Rafael**, with 74 grandly spacious rooms, 55 of them suites, in a Neo-Renaissance building. The lobby is a splash of marble, cherry, and ebony. Each guest room is individually designed, and all feature opulent interiors decorated with period pieces. Several suites open onto terraces with spectacular views of the city.

Neuturmstrasse 1, D-80331 München. Tel: 29-09-80; Fax: 22-25-39. DM 520–750.

If price is an obstacle but gentility and elegance remain a goal, then the ▶ **Splendid** is splendid indeed. Each of its 40 rooms is appointed differently, and service is so friendly and personal that the feeling of being in a hotel soon dissipates.

Maximilianstrasse 54, D-80538 München. Tel: 29-66-06; Fax: 291-3176. DM 160–390.

Nearby, in the quiet, gentified "Lehel" district, a couple of minutes' walk from the "Lehel" U-Bahn station or from Maximilianstrasse, is the dignified 25-room ▶ **Hotel Opera**, whose proprietor, Ernestine Lutz, has converted a turn-of-the-century apartment house into an Italianate-style palais. There is a small bar for hotel guests only, and the kitchen provides a scrumptious breakfast.

St. Anna Strasse 10, D-80538 München. Tel: 22-55-33; Fax: 22-55-38. DM 260–400.

Modern functional comfort, quiet surroundings, and personalized efficient service come together just off Maximilianstrasse at the ▶ **Hotel an der Oper**, which has 17 singles and 38 doubles.

Falkenturmstrasse 10, D-80331 München. Tel: 29-00-270; Fax: 29-00-27-29. DM 200–225.

The ▶ **Continental** is within easy walking distance of Königsplatz and the museums. The Baroque wood paneling in the public rooms is genuine, salvaged from a razed castle.

The antiques in the public rooms, restaurants, and many of the 134 guest rooms and 15 suites are collector's pieces. Discretion and personal service are stressed in this quiet luxury-class establishment.

Max-Joseph-Strasse 5, D-80333 München. Tel: 55-15-70; Fax: 55-15-75-00. DM 350–490.

The pedigree of the ▶ **Königshof** reaches back to 1862, when a baronial mansion in what was then still a verdant area between the Hauptbahnhof and the Karlstor, one of the city's old medieval gates, was converted into a hotel. As the spot is now the city's busiest square, the Geisel family, which has owned the establishment for two generations, could have left it as it was, assured that its 120 rooms would always be filled. But in the late 1970s they decided to elevate it into the top category by retaining a prize-winning architect and interior designer, who gave it a total overhaul: a dining room of chalked oak panels and hand-wrought bronze chandeliers, a lobby of tinted mirrors and stucco, carpeting everywhere, opulent guest rooms with floor-to-ceiling marble bathrooms, and nine suites with silk wallpaper and period pieces. "Lush" does not do it justice.

Karlsplatz 25, D-80335 München. Tel: 55-13-60; Fax: 55-13-61-13. DM 395–450.

The same spirit and the same family—the Geisels—prevail a block away at the slightly less pricey ▶ **Excelsior**, conveniently located within shouting distance of the Hauptbahnhof. In an old though completely modernized and renovated building, it offers some pleasant surprises: high ceilings and some bathrooms with windows facing the courtyard, providing natural light.

Schützenstrasse 11, D-80335 München. Tel: 55-13-70; Fax: 55-13-71-21. DM 295–370.

On the whole, though the railway-station neighborhood is grim, the reasonably priced ▶ **Drei Löwen** is a quiet, dignified oasis. A feeling of relief overcomes you the minute you enter the lobby and get a friendly greeting. It is enhanced by the cozy comfort of the 130 modern but individually appointed rooms.

Schillerstrasse 8, D-80336 München. Tel: 55-10-40; Fax: 55-10-49-05. DM 230–250.

The ▶ **King's Hotel**, just 200 yards from the station, is not a play on Munich's royal past. The proprietor of this moderately priced establishment, opened in 1988, is Hanna King, and she oversees it personally. Besides the usual comforts and conveniences, each of the 72 rooms has a canopy bed.

Dachauer Strasse 13, D-80335 München. Tel: 55-18-70; Fax: 55-18-73-00. DM 240–265.

No hotel could be more centrally or historically located than the ► **Platzl**, directly across the square of that name from the Hofbräuhaus and a five-minute walk from Marienplatz. Though the interior is new, with a wood-paneled decor reminiscent of a Munich inn, the exterior façade is left over from the Middle Ages. There are 167 rooms.

Sparkassenstrasse 10, D-80331 München. Tel: 23-70-30; Fax: 23-70-38-00. DM 274–398.

Also not far from the Viktualienmarkt and Marienplatz is the ► **Blauer Bock**, a bit of innkeeping history that's a boon for the budget-minded. A picturesque old *Gasthaus*, originally built as a church in 1300, it has been run by the same family since 1900. Of its 41 double rooms, however, only 24 have private baths.

Sebastiansplatz 9, D-80331 München. Tel: 23-17-80; Fax: 23-17-82-00. DM 150–165.

Schwabing

Whether the ► **Carlton**, only a few minutes' walk north of Odeonsplatz, is in Schwabing depends on where you draw the neighborhood's southern boundary. Still, this establishment, built in 1920, is a gem in the moderate bracket. Its 45 airy rooms, 17 of them doubles, are all exquisitely appointed in Baroque style and furnished with period pieces, and the service is refreshingly personal.

Fürstenstrasse 12, D-80333 München. Tel: 28-20-61; Fax: 28-43-91. DM 190–320.

Relatively new and functional, the ► **König Ludwig**, just off Leopoldstrasse north of the Siegestor, will give you the feeling of being in the middle of whatever Schwabing is about these days. The decor of its 60 rooms is vaguely Postmodern.

Hohenzollernstrasse 3, D-80801 München. Tel: 33-59-95; Fax: 39-46-58. DM 250–350.

Also north of the Siegestor and equidistant from Leopoldstrasse and the Englischer Garten, on one of Schwabing's old squares, the moderately priced ► **Astoria** will give you an even better sense of the district. A well-kept Jugendstil house, renovated in 1993, the hotel has 20 doubles and 10 singles furnished in ultramodern style and, along with the corridors, small lobby, and breakfast area, decorated with contemporary art (which changes frequently). Ilona Leven, the proprietor, makes sure the service is friendly and personal—and that service includes bicycle rental.

Nikolaistrasse 9, D-80802 München. Tel: 39-50-91; Fax: 34-14-96. DM 165–190.

Upper Prinzregentenstrasse

This carriage-trade neighborhood is easily accessible thanks to the U-4 subway line, and has a number of new hotels. The most luxurious, and priced accordingly, is the ▶ **Palace**, at the corner of Prinzregentenstrasse. All marble, stucco, deep pile, and plush, with period furnishings, the Palace exudes elegance.

Trogerstrasse 21, D-81675 München. Tel: 470-50-91; Fax: 470-50-90. DM 320–520.

The bill will be a little more reasonable a block away at the ▶ **Prinzregent**, right around the corner from the Stuck villa. Its lobby, bar, restaurant, and 68 rooms are all richly paneled with wood and have a rustic Bavarian country-style look. The service is exceptionally friendly and attentive.

Ismaninger Strasse 42–44, D-81675 München. Tel: 41-60-50; Fax: 41-60-54-66. DM 330.

Haidhausen

Here, too, new hotels are mushrooming, most of them branches of international chains. Though also located in a modern building, a welcome exception is the not-inexpensive ▶ **Preysing**, which is so close to the philharmonic hall that, given the hall's devious acoustics, you will probably hear the music just as well from one of the hotel's 60 plushly furnished rooms. For all its modernity, it sits atop a 14th-century vaulted cellar with one of the city's really fine restaurants, the **Preysing-Keller.**

Preysingstrasse 1, D-81667 München. Tel: 48-10-11; Fax: 447-09-98. DM 300.

For budget accommodations the ▶ **Hotel Stadt Rosenheim** is hard to beat in terms of convenient location: right across from the Ostbahnhof, the terminal for all S-Bahn connections, the U-5 subway, numerous bus lines, and the number 19 streetcar, which provides access to Karlsplatz. Not all of the 58 rooms have private baths.

Orleansplatz 6a, D-81667 München. Tel: 448-24-24; Fax: 48-59-87. DM 100–190.

DINING

Thomas Wolfe described Munich as "an enchanted land where one ate and drank forever." Little has changed. It is not only Germany's secret capital but also its culinary capital. The statistics of its gastronomic wonders are positively staggering. It has more *Gourmettempel*—"temples of haute cuisine"— with more Michelin stars, Gault-Millau toques, and similar badges of culinary supremacy than any other German city. *Gasthäuser* and *Gaststätten* (eateries and beer halls serving rustic German and regional Bavarian food) number more than 2,000. To them add some 320 Italian, 200 Balkan, and 100 Greek spots—a natural consequence of all the resident foreigners and the fact that the Italian and Slovenian-Croatian borders are only a few hours away. Twenty McDonalds make a concession to local taste by serving beer. On top of all this, there are more than 300 Konditorei-Cafés, most of which make their own calorific tarts, cream cakes, petits fours, confectionery, and chocolates. To eat and drink your way through the city would be a tour de force.

Haute Cuisine

Since the early 1970s, Germany has been in the throes of a culinary revolution aimed at changing the image of German cooking from rib-sticking and boring to artistic and creative, and Munich has been its epicenter. Its leader, ironically, was not a German but an Austrian strongly influenced by French teachers: Eckart Witzigmann. Herr Witzigmann was working as sous chef at Washington's Jockey Club when a wealthy Munich real-estate developer invited him to preside over the kitchen of a new restaurant with a concept of haute cuisine the likes of which Germany and Munich had never seen before. The restaurant was **Tantris**, Johann-Fichte-Strasse 7, in Schwabing, and in less than a year Witzigmann parlayed it into the country's most celebrated eatery. For Witzigmann, however, it was not only too large but too confining creatively. In 1978 he left and opened his own exquisitely elegant 40-seat **Aubergine**, at the northwestern Altstadtring at Maximiliánplatz 5, where his creativity reaches seemingly unattainable new heights with each day's changing menu. To eat here is as close to culinary perfection as you can get, though it does require a very fat wallet as well as some advance planning, sometimes several weeks in advance. Tantris is closed Sundays, Mondays, and public holidays; Tel: 36-20-61. Aubergine is also closed Sundays, Mondays, and public holidays; Tel: 59-81-71.

No less creative a genius in the kitchen is Otto Koch (the name means "cook"), proprietor and chef of the sumptuous **Le Gourmet**, Hartmannstrasse 8, near Marienplatz. Koch once aspired to be a psychologist, but his therapy on the plate, resulting in total bliss, surely surpasses any he might have dispensed on the couch. The treatment is heavenly, all the more because he applies his skill and imagination to nouvelle-style transformations of traditional and long-forgotten Bavarian recipes. Closed Sundays and Mondays. By reservation only; Tel: 212-09-05.

Two hotel restaurants have also achieved culinary stardom. One is the **Königshof**, where every dish is as much a feast for the eyes as for the palate. For reservations, Tel: 55-

13-61-42. The Preysing Hotel's **Preysing-Keller**, entrance at Innere-Wiener-Strasse 6, on an equal plane of perfection, offers the added pleasure of dining exquisitely in medieval surroundings. Open evenings only, closed Sundays and public holidays; for reservations, Tel: 48-10-15 or 11.

Game has always ranked as a delicacy in Bavaria and elsewhere in Germany, partly because most of the forests belonged to nobles and hunting was their jealously guarded privilege. But when a Witzigmann protégé prepares it, even the nobles bow. The master is Hans Mair, who owns and presides at **Halali**, Schönfeldstrasse 22, just off Ludwigstrasse. Here you dine amid the regal splendor of candelabras, heavy silver, and precious china and crystal in a wood-paneled room filled with antlers and other hunting trophies. Closed Sundays and lunchtime Saturdays; Tel: 28-59-09.

Bistros

One of Munich's new culinary vogues is the bistro, of which dozens have sprouted. Some actually call themselves that, others are just very small restaurants with creative international cooking. The best are located in and around Schwabing and Haidhausen. Alas, what distinguishes them from their French models is that they are rather expensive.

At **Le Cézanne**, Konradstrasse 1, the proprietor-chef is from Marseilles, the cuisine is classically Provençal and usually impeccable, the choice limited to half a dozen entrées, and the wine list is small but reasonable in price. Open evenings only, reservations recommended; Tel: 39-18-05.

The **Schönfelder Hof**, Schönfeldstrasse 15a, halfway between the Haus der Kunst and Ludwigstrasse, is a cozy, wood-paneled, candlelit inn, with seating in the garden on warm days. Bavarian and international dishes are prepared nouvelle style, and there is always a three- or four-course prix-fixe menu. Closed for lunch Saturdays; Tel: 28-53-57.

Käthe's Küche, Georgenstrasse 48, is on the ground floor of a 100-year-old Jugendstil apartment house in the heart of Schwabing. Owner Mike Maples and his wife, Barbara, are masters when working with lamb, hare, and salmon. Lunch and dinner served on weekdays; dinner only on weekends; Tel: 271-95-17.

Rue des Halles, Steinstrasse 18, right in the center of Haidhausen, is like a French corner restaurant, which should come as no surprise since two Frenchmen own and run it. A favorite of the *Schickeria* (fashionable) crowd, it tends to be a bit pricey, but the cooking is fine. Open evenings only, reservations a must; Tel: 48-56-75.

La Marmite, Lilienstrasse 8, close to the Deutsches Museum, is the creation of Luc and Gaby Hediard, who have

more respect for their guests' budgets than for their waist-
lines. Gaby does most of the classically French cooking, and
prices are reasonable. No credit cards; evenings only, closed
Saturdays and Sundays; Tel: 48-22-42.

Bavarian Fare

Traditional "German" dishes such as *Wienerschnitzel* and
Sauerbraten really aren't considered Bavarian, but *Leberknödelsuppe* (liver dumpling bouillon), *Kalbshaxe* (roast leg
of veal), *Schweinsbraten* (pork roast), *Weisswürste, Leberkäse*
(a meat loaf), *Semmelknödel* (breadcrumb dumplings), and
sauerkraut definitely are.

The *Weisswürste,* which tradition dictates must be eaten
before noon as a midmorning snack rather than as a meal,
are by consensus still best where they were invented, at the
Gaststätte Peterhof, Marienplatz 22, open daily 9:00 A.M. to
midnight; Tel: 260-80-97.

Owing to the Francophile bias of Michelin inspectors, it
will take a miracle for any real Bavarian Gasthaus to get a
star, but if the miracle happens, it will be at the **Straubinger
Hof**, Blumenstrasse 5, right by the Viktualienmarkt, where
the daily menu includes not only the standard dishes mentioned above but also more esoteric Bavarian specialties
such as *Züngerl* (tongue) and *Kutteln* (tripe). Closed Saturday evenings and Sundays; otherwise open 9:00 A.M. to 11:00
P.M.; Tel: 260-84-44.

At the **Augustiner-Gaststätten**, Neuhauser Strasse 16, right
along the main pedestrians-only shopping street that begins
at Marienplatz, the food is as genuine as the ambience is
gemütlich. The building, dating from the early years of this
century, was one of the few in Munich that suffered no
wartime damage. There are a number of cavernous rooms,
all rustic. The menu is voluminous and prices are moderate.
Open daily, 9:00 A.M. to midnight; Tel: 55-19-92-57.

The **Weinstadl**, Burgstrasse 5, right off Marienplatz, is in
Munich's oldest surviving building, a merchant's house dating from the 16th century; the inn itself has been in operation since 1850. What makes it all the more unusual is that
the cuisine—and the wines—include specialties from the
Rhineland Palatinate, adjacent to the French border, which
was once a Bavarian territory. Open daily from 10:30 A.M.
until midnight; Tel: 290-40-44.

You might call **Zum Alten Markt**, Dreifaltigkeitsplatz 3,
just off the Viktualienmarkt, "up-market Bavarian." That
goes for the prices as well as proprietor Josef Lehner's
offerings: international nouvelle creations along with traditional dishes such as filet of venison or sliced liver with
root vegetables. The small wood-paneled restaurant is a

gem of cozy, rustic interior decor. Open daily for lunch and dinner; no credit cards; reservations essential; Tel: 29-99-95.

Also just off the Viktualienmarkt is the intimate, wood-paneled, and rather smoky **Weinstube Holzbaur**, Frauen-strasse 10, a wine tavern specializing in Württemberg vintages and Swabian dishes. It's open weekdays from 4:30 P.M. until 1:00 A.M., Saturdays from 10:00 A.M. to 4:00 P.M., closed Sundays, and always crowded to bursting; Tel: 22-41-41.

Beer Halls and Gardens

Any large Gasthaus can be taken for a beer hall, if it is large enough, and any place with a few tables outside, shaded by trees, can be called a garden. The biggest and most colorful are, as previously mentioned, the **Hofbräuhaus**, the **Chinesischer Turm** in the Englischer Garten, and the **Königlicher Hirschgarten** near the Nymphenburg palace.

Add two more, both virtually adjacent to and operated by the breweries whose beer they serve. The **Löwenbräukeller**, on Stiglmaierplatz west of Königsplatz, can seat 7,000. The surrounding garden is, mercifully, somewhat smaller, but therefore crowded to bursting on warm summer evenings. The **Salvatorkeller** (Hochstrasse 49, close to Gasteig Philharmonic Hall), operated by the Paulaner-Thomas brewery, derives its name from *Starkbier* (strong beer), a potent, oily brew served for two weeks only during Lent. It was first brewed by the Franciscans of St. Paul's Abbey in the 17th century, with the idea that it would see them through the 40-day fast. They called it *Salvator* (beer of the Savior), though what kind of salvation was intended remains in doubt.

One of the most colorful spots is not a beer hall at all but a converted 19th-century suburban railway station, the **Isar Bräu**, Kreuzeckstrasse 23, just beyond the city limits in Grosshesselohe. The small brewery that operates it specializes in *Weissbier* (wheat beer)—which you can see being made right on the premises—and its own fruit brandies. The commendable Bavarian cuisine is honestly regional, the clientele drawn largely from the well-to-do southern Munich district of Solln. The S-7 line of the S-Bahn will take you there (by way of the "Grosshesselohe-Isartalbahnhof" station) in 20 minutes. Open daily, 11:00 A.M. to midnight; Tel 79-89-61.

In all beer gardens, incidentally, it is perfectly acceptable to bring your own food.

Konditorei-Cafés

Traditional *Kaffee und Kuchen* (coffee and cake) time is 3:00 to 5:00 P.M., and Müncheners certainly uphold the tradition, though most of these establishments open for Continental breakfast and serve all manner of other libations, and many remain open until 7:00 P.M. The best and most elegant, with deep upholstered chairs, sumptuous chintz-curtained surroundings, waitresses in black dresses with primly starched white aprons, and a mouth-watering selection of pastries, are within a block or two of Marienplatz. The ones to seek out are the **Café Kreutzkamm**, Maffeistrasse 4; the **Café Feldherrnhalle**, Theatinerstrasse 38; and the **Café Hag**, Residenzstrasse 26, which was once the confectionery shop by appointment to the Wittelsbach court.

BARS AND NIGHTLIFE

Considering that every beer hall, Gasthaus, restaurant, café, and even ice-cream parlor serves alcoholic beverages, bars and pubs are rare in Munich, although in vogue among the "fashionable people." The most chic spots are **Harry's New York Bar**, Falkenturmstrasse 9 off Maximilianstrasse south of the Residenz, open 4:00 P.M. to 3:00 A.M., closed Sundays; **Schumann's**, Maximilianstrasse 36, open 6:00 P.M. to 3:00 A.M., closed Saturdays; **Wunder-Bar**, Hochbrückenstrasse 3, open 8:00 P.M. to 3:00 A.M., closed Sundays; **Gratzer's Lobby**, Beethovenplatz 2–3, one block north of the Goetheplatz subway station, open weekdays from 5:00 P.M. to 1:00 A.M.; **Schnellinger & Hardt**, Innere Wiener Strasse 2 in Haidhausen, open daily except Mondays, 9:00 A.M. to 3:00 A.M.; and **Zum Weintrödler**, Brienner Strasse 10, right off Odeonsplatz, which also serves full meals daily from 5:00 P.M. to 6:00 A.M., Sundays from 10:00 P.M.

Nightlife in other forms—discotheques and nightclubs with shows—tend to have a patina of provincialism. The "in" discos of the moment—and moments are brief in Munich—are **P-1**, Prinzregentenstrasse 1, in the Haus der Kunst (closed Mondays, otherwise open 9:30 P.M. to 4:00 A.M.); **Maximilians**, Maximiliansplatz 31 (also closed Mondays, otherwise open 9:00 P.M. to 3:00 A.M.), preferred by the well-heeled *arrivée* crowd; and **Jackie O's**, Rosenkavalierplatz 12, near the Arabellapark station of the U-4 (open 10:00 P.M. to 4:00 A.M.), catering to the international business set.

Of the striptease places, the most established and expensive is **Maxim**, Färbergraben 33, just west of Marienplatz, open daily from 9:00 P.M. to 4:00 A.M.

Jazz is best at the **Schwabinger Podium**, Wagnerstrasse 1, Tel: 39-94-82; **Allotria**, Oskar-von-Miller Ring 3, Tel: 28-58-58; and **Unterfahrt**, Kirchenstrasse 96 in Haidhausen, Tel: 448-27-94. Programs change weekly, sometimes daily, and most jazz taverns open around 7:00 P.M. The **Oklahoma**, Schäftlarnstrasse 156 in the Thalkirchen district, close to Thalkirchen station on the U-3 line, is best for live country-and-western groups; Tel: 723-43-27.

SHOPS AND SHOPPING

To ask where the most interesting shops are in Munich is like seeking the forest through the trees. The entire city is a shop, with purchasing power high and prices for everything inflated to meet a seemingly insatiable demand. If there is such a thing as a bargain in Munich we have yet to find it, and chances are we never will.

The gilt-edged tour begins on Maximilianstrasse, where you will find every high-carat name from Bulgari to Yves St. Laurent. It has a little codicil called Perusastrasse, where the action includes Tiffany's and Etienne Aigner. Then turn right onto Theatinerstrasse and dash through the passageways to the parallel Residenzstrasse. At Odeonsplatz, turn left onto Brienner Strasse, where you again find yourself in the nine zeros bracket, and end up a couple of blocks down face to face with Cartier's. At this point, you will have walked perhaps one and a half miles and encountered every glittering name of international haute couture, sartorial splendor, footwear and leather goods, and jewelry.

Dotted between these branch outlets of global fame are the names of some of Munich's own: **Rudolph Moshammer**, Maximilianstrasse 14, a tailor and haberdasher who caters to those who dare to be different and can plunk down several hundred dollars for a shirt or a couple of thousand for something like a cashmere-and-silk sport jacket; **Gebrüder Hemmerle**, also at Maximilianstrasse 14, purveyors of their own extravagant jewelry designs to royalty and cinema stars; the **Bognerhaus**, Residenzstrasse 15, home of Willy Bogner's line of sports and casual wear; **Max Dietl's**, Residenzstrasse 16, the five-story fashion palace of Munich's most renowned couturier and tailor for both women's and men's wear; **Eduard Meier**, Residenzstrasse 22, a shop that has been cobbling for Europe's rich, powerful, and pampered since the 16th century; **Kunstring München**, Brienner Strasse 4a, a porcelain shop filled with Meissen, new and antique; and **M. Lange & Co.**, Brienner Strasse 1, a fashion house that sells only its own designs and creations, made to order or ready to wear.

More in the mainstream are the streets leading directly off Marienplatz: Kaufingerstrasse and **Neuhauser Strasse**, the main pedestrian mall, which leads all the way down to Karlstor and Karlsplatz; the **Tal**, which begins behind the Altes Rathaus; **Dienerstrasse** and **Weinstrasse**, which run parallel along the eastern and western sides of the Neues

Rathaus; and **Sendlinger Strasse**, which is slightly more affordable though rather trendy.

There are more than 300 antiques and bric-a-brac dealers in Munich, by no means concentrated in any single area. **Westenriederstrasse**, a long, narrow lane that extends from the Viktualienmarkt to the Isartor, is lined on both sides by bric-a-brac shops. **Ottostrasse**, which extends in a southwesterly direction from Brienner Strasse to Karlsplatz, is a good place to browse if you are in the market for authentic—meaning expensive—antique furnishings and applied art. Here, at number 11–13, is the Neuer Kunstblock, an entire building of dealers. **Türkenstrasse** in Schwabing is good for both bric-a-brac hunters and less demanding antiques collectors.

Auction houses, on the other hand, are not concentrated in any area. The local branch of Sotheby's is at Odeonsplatz 16; Christie's is at Residenzstrasse 27. **Hartung & Karl**, good for old books, manuscripts, and autographs, is located at Karolinenplatz 5a. **Karl & Faber**, major players on the Old Master as well as modern art scene, are at Amiraplatz 3, just off Brienner Strasse. **Wolfgang Ketterer**, good for Jugendstil applied art as well as modern art, operates at Brienner Strasse 25. **Rudolf Neumeister**, whose auctions are strong on both 19th-century German and 20th-century art, has showrooms and auction facilities at Barerstrasse 37. **Hugo Ruef**, interesting for folk as well as Old Masters and modern art, is based at Gabelsbergerstrasse 28. The Munich branch of Berlin's **Villa Grisebach**, specializing in 20th-century painting, is at Prannerstrasse 13.

"Finds" have already been found, however. That for which Munich ought to be best known—Biedermeier art and decorative art, Jugendstil, German classical modern, Art Deco, and even the rustic Bavarian folk art and furnishings of the 18th and 19th centuries—was all gobbled up years ago, and when it does go on the market again, either for direct sale through dealers or at auctions, prices are at international levels.

What, then, can you find in Munich that you cannot find elsewhere, and at prices still in line?

Loden Fashions, Trachten, Bavarian Handicrafts

Müncheners really do wear dirndls, lederhosen, Loden togs, and other variations on the Bavarian folk costume theme, all of which fall under the generic term of *Trachten*. They even wear such apparel to the opera, for which gown-length dirndls and tuxedos tailored like traditional peasant garb are fashioned. Munich without Trachten would be like Texas without ten-gallon hats and cowboy boots. And nowhere in

Germany are such duds more easily acquired, and at still-reasonable prices, than in the Bavarian capital.

One of the best addresses for folk fashions, and for genuine as well as replica folk artifacts (such as antique etched glasses, hand-painted schnapps flasks, lusterware jugs, pillows covered with old lace or embroidery, and antique peasant furniture), is **Wallach's**, Residenzstrasse 3, just a block up from Marienplatz via Dienerstrasse.

Loden-Frey, Maffeistrasse 7–9 north of Frauenplatz, an entire department store of top-of-the-line designer ready-to-wear men's and women's fashions, got its start in 1842. Johannes G. Frey, then 21, set up a mill with ten looms to produce *Loden,* a thick, felted woolen cloth cherished by Bavarian highland farmers for its warmth and waterproof qualities. Eleven years later he opened his first retail store, and today, under the direction of his great-great-grandchildren, the company is a Munich institution known worldwide for its handsome, sturdy Loden fashions—men's jackets, women's skirts, overcoats—all cut to meet the latest styles. You will also do well at **Ludwig Beck am Rathauseck**, sometimes referred to as the "Bloomingdale's of Munich" for its imaginative merchandising techniques—though not in the main store at the corner of Marienplatz and Dienerstrasse. Try, instead, their special *Trachten* division on Burgstrasse, right behind the main store. Lederhosen—a good pair made of the finest soft chamois can cost well over DM 1,000, but will last a lifetime—are still hand made and embroidered to order at **Leder-Moser**, Herzogspitalstrasse 7, and by **August Strauss**, Heiliggeiststrasse 2. The best place for *Gamsbärte,* the tufts of chamois hair worn on Bavarian and Tyrolean highlanders' hats (and resembling giant shaving brushes), is **Johann Bösl**, Hochbrückenstrasse 4, a tiny Trachten shop near the Hofbräuhaus, where regulars wearing all this garb show up at 9:00 A.M. for their first beer of the day.

SOUTHERN BAVARIA

By John Dornberg

To many people, Southern Bavaria is Germany incarnate. It is made up of two regions that also happen to be political provinces, Oberbayern and Niederbayern. Oberbayern, or Upper (higher-in-altitude) Bavaria, takes in the Alpine highlands south of Munich, stretching more or less from the Lech river eastward to the little Salzach river that, from Salzburg north, forms the border between Germany and Austria. Niederbayern (Lower Bavaria) is lower country, mostly flats and gentle hills, located generally north and east of Munich between the Inn river and the Danube, and again stretching to the Austrian border.

By any name, Southern Bavaria is *the* vacationland of Germany, as the annual invasion of visitors, both foreign and German, attests: on average 15 million, more than the population of all Bavaria. The majority arrive with travelogue expectations of a land of fairy-tale castles peopled by buxom dirndled maidens and bearded lederhosen-clad peasants yodeling from snow-capped Alpine peaks.

Granted, some of the clichés are true, though primarily in Oberbayern, and where they aren't, Bavarians fulfill them artificially. Well aware that they are sitting on a touristic gold mine, Bavarians assume that travellers like nothing better than to have their preconceived illusions affirmed. Many dress in *Trachten* (folk costume) that are about as genuine as American Western duds produced in New York's garment district. But there are also 18 regional folk-costume festivals each year, sponsored and arranged by the 130,000 Bavarians who belong to nearly 900 *Trachtenvereine* (folk-costume societies). The costumes on display at such festivals are heirlooms or meticulously reconstructed replicas, often costing thousands of marks and as distinctively representative of a

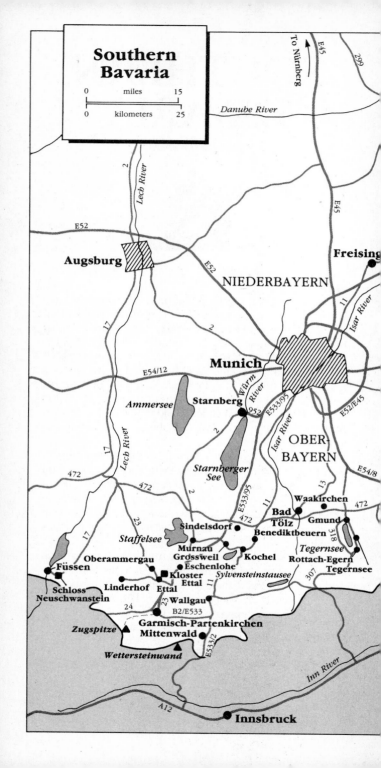

specific town or county as a Scottish kilt is of a clan. Unfortunately, many of Southern Bavaria's visitors see only the phony setups, missing out on the opportunity to view some of the region's authentic traditions and costumes. Also invisible to most travellers are the 4,000 village brass bands, more than 500 folk-music groups, and dozens of folk-dance ensembles, all doing their thing as it has been done for generations.

Most preconceptions about Southern Bavaria are part truth, part myth. Consider the notion that the region is a bucolic backwater. True, it does produce as much milk and cheese as Switzerland, but it is also the sun-belt region of Germany and home of the country's burgeoning aerospace industry. Leading electronics, electrical, machine-tool, automobile, engineering, optical goods, and petrochemical companies have their headquarters here. Then there's the sausage-and-beer legend. Sausages are indeed consumed in vast quantities in Southern Bavaria, where, moreover, two-thirds of West Germany's 1,700 independent breweries are located. But you will also find inns and restaurants applying the principles of nouvelle cuisine to traditional Bavarian recipes in refined surroundings.

While our discussion of the region covers some of the well-beaten paths and the best-known Alpine resort areas, which are certainly more than worthwhile—and many of which can be explored in one- or two-day trips from Munich—we also introduce you to a Bavaria—with its fascinating history, spectacular scenery, and centuries-old culture—beyond the myths and legends.

MAJOR INTEREST

Castles, fortresses, and churches
Folk festivals
Spectacular scenery
Summer and winter sports in the Alps
Spa towns
Gothic town of Landshut
Scenic beauty of Inn river towns
Ludwig II's reproduction of Versailles on the
    Chiemsee
Wassily Kandinsky and Franz Marc museums in
    Murnau and Kochel
Linderhof, Ludwig II's most elaborate palace
Passionsspiel at Oberammergau
Violin-making at Mittenwald

Bavarians are sometimes called the "Texans of Germany"— an allusion to the size of their territory, their inclination toward braggadocio, and their penchant for independence. History is to blame, for Bavaria has enjoyed a large measure of sovereignty, often complete, for nearly a millennium.

A powerful duchy whose ruling dynasty, the Wittelsbachs, tended to side with France instead of the other German mini-states in many European wars, Bavaria reached its greatest flowering thanks to Napoleon. In 1806 he proclaimed it a kingdom and virtually tripled its territory, so as to have a friendly buffer state between his realm and the Austrian empire. The monarchy outlasted Napoleon by more than a century—until 1918, when dukes and kings in general went out of style in a Götterdämmerung of revolution that briefly turned Bavaria into the world's second "soviet" republic. After that it became a "Free State" within Weimar Germany, then a part of the Third Reich, and ultimately joined today's Federal Republic—whose 1949 constitution, incidentally, has never been formally signed and ratified in Bavaria. It is still a "Free State," and more than just history sets it apart.

"In Bayern gehen die Uhren anders," other Germans say: "In Bavaria the clocks go counterclockwise." Bavaria is the only German federal state with a bicameral legislature. Its frontiers are marked by border signs proudly bearing the blue-and-white rhombuses and heraldic lion of the Wittelsbachs. It has its own border police and its own national anthem, with which the Bavarian Broadcasting Corporation signs off radio and television transmission each night. Small wonder that even Germans feel they are going abroad when visiting Bavaria, a sensation no doubt enhanced by the natives' predilection for regarding all non-Bavarians as foreigners.

Munich is a perfect base for exploring Southern Bavaria. A route generally northeast, along the Isar river, will take you into the heartland of Altbayern and the administrative district of Niederbayern—including the towns of Freising and Landshut. From there, heading southeast (or directly east from Munich), you can explore the charming old towns of the Inn river valley. The Bavarian Alps stretch along an east–west axis south of Munich—Berchtesgaden is at the eastern end—with much of the loveliest scenery and most of the picturesque towns within an hour's drive (about 100 km/62 miles) of the capital itself. This includes the Chiemsee (lake) and the Chiemgauer Alpen (Chiemgau Alps), the highlands directly south of Munich on the way to Garmisch-Partenkirchen, and the Zugspitze, Germany's highest peak.

FREISING AND LANDSHUT

Freising, on the banks of the Isar river, is so close to Munich (34 km/21 miles), to the northeast, that you can take an S-Bahn between the two (15 stops on the S-1 from Munich's Marienplatz; see the Munich chapter). Originally called Frisinga, the town was first mentioned in documents in 744 and was one of the great spiritual and ecclesiastical centers of southern Germany in the Middle Ages. Not only was it the seat of the archdiocese that includes Munich, it was also the residence of the 12th-century bishop Adalbert, uncle of Holy Roman Emperor Frederick Barbarossa, whose bridge over the Isar was destroyed by Henry the Lion's knights in 1157—an act that led to the official founding of Munich a year later.

Freising was a cathedral town from the mid-eighth century until 1821, when the see and archbishop's residence were moved to Munich. Its cathedral, the **Dom St. Maria und St. Korbinian**, on the Domberg, a ridge high above the town and river, is in its exterior essentials still the same building consecrated in 1160. The interior, however, has undergone several transformations. The original flat ceiling was replaced by vaulting in the Late Gothic period. In the early 17th century it was redecorated in Renaissance style. A hundred years later, in 1723, Cosmas Damian Asam and Egid Quirin Asam, the renowned Munich-based artist-architect brothers, gave it the lavish Rococo stuccowork and extravagant frescoes that it has today. The high altar, installed in 1625, once contained Rubens's *Woman of the Apocalypse*. The original is now in Munich's Alte Pinakothek; what you see here is a copy.

Behind the Dom, and connected to it by cloisters, is the **Benediktuskapelle** (Chapel of St. Benedict), also known as the Old Dom. Although it is a 14th-century structure of the High Gothic style, its pillars and vault ribs were covered with Baroque stuccowork in the 1700s. More pure in its Gothic forms is the **Johanneskirche** (St. John's Church), on the west side of the Dom, built between 1319 and 1321. The **Bischöfliche Residenz** (Bishop's Residence) next door, now a school, has exterior and interior decoration by François de Cuvilliés and Johann-Baptist Zimmermann.

For more earthly pleasure in Freising treat yourself to a hearty lunch of warm *Leberkäs* (meat loaf) or *Haxen* (roast shank of veal or pork) at the **Bräustüberl Weihenstephan**, Weihenstephan 1, west of the Domberg. The restaurant is attached to the Weihenstephan brewery, the oldest in the world, founded in 1040. To this day it produces the cream of Bavarian beers—which is quite a claim, since in Upper

Bavaria alone there are more than 600 independent breweries. Weihenstephan offers 12 beers on tap daily, including a tart, unfiltered Pilsner. The brewery is also a college-level training school for brewmasters.

Landshut, the first capital of Bavaria—38 km (about 24 miles) northeast of Freising by way of highway B 11 along the Isar or 72 km (45 miles) from Munich along Autobahn A 92—is one of the most beautiful and best-preserved Gothic towns in all of Germany. Its central area and two parallel main streets, called Altstadt and Neustadt, have scarcely changed since the 16th century.

Like Munich, Landshut was created through an act of force, when an Isar river crossing with its lucrative toll and duty revenues was moved a short distance upstream under the menacing protection of a fortress built by Bavaria's second Wittelsbach ruler, Ludwig-der-Kehlheimer, in 1204. Ludwig called the stronghold Landes Hut. Known today as **Burg Trausnitz**, this massive, much-expanded castle is situated on a bluff overlooking the city and is visible from miles away. Defensive and residential buildings were added during the 14th, 15th, and 16th centuries, and Italian artists and craftsmen were hired in the 1570s to embellish it in Renaissance style, turning it into a *Lustschloss* (pleasure palace). Duke Wilhelm V and Renate of Lorraine (whose costly wedding bash is commemorated in the glockenspiel at Munich's Neues Rathaus) spent their honeymoon here. Wilhelm lived in the castle 11 years before becoming duke in 1579, during which time he made it into an international meeting place for artists, actors, minstrels, and musicians. He also hired artisans recommended to him by Hans Fugger, one of the rich Augsburg merchants and bankers, to decorate Trausnitz. The most dazzling legacy of the era is the *Narrentreppe* (Fools' Staircase), frescoed with vigorous commedia dell'arte figures.

For all its impressive majesty and visibility, Trausnitz is dwarfed by **St. Martin's**, Landshut's 14th-century parish church and collegiate minster. The majestic brick church stands in the very center of town, on the Altstadt. The cast' looms directly above it on the bluff south of the city. Martin's may well be the only Gothic church that was work of a single architect. Not only is his name kno' Hans von Burghausen—but on the south wall, betwee' portals, there is a monument to him erected by workers and successors after his death in 1432. The 430-foot spire, completed in 1500, is the tallest bri' tower in the world. St. Martin's is not only huge— 300 feet long and 95 feet high—it is also rich i' 16th-century sculpture and carved stone port'

The *Landshut Madonna,* a larger-than-life-size figure carved in 1520, is its finest piece.

Landshut's two principal streets, Altstadt and Neustadt, run south to north from the foot of the castle hill to the Isar. Both are lined by richly decorated burgher and patrician houses. The most impressive structure is the **Stadtresidenz**, at Altstadt 79 (two blocks north of St. Martin's), a little city palace that the Wittelsbachs used when they considered Trausnitz castle too "suburban" for their mood. Duke Ludwig X admired the Palazzo del Té in Mantua during his visit to Italy in 1563, and hired builders and craftsmen from Padua to make him this replica in Landshut. Today the Italian Renaissance palace is a dual museum devoted to 18th-century applied art (the **Stadt und Kreismuseum**) and 16th- to 18th-century European painting (the **Staatliche Gemäldegalerie**).

A few yards south on a little side street, at Ländgasse 51, is the former ducal chancellor's house, **Beim Vitztumb**, where you can dine superbly in 15th-century surroundings. For a substantial Bavarian lunch there is also the moderately priced ▶ **Goldene Sonne**, at Neustadt 520, an old inn with 54 comfortable guest rooms. For more expensive, but romantic, overnight surroundings, consider the ▶ **Lindner Hotel Kaiserhof**, Papiererstrasse 2, idyllically situated on the west embankment of the Isar, just a two-minute walk from Landshut's historic quarter.

The historic quarter was also the scene of the most famous event in Landshut history—the marriage in 1475 of Duke George the Rich to Jadwiga, daughter of Poland's King Casimir V. To celebrate, the extravagant duke invited all of Europe's royalty and nobility and spent the equivalent of around DM 20 million to stage a week-long orgy, during which the guests and townsfolk consumed 333 roast oxen, 490 calves, 1,133 sheep, 1,537 lambs, 684 pigs, 11,500 geese, 40,000 chickens, and oceans of beer and wine. Every four years some 1,300 Landshuters don medieval costumes and stage reenactments of the "Landshuter Hochzeit." It is one of Bavaria's chief folk festivals, and although the original wedding was on November 19, the reenactment is staged during the summer for the benefit of visitors.

INN RIVER TOWNS

The Inn river rises in Switzerland's Graubünden canton, winds its way generally northeast through Austria's Tyrol, passes through Innsbruck, enters Bavaria near Rosenheim, a medieval mountain city some 56 km (35 miles) southeast of Munich, then continues its convoluted chalky-green course (first through Oberbayern and then Niederbayern) along the Austrian border before spilling into the Danube at Passau.

The Inn valley is at its most breathtaking and dramatic at **Wasserburg**, where the river makes a hairpin bend so sharp that this 850-year-old town appears to be a fortified island with the river serving as a moat. Its name, in fact, means "water fortress."

Located 50 km (31 miles) east of Munich along highway B 304, the incomparably picturesque town of Wasserburg is perfect for half a day of wandering through streets that take you back to a time long past. Ironically, the little city owes its splendid medieval appearance to economic misfortune. Founded in 1137, it became rich and powerful as a central junction on the vital salt-trade routes between the mines in the Bavarian and Tyrolean Alps and Bohemia and northern Germany. But in the 16th century the salt road was shifted southward to Rosenheim, and Wasserburg went into a decline that lasted hundreds of years. Lack of money prevented burghers from redecorating their houses, public buildings, and churches in later architectural periods, a practice that turned many other Bavarian towns into kaleidoscopes of Gothic, Renaissance, Baroque, and Rococo styles. Though it is lively enough today, you will find Wasserburg a perfectly preserved medieval gem.

On Kirchplatz, in the heart of the old quarter, stands the **Pfarrkirche St. Jakob** (Parish Church of St. James), built by Hans von Burghausen, the same master responsible for Landshut's minster. His parish church in Wasserburg is a classic example of 15th-century Gothic. Up the steep hill from St. Jakob in a westerly direction is the town's 12th-century fortress, rebuilt in 1526 by Duke Wilhelm IV—in part to compensate the town for its commercial troubles—who turned it into an occasional residence. Now used as an old-age home, the fortress is notable for its elaborately decorated reception hall. The **Rathaus** (City Hall), on Marienplatz, a few blocks east and downhill from the Burg, will give you a sense of Wasserburg's pride and wealth in the 15th and 16th centuries. It was a typical practice of the time to combine the town council chamber, a public ballroom, and a granary under one roof, and this curious trifold purpose has been preserved here. The councillors' chamber on the upper floor is richly decorated with intricately carve oak ceiling panels and allegorical murals.

One of the most unusual attractions in Wasserburg is **Erstes Imaginares Museum** (First Imaginary Museum) ir 14th-century Heilig Geist Spital (Holy Ghost Hospital) Brucktor. It contains some 500 masterpieces of world of them perfect replicas produced by the silk-screen of local artist Günter Dietz. Even sharp-eyed Picasso was unable to distinguish his original work from the copy Dietz had made. (Open daily except Mondays from 11:00 A.M. to 5:00 P.M., May through September; from 1:00 to 5:00 P.M. October through April.)

Altötting, 60 km (37 miles) downstream and northeast of Wasserburg by way of highways B 15 and B 12, is a world unto itself, due to its centuries-long role as a kind of German Lourdes. The **Heilige Kapelle** (Holy Chapel) on Kapellplatz, the center of town, draws up to 600,000 faithful each year. First mentioned in 877, the little church may well have existed much earlier: One legend has it that a seventh-century Bavarian count was baptized in it by Saint Rupert, a missionary monk. Until 1491 the round church was just a simple chapel in the Carolingian style. But then it became the repository of the *Black Madonna*—so-named because it is blackened with soot—a two-foot-high 13th-century wood carving of Mary, thought to have come from Alsace and believed to have miraculous powers. The figure has been kept in a richly decorated silver tabernacle since the 17th century. An almost-life-size solid-silver sculpture of Bavaria's Duke Max III Joseph, depicted as a ten-year-old, kneels before the shrine. It was an offering of thanks to the Madonna from his father, Elector Karl Albrecht, for the deliverance of the young duke from a serious illness in 1737.

Bavaria's Wittelsbach rulers have long been associated with the Heilige Kapelle, which is in effect a national shrine. The hearts of six Bavarian dukes and kings, two queens, two electors, and Field Marshal Tilly, the Bavarian hero of the Thirty Years' War, are kept in silver urns in wall compartments opposite the shrine. The most famous pilgrim of modern times was Pope John Paul II in 1980.

The exterior and interior walls of the chapel, as well as the sacristy of the adjacent 16th-century **Stiftskirche St. Philipp und St. Jakob** (Collegiate Church of St. Philip and St. James), are covered with offerings of thanks for deliverance from sickness and danger. Among them are hundreds of *Votiftafeln* (votive tablets), some of them five centuries old, and most of which are fine examples of folk art.

Given its role as a place of pilgrimage, Altötting hardly lacks for hotels and inns. The top spot is the ▶ **Hotel zur Post**, Kapellplatz 2, directly across the square from the Heilige Kapelle.

Sixteen kilometers (10 miles) southeast of Altötting, by way of an unnumbered country road, is **Burghausen**, a town in its own way as spectacular and photogenic as Wasserburg. Located on the left (west) bank of the Salzach river, a tributary of the Inn, this 1,000-year-old town is crowned on the cliff above it by the largest medieval fortress complex in Germany.

More than 1,200 yards long and almost a town in itself, the **Burg** is located atop a ridge between the Salzach and a little lake. Built over a period of centuries, starting in the 11th, the castle served a succession of Bavarian dukes who at one time or another held court here, as did Holy Roman Emperor Heinrich II. Most of the extant buildings, one of which contains a division of the Bayerische Staatsgemäldesammlung (Bavarian State Pictures Collection), date from the 13th to the 15th century. The castle, with its numerous buildings, could occupy an entire day, and since there is even more to see and do in Burghausen you may want to spend a night in the moderately priced ▶ **Hotel zur Post**, Stadtplatz 39, right in the center of the Altstadt, or the equally economical ▶ **Hotel Glöcklhofer**, Ludwigsberg 4, located on the castle hill at the entrance to the fortress.

Also on the Stadtplatz is the 14th-century **Rathaus**. Fifty yards away is the **Pfarrkirche St. Jakob** (Parish Church of St. James), and 150 yards farther south is the 16th-century **Spitalkirche Heilig Geist** (Church of the Holy Ghost). The narrow, winding, cobblestone streets of the quarter are lined by arcades and 16th- to 17th-century burgher houses. Thanks to the modern world of electronics and its own vast resources of silicon, Burghausen has become a major center of microchip manufacturing and is in the midst of an unprecedented period of prosperity that in turn is benefiting its abundance of old architecture with costly restoration and preservation. The renovated town now looks much the way it must have centuries ago.

THE CHIEMSEE AND THE CHIEMGAU ALPS

A leisurely and scenic 35-km (22-mile) drive south from Burghausen along the Salzach river leads to the Waginger See, a peaceful little lake, and the resort town of **Waging am See**, where the main attraction is the incomparable chalet-style **Kurhausstüberl**, Am See, which Gault-Millau considers one of the ten best restaurants in the country. Proprietor-chef Schuhbeck is omnipresent in Germany these days, both as a network television chef and on the pages of gourmet magazines. Though his approach is nouvelle, the cuisine is strictly regional Bavarian, and nearly all of his ingredients are supplied locally. Except Sundays, when he also serves lunch, the restaurant is open evenings only. Dinner for two will cost around DM 300 without wine, and reservations are a must. Tel: (8681) 40-09-12 or 400-90 (closed Mondays, Tuesdays, and six weeks in January–February).

From Waging it is a 35-km (22-mile) drive, generally westward by way of Traunreut and Altenmarkt, to Seebruck, at the northern end of the **Chiemsee**, the largest of the Bavarian lakes. Because it covers nearly 33 square miles, it is often referred to as the Bavarian Ocean. The duchy did indeed once have a navy and even a couple of grand admirals before Benjamin Thompson, a.k.a. Count Rumford, the American who became Bavaria's minister of war, reorganized the ducal forces in 1788. Of course, they sailed their boats on the Rhine; the Chiemsee was too shallow. This fact, however, does not deter thousands of summer and weekend sailors and windsurfers. The shore from Seebruck to Prien, on the southwestern side, is lined with inviting little holiday towns and villages.

As spectacular as the lake itself are Frauenchiemsee and Herrenchiemsee, two small islands reached by excursion boats, one of them a 1920s sidewheeler, from Prien.

Frauenchiemsee is so named for its 1,200-year-old Benedictine nunnery, one of the best-preserved medieval convents in Germany, and still active today. Saint Irmengard, a great-granddaughter of Charlemagne, was its abbess in the ninth century. Though much of the original eighth-century complex was destroyed in the tenth century by the Magyars during their raids into Bavaria, reconstruction began not much later, and the convent church as well as surrounding buildings, which are Romanesque in style, date from the 11th century. Renovations and excavations in the 1960s exposed portions of the earliest structures and some magnificent 12th-century frescoes that had been painted over.

Frauenchiemsee is also the name of the island's small fishing village, which became a favorite summer hangout of Munich painters and writers in the 19th century. They congregated to dine on *Renken,* a member of the trout family indigenous to the lake, and other charcoal-broiled fish at the colorful, cozy **Inselwirt**, a 200-year-old inn with a small beer garden where you can have lunch or supper in idyllic surroundings.

Herrenchiemsee, the larger of the two islands, derives its name from the Benedictine monks and canons who inhabited its monastery from the early eighth century until the Magyars laid waste to it in the tenth. Rebuilt in 1130, it became an Augustinian abbey that was later secularized in 1803. Only a few of its buildings survive, among them the

Gothic Pfarrkirche (Parish Church) and the 19th-century Altes Schloss (Old Palace), which has a lavishly decorated Imperial hall and a richly endowed library.

But what really draws the steamboat crowds to Herren-chiemsee is the **Neues Schloss** (New Palace), Ludwig II's extravagant replica of Versailles. Whatever the Dream King's romantic motivations for building his other castles, this one seems to have had a pragmatic purpose. From his first visit to Versailles in 1867, Ludwig had dreamed of building some-thing equally grand in Bavaria. He bought the island in 1873 to prevent its falling into the hands of real-estate speculators and five years later began his copy of Versailles, complete with a Hall of Mirrors, a staircase that is almost an exact facsimile of Louis Le Vau's and Charles Le Brun's Escalier des Ambassa-deurs, a suite of private rooms corresponding to the apart-ments of Louis XV, a fountain of Apollo, and a Latona fountain.

Ludwig II occupied the Herrenchiemsee palace on only one occasion, for ten nights in the fall of 1885—and when he was removed from the throne and died, in 1886, only the central block and one of the wings, since taken down, had been completed. But already the cost was more than that of Neuschwanstein (see the Romantic Road chapter) and Linderhof (see below) put together. To see what else was planned on Herrenchiemsee, visit the adjacent **König-Ludwig-II Museum**, with its exhibits of construction draw-ings and models.

In the Chiemsee region nearly every little *Gasthaus* (guest house) has a portrait of Ludwig. But considering his eccen-tricities, the vast sums he spent on building his dreams, and his notions of absolutism in an age of constitutional monar-chy, one would expect him to be regarded as anything but the folk hero he is. His admirers explain away this apparent contradiction by pointing out that he really did care for his subjects. His castle projects provided a great deal of employ-ment in Bavaria's most remote areas, and records show that he spent vast sums on charity. And, too, Ludwig's eccentricity was just the kind that mountain people understood.

Back on the mainland you are not far from the mountains. South of the lake are a number of spectacular routes and pretty villages that can be reached in an hour or two. Or you may wish to rest for a night in the Chiemsee area before venturing forth. Take the unnumbered country road south from Prien on the Chiemsee to **Bernau**, a distance of only 6 km (3½ miles). Prien abounds with hotels, inns, and pen-sions, and is a very busy lakeside and boating resort. Bernau is an even better choice to spend a night, and its best accommodations are at the   ▶ **Alter Wirt-Bonnschlössl,**

Kirchplatz 9, a dignified, moderately priced 19th-century inn with rustic wood-paneled decor, cozy guest rooms, and friendly hospitality.

Bernau is a good jumping-off point for the year-round attractions of the Chiemgau Alps. In summer, when the highland pastures, laced with stands of dark pine and spruce, are a velvety emerald green and the higher peaks rise chalky gray against the azure sky, the Chiemgau region attracts droves of hikers and climbers. Bernau, a mere 80 km (50 miles) southeast of Munich, can be crowded on weekends, summer and winter alike. From December through February, and sometimes into March, it is a winter resort area with an abundance of downhill and cross-country skiing facilities. These are Munich's *Hausberge* (backyard mountains), and they attract the multitudes who don't want to drive farther afield.

The beauty of the area outweighs any inconvenience caused by the crowds. One short and splendidly scenic route leads from Bernau through Aschau, past the dramatic Kampenwand massif, to the hamlet of Sachrang at the Austrian border. The entire drive is only 20 km (12 miles), but you could easily spend a day or two along the way. Though **Aschau** is a mere 5 km (3 miles) southwest of Bernau, you may want to spend the night here, for its 15th-century ► **Residenz Heinz Winkler**, Kirchplatz 1, is as historic as it is sumptuous. Post hotels in southern Germany go back to the 15th and 16th centuries when local butchers, who were also the village innkeepers, did double duty as "mailmen" by carrying letters and information as they made the rounds buying up livestock. In the 17th century, when the princes of Thurn-und-Taxis (see the reference to them under Regensburg in the Northern Bavaria chapter) started Europe's first postal service with express riders and stagecoaches, the butcher-innkeepers became the local postmasters, their inns the relay stations along the Thurn-und-Taxis routes. In time, the postal inns established reputations as the most comfortable places to stay. Aschau's is now in a very special category. Heinz Winkler, for more than 12 years the chef of Munich's Tantris restaurant, bought the hotel in 1991, expanded and totally renovated it, and has established his own outstanding eatery in its historic rooms.

On a cliff high above the town is **Burg Hohenaschau**, mightiest of the fortresses in the Chiemgau. The castle, first mentioned in 927, passed through various baronial hands, including those of the counts of Freyberg, one of whom transformed the uncomfortable digs into a Renaissance-style palace. The counts of Freyberg sold the property to the counts of Preysing, who lived in it from 1608 to 1853, at one point dismantling the Renaissance decoration and replacing it with Baroque. Still private property, it now belongs to the baronial Cramer-Klett family, who also operate a small brewery at the foot of the cliff, and can be visited during the summer months. Among the things to see on the guided tour is the monumental gallery of ancestors in the state ballroom of the main castle. It displays 12 larger-than-life-size statues on pedestals in ornately decorated surroundings. The chapel's Rococo interior, dating from the 18th century, is partly the work of Zimmermann.

Just beyond the castle the road passes the base station of the gondola lift up the **Kampenwand**, a 5,500-foot-high crenellated stone massif that is the landmark of the Chiemgau Alps. At the top of the gondola system there are numerous smaller chair lifts and T-bars to accommodate visitors to one of the area's most popular ski slopes. The gondolas operate in summer as well, transporting climbers and hikers, but beware: This is no mountain for amateurs. The sheer cliffs facing north toward the Chiemsee can be negotiated only by experienced, fully equipped alpinists.

From the Kampenwand the winding road climbs steeply through picture-postcard hamlets and dark evergreen forests to the Austrian border and the little town of **Sachrang**, whose main attractions are a Baroque parish church, winter lifts for intermediate-level skiing, a maze of cross-country tracks, and well-marked hiking trails.

The same road takes you back to the starting point at Bernau, a half-hour drive—unless you get caught in weekend traffic.

From Bernau there is an even more dramatic and scenic journey (26 km/16 miles) south through a different valley to the winter-and-summer resort town of **Reit im Winkl**. Everything is well posted, but for guidance it may help to know that the road (B 305, the Deutsche Alpenstrasse) passes through Grassau, Marquartstein, and Unterwössen, then rises steeply, with grades of up to 15 percent and many hairpin curves, for the final leg into Reit im Winkl.

Reit im Winkl is a summer hiker's joy and a winter skier's paradise, with miles and miles of cross-country *Loipen* (prepared tracks) as well as downhill trails. Because of its altitude and enclosure by craggy peaks up to 7,000 feet high, the **Winklmoosalm** (10 km/6 miles east of the center of town) is one of the best ski areas in Bavaria. It has an exceptionally long season, and with luck you will find good snow as early as November and as late as April. There are nearly two dozen chair lifts and T-bars, so lift lines are tolerably short, even on weekends. The road up to the Winklmoosalm is open in summer, but during the ski season you must leave your car at the Seegatterl parking lot and take a shuttle bus from there. Purchase of a pass to all the lifts includes the bus fare, and at the end of the day you can ski back down to the parking lot—a spectacular six-mile run that all but rank beginners can easily negotiate. Always popular, the Winklmoosalm became famous thanks to the daughter of a local innkeeper and ski-school operator, Rosi Mittermaier, who won the World Cup and two gold medals during the Winter Olympics in 1976. The area straddles Germany and Austria, and many of the lifts and trails criss-cross the border. If you want to spend a night on top, the best spot is the ▶ **Alpengasthof Winklmoosalm**, Dürrnbach-hornweg 6. In Reit im Winkl itself you will find very comfortable rooms and solid stick-to-the-ribs Bavarian food at the ▶ **Hotel Unterwirt**, Kirchplatz 2, adjacent to the parish church. There is less traffic and more fresh air and nature, as well as more sophisticated cuisine, at the ▶ **Hotel Steinbacher Hof**, Steinbachweg 10, at the foot of the *Sprungschanze* (ski jump).

From Reit im Winkl the **Deutsche Alpenstrasse** (German Alpine Road), one of Germany's more than 140 officially designated scenic driving routes, leads generally east through gorgeous mountain country to Berchtesgaden. It is a drive of 61 km (38 miles), all of it along B 305.

BERCHTESGADEN

Today the name of this idyllically situated town, tucked into the southeasternmost corner of Germany within shouting distance of Salzburg, conjures up recollections of Hitler. It was on the **Obersalzberg**, one of many high peaks surrounding Berchtesgaden, that Hitler had his vacation retreat and received foreign heads of state at the "Eagle's Nest." You can still see the ruins of the complex, with its guest houses, underground bunker system, and the barracks of Hitler's SS bodyguard detachment.

Berchtesgaden's history predates that dark period by nearly 850 years, and the town, rich in art and architecture as well as glorious Alpine scenery, offers far more than the legacy of Hitler's residence. It began around 1100 with an Augustinian priory and achieved prosperity through the mining and export of salt, the "white gold" of the Middle Ages. Today, Berchtesgaden preserves its prosperity as a summer and winter resort.

Much of the monastery remains, including the former **Stiftskirche Sts. Peter und Johannes** (Collegiate Church of St. Peter and St. John the Baptist), a Romanesque and Gothic structure in the center of town, at Schlossplatz. Built and decorated in stages from the late 12th through 16th centuries, its treasures include the sculpted tombstones of a number of priors, who were also princes and secular rulers, and the richly carved 15th-century choir stalls. The *Stift* (canonry), adjacent to the church, is now called the *Schloss* (palace): After secularization, Bavaria's Wittelsbach rulers took it over in 1818 and turned it into a summer palace. Exactly a century later, the last Wittelsbach king, Ludwig III, fled here from revolutionary Munich, and his son, Crown Prince Rupprecht, made it into his permanent home, filling it with treasures of art and applied art. It is still owned by the Wittelsbach family.

The **Schlossmuseum** inside the palace was once the vaulted 14th-century dormitory of the abbey's canons, and today houses the excellent art collection assembled by Rupprecht, who, it should be added, lived until 1952—long enough, so the story goes, to reject an offer by General George S. Patton, then U.S. military governor of Bavaria, to restore the monarchy.

Also worth seeing are **St. Andreas**, a 14th-century parish church with late-17th-century embellishments, on Schlossplatz, and the early-16th-century **Frauenkirche** (Church of Our Lady), on the river Anger.

Typical of Bavarian mountain towns are the painted façades of the burgher houses around **Marktplatz** and on **Metzgerstrasse**, the two central pedestrians-only shopping streets. This *Lüftlmalerei* (roughly, "open-air painting") uses trompe l'oeil to create three-dimensional effects and often transcends pure folk art: The scenes of monkeys parodying human passions and frailties around the windows of the Gasthaus zum Hirschen are masterpieces.

Salt is still mined in Berchtesgaden today; to see how it was done centuries ago, visit the **Salzmuseum**, Bergwerkstrasse 83 (east of the center), operated by the local mining company. Part of the fun is donning traditional miners' garb, sliding down wooden chutes into the shafts and tunnels, and seeing exhibits of old equipment. No less interesting is the **Heimatmuseum** (Museum of Local History), on Salzburger Strasse near the northern edge of town, with its rich displays of local craftsmanship, including intricate filigreelike wood carving and the brightly painted wooden boxes that are a local specialty. The **Berchtesgadener Handwerkskunst**, in the Heimatmuseum, is the best shop at which to buy them.

The landscape around Berchtesgaden, situated at the base of the 9,000-foot **Watzmann**, Germany's second-highest mountain, is spectacular enough, but nature seems to have outdone herself at the **Königssee**, 5 km (3 miles) south of town. This

crystal-clear mountain lake, surrounded by the steep faces of
the Watzmann, Jenner, and Götzenberg peaks, is the quintessence of dramatic Alpine scenery. Nonpolluting electric-
powered boats make excursions around the five-mile-long
lake, stopping off at St. Bartholomä, a little Baroque church on
the western shore. For winter sports, **Jenner mountain**, with
an aerial cable car and an abundance of chair lifts and T-bars
higher up, is your best bet.

Hotels and inns in every category abound in Berchtesgaden. For the best in chalet-style accommodations, with
breathtaking views of the mountains from virtually every
room, there is the ► **Hotel Geiger**, on Stanggass at the
southwestern edge of town. The 24-room ► **Hotel Fischer**,
Königseer Strasse 51, close to the railway station, is a slightly
more moderately priced chalet. The 100-year-old ► **Hotel
Wittelsbach**, Maximilianstrasse 16, is the best choice near
the center of the old quarter.

Accommodations are even more plentiful, ranging from
spartan to pampered luxury, in Bad Reichenhall, one of
Germany's oldest and most famous spa towns, 12 km (7½
miles) northwest of Berchtesgaden by way of B 20.

Bad Reichenhall

Legend has it that this gold-plated, gilt-edged health resort
was an Illyrian settlement long before the Romans arrived in
southern Germany. While there is little physical evidence of
either Illyrians or Romans, it is a fact that *hall* was the Illyrian
word for salt, and here, as in nearby Berchtesgaden, salt has
been, if not the spice of life, then certainly the resource that
gave (and still gives) Bad Reichenhall its riches and prosperity. The salinic mineral waters, guaranteed to cure whatever
ails you, and splendid mountain scenery attract the multitudes and also account for Bad Reichenhall's ornate Belle
Epoque architectural look.

For all the salty spa atmosphere, the little city's medieval
beginnings, like Berchtesgaden's, were as a priory. **St. Zeno**,
the church completed by Augustinian canons in 1228, is the
largest Romanesque structure in Upper Bavaria. Though
damaged by a fire in 1412, which resulted in the reconstruction of its interior in Late Gothic style, the exterior is classically Romanesque. The west portal is a remarkable piece of
masonry in red and gray marble, strongly influenced by the
style then prevailing in northern Italy. Be sure to see the
Romanesque **cloisters** in the adjacent monastery building.
On one of the columns there is a bas-relief of Emperor
Frederick Barbarossa, a patron of the abbey. Bad Reichenhall's parish church, **St. Nikolaus**—at the southern edge of

town on a square between Innsbrucker Strasse and Tiroler Strasse—is older, dating from 1181, and also worth a visit.

Fortunately, Bad Reichenhall offers more than its waters. As in all German spa towns, there is a well-tended, neatly manicured Kurpark, a Kurhaus with an auditorium for concerts and plays, and a plush **casino**, where the major attractions are roulette and baccarat. For a sophisticated meal, though not necessarily a local one, try the **Schweizer Stuben** at Thumseestrasse 11, on the west bank of the Saalach river at the southern edge of town, where the fare is a mixture of Swiss and Swabian.

The hotel scene is abundant in Bad Reichenhall, though comparatively pricey in every category. For grand-hotel elegance, the top address is the venerable ▶ **Steigenberger-Hotel Axelmannstein**, Salzburger Strasse 2–6, surrounded by its own park. Nearly directly across the street, just below where Salzburger Strasse becomes Ludwigstrasse, is the ▶ **Kurhotel Luisenbad**.

Unless you want to retrace your route or see more of the countryside, the fastest return route to Munich is the Salzburg–Munich Autobahn. Access to the highway is only 3 km (2 miles) from the center of Bad Reichenhall, and the distance from there is 136 km (84 miles).

THE HIGHLANDS
SOUTH OF MUNICH

Upper Bavaria is at its loveliest and most historic south of Munich, where the countryside, dotted with lakes, rises gently through foothills covered with verdant pastures and groves of evergreens, and farther south reaches dramatic heights in the Alpine ranges that divide Germany and western Austria.

A round-trip itinerary from Munich would entail little more than 240 km (150 miles) of driving, detours included. And though it is possible to take in the scenery and charming towns along the way in a day or a weekend, the area could also easily occupy you for a week, or even two.

The journey we suggest begins at Starnberg, 27 km (17 miles) south of Munich, and leads south through Murnau (on the Staffelsee), Kochel (on the Kochelsee), and Oberammergau; past the Ettal monastery, King Ludwig II's Linderhof château, and Garmisch-Partenkirchen, at the foot of the Zugspitze; then east to Mittenwald and northeast to Tegernsee and the little mountain city of Bad Tölz.

Starnberg, best reached by taking the Munich-to-Garmisch-

Partenkirchen Autobahn, is practically a suburb of Munich, and so are many of the other little towns around the **Starnbergersee**, Bavaria's second-largest lake, which on a wintry night can become as stormy as the Atlantic. Excursion steamers ply it from April through October, and like the Chiemsee, it is a popular weekend sailing and windsurfing spot.

It was in this lake that Ludwig II, accompanied by his psychiatrist-keeper Dr. Bernhard von Gudden, drowned mysteriously three days after his arrest at Neuschwanstein castle. It happened at **Schloss Berg**, 6 km (3½ miles) south of Starnberg on the lake's eastern shore.

To call Schloss Berg a castle stretches the term; manor house is more exact. Ferdinand Maria, the first Wittelsbach duke to become an elector of the Holy Roman Empire, bought it in 1676, surrounded it with a lovely park, and used it as a base for outings on the lake aboard an ornate ship called the *Buccentaur*. More than a century and a half later King Maximilian II rebuilt the mansion in Neo-Gothic Tudor style. It is still Wittelsbach property—octogenarian Duke Albrecht von Bayern, the present head of the family, lives in it a great deal of the time. But Schloss Berg is more than just a footnote to Bavarian and Wittelsbach history, thanks to the mysterious death of Ludwig II.

A first attempt to arrest the Dream King had been made the night of June 9, 1886, shortly after a commission of psychiatrists had ruled him incompetent. The doctors and some cabinet ministers and keepers arrived at Neuschwanstein but were themselves arrested by armed and angry highland peasants who had rallied to the king's defense. Ludwig decided to release them, but the next night they were back and forced him to surrender. He was taken to the castle, where a royal prison was already being constructed for him; he was to be locked up there, and the government of Bavaria was to go to his uncle, Luitpold. Three days after his arrival, Ludwig succeeded in being let out for a walk on the lakeshore, accompanied by Dr. von Gudden, the psychiatrist who had compiled the dossier and declared him insane. Several hours later both men were found floating dead in the water near the shoreline: Ludwig in shirtsleeves, Gudden fully dressed and with strangulation marks and other bruises suggesting he had died in a struggle.

To this day speculation as to what really happened has not subsided—not even the rumor that the fishermen who pulled the bodies out of the lake had actually hauled out wax dummies, and that the king had escaped to lead his dream life incognito for many more years in Italy or Switzerland.

The memorial cross, just offshore at the site where the bodies were found, was erected almost immediately and is the scene of annual pilgrimages by Ludwig admirers, as is the memorial chapel on the shore. The chapel, a Neo-Romanesque structure built by Julius Hofmann, Ludwig's favorite architect, was dedicated in 1896. Flowers and wreaths from Ludvicophiles grace its altar every day.

A good place to contemplate the mystery of the Dream King's demise is the terrace restaurant of the ▶ **Park und Strandhotel Schloss Berg**, at Seestrasse 17, virtually adjacent to the chapel. With its rustic public rooms and 27 bedrooms decorated with period furnishings, it's an enjoyable place to spend a night or two.

For a different slice of Bavarian life, continue south on B 2 in the direction of Garmisch-Partenkirchen, to **Murnau** and **Kochel**, where Wassily Kandinsky and Franz Marc founded the *Blaue Reiter* (Blue Rider) artists' circle. It is a drive of 46 km (28 miles) from Starnberg to Murnau, and from there about 15 km (9 miles) to Kochel heading east on an unnumbered side road.

The skylines of both towns are punctuated with onion domes and the steep saddle roofs of chalets. Tourism and highland dairy farming are their primary sources of income, and both towns are so studiedly picturesque that they seem to give a new dimension to the word *kitsch*. But there is nothing kitschy about the epochal art movement that began here.

The story begins in 1902 in Munich, where Kandinsky, then 36, having left a wife and a law practice behind in Moscow, had been living and trying to make his way as an artist since 1896. He was teaching at an art school and had befriended one of his students, Gabriele Münter. In 1908 the couple settled in bucolic Murnau, where Münter had bought a cozy three-story country house. Kandinsky painted their rustic furniture with peasant motifs and embellished the staircase with folkloric images of little horses and riders galloping up to the second floor, where he and Münter had their studios and bedroom. It was in Murnau that Kandinsky began his forays into nonrepresentational painting. His 1910 *Church in Murnau,* a brightly colored, abstract view of the town's 18th-century parish church of St. Nikolaus, was painted from the bedroom window of the house.

Also in 1910, Franz Marc, then 30, moved with his second wife, Maria, to the farming hamlet of Sindelsdorf, today a part of the town of Kochel. Marc, a native Münchener, was already a member of the new artists' federation that Kandinsky, Münter, Paul Klee, Alexej Jawlensky, Marianne von

Werefkin, Alfred Kubin, and others had launched in an attempt to break with the genre painting then admired in Munich.

Marc and Kandinsky became close friends, and with Murnau and Kochel less than an hour away by bicycle, visited each other almost daily. In March 1911 they forged plans to publish a yearly almanac for the circle, to be called *Der Blaue Reiter.* Many years later Kandinsky explained how the name came about: "Marc and I chose the name as we were having coffee on the shady terrace of his house. Both of us liked blue, Marc for horses, I for riders. So the name came by itself." The first and only edition was published in May 1912, with most of the preparatory work done in Murnau and Kochel.

The artistic idyll in the two villages might well have continued had World War I not intervened. Marc, a reserve lieutenant in the Bavarian army, was killed in action at Verdun in March 1916. His remains were brought from a battlefield cemetery for reburial in the Kochel village graveyard after the war. Kandinsky, fearing internment as an enemy alien, fled to his native Russia. He and Gabriele Münter met once in Stockholm, in 1915, and never saw each other again. In 1931 Münter moved back into the Murnau house and preserved it almost exactly as she and Kandinsky had left it. When the Nazis came to power and declared avant-garde artists "degenerate," some 130 of Marc's pictures were confiscated and destroyed. Kandinsky had left Münter a substantial lode, and to protect it she built a brick vault around the paintings in the basement of the Murnau house. In 1957 she donated this priceless collection—90 oils, 300 watercolors and drawings, 29 complete sketchbooks, four dozen of her own pictures, and numerous works by other Blue Rider artists—to the Städtische Galerie in Munich's Lenbachhaus, which got title to the house after Münter's death in 1962.

The **Münter-Haus**, at Kottmüllerallee 6, has been turned into a small museum. The entry hall, staircase, and second-floor rooms look almost the way they did when the two artists lived there, with all the furniture, personal belongings, and Kandinsky's collection of Bavarian clay pipes in place. In 1986 the **Franz Marc Museum** opened in Kochel. It features a collection of memorabilia; paintings by Marc's father, a Munich landscape artist; several early works by the artist as well as some of the fine abstract paintings he did between 1910 and 1914; and even some of his original woodcuts and proofs of the *Blaue Reiter* almanac. There is also a fascinating collection of paintings by Münter, Jawlensky, Werefkin, Klee, and other members of the Munich avant-garde, and Kandinsky's oil-on-cardboard study for that topsy-turvy view from the bedroom window of Murnau's St. Nikolaus church. The museum, which is clearly signposted, is just off highway B 11 on the way out of Kochel in the direction of Urfeld.

Because you cannot live on art alone, have lunch—or dinner and spend the night—at the ▶ **Hotel und Gasthof zum Rabenkopf**, Kocheler Strasse 23, in the suburb of Ried, 5 km (3 miles) northeast of the center, the neighborhood where Franz Marc had his house. It's delightfully cozy and rustic, the cuisine a blend of Czech-Austrian (proprietor-chef Jörg Slaschek and his wife Therese hail from Bohemia).

If you prefer to stay instead in Murnau, you will find delightful accommodations, with breathtaking views of the Alps from your room and exquisite nouvelle Bavarian cuisine, at the ▶ **Hotel Alpenhof Murnau**, Ramsachstrasse 8.

Two short side trips from Murnau and Kochel open up yet another dimension of this area. Near Grossweil, off the road between Murnau and Kochel, is the open-air **Dorfmuseum** (Village Museum), with 90 historic chalets and Alpine farmhouses where local people demonstrate handicrafts and depict Bavarian countryside life in the 17th through the 19th centuries. It is open from spring through fall.

An 8-km (5-mile) drive north from Kochel, on B 11, will take you to **Benediktbeuern**, site of the oldest Benedictine monastery in Upper Bavaria. Though founded around 747, the complex, which includes the church of St. Benedict, is largely 17th- and 18th-century Baroque, featuring frescoes, stuccowork, and embellishment by such masters as the Asam brothers and Zimmermann. The text of *Carmina Burana,* written here around the beginning of the 13th century, and set to music by Munich composer Carl Orff in 1937, was found in the monastery library.

To continue your journey through the highlands drive south on B 2 from Murnau for 12 km (7½ miles) to the village of Eschenloe and the ▶ **Hotel Tonihof**, Walchensee-strasse 42, one of the most picturesque and idyllically situated inns in the area. The cuisine here ranges from regional specialties (particularly the local lake trout) to nouvelle-style Bavarian with a French touch. The view of the Zugspitze and other peaks around Garmisch-Partenkirchen from most of the 25 rooms is stunning.

Just 7 km (4 miles) south of Eschenloe, B 2 intersects with B 23, the steep, winding road that leads up to the Ettal monastery, Linderhof, and Oberammergau.

Kloster Ettal, 7 winding km (4 miles) from the highway junction, is known as the Bavarian Temple of the Grail. The Benedictine monastery was founded in 1330 by Bavarian duke and Holy Roman Emperor Ludwig-der-Bayer to house

22 monks, 13 knights and their wives, and several widows. An Italian painting of the Madonna, brought to the monastery church soon after its completion in 1370, made it the most important pilgrimage center in the Bavarian Alps. The church, originally Gothic in style, was a 12-sided building modeled on the church of the Holy Sepulcher in Jerusalem. In 1710 Enrico Zucalli, the Swiss master architect, set to work remodeling the building in Baroque style. Later work by other masters, including Zimmermann, turned the huge domed minster into one of the finest examples of Rococo in Germany.

A scenic drive through a valley flanked by 6,000-foot peaks will take you to **Linderhof**, 13 km (8 miles) west of Ettal on B 23. This most elaborate of King Ludwig II's palaces, built in the 1870s, is the full expression of his love for the solitude of the mountains. It is open to the public during the summer.

Vaguely resembling the Petit Trianon at Versailles, Linderhof is a compact, dazzling white château in such a variety of Baroque styles from various periods and countries that it is hard to find a common denominator or pin down a model for it. Though the exterior, with its sculptures and bas-reliefs, seems blindingly ornate, by comparison with the interior it is actually restrained. Inside, the palace is a riot of Rococo, a flash of mirrors, a bewildering mix of rich tapestries and crystal chandeliers. The most impressive chambers are the mirror room and the king's bedroom. In the oval dining room there is a Grimm's fairy tale come true: a "magic table." Those who remember the story will recall the command, "Little table, serve dinner." Ludwig's table could be lowered through the floor to the kitchen and pantry below and there reset with dishes, thus allowing the reclusive monarch to dine without the intrusive presence of servants.

For all its ostentatiousness, Linderhof is not without charm, thanks to the beauty of its natural setting in the Ammerberge range and the fine formal French gardens surrounding it.

After the dining room, the greatest attractions here are the Moorish kiosk, a cast-iron pavilion walled with zinc plaques stamped in relief; and the Venus Grotto, inspired by the Blue Grotto at Capri and containing an artificial lake fed by an artificial waterfall and a stage hung with a backdrop scene from the first act of *Tannhäuser*. Equipped with hypocaustal heating, which can turn it into a sauna bath, and the first full electrical lighting in 19th-century Bavaria, the room can be illuminated with changing colors. On the lake, which had artificial waves, Ludwig kept two swans and a gilded boat, in which he was frequently rowed by a servant. Legend has it that he once attempted to stage the first act of *Tannhäuser* in the grotto, but the roar of the waterfall and the fickle acoustics of the place turned the orchestra into a cacophony of sound and left the singers inaudible.

To get to **Oberammergau**, 17 km (11 miles) north of Linderhof, drive back toward Ettal, take a left turn at the fork in the road about 10 km (6 miles) past the castle, and follow the signs into the center of the "Passion Play town."

Oberammergau, a year-round resort with excellent downhill and cross-country skiing facilities, is also famed for its wood carvers and *Hinterglas* artists. (*Hinterglasmalerei,* an art form unique to Bavaria, Croatia, and parts of Austria, is painting done directly on glass and in reverse.) It is worth a detour any time, but in a festival year it becomes a magnet for the entire world.

The origins of the *Passionsspiel* (Passion Play) in Oberammergau go back to the year 1633, when townsfolk first staged the play with amateur actors in gratitude for the plague's end and as a hedge against a new outbreak of it. Since 1680 the drama of Christ's Passion has been performed by locals every ten years. A presentation with a cast of hundreds, the play depicts Christ's journey to the Cross in 16 acts and is staged in a special festival house, the **Passionsspielhaus** on Theaterstrasse, which was built for the 1930 performance. During a Passion Play season there are 102 performances, each lasting five and a half hours, with a two-hour intermission for lunch. Actors must either be Oberammergau natives or have lived in town for at least 20 years. The text has often stirred controversy for its anti-Jewish lines.

Owing to the multitudes who converge on Oberammergau, tickets are at a premium—and so are accommodations during the summer festival season. A moderately priced choice is the ▶ **Hotel Alte Post**, Dorfstrasse 19, right in the center of town.

To leave town, follow B 23 back down the valley to the junction with B 2, where you turn right (south) for the 10-km (6 mile) drive to **Garmisch-Partenkirchen.**

This bustling, highly popular holiday town, the scene of the 1936 Winter Olympics, was once two separate communities, now incorporated into one. Located at the base of the 9,800-foot **Zugspitze**, Germany's highest elevation, it is a spot where nature outdoes herself. That is one reason why Garmisch-Partenkirchen is hopelessly overrun with visitors year-round. Other attractions are folk theater and folk-costume festivals, central to the local tradition, as well as some surprisingly romantic nooks and crannies in which you can wander and try to forget that one of the loveliest painted Baroque houses on Garmisch's main square now houses a McDonald's.

One of Europe's oldest and most scenic cog railways will take you up the Zugspitze, as will an aerial cable car. There are ski lifts at the top and usually enough snow to last through the entire summer.

Because it was once two separate towns, Garmisch-Partenkirchen has two postal inns, and in the summer months a 19th-century stagecoach still operates between them (and on excursions beyond). The ► **Posthotel Partenkirchen**, at Ludwigstrasse 49, is the more venerable of the two. It was registered as a monastery tavern in 1542, and the building itself is at least a century older. It is a jewel of *Gemütlichkeit* (coziness), with *Lüftlmalerei* (trompe l'oeil) frescoes on its façade; a wood-paneled, beam-ceilinged lobby and dining room; and an array of Baroque art and peasant handicrafts on display. Proprietor Otto Stahl serves sophisticated Bavarian food with a nouvelle touch. ► **Clausings Post-Romantik-Hotel**, at Marienplatz 12 on Garmisch's main square, is even more overwhelming architecturally—a squat, three-story house with a huge overhanging Alpine roof and a façade emblazoned with statues of various saints. From the terrace, heated and glass-enclosed in winter, you will have a perfect view of the Zugspitze. The dining rooms are invitingly cozy with mahogany paneling, plush Oriental carpeting, and an assemblage of art and heirlooms collected over the more than three centuries it has been serving travellers.

Mittenwald

One of Upper Bavaria's most scenic journeys is the 18-km (11-mile) drive east and south along B 2 to Mittenwald, nestled in a valley at the foot of the Wetterstein range, just 32 km (20 miles) north of Innsbruck, Austria.

A summer resort and winter sports center, though blissfully less crowded than Garmisch-Partenkirchen, this town of 8,000 (whose name means "in the middle of the forest") played an important role in the Middle Ages as a market center on the treacherous mountain trade route from Venice and the Adriatic to central and northern Europe. Mittenwald's fame rests even more on violin making, a local industry since 1683, when native son Matthias Klotz, whose statue stands on the main square, returned home from his studies with Nicolo Amati in Cremona, Italy, to open a workshop in his hometown.

Today Mittenwald is known not only as the source of some of the finest stringed instruments in the world but also as the site of the world's oldest, largest, most stringently demanding school for violin makers, the state-run Staatliche Geigenbauschule. Its graduates ply their trade in 40 countries on six continents.

Most people associate fine stringed instruments with Cremona, and Germany does not necessarily come to mind. But there is persuasive evidence that the first makers of violins and a related, somewhat earlier group of instruments known as viols or viola da gambas were actually Germans with Italianized names working in northern Italy. They, in turn, were second- and third-generation descendants and pupils of 15th-century lute makers from Füssen, near Neuschwanstein. When viol- and violin-type instruments—both played with bows instead of plucked with the fingers—made their debut in the Renaissance music world of the early 16th century, they were produced at first by these German lute makers, who passed on their craft to Italians.

Mittenwald's role in this began with Klotz. Born in 1653, the son of a well-to-do Mittenwald tailor, he was dispatched to Italy to learn the lute- and violin-making trade at the age of ten. The boy was accepted as an apprentice by Amati in Cremona, where two of his fellow students turned out to be Antonio Stradivari and Andrea Guarneri. Young Klotz spent two decades in Italy learning the craft from Amati and working for other masters, including Johann Railich in Padua. He also worked for a Tyrolean master, Jakob Stainer, at Absam, a town near Innsbruck. In those years Stainer's reputation equaled, and sometimes surpassed, that of Amati.

Klotz eventually returned to Mittenwald, married the daughter of a local weaver, and opened his own lute- and violin-making shop. He taught the craft not only to his own two sons, Georg and Sebastian, whose instruments were reputed to be of even higher quality than his own, but also to seven other Mittenwald youngsters. When he died, at age 90, in 1743, there were a dozen other master violin makers in town, and by 1800 the number had swollen to 80. There were also ten bow makers and any number of journeymen and amateurs who made instruments or parts for them, often as a winter vocation and as home- and pieceworkers.

In the early years after Klotz started the industry, the masters were also their own salesmen, travelling and selling their instruments as far as feet or horse could carry them. But by the middle of the 19th century, Mittenwald was producing thousands of stringed instruments for ultimate resale in places as far away as St. Petersburg and Cincinnati. The more the trade flourished, the more quality declined, along with the earnings of violin makers, who were now little more than assembly-line laborers. With the cheapest violins selling for as little as the equivalent of DM 3, Mittenwald gained a reputation for inferior, mass-produced instruments—a reputation that lasted well into the early 1950s.

This, along with the abominable pay, working conditions, and the deteriorating skills of the local craftsmen, was a source of concern to Bavaria's King Maximilian II. It was at his behest that the **Staatliche Geigenbauschule** was established in 1858. Now located in a three-story building on Partenkirchner Strasse, it is the oldest violin-making school in the world and by far the leading one. A state institution with free tuition, its students come from all over the world. Two graduates, a Korean and a German, have started private schools in Chicago and Salt Lake City. At no time does the student body exceed 50 to 60, and since it is a three-and-a-half-year program, only 12 new students are accepted each year, though there are usually 1,500 to 2,000 applicants annually.

Thanks to the school's success, Mittenwald's violin makers again rank among the best in the world, with their instruments fetching gold and silver medals at major international competitions, not to mention prices of $15,000 and more. Although the school and the workshops of Mittenwald's top masters are usually not open to visitors, the **Geigenbaumuseum** (Violin-Making Museum), at Ballenhausgasse 3, is. The museum is devoted to the local instrument-making craft and has a fine collection of old violins, violas, and cellos as well as lutes and other stringed instruments.

From Mittenwald our route leads northeast again to another beautiful lake, the Tegernsee. Drive north 12 km (7½ miles) from Mittenwald on B 2 and then take B 11 (B 2 forks left and leads back to Garmisch-Partenkirchen) to **Wallgau**. Here you can stop to have lunch or even spend a night at the ▶ **Hotel Post**, Dorfplatz 6, a postal inn since 1621, and run by the Neuner family for more than 350 years. Goethe stayed here, as did Elizabeth Taylor and Richard Burton. From Wallgau a memorably scenic toll road follows the Isar river eastward for some 20 km (12 miles) to the Sylvensteinstausee, an artificial lake-reservoir. From there it is 27 km (17 miles) northeastward along B 307 to **Rottach-Egern**, the southernmost town on the shores of the **Tegernsee**, as well as the most affluent.

The "developer" of the Tegernsee region was Bavaria's first king, Maximilian I, who in 1817 bought the secularized Benedictine monastery in the town of Tegernsee, on the eastern shore of the lake, and commissioned Leo von Klenze to convert it into a summer vacation palace. Munich's and Bavaria's nobility followed suit, building mansions and chalets. For Müncheners the Tegernsee is one of the most popular mountain recreation areas, with boating and wind-surfing in summer and skiing in winter.

Of Rottach-Egern's profusion of luxury and first-class accommodations, the most luxurious is the ▶ Hotel Bachmair-am-See, Seestrasse 47. It is also the oldest, founded in the early 19th century as a village tavern. It has been owned and managed by the Bachmair family for nearly 150 years. Beamed ceilings, paintings, old etchings, ecclesiastical art, and wide fireplaces lend this hotel an atmosphere of deep tradition and comfort.

Bad Tölz, our last destination, is 12 km (7½ miles) north-west of the Tegernsee by way of an unnumbered road from the lake's northernmost village, Gmund, to Waakirchen, then due west on B 472. Tucked into the Isar river valley and surrounded by peaks as tall as 5,000 feet, the town is a popular spa and year-round resort, thanks to its iodine springs. Its Marktstrasse, lined by 18th- and 19th-century houses with protruding saddle roofs and painted façades, is one of the most picturesque main streets in Upper Bavaria.

Should you happen to be in the area on November 6, be sure to visit Bad Tölz for the annual **Leonhardifahrt.** Pilgrimage processions in honor of Saint Leonard, patron saint of livestock, are held in various parts of Bavaria, but none provides as much folkloristic color as this one. Farm women, dressed in their finest local *Trachten,* ride in elaborately carved and painted peasant carts, each drawn by a team of four garlanded horses, followed by drummers, trumpeters, hundreds of highland farmers on horseback, lederhosen-wearing rifle squads, and brass bands in all their finery. The parade follows a traditional route and ritual dating from the 18th century, passing through the main streets of the town and up to St. Leonard Chapel on the **Kalvarienberg** (Calvary Mountain). The fencing around this little church is made of chains from barns and stables, presented as devotional gifts by farmers whose cattle have been saved from disease or accidents. Before heading back to town, the procession encircles the church three times. On the way downhill the horseback riders snap huge 12- to 15-foot whips, called *Goaslschnalzen,* over the heads of the women and children in the carts, to protect them against demons and evil spirits.

Hotel accommodations are always hard to come by during the Leonhardifahrt festival, so book well in advance. Try the ▶ **Hotel Jodquellenhof,** Ludwigstrasse 13–15, on the west bank of the Isar. Though pricey, it's the best spa hotel in town.

From Bad Tölz it is a quick 53-km (33-mile) drive due north on B 13 back to Munich.

GETTING AROUND

Though there is train and bus service to all the destinations in Southern Bavaria, it tends to be a bit slow and infrequent. Two exceptions are Freising and Starnberg: Freising is served by S-Bahn (number S-1) from Munich's Marienplatz every 20 minutes during the daytime, and is the last stop on that line; Starnberg can be reached by the S-6 and is 14 stops from Marienplatz.

The best way to get around Southern Bavaria is to rent a car in Munich. Stick to the roads given here, and take along a detailed road map or, before setting out from Munich, purchase the *H-B Bildatlas:* number 7 for Oberbayern and number 36 for Niederbayern. Even if you speak or read no German, these picture atlases are useful, as they contain very detailed maps showing all the little side roads and unnumbered highways of the areas described.

Although there are Autobahn expressways from Munich to Landshut, from Munich past the Chiemsee to Berchtesgaden, and from Munich to Murnau (the stretch into Garmisch-Partenkirchen is incomplete), they tend to be heavily travelled and are no way to see the countryside, as they bypass the most interesting towns and the best scenery.

ACCOMMODATIONS REFERENCE

The hotel rates listed here are 1994 projections for double-bed, double-occupancy rooms, with a range from low to high whenever possible. Prices are given in deutsche marks (DM). Basic rates are always subject to change, so please verify price when you are booking. Breakfast is usually included in the price of a room.

City area codes must be preceded by a zero if you are calling from elsewhere in Germany.

▶ **Alpengasthof Winklmoosalm.** Dürrnbachhornweg 6, D-83242 **Reit im Winkl.** Tel: (8640) 10-97. DM 86.

▶ **Alter Wirt-Bonnschlössl.** Kirchplatz 9, D-83233 **Bernau am Chiemsee.** Tel: (8051) 890-11; Fax: (8051) 891-03. DM 90–140.

▶ **Clausings Post-Romantik-Hotel.** Marienplatz 12, D-82467 **Garmisch-Partenkirchen.** Tel: (8821) 70-90; Fax: (8821) 70-92-05. DM 180–300.

▶ **Goldene Sonne.** Neustadt 520, D-84028 **Landshut.** Tel: (871) 230-87; Fax: (871) 240-69. DM 175.

▶ **Hotel Alpenhof Murnau.** Ramsachstrasse 8, D-82418 **Murnau.** Tel: (8841) 49-10; Fax: (8841) 54-38. DM 210–410.

▶ **Hotel Alte Post.** Dorfstrasse 19, D-82487 **Oberammergau.** Tel: (8822) 10-91; Fax: (8822) 10-94. DM 110.

▶ **Hotel Bachmair-am-See.** Seestrasse 47, D-83700 **Rot-**

tach-Egern. Tel: (8022) 27-20; Fax: (8022) 27-27-90. DM 300–500 (includes lunch or dinner).

▶ Hotel Fischer. Königseer Strasse 51, D-83471 Berchtesgaden. Tel: (8652) 95-50; Fax: (8652) 648-73. DM 210–230.

▶ Hotel und Gasthof zum Rabenkopf. Kocheler Strasse 23, D-82431 Kochel am See. Tel: (8857) 208; Fax: (8857) 91-67. DM 136.

▶ Hotel Geiger. Stanggass, D-83471 Berchtesgaden. Tel: (8652) 50-55; Fax: (8652) 96-54-00. DM 180–280.

▶ Hotel Glöcklhofer. Ludwigsberg 4, D-84489 Burghausen. Tel: (8677) 70-24; Fax: (8677) 655-00. DM 130–150.

▶ Hotel Jodquellenhof. Postfach 2169, Ludwigstrasse 13–15, D-83640 Bad Tölz. Tel: (8041) 50-90; Fax: (8041) 50-94-41. DM 300–370.

▶ Hotel Post. Dorfplatz 6, D-82499 Wallgau. Tel: (8825) 10-11; Fax: (8825) 16-58. DM 110–190.

▶ Hotel zur Post. Kapellplatz 2, D-84503 Altötting. Tel: (8671) 50-40; Fax: (8671) 62-14. DM 160–290.

▶ Hotel zur Post. Stadtplatz 39, D-84489 Burghausen. Tel: (8677) 30-43; Fax: (8677) 620-91. DM 135.

▶ Hotel Steinbacher Hof. Steinbachweg 10, D-83242 Reit im Winkl. Tel: (8640) 80-70; Fax: (8640) 80-71-00. DM 150–215.

▶ Hotel Tonihof. Walchenseestrasse 42, D-82438 Eschenloe. Tel: (8824) 10-21; Fax: (8824) 14-77. DM 158–198.

▶ Hotel Unterwirt. Kirchplatz 2, D-83242 Reit im Winkl. Tel: (8640) 80-10; Fax: (8640) 80-11-50. DM 157–385.

▶ Hotel Wittelsbach. Maximilianstrasse 16, D-83471 Berchtesgaden. Tel: (8652) 50-61; Fax: (8652) 663-04. DM 115–158.

▶ Kurhotel Luisenbad. Ludwigstrasse 33, D-83435 Bad Reichenhall. Tel: (8651) 60-40; Fax: (8651) 629-28. DM 285–330.

▶ Lindner Hotel Kaiserhof. Papiererstrasse 2, D-84034 Landshut. Tel: (871) 68-70; Fax: (871) 68-74-03. DM 200–275.

▶ Park und Strandhotel Schloss Berg. Seestrasse 17, D-82335 Berg am Starnberger See. Tel: (8151) 501-06; Fax: (8151) 501-05. DM 230.

▶ Posthotel Partenkirchen. Ludwigstrasse 49, D-82467 Garmisch-Partenkirchen. Tel: (8821) 510-67; Fax: (8821) 785-68. DM 220–280.

▶ Residenz Heinz Winkler. Kirchplatz 1, D-83229 Aschau im Chiemgau. Tel: (8052) 179-90; Fax: (8052) 17-99-66. DM 220–450.

▶ Steigenberger-Hotel Axelmannstein. Salzburger Strasse 2–6, D-83435 Bad Reichenhall. Tel: (8651) 77-70; Fax: (8651) 59-32. DM 320–490.

STUTTGART AND THE SWABIAN HEARTLAND

By Peter Hays

Early on most weekday mornings the whole of Swabia shifts relentlessly into high gear. By 7:00 A.M. towns, streets, and Autobahns are buzzing with traffic. Up in the hill country, school buses shuttle their way through bustling villages. The region's overall mood of urgency is captured in the blur of cyclists swooping past the pedestrians in Stuttgart's Schloss-garten, legs pumping like well-tuned pistons.

For decades Swabia, the industrial heartland of the federal state of Baden-Württemberg, was a leader among even the pacesetters of the fabled "Economic Miracle." Its automobile industry, which owes much to Swabian inventors Gottlieb Wilhelm Daimler and Karl Friedrich Benz, led the way. The pace of industry has stepped up of late and the state now prides itself on the lowest rate of unemployment in the republic's 16 *Länder* (states).

For a breather from all that dynamism, Swabians regularly head for the surrounding countryside, an escapist's boon. A web of signposted hiking trails totaling some 12,500 miles threads through vast forests, this landscape's recurring theme. The forests sweep south to the northern shore of palm-fringed Lake Constance on the border with Switzerland, popular among Central European vacationers from spring to autumn. In the west, the forests follow the meandering Danube as the river begins its course to the Black Sea. The more provincial Neckar, inspiration for

Swabian poets Friedrich Schiller, Eduard Mörike, and Friedrich Hölderlin, flows here, too. To the southeast, roughly between Biberach, Isny, Friedrichshafen, and Ravensburg, the coniferous and deciduous forest thins into coppice dotted with Baroque monasteries, churches, and palaces.

One of the biggest wooded areas in the north, the **Schwäbische Wald** (Swabian Forest) has sun-dappled trails and glades that easily match those of the Black Forest. It stretches to the **Schwäbische Alb**, a corrugated Jurassic limestone wedge of upland south of Stuttgart. This is the region's geological backbone, undulating northeast to southwest with peaks between 1,500 and 2,700 feet high.

Scores of subterranean streams and rivers percolate through the Alb's porous interior and well up in countless valleys, glades, and hollows, most spectacularly in the **Blautopf**, an azure pool in the monastery village of Blaubeuren. The huge ridge also generates thermal currents suited to the region's many model-airplane and glider enthusiasts. Hang-glider pilots regularly plunge from limestone pinnacles (near Neuffen, for instance) that tower up along the Alb's westerly rim.

You may wish to confine yourself to some of the less hazardous activities in the region. Recently, many municipal councils have gone to great expense to refurbish their *Altstadt* (old city) areas. To walk the newly recobbled alleys is to step back into a medieval world. Towns like Schwäbisch Gmünd were granted charters in the 12th century by the local Hohenstaufen dynasty, which produced several Holy Roman emperors, including Frederick Barbarossa. The battlements and moats still existing in the region are evidence of a protracted territorial tussle among hundreds of rival principalities, duchies, prince-bishoprics, counties, palatinates, city-states, and tiny independent farming communities owing allegiance only to the Holy Roman emperor. After the fall of the Hohenstaufen rulers in 1268, major and minor potentates spent centuries jockeying or fighting for supremacy. Unification finally was forced upon them in 1806, when Napoleon declared the then-dominant Swabian duchy the kingdom of Württemberg.

With such varied terrain to cover, your route needs to be woven rather than plotted—ideally, in a series of long loops. From Schwäbisch Hall head southwest via Schwäbisch Gmünd to the state capital, Stuttgart, and from there up the Neckar valley to the university town of Tübingen. Then shuttle across to the Schwäbische Alb and back down to the historic towns of Hechingen, Rottweil, and Donaueschingen before threading your way through Konstanz, Überlingen, Meersburg, and Friedrichshafen on the banks of Lake Constance. Your third and final loop, the Baroque Road, will swing you north and westward, back to your starting point.

MAJOR INTEREST

Medieval towns of Schwäbisch Hall and Schwäbisch Gmünd

Stuttgart
Altstadt and Markthalle
Artifacts of Roman occupation in Römisches Lapidarium
Daimler-Benz Museum
Staatsgaleries, with German Old Masters and contemporary art

Tübingen
University and Altstadt
Hölderlinturm

Schwäbische Alb Region
The Blautopf (mysterious spring-fed crater)
Wimsener Höhle (aquatic cave)

Hohenzollern Country
Castles in Hechingen and Sigmaringen
Ancient Roman artifacts in Rottweil
Source of the Danube at Donaueschingen

Lake Constance (Bodensee) Region
Konstanz
Islands of Reichenau and Mainau
Überlingen
Stone Age village in Unteruhldingen

The Baroque Road

Schwäbisch Hall

Do not be put off by the unprepossessing outskirts of this town, 68 km (42 miles) northeast of Stuttgart on B 14. A business belt is a postwar phenomenon around most Swabian towns. The **Altstadt** proper is on the bank of the river Kocher; enter it along Salinenstrasse and you'll be reminded of the saltworks that flourished here for centuries. The *Hall* in the town's name also derives from them. Brine was pumped from a deep well, then simmered in large pans in the Hallplatz, now a riverside parking lot, until only the crystalline salt was left. The industry began to decline in the 19th century after the discovery of salt deposits in nearby

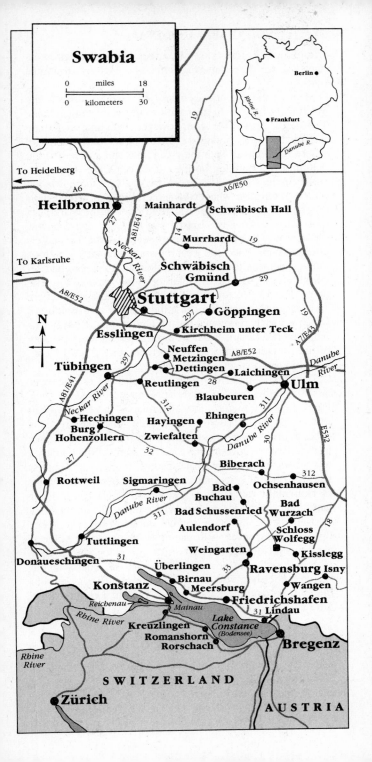

Wilhelmsglück. Tradition still decrees, however, that descendants of the salt-simmering families are given an annual pension.

Many of the old houses from Neue Strasse down to the Milchmarkt have been gentrified to the point of blandness. The Middle Ages come alive, however, in an uneven triangle bounded by the Marktplatz, Hafenmarkt, Keckenhof, and Obere Herrngasse. Note the chain links still attached to the half-timbered building on the corner of Obere Herrngasse and the main square: They were part of chains that cordoned off the **Marktplatz** whenever medieval knights settled their differences here. The last recorded duel in the Marktplatz took place between two brothers in 1523. Along the narrow cobblestone **Obere Herrngasse** are several particularly stately houses which reflect the wealth that accrued after generous municipal loans to various Holy Roman emperors had secured Schwäbisch Hall the status of a Free Imperial City. The poet Eduard Mörike lived with his sister at number 7. Obere and Untere Herrngasse meet at the **Gasthof zum Waldhorn,** which is locally renowned for the *tagliatelle* named after its Italian owner, Cesare. From the tavern's terrace there is a view of the Altstadt's ramparts, inadvertently unearthed by construction workers several years ago.

The town—presently with a population of just over 30,000—enjoys an annual relapse into the Middle Ages. From June to August, the Marktplatz's most prominent feature, 54 broad curving steps at **St. Michaelskirche,** is used as a slanting stage for the town's open-air theater festival. Past productions have starred some of the country's top actors in plays by Shakespeare, Brecht, and Schiller. Guests of honor sometimes include members of the house of Hohenlohe-Langenburg, relatives of England's Windsor family. Part of the former's palatial edifice, just up the road in **Neuenstein,** is open to the public. Those of lesser lineage staying at the ▶ **Romantik-Hotel Goldener Adler** in a room overlooking the Marktplatz can enjoy a royal view of the floodlit performance below, as can guests at the ▶ **Hotel Adelshof,** also on the square, which succeeds in blending its antique paneled and coffered interior with a full range of modern conveniences.

Schwäbisch Gmünd

Schwäbisch Gmünd is less than an hour's drive south of Schwäbisch Hall via the B 19 and B 298, and 52 km (33 miles) due east of Stuttgart on the B 29. A longer, scenic route, the *Idyllische Strasse* (Idyllic Road) between Main-hardt and Fichtenberg, skirts the **Murrhardter Wald**, one of the unsung corners of the Schwäbische Wald. Great waves of forest seem to roll toward the horizon, particularly after a thunderstorm has shrouded them in mist. At dusk, deer lope over patches of farmland; at dawn, tattered feathers in quiet clearings are the only remainder of some fox's midnight feast. The local farming folk are tough and independent. Their dialect is down-to-earth Swabian, which incongruously attaches the diminutive *le* to nearly every noun, and thus sounds strangely sweet to German ears. Strangers who linger long enough in a remote village like **Steinberg** are often invited to a *Hockele,* an impromptu gossip 'n' grub session at the end of the day. Bottles of the local *Apfelmost,* cider with a kick, are thumped down on long tables along with *Schärrkuchen,* savory pastries sprinkled with flakes of butter and cheese, and served straight out of the oven. For a wider range of rural fare, stop in at the **Gasthof Engel** in the little town of **Murrhardt**.

Schwäbisch Gmünd's main square, the **Marktplatz**, is 600 feet long, and a stroll across it is something of an expedition. The Baroque town-house façades around it appear standoffish and ornamental. As far as the original owners—wealthy merchants and craftsmen—were concerned, this was probably the desired effect.

As early as the 14th century municipal power passed from the local nobility to the guilds. The Swabians' entrepreneurial skill was admirably demonstrated in Gmünd by blacksmiths and cartwrights. As business slackened they turned their hand to forging scythes, and by 1580 were producing more than 270,000 a year, exporting them as far away as France and Spain. That trade dwindled during the devastating Thirty Years' War. Splendid isolation was never an option in those turbulent days, however substantial the town fortifications, and Gmünd suffered considerable damage during the Peasants' War in 1525 and the religious feuds that followed. The town was also drawn into the War of Spanish Succession and skirmishes in 1796 triggered by the French Revolution.

A sizable **Altstadt**, which survived World War II unscathed, still surrounds the Marktplatz. Two houses deserve special scrutiny. The **Kornhaus** (at the end of Kornhausstrasse), a lofty half-timbered tithe barn, dates from the 16th century. The **Fuggerei**, in the Münsterplatz, was a residence for visiting medieval VIPs. Its Romanesque façade was elaborated with half-timbered frills in the 15th century. Of the town's three main churches, the **Johanniskirche** (St. John's Church) is outstanding. If you sample an ice cream at the Italian-run

Café Margrit, you will have a wonderful view of the late afternoon sun gilding the finely sculpted hunting scenes on the façade opposite.

Several bits of stonework are left from the Hohenstaufen era. Some can be found down narrow Bühlsgässle. One whole wall of the **Grät**, an early medieval building, consists of *Buckelquader*, large chunks of quarried rock with the visible surface left unfinished. Period sleuths enjoy tracking down the roughly hewn masonry, which also crops up in Schwäbisch Hall and Vellberg. South of Schwäbisch Gmünd brown Staufer Route signs with their crown-and-lion logo lead to the village of **Hohenstaufen**, nestling below the ruins of one of the Imperial family's hilltop castles. A steep path snakes up to some fragments of ancient wall, another good example of *Buckelquader* and their uneven surfaces. Here, the various Hohenstaufen emperors had a superb view of a fraction of their territory. They spent very little time in their Swabian homeland, however; leading Crusades and vying with successive popes for European supremacy kept them down south. The Hohenstaufen Friedrich II was even crowned king of Sicily in 1198. The last Hohenstaufen, Konradin, was beheaded in Naples in 1268, and these ruins are the last memento of an overambitious family that faded into oblivion. Stuttgart is only half an hour west of Schwäbish Gmünd.

STUTTGART

A capital's inhabitants often have a supercilious attitude toward their country cousins. Stuttgart's 600,000 citizens are an exception to the rule. When Baden and Württemberg were unified into a single political region in 1952, Stuttgart became the new federal state's capital. But those busy postwar decades did not lend themselves to the development of cosmopolitan airs and graces. Stuttgarters instead buckled down to rebuilding their city. During World War II, more than 50 air raids had destroyed an estimated 75 percent of the Altstadt. Up on the **Birkenkopf**, a hillock near the city center, a mound of rubble 40 feet high was dubbed "Monte Scherbelino" (Mount Smithereens) by the locals. It has since been landscaped into a memorial park. And there has been considerable industrial success—today Bosch, Bauknecht, Daimler-Benz, IBM, Kodak, Leitz, and Porsche are based in Stuttgart. Tour guides even point out the Mercedes trademark rotating on top of the main railway station's tower as one of the city's major sights.

Today's Stuttgarters are a fascinating hybrid: children of

an industrialized society, proud of their rural heritage. If you arrive at the Hauptbahnhof (main train station), you will sense this. Look uphill from the station's main entrance toward a vineyard that slopes down the **Kriegsberg** into the heart of town. These dusty vines, one of the world's most surprising metropolitan sights, produce quite a reasonable red Trollinger wine. Property developers would love to grab them up, but because of their symbolic value they seem destined for survival. The steep valley that hems the city in on all sides used to be densely covered with vineyards. Like any ancient Neckar village downriver, Stuttgart still holds its *Weindorf* (wine festival) late every summer on Kirchstrasse and the Marktplatz.

Stuttgart's picturesque setting has its drawbacks, however. In summer, early-morning mist from the river mingles with exhaust fumes, and the resulting smog may not lift until well after noon. For the predominantly working-class community on the lower-altitude outskirts of the city, the days can be unbearably sultry. Those who are better off live up on the metropolitan basin's edge, in affluent districts such as Feuerbacher Heide, Degerloch, or Sillenbuch.

Stuttgart's yellow municipal trams run on seven main lines and link up with the underground Stadtbahn's network. VVS, the public transport authority, offers a very reasonably priced *Tagessparkarte,* or rover ticket, which entitles the bearer to a full day's use of its services. Short of hiring a plane there is hardly a quicker way to get your bearings than by tram-hopping. You have several options. Tram line number 5 climbs up to **Degerloch**, giving you a splendid view of the city. For a different view, you can also board the network's one and only cable car from Heslach up to the **Waldfriedhof,** one of the city's main cemeteries. It runs every quarter of an hour until 8:45 P.M. in summer and 7:41 P.M. in winter. Equally exciting is the cogwheel tram ride (number 10) from Marienplatz up to Degerloch. Late at night a cogwheel taxi takes over, at no extra charge. These rides, with their choice of vistas, also serve a useful purpose: It quickly becomes clear that historic Stuttgart is compact enough to explore on foot.

The Altstadt

Visitors with a sense of history start their walk at Schillerplatz. This was the city's nucleus, the site of the *Stuatgarten* (stud farm) owned by Luitolf, one of the dukes of Swabia, in the tenth century.

On the south side of the square is the moated **Altes Schloss** (Old Castle), built around 1320. The castle's deli-

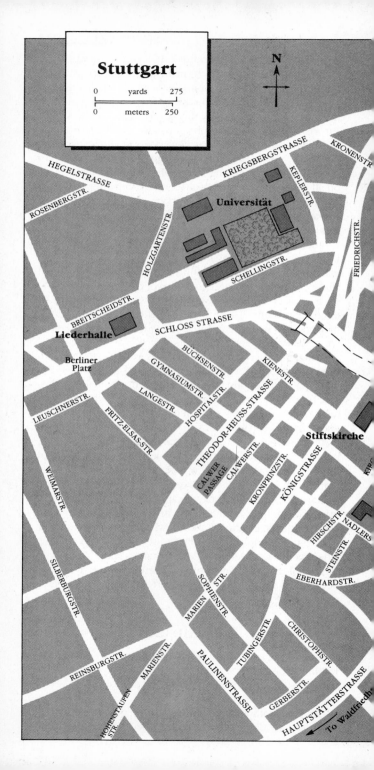

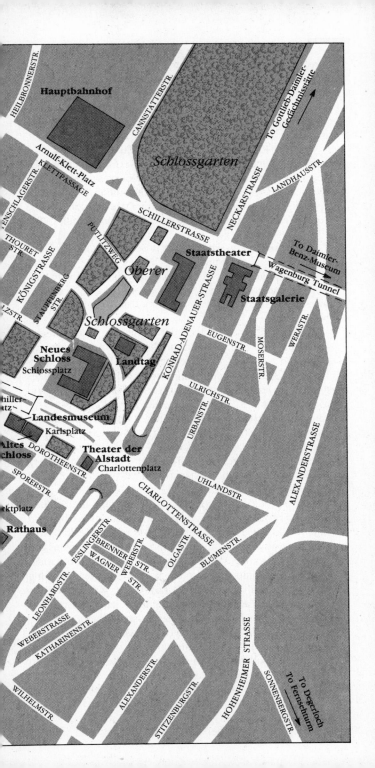

cately sculpted Renaissance arcades, added in the 16th century, frame weekend concerts held in the courtyard during the summer. Inside, the **Württembergisches Landesmuseum** has the former monarchy's crown jewels on display. Admission is free, as is the case in most of the other town museums, except for special exhibitions.

The **Alte Kanzlei** restaurant on the square specializes in a number of the region's staple dishes. *Gaisburger Marsch* (beef stew served with radishes and onions) and *Spätzle,* Swabia's version of pasta, are worth sampling. The open-air section of the restaurant juts toward the middle of the square with its statue of a pensive Friedrich Schiller; Tel: (711) 29-44-57.

Just behind cozy Schillerplatz is Schlossplatz, laid out to overwhelm. Its prim and proper **Neues Schloss** (New Palace), completed in 1807, embraces a symmetrical composition of segmented lawns, splashing fountains, and chestnut trees that could probably accommodate Trafalgar Square twice over.

This square amply reflects the past century's golden era. Pomp and circumstance became the order of the day when Napoleon elevated Duke Friedrich to first king of Württemberg, in 1806. Friedrich I commanded Württemberg's dukes to spend at least three months a year at court in Stuttgart and to address him as "Your Most Serene and Almighty Majesty." King and courtiers divided their time between Stuttgart and nearby Ludwigsburg, with its regal residence, **Monrepos**, and Baroque palace. The special Franco-Swabian relationship cooled appreciably in 1812: Of 15,000 Württemberg soldiers forced to join Bonaparte on his disastrous Russian campaign, only 300 returned.

Save a whole afternoon for a walk through the **Schlossgarten**, a broad ribbon of a park that extends more than two miles from the Hauptbahnhof to where the Neckar river snakes its way out of the city. Some very senior citizens can remember spotting Württemberg's King Wilhelm II out walking his own Pomeranians in the park and at first mistaking him for a royal servant in shabby livery. Wilhelm II was never keen to have his photo taken in military uniform, and his pacifist views incurred Prussian Kaiser Wilhelm's displeasure. After World War I, he was deposed by a "tearful revolution," his former subjects affectionately but firmly retiring him to palatial lodgings next to a 12th-century Cistercian cloister in **Bebenhausen**, north of Tübingen. There he soon became a regular in the Hirsch tavern, partial to a *Viertel* (quarter-liter) of wine. His wife, Charlotte, lived in Bebenhausen until 1946.

The park's sunbathers adhere to the Swabian level of

decorum: The nudist frolics seen in Munich's Englischer Garten never caught on here. Stuttgarters often round off their Schlossgarten walk by dropping into the **Mineralbad Leuze**. Pungent mineral water said to be good for the digestion and all sorts of ailments gushes out of three taps; you can help yourself to some with one of the ladles hanging on a chain. In fact, there is so much water to go around that it circulates copiously through the Leuze's pools and even rains out of a row of decorative fountains.

In the past, children from outlying villages fetched the "health water" in large cans. They came into town the old-fashioned way: down *Stäffele,* long flights of steps cut into the valley's flanks. The 306 Hasenberg steps and most of the other Stäffele are still used by joggers.

From the Leuze baths it is only a short walk to the **Wilhelma piers**, where the **Neckar-Personen-Schiffahrt**'s riverboats dock. There are two river cruises daily that go as far downstream as **Marbach**, Schiller's birthplace. The house the poet/playwright was born in is on Nikolastorstrasse. The **Schiller Nationalmuseum** (on the Schillerhöhe) has memorabilia associated with him.

Museums in Stuttgart

A dozen major museums in Stuttgart chronicle several millennia of history. At Schillerplatz you can go from one era to the next in minutes. The **Römisches Lapidarium**, in the Fruchtkasten, the city's medieval wine depot, shows artifacts of the Roman occupation. A few doors away, the **Württembergisches Landesmuseum** takes up the story in the third century when the Alemanni, the Swabians' West Germanic forebears, overran the Roman Limes and settled between the Neckar and the Danube.

Many Stuttgarters, more interested in revs per minute than revolutions, prefer over history an era that has pride of place in the city's consciousness: the hundred-odd years of automobile manufacture. On weekends pilgrimage-size crowds flock to the **Gottlieb-Daimler-Gedächtnisstätte** (Daimler Memorial) in Bad Cannstatt, a neighborhood on the north banks of the Neckar, and the converted shed in which Daimler, assisted by his friend Wilhelm Maybach, assembled the first high-speed gasoline engine in 1883. The exhibits include Daimler's workbench and tools. The little museum is open from May to October. There is also a much larger **Daimler-Benz Museum** on the car plant's grounds in the Stuttgart-Untertürkheim district on Mercedesstrasse. A full range of automobiles, from vintage to the very latest, is on display. From Gate 1 of the plant, a shuttle bus carries visitors to the museum, which is open daily except Mondays and public holidays year-round. One of Daimler's best customers was Consul Jellinek, who had a daughter named Mercedes. As a token of gratitude, the Swabian engineer named his first models after her.

The new wing of the **Staatsgalerie** (State Gallery), designed by the late British architect James Stirling, opened in 1984, and is the city's most entertaining piece of modern architecture. A flamingo-pink balustrade arches up to a slanted façade of local sandstone punctuated by broad, green-mullioned glass. Ivy has already spread up the walls of the inner courtyard, where art students sketch away in the shadows of statues. Lovers of contemporary art are treated to regular exhibitions of the new masters, including Georges Braque, Marc Chagall, Otto Dix, Oskar Kokoschka, Piet Mondrian, and Salvador Dalí. The gallery owns one of the country's most respected collections of Picassos.

Unfortunately, on Stuttgart's outskirts, slabs of concrete have replaced anything resembling a façade. One of the city's most obtrusive eyesores is the top-security prison in the Stammheim district, whose inmates once included members of the terrorist organization Rote Armee Fraktion. The **Fernsehturm**, Stuttgart's concrete television tower, much criticized on aesthetic grounds when it opened in 1956, has since been copied in Paris. Its restaurant, with magnificent views of the Alb and the Black Forest, is much frequented on weekends.

The Arts in Stuttgart

Bordering the Oberer Schlossgarten, the **Landtag**, Baden-Württemberg's glass-plated House of Parliament, faces the pillared **Staatstheater**. After their debates, the state deputies often dash over to catch a performance. The State Theater is composed of the **Grosses Haus** (1,400 seats), the **Kleines Haus** (851 seats), and the **Kammertheater**. The latter, also designed by Stirling and known for its experimental repertoire, is actually in the Staatsgalerie and is connected to the main building by a pedestrian subway under Konrad-Adenauer-Strasse. Guest performances by world-famous companies from abroad continue to bring the theater good reviews, and its own **Staatsoper** and **Stuttgarter Ballet** ensembles are popular in their own right. The Staatsoper was formed in the mid-18th century with the support of Duke Karl Eugen, an ardent patron. The ballet owes its present reputation to the late John Cranko and to Marcia Haydée, who took over in 1976 after "miracle-worker" Cranko's death.

The **Varieté Marquee**, featuring afternoon and early evening performances by jugglers, clowns, acrobats, and assorted other entertainers, is the closest Stuttgart gets to old-time music-hall entertainment. The theater performs in a tent opposite the Inter-Continental hotel at the moment, and its permanent 1993 site won't be known until early in the year. **Theaterle der Käsreiter** has moved from Stuttgart to Holzgerlingen, 19 km (12 miles) west of the city, where, in the **Gasthof "Waldhorn,"** it offers a repertoire of sketches and fairy tales performed in the unmistakable Swabian dialect. Some of the dialogues in the **Theater am Faden**, in Hasenstrasse, may be just as incomprehensible to Swabians, but the stars—intricately crafted marionettes—are worth seeing. The **Liederhalle**, on Berliner Platz, is the venue for big rock, jazz, and classical concerts. An adjoining congress center has just been completed.

Staying in Stuttgart

The postwar years here have ushered in a new generation of hotels geared to the needs of business travellers. Modern business conveniences—central location, 6:00 A.M. breakfast—generally rank higher on the list of priorities than, say, atmosphere. The leaders in the efficiency stakes include the ▶ **Steigenberger-Hotel Graf Zeppelin**, on Arnulf-Klett-Platz, and the ▶ **Inter-Continental**, at Willy-Brandt-Strasse 30. Both are ideally situated if you fancy joining executives for long prebusiness jogs in the Schlossgarten. Jet laggards opt for the ▶ **Stuttgart Airport Hotel** on the Randstrasse. However, farther to the west and north along the rim of Stuttgart's valley, hotel life gets more interesting. From the ▶ **Relexa Waldhotel Schatten**, on Magstadterstrasse, you can conveniently sidetrack to Duke Karl Eugen's 17th-century Rococo residence. The ▶ **Messehotel Europe**, at Siemensstrasse 33, is handy to the big trade fairs held up on the Killesberg as well as to **Perkins Park**, the city's longtime top disco.

Dining and Nightlife in Stuttgart

Spells of sultry weather assail the city from early spring to late autumn. But a redeeming feature of a hot, sticky day is that it often turns into a balmy night. When that is the case, early nightlife follows a simple traditional routine: several hours of starlit chat, regional wine served in squat *Viertel* glasses, and hearty Swabian food in a favorite *Gartenwirtschaft*. There are some 160 of these restaurants, which spill over onto pavements, courtyards, gardens, and parks. The huge **Amadeus**, on Charlottenplatz, has 400 seats; Tel: (711) 29-26-78. The elegant **Café Künstlerbund**, in the yard of a former orphanage, attracts an artsy-craftsy clientele to its site under the Schlossplatz's arcades; Tel: (711) 226-41-49. The **Kachelofen**, at Eberhardstrasse 10, tolerates casually dressed guests out on the pavement but not necessarily inside the restaurant proper. Closed Sundays; Tel: (711) 24-23-78. And the vine-draped **Rebgarten**, on Hohenheimer Strasse, has an admirable choice of wines. The **Kiste** on Kanalstrasse is one of the city's oldest and most popular *Weinstüben*.

Very little pub crawling takes place in Stuttgart, where patrons' allegiance to a regular *Wirtschaft* is likely to waver only after a change in ownership. These establishments all have an egalitarian feel, but telltale signs distinguish them. You are in pricey territory if the wine list differentiates between fruity Badener vintages and their drier Württemberg counterparts. Prices are most reasonable where you are offered five variations on the theme of *Maultaschen,* the Swabian answer to ravioli. Members of the moderately bohemian "in" crowd congregate in the candlelit **Litfass** (halfway down to the Rathaus underground station), but would never set foot in the **Weinstube Schellenturm**, at Weberstrasse 72, a favorite haunt of government officials. Closed Sundays; Tel: (711) 236-48-88. The Schellenturm got its name from the little bells stitched to the garments of the convicts who were formerly incarcerated here.

There are also Italian, Greek, Chinese, and vegetarian restaurants in Stuttgart. One of the few surviving fragments of the real Altstadt stretches from Fritz-Elsas-Strasse down the first hundred yards or so of Calwer Strasse. This is where businesspeople bring visiting associates for meals and deals. There is a row of popular restaurants: **Mira**, Calwer Strasse 46, Tel: (711) 29-36-30; **Da Vinci**, first and foremost a fast-serving pizzeria; **Fifty-Two**, at number 52, Tel: (711) 29-75-12; and **Bistro St. Germain**, at number 56, Tel: (711) 29-59-00. Invariably, their tables crowd the sidewalks, leaving just enough room for a thin trickle of pedestrians.

A sprinkling of discos, bistros, bars, peep shows, and nightclubs stay open into the wee hours. Observers attribute the state capital's straitlaced late-night style to Calvinist principles of the Reformation, and indeed, compared to other cities, Stuttgart manages only a blushing pink-light district, in the **Bohnenviertel**. Bounded by Charlottenstrasse, Esslinger Strasse, and Wagnerstrasse, this former low-rent area has seen seedier days. The professional classes have begun to move into the revamped terraced housing, and in streets full of dutifully fed parking meters, chic boutiques and wine parlors are fast replacing the *Stundenhotels,* where rooms are leased by the hour. Perhaps a slight air of mystery still surrounds bars like the **Nachtwächter** on Brennerstrasse, which serves its clients behind an opaque glass front. **Basta**, on Wagnerstrasse, is a middle-brow debating bistro where the day's newspapers, attached to long sticks, are scoured for financial tidbits and the like until well past midnight.

Shopping in Stuttgart

The Swabians' are allegedly tightfisted, but this is nowhere in evidence on Saturday morning's spending spree in **König-strasse**, Stuttgart's shopping haven. Converted from city moat to elegant boulevard during King Friedrich I's reign in the early part of the 19th century, the street is now a mile-long pedestrian zone flanked by department stores. On weekdays it dies a sudden death at 6:30 P.M., when the shops close. Evening shopping (until 10:00 P.M.) continues in the subterranean **Klettpassage**, opposite the main railway station. The city's glitterati pop into the **Calwerpassage** between Calwer Strasse and Theodor-Heuss-Strasse for their more pricey upmarket needs. In the neon-flecked fashion boutiques you pay that little bit extra for the prestigious labels. The pedestrian-zone **Schulstrasse** is in the same class. The Parisian-style **Flo** has already attracted its own "in crowd" in the recently completed **Karlspassage** shopping arcade. The burghers are especially proud of their ultra-modern consumerists' temple, the **Schwabenzentrum**, on Eberhardstrasse. The **Markthalle**, on Dorotheenstrasse, cele-brated its 75th anniversary in 1989; it's a cornucopia of fruit, vegetables, fish, meat, and spices. Outdoor markets are held on Tuesdays, Thursdays, and Saturdays on Schillerplatz and Marktplatz. And every Saturday, a flea market spreads over Karlsplatz.

TÜBINGEN

In its less modest moments Tübingen refers to itself as a supplier of "seminal thinkers." An occasional lapse into hubris is excusable. The University of Tübingen is one of the country's oldest and best respected, and its 25,000 students make up a third of the city's population. The Hohe Schule was founded in 1477 when Pope Sixtus IV granted permission to a minor aristocrat, Count Eberhard, to do so. In 1536 Duke Ulrich added the **Stift**, originally a college to train the Protestant vicars needed to replace the Roman Catholic priests ousted by the Reformation, and situated in a dissolved Augustinian monastery. Over the centuries the two merged into the present university. Graduates have included some outstanding figures: Philipp Melanchthon

(1497–1560), who succeeded his friend, Martin Luther, as leader of the German Reformation movement; the astronomer Johannes Kepler (1571–1630), who was one of the first to support Copernicus's theory of the solar system and also advanced his own formulae, confirmed by the Sputnik space probe three centuries later; and the philosopher Georg Wilhelm Friedrich Hegel (1770–1831). Hegel shared a room in Tübingen with the student poet Friedrich Hölderlin and the future philosopher Wilhelm Schelling. The poet Eduard Mörike and the novelist Wilhelm Hauff were also students here.

Although many departments have long since moved to modern buildings in the suburbs, the university's old core is still a photogenic jumble of half-timbered houses stretching down from Schloss Hohentübingen to the Neckar. Flotillas of swans and students in narrow flat-bottomed punts drift languidly past a skyline that is almost identical to the one shown in a 347-year-old copperplate etching by Mathäus Merian. Mörike waxed lyrical over the irresistible view from the **Eberhardsbrücke**: "My hands folded, as if of their own free will, and I felt my soul rejoice."

There are still a lot of romantics around, more than a million of whom visit Tübingen annually. (Tübingen is only 44 km/27½ miles south up the Neckar from Stuttgart.) The **Altstadt** is at its time-warped best early in the morning or very late in the evening, when the crooked lanes are empty. At the northern end of the Eberhardsbrücke turn down the path between the river and the **Zwingel**, the 13th-century remains of the town wall. Near the punt moorings, where willow branches trail in the Neckar, is the **Hölderlinturm**, a part of the old fortifications. Following a tragic love affair, theology graduate and tutor Hölderlin tumbled into the shadowy world of schizophrenia. In an act of charity, Ernst Friedrich Zimmer, a well-read carpenter who had been impressed by Hölderlin's novel *Hyperion,* took in the ailing man of letters as a lodger in the little tower above his workshop. There Hölderlin lived for nearly 40 tormented years. His lyrical genius was not fully appreciated until this century (Heidegger was one booster), when donations helped convert his refuge into a museum. Exhibits include first editions and some of the essays Hölderlin wrote as a university student.

Only 5,000 or so people actually live in the old part of town, no more than during Duke Karl Eugen's reign. The stately university buildings stand out from their half-timbered neighbors huddled above the Hölderlinturm. In 1477, the first 250 scholars studied, ate, and slept in the **Bursa**, on Bursagasse. In those days only Latin was spoken within the college walls, a rule enforced by a *lupus,* or supervisor. Now the Alte Bursa houses art, history, and philosophy seminars.

The university has always been known for its pugnacious brand of theologian. On July 14, 1793, Hegel, Schelling, and Hölderlin danced a boisterous *carmagnole* together to celebrate the fourth anniversary of the storming of the Bastille. Young Hölderlin's enthusiasm in particular seems to have waned as the French Revolution's atrocities became apparent.

The first women students were admitted to the university way back in 1904. In 1987 students proclaimed the university a "nuclear-free zone." Defiant graffiti line the Neckarhalde, a rambling lane in which several of the more militant ecology groups have their offices. Earnest political debate, a favorite student pastime in the evenings, is a public spectacle, witnessed in any of the *Gögenbeizen.* There are dozens of these wine taverns; the **Wirtschaft am Hölderlinturm**, down by the river, is one of the best known.

About 600 students, often resplendent in colorful caps and sashes, belong to centuries-old fraternities. Some members still indulge in initiation duels ruled legal by recent court decisions. The fraternities' traditional *Maisingen,* the singing of patriotic songs in the Marktplatz in May, sometimes leads to clashes with the less-conservative student faction. Under the town hall's Baroque-style gables, an astronomical clock has accurately recorded astral maneuvers, including solar eclipses, since 1511. Happily, its brilliant inventor, the mathematics professor Johannes Stöffler, was mistaken when he predicted the end of the world for February 25, 1524.

The town employs some 30 guides, many of them former academics who take visitors on individual tours. With a jangling bunch of keys they can get you into Tübingen's lesser-known nooks and crannies, including the **Karzer**, the tiny cell in which students had to spend hours or even days for minor offenses such as wearing the wrong attire. The brand-new **Stadtmuseum** on Kornhausstrasse is already renowned for its self-critical view of local affairs: Its inaugural exhibition was entitled "National Socialism in Tübingen." Two nice, moderately priced hotels offer pleasant lodging in the old city: ► **Am Schloss**, on Burgsteige, and the ► **Hospiz**, on Neckarhalde.

THE SCHWÄBISCHE ALB

East of Tübingen and more or less south of Stuttgart is the Schwäbische Alb, a high limestone plateau stretching from the Black Forest to the mountains of Bohemia. More than

175 million years ago it was part of a desert swept by scorching winds. As the millennia elapsed, the shifting surface compacted into a deep layer of red sandstone, which in turn disappeared under a gradually encroaching saltwater sea whose graveyard of shellfish and other crustaceans decomposed into limestone. Toward the end of the Mesozoic era, roughly 135 million years ago, the multitiered rock sandwich was topped off by three more strata of Jurassic limestone after yet another inland sea receded. In the course of seismic upheavals that ended 15 million years ago, the formation reared up into a rough version of the upland we know today. Modern geologists liken the Alb to an enormous leaky barrel. Over the ages water has seeped through the porous limestone and accumulated carbonic acid, which is steadily eroding a subterranean tracery of largely uncharted streams, rivers, lakes, and caves.

Slate from the Alb's Jurassic layer has been quarried for centuries. At the end of the 19th century, a young man named Bernhard Hauff was the first to probe the area for fossilized remains of the denizens of those primeval seas. Many of these specimens are in the **Staatliches Museum für Naturkunde** (Natural History Museum) in Stuttgart. The fossil hunt is still on. Collectors crack open slate shards with little hammers, usually discovering dozens of fossils, mainly of mollusks.

Dettingen/Kirchheim unter Teck

A particularly good view of the Alb, a shoal of dark humps beckoning southward, can be had from the cherry orchards overlooking Dettingen (south of Stuttgart to Metzingen, then east on B 28) and the neighboring town of Kirchheim unter Teck. Farmers in Dettingen pick fruit by hand from more than 10,000 trees. Part of the crop is traditionally distilled into *Kirschgeist,* a clear, fiery cherry brandy. Recently there has been a slump in production because of ever-higher duty and overhead, but many villagers nonetheless keep their cellars well stocked with their own moonshine. You can sample Kirschgeist at its best and punchiest in the **Gasthaus Grüner Baum**, the village's liveliest tavern, populated by a bunch of regulars versed in the coarser forms of Swabian humor. Genuine Kirschgeist generally comes in a bottle without a label, and is served in thimble-size glasses. Connoisseurs dab a drop on the backs of their hands and sniff it for quality.

Blaubeuren

Southeast of Dettingen, B 28 climbs toward Blaubeuren and Ulm into a less fertile region atop the Alb. The villages, clusters of red-roofed cottages in the upland's folds, look deceptively prosperous. The topsoil here is sometimes less than four inches deep. Rye and wheat grow only about half as tall as down in the Neckar valley. Rain falls frequently but percolates rapidly into the Alb's porous limestone innards. Despite a great deal of research, the exact location of many huge underground reservoirs is still anyone's guess. One subterranean river route was traced simply enough, however, when dye allowed to trickle into the ground in Laichingen and Suppingen during a heavy rainfall resurfaced three days later just west of Ulm in Blaubeuren's **Blautopf**, a small crater filled with water that turns a brilliant shade of blue during dry periods.

The Blautopf's spring bubbles away, and its water is channeled up at high pressure through a series of limestone caves. Attempts to swim down the latter have claimed the lives of several divers. Jochen Hasenmayer, the most successful to date, was equipped with six aqualungs and a turbine-driven propeller when, in 1983, he fought and wriggled his way through 3,000 feet of tiny caves and lofty caverns. Groups of five and more can watch a 45-minute video film of his exploit in the tiny poolside cinema.

Eduard Mörike found the intriguing blue pool "too wonderful to be adequately described." Its setting in a quiet valley has attracted generations of people who come to meditate and marvel. The first church here was built in the seventh century; a monastery was erected in 1085. The monks' cells are now used by a boarding school, and the magnificently sculpted **cloisters**, which frame an herb garden, are open to the public. Some of the 500-year-old frescoes, especially those in the **Margarethenkapelle** (Chapel of St. Margaret), serve as a backdrop for the graffiti of generations of young boarders.

Wimsener Höhle

Not all of the Alb's caves are restricted to intrepid explorers. A wooded ravine just off the scenic country road between Hayingen and, south of there on the B 312, **Zwiefalten**, camouflages the country's sole navigable cavern, the **Wimsener Höhle**. At the **Gasthaus Friedrichshöhle**, known for its trout dishes, you can rent essentials for the expedition: a guide and a flat-bottomed boat. Open April through October; Tel: (7373) 813. At the cavern's lip a Latin inscription commemorates a ducal visit by Friedrich von Württemberg in 1803. Nothing much has changed in the dimly lit cave since then. The boatman claws the clammy walls with his fingertips to propel the vessel. The interior is just big enough, if passengers duck their heads, for a 200-foot foray. Beyond that are darkness and silence, except for the eerie drip of water. What people remember most about their short cruise is a rock about halfway along shaped spookily like an old man's head.

Bad Buchau

The Alb's dry patches generate thermal currents that local gliders thrive on. Villages like **Hayingen**, on the southeast side of the Alb, have long, stubbly runways, called "airports," for their sailplane enthusiasts. Storks, flying in from Africa to breed, also benefit from the thermals. Generations of storks have homed in on the **Federsee**, a marshy lake at Bad Buchau (southeast of the Alb near Biberach) that the *Deutscher Bund für Vogelschutz* (German Society for the Protection of Birds) has kept as a bird sanctuary since 1911. In the 1960s Baden-Württemberg's population of itinerant storks dropped from 154 to 45, but recently there has been an upswing in their numbers. A mile-long boardwalk stretching out through the reeds provides a binoculars-aided view of some of the more than 200 bird species that congregate here. By autumn most of the birds, both parents and offspring, head for Africa. A few remain, to be fed through the winter by farmers in nearby Oggelshausen.

Hohenzollern Country

The facts of Prussian history are far removed from a fairy tale, although the royal family's last outpost, **Burg Hohenzollern**, suggests otherwise. Perched south of Tübingen at 2,700 feet on one of the Alb's westernmost pinnacles, the castle stabs the clouds with turrets that bring to mind knights in armor and damsels in distress. A narrow road winds up to the castle from **Hechingen**, its attendant town. Great echoing halls like the Grafensaal are a bit too monumental for domestic comfort. No one actually lived in Burg Hohenzollern until 1951, when Prussia's prince-in-waiting, Louis Ferdinand, and his wife, Kira, a great-niece of the last tsar, Nicholas II, brought a whiff of domesticity with them. Every summer the sound of children's laughter echoes through the castle. Princess Kira, who has since died, founded a charity for deprived Berlin youngsters, and the proceeds from an annual concert held in the Grafensaal go toward funding long therapeutic stays for them at the castle.

If a flag with the Prussian eagle is fluttering in the breeze, Louis Ferdinand is at home. During his sporadic stays the crown prince uses five of the castle's 250 salons, chambers, and banqueting halls. A retainer serves him breakfast, but Louis Ferdinand takes his other meals in the nearby **Burgschenke**, a restaurant that caters to nearly half a million visitors annually.

His employees address the prince as "Your Imperial Majesty," and their devotion borders on the effusive. One typical comment: "You could chop the prince into a hundred pieces and each bit would still be imperial." Prince Louis Ferdinand is a grandson of the last German kaiser, Wilhelm II. Although Prussia's royals were stripped of their political power at the end of World War I (along with the rest of Germany's aristocracy), within their own circles the hierarchies of old, as set down in the *Almanach de Gotha* (the Continent's peerage register), still hold.

The first castle on the present site was probably built in the 11th century. Although records are inconclusive, the original owners were probably forebears of the Hohenzollerns named Burchardinger. The seemingly impregnable castle has been wrested from the Hohenzollern grip twice: by Countess Henriette von Württemberg's army in 1423 and by French troops in 1744. It was rebuilt from ruins in 1846, when the Prussian and Swabian branches of the Hohenzollern family chose it as their joint ancestral residence.

At the foot of the castle rock you can take a shuttle bus up or opt for a steep walk through the woods. Crenellated walls lead up to the keep and the castle's Neo-Gothic melodrama of flying buttresses, rib and shaft ceilings, pointed arches, and stained-glass windows.

The treasures on display in the **Schatzkammer** (Treasury) include a bejeweled Prussian crown that Kaiser Wilhelm II had made in 1889. The **Christuskapelle** (Christ's Chapel) held the coffins of kings Friedrich Wilhelm I and Frederick the Great until August 1991, when they were transferred to Potsdam by train with a modicum of pomp and ceremony.

Hohenzollern territory extends south across the Alb to the town of **Sigmaringen**, an hour's drive down the B 32 and B 313 from Hechingen. **Schloss Sigmaringen**, seen from the Danube below, looks intimidating and aloof atop its sheer rock face. But its front section juts into the heart of town. In medieval times the castle's occupants must have felt particularly vulnerable during periods of unrest. This is hinted at by the array of helmets, maces, and heavy muskets you'll pass on the way into the keep. Fortunately for Sigmaringen, the ruling family's diplomatic skills usually averted major showdowns. Even Napoleon was successfully appeased. Portraits of his relatives still abound in the stuccoed interior, which was largely refurnished after a devastating fire in 1893. Prince Franz, who lives here with his family, turns up as a guest of honor at local soccer club functions and joins in the fun at meetings of the *Elferrat* (Carnival committee) wearing old Hohenzollern uniforms. The locals have nicknamed him *Eierprinz* (Egg Prince) because of the farm he owns and runs.

Rottweil

Rottweil, 35 km (22 miles) southwest of Hechingen via the B 27, is Baden-Württemberg's oldest town; exploring its past requires only some sensible walking shoes. Start down in the **Altstadt** on the banks of the Neckar. The river wends its way between the Alb's wooded flanks and the foothills of the Black Forest. Ancient Rome's empire builders risked a tentative settlement here that they called Arae Flaviae. From A.D. 73 on, the military encampment developed into a community. The **Römerbad**, remains of thermal baths on Holderstrasse, is one of several archaeological sites in the area. At the priest's house on Pelagiusgasse the housekeeper will unlock a vault door in the church opposite and guide you down to the stone pipes of a Roman central heating system. Rottweil's most prized antique was excavated in 1834: a brilliant Roman mosaic of 570,000 pieces depicting Orpheus playing a lute. It is now in the **Dominikanermuseum** (Am Kriegsdamm).

The **Hochturm** and the **Schwarzes Tor** (Black Gate) were key towers in the fortifications built during the Hohenstaufen era. For centuries Rottweil was a Free Imperial City with its own judicial and penal system, answerable only to the distant Holy Roman emperor. From 1418 on, trials were held at the **Hofgerichtsstätte** (High Court Chambers)—where you can see a replica of the judge's chair—next to the present *Landgericht* (Superior Court), on Königstrasse. The actual, finely sculpted *Hofgerichtsstuhl* is in the **Stadtmuseum Rottweil** on Hauptstrasse.

Its long spells of imperial grandeur help to explain Rottweil's strong sense of tradition. Local society is still very close-knit. Its members keep tabs on one another and their assessments rattle through the municipal grapevine at taverns like the **Zum Goldenen Becher** or cozy meeting places such as the **Café Armleder**, where slabs of *Schwarzwälder Kirschtorte* (Black Forest cherry cake) are served with great dollops of whipped cream.

The routine of everyday life disappears during Rottweil's annual **Fasnet**, the Alemannic version of Carnival that takes place toward the end of winter. For several high-spirited days more than 2,000 townsfolk cavort behind exquisitely carved wooden masks and hand-painted linen robes, which are usually handed down from one generation to the next. As officially sanctioned *Narren* (jesters), plied with endless rounds of Champagne during tavern breathers, they roam the town recounting the year's events with a satirical bite that convention would normally forbid. Depending on their period of origin, from pagan to Baroque, the expressions on the masks range from bland to ferocious. Disguise is maintained for the duration of revelries; even during meals their wearers raise the masks just enough for the intake of food. The two main parades are held on Fasnet Monday and Shrove Tuesday. At 8:00 A.M. sharp all the Narren prance through the Schwarzes Tor and then tour the town for nearly three hours, cracking long whips, vaulting along on poles, and showering spectators with pretzels and sweets. This is all meant to banish winter's evil spirits. The high-pitched whoops the Narren excel in have a pagan ring, reverberating from the distant days when the first Alemannic tribes arrived to spoil the Roman idyll.

Donaueschingen

First-time visitors to Donaueschingen, 31 km (19 miles) south of Rottweil on B 27, are usually intrigued by the Art Nouveau façades they encounter on a crosstown stroll from, say, Augustenstrasse to Sennhofstrasse. A fire raged through the town in 1908, and the **Stadtkirche St. Johann** (Church of St. John the Baptist), in the Schlosspark, was one of the few major Baroque buildings to survive. There are other reminders of the past here as well: In the **Karlsbau Museum** on Karlsplatz is the best preserved of the three known handwritten *Niebelungenlied* scripts, along with a fine collection of panel paintings, with works by Hans Holbein the Elder, on loan from the House of Fürstenberg, which has resided in the local **Schloss** since the 18th century.

The real crowd-puller is the **Donauquelle**, the source of the Danube, in the Schlosspark. The "glorious river" starts out on its journey to the Black Sea as a tiny spring bubbling into a shallow pool of water encircled by an ornamental railing. Hundreds of coins, thrown in by tourists, glitter on the pebble bed.

By the time it reaches Immendingen, 24 km (15 miles) down the B 33 and B 311 from Donaueschingen, the Danube has grown into a full-fledged river, its banks dotted with anglers. Here, near its westernmost end, however, the river seems almost to disappear altogether—one more surprise that the Alb has in store. Just east of Immendingen signs marked *"Donauversinkung"* lead to a secluded parking lot near the river. Head toward Möhringen on a narrow path, and you will watch the Danube slowly but surely peter out. After a couple of hundred yards there is just about enough Danube left to cover your feet. Then the last few puddles disappear and the river seeps away into the pebble bed, another case of the Alb at its most porous. The Danube resurfaces in Aach (on B 31), where Germany's biggest spring, the **Aachtopf**, bubbles. The dry riverbed, for its part, meanders on from Immendingen toward Tuttlingen, to be replenished by streams with, as yet, no waltzes named after them.

THE LAKE CONSTANCE AREA

Vineyards sloping down to crowded marinas on the north shore and snow-capped Alps towering to the south face each other across the waters of Central Europe's third-biggest lake. Its 160 miles of hilly shoreline, some 1,200 feet above sea level, are shared by Switzerland, Austria, Bavaria, and Baden-Württemberg, the latter claiming the lion's share. In summer the water temperature rarely drops below 70° F in the **Bodensee** (the lake's German name), which accounts for the subtropical vegetation that in places fringes this medium-altitude sun trap. Fierce winds from the mountains occasionally whip up formidable seas, but on the whole this is a lake popular with those who like their boating and bathing on the tame side. Widespread pollution threatened the waters more than a decade ago, but improved sewage treatment has saved the day for tourism. All sorts of publicity stunts were dreamt up to reassure doubters, including a photo of Count Bernadotte, who runs the island of Mainau, sipping a glass of lake water.

Konstanz

Getting your bearings in Konstanz is a challenge. The oldest part of this former Free Imperial City is a German enclave in Swiss territory linked by the **Rheinbrücke** to its new suburbs in Baden-Württemberg. Scores of one-night emigrés from Zürich and St. Gallen cross the frontier and head for its roulette tables, which are forbidden in their own country.

Judging by the thorough and costly face-lift the Altstadt recently received, its venerable buildings will survive well into the next millennium. A case in point is the **Obermarkt** (formerly the place of public execution). Thanks to several coats of blue and gray paint, the **Malhaus** looks only half as old as its Renaissance bays. In fact, the pharmacy on its ground floor has been in business since the 14th century.

That period will keep you in its grip all the way down Hussenstrasse to the **Schnetztor**, a former gate tower that looms over the half-timbered house in which Jan Hus is said to have spent three weeks in 1414 preparing to face the Council of Constance. The Bohemian teacher, preacher, and religious reformer had vehemently criticized church leaders, mainly on moral grounds. He was lured to Konstanz to defend his views with a promise of safe conduct. But the council interrogators threw him into jail, found him guilty of heresy, and burned him at the stake on what is now Tägermoosstrasse. The martyr's former rooms were turned into a museum in 1922.

Hus was held prisoner in the Dominican monastery, which one of the country's big hotel chains has since transformed into the deluxe ▶ **Steigenberger Insel-Hotel** on the edge of the Stadtgarten. A recent addition to the modern hotel scene is the ▶ **Hotel Halm** opposite the station. Its Arabian-style gourmet restaurant is particularly popular with the locals. Back on the waterfront, just a few crooked streets from the city center, you can enjoy a walk to the **Konzilgebäude**, built for the wealthy merchant class as its guildhall-cum-warehouse in 1388. Only 29 years later it was the venue for the council conclave that elected Cardinal Otto Colonna as Pope Martin V. A variety of conferences of a less momentous nature are still held in the main hall with its oak beams, pillars, and frescoed panels. The new **Archäologisches Landesmuseum** (Regional Archaeology Museum) on Benediktinerplatz delves even further back in time. Some of its artifacts are Celtic in origin, dating from the eighth century B.C.

Reichenau

From the little harbor at Konstanz, umpteen pleasure-boat cruises leave for destinations as distant as the Austrian town of Bregenz. In little more than an hour you can also travel by a roundabout but scenic water route to the island of Reichenau (only a few minutes' drive away via a causeway). As you pass beneath the Rheinbrücke, you will momentarily be on a continuation of the upper Rhine. A few hundred yards on, the channel widens into the branch of the lake, split into the **Gnadensee** and the **Untersee**, in which Reichenau basks.

Reichenau makes a first and lasting impression of sunlight glinting on greenhouse glass. The islanders export millions of cucumbers, tomatoes, and heads of lettuce annually. In this workaday setting, the three buttressed churches, all Romanesque in style, come as a surprise. **St. Georg** in

Oberzell is the oldest such example north of the Alps. Its foundations date to the ninth century. Recent restoration, carried out according to the methods of that era, used a mixture of plaster and ox blood.

Mainau

Within walking distance of modern Konstanz lies the more exotic of its two main islands, **Mainau**. Lennart Bernadotte moved into the Baroque island residence more than half a century ago. A trained agriculturist, the Swedish count spent years creating a botanical wonderland. Some 20 tons of bulbs are still planted annually. The season usually opens with an orchid show in the **Palmenhaus** (conservatory) toward the end of March, followed by the blossoming of rhododendrons, hyacinths, and more than 800 varieties of roses. Now and then King Carl Gustaf XVI, Bernadotte's great-nephew, drops in for a chat in the shade of Mainau's palm and citrus trees. A pedestrian causeway leads out to the island; a small entrance fee is charged.

Meersburg

Ferries for Meersburg leave from the Konstanz-Staad dock every 15 minutes, and at hourly intervals during the night. As you steam northeast across the lake toward the old harbor, steep green cliffs covered with neatly planted vines rise to meet you. Some vineyards date from the Dark Ages, like the castle from which the town gets its name. The **Meersburg** presides over a two-tier cluster of half-timbered houses, the **Oberstadt** (upper town) and the **Unterstadt** (lower town). Called Germany's oldest inhabited castle, the Meersburg was built in the seventh century at the command of King Dagobert I. Its fortifications withstood attack by the first-ever gunpowder cannons. In 1841 the author Annette von Droste-Hülshoff came here to stay with her brother-in-law, the owner, and wrote *Die Judenbuche* (*The Jew's Beech Tree*) and other works. Seven years later, after a lingering illness, she died in the castle. A small museum displays memorabilia associated with her, including the armchair in which she died.

With centuries of wine-growing experience, the local *Winzer* (vintners) have perfected several Müller-Thurgau and Ruländer wines. Special praise must go to the fruity lakeside Spätburgunder Weissherbst, equally delicious in its rosé hue or its alternative amber color. The lake's premier delicacy, freshly netted whitefish (called *Felchen* on local menus), goes well with every variety of Weissherbst. Meersburg is on the northern shore's well-travelled gourmet trail, where vacations are often planned as culinary expeditions. Good, reasonably priced cooking can be found in any of the older establishments. One such is the **Wilder Mann**, down on the harbor at Bismarckplatz 2, where latecomers, confronted by the locked town gates, used to stay more than 250 years ago; Tel: (7532) 90-11-12.

Überlingen

While Meersburg bursts at its medieval seams during the summer, serenity reigns in the cobbled lanes and squares of Überlingen (10 km/6 miles up the shore), only a couple of hundred years younger and endowed with such fine examples of Gothic and Baroque architecture as the **St. Nikolaus Münster** (Cathedral of St. Nicholas) and the **Rathaus**. Even on the busiest weekends, the wine taverns between Wiestorstrasse and Münsterplatz have enough elbow room for some serious sampling. A prowl through the Altstadt usually ends in the **Spitalkeller**, which has a selection of 65 wines in its cellars.

In the winter of 1904, ducal district doctor and medical counsellor Eduard Würth had a pavement of expensive Ticino gneiss laid from his favorite inn, the **Christophkeller**, to his house on Mühlenstrasse. Ever since, local connoisseurs have prided themselves on making stylish exits, whatever their degree of inebriation, after a hard night's wine tasting.

Unteruhldingen, 3 km (2 miles) east on B 31, warrants a stop. Archaeologists found remarkably well preserved remains of Stone Age and Bronze Age pile dwellings at the muddy bottom of the bay here. There was enough material to reconstruct a village on stilts, including such artifacts as a Stone Age oven and Bronze Age bellows. Long lines tend to form at the entrance to the open-air museum, however.

Friedrichshafen

The 14 km (8½ miles) between Friedrichshafen (east of Meersburg) and Romanshorn, on the Swiss shore opposite, comprise the widest part of Lake Constance. On hazy days, as the ferries, with their escort of squawking gulls, glide out of the harbor and fade into the distance, it is easy to see why lake transit burgeoned during the steamboat era. A regular ferry service between Friedrichshafen and the Swiss town of Rorschach began in 1824, with the steamer *Wilhelm* making a trial run on November 26. Buffeted by a storm, it still beat the sailboat carrying the day's mail by more than three hours. For decades Swabia had what amounted to a "Royal

Württemberg Navy" with captains decked out in full sword-toting regalia. Nowadays some three dozen diesel-engined ferries ply to and fro. They belong to the lake's "White Fleet," run as a joint venture by the Swiss, Austrian, and German railways.

A longish tramp steamer tour of the lake, with sorties into the hinterlands, is not expensive. The Deutsche Bundesbahn (German Federal Railways) offers a reasonably priced *Bodenseepass,* valid for 15 days, that entitles you to ride ferries as well as trains, buses, and cable cars on and around the lake.

Both passenger vessels and car ferries call at Friedrichshafen. The broad sweep of its palm-studded esplanade is a reminder that this town, the lake's only real industrial sprawl, was a sleepy little royal spa at the turn of the century. Its days as a center of aeronautical engineering were inaugurated by Ferdinand von Zeppelin. On July 2, 1900, the count's first dirigible, filled with hydrogen and powered by twin Daimler gasoline engines, took off from a floating hangar moored off the village of **Manzell.**

One whole floor of the **Bodensee Museum,** in the north wing of the Rathaus, is devoted to the Zeppelin saga. At the touch of a button, a trail of light crawls along a map of the airships' global routes.

THE BAROQUE ROAD

Bounded by Lake Constance and the river Danube (and, to the east, the Iller), Upper (southern) Swabia's gently sloping hill country lulls visitors into a pastoral, straw-chewing mood with its isolated farms, hamlets, and villages. All the more overwhelming then to step into the lavish Baroque spectacles within the area's abbeys, churches, mansions, and town halls. The vivid blues, pinks, and yellows of the celestial scenes on the vaulting are offset by dazzling white walls and pillars dripping with stucco ornamentation. Gilded cherubs and angels, lips parted joyously, float over superbly carved altars, choir stalls, and pulpits.

If you are more an admirer of, say, Norman architectural austerity, this is rich fare indeed. The region's Baroque architecture was born of the Counter-Reformation, instigated by the top echelons of the Roman Catholic Church in the 16th and 17th centuries. After the Reformation, roughly two-thirds of Austria, to which most of Upper Swabia belonged at the time, had turned to Protestantism. To add insult to injury, Protestant troops from Sweden and Württemberg wrecked a considerable part of the region's finest architecture during the Thirty Years' War. Large-scale rebuilding started toward the middle of the 17th century, when counts and abbots brought in painters, sculptors, and plasterers from as far afield as the Ticino. It was their goal to create imaginative and uplifting interiors that would help win back hearts and minds to the Roman Catholic faith. Their Baroque extravaganza here apparently did the trick, for most of today's Upper Swabians are Roman Catholic.

Plotting a route full of interesting examples of the Baroque style is easy enough. Endless permutations are possible, including the official **Schwäbische Barockstrasse** (Swabian Baroque Road) designated in 1966 (contact the German National Tourist Office for details). We suggest a looping run, less than 200 km (124 miles) in overall length, that will take you as far north as Ochsenhausen, near Biberach, and as far east as Eglofs.

A visit to the **Wallfahrtskirche St. Maria** (Pilgrimage Church of St. Mary) in **Birnau**, near Überlingen, will whet your appetite. The angels portrayed on the nave's frescoes are traditional enough. The *Honigschlecker,* in the transept, makes people smile; a stucco cherub holds a hive buzzing with golden bees and licks an apparently sticky index finger. This is Baroque at its most playful.

Drive southeast to Meersburg, then follow B 33 to **Weingarten**, less than an hour's drive to the northeast, where the **Pfarr- und Klosterkirche St. Martin und St. Oswald** (Parish and Monastery Church of St. Martin and St. Oswald) is an unusually monumental example of German Baroque. The original Romanesque basilica was demolished at the beginning of the 18th century so that 200 craftsmen and artists, including the renowned fresco painter Cosmas Damian Asam, could create what is often called "Swabia's answer to St. Peter's." The church is approximately half as big as the Vatican structure. Priests, choirboys, and Benedictine monks from the adjacent monastery have perfected a decelerated delivery for sermons, hymns, and psalms to accommodate the echoes from the back of the church.

A pleasant country road, which bypasses heavy traffic on B 32 and B 30, meanders from Ravensburg to **Aulendorf**. Opposite the tiny spa's elegant Hofgarten, the **Pfarrkirche St. Martin** (Parish Church of St. Martin) exemplifies Baroque's early and later phases. The life-size Madonna dates from 1656, the stucco ceiling in the nave from 1711. One of the altar shrines contains the bejeweled bones of Saint Felix, who was martyred in Rome. During the Middle Ages the local counts of Königsegg had the holy man's skeleton removed from Rome's catacombs and brought to Aulendorf.

Bad Schussenried, another of the region's spas, lies a few miles to the north. It, too, has several Baroque master-pieces. Connoisseurs regard the **Bibliotheksaal** (Library Hall), tucked away in a former monastery, as outstanding. Dominikus Zimmermann, one of Germany's most prolific Baroque artists, had a substantial hand in designing the library. Stucco heavens soar above balustrades, pillars, alabaster statues, and trompe l'oeil bookcases in a wing of the ex-monastery that now houses a psychiatric clinic. To get to the Bibliotheksaal, pay the nominal fee at the entrance gates and then follow the signs to Stationen 14–17. Psychiatric wards and the library are at opposite ends of a long corridor. (Bad Buchau and the Federsee are only about 5 km/3 miles to the north; see the Alb section above.)

If you keep to minor roads, Degernau and Ummendorf are the only two sizable villages on the way to **Ochsenhausen**, an unassuming town to the northeast heralded by the **Pfarr-kirche St. Georg** (Parish Church of St. George) and its slender bell tower on a hill. Until the end of the 15th century, the basilica was a prime example of the Gothic style. It is now as ornate as a wedding cake, as a result of rebuilding from 1725 onward. The adjoining palatial structure was a Benedictine monastery until 1803, the year Napoleonic edicts put an end to most of the monastic life in this region. The buildings have proven to be a godsend to local clubs. The former monks' quarters are occupied by a school for Baden-Württemberg's promising young musicians.

From Ochsenhausen south toward Wangen, follow the official *Oberschwäbische Barockstrasse* (Upper Swabian Baroque Road) signs, showing a tilted cherub's head on a bluish background. The **Schloss** in **Bad Wurzach** is now a boarding school run by two dozen monks of the Salvator order. School holidays are an ideal time to visit. From 8:00 A.M. until about 7:00 P.M. the monks leave the gates and the main door open, and anyone can stroll in. The building's staircase, its best-known feature, is another grand gesture of the Baroque, with Herculean torsos shouldering masonry and cherubs perched decoratively on the balustrades. The ceiling's fresco scenes are joyously pagan: Aphrodite, Zeus, Chronos, and other Greek deities seem to have just landed in a blaze of color.

Schloss Wolfegg, on a promontory between the Ach and Höll valleys, has belonged to the counts of Waldburg-Wolfegg since the 13th century. During the Thirty Years' War it was burned down by Swedish troops while the head of the family was away defending Konstanz and Lindau. Restoration was supervised by the 17th-century master plasterer Balthasar Crinner. His magnificent Baroque ceiling spans the

Rittersaal (Knights' Hall), a gallery flanked by 24 carved wooden knights representing prominent family ancestors. Unfortunately, the owners have stopped opening the Schloss to the public, at least for the time being.

Many smaller pieces of Baroque art are easily detachable, and thieves have frequently preyed on Upper Swabia's churches. The tiny market town of **Kisslegg**, just south of Schloss Wolfegg, had its **Pfarrkirche St. Gallus** (Parish Church of St. Gallus) wired with an alarm, but someone still made off with most of the cherubs on the choir stalls. Special alarms protect the church's "silver treasure": 21 shining statues of Christ, the apostles, and other biblical figures by the local artisan Christoph Mäderl. The silver can be viewed at close quarters only when a guide escorts visitors to the gallery. But by squeezing up against the opposite wall, you can catch a glimpse of the Christ figure from below.

Just south of Kisslegg is **Wangen**, with its surrounding sprawl of small factories. This is the biggest town on our Baroque itinerary, but the cobbled **Oberstadt** (Upper Town) offers sanctuary. Stroll in through the **Frauentor**, one of three remaining gate towers, and the traffic will suddenly abate. Much of the **Altstadt** is now a pedestrian zone. For the past 20 years a history-conscious town council has allocated part of its budget to restoration. Many of the painted façades speak volumes: From a seat at one of the open-air cafés in Herrengasse, you can peruse whole chapters of Wangen's history. Up on the Frauentor's outside wall, for example, Emperor Ferdinand is depicted holding an orb. As a Free Imperial City, Wangen owed allegiance to a succession of Holy Roman emperors. Ferdinand dropped in on the town with a retinue of 1,500, and municipal funds were greatly depleted by the ensuing days of merrymaking. The **Rathaus** and **Spitalkirche** (Hospital Church) are two more of Wangen's Baroque frills; the **Marktplatz** front of the Rathaus is decorated with cartouches, pillars, balconies, and gilded statuettes. In the back of the building is a conspicuous bulge under the ornate stonework: a segment of wall left over from distant imperial days.

Eglofs is little more than a sprinkling of farms some 8 km (5 miles) east of Wangen. Its elaborately stuccoed **Pfarr-kirche St. Martin** (Parish Church of St. Martin), however, will match most of what you have seen so far. You can enjoy a hearty meal in the **Gasthof zum Löwen von Josef Ellgass**, which looks onto the village square with its patrician fountain and elegant half-timbered houses. Closed Thursdays and Fridays; Tel: (7566) 578. Local families like Ellgass, Gollinger, and Egger are descended from forebears who were wealthy enough to qualify as *reichsfreie* farmers. In the 13th century that meant the little community was as autonomous as any of the Free Imperial towns. Later their privileges were rescinded, and a street called Freie Bauernstrasse is the only reminder of those decades of independence.

From Wangen it's a 15-km (9-mile) drive south to Lindau, at the eastern end of Lake Constance.

GETTING AROUND

Whether you plan a short trip into Swabia or a more thorough exploration of its heartland, Stuttgart is a good base from which to start. The state capital is linked by regular InterCity (IC) rail service with other major cities, and it is also a hub for Autobahns from Munich, Singen, Karlsruhe, Frankfurt, and Würzburg. The Stuttgart-Echterdingen airport had a distinctly provincial reputation for many years, but it has been upgraded, and domestic and international flights to and from Stuttgart-Echterdingen have increased in number. All the major car-rental agencies have desks at the airport and branch offices in even the smallest towns.

In general, motorists are pampered by a meticulously kept road network, with surfaces fit for an Autobahn. Be warned that the smooth ride encourages high-speed driving. Trunk road travel across the Swabian Alb's broad back is a pleasure, however. Traffic tends to build up only in the industrial sprawls around Stuttgart, Esslingen, Göppingen, Reutlingen, and Friedrichshafen. Lake Constance's northern shore road is also notorious for traffic jams during the summer months.

Roads are very well marked. Even the sites of minor tourist interest are well signposted. An exception is Greater Stuttgart, which makes no attempt at any semblance of a ring road and gives no warning that through traffic has no option but to struggle right down into the city basin and out the other side again.

A folk song that many Swabians know by heart immortalizes the regional railways and their plodding climbs up the Alb. Several of the trans-Alpine stretches, including Engstingen–Schelklingen (near Blaubeuren), have had their passenger services terminated. But enough lines remain in service for some extensive rail travel by *Bummelbahn* ("dawdle trains"), which stop at small country stations. One of the most scenic stretches meanders along the Danube from Tuttlingen to Ehingen. Fast, relatively direct rail links include Stuttgart–Rottweil and the Biberach–Ravensburg–Friedrichshafen run, which gives you access to the Lake Constance ferries described above.

ACCOMMODATIONS REFERENCE

The hotel rates listed here are 1994 projections for double-bed, double-occupancy rooms, with a range from low to high whenever possible. Prices are given in deutsche marks (DM). Basic rates are always subject to change, so please verify price when you are booking. Breakfast is usually included in the price of a room.

City area codes must be preceded by a zero if you are calling from elsewhere in Germany.

▶ **Hospiz.** Neckarhalde 2, D-72070 **Tübingen.** Tel: (7071) 92-40; Fax: (7071) 92-42-00. DM 135–180.

▶ **Hotel Adelshof.** Am Markt 12–13, D-74523 **Schwäbisch-Hall.** Tel: (791) 758-90; Fax: (791) 60-36. DM 190-230.

▶ **Hotel Halm.** Bahnhofplatz 6, D-78462 **Konstanz.** Tel: (7531) 12-10; Fax: (7531) 218-03. DM 250–390.

▶ **Inter-Continental.** Willy-Brandt-Strasse 30, D-70173 **Stuttgart.** Tel: (711) 202-00; Fax: (711) 20-20-12; in U.S., Tel: (800) 327-0200. DM 265–490.

▶ **Messehotel Europe.** Siemensstrasse 33, D-70469 **Stuttgart.** Tel: (711) 81-48-30; Fax: (711) 814-8348. DM 280–320.

▶ **Relexa Waldhotel Schatten.** Magstadterstrasse, D-70569 **Stuttgart.** Tel: (711) 686-70; Fax: (711) 686-79-99. DM 290–690.

▶ **Romantik-Hotel Goldener Adler.** Am Markt 11, D-74523 **Schwäbisch Hall.** Tel: (791) 61-68; Fax: (791) 73-15. DM 178–220.

▶ **Am Schloss.** Burgsteige 18, D-72070 **Tübingen.** Tel: (7071) 210-77; Fax: (7071) 520-90. DM 128.

▶ **Steigenberger-Hotel Graf Zeppelin.** Arnulf-Klett-Platz 7, D-70173 **Stuttgart.** Tel: (711) 204-80; Fax: (711) 204-8542. DM 345–445.

▶ **Steigenberger Insel-Hotel.** Auf der Insel 1, D-78462 **Konstanz.** Tel: (7531) 12-50; Fax: (7531) 264-02. DM 320–390.

▶ **Stuttgart Airport Hotel.** Randstrasse, D-70629 **Stuttgart.** Tel: (711) 790-70; Fax: (711) 79-35-85; in U.S., Tel: (800) 333-3333. DM 289–335.

THE BLACK FOREST

BADEN-BADEN AND FREIBURG

By Ted Heck

Ted Heck, a freelance travel and sportswriter who lived in Germany for five years, contributes regularly to magazines and newspapers. He returns to Germany every year.

Travellers come to Baden-Baden to bathe in thermal waters discovered by Roman soldiers or to gamble in the elegant casino. They are drawn also to the medieval attractions of the university city of Freiburg. But both these cities are on the western edge of the forest, and the rest of the Schwarzwald (Black Forest) is frequently shortchanged by tourists with checklists of castles, museums, beer halls, and shops.

For Germans, however, the mountainous, legend-filled Schwarzwald is a favorite place to spend holidays. They come to this stretch of pine and fir trees and mountain meadows for lengthy vacations in hotels or for weekends in private retreats where they can hike, wander in the woods—and take *die Kur* (the cure). The forest dominates the southwestern corner of Germany, running parallel to the Rhine river, which serves here as the boundary with Switzerland to the south (Basel is right across the river) and France (Strasbourg, Alsace) to the west.

Health bubbles up from mineral springs in the Black Forest. Germans suffocating in highly industrialized cities look to the region's spas and Kur houses to heal assorted ailments. Resorts such as Wildbad, in the northern part of the forest,

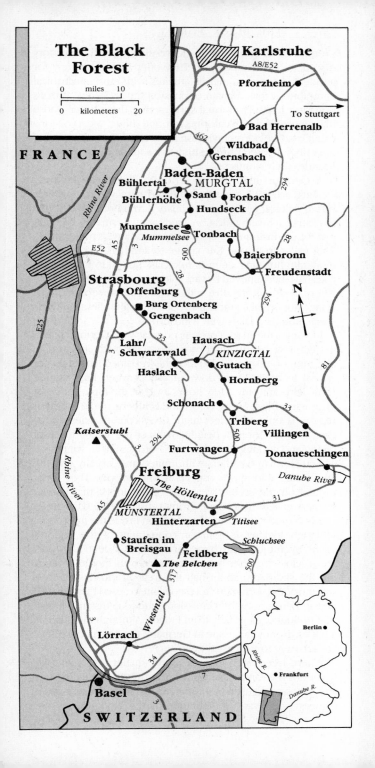

promise relief from rheumatic, respiratory, and circulatory disorders, even impotence. They offer motion therapy for accident victims and injured athletes, with more mechanical contraptions than a chain of physical fitness salons. Patrons don't just bathe in thermal springs; they drink water whose main ingredients are chlorine, salt, and sulfur. "Meet you for a drink" may be not an invitation for cocktails but for a quaff of hot mineral water. Unrefreshing as it sounds, many claim that it settles their stomachs.

A German need not be seriously ill to take the cure. Healing activities are supplemented with vigorous sports, varied cultural events, and culinary adventures. A week in a spa can be a healthy vacation, paid for by Germany's compulsory health-insurance system. Other vacationers prefer week-long walks from one Kur village to another. They lunch in mountain huts and sleep in first-class hotels, to which their bags have been moved by van. Hikers are encountered everywhere, and hills are alive with cyclists and horseback riders. Hang gliders make graceful swoops through valleys; sailboats share mountain lakes with windsurfers.

In winter the Black Forest is popular with German skiers, though few North Americans are seen; with an average elevation of less than 3,000 feet, the tree-lined slopes do not appeal to transatlantic downhill skiers when high-altitude snowfields are only a few hours away in the Alps. The most impressive Black Forest resort, the **Feldberg**, in the southern region, is only 4,900 feet high. Cross-country skiers, however, find the forest a delight. Many of the 14,260 miles of hiking and walking paths become Nordic trails in winter.

Non-German travellers with limited time usually give the area's cure and sports aspects a low priority. They focus instead on the scenic pleasures of the forest that Roman soldiers called Silva Nigra. From a distance the dark green trees do indeed look black—and from inside the forest, too. Although logging is a major component of the region's economy, lumberjacks have hardly made a dent. Tall trees are so close together here that the treetops merge to block out the sky. Sadly, about half the trees in the Black Forest suffer from *Waldsterben* (forest decline) caused by a mixture of acid rain, automobile emissions, and long-distance industrial pollution, especially from France. Although the blight is a hot environmental issue in Germany, the destruction is not yet apparent to the casual traveller.

Where trees open into meadows, quaint towns and villages dot the landscape. Some have historical significance and may have figured in internecine conflicts in times when princes ruled various segments of the land. Others are worth a look because of a folk museum or glassblowing studio or even a cuckoo-clock factory.

MAJOR INTEREST

Scenery, panoramas of forests and meadows
Mountain lakes and streams
Folk museums

Baden-Baden
Casino
Parks
Thermal baths

Freiburg
Old town
Cathedral
Museums

The Food of the Black Forest

The Black Forest is a regional culinary paradise, in part because of its proximity to France and Switzerland, in part because of 20 centuries of cross-cultural influences. Some of the finest restaurants in Germany are scattered throughout the forest's towns and villages, most of them in charming inns where cooking odors complement the Old World atmosphere.

Regional specialties range from such farmhouse fare as *Schwarzwald Schinken* (smoked ham), bread, cheese, and wurst, to various pork and veal plates, to delicately prepared *Forelle* (trout). A typical Gasthof menu will have a sturdy soup, perhaps a *Flädlesuppe* with floating pancake strips. The variety of hot and cold sausages is often surprising, and no two restaurants seem to make their *Hauswurst* (house sausage) the same way (and they guard their recipes).

Spätzle and other pastas are homemade, too. Typical main courses include various meat and fowl dishes with creamy sauces. Beef is usually on the menu, but rarely in the form of a large steak: Germans regard the cow primarily as a machine for making milk and cheese. Wild game is frequently offered, sometimes in a ragout of venison, hare, and boar, with wild mushrooms from the forest. Side dishes are mixed salads, potatoes, and red and green cabbage prepared in a variety of ways. Other members of the cabbage family are plentiful—and *Spargel* (asparagus), available in May, is a national passion.

Black Forest diners take wine with their meals, generally

from a local vineyard on the Badische Weinstrasse (Baden Wine Road), which runs through the Rhine valley between the river and the mountains. Beer, of course, is also a staple on Black Forest tables, served chilled but not ice-cold. Some beers require attention; ask for a *Pils vom Fass* (on tap) and you'll wait seven minutes while the bartender pauses several times to fill the stemmed glass and build a foamy head inch by inch.

Pastries and ice cream are popular desserts. The ice cream is served by the scoop, but often as part of an *Eisbecher,* a sundae smothered with fruit and whipped cream. A local specialty is *Schwarzwälder Kirschtorte* (Black Forest cake), a dense, chocolatey confection flavored with *Kirschwasser* (cherry brandy). The brandy is also popular as an after-dinner drink.

The challenge facing many visitors to the Black Forest is where to begin. Sightseeing strategy depends on available time, special interests, and points of access. Many travellers arrive in this southwestern corner of Germany from points north (Frankfurt and Heidelberg) or from Stuttgart to the east, and pass through the Karlsruhe area on the northern edge of the forest. From there, the international spa town of Baden-Baden, less than an hour south of Karlsruhe, is a good starting point—and it's there that we begin our coverage.

We follow Baden-Baden with two recommended motor trips into the forest. One is a scenic loop that begins on the **Schwarzwald Hochstrasse** (Black Forest Highway) and goes south to Freudenstadt and back. The other is a bit more ambitious, from Offenburg (west of Freudenstadt) through a series of small villages to medieval Freiburg, the other city we cover in detail, farther south.

Other suggested itineraries then follow for visitors who enter the Black Forest from the south—from Basel, Switzerland, for example—or from Swabia to the east.

BADEN-BADEN

Elegance still reigns supreme in Baden-Baden. For over 150 years this small (50,000 inhabitants) spa, located in a sheltered, verdant valley on the northern edge of the Black Forest south of Frankfurt and west of Stuttgart, has been one of Germany's most luxurious resorts. Its thermal mineral springs, discovered by the Romans, attracted the likes of the rheumatic Roman emperor Caracalla, who built the first baths here in the third century, but it was not until the 19th century that Baden-Baden began to attract large numbers of visitors. The spa's convenient location—close to France, the Low Countries, England, and several major German cities—and the advent of the railroad played a great part in its burgeoning popularity.

Kings, queens, nobles, and petty aristocrats initially set the social tone, converging on Baden-Baden—the "summer capital" of Europe's privileged classes—for a seasonal regimen that interspersed "taking the waters" with genteel promenades or carriage rides. When the famous Casino was opened in 1838 gambling quickly became as important a lure for visitors as the spa facilities. An opera house and other cultural attractions followed. Today Baden-Baden rivals Monte Carlo as a mecca for gambling, attracting a gilt-edged, international crowd of wealthy businesspeople and celebrities. It has also become an important meeting place for high-level politicians from around Europe, and hosts several international conferences a year. And, of course, it still remains a popular spa.

The French have left their imprint on Baden-Baden in a number of ways. Many of the 19th-century public buildings and churches were designed and financed by Jacques and Edouard Bénazet, French businessmen who were also responsible for the Paris Jockey Club's race course at nearby Iffezheim. In fact, what the Bénazets gave to Baden-Baden may account for its being left unscarred in World War II. After the war, when Germany was divided into occupation zones, the French selected Baden-Baden for their headquarters.

Although the main sights in Baden-Baden can easily be seen in half a day, it's a place that invites you to linger—whether to luxuriate in one of the ultramodern spa facilities, try your luck at the gaming tables, shop, or take your own leisurely promenade through its quiet flower-filled parks.

A small stream, the Oos, flows north through the city and divides the park area on the west bank—where the 19th-century buildings comprising the spa and casino facilities are found—from the commercial and residential areas on the east, or right, bank. The *Altstadt* (Old Town), with the baths and the castle museum, are on the right bank.

The main railroad station is Baden-Oos, a 20-minute drive north of town. Taxis into the city are available but the price is fairly steep. The number 1 and 3 buses will take you to Augustaplatz and the Haus des Kurgastes, the main tourist office, which is a good place to book a room, pick up maps and city information, and begin a walking tour. A pleasant alternative, if you are arriving by train, is to rent a bicycle at the station and pedal in via Rheinstrasse, which becomes Lange Strasse.

The Kurhaus and Casino

With its colonnade of white Corinthian columns, the center-piece of the west, or left, bank of Baden-Baden is the Neoclassical **Kurhaus**, built by Felix Weinbrenner between 1822 and 1824. Despite its name, the Kurhaus doesn't actually "cure" anything. It can, however, lift the spirits, for during the summer season there is always something going on, inside and out. Behind its stately portico is the famous Casino (*Spielbank*), numerous restaurants, and a variety of public rooms where concerts and society balls are held.

In the outdoor restaurant of the Kurhaus couples dance to music played by the casino band. The Baden-Baden Symphony and guest orchestras perform daily in a bandshell nestled among chestnut trees in the surrounding **Kurgarten** and also give concerts in the Kurhaus's opulent Weinbren-nersaal. To the strains of Brahms, who spent ten summers in Baden-Baden, you can shop in one of the exclusive boutiques clustered to the right of the bandshell. And as fortunes are being won and lost in the Casino, you can enjoy a pleasant and surprisingly affordable lunch or dinner at the **Boulevard** restaurant in the Kurhaus. The menu is wide-ranging and international in scope.

Anyone expecting slot machines and the blinding, garish, informal glitz of Las Vegas or Atlantic City may be severely intimidated by Baden-Baden's **Casino**. The late Marlene Dietrich described it as the "most beautiful casino in the whole world—and I have seen them all." Gambling here is a rather stately affair, a social art form carried on between 2:00 P.M. and 2:00 A.M. amid lushly theatrical surroundings that are more French than Teutonic. You must dress for it. You pay an entrance fee for the privilege (once inside, however, there is no obligation to gamble). And you must carry a passport.

The games—blackjack, roulette, baccarat, and, most recently, poker—are presided over by German croupiers who deal the cards and spin the balls for intervals of 30 to 45 minutes. The croupiers, who live on the winners' tips, work in conjunction with "judges" who carefully watch the proceedings at each table. The minimum value chip is DM 5, except for baccarat (DM 100); the maximum is DM 10,000. Most of the gamblers are German, French, and Arab.

If you're not tempted to roll the dice yourself, you can still have a look at the opulent gaming rooms by taking one of the guided tours, held daily between 10:00 A.M. and noon. The Casino in its present form was designed in 1854 by Jacques and Edouard Bénazet, who commissioned another

Frenchman, Charles Sechan, to decorate the interior. The dazzling theatricality of the place is no accident: Sechan was a set designer. For the Casino he created a series of lavish salons inspired by French royal palaces, the most notable being the gold-and-beige **Hall of a Thousand Candles**.

Exploring the West Bank

The other colonnaded building in the Kurgarten, adjacent to the Kurhaus, is the **Trinkhalle** (Pump Room), where locals and visitors alike congregate to sip hot mineral water or grape juice. The gallery, dating from 1842, is covered with frescoes depicting legends of the Black Forest.

From the Trinkhalle a pleasant walk heads north up the Michaelsberg to the peaceful **Stourdza-Kapelle**, a Neoclassical chapel built by Leo von Klenze in 1866 to house the body of a Romanian prince. Situated in a landscaped garden with a lake and waterfall, the chapel provides lovely views.

On Goetheplatz, just outside the Kurhaus, stands the Neo-Baroque **Stadttheater**, another French-designed building. The French composer Hector Berlioz inaugurated the theater in 1862 with the premiere of his opera *Béatrice et Bénédict*. In the park south of the theater, on Lichtentaler Allee, is the **Kunsthalle**, a small municipal art gallery that features travelling exhibits of mostly 20th-century art.

Lichtentaler Allee, planted with azaleas, maples, silver poplars, magnolias, gingkos, and other flowering trees and shurbs, is Baden-Baden's most beautiful promenade. In the spa's "summer capital" days, the carriages of Queen Victoria, Bismarck, and Napoleon III rolled along its leafy route. Passing various sports facilities (tennis courts, swimming pool, riding trails) and some of Baden-Baden's leading hotels, the avenue runs south alongside the brooklike Oos to the **Gönneranlage**, a charming period garden on the east bank with Art Nouveau fountains, pergolas, sculptures, and 350 varieties of roses. The onion-shaped dome visible from the rose gardens belongs to the **Russische Kirche** (Russian Church) on Lichtenthaler Strasse.

Continuing south on Lichtentaler Allee brings you to the Lichtenthal quarter, a former village that has been incorporated into Baden-Baden. The **Brahmshaus**, now a museum at Maximilianstrasse 5 in Lichtenthal, is the house where Johannes Brahms spent ten productive summers, beginning in 1865, composing such works as his Symphony No. 1 (also called the "Lichtentaler Symphony"). Not far from the Brahmshaus, on Klosterplatz, is the formidable **Kloster Lichtenthal**, a 15th-century abbey inhabited by Cistercian nuns. Their handicrafts and a selection of convent-brewed liqueurs are for sale in a shop in the main convent building. From Lichtenthal the number 1 bus will return you to Leopoldsplatz in the center of town.

The East Bank

If gambling, listening to music, sipping the waters, and promenading are the primary activities of Baden-Baden's west bank, shopping and soaking are the favorite pastimes of the east, or right, bank. Fashionable shops of every description line the pedestrian zone of **Lange Strasse** and **Gernsbacher Strasse**, across the Oos from the Trinkhalle, and continue on into the neighboring chestnut-tree-lined **Sophienstrasse**.

The rebuilt 17th-century **Rathaus** (Town Hall) on the western end of Gernsbacher Strasse was originally a Jesuit college. Next to it is Baden-Baden's largest church, the 13th-century **Stiftskirche** (Collegiate Church). In the chancel is an exquisite Gothic sandstone crucifix dating from 1467 and the ornate 18th-century trophy-laden tombstone of Margrave Ludwig Wilhelm of Baden-Baden.

But the real hot spots in this part of town are the baths. Thermal bathing is nothing new here: Beneath Römerplatz are the **Römische Badruinen**, ruins of the third-century baths built to soothe the bones of the emperor's weary Roman soldiers. Today half a million visitors a year use the bathing and sauna facilities of the Friedrichsbad and Caracalla-Therme on Römerplatz and the Augustabad on Gernsbacher Strasse.

The **Friedrichsbad** has been a therapeutic center for more than a century, offering various treatments, baths of different chemical compositions, and stimulating massages. You can sample the routine here in as little as two hours, sweating in the steamrooms, soaking in the pools, grunting under a wire-brush massage, dunking in an ice-cold tank, and then being swaddled in cotton sheets and blankets for a half-hour nap.

The ornate **Caracalla-Therme** features indoor and outdoor pools and romantic grottoes with warm water or cool. Built in the mid-1980s, the spacious facility sits above mile-deep thermal springs whose water comes to the surface at temperatures of 150 degrees Fahrenheit. With a ticket purchased from vending machines in the main lobby visitors can use the Caracalla's pools, saunas, solariums, and inhalatorium. An information desk helps first-time guests with details on lockers and additional services such as massages and mud wraps. Take a towel and bathing suit; they don't rent them. There's also a cafeteria with an outdoor terrace. (Open daily from 8:00 A.M. to 10:00 P.M.)

If you leave the baths with any energy, you can walk a short distance up the Florentine hill to the 15th-century Neues Schloss (New Palace) with its gardens and views over the town. The former margravial residence is now the home of the **Zähringer Museum**, its rooms decorated and furnished in an opulent Empire style.

Staying and Dining in Baden-Baden

▶ **Brenner's Park-Hotel and Spa** on Lichtentaler Allee, near the Kurhaus, is one of Europe's finest luxury hotels and a favorite of celebrities and well-to-do visitors. A classic, understated elegance characterizes the public halls, bedrooms, and spa facilities of this century-old Baden-Baden aristocrat. The hotel's vast, high-ceilinged **Schwarzwaldstuben**, with windows looking out onto the surrounding garden, features an extensive menu, white-glove service, and is considered one of the best hotel restaurants of Europe; for reservations, Tel: (7221) 90-00.

Also on Lichtentaler Allee, and splendidly situated in a park on the banks of the Oos, is the family-run ▶ **Allee-Hotel Bären**, where free admission to the Caracalla-Therme is included in the price of a room. The hotel's **Schwarz-waldstube** (not to be confused with the Schwarzwaldstuben in Brenner's) is a highly rated restaurant; for reservations, Tel: (7221) 70-22-22.

After Brenner's, Baden-Baden's other grand hotel is the ▶ **Steigenberger Europäischer Hof** on Kaiserallee, located on the Oos beside an 18-hole golf course and with a direct view of the Casino. There are views of the park from many of its 200 rooms. On the east bank of the Oos, the distinctive ▶ **Steigenberger Avance Badischer Hof**, on Langestrasse, is a former monastery whose roofed-over cloister now forms the hotel's dramatic lobby. This 100-room establishment is well run, carefully furnished, and top-of-the-line in price.

Baden-Baden's numerous hotels are not exclusively geared to the luxury trade. The small ▶ **Deutscher Kaiser**, on Merkurstrasse near Augustplatz, is family-run with well-equipped rooms and a *gemütliche Bier-und-Weinstube*. The moderately priced ▶ **Badhotel zum Hirsch**, on Hirschstrasse, and the ▶ **Hotel Colmar**, on Langestrasse, both face the action on the pedestrian zone but have quiet terraces out back. At the Badhotel zum Hirsch, water from thermal springs is pumped into each room and the bathtubs have separate faucets for mineral water.

The **Stahlbad** at Augustaplatz 2 attracts a devoted clientele who return for its French and German cuisine, exceptional wine list, and atmosphere. Nineteenth-century Boilly prints satirizing gourmands line the walls of this intimate, stylish restaurant located in an elegant mansion. Closed Sundays and Mondays; for reservations, Tel: (7221) 245-69. **Münchner Löwenbräu**, at Gernsbacherstrasse 9, just southeast of the Rathaus, offers hearty regional specialties, has an outdoor beer garden, and is open all week long; Tel: (7221) 223-11.

For *Kaffee und Kuchen,* an *Eis* (ice cream), or a glass of wine, stop in at the **Café-Konditorei König**, Lichtentaler Strasse 12; the pastries alone make it worth the trip, and the café itself is a Baden-Baden institution.

Some travellers to Baden-Baden prefer to stay in villages farther into the forest. A hotel that anyone will be happy with is the reasonably priced ▶ **Zum Rebstock** on the main street in the village of Bühlertal, about 15 minutes south of town. Ask for a room overlooking the patio.

THE SCHWARZWALD HOCHSTRASSE

One of the most popular auto trips through the Black Forest is from Baden-Baden to Freudenstadt on the Schwarzwald Hochstrasse (B 500). Along the way follow the signs from Baden-Baden southeast to Bühlerhöhe. If you can talk your way past the gatehouse without a reservation, the ▶ **Schlosshotel Bühlerhöhe** is worth seeing. This recently renovated castle offers first-class elegance (and charges royal prices to match). A favorite of world political leaders, the mountaintop complex also has a beauty farm and health clinic.

From Bühlerhohe the Hochstrasse south passes through Sand, past two small ski areas, then by Hundseck to the **Mummelsee**. For all the attention Germans pay to the Mummelsee, foreign visitors are certain to be disappointed with the tiny lake. Mermaids in earlier days may have come out of the lake at night to cook and clean for sleeping farm wives, but nowadays the legend has been supplanted by the lakeside souvenir shop. One saving grace of the shop is the food section, featuring Schwarzwald specialties. You can make a spur-of-the-moment decision here to have a picnic of air-dried beef, smoked ham, cheese, hearty bread, and honey. Take along a Riesling wine from the Bühlertal or one of the neighboring villages of Baden-Baden and have your picnic at an *Aussichtpunkt* (lookout point). On a clear day at the Mummelsee, you can see across the broad expanse of the

Rhine valley and pick out the famed Strasbourg cathedral in France.

Freudenstadt, about half an hour from the Mummelsee on the eastern side of the Schwarzwald mountains, is a 400-year-old city that survived two outbreaks of the Black Death and many wars. Shortly before V-E day, the city center was destroyed by French soldiers who set the town on fire.

The ravages of war have long since been repaired. Freudenstadt was founded when Duke Friedrich of Württemberg commissioned an architect to create a new town in the center of his realm as a haven for Protestant refugees from religious persecution by the Catholic Hapsburg rulers in Austria, the duke being allied with French Huguenots. The architect explains his plan to the duke in a painting in the Schickhardt room of the **Gasthof Dreikönig**, on Martin-Luther-Strasse, which is a comfortable place for lunch. (Another good choice is the **Ratskeller**, on the Marktplatz.)

Architect Schickhardt was a borrower—his **Stadtkirche**, on a corner of the market square, has Romanesque-style towers, Renaissance-style doors, and Gothic-style windows. It is an unusual church, having two naves: The congregation sits on two sides at right angles, men and women separated, with the pulpit in the juncture.

A museum in the **Stadthaus** depicts other aspects of Freudenstadt's past. An exhibit devoted to raft-making shows how trees were lashed together and floated down Black Forest rivers to the Rhine and on to Holland. (Many a vessel in the days of sailing ships had masts cut from the Black Forest.)

Take time in Freudenstadt to wander through the impressive shopping area. Two adjoining sections of arcades make a square more than 650 feet on a side. If the Schwarzwald is having one of its frequent showers, you can browse under cover in the many delicatessens and boutiques here.

A recommended return route to Baden-Baden is through the Murgtal (*tal* means "valley") on highway 462. The small town of Baiersbronn-Mitteltal has a noted restaurant in the **Kurhotel Mitteltal.**

The ride along the Murg river passes a hydroelectrical plant in Forbach, but of more interest is **Schloss Eberstein**, near Gernsbach. The restaurant in this 13th-century castle mixes the menu with history; medieval surroundings make food seem less important.

Look for the rock from which Count Wolf von Eberstein supposedly leapt into the Murg on horseback to escape his enemies. The *Grafensprung* (Count's Leap) is one of the legends depicted on the front wall of the Trinkhalle in Baden-Baden.

THE KINZIGTAL

If you have time for an overnight stay in the Black Forest, it should be on this route, which runs from Offenburg south-east up the Kinzigtal via route B 33 to Hausach, through Gutach south to Triberg, south from there to Furtwangen and Titisee on routes 500 and 31, and finally west on route 31 to the Rhine valley at Freiburg. (As with other recommended routes into the Schwarzwald, this one works just as well in reverse, starting in Freiburg.)

Offenburg, 43 km (27 miles) south of Baden-Baden and due west of Freudenstadt across the Schwarzwald mountains, is a picturesque place, with fountains and step-gabled buildings and a Baroque Rathaus. On the way up the valley you pass the imposing **Burg Ortenberg**, a castle sitting on a promontory of vineyards, with fruit trees in the foreground.

A few miles south of here, **Gengenbach** will charm you. Half-timbered houses are rarely so colorful. Among the sights are the stunning market square with outdoor restaurants, a maze of narrow side streets, a cloister, and walls and gates from medieval times.

The parking lot of the **Freilichtmuseum** at **Gutach** (south of Gengenbach on B 33) will be jammed with the cars of visitors to this open-air museum that re-creates Black Forest life of centuries ago. Original farmhouses with large sloping roofs that almost touch the ground were dismantled elsewhere in the Schwarzwald and reassembled here. The Vogtbauernhof, built in 1570 and the showpiece of the museum, gives a good picture of how an entire family, including grandparents, lived under the same thatched roof with their animals.

Along this route you may want to experience farmhouse living firsthand. Local tourist bureaus often list private homes that take in paying guests. But serendipity works, too. A *Zimmer Frei* (room free) sign pointing up a narrow lane can lead to an inexpensive night in a bona fide farmhouse such as the ▶ **Kaltenbach Bauernhof** near Hornberg. Cows are in the stable underneath, a hayloft on the other side of the bedroom wall, and a bathroom down the hall. Breakfast is served on a balcony with geranium-filled window boxes overlooking a meadow.

Triberg sits on the side of a mountain, its main street a long incline of shops, restaurants, and hotels, including the ▶ **Parkhotel Wehrle**, a charming establishment that serves gourmet meals, including more than 20 different trout dishes. Despite the old-fashioned look of the main building on the grassless thoroughfare, the Wehrle has an adjunct of modern villas with a park and swimming pool.

Triberg's **Heimatmuseum** (Local History Museum) is one of the most comprehensive in the Schwarzwald, with elaborate exhibits of costumes, clocks, musical instruments, wood carvings, and farm tools. A model of the surrounding countryside and the Schwarzwaldbahn shows how the railroad pierces the mountains with tunnels between Freiburg and Triberg. Murals on one floor record Black Forest industry, including its extensive mining operations. Showcases in the basement are filled with exotic minerals from the region.

Triberg's most popular attraction is its **Wasserfälle**. Although they are only 531 feet high, the falls are Germany's highest. The Gutach river cascades down the granite mountain in seven steps, its white water roaring through the forest. A walkway with guardrails allows visitors to follow the falls down through the gorge and on into town.

Once you leave Triberg (with its dozens of cuckoo-clock shops) do *not* be tempted to detour to Schonach *just* to see the world's largest cuckoo clock. The façade of a one-room house is a clock face, from which an insipid cuckoo emerges. Anyone who pauses to see it moves on, embarrassed for having taken the time. There are better things to see in Schonach.

A worthwhile detour from Triberg is to the **Uhrenmuseum** (Clock Museum) in **Furtwangen**, south on route B 500. Collectors are in heaven among the thousands of timepieces here, ranging from small gold pocket watches to pipe organs and player pianos that double as musical alarm clocks. There are cuckoo clocks here, too, but not as many as down the road at Titisee, a lively town popular with tourists.

Titisee (*See* means "lake") is said by many to be the most beautiful of the region's natural lakes, but that category leaves out the larger and more rustic **Schluchsee**, a lake to the south that was greatly enlarged by man. Moreover, Titisee teems with sightseeing cruise boats, rowboats, motorboats, and children's paddle-wheelers.

The ► **Maritim Titisee Hotel** on the lake offers a temporary haven for visitors who want to lunch in relative quiet. The hotel becomes a lodge in winter for skiers on the Feldberg, which is less than half an hour away.

From **Hinterzarten**, to the west of Titisee, as highway B 31 continues down the Höllental toward Freiburg, you get a completely different feeling: Vacationers stroll through the nature preserve, and day hikers in heavy shoes and knapsacks roam the hills. One trail goes by the ski jump, a long incline in a clearing in the woods that is used for competitions in both winter and summer (in warm weather jumpers land on plastic grass).

Hinterzarten's ▶ **Parkhotel Adler** is a coat-and-tie establishment of Continental graciousness situated in the village near the ski jump. The Adler's annex, the Schwarzwaldhaus, has seven rooms for dining, with varying international menus. A dance band plays in one of the rooms. The hotel's 500-year history includes an overnight visit in 1770 by 15-year-old Marie Antoinette on her way to Paris to marry the future Louis XVI. Her mother, Empress Maria Theresa, ordered the road leading through Hinterzarten leveled and widened for the entourage.

Anyone who wants to tarry in Hinterzarten does not have to invest in deluxe accommodations. There are many more humble but perfectly satisfactory places to stay. The ▶ **Waldheim** pension, a few hundred yards from the Adler, is plain but comfortable, and only half the price. The birds singing in the fresh morning air will be just as melodious.

The drive west to Freiburg on B 31 is best done in daylight. From Hinterzarten and Titisee it goes through the deep gorge of the **Höllental** (Hell Valley), where overhanging cliffs almost meet over the highway. A ride through the gorge on a century-old railroad is also a popular diversion. On one rocky precipice is a statue of a stag, the *Hirschsprung,* which in legend jumped across the gorge to avoid hunters.

FREIBURG

Freiburg, with 189,000 residents, is the largest city in the Black Forest and a thriving center of commerce. It is also a college town of 25,000 students; the philosopher Edmund Husserl worked here, as did the sociologist Max Weber, and Martin Heidegger taught at the university from 1927 to 1944. Despite extensive damage suffered in World War II (including a bombing run by the Luftwaffe), its medieval charm has been preserved.

Because Freiburg has assimilated surrounding villages, it has 1,600 acres of vineyards, more than any city in Germany. On the last weekend each June, during a four-day festival in the Münsterplatz, wines from these vineyards are sampled by the public.

Freiburgers know how to revel, as the number and variety of their festivals will attest. They boast of their *Fasnet* as one of Germany's better pre-Lenten carnivals, with bonfires on Shrove Tuesday and parades of jesters the day before. The May *Frühjahrsmesse* (Spring Fair) and October *Herbstmesse*

(Autumn Fair) both last ten days. *Weinkost* is a long wine-tasting event in mid-August. June visitors can take in the fortnight-long International Tent Music Festival.

Freiburg is a fairly easy city to get your bearings in. The Hauptbahnhof (railroad station) is on the west side of the inner city; trains run north and south between Karlsruhe and Basel. (A new high-rise hotel, the moderately priced ► In-terCity Hotel Freiburg, is next door to the station.) On the south side is the Dreisam river, flowing east to west. Most of what you want to see is in the area bounded by the railroad and the river and, on the east side, by the Schlossberg. This is the medieval **Altstadt** (Old City).

A good starting point is the Freiburg tourist information office on Rotteckring, several blocks east of the station and across the street from Colombipark. A palace in the park houses the **Museum für Ur- und Frühgeschichte** (Pre- and Early History Museum), with archaeological finds from the Paleolithic period to the Middle Ages. Next door to the tourist office is the modern-looking ► **Colombi Hotel**, costly but popular with business travellers.

Münsterplatz is where all travellers eventually congregate—with or without festivals. It is easy to spot; just look for the Gothic spire of the rose-colored **Münster** (Cathedral), the dominant feature of the Altstadt. Even if you don't include churches on your itinerary in other parts of the region, take time here to marvel at the artistry of the master builders, who began this church around 1200. A magnificent Gothic openwork spire soars above the religious friezes and life-size statues. Inside the church are stained-glass windows of incomparable beauty; pray for the sun to be shining through. The triptych on the high altar, by Hans Baldung-Grien, is widely acclaimed. The cathedral's imposing pipe organs are played in daily concerts (except Sundays) during the summer.

The area around the cathedral is often a marketplace of bright colors—flowers, vegetables, handicraft works, and *Gugelhopf* ceramic cake molds. When you tire of browsing, draw up a chair outside the ► **Hotel Oberkirchs Wein-stuben** and people-watch over a piece of *Zwiebelkuchen* (onion tart). Note the coat of arms on the dashing red **Kaufhaus** (Merchants' Hall) adjacent and its exotically tiled roof. Look up at the cathedral roof to the projecting gargoyles (one with his backside turned toward the bishop's house, said to convey the architect's contempt for the city fathers). Enjoy the street musicians if there are any about. Most are university students; the university itself is six blocks away in the middle of town.

Inside the Oberkirchs' dark-wood-paneled *Weinstuben*

and out, locals fork up their *Spätzle*. In May they make a ceremony of eating long white spears of asparagus. For dessert they might choose a piece of *Zwetchgentorte* (plum pastry), another specialty of the region. If you like the food and the location, the recently renovated Oberkirchs also has 50 beds at moderate prices.

Other points of interest in Freiburg: the Kaiser-Joseph-Strasse is a north–south street that separates the Münsterplatz on the east side from several worthwhile buildings on the west. At the Renaissance **Rathaus** (Town Hall) a carillon peals at noon, and a wedding party is not an unusual sight—you might even see a farmer's daughter emerge from under an arch of shovels. The **Martinskirche** (St. Martin's Church), also on the Rathausplatz, is a former Franciscan monastery that dates back to 1300. The **Haus zum Walfisch** (House of the Whale), nearby, has impressive Gothic doors. It was briefly the home of the Dutch humanist Desiderius Erasmus, who took refuge here at the height of the Reformation, which he opposed.

On Kaiser-Joseph-Strasse you are back in the 20th century amid arcades of modern shops. Streetcar tracks run down the middle of the street. The *Bächle,* shallow runnels lining both sides of the street, were formerly used to water livestock and as a fire precaution. More than four miles of these two-foot-wide mini-canals lace the town, clean enough to wade in (unfortunately, they act as traps to the unwary pedestrian).

The **Martinstor** on Kaiser-Joseph-Strasse is one of two surviving gates from the Middle Ages, when Freiburg was a walled city. It now guards a McDonald's. On the southeast edge of the Altstadt is the **Schwabentor**, the other old city gate, built around 1200. Paintings on the tower include one of Saint George, the city's patron saint. In this cobblestoned area are restored buildings, narrow streets, and a canal whose water was used in tanneries and gem-cutting workshops. One of Germany's oldest inns, the ▶ **Hotel zum Roten Bären**, is a short distance from the Schwabentor on Oberlindenstrasse. In business since 1387, the moderately priced Roten Bären (Red Bear) is proud of its atmosphere, bedrooms, and excellent kitchen.

The chief attraction in this vicinity is the **Augustinermuseum**, noted for its collection of art from medieval times to the present. The museum is located in a former monastery with a yellow Baroque exterior. Gargoyles and stained glass from the Münster are on display, as are gold and silver relics and a memorable collection of wood carvings by such Upper Rhine masters as Hans Wydyz. The museum's treasures also include paintings by Hans Baldung-Grien, Matthias Grünewald, Lucas Cranach, and others.

A city proud of its history and culture, Freiburg has many museums. Some of the more prominent are: the **Museum für Völkerkunde** (Ethnographic Museum), on Gerberaustrasse, near the Augustinermuseum; the **Museum für Naturkunde** (Natural History Museum), with Black Forest minerals, gems, flora, and fauna, in the same location as the Völkerkunde; the **Museum für Neue Kunst** (Modern Art Museum), featuring Expressionist and abstract paintings, on Marienstrasse; and the **Zinnfigurenklause** (Tin Figure Collection), in the Schwabentor.

THE WIESENTAL

For vacationers in Switzerland who want to add a day trip to Germany, the Black Forest is perfect, just a short distance across the Rhine from Basel.

Route 317, running northeast from Basel, leads through Lörrach along the river Wiese, where textile plants and lumber mills interrupt the landscape. As the road winds up the Wiesental, look for farmers cutting hay with scythes. Purple lupines and yellow buttercups make the hills look like a Pointillist painting. Deciduous trees that blaze with color in the fall ultimately yield at higher altitudes to dark evergreens. Some travellers consider this the sunniest and prettiest part of the Schwarzwald.

The goal here is the **Belchen**, a rounded mountain nearly a mile high, with wandering trails ringing its grassy peak. A ski lift on one side takes visitors up the steep hill. The view from the top is spectacular. The Feldberg and other mountains are identifiable in the distance; pastures of different shades of green roll down from the Belchen; tile roofs in small villages in the valleys reflect the sunlight. Sightseers can relax or have lunch after their walk on the balcony of the **Hotel Belchen**, the only large structure on the mountain, with a pleasant restaurant and welcome *Bier vom Fass* (beer on tap).

Continue the journey down the Münstertal west and north from the Belchen to **Staufen im Breisgau**, a village on the Neumagen river. Ruins of a castle destroyed in the Thirty Years' War tower over vineyards on the edge of town. Narrow gutters of running water flow before the gabled Rathaus, whose flower-crammed window boxes complement its mustard color.

Lunch or dinner in the nearby **Gasthof zum Löwen** is worth lingering over, if only for dessert. The chef has a heavy hand with the *Kirschwasser* in the *Schwarzwälder Kirschtorte* (Black Forest cake). (By now you may have noticed the many guest houses called *zum Löwen*—lion—and other animal names, and may wonder at the apparent lack of originality. Most people could not read in the Middle Ages when these houses opened, whereas symbols of lions, bears, and eagles were instantly recognizable.) In this particular Gasthof zum Löwen, you may be less interested in lunch than legend. Doctor Faustus, the medieval alchemist, whose deal with the Devil became the plot for Christopher Marlowe's *Doctor Faustus* and subsequent works by Goethe and Charles Gounod, lived here in the early 16th century. Baron von Staufen had invited the alchemist to town to use his skills in making gold. Faustus conducted his experiments in the Löwen. One day the house was rocked by an explosion and a terrible smell of sulfur filled the air. Everyone rushed to Faustus's room; he lay dead on the floor, his face blackened, his neck broken.

You can ponder the legend while driving back toward Freiburg on the Autobahn, past the vineyards of the **Badische Weinstrasse** (Baden Wine Road). Vintners here produce a variety of wines well known in Germany and increasingly on the lips of English-speaking connoisseurs everywhere: Riesling, Weissburgunder, Spätburgunder, Müller-Thurgau. Said to lift the spirits is a Silvaner from the Kaiserstuhl, an extinct volcano west of Freiburg. It is the wine to order at the **Schwarzer Adler** restaurant in Vogtsburg-Oberbergen, on the west side of the Kaiserstuhl. The dining room is considered one of the finest in Germany.

Other Parts of the Forest

Routes described above are oriented toward visiting the Schwarzwald from the *west* side—the Rhine valley and the major cities of Karlsruhe, Baden-Baden, and Freiburg in Germany, and Basel in Switzerland. But access points along the *eastern,* Württemberg, side of the state offer additional adventures, perhaps as side trips from the Stuttgart–Swabia area (see the preceding chapter).

It is a comfortable drive from Pforzheim on the Karlsruhe–Stuttgart Autobahn south to the spa town of **Wildbad**, where kings have come to seek a cure for rheumatism. Present-day businesspeople like the conference facilities (and mountaintop views) at the ▶ **Sommerberg Hotel**, which can be reached by car or funicular. For commercial travellers this hotel in the forest has all the amenities of a large metropolitan hotel. Its amenities include a big indoor pool, a sauna, and massage rooms. Popular in spring, summer, and fall for nature walks, the Sommerberg draws skiers in winter to its cross-country trails and lighted downhill slope.

Most Germans like a warm meal at noon, but for a cold plate try the *Vesperteller* at the **Hotel Bären**, on the main street of Wildbad beside the rushing Enz river. This wooden plate of sausages, cheese, and dark bread is the hearty fare a logger takes into the forest. (Your beer, of course, will be colder.)

From the Stuttgart–Bodensee (Lake Constance) Autobahn, it is a short jaunt from the Horb, Rottweil, and Villingen exits to destinations like Freudenstadt, covered above in the Schwarzwald Hochstrasse section.

GETTING AROUND

The vastness of the Black Forest makes transportation an important consideration. You can ride trains through the region on major service from Karlsruhe to Freudenstadt and on to Lake Constance. Scenic rail excursions run through the forest from several cities. Connections can be made from the main north–south rail route from Frankfurt to Basel, which runs through the Rhine valley past Baden-Baden and Freiburg.

It is even possible to see a bit of the Black Forest by streetcar. Residents of Karlsruhe, northwest of the forest, ride trolleys on day trips up into the hills to **Bad Herrenalb**, a spa with ruins of a 14th-century monastery.

Trolley and train rides offer vistas with comfort. So do buses, which operate from many cities near the forest, but you may find yourself at the mercy of a driver who gets commissions from souvenir shops. Not everyone relishes waiting an hour to watch hundreds of cuckoo clocks chirp on cue.

The ideal way to see the Black Forest is by automobile. Most visitors to the area who do not arrive by bus will rent cars at major airports in Frankfurt and Stuttgart in Germany or Zurich and Basel in Switzerland. By car, Baden-Baden is 179 km (111 miles) south of Frankfurt on the A 5 Autobahn; from Stuttgart, to the east, it is about 57 km (36 miles) on the A 8 to Karlsruhe, and another 39 km (24 miles) south from Karlsruhe on the A 5. From Strasbourg, 25 km (16 miles) to the southwest, take A 828/B 28 east across the Rhine to the A 5 heading north. Parking is available along Lange Strasse to the north or Lichtenthaler Strasse to the south.

Lufthansa is the major carrier to German cities, Swissair to Swiss cities. Many international carriers also offer service. Airlines offering service from the United States include American, Continental, Delta, TWA, United, and US Air. From the U.S., Balair, a public charter subsidiary of Swissair, offers direct flights to Basel at reduced rates.

When you pick up your rental car, get the largest-scale

road map you can find, as well as a panorama map of the Schwarzwald, a yard-long foldout relief map from which to choose one or more trips into the mountains. The map clearly shows points of access, whether you start in Baden-Baden, Freiburg, or from the Stuttgart Autobahn. It also indicates how easy it is to combine the Black Forest with a visit to Switzerland. It's also good for route-number guidance. Some tourist offices may have free English versions, but unfortunately, the map is not often found outside of Germany.

ACCOMMODATIONS REFERENCE

The hotel rates listed here are 1994 projections for double-bed, double-occupancy rooms, with a range from low to high whenever possible. Prices are given in deutsche marks (DM). Basic rates are always subject to change, so please verify price when you are booking. Breakfast is usually included in the price of a room.

City area codes must be preceded by a zero if you are calling from elsewhere in Germany.

▶ **Allee-Hotel Bären.** Lichtentaler Allee, D-76534 **Baden-Baden.** Tel: (7221) 70-20; Fax: (7221) 70-21-13. DM 180–340.

▶ **Badhotel zum Hirsch.** Hirschstrasse 1, D-76530 **Baden-Baden.** Tel: (7221) 93-90; Fax: (7221) 381-48; in U.S., Tel: (800) 223-5652. DM 250–280.

▶ **Brenner's Park-Hotel and Spa.** Lichtentaler Allee, D-76530 **Baden-Baden.** Tel: (7221) 90-00; Fax: (7221) 387-72. DM 474–1,104.

▶ **Colombi Hotel.** Rotteckring 16, D-79098 **Freiburg-im-Breisgau.** Tel: (761) 210-60; Fax: (761) 314-10. DM 350–370.

▶ **Deutscher Kaiser.** Merkurstrasse 9, D-76530 **Baden-Baden.** Tel: (7221) 27-00; Fax: (7221) 27-02-70. DM 155–185.

▶ **Hotel Colmar.** Langestrasse 34, D-76530 **Baden-Baden.** Tel: (7221) 938-90; Fax: (7221) 93-89-50. DM 145–170.

▶ **Hotel Oberkirchs Weinstuben.** Münsterplatz, D-79098 **Freiburg-im-Breisgau.** Tel: (761) 310-11; Fax: (761) 310-31. DM 195–250.

▶ **Hotel zum Roten Bären.** Oberlindenstrasse 12, D-79098 **Freiburg-im-Breisgau.** Tel: (761) 38-78-70; Fax: (761) 38-78-17; in U.S., Tel: (800) 826-0015; Fax: (206) 481-40-79. DM 220–250.

▶ **InterCity Hotel Freiburg.** Bismarckallee 3, D-72098 **Freiburg.** Tel: (761) 380-00; Fax: (761) 380-09-99; in U.S., Tel: (800) 223-5652. DM 171–191.

▶ **Kaltenbach Bauernhof.** Obergiesshof 34, D-78132 **Hornberg/Niederwasser.** Tel: (7833) 69-78. DM 45.

▶ **Maritim Titisee Hotel.** Seestrasse, D-79822 **Titisee-Neustadt.** Tel: (7651) 80-80; Fax: (7651) 80-86-03. DM 279–367.

▶ **Parkhotel Adler.** Adlerplatz 3, D-79854 **Hinterzarten.** Tel: (7652) 12-70; Fax: (7652) 12-77-17. DM 320–460.

▶ **Parkhotel Wehrle.** Markplatz, D-78094 **Triberg.** Tel: (7722) 860-20; Fax: (7722) 86-02-90. DM 140–330.

▶ **Schlosshotel Bühlerhöhe.** Schwarzwaldhochstrasse 1, D-77815 **Bühl.** Tel: (7226) 550; Fax: (7226) 557-77. DM 490–650.

▶ **Sommerberg Hotel.** D-75313 **Bad Wildbad.** Tel: (7081) 17-40; Fax: (7081) 17-46-12. DM 165–390.

▶ **Steigenberger Avance Badischer Hof.** Langestrasse 47, D-76530 **Baden-Baden.** Tel: (7221) 93-44-50; Fax: (7221) 93-44-70. DM 270–430.

▶ **Steigenberger Europäischer Hof.** Kaiserallee 2, D-76530 **Baden-Baden.** Tel: (7221) 93-30; Fax: (7221) 288-31; in U.S., (800) 223-5652. DM 270–470.

▶ **Waldheim.** Windeckweg 9, D-79856 **Hinterzarten.** Tel: (7652) 286; Fax: (7652) 451. DM 135–150.

▶ **Zum Rebstock.** D-77830 **Bühlertal.** Tel: (7223) 731-18; Fax: (7223) 759-43. DM 160–180.

CHRONOLOGY OF THE HISTORY OF GERMANY

Prehistoric Origins

Present-day Germany was the scene of human activity some 500,000 years ago, when early man hunted in the Rhine and Neckar valleys. The 50,000-year-old skeleton of a Neanderthal man, discovered in 1856 in a cave near Erkrath southeast of Düsseldorf, may be seen today in the Neanderthal Museum at the site. Bronze Age agricultural communities occupied southern Scandinavia, Jutland, and the North German Lowlands between the Weser and Oder rivers in the first millennium B.C. Utensils imported from the Mediterranean have been found in Iron Age graves.

- c. 600 B.C.: The northern Germanic tribes known as Teutons and Cimbrians migrate as far south as the Lower Rhine and Vistula. With tools and farming skills imported from Asia, these nomadic tribes push the Celts, who had initially migrated to the area, westward over the Rhine.
- 102 B.C.: The Teutons and Cimbrians invade Gaul and northern Italy but are decimated by the Romans.
- c. 50 B.C.: The German tribes settle more heavily in the area between the North Sea and the Central Uplands as far as the Limes, the Roman frontier that extends from the Rhine to the Danube.

The Roman Period

By the first century A.D. the Roman sphere of influence (read "control") extended well into the borders of present-day Germany, but, because of successive attacks by Germanic tribes, never very far or firmly beyond the Rhine and the Main. In and after 53 B.C. Julius Caesar led his troops all the way to the banks of the Mosel, the Neckar, and the Rhine, establishing garrisons at Cologne, Koblenz, Mainz, and Trier.

Trier's Porta Nigra (restored by Napoleon in the early 19th century) stands as perhaps the prime relic of Germany's Roman period.

- **A.D. 9**: Arminius leads his Cheruscans and other German tribes into battle, defeating 20,000 Roman troops near Osnabrück, Westphalia. Renamed Hermann during the nationalistic fervor of the 19th century, he becomes the first hero of German unity and freedom.
- **98**: Tacitus, in his *Germania,* describes for the first time the customs and beliefs of the Germanic people.
- **c. 200**: The Romans are unable to maintain a hold on Central Europe, as the tribes from whom the Empire recruited its frontier armies move further into Germania. The Alemanni, Franks, and Saxons emerge as dominant West Germanic tribes.
- **313**: With the Edict of Milan, Constantine I puts an end to Christian persecution. Trier becomes the "Second Rome," and site of the first bishopric in Germany.
- **c. 375**: The Huns of Central Asia attack the East Germanic tribes—the Goths, Vandals, and Burgundians—forcing them to move westward. The Slavic peoples move south into previously Germanic areas, and the West Germanic tribes gain control of the land between the North Sea and the Alps. The Franks, a tribal integration of Roman and Germanic communities, become the transitory link between Roman influence and the rise of German princedoms. The only Roman influence in the region is the Christian church.
- **400**: The Romans withdraw from Germany.

The Franks

Although boundaries shifted substantially, the empire of the Franks represented the transition of the Germanic territories from a loose conglomeration of Germanic tribes into what would eventually become the German Empire. Charlemagne (Karl-der-Grosse; 768–814) was responsible for the earliest large-scale attempt to unite the lands of Germany under one ruler, mostly through military victory and forced Christian conversion. The Frankish Empire incorporated what is today France, the Rhineland, the land between the North Sea and the Alps, and the Central German Highlands.

- **486**: Clovis of the Merovingian family is crowned king of the Franks. He subdues the Swabians (Alemanni) and unites most of the remaining West Germanic tribes (Bavarians, Thuringians, Franconians, Frisians, Saxons). His conversion to Christianity helps him to integrate the Germanic and conquered Roman peoples.

- **744**: Benedictine abbey founded at Fulda (near present-day Frankfurt-am-Main) by a follower of Saint Boniface. From this great center, Christianity and learning spreads to regional centers throughout central Germany: Cologne, St. Gallen, Aachen, and elsewhere.
- **788**: Charlemagne deposes Tasso of Bavaria and annexes his lands.
- **794**: Charlemagne establishes Aachen as the imperial court and intellectual capital of Europe, fostering what is considered to be the first great cultural renaissance after the collapse of the Roman Empire (the so-called Carolingian Renaissance).
- **800**: On Christmas Day in Rome, Pope Leo III crowns Charlemagne emperor of all the Romans, giving him jurisdiction over the new Empire of the West (formerly Gaul and Germania). Four years later, Charlemagne defeats the Saxons, extending his empire to the Elbe.
- **843**: The Treaty of Verdun divides the Frankish empire into three Carolingian dynasties: a western portion (later France); a central portion (the Low Countries, Lorraine, Alsace, Burgundy, Provence, and most of Italy); and an eastern portion, which ultimately becomes the German Empire and goes to Charlemagne's grandson, Louis I.
- **911**: Conrad I is elected king by the Frankish and Saxon dukes of the Eastern Kingdom. The end of the East Frankish kingdom as a Carolingian dynasty is accompanied by the complete separation of the Germanic tribes from the rest of the Frankish empire.

The Holy Roman Empire of the German Nation

The Holy Roman Empire survived until 1806, although the power struggles of the Middle Ages continually disrupted the unity hammered out by Charlemagne. His successors were unable to defend the Empire from the invasions of Arabs, Normans, Slavs, and Magyars. Because of the weakness of central authority, various German tribal duchies sought to build their own autonomy, giving rise to the manorial system and contributing to the growth of feudalism. Ultimately it was the power and organization of the Church over secular matters that kept the Holy Roman Empire at least partially intact, but this also led to a bitter power struggle between the imperial rulers and the papacy. Until the demise of the Holy Roman Empire, Germany remained a collection of small principalities and free cities.

- **919–936**: Heinrich (Henry) I takes the title of king and consolidates the realm. Germany is described as a kingdom ("Regnum Teutonicorum") for the first time.
- **936**: Otto I is crowned in Aachen by the archbishop of Mainz, which ensures him the powerful support of the Church.
- **962**: Otto I is crowned "King of the Franks and the Lombards" in Rome, becoming ruler of both Germany and the Holy Roman Empire.
- **1075**: Pope Gregory VII decides that lay investiture overseen by imperial officials acting as Church representatives must be ended. The pope excommunicates Henry IV, who is forced to submit to the pope two years later at Canossa. A struggle around the investiture issue lasts for fifty years, until a settlement is reached with the Concordat of Worms (1125).
- **1152–1190**: During the reign of the Hohenstaufen Friedrich I (Frederick Barbarossa), the term "Holy Roman Empire" first comes into use ("of the German Nation" will not be added until the 15th century). Throughout nearly forty years the empire is enlarged and internal peace is maintained.
- **1158**: Duke Henry the Lion founds Munich. His hold over Saxony and Bavaria—the last great independent German domain of the time—is eventually broken by Barbarossa.

The Merchant Princedom

The period following the Christian Crusades to win back the Holy Land from the Muslims (11th–13th centuries) was marked by an upswing in international commerce, building, and the arts. Economic life shifted from a barter to a money economy, foreign trade increased, and Free Imperial cities such as Hamburg and Lübeck became increasingly autonomous. The prosperity of the rising merchant class resulted in the establishment of merchant dynasties whose patrons began to build imposing town halls and churches. Knights returning from the Crusades were employed in the German colonization of eastern and southeastern Europe from the 12th to the 14th centuries.

- **1125–1350**: German colonization of eastern Europe.
- **1348**: The Black Death reduces the population of Germany from 14 to 10 million over the next century.
- **1358**: The Hanseatic League, a merchants' guild that links the majority of the towns throughout northern Germany and dominates Baltic trade, is formed. Lübeck is named its capital. (The city's Gothic Altstadt, still a gem, was recently added to UNESCO's World Heritage List.) The League's trading connections eventually extend from London to Stockholm, and from Bruges to Novgorod.
- **1356**: In an attempt to check the growing independence of the dukedoms and to prevent further disintegration of the empire, Hapsburg Emperor Karl (Charles) IV issues the Golden Bull, a decree authorizing seven electors to appoint the German sovereign.
- **1386**: Heidelberg University, Germany's oldest, is founded.
- **c. 1455**: Johannes Gutenberg, the inventor of printing from movable type, publishes the first printed Bible.

The Reformation

The 16th century was a time of social unrest and religious upheaval throughout Germany. Martin Luther, destined to become the father of the Reformation, opened a battle against the excesses and abuses of the Catholic Church that had far-reaching implications. Luther's belief in personal Christian freedom based on inner inspiration inspired the German peasants to demand a return of their ancient rights and led to their eventual (unsuccessful) revolt. (Luther himself denounced the peasants' demands.) As the Reformation spread through the efforts of Calvin and other Protestants, the Catholic Church launched the Counter-Reformation which culminated, nearly a century later, in the bloody Thirty Years' War, pitting northern Protestants against the Catholic south and affecting the whole of Europe.

- **1483**: Martin Luther is born in Eisleben.
- **1517–1522**: Luther posts his 95 theses on a door of the castle church at Wittenberg, burns the Papal Bull (the fundamental law of the empire), and translates the Bible into German.

- **1520**: Emperor Karl (Charles) V is crowned at Aachen.
- **1525**: The Peasants' War breaks out as Luther's battle against authority sows the seeds of social revolution.
- **1545–1563**: The Council of Trent, which established the basic doctrines of the Counter-Reformation, moves to reform Church abuses.
- **1618**: The Thirty Years' War breaks out in Bohemia and continues until the Peace of Westphalia in 1648. Results: the realignment of much of Europe, the laying waste and carving up of Germany, and an equal-rights guarantee to German Catholics and Protestants.
- **1640–1688**: Under Friedrich Wilhelm, the Great Elector, Brandenburg-Prussia begins its ascent to power.
- **1685**: Johann Sebastian Bach is born into a musically gifted family in Eisenach. Georg Friedrich Handel is born in Halle.

Prussia Ascendant

The ongoing competition for power in Germany resulted in the rise of two absolutist ruling dynasties: the Hapsburgs, who had recovered Austria as their stronghold at the end of the Thirty Years' War, and the Hohenzollerns, who were building a powerful state in Brandenburg-Prussia. Under Frederick the Great (Friedrich-der-Grosse; 1740–1786), Prussia forcibly acquired the Austrian province of Silesia and gained the status of a great European power, although it remained a component of the Holy Roman Empire ruled by the Hapsburgs. Berlin became a major European capital during this period, and German culture rose in prominence as the works of German artists, writers, composers, and philosophers ushered in the "Age of Enlightenment."

- **1701**: Friedrich, son of the Great Elector, gains the consent of the emperor to have himself crowned king of Prussia.
- **1733**: Munich's Asamkirche is built by the Asam brothers (Cosmas Damian and Egid Querin), creators of some of the most enduring examples of Baroque architecture and decoration.
- **1740**: Frederick the Great ascends the Prussian throne and makes Berlin into a major European capital. The "Linden" (today's Unter den Linden) is expanded into a grand boulevard in 1770 and the

palace of Sanssouci in Potsdam is built as his summer residence.

- **1749**: Johann Wolfgang von Goethe, whose tragedy *Götz von Berlichingen* will become the first major drama of the German literary movement known as *Sturm und Drang* (Storm and Stress), is born in Frankfurt-am-Main. Goethe's novels and plays culminate in the drama *Faust,* the masterpiece for which he is best known today.
- **1756–1763**: During the Seven Years' War Prussia, in cooperation with England, fends off the allied armies of France, Austria, and Russia.
- **1770**: Ludwig van Beethoven, whose creative genius as a composer will help to usher in the Romantic era in music, is born in Bonn. Georg Wilhelm Friedrich Hegel, whose philosophy of the Absolute will become the 19th century's leading system of metaphysics, is born in Stuttgart.
- **1781**: Immanuel Kant, founder of critical philosophy, in which he sought to determine the limits of man's knowledge, publishes *The Critique of Pure Reason*.
- **1786–1797**: During the reign of King Friedrich Wilhelm II of Prussia, Berlin becomes the "City of the Enlightenment." The Brandenburg Gate is completed in 1791 and becomes a symbol of the city.

Napoleon and the
Collapse of the Holy Roman Empire

To counteract governmental anxiety about the ongoing threat of French power following the French Revolution, Prussia, Austria, Russia, and England formed a coalition against Napoleon. After a brief period of peace in the early 1800s, Napoleon defeated the Austrian and Prussian armies at Austerliz and occupied several German cities. With the abolition of the Holy Roman Empire in 1806, Prussia became more independent and after 1815 began the process of political and economic modernization, challenging Austria for dominance in the German-speaking countries.

- **1795**: After their unsuccessful attempts to intervene in the post-Revolutionary affairs of France, Prussia and Austria are forced by Napoleon to sign the Peace of Bâle. Prussia promises neutrality and Germany loses the west bank of the Rhine to France.
- **1800**: Napoleon's troops occupy Trier.
- **1806**: The Holy Roman Empire officially ends with

the abdication of Hapsburg Kaiser Franz II as Holy Roman Emperor. The Confederation of the Rhine is formed when German states bordering on France unite under Napoleon. After the collapse of the Prussian military forces in the Battle of Jena and Auerstadt, Napoleon marches into Berlin and a two-year French occupation of the city begins.

- **1810**: The University of Berlin (which is to become Humboldt University during the GDR years) is founded by Wilhelm von Humboldt. Munich's first Oktoberfest is staged to celebrate the engagement of Crown Prince Ludwig and Princess Theresa.
- **1812**: Publication of the first of Jakob Ludwig and Wilhelm Karl Grimm's *Kinder- und Hausmärchen* (known to the English-speaking world as *Grimm's Fairy Tales*).
- **1813**: Napoleon's armies forced to retreat across the Rhine back into France. Richard Wagner is born in Leipzig.
- **1815**: The initial defeat of the French in the Battle of Nations in Leipzig is followed by the decisive Battle of Waterloo.

Revolution and German Unity

The defeat of Napoleon awakened in many Germans a strong sense of national pride and unity. The country's aristocratic and conservative military and political rulers, however, were determined to defeat liberalism (based as that was on Republican ideals) and return to their old system of absolute monarchy. The rapidly industrializing German Confederation experienced several decades of relatively quiet political activity, during which rapid advances were made in the fields of transportation and communication. But the underlying social demands for basic German rights and the question of independence and national unity finally came to a head in the 1848 revolution. When the revolution failed, the Austrian monarchy reimposed its sovereignty over the German Confederation and Prussia.

- **1815**: The Holy Alliance between Prussia, Austria, and Russia is signed on September 26, helping to preserve absolute monarchy. Under the conservative leadership of Prince Metternich, the Congress of Vienna carves up Europe anew and promotes the German Confederation, a Hapsburg-dominated confederation of 35 princely states and four free cities.
- **1819**: The Carlsbad Decrees usher in a period of

rigid censorship and press control with the intention of routing subversive elements.

- **1833**: The composer Johannes Brahms is born in Hamburg. Carl Friedrich Gauss and Wilhelm Eduard Weber invent the electromagnetic telegraph.
- **1834**: The German Customs Union (*Zollverein*) economically unites German merchants by creating a free trade area under Prussian leadership. Austria is excluded.
- **1835**: The first German passenger railways opens for service between Nürnberg and Fürth.
- **1848**: Revolution breaks out in Italy and spreads to all of Central Europe, threatening conservative monarchies. Friedrich Wilhelm IV of Prussia pledges his support for the unification of Germany and a short-lived German National Assembly is convened in Frankfurt. The law concerning the basic rights of the German people is passed, and a year later Friedrich Wilhelm IV declines the imperial crown offered him by the Frankfurt parliament.
- **1850**: The Frankfurt parliament is dissolved. A reactionary "imposed constitution" of the Prussian government takes effect on January 31 and remains in force until November 1918.

Bismarck and the German Reich

As Germany continued to industrialize, it became an economic rival to England, and also a center of great social conflict through the growth of the revolutionary Social Democratic movement, which the autocratic Bismarck declared illegal for 12 years. With the emergence of political thinkers like Karl Marx, and artists like the working-class Käthe Kollwitz, the writers Thomas and Heinrich Mann, and others associated with the Berlin Secession movement, cultural and intellectual life in this period began to transcend the conservatism and authoritarianism that had characterized so much of German history.

- **1862**: Otto von Bismarck is appointed prime minister of Prussia.
- **1864**: War breaks out between Denmark and Germany. Prussia annexes Schleswig and, in 1866, Holstein.
- **1866**: Germany defeats Austria, resulting in the foundation of the North German Confederation (which replaces the old German Confederation) and the dual monarchy of Austria-Hungary.

- **1867**: Käthe Kollwitz, graphic artist and sculptor, and ardent socialist and pacifist, is born. She becomes widely known for her powerful woodcuts and lithographs depicting the misery and hunger of society's dispossessed.
- **1867**: Karl Marx publishes the first volume of *Das Kapital*. (Frederick Engels will complete the work in 1885 and 1894.)
- **1869**: The Social Democratic Party is founded with leadership provided by August Bebel. In 1872 Bebel, along with Karl Liebknecht, is sentenced for plotting treason.
- **1870–1871**: The Franco-Prussian War results in the collapse of the French and, ultimately, in Bismarck's success in having Wilhelm I proclaimed German emperor at Versailles—completing the groundwork for the unification of Germany. Berlin becomes the capital of Germany.
- **1875**: Thomas Mann is born in Lübeck.
- **1876**: The Bayreuth Festival celebrates its premiere with Wagner's *Das Rheingold*.
- **1889**: Adolf Hitler is born in Braunau, Austria.
- **1890**: Emperor Wilhelm II dismisses Bismarck, who has challenged his authority, as Reich chancellor and Prussian prime minister.
- **1898–1909**: The German navy steadily grows in power until it equals the strength of the British navy.
- **1900**: Berlin's population reaches 1,900,000. The first subway line opens in 1902.
- **1901**: Wilhelm Conrad Roentgen, discoverer of the X ray, wins the first Nobel Prize for Physics.
- **1911**: Wassily Kandinsky and others found the *Blaue Reiter* movement of German Expressionist art in Munich.

World War I

For many observers, the Great War represented a German attempt to dominate Europe. The military conflict on the eastern front resulted in the defeat of Russia, while fighting on the western front ultimately led to German defeat. Although the war was not fought on German soil, it resulted in severe food shortages throughout the country and intensified political unrest.

- **1914**: The heir apparent to the Austrian throne is assassinated in Sarajevo on June 28, precipitating World War I. Germany declares war on Russia on

August 1, and on France two days later. On August 4, Great Britain declares war on Germany. Japan declares war on Germany on August 23.

- **1914–1918**: Fully mobilized, Germany fights the war on the eastern and western fronts. Berlin, the German capital, remains outside the front lines of fighting, but it proves increasingly difficult to keep the city stocked with food and rationing eventually goes into effect in cities throughout Germany.
- **1917**: The United States declares war on Germany, bringing the number of nations opposing Germany to 28. Hunger and war-weariness, compounded by political grievances, culminate in mass strikes in 1917 and 1918.
- **1918**: At war's end, Kaiser Wilhelm II is forced by the victorious Allies to abdicate. The November Revolution ends Hohenzollern rule in Germany, and Friedrich Ebert, the head of the Social Democratic Party is named chancellor of the Reich. In Berlin, Philipp Scheidemann, Social Democrat, proclaims the "German Republic" from the Reichstag.

The Weimar Republic

In its attempt to establish a democratic and republican government, the so-called Weimar government represented a break in the dominant traditions of German history. Residual issues from the war and the hostility of conservative groups conflicted with the reformist and radical impulses of the left and the cultural avant-garde. During the "Golden Twenties," Berlin—the capital of the republic—blossomed into the economic and cultural center of Germany as well.

- **1919**: Germany signs the Treaty of Versailles, which limits the army to 100,000 officers and men, although a "free corps" of soldiers remains. The Allies determine the total reparations bill in 1920. Rosa Luxemburg and Karl Liebknecht, the Communist leaders of the Spartacus League, are assassinated. Walter Gropius founds the Bauhaus school, noted for its unique style of functionalist architecture, in Weimar.
- **1920**: The Kapp putsch and Communist uprisings in the Ruhr industrial district help to spread a wave of lawlessness and disorder. A police operation against leftist radicals in Berlin ends with 42 dead, and the Reich government flees in the face of an attempted right-wing putsch in March.

- **1921–1923**: Large-scale strikes disrupt and paralyze Berlin. Political violence escalates and culminates in the assassination of Foreign Minister Walter Rathenau in 1922. The number of unemployed soars, and inflation, which reaches ludicrous proportions, is stabilized in 1923 when one new banknote (Rentenmark) is issued to replace 1,000 billion old paper marks. Hitler makes his first bid for power with the November 8–9 "Beerhall Putsch" in Munich.
- **1924–1925**: The Social Democrat Friedrich Ebert dies and Paul von Hindenburg is elected *Reichspräsident*.
- **1926**: Germany is admitted to the League of Nations.
- **1928**: The Brecht/Weill *Threepenny Opera* premieres in Berlin.
- **1929**: The Great Depression creates greater political and social tensions within Germany. Lübeck-born Thomas Mann receives the Nobel Prize for Liberature.

The Rise of Nazism and World War II

The economic crisis in Germany was a major factor in the rise of the Nazi movement, but the old authoritarian, nationalistic, and imperialistic attitudes of the country also provided a ripe environment for the National Socialist party to take control. As the brutal anti-Semitic political agenda of Adolf Hitler became apparent, thousands of German Jews—including many prominent artists, scientists, and politicians—fled the country to escape persecution. Millions of Jews and other "undesirable" minorities throughout Germany and the rest of Nazi-occupied Europe were systematically exterminated in one of the most horrifying chapters in world history. By the end of the war, Germany's major cities lay in smoldering ruins and Germany ceased to exist as an independent state.

- **1933**: On January 31, Hitler is appointed Reich chancellor. The Reichstag is burned on February 27. On October 14, Germany withdraws from the League of Nations. The National Socialist Party comes to power. Hitler receives dictatorial powers, and embarks upon the "Third (or 1000-year) Reich," a concept patterned after the Holy Roman Empire of the German Nation.
- **1934**: Hitler organizes the "Blood Purge" to rid the party of all opponents. On the death of President Hindenburg, Hitler is appointed Führer.

- **1935:** Universal conscription is established. The Nürnberg Laws deprive German Jews of citizenship, deny them all civil rights, prohibit them from marrying Aryans, and bar them from the liberal professions.
- **1936:** The Olympic Games open in Berlin's new stadium. Hitler storms out of the stadium when a black American named Jesse Owens wins four gold medals.
- **1938:** On November 9, synagogues and Jewish businesses throughout Germany are savagely attacked and destroyed in the officially organized "Kristallnacht." The Munich Pact marks the culmination of British and French attempts at appeasement, a policy based on the assumption that Hitler's aims are limited.
- **1939:** Germany invades Czechoslovakia and Poland. On September 3, Great Britain and France declare war on Germany.
- **1941:** Hitler invades the Soviet Union in June. In December, Hitler declares war on the United States following the bombing of Pearl Harbor.
- **1942:** The "final solution to the Jewish question" is adopted at the Wannsee Conference. The destruction of German cities by the Allies begins.
- **1943:** After Germany's large-scale defeat at Stalingrad, the National Socialists declare "total war" on February 18 in the Berlin Sports Palace. In November the Allied forces begin the steady bombardment of Berlin. Roosevelt demands an unconditional German surrender.
- **1944:** Allied troops land at Normandy and air attacks on Germany are intensified. An assassination attempt is made on Hitler's life by a secret resistance group around Colonel von Stauffenberg.
- **1945:** Churchill, Stalin, and Roosevelt meet at the Yalta Conference in February to determine the course of Allied occupation policy. Germany is invaded on two fronts, and major cities such as Dresden, Berlin, Cologne, and Leipzig are virtually destroyed by Allied bombing. Soviet troops reach Berlin on April 21. On April 30, Hitler commits suicide. Just over a week later, on May 8, the war in Europe ends with the Allied occupation of Germany. Berlin is partitioned into East (Soviet) and West (American, British, and French) zones, governed by the Allied Control Council. The Potsdam Agreement between the United States, Great Britain, and the Soviet Union divides the rest of Germany into occupation zones in August. The Nürnberg trials begin in November.

The Two Germanys

Having at first intended to govern conquered Germany as one unit, the victors divided it into two states as the Cold War intensified. The two separate states, the Federal Republic of Germany and the German Democratic Republic, developed with highly differing political, economic, and social systems.

- **1946**: The Iron Curtain (Churchill coins the term) rings down. From this time, the separate eastern and western zones develop in accordance with the desires of the Western states or the Soviet Union.
- **1948**: West German reindustrialization and recovery, the fabulous *Wirtschaftswunder* (Economic Miracle), gets under way, with U.S. assistance in the form of the Marshall Plan, or European Recovery Program. In June the establishment of the West German deutsche mark sparks an eastern currency reform. The Soviet blockade of West Berlin results in the Anglo-American airlift, which continues until May 12, 1949.
- **1949**: On May 23, the Basic Law for the Federal Republic of Germany is instituted and Bonn becomes the capital of West Germany. The German Democratic Republic (GDR) is established in the Soviet-occupied zone, with Berlin as its capital. NATO is founded.
- **1950**: The Görlitz Agreement between Poland and the GDR fixes the Oder–Neisse line as the border between the two states.
- **1953**: A strike by building workers in East Berlin develops into a popular movement throughout the GDR and is quashed by Soviet tanks.
- **1955**: Under the leadership of Chancellor Konrad Adenauer, the Federal Republic of Germany becomes a sovereign state on May 5. On May 9 the Federal Republic is admitted into NATO.
- **1957**: The Federal Republic joins other European countries in establishing the European Economic Community (now the E.C., the European Community).
- **1958**: The collectivization of agriculture in the GDR prompts a mass exodus to the West.
- **1961**: On August 13 Erich Honecker, head of East German security, oversees the construction of the Berlin Wall, sealing off East Berlin from West Berlin.
- **1963**: The first passes are issued to GDR citizens enabling them to visit relatives in the West.

- **1970**: West German chancellor Willy Brandt meets with the chairman of the GDR council of ministers, Willi Stoph, to discuss relations between the two Germanys.
- **1971**: The Four Powers Pact on Berlin guarantees the free movement of persons and goods between the western sector of Berlin and the Federal Republic. Chancellor Willy Brandt wins the Nobel Peace Prize. Erich Honecker becomes head of East Germany's ruling Communist party.
- **1972**: Munich hosts the Summer Olympics, a tragic event at which nine Israeli athletes are kidnapped and killed by Arab terrorists.
- **1973**: Both Germanys join the United Nations.
- **1975**: East Germany signs the Helsinki Final Act, recognizing human rights. Twelve thousand applications for emigration are filed and all are rejected.

Germany Reunited

The opening of the Berlin Wall in 1989 marked for East Germany the culmination of a wave of previously suppressed revolutionary sentiment across Central and Eastern Europe. The reforms of Mikhail Gorbachev and the underground, grassroots communication between citizens in East Germany lead to massive demonstrations against the repressive, Stalinist government of the GDR. Freedom of travel and an end to the East German secret police (*Stasi*) were among the demands. The events surrounding the opening of the East German border are all the more remarkable for being entirely unexpected. The initial euphoria has inevitably become subdued as the very real problems of reunification make themselves known, and the hard work of social, economic, and political restructuring begins.

- **1989**: In May, East German "vacationers" crowd into Hungary and continue across the newly opened border into Austria and West Germany. Gorbachev visits East Berlin in October for the 40th anniversary celebrations of the GDR. In November Erich Honecker is replaced by Egon Krenz as general secretary of the Communist party. Mass demonstrations are held in Berlin and Leipzig. The East German Politburo resigns and the Central Committee of the Communist Party recommends that a new government be formed. By November 9, East Germans are allowed to travel to West Germany without special visas. Hundreds of thousands of them pour into

West Berlin, and the two sides celebrate the opening of the Wall that had separated them for forty
years. Calls for full reunification with West Germany
continue. Erich Honecker and other top party members are placed under house arrest as details of
official corruption and abuse of power are made
public. Entry visas and compulsory exchange are
abolished for visitors to the GDR. On New Year's
Eve half a million people ring in a new decade for
Germany at the officially opened Brandenburg Gate.

- **1990:** The dismantling of the Wall continues as the
Allied side of Checkpoint Charlie, one of the two
crossing points into East Berlin, is removed in June.
East and West Germany adopt a single monetary
system on July 1, the same day that all border con-
trols in and around Berlin are suspended. The four
wartime Allies sign a document on September 12
relinquishing their occupation rights in Germany.
On October 3 the two Germanys are officially reuni-
fied as a single political entity and the GDR ceases to
exist. To escape an arrest order, Erich Honecker
enters a Soviet military base near Berlin. In December, Helmut Kohl becomes chancellor of a united
Germany in the first free nationwide elections since
Adolf Hitler was named chancellor of the Reich in
1933.

- **1991:** Berlin is made the new capital of Germany,
although the move is not expected to take place for
several years. Evidence of environmental destruction
under the government of the GDR is made public.
Erich Honecker is spirited out of Germany aboard a
Soviet plane. Tens of thousands of East Germans lose
their jobs as eastern Germany privatizes industry.
The former East German price constraints on basic
necessities such as food and housing are eliminated.
Neo-Nazi attacks take place in Berlin, Leipzig, and
other German cities.

- **1992:** Issues resulting from reunification continue to
dominate German politics. Erich Honecker returns
to Berlin to face charges of corruption and man-
slaughter involving shoot-to-kill orders against people attempting to flee across the former East German
border. Investigators uncover evidence that at least
350 people died trying to escape, twice the previously documented number. Manfred Wolf, former
head of East Germany's Stasi spy service, also returns
from Russia to face charges of treason, espionage,
and bribery.

Overriding predominantly West German opposition, the German Parliament votes to adopt a new post-unification law liberalizing a woman's right to obtain an abortion; the constitutional court places an injunction on the law going into effect until a ruling can be made on its constitutionality. In April, the powerful Union of Public Services goes on strike, disrupting basic services in several German cities. The number of refugees, most of them from Eastern Europe and seeking asylum in Germany, climbs toward 500,000, twice the 1991 number. Neo-Nazis demanding the expulsion of refugees stage riots and firebomb refugee housing in Rostock and several other eastern German cities. In September, the German government signs agreements with Romania and Poland that pave the way for Germany to deport tens of thousands of Poles, Gypsies, and other Romanians; similar agreements with Czechoslovakia and Bulgaria are planned. Former West German chancellor Willy Brandt, a Nobel Prize laureate for his work to overcome the postwar division of Europe, dies in October. In November, an estimated 300,000 Germans gather in Berlin to repudiate rightist violence, an event disrupted by militant leftists. When three Turkish women are killed in a firebomb attack in late November, the German government bans the Nationalist Front and the Deutsche Alternativ, two Neo-Nazi parties, and begins a wave of house searches and arrests. The German parliament votes in December to approve the Maastricht treaty of European union. In December the country's main political parties agree on a new law to make it harder for asylum seekers and refugees to enter Germany. German citizens hold mass rallies and candlelight vigils throughout the country to protest right-wing anti-foreigner violence.

- **1993:** Berlin loses its bid to host the 2000 Olympic Games. Ground is broken at Potsdamer Platz—once one of Europe's busiest urban spaces, then a part of the Wall's "death strip"—for what is soon to become one of Europe's largest construction sites. In October, after several years of vacillation, the government decides to complete the move of the German capital from Bonn to Berlin by the year 2000; Parliament is expected to move in 1998.

—Donald S. Olson

INDEX

August 1, and on France two days later. On August 4, Great Britain declares war on Germany. Japan declares war on Germany on August 23.

- **1914–1918:** Fully mobilized, Germany fights the war on the eastern and western fronts. Berlin, the German capital, remains outside the front lines of fighting, but it proves increasingly difficult to keep the city stocked with food and rationing eventually goes into effect in cities throughout Germany.

- **1917:** The United States declares war on Germany, bringing the number of nations opposing Germany to 28. Hunger and war-weariness, compounded by political grievances, culminate in mass strikes in 1917 and 1918.

- **1918:** At war's end, Kaiser Wilhelm II is forced by the victorious Allies to abdicate. The November Revolution ends Hohenzollern rule in Germany, and Friedrich Ebert, the head of the Social Democratic Party is named chancellor of the Reich. In Berlin, Philipp Scheidemann, Social Democrat, proclaims the "German Republic" from the Reichstag.

The Weimar Republic

In its attempt to establish a democratic and republican government, the so-called Weimar government represented a break in the dominant traditions of German history. Residual issues from the war and the hostility of conservative groups conflicted with the reformist and radical impulses of the left and the cultural avant-garde. During the "Golden Twenties," Berlin—the capital of the republic—blossomed into the economic and cultural center of Germany as well.

- **1919:** Germany signs the Treaty of Versailles, which limits the army to 100,000 officers and men, although a "free corps" of soldiers remains. The Allies determine the total reparations bill in 1920. Rosa Luxemburg and Karl Liebknecht, the Communist leaders of the Spartacus League, are assassinated. Walter Gropius founds the Bauhaus school, noted for its unique style of functionalist architecture, in Weimar.

- **1920:** The Kapp putsch and Communist uprisings in the Ruhr industrial district help to spread a wave of lawlessness and disorder. A police operation against leftist radicals in Berlin ends with 42 dead, and the Reich government flees in the face of an attempted right-wing putsch in March.

- **1867:** Käthe Kollwitz, graphic artist and sculptor, and ardent socialist and pacifist, is born. She becomes widely known for her powerful woodcuts and litho-graphs depicting the misery and hunger of society's dispossessed.
- **1867:** Karl Marx publishes the first volume of *Das Kapital.* (Frederick Engels will complete the work in 1885 and 1894.)
- **1869:** The Social Democratic Party is founded with leadership provided by August Bebel. In 1872 Bebe[l], along with Karl Liebknecht, is sentenced for pl[...]
- **1870–1871:** The Franco-Prussian War [...] collapse of the French and, ultimat[...] success in having Wilhelm I [...] emperor at Versailles—co[...] for the unification of G[...] capital of Germany[...]
- **1875:** Thomas M[...]
- **1876:** The [...]
- **1881:** [...] with Wa[...]
- **1888:** [...]
- **1898:** [...] Pru[...] power[...]
- **1900:** Be[...]
- **1901:** Wilhel[...] X ray, wins the [...]
- **1911:** Wassily Kan[...] *Reiter* movement [...] Munich.

World Wa[r...]

For many observers, the Great War re[...] attempt to dominate Europe. The milita[...] eastern front resulted in the defeat of Russ[...] on the western front ultimately led to Germ[...] though the war was not fought on German soil, [...] severe food shortages throughout the country a[...] fed political unrest.

- **1914:** The heir apparent to the Austrian thro[...] assassinated in Sarajevo on June 28, precipitat[...] World War I. Germany declares war on Russia o[...]

"*T*his is the granddaddy of travel letters... *Passport* emphasizes culture, comfort, and quality...it can glow with praise, or bite with disapproval."

Condé Nast Traveler

BUSINESS REPLY MAIL

FIRST CLASS MAIL   PERMIT NO 45660   CHICAGO IL

POSTAGE WILL BE PAID BY ADDRESSEE

PASSPORT NEWSLETTER®
350 WEST HUBBARD STREET
SUITE 440
CHICAGO, ILLINOIS 60610-9698